Making Inclusion Work

Frank Bowe
Hofstra University

Upper Saddle River, New Jersey
Columbus, Ohio

Library of Congress Cataloging-in-Publication Data

Bowe, Frank
Making inclusion work/Frank Bowe
p. cm.
Includes bibliography references and index.
ISBN 0-13-017603-6
1. Inclusive education—United States. 2. Children with disabilities—Education—United States. I. Title.

LC1201.B69 2005
371.9'046'0973—dc22

2004044844

Vice President and Executive Publisher: Jeffery W. Johnston
Acquisitions Editor: Allyson P. Sharp
Editorial Assistant: Kathleen S. Burk
Development Editor: Heather Doyle Fraser
Production Editor: Sheryl Glicker Langner
Production Coordination: Amy Gehl, Carlisle Publishers Services
Design Coordinator: Diane C. Lorenzo
Photo Coordinators: Cynthia Cassidy and Lori Whitley
Cover Designer: Bryan Huber
Cover Image: © VSA/Tom Renino; http://www.vsarts.org
Production Manager: Laura Messerly
Director of Marketing: Ann Castel Davis
Marketing Manager: Autumn Purdy
Marketing Coordinator: Tyra Poole

This book was set in Garmond by Carlisle Communications, LTD., and was printed and bound by Courier Kendallville, Inc. The cover was printed by The Lehigh Press, Inc.

Photo Credits: Scott Cunningham/Merrill, pp. 2, 6, 36, 78, 126, 135, 240, 244, 257, 284 (right), 340, 369, 373, 427, 433; Irene Springer/PH College, pp. 5, 284 (left); KS Studios/Merrill, p. 9; AP/Wide World Photos, p. 14; Anthony Magnacca/Merrill, pp. 20, 43, 51, 64, 85, 150, 154, 170, 198, 219, 230, 328, 332, 336, 366, 424, 428, 452; Barbara Schwartz/Merrill, pp. 32, 38, 95, 215, 518, 554; Pearson Learning, pp. 45, 506, 534; Lloyd Wolf/U.S. Census Bureau, pp. 68, 508; Silver/Burdett Ginn, p. 110; Todd Yarrington/Merrill, pp. 115, 162, 245, 264, 457, 465; Patrick White/Merrill, pp. 119, 267, 278, 354, 358, 384, 488, 513, 515; Ken Hammond/USDA, p. 125; courtesy of John Williams, p. 130; Anne Vega/Merrill, pp. 159, 391, 478, 510; Skjold/PH College, p. 177; Richard Haynes/Prentice Hall School Division, p. 204; courtesy of Altimate Medical/Easy Stand, p. 213; Tom Watson/Merrill, pp. 281, 441; courtesy of Homes for Easy Living Universal Design Consultants, p. 293; Courtesy of Pyramid Educational Consultants, Inc., p. 294; Jean Greenwald/Merrill, p. 324; David Mager/Pearson Learning, p. 350; George Dodson/PH College, p. 387; Ken Karp/PH College, pp. 396, 456; PH College, pp. 401, 565; Spencer Grant/PhotoEdit, p. 409; Shirley Zeiberg/PH College, p. 461; Andy Crawford/Dorling Kindersley Media Library, p. 502; UN/DPI, p. 524; Mazlan Enjah/Getty Images Inc. – Hulton Archive Photos, p. 531; Ken Karp/PH Photo, p. 550; Michelle Bridwell/PhotoEdit, p. 562; Rhoda Sidney/PH College, p. 572.

Pearson Education Ltd.
Pearson Education Singapore, Pte. Ltd.
Pearson Education Canada, Ltd.
Pearson Education—Japan
Pearson Education Australia PTY, Limited
Pearson Education North Asia Ltd.
Pearson Educacíon de Mexico, S.A. de C.V.
Pearson Education Malaysia, Pte. Ltd.

10 9 8 7 6 5 4 3 2 1
ISBN: 0-13-017603-6

Dedication

For Doran and Tom,
Whitney and Josh:
You make it all worthwhile.

Preface

Inclusion is an ideal, a goal toward which educators continually strive. Translating it into reality can be challenging. The task is not made easier when proponents offer platitudes instead of practical tools. Diane Bricker (2000) of the University of Oregon, a pioneer in inclusion, sadly observed, "Many of the outspoken advocates for inclusion are not in the classroom or community delivering services" (p. 18). This may be why so many articles and texts about inclusion fall short of helping teachers-in-training and classroom educators to make inclusion work.

This text offers a practical perspective. Over the years, I have had the privilege of helping to prepare a few thousand educators. Several contributed real-life perspectives to this text. Most of my current students work in local public schools while completing their degree at Hofstra. We talk in class about the problems they encounter. I go out into the field to observe them in their classrooms. After they graduate, many e-mail me to ask for suggestions. Together, these teachers and teachers-in-training have taught me as much as, if not more than, I have taught them. Such primary-grade teachers as Natasha Mattera and William Marzellier created highly effective techniques for making inclusion work. Similarly, such middle-school and secondary teachers as Kim Ballerini, Kelly Pleasants, and Lori Rosendale successfully integrated content knowledge and classroom-management expertise to help students with disabilities who were included in general education classrooms to reach rigorous state learning standards. Each chapter in this book opens with, and many also have within them, stories that Natasha, Will, Kim, Lori, Kelly, and other teachers (some of whom have been given fictitious names to protect their privacy) have shared with me—the problems they faced and the solutions they found.

Now employed in public schools as far north as Massachusetts and as far south as Florida, they have identified several "keys" to successful inclusion. Time after time, they told me that inclusion *could work* but that administrative obstacles were frustrating them. In school district after school district, the same basic mistakes appear: Principals announce in March that entire grades, or even whole schools, will "go inclusion" the following September. This simply does not allow enough time for teachers to be trained and for teams to plan together. Children are placed into inclusive classrooms because of administrative convenience, not because of the children's needs; inappropriate placements all but guarantee failure. Personnel preparation programs often do not teach the skills of collaboration; as a result, teachers often do not know how to share decision-making authority with other team members. These widespread concerns of working teachers helped to shape this book, because they tell us what *not* to do.

On the other side of the same coin, the experiences of working teachers tell us how to "make inclusion work." Teachers tell me, again and again, how important it is when school administrators provide the support that is needed for inclusion to succeed. Inclusion is implemented only after careful planning. New teachers require mentoring from veterans. Collaborating teachers need time to plan lessons. Children with disabilities are placed into inclusive classrooms when their unique needs may be met in those settings. Related-services personnel work closely with classroom teachers to "push-in" and not just to "pull-out." Teachers and teachers-in-preparation have also told me that they benefit when their college programs are revamped so that university faculty in special education work hand-in-hand with professors in general education, "walking the walk" and not just "talking the talk" about how to make inclusion work.

INTENDED AUDIENCE

This book is designed both for preservice and inservice use. It was conceived as, and remains, a text that is suitable for use at the undergraduate level, as well as at the graduate level. I strived for readability at the undergraduate level. It is my belief that this same readability will serve graduate students and practicing teachers well, too. That is because this text does not sacrifice comprehensiveness of coverage, including research in the field, in the interests of readability. The intent, and I hope that it has been achieved, was to be both authoritative in coverage and easily understood and applied.

UNIQUE FEATURES OF THIS BOOK

Making Inclusion Work has a number of features not found in other texts. For example, Part Six provides in-depth coverage of content subjects (English, math, science, social studies, etc.) all the way from early childhood through the secondary years. This is important for several reasons. Many teacher-training programs offer just one course on inclusion—students at the early childhood, elementary, middle-school and high-school levels all take the same course. It is important, too, because many middle-school and secondary educators say they need more guidance on "how to do inclusion" than they have received to date. It is also important because the push for inclusion is occurring at the same time as the push for higher learning standards. Inclusion will work only if special educators as well as general educators are familiar with national and state learning standards and with proven techniques for teaching content subjects.

Making Inclusion Work connects inclusion to broader efforts by preK–12 schools to respond to today's greater diversity. Educators are challenged by classes having far greater ranges of abilities, learning styles, and interests than was the case in past years. For example, in 2000 the number of young children who are of Hispanic origin for the first time exceeded the number who are African American (U.S. Bureau of the Census, 2001). This is happening at the same time that teachers are being asked to implement inclusion. Fortunately, research suggests that some of the *same* techniques that effective teachers use to meet the unique needs of children and youth who come from culturally and linguistically diverse families, who are homeless, and who are at risk for possible school failure for other reasons *also* are useful for educators wanting to respond to the needs of students with disabilities. Good examples are grouping and peer tutoring. In the "methods" chapters (Chapters 8 to 10) and in a wide-ranging Chapter 11 (on students at risk), *Making Inclusion Work* shows teachers how they can broaden the appeal of their instruction and heighten the success of students having a wide variety of needs and desires.

This book explains a relatively new way of thinking about, and doing, teaching: "universal design in education" (Bowe, 2000c). Universal design is widely misunderstood as simply a way of using technology in the classroom. It is, in fact, much more than that. Educators who practice universal design create their instruction, from the beginning, to reach children and youth with widely differing learning styles, preferences, strengths, and needs. Done right, universal design enhances instruction while also containing costs. Technology *is* a component of universal design, because today's technologies make universal design so much easier to do and so much more effective. That being said, it is again worth emphasizing that universal design is much more than technology. This text helps teachers to become proficient in this exciting new way of designing and delivering instruction.

Teachers-in-training as well as working educators need to know what the best, and most current, research has to tell us. They require this information in a form they can use. The material must be readable and it must be integrated so that they can connect it to their own experiences and daily teaching needs. This text draws upon several hundred very recent articles and books in a wide range of fields and presents this knowledge in a concise, readily understood form. The book adopts a conversational tone, even using "I" and "you" so as to make the information more accessible for readers.

Readability is also enhanced by the use of a number of pedagogical features. Every chapter opens with theme-setting vignettes, focus questions, and an introduction. Each chapter, too, concludes with bulleted chapter summaries and chapter-ending "Questions for Reflection." A wide variety of boxes offer first-person narratives on inclusion, lesson plans, sample IEPs, and the like, to illustrate material and to guide the reader's further study of important topics. You will find:

Teacher Strategies That Work
Student Strategies That Work
Technologies That Work
Resources That Work
Lesson Plans That Work
Research That Works

HOW THE BOOK IS ORGANIZED

Part One of *Making Inclusion Work* introduces inclusion, outlines the key provisions related to inclusion that are found in the Individuals with Disabilities Education Act (IDEA) and in section 504 of the Rehabilitation Act, and discusses how identification of students with disabilities occurs and how educators may avoid overidentification of members of ethnic and racial minority groups and children from low-socioeconomic status (SES) homes. Chapters 1 and 2 also explain how to write an Individualized Education Program (IEP).

Part Two describes the more common categories in special education. Chapters 3, 4, and 5 introduce specific learning disabilities, speech or language impairments, attention deficit disorders and attention deficit hyperactivity disorders, as well as mental retardation and emotional/behavioral disorders.

Part Three discusses less common disabilities, including blindness and vision impairment, autism, traumatic brain injury, and physical and health disabilities.

Part Four is devoted to techniques—the "methods" of teaching, managing behavior, and assessing student progress.

Part Five offers a "diversity" chapter that summarizes the effects of childhood poverty, minority group status, teen pregnancy, substance abuse, and other factors that may place children and youth at risk for school failure. That is followed by Chapter 12, on collaboration between educators and related-services personnel, paraprofessionals, family members, and students themselves. In Chapter 13, the book addresses transition from high school to life beyond high school.

The final section of the book, Part Six, surveys the "content subjects" of English and language arts, math, science, and social studies. Each chapter in this section opens by describing the national learning standards upon which state standards are based. Methods are then introduced for use in early-childhood or elementary classes and for use in middle-school or secondary classes.

ANCILLARIES

- *Instructor's Manual and Test Bank*—The Instructor's Manual is a comprehensive resource that includes chapter outlines, chapter objectives, key terms, and class discussion questions for each chapter. In addition, each chapter contains a test bank which includes true/false, multiple choice, and essay questions.
- *Computerized Test Bank Software*—The computerized test bank software gives instructors electronic access to the test questions printed in the Instructor's Manual,

allowing them to create and customize exams on their computer. The software can help professors manage their courses and gain insight into their students' progress and performance. Computerized test bank software is available in both Macintosh and PC/Windows formats.

- *Companion Website*—Located at *http://www.prenhall.com/bowe,* the Companion Website for this text has a wealth of resources for both students and professors, including a user guide. The Website provides updated information about the most recent changes in the federal law, the Individuals with Disabilities Education Act (IDEA). The *Syllabus Manager™* enables professors to create and maintain the class syllabus online while also allowing the student access to the syllabus at any time from any computer via the Internet. In addition, on a passcode-protected portion of the site, professors can access instructor resources for the text, including an online version of the Instructor's Manual, downloadable PowerPoint lectures, and additional resources for effective instruction.

  The student portion of the Website helps students gauge their understanding of chapter content through the use of online chapter reviews and interactive multiple choice and essay quizzes. The *Web Links* module contains links to all the Websites mentioned in the text and assists students in using the Web to do additional research on chapter topics and key issues. In addition, in the *Video Cases* module, students have access to in-depth activities that connect the *Inclusive Classrooms: Video Cases on CD-ROM* to chapter content. Finally, the *Message Board* feature encourages student interaction outside of the classroom.
- *Inclusive Classrooms: Video Cases on CD-ROM*—The CD-ROM that accompanies the text provides immediate access to living classroom examples of teaching and learning strategies for inclusion. These examples are video clips, grouped by topic and classroom, which give the preservice teacher a good picture of what inclusion looks like in a preschool, elementary school, middle school, and secondary school. In each classroom, you will see a lesson that clearly shows the impact of inclusion on supporting students with challenging behaviors (preschool), classroom climate (elementary), assessment and planning (middle), and partial participation and cooperative learning (secondary).

  Each classroom case contains nine video clips. In each case, you will see how children with learning disabilities, attention deficit disorders, and mild/moderate disabilities are successfully engaged in the classroom community and in learning. Because of the natural supports and inclusive stance of the teachers and schools, it may be difficult to identify which children are indeed identified as having disabilities or in need of other accommodations.

ACKNOWLEDGMENTS

My first acknowledgment must be to the teachers I helped to prepare. I am also very much indebted to colleagues of mine at Hofstra University, on Long Island. They believe in collaboration, as I do, and we practice it. Vance Austin, Rhonda Clements, Eduardo Manuel Duarte, Debra Goodman, George Giuliani, Judith Kaufman, Janice Koch, Max Hines, Maureen Murphy, Karen Osterman, Darra Pace, Diane Schwartz, Daniel Sciarra, Alan Singer, Sharon Whitton, Gloria Lodato Wilson, and Joan Zeleski in particular helped by sharing their knowledge. Hines, Murphy, Singer, and Whitton co-taught a course with me on collaborative teaching across content areas. Wilson and Lisa Gaeta deserve my thanks for preparing the Instructor's Manual.

At Merrill, editors Allyson Sharp and, before her, Ann Castel Davis, and senior development editors Heather Doyle Fraser, and before her, Gianna Marsella, made substantial contributions to the overall design and shape of the book. Thank you to the following reviewers: Thomas P. Lombardi, West Virginia University, emeritus; Mark Mostert, Regent University; Greg Conderman, St. Ambrose University; Janice Sammons, University of Arizona; David Majsterek, Central Washington University; Robbie Ludy, Buena Vista University; Gail Peterson Craig, University of Wisconsin—Superior; Elaine Traynellis-Yurek, Mary Baldwin College; and Bill Murphy, Bridgewater State College, deserve my thanks for reviewing each chapter as the manuscript was being written.

I also thank the copy editor, Keri Miskza and Carlisle Publishers Services production editor, Amy Gehl, who helped to create the finished product.

EDUCATOR LEARNING CENTER: AN INVALUABLE ONLINE RESOURCE

Merrill Education and the Association for Supervision and Curriculum Development (ASCD) invite you to take advantage of a new online resource, one that provides access to the top research and proven strategies associated with ASCD and Merrill—the Educator Learning Center. At **www.EducatorLearningCenter.com** you will find resources that will enhance your students' understanding of course topics and of current educational issues, in addition to being invaluable for further research.

How the Educator Learning Center Will Help Your Students Become Better Teachers

With the combined resources of Merrill Education and ASCD, you and your students will find a wealth of tools and materials to better prepare them for the classroom.

Research

- More than 600 articles from the ASCD journal *Educational Leadership* discuss everyday issues faced by practicing teachers.
- A direct link on the site to Research Navigator™ gives students access to many of the leading education journals, as well as extensive content detailing the research process.
- Excerpts from Merrill Education texts give your students insights on important topics of instructional methods, diverse populations, assessment, classroom management, technology, and refining classroom practice.

Classroom Practice

- Hundreds of lesson plans and teaching strategies are categorized by content area and age range.
- Case studies and classroom video footage provide virtual field experience for student reflection.
- Computer simulations and other electronic tools keep your students abreast of today's classrooms and current technologies.

Look into the Value of Educator Learning Center Yourself

A four-month subscription to Educator Learning Center is $25 but is **FREE** when ordered in conjunction with this text. To obtain free passcodes for your students, simply contact your local Merrill/Prentice Hall sales representative, who will give you a special ISBN to give your bookstore when ordering your textbooks. To preview the value of this website to you and your students, please go to **www.EducatorLearningCenter.com** and click on "Demo."

Brief Contents

Part Four
Teaching in the Inclusive Classroom 277

Part Five
Other Aspects of Teaching in the Inclusive Classroom 383

Part Six
Content-Area Instruction 477

Contents

Part Three

Part Four

Part Five

Other Aspects of Teaching in the Inclusive Classroom 383

Chapter 11
At-Risk, Culturally/Linguistically Diverse, and Gifted/Talented Students 384

Chapter 12
Collaboration 424

NOTE: Every effort has been made to provide accurate and current Internet information in this book. However, the Internet and information posted on it are constantly changing, and it is inevitable that some of the Internet addresses listed in this textbook will change. Visit the Companion Website (CW) for updates (http://www.prenhall.com/bowe) or use a search engine to learn the new addresses.

Special Features

Teacher Strategies That Work

Student Strategies That Work

Technologies That Work

Resources That Work

Lesson Plans That Work

Research That Works

Part One

Setting the Stage for Successful Inclusion

Part One of *Making Inclusion Work* presents the core knowledge that PreK–12 teachers of inclusive classrooms need in order to realize the potential of inclusion. In Chapter 1, we define the word "inclusion" as referring to education for students with disabilities in regular classroom settings for all or most of the school day. Inclusion often has failed to live up to its promise. This book is about how to make inclusion work.

We begin by explaining what educators need to know about the nation's landmark special-education law, the Individuals with Disabilities Education Act (IDEA). Much of the book's first chapter is taken up with a step-by-step review of what that law requires teachers and other educators to do. The key words are defined and illustrated. We look at labels—what they are, why and how we use them. We introduce the idea of "least restrictive environment" and explore how it forms a basis for inclusion.

In Chapter 2, we trace the steps toward inclusion. We begin with pre-referral interventions, or measures teachers of regular classrooms can take to meet children's needs short of referring those students for special education. We turn then to identification and the many issues surrounding that, notably the continued overidentification of children and youth from minority families. Assessing student needs and writing individualized plans for children and youth are then considered. The chapter concludes with a discussion of working with families, including due process procedures through which schools and families resolve differences of opinion about how best to serve children with special needs.

For more information about the IDEA—including recent updates on the law itself as well as federal and state regulations—go to the Companion Website at: http://www.prenhall.com/bowe

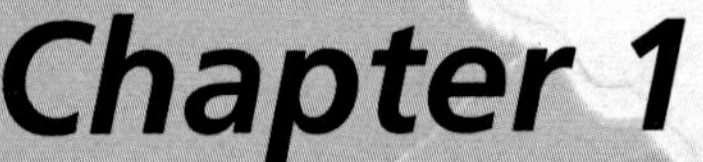

Chapter 1

The Ideas of IDEA

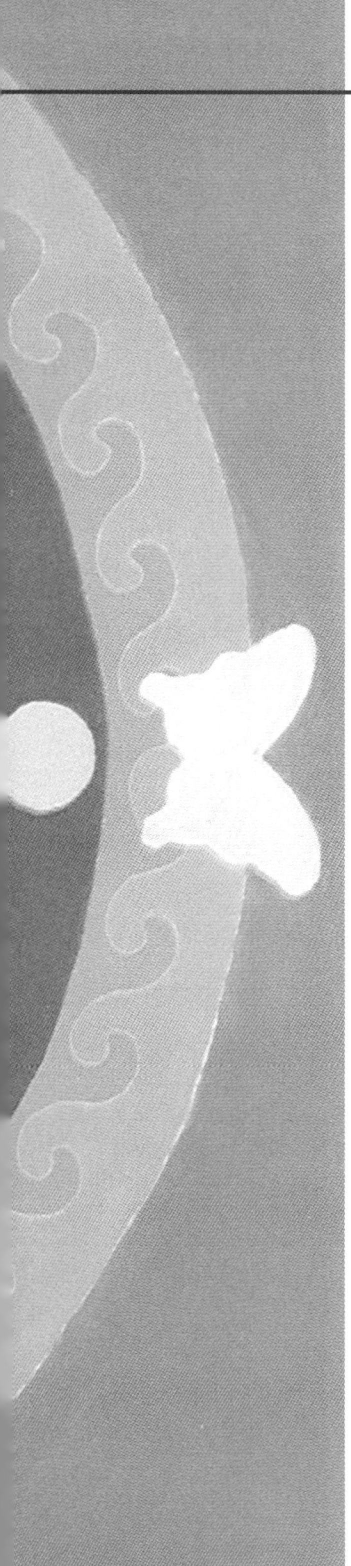

TERMS

inclusion
Individuals with Disabilities Education Act (IDEA)
full inclusion
socioeconomic status (SES)
mainstreaming
Regular Education Initiative (REI)
child with a disability
early childhood
labels
developmental delay
at risk
least restrictive environment (LRE)
supplementary aids and services
itinerant teachers
resource rooms
assistive technology devices
assistive technology services
supported education
appropriate
special education
related services
section 504
"504 children"

CHAPTER FOCUS QUESTIONS

After reading this chapter, you should be able to answer such questions as:

1. What are some different definitions for the word *inclusion?*
2. Who are *children with disabilities?*
3. Why do educators use labels to discuss children with disabilities?
4. What do we mean by *least restrictive environment?*
5. What is *special education?*
6. What are *related services?*
7. How can we serve children who have disabilities but who are not eligible under the IDEA?

PERSONAL ACCOUNTS

One teacher I helped to prepare, who was employed by a school district that wanted to "do" inclusion, recently told me about his experiences in piloting (starting the first class of his school in) inclusion:

> *Asked to teach an inclusion second-grade classroom, I was skeptical. I was nervous. Most of all, I wondered if I would lose patience with the program, my special education students, and myself. Was my teaching style flexible enough to handle all the different needs? Would I like teaching with another teacher by my side? How would it feel to share my classroom, my chalkboard, my bulletin board? Finally, I decided to give it a go. I volunteered for a nervous stomach for several weeks in August and September and, ultimately, for a priceless experience.*
>
> *My collaborative teacher and I quickly decided against any "pull-out" services for the special education students. We wanted the class to grow together and to bond. So we encouraged all the children to help each other out, to problem solve, and to organize themselves on their own. We found that the children were often more effective (and more efficient) problem solvers than we were!*

Their ideas were genuine and fresh. They created a sense of trust and warmth early in the school year. In time, they gave me a sense of trust, too. My team teacher and I also decided, early on, to be brutally honest with each other when it came to feelings and ideas. When you work side by side with one person for an entire year, that's a must. We learned to offer each other constructive criticism. We learned how vital it is to be flexible. My cooperative teacher and I now know how to help each other during a lesson, without interrupting or stepping on the other's toes.

Collaboration is, I now realize, the most under-rated part of inclusion. The coupling of two teachers—everything from philosophy of teaching to preferred colors of chalk— is a delicate process. Collaborative teaching is, I think, essentially a working marriage. That's why it is so important that teachers be able to form their own teams. My team teacher and I knew each other well. We respected each other. We were ready to be a team. It was also vital, I now see, that our building administrators were supportive. I felt "listened to" and "backed up" by my principal and supervising teachers.

My conclusion after this first year is that undergraduate students must *take at least one course in special education and/or inclusion. In fact, I would go so far as to recommend that anyone entering the teaching profession become certified in special education as well as in some other area. This is because reaching students with exceptional needs within the regular education classroom is now part of every teacher's job. The demands on educators are growing exponentially. Year after year, larger and larger numbers of students with disabilities are being educated in regular settings. It is up to us, as teachers, to prepare them to meet the new, higher learning standards.*

—Will

The same teacher, three years earlier, had described a very different view of inclusion at his school. Reading between the lines, you can see that the school administration was not then ready to "do" inclusion:

The superintendent and district special-education director decided in March 2000 that the district's main elementary school would "go inclusion" the following September. All of the elementary-age children with disabilities or developmental delays would be included, for all or most of the day, during the 2000–2001 school year. The building principal assigned regular and special educators to two-teacher teams to instruct the classes that would include such students. He did this on the basis of his perception that they would "get along well together." In response, the designated team members scrambled during the closing weeks of the 1999–2000 school year to find time to meet and to plan for inclusion. Feeling frustrated because these ad-hoc get-togethers did not leave them feeling prepared, they organized an inservice training session for themselves in July. Attendance was sporadic, because the district declined to pay them for their time during the summer months.

—Will

INTRODUCTION

This chapter opens with a "tale of two schools," one successful at inclusion, the other not. You can identify several reasons for their different outcomes. Other factors will elude you at present. However, as you read this text, more and more will become evident to you. By the time you complete *Making Inclusion Work,* you should have become very familiar with the key causes behind the success of one school and failure of the other. The intent of the "tale of two schools" is to begin our discussion of the topic of inclusion, and to set the stage for all that follows in this book.

The chapter then takes a quick look at its core subject, inclusion. What is inclusion? What is it not? We then step back to fill in background information necessary for a more complete understanding of inclusion. This leads us to a brief tour of the history of education law. That is followed by a discussion of the federal law, the Individuals with Disabilities Education Act (IDEA), which tells all of us involved in educating children with disabilities or developmental delays what to do and how to do it. This law defines which children are eligible for special education. The definition incorporates the concept of developmental delays and the much more controversial topic of labels.

Because IDEA does not even mention the word "inclusion," we must see what the law *does* tell us about placing children with disabilities in the "least restrictive environment" (LRE). The chapter then picks up other main themes of IDEA: an *appropriate* education, *special education, related services,* and *supplementary aids* and *services.* Finally, we look at a complementary law, *section 504* of the Rehabilitation Act of 1973, which helps us to educate some children we cannot serve under IDEA.

For more information about IDEA, LRE, and section 504, see the Companion Website at http://www.prenhall.com/bowe

A TALE OF TWO SCHOOLS

Below are two memos from building principals to teachers and other school staff members. The two memos are based upon actual statements, oral and written, by real school administrators. The memos themselves, however, are fictional. Read both. After you do, think about why it may be that inclusion was a failure at Forest Avenue School but became a success at Hasta Vista School. You may not immediately see the relevance of any specific comment in either memo. That's O.K. The impact of these factors will become apparent to you as you work your way through *Making Inclusion Work.* Think of it as a mystery or a detective story: As you read this book, write down the "clues" that are revealed to you. By book's end, you will have a better sense of what it all means.

Forest Avenue School

Memo from: Principal
Date: April 4
Re: Inclusion

In February, the district director of special education and I visited some "inclusion" schools. Clearly, this is the "coming thing." As I have said many times, Forest Avenue School is not going to take second place to any other local school.

The fictional Forest Avenue School.

Accordingly, we have decided that, effective September, Forest Avenue will "go inclusion" in grades 9 and 11. Only students with the labels "autism" and/or "mental retardation" will continue in separate classrooms and/or resource rooms.

Before school lets out in June, I will create two-teacher teams for each grade 9 or 11 classroom. After you learn who your partner will be, you might wish to plan get-togethers during the summer. I expect that the regular educators on each team will continue to do what they have done. The special educators on each team will be responsible for consulting about special needs and accommodations, about testing modifications, and about disciplining students. They will also tutor the special-needs students. As for speech/language pathologists, physical therapists, and other related-services personnel, I don't anticipate much if any change.

Your cooperation is essential to the success of this plan. I expect each of you to "sign up" with enthusiasm and commitment. If you do not, you will leave the grade and I will assign you to grades 10 or 12. Be advised that I fully expect those grades, too, will "go inclusion" a year from this coming September.

We will succeed, because we are Forest Avenue! If any child fails next year, we will deal with that on a case-by-case basis. However, knowing the spirit of excellence that pervades our school, I believe these failures will be few and far between.

Thank you.

Hasta Vista School

Memo from: Principal
Date: September 14
Re: Inclusion

Now that the day after Labor Day is behind us, and things have settled down a bit, I want to outline our plans for implementing "inclusion." The district director of special education and I visited some inclusion schools last spring. We were impressed with what we saw in some schools and distressed by what we viewed in others. So that every teacher, speech/language pathologist, and therapist at Hasta Vista can gain the kinds of insights we did last year, I am authorizing funds to employ substitute teachers and therapists for three (3) school days during the next three months. As you use these professional days to observe other schools, keep receipts for all ordinary and necessary expenses such as food, mileage, parking fees, and so on, and you will be reimbursed.

It is my hope, and that of the district director of special education, that by mid-December you will all have enough information about inclusion programs to

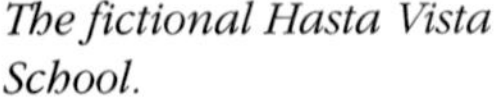

The fictional Hasta Vista School.

give the administration the guidance we will need from you. I am particularly interested in your observations about consultative versus collaborative teaming, mixed-ability groupings, and other instructional models. There are arguments for and against "push-in" and "pull-out" models for therapy. We need your input on that. We also need guidance about how to use assistive technology and about the new approach known as "universal design in education."

Please give me your recommendations about planning time during this coming summer and then during the implementation year next year. This includes inservice training. Are you willing to come to school during this coming summer to receive training on inclusion? (We will, of course, pay you for this additional work.) If not, we need to know in December so that we can arrange appropriate training for the spring months. What should this training include? We need your recommendations!

We at Hasta Vista have always prided ourselves on being a "family." We value input from parents and other caretakers. In that spirit, we will host a meeting of parents here at Hasta Vista next month to explain inclusion to the families of our students and to secure their input. In the same spirit, I invite all teachers who wish to participate in the inclusion program next year to self-nominate teams: one special educator and one regular educator on each team. Please explain why you believe the two of you would make a good team and describe how you would work together effectively. Please also document your conversations with speech/language pathologists, physical and occupational therapists, and other support personnel about push-in/pull-out services.

The placement team meetings scheduled for this coming spring (following the IEP team meetings) will recommend those children who are, in the judgment of parents, teachers, and other team members, suitable candidates for inclusion. The administration will then place highest priority on arranging for the supplementary aids and services, related services, and other supports that these children will require in inclusive settings next year.

I know this memo leaves many questions unanswered. Please consider this note, and our plans, to be a work in progress. We all have much to learn—starting with me!

Thank you.

WHAT IS INCLUSION?

The word "inclusion" does not even appear in IDEA. Nor does any related term, for example, inclusive education. Accordingly, there are no federal definitions for the word "inclusion." Educators have adopted a number of definitions over the years. Let us examine some of these in order to come to an understanding of the concept.

Most educators use the term **inclusion** to mean the placement of children with disabilities into general education classrooms for all or significant parts of the school day (e.g., Crealock & Bachor, 1995; Fuchs & Fuchs, 1994; York, Doyle, & Kronberg, 1992). Most, too, recognize that placements must be made in such a way as to follow federal law, the **Individuals with Disabilities Education Act (IDEA;** 20 U.S.C. 1400 *et seq.*). IDEA's two cardinal principles are appropriateness and individualization. As we will see later in this chapter, the law guarantees each child with a disability a public education that is "appropriate," that is, meets that child's unique needs. IDEA mandates that placement decision be made on a case-by-case basis, that is, individualized. Most special educators (e.g., Kauffman, 1993; Yell, 1995; Zigmond et al., 1995) acknowledge that inclusion, as emotionally appealing as it may be, does not override these two bedrock principles of IDEA. Inclusion, in their view, should be practiced in the public schools only when the unique needs of each child with a disability are met and when placements are made on an individualized basis. These considerations are important. When they are observed, inclusion is a powerful idea.

Balancing Competing Needs

This conception of inclusion is one that respects the power of the idea of inclusion while also recognizing its limits. There is much to be said for the integration of students with and without disabilities. By insisting that children with special needs be served in general environments, that is, in buildings and in rooms that are highly visible to members of the community, inclusion acts to increase public interest in, and enhance public oversight about, services for these children. Students with disabilities can benefit from inclusion in many ways. Notably, in an era of higher learning standards and high-stakes assessments, students with disabilities can be taught the same content as is provided to students without disabilities. At a time when school administrators and teachers feel "under the gun" to raise achievement in their schools, the fact that students with disabilities are tested, as are most other students, in districtwide and statewide assessments means that the central administration officials, building principals, and other educators in the school district are very interested in seeing that students with disabilities learn the required material and pass the high-stakes tests. Also significant is the fact that students with disabilities are exposed every day to the behavior of children and youth who do not have disabilities. They are given, that is, models to follow. So it is appropriate that inclusion is increasing. As Figure 1.1 shows, the number of students with disabilities who spend all or virtually all of the school day in inclusive classrooms has grown over the years. According to the most recent figures, those from the U.S. Department of Education's *Twenty-Sixth Annual Report to Congress on Implementation of the Individuals with Disabilities Education Act* (2004), 48% of all children and youth with disabilities who were served under IDEA were placed in inclusive classrooms.

That having been noted, the desire to integrate children must be balanced by respect for the other interests of these same children. IDEA forbids placing *groups* of children with disabilities into any setting, including the general classroom. Rather, the law speaks to *individualizing* all important decisions, including placement. Educators cannot simply say, as the principal of the Forest Avenue School did (see "A Tale of Two Schools," p. 5), that all students with disabilities except those with the labels "autism" and "mental retardation"

FIGURE 1.1 The Trend Toward Inclusion

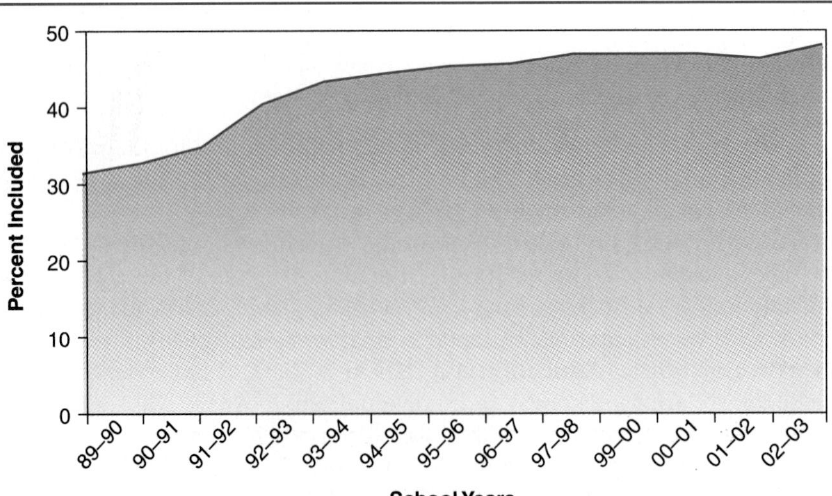

Sources: 14th Annual Report to Congress (for 1989–1990) through *26th Annual Report to Congress* (for 2002–2003) and *www.ideadata.org.* Table AB2, "Number of Children Ages 6 to 21 Served in Different Educational Environments," in each report, first column ("< 21% Outside Regular Classroom"). Data cover the 50 states and outlying areas.

The decision to place children into inclusive classrooms is made on a child-by-child basis.

will be placed into inclusive classrooms. Rather, the law tells us to make the placement decision anew for each child and to be prepared, each year, to change it if necessary. This is because the major purpose of schools is, after all, to *educate* children. If a child is denied an appropriate education, even though this child is placed in an inclusive setting, the child's best interests are not being served. That is why IDEA places limits on the extent to which it promotes the integration of children with and children without disabilities. This balancing of competing needs is one that is widely respected in education.

Full Inclusion

Some advocates have proposed quite radical conceptions of the meaning of the word "inclusion." To illustrate, Dorothy Lipsky and Alan Gartner (1996) advanced a definition of inclusion that they had first offered a year earlier (*National Study of Inclusive Education,* 1995):

> Inclusion is the provision of services to students with disabilities, including those with severe impairments, in the neighborhood school, in age-appropriate general education classes, with the necessary supports and supplementary aids (for the child and the teacher) both to assure the child's success—academic, behavioral, and social—and to prepare the child to participate as a full and contributing member of the society. (Lipsky & Gartner, 1996, p. 763)

This is a sweeping, even breathtaking, interpretation of the term "inclusion." That Lipsky and Gartner were more interested with this article in advocacy than in teacher training should be evident from the article's title ("Inclusion, School Restructuring, and the Remaking of American Society"). Let us break down their definition so as to appreciate its nature as an advocacy position. First, Lipsky and Gartner, in this definition, which is often called **full inclusion,** envisioned placement of *all* children with disabilities into general education classrooms. That violates the law's proscription against group placements. Lipsky and Gartner insisted that even children with very severe disabilities be educated in general classrooms. While some such children can be taught, at least during part of the day, in such settings, many require the more customized curricula, more intensive instruction, and more individualized attention they would receive in less integrated settings. Second, Lipsky and Gartner wanted children with disabilities to be placed into age-appropriate classes. Again, this is admirable and often achievable. However, some children benefit more when they are in classes where their abilities and needs match the curricula and the methods of instruction than when they are put into settings which may be age-appropriate but which are not content-appropriate (e.g., Bricker, 2000).

Finally, Lipsky and Gartner wanted general classrooms to meet children's academic, behavioral, and social needs. Yet again, this is sometimes doable. Often, though, children's needs differ so much from the needs of other children that general classrooms simply are not suitable for meeting those diverse needs. Consider, for example, children who need a great deal of extended and highly individualized instruction in basic life skills (self-care, self-feeding, self-dressing, and the like). Students with these needs deserve other placement options. They benefit from the requirement, in federal regulations, that all school districts make available, as needed, a continuum of alternative placement options. We will discuss the continuum in Chapter 2. For now, suffice it to say that under full inclusion the continuum ceases to exist. That could deprive many children and youth of the individualized instruction they require.

There is another danger with the ideal of full inclusion. When schools embrace full inclusion, they often fail (e.g., King-Sears & Cummings, 1996; Mamlin, 1999; Walther-Thomas, Bryant, & Land, 1996). Then, rather than realize that their failure was because they overreached, school officials typically conclude that inclusion is not doable. They then return to the way they used to do things. This pattern of short-lived trends, or fads, is one we have seen distressingly often in the history of American education (see, for example, Stewart [2001] on California's wild swings toward and away from whole language, and Wolfe [2001], on the history of American education). *Making Inclusion Work* is founded upon the belief that educators and students are far better served if more realistic goals are set. If done right, inclusion can be a success. Part of "doing it right" is to set reachable, rather than idealistic, goals.

HISTORICAL BACKGROUND

Forest Avenue and Hasta Vista schools were trying to carry out inclusion plans. Where did this idea of inclusion come from? To answer that question, we need to take a brief tour of history and of laws.

How Education Is Governed

Education for children with disabilities is run, to an extent unimaginable in general education, at the federal level of government. We need to devote a few moments to understanding why this is so. To begin, recall that elementary and secondary education in the United States is administered, almost exclusively, by state education agencies (SEAs) and by local education agencies (LEAs). The SEAs, or state departments of education, set the overall standards for students to meet, outline the scope and sequence of state-approved curricula, and certify PreK–12 administrators and teachers. The LEAs, or school districts, hire the administrators, teachers, and other personnel, establish rules for student conduct, and create school operating budgets. When you become a teacher, it will most likely be an LEA that employs you. The federal government plays a minor role, by comparison. Its major responsibilities are to encourage states to raise academic standards and to offer supplemental funding that helps schools to serve disadvantaged children. The federal presence in PreK–12 education increased, notably in the call for higher standards and in the use of technology in instruction, in the No Child Left Behind Act of 2001 (see *Education Week* front page stories April 7, 2004, and May 5, 2004). Even so, the federal role in public education in our country is still limited (e.g., Foster, 2004; Schemo, 2004).

Why Special Education Differs from General Education

Education for children and youth with disabilities or developmental delays is also founded on the Constitution's "general welfare" clause. There is, however, a major difference in how different levels of government carry out the nation's commitment to spe-

Resources That Work

Laws and the Schools

For more information on the Library of Congress's "Thomas" site, go to the Web Links module in Chapter 1 of the Companion Website.

You can find laws in many public libraries. Rules are a little harder to find as you may have to go to a law school library. Many laws and regulations are also available on the Internet. A useful starting point is the Library of Congress's "Thomas" Website.

A good summary of how federal and state laws affect public education is offered by Valente and Valente (2001) in their *Law in the Schools.* A primer on laws related to special education is provided by Turnbull and Turnbull (2000) in their *Free Appropriate Public Education: The Law and Children with Disabilities.* For shorter summaries of key laws, see Jennings (2000), about Title I, and Yell (1995), about special education law.

The laws themselves are collected in the *United States Code,* available in larger public libraries. Federal laws about education appear in the 20th volume of the U.S.C. The rules are collected in the *Code of Federal Regulations* (C.F.R.). Those for special education appear at 34 C.F.R. 300 (PreK–12) and at 34 C.F.R. 301 (Early Intervention).

---

cial education. With respect to PreK–12 children who have disabilities or delays, the federal level of government dictates, in highly specific detail, exactly what schools, parents, and children may and may not do. The role of the SEA is reduced in special education to one of complying with the federal mandates and of ensuring that the state's local schools do, as well. All 50 states have passed "me too" laws in which they promise to carry out the IDEA mandates. LEA's obey both federal and state rules under close supervision of state officials, although not always happily (e.g., Foster, 2004).

This difference is a function of history. Whereas a public education was offered to most students between the ages of about 6 and 16 (in some states) or 7 and 17 (in some others) as early as 1905 to 1915, that privilege was not generally extended to students with disabilities until some 60 years later. As recently as the early 1970s, local school officials routinely told parents of children with disabilities to send those children to state institutions or to expensive private schools. The fact that those special facilities often were located hundreds of miles away meant that these school administrators (who are, after all, agents of local governments) were disrupting families. And there was more: Private schools cost as much as $35,000 a year in today's dollars, or about as much as an Ivy League college.

What the local school officials were doing was, in fact, in violation of the United States Constitution. The Fifth Amendment to the Constitution holds that no person is to be deprived of his or her freedom, including the freedom to associate with other people, without due process under law. This amendment was also at root in the famous 1954 Supreme Court decision in *Brown v. Board of Education*. There, the Court said that segregating Topeka, KS, school students by race unnecessarily deprived those students of freedom. *Brown* laid some crucially important groundwork for what was to come, not only in race relations but also in special education (see such "50th anniversary" stories on *Brown* in the *New York Times'* [2004] and *Education Week's* [2004]). *Brown* also cautions educators to be realistic about the pace of change in public school systems. Today, over 50 years after the 1954 decision, America's schools are, on the whole, only marginally more integrated than they were then (e.g., Carnahan, 2003). While progress has been made, it has been uneven. Because inclusion of students with disabilities involves social change, it may also require many years to reach its potential.

Title I: Compensatory Services for Children from Low SES Families

One result of the *Brown v. Board of Education* decision was the enactment, in the mid-1960s, of the Elementary and Secondary Education Act (ESEA; 20 U.S.C. 2701 *et seq.*). Title I of this Act offers federal funds to help schools that serve large numbers of children from low **socioeconomic status (SES)** homes. Socioeconomic status is a measure of family wealth and income. Low SES families are poor as compared to other families.

This important law originated as part of President Lyndon Johnson's War on Poverty. It was one of the first federal laws on education. How the ESEA came about matters to us, because it presages what later happened with the IDEA. The Tenth Amendment to the U.S. Constitution states, "The powers not delegated to the United States by the Constitution, nor prohibited by it to the states, are reserved to the states respectively, or to the people." Because the word "education" is not mentioned as a federal responsibility, the Constitution gives that role to the states. What the ESEA of 1965 (Public Law [PL] 89-10) did was to exploit something else in the Constitution: the fact that the Constitution's section 8 gives to the Congress responsibility to "provide . . . for the general welfare of the United States." The ESEA, by focusing on the needs of children who are economically, educationally, or otherwise disadvantaged, seeks to advance the general welfare and thus to comply with the Constitution. As innovative as ESEA's Title I was, it made no mention of children with disabilities. For that to occur, a new interpretation of the Constitutional underpinnings of the *Brown v. Board of Education* case would be needed. It was not long in coming.

The Emergence of a Federal Law

PARC

What no one recognized until the 1970s when Thomas Gilhool, the great civil rights lawyer, advanced it on behalf of Pennsylvania parents whose children were mentally retarded, is that freedom of association includes the freedom of people with disabilities to associate with people who have no disabilities and the freedom of family members to associate with each other. The Fifth Amendment says that such freedom may not be abridged by government without having very compelling reasons. But that is what local administrators were doing. Pursuant to the Fifth Amendment, Gilhool argued that local government should make such recommendations *only* after exhaustive efforts are made to find ways to accommodate mentally retarded children in local schools.

In 1972, the Commonwealth of Pennsylvania conceded that he was right in *Pennsylvania Association for Retarded Children (PARC) v. Commonwealth of Pennsylvania.*

In a consent decree, the Commonwealth agreed to begin educating children with mental retardation, free of charge to the families, and usually in local programs. The agreement did not affect children who were not mentally retarded.

Mills

That same year, parents of children with a wide range of physical, sensory, mental, and emotional impairments persuaded a judge in Washington, DC, to order city schools to begin teaching children with all kinds of disabilities. This was decided in *Mills v. Board of Education of the District of Columbia* (1972).

PARC and *Mills* were both consent decrees. What this meant is that the agreements could not be appealed to higher courts (i.e., to U.S. Courts of Appeals and to the U.S. Supreme Court) and, for that reason, could not be extended, via litigation, to entire circuits (multi-state areas under the jurisdiction of a Court of Appeals) nor to the country as a whole. Rather, the legislative branch of government would have to extend it nationwide. In 1975, it did: Congress enacted PL 94-142, the Education for All Handicapped Children Act, later called the IDEA. The rest, as they say, is history (see Turnbull & Turnbull, 2000, for an in-depth review of that history).

The Trend Toward Inclusion

Exactly how teachers and other educators, working with parents, are to carry out the decision, first expressed in the *PARC* consent decree, that children with disabilities should be served in neighborhood schools, when possible, is a major topic deserving an extended

Teacher Strategies That Work

Welcome to the Real World, I

I am the sole teacher of a first-grade class of 18 students. Three of these students are English-as-a-second-language learners who receive pull-out services. Two of those three also have disabilities. One is a student with cerebral palsy and multiple other disabilities. He receives speech and language pathology services, occupational therapy, and physical therapy a few days a week. The other child (according to unofficial sources) had been classified as emotionally disturbed during preschool; however, for some reason he was declassified before entering my first-grade class. He came into my class clearly having many needs! All three are functioning way below grade level.

I referred these children to [the IEP] team at the beginning of the school year. The first child had his first IEP meeting in February. I brought a briefcase filled with work samples to make the case that this child needed more support in the classroom. Just this week (early April), seven full months after I first referred him to team, I received an aide to work with him. I am still waiting for the initial IEP meetings on the other two children.

I adapt all work for these children: spelling, class work, homework. I am constantly overwhelmed with the concern that I am not doing enough for them. I have spent many, many nights awake thinking of their well-being and evaluating myself to make their education the best it can be. That being said, I love every minute of it. I know where I need to keep growing. I just need the time to do it all!

What I have learned this year is that half of making inclusion work is making the right decisions at the right time. There are so many factors that go into getting things done for a student—most of them having nothing whatsoever to do with that child or his needs!

—Natasha

discussion (see Chapter 2). For now, let us make a few comments about the history of inclusion.

First, inclusion is a reflection of larger social trends. In the years preceding the enactment of PL 94-142, major efforts were undertaken to move people out of institutions and into community settings. Wolf Wolfensberger (1972) and others made a powerful case for "normalization," that is, for the creation of service-delivery environments that resemble those we find in our communities. In Wolfensberger's words, these are "means which are as culturally normative as possible, in order to establish and/or maintain personal behaviors and characteristics which are as culturally normative as possible" (p. 28). The implications for education are that children and youth with disabilities should attend neighborhood public schools whenever possible, they should be taught in much the same ways as are nondisabled students, and the aims of education should be similar for disabled and nondisabled students.

Mainstreaming

Translating the ideals into practical realities proved to be harder to do than some advocates had hoped. When what is now IDEA was first enacted in 1975, the prevailing attitude of administrators and teachers was that Congress could not possibly have intended what the words in IDEA section 612(a)(5), on the surface, seemed to mean. As we will examine in depth later in the chapter, this section has the law's requirements about placement of students with disabilities into regular settings, when appropriate. The law calls this the "least restrictive environment" (LRE). The initial thought, in 1975, was that this section must have a rather modest meaning. While some educators interpreted the language differently, the prevailing view was that this provision told schools to integrate students who have disabilities with students who have no disabilities into non-academic activities, such as lunch, recess, and the like. One word to describe this is **mainstreaming.** To do more, that is to integrate these students into content (subject) classes, would be to expect from children with disabilities more than many educators thought they could deliver. Thus, most children with disabilities continued to be placed into separate (self-contained) classes for most or all of the school day.

No one wants to return to the time when many people with disabilities were institutionalized in places such as Willowbrook, on Staten Island, in New York.

Regular Education Initiative

A few years later, in 1986, a new interpretation of the law's LRE provision emerged. This view was championed by Madeleine C. Will, at the time the Assistant Secretary for Special Education and Rehabilitative Services in the U.S. Department of Education. Will was not an educator; rather, she was a mother and an advocate. (Her son Jon had Down syndrome.) She was interested in furthering integration of students with and without disabilities, and she believed that this would not happen unless the general education teachers took responsibility for students with disabilities. That is why Will called her idea the **Regular Education Initiative (REI).** In a speech delivered in late 1985 (adapted for an article in the journal *Exceptional Children* in early 1986), she talked about breaking down barriers between regular and special education, so as to benefit children with learning disabilities and other mild conditions (Will, 1986). Will wanted to direct more funds to regular-education remedial and support services, in the hope that less would be required in special education: "This means special programs and regular education programs must be allowed to collectively contribute skills and resources to carry out individualized education plans based on individualized education needs" (p. 413).

Will's speech and article were widely misunderstood. At the time, commingling of resources (the spending of special-education dollars, that is, funds appropriated to carry out what is now IDEA, in regular education programs) was forbidden. So Will proposed "trials" (p. 414), or, to use Washington vernacular, "demonstration programs," as a way of exploring the delivery of some special services in regular education, yet not violating the ban on commingling of funds. Many in the audience thought she was dictating a solution that would require a lot of change on the part of general educators, without first consulting those regular educators. At the time, many educators felt they had enough on their hands with the "excellence in education" movement (e.g., Fuchs & Fuchs, 1994).

IDEA today allows some commingling in the interests of promoting integration of students with disabilities. The change was made to accept the reality that when "special" funds are used in general classrooms, *some* of the children benefiting will be non-disabled students, that is, children who are not "eligible" under the special-education law. This acceptance came in 1997, more than a decade after Will first proposed it.

In the years following 1986, REI came to stand for the proposition that students with *mild* disabilities (such as speech and language impairments, specific learning disabilities, and the like) should be integrated with students who have no disabilities *throughout the school day*. That only students with mild impairments would be considered for integration reflected the prevailing opinions of the times: Even in the late 1980s, many educators had difficulty imagining that the U.S. Congress would want them to integrate children with such severe disabilities as autism into general classes. It is worth noting here that nothing had changed in the law itself by 1986. What was different was the ways it was being interpreted.

Inclusion

Some special educators offered an even more radical view of this section in the late 1980s and during the 1990s. This third interpretation proposed that the law meant that students with *all* levels or severities of disabilities should be integrated with nondisabled students throughout the school day. Two words describe this third interpretation: *full inclusion* (Lipsky & Gartner, 1996; Stainback & Stainback, 1991; Taylor, 1988). It was immediately controversial, for much the same reason as REI had been: general educators, not to mention many special educators, were very skeptical that children with such severe disabilities as moderate to profound mental retardation and serious emotional disturbance could be appropriately educated in general classrooms.

What LRE Means

Actually, all three interpretations of the LRE section were, and are, wrong. This is because, as mentioned briefly above, the core ideas in IDEA are "appropriate" and "individualized." Each of the three successive renderings of what the law's LRE provision means proposed that *groups* of children having disabilities be placed in certain ways. This ignored the fact that the IDEA proscribes group placements. Rather, the law insists that placements be decided on a student-by-student basis, that is, individually. IDEA also guarantees each child with a disability an appropriate education. The three interpretations of IDEA's LRE language all overlooked this important fact.

IDEA

The Individuals with Disabilities Education Act (IDEA) tells us what to do when educating students with disabilities. Whatever your role in a public school—teacher, counselor, therapist, administrator, or parent—IDEA prescribes certain rights and privileges

Teacher Strategies That Work

Welcome to the Real World, II

Here's my day: I am in school officially from 8:20 A.M. to 3:00 P.M., but usually stay until about 6:00 P.M. I am usually planning/writing at home until 9:00 P.M., especially Mondays.

My student with behavior problems gets pulled out every day from 9:20 to 10:40. The student with cerebral palsy has occupational therapy for 40 minutes in the morning, 40 minutes of speech pathology before lunch, and 40 minutes of physical therapy at the end of the school day.

The three special-needs students get pulled out for 40 minutes every day for ESL. All 18 students have computer with me. They have science with another teacher in the afternoons. I get to teach them for one academic period in the morning and one in the afternoon.

This may sound like a dumb question, but how am I supposed to create a rhythm in my classroom, let alone teach the curriculum?

—Natasha

and proscribes others. Remarkably, it does all of this without ever mentioning, even once, the term "inclusion."

The text now turns to an exploration of the main ideas in IDEA, as it stands today. We start with a definition of the term "child with a disability." We do that because everything that follows assumes an understanding of who these children are.

Who Is a "Child with a Disability"?

Who are the early childhood/elementary and secondary students who are entitled, under IDEA, to receive an appropriate education in the least restrictive environment? The law calls each of them a **child with a disability.** The statute defines this term as follows, in section 602(3):

> a child (i) with mental retardation, hearing impairments (including deafness), speech or language impairments, visual impairments (including blindness), serious emotional disturbance (hereinafter referred to as 'emotional disturbance'), orthopedic impairments, autism, traumatic brain injury, other health impairments, or specific learning disabilities; and (ii) who, by reason thereof, needs special education and related services.

What This Means

The definition of a "child with a disability" has three parts, only two of which are obvious. It opens with the words "a child" by which it means a child between 3 years of age and exit from high school (typically between the ages of 18 and 21). We use the term **early childhood** to refer to children under age 9. At the other end of the range, when young people reach age 22, they "age out"—they are no longer "children with a disability."

The definition continues by offering a list of 10 categories or types of conditions. To be a "child with a disability," a student must have one or more of the 10 impairments. (The U.S. Department of Education requires states to report services provided to children who have one of 12, not 10, labels. The additional two are simply combinations: "multiple disabilities" and "deaf-blind." This reporting system complies with the law because children with one of those combination labels do in fact have "one or more" of the statutory 10 impairments.) Finally, and very importantly, being between the ages of 3 and 18 or 21 and having one of those conditions are not enough. The child must also "*need special education and related services*" because of the disability.

The terms "special education" and "related services" are discussed below. For now, note that "special education" means specially designed (custom-designed) instruction. This differs from standard, general education in that what is taught, how it is presented, and what the child does in class are all tailored to the child's unique needs. Thus, if a child has one of the conditions in the list but does *not* require special education, he or she is not a child with a disability under IDEA. This might include a child with a speech impairment, for example, whose condition does not limit her ability to benefit from general instruction. It might include a child whose epilepsy does not require specialized instruction. The term "related services" refers to non-instructional services a child needs to benefit from education. This might be services for a child with a hearing loss who, with the assistance of an FM assistive listening system, hears well enough to participate fully in the classroom. Similarly, speech and language pathology services are related services. (To anticipate a topic we will address at the end of this chapter, children who are not eligible under IDEA as "children with disabilities" may be eligible under another law, section 504.)

Why We Use Labels

The definition of "child with a disability" requires that children be given **labels** such as "deafness" or "specific learning disability." Unless children are assigned labels, IDEA funds may not be used to give them special services. This fact raises the sensitive issue of labeling children. Labels are controversial, and sometimes even harmful. Why, then, do we use them?

To Identify Children for Special Education Services

We use labels because only some children *qualify* for publicly financed special education services. To receive services under IDEA, children *must* be given a label. We use labels to identify eligible children and, by the same token, to exclude from publicly supported special education children who do not meet eligibility requirements. Thus, a child who is an "army brat" and for that reason has missed substantial amounts of schooling certainly needs supportive services. He is not, however, a child with a disability. We would serve him using other, non-special-education resources, for example, remedial instruction.

To Communicate Complex Ideas, Briefly

Educators also use labels because we need a way to *communicate* with each other in quite precise language. A good example is the first one given here: "deafness." What we mean when we use the label "deafness" is something very concrete. The U.S. Department of Education (1999a), in its regulations governing IDEA, defines the term this way:

> Deafness means a hearing impairment that is so severe that the child is impaired in processing linguistic, information through hearing, with or without amplification, that adversely affects a child's educational performance. (34 C.F.R. 300, section 300.7[c][3])

This definition contains 31 words. The definition refers to children who learn language principally through their eyes. As such, deafness differs from the broader term "hearing impairment," which is a loss of hearing that is not so severe as to impair significantly a child's acquisition of language. The definition of "deafness," then, calls our attention to the fact that the *educational* relevance of deafness lies primarily in its impact on the learning of language. A teacher could use the 31-word definition to explain this to another teacher. Alternatively, however, he or she could do that with just one word, deafness.

The labels "mental retardation," "emotional disturbance," and "specific learning disabilities," to name three other labels, similarly have very particular definitions. For example, educators use the term "mental retardation" when intellectual limitations of a certain severity occur during the developmental years (i.e., prior to age 18). They apply a different label when the age at onset is during the adult years (age 18 or later). As with the definition of deafness, this characteristic of labels—that they briefly and quickly communicate complex ideas—facilitates professional-to-professional communication.

The "Down Side" to Labels

As useful as labels often are, sometimes they can cause more harm than good. Educators and parents long have had an uneasy relationship with labels in special education. As far back as 1975, Nicholas Hobbs led a group of distinguished educators in exploring *Issues in the Classification of Children*. They were concerned about the accuracy of tests (especially the ways in which tests seemed to be biased against members of ethnic or racial minority groups), the use and misuse of labels, and similar matters. Such issues have continued to engage the attention of professionals and of parents in the years since that report was issued.

Labels May Communicate Information to Professionals, But Not to Others. While labels are useful for professional-to-professional communication as a tool of brevity, educators need to be sensitive to the fact that family members and many paraprofessionals may not know the nuances associated with those labels. In addition, labels may carry unintended meanings when used by professionals in communication with some members of culturally diverse backgrounds (Harry, Kalyanpur, & Day, 1999).

Stigma and Labels. Labels can be stigmatizing. This is especially true of such labels as "emotional disturbance" and "mental retardation." To illustrate, the national parent group representing families having members with mental retardation used to be known as the National Association for Retarded Children. Later, the organization changed its name to the National Association for Retarded Citizens, and then to The ARC. Today, it is known as The Arc of the United States. This latest nomenclature does not even hint at the word "retardation." The professional association in the same field, AMMR, formerly the American Association on Mental Retardation, has also been concerned about the label "mental retardation." For many years, the AAMR has conducted an intensive internal debate over those words.

A Myth About Labels. Some educators argue that we should not use labels because they stigmatize children (e.g., Stainback & Stainback, 1991). While that can be true, the more likely case is that the behavior of children with disabilities or delays calls attention to them and stigmatizes them long before labels are ever used (Kauffman, 1999). In other words, children stigmatize other children before adults do so with labels. We should not confuse effect with cause. The stigmas that are associated with labels results more from *our inappropriate use* of labels than from the labels themselves.

Labels Do Not Tell Us How to Teach. IDEA emphasizes the need for educators to identify and respond to the *unique needs* of children, not to their labels. The law does that for a reason: *labels do not tell teachers much about how to educate children.* That is, labels really are not very helpful in the classroom. Similarly, educators should not make placement decisions on the basis of labels (e.g., the U.S. Department of Education's [1999a] regulations on implementing the IDEA, at 34 C.F.R. 300[a][3]: "The services and placement needed by each child with a disability to receive FAPE [free appropriate public education] must be based on the child's unique needs and not on the child's disability."). That is, *educators should make decisions about what services to provide to a child, and on where to place that child, on the basis of the child's needs and not on the basis of a label.* Recall, for a moment, the "tale of two schools" in the beginning of this chapter (p. 5). Do you remember which principal said placement decisions would be made on the basis of labels? This is an example of how "clues" will be revealed to you as you continue through this text.

Labels of Convenience

Labels are something people give to children, not something children *have.* This distinction is important because educators at times will assign a false label to a child. This happens for political reasons. A good example is when parents refuse to allow their child to be assigned the label "mental retardation." This is a stigmatizing label in our society, so it is understandable that some parents will object to it. They may insist, instead, that the much less stigmatizing label "specific learning disability" be used instead. To take another example, the label; "emotional/behavioral disturbance" is fiercely resisted by many parents, who fear that others will blame them for having raised a child with such a condition. Rather than fight the parents, some educators give in and use a less-stigmatizing label. The fact that such "labels of convenience," to coin a term, do occur warns all of us not to make the mistake of assuming that children actually have the limitations that their labels claim they have.

"Delay" as an Alternative to Labels

As we will see later (see Part Two, p. 63), it is often the case with young children, especially preschoolers and children in the primary grades, that we just do not know precisely what is the problem. I recently observed the teacher whose story opens this chapter. A little girl in his class was working by herself, in a partially contained area. The teacher told me, during a break, that he was not sure why this girl had been unable, all year, to do much of her assigned work. A language other than English was spoken in the girl's home, he said. There were also domestic-discord issues at home. But did this girl also have an emotional or behavioral disorder? Certainly, she seemed to be highly anxious. She spent some 75% of the time I was there looking, not at her own work, but at the other children. She would then shyly glance at the teacher (or at me) and return to her task. Mere seconds later, she would be distracted again.

Making the decision, when she was just 8 years old, about whether she has a disability (let alone which disability) is problematic. She is, however, clearly developmentally delayed. **Developmental delay** is the label we use to describe an instance in which a child is developing through typical stages but more slowly than expected. An example might be a child aged eight who still clings to the mother's clothes when near strangers.

Delay: What It Means. Because of the stigmatizing nature of some labels, and to recognize the difficulty we often encounter with young children such as the little girl who spent most of her time watching other children, IDEA permits us to avoid the use of labels until children reach age 10. It does this in section 602(3)(B):

> CHILD AGED 3 THROUGH 9—The term "child with a disability" for a child aged 3 through 9 may, at the discretion of the State and the local educational agency, include a child—(i) experiencing developmental delays, as defined by the State and as measured by appropriate diagnostic instruments and procedures, in one or more of the following areas: physical development, cognitive development, communication development, social or emotional development, or adaptive development; and (ii) who, by reason thereof, needs special education and related services.

State Definitions. This language authorizes state governments to define the "delays" they will recognize as sufficiently serious as to qualify children for publicly supported special education services. The phrase "at the discretion of the State and the local educational agency" means that this decision to use "delays" rather than disabilities is *optional,* that is, not required. If a state selects this option, then all children who satisfy the state definition for delay in any given domain of development (cognitive, physical, etc.) would qualify for services. They would be, in other words, "children with disabilities" under IDEA. Note, however, that *if a state declines to adopt delays, LEAs may not, on their own, use delays to identify children.* Rather, the LEAs in that state must label children with one of the IDEA categories.

States were first permitted to elect the "delay" option during the 1997–1998 school year. The U.S. Department of Education's *21st Annual Report to Congress on Implementation of the Individuals with Disabilities Education Act* tells us that only eight states did this that year, and that just 1.3% of the children with disabilities in those states were identified with a delay rather than a disability-specific label (U.S. Department of Education, 1999c, iv). This may be evidence that educators tend to be fairly comfortable with labels, but more likely it reflects bureaucratic inertia: We should not be surprised if the number of states adopting this option and the number of children they use it with both increased in later years. The Department's *Annual Reports* are very valuable resources for you as a teacher of an inclusive classroom.

Person-First Language

Before we leave the topic of labels, a few observations may be helpful. Good practice is to adopt *person-first language* in your communications: child with a disability, individual

Teacher Strategies That Work

Using "Delay" as a Label

For more information on the U.S. Department of Education's Annual Reports, *go to the Web Links module in Chapter 1 of the Companion Website.*

Use "delay" when

1. The state permits use of delays in lieu of labels, AND
2. The child is under 10 years of age, AND
3. The developmental delay is sizeable enough to qualify under state rules (e.g., speech is 25% or more delayed compared to age norms), AND
4A. You are not sure what condition is responsible for the delay, **OR**
4B. You are confident of the underlying cause but the parents resist use of a specific label and/or the school district prefers not to use a specific label.

Labels are useful for professional-to-professional communication, when precision in terms is required, but may be harmful in other kinds of communication.

who has cerebral palsy, professor who is deaf, and the like. (A parking space may be handicapped, but people are not.) We use the term "disability" and not "handicap" to refer to the physical, mental, sensory, and other limitations that we encounter in special education. As for *when* to use labels, my practice is to use them in professional communication, such as in writing this textbook or in preparing reports for public agencies, that is, in instances where labels are necessary either for the sake of clarity of communication or for compliance with government rules—and *not* to use them in front of children.

Three Exceptions. There are three exceptions to the above rule that one should use person-first language.

The first relates to adults who themselves have disabilities. Just as it is acceptable for women (but not for men) to refer to other women as "girls," so, too, it is acceptable for persons with disabilities to refer to themselves and others by such terms as "crips" or "chairs." Some adults with disabilities have other reasons to use politically incorrect language. John Callahan, a syndicated cartoonist who uses a wheelchair, is one example. He deliberately uses shocking language as a way to "wake up" members of the general public, as in his book *Don't Worry, He Won't Get Far on Foot* (1990). The other exceptions have to do with the desires of people who are deaf and of those who are blind.

Individuals who are deaf and people who teach deaf children tend to be quite comfortable with the terms "deaf" and "deafness." During the late 1980s, while I chaired a Congressional commission that was examining the state of the art of education for deaf children and youth, I made a motion during a Commission meeting to adopt person-first terminology in all our reports. My motion was soundly defeated. That was because the deaf members and the hearing professionals alike who sat on the commission saw nothing wrong with such phraseology as "deaf people" or even "the deaf." The major self-advocacy organization in that field continues to call itself the National Association of the Deaf. Having been a member of that group for several decades, I cannot recall even one serious effort with the organization to change the name. In fact, the only change I have seen in recent years in the deaf community is the adoption by some people who were born deaf of the capitalized Deaf as their preferred term (distinguishing them from people who have hearing losses at the level of deafness but who do not share their passionate embrace of Deaf culture and of American Sign Language).

Similarly, the major organizations in blindness—the American Council of the Blind, the American Foundation for the Blind, and the National Federation of the Blind—have not changed their names in decades. I do not recall any time when any of these groups even entertained the idea of a name change. This reflects a level of comfort with the label "blind." In fact, the Federation proudly claims to be the "voice of the organized blind." Missing from that phrase, rather conspicuously, is any person-first sensitivity. Federationists do not think any is necessary.

Who Is Not *a Child with a Disability?*

Many children attending PreK–12 schools have special needs that are not related to disabilities, nor to developmental delays. Some come from families where other languages are spoken. These children may not have mastered the English language. Other children and youth lack important preparation because of personal or family factors, as when a serious illness keeps a child out of school for a lengthy period of time or when the family moves frequently. These children are not, for those reasons, children with disabilities. Rather, they are students in need of remedial services, which we may and should provide within the context of general education.

Some of these children may be at risk. In the IDEA, the term **"at risk"** refers to a child who does not have a disability and does not display a delay in development, but is perceived to be a child who might later develop a disability or a delay. This may be because the child's parents never completed high school or one or more parents is known to abuse controlled substances, among other possible factors. Unless and until a delay or a disability appears, however, the child is not a child with a disability. At-risk children are not eligible for special education and related services under IDEA. Infants and toddlers may be eligible for early intervention services under IDEA's Part C if the state in which the family resides elects to serve at-risk infants and toddlers. In other laws, the same "at-risk" term is used to refer to students who are at risk for school failure (see Chapter 11).

Least Restrictive Environment

We are now ready to examine what IDEA tells us about placement of children with disabilities. Recall that we said that the law does not even mention the word "inclusion." What *does* it say? The term the law uses to discuss placement issues is **least restrictive environment (LRE).** Here, in its entirety, is what the law says about LRE, in section 612(a)(5)(A):

> To the maximum extent appropriate, children with disabilities, including children in public or private institutions or other care facilities, are educated with children who are not disabled, and special classes, separate schooling, or other removal of children with disabilities from the regular educational environment occurs only when the nature or severity of the disability of a child is such that education in regular classes with the use of supplementary aids and services cannot be achieved satisfactorily.

This wording has remained unchanged since the law's original enactment in 1975 (PL 94-142). In fact, a Member of Congress once commented, during a public hearing on a reauthorization of this law: "You know, we can't change even a comma in this [passage]." He was correct (for rather obscure political reasons). The point is that this language, however confusing it may be, is very unlikely to be changed at any time in the foreseeable future. Accordingly, we need to understand it so that we may comply with its dictates. This means the paragraph deserves a lengthy and highly specific discussion.

What "LRE" Means

Let us begin by noting that this paragraph is the single most controversial provision in IDEA. Knowledgeable observers differ, often dramatically, in their interpretation of this passage. All I can do (all anyone can do) is to explain what I believe the paragraph means.

The LRE paragraph is the part of the law that tells states what they must do in order to qualify for federal financial assistance under the IDEA. Thus, the paragraph is to be obeyed by SEAs, which in turn assure the compliance of LEAs. The state agencies are told to be sure that when they provide financial assistance to LEAs, they do so in a manner that does not compromise the LEA's abilities to follow this LRE requirement.

There are really two parts to the quoted paragraph. If you mark the passage after the words "who are not disabled," you will divide it into its two sections. The first half of the paragraph is the part of most concern to us. It opens with five words: "To the maximum extent appropriate." These words are very important in understanding the LRE requirement. They remind us that IDEA *guarantees* all children with disabilities an education that is "appropriate." This assurance holds no matter where a child is placed. Thus, if a child with a disability were to be placed in a general classroom, but received there an education that was *not* appropriate (did not meet the child's unique needs), the LRE requirement would have been violated. This deserves repeating in different words: Children must not be put into settings where they will not receive an appropriate education, no matter how integrated such a setting may be. Yet again, in still other words, this time words written by the federal education agency: "Any setting, including a regular classroom, that prevents a child . . . from receiving an appropriate education that meets his or her needs . . . is not the LRE for that individual child" (U.S. Department of Education, 1992b, p. 49275).

Controversy

Looking now at the second half of the paragraph (beginning with ". . . and special classes . . . "), we find language that has confused whole generations of educators. On the surface, the wording might seem to say that children with disabilities should be educated in general classrooms and that they should be removed from such settings only when, and after, they failed to learn there. This is *not at all* what the language means. In order to appreciate this, you should re-read the second half of the paragraph, this time attending more to the language "only when the nature or severity of the disability of a child is such that education in regular classes with the use of supplementary aids and services cannot be achieved satisfactorily." This is, in my view, a complex way of saying what was said in the first part of the paragraph. The overriding rule is that these children must be given an appropriate education. If you see that such a child is not, and you cannot "fix" the instruction in that setting to make it appropriate, then you should find a setting where you *can* deliver an appropriate education.

Supplementary Aids and Services

Finally, notice the words "supplementary aids and services." (These words appear in the section 504 rules, as well. See "Section 504," p. 29) What does this mean? Section 602(a)(29) of IDEA defines the words in this way:

> The term "supplementary aids and services" means aids, services, and other supports that are provided in regular education classes or other education-related settings to enable children with disabilities to be educated with nondisabled children to the maximum extent appropriate in accordance with section 612(a)(5).

That helps. More useful, however, is guidance provided by the U.S. Department of Education, in its regulations interpreting the law (34 C.F.R. 300.28). These rules explain that **supplementary aids and services** means additional support services, beyond special education and related services, that may be required to assist a child to benefit from education. These may include itinerant teacher services, resource room services, and the like. Supplementary aids and services may also include assistive technology devices and assistive technology services, as well as the use of applied behavior analysis techniques.

To explain new terms mentioned above: **Itinerant teachers** are instructors who travel between different school buildings in a given school district, assisting children in these various schools. **Resource rooms** are special classrooms in regular school buildings in which small groups of children with disabilities receive tutoring and other supportive services. Some students spend the majority of the school week in resource rooms, receiving there not just tutoring but the bulk of their instruction in content subjects as well. Resource room services may also be "pushed-in" as when a resource room teacher comes to the child's classroom and provides instruction in the general classroom or an inclusion classroom. **Assistive technology devices** are hardware, software, and other technologies that help children with disabilities do the things that children with no disabilities do. For example, there are assistive technology devices that "speak" for the child, that "read" printed materials out loud, and so on. **Assistive technology services** are the steps that bring the devices to the child. These include identification of suitable products, acquiring those products, training the child and his teacher and parents to use it, repairing it, and the like. **Applied behavior analysis (ABA)** is a subset of behavior modification techniques. These include reinforcement of desired behavior and extinction of undesired behaviors. ABA and other behavior modification strategies will be discussed later in this book, notably in Chapter 9.

The point is that regardless of the fact that children with disabilities may be placed in general classrooms for most or all of the school day, they may still need, and if so must receive, other kinds of support. Supplementary aids and services, then, are steps that educators take to try to make general education settings more appropriate for children with disabilities. At times, they are exactly what is needed. Some educators prefer the term **supported education** over inclusion, in order to emphasize that what is needed for inclusion to work is the provision of needed supports in the general education environment (e.g., Hamre-Nietupski, McDonald, & Nietupski, 1992). At other times, no amount of such support services suffices to render an education appropriate under the law. In these latter instances, a change in placement may well be required. Such decisions are driven by the law's LRE paragraph, particularly by the words "to the maximum extent appropriate. . . ." These five words signal that the LRE mandate is subordinate in importance to the Act's guarantee of an appropriate education for all children with disabilities. *What really matters, under IDEA, is that each child receives an appropriate education; where that instruction takes place is relatively less important.*

A Principle, Not a Place

To answer now the question of what the least restrictive environment actually is, let us begin by saying this: *LRE is not a place. Rather, it is a principle* (section 601[c][5][C]). That it is a principle, that is, part of an overall educational philosophy, tells us to focus on the *process* and not just on the *product.* Stated differently, if we act to assure that a child receives an appropriate education, we have done our job—even if, as does sometimes happen, this child must be placed in a separate classroom in order to get such an education. In a review of legislation and litigation, Turnbull and Turnbull (2000) observed that "the courts more often than not chose the placement that offered the more appropriate education" over placements that offered more integration (p. 261). This reinforces the point: to adopt an analogy from card games, "appropriate" trumps "least restrictive."

The LRE Could Change. That the LRE is not a place also frees us to recognize what is in fact true: What the LRE is for any given child may be different from what it is for another child. Similarly, it could be different at different times for the *same* child. That is, the LRE

Resources That Work

Differentiating Three Key Terms

Special Education	***Related Services***	***Supplementary Aids and Services***
Adapted curriculum	Speech pathology	Resource room services
Adapted materials	Occupational therapy	Itinerant teacher
Adapted methods	Physical therapy	Behavior modification
Adapted modalities	Assistive technologies	Assistive technologies
	Sign-language interpreting	
	Counseling	
	Medical support services	

may change over time. The LRE for Julio during third grade may not be the LRE for his classmate Oween. It may not even be the LRE for Julio himself in fourth grade. Placement decisions are to be made on an *individual basis,* so much so that they may differ for a single child from year to year, or even within a single school year. If Oween's LRE in School District #14 is a regular classroom, but her family moves in mid-year to School District #15, Oween's LRE may *not* still be a general classroom. It may be that School District #15 does not have the kind of highly trained fourth-grade teachers that School District #14 has. The family may have to use due process procedures to secure a regular-classroom placement in the new district (see Chapter 2).

A Preference. A second important concluding observation is that LRE is a *preference.* All else being equal, we are to place children with disabilities into settings where they will be integrated with children who have no disabilities. This is because there are benefits associated with integration. However, as we have seen, all else may well not be equal. But if it is—if, that is, an appropriate education is available in two different settings—the fact that LRE is a preference instructs us to choose the more-integrated of those settings. (How to do that is discussed in "continuum of alternative placement options," in Chapter 2.)

Let me make all of this concrete. Consider one deaf child (we will call her Towanna). There is an excellent school for deaf children near Towanna's home. This special school was designed from the ground up to serve children who are deaf. All teachers, teacher aides, administrators, and even custodial staff sign; all alarm systems have both flashing-light and auditory signals; all phones are reachable through telecommunications devices for the deaf (TDD). Similarly, the deaf children attending this school do have opportunities to take the lead roles in school plays, to start on the athletic teams, and to serve as class president. Try as they may, neighborhood public schools which serve many hundreds of hearing children and one or a handful of deaf children cannot always assure that level of opportunity both in the classroom and in extracurricular activities. Towanna is not permitted, under the law, to attend that special school. This is because her local public school makes available, in separate classrooms and resource rooms, a level of instruction that is in fact "appropriate"—that meets Towanna's needs. It does not meet those needs anywhere near as comprehensively as does the special school. However, the issue is not one of comprehensiveness, nor of excellence. The LRE mandate requires that Towanna attend the local school because an appropriate education is available there. For her, a separate classroom in that school is the LRE.

Appropriate, Special Education, and Related Services

Other major ideas of IDEA include "appropriate," "special education," and "related services." We now define each of these important terms.

Appropriate

The core idea in IDEA is "appropriate." We have mentioned it several times in this chapter. The law guarantees that each child with a disability will receive an **"appropriate"** education. By that, it means an education that *meets each of the child's unique needs.* This mandate for an appropriate education is more sweeping than are IDEA's dictates about where these children are to be educated, or, for that matter, anything else.

The law introduces the term "appropriate" in IDEA's very first statement of its purposes. In Part A, section 601(d), the statute declares its initial purpose as being

> to ensure that all children with disabilities have available to them a free appropriate public education that emphasizes special education and related services designed to meet their unique needs and prepare them for employment and independent living.

We next encounter the term "appropriate" when IDEA defines the term "free appropriate public education." It does this in section 602(8):

> special education and related services that—(A) have been provided at public expense, under public supervision and direction, and without charge; (B) meet the standards of the State education agency; (C) include an appropriate preschool, elementary, or secondary school education in the State involved; and (D) are provided in conformity with the individualized education program required under section 614(d):

This definition is not particularly useful to us. It explains, rather redundantly, that "free" means free to the family. It then adds that an "appropriate" education complies with the standards set by SEAs, including teacher certification as well as scope-and-sequence curricula for the level of PreK–12 education involved. Finally, somewhat more usefully, it notes that an appropriate education follows the guidelines set forth in the child's Individualized Education Program (IEP) (see Chapter 2).

Special Education

To understand what the law means by "appropriate" we need to look at two other definitions. These are for the terms "special education" and "related services" that we encountered in the Act's statement of purpose. Section 602(25) tells us that **special education** means

> specially designed instruction, at no cost to parents, to meet the unique needs of a child with a disability, including (A) instruction conducted in the classroom, in the home, in hospitals and institutions, and in other settings; and (B) instruction in physical education.

This definition helps us in several ways. First, it is our source for the knowledge that an appropriate education "meet[s] the unique needs of the child." Second, it revealingly indicates to us that an appropriate education may, in fact, be provided in a whole range of settings. Thus, the law's guarantee that children with disabilities will be given an appropriate education may be carried out in many different places. Almost parenthetically, then, IDEA tells us that inclusion is of less importance than is appropriateness. In other words, what really matters, under the law, is what we do with children—not so much where we do it.

Related Services

In section 602(22), IDEA defines "related services" as transportation and such developmental, corrective, and other supportive services (including speech-language pathology and audiology services, psychological services, physical and occupational therapy, recreation, including therapeutic recreation, social work services, counseling services, including rehabilitation counseling, orientation and mobility services, and medical services, except that such medical services shall be for diagnostic and evaluation purposes only) as may be required to assist a child with a disability to benefit from special education, and includes the early identification and assessment of disabling conditions in children.

Briefly, **related services** are non-instructional services. Notice that the definition tells us that an appropriate education will include whatever such services a child may need in order to "benefit" from education. This helps us to more fully appreciate the meaning of the key term "appropriate."

"Benefit"

What does "benefit" mean? This is important. Does it mean that the child with a disability learns as much, as quickly, as do his or her classmates who do not have disabilities? Or does it mean something else? To answer this critical question, we need to leave IDEA briefly and turn, instead, to a major decision by the U.S. Supreme Court.

In *Board of Education, Hendrick Hudson School District v. Rowley* (102 S.Ct. 3034), the Supreme Court ruled that an appropriate education is one that just "meets" the child's needs, that is, allows the child to be promoted from grade to grade. At issue was whether the Westchester County, NY, school district had to provide a sign-language interpreter for Amy Rowley, a young girl who was deaf. When the case was first litigated, Amy had successfully passed first grade, despite not having an interpreter. The Court's 1982 decision was based on the ideas we have just discussed, so its reasoning should be familiar:

> According to the definitions contained in the Act, a "free appropriate public education" consists of educational instruction specially designed to meet the unique needs of the handicapped child, supported by such services as are necessary to permit the child "to benefit" from the instruction. Almost as a checklist for adequacy under the Act, the definition also requires that such instruction and services be provided at public expense and under public supervision, meet the State's educational standards, approximate the grade levels used in the State's regular education, and comport with the child's IEP. Thus, if personalized instruction is being provided with sufficient supportive services to permit the child to benefit from the instruction, and the other items on the definitional checklist are satisfied, the child is receiving a "free appropriate public education" as defined by the Act.

The Supreme Court, noting that Amy had passed first grade without interpreting services, decided that she was receiving an appropriate education without them. The court reasoned that Amy was "benefiting" from instruction because she was promoted from first to second grade. Certainly, that is a low standard for "benefiting"—but it was the standard in 1982, and remains the standard today. The purpose of what is now IDEA, the court said, was to enable children with disabilities, such as Amy Rowley, to "get in the door"—it was *not* to assure her the "best possible" education, or anything approximating that level of instruction. The law sets a *minimum* standard for educating students with disabilities. Having said that, we note that IDEA does not limit quality on the upside. Thus, SEAs and LEAs *may* offer services that exceed the *Rowley* standard. Some SEAs do; California is an example.

Take a few moments to read the nearby box, "Resources That Work: The Story of Amy." It is based on R.C. Smith's 1996 book, *A Case About Amy*. Smith researched this important, but painful, story over several years. In his book, he makes us feel that we "get to meet" all the main characters in the saga. For anyone interested in deafness, in special education, or simply in a good story, I strongly recommend his book.

Concluding Thoughts on IDEA

Funding for Special Education

In dollars, the financial contribution of the different levels of government is comparable between general and special education. In both instances, LEA's have paid a bit more than 45% of the costs, SEA's paid about 45% as well, and the federal government chipped in between 5% and 10%. In 2001 and 2002, the federal share grew significantly. However, it is still lower than the local or state shares. This makes sense, given our country's tradition of governing education primarily at the local and state levels. At the federal level, student financial aid for college is the largest education program. Of the programs relevant to us in this book, Title I is the largest federal program. It is followed closely by federal funding for such general-education programs as Goals 2000 (the national law calling upon states to set higher academic standards), the School-to-Work Opportunities Act (authorizing work-study programs that help students to relate their learning to the world of work), and the Carl Perkins Vocational and Technical Education Act (authorizing vocational education). The next-largest federal education program, by dollars, is special education (Halpern, 1999; National Center for Education Statistics, 2000; Odden, Monk, Nakib, & Pincus, 1995).

SECTION 504

Before we conclude this chapter, it is important to add a few comments about a civil rights provision that helps us to serve children who are not eligible under IDEA. That provision is section 504. Section 504 has affected the education of children with disabilities for more than a quarter century. In 1990, another law, the Americans with Disabilities Act (ADA; 42 U.S.C. 12101 *et seq.*), gave persons with disabilities additional civil rights. However, the

Resources That Work

The Story of Amy

[Board of Education, Hendrick Hudson School District v. Rowley, 1982, 102 S.Ct. 3034]

Nancy Rowley, Amy's mother, contacted her local elementary school, the Furnace Woods Elementary School, in Westchester, New York, in the spring of 1976. This was 18 months before her daughter Amy would be old enough to begin kindergarten. Nancy believed that by giving the school more than a year to prepare, she was maximizing the chances that Amy would be well-served. Being deaf herself, Nancy instinctively used a letter to make her case, so that she could be sure that her requests would be clear. As a teacher, she knew that bureaucracies act more quickly on formal written communications than on spoken ones. Nancy wanted no one to misunderstand her: Amy Rowley was a deaf girl, with deaf parents, whose native language was American Sign Language. Amy needed an interpreter in order to function well in a class filled with hearing children and taught by a hearing teacher. To buttress her argument, Nancy also sent an article by two nationally prominent experts in deafness, McCay Vernon and Hugh Prickett, both of Western Maryland College. The article, "Mainstreaming: Issues and a Model Plan" (1976) noted that lipreading was a very imperfect means of receptive communication: "If he [the deaf student] is a good lip reader, he may get from 5 to 20 percent of what the teacher says when the teacher's lips can be seen" (p. 10). That was under the best of circumstances; when the teacher moves around the classroom, or when other children speak, a deaf student understands even less. The facts, Nancy thought, were indisputable, and she fully expected Assistant Superintendent Charles Eible and Principal Joseph Zavarella to agree.

They did not. For an entire year, neither responded to Mrs. Rowley's letter. In the spring of 1977, they finally acknowledged her letter, telling Nancy that Amy could begin kindergarten that fall, but without the services of an interpreter. The following year, a District Committee on the Handicapped (today it would be called an Individualized Education Program [IEP] team) planned Amy's first-grade year—again without an interpreter.

Thus the battle was set. Cliff and Nancy Rowley requested a due process hearing. At that hearing, held in December 1978, they and the school presented their different views. The hearing officer sided with the school. Undeterred, the Rowleys appealed to the state review officer, a chief state schools official in the state, and he, too, agreed with the school in the spring of 1979. The Rowleys, as was their right under the law (then called the Education for All Handicapped Children Act), appealed to the federal district court level. Finally they won: In January, 1980, district court judge Vincent Broderick ruled that Amy was, indeed, entitled to an interpreter. He ordered the Furnace Woods Elementary School to provide her with one. Thus, at the beginning of her third-grade year, Amy finally got an interpreter.

But not for long. The school promptly appealed to the U.S. Court of Appeals. That court affirmed the district court decision. The school again appealed, this time to the U.S. Supreme Court. That Court agreed to take the case. Amy was now in the midst of her fourth-grade year. She continued to enjoy the use of an interpreter, under court order. That summer, in June 1982, the Supreme Court reversed the lower court rulings. Amy, it said, was *not* entitled to an interpreter. In brief, the Court reasoned that during Amy's first-grade year (when she did not have an interpreter), Amy successfully completed her work and was promoted to second grade. Thus, the education she received, *sans* interpreter, was in fact an "appropriate" one.

Therefore, Amy would not receive an interpreter for her fifth-grade year in the Hendrick Hudson School District. Cliff Rowley did what any father would do. Because no further legal proceedings were possible, he began to look for a school district which would be willing to provide an interpreter for Amy. In Mountain Lakes, New Jersey, he found one. The Rowleys moved in time for Amy to begin sixth-grade the following September. That school year, and every school year thereafter until Amy was graduated from high school, the public schools of Mountain Lakes gave her an interpreter (Smith, 1996).

Amy went on to complete college at Gallaudet University, in Washington, DC. She also earned a master's degree at Western Maryland College (now McDaniel College). While I was writing this book, Cliff e-mailed me to tell me she now lives in Wisconsin, is married, and teaches American Sign Language at the University of Wisconsin, Milwaukee, campus.

ADA explicitly declared that it did not amend, in any way, section 504. Thus, section 504 remains an important law for educators to understand and obey.

Two years before what is now IDEA was first enacted in 1975, Congress passed the Rehabilitation Act of 1973 (PL 93-112). The final section of that statute was a one-sentence statement to the effect that, henceforth, no American with a disability could be discriminated against simply because he or she was disabled, at any program that received federal funds. Section 504 thus is a *civil rights* declaration. It is not a publicly funded service program, so it carries with it no federal financing (schools may receive some state and/or local funding to help defray costs of serving children under section 504). Rather, it tells recipients of federal grants, notably including every public school system in the nation, as well as virtually every one of the country's 3,000-some colleges and universities, thousands of public libraries, and hundreds of airports to cease and desist in any acts of discrimination on the basis of disability.

In 1973, and even as late as 1977, when federal regulations were issued to explain the meaning of section 504, people did not quite know what to make of this one-sentence civil rights statute. What acts are discriminatory? Which acts are not? Who exactly are "handicapped persons" (the original term; the current one is "individuals with a disability")? And, of particular concern to PreK–12 educators, how does section 504 relate to IDEA? In 1977, the federal agency in charge of carrying out both section 504 and PL 94-142 answered those questions. In April of that year, the U.S. Department of Health, Education, and Welfare (HEW) issued its regulations governing section 504 (34 C.F.R. 104 has the current edition of these rules, as they apply to the U.S. Department of Education, a successor agency to HEW). In August of the same year, HEW released its rules articulating PL 94-142 (34 C.F.R. 300 has the current version of those regulations).

Section 504 and IDEA

In general, the relevance of section 504 to general and special educators today is that it provides a basis for instructing children with disabilities who do *not* qualify for services under IDEA. If you recall (you may refer back to "Child with a Disability" earlier in this chapter, p. 16), the IDEA definition includes a *list* of conditions, and also requires that children with one or more of these conditions *need special education and related services.* What happens to children who have medical conditions that are not on this list? What about children with IDEA-listed conditions who need such related services as physical therapy, but who do not require special education? In both instances, the children may be served under section 504. In fact, most children who are served under section 504 need "related services" because of their disabilities (e.g., students with cerebral palsy often require both speech pathology services and physical therapy services). To clarify this distinction, consider that all children who are eligible for services under IDEA are also eligible for protection under section 504, but the reverse is not true: some children who are eligible under section 504 are not eligible under IDEA. (See "Resources That Work: Section 504".)

The Section 504 Definition

Section 504 defines "individuals with a disability" in a three-prong definition. Bear in mind that this is, after all, a civil rights term; the definition reflects that. It is not a definition intended to define who may or may not receive publicly funded services. Children who qualify under this definition are sometimes, rather colloquially, referred to as **"504 children."** Briefly, the section 504 definition contains no list of conditions. It also contains no statement about "needing" special education and related services. These features of the definition are the "windows" that permit educators to serve children with disabilities who cannot be served under IDEA.

The three prongs of the section 504 definition provide that people may be eligible for protection against discrimination if they meet one of three tests: (1) they have a permanent medical condition that significantly limits one or more major life activity (going to school is a major life activity for children); (2) they do not have such a condition but they once did; or (3) they do not have such a condition but officials at publicly funded programs treat them as if they did. These prongs make sense if you bear in mind that the idea behind section 504 is that people could be victimized by discrimination in several ways. First, they could be denied services they need because of their disabilities. Second, they could be refused employment or other benefits and services because of something in their past—the fact that at some prior time they had a heart attack, cancer, or some other condition. Third and finally, they could be discriminated against because someone wrongly assumed that they had a disability. An example of this might be an individual who uses a hearing aid and with the aid's assistance hears well but who is incorrectly assumed to be deaf and for that reason is denied services.

Resources That Work

Section 504

Subpart D—Preschool, Elementary, and Secondary Education [Excerpts]

Source: 34 CFR 104.31 *et seq* (as most recently revised, *Federal Register,* "Nondiscrimination on the Basis of Disability in Programs and Activities Receiving Federal Financial Assistance," July 1, 1998, pp. 344–347).*

Sec. 104.3 Definitions.

(j) Individual with a disability means any person who (i) has a physical or mental impairment which significantly limits one or more major life activities, (ii) has a record of such an impairment, or (iii) is regarded as having such an impairment.

Sec. 104.33 Free appropriate public education.

(b) Appropriate education. (1) For purposes of this subpart, the provision of an appropriate education is the provision of regular or special education and related aids and services that (i) are designed to meet individual educational needs of individuals with disabilities as adequately as the needs of nondisabled individuals are met and (ii) are based upon adherence to procedures that satisfy the requirements of sections 104.34, 104.35, and 104.36.

(2) Implementation of an individualized education program developed in accordance with the Individuals with Disabilities Education Act is one means of meeting the standard established in paragraph (b)(1)(i) of this section. . . .

Sec. 104.34 Educational setting.

(a) Academic setting. A recipient to which this subpart applies shall educate, or shall provide for the education of, each qualified individual with a disability in its jurisdiction with individuals who are not disabled to the maximum extent appropriate to the needs of the individual with a disability. A recipient shall place an individual with a disability in the regular educational environment operated by the recipient unless it is demonstrated by the recipient that the education of the individual in the regular environment with the use of supplementary aids and services cannot be achieved satisfactorily. . . .

(b) Nonacademic settings. In providing or arranging for the provision of nonacademic and extracurricular services and activities, including meals, recess periods, and counseling services, physical recreational athletics, transportation, health services, recreational activities, special interest groups or clubs sponsored by the recipients. . . .

Sec. 104.35 Evaluation and placement.

(a) Preplacement evaluation. A recipient that operates a public elementary or secondary education program shall conduct an evaluation in accordance with the requirements of paragraph (b) of this section of any person who, because of a disability, needs or is believed to need special education or related services before taking any action with respect to the initial placement of the individual in a regular or special education program and any subsequent significant change in placement.

(b) Evaluation procedures. A recipient to which this subpart applies shall establish standards and procedures for the evaluation of individuals who, because of a disability, need or are believed to need special education or related services which ensure that: (1) Tests and other evaluation materials have been validated for the specific purpose for which they are used and are administered by trained personnel in conformance with the instructions provided by their producer; (2) Tests and other evaluation materials include those tailored to assess specific areas of educational need and not merely those which are designed to provide a single general intelligence quotient; and (3) Tests are selected and administered so as best to ensure that, when a test is administered to a student with impaired sensory, manual, or speaking skills, the test results accurately reflect the student's aptitude or achievement level or whatever other factor the test purports to measure, rather than reflecting the student's impaired sensory, manual, or speaking skills (except where those skills are the factors the test purports to measure.)

*Technical Note: The *law* uses the term "individual with a disability" while the *regulation* adopts the term "individual with a handicap." To avoid confusion, the author of this text adapted the above passage, using the language that appears in the Rehabilitation Act. For this reason, the above passage is slightly different from the federal rule.

How Schools Use Section 504

In the public schools today, the most frequent use of section 504 is to give children related services such as occupational or physical therapy, sign-language interpreting, and so on, when the children do not also need specially designed instruction. Thus, a child with a physical disability may learn as well and as rapidly as do other children, so does not require special education, but still does need the help of an occupational therapist to master self-feeding and self-dressing. Children and youth with attention deficit hyperactivity disorders (discussed in Chapter 3) frequently are identified as "section 504 children" because they require supplementary aids and services (defined on the previous page),

Resources That Work

IDEA v. Section 504

	Section 504	**IDEA**
Title	Rehabilitation Act	IDEA
Purpose	Nondiscrimination	Special education
Eligibility	Has a condition, did have one, or is falsely thought to have one.	Has a condition on the federal list; needs special education and related services; and is between the ages of 3 and 22
Applies to	Education (general)	Special Education
Implementation	IEP or "Section 504 Plan"	IEP
Local Official	Section 504 coordinator	District director of special education
Federal Enforcer	*Office for Civil Rights (ORC)* U.S. Department of Education	Office of Special Education Programs (OSEP) U.S. Department of Education

occasional tutoring, strategy instruction, and other services, but do not typically require the modified curricula, materials, and methods that constitute special education. Note that supplementary aids and services are included among the services schools must provide to "section 504 children." (See section 104.34 in "Resources That Work: Section 504.")

A second important use of section 504 is to protect children from discrimination by educators and by other children. An example is a child who is HIV-positive. People who test positive for the virus that causes AIDS do not necessarily have any symptoms and thus do not have any special instructional needs. Such needs surface after AIDS itself develops. While they are symptom-free, however, they may be harassed or shunned because of their HIV+ status. Such adverse actions are what section 504 is designed to forestall or prevent. Thus, if a child who is HIV+ were to be refused permission to join a French Club, the child and her parents would have a right of action against the school. Section 504 is what gives them that right.

The section 504 regulations note that Individualized Education Programs (IEPs) represent one way in which children may be served (34 C.F.R. 104.33[b][2]). Related services a child needs could be listed in such a plan. As an alternative, schools may prepare "504 plans," which are similar to IEPs but generally shorter and simpler.

CHAPTER SUMMARY

Inclusion

- Inclusion is an approach that balances competing priorities: the child's needs and the ideal of integration.
- Full inclusion is a more extreme position. It calls for *all* children with disabilities to be educated in general classrooms *all* the time.

How Education Is Governed

- The federal government dictates to state and local governments about special education. This is primarily because, for most of our country's history, children with disabilities were not educated appropriately.
- Title I is the major federal program that funds supplementary services for children from low SES families.
- *PARC* and *Mills* are the landmark court cases that led to IDEA.

IDEA

- IDEA defines "child with a disability" according to the child's age, the child's disability (label), and the child's need for special education and related services.
- Under IDEA, children may not receive special education services unless they are first given a label. "Delay" may be used as a label for this purpose.
- Labels also facilitate communication between professionals.
- Person-first language opens with nouns such as "children," "teachers," and "pilots." Only then is the disability mentioned.
- Educational decisions are to be based upon a child's *needs,* not upon a label.

Least Restrictive Environment

- IDEA's language about least restrictive environment (LRE) has not changed since the law was first written in 1975. What people *think it means,* however, has changed from mainstreaming to the Regular Education Initiative to inclusion.
- Often overlooked when educators talk about LRE is the fact that IDEA mandates that placement decisions, no less than other education decisions, be made on an *individual,* case-by-case basis.
- Supplementary aids and services are supports that help children with disabilities to succeed in regular educational environments.
- LRE is a principle. It is also a preference. However, another principle—that of "appropriate"—is more important than is LRE.

Child Protections

- IDEA guarantees that every child with a disability will receive an "appropriate" education, by which it means instruction and related services that meet that child's unique needs and that are outlined in an Individualized Education Program (IEP) written specifically for that child.
- Section 504 is a civil rights statute, one that provides for nondiscrimination on the basis of disability. Schools often use section 504 to serve children who are not eligible for IDEA services.

QUESTIONS FOR REFLECTION

1. Why do you think the Hasta Vista school is likely to do well with inclusion? What did the principal say that gives you confidence in the school's chances of success?
2. What are the major roles played in public education by state education agencies (SEAs)? By local education agencies (LEAs)?
3. How does the "general welfare" clause in the U.S. Constitution justify a federal law for special education? Why was such a justification needed?
4. What are the three elements to the definition of "child with a disability"? How can those components help you to make the decisions you will have to make about who is eligible for special education services?
5. Why is it important to make decisions based on children's needs and not based on their labels?
6. How can "supplemental aids and services" help us to "do" inclusion?
7. How does "mainstreaming" differ from "inclusion"?
8. In your own words, what is an "appropriate" education?
9. How does the three-part definition in section 504 of "individual with a disability" differ from the definition in question 4? Why is that difference potentially significant for a child who moves about in a wheelchair but learns in the same ways, at the same pace, and with the same materials as do ambulatory children?
10. What kinds of children may be eligible for services under section 504, but not under IDEA?

Chapter 2 *From Identification to Placement*

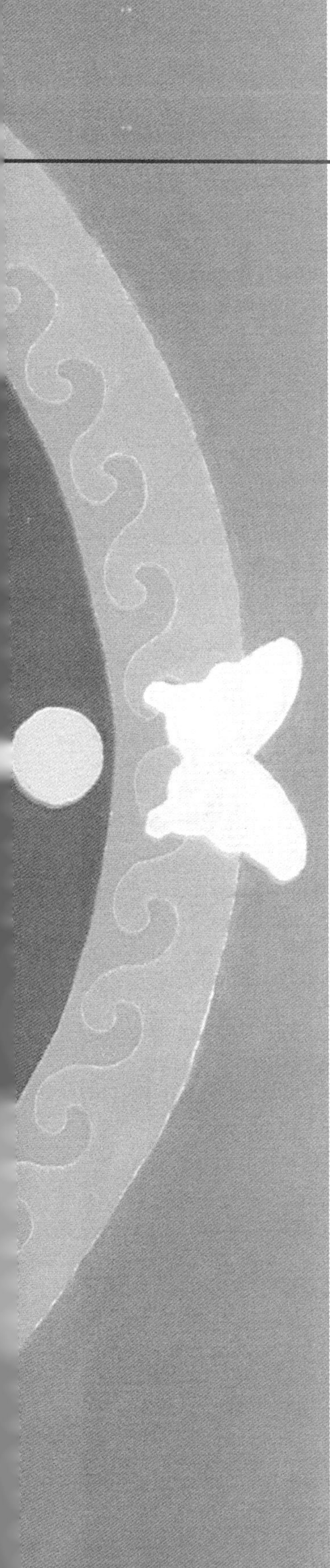

TERMS

referral
unique needs
pre-referral interventions
advance organizers
identification
Child Find
assessment
culturally sensitive
culturally competent
socioeconomic status (SES)
evaluation
Individualized Education Program (IEP)
extended school year (ESY)
due process

CHAPTER FOCUS QUESTIONS

After reading this chapter, you should be able to answer such questions as:

1. What kinds of pre-referral interventions may general educators try in general classrooms?
2. What are the major issues today with respect to identification of children for special education services?
3. When do teachers refer children for evaluation?
4. Why is overreferral of minority children, especially boys, into special education a concern?
5. What are the key components of an Individualized Education Program (IEP)?
6. How do educators decide "how much is enough" in the way of services for children?
7. How does IDEA's "LRE preference" play out as educators make placement decisions?

PERSONAL ACCOUNTS

An experienced teacher described this "introduction to inclusion":

> *Well, in mid-March, the principal announced that all of our fifth grade classes will "go inclusion" in September. It turns out that he and the district director of special education went on a few site visits last fall before we were even told about anything. We (the teachers) were not at all pleased about how the district planned and decided to move ahead. We had our first inclusion meeting the other day (April 2nd). The resource room, reading, and speech teachers were there, too. We briefly talked about the type of children who would go into the class. No decisions were made and hardly anything was accomplished. There was a lot of talking in circles. I did come right out and ask, "How are we defining inclusion?" I said that my idea of inclusion was a regular teacher and a SPED teacher collaborating together in one classroom. The resource room teacher laughed at that comment. She said there wouldn't be any chance of that happening! At most, she said, she would probably come into the room for one period each day. I learned later that there are no plans to train us in inclusion. We will be asked to make a decision: Teach in an inclusion class or leave the grade. It is coming no matter what.*
>
> —Lara

A teacher who was graduated from the Hofstra teacher-training program shared her concerns about one student's placement in her inclusive classroom:

> *I teach a first-grade class. One of my students has autism. He does not speak at all, not even one word. He has a one-on-one teacher assistant who works with him. Most of the time, she teaches him things the rest of us in the class are* not *working on. A lot of this is tracing work: he traces what she draws. This really bothers me—if he's in our class, he should be doing what we're doing. It also upsets me that the* least *well-trained adult in the room is the one who works with this child, the child who has the* most *challenging needs.*
>
> *At this point, in the middle of the school year, he can finally write his name. If you ask him to point to a number up to 20, he can do that. That's about it. There's* nothing *else that he has learned this year, at least not that I am aware of. He's clearly not "with us" despite being in the room every day. He's here because of his mother. She has been known to tell people that he is not autistic. The principal of our school never goes against the parents, so he's included simply because the mother is in denial.*
>
> *I plan to tell the IEP team that I believe the placement is not providing an "appropriate" education for this little boy at this time. We have done all we can in my classroom to make the placement work, and it hasn't worked. I hope that the parents and my principal realize that it is not always possible to meet the needs of a child in an inclusive setting. This is, after all, why the federal regulations require that a full spectrum of placement options be available. Some children, at some points in their PreK–12 years, simply need the more intensive services that are available in other settings.*
>
> —Shalinie

INTRODUCTION

General and special education teachers, as well as teachers-in-training, consistently report that they want, and need, specific information in order to succeed in inclusive classrooms (Austin, 2000; Kamens, Loprete, & Slostad, 2003; Langone, 1998). This chapter addresses key "skills and knowledge" areas rated as important by teachers and teachers-in-training. Educators first make preliminary identifications of children who seem to be struggling to learn. They initiate *pre-referral interventions,* or steps to try to resolve those problems in the regular classroom. Formal *identification* occurs when a teacher believes that the child's problems may be disability related. Identification includes Child Find, teacher identification, and pre-referral interventions in the regular classroom. Because so many concerns have been expressed about issues related to race, ethnicity, and other "diversity" issues at the identification stage, we devote considerable attention to these matters in our discussion of identification.

Once a child has been identified as potentially eligible for services under the Individuals with Disabilities Education Act (IDEA), the next step is a **referral** for evaluation. If the IEP team (in some school districts, this is called a multidisciplinary team or MDT) agrees to accept the referral, it notifies parents and solicits their permission for *evaluation.* The purpose of evaluation is to establish eligibility for IDEA services.

If the evaluation shows that the child is, indeed, eligible for IDEA services, an *assessment* is then performed. Assessments seek to identify the child's strengths and needs so that individualized instruction may be planned. That planning takes place during the process of writing an Individualized Education Program (IEP). Regular and special educators, as well as therapists, counselors, and other professionals help to write IEPs. It is a major responsibility of each. That is why this chapter includes an extensive explanation of the IEP writing process.

Finally, a placement team makes the *placement* of the child. The IEP team may be the placement team. In other instances, a separate team convenes to determine the placement. Obviously, placement is very important in any book about inclusion. The most important guideline for educators is to make placement decisions on a child-by-child basis, that is, individually. You will recall, from Chapter 1, that an appropriate education is "designed to meet their **unique needs**" (emphasis added). The unique needs of children with disabilities are the needs they experience in educational settings because of their disabilities. The use of the word "unique" highlights the fact that children with disabilities are different, one from another, and that the needs of each must be considered individually. No decision about a child may be made on the basis of the child's disability or on any other grounds save one: that particular child's needs (34 C.F.R. 300.340–350). This applies with special emphasis to placement decisions. The U.S. Department of Education's regulations for IDEA contain the following statement about individualizing placements, which is so important it is bolded here:

> **The overriding rule in this section is that placement decisions for all children with disabilities, including preschool children, must be made on an individual basis. . . . If the placement team determines that even with the provision of supplementary aids and services, the child's IEP could not be implemented satisfactorily in the regular educational environment, that placement would not be the LRE placement for that child at that time.** (34 C.F.R. 300.552)

PRE-REFERRAL INTERVENTIONS

If a teacher notices a child having a problem of some kind, the first step is to initiate interventions designed to help the child solve that problem. We use the term **pre-referral interventions** for measures that educators take in the regular classroom. It is, in many ways, an unfortunate term. The suggestion in the phrase is that referral to special education will follow those interventions. In reality, the intent actually is to *avoid* unnecessary referrals to special education. Rather, the goal is for the educator, perhaps aided by a child study team, a counselor, or a special educator, to "find out what works" in the regular classroom. One approach might be called: SHOOT-AIM-FIRE. That is, make a change. If it doesn't work, adjust your target and try again. The important thing is to *try something*.

What to try depends on what the problem is. A child who is continually out-of-seat may be given assignments, such as running errands, handing out worksheets, cleaning the blackboard, and so on. The child may also be allowed to stand from time to time, or even to walk around the room while reading an assignment. These examples illustrate the nature of pre-referral interventions: They are steps, often small ones, that teachers take in an effort to solve the problem *within* the regular classroom. Another pre-referral intervention is to give the child tasks related to the child's areas of interest. If Rosalie is fascinated by women's soccer, for example, the teacher might allow Rosalie to write about countries having outstanding women's soccer teams (geography), determine how many wins would be required for a third-place team to win the regular season title (math), and the like. Students who seem to be "low-achieving" or "at risk" may do dramatically better when given the opportunity to work in their areas of high interest (see Chapter 11).

Other pre-referral interventions include *scaffolding,* in which teachers give students some structure on which to "hang" the information they are learning. Scaffolding can be very useful in the teaching of literature, for example (see Chapter 14). Similarly, **advance organizers** such as the vignettes that open this book's chapters and the chapter summaries

Pre-referral intervention includes observations by a peer, followed by that peer's suggestions to the classroom teacher.

at the end of each chapter can help students to focus their attention. Both are tried-and-true methods from special education. They are helpful, however, for *any* child who is experiencing difficulty.

McCarney and Cummins (1988), in *The Pre-Referral Intervention Manual: The Most Common Learning and Behavior Problems Encountered in the Educational Environment,* offered a wealth of assistance. Nearly 200 problems are described in this book, with a dozen or more interventions outlined for each. In addition, teachers should talk with other educators, including those who worked with the child in previous years as well as others now teaching the child, for suggestions on "what works" with that particular child. If the child's problems are related to behavior, teachers could implement well-documented behavior-modification techniques, such as rewarding "good" behavior and ignoring "bad" behavior. Educators might meet with parents to share concerns and solicit advice. Teachers could also bring the child's problem(s) to the attention of a child study team (sometimes called a pupil personnel team; Pierangelo & Giuliani, 1998).

That the kinds of pre-referral interventions recommended by Pierangelo and Giuliani can be effective was demonstrated by Fuchs and Fuchs (2001), who provided expert help to Mainstream Assistance Teams in local public schools that "dramatically decreased special education referrals" (p. 1). The Fuchs recommended that teachers actively involve family members in helping to understand a child's behavior and in planning interventions that could be made both at home and at school. These researchers added that an essential element for success is "a key individual" (p. 12) in the school who places priority upon pre-referral interventions, makes sure that teachers receive the explicit guidance they need, and arranges for successful teachers to receive recognition. Teachers needed *practical and specific recommendations and recognition by administrators/peers/parents* for their efforts. Such steps were suggested by Fuchs, Fuchs, and Bahr (1990) in an earlier report on mainstream assistance teams. They include teacher-student contracts as well as techniques of behavior modification. Teachers need guidance on promoting student self-monitoring as well.

If such steps do not solve the student's problems, teachers may recommend that a child receive remedial instruction (say, in math or reading) and, if needed, in-school counseling. Educators may also refer a child for hearing and/or vision testing, as well as for a broader medical evaluation. You may refer the student to a school-based child study team for evaluation for Title I or other remedial services (see Figure 2.1). The National Center on Educational Outcomes (2001) offers an online document, "Crosswalk of Title I and IDEA

FIGURE 2.1 Steps from Identification to Placement

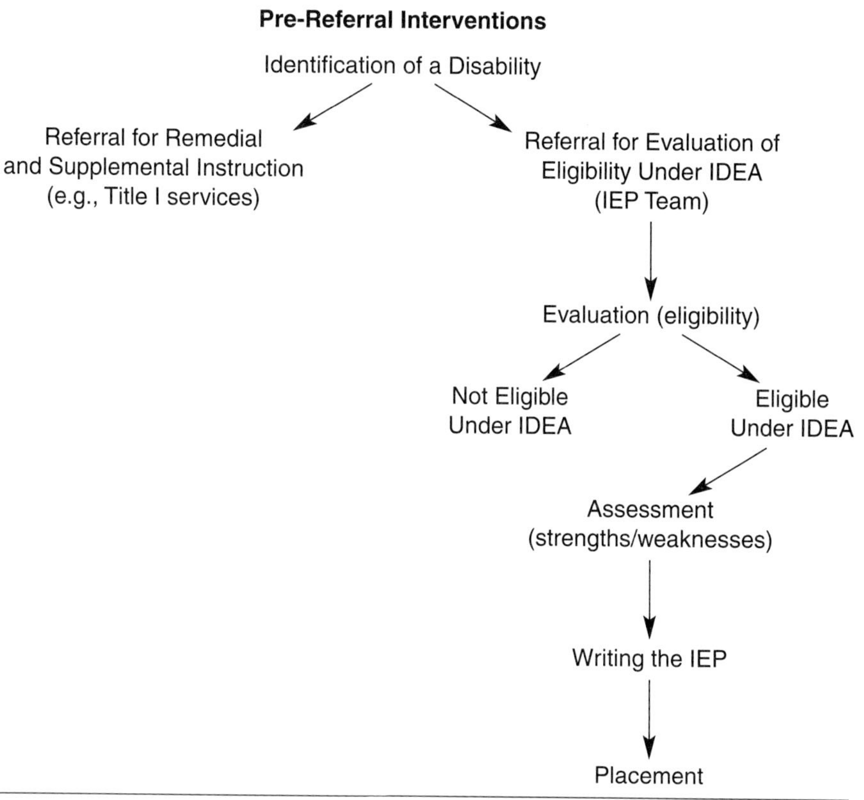

Assessment and Accountability Provisions for Students with Disabilities," that may help you to learn and follow the requirements of Title I and of the IDEA. Supplemental services such as remedial instruction keep the student within the general education "system." They are "pre-referral interventions" you should attempt before initiating a referral to special education.

IDENTIFICATION

We use the word **identification** to refer to the process of locating children who may be eligible for IDEA services. Some identification occurs as part of **Child Find,** the outreach and screening efforts through which public schools, working with hospitals, pediatricians, social service agencies, and parents, identify potentially eligible infants, toddlers, children, and youth. These steps are required by the IDEA (sec. 612[a][3] and sec. 635[a][5]; see also 300 C.F.R. 300.125 and 303 C.F.R. 321). Child Find was instrumental in bringing children with special needs into special education during the first decade after what is now IDEA was passed in 1975. In recent years, it has been less important in identification. This is because many children are now identified in other ways, notably through the early intervention services authorized by IDEA Part C (Infants and Toddlers with Disabilities) and by IDEA Part B Section 619 (Preschool Grants), through parent identification, and through teacher identification.

Most identification today occurs as a result of *teacher* identification. General educators notice that some children in their classrooms appear to be having particular problems. The teachers then monitor the children's progress, noting (among other things), What are the specific problems? When do the children usually have these problems? How often do these problems occur? These notes document educator efforts at *informal identification*. Teachers then take additional steps, referred to as *formal identification*. These measures include using teacher-made and other tests. The purpose of formal identification is to illustrate to educators that some children indeed have problems (McLoughlin & Lewis, 2001).

Identification by teachers continues with **assessment** (the process of gathering data so as to make a decision). We will have much more to say about teacher assessments in Chapter 10. For now, teachers collect information so as to understand *exactly what the problem is.* Questions asked include: Is this a problem related to attendance? To personal/family issues? To lack of effort? Or is this a disability-related problem? The focus is strictly educational. Teachers do *not* do these assessments to identify causes, nor to assign labels (McLoughlin & Lewis, 2001).

Informal Assessment

Educators may watch the child closely for a few weeks. Such observation is the most-used assessment technique, according to McLoughlin and Lewis. Teachers may notice that problems occur most often on Mondays or right after a vacation. This would suggest the possibility of problems at home. Teachers may try different teaching methods. If the child experiences problems when asked to read out loud, but not when asked to read silently, this may be an indication of a possible learning disability such as dyslexia. Alternatively, if the child has trouble following oral directions, but not when obeying written instructions, this suggests the possibility of deafness or other hearing impairment. Educators may give the child a number of tasks to perform. If the child has difficulty sustaining attention for more than a few minutes, or if she quickly becomes frustrated, there may be an underlying attention deficit hyperactivity disorder or perhaps an emotional disturbance (see Chapters 3 and 5).

There are other means of informal assessment. Educators may review the child's school records. These might indicate sporadic, attendance patterns, chronic lateness, or frequent disciplinary action. Such information may help the educator to understand that at least some of the child's problems may be personal/familial in nature. Teachers may make use of informants, that is, people who know the child. Teachers may meet with the child's other teachers and previous teachers. And they may meet with the child's family. Such informants may complete rating scales, questionnaires, and/or interviews. In these efforts, teachers may tell informants, "Khalid's academic performance this fall has been rather erratic. I am trying to understand why. I need your help. Anything you tell me will remain confidential. Thank you."

Formal Assessment

At times, further diagnosis is necessary. Teachers may then make use of formal diagnostic tests. Families must be notified, in advance, of plans to test children. These tests are in-

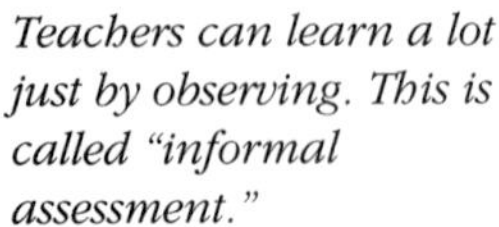

Teachers can learn a lot just by observing. This is called "informal assessment."

dividually administered. They are designed to identify not only whether there is a problem but also the specific nature of that problem. A good source on diagnostic instruments is that of Pierangelo and Giuliani (1998). These authors discuss intelligence tests, achievement tests, perceptual measures (visual, auditory, visual-motor, etc.), psychological instruments, speech/language assessments, and the like. In each case, specific tests are identified, addresses for test publishers given, tests described, and scoring measures outlined. Many of these tests may be given by teachers. Others call for administration by psychologists, speech-language pathologists, or other professionals.

Diversity Issues in Identification

Overidentification of children and youth occurs when educators mistakenly "identify" students as having disabilities when they do not. It is followed by overreferral, meaning that students are inappropriately referred to special education. Overidentification and overreferral are major, long-standing problems in American public education (e.g., Sorrells, Rieth, & Sindelar, 2004). Overton (2000), in his text on assessment, highlights these as national concerns. One issue, which affects identification of some disabilities more than of others, is gender. Teachers in K–12 schools tend to be female. Students who are classified as having disabilities, however, generally are male (see Figure 2.2).

Another reason that overidentification appears to occur is because some educators are inexperienced at differentiating disabilities from other factors (see "Resources That Work: What is NOT a Disability," on p. 40). To illustrate, some teachers are more tolerant of acting-out behavior than are others, and thus less likely to refer a child for evaluation on suspicion of attention deficit hyperactivity disorder (e.g., Greene, 1995; Tournaki, 2003).

Solving our diversity problems begins with steps to reduce overidentification. Recalling that most identification currently is done by educators, we must ask: Why does overidentification occur? In part, it happens because school administrators and teachers frequently lack training about economic, racial, ethnic, and other kinds of diversity. Too often, they are neither culturally sensitive nor culturally competent. Duarte and Smith (2000) went so far as to charge many educators with being culturally indifferent, that is, neither knowing much about cultural diversity nor caring much about it. **Culturally sensitive** educators have examined their own cultural biases and thus are attuned to the fact that other, equally valid, cultural beliefs exist. **Culturally competent** teachers have developed skills that enable them to relate well with people from other cultures. They know how

FIGURE 2.2 Gender of Secondary-Age Students with Disabilities, By Disability Category

Disability	Male (percent)	Female (percent)
Learning disability	73.4	26.6
Emotional disturbance	76.4	23.6
Speech/language impairment	59.5	40.5
Mental retardation	58.0	42.0
Other health impairment (Includes ADD/ADHD)	56.0	44.0
Deafness	54.5	45.5

Source: Table II-4, *Twentieth Annual Report,* U.S. Department of Education, 1998, p. II-26. Data source: *The National Longitudinal Transition Study of Special Education Students: Statistical Almanac,* Vol. 1, by K. Valdes, B. Williamson, and M. Wagner, 1990, Menlo Park, CA: SRI International.

Resources That Work

What Is NOT a Disability

You may notice learning problems and delays in development among your students. These should cause you to begin pre-referral interventions in which you try a variety of measures to help these students.

If those steps do not produce results, you may desire to refer the students to the IEP team for evaluation as children with disabilities. Before you do, however, it is important to rule out other possible causes. These will help you to reduce overreferral to special education.

The following are *not* indications of possible disability:

- The child comes from a Spanish-speaking family and, in tests administered in English, displays linguistic problems. These are not speech and language impairments (SLIs). If it is an SLI, the child will demonstrate linguistic difficulties in both languages. Before considering referral to the IEP team, arrange for the child to take language tests that are administered in Spanish. You may later arrange for the child to receive services from the school's program for Limited English Proficiency (LEP) services.
- The child appears listless and, at times, depressed. This probably is not emotional disturbance. Children may exhibit these feelings as a result of divorce, breakup with a boyfriend or girlfriend, or simply by virtue of being of middle-school or high-school age. Before referring the child to the IEP team, arrange for counseling and social work services.
- The child receives a score between 75 and 100 on an individually administered IQ test. This is not a child with mental retardation. To qualify for that label, the IQ test score must be below 70 or 75, and must be accompanied by behavior characteristics common to individuals who are mentally retarded.
- A teenager who lives in an inner-city housing project walks and talks in a manner that a suburban female teacher interprets as threatening. This is not emotional disturbance. Rather than referring this teen to special education, the teacher is better advised to talk with the student along the following lines: "In my classroom, you are not in danger. There is no need to use body language to signal your 'no fear' attitude. That attitude may well serve a functional purpose in your neighborhood, but it has no place here."

to adjust their teaching so that students from other cultural backgrounds are comfortable and ready to learn. They do not mistake linguistic needs for speech and language impairments.

Social Class

With respect to inclusion and to special education, the most important "diversity" characteristic is social class. Many educators, including many professors and researchers, think that the core issues in diversity are those of race and ethnic group status. However, the evidence is that overidentification and overreferral of minority-group members occurs primarily when family income and wealth are *also* involved, that is, when children come from families that are of lower socioeconomic status than is typical of the school district as a whole. That was a key conclusion from an impressive study by Oswald, Coutinho, and Best (2001).

For more information on the study by Oswald, Coutinho, and Best (2001), go to the Web Links module in Chapter 2 of the Companion Website.

A few words of explanation about **socioeconomic status (SES):** We say families are of "high SES," by which we mean that their wealth and annual incomes are higher than average, "middle SES," by which we mean having "middle class" assets and salaries, and "low SES," by which we mean being "poor."

Social class is a diversity issue because a far greater proportion of children with disabilities than the teachers who instruct them and than their classmates without disabilities come from low-SES families. Nearly three in every ten (28%) children aged 3 to 21 who have disabilities come from families having below-poverty income levels, according to the *National Health Interview Surveys* conducted by the National Center for Health Statistics (NCHS 1998), in 1996 (the most recent year for which data were available). That compares to 19% of children in the same age range who do not have disabilities (National Center for Education Statistics, 2000). The term "poverty" refers to family incomes in 2000 that were below $17,600 for a family of four (Lamison-White, 1997).

For more information on family incomes and national poverty levels, go to the Web Links module in Chapter 2 of the Companion Website.

Public school teachers, by contrast, have incomes that place them comfortably within middle-SES levels. To illustrate, the American Federation of Teachers (AFT), which annually queries state education departments, has reported that the average salary for K–12 classroom teachers in 1998 was $39,347. Some made more than $100,000 a year (AFL-CIO, 2000).

Low SES is associated with a number of factors that affect the education of children. First, many low-SES families are single-parent households, most headed by a woman. The NCHS data show that 62% of children with disabilities coming from such one-adult households lived in poverty (significantly more than the 38% of children with disabilities who came from two-parent households). Single-parent households often are under great stress as the adult juggles work, child-care, and many other responsibilities. One result is less time for parental assistance on a child's homework. Second, the women heading these one-adult families likely are not well-educated; in the typical case, they dropped out of high school after becoming pregnant (Lerman, 1996). When adults do not possess even a high-school diploma, studies have shown that their ability to help children to learn is limited (Brody & Flor, 1997).

For you as a teacher, these facts suggest that when you see a child having problems learning, you should look into the family's SES and head of household information as possible explanatory factors, rather than assuming that there must be a disability. Low-SES families may experience considerable stress (paying the rent, putting food on the table), especially when only one adult heads the household. Not surprisingly, children from such households may be anxious. That, in turn, may manifest itself in short attention spans, unwillingness to assign importance to academic matters, and even difficulty trusting adults. These considerations should focus your attention on ways you can help the child *outside* of special education. Until you have ruled out these factors, you should not entertain assumptions of possible learning disabilities, mental retardation, or attention deficits. If you wish to increase your sensitivity to the pressures faced by low-SES families, reading Barbara Ehrenreich's *Nickel and Dimed: On (Not) Getting by in America* (2001) and her earlier *Fear of Falling: The Inner Life of the Middle Class* (1990) will make you more aware of how middle-SES and low-SES families differ in their experiences.

Race and Ethnicity

The "white" nature of most K–12 schools is reflected in many ways (see Figure 2.3). Students are rewarded for sitting upright, working quietly, and speaking only when recognized. Verbal communication is acknowledged, but nonverbal communication often is ignored. Some African-American teens sit at angles, work with others, engage in call-and-response speaking behavior, and use nonverbal communication as an essential and habitual part of their expressive behavior. The conflict between these two norms of behavior shows up in grim statistics: more than members of any other racial group, African

FIGURE 2.3 What Makes Schools Seem to Be "White"?

Duarte and Smith (2000), among others, have complained about the "white" nature of many public schools. What do they mean by those accusations?

1. The fact that most principals and teachers are themselves white. It is not so much that they are white that bothers Duarte and Smith. Rather, it is that so few of these white educators are culturally *sensitive* to other ethnic and racial group norms. In fact, it is more even than that: they are concerned that so few white teachers *care* about cultural diversity and are willing to learn how to be culturally competent.
2. In fact, Duarte and Smith contend that there is a dominant discourse within our public schools which "sanctions" and thus propagates cultural ignorance. They see this as a "power play" in which the dominant white culture imposes its will within the schools.
3. The almost Teutonic obsession of public schools with starting "on time" is another concern. Some racial and ethnic cultures have a different perspective on time, such that it is more important that all expected participants are present before the meeting begins than it is that the session start at some predetermined time.

Americans are disciplined, suspended, and expelled (Townsend, 2000). They are also removed in disproportionate numbers from general classrooms by means of referral into special education. The two disability labels they are most likely to be given (mental retardation and emotional disturbance) also happen to be labels that are associated with placement into separate classrooms. The result is de facto, if not intentional, segregation by race (Artiles & Trent, 1994).

Among many African Americans, schools are "white" institutions, which makes them hostile environments (Duarte, 1998; Townsend, 2000). This may be why relatively few African Americans enter the teaching profession. While 17% of all K–12 students are African Americans (National Center for Education Statistics, 2000), just 8% of teachers are (Wald, 1996). In special education, the disparity is similar: 16% of students but 10% of teachers (Cook & Boe, 1995). Projections suggest that the divergence is widening, because just 9% of teachers-in-training were African American in 1995 (American Association of Colleges for Teacher Education, 1999). King (1993) also referred to the imbalance as extreme and worsening. Today, it is even more disturbing.

To illustrate, the U.S. Department of Education's *20th Annual Report to Congress on Implementation of the Individuals with Disabilities Education Act* (1998) observed that African-American K–12 students were given the label "mental retardation" at a 2.6% rate versus just 1.2% of white, non-Hispanic students, or more than twice as often. They were labeled with "emotional/behavioral disorder" at a 1.1% rate versus a 0.8% rate for white, non-Hispanic students. The same report indicated that 54% of students identified as mentally retarded and 32% of those labeled with emotional/behavioral disorders were educated in separate classrooms. These patterns are particularly troublesome because, as we will see later (Chapter 5), students with those two labels tend to be placed in noninclusive settings.

These facts should caution you to exercise care in interpreting behavior of African-American students, especially males. There are specific steps you can take to avoid over-identification. If you recognize that the natural mode of speaking for many African-American students includes body movements, and that the behavior for some African-Americans in church typically features call-and-response actions, you will be less likely to misinterpret their actions in your classroom as threatening or as disrespectful. You will not be insulted if they do not sit upright in class. You will not be bothered if they do several things at once. You will be more willing to give them opportunities to move about at frequent intervals throughout the day, thus reducing disruptions in your classroom (Townsend, 2000). All of these techniques will help you to educate these students in an inclusive setting while still meeting their needs. The nearby box, "Teacher Strategies That Work: Cultural Sensitivity and Cultural Competence," offers some guidelines.

Teacher Strategies That Work

Cultural Sensitivity and Cultural Competence

1. Consider your own cultural beliefs. Which of those are important to you in your role as an educator? Which could you bend or suspend, if needed, in deference to different beliefs on the part of students?
2. Learn a second language, especially Spanish.
3. If a child comes from a single-parent household, see if homework could be done at school and/or a later departure for home could be arranged, so the child has adult supervision while doing homework.
4. If the child comes from a single-parent household, consider telephoning the parent at times convenient to the parent, in lieu of face-to-face parent-teacher meetings.
5. If the child comes from a low-SES household, consider teaching/counseling the child to think in terms of long-range goals and to become skilled at deferring gratification.
6. If the child comes from a low-SES family, be sure the family is aware of Supplemental Security Income (SSI).
7. Provide opportunities for physically active, rather than in-seat, ways to demonstrate learning, especially for boys.

The child's work in the classroom is included in the materials that a teacher forwards to the IEP team in making a referral for evaluation.

REFERRAL

Referral to the IEP team is made when the teacher concludes that the appropriate next step is a formal evaluation of a child's possible eligibility for special education. (As mentioned earlier, this team has different names in different states. In New York State, it is called the Committee on Special Education. In other states, it is known as a multidisciplinary team, or MDT. Yet other states use different names.) The referral request must be accompanied by documentation. Included must be the child's name and other identifying information, the referring teacher's name, what problems the child is experiencing, why the teacher believes the child may be eligible under IDEA, and what pre-referral interventions the teacher made, with what results (including outcomes of any meetings with parents). The nearby box, "Teacher Strategies That Work: Identifying a Child with a Disability," offers some guidance.

IDEA requires that families be notified when the school intends to evaluate the child. The request is to be made in lay terms (understandable language) and in the family's native language, if feasible (34 C.F.R. 300.503, 505). Written permission from the family must be secured. Sometimes, parents, guardians, and other family members need reassurance about the nature and purpose of the evaluation and how results will be used. For this reason, teachers and IEP team members should give family members every opportunity to learn about the evaluation process before they are asked to consent to it. Despite such consultations, families at times decline to give their permission. In such instances, the school should ask for mediation and other due process measures, such as an impartial hearing, seeking the decision of an independent official to waive the parental consent requirement' (see "Due Process," p. 56; see also, Pierangelo & Giuliani, 1998). The school needs to take those steps because of IDEA's guarantee of an "appropriate" education for all children with disabilities. Schools cannot do so unless they know who those children are.

EVALUATION

Evaluation is the process of determining whether or not children qualify under IDEA as a "child with a disability." To be eligible, the student must meet the law's definitional requirements. Specifically, the child must be of school age (generally, between the ages of 3 and 22), have one of the disabilities recognized under the law, and, because of that disability, or those disabilities, need special education and related services (see Chapter 1).

Teacher Strategies That Work

Identifying a Child with a Disability

1. Is the child between 3 years of age and leaving high school?
↓ ↓
Yes No > If under age 3, the child may be eligible as an "infant or toddler with a disability" for IDEA Part C services. If graduated from or dropped out of school, the child may be eligible as an "individual with a disability" for section 504.

2. Does the child have one or more of these conditions: specific learning disability, speech/language impairment, mental retardation, emotional disturbance, other health impairment, visual impairment including blindness, hearing impairment including deafness, orthopedic impairment, autism, or traumatic brain injury?
↓ ↓
Yes No > If the child has a condition not on the list, could be eligible under section 504. If the child has non-disability special needs, may be eligible for general-education support services.

3. Does the child need special education and related services because of the condition?
↓ ↓
Yes No > May be eligible for related services and/or civil rights protection under section 504.

Most states have adopted the federal definition without change; some, however, have made (usually minor) alterations. You should check with your district director of special education about the state definition.

When mental retardation is suspected, the IEP team may order an individually administered intelligence test. This may be the Wechsler Intelligence Scale for Children (WISC-III; Wechsler, 1991), or some other such test (see Pierangelo & Giuliani, 1998). If emotional disturbance is possibly involved, the IEP team may request that a psychologist perform an evaluation. When a hearing loss is believed to exist, the IEP team may direct an audiologist to test the child's hearing. The team then assembles the reports, invites the testing professionals and the child's teacher(s) to comment, and applies the applicable definition so as to determine eligibility. The federal definitions for various disabilities are given in Parts Two and Three (Chapters 3–7).

If the child meets the requirements of a "child with a disability," then the IEP team must designate the child as eligible for IDEA services. The IDEA's guarantee of an "appropriate" education applies to *all* children with disabilities. No child, no matter how severely or multiply disabled, may be denied a public education. The most famous case in which federal courts reaffirmed this zero-reject principle was *Timothy W. v. Rochester School District,* a 1989 case involving a boy with very severe and multiple disabilities. The New Hampshire school district had requested permission to decline services to Timothy, on the grounds that he appeared to be uneducable. The federal appeals court firmly instructed the school district to find ways to teach Timothy. Even though the court recognized that a very individualized instruction was going to be necessary in order to help Timothy to learn, the court ruled that IDEA requires local schools to custom-design an education for him.

Once the child is determined to be eligible, the next step is for the IEP team to conduct an assessment. This is a more comprehensive data-collection process than is done by individual teachers (see "Identification," p. 37).

ASSESSMENT

Why do educators and IEP teams do assessments? There are four reasons. Two have already been discussed: to help teachers make pre-referral classroom decisions and to help IEP teams make eligibility determinations. The others: to help make post-referral classroom decisions and to support accountability/outcome decisions (Salvia & Ysseldyke, 1998). The

Program planning is greatly aided by teacher assessment of children's strengths and needs.

last is academic assessment, which we will address later. Our focus here is on the third use: assessment to help identify what should be done in the classroom after referral to the IEP team. McLoughlin and Lewis (2001) refer to this purpose as "program planning" (p. 8).

This use of assessment focuses upon the child's strengths and weaknesses. The IEP team wants to know what the child's unique needs are. It is also vital for the team to know what capabilities and resources the child possesses that may help him to succeed in school. These kinds of information are essential prerequisites for the preparation of an IEP. The team is attempting to identify the child's needs for special education services, for related services, and for supplementary aids and services. (All three were defined earlier in Chapter 1.) They are central components of the Individualized Education Program.

The assessment conducted by the IEP team is designed to answer such questions as: What is the child's school-related problem? Is the problem a function of the child's disability? How is the child performing academically (strengths/weaknesses)? What is the child's level of intellectual functioning? Of behavior functioning? What special-education services does the child need? What related services does the child require? What frequency/intensity of related services are necessary to meet the child's needs? What supplementary aids and services would be required to support the child in a regular classroom? (McLoughlin & Lewis, 2001). As you will see, the answers to these questions are needed before the IEP team can complete the plan.

INDIVIDUALIZED EDUCATION PROGRAMS

IDEA calls the annual planning document prepared for each child with a disability an **Individualized Educational Program.** This is usually abbreviated as IEP. General as well as special educators are expected to take part in developing and carrying out IEPs. Doing those things is a key component of the "skills and knowledge" teachers require. For that reason, we examine them in detail.

Planning, Writing, Implementing, and Revising IEPs

The meeting of teachers, related-services professionals, school-district personnel, and parents to plan an IEP may be a teacher's first encounter with a child who has a disability. At the secondary level, a teacher often will meet the child; at the early childhood/elementary level, a teacher will "meet" her through school records and the observations of current and past teachers and other personnel, as well as the parents. IEP meetings are held in the spring, usually March and April, in many school districts. They may also be called—at *any* time—by parents and/or by school officials, to review and/or revise the plan.

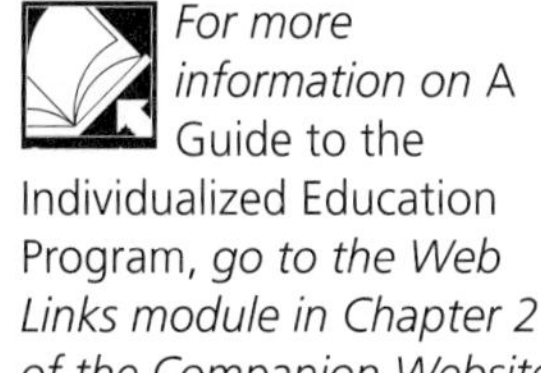

For more information on A Guide to the Individualized Education Program, *go to the Web Links module in Chapter 2 of the Companion Website.*

A CD-ROM on writing IEPs is offered by Prentice Hall/Merrill Education: *Developing Quality IEPs: A Case-based Tutorial.* In addition, *A Guide to the Individualized Education Program* has been provided by the U.S. Department of Education. While helpful, these materials are rather cursory in nature. The focus is more upon the mechanics of writing IEPs than on the thinking processes involved. Because the key is understanding how to write effective IEPs, this section focuses upon how and why educators do what they do when they write IEPs.

The IEP Team

Who is on an IEP team? The U.S. Department of Education's regulations (34 C.F.R. 300.344) explain that membership consists of

1. the child's parents;
2. at least one general education teacher (if the child is, or is expected to be, taught in general classes for at least part of the school day);
3. at least one special educator;
4. a representative from the school district;
5. someone who can explain evaluation results (this could be 2, 3, or 4, above);
6. others whose presence is desired by parents and/or school officials (this might include, for example, such related-services personnel as a speech/language pathologist); and
7. the child, if appropriate (generally, if age 14 or older and able to participate meaningfully).

Ideally, the child's current teacher(s) *and* the teacher(s) expected to work with the child during the following school year will attend these meetings. Beginning when the child is 16, or earlier if suitable, a state or community agency that will offer post–high-school services may also be represented on the IEP team (because that agency needs to agree to pay for such services).

In many instances, the IEP team contains between 6 or 7 people. The U.S. Department of Education has argued that small groups are better than large ones, for several reasons. First, parents are more likely to participate actively in small groups but may be intimidated in large ones. Second, the meetings themselves are much easier to set up when only a few people's schedules must be coordinated than when many persons' time must be arranged. Third, small meetings are less costly to school districts, simply because virtually all participants are salaried personnel. Finally, small meetings tend to be more productive and less "political" (U.S. Department of Education, 1992a, p. 44835).

The Teacher's Role on the IEP Team

For our purposes in this book, the involvement of teachers is of most interest. IDEA calls for the participation of "at least one regular education teacher" if the child is expected to be placed in general education settings for all or part of the school day or year (section 614[d][1][B]). In section 614(d)(3)(C), IDEA as amended in 1997 added

> The regular education teacher of the child, as a member of the IEP team, shall, to the extent appropriate, participate in the development of the IEP of the child, including the determination of appropriate positive behavioral interventions and strategies and the determination of supplementary aids and services, program modifications, and support for school personnel consistent with paragraph (1)(A)(iii). [Note: That paragraph refers to the special education, related, and supplementary services to be provided; see Figure 2.4.]

In Appendix A accompanying its March 1999 regulations for the IDEA Amendments of 1997, the U.S. Department of Education (1999a) added, in item number 24, that the general educator need not participate in all IEP meetings nor remain in the room for the entire duration of any one meeting. This is because the law, in section 614(d)(3)(C), calls

FIGURE 2.4 IEP Contents

[IDEA Section 614(d)(1)(a)]

(i) a statement of the child's present level of educational performance, including
  (I) how the child's disability affects the child's involvement and progress in the general curriculum, or
  (II) for preschool children, as appropriate, how the disability affects the child's participation in appropriate activities;

(ii) a statement of measurable annual goals, including benchmarks or short-term objectives, related to
  (I) meeting the child's needs that result from the child's disability to enable the child to be involved in and progress in the general curriculum; and
  (II) meeting each of the child's other educational needs that result from the child's disability;

(iii) a statement of the special education and related services and supplementary aids and services to be provided to the child, or on behalf of the child, and a statement of the program modifications or supports for school personnel that will be provided for the child
  (I) to advance appropriately toward attaining the annual goals;
  (II) to be involved and progress in the general curriculum in accordance with clause (I) and to participate in extracurricular and other nonacademic activities; and
  (III) to be educated and participate with other children with disabilities and nondisabled children in the general class and in the activities described in clause (iii);

(iv) an explanation of the extent, if any, to which the child will not participate with nondisabled children in the general class and in the activities described in clause (iii);

(v) (I) a statement of any individual modifications in the administration of State or districtwide assessments of student achievement that are needed in order for the child to participate in such assessment; and
  (II) if the IEP Team determines that the child will not participate in a particular State or districtwide assessment of student achievement (or part of such an assessment), a statement of
    (aa) why that assessment is not appropriate for the child; and
    (bb) how the child will be assessed;

(vi) the projected date for the beginning of the services and modifications described in clause (iii), and the anticipated frequency, location, and duration of those services and modifications;

(vii) (I) beginning at age 14, and updated annually, a statement of the transition service needs of the child under the applicable components of the child's IEP that focuses on the child's courses of study (such as participation in advanced-placement courses or a vocational education program);
  (II) beginning at age 16 (or younger, if determined appropriate by the IEP Team), a statement of needed transition services for the child, including, when appropriate, a statement of the interagency responsibilities or any needed linkages; and
  (III) beginning at least one year before the child reaches the age of majority under State law, a statement that the child has been informed of his or her rights under this title, if any, that will transfer to the child on reaching the age of majority under section 615(m); and

(viii) a statement of
  (I) how the child's progress toward the annual goals described in clause (ii) will be measured; and
  (II) how the child's parents will be regularly informed (by such means as periodic report cards), at least as often as parents are informed of their nondisabled children's progress; of
    (aa) their child's progress toward the annual goals described in clause (ii); and
    (bb) the extent to which that progress is sufficient to enable the child to achieve the goals by the end of the year.

for the general educator to take part only in certain decisions. Notably, the general educator should contribute to decisions about (1) what supplementary aids and services are needed, (2) what program modifications are required, (3) what support from other school personnel is necessary, and (4) what behavioral interventions and strategies are appropriate.

In an "OSEP Brief: Regular Education Teachers as IEP Team Members," also issued in March 1999, the Department commented that the general educator is expected to take part in team consideration of the child's current and anticipated involvement in the regular curriculum. The Department added that the general educator must have access to the child's IEP in order to be an effective team member (U.S. Department of Education, 1999b).

The Family's Role on the IEP Team

Family members are always invited to attend IEP team meetings. They must be notified in advance about all such team meetings. Whenever feasible, this should be 30 days' advance notice. The notice must be in the family's native language, if possible (exceptions are made for languages that are very uncommon in the United States). These parental roles are explained in the U.S. Department of Education's (1999a) rules for IDEA.

Family members are the only participants at IEP team meetings who can independently challenge the school district about IEP team decisions. No teacher, counselor, or therapist enjoys that right. This places the family in a unique role. Bear in mind that IEP team meetings are *not* sessions where votes are taken. It is not a matter of majority vote. (If it were, of course, parents would often be out-voted.) Rather, IEP team meetings are opportunities for discussion and for communication. The responsibility to provide an appropriate education that carries out the IEP rests with the LEA, that is, with the school district. If the LEA were to fail to do so, families may use due process to challenge the school district. Parents do not actually fight the IEP team in due process. Rather, they confront the LEA. Notice, for example, how the court cases mentioned in this book are named: *Timothy W. v. Rochester School District, Mills v. Board of Education of the District of Columbia,* and so on. We will explore this in further detail (see "Due Process," p. 56).

IEP Contents

The contents of an IEP (see Figure 2.4) are specified in IDEA (sec. 614[d][1][A]). These are *annual* plans: IEPs outline what will be done the following school year (September to June).

In essence, IEPs contain:

1. The child's present level of educational performance.
2. Measurable annual goals.
3. Special education, related services, and supplementary aids and services to be provided.
4. The extent, if any, that the child will participate in the general curriculum.
5. Test modifications that will be used.
6. Start date and duration of services.
7. Transition services.
8. How progress toward goals will be measured and parents informed.

Let us take these one-by-one. You may find it helpful to refer to Figure 2.4, which contains the law on IEPs, and Figure 2.5, which contains an example of an IEP for illustrative purposes, as you read the following.

1. *The child's present level of educational performance.* Sensibly enough, the law calls for an IEP to open with a statement of the child's needs. In this first part of the IEP, the team records its consensus about what the child most urgently requires in order to benefit from instruction. The team also enters the child's strengths, interests, and achievements. That is because the word "educational" is to be broadly interpreted, it refers to all of the many areas of child development that affect learning. These needs and strengths, taken together, constitute the child's "present level of educational performance." The needs are the reasons

FIGURE 2.5 Illustration of an IEP

Individualized Education Program

Student's Name: Emil Gerardi D.O.B.: 4/14/89

Student's Address and Home Phone Number: 510 North Main, 557-1500

Parents/Guardian(s) Name(s): Bob and Judy Gerardi

Parents/Guardian(s) Address(es) and Phone Number(s), if different from Student's: N/A

Date of Latest Meeting to Prepare/Revise This IEP: 4/3/04

I. Present Educational Performance

Emil requires short assignments and frequent brief breaks. He also requires consistent reinforcement of appropriate behaviors. Thus, he needs structure throughout the school day. These needs are not expected to preclude his participation in general academic classes this coming school year. Emil also needs to begin to explore career options and to be exposed to work sites.

WISC-III 12/3/02

Verbal Score	98	42nd Percentile
Performance Score	90	20th Percentile
Full Score	94	30th Percentile

Social/Emotional Development

Relations with Peers	Not age appropriate
Relations with Adults	Not age appropriate
Self concept	Age appropriate
Adjustment to school	Not age appropriate

[This section describes the child's needs. Include specific details about how the child's disability affects or does not affect the child's potential participation in the general (regular) curriculum, alongside children the same age who have no disabilities.]

II. Goals

By June 25, 2004, Emil will demonstrate age-appropriate behavior in the classroom, in the halls, and in the playground, both with students and with adults. Largely as a result, Emil will have passed the ninth grade achievement tests. He will have spent at least 80% of the school week in integrated environments, with only periodic counseling and other support services designed to help him to self-monitor and self-reinforce. Progress will be evidenced in B or better grades in each marking period and in continually reduced amounts of time spent in out-of-classroom counseling and other support services as the year proceeds.

[Explain, in behavioral terms, what the child is expected to be capable of doing by the end of the school year. You may include benchmarks, or progress indicators, that will "flag" problems or, alternatively, will signal the child is on the right path.]

III. Services

Emil will receive counseling 2 × 30 min./week to help him to learn to control his emotions and impulses. Each of his subject-matter teachers will be trained by the beginning of the school year in behavior-modification techniques; they will reinforce appropriate behavior that Emil demonstrates and ignore inappropriate behaviors. They will also permit Emil to stand and move around the room for brief periods of time during class periods.

These teachers will meet biweekly to coordinate their activities. Every Friday afternoon, Emil will participate in a work-study program that will expose him to expectations of behavior in the workplace.

[Special education and/or related services and/or supplementary aids and services *must* be provided in response to each of the needs identified in part I, above. Related services must be specified as to frequency and length (e.g., 3 × 30 min.).

IV. Extent, if Any, to Which the Child Will Not Participate with Nondisabled Children

Emil is expected to participate in general education classes except for 2 × 30 min./week counseling sessions outside those classrooms. Those sessions are necessary so that Emil can internalize societal expectations and acquire self-monitoring and self-reinforcement capabilities. If he did not leave general education classes for these sessions, Emil might well not be successful in his academic work this year.

[If this child will be served outside the general classroom for all or part of the school day, explain briefly why that is necessary. "Special factors" such as a deaf child's needs for communication in sign language may be noted here.]

continued

FIGURE 2.5 Illustration of an IEP *(continued)*

V. District-Wide and State Assessments

Emil will take all ninth-grade assessments, but in a separate room so that he gets a 10-minute break every 20 minutes. Extended test-taking time is approved.

[If the child will take such tests, with modifications, identify those adjustments; if not, then state "Child does not require test modifications" or words to that effect. If the child is to be exempted entirely from such tests, justify that and explain how he/she will be assessed.]

VI. Start Date and Duration

Emil will not receive extended school year (ESY) services because his parents have arranged for his attendance at a sports camp during July and August 2004.

[Note if extended school year services are anticipated and, if so, justify them as needed.]

VII. Transition

Emil will receive counseling and will participate in a work-study program; both of these services are intended to assist him to acquire behaviors he will need on the job and in everyday life after he leaves high school. Emil may attend any IEP team meeting he wishes.

[If the child is 14 or older, transition services must be described; if the child is under age 14, such services *may* be detailed, if the IEP team believes that is proper.]

VIII. How Progress Will Be Measured and Parents Informed

Emil's parents will be advised, via e-mail and/or phone messages from the school guidance counselor any time Emil's behavior results in disciplinary action. The parents will also be told, in the same ways, any time Emil's behavior results in special commendation by a teacher or other school official. Other than these steps, Emil's progress will be reported on regular six-week report cards.

[If regular report cards will suffice, say that; if not, explain how and how frequently progress toward goals will be assessed and parents advised of such progress.]

Note: Figure 10.5, in Chapter 10, shows how Emil's progress toward the goals in this IEP might be tracked and reported by his teacher.

for, and justification of, the special education services, related services, and supplementary aids and services that will be entered into section 3 of the IEP.

The 1997 IDEA Amendments require that this first section of the IEP focus especially upon "how the child's disability affects the child's involvement and progress in the general curriculum" (section 614[d][1][a][I]). This is one of the ways in which the law expresses a preference for integration of students with and without disabilities. IDEA creates a preference for placement of children with disabilities into general classrooms. The law conditions this preference by allowing IEP teams to explain why such environments would not be suitable for particular children for all or part of the school day. The preference also appears in the IEPs goals section (section 2 of the IEP), its services section (section 3), and its "general where" section (section 4). In each instance, teams may set aside the preference if they believe it is not appropriate. In legal terms, the LRE principle is a rebuttable presumption. Turnbull and Turnbull (2000), in their text on the law and special education, explained that children with disabilities have the right to an education in an integrated setting *unless* the instruction they would receive if placed there violates their higher-order right to an appropriate education.

In section 614(d)(3)(B), IDEA 1997 required IEP teams to take into consideration "special factors" that may affect some children with disabilities. This includes the language and communication needs of children who are deaf, the behavioral support needs of children with emotional disturbance, and the technology needs of children who are blind. Consider, for example, a child who is deaf. Section 614(d)(3)(B) calls upon the team to take into consideration "the child's language and communication needs, opportunities for direct communications with peers and professional personnel in the child's language and communication mode, academic level, and full range of needs, including opportunities for direct instruction in the child's language and communication mode."

IEP meetings are more about family-educator communication than they are about taking votes.

This is quite a lengthy list. That is because there is a long history of serious concern about whether integration of deaf and hearing children may actually be "excluding" children who are deaf, largely because the most natural language for many deaf children is American Sign Language (ASL). The team must carefully weigh the special needs of such children before concluding that general classrooms do in fact provide appropriate services for them.

How the child's unique needs are written in this section of the IEP is very important. It would make sense for the most critical needs to be entered first; that is, the child's different needs should be prioritized. The words used should clearly present the *child's* needs—not the teacher's, not the school's, and not the parent's. This section is one place where you can make good use of what Mager (1997) has taught, by selecting words that unambiguously describe the child's needs.

This initial section of the IEP is often a source of tension between parents and professionals. Indeed, sometimes this section becomes a subject of due process, as parents challenge the LEA through mediation and legal channels. The IEP statement of needs can become contentious because identifying, and placing in priority order, the unique needs of a child are steps that lead so directly to goals, services, and placement.

For a general educator, this section of the IEP forces attention to the "fit" between what is needed by this particular child and what is planned to be taught in that particular class during the next school year. Teachers who are not dually certified will often need to consult with special educators to address the question: "How can this need be met in a general classroom?" It is very important that general educators *not* jump to conclusions here. With modifications, adaptations, supplementary aids and services, and so on, needs that at first glance appeared irreconcilably different from typical needs may, in fact, be met in a general classroom. This is where the special educator makes a strong contribution: He articulates *how* unique needs may be met.

On the other hand, there may be times when the "disconnect" between unique needs and typical needs is very strong. To illustrate, consider a child who has great difficulty comprehending other people's thinking. (This often happens with children who have severe autism, for example.) If the class is one on appreciating literature, or on interpreting music—two subjects that require well-developed skill in empathy—it may be that the gap is too great to be bridged, even with support services. If so, this fact should cause you to consider placements other than a general classroom. Some children, in some school years, simply cannot be served adequately in an inclusion setting (34 C.F.R. 300.552).

2. *Measurable annual goals.* These are school-year goals. The question being answered in this section of the IEP is "What can we expect Mei-Lin to do in June?" Notice, too, that IDEA explicitly calls for goals to be stated in "measurable" terms. This is where so many IEPs fail—miserably. They feature annual goals on the order of "Mei-Lin will be more independent" or "She will know her colors." Stated in these ways, those goals are not measurable. For example, what exactly does it mean for Mei-Lin to be "more independent"?

As with needs, this section forces educators to confront the "fit" between unique goals and typical goals. Once again, general educators may find themselves turning to special educators and asking "Can Mei-Lin actually meet this goal in one school year?" and "If she can, what services will she need to get there?" This "fit" also figures in the IEP team's goal-setting work because the team must see if the child's goals may be met in general educational environments.

IDEA calls for "benchmarks or short-term objectives" to be entered in this section of the IEP (section 614[d][1][ii]). These are intermediate goals for shorter time periods, such as a month or a marking period. They are signposts along the way. With their aid, teachers can make sure that the child is in fact progressing toward the annual goals, at an acceptable pace.

3. *Special education, related services, and supplementary aids and services to be provided.* This section of the IEP specifies how a school will help the child to reach the goals set forth in the plan, including the goal "to be involved and progress in the general curriculum." As with needs, the services section often occasions parent-team conflicts. Some services are readily available and routinely offered in some settings, but may be much more difficult to offer and thus more rarely provided in other settings. At times, school officials will resist parent suggestions on services, fearing that costs would rise. At other times, teachers may fear that certain services may disrupt the classroom. It may even be that some services may be perceived as giving the child an unfair advantage over other students (extended test-taking time is one possible example).

Special education means, as we saw in Chapter 1, custom-designed instruction, including adapted materials, different methods of teaching, and similar steps. Related services are non-instructional support services, including occupational and physical therapy, speech and language pathology services, and the like. Supplementary aids and services include assistive technology devices and assistive technology services, the use of behavior modification techniques, the assistance of an itinerant teacher, the use of a resource room, and similar steps. This section of the IEP specifies *all* of the kinds of services that will be provided. That is a major reason for the presence at the IEP team meeting of a local school official, who can confirm that the district will provide, and pay for, all such services.

The frequency and duration of periodic services *must* be specified. Thus, if speech and language pathology services are to be provided, they may be entered in this section together with the notation "3 × 30 min." (that is, three times weekly for 30 minutes per session). In section 300.347(a)(6A) of its March 1999 regulations implementing the 1997 IDEA Amendments and in item number 35 of Appendix A accompanying these rules, the Department noted that the amount of services must be specified in this section of the IEP so that the school district's financial commitments are clear to all IEP team members, especially to parents. The frequency and duration should be specific, particularly in the amount of time services will be provided. A range (e.g., 30 to 45 minutes per session) is allowable *only* if the IEP team decides that the child's needs require that the duration vary from session to session (U.S. Department of Education, 1999a).

How do you decide "how much is enough?" The standard set by IDEA calls for services that "meet" all the unique needs of the child with a disability. The word "meet" was featured in the U.S. Supreme Court's 1982 decision at Rowley (see Chapter 1). Notice that the IDEA wording "designed to meet the unique needs" of the child was interpreted, by the Court, to mean that the child will "benefit" from the instruction. Elsewhere in its decision, the Court explained that children demonstrate that they "benefit" when they are promoted from grade to grade.

That is a low standard. IDEA calls for "just enough" services so that the child is granted access to, and passes in, early childhood/elementary and secondary public education. Thus, if Eddie needs speech and language pathology twice a week for 30 minutes each time in order to maintain passing grades, that is what IDEA requires for him; if Jennifer needs just one weekly session of 30 minutes duration, that is what she is to receive. Balancing this fairly low level of required services is IDEA's insistence that *all* of the needs specified in the IEPs opening section be met. An education that does meet each such need is an "appropriate" one.

The standard under section 504 is a higher one (see Chapter 1). Under section 504, the amount and quality of services must be "designed to meet individual educational needs . . . as adequately as the needs of [other] children are met" (34 C.F.R. 104.33[b]). The "as adequately" standard was adopted because section 504 is a non-discrimination statute. Public schools may not discriminate against individuals with disabilities by providing to them services that are lesser in kind or quantity than those that the schools offer to non-disabled persons.

4. *The extent, if any, that the child will not participate in the general curriculum.* Here we see the IDEA "preference" in its most explicit form. The law requires IEP teams to enter, in this fourth section of the plan, an explanation for why a given child will not take part in regular school activities. No such justification is required when the IEP team *does* expect the child to do so. Note the wording *"extent, if any"*: the team is expected to justify not only a child's non-participation in all or some general school activities or programs, but also the extent of such non-participation. That is, if a lesser degree of non-participation than the team recommends is possible, the team needs to explain why that greater integration is not desirable. How does one justify non-participation in some or all general activities? By noting that the instruction the school district can make available in more integrated, general school environments will not result in an "appropriate" education for the child. This, again, calls upon the concept of "rebuttable presumption" (op. cit.).

Nonetheless, it is important that you realize that this is *not* to be a statement of the "least restrictive environment." Rather, it is a general statement of intent, justified (as needed) if the IEP team does not anticipate integration for all or part of the school day. The LRE for this child for the next school year is decided later, *after* the IEP has been developed and signed by all appropriate parties. (Were the LRE to be placed in the IEP, this would require that the IEP team reassemble if it proved necessary to change the placement. That would be time-consuming. Fortunately, it is unnecessary. The placement decision follows the completion of the IEP. It is a separate decision; 34 C.F.R. 300.552.)

You will often find that the first page of a child's IEP does note placements. That is fine. This first sheet is actually completed by the placement team (see "Making the Placement Decision," p. 59) *after* the IEP itself is written. The fact that the placement(s) appear on the first sheet, and that this sheet is stapled to the IEP, does not violate the requirement that the placement decision follow completion of the IEP.

5. *Test modifications that will be used.* In this section of the IEP, the team enters its consensus about whether any modifications or adaptations in testing will be provided.

Teacher Strategies That Work

Justifying Non-Participation in Some Activities

Activity	Justification
Ninth-grade algebra	Student requires practical, real-world math experiences (making change, etc.).
Ninth-grade English	Child reads significantly below age level.
Tests in classrooms	Child requires substantially longer time periods to complete tests.
Music	Child cannot hear.

This includes regular class tests as well as district-wide assessments. If no modifications or adaptations are noted here, none may be offered in high-stakes tests. The box "Teacher Strategies That Work: Test Modifications," describes some adjustments. This is an area in which general educators should consult with special educators, to answer the questions: "Are modifications or adaptations necessary? Are they feasible and available? Would they confer an unfair advantage on this child as compared to her peers?"

6. *Start date and duration of services.* Usually, this is a short, perfunctory statement: "September 5 to June 15" or similar terms. For some children, however, **extended school year (ESY)** services will be provided. In most States, ESY services are offered if it is known that the child will regress during the summer months if services are not continued during that period. The ESY period generally is from early September to mid-August.

7. *Transition services.* IDEA requires that transition services be specified for all children with disabilities who are age 14 or older as of the following school year. That is largely why the law also calls for participation in IEP team meetings by "the child, if appropriate" and because students of high-school age should take part in planning their own futures. This includes attending IEP meetings so as to advocate for themselves.

This seventh section is a very important element of the IEP of any secondary-age student. As a general rule, secondary schools have done very poorly in planning and carrying out transition services (e.g., Hasazi, Furney, & DeStefano, 1999; Repetto & Correa, 1996; Valdes, Williamson, & Wagner, 1990).

Once again, general educators should consult with special educators to answer the questions: "What services are needed so that the child will be most likely to succeed in his or her chosen post–high-school life? How can our school provide those services?"

8. *How progress toward goals will be measured and parents informed.* Sometimes, this section is a brief one: "Progress will be assessed through teacher-made and standardized testing. Parents will be informed by means of report cards at the end of each marking period." At other times, however, more detailed statements are needed. If, for example, one of the child's most important needs is to acquire self-care skills (something not usually measured in the public schools and not generally reported to parents), it is important to specify how the child's growing competence in that area will be measured and how parents will be kept abreast of that progress. Another change may be called for with some children: Frequent teacher-parent contact, as often as daily, can make a big difference with many young children and with children of any age who have severe behavioral disorders (Kauffman, 1999).

Teacher input is particularly important in these elements: (1) Current educational performance (needs); (2) Annual goals; (3) Services; and (8) How progress will be measured and reported.

The child's current teachers know the child's needs, what goals are reachable, and which services are necessary. The teacher(s) who will instruct the child during the next school year know what services they can provide and how they can, and prefer to, assess progress and report it to parents.

Teacher Strategies That Work

Test Modifications

Regular Testing Environment

Morning-only tests
Large-print test booklets
Sign-language interpreter for oral instructions and for any questions

Separate Testing Environment

Small-group or even one-student test room
Carrel to minimize distractions
Extended time with or without breaks
Speaks rather than writes responses; scribe records answers
Types rather than hand-writes responses
Use of spell-checker permitted

TEACHER-FAMILY COMMUNICATION

The chapter on collaboration (Chapter 12) discusses teacher-family relationships. A few words are appropriate here, however. Family members want only the best for their children, in virtually every case. This includes parents of children with disabilities or delays in development (see, for example, Skinner, Bailey, Correa, & Rodriguez [1999], who wrote about Latino mothers and how these women respond to children's disabilities).

Family members may resist the idea that their child "has a problem." This is understandable. Also understandable would be defensiveness on their part. Accordingly, if you know of or suspect a disability or delay, you should be careful in your choice of words when communicating with family members. Experienced teachers suggest that you establish positive relations with family members at the beginning of a school year. By talking with parents when good things happen, and not only when bad things do, you open lines of communication with them that will make them more receptive to bad news later. Teachers also suggest that you begin discussions of problem areas by asking questions along the lines of: "Have you noticed that Susie seems to have difficulty concentrating on some tasks?" If the parent acknowledges a possible problem, experienced teachers suggest that you pursue the matter by using "we" words, such as, "Let's see if we can find a solution to this problem." This wording signals to the parents that you are working *with* them both on problem identification and on problem solving; that is, you are assuming, with the parents, joint ownership of the problem. This will reduce parental defensiveness. Turnbull and Turnbull (2001), in their text on families, offer additional insights into how teachers may empower parents.

Experienced teachers also urge that you adopt sensitive language. Do not use labels unless you are sure that the family members define those words the same way you do. Rather, use words describing the *child's needs*. Family members usually are accustomed to thinking and talking about needs; after all, needs are central to the way IEPs are written. By focusing on what the child needs, and not on a label, you keep the discussion on a practical level, avoiding unnecessary emotions. As a teacher, you need to bear in mind that family members enjoy the right to see *everything* in the child's school records. Thus, anything you insert into the child's personnel file may be, and probably will be, read by family members at some point in time. For this reason, you should exercise sensitive language in everything you write for inclusion in the file. This includes using person-first language, avoiding unnecessary use of labels, and the like.

On occasion, you will encounter family members who seek labels for children who do *not* have disabilities. They may have heard, perhaps from other families, that extended test-taking time, individualized instruction, and other "benefits" are available for children who are given labels. The decision as to whether or not to evaluate a child, and whether to assign a label, is not yours as a teacher. Rather, those responsibilities rest with the IEP team. Any family member enjoys the right to request that the IEP team assess a child's eligibility. It may be that you would be part of such a meeting, in your role as the child's teacher. If so, you may wish to explain to overly aggressive family members that you will be speaking out against identification because special education services are, by federal law, reserved for children with disabilities, as defined in that law, and it is your opinion that this is not such a child.

Among the rights enjoyed by parents, guardians, or other family members of children with disabilities are the right to receive "prior written notice" (sent at least 30 days before any important meeting). This notice must be in the parents' native language unless that native language is very unusual in the United States. No major decision may be made about a child with a disability prior to such a meeting. Thus, the advance notice will tell family members that a decision has not yet been made, but will be, and invites them to attend. They have the right to bring with them anyone they wish, even a lawyer. The date and time of the meeting may be changed if the initial plan is not convenient for the family. In addition, if necessary, a teleconference call may substitute for an in-person session.

If the child has been tested, evaluation results should be communicated to the family in advance of the meeting, together with a "plain English" interpretation of what the numbers mean. If the school district is proposing to (a) begin special-education services, (b) change current services, or (c) refuse to provide special-education services, the prior written notice must lay out what options the family has. Notably, these include "procedural safeguards" (due process) steps. We now review these, from the family's perspective.

DUE PROCESS

Due process, also called "procedural safeguards," refers to the ways in which IDEA permits family members to challenge school districts about how children will be educated. These parental rights emerged because the U.S. Congress recognized that IDEA would not even exist were it not for parents of children with disabilities, who brought the original cases that led to the law, notably *PARC* and *Mills* (see Chapter 1).

Parents, guardians, and other family members of special-education students are granted by IDEA the privileges both of taking part in the making of decisions about how and where children will be educated (that is, these persons are members of the IEP team) *and* of challenging the school district (LEA) on any substantial decision about their children. No other member of the IEP team is given this special standing. (The LEA as a whole may challenge the family through due process, but no one district employee, acting alone, may.) Family members may agree with the IEP team on all major decisions, in which case they will sign the IEP. However, if family members strongly disagree about any provision in the plan, they have the option of (1) signing it, with a notation on the area of disagreement, or (2) refusing to sign it. In either event, they may pursue the matter through due process. The steps they may take are outlined in section 615 of Part B in IDEA.

They may begin with mediation, which is voluntary on both sides. In mediation, a qualified individual talks with school officials and with the family, attempting to create a compromise in which both parties win something and can walk away with a "victory." If mediation fails, or if the family refuses mediation, the next step is an independent hearing officer (IHO). This person is "independent" in the sense that he or she is not employed by the local school district. IHOs do not seek compromises; rather, they make decisions, favoring one side or the other. The losing party may appeal to a state review officer (SRO), again someone who does not work for the local school district. SROs, like IHOs, make decisions. The losing party, whether the family or the school, may appeal again, this time to federal courts. They begin at the district court level, proceed to the appeals court level, and finally reach the U.S. Supreme Court.

School-family disputes sometimes take a long time. The *Rowley* case, for example, dragged on for more than five years (see Chapter 1). Throughout the period of dispute, the family enjoys the right to have the child stay put. That is, the child will receive appropriate educational services during the time family members and school officials are in due process. Usually, this means that the child continues receiving whatever special education and related services he or she was getting before the dispute began. Alternatively, it will mean whatever such services the school and family members agree upon will be offered in the interim. For example, the family and the local school district might concur that while the dispute continues, the child will be placed in a separate classroom. We will look now at the placement process.

PLACEMENT

After the IEP has been written, the IEP team may converge again to decide upon placement; as an alternative, another group, the placement team, does so. The U.S. Department of Education's rules for IDEA explain that the team making placement decisions

FIGURE 2.6 Continuum of Alternative Placements

General Classrooms	*Resource Rooms*	*Separate Classrooms*	*Special Schools*	*Home/Hospital 34 C.F.R. 300.26 and 300.351*

consists of "a group of persons, including the parents, and other persons knowledgeable about the child, the meaning of the evaluation data, and the placement options" (34 C.F.R. 300.552). As already discussed (IEP Contents, item 4), the IEP does not indicate the placement. Rather, the IEP document must be finished before placement is considered (34 C.F.R. 300.552). The 1997 IDEA Amendments emphasized that parents must be part of the team that decides upon placement. This is true even if the IEP team is not the placement team; parents may be members of whatever team *does* make placement decisions.

The team begins by considering the continuum of alternative placement options. This continuum is always presented the same way (see Figure 2.6). On the far left is the General Classroom. It is followed, reading from left to right in turn, by a Resource Room, a Separate Classroom, and a Separate School. Home or Hospital placements are always on the far right of the continuum. The U.S. Department of Education, in its regulations for IDEA, requires school districts to make available the full continuum of options, to the extent that any child needs any of those alternatives (34 C.F.R. 300.551). Despite being ordered in this way, from left to right, the options are *value neutral.* While it is true that IDEA presents a rebuttable preference for settings that are integrated, it is also true that no placement is preferable to any other placement *until* you are considering a specific child. IDEA insists upon individualization of placements. That is why this scheme is called a "continuum" and not a cascade. (Under the cascade model [Deno, 1970], the more left an option is, the better.) That the cascade interpretation is incorrect should be evident when you consider that for some children, a general-classroom placement would result in provision of an inappropriate education. How, then, could such an option be, *ipso facto,* "better" than a resource room?

School districts must make available the full range of alternative placement options (34 C.F.R. 300.551). This does not mean that every placement type must be physically located within the school district. It *does* mean that the school district has, or is prepared to enter into, contracts with other school districts or programs to make a specific placement option available for a particular child who needs that option.

Placement decisions must be made on the basis of a *child's needs.* The question is, "Can this child's needs be met here?" No other basis for decision making is permitted by IDEA. That includes "administrative convenience." To illustrate, the author has been in meetings where a district administrator made comments like "All our special classes are filled" and "We want each class to reflect the district's demographics, so we will not put more than two special-needs children into any one inclusive classroom." The former statement has nothing whatsoever to do with the needs of any child with a disability. It is not a lawful basis for making placement decisions. The latter is a more noble sentiment but it, too, is not lawful. The placement team must focus on *one child at a time* and make decisions based solely on whether that child can receive an appropriate education in a particular setting.

Some administrators dislike this, preferring to follow a more "neat and orderly" pattern in which a certain number of children are placed in particular environments (i.e., just enough to "fill" the room). But that would be decision making on the basis of *groups* of children. IDEA proscribes such processes. Going about things on a child-by-child basis may seem to be more "messy" from the administrative point of view. But in any decent-sized school district, the end result is likely to be that similar numbers of children end up in each placement. The law of large numbers works that way. *Which* children are placed in *which* settings will differ, depending on whether a child-basis or a group-basis decision-making model is used. And that is exactly the point: by focusing on what each

Resources That Work

Examples of Unique Needs of Children with Different Disabilities

Need	***Possible Disability(ies)***
Highly structured environment, with few unexpected changes	Autism, E/B, ADHD, traumatic brain injury (TBI)
Consistent reinforcement of desired behaviors	Autism, E/B, ADHD, specific learning disabilities (LD), TBI
Hands-on, physical, concrete learning experiences	MR, autism, ADHD, LD, deafness
Multisensory input (e.g., auditory, visual, tactile)	Deafness, blindness, MR
Frequent breaks between on-task activities	E/B, ADHD
Carrels for study, test-taking	E/B, ADHD, some LD
Advance organizers	LD, deafness
Much repetition, many examples	LD, deafness, MR
Assistive technology	Blindness, CP, deafness
Teacher-highlighted key words in reading materials	LD, deafness
Tutoring and extra help with math	LD, MR
Counseling	E/B, ADHD, TBI
Extended test-taking time	MR, E/B, deafness, LD, ADHD
Scribe to write test answers	Blindness, some LD, MR
Instruction and practice in life skills areas (e.g., self-care)	MR, autism, blindness, TBI

child needs, the team places each in a suitable setting. The administrator's group-based process would result in some children being placed where their needs cannot be met.

The placement team begins its task by examining the general classroom. The question being asked is, "Can an appropriate education be offered this coming school year to this child in this setting?" That is, the decisive factor is whether all of that child's unique needs will be met in a satisfactory manner in the general classroom (see the box, "Resources That Work: Examples of Unique Needs of Children with Different Disabilities"). If the answer to that question is "yes," then this is a suitable placement, and the team selects it.

If, however, the answer is "no," then the placement team considers whether changes can be made so that the setting becomes a suitable one. This means bringing into the general classroom whatever special education, related services, and/or supplementary aids and services are required so that all of the child's needs are met. Given such additions, the question becomes, "Can an appropriate education now be provided in a general classroom?" There will be instances when the answer continues to be "no." In such cases, the team cannot make the placement there. IDEA forbids provision of an inappropriate education to children with disabilities. Recall that in the vignette that opened this chapter, Shalinie reported, "The principal of our school never goes against the parents." This was her shorthand for saying that the school where she works and the placement team did not follow this requirement. Rather than risk upsetting parents, they made a placement that clearly was not appropriate. Shalinie, as the child's teacher, was left to cope with the consequences.

What should have happened was the placement team would turn its attention to the next left-most placement, in this case, a resource room. Again, the question is posed: "Can an appropriate education be delivered this coming school year to this child in this resource-room placement?" If the answer is "yes," the team makes the placement there. If it is "no," then the team considers whether adding additional special education, related services, and/or supplementary aids and services could render this placement a suitable one. If the answer continues to be "no," then the team moves to consider a separate classroom placement. The nearby box, "Teacher Strategies That Work: Making the Placement Decision," illustrates the process.

For some children, an appropriate education cannot be provided by a particular school district during a given school year, even in a separate classroom. For such children,

Teacher Strategies That Work

Making the Placement Decision

1. Has the IEP been completed?
   ↓ Yes
   ↓ No > Complete it first.
2. Make all placement-related decisions on the basis of the child's needs.
3. Begin by examining the general classroom setting age peers with no disabilities attend:
   Can the setting offer an appropriate education, without modifications?
   ↓ Yes > Make the placement.
   ↓ No > Can special education, related services, and/or supplementary aids and services be added that will result in appropriateness?
   ↓ Yes > Make the placement.
   ↓ No > Move to 4.
4. Examine the resource room as the main placement, supplemented by some time in regular or separate classrooms:
   Can the setting offer an appropriate education, without modifications?
   ↓ Yes > Make the placement.
   ↓ No > Can special education, related services, and/or supplementary aids and services be added that will result in appropriateness?
   ↓ Yes > Make the placement.
   ↓ No > Move to 5.
5. Examine the separate classroom as the main placement, supplemented by some time in regular or special classrooms, or as the single placement:
   Can the setting offer an appropriate education, without modifications?
   ↓ Yes > Make the placement.
   ↓ No > Can special education, related services, and/or supplementary aids and services be added that will result in appropriateness?
   ↓ Yes > Make the placement.
   ↓ No > Move to 6.
6. Examine the separate school as the main placement, supplemented by some time in regular schools, or as the single placement:
   Can the setting offer an appropriate education, without modifications?
   ↓ Yes > Make the placement.
   ↓ No > Can special education, related services, and/or supplementary aids and services be added that will result in appropriateness?
   ↓ Yes > Make the placement.
   ↓ No > Move to 7.
7. Examine home/hospital settings as the main placement, supplemented by some time in regular or special schools, or as the single placement:
   Can the setting offer an appropriate education, without modifications?
   ↓ Yes > Make the placement.
   ↓ No > Can special education, related services, and/or supplementary aids and services be added that will result in appropriateness?
   ↓ Yes > Make the placement.

the team must consider out-of-district placements such as separate schools. In very few instances will a team actively consider a home or hospital placement. Usually, those are limited to instances where a child is medically fragile, technology dependent, or has other very serious medical needs.

Regardless of the placement chosen for the beginning of the school year, if the team determines that it is in fact not offering an appropriate education for the child, the team must revisit that placement decision. It may be that the placement can be "saved" by the addition of support services. If not, a change in placement must be made. This may occur at *any time* during the year. The bottom line is that schools are not permitted to provide an inappropriate education to a child with a disability.

CHAPTER SUMMARY

Pre-referral Interventions

- The goal of pre-referral interventions is to try different things in the general classroom. Often, that is all that is required to solve student problems. Referral for evaluation by the IEP team should not be made until teachers exhaust their repertoire of pre-referral intervention strategies and tactics.

Identification, Assessment, and Evaluation

- Identification is most often made by teachers in general classrooms.
- Assessment is the collection of data so as to make a decision. Tests are only one kind of assessment. Teachers also use observation, rating scales, and record reviews, among other steps.
- Overidentification of low-SES and minority children is a major problem in American education. Overidentification refers to "identifying" (and then referring to special education) children who do not have disabilities. It seems to occur most often when educators' backgrounds differ substantially from students' backgrounds.
- SES status, rather than race or ethnicity, seems to be the bottom-line factor behind much overidentification. Children from low-SES families often are eligible for Title I and other support services. These should be tried before referral to special education is made.
- Evaluation, for purposes of this book, is the process of determining eligibility under IDEA. Assessment, by contrast, looks not at eligibility issues but rather at academic ones, such as what a student's strengths are.

IEPs and IEP Teams

- Small, rather than large, IEP teams are preferable, both because team meetings are easier to set up and because the sessions are less intimidating for many families.
- General educators are required to participate in IEP team meetings for specific agenda items, notably (1) what, if any, supplementary aids and services will be needed to support the placement, (2) what teaching and other program modifications will be required, (3) what support from other school personnel, including related services professionals, will be needed, and (4) what behavior modification techniques will be used.
- IEP teams must consider certain "special factors" when preparing IEPs for children who are deaf or hard of hearing, who have emotional disturbances, or who are blind or visually impaired.
- To answer the question, "How much is enough?" about services for children, the standard set by the law is that of "appropriate" enough to "meet" the child's unique needs, no more and no less.
- The IEP team writes a "justification" statement if the child is *not* expected to be educated in an inclusive setting. No such justification statement is required if an inclusive placement is anticipated.
- Placement is discussed and decided *after* the IEP is completed.

QUESTIONS FOR REFLECTION

1. How do teachers identify students as potentially eligible for services under IDEA?
2. What does the term "culturally indifferent" mean to you? How could a culturally indifferent teacher improve?
3. Do you think a school district realistically could solve its diversity problems by filling all teacher openings with members of minority groups, males, and adults with disabilities?
4. Explain the rules on family notification of a planned evaluation.
5. Why is assessment so important in special education?
6. What are three advantages of small, as opposed to large, IEP meetings?
7. What "special factors" must an IEP team consider on behalf of a child who is deaf?
8. In which three sections of the IEP does IDEA's "preference" become an issue?
9. What could you do, in the IEP meeting, to ensure adequate transition services for a child with mental retardation, notwithstanding strong state pressure for higher learning standards?
10. What is the overriding rule about placement?

Part One Endnotes

Making Inclusion Work . . . The Story So Far

In Part One, we outlined IDEA. The keys to making inclusion work within this law include these ideas:

- IDEA requires that each child with a disability receive educational and related services that at least "meet" his or her unique needs. Any placement, even inclusion in a general classroom, cannot result in an education that fails to rise to that standard.
- Placement decisions, as well as other decisions about children with disabilities, must be made on a one-by-one basis. These must be *individualized* decisions.
- Educators should use labels only as required (as part of eligibility determinations). In all other instances, educators should base decisions on children's unique *needs,* not on their labels.
- Given that the child's unique needs are met, placement should be made in a setting that gives the child opportunities to interact with children without disabilities. This is the value behind the law's preference for placement in the least restrictive environment.
- Because children change over time, the LRE for a given child at one time may not be the LRE for the same child at some other time. The LRE is a principle. It is not any particular place.
- Children and youth who do not qualify for IDEA services may qualify for protection under section 504. Section 504 is a nondiscrimination statute. There is no list of conditions, no "needs special education and related services" requirement, and no age limitation in section 504.
- Overidentification of children and youth is a major problem in public education today. Educators should take care not to classify as disabled children who have no disabilities. Cultural competence is a key to this. Educators need to recognize how family economic conditions, ethnic status, race, and other variables may place children at risk for school failure, and must arrange for appropriate services to help those children succeed in school.
- Pre-referral interventions are essential steps in helping to prevent overidentification. Educators should consult widely with people who know the child, try different strategies and tactics, and arrange for remedial instruction *before* initiating a referral for evaluation by the IEP team.
- Participation by general and special educators, as well as family members, in writing the IEP is essential so that an effective plan of action is developed, one that everyone is committed to carrying out.
- Families have the right to contest decisions made about their children. These due process rights (also called "procedural safeguards") are central to IDEA. However, if the IEP team functions as a forum for free and open communication (as it should), many due process complaints can be avoided.

Part Two

Students in the Inclusive Classroom with Higher-Incidence Disorders

Part Two focuses upon students with disabilities who are included in general classrooms *and* who have high-prevalence disabilities. By "high prevalence" we mean that they are large in number, as compared to children and youth with other disabilities. Students with these common disabilities account for over 90% of all students with disabilities in the public schools today.

Chapter 3 looks at specific learning disabilities and attention deficit hyperactivity disorders. Chapter 4 focuses upon speech or language impairments (SLI). These disabilities are "mild" in the sense that accommodating the needs of children and youth with these conditions is relatively straightforward. Chapter 4 also discusses a low-prevalence disability category, that of students who are deaf or hard of hearing. This is because of the commonality of needs between SLI and hearing impairment; that is, both typically require related services from speech and language pathologists.

Chapter 5 examines two high-prevalence disabilities that are more challenging: mental retardation and emotional/behavioral disorders. Mild mental retardation can pose significant problems for inclusive teachers, particularly at the secondary level. Moderate, severe, and profound mental retardation are even more difficult to accommodate in inclusive classrooms. Much the same may be said about emotional/behavioral disorders, which tend to be severe.

Chapter 3 Learning Disabilities and Attention Deficit Hyperactivity Disorders

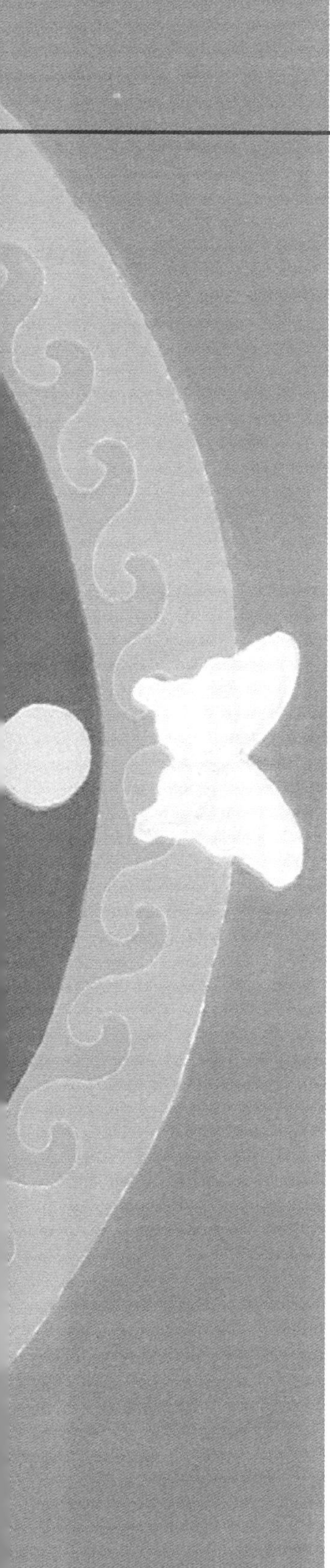

TERMS

attention deficit hyperactivity disorder (ADHD)
mild
co-morbid
Other Health Impaired (OHI)
automaticity
specific learning disabilities (SLD)
metacognition
phonemic awareness
number sense
reading disabilities (RD)
dyslexia
dyscalculia
dysgraphia
embedding
early intervention
Direct Instruction (DI)
phonemes
phonics
graphemes
mnemonics
manipulatives
universal design
speech synthesis
scaffolding
speech recognition
peer tutoring

CHAPTER FOCUS QUESTIONS

After reading this chapter, you should be able to answer such questions as:

1. What are learning disabilities?
2. How are learning disabilities diagnosed?
3. How are learning disabilities like attention deficit hyperactivity disorders? How are they different?
4. What strategies work for students with learning disabilities who are in the inclusive classroom?
5. What are the three basic types of attention deficit hyperactivity disorders?
6. What are some controversies surrounding the use of medication for attention deficit hyperactivity disorders?
7. What strategies help teachers of inclusive classrooms to manage the behavior of students with attention deficit hyperactivity disorders?

PERSONAL ACCOUNTS

A young woman I taught, who had a learning disability, told me about the importance of family, teacher, and peer support in helping her to succeed in school. As you read her story, notice the kinds of challenges she had, the different services she received, and the persistence she needed to succeed. This chapter will elaborate on these.

> *In my first few years of elementary school, I had no trouble making friends. As I started learning how to read, however, my struggle began. In third grade, my parents noticed a change. I would avoid doing homework and dreaded going to school. After many tests and meetings with school officials, I was diagnosed as having learning disabilities. Getting the school to recognize this fact took another eight months of fighting by my parents against the school district. Finally, an IEP was prepared. It noted that I had difficulty with short- and long-term memory, with sequencing, and with inferential reasoning (drawing conclusions*

from disparate sets of facts). I was then placed, for most of middle school, in lower-ability classes. This upset me, because it separated me from my friends. That really motivated me to improve my grades. I went to the resource room one period every day, instead of taking a foreign language. I took exams there, too. Someone read directions out loud to me (and sometimes the questions, as well). My tests were untimed. Spelling errors were overlooked in grading my tests. All of this helped.

But I did much, much more. Every school day when I returned home, I started another school day, this one called "homework." My mom looked over my homework assignments and then helped me set up a schedule. I did writing assignments first. All reading and math was saved until after dinner, because my dad would be home to help me. I also signed up for private tutoring. Even with these adjustments, the struggle to keep up was exhausting. I would often become frustrated. There were many times I wanted to give up. But I'm glad I didn't! I got an academic achievement award in eighth grade. Four years later, I graduated. I was so proud of myself! We were allowed to say something while we were on stage. I just said, "Mom and Dad, thank you for all your help and support!" And I meant it!

—Dana

Another former student noted that support services can also be vital for many children and youth with attention deficit hyperactivity disorders, such as her brother. In her story, you will observe difficulties in organizing and completing assignments—these are characteristic of students with attention deficit hyperactivity disorders. Teacher-created structure is often the key to success in inclusive settings for such students.

My brother has attention deficit disorder. In elementary school, he had a hard time learning because he was so disorganized. My parents and the school team decided to place him in a regular classroom, with a resource room pull-out. The teachers would send notes home together with homework, so communication between school and family was very good. However, when he went to middle school, he no longer received resource-room services. There, and especially in high school, notes came home from teachers saying that he did not come prepared to class, did not do his homework, and was acting up. So my parents spent a lot of time with him on homework. Eventually, he learned to organize his work. He did especially well in subjects like computer engineering, which he loved because it is so hands-on.

—Claudia

These two personal accounts offer perspectives on learning disabilities and attention deficit hyperactivity disorders. They highlight issues to be discussed in this chapter. Notice that both Dana and Claudia's brother needed support services in order to succeed in school. Dana needed help with reading and with remembering facts and organizing them. Claudia's brother also required assistance in organizing. Their families had to provide a lot of the needed help themselves. They also had to advocate for school-provided support services. As a classroom teacher, you likely will have students with learning disabilities and attention deficit hyperactivity disorders, because both are prevalent (high in number). You will be responsible to meet their needs, although you may call upon specialists to help you as needed.

INTRODUCTION

Specific learning disabilities are the most common conditions among students who are classified as eligible for special education. Almost half (48%) of students with any label had the label "specific learning disabilities" as of the 2002–2003 school year (Table AA3 of the *26th Annual Report to Congress on Implementation of the Individuals with Disabilities*

Education Act, 2004). What students with these conditions need to be successful in school varies depending on what kinds of learning disabilities they have. There are several types of learning disabilities, each affecting one or a few academic activities but not others, which is why the word "specific" is used. In his best-selling 2002 book, *A Mind at a Time,* Levine emphasized that many difficulties are very narrow in scope, affecting, for example, handwriting but not any other academic skill area. Some children and youth have difficulty with reading, some with math, some with planning, and some with understanding what they hear. Most, however, can learn effectively in inclusive classrooms, with the proper support. Also quite common are **attention deficit hyperactivity disorders (ADHD).** These, too, come in different forms. Children and youth with ADHD/I are primarily inattentive, while those with ADHD/HI tend to be hyperactive and impulsive. There also is a third, combined type, ADHD/C. As is the case with students having learning disabilities, most children and youth with attention deficit hyperactivity disorders can succeed in an inclusive classroom if given the support they need.

For more information on specific learning disabilities based on the U.S. Department of Education Twenty-Sixth Annual Report, *go to the Web Links module in Chapter 3 of the Companion Website.*

In this chapter, we discuss learning disabilities (LD) and attention deficit hyperactivity disorders. We do this because the two categories are presumed to be neurological in nature. That is, they have to do with wiring in the brain. This is why Silver (1998, 1999), an expert on both disorders, considers LD and ADHD to be related but different conditions.

The two disabilities have five things in common (see Figure 3.1). First, as mentioned, they are both presumed to be neurological in nature. Second, both are high-prevalence disabilities. You are very likely to see students with these disabilities in your classrooms. Third, they are, by comparison to many other limitations, "mild." In this book, the word **mild** means that students usually can adapt successfully in inclusive classrooms, with modest teacher adaptations. The needs of children and youth with mild disabilities vary tremendously. Most can achieve or even excel academically with minimal support. Others, however, will need many years of assistance just to survive in school. Fourth, many students with these disabilities have intelligence in the typical range. It is important to bear in mind that intelligence tests produce information on *measured* intelligence. The reported IQ scores of students with learning disabilities and those with ADHD may be lower than their true levels of intelligence, because their conditions may interfere with performance on the tests. Fifth and finally, the two kinds of conditions often occur together. They are, in educational jargon, **co-morbid** because often one student has both disabilities. About one student in every three who has ADHD also has a learning disability (Silver, 1998).

Learning disabilities differ from attention deficit hyperactivity disorders in five major ways. First, specific learning disabilities is a category in the law, the Individuals with

FIGURE 3.1 LD and ADHD: Similarities and Differences

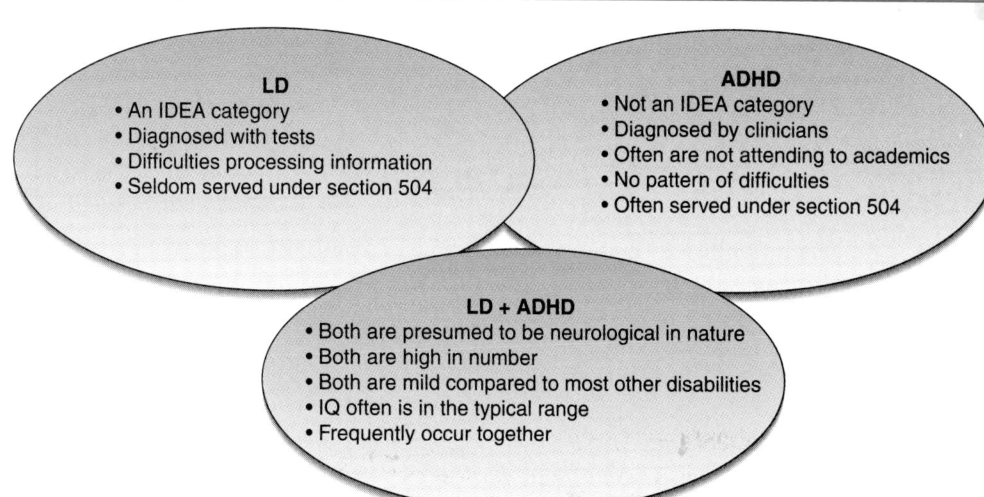

There is nothing about the appearance of students with learning disabilities and those with ADHD that makes them look different from other students.

Disabilities Education Act (IDEA). ADHD, by contrast, is not an IDEA category in itself. Rather, children and youth with these disabilities are either classified as **Other Health Impaired (OHI),** making them eligible for IDEA services, or are, instead, served under section 504 of the Rehabilitation Act (see Chapter 1). Second, learning disabilities are diagnosed using individualized tests. Attention deficit hyperactivity disorders, by contrast, are diagnosed through the taking of a personal history and through observations of the child. Third, students with learning disabilities typically have difficulty in processing information, that is in making sense of what they see and hear. They are paying attention. Children and youth with attention deficit hyperactivity disorders, by contrast, commonly do not give full attention to academics. Those who are inattentive may seem to be daydreaming, while those who are hyperactive may be preoccupied with their own activities. Fourth, students with learning disabilities often are challenged on comprehension of information, on the mental processing of that information, and on basic intellectual tasks, notably in automaticity with phonemes and numbers (Fuchs, Fuchs, Mathes, Lipsey, & Eaton, 2000; Miller & Felton, 2001; Shaywitz & Shaywitz, 1993; Wadlington, 2000). **Automaticity** refers to speed of response. "Automatic" behavior is very high-speed, either because of the ways in which our brains work or because skills have been overlearned. Children and youth with LD may respond more slowly to new information than do others. Students with ADHD, by contrast, exhibit no particular pattern of deficiencies. Fifth, and finally, students with ADHD often are served under section 504, while those with LD rarely are. This is not just a matter of IDEA categories. Rather, it is an issue of eligibility. As you read in Chapter 1, children and youth who do not require both special education and related services generally do not qualify under IDEA. They may, however, meet the different requirements under section 504.

SPECIFIC LEARNING DISABILITIES

The most prevalent (highest in number of children and youth) disability label is **specific learning disabilities (SLD).** Notice the plural: There are several types of learning disabilities. This text primarily will use the term "learning disabilities" and the abbreviation "LD" from this point forward.

Definition

LD is the only category that is defined in the Individuals with Disabilities Education Act (IDEA) itself. All others are defined in federal regulations (U.S. Department of Education, 1999a). Section 602 of IDEA contains the statutory definition:

> The term "specific learning disability" means a disorder in one or more of the basic psychological processes involved in understanding or in using language, spoken or written, which disorder may manifest itself in imperfect ability to listen, think, speak, read, write, spell, or do mathematical calculations. Such term includes such conditions as perceptual disabilities, brain injury, minimal brain dysfunction, dyslexia, and developmental aphasia. Such term does not include a learning problem that is primarily the result of visual, hearing, or motor disabilities, of mental retardation, of emotional disturbance, or of environmental, cultural, or economic disadvantage.

Under the latest IDEA amendments, IDEA adds that local education agencies (school districts) are *not* required to use discrepancy in determining whether or not a given child has a specific learning disability. The term "discrepancy" was used by the U.S. Department of Education in its regulatory definition (1999a, section 300.7[10]). Under those rules, school districts were required to establish that a discrepancy existed between ability and achievement. The federal regulations left it up to states to determine the required size of the discrepancy. You should check with your state's department of education to see if a discrepancy requirement continues to be in effect. The new amendments to IDEA also call for a process that determines if a child responds to "scientific, research-based intervention." If a student does, the school district may rule that there is no specific learning disability, but rather a prior failure to provide adequate instruction.

The Department's regulations will need to be revised to reflect the amendments to the law. This may require a year or two. Likely to survive, from the old regulations, is an *exclusion clause* such that the LD label may be applied if a child's poor academic achievement cannot otherwise be explained. Thus, intelligence, hearing, vision, and the child's other faculties generally are unimpaired and the child has had an adequate opportunity to learn. Also probable in any new federal regulation is a rule continuing to forbid use of any one test for purposes of identifying a student as having a learning disability. The intent is to require that school districts and IEP teams tap a variety of measures before determining that a child has a specific learning disability.

Problems with This Definition

The Department's definition of learning disability has been controversial for several reasons. The discrepancy requirement was widely viewed as being both unnecessary and misleading. In particular, it was cited as the key cause of the "wait to fail" model that postpones services until children are as old as nine or ten (Lyon, 2002; Lyon et al., 2001; Silver, 2002). Continuing a long history of efforts to devise better definitions, the Department in late 2001 sponsored a Learning Disabilities Summit that examined issues surrounding definition and identification of children and youth with LD, after which it charged a newly funded Center on Learning Disabilities to review state and local practices in this area as well as research in the field (*Federal Register,* July 6, 2001).

Lyon et al. (2001) identified some issues with the then-current federal definition. First, the Department's definition assumed, incorrectly, Lyon et al. contended, that learning disabilities have neurological but *not* environmental causes. In fact, Lyon et al. noted, research shows that environmental factors often are involved. Poor teaching often is a precipitating factor in LD. Thus, the difficulties that children encounter with reading and writing *can* be explained, in part, by factors other than LD itself. This violates the regulation's "exclusion" requirement, according to Lyon et al. Second, the discrepancy formula may overidentify children (mis-diagnosis). Better, Lyon et al. argued, would be to focus upon differences between children who have been provided early and intensive instruction: Only those who still display great difficulty in learning should be classified as having learning disabilities. Third, the discrepancy requirement has the effect of delaying definitive diagnosis until about age nine. It takes until that time for intelligence and achievement tests to be administered and for a discrepancy between a child's results on both to be discovered. As Lyon (2002) put it in Congressional testimony, "Because achievement failure sufficient to produce a discrepancy from IQ cannot be reliably measured until a child reaches approximately nine years of age, the use of the IQ-achievement discrepancy literally constitutes a 'wait to fail' model" (p. 3). That is because the requirement to establish a discrepancy has the perverse effect of postponing intervention that could help the child.

Ten national organizations interested in learning disabilities reached consensus in mid-2002 that the statutory definition (the one in the law itself) was satisfactory but that the Department's regulations should be changed to remove ability-achievement discrepancy (*Specific Learning Disabilities: Finding Common Ground*). The Learning Disabilities Association of America (LDA), the Council for Exceptional Children's (CEC) Division for Learning Disabilities, the International Dyslexia Association (IDA), and other groups agreed that discrepancy formulas are not reliable nor are they valid. Instead, these organizations recommended that identification of learning disabilities in children and youth should feature a comprehensive evaluation that emphasizes a problem-solving approach and includes multiple measures, different sources of information, and clinical judgment. This is exactly what Congress did in its most recent IDEA amendments.

Characteristics and Types

The 10 organizations interested in learning disabilities that reached consensus in 2002 about defining LD agreed that learning disabilities are neurological disorders that are characterized by intra-individual differences. That is, children and youth with LD vary within themselves more than do most other students. Each such individual has at least one core cognitive deficit, or disorder in a basic psychological process.

Students with LD tend to have unusual difficulties in comprehending what they read and, less often, what they hear. They may also be limited in their ability to process information, particularly if speed is important (Deshler, Ellis, & Lenz, 1996; Fuchs et al., 2000; Miller & Felton, 2001). The word **metacognition** is often used in this context. Metacognition is, literally, "thinking about thinking." That is, it is a mental process that people use to sort out, prioritize, and evaluate information they hear or read. One major characteristic of students with learning disabilities is that they often have difficulty with, and thus require explicit instruction in techniques of, metacognition (Meltzer, 1993; Silver, 1998).

Some children and youth with learning disabilities display difficulty in combining and separating phonemes, that is, in phonemic awareness, in number sense, and in organizing what they read, what they write, and what they calculate (Levine, 2002; Shaywitz et al., 1998). **Phonemic awareness** is the set of abilities to separate and combine phonemes. It is explained in the section titled "Instructional methods" (p. 79). For now, you may think of phonemic awareness as a set of abilities that help us to identify sounds within words, to separate those sounds, and to combine them. **Number sense** is a fundamental ability to use numbers. It is similar to phonemic awareness in that it seems to be "automatic" in many children. Disorders of phonemic awareness, number sense, and other basic psychological processes are "specific" in students with specific learning disabilities in that a child or youth typically will demonstrate deficiencies in one or a few such areas, but not in others. Thus, a child who is deficient in phonemic awareness may not be deficient in number sense, and vice versa.

As the word "specific" suggests, children and youth with LD may have challenges with particular kinds of mental activities, but not with others (see Figure 3.2). Some face difficulties with input. This may be visual input, in which case there may be a *visual perceptual disability*. Another child, also classified as having a learning disability, may instead have an *auditory perceptual disability* that causes him to misunderstand what he hears. Quite common, in both cases, are difficulties distinguishing between figure and ground (that is, between signal and background). Children and youth may not quickly identify the critical information. They have learning disabilities related to *figure-ground* issues. Yet other children with LD have difficulties with *sequencing* (that is, following a series of steps in the right order) or other kinds of integration of new information. Limitations in short-term memory are common. Still others identified as having LD may have *language disabilities*, including *reading disabilities* (Silver, 1998). Importantly, children and youth who display one kind of difficulty do not necessarily have problems with other kinds of men-

FIGURE 3.2 Types of Specific Learning Disabilities

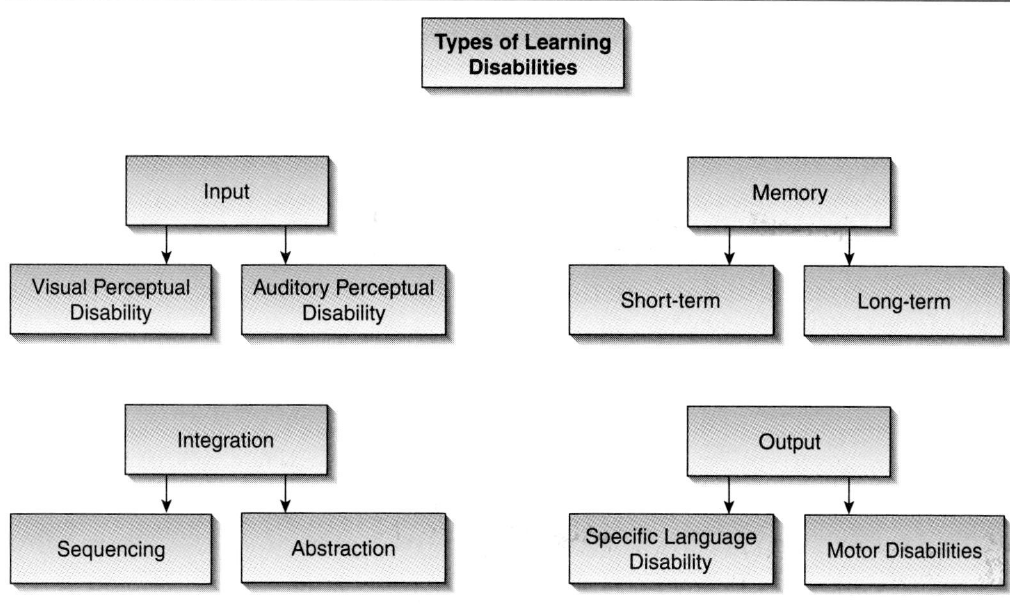

Source: Data from Silver (1998, 2001).

tal tasks. That is why the official term is "specific learning disabilities"—to alert us to the fact that the disorders are very specific in nature.

Characteristics

Learning disabilities may be mild, moderate, or severe. Students differ, too, in their coping skills. Some learn to adjust to LD so well that they "pass" as not having a disability while others struggle throughout their lives to do even "simple" things. Despite these differences, LD always begins in childhood and always is a life-long condition (Levine, 2002; Silver, 1998; *Specific Learning Disabilities Finding Common Ground,* 2002).

Learning disabilities may be understood by contrasting mental functions in children who have and those who do not have LD. Most children can trust what they see and hear. Those with learning disabilities, however, may learn that they cannot rely on that input (e.g., Silver, 2001). Most children enter school possessing a good sense of the sounds of their native language. They can make sense of what they hear and they can combine sounds into recognizable words. That is, they possess phonemic awareness. They can also count at a basic level and tell the difference between "a few" and "many." In other words, they have good number sense. These children have mastered the most basic tasks of language and of mathematics. By contrast, children with LD tend to have severe and long-lasting limitations with these fundamental tasks (Shaywitz et al., 1998).

Key characteristics of individuals with LD include

- difficulties understanding in a specific modality (e.g., reading print, say, or comprehending what they hear);
- academic concerns, particularly with basic skills such as phonemic awareness and number sense, and in metacognition (awareness of one's own learning styles, strengths, and weaknesses);
- social awkwardness;
- challenges in organizing their work and their time.

Many students with LD have mental processing difficulties, despite intelligence that is usually in the typical range (e.g., most have IQ scores between 85 and 115). As already briefly suggested, their reported IQs may understate their actual intelligence, especially if the test is timed. The difficulties these children have vary from child to child. The word "specific" points to the fact that some students have difficulties in reading, especially in reading out loud, while others do not. There are, nonetheless, some characteristics that many students with LD have in common. Particularly an issue is metacognition. Many children and youth with LD are not skilled at understanding what they know and how they learn best. They are sometimes described as deficient in academic skills, notably in monitoring and checking their own work. They may be particularly weak in following multistep procedures. They may overlook a key step, or may perform the steps in an incorrect sequence. They may not use active strategies for learning and memory that their peers routinely adopt (Deshler et al., 1996). Many students with LD have limitations in organizing their own work. In math, children and youth with LD may add when they should subtract. Their spelling often is poor. Algozzine, Beattie, Audette, and Lambert (2000) bluntly summarized these characteristics:

> Cognition is how we think. Many children with learning disabilities need to be taught how to think. They need strategies for tasks such as organization, test taking, and remembering facts. They do not think how to approach a task. Some students with learning disabilities think that they will fail before they even attempt a task. If they do perform well, many times these students will attribute it to luck or level of difficulty of the task (e.g., too easy). If they do poorly, they will attribute it to their own lack of ability or effort. (p. 161)

Students with LD may appear to be socially awkward, especially when the "unwritten rules" of social engagement call for immediate responses. They may not respond appropriately to what others say. Frequently, their self-esteem is low (Bos & Vaughn, 2002; Deshler et al., 1996; Meltzer, 1993). Some students with LD lack the self-confidence required to persist in a task. They need teachers and family members to both explain exactly what the difficulty is and to identify strategies and tactics that will help to solve that problem. However, children and youth with LD differ greatly from each other. No generalization, including this one, applies to all such students. Many, such as Dana in the chapter-opening "Personal Accounts," will persist to extraordinary lengths; despite frustrations—they will tackle even the most daunting task!

One way to think about LD is to recognize that *all of us* display difficulties characteristic of learning disabilities at some times. Especially when we are tired, we may not process words we read on a page or may not pick up quickly on words we hear. We may do the steps of a task out of order. These are concerns that some people with learning disabilities have—*virtually all the time* and *to a much more severe degree.* LD is a life-long condition that often causes severe limitations in these mental tasks. Also worth bearing in mind is that all of us have weaknesses as well as strengths. The major difference between adults and children, contends Levine (2002), is that adults can choose activities, including work, that tap strengths rather than weaknesses, whereas children cannot.

Types

Studies using functional magnetic resonance imaging (fMRI) have demonstrated notable differences in the ways that the brain of individuals with LD function as compared to those of people without LD (e.g., Shaywitz et. al., 1998). This is why all definitions refer to presumed neurological deficits. However, there are distinct types of learning disabilities.

LD may be classified according to the basic psychological processes involved. Most prominent are reading disabilities. There are other, less common, variations, notably disabilities related to written expression and oral expression (Lyon, 2002), short- and/or long-term memory, organizational skills, mathematics, map/illustration reading, and comprehension of what is heard (Hallahan, Kauffman, & Lloyd, 1999). Silver (1998, 2001) distinguishes specific kinds of learning disabilities according to the following scheme:

- *Input:* Visual perceptual disabilities and auditory perceptual disabilities
- *Integration:* Sequencing disabilities and abstraction disabilities
- *Output:* Language disabilities and motor disabilities

These types of learning disabilities are outlined in Figure 3.2.

Input. According to Silver (1998), visual perceptual disabilities may cause students to perceive letters on a page as reversed or rotated. They may also produce difficulties in distinguishing between figure and ground, that is, between the more important information on a page and the less important. These conditions may also lead to figure-ground difficulties, as in attending to the key content on a page and ignoring the less-important illustrative information.

Input disabilities related to hearing, what Silver called auditory processing disabilities, cause students to be unsure about what they have heard (Paton, n.d). That is, were you to say, in class, "*The Catcher in the Rye* is a classic coming-of-age story," students with auditory processing disorders might be confused. "Did I hear 'The Hacker in the Rye' or was it 'The Catcher in the Sky'?" While you continue with more sentences, these students are still trying to figure this out. These students also have problems picking out your voice from the many ambient sounds in the room.

Integration. Once information has been heard and/or seen, it needs to be processed in the brain. Some children and youth with learning disabilities may mis-order the sequence of events or of steps to solve a problem. These are sequencing difficulties. Others may have trouble extracting the general rule from a series of particular facts. This is the issue that Dana referred to, in "Personal Accounts," as inferential reasoning.

Memory. Dana also reported having other difficulties that Silver classified as memory difficulties. According to Silver (1998, 2001), people with LD are more likely to have concerns with short-term than with long-term memory. He explained that children and youth with these limitations need to concentrate upon new information, and to repeat it continually, in order to keep it in short-term memory. If their attention is disrupted, the information may be lost. As a teacher, you might notice a student with LD taking notes on your lecture. If so, this should cue you to pause, repeat what you said, or give examples (see "Instructional Methods," p. 79). That is because this student may not hear what you might say while she is taking notes.

Output. Silver (1998, 2001) distinguishes between spontaneous and demand output. He explains that people with LD rarely have problems with spontaneous output. However, when output is demanded, they may display real difficulties. Another kind of output issue involves motor activity. Since we move our muscles in response to mental signals, motor disabilities may cause people to stumble or to write illegibly.

Of the learning disabilities Silver discussed, researchers have devoted most attention to input (particularly visual processing) and output (especially demand). **Reading disabilities (RD;** sometimes called dyslexia) is a disorder affecting reading, especially oral reading. RD is by far the most common type of LD, accounting for some 80% of instances (Lyon, 2002; Shaywitz et al., 1998). According to the International Dyslexia Society (formerly known as the Orton Dyslexia Society), **dyslexia** is defined as "a specific language-based disorder of constitutional origin characterized by difficulties in single-word decoding, usually reflecting insufficient phonological processing" (*http://www.interdys.org*). Dyslexia, explained Shaywitz (1996), "reflects a deficiency in the processing of the distinctive linguistic units, called phonemes, that make up all spoken and written words" (p. 98). In other words, students' difficulties relate to phonemic awareness. Shaywitz's work has focused especially upon demand output, as when people are ordered to read out loud. She has vividly illustrated with the story of a medical student who had mastered a demanding curriculum yet could not accurately read aloud from a simple list (Shaywitz, 1996; see also D'Arcangelo, 1999).

Although researchers agree upon the importance of input and output as dimensions of reading disabilities, they disagree over terminology. Lyon et al. (2001) suggested that the term reading disabilities be used in lieu of dyslexia. These researchers explained RD as learning disabilities related to basic reading skills and reading comprehension. Many experts now shun the use of the term dyslexia, contending that the term is not descriptive and thus not helpful. They recommend use of the term reading disabilities (e.g., Lyon et al., 2001; Lyon, 2002). Silver (1998, 2001) preferred the term "specific language disability," and discussed expressive language disabilities and receptive language disabilities as subtypes. Others seek to avoid using any terms. Levine (2002), for example, devoted 300 pages to explaining, in considerable detail, a broad variety of learning difficulties. Only in his final chapter did he begin to use labels, explaining; "Labeling is reductionistic. It oversimplifies kids . . . Labeling can be dehumanizing; it can consume a person's entire identity" (p. 328).

Another kind of LD, which affects the learning and use of mathematics, is often called dyscalculia. According to Hallahan, Kauffman, and Lloyd (1999), **dyscalculia** refers to difficulties using arithmetical symbols and performing computations. Dyscalculia is somewhat controversial. Experts note that people with LD may experience difficulty when they do math work because math problems frequently are presented in prose. That is, the students' difficulties may not be math-related at all. Other authorities insist that dyscalculia is indeed a distinct disorder, apart from dyslexia. They cite evidence that some students with LD display difficulties with math even when problems are not posed in words (Hallahan, Kauffman, & Lloyd, 1999; Shaywitz & Shaywitz, 1993). Whether or not experts believe that this disorder is entirely distinct from dyslexia, they agree that many, if not most, students with learning disabilities have notable difficulties with math (*http://www.ldonline.org*). Math is, after all, a symbolic language. It makes sense that children who have difficulty with the symbols of one language may have difficulties, as well, with symbols of another (Roditi, 1993). As is the case with dyslexia, many experts prefer not to use the term dyscalculia because, they say, the word is ill-defined.

Dysgraphia is a writing disability, affecting students' abilities to form letters or compose sentences/paragraphs. It can limit a student's ability to do something as simple as writing the letters of the alphabet from memory. Dysgraphia often goes undiagnosed or is confused with dyslexia (which affects reading rather than writing). Silver (1998, 2001) does not use the word dysgraphia, preferring to refer, instead, to output disabilities, specifically expressive language disabilities and fine motor disorders.

Commonalities. Regardless of specific types of LD, individuals with learning disabilities often have much in common. Researchers have found differences in the brain wiring of people with LD as compared to others (Galaburda, Menard, & Rosen, 1994; Livingstone, Rosen, Dislane, & Galaburda, 1991; Shaywitz et al., 1998). In addition, people with LD generally have average intelligence or better.

Differences. People with LD are remarkably different from each other. One student engaged in mirror writing. She wrote her test answers on transparency sheets, telling the

Research That Works

Myths About Reading Disabilities or Dyslexia

Yale researcher Sally Shaywitz (1996), based upon her research, dispelled several myths:

- Backward writing and letter reversals are, in fact, *not* characteristic of children with reading disabilities or dyslexia. These children have difficulty *naming* letters and reading out loud, not (because of dyslexia) in writing letters or words.
- Eye training has *not* been shown to be an effective treatment. The difficulties children with dyslexia have are rooted in the ways their brains work, not in their eyes or optic nerves.
- Dyslexia *may not* actually be more common among boys than girls. It is *identified* more frequently among boys (that is, boys are more likely to be labeled), but such identification may be biased.
- Dyslexia is *not* something people "grow out of." They generally do, however, learn coping strategies that allow them to function effectively as adults despite dyslexia.
- People with high levels of intelligence *can* in fact have dyslexia.

teacher to turn them over and place a sheet of white paper behind them so that her answers could be read. Although everything she wrote by hand was done in this way, she typed and read in the usual manner. Another student told her teacher that she could not simultaneously listen to him speak and read what he wrote on a board or on an overhead. Neither of these students required additional time to complete tests. A third student, however, needed two times the usual test period to complete her mid-term and final exams.

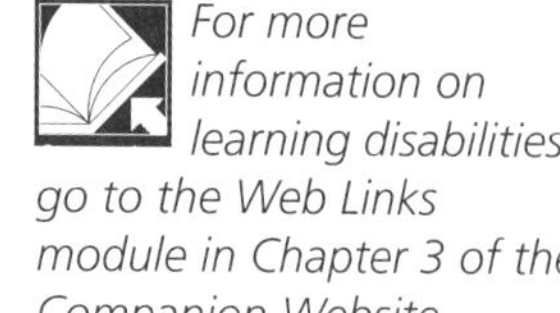

For more information on learning disabilities go to the Web Links module in Chapter 3 of the Companion Website.

Co-Morbidity. Learning disabilities often occur together with other conditions. That is, LD is frequently co-morbid with other limitations. For example, as mentioned earlier, ADHD may occur among children and youth who have learning disabilities. Silver (1998, 1999) estimated that about one-third of students with one condition also have the other. In addition, some students with LD may mis-read facial expressions and/or misunderstand what is said to them by other children, especially in social settings (Dimitrovsky, Spector, Levy-Shiff, & Vakil, 1998; Kravetz, Faust, Lipshitz, & Shalhav, 1999). These behaviors may lead them to withdraw from social interactions and perhaps even be diagnosed as having emotional/behavioral disorders. Finally, some speech and language impairments (SLI) co-occur with LD. We will discuss SLI later in this book. For now, however, SLI features limitations in speech (e.g., articulation, fluency) and/or in language (e.g., aphasia and other word-finding problems). LD, by contrast, is a much more complex disability, one affecting comprehension, information processing, and much more—not just speech and language.

In addition to co-morbidity with other disabilities, children and youth with LD may have limitations that place them at risk for school failure. There is some evidence that young people with learning disabilities self-medicate by abusing controlled substances more than do most students (Center on Addiction and Substance Abuse, 2000). Drop-out rates, as well, are higher than with most other labels (U.S. Department of Education, 2001, Table AD1). Substance abuse and dropping out are discussed in Chapter 11.

Prevalence

As shown in Figure 3.3 (based upon placements reported in the *26th Annual Report*, U.S. Department of Education, 2004), nearly half of all students with the LD diagnosis

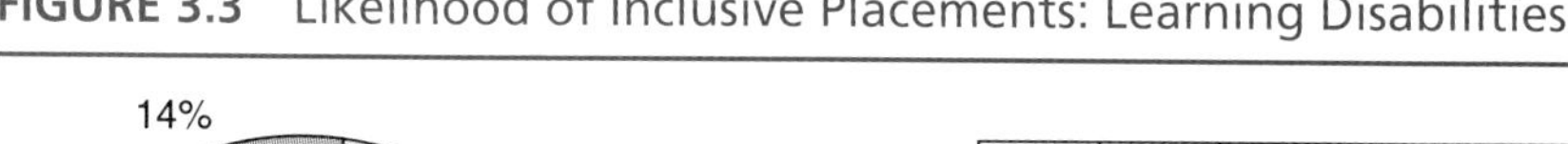

FIGURE 3.3 Likelihood of Inclusive Placements: Learning Disabilities

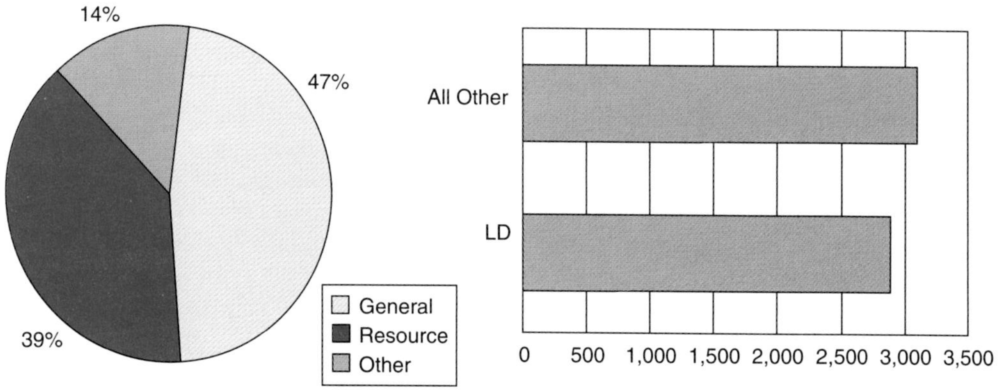

Students with the "specific learning disabilities" label comprise almost half (48%) of K–12 students with any classification. They number 2,870,000, according to the *26th Annual Report* (U.S. Department of Education, 2004). About half of them (47%) were placed into inclusive environments for all or virtually all of the school week (spending less than 21% of the time in other settings). The two charts above illustrate these data.

Source: Based on placement reports from the *26th Annual Report to Congress on Implementation of the Individuals with Disabilities Education Act*, 2004, U.S. Department of Education, Washington, DC: Author.

FIGURE 3.4 Prevalence of LD: K–12

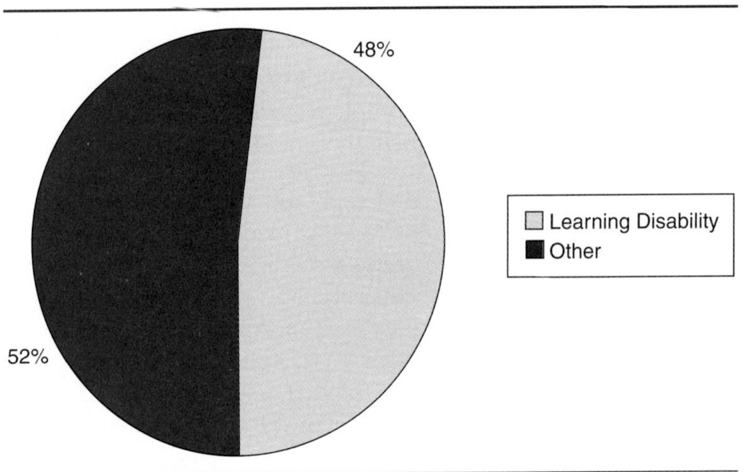

Source: Based on placement reports from the *26th Annual Report to Congress on Implementation of the Individuals with Disabilities Education Act,* 2004, U.S. Department of Education, Washington, DC: Author.

attend general classrooms all or virtually all of the school day. In addition, LD is the most prevalent of all classifications, at 2,870,000 K–12 students in the 2002–2003 school year, or 48% of those with any label (see Figure 3.4). In fact, so common are specific learning disabilities that we can talk meaningfully about how frequent they are vis-à-vis the entire K–12 school population—6%.

For more information on prevalence data based on U.S. Department of Education Twenty-Sixth Annual Report, *go to the Web Links module in Chapter 3 of the Companion Website.*

Among school-age children and youth, LD has been least-often identified among young children. Looking only at those aged 6 through 8 (the primary grade years), those with the label "specific learning disability" comprised 23% of children with any label, during the 2002–2003 school year. The number climbs steadily as children age, however. If we look at the older elementary students, those aged 9 through 11, served during that school year, we see that students with LD represented 51% of students having any label (U.S. Department of Education, 2004). Likely, these figures reflect the use in recent years of a discrepancy formula that has the effect of delaying diagnosis until about age nine (Lyon et al., 2001; Lyon 2002).

LD is most prominent among middle-school and secondary students: 61% of students aged 12–18 who are classified with any label have this one (Lyon et al., 2001; Lyon 2002) (see Figure 3.5). This is probably because diagnosis becomes increasingly definite as children enter the middle-school and high-school grades (see "Diagnosis and Assessment," p. 77). Some children identified as "speech and language impaired" during the elementary years are later found to have, instead, learning disabilities, and so are re-classified as LD during the middle- or high-school years. Importantly, as academic demands grow, from elementary to middle to high school, the effects of learning disabilities become increasingly apparent. For this reason, the greater prevalence of LD at the secondary level may reflect the increasing difficulty of academic work there, as compared to lower levels of schooling.

LD occurs about as often among different racial and ethnic groups as would be expected given the population distribution of these groups: 58% of PreK–12 students with this label are Caucasian, while 19% are of Hispanic origin and 19% are African American (U.S. Department of Education, 2004). There is some overrepresentation of minority groups in this category. It may be that families of low socioeconomic status (SES) tend to read less to young children. Because African Americans are more prominent among low-SES populations than are Caucasians, the appearance is created of racial overrepresentation. The reality, however, is that the underlying causes are more economic than they are racial (e.g., Fujiura & Yamaki, 2000).

FIGURE 3.5 Prevalence of LD: High School

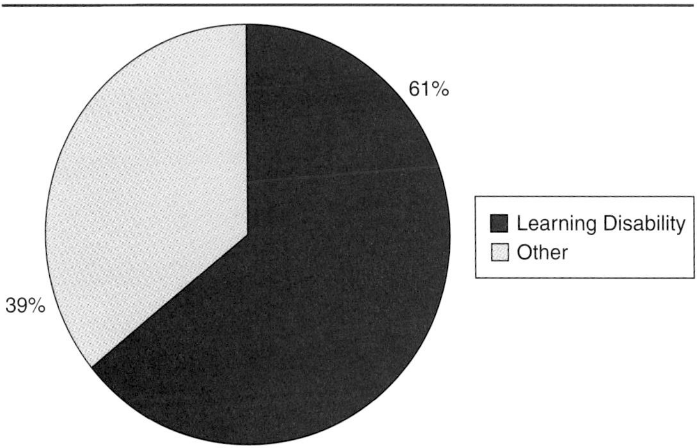

Source: Based on placement reports from the *26th Annual Report to Congress on Implementation of the Individuals with Disabilities Education Act,* 2004, U.S. Department of Education, Washington, DC: Author.

Diagnosis and Assessment

The diagnosis of LD is based upon individualized assessment instruments. Evaluators determine that a child is having academic difficulties that cannot be explained by other factors (e.g., mental retardation, lack of education opportunity, etc.). With respect to reading, they may use timed tests to distinguish children with LD from peers who are delayed in reading for other reasons (e.g., Felton, 2001; Fuchs et al., 2000). In this as in other ways, assessors "test for everything else" before seriously considering the possibility of LD. A child's hearing, vision, and intelligence are all tested, for example. This carries out the "exclusion" requirement in the definition.

If the state continues to require school districts to demonstrate discrepancies, evaluators would then establish that a discrepancy exists. The size of the discrepancy required to satisfy the definition of "specific learning disability" varies from state to state; a 50% discrepancy is common, as is a one or two standard deviation discrepancy. This difference is between aptitude and achievement subscales of the individually administered Woodcock-Johnson III (see Pierangelo & Giuliani, 1998) or between intelligence tests (such as the Wechsler Intelligence Scale for Children, WISC-III; Wechsler, 1991) and achievement tests (such as the Basic Achievement Skills Individual Screener, BASIS; Sonnenschein, 1983).

While testing to establish a discrepancy is controversial, assessment to identify precisely the nature of the child's needs is not. Experts are adamant in insisting that evaluators employ a broad range of probes, looking not just at reading but at each element of the reading process (decoding, comprehension, etc.), not just at writing but at each component of the writing process (letter formation, spelling, mechanics, organization, etc.). The child's weakness may be confined to just one of those parts of larger processes (Levine, 2002; Silver, 1998). The 10 national organizations that reached consensus in 2002 recommended a comprehensive evaluation be used. The groups supported the problem-solving approach that was featured in the federal law "No Child Left Behind" (PL 107-110). That is, intensive and scientifically based instruction should be offered early (during the preschool and kindergarten years, as well as in the primary grades). Children who fail to achieve despite such interventions may be candidates for identification as having learning disabilities (*Specific Learning Disabilities: Finding Common Ground,* 2002).

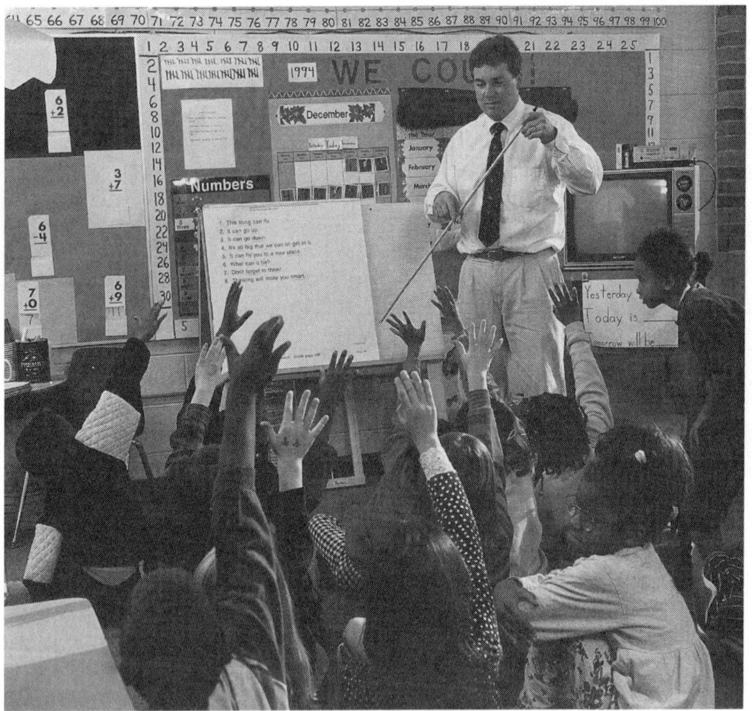

The principles of universal design, illustrated here by the principle of offering information in more than one modality, are very useful in teaching students with LD and many with ADHD.

Causes

The professional literature emphasizes biological causes, although these are not well understood. We do know that LD tends to run in families. Silver (1998) estimated that about 50% of instances of LD are hereditary. He wrote that the causes in other cases are not well known. Some experts point to environmental causes. In these instances, LD is seen as emerging, in part, from poor teaching and/or from lack of opportunities to learn at home. There may be other environmental causes, as well (e.g., brain injuries). As you will recall the official definition from the U.S. Department of Education states that LD may not be due *primarily* to environmental factors; it does not completely exclude such causes, however. Children may inherit from one or both parents a tendency toward LD. That would be a biological cause of a *tendency.* What may trigger that tendency, turning it into a disability, is the environment, such as the parent's failure to read to the child (Lyon et al., 2001).

Genetic Factors

LD may have genetic or other medical causes (e.g., Bender, 1998; Smith, 1998). Many learning disabilities are inherited. These conditions run in families. However, the particular *ways* in which LD affects family members often differ. For example, one woman was unable to listen to conversation and simultaneously take notes. Her son could do those things with ease, but he frequently mis-spoke when he attempted to read out loud. These differences may reflect environmental influences (genes often affect us differently depending upon other, non-genetic factors) (Hallahan, Kauffman, & Lloyd, 1999).

Environmental Factors

In some instances, LD may be due to brain injuries at the pre-, peri-, or post-natal stages of development. Notable among those are fetal injuries caused by maternal drinking; fetal alcohol effect (FAE) and fetal alcohol syndrome (FAS) are leading causes of learning disabilities (Wekselman, Spiering, Hetteberg, Kenner, & Flandermeyer, 1995). As few as one drink each day could prove harmful to the fetus (Bender, 1998; Smith, 1998). There is some evidence that stressful pregnancies are linked to language difficulties (Kotulak, 1993).

Resources That Work

Readings About LD

- *Learning a Living: A Guide to Planning Your Career and Finding a Job, for People with Learning Disabilities, Attention Deficit Disorder, and Dyslexia,* by D. Brown, 2000, Bethesda, MD: Woodbine House. As the title indicates, this is a guide for teens and young adults. The author has a learning disability.
- *Learning Disabilities & Life Stories,* by P. Rodis, A. Garrod, and M. L. Boscardin (Eds.), 2001, Needham Heights, MA: Allyn & Bacon. A collection of autobiographical stories.
- *Introduction to Learning Disabilities,* by D. P. Hallahan, J. M. Kauffman, and J. W. Lloyd, 1999, Needham Heights, MA: Allyn & Bacon. A textbook for teachers and teachers-in-training.
- *The Misunderstood Child,* by L. B. Silver, 1998, New York: Times Books. Third edition. The author is an authority on the topic.

After children are born, drinking water or ingesting paint with lead may also cause LD. As noted earlier, failure to teach or inadequate opportunities to learn are other environmental causes. Learned helplessness, academic difficulties, and problems reading out loud may result from poor teaching.

Instructional Methods

Research on ways of teaching students with LD has produced strong support for Direct Instruction, behavior modification, and strategy instruction. Also documented as effective are teaching approaches that feature pauses between key ideas, repetition of important information, and illustrations or examples. Also accepted by most educators are methods of teaching phonemic awareness and phonics.

Strategies in Early Childhood and Elementary School

First, we look at strategies for young children. Almost half (48%) of elementary students who have learning disabilities were educated in inclusive settings for all or virtually all of the school week during the 2001–2002 school year, according to the *26th Annual Report* (U.S. Department of Education, 2004, Table AB3). For this reason, elementary school teachers can expect to encounter such students frequently. Elementary-age students with LD who are not in regular classrooms all or most of the school day generally are in resource rooms or separate classrooms. This is because they need specialized instruction.

Methods: Early and Intensive Intervention. At the early childhood level, **embedding** special education and related services into ongoing activities is strongly recommended by experts in **early intervention** and preschool special education (e.g., Dunst, Bruder, Trivette, Raab, & McLean, 2001). The technique involves, as the name suggests, inserting specialized instruction while the child is doing something of interest to her. Thus, embedding integrates extra assistance naturally as part of a child's everyday activities. This approach allows educators to include young children with special needs into regular programs while also offering the additional assistance those children need.

Early instruction is widely recommended for children with LD, especially in reading and in math. The fact that diagnosis often is delayed for reasons having to do with methodology (see "Diagnosis and Assessment," p. 77) distresses many educators. As a teacher of an inclusive classroom and as a member of an IEP team, you may consider enrolling young children with LD in "Early Reading First" and "Reading First" programs authorized under the federal "No Child Left Behind Act." These programs are designed to help all children learn to read by third grade, by employing such scientifically based interventions as training in phonemic awareness, phonics, fluency, vocabulary, and reading comprehension. The Learning Disabilities Association of America, other national organizations (*Specific Learning Disabilities: Finding Common Ground,* 2002), and Lyon et al. (2001) strongly

For more information on the No Child Left Behind Act, go to the Web Links module in Chapter 3 of the Companion Website.

recommended that students with reading disabilities and other kinds of LD participate in such programs.

The idea is that scientifically based instructional methods, such as Direct Instruction, should be offered on an intensive basis early in the education of all children. This work should be done by pre-referral teams. These groups are variously known, in different school districts, as teacher assistance teams, pre-referral teams, mainstreaming assistance teams, school-based consultation teams, and the like (e.g., Fuchs, Fuchs, & Bahr, 1990). We discussed such teams in Chapter 2. Individualization of instruction should be based upon the lack of response by some children. Student progress must be documented both in regular and in individualized instruction. Families should have the option of requesting referral to special education if such early and intensive instruction is not made available, or if it proves to be ineffective.

Methods: Direct Instruction. Particularly supported in the literature is **Direct Instruction (DI).** This approach tells educators to explicitly teach skills and content, to test children on their mastery, to re-teach as indicated by those assessments, and to review material frequently over time (Gersten, Carnine, & Woodward, 1987). This strategy features to-the-point teaching, followed by assessment to identify what children do not yet know, re-teaching of those elements, and periodic review. It may include teaching in phonics and in phonemic awareness. Direct Instruction may also be used in teaching math and other subjects (Roditi, 1993). DI should focus upon the most basic academic skills, such as the connections between sounds and letters and fundamental number sense.

The SCREAM approach (Mastropieri & Scruggs, 2000) is one way to implement Direct Instruction at the early childhood and elementary levels. The acronym stands for *s*tructure, *c*larity, *r*edundancy, *e*nthusiasm, *a*ppropriate, and *m*aximized engagement. SCREAM is a way of planning your teaching so that your instruction is highly organized and clear, offering plenty of examples and repetition of key ideas, delivered with energy and positive reinforcement, and featuring opportunities for questions and for feedback.

Methods: Notetakers and Pauses During Lectures. Many students with LD have difficulties with short-term memory. They must concentrate hard to keep new information in short-term memory and must repeat it continuously while writing it down. One effect of these needs is that students may not fully be comprehending your lecture while they are taking notes. To avoid these problems, you might wish to assign a fellow student to be a notetaker. Alternatively, the student may take his/her own notes on a laptop or desktop PC. LD expert Gloria Wilson (personal communication, October 25, 2002) reports that students she has taught can keep up with lectures if they type, rather than hand-write, class notes. If such steps are not possible, you may pause after each major idea. Pauses may take any of three forms: silence, repetition, and examples. Thus, after saying something important, you may cease lecturing for a minute or two. As an alternative, you may immediately repeat what you just said. The third option is to offer an illustration of the key idea. Finally, you may offer important information in "redundant modalities." Thus, if you say something important, the same facts should be offered visually; if you write something important, say it as well. All four of these tactics give students with LD the time they need to write down the important information or eliminate that need altogether.

Methods: Phonemic Awareness and Phonics. Because children with RD typically are lacking in phonemic awareness and in phoneme-grapheme correspondence, explicit teaching in these areas is strongly recommended. The National Reading Panel (2000), a distinguished body of experts, found that research powerfully supports the teaching of phonemic awareness to young children with or without disabilities. The group explained that phonemic awareness is a set of abilities to separate and combine phonemes. Phonemic awareness lets us identify sounds within words ("What is the middle sound in fat?"), to count those sounds ("How many different sounds make up the word Juanita?"), to know which sounds repeat in different words ("What sounds are common to all the following: bat, fat, cat?"), to combine phonemes into words ("What word do I make if I add /s/ to /o/ and then to /m/?"), and to take sounds out of words ("What word remains if I take away the /t/ from boot?"). **Phonemes** are the smallest units of sound that listeners can distinguish. There are 52 phonemes, including diphthongs such as /ai/ (Plante & Beeson, 1999). In the teaching approach known as **phonics,** educators help children to establish the connections between phonemes and their written representations, called **graphemes.** There are 36 graphemes (the 26 letters, plus the numbers zero through nine).

For more information on the National Reading Panel's research on phonemic awareness, go to the Web Links module in Chapter 3 of the Companion Website.

The abilities to separate and combine phonemes appear to be innate. That is why these mental abilities seem so "basic" and "simple" to most of us. They are, however, precisely the kinds of tasks with which children and youth with LD often have difficulty. For them, there is no automaticity to these skills (Fuchs et al., 2000).

What is the difference between the "phonemic awareness" and "phonics"? *Phonemic awareness* is a mental ability, one most of us possess at birth, that equips us to pull apart the different phonemes in the speech we hear and to put together different phonemes to make the words we speak. *Phonics,* by contrast, is a method of teaching, one we use to instruct children to "sound it out" when they encounter new words on a page. We will discuss phonics and phonemic awareness in greater depth in Chapter 14.

Methods: Strategy Instruction. We noted earlier that many students with learning disabilities have difficulties with multistep procedures. Students with specific learning disabilities are repeatedly shown in studies either to lack knowledge of appropriate strategies or, if they do know these, to fail to apply them suitably (e.g., Cawley et al., 2001; Maccini & Gagnon, 2000). That is why much of the professional literature recommends teaching explicit strategies, also known as **mnemonics,** to these children and youth. The intent is to give students an easy-to-remember acronym that cues them on the steps to be followed, and in what order. If, to illustrate, a student needs to remember a four-step procedure, memorizing a string comprised of the first letters of each step helps to ensure that no step is overlooked. For example, the PENS sentence-writing mnemonic strategy (Ellis & Colvert, 1996) tells children and youth to first *p*review ideas (decide what they want to say), then *e*xplore words (find the words they will require to express their thoughts), *n*ote words (be sure all required words are in the sentence, that the first word is capitalized, etc.), and *s*ee if the sentence is OK (proofread it). This illustrates the power of the idea: If students create acronyms that they can remember, and that trigger their memories for the steps of a process, they will be much more likely to perform all steps, in the correct order.

Students who do not have learning disabilities often come up with such strategies on their own. However, those who do have learning disabilities often need to be trained in these techniques. Lederer (2000), who was instructing elementary students having learning disabilities, reported needing to teach them how to ask good questions and make intelligent predictions about a text, how to monitor one's own learning, and how to summarize information. Explicit instruction in strategies for learning and memory is something else that many students with LD require. Because many children and youth with LD do not make effective use of textual cues, they need training to take advantage of heads, subheads, boxes, and other features of textbooks. If necessary, technology can assist. The Center for Applied Special Technology (CAST), in Massachusetts, has pioneered ways to use electronic versions of texts so as to give a student unadorned material (e.g., boxes, graphs, etc., are hidden). Other ideas on teaching strategies are offered in "Student Strategies That Work: LD."

For more information on other assistive technologies and resources, go to the Web Links module in Chapter 3 of the Companion Website.

Many students with LD benefit greatly from being shown "memory tricks" and other strategies for learning and for test taking. While such tactics are helpful for all students, the evidence is that those with LD tend not to learn them on their own, for which reason explicit instruction is needed (e.g., Hallahan & Kauffman, 2000). The

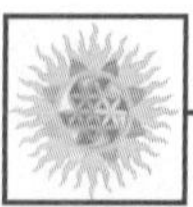

Lesson Plans That Work

Teaching Reading to a Young Child with LD

Assess, Then Teach

Children with learning disabilities (LD) *differ* so greatly one from another that you *must* begin by identifying the specific area(s) in which the child is having difficulty. Some children with LD are limited in their ability to read out loud. Others think they are seeing letters "float" on the page (turning upside down, moving left to right, etc.). Yet others routinely confuse "b" with "d" and "p" with "d" on the page. Here, we will focus on a young child (say, eight years old) who does not yet get the idea of phoneme-grapheme relation (e.g., "doesn't know her letters"). Let us call her Brenda. Clay's Running Record and the Goodmans's Miscue Analysis are two good tools to help you to understand what the child is doing. Both are discussed later in this chapter.

Young children seldom can tell you exactly what they are seeing and doing. You must try this, try that, until you see what works. You might use oral exercises such as those in the boxes, "Teacher Strategies That Work: Phonemic Awareness" and "Teacher Strategies That Work: Phonics" (both in Chapter 14). For example, you could say out loud to her many sets of three or four words, asking her what the one sound in common is. You might speak many other series of words, asking which one is out of place (does not belong in the set). All of this will help you to see if the underlying problem has to do with phonemic awareness or if the fundamental problem lies elsewhere.

You might ask Brenda to place a ruler under the line she is reading. See if this helps. You might even give her similar-looking letters in different colors (e.g., "b" in red and "p" in black). See if that helps. (It probably won't, but it is worth looking at.) You might call her attention to pictures in a story and ask her to talk about those pictures. Can she make up a story based on those pictures? What you are seeking here is to find out if making use of contextual clues (concept maps) helps Brenda with her reading. (It is possible that she usually ignores those pictures. Students with LD often do not make effective use of context when reading.)

Use Direct Instruction

When you know precisely where it is that Brenda is having difficulty, you should explicitly teach her how to do what she needs to do (e.g., to distinguish "b" from "p" or whatever the problem is). As we will see in Chapter 8, the keys to direct instruction are clear teaching of an idea, lots of practice, regular testing, re-teaching as needed, more practice, and (later) more testing. Be prepared to spend a *lot* of time teaching. If phonemic awareness is an underlying problem area, do a great deal of rhyming work with Brenda. Read (and encourage her parents to read) to her Theodore Seuss Geisel's "Dr. Seuss" books such as *The Cat in the Hat.* Sing a lot of songs with rhymes in them. All of this should help Brenda to recognize sounds. It will also support her learning of how printed letters and letter combinations stand for those sounds. Use **manipulatives**—have Brenda cut out letters, paste letters, and otherwise use letters in her drawings and other activities. These exercises give her multisensory input. Ask Brenda questions, and have her make predictions, about stories you read to her. These steps will help her to learn how to make good use of contexts and how to bring her own knowledge to the reading endeavor. They will also expand her vocabulary, which will help when she finally learns her letters.

Provide Support as Needed

Use Center for Applied Special Technologies eReader (see Chapter 8) to provide support for Brenda when she reads (the software speaks words out loud, offers choice of colors, etc.). Give Brenda a paper-board ruler or bookmark to use while she reads (if that is something that improves her reading). Assign a "reading buddy" to do peer tutoring with Brenda, both during school hours and at other times. If Brenda begins to read silently, but still has difficulty reading out loud, you should avoid calling upon her to read out loud until she becomes fluent and confident in silent reading. The eReader program is one example of assistive technologies that can help students with specific learning disabilities. SchwabLearning refers to these as "bypass strategies" because they help children to "bypass" initial difficulties.

For more information on CAST's eReader, go to the Web Links module in Chapter 3 of the Companion Website.

Center for Research on Learning, at the University of Kansas, recommends strategy instruction in these areas:

1. *Paraphrasing.* How to rewrite a story or a text passage into your own words.
2. *Self-questioning.* How to monitor your own understanding.
3. *Imaging.* How to visualize a scene or event to help store and retrieve information.
4. *Decoding unknown words.* How to attack new words to discover what they mean.
5. *Mnemonics.* How to create your own mnemonics to help you recall information.
6. *Error monitoring.* In writing, how to analyze your own work to spot and correct errors. *(http://www.ku-crl.org)*

Student Strategies That Work

LD

As you saw in the "Personal Accounts" opening this chapter, students with LD often need to identify, learn, and practice self-advocacy and self-help strategies. Dana had to recognize her need for support services, even if this temporarily removed her from the classes her friends attended. Together with her family, she advocated for these special-education services. She also had to learn that she was weak in short- and long-term memory, in sequencing, and in inferential reasoning. That self-awareness enhanced her metacognition (ability to think about her own thinking and learning processes). Perhaps most important, Dana recognized that learning would take more time and effort on her part than she observed among her friends. She knew that she would need to make some sacrifices. To her credit, she did. In these ways, Dana helped herself and became her own best advocate.

Involvement of the student is essential, according to Levine (2002). At all stages, from initial identification of problems through implementation of strategies to improve learning, children and youth should be fully informed partners with teachers and parents. Children and youth frequently have a keen understanding of their own problems, although they tend to over-generalize, conceptualizing their difficulties as more pervasive than they actually are (Levine, 2002). Students also may come up with imaginative strategies to circumvent or solve their problems. Recommended steps (Jensen, 1998; Levine, 2002) include

- Do a thorough review of the child's learning and memory patterns. What *specifically* does the child have difficulty doing? Levine emphasized the need to target exactly the issue areas (e.g., not just "reading" but reading what kinds of materials? under which conditions? at what times of the day? etc.).
- Document past successes and failures (child history, family history if relevant).
- Try many strategies and tactics to see which the child does well and which present problems.
- Explain to the child that *everyone,* including very successful adults, have areas of strength and of weakness. Identify for the child his specific strengths and weaknesses. Help the child feel good about the strengths. Explain that there are ways to respond to the weaknesses and that the team (teacher, family, child) will work together on these approaches.
- Try alternative strategies and tactics. See which ones are effective for the child.
- Work with the child on ways to implement successful strategies and tactics. This might include, for example, creating and using a "to do" list on a card. This convenient reminder list may assist the child in carrying out the strategy, not overlooking any steps.
- Document progress. Records are essential. Periodically, review results with the child. Motivation to persist likely will increase once the child sees concrete evidence of improvement.
- Periodically review and reassess. It may be that strategies and tactics that worked in elementary school, for example, may no longer be effective in middle school.

Some approaches require the student to make requests for accommodations such as extra time for tests. Once the child recognizes that a certain accommodation is both necessary and effective, he needs to request it. Teachers and family members need to monitor to be sure that accommodations which are written into the IEP are in fact provided. When the student reaches secondary school, training in self-advocacy should be offered as part of transition services. This is because self-advocacy is an essential skill in postsecondary education and in the workplace (see "Strategies in Transition to Adult Life," p. 88). In college and at work, people with LD must request accommodations. They cannot depend, as can PreK–12 students, upon a team of professionals to make those arrangements for them. Rather, they need to express their needs in understandable terms, including what products and services are available to meet their needs.

In math, students with LD often lack automaticity in basic number facts. That is, they have not over-learned addition, multiplication, and other rules and routines and do not promptly apply them when needed. Roditi (1993) recommended that Direct Instruction be used to develop such automaticity. She also urged use of DI to help students to identify the nature of a problem, recognize patterns, organize information, self-monitor, and self-correct. DI lends itself well to such strategy teaching, because it features explicit instruction in the tactics, testing of the student to ensure mastery, re-teaching of unlearned information, and periodic review.

Methods: Behavior Modification. Learning how to self-motivate is a key to success for many students with learning disabilities. Some may appear to be unmotivated, perhaps because of past failure. Motivation increases when students possess both content beliefs ("I can learn this stuff") and context beliefs ("The strategies that I have acquired will work in this class, with this teacher"). Such beliefs activate intrinsic motivations (Ford, 1992).

For some students, external motivators can help, as well. Experts on behavior modification in classrooms recommend that teachers praise students when they do something right, but ignore behavior that is not appropriate. Students with LD are like most other students in enjoying recognition for work well done, for example, stars, tokens, praise. Because learning disabilities tend to make school work frustrating for these children and youth, "presentation reinforcers" like these give them something to look forward to in the school day. Other students appreciate, after they have done something particularly well, being excused from an onerous task. Such "removal reinforcement" can be a relief. Students with reading disabilities, for example, may dread having to read lengthy materials. Telling them that they have earned the right to skip such an assignment could be a powerful reward.

Methods: Universal Design and Technology in the Classroom. When you change the way you teach so that your instruction reaches different students in different ways, you are practicing **universal design** (Bowe, 2000c). This is a way of preparing to teach, and a way of teaching. Generally, the idea is to design your instruction *from the start* so as to respond to the diversity of needs, interests, and preferences that you will encounter in an inclusive classroom.

The term "universal design" was first used in architecture. There, it was used to develop "visitable" houses, for example, homes that are accessible to all generations (babies in carriages, very small children such as toddlers and preschoolers, senior citizens using walkers or wheelchairs, etc.). The term refers to designing something (a house, a classroom building) so that people of different sizes, with very different needs, can use it. Later, the principles of universal design were applied to the design of consumer products, such as Friendly Fit™ or OXO Good Grip™ forks and spoons.

As applied to education, universal design emphasizes the need for *teachers* to be proactive in advance of instruction. The essential idea is to create alternative versions of instructional materials and to allow students to adopt alternative ways of interacting with them. Universal design in education is a way of planning. The key is to ask the right questions. As a teacher in an inclusive classroom, you need to deal with a broader range of abilities and interests than do most teachers. Some students are visual learners; others learn better by listening. Some work best on their own; others like to work with a partner or two. Some are good with abstract ideas; others do better when concepts are translated into concrete realities. Students with learning disabilities are particularly likely to respond better if you offer them options.

Universal design encourages you as a teacher to ask questions such as Can I make this more visual (perhaps by showing a video, displaying a map, using concept maps, etc.)? Can I offer an auditory learning experience (perhaps by letting students listen to a politician's speech, sing a song popular in another culture, etc.)? Can I make this idea more concrete (perhaps by discussing school and class rules, talking about a recent event in the neighborhood, etc.)? Can I arrange for participatory learning (perhaps by assigning groups to investigate an issue, putting on a play in which students portray historical characters, etc.)? Can I use community-based learning opportunities (perhaps by taking students to a store where they order items and make change, visiting a local museum, etc.)?

Universal design in an inclusive classroom, then, calls for you to make information available in more than one modality. The technical term for this is *redundancy.* You should plan redundancy *in advance* of actual instruction. Many teachers prepare lectures on home and office PCs. This means that these lectures are in electronic form from the beginning. It takes just a few seconds to copy them to a floppy disk, or two. In a few seconds more, you could post them to a personal or course Web site. Now, why would you do these things? A lecture on disk or on a Web site can be listened to by a student whose home PC is equipped with speech synthesis hardware and software. It can also be read at leisure, with whatever aids work for a student (e.g., highlighting).

Speech synthesis is computer talk: the student tells the software what to read, how fast to read it, and whether or not to speak out loud the punctuation marks. The hardware is the speaker that does the actual talking. With speech synthesis, students can listen to texts in addition to, or instead of, reading them. Many school texts are now available as e-texts (electronically published versions). You may check with the publisher of texts you adopt for your class. Recordings for the Blind & Dyslexic provides thousands of texts, including the popular *Harry Potter* series as well as standard textbooks, in electronic form. These are made available to children and youth who have registered with the organization. E-texts may be searched as well as listened to: Students can use the search-and-replace or find features of word processing software to locate specific words or phrases. This can be a real help during studying or while writing a term paper.

For more information on the Recordings for the Blind & Dyslexic organization, go to the Web Links module in Chapter 3 of the Companion Website.

As this illustrates, you can make good use of today's technologies to improve instruction for students with LD. Notice, first, that the popular word processing programs (Microsoft® Word® and Corel® WordPerfect®, among others) have highlighting and font color options. Teachers can highlight key words, phrases, and math symbols in yellow. You can also use red or other different colors for specific symbols, letters, or even entire sentences. In addition, you can insert "comments" into a document, identifying each comment by your initials and a comment number (e.g., fgb12).

Suppose, for example, that a student turns in a composition. You can highlight changes you want made. You can also identify (in red) additions that you recommend. You may cross out deletions you recommend, using overstrike characters. In math, highlighting and/or using red may help if your student tends to perform the wrong function. To illustrate, if you have taught subtraction to your class in recent weeks but are giving a quiz that includes problems in addition, you might want to use a red-color font for the plus sign to make sure the student does not overlook it. These colors do not come out in a black-and-white printer, of course, but they do show in electronic documents. You may e-mail those to your student, at home or at school.

If your school licenses the class management software Blackboard®, you will be able to do even more. This program enables you to compare the first draft of a student's story to the second draft of that story. You can also compare your edited version of the second draft to the student's submission of a third draft. The software places one document on top of the other document, allowing you to see which changes the student did and did not make.

For more information on Blackboard®, go to the Web Links module in Chapter 3 of the Companion Website.

Another software program, Inspiration®, lets students organize their work. Experts on technology and disability have found this software to be particularly helpful for students with LD. Young children who are not yet comfortable with words may use Kidspiration™, which is similar but uses symbols and pictures much more than does Inspiration. It also "talks" with text-to-speech capabilities. These programs let children and youth use a template, or

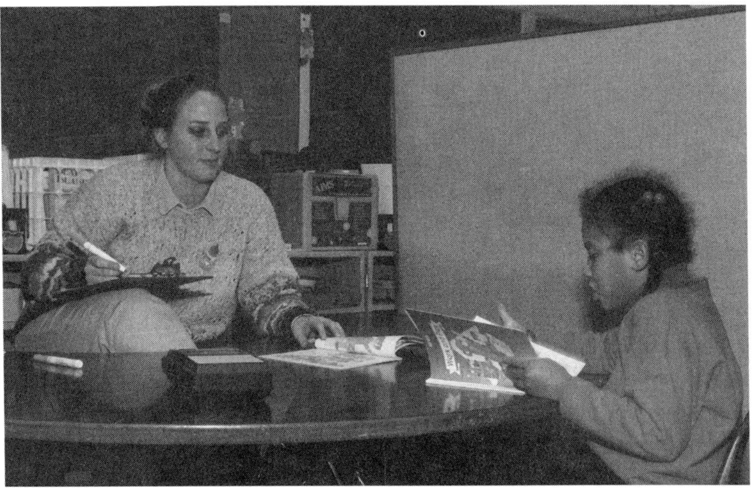

One-on-one tutoring and other supplemental aids and services are valuable for children and youth who have specific learning disabilities.

For more information on Inspiration®, go to the Web Links module in Chapter 3 of the Companion Website.

professionally created boilerplate, for each topic or chapter and to connect the balloons in the template to each other in a systematic way. Templates (Inspiration offers several for language arts, several for science, etc.) facilitate essay-writing. Teachers and tutors may also use these to organize assigned reading, so the student has an outline to refer to while reading. The box, "Technologies That Work: LD," was created, in part, using Inspiration.

Strategies in Middle School and High School

For more information on U.S. Department of Education's Annual Reports, *go to the Web Links module in Chapter 3 of the Companion Website.*

We turn now to strategies with older children and youth. According to the *26th Annual Report* (U.S. Department of Education, 2004, Table AB4) 46% of middle-school and high-school students with the label "specific learning disabilities" spent virtually all of the school week in inclusive settings. As was the case with respect to elementary students, most of those with LD who were not in regular classrooms spent most of their time in resource rooms. Another important fact about LD at the secondary level, as noted earlier, is that 61% of all secondary students with any label had the LD label, versus just 39% at the elementary level (ibid., Table AA7). For both of these reasons, teachers in secondary schools can anticipate having sizeable numbers of students with learning disabilities.

For more information on testing and accommodations provided by The National Center on Educational Outcomes, go to the Web Links module in Chapter 3 of the Companion Website.

Methods: Test-Taking Accommodations. The IEPs of students with LD often include provisions for accommodations to be offered during tests. This includes high-stakes tests such as those required by the No Child Left Behind Act (annual assessments of math and reading in grades three through eight) and tests required for graduation. Ideally, the IEP identifies precisely what accommodations are needed (e.g., if extra time is required, how much additional time?). If not, teachers should work with students to determine the necessary adjustments. This may involve some trial-and-error. Those experiments should be performed during low-stakes tests. In addition, students should receive practice in taking tests under the IEP-required conditions before taking a high-stakes assessment. In 2002, both the College Board (which offers the SAT examinations) and the American College Testing Program, now known as ACT, which owns the ACT test, announced that they would no longer "flag" the scores of students who took the tests with accommodations.

Methods: Strategy Instruction. Many middle-school and high-school students with learning disabilities are especially vulnerable to embarrassment. Wrote Levine (2002): "From the moment a kid gets out of bed in the morning until she is securely tucked into her quilt at night, she has one central overwhelming mission, the avoidance of humiliation at all costs" (p. 286). Teachers and learning specialists need to work with students to identify, practice, and perfect strategies and tactics that will prevent or ameliorate embarrassment. One that Levine recommended is for teachers to announce, the first day of class, that every student will be treated differently because there are all kinds of minds. This may mean that one student will do more reading than others do, but less writing. Such announcements go a long way toward removing the stigma of accommodations such as extra time for tests. Levine also commented favorably upon the practice of many teachers to assign additional tasks to students who receive academic accommodations. A student who is allowed to write a 2-page rather than a 5-page paper, for example, might be assigned an extra book to read. Such "payback" (Levine, 2002, p. 281) tends to be quickly noticed by other students, reducing stigma.

Methods: Scaffolding. Because many students with LD need help in organizing the work, you may wish to offer them scaffolding. **Scaffolding** is structure. It may take the form of a lecture outline. Given to students prior to the lecture, it cues them to each topic and helps them to organize their class notes. Scaffolding for assigned reading might include definitions for key terms, a summary or synopsis of the content, and similar kinds of "hooks" upon which students may "hang their learning" as they work through the assignment. Teachers need to be prepared to provide much more scaffolding at the secondary level than is needed in elementary schools. This is because students, faced with academic work in as many as seven or even more courses, will quickly become overwhelmed unless given some structure to help them organize.

Technologies That Work

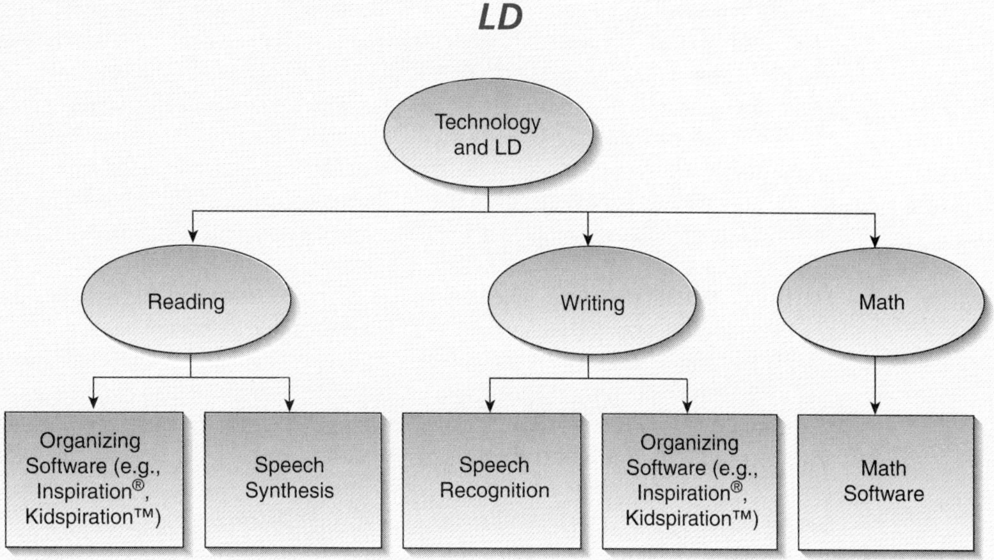

Speech recognition (speech-to-text, or computer "hearing" capabilities) can also be useful for some students with LD. A limited speech recognition program is built into Apple®'s operating systems. Low-cost programs for PCs also are commercially available. Notable among those are Via Voice™ from IBM and Dragon Naturally Speaking®. With speech-recognition programs, students may enter text simply by talking. You may find that they submit longer, more complex essays when they can create these using speech recognition than they do when they must write by hand or type. The major limitation, with respect to children and youth with LD, is that speech recognition programs inevitably make errors. There are sounds that the programs do not understand and words they confuse with other words. The systems offer drop-down menus for purposes of correction. Unless the student knows what the correct response is, however, such menus are of little help. This is a significant issue for some students with LD. They may require much training before they can make effective use of speech-recognition software.

Special software often helps students with LD. For example, IntelliTools® offers a variety of math programs teaching number concepts (addition, subtraction, place value, etc.) as well as IntelliMathics™, which is a problem-solving tool with onscreen manipulatives. These software programs may be particularly useful for children and youth with learning disabilities.

For more information on Via Voice™ and Dragon Naturally Speaking®, go to the Web Links module in Chapter 3 of the Companion Website.

For more information on IntelliTools®, go to the Web Links module in Chapter 3 of the Companion Website.

Speech synthesis, speech recognition, and special software all have proven to be valuable for students with LD. However, it is important to emphasize, again, how variable these students are.

Some neither need nor benefit from any of these technologies. Other students perform at much higher levels when provided with these programs. Most seem to fall somewhere in the middle: they gain some support from these technologies but they continue to require tutoring and assistance from educators. To illustrate, one student needed four hours to take a test without the help of speech synthesis and two hours to complete a similar test with that assistance. Still, she required much more time than did her fellow students, who finished those tests in less than one hour. For all of these reasons, it is important that you not expect too much from computer-based accommodations. They are valuable, but they do not eliminate the effects of learning disabilities.

Allowing students with LD to use PCs, including laptops and such special-purpose devices as AlphaSmart's Dana, both in test-taking and in note-taking, can make a real difference. For skilled typists, keying on a computer keyboard is a far more automatic process (that is, a much less cognitive one) than is writing by hand. Some students do much better writing on a computer keyboard because they can focus their mental energies upon the content of the course lecture or examination. Nonetheless, even those students likely will be best served if offered a scribe to write notes in class and/or write answers in a test book.

For more information on AlphaSmart's Dana, go to the Web Links module in Chapter 3 of the Companion Website.

Methods: Pacing Your Instruction. Because much learning disability relates to processing rapidly changing information, you may pause *between ideas*. If you do not, some students will still be processing your first thought and miss your second (and perhaps your third). Many students with LD cannot pay attention to what you say if they are taking notes on something you already said. This is not true of all such children and youth, but it happens often enough that you might make a practice of pausing when you see them writing notes. A related tactic: After articulating a key concept, give an example. This has the effect of pausing between ideas. A third: Display key ideas visually while also talking about them. This "redundancy" assures that students receive information in modalities most appropriate for them. Students with reading disabilities can listen in addition to reading.

Methods: Peer Tutoring. The technique of **peer tutoring,** which has a fellow student working one-on-one with a student with LD, has much research behind it (e.g., Greenwood, 1997). The big advantage of the method is that it facilitates individualization of instruction. The peer can concentrate upon doing what *that* student needs, which may be difficult for you given that you likely have 25 other students. The key to success with peer tutoring is for you to provide training and explicit instructions for the peer tutor. Peer tutoring offers students the time they may need to process information, to understand it, to test their ideas against others' perceptions, and to apply it to solving problems (Levine, 2002).

Methods: Mathematics Instruction. Research shows that math drill-and-practice routines are of little help to students with LD. Rather, explicit teaching strategies are recommended (e.g., University of Kansas Center for Research on Learning at *http://www.kucrl.org*; Roditi, 1993). Researchers urge you to teach students how to attack math problems-in this way:

1. Conceptualize the problem (Is this a problem of addition? Of subtraction?).
2. Organize details (Separate relevant facts from irrelevant ones).
3. Brainstorm ways to attack the problem, then plan your approach.
4. Do the math.
5. Check your work. (Roditi, 1993)

In addition, instruction on number sense often is needed well into the middle-school and even later school years (Gersten & Chard, 1999). Students with LD continue to make math errors in the most elemental aspects of calculation and problem solving. This is why they need continued support and instruction in those skills.

For more information on IntelliTools®, go to the Web Links module in Chapter 3 of the Companion Website.

Methods: Technology in the Classroom. You may acquaint middle-school and high-school students with LD with technologies that may help them. IntelliTools® offers IntelliTalk™, which is a talking word processor. This product can greatly facilitate writing, because it speaks out loud what the student types. Children and youth may elect to have words spoken as soon as they are typed; sentences may be narrated as soon as a period is entered. See also "Technologies That Work: Learning Disabilities" and "Methods: Universal Design and Technology in the Classroom" under "Strategies in Early Childhood and Elementary School."

Methods: Social Strategies. Explicit instruction on the rules of social discourse (e.g., turn-taking, the awkwardness of pauses) and in tactics for social interaction (e.g., re-stating what someone else says, asking questions) is recommended by the Kansas researchers (*www.ku-crl.org*). Their "SCORE Skills" strategy helps students learn to help each other, extend compliments, ask questions, suggest changes, and control their impulses (Deshler et al., 1996). A key is to give students plenty of practice in non-threatening social situations, so that they may become proficient in use of such strategies.

Strategies in Transition to Adult Life

Many PreK–12 students with LD continue their education at institutions for postsecondary education. Others begin working after high school. In both cases, they quickly discover that they must continue to deal with the written word, with math, and with social-interaction issues. That is why training during the secondary years to help them to prepare for these post-high-school challenges can be so helpful. IDEA refers to this training as "transition" (see Chapter 2).

Methods: Improving Social Skills. Employment typically requires people to be effective team members. Workers need to show respect to others, assume a fair share of the burden, and communicate regularly and fully to other team members. These are skills that are not always taught in school. Particularly during the secondary years, students are assessed on their individual achievement, not on a group's success. This may be a factor in the research finding that when workers with learning disabilities lose their jobs it often is because they were not good team players, rather than because they did not perform their individual roles (Blackorby & Wagner, 1996). This knowledge is information we should "feed back" into our schools. Transition services should include explicit instruction, and plenty of practice, in working on teams.

Methods: Preventing Dropping Out and Delinquency. Many youth with LD drop out of school, hoping to escape the daily frustration they experience in academics. The drop-out rate among these students is high (higher, in fact, than is the case with any disability other than emotional/behavioral disorders; U.S. Department of Education, 2001). After dropping out, these young people discover, to their chagrin, that these same "school subjects" are required for life outside of schools. That is, dropping out of school does not allow them to escape reading, writing, and mathematics. While most (71%) young adults with learning disabilities do have jobs (Blackorby & Wagner, 1996), just 45% of them earn more than $6 an hour, largely because as drop-outs many qualify only for minimum-wage jobs.

Some drop-outs, unable to make ends meet, turn to crime (e.g., Bryan, Pearl, & Herzog, 1989; Keilitz & Dunivant, 1986). A few are even educated in correctional institutions for parts of their PreK–12 years. The *21st Annual Report* (U.S. Department of Education, 1999c), in its Section II, offered a good summary of strategies educators may use to serve those young people, notably to strengthen students' ties to school (e.g., via school-based clubs and activities) and to make instruction meaningful and useful "in the real world" by tying academics to ways in which adults use it. The larger issue is taking steps to prevent delinquency altogether. This includes measures to prepare high-school age students with LD for successful living in the community, including such vital skills as working, making change, and paying rent.

Methods: Preparing Students for Success in College. About three in every ten students with learning disabilities continue their education at postsecondary institutions (Blackorby & Wagner, 1996). During the 1998–1999 academic year, an estimated 63,000 college freshmen reported having LD. They comprised some 3.5% of all college freshmen that year, and 41% of freshmen reporting any disability (Henderson, 1999). These freshmen were more likely to attend two-year (52%) than four-year (47%) institutions of higher education.

Transition services provided during the secondary-school years to students with LD who expect to go to postsecondary programs may prepare these youth for the greater personal responsibilities they will have at college. They will not be offered any support services unless they first *self-identify* themselves to the institution. Generally, this means contacting the college "special services office" or "504 coordinator." The college may, and usually will, require documentation of the disability (e.g., reports of psychologists or physicians; evidence that a PreK–12 school classified the student; etc.). It will be up to the student to request whatever accommodations he believes are necessary. This is a marked change from PreK–12 schools, where all of these responsibilities (identifying students, selecting accommodations) rest with IEP teams, not with students. The HEATH Resource Center, at George Washington University, offers a useful guide to programs at various colleges and universities that are designed to smooth the entry of students with LD into postsecondary education.

For more information on the HEATH Resource Center, go to the Web Links module in Chapter 3 of the Companion Website.

ATTENTION DEFICIT HYPERACTIVITY DISORDERS

All of us are hyperactive, impulsive, and/or inattentive at some times. If you are highly stimulated and anxious (think of how you felt while waiting to learn your score on a very important test), you may jump from thing to thing, finishing none. That is, you would be hyperactive. If you are anxious to start something, feeling under pressure, you may act without really thinking through what you're doing. You would be impulsive. If you are very tired and reading a boring assignment before falling asleep, you may be inattentive. Children and adults who are diagnosed with attention deficit hyperactivity disorders, however, behave in those ways *routinely*.

This chapter addresses ADHD as well as LD. We do so for several reasons. Briefly, ADHD and LD are both high-prevalence conditions that teachers of inclusive classrooms are likely to see. The two frequently occur in the same child; they are, that is, co-morbid. Silver (1998) estimated that 20% of children and youth with LD also have ADHD, while 30% to 50% of those with ADHD also have LD. Both conditions are "mild" in the sense that they tend to respond well to interventions provided in regular and inclusive classrooms, particularly if they receive there the supports they require (called "supplementary aids and services"; see Chapter 2).

There are, however, significant differences between LD and ADHD. Perhaps the simplest, and best, way to distinguish between them is this: In LD, information does get into the brain, whether through the eyes, the ears, or both. The child has difficulty processing and remembering data. In attention deficit hyperactivity disorders, by contrast, the information may never even get to the brain. As Silver (1999) put it, LD affects a child's ability to learn while ADHD limits the child's availability to learn. Whether because they are inattentive to your lecture or to their reading or because they are so physically active that their attention is directed toward their (the inattentive type) activities rather than toward academics (the impulsive/hyperactive type), or both, people with ADHD tend to miss out on much academic information. Another area of difference is that children and youth with ADHD may require less special education and other modifications in instruction than do those with LD. They most need, and benefit from, a structured classroom and shorter-than-usual lessons and test periods. For that reason, many with ADHD do not qualify for services under IDEA but are eligible for services under section 504. Only students who need both special education and related services qualify under IDEA. Section 504 contains no such requirement (see Chapter 1).

Definition

IDEA does not recognize ADHD as a classification; accordingly, neither the law nor its regulations define the term. Students with ADHD may, however, qualify for services under the IDEA, in the category Other Health Impaired (OHI). The regulatory definition notes that OHI includes ". . . limited alertness with respect to the educational environment that. . . is due to. . . attention deficit disorder or attention deficit hyperactivity disorder. . . " (U.S. Department of Education, 1999a, section 300.7[9]).

The American Psychiatric Association (APA), in its *Diagnostic and Statistical Manual of Mental Disorders,* 4th edition (*DSM-IV*), defines ADHD in terms of the symptoms displayed. This is a clinical definition rather than an educational one. That is, it is designed for use by clinicians such as physicians or psychologists, rather than by teachers. The criteria, which are summarized in figures 3.6 and 3.7, state that the child

- fails to attend to details,
- fails to sustain attention to a task,
- has difficulty organizing,

FIGURE 3.6 DSM-IV Criteria for ADHD/I (Inattentive)

1. Inattention: At least six of the following symptoms of inattention have persisted for at least six months to a degree that is maladaptive and inconsistent with developmental level:
   a. Often fails to give close attention to details or makes careless mistakes in schoolwork, work, or other activities.
   b. Often has difficulty sustaining attention in tasks or play activities.
   c. Often does not seem to listen to what is being said to her.
   d. Often does not follow through on instructions and fails to finish schoolwork, chores, or duties in the workplace (not due to oppositional behavior or failure to understand instruction).
   e. Often has difficulties organizing tasks and activities.
   f. Often avoids or strongly dislikes tasks (such as schoolwork or homework) that require sustained mental effort.
   g. Often loses things necessary for tasks or activities (e.g., school assignments, pencils, books, tools, or toys).
   h. Is often easily distracted by extraneous stimuli.
   i. Is often forgetful in daily activities.

Source: Reprinted with permission from the *Diagnostic and Statistical Manual of Mental Disorders,* Text Revision, Copyright 2000. American Psychiatric Association.

FIGURE 3.7 DSM-IV Criteria for ADHD/HI (Hyperactive/Impulsive)

1. Hyperactivity/Impulsivity: At least six of the following symptoms of hyperactivity/impulsivity have persisted for at least six months to a degree that is maladaptive and inconsistent with developmental level:

   Hyperactivity:
   a. Often fidgets with hands or feet or squirms in seat.
   b. Leaves seat in classroom or other situations in which remaining seated is expected.
   c. Often runs about or climbs excessively in situations where it is inappropriate (in adolescents or adults, may be limited to subjective feelings of restlessness).
   d. Often has difficulty playing or engaging in leisure activities quietly.
   e. Often talks excessively.
   f. Often acts as if "driven by a motor" and cannot remain still.

   Impulsivity:
   g. Often blurts out answers to questions before the questions have been completed.
   h. Often has difficulty waiting in line or awaiting turn in games or group situations.
   i. Often interrupts or intrudes on others.

Source: Reprinted with permission from the *Diagnostic and Statistical Manual of Mental Disorders,* Text Revision, Copyright 2000. American Psychiatric Association.

- is easily distracted,
- often leaves seat in a classroom or in other settings where seating is expected, and/or
- often blurts out answers without even waiting for the question to be completed.

The *DSM-IV* continues by noting that these symptoms appear before the child reaches age seven and that at least some of them are displayed in two or more settings (e.g., school and home). More information on these criteria are offered in "Diagnosis and Assessment", p. 98.

Resources That Work

ADHD and Section 504

Under the IDEA, children diagnosed with an attention deficit hyperactivity disorder who require special education and related services because of the condition may be served using the label "Other Health Impaired" (OHI). Those who do not require such services may, instead, be served under section 504.

To read the federal government's memorandum authorizing services for children with ADHD, as well as other ADHD information, go to the Web Links module in Chapter 3 of the Companion Website.

Four brief texts offer helpful information:

- *An ADHD Primer,* by L. L. Weyandt, 2001, Needham Heights, MA: Allyn & Bacon. A good "primer."
- *ADHD: Achieving Success in School and in Life,* edited by B. P. Guyer, (Ed.), 2000, Needham Heights, MA: Allyn & Bacon.
- *Dr. Larry Silver's Advice to Parents on ADHD,* 2nd ed., by L. B. Silver, 1999, New York: Times Books.
- *Attention Deficit Diodes: Assessment and Teaching,* by J. W. Lerner, B. Lowenthal, and S. R. Lerner, 1995, Pacific Grove, CA: Brooks/Cole. Features a helpful resources section.

Problems with This Definition

The APA criteria are problematic in some ways. First, the definition is not easy for educators to apply. It is a clinical one, intended for use by physicians and psychologists. Second, the symptoms themselves are subjective. Whether they are severe enough and frequent enough to merit referral to an IEP team or to a 504 team may depend as much upon the values of the observer as upon the behavior of the child. For one teacher, "often leaves seat" means 2 or 3 times a day while for another it means 20 or 25 occurrences daily. In these ways, the ADHD label may be criticized for lack of objectivity and for potential for being abused, particularly by families seeking to qualify the student for extra time in taking high-stakes tests (e.g., Armstrong, 1995; Breggin, 1998; Shaywitz & Shaywitz, 1993). However, Silver (1999) claimed that such abuse is rare.

Characteristics and Types

Whether because they are hyperactive or inattentive, people with ADHD frequently fail to notice important information. They may appear to be in a rush to complete a task before they understand what they are supposed to do. Alternatively, they may seem to be daydreaming. As this suggests, attention deficit hyperactivity disorders come in three varieties: Primarily inattentive (ADHD/I), primarily hyperactive/impulsive (ADHD/HI), and a combined (ADHD/C) type (American Psychiatric Association, 1994).

Characteristics

One frequent trait of students with attention deficit hyperactivity disorders is that they are consistently inconsistent. They may do well in the morning, yet badly in the afternoon. They may pass a test one day that they fail a few days later. For this reason, many students with ADHD have a record of academic difficulties, particularly in sustaining effort over time, in planning ahead, and in detail work (Weyandt, 2001). In the middle-school and especially the high-school years, the demands on them for consistency will only increase. Silver (1999) reported upon evidence that weaknesses in working memory (the memory we use while we are working on a problem) may be characteristic of people with ADHD. No evidence suggests long-term memory deficits, however (Weyandt, 2001).

It is important to recognize that not all children identified as having ADHD will display all or even most of the following common characteristics. Most will, however, display more than one:

- underarousal, resulting in inattention, at one extreme, and hyperactivity (novelty-seeking) at the other
- difficulty sustaining attention for long periods of time

- social awkwardness and difficulty making and keeping friends
- academic deficiencies

Experts are not sure why these students tend to be underaroused and easily bored. Researchers studying a worldwide population sample of 600 people recently reported that underarousal may be based upon a genetic mutation that probably arose tens of thousands of years ago (Ding et al., 2002). It appears in people with ADHD and also those who are unusually attracted to novelty-seeking behavior. The researchers proposed that the mutation was positively selected (that is, increased in prevalence among humans) because it conveyed greater alertness and thus helped people to survive.

Those with the inattentive variety often miss social cues, simply because they're not paying attention. Such cues can be crucial in the making and keeping of friends. Children with the hyperactive/impulsive variety often blurt out comments, some of them offensive, without first thinking of the possible consequences. It only takes a few such insults or snide remarks to cause them to lose friends. This matters greatly because friends are vital in maintaining students' feelings of connectedness to and satisfaction with school (see e.g., Osterman, 2000).

Many students with ADHD become exhausted trying to focus. ADHD is a medical or biological condition. The brains of these children function differently. They really have to work to do many mental tasks that most of us do without much apparent effort. Accordingly, many students with ADHD have a record of academic difficulties. Their grades are lower, and their suspensions or other punishments for disciplinary infractions are greater than would be anticipated based upon other factors, such as intelligence, socioeconomic status, and the like (Weyandt, 2001).

Students with ADHD, especially those who are also oppositional defiant (see "Co-Morbidity," p. 96), may refuse to go to counseling or, if forced to do so, will resist the counselor's help. You may need to allow such individuals to be "pulled out" of your classroom to see a counselor. You may also arrange for them to hand in an assignment unobtrusively, that is, out of the sight of other students. One teacher told her students who were ADHD and oppositional defiant to attach their assignments to e-mails addressed to her. This neatly ensured that other students did not see these youth hand in their homework.

Weyandt summarized characteristics widely attributed to ADHD. Her list appears in Table 3.1. Any of these, as well as any of the characteristics just discussed, may limit performance on an IQ test, as well as on any other test. For this reason, measured IQ for students with ADHD may not reflect actual ability.

Types

Children who are inattentive (ADHD/I; sometimes labeled "ADD") tend to be "unavailable for learning" because they are not attending to lectures or other academic information; it is as if they are daydreaming. Children with hyperactivity (ADHD/HI; frequently referred to as "ADHD") often do not acquire information for a different reason: They are so busy doing other things. Less common is the combined type (ADHD/C), in which students display a range of behaviors characteristic of both of the other types.

Commonalities. The major commonality among students with these different forms of ADHD is that they miss out on instruction when not attending to the teacher. They also tend to overlook key elements in a prose story or in a math problem. They may blurt out an answer even before you finish asking the question. The different forms of ADHD relate to *why* they miss out on or overlook information. Those who are impulsive cannot restrain their impulse to "cut to the chase" while those who are inattentive simply overlook aspects of the information. Those who are hyperactive may be so preoccupied with physical activity that they don't give the problem the attention it requires. Another commonality is that most, but not all, children and youth with ADHD respond well to medication. This topic deserves an extended discussion.

TABLE 3.1 Common Characteristics of Individuals with ADHD

Early Childhood

Excessive activity level
Talking incessantly
Difficulty paying attention
Difficulty playing quietly
Impulsive and easily distracted
Academic underachievement

Middle Childhood

Excessive fidgeting
Difficulty remaining seated
Messy and careless work
Failing to follow instructions
Failing to follow through on tasks
Academic underachievement

Adolescence

Feelings of restlessness
Difficulty engaging in quiet sedentary activities
Forgetful and inattentive
Impatience
Engaging in potentially dangerous activities
Academic underachievement

Adulthood

Feelings of restlessness
Difficulty engaging in quiet sedentary activities
Frequent shifts from one uncompleted activity to another
Frequent interrupting or intruding on others
Avoidance of tasks that allow for little spontaneous movement
Relationship difficulties
Anger management difficulties
Frequent changes in employment

Source: From *An ADHD Primer* (p. 17), by L. Weyandt, 2001, Boston: Allyn & Bacon. Copyright © 2001 by Pearson Education. Reprinted with permission of the publisher.

Medication and ADHD

More so than is the case with any IDEA category other than emotional/behavioral (E/B) disorders, medication is an issue with respect to students with ADHD. For children who need it, medication can make a difference. The drugs are not a cure. Symptoms reappear quickly if medication is stopped. Thus, the medication treats symptoms rather than the underlying disorder.

The most commonly used ADHD medications are Ritalin® and Adderall®. The prevailing evidence is that these drugs generally are safe for human use. Ritalin has been used for many years and its side-effects are known to be rather mild, as compared to many other drugs. Ritalin is available in a generic form, known as methylphenidate. Also commonly prescribed are Dexedrine® and Cylert®. The newest is Focalin®.

The decision to medicate or not is one that is made by families in consultation with their physicians. Teachers neither prescribe medications nor give them to students. What follows is information that relates to your role in the classroom.

First, the medications used with children and youth who have ADHD treat that condition. They are not intended to have, and do not have, any beneficial effects on co-morbid disorders. This fact is of major importance to teachers. If a student in your class has ADHD and also a learning disability, you must bear in mind that the medication treats only the ADHD, not the LD.

For reasons we do not fully understand, none of these medications help an estimated 25% to 30% of individuals with attention deficit hyperactivity disorders. Silver (1999) suggested that these persons may not in fact have ADHD. That is, they may have been misdiagnosed.

Many family members resist medication. Some may not wish to have their children "on drugs" as a matter of principle. Others worry that if their children begin using drugs, they may "graduate" to more deleterious substances. Yet others express concerns about side-effects. The evidence is that ADHD medications are well-tested, well-understood, and known to have few and rather minor side-effects. One reported side-effect is a temporary stunting of physical growth (Jensen et al., 1994). However, this side-effect is not well documented and, at any event, usually is minor (about one inch; Silver, 1999). Other reported side-effects include some loss of appetite, some difficulty sleeping, and stomachaches or headaches. All tend to be temporary, disappearing within weeks. If they persist, the likelihood is that the dosage needs to be adjusted or the time of administration of the medication changed (Silver, 1999). That being said, Levine (2002) suggested that medication be given only when it is necessary and then only for as long as it continues to be needed.

Other families give children and youth a "break" from medication, often on weekends and during vacations. They may do this because some students who use these medications find the side-effects to be significant. In fact, some refuse to take the pills altogether. Others "forget" to take their medication on a regular basis (the mid-afternoon dose is frequently missed). Aside from such side-effects as a reduction in appetite, a delay in growth, and some difficulty in sleeping, some children and youth report a general sense of being "off"—not quite right. Silver (1999) is adamant that there is no medical justification for "vacations" from medication.

Until recently, the big difference between Ritalin® and Adderall® is that the latter lasts for virtually the whole school day (about six hours), while the former wears off by about lunch time. In recent years, however, many children and youth have switched to a "time-release" version of Ritalin (SR-20, for "sustained release" and 20 mg strength). These time-release versions last six to eight hours. However, if the surface of the SR-20 tablet is broken (e.g., crushed, chewed, cut), the release time may be as short as three hours (Silver, 2002). Dexedrine® lasts four or eight hours, depending on the version. Cylert® comes only in a

Teaching students with ADHD often includes behavior management, notably instruction and practice in following rules of interpersonal conduct.

long-lasting form. It is designed to be administered once a day and to last a full 24 hours. Focalin®, from the same company that makes Ritalin, supposedly is twice as powerful as Ritalin, thus dosages are half as large. Focalin is said to last four hours.

As a teacher, you need to be alert to signs that medication was under- or over-prescribed, for example, that children are unusually "hyper" on the one hand or sleepy on the other hand. You may report those effects to families, which may, in turn, decide to adjust dosage and/or times of administration of the medication. If families give children "medical vacations," you may anticipate that Monday mornings will be stressful for you, because students may be unusually active, impulsive, or inattentive. Generally, by mid-day Monday, the effects of the medication return in full force.

Properly prescribed and taken as directed, the medications generally work. They are most effective, however, in *combination with behavior modification* (Richters et al., 1995). Behavior modification alone has a modest impact. Researchers have pointed out that behavior modification is effective in settings where it is employed (e.g., behavior modification in the classroom has little impact at home; Pelham, Wheeler, & Chronis, 1998).

School personnel often dispense ADHD medications. This has been particularly true in years past with respect to Ritalin® or its generic equivalent methylphenidate, because these last only half the school day. You would see children lining up outside the school nurse's office about noon or 1 P.M. There is some evidence that not all such school staff have been trained in proper administration of ADHD drugs. Lay personnel may unintentionally over-medicate children, leading to distressing numbers of overdoses (White & Yadao, 2000). This is less of a concern today, because time-release versions last the whole school day.

Still a concern, however, is the large and growing number of children and youth taking such medications. A report (Zito, Safer, dosReis, Gardner, Boles, & Lynch, 2000), published in the *Journal of the American Medical Association* (JAMA), found a "dramatic" increase in prescriptions for very young children (2 to 4 years of age). Little is known about how such medications work in children that young (Jensen, et al., 1994). An earlier study by some of the same researchers (Safer, Zito, & Fine, 1999) reported a "great increase" among children aged 5 through 14.

Some children with ADHD are also prescribed antidepressants, which tend to last the full day and thus to smooth out the ups and downs of stimulants. This means that children are on multiple medications. Zito et al. (2000) and Safer et al. (1999) warned that our knowledge of the long-term effects of antidepressants on young children is weak. One known effect is sluggishness or difficulty awakening from sleep or a nap (Silver, 1999).

Differences

Those who are inattentive, generally girls, may be underidentified. Teachers often think that these students are "just shy" and because these students do not disrupt the instruction in the classroom, may not refer them for evaluation (Silver, 1999). By contrast, those who are hyperactive and/or impulsive, usually boys, force themselves upon a teacher's attention. This may result in referral and then to identification (Weyandt, 2001). These referral patterns—which show boys being identified by a 3-to-1 or even higher margin over girls—do not reflect the underlying situation. More and more girls are now being found to have ADHD (Robinson, Skaer, Sclar, & Galin, 2002). The likelihood is that gender is an area of difference in ADHD in *type* rather than in prevalence. Finally, as is the case with LD, there are different levels of severity of ADHD.

Co-Morbidity

About one in three students with ADHD also have an LD (Silver, 1998). Others speculate that the proportion may be as high as 70% (Mayes, Calhoun, & Crowell, 2000). Emotional/behavioral disorders, including obsessive compulsive disorder, oppositional defiant disorder, conduct disorder, and anxiety, may also be co-morbid with LD (Bussing, Zima, & Forness, 1998; Green et al. 1999; Silver, 1998). These terms will be defined in the chapter on emotional/behavioral disorders and mental retardation. The vignette, "Robbie," features a student with ADHD and oppositional defiant disorder (ODD).

Clearly, large numbers of children and youth with ADHD also have another disability. This is a point that Silver (1999) emphasized. Teachers, as well as family members, often must deal with not one but rather two or more disorders. It is important that they distinguish between the conditions, understanding what services are required for each. Often, counseling is a recommended related service, not only to help the student to cope with ADHD but also to assist in treatment of emotional disabilities, conduct disorders, and ODD.

Robbie: A True Story About ADHD and ODD

Robbie is a sixth-grader diagnosed with ADHD/HI and ODD. He is included in a regular classroom at Central Avenue Middle School. Robbie's mother is described by his teacher as "quite adept at making excuses for her child." This year, for the first time, Robbie received medication for his condition. Yet, the teacher says, it is not regularly given to Robbie at home ("I know the days when he comes in without it!"). Robbie's teacher described her experiences with Robbie in this way: "The word 'problematic' does not begin to describe Robbie. He is easily angered, resistant, and defiant. Even during my most exciting lessons, he is easily distracted—and he is actively distracting my other students from the lesson. He taps his desk. He strolls and skips around the room. He makes guttural noises. He forgets what he has learned and forgets what his assignments are. He is easily overwhelmed by the curriculum. Then he threatens those around him. All in all, his behaviors mimic those of a feral child—a child raised by wolves. Robbie once told me, 'I should kill you.' Last year, at the elementary school, he even tried to flush a third-grader down the toilet. I am now embarrassed to admit this, but I almost gave up on educating this child."

But she did not. "He was reading on a 12th-grade level! Robbie was an extremely intelligent boy. I told him as much. I saw promise in him and made him live up to small challenges. I gently guided him. I made sure he knew when 'enough was enough.' I gave him structure that he did not get at home. I fed him. I loved him. And, as any human would do, eventually he warmed up and came to trust me. The fact is that Robbie did not learn in traditional ways. He was technical, kinesthetic, and tactile. He was a problem solver. I turned traditional writing exercises into kinesthetic activities he could succeed with, then built on those to teach him more traditionally."

Settling upon a placement and a set of services for Robbie for seventh grade required months of debate between the school and Robbie's mother. There were two problems. First, his mother did not trust the educators. Second, the services she wanted for her son were costly. Throughout the several weeks of negotiations, the building principal, Mr. Smith, made a point of keeping Robbie's mother appraised of his progress. Eventually, he noticed a change in attitude on her part: She no longer seemed to think the school district was telling her what to do, but now appeared to believe that the principal and others were genuinely seeking solutions. She felt like a member of the team.

With Robbie's mother's active cooperation, the IEP team made rapid progress. She agreed to give Robbie medication on a strict daily schedule at home and also to learn applied behavior analysis techniques so she could reinforce appropriate behaviors. The school, in turn, agreed to assign a trained special educator as a team teacher in the seventh-grade classroom. Robbie will have a behavior plan that will include twice-daily assessments. If he meets his goals, he will have his choice of rewards. Although paying two salaries instead of one was a "hard sell" to the central administration, according to Mr. Smith, the superintendent herself signed on to the agreement.

Will it all work out for Robbie next year? No one knows. But at least he will be given a chance.

—Evelyn

Prevalence

Attention deficit hyperactivity disorders may affect as many as 3% to 7% of all children (Barkley, 1990; Silver, 1999). Other estimates put the proportion as high as 9% of all children and youth (e.g., Wasserman et al., 1999). States do not report to the U.S. Department of Education how many children with ADHD they serve under IDEA. Rather, states report the number of students classified under OHI, which includes ADHD but also has such conditions as epilepsy, asthma, cancer, AIDS, and many others. States also do not report to the Department on the number of children and youth served under section 504. For these reasons, the *Annual Reports* issued by the Department do not contain figures for the label ADHD. The latest report, the *Twenty-Sixth,* shows a total of 393,000 children and youth aged 6 to 21 with the OHI classification, as of the 2002–2003 school year (U.S. Department of Education, 2004). OHI thus is the fifth-largest category (after "the big four": LD, speech and language impairments, mental retardation, and emotional disturbance).

A common misconception is that because ADHD is one of many conditions in the OHI label, this means that at most some 390,000 students have ADHD. That would not be correct. The reason is that many children and youth with ADHD are served under section 504 rather than under IDEA. In fact, schools did so for many years until they were told that they could serve these children under IDEA, using the category "OHI." A decision made by the U.S. Department of Education in 1991 explained that schools and state education agencies may serve children and youth with ADHD under either statute (Davila, Williams, & MacDonald, 1991; *http://www.add.org/content/legal/memo.htm*). We do know that ADHD is the most common neurobehavioral disorder of childhood and one of the most frequent chronic health conditions of any kind in school-age children (American Psychiatric Association, 1994; Weyandt, 2001). This suggests that the number of students aged 6 to 21 with ADHD is quite high, certainly larger than 390,000.

The size of the population of OHI-classified students has exploded in recent years. This growth reflects the tremendous increase in the number of PreK–12 children identified as having attention deficit hyperactivity disorders. The other OHI conditions are not growing nearly as fast. According to the *21st Annual Report* (U.S. Department of Education, 1999c), the number of elementary-age children in the OHI category grew by 308% between 1988 and 1998. Similarly, the number of high school-age students in this classification increased by 286% during that 10-year period. No other label has shown such huge growth as has the OHI category.

Other evidence, from outside the public schools, supports these reports. A major national study looking at trends in office visits and pharmacological prescriptions reported that both showed large increases among children and youth aged 5 to 18 between 1990 and 1998, especially among girls. This clinical evidence suggests that ADHD is being diagnosed much more often among girls than was the case in the past. The rapidly rising rate among girls may help to explain the overall surge in the size of the population (Robinson et al., 2002).

Among school-age children, psychotropic medications are prescribed for boys over girls by a 3-to-1 margin (Safer et al., 1999; Zito et al., 2000). However, the gap narrowed in the 1990s (Zito et al.), as more girls were given ADHD diagnoses and then were given medication. This is consistent with the suggestion of several experts that the gender differences are artificial, reflecting referral bias more than actual difference in prevalence (e.g., Silver, 1999).

Diagnosis and Assessment

Diagnosing ADHD is performed on the basis of reports from family members, educators, and others (e.g., a personal history of the child) and of observations of the child's behavior. The usual practice is for attention deficit hyperactivity disorders to be diagnosed by physicians (frequently psychiatrists or pediatricians), although diagnosis could be made by a psychologist or other qualified person or team of persons, including social workers and educators. The American Academy of Pediatrics issued guidelines for diagnosing ADHD in children aged 6 to 12 in May 2000. These practice guidelines call for children to exhibit symptoms that affect their academic and/or social functioning in at least two settings (generally, home and school; *http://aappolicy.aappublications/cgi/content/full/pediatrics;105/5/1158*). The guidelines tell primary caregivers to follow the criteria of the American Psychiatric Association (1994), in its *Diagnostic and Statistical Manual of Mental Disorders,* 4th Edition (*DSM-IV*).

The APA said that symptoms should appear prior to the age of 7: Because ADHD is neurological, its effects will be evident at an early age (*http://www.aap.org/*). However, according to a survey of parents by Children and Adults with Attention-Deficit/Hyperactivity Disorder (CHADD), an advocacy group, diagnosis often occurs as late as age 10 or 11 (*http://www.chadd.org/fs/fs1.htm*). Diagnosis may occur at any age.

It should be clear from all of this that diagnosis requires the collection of information as well as observation of the child. That is, a multimodal assessment is needed (Silver, 1999; Weyandt, 2001). Levine (2002) cautioned assessors and family members alike to look first at LD. Children and youth who are frustrated because they have not been given the tools they need to cope with LD may act out; before diagnosing ADHD, Levine said, this possibility needs to be investigated. DuPaul and Stoner (1994) offered a five-stage model for assessment (see Figure 3.8).

Distinguishing ADHD/HI from Typical Behavior and from E/B

This multistep process clearly has elements that are subjective and call for evaluator judgment. Distinguishing ADHD from age-appropriate behavior can be challenging. Some observers have questioned the lack of objectivity of ADHD assessment, even going so far as to suggest that ADHD does not exist (e.g., Armstrong, 1995; Breggin, 1998). These critics noted that children and youth who do not have ADHD will at times display inattention, impulsivity, and hyperactivity. They may be inattentive in class when tired or when worried about something. They may be impulsive when excited. And they may be hyperactive when stimulated by caffeine or when anticipating an upcoming event (e.g., a football game against a rival school). For these reasons, overidentification may occur, especially of boys.

Evaluators must distinguish between behaviors that are typical, on the one hand, and behaviors that signal ADHD, on the other. One factor they use is pervasiveness. With ADHD, such behaviors are of long standing. They are persistent. With children and youth who do not have ADHD, by contrast, these behaviors are atypical and sporadic. Another is age-appropriateness. A third is the environment: ADHD-caused behaviors occur in different settings, under different circumstances, while typical children tend to be inattentive and/or impulsive only under unusual conditions.

Teachers and teachers-in-training sometimes ask how they can distinguish ADHD/HI, on the one hand, from emotional/behavioral disorders, on the other. In general, students with ADHD/HI do not hurt themselves or other students, physically or emotionally. The behavior they exhibit is normal behavior—it just occurs much more often than in typical children. Medication frequently makes a dramatic difference for these children and youth. Students with E/B disorders, on the other hand, often do harm themselves and others, both physically and emotionally. Their behavior frequently is not typical at all: It is very different in nature from that of other children of the same age and of students in similar situations. Some children and youth with E/B disorders are oblivious of the effects of their behavior on others. While many students with E/B require medication, the drugs tend to alleviate the more extreme and bizarre behavior, rather than to allow the individual to display behavior characteristic of typical children. In all of these ways, ADHD/HI is a much less severe condition than are E/B disorders. That being said, diagnosing students with one or the other condition remains a judgment call in many cases, requiring the expertise of a trained psychologist or psychiatrist (Kaufman, 2001; Kerr & Nelson, 1998).

FIGURE 3.8 Five Stages of the School-Based Assessment of ADHD

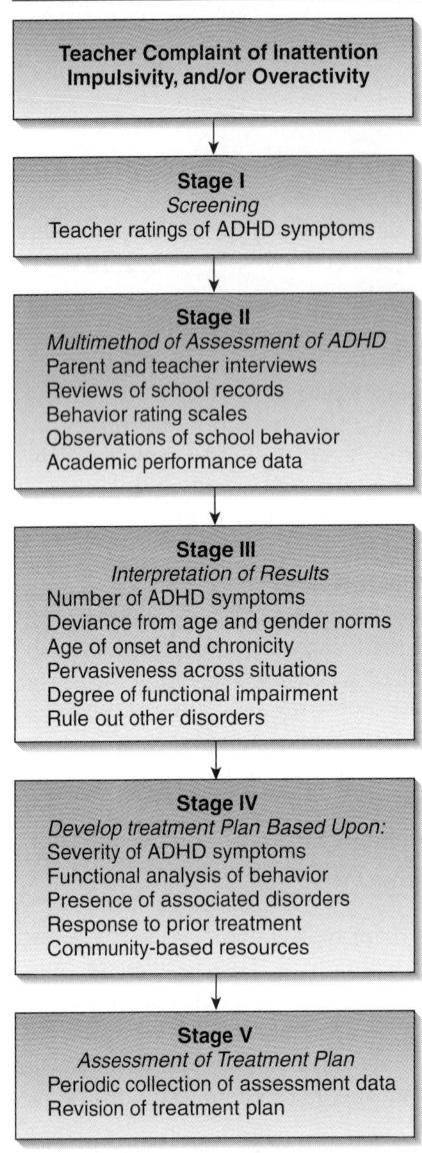

Source: From *ADHD in the Schools: Assessment and Intervention Strategies,* 2nd edition, (p. 32), by G. J. DuPaul and G. Stoner, 2003, New York: Guilford Press. Reprinted with permission.

Causes

The cause(s) of any one child's ADHD is difficult to determine. Most ADHD appears to be genetic in nature, that is, either inherited from parents or grandparents or rooted in some genetic event or mutation during gestation. There are almost certainly other causes, but these are not well-understood. In general, ADHD is conceived as a neurological condition with neurochemical, neuroanatomical, neuropsychological, and neurophysiological causes, rather than environmental ones.

Genetic Factors

The taking of a family history frequently reveals that a relative of the child was identified, by school or family or both, as "hyper" or "always getting into trouble" (to use terms people once applied to what we now call attention deficit hyperactivity disorders). Silver (1999) reported that 50% of instances of ADHD are hereditary (that is, they run in families). This is why the taking of a family history is part of the evaluation of ADHD in children.

As for the other 50% of instances, many may be genetic but non-familial. That is, there may be variations in the amount of critically important chemicals known as neurotransmitters in the brain. Researchers disagree over whether there are too many or two few such neurotransmitters. Some investigators have suggested that the brains of people with ADHD contain unusually large amounts of the neurotransmitter dopamine. Dopamine modulates movement and emotion in the brain. Apparently, people with attention deficit hyperactivity disorders over-produce dopamine. Researchers have been able to count dopamine transporters, using functional magnetic resonance imaging (fMRI) and other techniques of brain mapping (Vaidya et al., 1998). Others, however, speculate that too *little* of the transmitter may be present (Guyer, 2000).

Regardless of who is right on this issue, Vaidya et al. showed that what Ritalin® does is to bind to dopamine transporters. They also demonstrated that Ritalin has different effects on the brains of people with and without ADHD. Guyer (2000) reported that what Ritalin and other drugs do is to raise those amounts to a more typical level.

Environmental Factors

According to Silver (1999), causes for other instances of ADHD are not well known. Maternal drinking is one possible cause (Wekselman, et al., 1995). There may be other non-genetic factors, notably maternal use of prescription and illicit drugs during pregnancy. Perhaps ingestion of lead, whether from the dust of lead-based paint or from old water fountains, is another cause.

We do not have a firm understanding of how modern culture may or may not be increasing the incidence and prevalence of ADHD. There is certainly no lack of possible causative factors. Television, from *Sesame Street* to MTV, accustoms children to very rapidly changing stimuli. Computer games require instant reactions. In the increasingly common two-income families, parents may not provide adequate supervision of children. Foods we eat contain more additives than they did in past years. Young children may have fewer opportunities to engage in stimulating physical activity. As one example of that, a 2-year-old today typically has spent 500 hours in a car seat, versus just 200 hours in a car in 1960 (Jensen, 1998). However, research has yet to connect these cultural changes to ADHD.

Many popular beliefs about what causes ADHD have been dispelled by research. See the box, "Research That Works: Myths About ADHD."

Research That Works

Myths About ADHD

Weyandt (2001), drawing upon her own and others' research, dispelled several myths about ADHD:

- ADHD conditions do in fact exist. They are genuine medical disorders. The contentions of such critics as Armstrong (1995) and Breggin (1998) notwithstanding, there is evidence that the brains of people with ADHD do function somewhat differently than do those of people without ADHD.
- ADHD is a life-long condition. People do not "grow out of it," as was once believed. What many individuals do is to learn how to deal with the condition and how to minimize its effects in their everyday lives.
- ADHD is not caused by dietary deficiencies. Only a very few individuals with ADHD are sensitive to food additives.
- Sugar does not cause ADHD. There is no medical evidence to support this contention.
- ADHD is not caused by poor teaching nor by poor parenting. Those may exacerbate a condition, making symptoms worse than they would be with good teaching and strong parenting, but they do not produce ADHD.

Instructional Methods

The best evidence is that a *combination* of medication and behavior modification works best with most children and youth who have ADHD (Jensen, Vitiello, Leonard, & Laughren, 1994; Kolko, Bukstein, & Barron, 1999; *http://www.add.org/content/abc/factsheet.htm*). We discussed medications earlier ("Medication and ADHD," p. 94). The discussion which follows focuses upon behavioral interventions, including classroom rules, and other non-medical interventions.

Strategies in Early Childhood and Elementary School

Teachers of young students with ADHD may monitor medication, practice the teachings of behavior modification, and set and enforce classroom rules. Research suggests that relatively minor modifications in teaching strategies and tactics can help these children. Your focus, then, should be upon classroom and personal behavior management.

Methods: Behavior Modification. As a teacher, you should remember that all of us, including students with ADHD, respond strongly to internal motivations. Our brains are rewarded when exposed to novelty, when given opportunities to solve puzzles, and when bathed in the hormones associated with pleasure (Jensen, 1998). These facts may be used by teachers to increase student attention to and engagement in academic activities. It is not necessary to rely only on external reinforcements. Indeed, behavior modification research clearly shows that benefits are long-lasting only when people self-reinforce, that is, internalize and self-administer rewards.

The research demonstrating the effectiveness of ADHD medication also noted that it is most efficacious when used in combination with behavior-modification techniques, notably reinforcement of desired behavior and non-reinforcement of non-desired behavior. The key is to be consistent. When a student with ADHD sustains attention to a task, completes a lengthy assignment, and/or obeys classroom rules, you may praise that student. By the same token, you need to recognize that the condition does make attending more difficult for these students than is the case with most students. For this reason, you may anticipate some disruptions in your classroom. Fortunately, these tend to be relatively minor.

Best practice in behavior modification tells you to ignore such misbehavior and to arrange with fellow students for them to ignore it, as well. This can be easier said than done! However, it is critical that you not "punish the victim" by imposing dire consequences on these students for occasional breaches of classroom rules (Kerr & Nelson, 1998; Zirpoli & Melloy, 2001). You should also encourage students to develop, and use, intrinsic sources of motivation. By finding real-life meaning in academic material, children and youth with ADHD can greatly increase their ability to attend to such information (see "Teach Strategies").

Methods: Clear and Enforced Rules. You may set clear rules for the classroom—and enforce them consistently. Again, this can be easier said than done. Even experienced teachers vary from day to day in how much they follow their own intentions. That is why behavior modification experts suggest that you have a co-teacher or other colleague monitor your classroom on occasion and remind you when you fail to adhere to your own rules (Martin & Pear, 2003).

For behavior modification to be effective, "desired" behavior must be known to the students. Children need to be familiar with what you expect from them.

- Step one is to create clear, understandable rules. These should be framed in positive terms (e.g., "remain in seat unless excused").
- Step two, experts in classroom management recommend, you may review class rules daily, taking perhaps five minutes each morning to do so (e.g., Kerr & Nelson, 1998).
- Step three is to enforce them consistently. This step can challenge even experienced teachers. We all want to attend to movement and to unexpected events. You need to

discipline yourself in order to reinforce what you want to see and to ignore what you don't.

Some bending of the rules can be helpful. It is reasonable to accommodate special needs, as long as such accommodations do not disrupt the classroom. Students who are hyperactive may perform better if allowed to get up and walk around on occasion. You may explain to the class that "Johnny needs to be up and around sometimes" to make it clear that such behavior is an allowed exception.

Methods: Teach Strategies. At the early-childhood and elementary levels, *you* often need to organize the student with ADHD. You may introduce academic topics by relating these to your students' lives (including their hoped-for future lives). You may also assemble what the student needs, remove distractions, provide a check-list of steps to perform in order, and the like. Teach the child to check off each task after it is completed. Over time, train her to assume responsibility. This includes self-monitoring of on-task performance and to self-reinforcing for sustained behavior. You can also teach effective study skills, such as minimizing distractions.

Attention to academic tasks increases when threats and distractions are minimized, when instruction features at least some novelty, when we are primed to look at or for something very specific, and when time is made available to process newly acquired information (Jensen, 1998). Very important in attention are emotions (Damasio, 1999). We all have six basic emotions: joy, fear, surprise, disgust, anger, and sadness (Ford, 1992; Jensen, 1998). Teachers and students themselves can tap into surprise and disgust during the course of a given school day. We tend to remember what surprised us and what annoyed us. Joy and anger, too, may be generated on occasion to heighten attention. Joy accompanies the successful completion of a challenging task. Anger is an emotion you might trigger by telling a story that generates annoyance among your students and then by solving the problem posed in the story. In this case, the anger they felt when they first heard the story will help them to remember the solution. Other keys for you as a teacher are to create a safe learning environment (one that eliminates threats and reduces distractions), to surprise your students by doing the unexpected and by varying routine, to highlight important information, and to arrange for "quiet time" during which students may talk among themselves and otherwise use what you have taught them. Similarly, you need to help students with ADHD to take steps on their own to reduce distractions, to surprise themselves, to make good use of textbook features and other indications of what's important, and to process new information.

Methods: Shorter Activities and Assignments. With young children, you may need to keep activities brief. Students with ADHD typically have short attention spans. They may do much better in shorter sessions, with breaks, than in longer ones. Indeed, you may find that by taking steps such as these you improve learning among *all* your students. In addition, more complex assignments may be given during the morning hours. This is because the attention spans of students with ADHD tend to be longer in the morning and also because some such children and youth neglect to take their medication after lunch.

Methods: Modifying the Environment. You may need to reduce distractions for the student with ADHD while also minimizing the likelihood that the child with ADHD will distract other students. As an example, you may seat a child with ADHD away from windows and doors. In more extreme cases, you might seat a child at a carrel or kiosk.

Similarly, you can reduce distractions and ameliorate temptations by giving students with ADHD specific tasks to perform during "transition times"—when one activity ends and the next has not yet begun. These are the periods when children and youth with ADHD are most likely to act out. By giving them assignments (e.g., to clean up, to prepare the room for the next activity) you focus their attention on a specific activity and at the same time give them opportunities to be "up and about" in the classroom.

Technologies That Work

ADHD

Computer games that teach academic skills offer important advantages, because they are fast-paced, because they require the student to participate actively in learning, and because most are multimodal (students see action, read text, and listen to spoken narration and sound effects). There are many hundreds of software programs available that teach math via sports-based games, that teach geography via action games, that teach science through high-resolution graphics and computer-generated images of nature, and that teach English through a wide variety of activities. For example, math games and other activities are available through the Web site "Math Explorer" at *http://www.resource2000.org/math_explorer.htm*. The computer game "Lemonade Stand" teaches elementary students how to run a profitable business. Computer simulations such as those offered at "Visual Physics" can hold the attention of even hyperactive students (*http://library.advanced.org/10170.main.htm*). A key is to select software that requires active participation by the student.

Finally, you may "modify the environment" by tapping gently on the desks or by calling out the name of the student who has the inattentive variety of ADHD. Such steps are small, but they can be effective in "bringing them back" to your lecture.

Methods: Additional Time for Assignments and Tests. If specified in the student's IEP or section 504 plan, you should allow extra time for completion of assigned work and for the taking of tests. Whether to permit these, and what amounts of time to allot, usually will be indicated in the IEP/504 plan. You should not extend extra time for high-stakes tests if that is not indicated in the approved plan.

Methods: Technology in the Classroom. Computer games and other computer-based activities can offer the fast-paced, multimodal activities that many students with ADHD find appealing. The box, "Technologies That Work: ADHD," offers some ideas. There are many others that you should explore. Note, too, that the highlighting and font color functions in popular word-processing software programs that were discussed earlier (see "Methods: Technology in the Classroom" under "Specific Learning Disabilities," p. 88) can help with ADHD students as well. This is because the color calls the student's attention to specific elements of a text or problem. Students who are inattentive and those who are impulsive thus are less likely to overlook important information.

Strategies in Middle School and High School

Medication, behavior modification, and clear rules are as important at this level as they are in the lower grades. Also critical is frequent breaks from demanding academic work. You may find *ADHD in Adolescents* (Robin, 1998) to be helpful in framing strategies to use in middle school and high school.

Methods: Medication and Behavior Modification. Medication alone is often very helpful for youth as it is for younger children. However, the evidence is that in this age group, as with younger children, a *combination* of behavior modification and medication works most effectively (e.g., Jensen et al., 1994). Teachers have most control over behavior modification. As with younger children, a key is for you to be consistent. You might ask a co-teacher, paraprofessional, or other colleague to observe you, perhaps once in the fall and once in the spring. This person could use a checklist to note how you handled each instance of desired and undesired behavior in your classroom. You may well be astonished how often you failed to reinforce good behavior and how frequently you violated your own rule of ignoring disruptive behavior. That is why periodic observation can help you "keep on track" in your program of behavior modification.

Methods: Frequent Breaks. Because academic demands upon middle-school and high-school students typically are heavier than are those on early-childhood and elementary students, the accommodation of reducing the length of assignments and of offering breaks is even more common at this level than in the lower grades. These adjustments recognize the fact that there are medical reasons why sustaining attention for long periods of time is harder for students with ADHD than it is for others.

Methods: Additional Time for Assignments and Tests. How long is "long enough" will vary from child to child. You may consult the child's IEP for information. The IEP Team should have specified in the plan how much time is enough for a test; that information offers you guidance for assignments as well. With respect to test accommodations, recall that frequent breaks in and extended time for high-stakes tests may not be provided for a student unless such are specified in the child's IEP (see Chapter 2).

Methods: Clear and Enforced Rules. At the middle-school and high-school levels, you may be able to rely upon clear, consistently enforced rules, because the students will have learned how to control their behavior more effectively than is the case with early-childhood and elementary students. This means that you may not need tangible reinforcers such as tokens as much as do early childhood/elementary teachers. Nonetheless, standing beside a student with ADHD can still be an effective tool, as can requiring the student to orally repeat instructions and rules so as to satisfy yourself that those are understood.

Methods: Peer Tutoring. Many students with ADHD require frequent "reminders" or prompts to sustain attention to a task. Peers can provide those. You should take time to train the peer on what you expect—and should also find ways to reward the peer (e.g., excusing him from some other assignment).

Methods: Teach Strategies. In contrast to early-childhood and elementary students with ADHD, who generally need external monitoring and reinforcement, middle-school and high-school students with ADHD can lengthen their attention spans, reduce their impulsivity, and control their hyperactivity, at least to some extent, on their own. Doing this requires that they learn, and regularly practice, strategies for self-management. You might teach them, for example, to indicate a need they have to complete one task before beginning another. See "Student Strategies That Work: ADHD."

Strategies in Transition to Adult Life

The major emphasis in transition, for individuals with ADHD, is that of increased responsibility for their own behavior. For this reason, transition services provided during the secondary years should emphasize instruction in, and practice with, behaviors expected in the post-high-school years, notably social interactions, organizing time and materials, and taking necessary medications.

Methods: Social Development. Students with ADHD often need training and lots of directed practice in dealing with social situations. Skills in social interactions can help to prevent students from dropping out, by strengthening their connections to school. Such skills also are vitally important for success in the world of work. Programs teaching such capabilities have been developed at the University of Kansas.

For more information on the University of Kansas Center for Research on Learning, go to the Web Links module in Chapter 3 of the Companion Website.

Methods: Teach Organizational Skills. Life after high school tends to be far more unstructured than is that during high school. That is why it is vital, during the secondary years, to develop the skills of students with ADHD to create their own structure. A key teaching tool is to give these children a structured environment in school, one that has firm and consistent rules. Gradually, such externally imposed structure may be withdrawn. At the same time, students should be trained on strategies for controlling their behavior themselves. In this way, when teacher and parental controls are removed, the young people will be equipped to function appropriately and successfully.

For more information on the HEATH Resource Center, go to the Web Links module in Chapter 3 of the Companion Website.

Student Strategies That Work

ADHD

The story about Claudia's brother, in the chapter-opening "Personal Accounts" section, illustrated the importance of self-advocacy for young people with ADHD. There is much that these individuals can do to alleviate the effects of their conditions on their everyday lives. Claudia's brother, for example, found that he was far more organized and much more successful in hands-on activities than in theoretical ones. He learned this by engaging in self-monitoring. He learned to notice when his attention is waning and to identify activities where his attention typically flagged. He learned how to self-praise, to reinforce himself for sustained attention and for successful completion of a task. With help from his family and teachers, Claudia's brother gradually built up effective study skills, such as minimizing distractions. Something as simple as turning off the radio, the TV, and the stereo while he studied at home or in the college dorm room yielded striking results.

Similarly, children and youth with ADHD who have short-term memory difficulties must learn that they require continued concentration and much repetition in order to keep new information in their short-term memory. More so than is true with other students, they may lose this information if distracted. What helps to reduce distractions may vary from child to child. Some students find that background music serves as "white noise" while they study, making them more attentive despite environmental sounds (Silver, 1999). At the middle- and high-school levels especially, students with ADHD need to identify the strategies that work for them.

Drawing upon research on how the brain works (Damasio, 1999; Jensen, 1998; Silver, 1999), here are some strategies that may be effective as methods to increase attention. What works for one child may not help another (Levine, 2002) so you and your students should try alternative approaches:

- Minimize distractions. Many students with ADHD find that playing background music helps them to attend to academic work (Levine, 2002).
- Reduce threats. Giving students a "practice test" a few days before an important test can reduce anxiety. Enforcing rules that forbid harassment, teasing, and so on, makes the classroom a safer environment. When students feel secure, their bodies and their minds are much more ready for learning than when they feel real or impending threats.
- Connect lessons to meaning. There are two basic types of meaning for most human beings: surface meaning and deep meaning (Ford, 1992). In the former, we know the meaning of a term in that we can define it. In the latter, we know its meaning because we have had personal experience with it and we have an emotional attachment to it. In general, people attend much more to new information that they can connect to their own lives—that is, to data that hold or have the potential of giving deep meaning.
- Engage in physical activity. Even a little—standing up, walking around, stretching—can help us to "wake up" and be more attentive. This is because our bodies and our minds are intimately connected. The hormones and bodily symptoms that give us homeostasis are very powerful influences on attention and learning (Nuland, 1997).
- Employ "teasers" (Jensen, 1998). All-news channels on television (e.g., CNN, CNBC, MSNBC, etc.) make frequent use of teasers to keep viewer attention. These are short, one- or two-sentence, previews that invoke viewer curiosity. Anchors pose questions rather than answering them. These questions relate to viewers on a visceral level or make them curious. You can use the same techniques in your classroom. Your students may, too, in their own study. For example, you or the student may pose a question that has relevance (e.g., when studying division, the question may be "How can I figure out if I can afford a new car?" or "Jorge makes $35,000 a year, yet he was able to buy an expensive car this week. How did he do that?").
- Vary the routine. Novelty increases attention. Do things in a different way. Surprise yourself and your students. To make learning more memorable, use community-based experiences (on-site instruction).
- Use opening and closing rituals. Clapping hands or singing signals a change, quickening the pace of activity as everyone wraps up what they were doing.

For more information on the National Center for the Study of Postsecondary Educational Supports, go to the Web Links module in Chapter 3 of the Companion Website.

For those planning to attend college, the HEATH Resource Center, at George Washington University, identifies some programs with specific offerings for students with ADHD. These include some pre-college programs that are specifically designed to help young people to structure their time productively. Also helpful for secondary educators are resources provided by the National Center for the Study of Postsecondary Educational Supports, at the University of Hawaii.

Methods: Help Students Assume Responsibility for Medications. Counseling about the need to take their medication is an essential step for many high-school students with ADHD. While parents, teachers, and others can and do monitor them in school and ensure that they take their medications on time, such structure may well be lacking when they graduate, drop out, or age out of school. To take just one example of the possible consequences: Given that as many as 9% of all Americans may have some kind of ADHD (Wasserman et al., 1999), imagine that as many as 9% of drivers on the road may be inattentive or impulsive or both! Defensive driving requires that drivers be both attentive and in control of their vehicles.

Silver (1999) expressed optimism that most young people with ADHD can manage the transition to adult life if given the necessary support services. He noted that many individuals learn to moderate their impulsiveness, inattention, and/or hyperactivity as they mature. Some even see a dramatic reduction in symptoms after puberty. It is not uncommon, Silver wrote, for people to attenuate the effects of ADHD to small effects, such as twirling hair, drumming fingers on a desk, and the like. Often, individuals learn what works for them and create their home and work environments around those strategies. One example was offered earlier: Some people with ADHD find that quiet background music reduces the distraction of ambient noises, enabling them to concentrate better.

CHAPTER SUMMARY

Learning Disabilities

- The official definition for "specific learning disability" has three elements: a presumed neurological deficit, exclusion of other explanations for their learning problems, and a discrepancy between ability and achievement. The definition is controversial.
- Students with LD have several characteristics in common: IQ scores that generally are within the "typical range" (85 to 115), difficulty in processing new information, and limitations in short-term memory.
- The most common learning disabilities are reading disabilities (formerly called dyslexia).
- Diagnosis of LD involves use of individualized tests of intelligence and of achievement.
- Direct Instruction in phonemic awareness, in phonics, and in number sense may help many students with LD.
- Scaffolding, strategy instruction, and repetition/pauses also may help.

Attention Deficit Hyperactivity Disorders

- Attention deficit hyperactivity disorders are defined according to symptoms discovered during the taking of a family and personal history and during observations. Inattention, impulsivity, and/or hyperactivity must be displayed more than is age-appropriate, in more than one setting, and to an extent that it interferes with learning and other daily functions.
- Attention deficit hyperactivity disorders differ from LD primarily in that information reaches the brain in LD, but may not when children have attention deficit hyperactivity disorders. They may be inattentive or engaged in other activities.
- Other Health Impaired (OHI) is the IDEA classification generally used when students with attention deficit hyperactivity disorders require special education and related services. If they do not require such help, they may be served under section 504.
- Diagnosis primarily relies upon the taking of a personal and family history, together with observations of the child, preferably in more than one setting.
- Teachers need to be alert to the fact that many students with attention deficit hyperactivity disorders have been prescribed two or more medications. If children seem to be drowsy or otherwise adversely affected by these drugs, teachers should alert parents.
- Behavior modification, abbreviated activities and test sessions, and clear class rules are the most frequent interventions used when children and youth have attention deficit hyperactivity disorders.
- Secondary students with attention deficit hyperactivity disorders often need counseling as well as supervised practice to acquire skills they need for success in school and, later, in work. Such services may reduce the high drop-out rates of this population.

QUESTIONS FOR REFLECTION

1. What does the fact that all of us, at some time, display some of the behaviors discussed in this chapter tell you about the nature of learning disabilities and of attention deficit hyperactivity disorders?
2. Why is the definition of LD controversial?
3. How might characteristic difficulties in organizing/planning, reading social cues, and so on, contribute to problems in adjusting to adult life for persons with LD?
4. What interventions are effective in teaching students with LD?
5. How do learning disabilities differ from attention deficit hyperactivity disorders?
6. Why is the APA's definition of ADHD controversial among many educators?
7. What would you tell a parent who asks your opinion about medicating a child?
8. Why might computer software that teaches academics through games be potentially helpful for many students with ADHD?
9. What kinds of strategy instruction might be particularly useful for youth with ADHD?
10. Which disabilities discussed in this chapter often are co-morbid?

Chapter 4 Communication Disorders

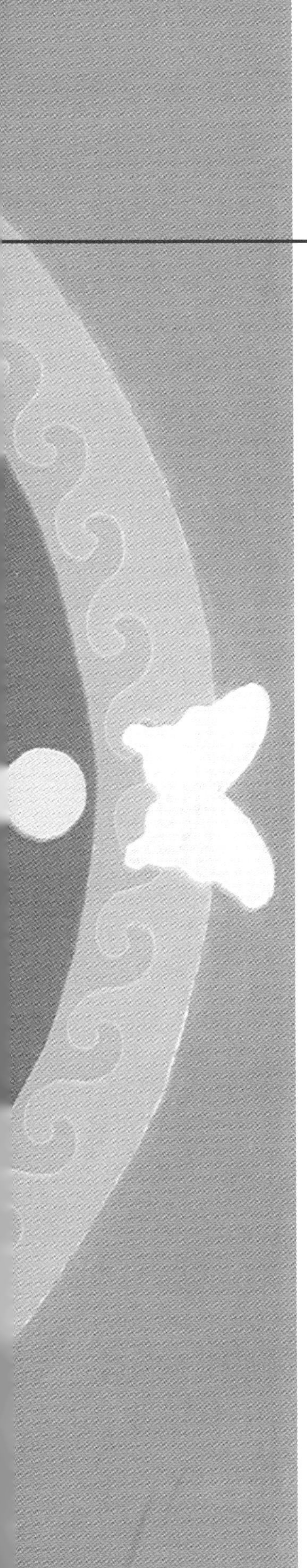

TERMS

Communication disorders
speech
prosody
language
phonology
hearing
speech or language impairment (SLI)
morphemes
syntax
semantics
pragmatics
stuttering
apraxia
aphasia
clinical judgment
elaboration
self talk
parallel talk
miscue analysis
augmentative and alternative communication (AAC)
hard of hearing
cochlear implants
deafness
American Sign Language (ASL)
Deaf culture

CHAPTER FOCUS QUESTIONS

After reading this chapter, you should be able to answer such questions as:

1. How is speech different from language?
2. What are the most common kinds of speech impairments?
3. Why are so many children with speech or language impairments de-classified (found no longer to be eligible for special education)?
4. Speech and language impairments often co-occur with which other disabilities?
5. How can teachers improve language development among young children?
6. Why is captioning a good technology for use by teachers of inclusive classrooms?
7. How can you work effectively with a sign-language interpreter in the classroom?

PERSONAL ACCOUNTS

One woman from upstate New York reported upon her unexpected experiences with a speech impairment. Betty's recollections highlight the social expectations for speech in our society:

> *For two weeks, I briefly entered the world of those who cannot speak. A severe case of laryngitis left me with no voice. There must be something universal about whispering back when someone whispers at you. Almost everyone started whispering when they realized I couldn't talk. Perhaps it goes back to a primeval urge for safety. Be silent if others around you are silent, even if you don't know why. Or maybe it's a social response—to match the volume of your speaking voice to that of those around you. Maybe it reminds us of those times we came barreling through a classroom door talking and laughing, only to be caught up short, embarrassed, in a silent room. Fortunately, I hadn't broken my wrist at the same time as I lost my voice. It is a blessing to be able to write. While I couldn't use the phone, having e-mail made connecting with friends and colleagues so much easier.*

In doing errands, before I approached a sales person I would write down what I needed and any questions that I had. I also noted that I had laryngitis and couldn't talk. Several people, when I gave them my written notes, would then answer me by whispering, which only made it harder for me to understand them. One person read my note and then started using sign language with me, as if I also couldn't hear. Once I mimed that I could hear just fine, she switched and spoke in a normal tone of voice. Another person took to writing notes in response to me. A few people made really bad sexist remarks about how if someone could bottle my laryngitis and sell it to husbands, they'd make a lot of money.

When driving teenagers to a movie, because I couldn't speak, all four teens sat in silence during the 10-minute drive. Ordinarily, they wouldn't even have involved me in their conversation with each other. Because I couldn't talk, it put a damper on their own talking.

Going through the check-out line in the grocery was odd. I couldn't add those little responses (plastic is fine, yes I have a keytag card, thank you) that help to make the interaction less impersonal.

I found that I really appreciated my friends who would keep talking and tell me about what was going on in their lives. Even though I couldn't speak, I was still very much interested in hearing from them.

Being without a voice for two weeks was a mere brush with speech impairment. I had every confidence that I would be regaining my voice. This is obviously a very, very different experience than that of someone who is unable to speak long term. I learned some things that, I hope, will make me a better friend to someone who cannot speak. I also learned much about the "quirks" in social interactions, including my own.

—Betty

Troy is a teen with an expressive language impairment. In their text for speech/language pathologists, Plante and Beeson (1999, pp. 152–155), trace Troy's progress over an eight-year period. Some excerpts show his difficulty in finding the words he wants to use, in making himself understood, in introducing characters and topics before discussing them, and in telling a narrative with a beginning-middle-end structure. He relies heavily upon sound effects and general-purpose words like "owie."

Troy at age 4:

Troy: This the fireperson. This the bell (indicating the fire alarm).
Mother: Does the bell ring in an emergency?
Troy: No. The bell, it has . . . the car come out.
Mother: The cars come out when the bell rings?
Troy: (nods) The telephone do that too!

Troy at age 12, telling the plot of a movie he saw:

It was hilarious. He didn't put the . . . um . . . 'owies.' He only put the best 'owie.' No, that was the second best 'owie.' The first was when the rope that he went down was soaked in some kind of thing . . . that makes fire go on . . . makes it go faster and they were on the rope and say 'Hey Harry, are you there?' No, that's Clorox, or something like that. (Speaks for a movie character.) 'Oh guys' (sound effect of guys falling). 'Get up! Get up!' (sound effect of guys yelling and hand gestures.) Then there's like a bridge and they fall right through and they get covered with all kinds of . . . sticky stuff.

A young woman received a cochlear implant on February 21, 2002. She describes her experiences:

Each person's experience with cochlear implants is unique, except for one thing—it takes a lot of patience, and then more patience, to adjust to the new world of hearing.

> *Doctors and audiologists at the New York University Cochlear Implant Center conducted extensive hearing tests and X-rays to determine if I was a candidate for the cochlear implant. Although I'm deaf in both ears, I have benefitted somewhat from the use of a hearing aid in one ear, which gave me general sound but not enough to understand speech or music. I have always relied mostly on lip reading. They all agreed that I would make an excellent candidate. Still, these specialists shied away from telling me just how well my implant would perform. Something I didn't have to consider was the cost: while the entire expense was about $45,000, my health insurance paid for all of it. Most policies will, I'm told.*
>
> *The procedure requires an overnight stay, and aside from the normal risks of any surgery, a cochlear implant also has post-operational risks, as well as side effects. The most draining side effects are tinnitus, or the perception of ringing in the ear, and vertigo, which occurs because the part of the ear that controls equilibrium is out of whack. Between the piercing ringing and the vertigo, for the first week of my recovery I sometimes felt like I was being hurled through the air in a giant space pod, listening to an imaginary rendition of Verdi's* Falstaff. *It was pretty surreal.*
>
> *Once my scar healed (after about three weeks), I was ready for my audiologist to turn on the implant. She programmed the device to give me sound at a comfortable volume. I heard sound immediately but everyone whose voices I heard sounded as if they had just sucked helium. Soon, people sounded more natural, and I stopped visualizing them as Donald Duck. When friends ask what they can do to help, I say, "Just talk." This, of course, leads to entire conversations about Britney Spears's love life, but I don't mind. I'm hearing things that I never did before, such as birds, raindrops, or burgers sizzling on a grill.*
>
> *This isn't perfect. While I can hear more general sounds than I used to, I can't quite decipher other people's speech yet without also reading their lips. That will come, I think. I can't wait.*
>
> —Suzanne

These stories introduce the three topics of this chapter: speech, language, and hearing. Impairments in those areas are collectively referred to as communication disorders. As Betty's story illustrates, any speech impairment can make social interactions awkward. Notice, too, Troy's word-finding problems. Those difficulties are typical of aphasia, which we will discuss in this chapter. Finally, some 40,000 people have received cochlear implants, as did Suzanne. These help individuals with hearing losses to hear better than they can with hearing aids. Still, as we will see in this chapter, the implants continue to be controversial, for a number of reasons.

INTRODUCTION

Communication involves three basic processes: language, speech, and hearing. Language is a set of symbols and rules for combining them. Speech is the oral means of delivering language. Hearing is awareness of sound, distinguishing between different sounds, and processing those sounds rapidly.

Communication disorders is the general term for limitations of speech, language, and/or hearing. Speech impairments involve articulation, fluency, or voice. Language impairments may be present at birth (perhaps due to a genetic mutation) or acquired later (as from a head injury). Hearing losses may be conductive or sensorineural. Figure 4.1 outlines these types of communication disorders.

Communication may take place in a variety of ways. People commonly speak to express themselves and listen to understand others. However, neither modality is necessary. We can write or sign, rather than speak. We can read text or signs, instead of listening.

FIGURE 4.1 Types of Communication Disorders

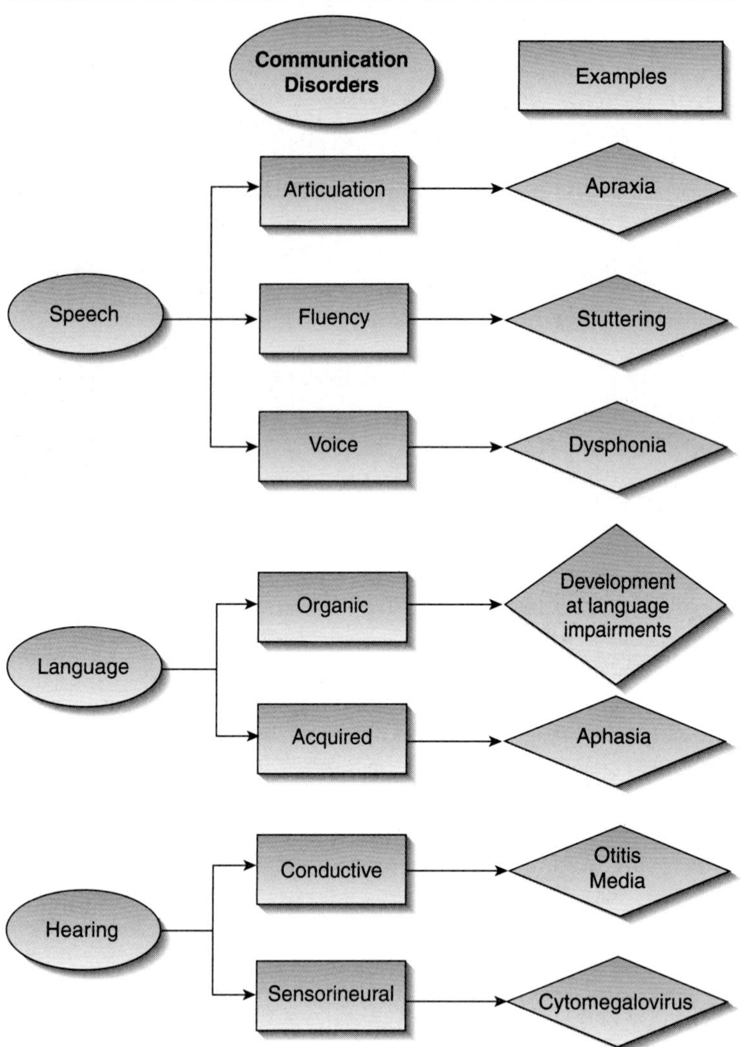

Speech is not language, and language is not speech. One may have speech but not language: Parrots may talk but they do not convey meaning through voice. One may have language without speech: People may write or they may sign, both of which are activities in which they express language. Sign language is a highly articulated and very sophisticated language that is played out in space by the use of arms, hands, fingers, and facial expressions. It has a complex system of formal rules, just as English does. For historical reasons, American Sign Language (ASL) more closely resembles French in its structure than it does English.

Hearing is critical for the development of both speech and language. Most people learn to speak after hearing others speak. They also monitor their own speech production in order to improve the clarity of their production.

SPEECH

Hall, Oyer, and Haas (2001) define **speech** as "the actual movements of the speech organs that occur during the production of various speech sounds" (p. 34). Speech is a developmental activity. It is something we learn during the early childhood years. Typically,

Hearing aids (such as the one worn by the boy on the right) amplify sound but typically not clearly enough to make speech comprehension possible through the ear alone.

3- or 4-year-old children are understandable only to immediate family members, until they begin formal schooling. During their first years in school, the quality and clarity of their speech improves dramatically. This occurs as the children realize that they must articulate more clearly to be understood by non-family members. Intervention by a speech/language pathologist at these ages usually is necessary only if the child's speech is very different from those of age peers.

Pathologists typically rely upon extended practice in clear speaking more than anything else. This is because speech is largely motor in character. It is not something that responds well to intellectual understanding nor to desire or intent. This can make speech pathology sessions frustrating for children and youth.

Speech uses changes in frequency, known as **prosody,** to convey important information. Prosody may be described along three dimensions (Plante & Beeson, 1999): tempo, rhythm, and intonation. Tempo is the speed of speech. We tend to talk more rapidly when we are excited and more slowly when we want to emphasize something. Rhythm is the flow of speech. People who stutter at times display disturbed and otherwise irregular rhythm. Intonation is the rise and/or fall of frequency (pitch). We tend to use rising pitch with questions and flat or falling pitch with statements of fact.

LANGUAGE

Language is a set of symbols and the rules for using them to express meaning. It is, as is speech, a developmental activity. Children typically learn a rule (i.e., /s/ signals plural) and apply it to all instances; only later, do they learn exceptions (i.e., men, not mans). Children's development of language abilities occurs in two dimensions: receptive and expressive. Typically, young children can understand far more language than they use in their own expressive communication. When we talk about language, we often use Bloom's (1988) taxonomy. Bloom characterized language along three dimensions: form, content, and use (see Figure 4.2). The *form* of language incorporates **phonology** (the sounds of speech, called phonemes), syntax (the structures of sentences), and morphology (meaning, in morphemes). Phonemes are the smallest units of speech sounds. To illustrate what Bloom means by syntax, syntactical rules tell us how to construct a sentence so its meaning is understandable: "Elsie beat Tom in the race of class president" or "Tom was beaten by Elsie in the race for class president." "Tom beat Elsie in the race for class president" means something very different. The *content* of language includes semantics (denotative

FIGURE 4.2 Bloom's Taxonomy of Language

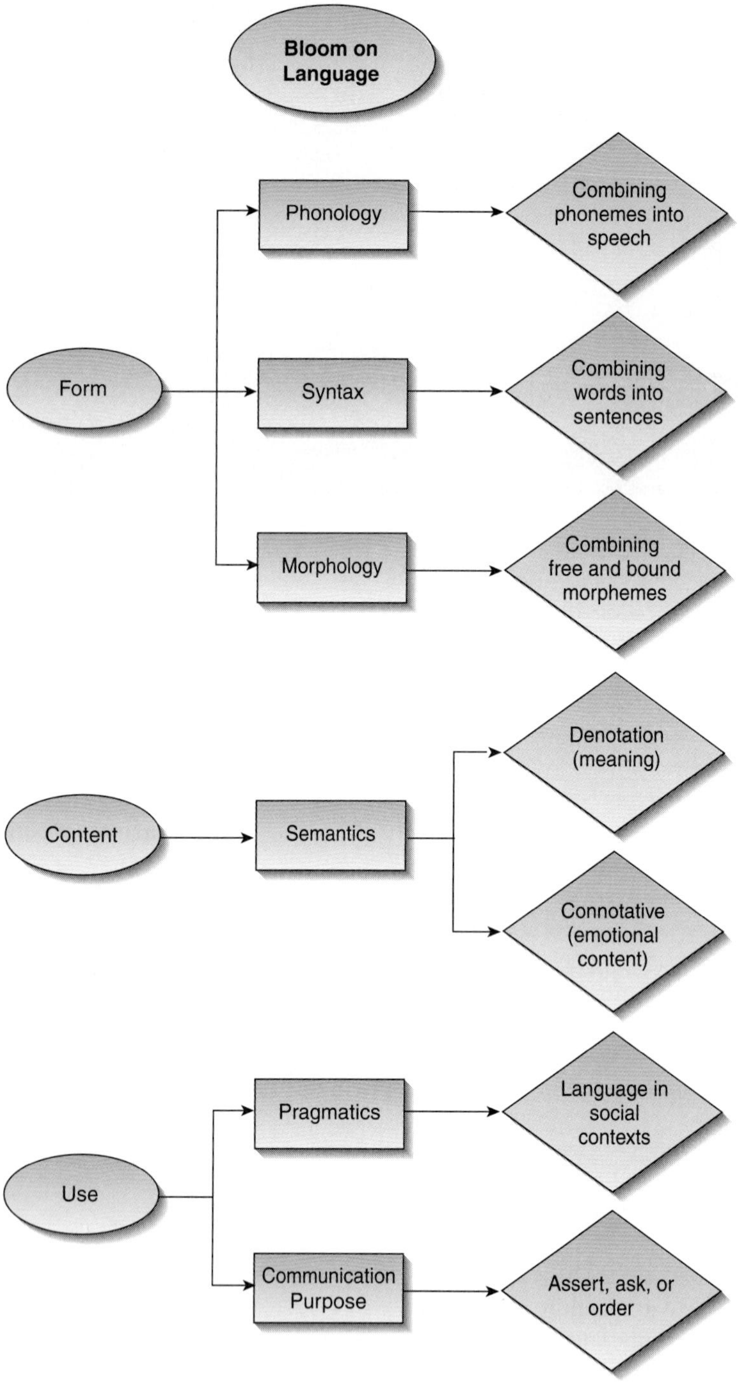

Source: Data from Bloom (1988).

or dictionary meanings and connotative or emotional meanings). For example, "the apple of his eye" taps the connotative meaning of the word "apple" as something that is appealing and appetizing. The *use* of language includes pragmatics (social aspects of language) and communication purpose (to assert a fact, to make a request, to command that something be done). Thus, I might say something like, "May I be excused for a moment?"

to use the rest room when I'm a guest at someone's house, but would just say, if anything, "Excuse me" when I'm in my own home.

The more we use language, especially the more we read, the better we become in our use of language. Therefore, practice—especially reading, more reading, and yet more reading—can help students to accelerate their language development. Unlike speech, which is largely a motor activity, facility with language is a skill that can be attacked intellectually. People can set themselves to increasing their vocabulary, to improving their skill with grammar, and to enhancing the clarity of what they write and say. That is, mental ability makes a difference in language more than is true with speech.

HEARING

Hearing is awareness of sound, the ability to distinguish one sound from another, and the competency to process sounds that follow each other rapidly (Plante & Beeson, 1999). People hear sounds as being loud or soft in intensity and as being high or low in frequency. Loudness or (to adopt the strictly correct terminology) sound intensity is measured in decibels (dB). A whisper is about 10 to 20 dB, conversational speech about 50 to 70 dB, a dog barking nearby 80 dB, and an outboard motor on a rowboat 100 dB. As this suggests, decibels are measured on a logarithmic scale. You can appreciate that by considering that a motor on a boat you're sitting in is not 10 times as loud as a whisper. In fact, that motor is a good 100,000 times as loud. The loudest sound people can listen to without experiencing pain (120 dB) is fully one million times louder than the softest sound people can perceive (0 dB; Kelly, 1985). Frequency is a measure of pitch. Sounds that people can perceive vary from low (about 200 or 300 cycles per second, or Hertz [Hz] in frequency) such as vowels to high (4,000 to 8,000 Hz) such as consonants. The "speech range" is 500 to 2,000 Hz because most speech sounds occur in that frequency range.

For more information on the American Speech-Language-Hearing Association, go to the Web Links module in Chapter 4 of the Companion Website.

Classroom acoustics should be a concern of all teachers of inclusive classrooms. Many teachers are surprised to discover that ambient noise in a classroom can be as loud as conversation. The American Speech-Language-Hearing Association (ASHA, *www.asha.org*) recommends that an unoccupied classroom should not have noise in excess of 30 dB. However, tests show that in actuality an unoccupied classroom often has sounds that exceed 60 dB. That is at the loudness of conversational speech—and this is in an *un*occupied classroom! ASHA recommends that the teacher's voice be some 15 dB above the level of ambient noise in the classroom. This often does not happen, particularly when children are moving around, when they are talking with each other, and when outside noises intrude into the classroom. If you sometimes think that your students are not paying attention, it might just be that they can't hear you (see "Hearing Impairments/Instructional Methods," p. 139).

SPEECH OR LANGUAGE IMPAIRMENTS

Speech and language impairments (SLI) include such disorders as stuttering and other dysfluencies, cleft palate, and other speech-related conditions, as well as syntax errors (saying "He hit her" when "She hit him" is meant), aphasia (unusual difficulty in using words), and other language-related conditions.

Children, and to a lesser extent adolescents, may have or develop any of a wide range of speech and/or language disorders. In fact, most children exhibit irregularities in both speech and language during the preschool years. It is only when speech problems fall outside the "usual range" that we identify children as having speech and/or language disabilities. In addition, difficulties with speech and language are often secondary to other disorders. See the nearby box, "Research That Works: Myths about Speech Impairments."

Research That Works

Myths About Speech Impairments

Plante and Beeson (1999) disprove several myths about speech impairments. Listed are the facts:

- Speech and language are not the same thing. Rather, speech is just one means of expressing language.
- Speech quality is not well correlated with intelligence. In fact, people with below-average and above-average intelligence can speak equally clearly. This is because speech quality is very much a function of muscles and fine-motor control, more than it is a function of intelligence.
- Errors of articulation and of fluency are not necessarily indications of speech and language impairments. In fact, most young children commit both types of errors. Some mispronunciation and some stuttering is quite normal until young children master the sounds of the language and until the many muscles involved in speech mature.
- Stuttering is not necessarily a condition that is readily ameliorated. In fact, some people who stutter as children still stutter as adults, despite years of speech/language pathology services.
- Speech is the not the only acceptable mode of expressive communication. In fact, nonverbal communication (including "body language") is universally used by humans. Sign language is a non-vocal means of communicating. Some people use augmentative and alternative communication systems. All of these are acceptable means of communicating.

Definition

The U.S. Department of Education's regulations for Part B of IDEA (1999a) define **speech or language impairment (SLI)** as "a communication disorder, such as stuttering, impaired articulation, a language impairment, or a voice impairment, that adversely affects a child's educational performance" (34 C.F.R. 300.7[c][11]). Notice that the definition ends with the words, "that adversely affects a child's educational performance." Many of the regulatory definitions of disabilities contain these, or similar words. The phrasing refers to the fact that, to be eligible for services under IDEA, children must need special education and related services. This idea should be a familiar one from our discussion earlier (see Chapter 1).

Problems with This Definition

The federal definition for "speech or language impairments" is relatively unambiguous as compared to some other definitions that the U.S. Department of Education (1999a) has adopted. Nonetheless, it could be clearer. The definition does not explicitly exclude situations in which children do not speak English well, because it is their second language. The Department's rules do add elsewhere (34 C.F.R. 300.534) that if the underlying factor is limited proficiency with English, the student does not satisfy the definition for SLI. Not all educators know this, however. Indeed, school districts often mis-classify such children as SLI. The definition could be improved, as well, were it definitively to rule out speech and language delays that are within the normal range. Because many young children display delays in one or both areas, considerable overidentification occurs in early intervention (IDEA Part C) and preschool (IDEA Part B) programs (Bowe, 2000a).

Characteristics and Types

Speech and language disorders tend to be "mild" in that they produce relatively minor effects on academic achievement, so the vast majority (87%) of PreK–12 students with this classification are placed into inclusive classrooms. That is the highest percentage of all 10 labels, suggesting that SLI limitations are less disabling than are other conditions. According to the *26th Annual Report,* most of the rest spend considerable time in such settings and some time in resource rooms. Most (70%) of PreK–12 students with the SLI label are boys (U.S. Department of Education, 1999c). That is not too surprising, since girls traditionally have been better than boys in verbal activities (e.g., Tompkins, 2002).

Characteristics

Speech and language impairments are common as secondary conditions to other disabilities, notably hearing impairments, specific learning disabilities, and mental retardation (see "Co-Morbidity," p. 121). However, some children and youth have SLI as their primary classification.

Speech Impairments. Persistent and severe speech impairments involve errors of articulation, or the production of sounds. Many speech impairments are violations of the rules of phonology, or the conventions for combining sounds into words we recognize as acceptable in the language. Some children will drop unstressed sounds from words (producing, for example, "member" when they mean to say "remember"). This is familiar as a source of nicknames (i.e., a Lisa is known to her family as "Leese"). Yet others are instances of problems in fluency, the most prominent of which occurs with stuttering.

Speech is a motor activity, one that involves the very fine coordination of hundreds of muscles. It is something most people do at a preconscious level (Shaywitz, in D'Arcangelo, 1999). For these reasons, fluency in speech is not readily amenable to intellectual focus. Rather, it improves through practice. For this reason, much of what speech and language pathologists do in their sessions is drill-and-practice. Anyone who has had speech pathology services can attest to how repetitive these sessions often are. The important idea is that the ability to speak well is not highly correlated with intelligence, nor with desire.

Language Impairments. Language impairments occur along four parameters identified by the American Speech-Language-Hearing Association (ASHA), in addition to that of phonemes (which we discussed earlier in this chapter): morphology, syntax, semantics, and pragmatics. **Morphemes** are the smallest units of meaning, so morphology is the study of meaning. We typically indicate plural, for example, by adding an "-s" at the end of a word and past tense by using the suffix "-ed." **Syntax** is the use of word order to indicate meaning: "She chased the dog," for example, means something quite different from "The dog chased her." **Semantics** is similar to morphology in that both deal with word meanings (some experts subsume semantics as one element of morphology). In general, semantics is the ability to choose and use the right words to express one's meaning and to recognize how others do so. Finally, **pragmatics** is the social use of language, i.e., knowing that one does not say the same things to a teacher that one says to a romantic partner (ASHA; *http://www.asha.org*).

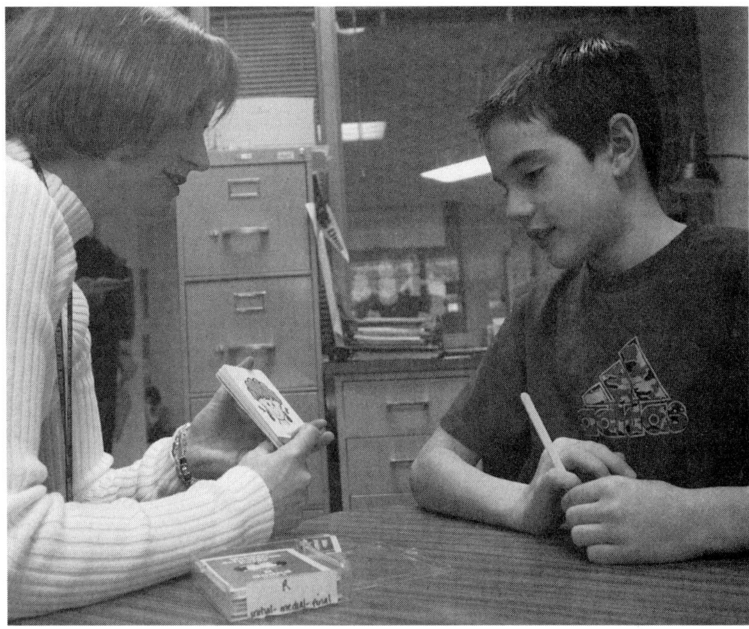

Speech-language pathologists offer one-to-one or one-to-few sessions, typically on a pull-out basis, but may also push into the classroom.

Types

As a teacher in an inclusive classroom, you are most likely to see students who stutter. **Stuttering** is a speech impairment characterized by repetition and elongation of sounds and by sudden disruptions in fluency (Plante & Beeson, 1999). Cleft palate is another impairment of articulation. This is a physical condition usually treated surgically that, despite surgical intervention, often limits childrens' ability to articulate clearly. Speech impairments also include severe apraxia and other phonological disorders (impairments of articulation), as well as dysphonia (impairments of voice). **Apraxia** is an inability to perform a learned movement, despite the fact that the muscles involved in that movement are intact. A brain injury, occurring before, during, or after birth, produces a lesion in the neural pathways that contain the learned movement. In severe cases, speech is affected (National Organization for Rare Disorders, *http://www.rarediseases.org*).

Language impairments include disorders of syntax and morphology. Students sometimes do not know how to combine words into acceptable English sentences (syntax-related limitations) or how to combine free and bound morphemes (morphology-related problems). A free morpheme is one that can stand alone (e.g., "tree") while a bound morpheme must be attached to another morpheme (e.g., "s"). Generally, impairments of syntax and morphemes may be treated successfully and quickly by speech and language pathologists. Language impairments may also be more intractable, as when **aphasia** occurs. This is an acquired language disorder which usually occurs as a result of damage to the brain (e.g., a traumatic brain injury or a stroke). People might say "fife" or "light" when they mean "life" and make other word-finding errors. Most cases of aphasia occur later in life, often following a stroke (Plante & Beeson, 1999). However, aphasia can also appear during childhood (when it is known as developmental aphasia). The box "Research That Works: Myths About Language Impairments" offers some additional information about aphasia.

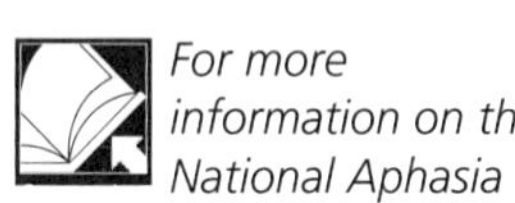

For more information on the National Aphasia Association, go to the Web Links module in Chapter 4 of the Companion Website.

Commonalities. Impairments of language frequently show up in speech patterns, because speech is a primary means by which people express language. Teachers need to distinguish the one from the other. That is because the interventions that are effective differ depending on the condition. If you need help, ask a speech/language pathologist working in your school (see "Resources That Work: How to Collaborate with a Speech/Language Pathologist," p. 127).

Research That Works

Myths About Language Impairments

A major language impairment is aphasia. The National Aphasia Association assembled a quiz with which visitors to its Web site could test their knowledge about aphasia. The questions were based upon common myths. The following are facts that dispel those myths:

- Aphasia is a word-retrieval impairment that manifests itself primarily when people speak. However, it *can* also limit a student's ability to write, read, and understand the speech of others.
- Aphasia usually has a sudden onset, generally following a stroke or a traumatic brain injury. However, developmental aphasia, which appears over time, has also been documented in children.
- Children and youth with aphasia usually have no impairments in general cognitive ability. They know what they have learned about history, math, science, and literature. The problems they experience because of aphasia are in retrieving the specific words they need to use to express that knowledge.
- Strokes or head injuries occur not only among adults but also among children. For this reason, sudden-onset aphasia appears in children as well as in adults.
- People can experience temporary aphasia. The condition is not always permanent. Two to three months following a stroke or head injury, many people recover functions that were impaired, including word-retrieval abilities.
- Individuals with aphasia sometimes do have noticeable physical impairments. This most often occurs on the right side of the body. That is because the left side of the brain, which is dominant for language, controls the opposite side of the body. Thus, damage to the left hemisphere can lead both to language impairments and to right-side physical limitations.

Differences. Apraxia and aphasia sharply illustrate differences between speech impairments and language impairments. Children with apraxia usually have a solid command of the language. If you give them an order, they understand it and can follow it. What they frequently cannot do is to produce speech sounds. That is, they cannot speak despite apparently having the necessary physical equipment (e.g., vocal cords, muscles to control those, etc.). Individuals with aphasia, by contrast, may not have a secure grasp of the language. They know what they want to say, but they can't find the right word in their mental "word bank." Another difference is children with speech impairments may have physical limitations (e.g., cleft palate, cerebral palsy, the hypotonia characteristic of Down syndrome) which may be ameliorated, at least partially, by surgery. Language impairments, by contrast, rarely yield to surgical interventions.

Co-Morbidity. Speech and language impairments may be secondary to other disabilities. These limitations commonly appear with such conditions as specific learning disabilities, mental retardation, deafness or other hearing impairment, autism, cerebral palsy, and others. That is, SLI frequently is co-morbid with other conditions. Many students with mental retardation display limitations of speech. This is particularly true of persons with Down syndrome, because hypotonia (unusually loose muscle control) is one aspect of the syndrome. Children who are deaf or hard-of-hearing regularly exhibit speech that is both delayed in development and quite different in nature from that of "hearing" people, as well as language that is impoverished both in vocabulary and in syntax and grammar. Similarly, people who have cerebral palsy typically speak slowly and with difficulty. In all three instances, IEP teams classify students according to the primary disability (mental retardation, hearing impairment, cerebral palsy) but note the presence of the secondary speech/language disorders. Often, too, children with two or more impairments are first identified with the SLI label, because speech and language impairments are visible during the early-childhood years and because delays in speech and/or language often are the precipitating events that cause families to bring young children to clinics and schools for evaluation. Only later, after extensive testing, does it become evident that there is another condition as well. This often occurs with mild mental retardation, which frequently is not identified until the child begins formal schooling.

Prevalence

Speech and language impairments (SLIs) are the second most-prevalent conditions in PreK–12 schools, among those that are counted separately. A total of 1,100,000 students aged 6 to 21 was reported in the *26th Annual Report* (U.S. Department of Education, 2004, Table AA4) for the 2002–2003 school year. A remarkable 89% of students with the SLI label were of elementary-school age (6 to 11). Stated differently, just 100,000 of the more than one million PreK–12 students with this label were of secondary age (12 to 17). Figure 4.3 displays the distribution. This pattern appears to reflect two factors. First, SLI is often used as a "place holder," while educators determine exactly what the problem is. For example, specific learning disabilities (SLD) present some of the same symptoms as do SLI impairments but commonly are identified later. When definitive testing reveals the existence of SLD, the label is changed. Second, SLI is the mildest of the conditions recognized in the law. Students with this label frequently benefit so much from special education and related services that they are declassified, that is, evaluated and found no longer to be eligible under the Individuals with Disabilities Education Act (IDEA).

About two-thirds (68%) of PreK–12 students with the SLI label were white, 12% were black, and 16% were of Hispanic origin, according to the *22nd Annual Report* (U.S. Department of Education, 2000b, Table AA3).

Diagnosis and Assessment

The *Diagnostic and Statistical Manual,* 4th edition (*DSM-IV;* American Psychiatric Association, 1994) describes impairments of speech as age-inappropriate omission or substitution

FIGURE 4.3 Students with Speech/Language Impairments

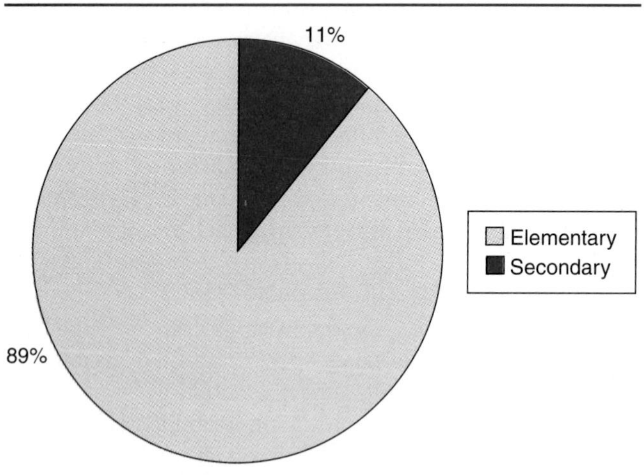

Source: Adapted from Tables AB3-AB4 in the *26th Annual Report*, 2004, U.S. Department of Education, Washington, DC: Author.

of sounds during speech and of speech sounds being inappropriately made. *DSM-IV* characterizes language disorders as "expressive" or "receptive-expressive" in nature. Both are diagnosed by comparing development to that of same age peers. Disorders of expressive language are characterized scores on standardized measures of expressive language that are substantially below scores for verbal intelligence and for receptive language. Notably, there are small vocabularies, errors in vocabulary (choosing the wrong words to express meaning), short sentences, simplified grammar, and unusual word order. Disorders that are "mixed receptive-expressive," according to the *DSM-IV,* include the above but add impairments in comprehension of language, particularly of expressions that indicate space (above, under, etc.) and relations (if-then, etc.).

It should be clear from all of this that considerable **clinical judgment** is involved in diagnosis. That is, much of the diagnostic process relies upon the clinician's discretion in determining that behaviors are not typical of the child's age group. Speech-language pathologists look at childrens' ability to complete rhymes, identify the sounds of a word (phoneme segmentation), and comprehend what is said to them. For example, they may identify apraxia after noting a marked discrepancy between a child's ability to understand speech and his ability to produce it.

While diagnosis and assessment of SLI limitations can be challenging, it is more straightforward than is the case with specific learning disabilities (see Chapter 3). Speech and language impairments and delays in development are quickly noticed by family members, who rapidly bring the child to diagnosticians for evaluation. SLD, by contrast, usually becomes evident only after children begin doing academic work. Similarly, there is no discrepancy requirement to meet to satisfy the SLI definition, as there is with SLD. This, as it happens, makes a major difference. Diagnosticians can identify SLI disabilities at much younger ages than is the case with SLD.

For more information on ASHA's documentation on how children are classified with SLI, go to the Web Links module in Chapter 4 of the Companion Website.

Educators sometimes inappropriately apply the SLI label. Children who come from homes where a language other than English is spoken are not, for that reason, "speech and language impaired." To qualify for that classification, children must demonstrate disorders in *both* languages. Similarly, people who speak African-American English (also referred to as "Black English" or as "Ebonics," the latter term being a combination of the words "ebony" and "phonics") do not, on that basis alone, have SLIs. Rather, this is usually considered to be a dialect of English or even a language of its own (Hall, Oyer, & Haas, 2001).

Causes

Speech and language impairments may be caused by organic/physical factors, as when aphasia results from a head injury. More frequently, however, SLI limitations result from environmental factors, as when parents and other family members fail to model clear and accurate speech or language patterns.

Genetic Factors

Some speech impairments may be caused by physical conditions, as with cleft palate. This occurs when facial tissues do not fuse appropriately during fetal development. It may happen due to a genetic mutation, a non-inherited condition. Plastic surgery often repairs the damage. However, even after such interventions, children may have difficulty articulating clearly.

A technical overview of the physiology of speech is offered by John Palmer in *Anatomy for Speech and Hearing* (1993). That review is particularly impressive in the way it graphically presents a convincing case that many small muscles are involved in the speech act. These muscles must mature before speech becomes consistently clear and articulate. For this reason, Palmer's book is a good reference to pull if a parent is unduly concerned about the speech of a young child. It can help you, as the child's teacher, to explain that there likely is no organic impairment. Rather, the parent should just give the child more time.

Environmental Factors

Many speech and language impairments, such as stuttering, may be caused, in part, by the environment. When children feel they must rush to complete a statement before being interrupted by a sibling, for example, they may begin to stutter. Parents may prevent this by insisting upon "one person at a time" rules in the home. Family members may take other steps as well. In families of middle or upper socioeconomic status (SES), adults tend to use, and to expect children also to use, clear pronunciation of words, in standard English. Additionally, such homes tend to be characterized by **elaboration.** That is, when an adult tells a child "No!" a reason is given. Language is used to explain events. Too often, lower SES homes are not characterized by similar emphases upon the use of speech and language for communication purposes. Rather, the "No!" may stand on its own, unexplained.

A hearing loss may lead to a speech impairment, for one or both of two reasons. First, the child may not hear the speech of others clearly, so she may not benefit from the modeling they offer of clear speech. Second, the child may not hear her own speech well enough to monitor and improve it. Down syndrome may cause speech impairments because one aspect of the syndrome is hypotonia in muscles (looseness; the opposite of hypertension). Cerebral palsy may cause impairments of speech because the motor cortex sends irregular and spasmodic signals to the muscles, including the many muscles involved in the speech act.

Language impairments may have organic roots, as with aphasia, where certain parts of the brain are damaged to the point that the individual is not able to use language naturally. A good discussion of neurophysiological conditions affecting language may be found in Antonio Damasio's *The Feeling of What Happens* (1999). Damasio's treatment differs sharply from that of Palmer (1993). Whereas Palmer focuses upon anatomy, Damasio helps us to understand how all the parts function together, both in speech and in language. Damasio has an engaging style that makes his book relatively easy to read.

Instructional Methods

SLI impairments, being "mild" by comparison to other IDEA disabilities, tend to respond quickly to relatively modest interventions. Speech/language pathology services, combined with conscientious follow-through by teachers of inclusive classrooms, can make a real difference. This is why many students are declassified (found no longer to be eligible for special education) before entering middle school or high school.

For more information on the U.S. Department of Education's Annual Reports, go to the Web Links module in Chapter 4 of the Companion Website.

Strategies in Early Childhood and Elementary School

Looking first at young children, we see that, according to the *26th Annual Report* (U.S. Department of Education, 2004, Table AB3), 90% of students aged 6 to 11 inclusive with speech or language impairments were educated in inclusive classrooms for all or virtually all of the school week. Thus, students with SLI are the most integrated (i.e., most likely to be in inclusive settings) of elementary students having any label. Figure 4.4 shows the likelihood of inclusive placement in K–12 settings.

At the early-childhood and primary-grade levels, impairments of speech are both common and normal. Young children have particular difficulty with certain sounds. In particular, the /zh/ phoneme (as in "measure"), the /s/ sound, and the /v/ sound are challenging even for 7- or 8-year-olds. Similarly, the /r/ phoneme and the /ch/ sound are difficult for many 6-year olds. That is why cartoons have characters saying "wabbit" (Sander, 1972). Accordingly, there is no need to refer a young child for speech/language pathology services unless and until the impairments of speech are uncharacteristic of children that age and do not resolve themselves on their own. As for language, facility improves rapidly during the primary grades. It is quite normal for young children to display irregularities in the use of language or imperfect mastery of the many rules of a language. Again, referral for evaluation is not necessary unless language development is seriously delayed or significantly deviant in nature, in the judgment of an experienced speech/language pathologist.

Methods: Model Speech. If you have a child with a speech impairment in your classroom, you should model both correct and, occasionally, incorrect speech patterns. Thus, with a child who stutters, you should display both fluent and dysfluent speech. The reason for showing dysfluent speech is to demonstrate to the student, and to his classmates, that occasional dysfluencies (e.g., "uh" and "you know") are acceptable behaviors. This should lower tension in the child and should ameliorate teasing by classmates. Stuttering is a case in point. Some very bright, highly motivated people continue to stutter despite many years of therapy. One, the writer John Williams (2000a), tells his story in the nearby vignette ("John: A True Story of Stuttering"). It is important for teachers not to blame the stutterer. Rather, teachers should slow down their own speech, model fluency, and also model dysfluency (i.e., by naturally saying "uh," "well, . . . " and the like), ask the child to cease other activities when speaking, and ignore any stuttering the child does produce.

FIGURE 4.4 Likelihood of Inclusive Placements: Speech and Language Impairments

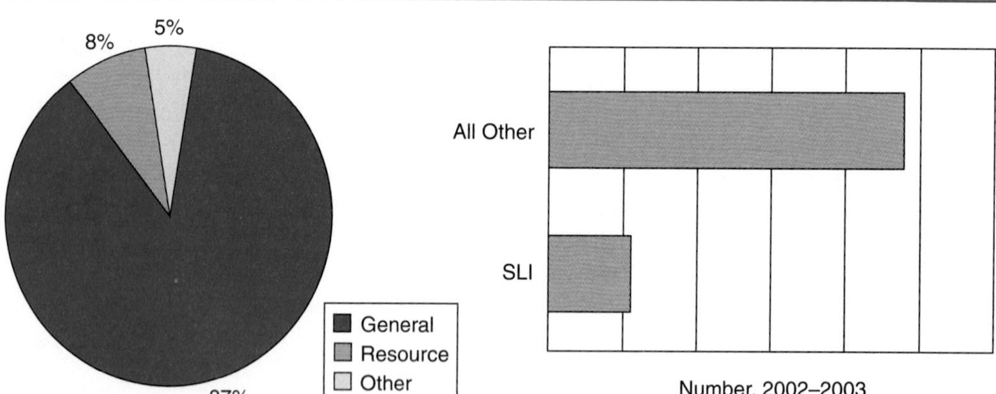

Students with the "speech and language impairments" label comprise nearly one in every five (18.5%) of K–12 students with any classification. They number 1,110,000, according to the *26th Annual Report* (U.S. Department of Education, 2004). Nearly all of them (87%) were placed into inclusive environments for all or virtually all of the school week (spending less than 21% of the time in other settings). The two charts above illustrate these data.

Source: U.S. Department of Education (2004).

JOHN: A TRUE STORY OF STUTTERING

John Williams.

How Stuttering Has Changed My Life, *by John Williams*

I've had to learn to accept it as part, but not all, of me.

The same questions always seem to come up whenever people first realize that I stutter. How long have you had this? Has your stuttering ever embarrassed you? And for those who know something about stuttering, there are follow-up questions: Have you ever used a metronome? Do you favor using a text-to-speech artificial device to avoid the embarrassment of stuttering? What was my most effective form of speech therapy?

I have stuttered for 46 of my 55 years. I have detested it, feared it, been consumed, frustrated, and, yes, embarrassed by it. I have used it like a warrior's shield going into battle. I have been psychologically and personally wounded by it. There have been thousands of occasions after I have constantly blocked severely when I have been physically spent, totally.

For 25 years, I tried different therapies to control my stuttering. Early on, therapists gave me plenty of advice on ways to stop it. Speaking in a rhythm using various methods was one of the earliest therapies. One therapist suggested I swing my arms back and forth so I could speak to the rhythm of rocking limbs. I tried. It certainly brought a lot of attention—but no fluency. I discarded it quickly.

TOE TAPPING. Another rhythm method was to learn to speak to the beat of my index finger. This was easier to do but still noticeable and embarrassing, though somewhat effective. One day while practicing this method, a friend sitting next to me in school reached over and placed his hand on my tapping finger. I was horrified. My security blanket was gone. Suddenly, I stuttered more when I did not use it. The incident made me realize that tapping was a false crutch that made me more self-conscious of my stuttering.

Another method to develop a fluent speaking rhythm was moving the largest toe on each foot up and down. After 10 minutes, I would alternate feet. This was effective but physically tiring. My toes quickly became sore. And I never mastered the rhythm in my left big toe on the same level of proficiency I did with my right big toe. Go figure.

Three times in my life, I turned to a metronome. Speech therapists told me it was a great tool for becoming fluent. A metronome is an instrument often used by piano players to develop a rhythm. A needle-pointed stick sits in the center of a platform, and it moves at various speeds to the left and to the right, producing a tick-tock noise. The idea for a person who stutters is to develop a rhythm of speaking according to the speed of the needle. When the needle moves slowly, you speak slowly. When it moves at a moderate pace you speed up your rhythm, and when it moves quickly you quicken your speed.

MISGUIDED THERAPIES. I saw a fresh demonstration of a metronome three months ago, with a teenager who stutters. When the metronome was ticking, the young man fluently spoke and read. When it stopped ticking, his fluency vanished. And there's the rub with me: What's the therapeutic value in a metronome when you're unlikely to use it anywhere but in a one-on-one situation with a speech therapist. I don't believe this is a practical control for stuttering. In fact, I don't believe in any of these rhythm methods.

I've seen people who stutter severely use artificial speech to speak for them. When meeting people, they have programmed phrases such as "Hello. I am Joe Smith. I am pleased to meet you." Other phrases give more information about the person.

Some people who stutter use text-to-speech products when ordering in restaurants, when speaking to someone on the telephone, to give speeches, or in other situations. I think it's misguided therapy and shouldn't be encouraged. What happens if the computer breaks down? Who will speak for the person then? Such crutches, I believe, only deepen the stuttering condition and make it more difficult for the person to speak in everyday situations.

LESSONS LEARNED. I used a computer to learn more about stuttering and to help me control it. I'm grateful for the results. Because of what I learned, I have fluency, though not always. The best therapy for me involved

1. Accepting my stuttering as part of me, but not all of me. Stuttering has an impact on my speaking ability but not on the way I think, write, create, manage, and work.

2. Challenging myself to be as fluent as I can whenever I can. This is not easy. It's the most difficult challenge I have ever faced. I know I can be fluent, and when I am, I feel positively wonderful. I practice fluency by concentrating on what I am saying and then reminding myself to be fluent.
3. Accepting the situation that, at this stage in my life, my stuttering is too much a part of my speaking pattern, and I know I will never be fluent.
4. Since I can't hide my stuttering, I won't tolerate it interfering with my livelihood, when I write this column or perform other job-related tasks. My editors, to their credit, expect me to do my job. When I talk to someone famous, they expect me to do my own talking. Either I do my job, or I fail.
5. I do not fear stuttering. O.K., so sometimes I speak too much and too often. I take every occasion to speak because I want to show people who don't stutter that I have a working mind. And I want to set an example for people who stutter and need to speak, but too often don't.

I know people who have stuttered but became fluent. I encourage people who stutter to work with a speech therapist. I encourage children who stutter to get speech therapy at stuttering's onset. I urge parents, teachers, friends, and fellow students to work with the child who stutters so he can become fluent. I urge adults who stutter to use their natural voice to speak often and to strive for fluency. And I advise people to take advantage of the times they live in and make wise use of technology to help control their stuttering.

Source: From "How Stuttering Has Changed My Life," by John Williams, April 12, 2000, *Business Week Online,* retrieved on 4/12/00. From *http://www.businessweek.com/bwdaily/dnflash/apr2000/nf00412b.htm*. Reprinted with permission from *Business Week*.

Methods: Teach Phonemic Awareness and Phonics. Phonemic awareness is a set of abilities to put phonemes together and to pull them apart. Thus, in phoneme segmentation, children can answer such questions as, "What is left if I take the /b/ sound away from 'brick'?" Rhyming, alliteration, and blending are all good ways to develop childrens' abilities in phonemic awareness. The Dr. Seuss books, such as *The Cat in the Hat,* are excellent for this purpose because they are rich both in rhymes and in alliteration. Phonics is a method of teaching that calls upon children to relate graphemes (letters) to phonemes (sounds) so as to decode unfamiliar words. The idea is that children can "sound it out" so as to understand a printed word. These two strategies were recommended by the U.S. Department of Education for use in Early Reading First and Reading First programs.

Peer tutoring has much research behind it.

Resources That Work

How to Collaborate with a Speech/Language Pathologist

Teachers of inclusive classrooms often complain that "pull-out" disrupts their teaching—and they most often blame speech/language pathologists. A less disruptive option is for the pathologist to "push-in," that is, to come into the classroom and work with the child there. As the teacher, you can collaborate with the pathologist to minimize disruption. While some pulling out may be necessary, at least some services can be provided via pushing in.

Experienced teachers suggest that you ask the speech/language pathologist what interventions you can implement yourself. The pathologist may suggest, for example, that you be alert to, and reinforce, the same behaviors during class that he does during sessions. Similarly, the pathologist can tell you how you, and the student's classmates, should respond to a child's speech and/or language errors during class. You may, for example, demonstrate patience in waiting for a student to complete a comment and, by modeling that behavior, lead fellow students to be patient, as well. Or the pathologist may suggest, instead, that you prompt the student by modeling the appropriate speech or language.

Teacher interventions are particularly important with language impairments. The rules of English need to be applied, and frequently practiced, before they become habit. This means enforcing Direct Instruction: explicit teaching of rules, considerable practice, review of outcomes, re-teaching in areas of weakness, and further practice and review. Avoiding errors of agreement in number ("When a student is tired, they [sic] make mistakes.") and the like requires focused attention. Students often make those mistakes in their writing, but less frequently, oddly enough, in their speaking. This is a good example of how a writing sample helps you to detect misunderstandings. You should coordinate with the speech and language pathologist, who will most likely have many quite creative suggestions on how to help children to acquire mastery in these areas.

Here is what one teacher reported after she consulted with a speech/language pathologist:

> *Juan could barely say four syllables without stuttering. It was painful to watch. I knew he was getting speech pathology services. What happened while he was in my classroom, however, was my responsibility. I set some rules the first week of class, and stuck to them all year long. First, I never called upon Juan unless he raised his hand. If he did, I always called upon him. As soon as I did, I immediately walked over to stand near a student or students I believed might laugh at him. If anyone teased him, I fixed her with a stern stare. I gave Juan all the time he needed to complete his statement. I never interrupted him and never tried to "finish his thought." I also made a point of modeling dysfluencies myself. That is, I consciously inserted "um," "ah," "well, you know," and similar sounds into my own sentences. In this way, I was letting Juan know, and the rest of the class, too, that occasionally dysfluent speech was perfectly acceptable. Did all this help? I think so. In the Spring, Juan came up to me in the hallway after school and said, "You always made me feel I could speak up in class. Thanks!"*

Methods: Elaboration. When you expand upon what a student says, providing a rich model, you are practicing what professionals in speech and language disorders refer to as elaboration. It is a well-regarded technique (e.g., Tompkins, 2002). That is because it offers incidental instruction at the moment the student is interested in it (which is why he was talking about it). In fact, elaboration is one of the major approaches of early childhood special education. If you watch early intervention specialists and preschool special educators at work, you see them *embedding* instruction into ongoing activities. They "embed" or insert special education, notably elaboration, as children play, color, or snack.

Methods: Self Talk. As you do something, "talk it out" so students learn the words that are connected to the activity. **Self talk** has you articulating your thoughts as you do something. This is an example of teaching language in *purposive contexts*. That is, the instruction is relevant to the context. Children who have delays in language development are especially in need of this kind of incidental learning. Many do not get it at home: Adults around them may issue one- or two-word orders (e.g., "No!" or "Not now!") without elaborating. This kind of linguistic impoverishment is most common in low-SES homes. Thus, children from such homes are in particular need of self talk and other kinds of elaboration-based interventions.

Methods: Parallel Talk. In this technique, you provide a running commentary as the *student* does something. You use the words that apply to that situation. **Parallel talk** helps

Technologies That Work

Speech

Important software and hardware products that may help students with SLI include "speech synthesis" and "speech recognition" technologies. This box discusses speech synthesis. Speech recognition, or machine hearing, is reviewed in greater detail in "Technologies That Work: Language," later in this chapter.

Speech synthesis is machine talk. All Apple Macintosh™ computers have the hardware and software required to produce computer speech. Some IBM-compatible PCs do, as well. One well-regarded speech synthesis offering is outSPOKEN from ALVA Access Group. Versions are available both for Windows® and for the Macintosh. Another product with speech synthesis is IntelliTalk from IntelliTools. It is also available from RJ Cooper & Associates. Two free ones are Clip & Talk and Speech 1.0.

Many educational software programs and games feature speech output. Generally, today's speech synthesis is quite human-sounding. Users often have a choice of voice (children's voices, women's voices, Spanish-accent voices, etc.). This can matter if the program is to be used as the child's voice. Just as we all are sensitive to how our voices sound, so too are students who use machines to speak for them. You should give the individual considerable discretion in selecting the voice.

Speech recognition is machine hearing. While another box discusses this technology in more depth, it is mentioned here because it may offer important advantages for students who have speech limitations. Examples are Dragon Naturally Speaking from ScanSoft and Via Voice from IBM. A key for teachers to recognize is that these programs respond to the voice of the person who trained them. Neither requires perfect speech. As long as the individual speaks consistently, as compared to when he trained the software, the programs will recognize that person's speech. This can be a real problem for individuals who do not speak consistently. Many children and youth with cerebral palsy, for example, can be inconsistent in the ways they speak. This is a simple matter of the nature of the disability: It limits the individuals' fine-motor control of the many muscles involved in speech production.

For more information on speech synthesis software, go to the Web Links module in Chapter 4 of the Companion Website.

For more information on speech recognition software, go to the Web Links module in Chapter 4 of the Companion Website.

the student to acquire the words that go with what she is doing. It works, perhaps even better than self talk, because words are taught when the student is interested in them. It also lowers the demands on the student to generalize, which would be higher were the instruction offered at one time and in one situation but required from the student at another time and in a different situation. This is another example of teaching language in purposive contexts.

Methods: Assess, Then Teach. You might begin each school year by giving assignments requiring extensive expressive-language samples. Younger children may be permitted to speak their stories; older ones could write them. You would then analyze the corpus of output, looking for syntactical and other errors, asking yourself, "What rules would produce this outcome?" That review may show you what to teach. The key for you as a teacher of an inclusive classroom is to discover what rules must have been used by the child to create that language. This tells you what strategies the child uses to generate language, and which she does not know.

Methods: Miscue Analysis. A variation on this is miscue analysis. It is a well-researched technique (Goodman, Goodman, & Hood, 1989). In **miscue analysis,** teachers note what children do while reading aloud. They use copy editors' marks to designate those behaviors. Despite the name, not all "miscues" are errors. Some are spontaneous corrections made by the child during active reading. A handbook for teachers that illustrates the method was written by Debra Goodman (1999): *The Reading Detective Club* uses copious examples to show how teachers can be "detectives" in discovering what children do and do not know about language.

Briefly, the intent in miscue analysis is to uncover what strategies students use as they read developmentally appropriate reading materials. Students typically use a variety of strategies as they actively attack a text. One key difference between good readers and poor readers is that the former apply more strategies as they read. One such strategy is to use syntactical cues. For example, do your students show knowledge of the function and use of prefixes, suffixes, and the like? If not, you know to teach such word-attack skills as separating a long word into its prefix, core, and suffix. Goodman (1999) illustrated these tactics with nonsense sentences. One example is "The mampy gruffle parstinked the bixton sirky snupples piskfully" (p. 16). Syntactical cues tell you that "mampy" must be an adjective, "gruffle" a noun, "parstinked" a verb, and so on. If your students cannot use such cues to identify the parts of speech in a nonsense sentence, you know exactly what syntactical strategies to teach.

Similarly, miscue analysis looks at what reading experts call "semantics": do children demonstrate an understanding of the world around them and an ability to use that information to understand what they read? To assess whether students have the semantic knowledge required to make sense of a text, you should see if they make reasonable predictions about the story. One characteristic of developmentally appropriate reading materials is that they are predictable: Young children can anticipate what will happen in the story. They can look at the cover illustration, read the title, and so on, and make logical predictions based on their knowledge of how the world works. They can revise their predictions as they read the story. To appreciate the importance of semantic cues, you might recall your own experience while trying to read a computer-program manual or a legal contract. Even very good readers lack the knowledge required to understand insurance contracts or other technical materials.

Miscue analysis also examines student use of pragmatics. Pragmatic knowledge relates to the "unwritten rules" of social behavior and to how we as human beings respond to different circumstances. We use more formal language in school than we do in the playground. We write differently than we talk. You can see if your students laugh as they read of a child using colloquial language when addressing the school principal, for example, or if they understand why Tom Sawyer changes his speech pattern depending upon whether he is addressing Aunt Polly, Becky, or Huck. If not, teaching these social rules will help your students to become better readers.

Resources That Work

Speech and Language

The major professional organization of speech/language pathologists is the American Speech-Language-Hearing Association. ASHA recently added the word "language" to its name, to emphasize the growing interest of speech/language pathologists in language disorders. The association, however, retained "ASHA" as its acronym because it is so well known. ASHA is a very large organization, with many resources for teachers and for teachers in training. Its Web site, for example, offers good news coverage, including items on federal laws and regulations, as well as a wide range of reading materials (10801 Rockville Pike, Rockville, MD 20852; *http://www.asha.org*).

Another organization of interest to teachers is the National Aphasia Association (NAA). This association offers information both about aphasia and about similar but different conditions, such as apraxia. NAA is based in Manhattan (156 Fifth Avenue, New York, NY 10010; *http://www.aphasia.org*). An obvious question NAA addresses at its site is what individuals with aphasia, therapists, and teachers can do. How can people get around word-finding problems? The association reports that, sadly, interventions of documented effectiveness are few and far between. Approaches that begin by specifying *precisely* what the problem is, where in the brain the lesion (damage) is located, and how that part of the brain normally functions, hold promise. Armed with such specific information, therapists and teachers could design individualized teaching approaches. The Association notes, too, that research supports interventions based upon attention. If teachers and therapists can enhance attention by students with aphasia, language use improves, as well. However, NAA remains skeptical of drug-based treatments, saying that evidence of efficacy is scarce. Interested readers are referred to a review of literature by Randall Robey (1998) of the University of Virginia. Robey's meta-analysis (review and analysis of earlier studies) examined 55 studies, finding some evidence for certain interventions but cautioning that much more remains to be learned.

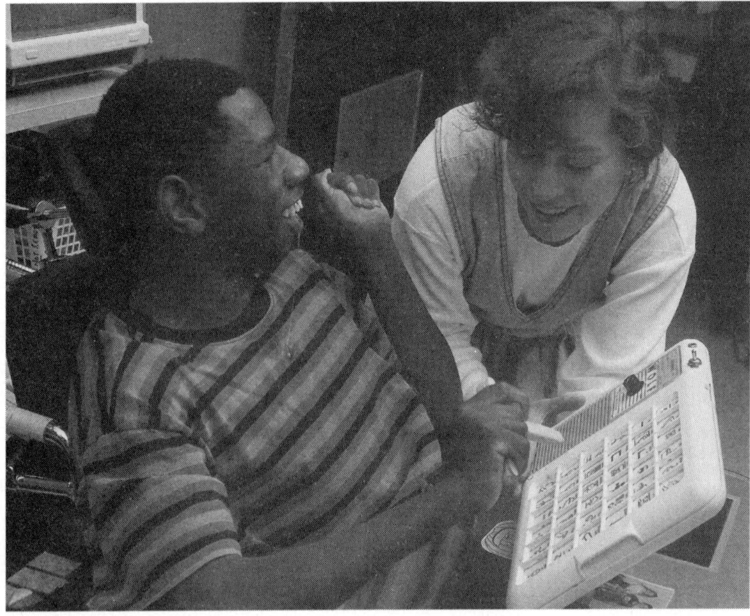

Communication boards, some of which are electronic, offer a "voice" for students who do not have comprehensible speech.

For more information on DynaVox® Systems, go to the Web Links module in Chapter 4 of the Companion Website.

Methods: Teach Students to Use Communication Technologies. The words "communication technologies" need to be understood broadly. While much attention has been devoted to high-tech machines such as the DynaVox, much more low-tech alternatives are also available. Students may use **augmentative or alternative communication (AAC)** technologies. As the name suggests, these are high- and low-tech devices that supplement or replace standard means of communication. AAC products include the high-tech DynaVox® and DynaMyte® machines distributed by DynaVox® Systems as well as the low-tech products collectively referred to as Picture Exchange Communication System, or PECS. The DynaVox Systems machines are electronic communication aids that produce computer speech. Children who need augmentative and alternative communication technologies to express themselves need to learn how to use these products. Usually, you as the teacher and family members also need to become familiar with the technologies. PECS is really not technology at all, but rather a process in which children communicate with others by pointing to or giving that person a picture (hence the name "picture exchange communication system").

Methods: Insist on Writing. Using these kinds of technologies, even students with severe speech and/or language disabilities can produce written work. It is essential for teachers of inclusive classrooms to require these students to write, just as they expect other students to do. Vygotsky (1978) taught us that children use language to work their way through new information. Writing about something helps us to learn it. Writing requires us to organize our thoughts, to express them clearly. Good teachers encourage children to work through these steps—regardless of whether the students are writing with a pencil, a pen, a computer, or a DynaVox®. As they do, teachers recognize the metacognitive strategies children are using and tap this knowledge to help children to learn better. Excusing children from writing tasks robs them of these beneficial experiences.

This is an example of *universal design,* an idea introduced in the previous chapter. As you may recall, redundancy is a key feature of universal design. By making use of augmentative and alternative communication technologies and methods, you are providing students with more than one way to do their work, in this case to write essays, reports, and other papers rather than being excused from such tasks.

Strategies in Middle School and High School

Examining now secondary-school students, we see that the *26th Annual Report* showed that 71% of students aged 12 to 17 with the SLI label were taught in regular (inclusive) classrooms all or almost all of the school week during the 2001–2002 school year (U.S. Department of Education, 2004, Table AB4). However, because the number of students with this label is far smaller at the secondary than at the elementary level, regular educators are less likely to see them in high schools than in elementary schools. Most speech and language disorders, except for stuttering, tend to be resolved by the high-school years, unless these problems are secondary to another condition.

Methods: Phonemic Awareness and Phonics. Some teachers in middle school and high school may think they may ignore the techniques of phonemic awareness and phonics that were discussed earlier ("Strategies in Early Childhood and Elementary School"). In fact, many students with learning disabilities, SLI, deafness and other hearing impairments, and some other disabilities may continue to help in these areas. Instruction and practice in phonemic awareness and in phonics may be required, on behalf of particular students, *at virtually any level of instruction.* The National Reading Panel (2000) and others (e.g., Plante & Beeson, 1999) urge teachers of inclusive classrooms to assess each child individually. For some, continued intervention will be required.

As with teachers at the earlier grade levels, it is not just that teachers of inclusive classrooms must know how to teach phonemic awareness and phonics. It is equally important that they know *when* to teach these. The "test-teach-test" approach will help you know that. You should, that is, "assess, then teach" just as do teachers in early childhood and elementary education. Also helpful will be comments by the IEP team when it prepares the student's IEP. Hopefully, the team will give you a sense of how much attention still needs to be given to phonemic awareness and phonics at these higher grade levels.

Methods: Wait Time. After you say something important, or ask students a question, give them time to process the information and prepare any responses they may wish to offer. Students with speech and language impairments, as well as many with learning disabilities, often need wait time (Bos & Vaughn, 2002).

Children and youth with aphasia, a word-retrieval condition, frequently need additional time. Variations on "wait time" include offering cues, such as the initial sound of the desired word, and rephrasing the question or statement so that students may respond in a different way (e.g., by saying "Yes" or "No").

Methods: Teach Writing in Context. Writing at the secondary level increasingly is writing *for a specific purpose.* We write in one way to send a friendly note to a relative, in a different way to communicate with a friend, and in a third way to apply for a job. We write differently when we are creating a short story than when we are writing a piece for the school newspaper. It is vital that students with SLI limitations gain experience with all these different kinds of writing. An important advantage is that these students may find such writing to be much more highly motivating than the more generic kinds of writing that are characteristic in elementary school. Precisely because of their speech and/or language limitations, they may require this additional motivation in order to persist in the challenging work of becoming good writers.

The ability to write for different purposes and different audiences is of great importance in reform curricula. Science, social studies, and other content areas are taught today by having students not only read a remarkable variety of materials, ranging from historical documents to scientific journal articles, but also to write in the styles and formats of such documents.

The aim is for students to achieve "deep understanding" (Morocco, 2001, p. 7) of imagery, metaphor, and point of view, not to mention maps, diagrams, and formulas. This is best done not merely by reading these but by producing them, as well. This is what literacy is all about: *using* language in meaningful ways to accomplish things important to the student.

Methods: Develop Reading Comprehension. Reading for understanding is, if anything, a skill more vital at the middle-school and secondary-school levels than in earlier grades. More and more, it is essential that students comprehend the "main idea." Less and less critical is that they know each individual word that they read. Goodman (1999) decried instruction that focuses upon accuracy in reading, contending that it is more important that children understand the ideas in what they are reading than that they get every word right. Strategies for reading comprehension focus upon understanding, remembering, and communicating information that is read. Research has identified some strategies that are known to help students, notably pre-reading activities that introduce a topic, group discussion, and ways of using context (known words in the sentence, illustrations that accompany the story, etc.) to figure out unfamiliar words.

Reading for comprehension has an important side-effect. When students understand a story, they feel good about it. They tend to gain confidence. They begin to think of themselves as "good readers"—which leads naturally to more reading. That, in turn, further strengthens their reading skills. By contrast, children who focus upon their failures in reading tend to avoid additional reading. That, in turn, causes them to fall further and further behind their peers.

Strategies in Transition to Adult Life

While speech and language pathology services are made available free of charge for eligible students during the PreK–12 years, this is not the case at the postsecondary level, nor in the adult work place. Accordingly, students must either work out their own coping strategies or identify affordable sources of continued sessions. Many do. According to the National Longitudinal Transition Study (Blackorby & Wagner, 1996), a large proportion (49%) of students labeled SLI during the PreK–12 years continued on to postsecondary education. Similarly, a higher percentage of adults with SLI who had been out of high school for 3 to 5 years were competitively employed (65%) than was the case for adults with any other label except for specific learning disabilities (71%). These findings reflect, again, the "mild" nature of speech and language impairments.

Methods: Teach Survival Words and Phrases. Which words *must* students learn? This question becomes a critical one when teaching students who are deaf or hard of hearing, as well as those who have mental retardation, many who have learning disabilities, and some with SLI. There is considerable consensus around certain "survival" words and phrases. Polloway and Polloway (1981) listed many of the most important of these.

Tables 4.1 and 4.2 offer some of their recommendations. Notice that most of these words and phrases are important for safety and for getting around in the community. Teachers should take whatever steps are necessary to ensure that children with disabilities master these words and phrases. University of Texas special-education professor David Katims (1999) was particularly adamant on this point with respect to instruction for students with mental retardation: "[T]he lack of content on literacy instruction for people with mental retardation in contemporary textbooks is deplorable" (p. 14).

TABLE 4.1 20 Survival Words

1. Poison	11. Women
2. Danger	12. Warning
3. Police	13. Entrance
4. Emergency	14. Help
5. Stop	15. Off
6. Not	16. On
7. Walk	17. Explosives
8. Caution	18. Flammable
9. Exit	19. Doctor
10. Men	20. Go

Source: From "Survival Words for Disabled Readers," by E. A. Polloway and C. H. Polloway, 1981. *Academic Therapy, 16, Issue 4,* pp. 443–448. Copyright 1981 by PRO-ED, Inc. Adapted with permission.

TABLE 4.2 20 Survival Phrases

1. Don't walk	11. Rest rooms
2. Fire escape	12. Do not touch
3. Fire extinguisher	13. Do not use near open flame
4. Do not enter	14. Do not inhale fumes
5. First aid	15. One way
6. Deep water	16. Do not cross
7. External use only	17. Do not use near heat
8. High voltage	18. Keep out
9. No trespassing	19. Keep off
10. Railroad crossing	20. Exit only

Source: From "Survival Words for Disabled Readers," by E. A. Polloway and C. H. Polloway, 1981. *Academic Therapy, 16, Issue 4,* pp. 443–448. Copyright 1981 by PRO-ED, Inc. Adapted with permission.

In this, as in so many areas, collaboration between educators and related-services personnel is essential. One technique introduced later in this book that is directly applicable to the teaching of survival words and phrases is *community-based instruction,* or, as Langone (1998) called it, "situated learning" (see Chapter 8). The idea is to take students out into the community and teach them essential words and phrases as they find them (e.g., on street signs). The task of generalizing instruction is made much easier in this way. Orientation and mobility specialists, occupational therapists, and speech/language pathologists can assist teachers in such field-based instruction.

Methods: Accept Other Means of Expressive Communication. Stuttering is for many people a life-long frustration. The IEP team may plan transition activities in which the student is encouraged to develop and learn effective coping strategies. Consider, for example, the dilemma of Peter Kupferman (Copeland, 1998). For him, the /p/ sound triggered stuttering. He even found himself nodding to the name "Paul" just to relieve his suffering as he tried, in vain, to say "Peter." People like Peter Kupferman need to identify strategies to deal with such situations at work, in social settings, and of course in school.

You should allow students *options* in how they participate in class discussions and answer teacher-posed questions during lectures. Children who stutter or who have other speech dysfluencies may be permitted to jot down comments and answers on a sheet of paper, and give you that. Children and youth with severe disabilities (such as cerebral palsy or mental retardation) may communicate via speech or AAC products, but may also do so via gestures, facial expressions, and bodily movements. Again, these are examples of universal design in education.

HEARING IMPAIRMENT, INCLUDING DEAFNESS

Relatively small numbers of PreK–12 students are deaf or hard of hearing. Hearing loss is most common among people who are much older (e.g., in their 60s to 80s) than it is among school-age children. (The pattern among people who are blind or have low vision is very similar.)

A major variable with respect to hearing impairment is age at onset: A hearing loss that occurs during the teen years (perhaps to a rock band member after prolonged exposure to excessive noise) will have minimal effects on language and on speech, whereas one that happens at or near the time of birth may have profound effects on both. The other key variable is severity of the loss. In general, impairment of the inner ear (cochlea, auditory nerves) has a much greater impact on the development of speech and language than does one of the outer or middle ear (auditory channel, small bones of the inner ear, stapes).

Technologies That Work

Language

Some students may find that speech recognition software helps them to write much longer pieces than they would compose by hand or by typing. Particularly helpful for students with language impairments are speech recognition programs that also offer speech output. That is, these programs both "hear" and "talk." The two most prominent vendors are those mentioned earlier: Scansoft, which offers Dragon Naturally Speaking Preferred, and IBM, which has Via Voice Pro Enterprise®. These work with virtually all popular applications, from Word® or WordPerfect® to Excel® to Web browsers and e-mail programs. They also feature speech synthesis. Students may listen to text that they have entered via voice.

Speech recognition software requires user training. That can vary from just five minutes to as long as two hours. Children and youth may read vendor-provided text into the microphone. This process can be speeded up considerably by using a program that comes with a large built-in vocabulary. Versions are available for different uses (e.g., for writers, for lawyers, for medical practitioners). Performance can also be enhanced by purchasing a high-quality microphone. And reducing ambient noise helps, as well. The programs typically are advertised as responding correctly to as much as 95% of what is said to them by the person who trained them. But this is under ideal conditions (no other sound in the area, etc.). It also is somewhat misleading. On a typical page of word-processed text, a 95% success rate translates into 8 to 12 errors per page. Each of those mistakes must be corrected. That slows down the effective dictation speed from an advertised 150 words per minute to perhaps 30 words per minute (see Microsoft's "In Depth" report on speed recognition at *http://www.microsoft.com/office/evaluation/indepth/speech.asp*).

Computers equipped with speech recognition software can respond in one of two ways when someone speaks. The first is that the spoken command may be obeyed. People may launch a program, open an e-mail message, save a written document, and so on, by issuing voice commands. This may occur when a student says, for example, "Indent this paragraph. Now bold this paragraph." In these instances, the program carried out the spoken instructions. Quite different is text insertion via speech. In that case, the words spoken are placed into the Word® or WordPerfect® document that the student is writing. Thus, the two sentences "Indent this paragraph. Now bold this paragraph." would appear in the student's paper.

Speech recognition programs used with word-processing software do not actually "write" for the student. Rather, the software programs make the writing task easier by responding to voice. This eliminates the need to spell out words. That being said, there are some significant limitations. First, the programs do not do well in punctuating compositions. That will come, with time, but today's programs are limited in their abilities to, if you will, "understand" what is a sentence (thus, automatically capitalizing the first word and inserting a period after the last word) and what is a question (automatically placing a question mark at the end). Second, the programs make mistakes.

A different kind of program is "word prediction" or "word expansion" software. Word prediction programs complete a word, phrase, or even a sentence after the student enters a few letters on the keyboard or using some other input device. Examples are Aurora 3.0 for Windows and Speaking Dynamically™ Pro. The first is software specifically for word prediction. The second is a speech synthesis program which includes a word-prediction feature.

Inspiration™ is another type of program that may help students with language impairments. This software was mentioned in Chapter 3. A sister program from the same company, intended for children with less well-developed language skills, is Kidspiration™. Children can use symbols in place of words. They may organize a concept map in which they place symbols in different positions to indicate above, beside, below, and so on, even if they do not know those positioning words.

For more information on speech-recognition and speech-output software, go to the Web Links module in Chapter 4 of the Companion Website.

For more information on word prediction software, go to the Web Links module in Chapter 4 of the Companion Website.

For more information on Kidspiration™, go to the Web Links module in Chapter 4 of the Companion Website.

When someone is referred to as being **hard of hearing,** the general meaning is that this individual *can* understand *some* conversational speech through the ear alone, usually with the help of hearing aids, AM/FM listening systems, or other assistive listening devices. How much the individual comprehends varies widely. It depends upon how well she knows the people speaking, whether she knows the topic of conversation, whether environmental noise (ambient sound) interferes with efforts to follow someone's speech, and other factors, such as whether he or she can see the speakers well

Students who are deaf or hard of hearing typically do best when offered visual means of instruction (sign language, fingerspelling, gestures, manipulatives, graphic arts, etc.).

enough to be able to use lipreading to augment residual hearing. Of special importance to educators, it also varies according to how much auditory training (aural rehabilitation) the person has had, how well chosen and well fitted the hearing aids are, and similar considerations.

Deafness, on the other hand, is the inability to understand *any* conversational speech through the ear alone, even if state-of-the-art listening devices are employed. To comprehend what is spoken, people who are deaf need to use their eyes. Some are good at lipreading, particularly when they are familiar with the speaker and also know the topic being discussed.

Teachers in inclusive classrooms are increasingly likely to see children who have received **cochlear implants.** These are devices that are surgically inserted into the head and connected to the cochlea (the coiled, "snail-like" part of the body's hearing mechanism). McKinley and Warren (2001) offered a good primer on cochlear implants, explaining not only the technology but also the biology of hearing. Thousands of young children have received implants in recent years. The results vary greatly: Some children continue to function as deaf children, showing little improvement in hearing ability, while others become able to use the telephone (Marschark, Lang, & Albertini, 2001). When cochlear implants (see "Technologies That Work: Cochlear Implants") work as designed, and when the children receive the ongoing training they need to benefit from them, the results can be remarkable. However, children with cochlear implants *continue to be hearing impaired.* As much as parents may wish to deny it, these children do not become "hearing children" by virtue of implantation (McKinley & Warren, 2001).

Definition

As noted earlier (see Chapter 1), the U.S. Department of Education's (1999a) regulations for IDEA define **deafness** as "a hearing impairment that is so severe that the child is impaired in processing linguistic information through hearing, with or without amplification, that adversely affects a child's educational performance" (34 C.F.R. 300[c][3]). The rules define the term "hearing impairment" in these words: "an impairment in hearing, whether permanent or fluctuating, that adversely affects a child's educational performance but that is not included under the definition of deafness in this section" (34 C.F.R. 300[c][5]). Thus, the federal regulations contain two separate definitions, one for deafness and another for hearing impairments. We do not see this with blindness and low vision.

Technologies That Work

Cochlear Implants

Cochlear implants include a microphone that picks up sound and a speech processor that codes that sound into electrical signals. Those signals are transmitted to an implant, surgically inserted in the skull, which in turn stimulates the hearing nerves of the brain (the VIIIth nerve). Typically, cochlear implants help individuals who have very severe or profound losses of hearing in both ears and who do not benefit sufficiently from hearing aids.

Some 40,000 cochlear implants have been performed worldwide. Typically, recipients can hear sounds they could not hear before, but only some become able to understand speech without lip reading as described in the chapter-opening "Personal Accounts."

Illustrations of cochlear implants and short videos about how they work are available at *http://www.cochlearimplant.com* and at *http://www.cochlearimplants.com*. These are both commercial sites; the former is that of Clarion® and the latter is that of Med-El®. More information, including a back-and-forth debate between advocates of deaf people and of hard-of-hearing individuals is offered at *http://www.pbs.org/soundandfury/*. A Q&A (e.g., "Am I A Candidate for a Cochlear Implant?") is posted at *http://www.shhh.org/cochlear/cochlearad.cfm*.

The key guidance for teachers is to not assume that a cochlear implant makes a deaf child "hearing." It is much more likely that a deaf child will begin to function as if he were hard of hearing. Teachers should work closely with audiologists and with speech/language pathologists to provide these children with ongoing support, especially on language acquisition. As recommended throughout this book, the necessary related services (speech and language pathology, aural rehabilitation, etc.) should be "pushed-in" whenever feasible. That way, the related-services personnel can help the child to make maximum use of the implant where it is most needed: in the classroom. Some students with cochlear implants continue to need the services of interpreters. Supports of these kinds can easily make the difference between succeeding in an inclusive setting and failing there (Marschark, Lang, & Albertini, 2001).

Recent news reports have linked unfortunately large numbers of cochlear implants with cases of meningitis. The federal Food and Drug Administration, together with the Centers for Disease Control and Prevention, and such private-sector organizations as ASHA have investigated reports of meningitis occurring with cochlear implant recipients. Although most states require physicians to report meningitis cases, state health departments often do not identify whether these cases involved a cochlear implant recipient.

So what's next? Researchers at the University of Michigan reported early in 2002 on the successful effort to resurrect nerve function in the ears of animals that had been deafened for investigatory purposes. Josef Miller, Richard Altschuler, and colleagues pumped nerve growth factors into laboratory animals for a month. Not only did hearing nerves grow, but the cochlear implants that were later given to the animals functioned much better than with control animals. Experiments with human subjects are planned for coming years.

For more information on meningitis cases involving cochlear implants, go to the Web Links module in Chapter 4 of the Companion Website.

The reason is that deafness is unique educationally (Bowe, 2000a). The very nature of instruction, as practiced in the public schools of this nation and most other nations, is one featuring a great deal of oral speech by the teacher. There are few classes in which the most commonly heard voice is not that of the teacher. Deafness, by definition, prevents people from understanding that speech—all of it, all day, every day. It has done that every day since onset. Most children who are deaf or hard of hearing have had the hearing impairment from birth or shortly thereafter. The technical term used to refer to this is "prelingual" ("pre" meaning "before" and "lingual" meaning "the development of language"). Language is usually learned most easily, and most rapidly, during the early-childhood years. Thus, early-onset deafness not only hinders day-to-day participation in a classroom but (and this may actually be more significant) it produces serious deficits in mastery of the language. The significance of this fact is schools teach virtually every subject through that language.

Characteristics and Types

Students with impairments of hearing tend to be most vulnerable with respect to mastery of the English language. Any degree of hearing loss can limit acquisition of linguistic competency. While deafness has more severe impact than do lesser degrees of hearing impairment, even students who are hard of hearing commonly display restricted vocabularies. In addition, interaction with hearing peers, with teachers, and with family members can be painfully difficult. This may lead to social isolation in neighborhood schools. That is one reason some experts refer to inclusion as, for many deaf students, exclusion (e.g., Moores, 1993).

Characteristics

Children and youth who are deaf, and to a lesser extent those who are hard of hearing, learn and function visually. That is, their interactions with the world around them are mediated almost exclusively through their eyes. This has several implications for teachers. First, while sound travels in many directions at once, and can navigate around walls, light does not. People who rely on vision must maintain a direct line-of-sight in order to receive information. This means not only front-row seats (for a good view of the teacher) but also rules of speaking in the classroom which require people to identify themselves and wait until the deaf or hard-of-hearing person is looking at them. There is another effect, one much less well-known: processing communication through the eyes and the visual cortex requires much more attention than is true of auditory processing. This is why you will so often see a deaf or hard-of-hearing student "get" a joke or other message a few seconds after hearing students do. It is also why deaf and hard-of-hearing students benefit by being given a "vision break": lipreading and watching an interpreter is hard work! Luckner, Bowen, and Carter (2001) and Easterbrooks and Baker (2001) suggested many of the steps outlined here for making instruction more visual.

Most children and youth who are deaf, and many who are hard of hearing, use **American Sign Language (ASL)** or some other manual communication system. ASL is a language of its own, on a parallel with English, French, and Japanese. It has its own grammar and other rules. Signed English is similar to ASL in that it makes use of hand shapes, facial expressions, and space to convey meaning. However, in Signed English, the grammar is that of English. People tend to use Signed English when they are also speaking, ASL when they are not speaking. Many people who are deaf use both ASL and Signed English. They also employ other modalities in communication, notably nonverbal communication (including facial expressions, natural gestures, and body language).

Teachers of students who are deaf or hard of hearing need to remind themselves of a simple truth: These are people, not just learning machines. This fact suggests that schools and teachers be sensitive to the social and emotional needs, and not just to the academic development, of these students. We will discuss this matter in "Issues in Middle School and High School," because it is most pressing at that level of education.

Many students who are deaf proudly support **Deaf culture.** This philosophy teaches that people who are deaf are best understood as users of a different language. That is, Deaf culture de-emphasizes the disability in favor of focusing on linguistic differences. Some educators have adapted Deaf culture to instruction, creating an approach familiarly known as "bi-bi" (short for "bilingual, bicultural"). While the idea is in many ways appealing (see e.g., Pittman & Huefner, 2001), it is not likely to be used in inclusive classrooms. This is so for several reasons. First, only a small fraction of deaf students (the 10% who have deaf parents) can be said to be native users of ASL and to have grown up in a home where Deaf culture is the "native culture." Second, bi-bi instruction requires knowledge about deafness and ASL that is possessed by very few regular education teachers. Rather, bi-bi is a teaching approach that is more likely to be found in self-contained classrooms or in special schools for deaf students.

By contrast, students who are hard of hearing seldom adhere to any particular "culture." Rather, they work as individuals, relying heavily on lipreading, hearing aids, and other technologies such as assisitive listening systems.

Types

Hearing impairment exists along a continuum. At one end is near-average hearing. Impairments of hearing below about 40 dB in the speech range (500 to 2000 Hz) are quite common today, largely because of environmental factors (e.g., loud music). Such losses do

Resources That Work

Organizations of Deaf and Hard of Hearing People

The major consumer organization on deafness is the National Association of the Deaf. The NAD was founded in 1880, making it the oldest self-help organization created by any group of Americans with disabilities. Today, the association has affiliates in all 50 states, as well as in the District of Columbia. The NAD focuses its energies upon protecting the human and civil rights of people who are deaf or hard of hearing. It has a nationally renowned Law and Advocacy Center that represents members' interests in Washington, DC, and also works with local lawyers to represent individuals who are deaf or hard of hearing in litigation over issues involved in employment, insurance, education, and other matters. The NAD publishes a bi-monthly magazine and hosts a biennial conference.

With respect to people who are hard of hearing, the counterpart group is Self Help for Hard of Hearing People (SHHH). SHHH has chapters in all 50 states and many county/local affiliates as well. The organization was founded in 1979 by Howard ("Rocky") Stone, a long-time official with the Central Intelligence Agency who was himself hard of hearing. The organization publishes a bimonthly magazine and hosts a biennial convention.

For more information on the National Association of the Deaf, go to the Web Links module in Chapter 4 of the Companion Website.

For more information on the SHHH and Rocky Stone, go to the Web Links module in Chapter 4 of the Companion Website.

not qualify children for the category "hearing impairments, including deafness." Rather, more severe impairments, which render students "deaf" or "hard of hearing" are included.

Deafness. Deafness is the inability to understand any conversational speech through the ear alone, even if state-of-the-art listening devices are employed. As suggested earlier, the most notable effect of childhood deafness appears in language acquisition. About one in every five (20%) deaf students, or some 2,000 annually, leave school reading at or below second-grade levels (Dew, 1999). As adults, many of these individuals become known (due to the fact that the rehabilitation system evaluates clients on their levels of functioning) as "low-functioning deaf" (LFD) persons. Because of their extremely low reading competencies, and other problems, adults who are LFD typically are unemployed. Another 3,500 youth who are deaf leave secondary school with reading competencies between second- and fourth-grade levels. Even under a generous fourth-grade or better reading standard, just 2,300 annual school leavers could benefit from postsecondary programs (Dew, 1999).

Other Hearing Impairment. In the public schools, more students are hard of hearing than are deaf. Children and youth who are hard of hearing have impairments of hearing that fall short of deafness, yet are more severe than mild losses. A frequent concern is tinnitus, or "ringing in the ears" (see the box "Student Strategies That Work: Hearing," p. 146). Another is excessive noise in the classroom (see "Strategies in Early Childhood and Elementary School/Improve Classroom Acoustics," p. 140).

Prevalence

The *26th Annual Report* (U.S. Department of Education, 2004; Table AA3) noted that 72,000 students between the ages of 6 and 21 inclusive were classified as having hearing impairments or deafness, in the 2002–2003 school year. These children and youth comprised just over 1% of PreK–12 students with any label. Thus, hearing impairment is one of the less common disabilities in the public schools. On the other hand, roughly three times as many students have hearing impairments as have visual impairments. There is no disproportionate representation of racial or ethnic groups in this category; that is, the same percentages are of Hispanic origin, white, and so on, as obtained in the general population as a whole (*22nd Annual Report,* 2000b, Table AA3).

Teacher Strategies That Work

Special Factors

Linguistic needs—American Sign Language (ASL)
Linguistic needs—Intensive instruction in reading/writing of English
Linguistic needs—Easy-reader version of textual materials
Linguistic needs—Highlighted key words in assigned reading materials
Social needs—Opportunities to play with other children who know and use ASL
Social needs—Opportunities for full participation in extracurricular activities
Communication needs—Classroom media that is captioned
Communication needs—Sign-to-voice interpretation (interpreter speaks out loud the message signed/fingerspelled by student)
Communication needs—Voice-to-sign interpretation (interpreter signs and fingerspells what the teacher and other students say)
Communication needs—One-at-a-time speaking rule in classroom
Communication needs—Front-row seat

Causes

Genetic Factors

Hearing impairment is occasionally inherited; there are entire families where grandparents, parents, aunts, and uncles are all deaf. Thus, some 10% of PreK-students who are deaf have deaf parents and use American Sign Language (ASL) as their native language. Deafness is only inherited if both parents have the same recessive genetic characteristics or if one passes on a dominant gene.

Environmental Factors

The other 90% have parents whose hearing is not impaired. This is significant for several reasons. First, these parents do not know sign language when the child is born; many do not even learn it before the child begins kindergarten. Second, being "hearing," these parents tend to want to "cure" the child's deafness, for which reason they may eagerly embrace cochlear implants and other surgical and non-surgical technologies. Causes range from congenital cytomegalovirus (CMV), which can also produce blindness or visual impairment, to low birth weight, to maternal rubella (German measles). CMV is a major cause of hearing impairment. This virus can remain dormant for many years; pregnancy can "release" it, and it can pass through the placenta to infect the fetus. Low birth weight is a danger to newborns in many ways. We saw earlier that it is a factor in cerebral palsy and we will see later that it is also associated with visual impairments. In maternal rubella, the mother contracts measles while she is pregnant; the fetus can be harmed by this illness.

Instructional Methods

IDEA requires that IEP teams take into consideration "special factors" when planning services for students who are deaf or hard of hearing. The nearby box, "Teacher Strategies That Work: Special Factors" outlines some of those issues.

Strategies in Early Childhood and Elementary School

We look first at young children. According to the *26th Annual Report* (U.S. Department of Education, 2004, Table AB3), 46% of deaf or hard-of-hearing elementary students were served in inclusive settings all or most of the school week in the 2001–2002 school year. Many of these are hard of hearing rather than deaf; the *Annual Report* does not disaggregate the number of deaf students from the number of hard-of-hearing students, so we cannot be sure. The bulk of the rest (28%) were placed in separate classrooms in neighborhood public schools.

Methods: Improve Classroom Acoustics. According to the Acoustical Society of America (ASA), ambient sound levels in many classrooms adversely affect learning. This is particularly true of students with hearing impairments. However, *all* students may have difficulty hearing if background noise exceeds 35 dB. ASA published standards in 2002 that were developed in conjunction with the American National Standards Institute (ANSI) and the U.S. Architectural and Transportation Barriers Compliance Board (ATBCB). Known as ANSI S12.60-2002, the standard sets criteria for maximum background noise (35 dB) and reverberation, a measure of reflection of sound waves off of walls and ceilings (0.6 to 0.7 seconds). Both apply to unoccupied classrooms and to classrooms having students with and without hearing impairments. The standards are voluntary unless and until they are adopted by a standards-setting body, such as a state or county standards bureau or the ATBCB. Copies of the standards may be secured through the ASA's Web site at *http://asa.aip.org*, or via e-mail at asastds@aip.org. The ATBCB, a small federal agency, may be reached via its Web site at *http://www.access-board.gov*, or via e-mail at baquis@access-board.gov.

Good design can help bring classrooms up to the standards. "Classroom Acoustics: Listening vs. Learning," a video showing innovative classroom designs, is available from the Educational Audiology Association via the association's Web site at *http://www.edaud.org*, via e-mail at eaa@L-Tgraye.com, or via phone at 1-800-460-7322. As a classroom teacher, you may also use amplification equipment. At Ocoee Middle School, near Orlando, Florida, a new infrared system amplifies teachers' voices by up to 12 dB, according to how loud ambient noise is. Most other schools that have classroom amplification, generally for students with hearing impairments, use FM channels. However, FM systems are subject to interference from other sound sources. Self Help for Hard of Hearing People (SHHH) recommends installing a loop around the room. The difference between loop systems and traditional hearing aids is that in a looped classroom, what is amplified is only the voice speaking into a microphone, whereas hearing aids amplify most any sounds in the environment. Loop systems send sounds to receivers students wear, which look somewhat like large hearing aids. Looping a room so as to improve acoustics is an example of universal design in education: It is a step you take that has the potential of helping all your students.

For more information on the ATBCB and SHHH, go to the Web Links module in Chapter 4 of the Companion Website.

Methods: Use Other Technologies. The ATBCB and SHHH recommend that alarms and alarm systems in schools provide visual as well as auditory alerts. Strobe lights are common. The key is to place these alarms where other information typically is not available to guide a child who is deaf or hard of hearing. Thus, a rest room is a good location for a visual alarm device. A hallway may not be, because the child will see other people reacting to the auditory alarm. In addition, at least one public-use telephone should be equipped with a telecoil. Such "hearing-aid compatible" phones "leak" electrical signals, which hearing aids can pick up.

Methods: Linguistic Enrichment. Students who are deaf present two substantial challenges to teachers of inclusive classrooms. First, they bring with them, in virtually every instance, a very limited command of the English language. Both vocabulary and knowledge of syntax and grammar likely are deficient. Second, they do not understand the words that are spoken in the classroom. Teachers often can comprehend the latter problem, and recognize how to solve it: employ an interpreter and enforce a one-speaker-at-a-time rule that slows down classroom conversation, gives the deaf student a chance to identify the speaker, and offers this child opportunities to contribute to the discussion. Appreciating the former problem is, for most teachers and teachers-in-training, much more difficult. They find it hard to grasp the extreme deficits of language that are characteristic of students who are deaf. Only after they teach such students do they begin to see the implications.

Prominent among these is that many deaf students cannot independently read assigned textbooks. Some have difficulty even with short newspaper or Internet stories. Their problems go beyond vocabulary. Syntax and grammar often are poorly understood.

You might, for example, ask a "Who" question only to get a "What" answer. To illustrate, suppose you and the student were looking at a picture. You might ask, "Who is riding the horse?" The student might respond, "Pal" (the name of the horse). Clearly, the student in this instance did not have a solid enough grasp of how the English language works to understand what you were asking.

Methods: Intensive Instruction in Reading. While some students who are deaf read at high levels, most do not. Fourth- or fifth-grade reading levels are common (Bowe, 2002b; Paul & Quigley, 1994). It is a long-standing problem. Research dating back 30-some years (e.g., Stuckless & Birch, 1966; Vernon, 1967) shows that many deaf students reach just third- or fourth-grade reading levels by age 13 or 14 and then plateau at that level throughout the high-school years. These dismal results continue today (Bowe, 1988; Braden, 1994; Paul & Quigley, 1994). This is a serious concern because much higher reading levels are required for employment in virtually every occupation (see, for example, the 2002–2003 Occupational Outlook Handbook, online at *http://www.bls.gov/oco/*). Similarly, vocational/trade schools typically require sixth-grade reading levels (Annette Reichman, Rehabilitation Services Administration, personal communication, March 15, 2001). As a result, many deaf school adults cannot find gainful employment. Instead, they rely upon Supplemental Security Income (SSI), a welfare-like benefit program intended to bring their incomes up to the poverty line. As of April 2002, a total of 54,000 adults with deafness as their primary disability were SSI recipients (Phil Landis, Social Security Administration, June 19, 2002, personal communication).

Raising the levels of reading among children and youth who are deaf is a challenge for teachers. Experts recommend the use of active learning strategies, that is, experiences which engage the child's attention and emotions, leads to better reading than does isolated instruction devoid of experiential meaning. In interviews with deaf students who were successful in a competitive college environment, Toscano, McKee, and Lepoutre (2002) found that early parental instruction, a rich linguistic environment at home, early and sustained instruction in strategies to attack written texts, and an enjoyment of reading were the common characteristics. Easterbrooks (2001) reported upon language-instruction practices recommended by veteran teachers of deaf and hard of hearing students. These included modeling appropriate language, hands-on activities, visual aids and prompts, and peer-to-peer tutoring. The Clarke School for the Deaf offers a curriculum that provides an illustration of active learning (deVilliers, Buuck, Findlay, & Shelton, 1994). Another example is provided by the Lexington School for the Deaf, in Queens, New York. Lexington's K–12 curriculum features a conceptual framework for active learning. The approach stresses development by students of cognitive foundations, attitudes, and problem-solving skills that enable them to learn—in school and out. At Lexington, assessment of student progress calls for the students to apply rather than just report information. All of these approaches feature active learning.

For more information on the No Child Left Behind Act, go to the Web Links module in Chapter 4 of the Companion Website.

The federal No Child Left Behind Act (PL 107-110) offers promise for improving the reading abilities of young children who are deaf or hard of hearing. Early Reading First and Reading First are programs for PreK–3 students. Both emphasize use of research-documented approaches to the teaching of reading. Those interventions include strategies such as phonemic awareness, phonics, vocabulary development, reading fluency, and reading comprehension. Policy guidance from the U.S. Department of Education defines "reading" as "a complex system of deriving meaning from print" that requires knowledge of phonemes, graphemes, vocabulary, and word-decoding skills, as well as information about the world so that children can construct meaning. Both Early Reading First and Reading First must, by law, feature instruction based upon research in these areas.

The smaller of the two new programs is Early Reading First. Targeted at preschoolers (3 to 5 years of age, inclusive), this program focuses upon letter recognition, phoneme-grapheme relations, and vocabulary development. Preschool educators are expected to engage children in conversation aimed at developing strong expressive and receptive vocabularies and to include stimulating yet appropriate pre-reading materials in the classroom. Early Reading First also includes testing and other screening procedures intended to identify, rapidly, young children who need intensive instruction in order to enter kindergarten ready to learn to read. Two good resources for teachers are *Phonemic Awareness in Young Children* (Adams, Foorman, Lundberg, & Beeler, 1998) and *Preventing Reading Difficulties in Young Children* (Snow, Burns, & Griffin, 1999). The Adams et al. text features "how to" methods for preschool teachers, while the Snow et al. book (which may be read online, at no charge) identifies factors that may place young children at risk of not becoming fluent readers.

Methods: Intervene Early. Action during the child's early years is essential, not just for reading but also for virtually everything else. The nature of education in public schools today is that content is taught through language. Whether students are learning math, chemistry, geography, or history, they do so by reading and writing in English. Recent research on the brain reveals that the language-learning capacities of the brain are altered by experience. By about age 11 or 12, if linguistic experiences have not activated those potentials, the brain in effect turns them off. Thereafter, learning a language is far more difficult than it is in the early-childhood and childhood years (Banikowski & Mehring, 1999; Jensen, 1998).

Particularly useful in the child's early years is a technique known as embedding. In this approach, educators take advantage of a young child's involvement in an activity or object and use that interest to teach language in (see e.g., Dunst, Herter, Shields, & Bennis, 2001). Yore (2000) discussed the technique as used to teach science to deaf students. Noticing that a young child is playing with a ball, for example, a parent or teacher would introduce the words and signs associated with ball-playing (e.g., ball, throw, catch, round, red, hand, etc.). These words would be taught in context, where they hold meaning. As mentioned earlier, family members and teachers may also use elaboration, self talk, and parallel talk, three other well-documented interventions. In elaboration, the adult explains decisions rather than just giving orders. This helps to provide a rich linguistic environment for the young child. A variation is self talk. Here, the adult "talks out loud" while he does something (e.g., "I know I put that crayon somewhere. Did I place it on the table? Did I put it in the box in the corner?"). Self talk is particularly useful in helping children to understand adult decision-making processes because it lets them "see inside your head" while you work through a decision. Parallel talk has the adult giving the child words that go along with what the child is doing (e.g., "I see that you drew a house there. That's a large house. I wonder what kind of roof it has? Is it a slate roof, a wood roof, or some other kind of roof? Who's in the house now? Which room are they in? What are they doing?").

Methods: Teach Vocabulary in Context. A related approach that has been scientifically validated is to provide concentrated instruction and plentiful experiential opportunities to develop conversational as well as reading and writing vocabularies. Traditionally, educators of deaf children have taught vocabulary words explicitly, often out of context. They typically employed some variation of Direct Instruction (Gersten, Carnine, & Woodward, 1987), which features teacher-led instruction followed by student practice, testing to identify areas of weakness, reteaching as required, and periodic review and testing over the course of the academic year. Direct Instruction is a well-validated strategy. However, recent research shows that vocabulary is best acquired incidentally, while the child is doing something else. This makes sense. When words are learned as part of an experience, they tend to be remembered as associated with that experience. The sights, sounds, bodily motions, and emotions of the experience are connected to the words, thus offering the brain numerous pathways to store and later to retrieve the word and its meanings. None of those advantages accrue when vocabulary is taught in isolation.

Methods: Miscue Analysis. Another well-researched technique draws upon what all good teachers do, especially at the beginning of a school year: collect from each student a corpus of self-generated language. This language may be written, signed, or spoken. The teacher analyzes the corpus to discover what rules must have been used by the child to create that language. This tells the instructor what strategies the child uses. Nielsen and Luetke-Stahlman (2002) showed how important regular assessment was in one deaf child's progress toward reading at grade level in sixth grade. Also writing about teaching deaf students, White (2002) highlighted the importance of assessment: "Indeed, discovering what a child knows and does not know about English is the starting point for all instruction" (p. 65).

Chaleff and Ritter (2001) outlined how miscue analysis may be used with students who are deaf or hard of hearing. First, they recommended, sessions should be videotaped, because teachers do not always catch all student miscues during live reading. Second, teachers should be alert to fingerspelling as a possible indication that the child does not know a written word. Chaleff and Ritter suggested that teachers request, after a reading session, that the child retell the story. The intent in retelling is to assess the child's comprehension of the story as a whole. White (2002) added highly specific ways of assessing deaf children's abilities to use semantic and syntactic clues to attack 13 subsets of verbs (Table 1, pp. 70–71). These tell educators which strategies students need to learn.

With many young deaf and hard of hearing children, strategies for attacking text must be taught explicitly. The need for this is not common knowledge. Goodman (1999), for example, drawing upon 15 years of experience in teaching students with unimpaired hearing, asserted that "We don't have to teach kids the rules and patterns of English grammar before they become readers and writers" (pp. 17, 19) because "As language users, we know these rules and processes *implicitly*" (p. 25; emphasis in original). Regular and special educators who are not experienced in teaching deaf students need to recognize that such "implicit" competencies develop only when young children are exposed to rich linguistic environments and have intact sensory faculties. We will discuss miscue analysis in much more detail later (see Chapter 14).

Methods: Provide Captioning. A major help in enriching linguistic input for these students is captioning of videos and movies. Captioned versions of educational and other videos are now widely available. Captioning of educational media is often available to classroom teachers at the touch of a button. Television receivers made or distributed after July 1993 are equipped with built-in caption decoder circuitry (P.L. 101-431, the Television Decoder Circuitry Act of 1990). Most TVs in use in American K–12 schools are so equipped. Depending on the model, the teacher touches a button on the monitor or one on a remote control unit, selects Caption I or the equivalent, and exits the control panel. Half of all broadcast and cable-cast television programming is captioned, pursuant to requirements in the Telecommunications Act of 1996 (PL 104-104) and implementing rules of the Federal Communications Commission (FCC), which call for 50% of all new programming to be captioned as of January 2002.

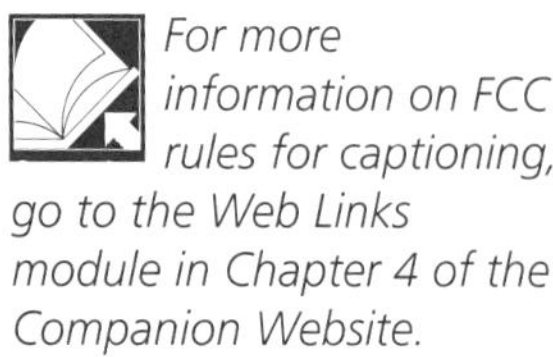

For more information on FCC rules for captioning, go to the Web Links module in Chapter 4 of the Companion Website.

However, the same cannot be said of educational videos and DVDs. Most such media are produced by private companies. These vendors are subject to title III of the Americans with Disabilities Act (PL 101-336) which requires, among other things, that communications be made accessible to and usable by persons with disabilities, if readily achievable. Public schools are subject to Title II of the ADA, which requires them to make their communications accessible to and usable by persons with disabilities. Finally, videos and other media that are developed using federal financial assistance are to be made accessible to and usable by persons with disabilities, pursuant to regulations promulgated by the U.S. Department of Education (20 U.S.C. Sec. 1404). The Captioned Media Program (CMP) (*http://www.cfv.org*) and the Media Access Group at WGBH (*http://www.wqbh.org*) estimate that as few as 15% of educational media are distributed with captions or subtitles, apparently because state and local education agencies do not insist upon captioning. For this reason, classroom teachers wishing to show captioned videos or DVDs must explicitly order ones with captions.

Deaf students generally can understand only videos or films that are captioned. Even when captioned versions are provided, many of these students will struggle to follow the story. Offering a printed script for them to study, perhaps with a family member or a peer tutor is a good supplementary measure. Students who are hard of hearing often can understand parts of non-captioned movies or films. However, even those with good residual hearing often benefit from having the captions as a backup source of dialog. That is why captioning is an example of universal design in education: It potentially can help *any* student, including those with no impairments of hearing.

Methods: The "Straws" of Language. Recalling our earlier discussion of the "language gene" believed to be on Chromosome 7 (see Chapter 3), another teaching technique might be to provide the student with extensive examples of different linguistic structures. The "language instinct" (to use the term popularized by Pinker [1994]) seems to work when the brain receives input that consists of individual sentences. The gene has evolved to use such "straws" to construct a "house" of grammar and syntax. Individuals who are deaf or hard of hearing have this genetic capability. The reason it often does not work for these persons as it does for people who have normal hearing seems to be this: The input they receive is fragmented and partial rather than complete. For that reason, the syntax and grammar it constructs are faulty. If this interpretation of the language problems facing many deaf and hard of hearing individuals is correct, as I believe it is, a solution suggests itself: Provide these students with copious examples of complete, correctly formed sentences. A great deal of such input is needed, as it is for everyone. Children with unimpaired hearing, after all, create their mental models of syntax and grammar only after hearing many thousands of sentences.

The work of Pinker (1994) suggests, too, that directly teaching grammar and syntax probably would not be effective. The "language gene" does not respond well when presented with rules. Rather, it needs discrete illustrations of a rule in effect. It then generates the rule. The difference between the two may be familiar to you if you think in terms of logic. Inductive reasoning is the deriving of a principle (here, a rule of language) from particular instances. The "language instinct" works in this way. What apparently does not work is deductive reasoning, that is, inferring from a principle or rule to specific applications. Attempts to teach language to deaf and hard-of-hearing students by providing them with instruction about rules has been tried for many years. The results have been very disappointing (Bowe, 1998a; Bowe 2002b). The work of Pinker (1994) and other followers of the linguistic pioneer Noam Chomsky (1965, 1972) provide an explanation for why those efforts have largely failed. Will teaching language inductively make a real difference? The likely answer is that it will help, but that other steps are needed as well. After an exhaustive review of research literature on the topic, Marschark (2001) concluded: "For many people, the most frustrating finding concerning language development of children who are deaf is the fact that we have not yet found the approach that supports development across the domains of social functioning, educational achievement, and literacy. A single such approach is unlikely. . . ." (p. 37).

Methods: Provide an Interpreter. Employment of an interpreter in the classroom can be of significant help. That is because a qualified interpreter can make visual virtually everything in the room that makes sound, including conversational speech. The word "interpret" means translation between English and ASL. Figure 4.5 illustrates the differences between the two languages. ASL has its roots in French (it was brought to the United States by Laurent Clerc, a deaf Frenchman), so its structure has more in common with French than with English. In general (there are exceptions, as there are with any language) ASL opens a statement with the most important sign (word). Notice, in Figure 4.5, that the first statement begins with the sign TRAIN (we follow the usual custom of designating signs by using all caps) because for that sentence the key word is "train." Similarly, the second sentence opens with the sign CHICAGO. While the ASL versions, in all caps, may appear to you at first glance to be simpler than English, this is misleading. ASL is a rich, fully fea-

Technologies That Work

Captions

Considerable research demonstrates that captions may enhance comprehension of educational materials by K–12 students who do and who do not have hearing impairments (e.g., Lewis & Jackson, 2001). This is particularly true because the speed in which captions are displayed may range from as low as 60 words per minute (wpm) for programming intended for preschoolers (e.g., *Sesame Street*) to as high as 250 wpm for programming intended for highly literate adults (e.g., nightly news programs Jensema & Burch, 1999). Students in middle school and high school, both deaf or hearing, have been shown to comprehend captions at all of these speeds. Jensema and Burch (1999), for example, tested deaf and hearing students aged 11 to 19 with videos captioned at speeds ranging from 80 wpm to 220 wpm, finding no significant differences by speed in student reading comprehension. In another study, this one of 578 deaf, hard-of-hearing, and hearing persons aged eight to eighty, Jensema (1998) found that the average "O.K." speed (comfortable; neither too slow nor too fast) was 145 wpm, which the researcher reported as nearly identical to the 141 wpm speed found in TV programs.

A smaller but still impressive body of research shows that English language learners (ELL; also ESL) may benefit when videos are captioned (Bean & Wilson, 1989; Spanos & Smith, 1990). Comprehension and vocabulary may both increase among ELL students, particularly when the vocabulary to be learned and remembered is challenging (Garza, 1991; Huang & Eskey, 2000). Adults with lower-than-average levels of reading ability despite unimpaired hearing have also been shown to benefit from captioned videos. Rogner (1992), for example, demonstrated such effects with functionally illiterate adults.

Educational videos and popular movies, are widely available in captioned form. Popular movies are available as soon as five to six months following initial release into theaters. If you search through a school library or a local video rental store, look for small symbols that designate captioning. On most video boxes, these will be two lower-case letter c's  or a symbol that looks like a Q: Q. In newspaper TV/radio schedules, captioned program typically are identified with a small (often a circle) letter "c."

For more information on finding captioned films and videos, go to the Web Links module in Chapter 4 of the Companion Website.

FIGURE 4.5 American Sign Language v. English

ASL Sign Order	English Word Order
TRAIN GONE SORRY	The train already left the station, unfortunately.
CHICAGO TOUCH NEVER ME	I have never been to Chicago.
SEE-FINISH DRAMA	I have already seen that play.
HOW HAPPEN ACCIDENT HOW	How did that accident occur?

tured language that makes extensive use of space, facial expressions, and other visual communications means. Indeed, ASL often can convey more meaning, with more subtlety and nuance than can English.

The contributions that realistically can be made by interpreters in inclusive classrooms should not be overstated. First, the difficulties deaf students typically have with the written form of English do not disappear just because an interpreter is in the room. The student still has to read textbooks, test questions, and the like, on her own. Second, the demand for interpreters in the public schools far outpaces the supply of qualified persons. For this reason, many of the interpreters who are employed in PreK–12 schools are better described as "signers" than as "interpreters." Stated differently, they convey some or even most of what is said in the classroom, but they often fall seriously behind or even omit entire sentences. Third, many schools wrongly classify interpreters as "teacher aides." The low salaries paid to teacher aides further depresses an already small supply of potential interpreters for public schools (Bowe, 1988b).

You need to observe certain practices when working with an interpreter in the classroom. First, as just implied, be alert to the fact that a "signer" may not communicate your

Student Strategies That Work

Hearing

Included students who are deaf or hard of hearing may ease some of the social isolation they feel in inclusive classrooms by developing an active social life outside of school. Virtually every city has a sizeable population of young people who are deaf or hard of hearing. Word-of-mouth, facilitated today by instant messaging and e-mail, often suffices to identify such individuals. They can make plans to get together on Friday nights, over the weekend, during holidays, and during summer vacations. In smaller communities, where there may not be even one other deaf teenager, the challenge is greater. Even there, however, today's technologies may come to the rescue. High-speed Internet connections, known as "broadband" communications, enable people to see each other over phone or cable lines. Many PCs today come equipped with a video camera. If not, one may be purchased at a computer store for as little as $40. Using these cameras, and a broadband connection, young people who are deaf can sign to each other on the phone.

Although people who are hard of hearing are much more numerous than are individuals who are deaf, this is not the case with children and youth. The vast majority of hard-of-hearing Americans are much older, in their 60s, 70s, or 80s. This fact makes it, if anything, harder for young people who are hard of hearing than for youth who are deaf to foster an active social life. The unfortunate result is social isolation. Technology can help. Theatres, auditoriums, and other places of public assembly often are "looped" and thus work with FM or AM receivers. Loop-equipped plays, movies, and other events are much easier to follow for individuals who are hard of hearing than are non-loop-assisted offerings.

Tinnitus ("ringing in the ears") is a common complaint of individuals with hearing impairments, whether deaf or hard of hearing. The problem has been studied for many years. Over time, we have learned that tinnitus may be caused by blood pressure, kidney disorders, diet, or allergies. Drinking alcohol, smoking, and exposing yourself to loud noises all can make tinnitus worse. Tinnitus may also appear as a side-effect of medications people take for other conditions. An otolaryngologist (ear, nose, throat doctor) can diagnose the condition and make recommendations. Much information that will help students and families deal with tinnitus on a day-to-day basis has been collected online. Several hundred articles, book chapters, and so on, on the topic are available at Medline *http://www.nlm.nih.gov/medlineplus/tinnitus.html*. What these suggest, in aggregate, is that people who are deaf or hard of hearing can, to some extent, prevent or at least forestall for many years the appearance of tinnitus. For example, people can wear maskers (electronic devices that make tinnitus less noticeable by producing other sounds that mask the "roaring" of tinnitus). The key is to take responsibility for tinnitus and seek answers.

full lectures. Second, try to remember to pause occasionally between sentences, to give the interpreter time to catch up with you (people tend to speak much faster than interpreters can translate). The interpreter needs to hear the complete sentence in order to sign it. Pausing between words does not help. Third, always speak directly to the deaf student; the fact that this student looks not at you but at the interpreter is irrelevant. The child is your student; talk to her as you would talk to any other student. Among other things, this means not saying (to the interpreter), "Tell him . . . ."

Strategies in Middle School and High School

Looking now at middle-school and high-school students, we see that 42% of students who are deaf or hard of hearing were placed, during the 2002–2003 school year, into inclusive settings for all or virtually all of the school day (U.S. Department of Education, 2004). This is about the same proportion as obtained in elementary schools (46%). The others were educated in separate classrooms or even in separate schools, such as state schools for deaf students. Larger numbers at this age level attend separate day or residential schools than is the case at earlier grade levels. That is because deaf teenagers are, after all, teenagers. As is true of most teens, they prefer to be among others like themselves. Teens are far more "cliquish" and far more critical of interpersonal differences than are elementary-age children. This same pattern works on the other side, too: Teens who are deaf or hard of hearing are much more interested in socializing than they were when they were of elementary age, and for that reason are far more attracted to others who are deaf or hard of hearing, with whom they can feel comfortable. For them, being one of a small handful of deaf students in a large "hearing" high school can be isolating. Accordingly, the appeal of separate schools may grow during the teen years. Such schools may offer a richer social life, thus helping these young people to develop into more well-rounded adults.

Methods: Promote Social Development. For those who remain in inclusive settings, teachers should work to foster social and emotional growth. It is important for schools (and for teachers) to identify appropriate social activities so that deaf and hard-of-hearing teens may develop socially, and not just academically. To illustrate, providing an interpreter so a deaf student may take an active role in a school play could make a very big difference in that student's social development.

Methods: Support for Students Who Are Hard of Hearing. For these reasons, and for some others as well, you are more likely to encounter, in inclusive settings at the secondary level, students who are hard of hearing rather than deaf. One of the other reasons is that hard-of-hearing students are easier to integrate into regular classrooms than are deaf students. These students usually can understand at least some of what is said. They benefit greatly from auditory listening systems ("loops") that amplify speech that is spoken into a special transmitter. They also benefit from one-speaker-at-a-time rules, because they can then lipread the speaker. Such lipreading adds greatly to their comprehension. Although the linguistic competencies of students who are hard of hearing are limited in comparison to "hearing" students, they generally are measurably better than are those of deaf students. Thus, they are more likely, on the whole, to be academically successful than are deaf students.

Strategies in Transition to Adult Life

Methods: Prepare for College. Students who are deaf or hard of hearing often continue on to postsecondary education. They benefit from the availability of specialized programs, including Gallaudet University (the world's only college exclusively for deaf students), the National Technical Institute for the Deaf (on the campus of the Rochester Institute of Technology, in upstate New York), and other programs such as the consortium of colleges and universities administered by the University of Tennessee at Knoxville. Despite all of these unique programs, the drop-out rate of these students from postsecondary institutions is very high (approaching three out of every four who begin study at such programs; Bowe, 1988).

If your students intend to matriculate at postsecondary institutions, it is urgent that their IEP's reflect these goals, as early as age 14. Intensive preparation, emphasizing mastery of the written form of English but also featuring visits to and study about the different postsecondary programs, should be provided as part of the students' transition planning. Particular emphasis should be placed upon ensuring that the students receive the academic preparation they need to successfully complete high-school work, including the new state-wide tests.

Methods: Teach Pragmatics. Whether your students plan to go to college, go to work, or go into the community to live independently, they need to know what the "unspoken rules" are that govern conversation. These rules are unspoken for a reason—they are rarely taught in school. While students with unimpaired hearing will pick them up, almost unconsciously, this may not occur with those who are deaf or hard of hearing. The effects of this lack of knowledge have been documented: Deaf and hard of hearing adults, as is true with adults having other disabilities, generally encounter difficulty in college, in work, and in the community not so much because they lack specific skills (in, respectively, studying, performing the job tasks, doing housework) as because they fail to master the pragmatics of social interaction. This is most evident in employment. If they are fired, more often than not, it is because they did not follow the unspoken rules of communication with bosses, co-workers, and customers or because they did not follow the "unwritten rules" of the workplace (e.g., Blackorby & Wagner, 1996).

That is why explicit instruction in pragmatics, or what people say in different situations, and in other unspoken and unwritten rules is so important with this population. A good way of teaching these is through role play. In this way, your students gain experience as well as practice in following these rules. They learn those rules by adhering to them.

CHAPTER SUMMARY

Speech and Language Impairments

- Stuttering usually has no identifiable cause. It is often a life-long condition. Teachers can help by modeling fluencies and by showing acceptance of dysfluencies.
- Other than stuttering, most speech impairments tend to be resolved before children leave the elementary grades.
- Students with speech or language impairments (SLIs) are the group most likely to be served in inclusive classrooms.
- Other than stuttering, most speech impairments tend to be resolved before children leave the elementary grades. One exception is severe apraxia, in which children know what to say but do not say it.
- Students with SLI's are the group most likely to be served in inclusive classrooms.
- Push-in often can work for teachers and speech/language pathologists. That is because they tend to be less disruptive. At times, however, pull-out is necessary.
- Aphasia is a word-finding impairment of language. Few interventions help all persons with aphasia. Rather, the literature suggests that treatments be customized on a one-by-one basis. Even then, they may be of limited efficacy.

Hearing Impairments, Including Deafness

- Any degree of hearing impairment can have significant negative effects in education. That is because classrooms feature so much talking, most of it by the teacher.
- Because classrooms tend to be noisy environments, you should consider asking your principal for a loop system. The loop picks up only the voice spoken into a microphone. For this reason, ambient noises are not amplified. The result can be noticeably better performance by your students.
- The number-1 concern of teachers of deaf and hard of hearing children is language development. This is because schools tend to teach *everything else* through language: biology, history, geography, and so on. Unless and until students who are deaf or hard of hearing master the language, they will struggle with other subjects as well.
- Captioning is a readily available technology for teachers of inclusive classrooms. It also costs nothing. Captioned media can enrich the learning experience of children—and not only those with hearing losses.
- If an interpreter is working in your classroom, you should speak as if the interpreter were not present. That is, you should talk directly to your students, whether deaf or not. When a deaf student signs, and the interpreter voices for that student, you should look at the student.

QUESTIONS FOR REFLECTION

1. What are some reasons why 88% of PreK–12 children with the SLI label are between the ages of 6 and 11 (that is, that few are aged 12 to 17 inclusive)?
2. Why is stuttering the one speech impairment you should not expect all students to "grow out of" despite intensive, long-term speech pathology services?
3. What is apraxia? How could you help a child with apraxia to express himself or herself?

4. What is aphasia? How would you differentiate it from a speech impairment?
5. Thinking about how educators diagnose and assess specific learning disabilities (see Chapter 3) versus how they diagnose and assess SLI, explain (a) why many children eventually found to have SLD are first classified as having SLI and (b) why students with the SLD classification are more prevalent in middle school and high school.
6. Why is it a problem for teachers that classrooms, even when not occupied, are noisy? What can you do about unwelcomed environmental noises?
7. How would you use miscue analysis with deaf students, many of whom do not speak intelligibly?
8. Can you identify a reason why many young people who are deaf may prefer to attend a separate, deaf-only high school?
9. What kinds of students, other than those who are deaf or hard of hearing, might benefit from captioned educational media?
10. Looking at Tables 4.1 and 4.2, why do you think most educators agree with Polloway and Polloway (1981) that *every* student, no matter how severely disabled, should be able to read these words and phrases?

Chapter 5 Mental Retardation and Emotional/Behavioral Disorders

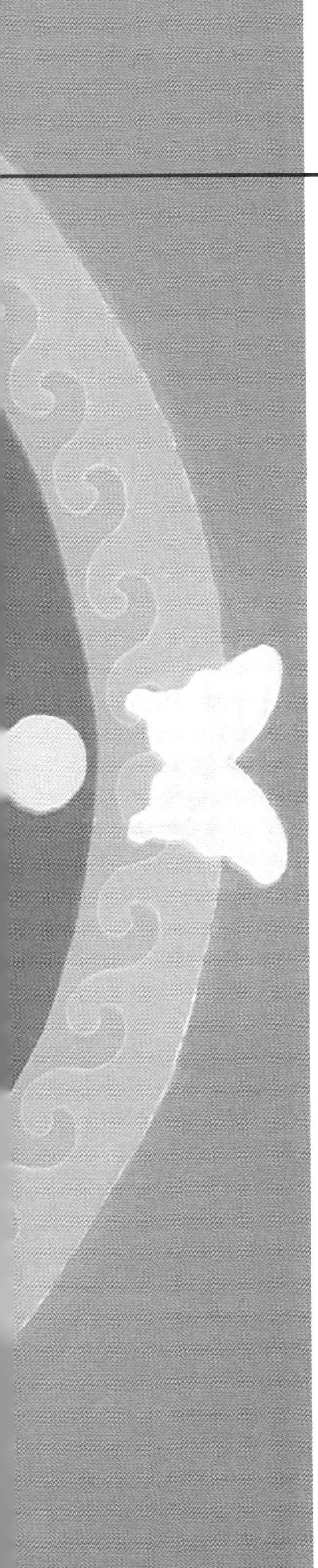

TERMS

severe disability
multiple intelligences
mental retardation (MR)
supports
Down Syndrome
generalizing
Fragile X Syndrome
functional curriculum
task analysis
Supplemental Security Income (SSI)
emotional disturbance
conduct disorder (CD)
oppositional defiant disorder (ODD)
anxiety disorder
mood disorders
schizophrenia
eating disorders
simulations

CHAPTER FOCUS QUESTIONS

After reading this chapter, you will be able to answer such questions as:

1. What is "significantly subaverage" intelligence?
2. In what ways is intelligence a socially defined concept?
3. How does "mild" mental retardation differ from "moderate," "severe," and "profound" MR?
4. Why is teaching life skills so important in the education of students with mental retardation?
5. What is *excluded* in the federal definition of "emotional disturbance"? Why is that significant?
6. In what ways is that definition a subjective one? Why might this matter?
7. What are some prominent techniques that experienced teachers recommend be used with students who have emotional or behavioral disorders?

PERSONAL ACCOUNTS

Kim Ballerini, a graduate student in secondary education (English) at Hofstra, taught a brief poem to a 14-year-old student with Down Syndrome. Mark was included for ninth-grade English and social studies at his neighborhood public school. The poem is about the soul, and includes language about birds, flight, and stars. Even though it is one of Walt Whitman's shorter ones, the poem was a challenging assignment for this young man. Making the task more difficult was the fact that his social studies class had just finished a unit on the Holocaust. Kim had to spend the first 15 to 20 minutes of each session waiting while Mark looked under the table, checked the locked status of each door, and looked out each window. "He was convinced," Kim told me, "that the Nazis might come after him." This young man knew, in one part of his brain, that the events of the Holocaust transpired more than a half-century ago. That knowledge, however, was intellectual in nature, devoid of emotional content. Far more powerful in directing his action was the emotion-laden information, stored more deeply in the brain, about the danger posed for ordinary citizens by the Nazi SS forces. By being persistent, Kim eventually succeeded in teaching Mark the poem. She was delighted that he was able to generate what she called "beautiful insights" about Whitman's poem.

A former student relayed this experience while working at a special school for emotionally disturbed youth:

> *Last year and this, I worked at Crossroads in Little Village. The program serves children and youth of all ages (6 to 21) who were referred here by their home school districts. The hope is that these students will learn enough about controlling their own behavior so as to permit return to the referring district. Some children and youth do in fact return. For many others, however, Crossroads is a "final stop." If they do not make it here, they may be sent to institutional settings such as mental health hospitals. What struck me most about the teens with whom I worked is how aware they were of their own situations. Again and again, they said things like, "You know, I really blew it. I can't even remember the fights I've had—and I've had one or two virtually every day—nor why I started them. That's how minor they seem now. The net result, though, is that I'm not going to be a high school graduate. That's a bummer. Even if someone wants to hire me, I'm afraid they'll call the school district, and call here as well. That'll probably be the end of that." Sadly, they're right. The reason I came to Hofstra for my Master's degree is so I can learn how to help these kids while there is still time!*
>
> —Juanita

These stories highlight some important information that will be discussed in this chapter. Notice, for example, how powerful emotion-filled experiences were for Mark. As a teacher, you may well find that students with mental retardation will learn and remember information that has an emotional component to it. Kim's account also introduces the idea of persistence in instruction. Much repetition and a wide variety of experiences may be necessary before a student with mental retardation acquires and retains new information. Juanita's story offers a different perspective. She is a teacher in a separate school, one specializing in instruction for students with emotional and behavioral disorders. Juanita was struck by how strongly her students wish, in retrospect, that they had been taught, while still placed in neighborhood school classrooms, how to control their behavior. This chapter will describe ways that teachers of inclusive classrooms can mobilize non-disabled students to help children and youth with emotional/behavioral disorders to behave more appropriately in the classroom.

INTRODUCTION

Chapter 5 continues our consideration of very common disabilities. Mental retardation (MR) and emotional or behavioral (E/B) disorders differ from the conditions reviewed in the previous two chapters in that MR and E/B disorders tend to be more severe conditions. In this book, a **"severe disability"** is one that is difficult to accommodate in inclusive or regular classrooms. This is not to say that children and youth with severe disabilities cannot be integrated into such settings. Many can be. It is to say, rather, that meeting their needs in inclusive or regular classrooms is much more challenging for educators than is the case with students whose disabilities are milder.

All of this raises the interesting question, "What about mild mental retardation?" We will address that question in this chapter, notably in Table 5.1 and in the section titled "Characteristics and Types." Briefly, mild mental retardation is *not* mild in comparison with other disabilities. Rather, it is mild only in comparison to moderate, severe, and profound mental retardation. The word "mild" is misleading, largely for historical reasons. Until the mid-1970s, mental retardation was usually defined to include persons with IQ scores below 85. This meant that individuals having measured IQs in the 70–85 range were considered to be "mildly" mentally retarded. Since that time, only people with IQs below 70 or 75 have met the criteria for classification. This is reflected in the use, in virtually all definitions of mental retardation, of the words "significant subaverage" intelligence. In this

FIGURE 5.1 MR and E/B Disorders: Similarities and Differences

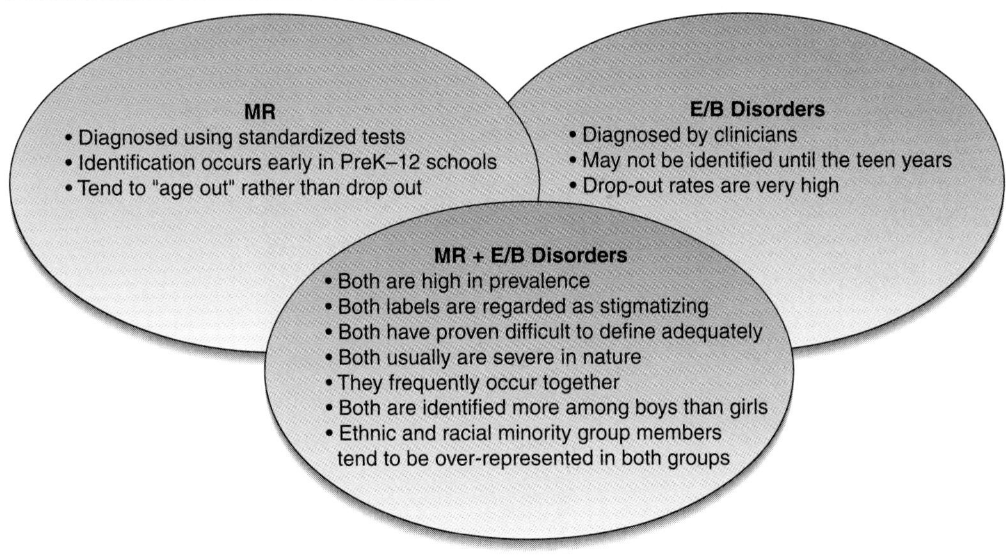

FIGURE 5.2 "Big 4" v. All Others

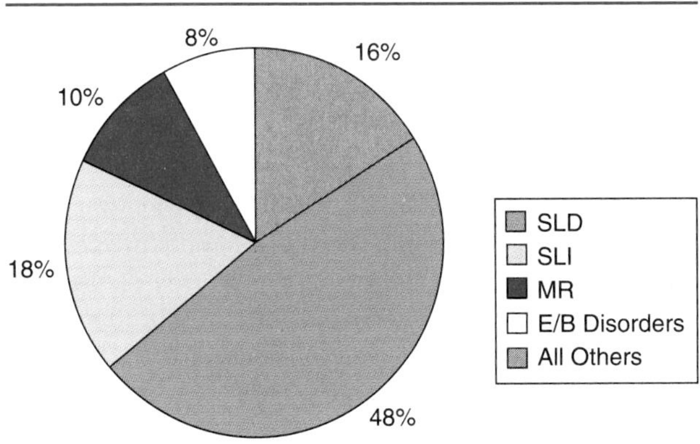

Source: Data from *The 26th Annual Report,* by the U.S. Department of Education, 2004, Washington, DC: Author.

context, "subaverage" would refer to IQ scores of 85 or below and "significantly subaverage" to 70 or below.

We discuss MR and E/B disorders together in this chapter because children and youth with these conditions have nine things in common (see Figure 5.1). First, both are high in prevalence. These are both large categories. They are two of the "Big Four" (see Figure 5.2 and Table 5.3, p. 171). In fact, from all available evidence, more children and youth have these conditions than are identified as such in the public schools. This is probably because of the second similarity: Both MR and E/B disorders are considered to be stigmatizing labels. Third, defining each has challenged professionals. There is a long history of contention behind the currently used definitions in each area. Fourth, both are generally severe in nature, as compared to other IDEA disability groups. Fifth, there is considerable co-morbidity in these populations. That is, emotional disturbance occurs more often among mentally retarded individuals than among non-mentally retarded persons; similarly, mental retardation is more frequent among students with E/B disorders than among students with no emotional disturbance. Sixth, children and especially youth with these disorders are placed in separate classrooms more often than are students with many other conditions. Seventh, there is a definite gender pattern in each category. Children and youth with MR or E/B disorders are more likely to be male than female: 60% of

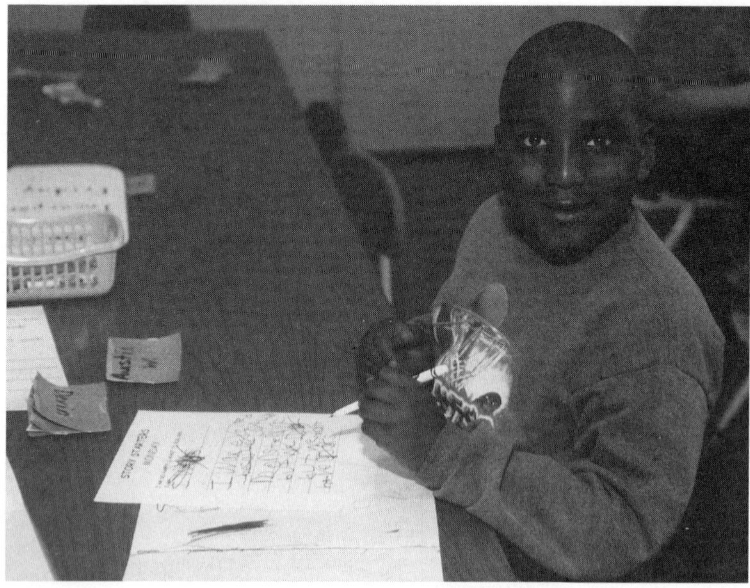

Students with the disabilities discussed in this chapter tend to come from families of lower socioeconomic status (SES) and of ethnic/racial minority group membership.

those with the MR label and a remarkable 80% of those with the E/B disorders label are boys (U.S. Department of Education, 2002). It may be that educators, being predominantly female, overidentify these conditions in boys and underidentify them in girls. Eighth, as compared to students with the conditions discussed in Chapters 3 and 4, those considered in this chapter are much more likely to be members of ethnic or racial minority groups and to come from homes of low socioeconomic status (SES). Ninth and finally, many instances of MR and of E/B disorders are caused by their own parents or other family members. This is not always the case. However, we know that parental neglect and abuse of children can produce mental retardation and emotional disturbance.

There are three main differences between the two categories. First, MR is diagnosed using standardized tests. E/B disorders, by contrast, tend to be identified by trained professionals on the basis of observation and the taking of a personal history. Second, MR is almost always diagnosed by the time a child reaches the primary grades (i.e., before third grade) while E/B disorders may be identified much later. In part, this is because E/B disorders are more subjectively defined and in part because age at onset may be at any age. Third, students with MR tend to remain in K–12 schools until they age out at 22 years of age, while students with E/B conditions are, as a group, the most likely to drop out of school (U.S. Department of Education, 2002).

MENTAL RETARDATION

Intelligence is a socially defined construct, one that we use to discuss how people vary in culturally important ways, notably in their ability to learn, remember, and adapt to different circumstances (American Psychiatric Association, 1994; Gardner, 2000). Understood in this way, intelligence is a broad concept. It incorporates much more than "school smarts"—that is why we talk about people possessing "street smarts," artistic "genius," and "basketball smarts." Intelligence might best be viewed as a set of abilities to attend to, manipulate, understand, and apply different kinds of information (e.g., Anatasi & Urbina, 1997).

The kinds of intelligence of most interest to educators are those most directly related to success in school. These are the kinds of "smarts" that are assessed using intelligence tests. Results of those tests, expressed as IQ scores, are useful in predicting success in school. Such instruments are based upon a construct or idea that we call "general intelligence." By that, we mean the kind of intelligence that helps students do well in school (such as seeing relationships between numbers and words, working rapidly, learning and remembering a wide variety of facts, etc.). IQ tests are much less helpful in predicting success in other areas of life, including work and social interactions (Baumeister, 1987). David Wechsler (1991), author of some of the most widely used IQ tests, himself has acknowledged this fact. However, we do not have well-established tests for most other kinds of intelligence.

Measured intelligence is distributed along a continuum. Within this range, a score of 100 on the Stanford-Binet IV (Thorndike, Hagen, & Sattler, 1986) or the Wechsler Intelligence Scale for Children (WISC III; Wechsler, 1991) is the mean, or the arithmetic average. About two-thirds of people taking one of these tests score between 85 and 115. All of them have measured intelligence that is within the "average" range. Intelligence test scores that are 30 points or more below or above the mean, by contrast, are outside that range. We tend to call people with very high IQs (above 130) "bright" and those with very low IQs (below 70) "mentally retarded." Table 5.1 outlines the different levels of mental retardation as understood with respect to measured intelligence.

Howard Gardner (1983) proposed that there are seven different intelligences, rather than one. He believed that people differ according to their "smartness" about words, logic, pictures, bodies, music, people, and self. Recently, this theory of **multiple intelligences** was expanded to add an eighth kind of intelligence (Gardner, 2000).

Verbal/Linguistic intelligence involves reading, writing, and public speaking. Logical/Mathematical intelligence is a pattern-seeking fluency, one we use to manipulate objects and to use with numbers. Visual/Spatial intelligence has to do with directionality (knowing where we are, where we parked the car) and with color, texture, and shape. Interpersonal intelligence concerns understanding other people, while Intrapersonal intelligence is "knowing thyself." Bodily/Kinesthetic intelligence helps us to use body language, facial expressions, and other forms of nonverbal communication. Musical/ Rhythmic intelligence is self-explanatory. Most recently, Gardner has proposed a Naturalist intelligence that has to do with recognizing different species and in using knowledge of nature in science or farming. As appealing as Gardner's ideas may be, the fact is that the Stanford-Binet and Wechsler scales are the standard, the proverbial Coke and Pepsi, in the field. This makes it difficult for new tests, including those devised to tap Gardner's dimensions, to gain acceptance.

There is yet another way to look at the socially constructed nature of intelligence. In today's information-age economy, the ability to obtain, process, and use the flood of information that comes at each of us every day is valuable. To appreciate this, imagine, for a moment, another economy: that of a band of hunter-gatherers. This group is forever on the move, following a herd of animals. Because the group is perpetually in motion, its members carry with them only what they absolutely need. That does not include much written information, if any at all. A low-IQ member of this peripatetic assemblage of people would not necessarily be disadvantaged. The number and variety of tasks this person would need to learn and know is well within the range of his capabilities. A very "intelligent" member of the group actually could be at a disadvantage in such a society: He might become frustrated by the fact that the hunter-gatherer culture does not permit careful, extended study of much of anything, and, more generally, it does not foster the development of a sophisticated civilization (Bowe, 1978, pp. 2–4; Bronowski, 1973). This example illustrates how our understanding of "intelligence" can vary over time.

The role of emotion in learning and memory has attracted much attention recently (Levine, 2002; Damasio, 1999). As was illustrated in one of the "Personal Accounts" opening this chapter, when an experience is accompanied by strong emotion, events become much more memorable. This knowledge can help educators to teach important information to students with mental retardation.

Definitions

Experts differ sharply over how **mental retardation (MR)** should be defined. The two most important definitions are those of the U.S. Department of Education (1999a) and of the AAMR (Luckasson et al., 2002). Generally, the Department's definition weights the environment less heavily than does the Association's. However, the two definitions have much in common. Indeed, the Department's definition is based upon an earlier (1983) AAMR definition.

The *official definition,* that of the Department of Education (1999a), is

> Mental retardation means significantly subaverage general intellectual functioning, existing concurrently with deficits in adaptive behavior and manifested during the developmental period, that adversely affects a child's educational performance. (34 C.F.R. 300.7[c][6])

The key elements of this definition are (1) the score the child receives on an individually administered test of intelligence, such as the WISC-III, is 70 or below; (2) the child behaves much like children some two or more years younger do ("deficits in adaptive behavior"); and (3) the age at onset (the age of the individual when MR began) was "during the developmental period" (e.g., prior to 18 or at least prior to 22). The Department's definition concludes with the words "that adversely affects educational performance." As with other definitions in the Department's rules, this refers to the fact that children are eligible for services under IDEA if, and only if, they "need special education and related services."

The 2002 AAMR *definition* is different in subtle but important ways:

> Mental retardation is a disability characterized by significant limitations both in intellectual functioning and in adaptive behavior as expressed in conceptual, social, and practical adaptive skills. This disability originates before age 18. A complete and accurate understanding of mental retardation involves realizing that mental retardation refers to a particular state of functioning that begins in childhood, has many dimensions, and is affected positively by individualized supports. As a model of functioning, it includes the contexts and environments within which the person functions and interacts and requires a multidimensional and ecological approach that reflects the interaction of the individual with the environment, and the outcomes of that interaction with regards to independence, relationships, social contributions, participation in school and community, and personal well being. (Luckasson et al., 2002)

The major features of this definition are (1) MR is a "disability." The Association was at pains to say that mental retardation is not something people have. It is not static. Rather, MR is seen as a state of functioning, one that varies as particular people navigate different conditions and demands and as they receive more or fewer supports. The "five assumptions essential to the application of the definition" are

1. Limitations in present functioning must be considered within the context of community environments typical of the individual's age peers and culture.
2. Valid assessment considers cultural and linguistic diversity as well as differences in communication, sensory, motor, and behavioral factors.
3. Within an individual, limitations often coexist with strengths.
4. An important purpose of describing limitations is to develop a profile of needed supports.
5. With appropriate personalized supports over a sustained period, the life functioning of the person with mental retardation generally will improve. (AAMR, *http://www.aamr.org/Policies/faq_mental_retardation.shtml*).

Continuing with the key aspects of this definition, (2) "significant limitations" in intellectual functioning refers to measured functioning, that is, at least two standard deviations (S.D.) below the mean. With respect to measured intelligence, this means IQ scores of 70 or below. That is because the S.D. associated with IQ tests is 15 points. The Association pointed out that the standard error of measurement (S.E.M.) of the most popular IQ tests is 5 points. S.E.M. is a measure reflecting the fact that error is inevitable in testing. Thus, a score of 75 could be accepted under this definition (the "true" score could be 70, with the error of 5 points within the S.E.M.). (3) "Significant limitations" in adaptive behavior, similarly, are scores of two or more S.D. below the mean in instruments that assess adaptive functioning.

AAMR is much more interested in support issues than in IQ score-based issues. By **"supports,"** the Association means types of assistance and extent or degree of such help.

TABLE 5.1 Measured Intelligence

Level	IQ Score Range	Percent of All with MR	Level of Functioning
Mild	50/55 to 70/75	85	• Potentially can reach 6th grade achievement levels • Can acquire vocational skills and get a job
Moderate	35/40 to 50/55	10	• Potentially can reach 2nd grade achievement levels • Can care for themselves at times, with help
Severe	20/25 to 35/40	3 or 4	• Potentially can learn some preacademic skills • Can signal need for help in everyday living
Profound	Below 20/25	1 or 2	• Potentially can show improvement in motor, communication, self-care skills • Usually need 24/7 support on a one-on-one basis

Source: From *Diagnostic and Statistical Manual of Mental Disorders,* 4th ed., American Psychiatric Association, 1994, Washington, DC: Author.

To illustrate, professionals, family members, and others may provide instruction, therapy, and even hands-on step-by-step guidance. AAMR seeks to have professionals differentiate degrees of support in nine areas of functioning (see Table 5.2). That is a major expansion from the 1992 AAMR definition, which was the first to advance the concept of supports (Luckasson et al., 1992). The key, according to the Association, is that focusing upon supports identifies the kinds and amounts of services required to individualize instruction and other kinds of assistance. Periodic assessments of a person's need for supports also highlights how people's needs change over time and in different contexts and environments. For these reasons, AAMR prefers that the focus shift away from levels of measured intelligence (see Table 5.1) and toward systems of support (see Table 5.2).

There are *other definitions,* as well. Perhaps most notably, in 1997 Stephen Greenspan offered a definition that returned to the 1983 AAMR's use of four ranges of severity (mild, moderate, severe, profound), based upon IQ test scores. He added a new wrinkle to his definition: a multiple-intelligences scheme that borrowed from Gardner and recognizes conceptual (the kind of intelligence tapped by IQ tests), practical (street smarts), and social (interpersonal) intelligences.

> The term mental retardation refers to persons widely perceived to need long-term supports, accommodations, or protections due to persistent limitations in social, practical, and conceptual intelligence and the resulting inability to meet intellectual demands of a range of settings and roles. These limitations are assumed in most cases to result from abnormalities or events occurring during the developmental period, and which have permanent effects on brain development and functioning. (Greenspan, 1997, p. 186)

In its *Diagnostic and Statistical Manual of Mental Disorders,* 4th edition (*DSM-IV*), the American Psychiatric Association (1994) defined mental retardation as a behavioral syndrome related to intelligence scores of 70 or below, an age at onset of 18 years or earlier, and impaired ability to cope with the demands of everyday life (notably communicating, caring for self, living at home, relating to others, using community resources, and working). Finally, the American Psychological Association (1996) offered a definition which was very similar to the earlier AAMR definition (1983) in that it features four levels of MR (see Table 5.1).

Similarities and Differences in the Definitions

The themes that repeat themselves, regardless of definition, are (1) a developmental perspective, (2) measured IQ that is 2+ S.D. below the mean, and (3) inclusion of behavior as

TABLE 5.2 Systems of Support

The AAMR identifies nine (9) areas in which individuals with mental retardation may require support from others. In each case, that support may be at one of four degrees of intensity. Thus, there are dozens of permutations possible. This permits professionals to fine-tune their assessments of the functioning of individuals with disabilities.

Areas of Support	Levels of Support
Human Development (e.g., motor skills) Education (e.g., academics) Home Life	Intermittent (e.g., training, prompts, and in-person assistance is only required on occasion)
(e.g., eating food) Community Life (e.g., using mass-transit buses) Employment (e.g., work and teamwork)	Limited (e.g., training, prompts, and in-person assistance are required at predictable times such as when first doing a job)
Health/Safety (e.g., diet, taking medication) Behavior (e.g., socially appropriate, context appropriate) Social Activities	Extensive (e.g., training, prompts, and in-person assistance are needed on a non-time-limited basis)
(e.g., recreation, leisure) Protection and Advocacy (e.g., self advocacy)	Pervasive (e.g., in-person assistance is required constantly and at a high-intensity level)

Sources: Based on data from *Mental Retardation: Definitions, Classification, and Systems of Support,* 9th ed., by Luckasson et al., 1992, Washington, DC: American Association on Mental Retardation; and *Mental Retardation: Definitions, Classification, and Systems of Support,* 10th ed., by Luckasson et al., 2002, Washington, DC: American Association on Mental Retardation. Adapted with permission from American Association on Mental Retardation.

well as measured IQ. All of the definitions reviewed above call for mental retardation to occur during a person's developmental years. If intellectual deficits occur for the first time after age 18, we do not use the term "mental retardation." Rather, we might use "traumatic brain injury" or some other term such as "dementia." The intent is to reserve the MR label for instances where a person's formative experiences (childhood and adolescence) are affected. The fact that 18 is sometimes used and that 22 is used at other times is of relatively little importance because most MR occurs prior to, at, or shortly after birth. All definitions call for measured IQs to be 70 or below. The AAMR allows scores to be as high as 75 but that is to incorporate known errors of measurement and not because of any substantive difference in how MR is understood or defined. All definitions refer to adaptive behavior. The differences are matters of emphasis: Some definitions give relatively more weight to this than to measured IQ than do other definitions. Notably, AAMR stresses the importance of identifying and assessing need for supports more than do the other definitions (see Table 5.2).

Problems with the Definitions

The several definitions of mental retardation require measures of adaptive functioning. This is particularly true of the AAMR definition. Other than the Vineland Adaptive Behavior Scales and the AAMR Adaptive Behavior Scales-School Edition (see "Diagnosis and Assessment," p. 162), we have few suitable measures for assessing behavior in many of the key areas, notably home life, community life, health/safety, and self advocacy (Pierangelo & Giuliani, 1998; Wicks-Nelson & Israel, 2000). Thus, while AAMR calls for scores at least two S.D. below the mean on standardized instruments of adaptive functioning in the areas of conceptual, social, and/or practical behavior, educators may find this to be a more idealistic than realistic requirement. Worse, AAMR insists that "valid assessment considers cultural and linguistic diversity" as well (AAMR, *http://www.aamr.org/*

A functional curriculum, unlike the general curriculum, emphasizes instruction in activities of daily living.

Policies/faq_mental_retardation.shtml). Few tests are accepted as being culturally and linguistically valid (National Center on Accessing the General Curriculum, *http://www.cast.org/ncac*; *Minority Students in Special and Gifted Education; http://www.nap.edu/catalog/10128.html*). Finally, educators and clinicians such as psychologists may have problems communicating with each other because the *DSM-IV* relies upon classification according to IQ scores while the AAMR definition de-emphasizes such scores.

Characteristics and Types

Most mental retardation is mild rather than moderate, severe, or profound. Whatever the level of MR, educators need to recognize that children and youth with the MR label very frequently have other conditions as well. This is well-known with respect to **Down Syndrome,** the non-inherited genetic disorder that produces, in addition to mild or moderate MR, a phalanx of other disorders, notably affecting the heart, and physical and facial features. The issue goes beyond Down Syndrome, however. Research conducted by the Shriver Center for Developmental Disabilities, at the University of Massachusetts, reveals that persons with MR often have under-diagnosed conditions affecting the gastrointestinal system, hearing, vision, respiration, and physical strength (Voelker, 2002a). For example, a wide range of characteristic problems related to the palate, lips, tongue, and teeth have been reported (Desai, 1997).

SUJEET: A TRUE STORY ABOUT DOWN SYNDROME

Sujeet Desai, a music student, delights in dispelling people's preconceived ideas about individuals with Down Syndrome. Growing up near Syracuse, NY, he attended neighborhood public schools. Sujeet was graduated with a high-school diploma after earning National Honor Society recognition and several appearances on the school's honor roll. That academic achievement is attributable, Sujeet's father told me, to his dedication to his school work. As remarkable as it is, that is just the beginning of Sujeet's record of accomplishment.

He plays four instruments (violin, piano, clarinet, and bass clarinet) well enough to be a member, for 5 years, of the school band and also to give solo performances to a variety of audiences in northern New York State. As a high-school student, he took some music courses at Syracuse University, as part of his school's efforts to offer special education students opportunities for transition from school to life beyond high school. Sujeet was also active in sports while in high school, earning a black belt in Tae Kwon Do. In the 1999 Special Olympics, he won two silver medals in aquatics.

Sujeet lists as a goal earning enough money to buy a car like his older brother. He also wants to continue to play music in public, both in solo performances and as part of a band.

Sujeet's mother Sindoor wrote a review of literature about Down Syndrome for a journal aimed at dental professionals. As a dental professional herself, she knew that dentists and oral hygienists worldwide need factual information about the cardiac, immune, musculoskeletal, and orofacial aspects of Down Syndrome.

For more information on literature involving Down Syndrome, go to the Web Links module in Chapter 5 of the Companion Website.

Mild MR

Teachers in inclusion classrooms are most likely to see students with mild MR (generally, IQs between 70 or 75, on the high end, and 55 on the low end). That is for three reasons. First, most MR is mild. Some 85% to 90% of all individuals with mental retardation are considered to have mild MR. Second, children and youth with mild MR are far more readily accommodated in general education settings than are students with more severe MR. This is because they usually can learn at least some academic information and can understand and obey most classroom rules, notwithstanding the fact that they need far more time, and much more repetition, to do so than is the case with most children and youth. Third, family members tend to advocate for inclusion more than is true with respect to many other IDEA categories of disability.

For more information on an advocate group for MR, The Arc, go to the Web Links module in Chapter 5 of the Companion Website.

Students having mild MR usually are well aware that they learn more slowly than do most other children and that their behaviors tend to make them less well-accepted by other students (Turnbull, Turnbull, Shank, Smith, & Leal, 2002). For these reasons, they pay close attention to what others do in the classroom. This is an argument for inclusion, because what they see modeled generally is acceptable classroom behavior. The opposite side of the same coin is that students with MR who are included may be distracted from academics by this very attention to the behavior of other students.

Individuals with MR suffer when distracted more than do most other students, because they are less able simultaneously to attend to two events at once. Similarly, the characteristically high levels of susceptible to influence may get them in trouble, as when age peers unscrupulously trick them into unwitting violations of school and/or societal rules.

Working Memory. Individuals with mild MR tend to have difficulty with short-term memory. However, once they learn something, they generally remember it. Hallahan and Kauffman (2000) prefer the term "working memory" to short-term memory. One young woman who works at a Marriott hotel, cleaning many dozens of rooms, keeping them immaculate day after day, needed many weeks of on-the-job training on each of the specific tasks involved (emptying the contents of trash cans into large canisters, moving the canisters from room to room, taking filled canisters down the freight elevator to depositories, etc.). Considerable additional time was then required to teach her the skills in combination. Once she mastered these, however, she became a valued employee who today is relied upon to do her job consistently, day after day.

Other Characteristics. People with mild MR can learn to apply learned behaviors in different settings. They need help, and much practice, however. **Generalizing** is when a student learns something in your classroom, then is able to do it in another classroom, or at home. Attention spans tend to be fairly short. In other words, individuals with mild MR may be easily frustrated and readily distracted. They tend to display immature behavior in social settings. With respect to motivation, many are strongly motivated to "become smart," which is why they may continue coming to school until they "age out" at 22 years of age (Turnbull, et al., 2002). Individuals with mild MR both need and benefit from adaptive physical education. Adaptive physical education can meet the needs of many of these children and youth, particularly those with Down Syndrome, while also training them on productive ways to make use of leisure time.

Moderate, Severe, and Profound MR

Teachers of inclusive classrooms are much less likely to see students with moderate, severe, or profound mental retardation than they are to see children and youth with mild MR. Students with moderate MR tend to have much greater difficulty with academic information than do those with mild MR. Many never learn more than very elemental academics. They need considerable help to master even basic material. That's why these students tend to receive instruction in self-help, in self-care, and in other "activities of daily living," such as grooming, using restroom facilities, riding the bus, and making change in a store. Urgent is instruction in ways of communicating their needs and desires. This may mean learning to signal that they need help by, for example, raising a hand. It may also mean becoming skilled in using a Picture Exchange Communication System (PECS) or a communication board (see "Technology That Works: MR"). A thorough overview of techniques of teaching self-help skills, including communication, is offered by Wehman and Kregel (1997) in their *Functional Curriculum*. For students with moderate or severe mental retardation learning these skills can take a lot of time, and occur only after repeated failure. Many will need assistance from others even after receiving extensive training in self-help tasks. That is why educators strive to help these persons to indicate their needs and to assist others in meeting those needs (Dever & Knapczyk, 1997).

Co-Morbidity

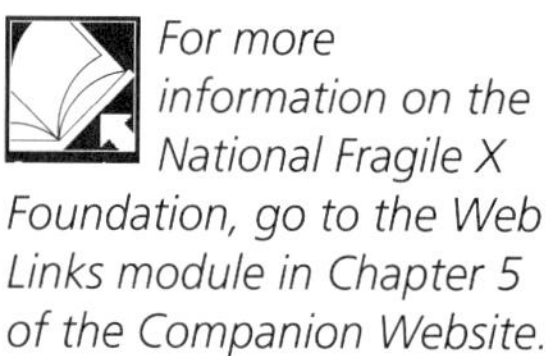
For more information on the National Fragile X Foundation, go to the Web Links module in Chapter 5 of the Companion Website.

Many children with mental retardation also have other conditions. Those with Down Syndrome, for example, typically have hearing impairment (some 68%), congenital heart disease (about 50%), and vision loss (some 35%; Roizen, 1997). Children who have mental retardation because of Fragile X syndrome may also have learning disabilities and/or attention deficit disorders. For these reasons, teachers must be vigilant about hearing, vision, LD, and ADHD as possible causes of academic difficulties. Cardiac conditions typically surface later in life, and are frequently the cause of death, generally for those in their 40s or 50s. Other physical disabilities, such as cerebral palsy and epilepsy, often co-occur with MR (Singh, Oswald, & Ellis, 1998).

Co-morbidity with emotional or behavioral conditions is particularly disturbing. Voelker (2002b), writing in an editorial in the *Journal of the American Medical Association,* reported, "Experts currently estimate that emotional, behavioral, and psychiatric disorders are three to four times more common in people with MR and developmental disabilities than they are in the general public" (p. 433). Human Rights Watch offered another, equally troubling, perspective. Before the U.S. Supreme Court's decision that execution of convicted criminals who are mentally retarded was unconstitutional, announced June 20, 2002, the organization compiled information about death-row inmates with mental retardation. Their report shows that the mother of one death-row inmate, who was mentally retarded, tortured him, tying him to the rafters, and stuffing him in a sack which was then swung over a fire. The father of another kicked him, punched him, and beat him with electrical cords. A third was beaten with belts and cords by his mother and stepmother; his mother also once hit him on the head while he was sleeping (Human Rights Watch, 2001, *http://www.hrw.org/reports/2001/ustat/ustat0301-01.htm*). These accounts help to show why some individuals with mental retardation also become emotionally disturbed. In some instances, familial poverty is at the root both of the MR (because of malnutrition) and of the abuse by family members (perhaps because of parental frustration and anger; e.g., Park, Turnbull, & Turnbull, 2002).

Prevalence

For more information on the U.S. Department of Education's Annual Reports, *go to the Web Links module in Chapter 5 of the Companion Website.*

According to the *26th Annual Report* (U.S. Department of Education, 2004, Table AB3), the category of mental retardation was the third-largest group, with 590,000 students aged 6 to 21 being served during the 2002–2003 school year. These children and youth comprised 10% of students with any label. To help place these statistics into context, Figure 5.2 and Table 5.3 offer summaries of the "Big Four" categories, plus Other Health Impaired

Down Syndrome features a number of physical characteristics in addition to mental retardation.

(OHI), which includes attention deficit disorders. As the table illustrates, only specific learning disabilities (SLD) and speech/language impairments (SLI) are larger categories than MR.

About 40% of PreK–12 students with the MR label are ages 6 through 11. Some who otherwise would have been classified with MR may have been given a less-stigmatizing label, such as speech/language impaired (SLI), while further testing was done. Such testing usually has been completed by the time children enter middle school and certainly by the time they begin high school. This may help to explain why 60% of K–12 students with the MR label are aged 12 through 18.

During the 1997–1998 school year, one-third (34%) of students with the label "mental retardation" were African American, 11% were Hispanic American (persons of Hispanic origin, who may be of any race), and 53% were non-Hispanic white (U.S. Department of Education, 2000b, Table AA3). These proportions are quite different from those we saw in Chapter 3. Specifically, the proportion of African-American students with the MR label is roughly double what one would expect from population demographics alone (African Americans are 15% of all K–12 students). This overrepresentation is controversial. Many experts argue that it reflects school climate, bias in testing, and even racism in the public schools (e.g., National Alliance of Black School Educators and Council for Exceptional Children, 2002), while others insist that it results largely from the lower socioeconomic status of many African Americans (e.g., Artiles & Trent, 1994; Fujiura & Yamaki, 2000). Similar overrepresentation occurs in the E/B disorders category. See "Research That Works: Overrepresentation" later in this chapter.

Diagnosis and Assessment

Mental retardation is assessed first by use of an individual test of general intelligence. Most used are the Wechsler scales of intelligence. These include the Wechsler Preschool and Primary Scale of Intelligence (WPPSI-R), the Wechsler Intelligence Scale for Children-III (WISC-III), and the Wechsler Adult Intelligence Scale-III (WAIS-III). Also used is the Kaufman Assessment Battery for Children (K-ABC). The WPPSI-R is used with children at the preschool and kindergarten levels, the WISC-III with children and youth aged 6 to 16, and the WAIS-III with youth aged 16 and over (Pierangelo & Giuliani, 1998). The Stanford-Binet Intelligence Scale is also used. It is appropriate for children and youth aged two or over.

A score of two S.D. below the mean (70 or, at times, 75 or lower) is required in most states. The K-ABC is well regarded as predicting academic success about as well as does the WISC-III (Anastai & Urbina, 1997). Intended for use with children between the ages of 2 and 12, it assesses abilities in sequential processing (step-by-step) and simultaneous processing (integration of information).

Also necessary are assessments of adaptive functioning. Widely used are the Vineland Adaptive Behavior Scales. These are interviews and rating scales for use by teachers and family members. They assess functioning in the areas of communication, daily living, socialization, and motor activities. The AAMR Adaptive Behavior Scale-School (ABS-S:2) may also be used. This well-regarded test includes measures of self direction, responsibility, and social engagement, among others. Other tests of adaptive behavior are described by Pierangelo and Giuliani (1998). Teachers of inclusive classrooms also need to recognize that some students labeled as having MR were in fact misdiagnosed. As was mentioned in Chapter 2, school officials in mid-SES districts at times overidentify children from low-SES families as being mildly mentally retarded. Such misdiagnosis is unfortunate. For you as a teacher, the key is to be aware that overidentification can and does occur. A signal to which you should attend is student behavior that is noticeably higher than is characteristic of mild MR. If you have a student who has been labeled mildly mentally retarded but whose behavior belies thc label, you should ask the IEP team to reassess the child.

Causes

The number-one most-reported cause of mental retardation is "unknown"—an identifiable cause cannot be identified in most instances, particularly of mild MR (Luckasson et al., 2002). That being said, mild MR is most common among children who come from poor families (AAMR, *http://www.aamr.org*). Park, Turnbull, and Turnbull (2002) discussed the many ways in which familial poverty could lead to MR in childhood: hunger, malnutrition, family stress, underutilization of health-care care services especially by pregnant women, and so on. Severe and profound MR, by contrast, occurs at all SES levels and is more likely to have uncontrollable causes.

Genetic Factors

Mental retardation is less likely to have genetic than non-genetic causes. **Fragile X syndrome** is the number-one inherited genetic cause of mental retardation in males. As you may recall from your biology studies, males have one X and one Y sex chromosome. Females, by contrast, have two X chromosomes. Thus, if an X chromosome is damaged, the effects are much more likely to be seen in males than in females. This may be why three in every five (60%) PreK–12 students with the MR label are boys (U.S. Department of Education, 1999c). Fragile X syndrome features severe MR (with IQ scores as low as 35 to 40), mild learning disabilities, hyperactivity, and/or autistic-like behaviors such as hand flapping and hand biting. The behaviors, particularly in the areas of attention and compliance with directions, concern many teachers (Hatton et al., 2000). A striking decline in measured IQ between the ages of 10 and 15 has been reported to be associated with the syndrome (State, King, & Dykens, 1997). Fragile X syndrome is also characterized by unusual elasticity in connective tissues. That is why the faces of people with Fragile X are long, the ears are large, and the fingers are double-jointed. The syndrome affects about 90,000 Americans; the incidence (number of new instances annually) is about 3,000, or some one per thousand live births (National Fragile X Foundation, *http://www.fragilex.org*).

Down Syndrome, by contrast, is a non-inherited genetic cause of mental retardation. The condition usually results from errors during meiosis (cell division). In these cases, the genome mistakenly makes three, rather than two, copies of the 21st chromosome during division. This "trisomy 21" results in mild to moderate mental retardation, in most instances. A few instances result from unbalanced translocations of chromosome 21. The characteristic facial "look" of Down syndrome includes eyes that seem to slant upwards and a sometimes protruding tongue. Other features include hypotonia in muscles ("softness" or low muscle tone) and cardiac irregularities. About 250,000 Americans of all ages have Down syndrome (National Down Syndrome Society, *http://www.ndss.org*).

Environmental Factors

Maternal consumption of alcohol during pregnancy is recognized as the number-one cause of mental retardation in the United States; it is also a completely preventable cause (Bauer, 1999). Whether expressed through fetal alcohol syndrome (the more severe form) or fetal alcohol effect (the less severe kind), the results include, in addition to MR, some specific learning disabilities, some attention deficit disorders, and some emotional/behavioral conditions (Bagheri, Burd, Martsolf, & Klug, 1998; Weinberg, 1997; Wekselman et al., 1995).

AAMR identifies family factors, such as nutrition, social interaction, and adult stimulation of and interaction with children as key causes of mental retardation. It is largely because of daily meals, regular medical care, and intellectual stimulation that Head Start and other comprehensive early intervention programs have demonstrated such impressive results with young children who come from poor families (Martin, Ramey, & Ramey, 1990; Zigler & Valentine, 1979). Mental retardation may also be caused by poor prenatal care, infections during pregnancy (e.g., Rubella), and physical abuse. Historically, a major cause has been lead. Children may ingest lead in drinking water. The pipes bringing water into buildings may have lead in the solder connecting them; brass faucets may also contain lead. Children might also eat the dust of lead-based paint. Although lead-based paint was banned in the United States in 1978, many buildings still have the old paint. When a home or school is renovated, the lead may be released into the air as dust.

Instructional Methods

Teaching students with mental retardation involves much repetition, multi-sensory input, peer tutoring, and activity-based learning (including on-site or community-based learning). Perhaps most important is selection of content. Because these students take so much more

Resources That Work

MR

A great deal of helpful information about teaching students with MR is available for teachers of inclusive classrooms. This includes comprehensive textbooks, such as Beirne-Smith, Ittenbach, and Patton's (2002) *Mental Retardation* and Wehman and Kregel's (1997) *Functional Curriculum.* Beirne-Smith et al. is particularly useful for a full range of educational interventions, including those applicable to inclusive classrooms. Wehman's text is more specific in its presentation of "functional" or alternative curricula and materials.

AAMR publishes a well-regarded journal, *Mental Retardation,* as well as a variety of other publications. The major parent-based organization, The Arc, offers a wide range of resources at its Web site, *http://www.thearc.org.* This site is especially relevant for teachers and family members who wish to advocate on behalf of persons with MR and who wish to teach young persons with MR how to self-advocate. Another resource is the small federal agency known as the President's Committee on Mental Retardation (PCMR). A unit of the Department of Health and Human Services (HHS), it has a Web site at *http://www.acf.dhhs.gov/programs/pcmr/.*

A nationwide network of Mental Retardation Research Centers (MRRCs) is sponsored by the National Institutes of Health (NIH). For example, the MRRC at the University of Colorado is investigating the co-morbidity of MR and E/B disorders such as schizophrenia. The 15 MRRCs currently being funded are listed and described at Mental Retardation and Developmental Disabilities (MRDD) Branch, *http://www.nichd.nih.gov/cdbpm/MRDD/MRDD.htm.*

Some resources that do not specialize in MR nonetheless provide much information that is helpful. The Transition Research Institute at the University of Illinois (113 Children's Research Center, 51 Gerty Drive, Champaign, IL 61820) is one example. This research center has done important work on transition from school to life after school. Another university-based center is the Institute on Community Integration, located at the University of Minnesota (109 Pattee Hall, 150 Pillsbury Drive SE, Minneapolis, MN 55455).

time than do others to learn, deciding what to teach is a key decision. You likely cannot teach them everything in your syllabus. That is why answering the question, "What is worth teaching?" is perhaps *the* major decision facing you as a teacher. Ideally, the IEP will answer this question for you. If not, you need to assess the student's capabilities and knowledge, discuss goals and objectives with the family, and make some fundamental decisions.

Probably the threshold decision for teachers of inclusive classrooms is "Academic or Functional Curriculum?" That is, you need to decide whether your emphasis, with respect to the student with mental retardation, is going to be on academics (generally, the content you will cover with other students) or on functional matters. A **functional curriculum** (also called an "alternative" curriculum and, by the Council for Exceptional Children, an "independence" curriculum) stresses instruction in practical survival and independent-living skills. It is very different from the general curriculum. Generally, a functional curriculum is followed in separate classrooms rather than inclusive classrooms. However, the IEP team may have determined that an inclusive classroom was the appropriate placement for other reasons (e.g., social development), in which case you would be expected, as the teacher of an inclusive classroom, to incorporate a functional curriculum into your plans for the class. See "Teacher Strategies That Work: Functional Curriculum" in the nearby box.

Strategies in Early Childhood and Elementary School

We first examine teaching strategies and tactics at the elementary level. During the 2002–2003 school year, fully 14% of elementary-age students (i.e., those 6 to 11 years of age) having the MR label were taught in inclusive settings all the time or very nearly so. An additional 31% were in inclusive classrooms for part of the school week (Department of Education, 2004, Table AB3). That 14% were in general classrooms is striking. It is more than double the proportion of just a decade ago. The balance of elementary students with the MR label were taught in separate classrooms and a few in separate schools. Figure 5.3 illustrates the likelihood of placement for K–12 students with MR into inclusive settings.

Parents of children with mental retardation, especially those who are of elementary age, are some of the most fervent advocates of inclusion. Usually, this is because they value highly the potential of general classrooms to develop the *social skills* of their children (e.g., Palmer, Borthwick-Duffy, & Widaman, 1998). Not all parents agree. These other parents believe that it is their role, not the school's, to nourish social skills. They want

FIGURE 5.3 Likelihood of Inclusive Placements: MR

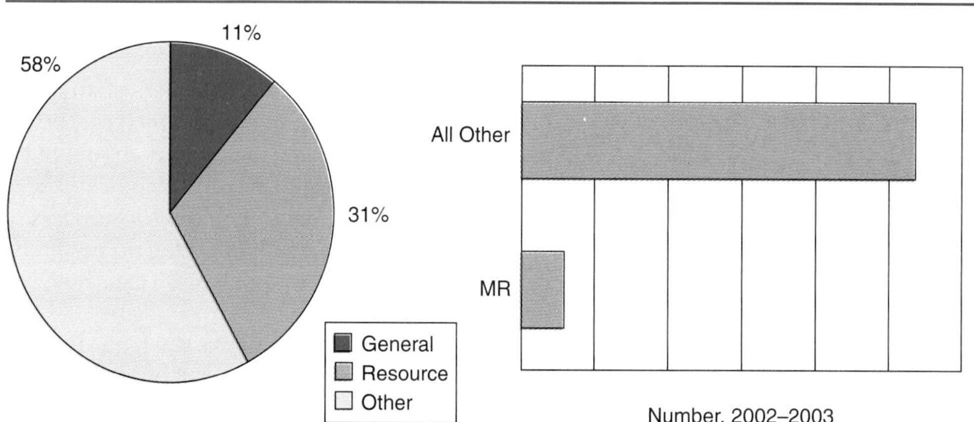

Students with the "mental retardation" label are one in every ten (10%) of K–12 students with any label. They number 590,000, according to the *26th Annual Report* (U.S. Department of Education, 2004). Of them, about one in every nine (11%) were placed into inclusive environments for all or virtually all of the school week (spending less than 21% of the time in other settings). The two charts above illustrate these data.

Source: From the *26th Annual Report,* by the U.S. Department of Education, 2004, Washington, DC: Author.

Teacher Strategies That Work

Functional Curriculum

If the IEP of a student with mental retardation specifies instructional goals and objectives related to the acquisition of practical and survival skills, you may need to adopt components of what some experts call a "functional" curriculum. This curriculum features instruction (often *in situ,* or in the community) in such things as using self-care, following balanced food plans, riding public transportation, ordering food at a fast-food restaurant, making change, budgeting scarce resources, opening and maintaining a checking account, paying rent and other regularly due bills, and the like. What these have in common is that they are *not* usually taught in inclusive classrooms. The assumption is made that most students will learn these things from family members or on their own. That is a valid assumption with respect to most students. However, many individuals with MR need additional and highly explicit instruction as well as extensive practice opportunities in order to master these skills and competencies.

Such instruction is the sole topic of a text edited by Paul Wehman and John Kregel. Their *Functional Curriculum for Elementary, Middle, and Secondary Age Students with Special Needs* (1997) offers in-depth discussions of ways to teach self-determination and other aspects of self-advocacy, functional academics (e.g., math and English specifically for everyday living), peer relations, self-care, and living in the community. Wehman and Kregel's book emphasizes that functional academics cross the traditional lines and are taught in different places, as when time-telling skills are taught at home, in school, at work, and in the community. Similarly, money skills are taught in restaurants and fast-food establishments, in stores, at pay phones, on the bus, and so on.

What Every Special Educator Must Know (2000), from the Council for Exceptional Children (CEC; 1920 Association Drive, Reston, VA 20191-1589) describes the "Individualized Independence Curriculums" recommended by CEC for teacher training programs. You may also visit the CEC Web site and enter, in the Search box, "Independence Curriculum." The page outlines what teachers-in-training should be taught to do. The topics and themes are also revealing as to what practicing teachers should do in the classroom. Another good resource is the Life Centered Career Education program. This one is specific to transition from school to work and to living independently in the community (*http://www.cec.sped.org/bk/catalog/transition-lcce.html*).

For more information on the "alternative" curriculum and the Council for Exceptional Children, go to the Web Links module in Chapter 5 of the Companion Website.

For an illustration of functional curriculum in the community, go to the Web Links module in Chapter 5 of the Companion Website.

schools to teach their children knowledge and skills about practical, "real-world" matters (like making change and riding the bus) so their children can function more independently at home and in the community. Such information seldom is conveyed in general classroom settings, but is a fixture of separate classes specifically designed for children with mental retardation. That is why these parents are less supportive of inclusion.

Methods: Select What Is "Worth Teaching" These Students. As a teacher of an inclusive classroom having a student (or several students) with mental retardation, you should review the student's (or students') IEP materials with care. These documents should highlight the priorities identified by the team. Some IEPs will emphasize instruction in social skills, while others will stress intensive work on academics. Many IEPs call for students to be instructed in learning strategies. This is because individuals with MR often do not know and use learning and memory techniques that other students routinely use (e.g., Butler et al., 2001; Parmar et al., 1996).

You should take your cue from the IEP. It will tell you what is worth teaching. To illustrate why this is so critical, consider the fact that students with MR may still be struggling in June with information that other students mastered in October. In one kindergarten class, for example, all the children but one knew everyone's name within 6 weeks. The child with MR was still learning those names when school let out for the summer vacation. This highlights the need to make firm decisions. To continue with this example, is it worth teaching that child the names of his classmates? Would the time be better used teaching him other things?

Methods: Perform an Ecological Assessment. The word "ecology" refers to the environment. Broadly defined, it is all of the resources available to you in the classroom, the school as a whole, and the surrounding community. You should begin by taking an inventory of such resources. Which people, rooms, buildings, and facilities potentially could help? If, for example, you plan to teach your class about heat, you need to learn how the classroom is heated and how other buildings and facilities nearby are heated. Where are the companies that provide oil and gas heating services located? Are the managements of those companies amenable to hosting a class visit? To sending an employee to do a "show and tell" in your classroom? You also need to do another kind of ecological assessment, as illustrated in the next section.

Methods: Assess, Then Teach. Individuals with MR have strengths as well as weaknesses. That is, they have resources. Evaluating those is another kind of "ecological assessment." It is imperative, before beginning to teach a young student with MR, to learn what that student already knows and can do (Mercer & Mercer, 1998). The IEP should offer you insights. These may be general ideas, however. Your own assessments likely will give you much more specific information that relates directly to what you plan to teach. Once you know where your student stands vis-à-vis your curriculum, the next step is to do a **task analysis.** This is a detailed extraction out of each skill of the specific sub-skills of which it is comprised. Thus, taking off a jacket in the morning may involve as many as a dozen small steps (e.g., releasing each button, pulling each arm out of its sleeve, etc.). Research conducted 20-plus years ago by Marc Gold, Tom Bellamy and others convincingly showed that complex behaviors can be mastered by individuals with mental retardation, including persons with severe MR, if these behaviors are taught step-by-step following a task analysis (e.g., Bellamy, Horner, & Inman, 1979; Gold, 1973).

Methods: Early Intervention and Preschool Special Education. The evidence is strong that early and intensive instruction can help young children with mental retardation. U.S. General Accounting Office (2002) reported that in Pennsylvania fewer than half of the young children who received early intervention services when they were under 3 years of age (1991 to 1995) needed special education when they entered the public schools (1996-1997). In Delaware, about half of the children who received preschool special education services between 1997 and 1999 entered general (rather than special) K–12 education programs. Both groups included young children with MR. Similarly, Hatton et al. (2000) documented positive outcomes of early intervention services for boys with Fragile X syndrome. Particularly helpful with young children in inclusion settings is the strategy of naturalistic instruction known as "embedding" (see Chapter 3). In embedding, children with MR participate in the same activities as do their age peers, but receive additional instruction and therapy during those activities (Dunst et al., 2001). Concluded Beirne-Smith, Ittenbach, and Patton (2002), in their text *Mental Retardation,* "The importance of naturalistic instruction cannot be overemphasized" (p. 287). That is because embedding offers instruction during regularly occuring activities, draws upon the child's own interests as motivators, and offers natural reinforcers.

Methods: Direct Instruction. Very well documented in the literature (see "Research That Works: Scientifically Based Interventions") is the approach known as Direct Instruction (DI). As you may recall from Chapter 3, this strategy involves explicit teaching of information, testing, re-teaching of material, and periodic review. It is often used with behavior modification to direct the attention of children and youth with mental retardation to the task at hand.

Experts on MR caution that the popular constructivist (discovery learning) approaches, where teachers facilitate instruction by providing and arranging materials but avoid direct teaching, are of limited utility for many children and youth with MR (e.g., Beirne-Smith et al., 2002). Actually, constructivist methods have their place but in conjunction with, rather

Research That Works

Scientifically Based Interventions

A rich body of literature, dating back several decades, supports the use of what are called "scientifically based" interventions. Simply, these are strategies and tactics that have been tested by scientists working hand-in-hand with teachers. The evidence in favor of these techniques is not merely anecdotal. Rather, these approaches have been shown to work *and* to be more effective than are competing applications.

A good example is *Direct Instruction.* As long ago as 1987, Gersten, Carnine, and Woodward summarized 25 years of research on DI. The evidence that DI works with students having MR is impressive. A very wide variety of academic and life skills have been taught using the approach. It has proven its value in early childhood (e.g., Goodman, 1992) and secondary school (e.g., Gersten, Keating, Yovanoff, & Harniss, 2001).

Another example is *behavior modification.* Again, several decades worth of research demonstrates that presentation (positive) reinforcement, in particular, is highly effective with children and youth having MR. Indeed, Wicks-Nelson and Israel (2000), reviewing intervention techniques, reported that "The single most important innovation in treating retardation has been the application of behavioral techniques" (p. 281). They reached that conclusion because behavior modification keeps the child on task, reinforces desired behavior, and supports generalization of learning.

Research on *embedding* (also known as naturalistic instruction) is also convincing. This technique helps children with MR to learn in inclusive settings because it does not require separate instruction, special materials, or highly trained educators. Rather, embedding allows students with MR to participate in the same activities, at the same time, as do other children, using the same materials, and being helped by the same professionals. Naturalistic instruction taps the interests of the child, at the time the child is engaged in pursuing those interests (Dunst et al., 2001; Beirne-Smith et al., 2002).

than in place of, DI. You might, for example, use DI to train a student how to perform a task, and then step back to allow this student and a peer to apply that task in discovery learning.

Methods: Tap Emotions. We saw in a chapter-opening story about Kim and Mark that emotion often plays a major role in learning by individuals with MR. Researchers and educators alike have become much more aware in recent years of the power of emotion in cognition (e.g., Damasio, 1999). On the one hand, shame can have "devastating effects on ensuing motivation and related goal-striving behavior" (Turner, Husman, & Schallert, 2002, p. 80). These researchers added, "Shame proneness is a dispositional tendency to interpret outcomes as a failure and to blame the (whole) self in a negative way for the perceived failure. Individuals prone to having feelings of shame are inclined to make internal, stable, and global attributions for negative events" (p. 82). Their words recalled Weiner's (1985) three-part attributional schematic, in which the causes of failure may be seen as internal or external ("It's my fault" or "It was out of my hands"), controllable or uncontrollable ("I could have done better" or "I did my best, but the test was just impossible"), and stable or unstable ("What happened is going to keep happening" or "This was a fluke; it will be better next time"). According to Weiner, individuals who perceive failure to be internal, uncontrollable, and stable will respond to shame by ceasing to strive toward their goals. Many experts believe that persons with MR tend to be particularly susceptible to shame because they do see failure as internal, uncontrollable, and stable (e.g., Beirne-Smith et al., 2002). On the other hand, joy is an emotion we enjoy revisiting. We feel joy when we succeed. And we avoid feeling shame if we believe that our lack of success is temporary and can be attributed to non-personal factors. This is why experts relentlessly emphasize the need for teachers to identify ways students can succeed. As Marc Gold (1980) put it, you should "try another way." Similarly, Mel Levine (2002) and Larry Silver (1998) urged teachers and parents alike to give children and youth specific strategies and tactics they can use to succeed.

Methods: Use Creative Repetition. Because of their characteristic limitations with short-term memory, children and youth with MR tend to require much repetition before information is learned. Simple repetition should be avoided in favor of what we might term "creative

Technologies That Work

MR

Very few computer software programs are designed specifically for students who have MR. However, you can find a wide range of offerings that are suitable for use with such children and youth. The key is to look for *multisensory* programs—software that provides information both visually and auditorially and programs that provide opportunities for experiential learning. Especially helpful are software programs that require the user to become active in learning and that offer immediate and appropriate feedback. In selecting such software, you need to perform a delicate balancing act between offerings that are (to adopt Vygotsky's terminology) at the student's zone for proximal development and those which are "too babyish" for students of that age. Special educators who have experience teaching students with MR can make good suggestions.

One might think that captioned television programs, movies, and so on, would be useful for students with MR. This makes logical sense, since the captioning offers a visual version of what is spoken, hence realizing the goal of multisensory input. However, the speed at which captions are displayed for TV programs and movies generally is too high. Such programs as *Mr. Rogers Neighborhood* and *Sesame Street* are captioned much more slowly, at the rate of about 60 words per minute. However, the content of such programming fails the "too babyish" test.

repetition," meaning that you should repeat the same content but in different ways. Gold's "Try Another Way" methodology was based on his contention that if persons with MR do not learn something, it is because we as educators have failed to teach it. If something is worth teaching, it is worth teaching in a wide range of ways until the student learns it. This may mean using manipulatives that the student can feel and move, mnemonics the student can use to remind himself of the steps of a process, songs he can memorize to remember information. It may mean community-based instruction, which can offer memorable experiences "in the real world" while minimizing the cognitive demands of generalizing knowledge and skills from one setting to another. It may mean using colors to help the student to differentiate one piece of information from another. The key is to be creative, and keep trying!

Methods: Use Sign Language. It is well-established that students with mental retardation tend to attend more, learn better, and remember more readily when they receive information in more than one modality. This is why good teachers say what they write, write what they say, and have children physically participate in learning activities. It is also why some teachers sign to children with MR. Manual signs often are concrete, so are readily understood even if the spoken words they accompany are not. The sign for "stop," for example, vividly shows a hand stopping. The sign for "milk," similarly, is directly connected to how a farmer milks a cow. For this reason, signs may be understood by students with MR even when vocal instruction is not. Research shows that signing in inclusive classrooms can help such children (e.g., DiCarlo, Stricklin, & Banajee, 2001; Grove & Dockrell, 2000). In addition, some children and youth with MR do not have speech that is readily intelligible to others. For this reason, they may make themselves understood more effectively by forming signs than by speaking words (Beirne-Smith et al., 2002).

Signed English, a method in which signs follow the English word order, probably will be easier to use than American Sign Language, which has its own grammar. Classes teaching basic skills in signing are offered in every state, every metropolitan area, and many suburban and rural areas.

TANIKA: A TRUE STORY ABOUT MENTAL RETARDATION

Tanika is a 4-year-old girl who was born with Down Syndrome. She is the second child of two parents, both of whom work. The diagnosis was made by the mother's OB-GYN physician shortly after birth. There was no prior history of mental retardation in the family. However, pre-natal consultations between mother and doctor had included chorionic villus sampling (CVS) testing at 10 weeks gestation, due to the mother's age (39). The test results indicated that Down Syndrome was a possibility. For reasons related to religion, the prospective parents elected to proceed with the pregnancy.

Shortly after birth, Tanika's hearing and vision were tested. Children with Down Syndrome often have hearing and vision impairments. Both sets of tests were conducted even before mother and child left the hospital for the first time. Tanika's parents know they also need to monitor her heart, because cardiac conditions frequently occur as part of the syndrome. Indeed, most deaths of children with Down Syndrome are related to heart conditions and occur during the first five years of life (Bowe, 2000a).

Tanika's intelligence cannot be ascertained with much specificity, due to her age. However, MR at the mild level already is evident. She was delayed in talking, saying her first distinct words at 19 months. Her speech is still "sloppy" (to quote her mother), largely because of the hypotonia (reduced tension) of Tanika's muscles, including those used in speech. Nonetheless, Tanika has little difficulty making herself understood to her parents and to her older brother. An outgoing, open and friendly little girl, she uses vocalizations, pointing, facial expressions, and some signs to express herself. She takes particular delight in making the signs for "no" and for "play" and she much enjoys singing nursery rhymes.

This fall, Tanika will be enrolled in a special-education preschool program for the first time. Her Individualized Education Program (IEP) specifies that Tanika's main goals for the upcoming school year are in the areas of socialization (learning to play with other preschoolers, learning to take turns) and in preacademics. The plan was prepared by an IEP team consisting of an early childhood special educator, an audiologist, a speech pathologist, and a physical therapist. From these professionals, her parents understand that they need to continue to provide an intellectually stimulating environment at home, including spoken words to describe things that Tanika does, elaboration to explain why decisions affecting her are made, and labels affixed to objects in her room and around the house. The family uses "manipulatives" (objects that Tanika can see and touch) to teach her both number sense and pre-reading skills.

Methods: Teach Adaptive Skills. The knowledge and competencies that the IEPs of students with mental retardation call for may not be part of the curriculum for a general classroom. Morse and Schuster (2000), for example, reported upon efforts to teach elementary-age children with moderate MR how to shop for groceries. Their 16-page article, published in a major journal, went into considerable detail about exactly how they

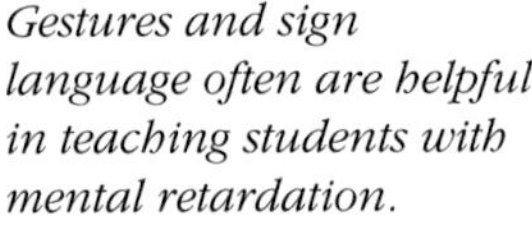

Gestures and sign language often are helpful in teaching students with mental retardation.

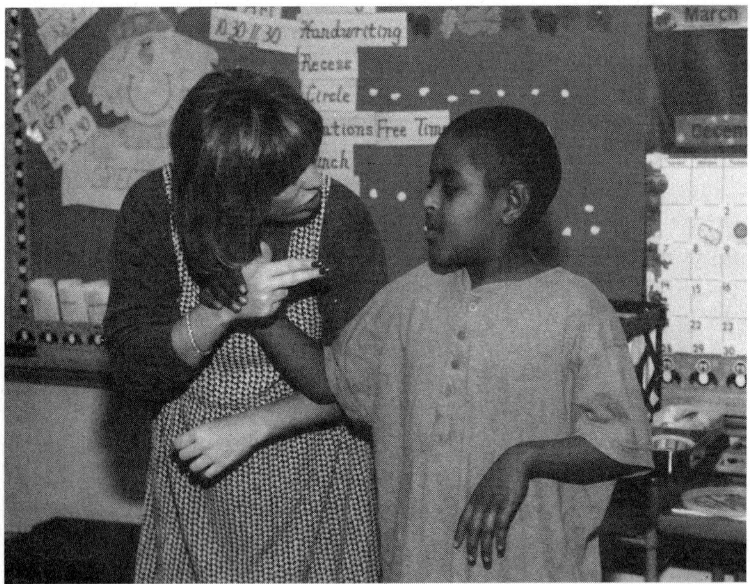

instructed 10 children to perform 28 subtasks involved in successfully purchasing two items at a grocery store. The authors reported needing as many as nine hours to teach these steps. Any general educator reading this article likely would be impressed by how utterly different it is from anything she does in the classroom; these simply are not things that are taught in most PreK–6 schools. Even if they were to be, few general educators would "task analyze" a project like this into 28 distinct steps and teach each until mastered.

This crystallizes the crux of the matter: How can we at one and the same time integrate students with MR into regular classrooms and also give them the extended, direct instruction they need, particularly on subjects that are not otherwise taught in those classrooms? It may not be possible in many, even most, cases. The problem is even more complex at the secondary level, as we will discuss later.

Methods: Enlist a Special Educator as a Collaborating Teacher. The Division on Developmental Disabilities (DDD) of the Council for Exceptional Children (CEC) is a major professional association. In the late 1990s, DDD issued a statement of its collective position on inclusion (Smith & Hilton, 1997). Neither completely endorsing nor totally opposing inclusion, the organization focused on the fact that inclusion cannot be successful with children and youth who have MR unless teachers and other personnel are properly trained and supported. The association was concerned that many general educators continue to hold negative attitudes about people with MR. For their part, special educators need to be prepared for roles that are very different from those they may have been trained for in past years. The DDD noted that the job of a special educator who teaches a separate ("self-contained") class is radically different from the responsibilities of a special educator who team teaches or otherwise collaborates in a general classroom. According to the association, relatively few teachers who are state-certified as educators for children with mental retardation have received training in collaboration in the teaching of general-education content subjects. We will discuss collaborative teaching later in Chapter 12.

For more information on the DDD of the CEC, go to the Web Links module in Chapter 5 of the Companion Website.

Strategies in Middle School and High School

We now turn our attention to older students with mental retardation. Some 10% of secondary students (those aged 12 to 17) who had the MR label spent all or virtually all of the school week in regular classrooms; another 32% spent part of the week in such settings (U.S. Department of Education, 2004, Table AB4). The proportion spending most or all of the time in inclusive settings thus was lower at the secondary-school level than at the elementary-school level. That is understandable: Instruction at the high-school level is more academic, and often more conceptual or symbolic, than is instruction at the early childhood/elementary level. Thus, it can be more challenging for students with MR. However, because MR is the third-largest of IDEA's 10 categories, even a 10% rate of inclusion means that secondary teachers will see more young people with this label in inclusive settings than students with such labels as hearing impairment, vision impairment, or autism. Table 5.3 offers numbers illustrating the size of the MR population (although the figures

TABLE 5.3 Prevalence Figures

	SLD	SLI	MR	E/B	OHI
Number	2,817,148	1,074,548	611,076	463,262	220,831
Percent	6	2	1	1	0.5
Percent SPED	51	20	11	8	4

Note: "Percent" means percent of all PreK–12 students (N = 46,349,803) as of July 1998. "Percent SPED" means percent of all PreK–12 students with any label (N = 5,541,166). "OHI" means "Other Health Impaired" and includes attention deficit disorders. Data are for the school year 1998–1999.

Source: Data from the *22nd Annual Report,* U.S. Department of Education (Tables II-2 and II-3), 2000b, Washington, DC: Author.

in that table come from the 1998–1999 school year, the numbers are quite stable from year to year, making the relationship between them consistent). To appreciate the size of the MR group, refer back to Figure 5.2 (p. 153), which compares the "Big Four" categories with those for lower-prevalence conditions.

Methods: Assess, Then Teach. Students with MR differ greatly in what they know, especially by the middle-school and high-school grades. What they have learned depends greatly upon what kinds of experiences they have had, how successful prior-year teachers were in instructing them, and how supportive their families have been of their academic work. All of this suggests that you need to assess before teaching (Mercer & Mercer, 1998). Properly performed, assessment will also tell you *how* a given student learns. That information can be invaluable for you as a teacher.

Methods: Use Peer Tutoring. It is difficult for a teacher to individualize instruction in a large classroom, especially when a large amount of content must be covered in a short class period. This is why peer tutoring is an approach that you should consider. A peer can instruct a student with MR one-on-one, repeating steps as needed, reacting immediately to errors and misunderstandings, and reinforcing success. Particularly well-supported in the literature is "reciprocal" peer tutoring (Greenwood, 1997). Students take turns being the "tutor" and the "tutee" which has the important advantage of giving the student with MR a chance to tutor a non-disabled student. Such opportunities may be treasured because they are so rare (Mortweet et al., 1999). A key is to prepare the student with mental retardation ahead of time, rehearsing privately as needed until the student masters the material.

Methods: Teach Life Skills. The new emphasis on "learning standards" has exacerbated what was already an inhospitable environment for many young people with MR, because the emphasis today is upon preparing high-school students for college. While this makes sense—about two-thirds of American high-school graduates continue on to some form of postsecondary education—the vast majority of students with MR will go, instead, into the workforce or into a day activity center (Dever and Knapczyk, 1997; Henderson, 1999). These individuals need not only to learn about the nature of work but also about surviving in the community. They need to learn "life skills": how to use public transportation, how to make change, how to dress for work and shopping, and a dizzying variety of other things. Virtually none of them are included in any state's new, higher learning standards.

We therefore have a real problem—one worth extended discussion here. It is the nature of MR that significant amounts of time are required to teach even the simplest things (recall that Morse and Schuster [2000] devoted nine hours to teaching students to shop for just two items). Yet we have structured our secondary schools so that precious little time is available during the school day to teach these non-academic or "life-skills" tasks. Students with MR who are included in regular classrooms will spend virtually all day, every day immersed in complex academic subjects, such as chemistry, algebra, and great literature. (See Part Six for discussions of these subjects.) None of that work prepares them for the lives most will actually live once they leave high school.

Dever and Knapczyk (1997) were especially vehement in their criticism of efforts to include students with MR at the secondary level:

> One reason that inclusion programs may fail to meet the needs of students with mental retardation is that the curriculum used in general education focuses mostly on getting young people ready for college, even when it is "watered down" in courses like Pre-Algebra and General English . . . . Traditionally, persons with mental retardation have fared very badly in this system. (pp. 2, 14)

Dever and Knapczyk, instead, supported a curriculum that is both functional and age-appropriate, geared specifically to teaching, in the community itself, the practical skills of survival on an everyday basis. These skills might include personal hygiene, appropriate dress, keeping to a schedule, making and keeping a budget, and performing work that employers willingly pay to have done. This real-world focus led Dever and Knapczyk to propose their own definition of MR: "A person with mental retardation is someone who requires specific training in skills that most people acquire incidentally and which skills enable people to live in the mainstream of the community without supervision" (p. 26). Dever and Knapczyk insisted that every individual associated with a person with MR (family member, friend, neighbor, co-worker, etc.) must be a teacher for that person. The aim, they stated, is for the person to function independently.

Beirne-Smith et al. were more optimistic about inclusion. Nonetheless, they echoed some of the caution expressed by Dever and Knapczyk (1997), writing, "When placement decisions are made judiciously and reviewed routinely, the goal of providing the most beneficial services to students who are mentally retarded with minimal segregation from their peers is attainable" (p. 366). This is careful wording. They added, "Instructing students who are mentally retarded in the general classroom requires teachers who are highly skilled and sensitive to those learners' needs" (p. 366). These teachers must be supported by special-education teachers, itinerant teachers, paraprofessionals, and related-services personnel who provide supplemental instruction and one-to-one tutoring as needed.

Student Strategies That Work

Self-Advocacy

Critical skills for students with MR to acquire, with your help, are those of self-determination and **self advocacy.** The term "self-determination" refers to making key decisions about one's own life. Not all persons with MR can do everything themselves, but virtually all can decide who should do those things, when, and how. Articles that provide teachers with important information include those by Martin, Marshall, and DePry (2001) and by Wehmeyer and Schalock (2001). The *Journal of Disability Policy Studies* devoted an entire issue (vol. 13, no. 2) to self-determination. That issue included eight articles providing a wealth of useful information about self-determination and young people with disabilities.

Central to training about self-determination is helping students to understand their own needs and limitations. Early childhood and elementary students may not appreciate these, meaning that teachers and family members need to make most key decisions. However, beginning in middle school and certainly in high school, students should be given opportunities to make decisions for themselves. A first step, explained Martin et al. (2001), is to set personal short- and long-term goals. As the teacher, you should consult with the student's family about these. Children and, especially, youth need to learn how to make progress toward those goals and how to measure that progress over time. They must acquire skills in adjusting strategies and tactics so as to remain on target toward their goals. At times, they may need to re-reevaluate and even change those goals. Throughout, students must recognize which steps they can do alone, which they can do with assistance, and which they cannot do at all (Milthaug, 1998). They should be granted by family members and teachers alike increasing independence in making decisions about who should assist them, when, and how.

For more information on teaching self-determination, go to the Web Links module in Chapter 5 of the Companion Website.

Martin et al. (2001) convincingly argued that high-school-age students, including those with MR, can and should assume the risks that come with self-determination. This is important at the secondary level because once they leave high school, these young people will be expected to be both responsible and accountable. You need to prepare them—and to urge their other teachers, their counselors, and other professionals to offer them additional opportunities to learn personal responsibility.

Self-advocacy is standing up for one's rights and requesting what one needs. Individuals with disabilities enjoy certain civil rights in 21st-century America, including the right to nondiscriminatory treatment in service programs, in transportation, in housing, and in employment. Virtually all of these rights are enforced, primarily, through self-advocacy. That is, people have to complain when rights are violated (Bowe, 2000b). Training in self-advocacy includes instruction in what those rights are and how to file complaints. A good way to begin such instruction is to prepare students for their first IEP team meetings. They may need several weeks to several months of preparation in order to understand the IEP process, learn what their options are, recognize their preferences, and learn to advocate for those in a room filled with adults. Later, as they participate in work-study, job-search, and other transition activities, they need to know what their rights are (e.g., for accommodations they need) and how to advocate for these rights.

Learning to be assertive without being aggressive is one part of such preparation. So, too, is learning how to communicate clearly, logically, and convincingly. Learning the art of negotiation is also part of this work. Much of this kind of training can be provided in social studies units and classes (see Chapter 16). If not, it must be offered during transition programming.

Methods: Use Behavior Modification. It is equally as important for teachers in the middle-school and high-school grades to set and enforce clear rules as it is for educators in the elementary grades. You should reinforce behavior you want to see more of and ignore behavior you wish to extinguish. This is harder for many teachers to do than they realize. That is why a good idea is to have a colleague observe you at least once every fall and once every spring. Even better is to have that colleague videotape you in the classroom. You may be surprised to find that, contrary to your beliefs and plans, you do in fact give much more attention to undesired behaviors than to desired ones.

Methods: Use Children's and Adolescent Literature to Improve Classroom Climate. Mary Ann Prater (1999) has identified juvenile literature suitable for use by teachers who have students with MR included in their classrooms. She reviewed 68 books for children and adolescents. Prater's review is helpful because she identified literature that portrays persons with MR in a positive light, works that illustrate relationships between children who do and do not have MR, and books that show characters with MR as making contributions to their communities. She also warned teachers about literature that should be avoided because of negative portrayals of persons with MR.

Methods: Offer Community-Based Instruction. When Morse and Schuster (2000) sought to instruct students with MR in techniques of shopping, they did it on-site (in the grocery store). Advantages of *in situ* instruction are several. First, the behavior is learned in the kind of setting where it will be used. This reduces the demands on students for generalization. Second, the novelty of learning outside the classroom alone makes the experience more memorable. Third, this kind of learning tends to emphasize physical activity and not just abstract knowledge. For that reason, it taps into physical, sensory, and, often, emotional pathways to learning.

Strategies in Transition to Adult Life

Methods: Teach Independent Living Skills. It should be evident from the preceding discussion that individuals with MR often need considerable support in order to live independently, or semi-independently, in the community. The more experience and training they receive during the PreK–12 years the less they will require after they leave school. Rud and Ann Turnbull, well-known authorities on special education (Turnbull & Turnbull, 1997; Turnbull et al., 2002), have described how their son created what was for him a meaningful life by combining activities of work, recreation, community service, and family life. An individual with MR, Jay Turnbull would not have been as successful in these endeavors had he not benefitted from transition services during his school years.

Methods: Acquaint Students and Families with Supplemental Security Income. For many adults who have MR, earning more than minimum wage is the exception rather than the rule. For this reason, many need **Supplemental Security Income (SSI).** As the name implies, SSI "supplements" earned income, bringing the person's total income to about the poverty line. In most states, SSI eligibility qualifies people for Medicaid as well. That is important because many low-wage jobs do not include medical benefits. That being noted, many adults with MR live lives that they find to be rewarding. Often they take considerable pleasure in performing routine functions on the job. Many make friends easily. This is particularly true of persons with Down syndrome. We will discuss SSI and Medicaid later in Chapter 13.

Methods: Offer Work-Study Opportunities. School-to-work transition services, provided during the secondary-school years, can be valuable not only to students with MR or other disabilities, but to the full range of high-school students. Hughes, Bailey, and Mechur (2001) reviewed a large body of research evidence for their report, *School-to-Work: Making a Difference in Schools.* Published by the Institute on Education and the Economy (IEE) at Columbia University's Teachers College, the report showed that student participation in school-to-work programs can reduce dropping out, increase college enrollment, and accelerate maturity for *most* young people. These findings surprised some observers, who anticipated that school-to-work programs might be associated, instead, with weaker ties to school, lower interest in postsecondary education, and diversion of student interest toward activities that offer short-term attractions but confer few long-term benefits.

The IEE found that school-to-work programs feature learning in context and constructivist education. Elsewhere in this book, we have referred to "learning in context" as "situated learning" and "constructivism" as opportunities for students to construct their own meaning or knowledge. School-to-work programs characteristically involve brief visits to work sites and job shadowing, followed by paid or unpaid work experience that is linked to school instruction.

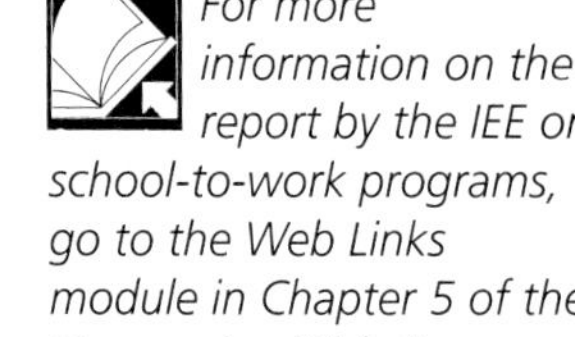

For more information on the report by the IEE on school-to-work programs, go to the Web Links module in Chapter 5 of the Companion Website.

EMOTIONAL OR BEHAVIORAL DISORDERS

When we talk about emotional or behavioral (E/B) disorders, we are discussing conditions that cause children and youth to display behavior that differs markedly from the kinds of behavior that are characteristic of persons of the same age and under the same circumstances. In general, we understand E/B disorders to refer to thinking and/or behavior that is disconnected from reality or that is very atypical. Thus, children who laugh joyously one moment and cry hysterically a moment later would be considered to be very different from typical children. Most of us move from one extreme to the other much more slowly, transitioning first through some intermediate stages or emotions. Similarly, a child who displays no reaction when a peer is seriously injured is showing behavior that most of us would consider not to be typical.

As many as one out of every ten school-age children may have emotional conditions that could impair their learning and development. Many of these are not diagnosed. Others are untreated or poorly treated, so concludes a major report from the United States Surgeon General, *Report of the Surgeon General's Conference on Children's Mental Health: A National Agenda* (2001). From these findings, the Report's authors urged, we should *not* conclude that the solution of choice is to identify these children, or most of them, as E/B disordered and then to serve them under IDEA. Rather, the approach should be to provide appropriate services, insofar as possible, within the *general* education system in the public schools while, at the same time, making suitable use of the services offered by community mental-health agencies.

Definition

Disorders of emotional functioning are defined by reference to a cultural standard of "normal" as that standard is interpreted by the observer. Thus, definitions in this area are subjective. Behavior that one observer considers to be well within the parameters of acceptability might strike another observer as outside those bounds. The U.S. Department of Education's (1999a) regulations for IDEA define the term **"emotional disturbance"** in these words:

> (i) a condition exhibiting one or more of the following characteristics over a long period of time and to a marked degree that adversely affects a child's educational performance: (A) An inability to learn that cannot be explained by intellectual, sensory, or health factors. (B) An inability to build or maintain satisfactory interpersonal relationships with peers and teachers. (C) Inappropriate types of behavior or feelings under normal circumstances. (D) A general pervasive mood of unhappiness or depression. (E) A tendency to develop physical symptoms or fears associated with personal or school problems. (ii) The term includes schizophrenia. The term does not apply to children who are socially maladjusted, unless it is determined that they have an emotional disturbance. (34 C.F.R. 300.[c][4])

Notice that this definition includes, as do other regulatory definitions offered by the U.S. Department of Education, the by now familiar words, "adversely affects educational performance." As it does elsewhere, this wording refers to the fact that, to be eligible for IDEA services, students must "need special education and related services."

Exclusion

The federal definition excludes students "who are socially maladjusted," by which it generally means persons with conduct disorders. This exclusion is based on the idea that while educators may disapprove of the students' choices, the making of such decisions is not in itself evidence of a disorder. Thus, the intent in the definition is to say, "Students who adopt subgroup norms are not for that reason emotionally or behaviorally disordered. They may be determined, on other grounds, to be emotionally disturbed, in which case they may be classified in this category."

Problems with the Definition

This definition is a troublesome one. The Department tried, in the early 1990s, to develop consensus around a better definition (U.S. Department of Education, 1993a). When that effort failed, it kept the earlier one. Among the features of this definition that make it so widely disliked is the subjective character of several of its key elements (Forness & Kavale, 2000). Notice, for example, the wording "to a marked degree." While the intent is clear to exclude disorders that fall within normal ranges, the fact is that different observers will interpret these words differently. That may lead to inappropriate overidentification of children who come from different ethnic and/or racial backgrounds than do the evaluators and other educators who make the classification decisions.

Particularly problematic is the definition's exclusion of "social maladjustment" despite the fact that the definition *includes* "inability to build or maintain satisfactory relationships with teachers or peers." The exclusion of "social maladjustment" apparently is an effort to disqualify students who have conduct disorders, perhaps on the grounds that such individuals elect to disobey societal rules. Forness and Kavale (2000) emphatically argued that conduct disorders are legitimate E/B conditions.

Also subjective are the words "inappropriate types of behavior or feelings under normal circumstances." Observers differ in their opinions about what kinds of behavior are appropriate, and which are inappropriate, under everyday conditions. The intent of this wording is to make the point that emotional or behavioral disorders often manifest themselves under circumstances that most of us do not respond to in those ways. Similarly, this language emphasizes that behavior that may be objectionable in some situations can be easily understood, and accepted, when displayed as a result of very unusual conditions.

The words "over a long period of time" are less subjective. The U.S. Department of Education explains that this phrase generally refers to behavior that persists for at least six months. The intent is to rule out temporary shifts in mood that are due to common elements of everyday life, such as parental divorce, loss of life by a friend, and so on (U.S. Department of Education, 1999a, 34 C.F.R. 300.7[c][4]). Most of us regard as quite normal temporary feelings of depression or of anger when a close relative or friend dies unexpectedly. Were such feelings to persist many months later, however, most of us would become concerned about the young person's mental health.

The language "inability to learn that cannot be explained by intellectual, sensory, or health factors" serves as an exclusion factor. Before the E/B disorders label may be assigned, IEP team members must be sure that other considerations do not suffice to explain the observed behavior. For example, a hearing loss might account for the fact that a student does not obey instructions and/or appears to "be in a world of his own." Similarly, students who do not comprehend rules or directions because they are mentally retarded should not wrongly be classified as having emotional or behavioral conditions. Poor health may lead to frequent absences from school which, in turn, may produce frustration that is expressed in antisocial behavior. Again, the IEP team needs to rule out such effects.

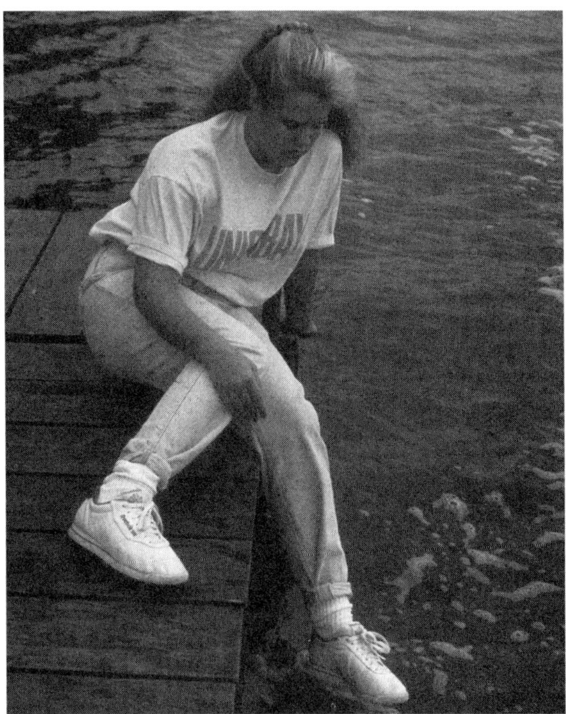

Internalizing is most often found among females who have emotional or behavioral (E/B) disorders.

Some experts have continued to support an alternative definition that was proposed a decade ago by a coalition of organizations representing professionals and family members interested in emotional disorders. This definition highlights the facts that E/B disorders are characterized by behaviors that are *very different from those of age peers under the same or similar circumstances,* that they can in fact co-exist with other conditions, that conduct disorders are in fact E/B conditions, and that diagnosis should proceed (as is the case with MR and SLD; see Chapter 3) under a two-step procedure where the clinical diagnosis is paired with evidence of academic underachievement (Forness & Kavale, 2000). This alternative definition refers to currently used diagnostic terms (e.g., schizophrenia, affective disorders, anxiety disorders) rather than the outdated terminology in the official definition (e.g., social maladjustment).

Characteristics and Types

Children with E/B disorders are often at risk of dropping out of school, according to David Offord, M.D., who presented at the Surgeon General's conference on childhood mental health. He reported that most children with mental-health problems come from mid-SES families, but that those who are raised in low-SES families are at heightened risk for mental illness. Depression and anxiety, two common E/B disorders, long have been associated with attempts at suicide. According to the American Foundation for Suicide Prevention (*http://www.afsp.org*), aggressive behavior preceded 54% of suicides among males and 36% among females; anxiety had been expressed or shown by 27% of males and 28% of females; and other mood disorders had been observed in 60% of males and 68% of females.

Characteristics

Young people with E/B conditions tend to have fewer friends than do others. Children prefer as friends peers who are "dependable" or "reliable"—who are much the same day in and day out. They become wary of peers who are unpredictable. Similarly, children and youth generally like peers who are open and approachable. They tend to avoid peers who are overly shy. They will also steer clear of violent peers.

Elementary and secondary students who have E/B disorders tend to do poorly in school. Their intelligence tends to be in the typical range, or slightly below (e.g., 85 to 100). When they have academic problems, it usually is because they have difficulty sustaining attention to a task over a long period of time. This group also has very high absenteeism rates, very high tardiness rates, very high rates of failing one or more courses, and very high drop-out rates (U.S. Department of Education, 2000b).

Many students with emotional disturbance take medication for their conditions. As the teacher of an inclusive classroom, you need to be alert to side effects of these drugs. You are most likely to see sedatives (for depression), stimulants (for ADHD), and, on occasion, tranquilizers (for psychosis).

Types

Emotional and behavioral disorders are classified generally as *externalizing* or *internalizing*. Among the major externalizing conditions are **conduct disorder (CD)** and **oppositional defiant disorder (ODD).** According to the American Psychiatric Association (1994), in its *Diagnostic and Statistical Manual,* 4th ed., CD features aggression toward people, destruction of property, deceitfulness, and repeated violation of societal rules. The term "delinquency" is used when those behaviors violate laws. Oppositional defiant disorders are characterized by active refusal to comply with orders from authority figures, frequent temper tantrums, and habitual blaming of others for their problems. Forness, an expert in this area, described conduct disorders as persistent patterns of behavior that involve injury to people, damage to property, violation of societal rules, and other kinds of aggression (Forness, Kavale, King, & Kasari, 1994; Forness, Kavale, & Lopez, 1993). Children with ODD may say they know they are not to do something, but the very knowledge that it is forbidden makes doing it irresistible. Conduct disorders and oppositional defiant disorders are frequently co-morbid (occurring in the same individual), in which case ODD typically precedes CD (Wicks-Nelson & Israel, 2000). If you reread the story of "Robbie" in Chapter 3, you will get a good picture of ODD co-morbid with ADHD.

Some important internalizing conditions are mood disorders such as **anxiety disorder** and *depression*. Both anxious and depressed individuals tend to react negatively to ambiguous signals. In the case of anxiety, people react to possible future events. Persons who are depressed react more strongly to past events. Anxiety disorders include separation anxiety, avoidance behavior, and chronic anxiety. These conditions are characterized by unusual anxiety, nervousness, and impaired functioning (American Psychiatric Association, 1994). Individuals who are anxious will often cease productive activities when they perceive themselves to be, or about to be, threatened. People who are depressed have already lowered such efforts. The two conditions often occur together. Some reports suggest that when they are co-morbid, anxiety usually precedes depression (e.g., Wicks-Nelson & Israel, 2000). **Mood disorders** also can occur in children, adolescents, and adults (Klein, Lewinsohn, Seeley, & Rohde, 2001). These all are serious conditions (Harrington, 2001b).

Other key internalizing conditions include schizophrenia and *eating conditions*. **Schizophrenia** is a serious mental illness in which people may become convinced that the environment holds personal messages for them. For example, they may "hear voices." Coleman (1996) described the condition as featuring inappropriate affects (emotions), disinterest in people and objects in the environment, and inappropriate speech. For many years, psychiatrists and other mental health professionals refused to believe that children could develop schizophrenia, because Freud taught that the ego development required for its development did not emerge until adolescence (Coleman, 1996; Harrington, 2001a). Today, we know that schizophrenia can and does occur in children, but that it is relatively rare prior to adulthood (U.S. Department of Health and Human Services, 2001). **Eating disorders** include anorexia nervosa and bulimia nervosa. Once widely dismissed, these are now recognized as potentially serious because the compulsive dieting and/or overeating signal a distorted sense of self. They are among a number of anxiety disorders.

Students tend to express emotional or behavioral disorders differently according to gender. Fully 80% of students with the emotional disturbance label are boys (U.S. Department of Education, 1999c). That may be in part because boys tend to externalize, that is, to act out in ways that classroom teachers view as aggressive (Coleman, 1996). This is particularly true of secondary-age boys, who, being much larger and stronger than elementary-age boys, may appear more threatening to teachers, especially to women teachers. Girls, by contrast, tend to internalize, for example, to withdraw. Their disturbances often take the form of anxiety, schizophrenia, phobias, and depression, all of which are internalizing disorders (e.g., Klein, Lewinsohn, Seeley, & Rohde, 2001). Their teachers may regard them as being "very shy" but, because that "shy" behavior is not disruptive in the classroom, may not refer them to the IEP team for evaluation. These gender differences are tendencies, not invariable divergences: Boys sometimes withdraw into themselves and girls at times engage in violent attacks on property and people. Adolescent girls, for example, sometimes do have conduct disorders (e.g., Pajer, Gardner, Rubin, Perel, & Neal, 2001), although this condition is male-dominated. Pajer and her colleagues estimated that as many as 10% of mid-adolescent girls have conduct disorders and that this may be the second most-prevalent diagnosis among teen women (after depression).

Co-Morbidity

Individuals with E/B disorders may also have specific learning disabilities. Some also have ADHD. A substantial number abuse controlled substances. These co-morbidities may explain, in part, the apparent undercounting of children and youth with emotional disturbance: The students are classified, not as emotionally disturbed, but rather as LD or ADHD, both of which are much less stigmatizing labels. Teachers should also be aware that different kinds of E/B disorders may co-exist. Anxiety and depression often are co-morbid (anxiety usually occurs first, with depression following). Both conditions make people react negatively to ambiguity. Individuals who are anxious tend to respond most rapidly to new instances of possible threat while those with depression often are responding to past incidents (Pury, 2002). People who are internalizers are more likely than are others to also have conduct disorders. Similarly, conduct disorders and oppositional defiant disorders are highly co-morbid, and both often co-exist with ADHD (Wicks-Nelson & Israel, 2000).

Prevalence

The *26th Annual Report* (U.S. Department of Education, 2004 revealed that the category of emotional/behavioral disorders was the fourth-largest group, with 480,000 students aged 6 to 21 being served in the 50 states, the District of Columbia, and Puerto Rico, during the 2002–2003 school year. They were 8% of students with any label. (In fact, at the secondary level, they comprised 12% of all students classified with any disability.) As for placements, 29% were in regular classrooms, 23% in resource rooms, and 31% in separate classrooms within neighborhood school buildings. The balance were in separate schools; some were in prisons or other disciplinary settings. The proportions by type of placement were quite similar at the elementary and secondary levels. About one in every four (26%) are African American, compared to 61% who are non-Hispanic white. The group is, thus, somewhat more racially and ethnically diverse than most, but less so than the category of mental retardation (U.S. Department of Education, 2000b, Table AA3).

Undercounted?

Although some segments of society may be overrepresented in this category, and although nearly one-half million students comprise a sizable population by any measure, the students identified with the E/B disorders label are nonetheless widely recognized to represent *only some* of a much larger group of students. This category, much more so than any other, is well-known as being much bigger on an unofficial basis than on an official one (e.g., Kauffman, 2001). The Department's *20th Annual Report* (1998) noted that official prevalence of E/B disorders has always been about one-half to one-third of the predicted rates. The Surgeon General's report estimated that one in ten school-age children has a diagnosed or undiagnosed mental illness. Given a PreK–12 population in 2001 of 53 million children, that translates into more than five million children and adolescents. Another report suggested that as many as 16% of school-age children and youth may have mental-health disorders (Roberts, Attkisson, & Rosenblatt, 1998). If that is correct, this implies a population of more than eight million PreK–12 students. Why, then, are fewer than one-half million (480,000) PreK–12 students identified under IDEA as having emotional or behavioral disorders? There are several possible explanations.

Emotional and behavioral disorders are, in many ways, social constructs (as is mental retardation). The federal definition (given earlier) makes subjective judgments inevitable. That gives family members an opening to challenge this label. Many parents regard the E/B disorders label as highly stigmatizing. E/B problems are widely known, by professionals and lay people alike, as being caused, in many instances, by parental behavior (Coleman, 1996; Harrington, 2001a; Kauffman, 2001; Klein et al., 2001).

Research That Works

Overrepresentation

Why are members of racial minority groups overrepresented in special education, especially in the MR and E/B disorder categories? Are such disabilities actually higher in minority groups than in the majority group of Caucasians? If so, our nation must strive to solve the underlying medical and social problems, including access to medical care, poverty, and the like. Alternatively, suppose that disability rates are not in fact higher in some races than in others. That would lead us to ask: Is the reported overrepresentation due to discrimination in the schools? If the answer to that question is yes, then we need to redress such discrimination in the nation's schools. According to the U. S. Department of Education (2000b), in its *22nd Annual Report,* African-American students were 2.9 times as likely as were white students to be given the MR label and 1.9 times as likely to be given the E/B disorders label.

Oswald, Coutinho, and Best (2001) examined these issues. They studied data collected by two units of the U.S. Department of Education: the Office for Civil Rights (OCR) and the National Center for Educational Statistics (NCES). The researchers discovered some unexpected correlations. They found that minority students, notably African Americans and Native Americans, were probably overidentified with E/B disorder or MR labels *if these students resided in mostly white school districts.* Oswald et al. also discovered that minority students were probably overidentified, again with E/B disorders or MR labels, *if they resided in relatively wealthy school districts.* Thus, discrimination by school officials is a possible causative factor in the reported overrepresentation. Minority, low-SES children may be overidentified by mostly white, mid-SES educators. But familial poverty is a direct cause itself, independent of any discrimination in the schools. When children are raised in low-SES families, they see doctors less rapidly after becoming ill or having an accident, they eat less nutritious meals, and so on.

The National Alliance of Black School Educators (NABSE) and the Council for Exceptional Children (CEC) jointly issued a report, *Addressing Over-Representation of African American Students in Special Education,* in mid-2002. The organizations agreed that overrepresentation may occur because (1) instruction is not individualized to respond to the learning strengths and needs of African-American students; (2) identification and referral processes are ineffective, notably because standardized tests that are biased against African Americans are used; (3) teachers have not been trained in cultural competency and cultural sensitivity; and (4) school administrators do not recognize that a problem exists, thus do not act to solve it. NABSE and CEC prepared a chart offering recommendations for change (see Figure 5.4).

In particular, teachers of inclusive classrooms need to be aware that African-American males may be highly sensitive to what Franklin (1998) referred to as "micro-aggressions"—seemingly minor but frequent incidents of being ignored or "dissed" in the hallway, in the classroom, and in the school as a whole. Such daily hassles may be interpreted as indicators of ethnic/racial prejudice. This cultural tenet may make African-American males especially vigilant about their interactions with others, notably with whites. Measures they perceive as self-protecting are not, and should not be interpreted as being, indications of emotional disturbance. Rather, they are culturally appropriate behaviors (Whaley, 1998). Teachers should not over-react by referring African-American males to special education and/or to counseling.

For more information on the study by Oswald, Coutinho, and Best, go to the Web Links module in Chapter 5 of the Companion Website.

For more information on the NABSE and the CEC, go to the Web Links module in Chapter 5 of the Companion Website.

This may be why parental involvement in the schools is lower in this category than in many others. There is no parent group advocating for this population with anything approaching the vigor and presence of parent associations in the areas of mental retardation, for example, or of deafness (Coleman, 1996). Recall from our discussion earlier in Chapter 1 that school districts will, at times, change labels rather than contest parents through due process. This happens often enough that some IEPs contain "labels of convenience." The relevant point here is that the IEPs of some children and youth who have E/B disorders may not contain this label, but rather one regarded by parents as less stigmatizing.

Second, the 50 states and the District of Columbia are free to use their own definitions for this category, as long as the state definitions are "not inconsistent" with the federal one. That some states may be undercounting students with E/B disorders is strongly implied by Figure 5.5. Students with conduct disorders are eligible for services in some states but not in others. This is one reason for the huge disparity in identification rates. Based upon

FIGURE 5.4 Addressing Overrepresentation Through School Climate

RECOMMENDATIONS	Extent to which we do this...			
Administrators can establish a positive school climate that prevents and reduces the over-representation of African American students in special education by...	All of the time	Sometimes, needs improvement	Not at all, need a plan	Not applicable to our school/district
ADDRESSING HARMFUL BIASES				
Support school staff in accepting the responsibility for supporting achievement for all students.				
Obtain membership in organizations that promote equitable education and provide instructional strategies for all students (e.g., NABSE, National Association for Bilingual Education) and prominently share materials obtained from such groups with all stakeholders.				
Discuss unfounded biases with staff members—and let staff members know that disrespectful responses to any child, regardless of cultural background, ethnicity, and/or socioeconomic status will not be tolerated on the school campus.				
ENSURING CULTURAL COMPETENCE				
Establish school and district-wide professional development training in cultural competence.				
Work with community members and institutions of higher education to identify a cultural competence training program that will meet the needs of your community.				
Include students in school and district-wide professional development on cultural competence.				

continued

	Always	Sometimes	Not at all	NA
ENSURING CULTURAL COMPETENCE (continued)				
Identify and use multiple assessment tools and strategies that are research-based and culturally competent.				
Provide school and district-wide training in the administration of assessment tools and methods that consider the student's culture and background.				
Assign personnel who are knowledgeable about students' cultures to conduct assessments.				
Ensure that high stakes tests have been validated for the purpose for which they are used and have been standardized on populations of students similar to your own.				
Schedule visits to students' homes and neighborhoods to learn more about them and their cultures.				
Provide training to employees before making home visits.				
Include skills that demonstrate cultural competence on teachers' exams for employment in your district.				
Enlist the help of community members and higher education personnel in developing standards and skills for school staff in becoming culturally competent and assisting all students in accessing the general curriculum.				
Assign task forces to suggest ways staff members may retool their skills.				
Tap into the expertise of community members who may be knowledgeable about African American and other cultures represented in your student population.				
Encourage the state licensing agency to require course work in areas such as multicultural education, cultural competence, accessing the general education curriculum, and improving student achievement for all students by improving instructional strategies.				
Hire personnel who demonstrate cultural competencies.				

*Note: *IDEA does not require the use of recommendations.*

Source: Copyright 2002 by the Council for Exceptional Children. From the Council for Exceptional Children (CEC) from *Addressing Over-representation* (2002).Reprinted with permission.

FIGURE 5.5 State Variations in Prevalence of E/B Disorders

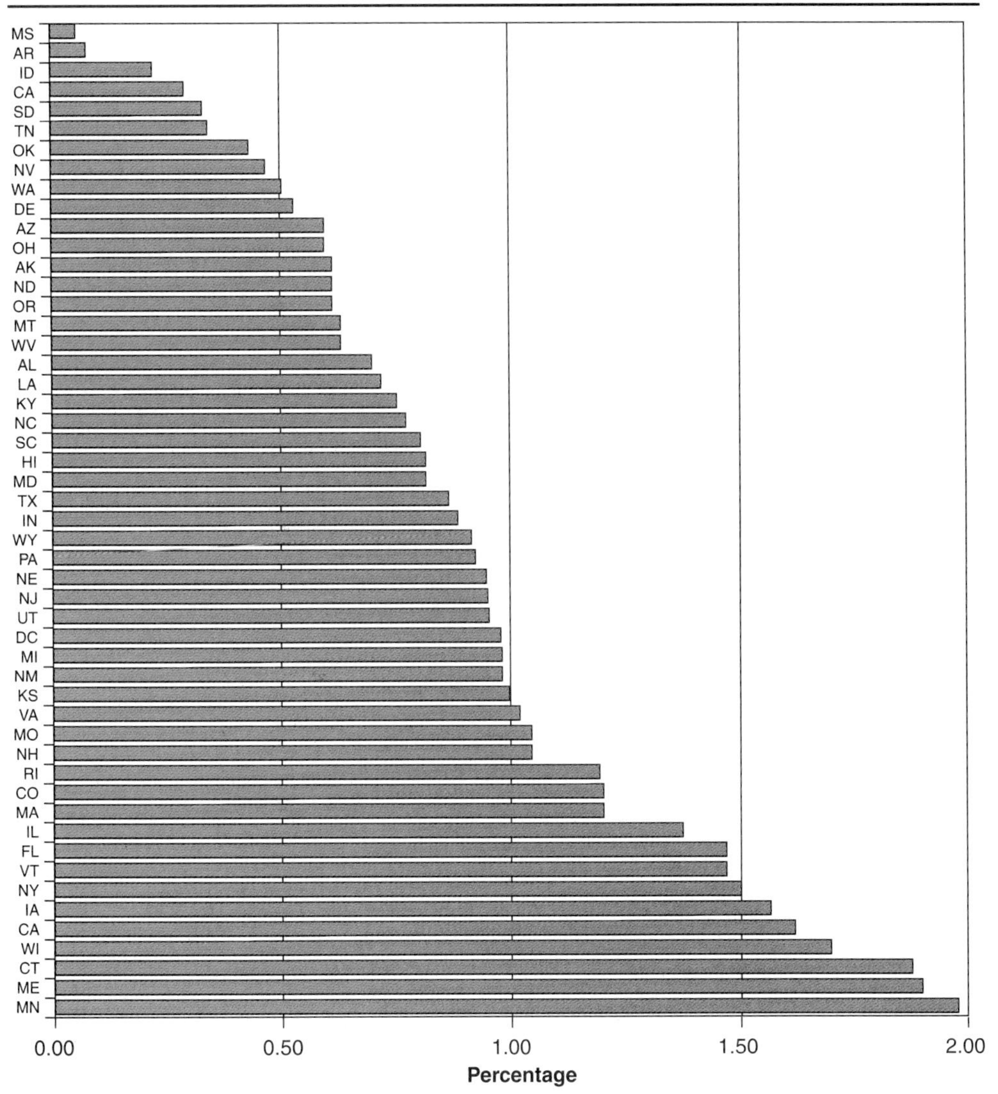

Source: From the *20th Annual Report* (Figure II-10), by the U.S. Department of Education, 1998, Washington, DC: Author.

Figure II-10, in the *20th Annual Report* (Department of Education, 1998), the chart shows an astounding 33-fold difference in proportions of students aged 6 to 21 who were identified in different states as having emotional or behavioral disabilities. One state (Minnesota) counted 33 times more students, per capita, than did another state (Mississippi). The only logical explanation for the dramatic differences from state to state is that states apply divergent criteria for identification. That is, some apparently include "conduct disorders" while others do not; some apply stricter standards for "inappropriate behavior" than do others.

Third, the definition used for this label specifically and explicitly rules out what it calls "social maladjustment." As just noted, it seems that this part of the definition is not always followed by the states. Fourth, when students who have attention deficit disorders also display oppositional defiant disorder, or evidence other kinds of behavioral needs, they tend to retain their label (in this case, that of "Other Health Impaired" or OHI) despite the fact that their behavioral problems may be quite severe. This is, in part, a function of the fact that the OHI label is much less stigmatizing than is the E/B disorders label. The result is that these students are *not* counted as being among those in the category "emotional or behavioral disorders."

Diagnosis and Assessment

Emotional or behavioral disorders are diagnosed by professionals on the basis of observation, personal and family history, and, at times but not always, tests and other assessments. Clinical judgement is important in virtually every instance. This means that the evaluator's biases may affect assessment. Behavior that one clinician regards as clearly outside the boundaries of "typical" or "normal" may strike another clinician as well within that range. Telling the difference between a teen who is distressed because of family instability and one who is clinically depressed for physiological reasons is not easy. It requires the taking of a family history and observation in different settings over a considerable period of time.

Emotional conditions exist across a broad spectrum from mild to very severe. In fact, the spectrum is even larger than this suggests, because some children and many more adolescents who are *not* emotionally disturbed may be treated by educators as if they were (see Chapter 11). Compounding the problem is the relative lack of valid and reliable instruments for assessment and evaluation.

Psychologists frequently identify emotional disorders by referencing the criteria in the American Psychiatric Association's (1994) *Diagnostic and Statistical Manual,* 4th ed. (*DSM-IV*). For example, oppositional defiant disorder (ODD) is described as being characterized by temper tantrums, arguing with adults, defiant refusal to comply with rules, and a persistent tendency to blame others when things go wrong. *DSM-IV* describes conduct disorders (CD) as aggression toward people, destruction of property, theft, and serious violations of school and societal rules. Anxiety is assessed on the basis of excessive worry, restlessness, fatigue, difficulty concentrating, irritability, and disturbed sleep. It should be evident from these characteristics that considerable examiner discretion is involved.

In education, the additional variable is underachievement (in the definition, "adversely affects educational performance"). In addition, psychologists working in schools must exclude "social maladjustment" and must also determine that the educational underachievement is not attributable primarily to other disabilities (e.g., to mental retardation).

Causes

Emotional or behavioral disorders come in many forms. Not surprisingly, then, they have many causes. We do not always know what cause(s) operated in every individual instance. Depression and schizophrenia may have biological roots, notably variations in the amount and behavior of neurotransmitters in the brain (Ridley, 1999). Childhood anxiety seems to be in part a function of inborn temperament but more powerfully a result of how children are raised. Those who are abused (physically, sexually, psychologically) and those who are neglected are at special risk of mental illness. Research that starts with the identities of students classified as emotionally disturbed and tracks back to find possible causative factors in their pasts tends to identify biological roots for E/B disorders. However, research that begins with a large sample of non-classified children and follows them forward often finds, instead, that environmental factors seem to be at cause (Forness & Kavale, 2000). In summary, emotional disturbance is now recognized as having multiple causes.

Genetic Factors

Schizophrenia, psychosis, and some other E/B disorders are known to be at least partially inheritable. Fragile X syndrome, which sometimes results in E/B disorders, is also genetic in nature. In addition to mental retardation and learning disabilities, it sometimes results in E/B conditions (The National Fragile X Foundation, *http://www.fragilex.org*). Cravchik and Goldman (2000) summarized what genome research is revealing about genetic predispositions to emotional conditions. They reported that neurochemical transmitters such as dopamine and serotonin are now understood to play large roles in predisposing people to E/B disorders.

Environmental Factors

Emotional or behavioral disorders often arise after sustained periods of time when adults, notably family members but also educators, fail to set limits and to enforce rules. Whether because they are inattentive to the child's behaviors, because they themselves accept such behaviors as normal, or because they prefer not to become involved, these adults may permit aggressive behavior to occur without consequences for the child. The result is increasingly aggressive behavior. Eventually, the behavior attracts adult attention. By that time, however, the behavior is well-entrenched. Patterson and his colleagues have convincingly demonstrated this process in research spanning more than a decade (e.g., Patterson & Capaldi, 1991). A similar pattern may lead to internalizing behavior. Parents, other adults in the family, and educators may simply overlook evidence that a child is unnaturally withdrawing from social contact (e.g., "She's just shy. Leave her alone.").

When parents insist upon unrealistically high expectations for their children, when parents are abusive (whether emotionally, physically, mentally, or all of these), and when parents are "not available" to their children (as when two-career families spend little quality time with children), E/B conditions may result (Coleman, 1996). The temperament of a baby, child, or youth may interact with the temperament of a parent such that the parent regards the child as having a "difficult temperament." In time, child-parent conflicts may even lead to emotional disturbance in the child. These are all other ways in which parental behavior may cause E/B disorders.

Brain damage, whether from severe malnutrition, from illnesses that produce high fevers, or from injuries such as traumatic brain injury, may also lead to E/B disorders (Park, Turnbull, & Turnbull, 2002). E/B conditions may also be caused, but less commonly, by mistreatment at the hands of siblings, adult caretakers, and other persons who play significant roles in a child's life, such as the coach of an athletic team. In many instances, we cannot identify causes with any degree of confidence (Kauffman, 2001).

Another widely recognized cause of E/B disorders is maternal consumption of alcohol. We saw earlier that drinking by pregnant women has also been associated with childhood mental retardation, some specific learning disabilities, and some attention deficit disorders. Secondary conditions connected to fetal alcohol syndrome or fetal alcohol effect include mental health problems, disrupted school experience, trouble with the law, confinement, inappropriate sexual behavior, and alcohol/drug problems (U.S. Department Education, 2000b, p. I-20).

Instructional Methods

The behavior of students with E/B disorders often challenges teachers of inclusive classrooms. There are several critically important strategies that experts recommend. One is to make sure that your language clearly distinguishes between the student and the behavior. You should make clear what behavior you accept and what behavior you do not accept. However, the words you use should not extend unnecessarily to the student himself. Experts urge that you use sentences like "Jose, I'm delighted to see that your text is open to the right page" (which pinpoints the behavior) rather than structures like "Jose, I'm so impressed with you. You're such a great person" (which evaluates him as an individual). If you as the teacher assess the child himself, even positively, you suggest that a future evaluation may occur, as well. This may be threatening to a child. If, however, you make it clear that your assessments are strictly limited to behavior, the child may not feel as vulnerable.

A second strategy applicable at different age levels is to make good use of peers. Many children and youth with E/B disorders will respond better to their peers than to adults, especially authority figures. Peers can model acceptable behavior and can give approval that students with E/B disorders value. A third is to teach students ways to behave.

One reason children and youth with emotional disturbance often behave in unacceptable ways is simply that they do not know other, more socially acceptable, ways of behaving.

Strategies in Early Childhood and Elementary School

We look first at younger students with E/B disorders. At the elementary level, 30% of students with the E/B disorders label are taught in inclusive classrooms all or most of the school week, with another 21% spending at least part of the week in such environments (U.S. Department of Education, 2004, Table AB3). Thus, as a teacher in an inclusive classroom, you can expect to have the opportunity to help some of these children. A large proportion (45%) is usually placed in separate classrooms, separate schools, or other non-inclusive environments. Figure 5.6 illustrates the likelihood of inclusive placements for K–12 students with the E/B label.

Methods: Intervene Early. Public schools tend not to take E/B disorders seriously until the behavior can no longer be managed by the general classroom teacher. Even then, the usual response of the school is to discipline the child. If that does not "solve the problem," referral may be made to special education. Steve Forness made that point at the Surgeon General's 2001 conference on childhood mental illness. Dr. Forness cited results from a study he had conducted with a colleague in California. They had examined 13-year-old youths. Despite the fact that E/B problems had been identified by the parents as early as 3.5 years, and by school personnel as early as five years (e.g., during kindergarten), the first documented intervention by educators occurred at a mean age of 6.5 (the middle of first grade). The initial referral for special-education services took place at 7.8 years (toward the end of second grade). The typical classification, however, was that of specific learning disabilities. Only at the mean age of 10 (fourth grade) did these children finally begin receiving appropriate services. These findings should disturb any educator or teacher-in-training.

Dr. Forness recommended that elementary teachers be trained on how to recognize early symptoms of E/B disorders. He further suggested that elementary schools adopt more positive, proactive interventions, rather than continuing to rely on discipline, suspension, and expulsion. Kauffman (1999), another expert, has deplored the extent to which educators "prevent the prevention" of E/B disorders. That is, teachers, counselors, and administrators tend to *overlook* behavior in young children that is known to signal

FIGURE 5.6 Likelihood of Inclusive Placements: E/B Disturbance

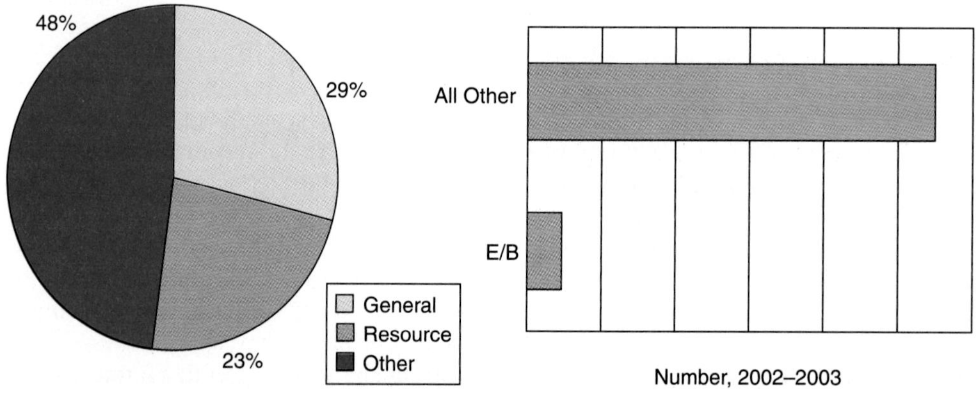

Students with the E/B disorders label comprise about one in every 12 (8%) of K–12 students with any label. They number 480,000, according to the *26th Annual Report* (U.S. Department of Education, 2004). Of them, 29% were placed into inclusive classrooms (spending less than 21% of the time in other settings). The above two charts illustrate these data.

Source: From the *26th Annual Report,* by the U.S. Department of Education, 2004, Washington, DC: Author.

possible mental-health needs, *postpone* early interventions to respond to those needs while they are still manageable, and *fail* to use well-documented methods of behavior modification to change children's behavior. As a result, he concluded, educators not only do not prevent E/B disorders but actually and unintentionally make matters worse. (We will discuss disciplinary measures later in this book; see Chapter 9.)

Methods: Collaborate with Other Professionals. If you have a student with an E/B disorder in your classroom, you should look for opportunities to collaborate. The school counselor is an obvious partner. You should seek her advice on handling behavior issues, refer your student to her for one-on-one and group counseling as appropriate, and ask her to join you when you meet with family members. Less readily available, because most schools do not have them on staff, are creative art therapists. They are trained in techniques of working with individuals who have emotional disorders, including play therapy, art therapy, and counseling. These professionals often work on an itinerant basis (that is, traveling from school district to school district). You can identify those near you by contacting the American Art Therapy Association (*http://www.arttherapy.org*; 1202 Allanson Road, Mundelein, IL 60060). The AATA will put you in touch with state association presidents who will, in turn, find those who are geographically proximate to you.

You should not stop at the classroom door, however. Other professionals can help you to extend your reach to include the school as a whole. When the building principal and other teachers place as much emphasis upon the setting and enforcement of fair rules as you do in your classroom, the likelihood that your student will display appropriate behaviors in and out of class increases. Even beyond the level of the school, you can enlist the support of the community. If, for example, your student is motivated by the chance to play video games, you might make arrangements with the manager of a neighborhood game establishment to honor tokens you give your student as "cash" good for playing games. Similarly, you could arrange with the student's family to honor such tokens as good for game-playing time at home.

Methods: Counseling. One professional with whom you should definitely collaborate is the school counselor. Counseling is a major related service that can help many students with E/B disorders. Many school counselors are familiar with the lessons science is teaching us about the "power of the placebo." The fact that most of us have "stories" that we tell ourselves and others—stories in which we relate our illnesses or disabilities to our lives—offers a tool teachers can use. Howard Brody, in *The Placebo Response* (2000), suggested that by helping others to construct different stories, specifically stories in which we proclaim our ability to rise above these conditions, teachers and counselors might make dramatic differences in students' lives. The very fact that someone listens to a student, shows concern about him, and draws out positive responses to a disability or illness can be as helpful as is medication or psychotherapy. This is why sugar pills (placebos) so often "cause" people to feel better and even to recover quickly from illness. The lesson is clear; make a point of noticing a child or youth, listen to her, and generally treat her as a significant human being. To reinforce the point, consider that the young men who precipitated the violence at the Columbine (CO) and Paducah (KY) high schools said that they had been teased mercilessly and bullied, but that no one had listened to them. As this illustrates, counseling can be effective in helping internalizers to develop effective responses to real and perceived threats, making such abrupt, if delayed, eruptions less likely.

Methods: Set and Enforce Clear Rules. As the teacher you need to *set clear rules* in your classroom and to *enforce* those. Students with E/B disorders very much need to know what the rules are. They will be less likely to cause problems in the classroom if they perceive the rules to be both comprehensible and fairly applied. More than are other students, they tend to be highly sensitive to teacher behavior that they perceive to be unfair. Best are rules that students themselves helped to set. What is perhaps most crucial is that if consequences are attached to rule violations, you *must* promptly and consistently invoke those consequences. As we saw earlier (in the "Causes" section), it is precisely the failure of adults to set and enforce rules that often contributes to the development of E/B disorders in the first place. We will discuss techniques of managing the classroom in much more detail later in Chapter 9.

Methods: Teach Strategies. Many students with E/B disorders display unacceptable behaviors because they do not have acceptable ones in their repertoires. This is why a crucial component of instruction for these children and youth is to teach them more appropriate ways of behaving. This includes the old standby "count to three" as well as "consider other possible explanations before assuming someone is affronting you" and "turn the other cheek." Direct Instruction (DI) should be used to teach these alternative behaviors and plenty of time allotted for practice in applying the new skills.

There is some controversy over whether DI or more constructivist approaches have better long-term outcomes, including for students having emotional disorders. A large-scale follow-up study of 15-year-olds who had participated in a preschool program for disadvantaged children (Schweinhart, Weikart, & Larner, 1986) suggested that those who were taught using DI as 3- to 5-year-olds were less likely, as 15-year-olds, to have engaged in juvenile delinquency activities than were age peers whose preschool instruction was more open, cognitive-based, and discovery-oriented. Replicating key parts of the study 16 years later, Mills, Cole, Jenkins, and Dale (2002) looked at 171 15-year-olds, 60% of whom had E/B classifications. They failed to find any evidence of program effects. Rather, their results showed that delinquency was most common among male students, especially those from ethnic and racial minority groups. Looking back at the Schweinhart et al. data, Mills and his colleagues found similar gender and ethnicity effects in the earlier data. They concluded that "the most parsimonious explanation for the different results in the two studies lies in the gender differences between the two samples" (p. 93). That is, different numbers of males in the two program models and in the samples at the time of preschool education versus the time of follow up accounted for most of the variance. Mills et al. concluded that both DI and discovery learning have beneficial effects for students in special education.

Methods: Create and Maintain an Orderly Environment in Your Classroom. Experienced teachers report that when the classroom is well-organized and when a firm schedule of activities is maintained, things go much more smoothly. When everything is in its place, there are fewer interruptions and disruptions in instruction. In addition, students with E/B disorders are less likely to "act up" during transition times (between the end of one activity and the beginning of the next) when teachers plan ahead (by, for example, assigning such students specific tasks to perform during those times).

Methods: Use Behavior Modification. As this suggests, consistent application of the well-documented principles of behavior modification is of critical importance when teaching students with E/B disorders. Why, then, do so many teachers not apply these interventions? The nearby box, "Teacher Strategies That Work: E/B Disorders" explores this quandary.

Strategies in Middle School and High School

We turn now to older students with E/B disturbance. About two-thirds (66%) of all PreK–12 students with this label are of secondary age (12 to 17 years of age inclusive). E/B conditions thus have the opposite age pattern of speech and language impairments (see Chapter 4). Despite this fact, secondary teachers actually are less likely to see students with E/B disorders in inclusive classrooms than are elementary teachers. That is because, according to the *26th Annual Report,* just 28% of secondary-age students with this label were educated in general classrooms all or most of the time (Table AB4). This proportion is slightly lower than that at the elementary level (30%). It reflects a regrettable phenomenon in American public schools, now less common than it once was: Students with E/B disorders tended to be placed into

Teacher Strategies That Work

E/B Disorders

The research evidence is compelling on the value of using presentation (positive) reinforcement (e.g., Curwin & Mendler, 2001). Studies have also questioned the real value of punishment (e.g., Kauffman, 2001). Still, teachers persist in using punishment more than they do presentation reinforcement.

Maag (2001) outlined reasons why educators so often ignore the mountain of research evidence that presentation (positive) reinforcement works, relying instead on punishment. Citing Kohn (1993), he observed that teachers tend to hold the same beliefs as do most American adults, including parents. These popular tenets say that punishment works, is easy to use, and is "just common sense." In reality, Maag contended, punishment often does not work, causes problems in the days and weeks that follow, and violates all that psychology has learned about people.

We all work for presentation reinforcements: pay, praise, recognition by our peers, and the satisfaction of a job well done or a mystery solved. Children are motivated by much the same desires. Teachers, then, argued Maag, should give students what they will work to get: praise, social recognition, and pay (in the form of free time, tokens, etc.). By contrast, we all avoid situations in which we are routinely punished. Children do, too, argued Maag. For that reason, teachers should avoid punishing children whenever other options are available.

Schools have tended to adopt a negative approach. The typical reaction of public schools when students exhibit unacceptable behavior is discipline, followed by suspension and then expulsion. These school policies may be popular with local taxpayers and school board members, but evidence that they are effective in helping students with mental-health needs is lacking (see, for example, Bowe 2000a; Forness, Kavale, & Lopez, 1993). Student response to such zero-tolerance policies may also be negative. They may feel that the increased scrutiny and what they perceive as overreaction by school officials to harmless pranks are "ruining high school" for them (Leland, 2001, p. 6).

Teachers are not alone in using methods that research has largely discredited in lieu of research-proven techniques. Many community mental-health practitioners, too, persist in using non-research-validated approaches, according to Tim Lewis of the University of Missouri and John Weisz of UCLA, both of whom presented at the Surgeon General's conference. Weisz insisted that there is little evidence that psychotherapy is any more helpful than is talking with a good friend.

Technologies That Work

E/B Disorders

By comparison to the plentiful technologies that are available to help students with many other conditions, those designed for students with E/B disorders are relatively few in number. Edmark sells "Strategy Series," software that teaches strategic thinking and problem-solving skills. Available for PCs and Macs, the Strategy Series programs retail for about $25. IEP Resources markets "Life Skill Game Package," a set of board games for special education students age 10 and over. Six games cover self-control strategies, social skills, safety signs, functional words and symbols, and social skills at work. Brain Train sells "Brain Train Volume 1: Basic Cognitive Skills (Enhanced Editions)," described as cognitive/behavioral software offering exercises in visual and verbal memory and in basic vocational skills. Available for PCs, it costs about $100. Software programs of these kinds can be helpful in extending the in-person support of counselors and teachers.

For more information on the software discussed in the "Technologies That Work" box, go to the Web Links module in Chapter 5 of the Companion Website.

more and more segregated (e.g., less and less inclusive) settings as they get older. General educators too often decided to "solve" the problems posed by the presence of such students by referring them out of inclusive settings.

Methods: Teach Strategies. You cannot assume that students know what to do, even after they have had years of schooling (e.g., Ferretti, MacArthur, & Okolo, 2001). Youth as well as children who have E/B disorders often need help in selecting and using appropriate strategies. As is true at the elementary level, teachers should use Direct Instruction (DI) to teach acceptable behaviors. At the middle-school and high-school level, you can make effective use of peer tutors. This is because teens tend to value the opinions of their peers and to want to please peers more than is the case with adults. Peers who model different ways of dealing with anger or frustration, and peers who explicitly teach adaptive behaviors, can supplement your efforts and those of a school counselor. Among other strategies, students need to learn to ignore provocative comments, to count to 10 before responding to perceived affronts, and to think of alternative explanations for others' behavior before assuming the worst. Explicit teaching of the key steps in problem solving can prove to be very helpful. This includes identifying the problem, brainstorming solutions, selecting one as the most appropriate solution, and carrying out the steps of that solution.

Methods: Model Your Thinking and Problem-Solving Behavior. You should "talk out loud" to explain why you do what you do. This "makes your thinking visible" for students. For many children and youth with E/B disorders, this articulation of rational behavior may be eye-opening. They did not see this at home. Rather, they were confronted with seemingly abrupt and even irrational behavior by the adults in their home environments. This is particularly true of children from low-SES families. It is very important for *any* child or youth, and particularly for those who have E/B disorders, to understand how well-adjusted adults maintain their demeanor, keep their temper, and deal with frustration. If, for example, you become frustrated with a student's seeming inability to learn something, verbalize your thoughts and your decision-making process. You might say, for example, "I feel a rising sense of annoyance here. I need to step back and count to three. One. Two. Three. Let me see here. What are some reasons Maria may not be doing this right? Quite possibly, I have not taught it. Or maybe she knows what to do but forgot it. At any event, maybe I'm really annoyed at myself, and not at Maria." Similarly, by "talking out loud" as you make a decision in the classroom, you model problem-solving behavior. Again, this may be "news" to some of your students. They need to "see into your head" to learn how you set priorities, decide on a plan of attack in a math problem, or make other decisions.

Methods: Use Simulations. A **simulation** is a learning activity that offers an artificial reality. An advantage of the method is that the artificial reality does not pose dangers for the student or for others as would a real-life situation. Some experiments, particularly in chemistry and physics, are potentially dangerous to student experimenters; by simulating them on a PC, that danger is removed. Simulations, however, need not be computer-based. A good example is a scene from a play. As acted out in the classroom, that scene portrays characters wrestling with powerful emotions. Such a simulation allows students to experience, vicariously, those powerful emotions. Another example is role playing. Here, students take on different roles (e.g., an advocate for developing a vacant lot, an advocate for turning that space into park land).

Methods: Use Advance Organizers/Scaffolding/Manipulatives. Special educators have made good use, with students having E/B disorders as well as with other children and youth, of *advance organizers, scaffolding,* and *manipulatives* (e.g., Mastropieri & Scruggs, 2000). Advance organizers help students to organize their study, by highlighting important ideas, outlining chapters, and so on. Scaffolding is a teacher- or textbook-provided structure, such as an outline or map. Manipulatives are objects you can hold in your hands. They help to make abstract ideas concrete. These three supports help students with E/B disorders to focus upon academic material, sustain attention, and complete assignments rapidly. Actually, they also have the potential to assist *other* students, including those with no disabilities. That is why using advance organizers and other supports is an example of universal design in education.

Methods: Shorten Class Units and Test Sessions. Research shows that many students with E/B disorders perform at a higher level when they are required to sustain attention over shorter rather than longer periods of time. This suggests that you consider abbreviating lessons, offering more short ones, and that you break up into smaller sessions any lengthy test you administer (National Center on Education Outcomes, *http://www.education.UMN.edu(NCEO)*.

Student Strategies That Work

Self-Monitoring

Students with E/B disorders need to acquire skills in self-monitoring, particularly as they enter their teens. As a teacher, you need to bear in mind the unfortunate high drop-out rates of this population. Among those aged 14 to 21, dropping out is particularly common at ages 16, 17, and 18 (U.S. Department of Education, 2002, Table AD2). Thus, you should not wait to teach students how to monitor the side-effects of drugs they take, how to monitor their reactions to frustration, and (for internalizers) how to overcome their shyness.

Self-monitoring involves, first, knowledge about what "should be happening" (what side-effects of medication are to be expected, what responses to perceived affronts are appropriate, and what she should do in order to be an active member of a group). To continue, self-monitoring includes the assumption of responsibility for one's own self. That can be a big step, especially for youth who habitually blame others for their problems. It relates to monitoring the effects of what one does, so that the individual learns from experience.

The effectiveness of "think aloud" strategies was demonstrated as long ago as the 1970s at a summer camp for aggressive boys (Camp, Blom, Herbert, & Van Doornick, 1977). Building upon the work of Albert Bandura (1977), a pioneer in the area of observational learning (learning by watching models behave appropriately), this camp taught young males to stop before acting impulsively. They saw models being taught by adults how to think aloud, after which the models demonstrated that behavior and then were rewarded for doing so. The key was for the boys to whisper to themselves, and later just to mentally talk to themselves, before acting. As this work shows, self-monitoring behavior can be taught and perhaps is most effectively taught using peer tutors.

Methods: Enlist Peers. When students with emotional or behavioral conditions remain in inclusive settings, they continue to observe appropriate behavior by their age peers. They remain under effective peer control, as well, because their age peers demand that they "behave." These two factors tend to have the effect of curtailing inappropriate behavior on the part of students with E/B disorders. This remains true only if you, as the teacher of an inclusive classroom, insist on fair and equal treatment. In particular, you should make sure that peers do not tease or otherwise harass students with E/B disorders, including those who are internalizers.

The potential value of peers goes beyond modeling. When peers are trained as tutors to teach appropriate behaviors, the effects can be even more positive—not only do students being tutored improve in behavior but the tutors themselves (including those who have E/B disorders) also display enhanced social skills (e.g., Blake, Wang, Cartledge, & Gardner, 2000). When, on the other hand, students with these conditions are placed into special environments, they see inappropriate behavior by their peers, every day. They are, in addition, encouraged by their peers to participate in such activities. Separate placements may, then, have the perverse effect of actually making things worse.

Methods: Use Other Resources. Schools usually make inadequate use of community mental-health agencies (Forness, Kavale, & Lopez, 1993). Educators tend to reach out to mental-health professionals in times of crisis (i.e., a suicide by a student) but not to create ongoing, routine referral relationships. According to the Surgeon General's report (2001), the average visit of school students to community mental-health agencies lasts just 15 minutes. Return appointments often are not kept. In part, this is traceable to the fact that the *school* does not require such follow-up visits. As a teacher of a student with an E/B disorder, you do not have the luxury of ignoring community resources. Rather, you should identify them (refer back to "ecology assessment," section under "Mental Retardation"), establish connections with them, and, as needed, refer students and families to them.

In a report on substance abuse among persons with learning disabilities, ADHD, and E/B disorders, the Center on Addiction and Substance Abuse (2000) noted that children and youth with these disabilities may use drugs initially for reasons connected to novelty-seeking, as do other young people. Continued use, however, may be related to a desire to self-medicate, so as to relieve stress and frustration. Yet other abuse may be tied to attempts to cope with the negative consequences, both in school and out of school, of

Teacher Strategies That Work

Homework

Students with E/B disorders often have tension at home. The relationship between the student and adults at home may be antagonistic, and thus interfere with completion of homework. There may not even *be* an adult at home during after-school hours. (Indeed, these factors may have caused the E/B condition itself.) Research suggests that you

- Assign a peer tutor to work with the student, and require that at least some homework be completed during study hall or homeroom, with that peer tutor's assistance.
- Encourage your school to offer after-school sessions specifically for homework, with teachers earning release time.
- Communicate, clearly, what the homework requirements are. Both parent and child should know exactly what is expected and when it is due to be completed.
- Individualize the homework, so it is "doable" by each student.
- Structure the homework, making it easier to follow directions.
- Allow alternative responses (let a student speak answers into a tape recorder, for example).
- Assign homework in small amounts.
- Be available via e-mail to your students during evening hours, if they have questions about homework.
- At the end of each week, reinforce homework completion (public recognition, tokens, etc.). (Epstein, Munk, Bursuck, Polloway, & Jayanthi, 1999)

their conditions. Regardless of student motivation, the report concluded, educators are well-advised to provide young people with *more acceptable and more effective alternatives*. By helping these students to improve their academic work and to enhance their interpersonal relations with others, teachers, and counselors may reduce substance abuse.

Strategies in Transition to Adult Life

Methods: Reduce Drop-Out Rates. Students with emotional or behavioral disorders drop out of high school at higher rates than do students with any other disability conditions. The effects of these high drop-out rates are quite dramatic. Let us illustrate by comparing school attendance and dropping out by students labeled with MR (who tend to have low drop-out rates) and those labeled with E/B disorders. If you examine the prevalence rates by age of MR (the third-largest category) and that of E/B disorders (the fourth-biggest group), you will see that the numbers enrolled in school are roughly identical among students who are 16 years of age. By age 17, the number with E/B conditions is 13% smaller than is the number with MR. By age 18, the number is 46% smaller. And by age 19, it is 68% smaller (U.S. Department of Education, 1999c). The reason is differences in rates of dropping out of school. That is, teens with E/B drop out of school at rates that are far higher than those of students with MR.

When young people with E/B disorders lack a high-school diploma, they are at risk for great difficulty in the adult world. Within three to five years after dropping out of school, nearly three in every four (73%) have been arrested. That compares to 58% who were graduated from high school. A major reason for these troubles with the law is that so few were employed. Even among the minority that did find, and keep, jobs in the years after dropping out, earned incomes rarely rose much above minimum wage (Blackorby & Wagner, 1996). The result can only be described as a vicious cycle. Many of these young people recognize it as such (see, for example, the chapter-opening "Personal Accounts" section).

The good news is that General Educational Development (GED) programs may be more tolerant than are K–12 schools of behavior commonly displayed by young people with E/B disorders (e.g., Scanlon & Mellard, 2002). For this reason, GED programs may offer a much-needed second chance for these individuals.

Methods: Teach Decision-Making Skills. While it is important for everyone to know and practice techniques for making good decisions, individuals with E/B disorders are particularly in need of help in this area (e.g., Kauffman, 2001). To illustrate, recall that Franklin

(1998) and Whaley (1998) highlighted the fact that some people, particularly African-American males, may misinterpret everyday incidents as personal affronts. Rather than respond impulsively with aggression toward the supposed offender, young people should train themselves to pause, consider alternative possible explanations for what happened, and resist the temptation to attribute others' behavior to racism or other kinds of prejudice. As this suggests, good decision making starts with defining the problem. The next step is to consider alternatives. A third is to weigh consequences of different courses of action. A fourth is to remind yourself of what really matters to you (the higher goal). Only then should a decision be reached.

Methods: Be Honest. Reflecting upon a long career in special education, notably with students having E/B conditions, Kauffman (2001) urged teachers to be candid and open when communicating with young people. Whenever possible, positive rather than negative words should be used. These suggestions may appear to be obvious; yet it is Kauffman's experience, as it is mine, that teachers tend to forget these simple rules. Kauffman also urged teachers to help students with E/B to develop capabilities in "play, work, love, and fun . . . nearly the essence of satisfying and meaningful existence" (p. 533). Children and youth with E/B disturbance too often do not know how to play and have fun, how to perform productive work, and how to love themselves and others, contended Kauffman. Being honest includes acknowledging the central importance of these in our own lives and, thus, in the lives of the students we educate. We should not be content just to teach academics.

CHAPTER SUMMARY

Mental Retardation

- Intelligence is a social construct. "General intelligence" helps students do well in school. IQ tests attempt to measure this kind of intelligence.
- Howard Gardner's theory of multiple intelligences proposes that there are at least eight different intelligences, maybe more.
- Experts differ greatly over how to define mental retardation. Some rely heavily on IQ test scores, while others prefer to look, instead, at how individuals behave in "real life." MR is generally understood to refer to IQ test scores of 70 or below.
- The short-term memory and generalization tends to be poor with many persons having mental retardation. They may be readily frustrated and easily distracted. Many have difficulty in social situations.
- Fragile X syndrome is both genetic and inherited. Down Syndrome, by contrast, is genetic in origin but is not inherited. Rather, it usually results from an error in copying during meiosis (cell division).

Emotional or Behavioral Disorders

- The federal definition for emotional disturbance is widely recognized as inadequate. However, consensus has yet to form around a better definition. Most experts look for behavior that is atypical for persons of that age and for that situation.
- In many instances, emotional or behavioral disorders may be caused, directly or indirectly, by family members. Only a few conditions, notably schizophrenia and depression, are known to have genetic components. Most have multiple causes (inadequate parenting plus deleterious peer influences, for example).
- Conduct disorders involve violence and damage to property. Sometimes, people elect to engage in such behavior (e.g., because a gang expects it). In such instances, we cannot meaningfully say the individual is E/B disordered.
- Research strongly favors positive behavioral interventions. Many schools, by contrast, rely much more heavily upon punitive measures.

QUESTIONS FOR REFLECTION

1. What is meant by the idea that intelligence is a "socially constructed" concept?
2. What are some examples of "systems of support"?
3. To what kinds of experiences would you *avoid* exposing a student with mental retardation?
4. How could familial social class affect a child's intelligence?
5. How do the two "genetic" causes (Fragile X syndrome and Down Syndrome) of mental retardation differ?
6. Why might the number of PreK–12 students with E/B conditions be much larger than is reported in official statistics?
7. Why is defining "emotional or behavioral disorders" so problematic?
8. What interventions do experts recommend to prevent or ameliorate E/B disorders?
9. Why does dropping out of school expose students with E/B disorders to so much difficulty as adults?
10. How do educators, to adopt James Kauffman's (1999) terms, often "prevent the prevention of" E/B disorders?

Part Two Endnotes

Making Inclusion Work . . . The Story So Far

In Part Two, we learned the keys to making inclusion work include these ideas:

- Provide support services that students with specific learning disabilities (SLD) require. Because these children and youth account for 51% of all students with disabilities (62% at the secondary level), no inclusion program can succeed unless at least one teacher, preferably several, have expertise in this area.
- Treat the secondary conditions that often accompany SLD. Children and youth with SLD may also have oppositional defiant disorder (ODD) and many have attention deficit disorders (ADHD).
- Recognize that ADHD conditions are genuine—these are not just "bad kids"—and deserving of support and of accommodations in the classroom and during high-stakes tests.
- Provide speech/language pathology services for students with speech or language impairments (SLI). The evidence is that many of these students benefit considerably from those services.
- Acknowledge that schools traditionally have overidentified members of minority groups as mentally retarded (MR) or emotionally or behaviorally (E/B) disturbed. Educators need to become culturally competent and culturally sensitive in order to avoid misidentification.
- Teach students with MR and E/B disorders in the community when feasible, to reduce problems of generalization and to increase hands-on learning opportunities.
- Provide training in independent living for youth with MR and E/B disorders, in recognition that these students typically need considerable instruction and practice in these vital skills.
- Attend to unacceptable behavior early (preferably during the early childhood as well as the primary grades) and offering school-wide and other interventions immediately, rather than waiting in the hope that the problems would disappear.
- Offer push-in services when feasible for students with physical, health, and sensory disabilities, to avoid the problems associated with pull-out services.
- Teach students how to be good team members and then give them opportunities to participate in cooperative-learning activities.
- Understand that without the appropriate support, inclusion may effectively be exclusion for students who are deaf or hard of hearing because they are surrounded by people who communicate differently from the ways they do.
- Speak aloud every word and symbol that is written on a board, displayed on an overhead or a slide, and printed in a handout, so that students who are blind or have low vision may keep pace with instruction. Such steps also help students who prefer to learn by listening.
- Look for subjects of high interest to slow learners.
- Become culturally competent and culturally sensitive so as to make school more inviting for members of ethnic and racial minority groups.
- Arrange activities that teens find attractive for after-school hours, to reduce delinquency.

Part Three

Students in the Inclusive Classroom with Lower-Incidence Disorders

Part Three discusses students with disabilities who are included in general classrooms *and* who have low-prevalence disabilities. By "low prevalence" we mean that they are few in number, as compared to children and youth with other disabilities. Students with these uncommon disabilities account for fewer than 10% of all students with any disabilities.

Chapter 6 explores physical, health, and vision impairments. Included are cerebral palsy and spinal-cord injuries, epilepsy and AIDS, and blindness. It also contains the book's most complete discussion of the "pull-out/push-in" controversy over where to deliver related services. Chapter 7 focuses upon autism and also on severe or multiple disabilities (such as mental retardation combined with another condition).

Some students with low-prevalence disabilities can succeed in inclusive placements. This is the case, for example, with most children and youth having health impairments. Other K–12 students with low-prevalence conditions, however, seldom can be fully accommodated in inclusive settings. This is because their needs are so severe and the services they require are so different from what is usually offered in the general curriculum.

One common theme in serving the children and youth discussed in Part Three is the need for collaboration between classroom teachers and other school personnel. We devote an entire chapter (Chapter 12) to techniques for effective collaboration. You may wish to consult that chapter while reading Part Two chapters.

Chapter 6 *Physical, Health, and Vision Impairments*

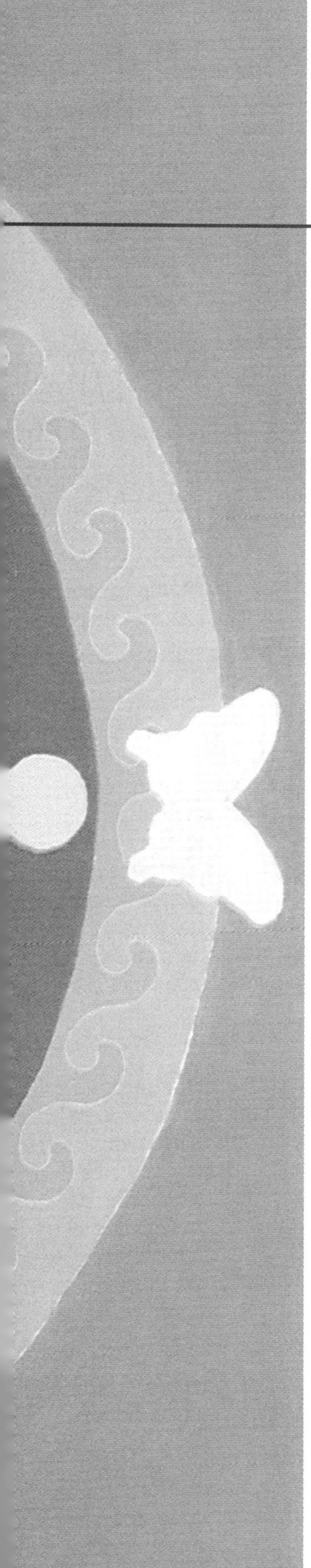

TERMS

orthopedic impairment
traumatic brain injury (TBI)
visitability
physical therapy
occupational therapy
experiential deprivation
positioning
technology abandonment
speech-language pathology
family services
service coordination
social work services
counseling
respite services
visual impairment including blindness
blindness
screen readers
listserv
e-texts

CHAPTER FOCUS QUESTIONS

After reading this chapter, you should be able to answer such questions as:

1. What does the term "orthopedic impairments" mean?
2. Why is pull-out an issue with the populations discussed in this chapter?
3. Why are many students with mobility limitations sent to out-of-district schools?
4. What disabilities other than ADHD comprise the category "Other Health Impaired"?
5. Why is diabetes in childhood and adolescence of growing concern among educators and family members?
6. Why do you think students who are blind or have low vision are the most likely to be graduated from high school and to go to college of those with any disability listed in the IDEA?
7. How can a teacher of an inclusive classroom identify the needs of a student who is blind?

PERSONAL ACCOUNTS

Breanna, who is 4 years old, has cerebral palsy (CP). Her mother, Trellis, described Breanna's needs and her efforts to help the little girl in an article by Whinnery and Barnes (2002), from which this account was drawn:

> *Breanna became sick with meningitis and encephalitis at three weeks of age. As a result, she has CP. In her case, CP is characterized by a mixture of high and low muscle tone, limited strength for standing and sitting, and difficulty holding her head up. Breanna's mother Trellis began by doing virtually everything that Breanna could not do. This included carrying Breanna from room to room as well as dressing, feeding, and bathing Breanna. In time, spurred by a doctor's prediction that Breanna would never walk alone, Trellis initiated physical therapy activities in the home. She soon discovered, to her distress, that Breanna would sometimes resist those training exercises. Trellis was also becoming exhausted from carrying Breanna.*

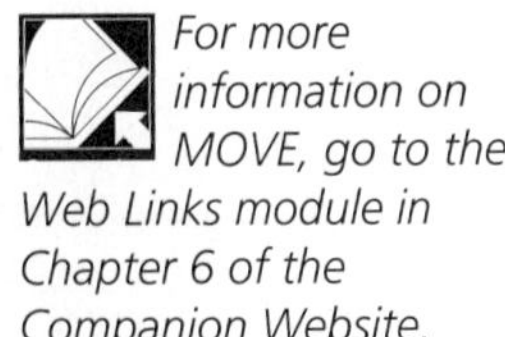
For more information on MOVE, go to the Web Links module in Chapter 6 of the Companion Website.

After watching a videotape about Mobility Opportunities Via Education (MOVE), Trellis met with two university professors to explore this curriculum. The basis, Trellis learned, was for the child to move for a purpose and in natural contexts. From that point on, Trellis used Breanna's inherent motivation to encourage her to move. If the two were in the living room, for example, and Breanna wanted to play a game that was in her bedroom, Trellis would help Breanna to stand—but then would insist that Breanna walk with her, side-by-side, to the bedroom. At the beginning, the most steps Breanna could take with her mother supporting her arms was 20. About a year later, Breanna was taking as many as 500 steps to get where she wanted to go. One day, walking along the road, Breanna looked at her grandparents' house. It was clear that she wanted to visit. With minimal support from Trellis, Breanna walked 600 feet, almost to the front door of the house, before she could walk no more.

Trellis says that there are many benefits for Breanna from this increased independence of mobility. Breanna is stronger now, better able to support her own weight. Her hips, once determined by a doctor to require surgery, are now much better aligned to the rest of her body; the doctor has stopped talking about surgery. Breanna also has better balance and control over her body.

Erin English, an 18-year veteran teacher in the Forest Hills school district in Anderson Township, OH, won an educational inclusion award in 2002 for her work with Emily Pennington, a first-grader who is blind. Mrs. English painted maps with puffy paint so that Emily could feel them. She brought worms to school so Emily and her classmates could feel them during a lesson about worms. She hired a teacher's assistant who was skilled at translating classroom materials into Braille. Mrs. English learned just enough Braille herself to be able to tell Emily when she was making mistakes. Emily taught her something, too. Mrs. English learned that she had to be much more verbally specific when giving directions and when reviewing materials in class. She had to articulate in speech everything that went on the blackboard or was displayed on an overhead. Mrs. English persuaded the school district to purchase a $2,000 Braille 'n Speak device that let Emily take notes and write essays. The machine uploads text into a PC, which can then send it, in English, to a printer so Emily could hand in a report that Mrs. English could read. The product greatly helped Emily. By the time she finished first grade, she could read at the fourth-grade level. Her sighted classmates scrambled to sit beside her because Emily was a walking dictionary. She could spell anything! (Kranz, 2002)

These stories illustrate two of the many disabilities discussed in this chapter. Breanna's cerebral palsy (CP) is one of the physical disorders recognized as "orthopedic impairments" in the rules governing implementation of the Individuals with Disabilities Education Act (IDEA). Breanna requires multiple services. This is typical of children and youth with orthopedic impairments. That is why most children and youth with CP qualify for assistance under IDEA. CP is also an immediately noticeable condition.

Emily was successfully included in a first-grade classroom because her teacher was willing to take a few extra steps and because the school district acquired assistive technology devices that Emily needed.

INTRODUCTION

Chapter 6 addresses disabilities that are much less prevalent than are those discussed in Chapters 3 to 5. Physical disabilities (referred to as "orthopedic impairments" in IDEA) are uncommon among school-age children. Vision impairments, including blindness, are even rarer in the PreK–12 population (U.S. Department of Education, 2004). Bearing in mind that 2,870,000 students between the ages of 6 and 21 inclusive have the label "specific learning disability" while about 1,110,000 are classified as having "speech or language impairments," consider the corresponding numbers for the conditions discussed in this chapter: 74,000 (orthopedic impairments), 26,000 (vision impairments, including blindness), and 21,000 (traumatic brain injury). While the category "Other Health Impaired" (OHI) is fairly large at 392,000 students, the bulk of that group is children and youth with attention deficit hyperactivity disorders (ADHD), which were discussed in an earlier chapter. Figure 6.1 compares low-prevalence disabilities to high-prevalence conditions. As the chart shows, all low-prevalence disabilities taken together account for just 10% of PreK–12 students having any label.

While they may be few in number, students with the disabilities reviewed in this chapter tend to be educated in inclusive classrooms. In this respect, they differ sharply from those discussed in the next chapter. To illustrate, 46% of students classified as having orthopedic impairments are educated in regular classrooms all or virtually all of the school week (meaning, they spend less than 21% of the school week outside of regular classrooms), with another 23% splitting time between such settings and resource rooms. The corresponding figures for those with a traumatic brain injury are 32% and 28%, respectively. Among students with OHI, 50% are in the general classroom all or most of the time and another 31% part-time. Finally, 52% of students classified as blind or visually impaired are in general classrooms all or virtually all of the school week, with an additional 17% in such settings part of the school week (U.S. Department of Education, 2004, Table AB2).

For more information on the tables and charts from IDEA's Annual Reports, *go to the Web Links module in Chapter 6 of the Companion Website.*

This chapter presents disabilities that vary so much that generalization about them is difficult. Some conditions discussed in this chapter are relatively mild, some relatively severe. Several have consistent and long-lasting effects on children and youth, while others manifest themselves on an irregular basis. That is, unlike most disabilities reviewed in this book, some considered in this chapter, notably several health conditions, create "episodes" or periodic crises from time to time. Some disorders are immediately visible to other people. Others are not noticeable, except during an attack.

FIGURE 6.1 Low vs. High Prevalence Disabilities

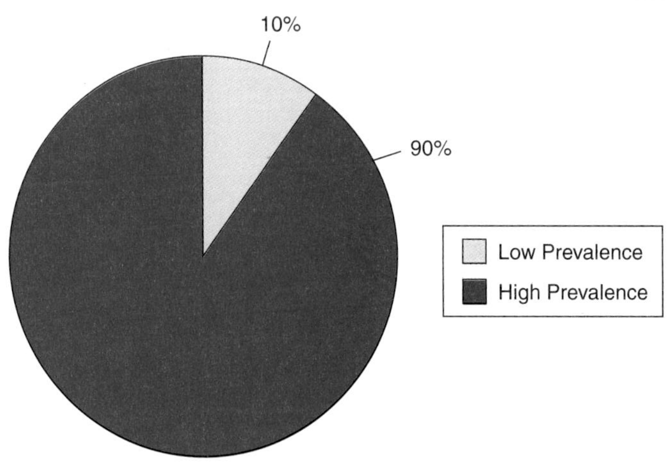

Source: From the *26th Annual Report,* U.S. Department of Education, 2004, Washington, DC: Author.

ORTHOPEDIC IMPAIRMENTS AND TRAUMATIC BRAIN INJURY

Students with physical disabilities who are served under IDEA usually are given one of four labels. First, they may have the label "orthopedic impairments," which is the term the law uses to refer to conditions most people consider to be "physical" in nature, such as CP. Second, they may have the label "traumatic brain injury" (TBI), which is a relatively new classification, having been added in 1990. Third, some are given the label of another disability which the Individualized Education Plan (IEP) team considers to be the child's primary classification. This may happen, for example, when a student has a specific learning disability and also has a cardiac disorder. Fourth and finally, if students have a physical condition and also have a second significant or co-equal disability, they may be given the fourth label, "multiple disabilities." That category is reviewed in the next chapter.

Section 504 is important for many students with physical disabilities (Bowe, 2000b). About half of PreK–12 students who have these conditions are eligible for IDEA services, using one of the labels introduced above. Others are served, instead, under section 504. To be eligible for services under IDEA, students *must* require special education and related services; section 504 imposes no such requirement.

Definitions

Here, we will look briefly at two definitions, that for orthopedic impairments and that for traumatic brain injuries. Both definitions appear in the federal regulations, rather than in IDEA itself.

The U.S. Department of Education's (1999a) rules for IDEA say that an **orthopedic impairment** is

> a severe orthopedic impairment that adversely affects a child's educational performance. The term includes impairments caused by congenital abnormality (e.g., clubfoot, absence of some member, etc.), impairments caused by disease (e.g., poliomyelitis, bone tuberculosis, etc.), and impairments from other causes (e.g., cerebral palsy, amputations, and fractures or burns that cause contractures). (34 C.F.R. 300[c][8])

The Department's definition begins with the now-familiar words "that adversely affects a child's educational performance." As with other definitions in the Department's rules, this refers to the fact that children are eligible for services under IDEA if, and only if, they "need special education and related services." The rest of the definition clearly refers to physical conditions. This label generally is used when children have spinal cord injuries (SCI), spina bifida, muscular dystrophy (MD), CP, or some other such mobility-related disability.

Traumatic brain injury (TBI) is defined as

> an acquired injury to the brain caused by an external physical force, resulting in total or partial functional disability or psychosocial impairment, or both, that adversely affects a child's educational performance.
>
> The term applies to open or closed head injuries resulting in impairments in one or more areas, such as cognition; language; memory; attention; reasoning; abstract thinking; judgment; problem-solving; sensory, perceptual, and motor abilities; psychosocial behavior; physical functions; information processing; and speech. The term does not apply to brain injuries that are congenital or degenerative, or to brain injuries induced by birth trauma. (34 C.F.R. 300[c][12])

Notice in this definition that TBI may result in a wide variety of problems. Thus, while the injury itself is a physical one, the fact that it occurs in the brain produces a range of behavioral and mental effects. That is why the definition focuses upon issues most of us would regard as cognitive in nature.

Problems with These Definitions

The Department's definition for orthopedic impairment does not explicitly include several physical disabilities that are much more common than are some that the definition does mention (amputation, clubfoot, etc.). Notable among these are spina bifida and spinal cord injury (see the section titled "Types"). The definition for TBI, by contrast, is quite inclusive and current. Note that the definition refers to memory and attention, as well as to sensory limitations. In many cases, heightened sensitivity to light and to sounds fades about a year after the injury. Personality alterations, however, can be permanent. The definition does not distinguish between short- and long-term effects.

Characteristics and Types

Orthopedic impairments are physical in nature, affecting mobility. CP, onc of the major orthopedic impairments, can also limit expressive communication. An important variable in orthopedic impairment is the age at onset. CP, for example, is virtually always present from birth or shortly after birth. SCI, by contrast, typically occurs in adolescence or early adulthood. TBIs have effects that also vary by age at onset.

Characteristics

It is difficult to generalize about such a broad spectrum of limitations. People with physical disorders, speaking generally, tend to learn in the same ways, and at the same pace, as do students with no disabilities. This fact is important to note. Although the appearance of someone sitting in a wheelchair, walking with crutches, or displaying the uncoordinated, jerky motions characteristic of CP may seem to signal that this is a person with special instructional needs, the more significant fact for an educator is that most such students do not require you to teach differently. This is why so many are "504 kids" (see Chapter 1). To illustrate, someone with MD (an orthopedic impairment) may bring his own chair into your class. Once there, however, he learns in the same ways as does any other student. The major exceptions to this general rule are (1) students who have secondary conditions in addition to orthopedic impairments and (2) children and youth who have a *recent* TBI.

Types

The most common physical disabilities in the orthopedic impairments category are *cerebral palsy, spinal cord injury, spina bifida, muscular dystrophy,* and *amputations.* CP produces jerking motions in the arms and/or legs, in one version (athetoid), and very stiff limbs, in another (spastic). A SCI limits movement and sensation in the legs (paraplegia) and in the arms, hands, and fingers (quadriplegia). About half of all people with a SCI have paraplegia and half have quadriplegia. Spina bifida is a spinal cord injury that is present from birth. Both SCI and spina bifida vary in effects depending upon where along the spinal column the injury occurred. In MD, the body attacks its own muscles. In time, the muscles weaken. MD is often fatal in early adulthood, frequently from a heart attack (the heart is a muscle). Amputation is removal or, occasionally, an inborn lack, of a limb.

Traumatic brain injury is a disability with a wide variety of effects. Some are temporary. This includes fatigue and irritability. It may also include extreme sensitivity to light (the individual avoids being near bright lights or other strong visual stimuli) and/or sound (the person has difficulty being around a lot of people, because the input from so many sounds is disorienting). In instances in which the TBI involved the temporal lobes on either side of the brain, the individual may experience great difficulty or even inability to learn new information. These effects generally subside about a year after the injury. If the injury occurred in the frontal lobe, effects may be seen in difficulties planning and carrying out a course of action.

Other effects of TBI are long-lasting. Personality is a striking example. People who have been outgoing all their lives may suddenly be very shy; the opposite may occur as well. Men and women have been known to show very different tastes in preferred activities, in food, and in friends, after as compared to before the injury. This is a permanent alteration. It can be very unsettling for the individual, for his or her family, and for peers to see Brynn—who was a very extroverted young woman prior to the injury—now shun school clubs and weekend parties in favor of staying home to read or watch TV, to watch her now dress herself in a completely different style of clothing than she used to wear, and to see that she has very different tastes in food and drink. Such personality changes may mean the loss of friends. While this may be understandable—the individual formed those friendships on the basis of shared interests which may no longer be shared—it can also be traumatic. Losing one's social support system soon after sustaining a TBI can be a serious setback.

These effects appear when a TBI is severe. While brain injuries are common in children and youth, most are mild and are transient in nature. The human skull is very effective in protecting the brain. That is why, fortunately, relatively few PreK–12 students have permanent effects from a TBI (National Center for Injury Prevention and Control, 2001).

Commonalities. CP, SCI, SB, and MD all affect gross-motor movements. CP and quadriplegic SCI also affect fine-motor movements in the fingers and hands. As mentioned earlier, TBI shares one similarity with CP: The site of the lesion is in the brain. Unless mental retardation is a secondary condition, persons with orthopedic impairments should not be limited in ability to learn and remember. The major variable with respect to how much someone with an orthopedic impairment will learn, and how rapidly, is attendance. A recent SCI and a recent TBI may require lengthy absences, due to hospitalization and/or physical rehabilitation sessions.

Many children and youth with visible physical conditions learn in the same ways and at the same speed as do students without such disabilities.

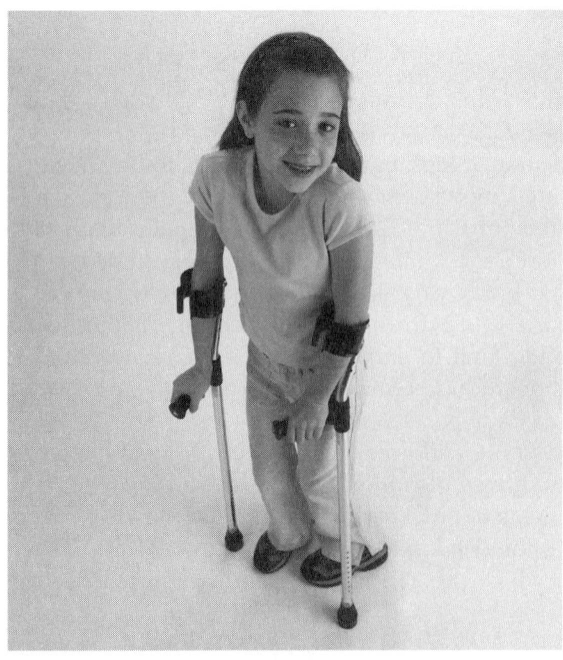

Differences. CP is the only one of the orthopedic impairments that commonly affects speech. The other four involve impairments of the body itself, either the spinal cord (spina bifida, SCI) or a limb (amputation). Spina bifida occurs before or at birth, while SCI happens during childhood or adolescence. MD and amputation both involve the musculoskeletal system. Only MD of the conditions reviewed in this section generally is fatal.

TBIs are different from orthopedic impairments in many ways. First, many children and youth having TBI are not limited in mobility. Second, as previously noted, a TBI can effect a personality change. No other disability alters personality as dramatically and as quickly as does TBI.

Co-Morbidity. CP often co-occurs with mental retardation and, less frequently, with impairments of hearing and of vision. These other conditions result from the same causes—oxygen deprivation in the brain, prematurity and low birth weight, and insufficient care and monitoring during the pregnancy. Usually, vision impairment is rather mild, requiring glasses; hearing loss, too, tends to be mild or moderate, treatable with hearing aids. Spina bifida is a condition that can lead to mental retardation because of fluid build-up in the brain. That is why children with this disability often receive a shunt, which drains the fluid and removes it from the body. As for SCI, if the accident was particularly severe, there may be a TBI in addition to the SCI.

Prevalence

According to the *26th Annual Report* (U.S. Department of Education, 2004, Table AB2), the categories of orthopedic impairments and traumatic brain injury both are relatively small. A total of 74,000 students between the ages of 6 and 21 inclusive (that is, up to age 22) were reported as having orthopedic impairments in the 2000–2001 school year. While they are small in number, nearly half (46%) of those who do have this classification spend all or virtually all of the school week in general classrooms (see Figure 6.2). Just 21,000 children and youth were classified as having TBI. Together, orthopedic impairments and TBIs account for just 1.5% of students identified with any label.

FIGURE 6.2 Likelihood of Inclusive Placements: Orthopedic Impairments

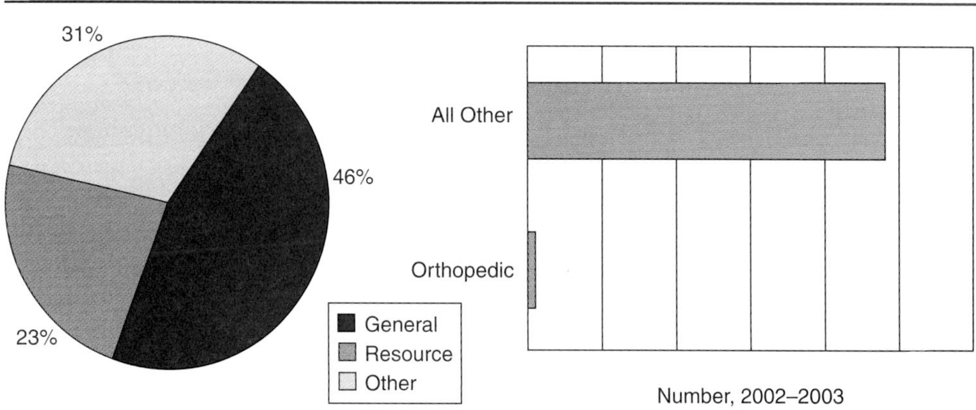

While students identified with "orthopedic impairments" label are relatively few in number at 74,000 out of 5,946,000 reported for the 2002–2003 school year (*26th Annual Report*), those who do have this classification tend to be placed into inclusive environments. The *Annual Report* shows that 46% were in general classrooms all or almost all of the school week (spending less than 21% of their time in other environments). The two charts above illustrate these data.

Source: From the *26th Annual Report,* by the U.S. Department of Education, 2004, Washington, DC: Author.

Diagnosis and Assessment

The diagnosis of conditions discussed in this section generally is performed by physicians, following medical criteria. Most disabilities in the orthopedic impairments category are well-defined. Diagnosis is objective, with little room for judgment. These disorders produce visible symptoms. In these ways, diagnosis is different than it is with more subjective cases, notably specific learning disabilities and emotional disturbance.

Assessment, because it involves determining eligibility under IDEA, is something the IEP team may discuss. The law requires that children and youth need both special education and related services in order to be classified. Some students with orthopedic impairments, particularly those with mild conditions, may not require special education. Very few may not even need such related services as special transportation, occupational therapy, and the like. In the event that a particular student does not require special education or related services, the IEP team may designate the child as eligible under section 504. This step would permit the delivery of related services. It also would protect the student against discrimination on the basis of disability, including harassment. This can be an issue because some orthopedic impairments, notably CP, are highly visible.

With respect to TBI, there is a risk of underidentification. Mitch's teachers noticed a change in his behavior when he was in eighth grade. He had been an outstanding student in sixth and seventh grades. Now, however, his grades were slipping, he seemed irritable, and seemed to be unable at times to remember recently learned information. Checking into the situation, his teachers learned that Mitch had been hit by a ball over the summer. His parents were not told by the hospital about any lasting effects, so they had not reported the incident to the school. This was an instance of a TBI not being identified until alert

Research That Works

TBI

Researchers suspect that a much larger number of traumatic brain injuries occur each year than are apparent from official government figures. The U.S. Department of Education (2004) reported that just 21,500 PreK–12 students were identified during the 2002–2003 school year as having TBI. Other data sources point to much higher prevalence rates. According to the National Center for Injury Prevention and Control (2001), as many as 400,000 children and youth are treated each year in hospital emergency rooms after trauma-related incidents, 29,000 are hospitalized, and 3,000 die. The Research and Training Center on TBI (RTC/TBI) has estimated that if proper screening were performed, it is possible that as many as 500,000 school-age students could be found to have a brain injury that has some effect on their academic performance (Mt. Sinai School of Medicine, 2003, *http://www.mssm.edu/tbinet*).

The RTC/TBI suggests that the Brain Injury Screening Questionnaire (BISQ) be completed if educators suspect a possible brain injury. This is an interview-based instrument. It may be self-administered. There are three parts to the questionnaire. Part one identifies the many different ways in which a TBI may be sustained. Completing this section might prompt a student, a parent, or a teacher to recall a recent incident. This is what happened with Mitch, the eighth-grader who had been hit by a ball over the summer (see "Diagnosis and Assessment"). Part two lists 100 symptoms, of which 25 have been identified as connected with TBI. Part three raises other possible causes, such as medication. The BISQ is intended for use with students aged 14 or over. A pediatric version is also available for use with younger students. Positive results from the BISQ should lead to a neurological examination that will confirm the diagnosis.

What symptoms should teachers look for? According to the RTC/TBI, possible indicators include deficits in attention and memory (e.g., inability to concentrate in a sustained manner as the child previously was able to do), new behavior (e.g., restlessness, fatigue, irritability that was not characteristic of the child in prior years), and psychological functioning (e.g., depression, withdrawal, or rage that is atypical for the student). Research shows that fairly simple adjustments can make a big difference. Changing the student's seating to reduce distractions can help. Use of memory aids, such as a schedule for the day or a "to do list," is also suggested. The student should be permitted frequent breaks throughout the school day. Teachers may prepare advance organizers, concept maps, and other tools that they use for students with specific learning disabilities (see Chapter 3).

For more information about the BISQ, go to the Web Links module in Chapter 6 of the Companion Website.

FIGURE 6.3 Functional Area of the Brain

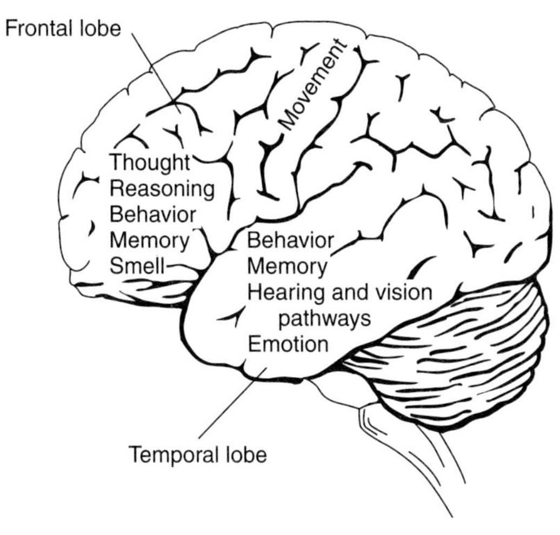

teachers acted to help get Mitch the services he needed (National Center for the Dissemination of Disability Research, 2002). See "Research That Works: TBI" for more information.

In addition, with TBI the need for *ongoing* assessment is unusually high, especially in the first two years post-injury. This is for two reasons. First, the effects of a TBI may not become evident until a child develops a bit more and is expected to do different things. Eight-year-olds are not expected to show competence in abstract reasoning; 15-year-olds are. For this reason, an injury to the frontal lobe (see Figure 6.3) that seems innocuous at the time (age 8) later reveals its effect (age 15). It is also because the individual's cognitive functioning can change dramatically and rapidly (Mt. Sinai School of Medicine, 2003 *http://www.mssm.edu/tbinet*) and because TBI can alter a student's personality. Regular assessment, including counselors' evaluations as needed, will pick up such issues in time for educators and family members to respond to it.

Causes

CP has numerous causes, most prominent among them prematurity and its accompanying low-birth weight, and oxygen deprivation in the brain during fetal development and/or during birth. In spina bifida, the spinal cord does not close during fetal development. As a result, there is an opening in the spinal cord (the term "bifida" means "divided into two"). SCI is similar, but occurs well after birth. Among PreK–12 students, spinal-cord injuries are most common in the mid-teen years. Sporting events, automobile and other transportation accidents, and diving/swimming accidents are among the most common causes.

Genetic Factors

Some impairments in these categories have genetic origins, generally in the form of mutations (i.e., MD, which is caused by a genetic mutation such that a protein critical to maintaining muscle integrity is not produced by the body in sufficient amounts). CP has no genetic causes, except in one rare case (United Cerebral Palsy Associations, 2004, *http://www.ucpa.org*). TBIs, by definition, do not have genetic causes.

Environmental Factors

CP can occur because of injuries during the pre-, peri-, or postnatal periods (that is, before, during, or immediately after birth). One known cause of spina bifida is folic acid insufficiency in the mother while she is pregnant. For whatever reason, CP is known to be associated with low birth weight. Twins often are born at low weights and CP is more common in those instances than in single births. However, it is not clear whether the low birth weight is causative of the CP, or if both result from some third factor. Many instances of CP have no known cause (United Cerebral Palsy Associations, 2004, *http://www.ucpa.org*). A SCI may result from bicycle, motorcycle, automobile, or other (e.g., airplane, boat) transportation accidents (the most common group of causes), sporting injuries (the second most-common segment), or falls.

TBI is caused by many of the same events. The difference is that the brain, rather than the spinal cord, is injured. Many cases of TBI result from incidents at home. These may go unreported, especially if the family wants to protect its privacy. Even mild injuries may affect cognitive functioning. What specific effects a TBI has depends largely upon where the injury occurs. It also depends upon whether the injury is an "open" or a "closed" TBI. In an open injury, the skull is penetrated; in a closed one, it is not. Closed head injuries may produce more diffuse effects. This is because pressure builds within the skull without an outlet. In open head injuries, by contrast, the damage tends to be localized at the site of the injury.

Amputations may have several causes. Worldwide, the most frequent is stepping on a land mine. Thousands of live mines remain hidden, mostly in areas ravaged by recent warfare. In the United States, a common cause is diabetes. Without proper treatment, diabetes can necessitate a leg amputation. Occasionally, a limb will be amputated as part of an effort to contain the spread of cancer in the body.

Instructional Methods

Strategies in Early Childhood and Elementary School

Of the 36,000 children between 6 and 12 years of age who were classified as having orthopedic impairments during the 2002–2003 school year, half (51%) were placed in inclusive classrooms all or virtually all of the school week. Another 21% split time between those rooms and resource rooms. About the same proportion (26%) were educated in separate classrooms. Just 7,800 students aged 6 to 11 inclusive who had the TBI classification were identified in the *26th Annual Report*. Of them, 28% were placed into regular classrooms all or most of the school week, with another 37% splitting time between such settings and resource rooms. About one in three (28%) were educated in separate classrooms in neighborhood schools.

Methods: Collaboration with Related Services Personnel. Students with orthopedic impairments often require such related services as *physical therapy* (PT) and/or *occupational therapy* (OT). Figure 6.4 compares and contrasts physical and occupational therapy. Teachers need to learn what these specialists do. In very general terms, physical therapists work on larger bodily movements and strive to maintain health. While occupational therapists sometimes do those things, too, they tend to focus upon helping children to do the things children must be able to do (dressing themselves, eating, grasping and

Resources That Work

Physical Disabilities

Individuals with orthopedic impairments, and many with TBI, need a wide variety of services and products. There is an impressive range of resources to help meet their needs. However, many more are required.

Housing

The most pressing transition-related need for many who use wheelchairs is housing. The National Council on Disability (NCD), a small independent federal agency, repeatedly has reported that laws on accessibility in housing are weak and that enforcement of those laws has been even weaker. To illustrate, NCD (2003) found that the budget for enforcement at the U.S. Department of Housing and Urban Development (HUD) of section 504 and of the Fair Housing Amendments Act (FHAA) of 1988 declined steadily from 1989 to 2002, even as the demand for accessibility in housing rose dramatically. Complaints about discrimination on the basis of disability comprised nearly half (42%) of all complaints at HUD. On average, the agency takes 500 days to review and act on complaints, five times as long as required by the FHAA. NCD also charged that the agency does little to publicize disability rights (NCD, 2003).

Fortunately, a Technical Assistance Collaborative (TAC), based in Boston, specializes in housing and persons with disabilities. It offers information both online and in print that explains housing options in plain language. This includes material about rent subsidies (section 8), public housing project (section 811), and vouchers. The Web site is *http://www.tacinc.org* and the mailing address is One Center Plaza, Suite 310, Boston, MA 02108.

Because the housing situation remains so dire for many persons with physical disabilities, and because federal laws are not likely to improve the situation any time soon, local advocacy becomes essential. A good resource for educators and family members is the Independent Living Resource Utilization (ILRU) center in Houston (*www.ilru.org*). ILRU offers updated information on 600+ local advocacy centers. ILRU publishes a compilation of information about those independent living centers every January. Because the centers move so often, the directory is valuable. Another good resource for local advocacy in housing is Concrete Change. Based in Georgia, it began the "visitability" movement. Interested persons may e-mail the organization at concretechange@yahoo.com. Another site of interest on visitability is the listserv at the State University of New York at Buffalo: *http://www.ap.buffalo.edu/~rercud*.

People who need accessible housing need to become forceful advocates for community change. The newest wrinkle in accessible housing is the 16-year-old movement known as **"visitability."** This movement is a local one. Naperville, IL, Pima County, AZ, and some communities near Atlanta, GA, have local ordinances requiring no-step entrances, wide front doors, and ground-floor rest room access in new one-family homes. These cities and towns are unusual in that the rules cover private as well as public (government-financed) housing. However, a visitable home is not necessarily an accessible one. The visitability standard is one seeking to assure that a relative or friend could visit in a private house, rather than live there. Concrete Change, the not-for-profit advocacy organization that began the visitability movement, defines visitability as comprising the following features:

1. no steps to the main entrance of the home
2. doors at least 32" wide throughout the first floor
3. basic access to a bath or half bath on the main floor (Concrete Change, 2004).

It is clear from this description that visitability is but a step in the direction of accessibility in housing. Information and assistance on accessible housing are available from the Technical Assistance Collaborative.

Services

IDEA provides for occupational and physical therapy services to be arranged for and provided to children and youth while they are in high school. There is no comparable law covering post–high-school services. Many individuals with physical disabilities continue to need occupational and physical therapy (OT/PT) services after leaving high school. Medical insurance plans, including Medicaid, typically cover some OT/PT sessions. Qualified individuals may be located through their professional associations. Physical therapists are represented by the American Physical Therapy Association. The counterpart group for occupational therapists is the American Occupational Therapy Association.

The National Easter Seals Society is a major resource on physical disabilities. Headquartered in Chicago, it has affiliates throughout the country. These direct-service programs offer training, counseling, parent information, and referrals to appropriate agencies for meeting specific needs.

Gene therapy holds great promise of someday ameliorating or even curing many of the conditions discussed in this chapter. A very good primer on gene therapy, including basics about the science and cautions about the near-term applicability of the "breakthroughs" reported weekly in the popular press, is offered by the University of Pennsylvania's Institute for Human Gene Therapy at *http://www.uphs.upenn.edu/ihgt*.

Creative Arts

VSA arts, formerly known as Very Special Arts, sponsors national, state and local exhibitions for graphic artists, musicians, and other artists. It also provides biographies and portfolios about and by artists with disabilities.

Other

Other resources are disability-specific. The key organization on CP is the United Cerebral Palsy Associations; the "s" at the end signals that this is a coalition of many state- and county-based groups which also have the name United Cerebral Palsy Association. For information on TBI, two good resources are the Brain Injury Association and the HEATH Resource Center. HEATH, formerly a unit of the American Council on Education, has an online publication, *The Student with a Brain Injury,* which is helpful for teachers. Also helpful are several Web pages at the Research and Training Center on TBI, at *http://www.mssm.edu/tbinet/*. The Spina Bifida Association of America is an excellent resource not only on spina bifida but also on SCI. The United Nations sponsors the "Adopt-a-Minefield" program that seeks to clear fields of land mines. The Amputation Coalition of America (ACA) is an outstanding source of information for amputees and their teachers.

For more information on organizations, associations, and services discussed in the "Resources That Work" box, go to the Web Links module in Chapter 6 of the Companion Website.

FIGURE 6.4 Physical and Occupational Therapy

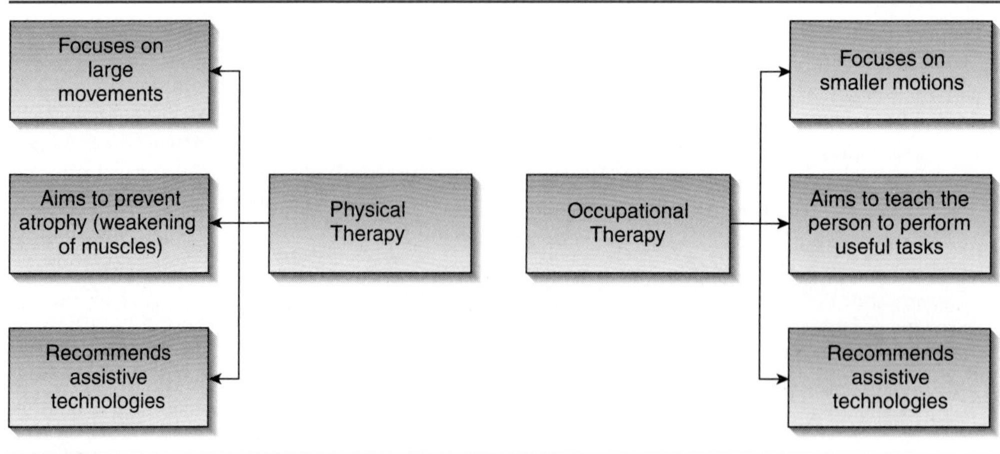

holding a pen, etc.). Both physical and occupational therapists are trained in assistive technology devices and assistive technology services; they can identify products that children can use, from wheelchairs to computer peripherals. Teachers of inclusive classrooms need to develop effective modes of collaboration with these professionals.

The U.S. Department of Education's rules for IDEA define **physical therapy** as

> services to address the promotion of sensorimotor function through enhancement of musculoskeletal status, neurobehavioral organization, perceptual and motor development, cardiopulmonary status, and effective environmental adaptation. These services include . . . Providing individual and group services or treatment to prevent, alleviate, or compensate for movement dysfunction and related functional problems. (U.S. Department of Education, 1993a)

It should be evident from this definition that much physical therapy needs to be conducted on its own. Physical therapists aim to maintain the child's physical capabilities (that is, to prevent muscle atrophy, or wasting away from non-use). With many children, especially those who have CP, positioning is a vital service. Supports need to be designed, made, and installed to help the very young child to sit, stand, and eat/drink. Physical therapists also help very young children to balance themselves when seated or standing, as well as how to move despite physical limitations. Toddlers may "ride" oversized balls in order to develop the ability to balance. As these examples suggest, much PT requires special sessions and even special facilities.

The Department's regulations define **occupational therapy** in these words:

> (i) services provided by a qualified occupational therapist; and (ii) includes—(A) improving, developing, or restoring functions impaired or lost through illness, injury, or deprivation; (B) improving ability to perform tasks for independent functioning if functions are impaired or lost; and (C) preventing, through early intervention, initial or further impairment or loss of function. (U.S. Department of Education, 1999a)

As this definition makes clear, OT focuses more upon practical, everyday skills than does PT. While occupational therapists can do many of the things that physical therapists do, occupational therapists tend to concentrate more upon functional abilities. An example is dressing. Some young children have great difficulty buttoning shirts. Occupational therapists know what adaptive devices are available to make this task easier (e.g., hooks) and what bypass methods may be used (e.g., shirts with no buttons). Similarly, occupational therapists can help young children to turn the pages of a book, either independently or with the help of an adaptive device. By contrast, physical therapists tend to focus upon helping young children to maintain the physical abilities they possess and to perform gross-motor activities such as walking or running.

Methods: Enriched Experiences. Parents, other relatives, and friends often overprotect young children with physical disabilities. The child is not allowed to explore in the house, in the yard, and in the community as are other young children. The result is **experiential deprivation.** This is particularly serious with young children because movement is central to learning in the pre-kindergarten years (Bowe, 2004). For this reason, educators should "make an extra effort" to provide opportunities for preschoolers, kindergartners, and primary-grade students with physical disabilities to move around. They should be able to experience "danger" as do other young children. Equally important, they must have opportunities to alter their environment. That is how children learn cause and effect. This is why low- and high-tech products that teach cause and effect are so important (see "Technologies That Work: Orthopedic Impairments"). We will revisit experiential deprivation later in the "Vision Impairment," section, p. 227.

Methods: Alternative Curricula. The chapter-opening "personal account" about Breanna mentioned the MOVE curriculum. This approach is one of several alternative curriculua. Mobility Opportunities Via Education (MOVE) was developed by MOVE International. With students having orthopedic impairments, the MOVE curriculum serves as a way to integrate PT and OT into the academic curriculum. It is woven into everyday activities, rather than being something separate. When used with students having severe or multiple disabilities, the MOVE curriculum may be the core scope and sequence. As we will see in Chapter 8, some such students cannot pursue an academic curriculum.

With many children and youth having orthopedic impairments, as was suggested in the story about Breanna, MOVE taps students' motivations. Thus, rather than consider movement to be something reserved for PT and OT sessions, MOVE regards it as part of the everyday classroom curriculum. Children move when they want to move—so that they can *do* something. Breanna's story illustrated the power of motivation. She resisted special sessions of physical therapy. However, when she wanted to play a game in another room, or visit her grandparents, she was highly motivated to move in order to "get there and get started." A third feature of the MOVE curriculum is that it focuses upon skills and competencies that have real-life value for children and youth. Unless the students will be expected to be able to do something as adults, reasoned the MOVE curriculum developers, why teach it when they are children (Snell and Brown, 2000)?

Methods: Teach Keyboarding. Students with CP and some other orthopedic impairments need to develop keyboarding skills even more than do students with no disabilities. This is because so many assistive technology devices require keyboarding skill. These students can produce much better output on the computer than they could by hand—but only if they learn keyboarding skills, including those needed to use augmentative and alternative communication devices.

Children and youth with CP, quadriplegia, and other physical disabilities may benefit from a keyguard. Keyguards are plastic coverings that fit over the keyboard. There are cut holes in the plastic above each key. The main function of a keyguard is to prevent the student from striking the wrong key(s). Typing with a keyguard is slower than typing without one, but the increased accuracy made possible by the keyguard more than makes up for that slowness. Another function of keyguards is to offer a resting place for the hands. Keyguards can be costly (as much as $150).

For more information on sources that provide keyguards, go to the Web Links module in Chapter 6 of the Companion Website.

They can also key with a mouthstick, head wand, or other alternative input device. Professionals need to identify one muscle that the individual can reliably control. This may even be an eyebrow. With the advent of powerful speech recognition software, the person may only need to be able to speak in a consistent manner. Twenty years ago, computer software that "hears" cost between $5,000 and $20,000. Today, much better programs retail for about $100. An occupational therapist or physical therapist can evaluate the individual's abilities to see what kind of product is most useful.

For more information on assistive technologies, go to the Web Links module in Chapter 6 of the Companion Website.

Instruction in keyboarding often begins in the primary grades (up to and including third grade; Tompkins, 2002). Frequently, it happens, as well, at home, usually on an informal basis. The days when keyboarding was taught for the first time during high-school typing classes are long gone! Computer software is widely available and inexpensive. Highly animated, game-like programs are used with younger children. By the time students reach middle school, they should be accomplished typists. Such programs as "Mavis Beacon Teaches Typing" can be used at this level.

At all levels, students should be taught techniques for reducing fatigue and preventing injury (e.g., carpal tunnel syndrome). These techniques should become habit over time. They include sitting up straight, facing the keyboard and the screen, with feet flat on the floor. Breaks every 15 or 20 minutes are important. Typists should stand up, stretch, walk around, and in general do things very different than typing. After a short period (perhaps 2 minutes), they may return to keyboarding again.

Methods: Accommodations. Students with orthopedic impairments may benefit from having an extra set of textbooks for use at home (to avoid the need to carry those books, as in a backpack on a wheelchair), additional room around the desk in the classroom (to place crutches or other devices and/or to allow turn-around space for maneuvering a wheelchair), extra rest time, and the like. Children with CP may benefit from help from fellow students, who take notes in class, turn pages of a text, and so on. Decisions about these accommodations should be made by the IEP team. If no mention is made in the IEP of such adjustments, and you believe they are needed, you should alert the IEP team.

An important set of accommodations for students with CP and some other orthopedic impairments, notably muscular dystrophy, is **positioning.** The term refers both to what teachers and therapists do to help the child to sit, so that the body is supported and so the student can perform school tasks such as writing, and to the products that assist the child to maintain proper positioning. Children and youth may need specially designed wheelchairs to support their posture, help them stay alert, and enable them to eat, swallow, and speak. This is much more than simply picking the right wheelchair. Custom-made adaptations often are required. These may be available at a nearby UCP or Easter Seals program. The first step is for a physical and/or occupational therapist to conduct an evaluation of the child's posture and positioning needs. The second is for a "shop" to create the needed supports. Many UCP and Easter Seals programs have customizing facilities on-site or under contract.

For more information on UCP and Easter Seals programs near you, go to the Web Links module in Chapter 6 of the Companion Website.

The kinds of accommodations that a child or youth with TBI may require vary greatly. In many cases, the first year post-injury features heightened sensitivity to sights and sounds. Some people report that they "can't stand" to be in a restaurant or other gathering place because they are unable to screen out the many environmental noises they hear in such settings and the many visual stimuli competing for their attention. This need to build up the ability to attenuate environmental stimuli is one reason that return to the school building is sometimes postponed until at least one year after the injury occurs. While the student remains at home or in a rehabilitation facility, therapists will gradually increase exposure to lights and noises so that the individual can adjust to them. In other cases, young people need to re-learn problem-solving skills (Kendall, Shum, Halson, Bunning, & The, 1997). For these reasons, accommodations for students having recent TBI should be reviewed at least every six months, to reflect the fact that their needs likely will change (Mt. Sinai School of Medicine, 2003, *http://www.mssm.edu/tbinet*). While the law requires IEPs to be reviewed at least annually, in this case twice-yearly reviews make more sense, at least until the condition stabilizes.

Methods: Pull-Out and Push-In Services. CP is probably the disability most likely to require a range of related services. Early childhood or elementary students with CP receive speech pathology, occupational therapy, physical therapy, and special transportation services. They, as well as many with other physical disorders, often are *pulled out* for related services. Pull-out services can be, and often are, disruptive both for the student and for the teacher. For this reason, many experts recommend an alternative service pattern, called "push-in" (Barnes, Schoenfeld, & Pierson, 1997; Bowe, 2000b). The difference is a central

Technology That Works

Orthopedic Impairments

Some students with orthopedic impairments, notably many with CP or quadriplegia (a form of SCI) benefit from technologies in the use of computers. The major applications are speech synthesis, speech recognition, and combinations of the two.

In all instances, it is vital for teachers of inclusive classrooms to take steps to prevent **technology abandonment.** Children may abandon technologies for several reasons. First, they may resist products they did not have a role in choosing. This is particularly the case with respect to speech synthesis programs or products intended to serve as the child's "voice"—because few things are more personal than one's voice. Second, students may stop using a product that they find difficult or cumbersome to operate. Third, they may turn away from a product because it is not quickly repaired. All of those problems are avoidable. Children and youth, as well as family members, should be consulted, in advance, about technology purchases. Many software programs are available on the Web, frequently with a 30-day trial period. Teachers should select that option so that the student can "play with" the program before it is purchased. Educators also need to determine, prior to acquiring a product, who will repair it, how rapidly, and how well.

Another option is to visit a nearby center that displays and demonstrates assistive technologies. A nationwide network of such centers is operated by the Alliance for Technology Access. The mission of ATA is to bring assistive technologies to children and families. The Alliance consists of 40 not-for-profit technology resource centers located around the country. The centers also have lending libraries through which children, youth, and families may "try it out" before purchasing a product. Most centers have paid staff members who are themselves individuals with disabilities, as well as other staff who are family members of persons with disabilities. Many United Cerebral Palsy Associations local affiliates also have assistive technology centers. Finally, Lekotek specializes in toys. There are many Lekotek-affiliated centers around the nation.

For information on tools and software applications for speech synthesis, speech recognition, and communicators refer back to the "Technology That Works" boxes in Chapters 3 and 4.

Wheelchairs and Other Mobility and Support Equipment

A remarkable variety of wheelchairs is now available commercially. These range from standard chairs intended for use indoors to lightweight sports chairs designed for recreational and outdoor use. The chairs may also be customized. Many children and youth with CP or MD need such adaptations because their bodies need to be supported while they are in the chair. MOVE International and its affiliated manufacturer offer many kinds of "standers," or devices that support a student who is upright. Some standers come equipped with very large wheels while others have small ones. Selection of appropriate equipment for a child or youth thus is much more complex a task than it was just a few years ago. An occupational or physical therapist needs to conduct a thorough evaluation, not only of the child's specific physical needs but also of what the child is expected to be doing at the school.

Artificial Limbs

With respect to amputation, today's bionic limbs provide remarkably life-like capabilities. Some might actually function better than the original ones (e.g., Savage, 2001). Perhaps the best-known of companies selling artificial limbs is Motion Control, distributors of the Utah Arm. In addition to this myoelectric above-elbow prosthesis, the company offers the Procontrol 2 for people with below-elbow amputations. Otto Bock Health Care distributes a wide variety of prosthetic hands.

For more information on the organizations, companies, and distributors discussed in the "Technologies That Work" box, go to the Web Links module in Chapter 6 of the Companion Website.

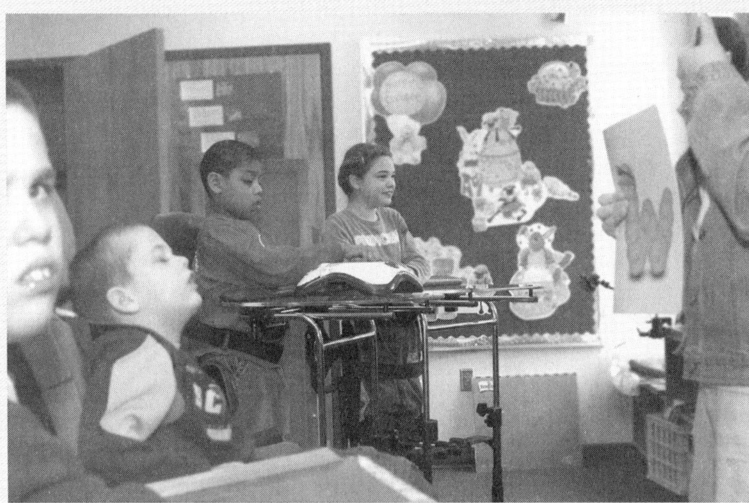

Mobility aids and other assistive technologies are critical to the successful inclusion of students with physical disabilities into general classrooms.

FIGURE 6.5 Pull-Out and Push-In

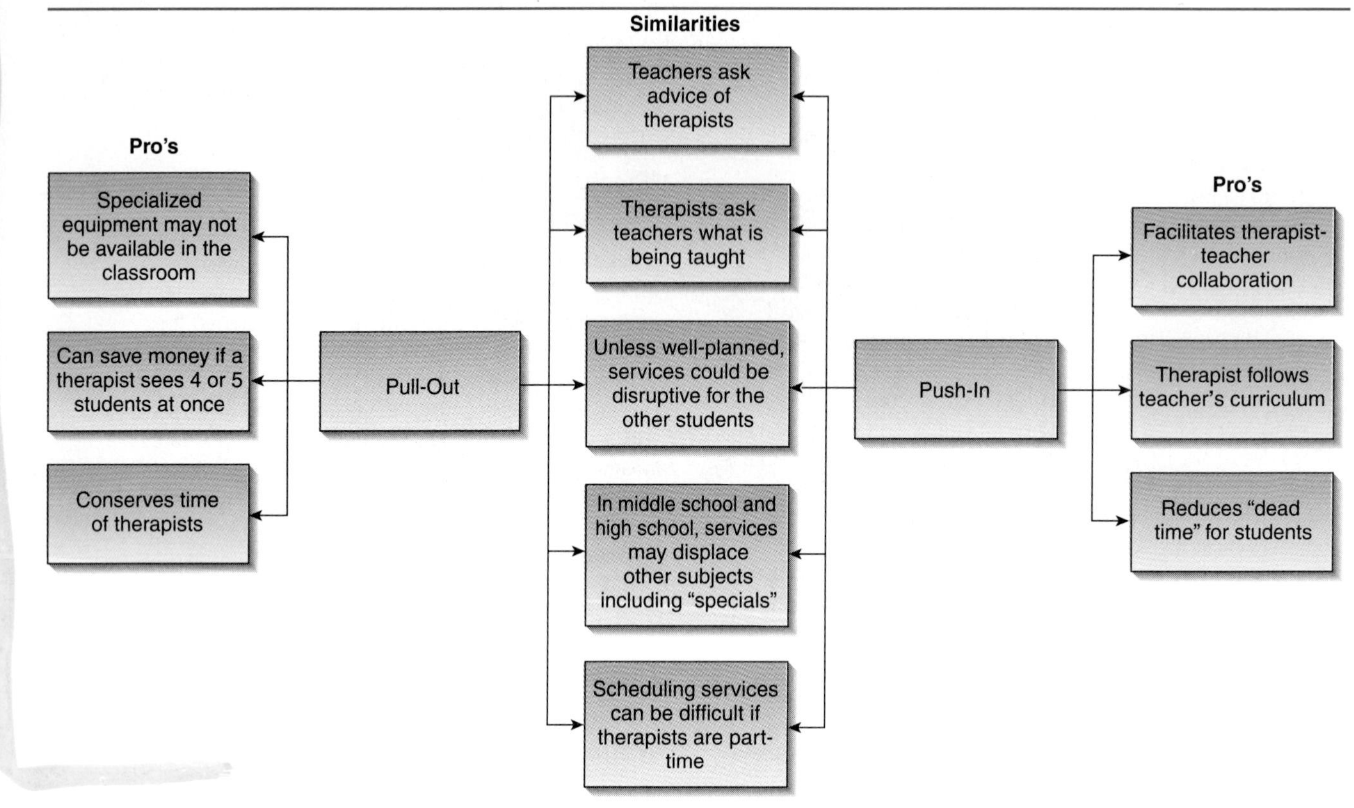

one. In push-in, the related-services professional comes to the child, in the classroom, and provides the services there. Pull-out, by contrast, has the child travel to the therapist's office or special-purpose room. Figure 6.5 compares push-in and pull-out.

Push-in services have several advantages over pull-out services. First, they promote collaboration between teachers and therapists. When speech pathologists, occupational therapists, orientation and mobility specialists, and physical therapists come to the classroom, they enter an environment the teacher has designed for instructional purposes. This has several effects, all good. Push-in naturally encourages related-services personnel to fashion their offerings in conjunction with the teacher's lessons. That is, the sounds and words the speech pathologist teaches can be selected from the classroom teacher's current lessons. Occupational and physical therapists can design physical activities that build upon what the class already is doing. For example, the therapists could lead the child in "acting out" a story that the teacher recently read to the class. Similarly, the related-services personnel can train the teacher to follow-up on what is done during therapy. For example, a speech pathologist might scribble a note to the teacher about a child with CP who is having difficulty enunciating words: "Tell him to take a deep breath and stop any other activity before allowing him to speak up in class."

Other advantages of push-in have to do with time. Push-in reduces the wasted time of pull-out (the time when the child physically leaves the classroom, travels to the therapy area, and then returns). In addition, push-in all but eliminates "transition time"—as any experienced teacher knows, the "dead time" between the end of one activity and the beginning of the next is problematic, because it tempts children to "act out." In sum, push-in minimizes time out of the classroom. Children who need considerable related services, as do many discussed in this chapter, suffer greatly if they are continually being taken out of the classroom.

On the other hand, push-in can be more costly for schools than pull-out. If a physical therapist can serve four or five students at one time in a pull-out session, but just one

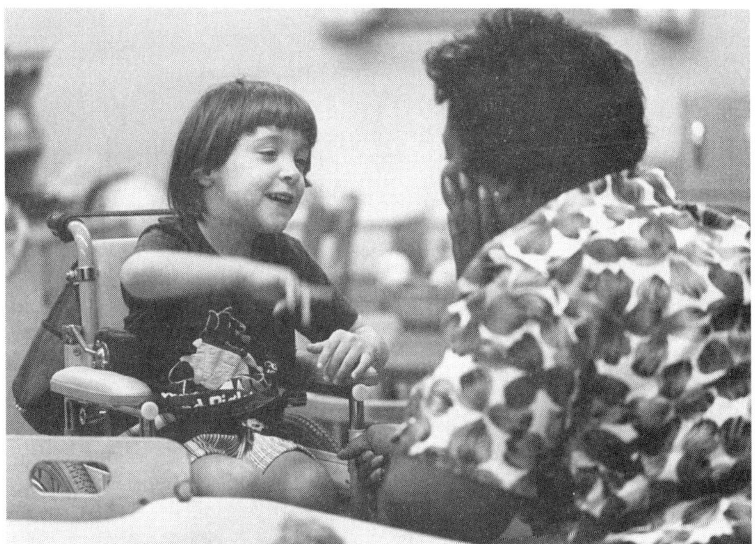

Sign language often can supplement speech to enable children and youth with cerebral palsy to communicate effectively.

at a time by pushing in to an inclusive classroom, it may be more cost-effective for the school to adopt a pull-out model. The pull-out/push-in discussion is important. We will continue to address it under "Strategies in Middle School and High School."

RONAN: A TRUE STORY ABOUT AMPUTATION

The world-famous Irish tenor Ronan Tynan stands on two prosthetic legs after amputation in 1980. Ronan had been born, in Kilkenny, Ireland, 20 years earlier, with a condition that caused his fibulas, the bones that support the body between the knees and the ankle, to be misformed. From the time he first began to walk, Ronan needed braces and other supports on his legs. Even with those aids, he sometimes had temporary paralysis, and even blindness, from the pressure placed on his nerves. He also lived with constant headaches and severe back pain. At age 20, a motorcycle accident forced amputation of both legs.

After the operation, he felt much better, so much so that he attended national and international sporting events for people with disabilities, including the Olympics in New York and Seoul, South Korea. He won 18 gold medals and set 14 world records for athletes with disabilities. Later, in 1994, he completed medical school. Ronan set up a practice in sports medicine in his native Kilkenny. Then, in 1999, he joined Anthony Kearns and John McDermott at a Dublin concert. Billed as the "Three Irish Tenors," they enjoyed immediate success. Today, having given his medical practice to two other doctors, Ronan tours the world, performing for audiences that may not even know that his legs are not his. (Schleier, 2000)

For more information on Ronan Tynan, go to the Web Links module in Chapter 6 of the Companion Website.

Strategies in Middle School and High School

Among students aged 12 to 17 inclusive who were served under IDEA during the 2002–2003 school year, 32,700 were classified as having orthopedic impairments and 11,500 as having a TBI. Those with orthopedic impairments were placed in regular classrooms (43%), combination regular and resource rooms (25%), and separate classrooms (27%). Among those with a TBI, the percentages, respectively, were 29%, 35%, and 27% (U.S. Department of Education, 2004, Tables AA5 and AB4).

Methods: Collaboration with Related-Services Personnel. Collaboration with occupational and physical therapists, as well as with speech-language pathologists, is as important at this level as it is in early childhood and elementary programs. Regardless

Student Strategies That Work

Improving Public Attitudes

CP, spina bifida, SCI, and MD are immediately visible, CP even more than the others because of limb movements. Other physical disabilities are only occasionally visible. Leg amputations may be hidden by pants, socks, and shoes. Research shows that public attitudes toward disability are inversely correlated with visibility: The more visible the condition, the more negative are public attitudes (Yuker, 1994). For this reason, students with visible conditions need to learn to deal with those attitudes. A TBI, by contrast, generally is not visible, but manifests itself through personality and behavior changes over time. Many health disabilities, from cancer to cardiac conditions to epilepsy, are noticeable only sporadically (during an attack). Blindness and visual impairments are quite visible. However, in the case of people who are blind or have low vision, another factor identified by Yuker as powerfully influencing attitudes comes into play: information, including prior contact. Most Americans feel that they "understand" blindness (from having to move around in a room when the lights are out and from seeing people who are blind or from watching TV programs and movies about them). Yuker's research therefore places disabilities on a spectrum with respect to public attitudes. Most favorably viewed is blindness and visual impairment, followed by conditions that are largely invisible but about which most Americans have some knowledge (asthma, cardiac conditions). Least favorably seen are highly visible disorders about which the general public lacks knowledge (notably CP) and conditions that are often fatal and thus frightening (cancer, AIDS).

Wherever along this spectrum a student's disability stands, children and youth need to learn strategies for dealing with members of the general public. Those persons are or will be their bosses and co-workers, neighbors, bankers, shopkeepers, and even prospective spouses. What does the research of Yuker and others who specialized in studying attitudes toward disability have to offer to these students?

First, information and contact help. The more visible the student is, and the more he finds ways to inform peers and adults about himself, the more comfortable people will be. By being "out and about" in the school and in the community, the student will raise the general level of awareness both about himself and about his needs. Yuker's studies show that when members of the general public feel competent about what to do in the presence of someone with a disability, public attitudes become more positive. A key, then, is for the student to make known what help, if any, the student needs and desires. This information assists people in understanding what they should do and thus increases their comfort level. Yuker reported that when students with disabilities are successful in school, attitudes toward them improve. This makes sense: People tend to admire achievers, particularly if they are known to have overcome some obstacle.

Positive attitudes toward oneself increase the likelihood of positive attitudes on the part of others. A sense of humor, too, helps a great deal. By demonstrating that he can laugh at problems, the student helps people feel at ease. By the same token, a sense of anger can put off members of the general public. People become upset when confronted with rage, especially if they feel "I was only trying to help," and if they cannot understand the reason for that rage.

Teachers have a major role to play in helping to improve attitudes toward disability in public schools. After talking with the students most affected, educators should provide factual information about disabilities. They should set the example by showing tolerance and by offering assistance when requested. Teachers must also enforce a "no harassment" policy in the classroom and in the school. The U.S. Department of Education has made clear (Cantu & Heumann, 2000) that harassment on the basis of disability is just as unacceptable as is harassment on any other basis (sex, race, ethnicity, religion, etc.).

of whether related services are push-in or pull-out, teachers should work closely with related-services personnel, in a collaborative fashion that reflects mutual understanding and respect. The urgency of cross-disciplinary collaboration has been highlighted by recent surveys. One, which queried PreK–12 school administrators, university personnel-preparation professors, and special educators found concern in all three groups that certified special educators were not prepared to meet some of the major needs of children and youth with physical disabilities (Heller, Fredrick, Dykes, Best, & Cohen, 1999). Specifically, weaknesses were identified in the areas of assistive technologies and of teaching reading to non-vocal students. The implications are serious for general educators, who have even less pre-service training in these areas. The expertise of physical and occupational therapists is required to meet those needs if teachers cannot.

What used to be called "speech pathology" is now known as "speech-language pathology" to reflect greater emphasis upon language development. The federal rules define **speech-language pathology** services in these words:

(i) Identification of children with speech or language impairments; (ii) diagnosis and appraisal of specific speech or language impairments; (iii) referral for medical or other professional attention necessary for the habilitation of speech or language impairments; (iv) provision of speech and language services for the habilitation or prevention of communicative impairments; and (v) counseling and guidance of parents, children, and teachers regarding speech and language impairments. (U.S. Department of Education, 1999)

Speech-language pathologists work on (1) speech, (2) language, and (3) eating and swallowing. In the latter efforts, they take steps much like those performed by occupational therapists. Pathologists may also recommend assistive technology devices.

Methods: Adapted Physical Education. IDEA specifically notes that the term "special education" includes adapted physical education. For now, notice that specialists in this field are few and far between. At the secondary level, students are served by physical education teachers. Many students with orthopedic impairments need accommodations in such classes. Physical educators may need to call upon occupational and physical therapists if adapted physical educators cannot be located in the local area. In early childhood and elementary school, inclusive classroom teachers typically instruct the class for physical education. The help of occupational and physical therapists is essential in that connection.

Many people with SCI or amputation are physically active. This may be because they had led an active life prior to the injury. It may also be what psychologists call overcompensation. As you read the vignette about the singer Ronan Tynan ("Ronan: A True Story about Amputation"), notice that he was active physically even before his legs were amputated (in, characteristically, a motorcycle accident) and that he continued to be afterwards (even choosing, as his medical specialty, sports medicine). Another amputee, Tim Whittaker, climbed Mt. Everest. His occupation was physical education teacher. The importance of these decisions, for educators, is self-evident. First, the desire to engage in sports can be highly motivating for these students, creating "teachable moments." Second, post-injury adjustment may be difficult. These young people have defined themselves largely in terms of their physical capabilities. Unless they can recover those abilities, at least in part, they may feel deprived of their "former selves." This heightens the importance of sports wheelchairs, bionic limbs, and other state-of-the-art technologies for these adolescents.

Resources That Work

Readings and Videos About Physical Disabilities

Sometimes, teachers of inclusive classrooms can facilitate the acceptance by peers of a student with a physical disability by assigning disability-related readings or screening a video about orthopedic impairments. Here are a few recommendations:

Younger Students

Rebecca Finds a New Way: How Kids Learn, Play, and Live with Spinal Cord Injuries and Illnesses, by Connie Panzarino and Marilyn Lash, 1995, DUNE Publishing, Bethesda, MD: National Spinal Cord Injury Association (6701 Democracy Blvd, #300-9, Bethesda, MD 20817).

Speedway Sam: A Book About Spinal Cord Injury for Children, University of Alabama at Birmingham, Spain Rehabilitation Center (1717 6th Avenue South, Birmingham, AL 35233).

Older Students

Still Me, by Christopher Reeve, 1998, New York: Random House. This autobiography of Christopher Reeve may engage the interest of teens who have seen him in *Superman* movies. Reeve's story includes a rare look into how people with quadriplegia (a form of SCI) do everyday tasks. The actor and director recently continued the story with a 2002 update, also from Random House, *Nothing is Impossible: Reflections on a New Life.*

You're Not Alone, 3rd ed., 2002, Oklahoma City: Scott Sabolich Prosthetic & Research Center (9801 N. Broadway Extension, Oklahoma City, OK; http://www.scottsabolich.com). The 3rd edition of this book profiles 38 amputees.

Nancy's Special Workout, by Nancy Sebring, Camarillo, CA: n.d., Avenues Unlimited Inc. (1199 K Avenida Acaso, Camarillo, CA 93012). Video by occupational therapist Nancy Sebring, for children and adults who use wheelchairs.

Methods: Push-In and Pull-Out. Despite the advantages of push-in that were discussed in the section "Strategies for Early Childhood and Elementary School," the practice of pull-out continues, largely because of administrative convenience. This is particularly true at the secondary level. When children who need these services are included in various classrooms, it is easier for the therapist to collect them in a separate room and serve them there, together. Principals and other administrators may prefer pull-out because it is less costly for a therapist to work with four or five students at once than it is for the therapist to help each child sequentially. Many of these therapists are consultants or independent contractors who come to the school periodically. This makes teacher-therapist collaboration difficult.

The issue of push-in versus pull-out is more complex at the secondary level than it is at the early childhood/elementary level. This is because of the schedule. Rather than having one day-long class with one teacher, high-school students attend as many as 10 class periods, each with its own instructor. Accordingly, related services may well consume the entire period of some subject. In many schools, the practice is to schedule related-services sessions in lieu of "specials" such as music or art. Full-period substitution is unfortunate for several reasons. First, it all but eliminates contact between subject-matter teachers (of English, math, science, music, etc.) and related-services personnel, thus depriving both sets of professionals of the benefits of collaboration. High-school teachers are much less likely than are elementary teachers to learn new and helpful techniques from therapists. Second, students with physical or health impairments are as much in need of the enrichment that music, art, and other "specials" can offer as are other students.

Methods: Building Accessibility. Another issue that is more pressing at the secondary than at the early childhood/elementary level is that of building accessibility. PreK–6 students tend to spend nearly all of the school day in one room, venturing only occasionally to other rooms (e.g., cafeteria, rest rooms, gym). At the secondary level, however, students are in different rooms virtually every hour of the school day. This makes the physical accessibility of the school building more of a concern. Federal law on the issue of physical accessibility of public schools is not very helpful. It requires public schools to make an appropriate education available to students with mobility needs, but does not require that neighborhood school buildings be accessible to those students. (Only new construction, including renovations, is required to be barrier-free.) Many school districts refer children with mobility needs to out-of-district settings rather than make accessibility renovations. Year after year, these schools postpone spending on building accessibility modifications, preferring to incur the transportation and other costs involved in out-of-district placements. It is actually more sensible, and in the long run less costly, to make the neighborhood school building accessible and to keep the student there. In addition, once the building is accessible, future students with mobility limitations may be kept in that school, saving the district money (Bowe, 2000b).

Methods: Flexibility in Scheduling. Middle-school and high-school students move from room to room throughout the school day. It may require much more time for a young person with CP or MD to make those trips. A good adjustment is to excuse the student several minutes before the end of any class period. This not only offers the required additional travel time, but it also enables the student to move without having to navigate through many hundreds of ambulatory students in the hallways.

Methods: Test Accommodations. Middle-school and high-school students with orthopedic impairments and some with a recent TBI may require accommodations in assessments. There are many options. These include additional time to take a test, a scribe to write answers, a separate test room to permit the student to use a PC to write answers without distracting other students, and (particularly for MD), frequent breaks in lengthy test sessions.

Strategies in Transition to Adult Life

Students with orthopedic impairments and those with TBIs may need considerable support in planning the transition from high school to life beyond high school. In particular, locating accessible and affordable housing can be a challenge. That is because very few single-family houses, and few apartment or condominium buildings, are accessible to people using wheelchairs. It is also because there is a chronic shortage in most parts of the country of affordable housing. It has been estimated that as few as 1% to 2% of private homes are wheelchair-accessible. Among buildings that have apartments and condominiums, only those constructed for first occupancy after March 13, 1991, are required by federal law to be accessible for persons using wheelchairs. Renters and buyers must pay for changes required in older buildings (Bowe, 2000b). For all of these reasons, families and teens may need to plan far ahead for housing alternatives.

Methods: Independent Living. The major concern with respect to adulthood, for people with physical disabilities, is the creation of an independent life (Bowe, 2000b; Turnbull, Turnbull, Shank, Smith, & Leal, 2002). Much thinking and planning is required before people with serious physical conditions can run their lives effectively. Transit routes must be identified to the workplace, community stores, and places of recreation. In many instances, continued medical care must be arranged. People with SCI, for example, sometimes need immediate attention from highly trained caregivers to prevent or ameliorate pressure sores and such other concerns as autonomic dysreflexia (a bladder distension). Secondary teachers need to include such matters in the IEPs of high-school students with physical conditions.

Methods: Support for Transition to Postsecondary Education. The proportion of students with physical disabilities who continue on to postsecondary education is higher than is that for students with disabilities in general (e.g., Valdes, Williamson, & Wagner, 1990). In fact, it is among the highest, although students who are blind or have low vision attend college at a higher rate. The fact that most students with orthopedic impairments have few difficulties learning academic material means that if their mobility and living needs are met, they can be successful at the postsecondary level. A key is planning so as to identify accessible housing, find lift-equipped bus transportation, and meet other mobility-related needs on campus.

For more information on adapting motor vehicles for persons with physical disabilities, as offered by the U.S. Department of Transportation, go to the Web Links module in Chapter 6 of the Companion Website.

For many college students and workers who have physical disabilities, a car or van is essential for transportation. All three American automobile companies run programs on accessible driving. Ford, for example, has a "Mobility Motoring Program" that features loans for converting vans and cars ("Mobility Financing"), roadside assistance, and referrals to companies specializing in van and car conversions.

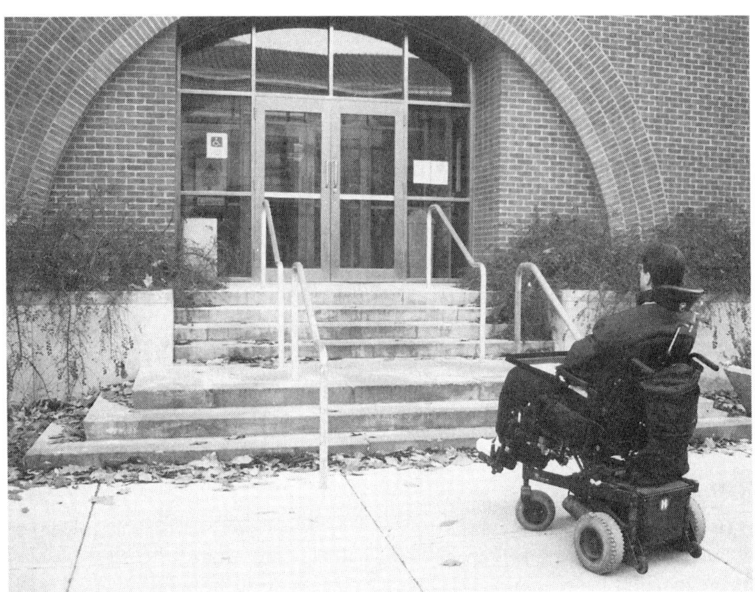

Across the United States, surprising numbers of elementary, middle school, and high school buildings are not physically accessible.

OTHER HEALTH IMPAIRMENTS

The IDEA category of "Other Health Impaired" (OHI) includes a wide variety of health conditions. The category is dominated, however, by ADHD—Attention Deficit Disorders and Attention Deficit Hyperactivity Disorders. Those disabilities were discussed in Chapter 3. Our focus here is upon non-ADHD health conditions.

Section 504 is important for students having health impairments, in large part because many health conditions have only mild or moderate effects on learning. Epilepsy, for example, generally is controlled by medication. Persons who test positive for the Human Immunodeficiency Virus (HIV) usually have no symptoms and, thus, learn in the same ways and at the same pace as do others. Children who have AIDS, however, often do display symptoms. About two-thirds of people with AIDS can benefit from the new "cocktail" of drugs, to the extent that their major symptoms disappear while they remain on the drug regimen. The others, however, suffer increasingly debilitating effects of this chronic health condition (Bowe, 2000b). One sad characteristic of children who are HIV-positive or have AIDS is that virtually all of them have mothers who themselves have AIDS. This means that AIDS is a family tragedy, with tremendous implications not only for the child but for the family itself. The mothers (who, statistically speaking, are often single) need considerable support and understanding. The child may well need a great deal of counseling and other help to cope with the mother's deteriorating health and, then, her death (Bowe, 2004).

Definition

The regulations define OHI as

> having limited strength, vitality, or alertness, including a heightened alertness to environmental stimuli, that results in limited alertness with respect to the educational environment, that—(i) is due to chronic or acute health problems such as asthma, attention deficit disorder or attention deficit hyperactivity disorder, diabetes, epilepsy, a heart condition, hemophilia, lead poisoning, leukemia, nephritis, rheumatic fever, and sickle cell anemia; and (ii) adversely affects a child's educational performance. (34 C.F.R. 300[c][9])

Problems with This Definition

Some of this is familiar from the discussion of ADHD in Chapter 3, notably the wording about "heightened alertness to environmental stimuli." The OHI classification is commonly used when children need both special education and related services because of such health conditions as AIDS, epilepsy, or asthma.

Characteristics and Types

Health impairments range from chronic conditions that have minor or sporadic effects on learning to some which have catastrophic effects. Asthma, diabetes, and epilepsy generally do not necessitate special education services. That is generally true of many OHI conditions. Health impairments that have very significant effects on education may be placed in the "multiple disabilities" category that is discussed in the following chapter. This has the effect of reserving the OHI category for conditions that are mild or moderate in nature.

Information about health conditions is widely available. Bowe (2000b), for example, summarizes what is known about many health impairments and reviews how those affect education. This text will provide brief synopses of the more common conditions only.

Characteristics

Children and youth with health impairments tend to miss school periodically, usually because of a flare-up in the condition and sometimes because of hospitalization. Many must take medication. Educators need to work with school nursing personnel and with family members to monitor medication (e.g., to alert the family if the child seems to be drowsy or seems not to be taking the required medication). In most other respects, however, teaching students with health impairments is not qualitatively different from teaching other children. Most students in this category do not require specially adapted instruction.

Types

For more information on the American Lung Association, go to the Web Links module in Chapter 6 of the Companion Website.

Asthma is a common disorder in children and youth, so common in fact that most teachers will have one or two students with asthma or an asthma-like condition in their classes. Asthma, according to the American Lung Association, is a reversible obstructive airway disease. The word "reversible" is important, suggesting that if triggers (environmental factors that set off a reaction, such as dust) are removed, the condition will improve. Children with asthma frequently have allergies, as well. Asthma has several effects on education. Absenteeism is one. If a child has an asthma attack, she may be absent from school for several days. Moving from class to class may be another. Severe asthma can make walking a few hundred feet as exhausting as running a mile may be for children who do not have the condition. Sensitivity to environmental pollutants is a third. Educators may need to check the environmental quality both inside the school and in the playground to be sure that factors which trigger asthma attacks are not present.

Diabetes is a chronic health condition that is of growing importance in PreK–12 schools. This is because ever-larger numbers of children and youth are obese. Type 2 diabetes (once known as "adult-onset diabetes" because it was known to occur to people in their 40s or 50s) is now occurring in children and adolescents. Fast foods are often blamed for this phenomenon. The much less-common Type 1 diabetes continues to strike children. A very different disorder, it is not connected to diet. Insulin injections are needed several times daily to control Type 1 diabetes. People with either kind of diabetes must eat at regular intervals and must follow doctor instructions about medication. Properly controlled, diabetes need not limit students in school. However, the long-term effects of diabetes, if not controlled, are very serious. Diabetes is the number-one cause of blindness in the United States. Adults with diabetes are more than twice as likely to have heart attacks as are other adults. Diabetes is a leading cause of amputations, particularly of a leg (American Diabetes Association, *http://www.diabetes.org*). For all of these reasons, diabetes is a "ticking time bomb" that should be taken seriously in children and youth.

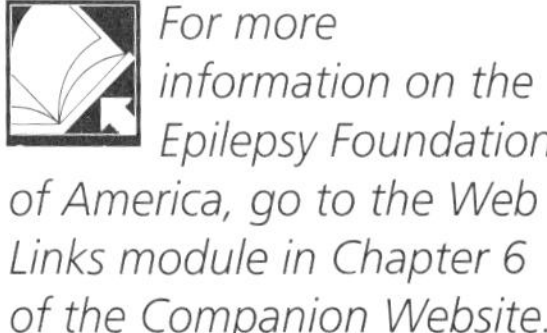

For more information on the Epilepsy Foundation of America, go to the Web Links module in Chapter 6 of the Companion Website.

Epilepsy is the word used to describe a variety of conditions that produce electrical discharges in the brain ("seizures"). While some children have a very occasional seizure, perhaps because of a TBI, the term "epilepsy" is reserved for instances in which seizures are frequent. Absence seizures (once called "petite mal seizures") are brief interludes during which the student is unaware of his surroundings. These commonly are over within seconds. Tonic-clonic seizures (previously known as "grand mal seizures") are more familiar. They can cause a person to fall, thrash on the floor, and lose consciousness. Most epilepsy today can be controlled with medication. Many people with epilepsy will go months or even years without any seizures. For this reason, PreK–12 students with epilepsy are more often "504 kids" than "children with disabilities" under IDEA. Their main need, other than medication, is to be protected against discrimination from peers and adults who fear the condition, because they do not understand it. The Epilepsy Foundation of America is an impressive resource.

AIDS is relatively uncommon in American children and youth. More, but still rather few, are *HIV+*. The key difference between the two: people with AIDS have symptoms, while those who are HIV+ do not. The designation HIV+ is given if someone "tests positive," which means that the antibodies the body produces to fight the HIV virus are detected. Accordingly, students with AIDS often meet the requirements of IDEA, because the condition has effects on their education. Those who are HIV+, however, do not require special education nor related services so are not eligible for IDEA. They do meet the requirements of section 504. Perhaps the biggest issue for children and youth who have AIDS or are HIV+ is discrimination on the basis of disability. They may be shunned, harassed and excluded from activities by children and adults who fear the condition but do not understand it. That is why section 504 is particularly crucial for these students: It bars discrimination against them on the basis of their conditions.

Cancer, including leukemia, is relatively rare among PreK–12 children. By one estimate, it occurs in one child per 600 (Stiller, 1992). That would produce a prevalence among school-age children of approximately 15,000. To place the number into context, it is about the same as that for TBI, the least-common of all the IDEA categories. Cancer can be fatal. It can also be treated. The effects vary by type of cancer, by how rapidly it is diagnosed, by how quickly and thoroughly it is treated, and by other factors as well.

Cardiac conditions are uncommon among school-age children and youth. It is one element of Down Syndrome (discussed in Chapter 5). Students with heart conditions need to take prescribed medication. They may also be excused from vigorous exercise (e.g., some physical education activities). On occasion, the disability necessitates absence from school, typically for treatment but sometimes for hospitalization.

Sickle-cell disease (including sickle-cell anemia) is a blood disorder that primarily affects African Americans. Sickle-cell disease is rare, affecting one per 400 African-American children and youth. It has serious effects, however. The most common is chronic pain. Another is periodic and often-lengthy absenteeism, following "episodes" or attacks (Nuland, 1997). During those episodes, people with sickle-cell disease often require heavy doses of pain killers. For this reason, teachers should not expect children and youth to be able to study while in a hospital. Rather, it makes more sense to schedule make-up sessions and make other arrangements following the student's release from the hospital.

Multiple sclerosis (MS) has wide-ranging effects, from a general lack of energy (lethargy) to numbness and nerve tingling ("pins and needles" sensations) to blindness. It is one of the more common disabilities among adults, at 350,000 nationwide. MS affects relatively few (about 15,000) children and youth. Doctors once suspected that stress causes MS.

Commonalities. Students may require related services and they may need flexibility in scheduling of activities, but they tend not to need specially modified instruction as a result of health impairments. The major exception is when health conditions force lengthy absenteeism.

Differences. The disorders in this category are more different than similar. Some health disabilities are potentially life-threatening (AIDS, some cancers, sickle-cell disease). Others are not. Some are more likely to be severe during adulthood than during the PreK–12 years (diabetes, MS).

Co-Morbidity. Students who have ADHD sometimes have seizures, as do some with TBI. As noted, children and youth with Down Syndrome commonly have cardiac conditions. We also mentioned that uncontrolled diabetes may lead to blindness, leg amputations, and cardiac conditions.

Prevalence

According to the *26th Annual Report* (U.S. Department of Education, 2004, Table AA3), students with OHI numbered 392,000 during the 2002–2003 school year. However, as noted earlier, many with the OHI label have ADHD. The data in the *Annual Reports* do not permit us to know how many students have which conditions, so we cannot say how many have impairments other than ADHD. What we do know is that ADHD has been increasing rapidly (up 16% between 1999–2000 and 2000–2001 alone). No other disorder in the OHI category is growing that rapidly. Whatever the number of students with non-ADHD health conditions, they tend to be educated in inclusive environments (Figure 6.6).

Just 200 American newborns were HIV+ or had AIDS in 2001. That was down from 4,000 in 1994. We can thank vigorous treatment for infected pregnant women and vigilant

FIGURE 6.6 Likelihood of Inclusive Placements: Other Health Impairments

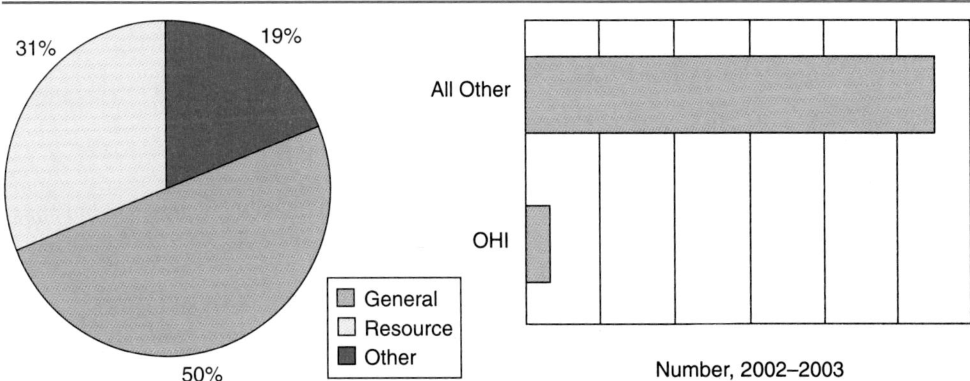

Students identified with the "other health impairments" label are fairly large in number at 338,000 out of 5,946,000 reported for the 2002–2003 school year (*26th Annual Report*). They also tend to be placed into inclusive environments. The *Annual Report* show that 50% were in general classrooms all or almost all of the school week (spending less than 21% of their time in other environments).

Source: From the *26th Annual Report,* by the U.S. Department of Education, 2004, Washington, DC: Author.

observation of "universal precautions" in schools, hospitals, and other programs for this remarkable progress against a deadly virus (Centers for Disease Control & Prevention, 2004, *http://www.cdc.gov*).

Diagnosis and Assessment

Most health conditions are physician-diagnosed. There is little for the IEP team to question or debate in the face of a doctor's report on epilepsy, asthma, or OHIs. Assessment, which is the process of determining eligibility under IDEA, is another matter. Many students with health conditions do not require special education. For this reason, many children and youth with health conditions are "504 kids." Notably with respect to health conditions, section 504 is a non-discrimination provision. It bars discrimination on the basis of disability. A child who has an occasional seizure may not, for that reason alone, be harassed, denied permission to participate in a sport or in an extracurricular activity, or placed into a separate classroom.

Causes

Each health impairment has several possible causes. Typically, there is a genetic predisposition that renders some individuals more susceptible than others to developing a disorder. Experts do not always know what environmental factors trigger that susceptibility. In many instances, "unknown" remains a prominent cause.

Genetic Factors

Sickle-cell disease clearly has genetic origins. It is caused by a recessive gene. Some cancers are known to be genetic, in that they are familial or hereditary (Quesnel & Malkin, 1997). There may be genetic predispositions for asthma, cardiac conditions, and diabetes. Most health impairments, however, seem to have environmental rather than genetic causes. MS is an example.

Environmental Factors

Epilepsy can be caused by the same accidents that cause TBI and SCI; it is a frequent secondary condition to both. Other cases of epilepsy, as with most conditions in these categories, occur prior to, at, or immediately after birth. Many have no known causes (Epilepsy Foundation of America, *http://www.efa.org*). When children are HIV+ or have AIDS, it is virtually always because of maternal-fetal transmission. Thus, while it is inborn, it is not genetic in origin.

Instructional Methods

Students with health impairments frequently require related services (nursing services, physical therapy, special transportation). They less often need special education services.

Strategies in Early Childhood and Elementary School

According to the *26th Annual Report* (U.S. Department of Education, 2004, Table AB3), students aged 6 to 11 inclusive who were classified as OHI were educated in regular, resource, and separate classrooms in the following proportions: 51%, 31%, and 16%. Thus, teachers of inclusive classrooms can anticipate teaching some such children.

Methods: Embedding Instruction. Embedding means inserting specialized instruction into ongoing activities. The idea is to take advantage of a "teachable moment." This concept lies at the heart of the MOVE curriculum, which was discussed earlier. Diane Bricker and her colleagues (1998), writing about early childhood instruction, defined embedding as follows:

> a procedure in which children are given opportunities to practice individual goals and objectives that are included within an activity or event in a manner that expands, modifies, or adapts the activity/event while remaining meaningful and interesting to children. (Bricker, Pretti-Frontczak, & McComas, 1998, p. 13)

Thus, embedding is a way to help young children to reach goals in a non-disruptive way. The key is to examine carefully what the early intervention program (for infants and toddlers), the preschool program (for children aged 3 to 5 inclusive), the kindergarten class, or the primary-grade class does during any given time period, day, or even week. Those activities potentially offer opportunities for learning. Seizing those opportunities to deliver the extra help infants and toddlers with disabilities need is what makes embedding so helpful. The value of embedding was illustrated in the chapter-opening account about Breanna. Rather than offer physical therapy and related services to Breanna in separately scheduled sessions, her mother made them part of what Breanna wanted to be doing at any given part of the day. As Trellis's story showed, Breanna was highly motivated to get to the location in which those activities were to take place. As a result, she learned more, faster, than she would have under more traditional approaches.

Early childhood program staff work closely with families. There is an impressive array of family activities that may be tapped for embedding special instruction. Families typically take their children shopping, biking, hiking, and to playgrounds and other locations in the community. Each offers chances to teach young children the words associated with an activity. They also provide natural opportunities for teaching children to take responsibility for themselves, to make decisions, and to manipulate a wide variety of objects. Especially because so many young children with physical disabilities are experientially deprived by caretakers, it is important for educators to "go the extra mile" to ensure that such learning opportunities are not missed. Importantly, embedding requires little additional staff, and thus is economical.

Methods: Collaboration with Related-Services Providers. Early intervention services include services provided directly to family members, and not just services for infants and toddlers with disabilities. This is why the written plans are called Individualized *Family Services* Plans (IFSPs). These **family services** may help families to identify resources available to them, to prioritize their needs, and to learn skills of effective parenting. A vital component of early intervention is the work of the service coordinator. This person is named in the IFSP (often with her phone number and e-mail address). **Service-coordination** services include, as the name implies, coordinating, on behalf of the family, services from a variety of local, county, and state agencies. Often, families find themselves being shuttled from agency to agency, searching in vain for assistance. A service coordinator is a professional at "cutting through red tape" and getting those agencies to deliver services to families. A related term is **social work services.** Social workers are trained to know what different state, county, and local agencies do and do not offer, and how to qualify families for help. **Counseling** services may be provided for adults in the family and for siblings. Some early intervention and preschool programs offer **respite services** in which adult caregivers are offered an afternoon or even a weekend "off" as professionals care for the child. Such services can be invaluable, particularly when young children have severe health conditions disorders.

In the school, nursing services may be required, particularly if a child is taking medication. Heller et al. (1999) found that even certified special educators frequently reported that they were not skilled in helping students to monitor their use of medication. Children and youth with sickle-cell disease frequently live with great pain. Pain increasingly is recognized as a chronic health condition. In 2001, the American Medical Association, the American Hospital Association, and other health groups recognized chronic pain as "the fifth vital sign," together with temperature, pulse, respiration, and blood pressure. Accordingly, the associations urged, pain should be monitored by nurses and other health care professionals on a regular basis. Cancer, diabetes, epilepsy, and other health conditions often require children and youth to observe strict schedules for the taking of medication. The role of the teacher is largely limited to monitoring. If you believe that a child is under- or overmedicated (because, for example, he is unusually drowsy), you should alert a school nurse and share your observations with the child's family. The Epilepsy Foundation of America's Web site offers a very helpful library and the opportunity to direct questions to expert physicians. Its "Answer Place" is particularly useful to educators (*http://www.efa.org/answerplace*), including what teachers should do in the event of a seizure.

The state of Georgia decided in 2002 to allow students with asthma to self-administer medication. This removes the necessity for these students to leave the classroom to visit a school nurse. The state law, known as Senate Bill 472, absolves school employees of any liability for injuries that result from such self-medication. The law, popularly referred to as the "Kellen Edwin Bolden Act," after the young man whose advocacy led to its enactment.

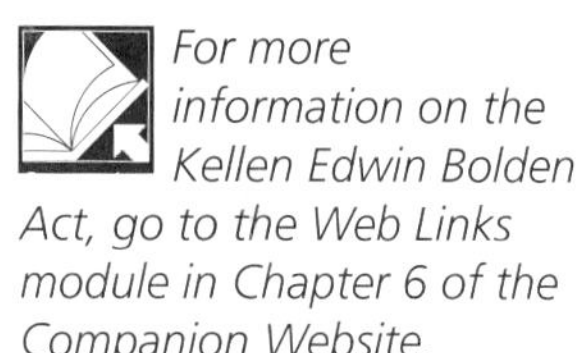

For more information on the Kellen Edwin Bolden Act, go to the Web Links module in Chapter 6 of the Companion Website.

While this is useful, asthma can be a serious medical condition. Teachers and school nurses need to remain vigilant for any indications of problems, even if a student has permission to self-medicate.

Methods: Ensure That the Classroom Is Safe. Most schools and other community resources routinely practice "universal safety precautions" (e.g., no touching of blood or other bodily fluids). That is why the number of new cases of HIV and AIDS in school-age children is actually lower than it was five or ten years ago (The Centers for Disease Control and Prevention, *http://www.cdc.gov*). Further progress requires that teachers continue to observe those practices. With respect to epilepsy, occupational and physical therapists often recommend that you examine the classroom and any other areas you plan to use, looking for any sharp and protruding objects. To make the area "safe," these should be removed or, at minimum, shielded. Such steps can help to prevent injury were a seizure to occur. Otherwise, teachers should allow a seizure to run its course (The Epilepsy Foundation of America, *http://www.efa.org/answerplace*). (For children with asthma, "safe" may mean a room with little dust [including chalk dust], plants that release pollen, and cleaning chemicals. These are all "triggers," or factors that may cause an asthmatic episode.) A national survey of school administrators, university professors, and special educators that Heller and her colleagues (1999) conducted found that many teachers felt unprepared to deal with different kinds of seizures. If you do not feel adequately trained in this area, you should consult with a school nurse.

Strategies in Middle School and High School

Students in middle school and high school who are classified with OHI tend to be integrated into regular classrooms much as are their younger counterparts. The proportions placed in general, resource, and separate classrooms, respectively, are 49%, 32%, and 14% (U. S. Department of Education, 2004, Table AB4). These figures are virtually indistinguishable from those in elementary school.

Methods: Integrating Health Care into the Curriculum. While virtually all middle-school and high-school students take courses on health, these typically do not address the special health-care needs of students having health impairments. They also do not tell teachers how to integrate health care into the curriculum. If a student in one of your classes has a health impairment, it is important that both you and the student locate reliable sources of information. You also both need to identify on-site personnel who can provide emergency assistance as needed. Both of you should do some planning. This involves asking questions that are uncomfortable. What, for example, would be done if a student having sickle-cell disease were to have an "episode" during school hours? You should ask the student what arrangements her family has made with private practitioners, including physicians with admitting privileges at local hospitals. If the required expertise to meet the special needs of persons with sickle-cell disease is not available locally, have arrangements been made for consultation with a specialist in the field? You should also ask the student and her family what they would like for you to do in the event of such an episode. Finally, you and the student need to explore whether, and to what extent, she would like for you to integrate information about sickle-cell disease when you discuss health, specifically blood, in the classroom. Some students will want to maintain privacy about blood disorders, while others will take comfort in knowing that peers are at least aware of the disorder and consequently less likely to be fearful about it.

Heller and colleagues (1999) found that even certified special education teachers reported being inadequately trained in these areas. That suggests that *general* educators, including many teachers of inclusive classrooms, may be even more lacking in preparation. Whether a student has epilepsy or some other seizure condition, a cardiac condition, diabetes, cancer, asthma, or AIDS, teacher-student discussions should be frank and open. What does the student desire for you to say and do? What medications is the student taking and what side effects are possible?

Methods: Counseling. Some students with health conditions, notably epilepsy, confront a dilemma. They can "pass" as unimpaired most of the time. Today's medications are highly effective in controlling seizures. For this reason, epilepsy may be apparent to educators and peers only once or twice during a student's period of enrollment in a middle school or high school. However, were a seizure that they did not expect occur, those teachers and classmates may be startled. Hence, the dilemma: Should the student tell educators and peers about the condition in advance of an episode? Doing so minimizes emotion (the discussion can be straightforward, even clinical, because no one is upset). Adolescents may resist this, however, fearing embarrassment. Regardless of the student's final decision, the issue should be discussed, preferably with a trained counselor or psychologist. These professionals can assist the student to think through the pro's and con's. Together, they may decide that the best course of action is for the student to explain the condition in advance to a trusted teacher and a close friend. That way, should a seizure occur, at least one or two people present will recognize what is happening and reassure the others. Similar considerations may apply with respect to asthma and diabetes.

Strategies in Transition to Adult Life

Whether they will continue on to college, go to work, or live in the community, students with health impairments need to recognize that they will be expected to assume responsibility for their needs, including medication.

Methods: Teaching Self-Care. During the middle-school and secondary years, educators and family members should gradually increase the extent to which students care for their own needs. They should be made aware of those needs and of the possible consequences of not meeting those needs. Thus, students with asthma, diabetes, and other health conditions should be prepared for eventual self-care. This includes learning how to keep up with the rapidly advancing state-of-the-art in medical care for their disorders. There are new ways for people with diabetes to take insulin, for example. Similarly, new and improved interventions for many kinds of cancer are being discovered each year. Persons who are HIV+ or have AIDS need to become thoroughly familiar with the "cocktail" of drugs and to learn how to comply with the strict regimen required to take those medications. Individuals with epilepsy need to acquaint themselves with state regulations about driver licensing. Generally, if there has been no seizure for five years, individuals with epilepsy may qualify for a driver's license. However, rules vary widely and change occasionally, so students should become familiar with current requirements.

Students should also become at least familiar with other common health conditions. Individuals with diabetes are at risk of developing visual impairments. Many who have diabetes do not know it. Any student who is obese should be alerted to the possibility of diabetes and shown how to monitor blood sugar. Similarly, anyone with a TBI should be aware that epilepsy-like seizures may occur. They need to know what to do if one were to happen. The important point for students is that once they are graduated or age out from high school, they no longer will have the luxury of knowing that others have legal responsibilities to take care of them. Whether in college, at work, or in a community apartment, they will be responsible for their own needs.

VISION IMPAIRMENT, INCLUDING BLINDNESS

A very small number of PreK–12 children have significant impairments of vision. While many wear glasses or use contact lenses, the definition of "visual impairments" is that these prevent people from seeing normally *despite* use of available corrective devices. Until the 1970s, the nature of blindness and low vision and the nature of education as practiced in the public schools effectively combined to necessitate separate schooling for many children and youth. This was because educational materials, chiefly textbooks, were available only in print. Some children who were blind did successfully navigate the public schools, but they did so because of an "army" of volunteers: people who painstakingly transcribed texts into Braille. That was an enormous effort, by any measure, as Harold Krents (1972) memorably described it in *To Race the Wind.* Such resources as the American Printing House for the Blind, the American Foundation for the Blind, and Recordings for the Blind (as it was then known) could and did convert to Braille commonly used textbooks, but none could do so for every book and every article used in the fiercely independent schools of America's 15,000 school districts.

Definition

The U.S. Department of Education's (1999a) definition of **"visual impairment including blindness"** is "an impairment in vision that, even with correction, adversely affects a child's educational performance. The term includes both partial sight and blindness" (34 C.F.R. 300[c][13]). As mentioned earlier, impairment of vision is measured *with appropriate corrective devices,* including glasses. The intent is to identify only children whose vision remains impaired despite the use of such products. The term **"blindness"** generally refers to vision that is 20/200 or worse, as measured on a Snellen chart. That is, individuals who are blind must stand within 20 feet of the chart to be able to read what people with unimpaired vision can read while standing 200 feet away. People with low vision (what the definition refers to as "partial sight") have Snellen-chart numbers between 20/70 and 20/200.

Problems with This Definition

Snellen chart measurements are not particularly helpful in PreK–12 schools (except for reading things written on a blackboard, displayed using PowerPoint® slides, or shown using an overhead projector). That is why educators often use different ways to describe vision impairments.

Characteristics and Types

For more information on Recordings for the Blind & Dyslexic, go to the Web Links module in Chapter 6 of the Companion Website.

Most meaningful to educators is the answer to this question: "How does this child learn?" Some students benefit from enlargement and from sharp contrast between foreground and background (i.e., black letters on a white sheet). Other students, including many who are blind, learn best through their hearing. These students typically prefer to listen to material, that is, taped books from Recordings for the Blind & Dyslexic, computer speech synthesis, and the like. Yet other students prefer to use the sense of touch. They benefit when materials are presented in Braille. They also like to take notes using mechanical or electronic Braille writers. See the nearby box, "Technologies That Work: Vision Impairment."

Characteristics

Children and youth who are blind tend to rely heavily on their sense of hearing if it is not impaired. They also make good use of the sense of touch, again if that is not impaired. Some factors that cause blindness may also produce a hearing loss. Diabetes, which is a major cause of blindness (albeit among adults rather than children), can limit tactile sensitivity so much that people become unable to read Braille effectively.

Types

People who are blind generally have some residual vision. That is why a distinction is made between "legally blind" (20/200 vision) and "totally blind" (no residual vision remains). The other distinction is between blindness and low vision.

Prevalence

The *26th Annual Report* indicated that just 0.5% of PreK–12 students have notable impairments of vision. A total of 26,000 students between the ages of 6 and 21, inclusive, were identified with the label "visual impairments" because they were blind or had low vision. To place these numbers into context, fewer K–12 students are classified with visual impairments than have any other label in IDEA other than TBI and deaf-blindness. Another comparison may help: About one-third as many school-age children have impairments of vision as have hearing impairments. However, half of those with this label spend all or virtually all of the school week in inclusive settings (Figure 6.7).

Diagnosis and Assessment

Blindness and other levels of vision impairment are diagnosed by specialists; notably ophthalmologists and optometrists. The IEP team generally will accept such diagnoses. The major question before the IEP team will be whether the child is eligible for IDEA services. As with other classifications, the major issue is whether both special education and related services are necessary. Young children with vision impairments often require specialized instruction in order to learn how to use assistive technologies, how to read and write in Braille, and the like. A vision teacher may offer such services. In addition, related services such as orientation and mobility instruction may be needed. Older students, however, may no longer require special education. In such an event, they may be found to be eligible

FIGURE 6.7 Likelihood of Inclusive Placements: Visual Impairments

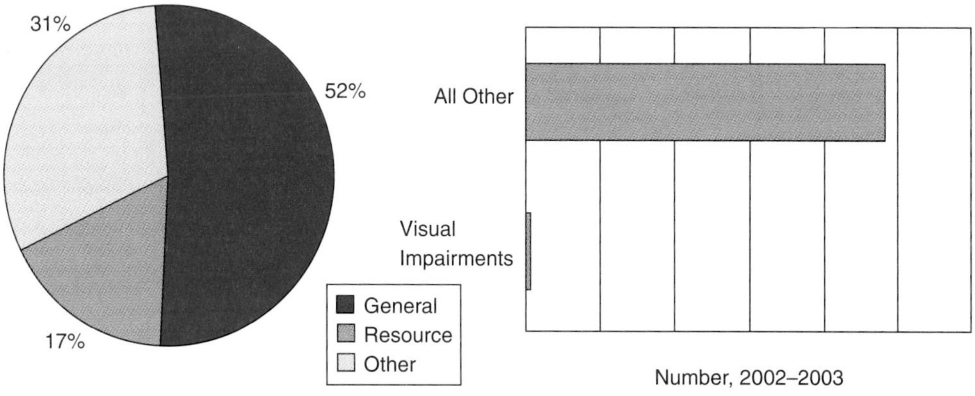

31%
52%
17%
All Other
Visual Impairments
General
Resource
Other
Number, 2002–2003

Students identified with the "visual impairments, including blindness" label are small in number at 26,000 out of 5,946,000 reported for the 2002–2003 school year (*26th Annual Report*). However, they tend to be placed into inclusive environments. The *Annual Report* shows that 52% were in general classrooms all or almost all of the school week (spending less than 21% of their time in other environments).

Source: From the *26th Annual Report,* by the U.S. Department of Education, 2004, Washington, DC: Author.

for section 504. That would ensure the uninterrupted delivery of related services, such as technologies required for participation in assessments.

Causes

It is unusual to find children born blind in families where one or both parents also are blind. Rather, the kinds of conditions that cause deafness or other hearing impairments (e.g., the CMV virus, maternal rubella, etc.) are also implicated in many instances of vision impairment. CMV (cytomegalovirus), for example, is a known cause of deafness (see The Centers for Disease Control and Prevention, *http://www.cdc.gov/ncidod/diseases/cmv.htm*).

Genetic Factors

Many causes of childhood blindness or low vision remain unknown. A few undoubtedly are genetic in origin, such as retinoblastoma (a malignant tumor in the retina) and congenital cataracts. Diabetes is a major cause of blindness, but usually in persons much older than PreK–12 students. There may be a genetic predisposition for diabetes.

Environmental Factors

These include low birth weight and maternal rubella. Prematurity, which co-occurs with low birth weight, is a growing cause. Blindness is also caused by retinopathy of prematurity (previously called retrolental fibroplasia). In years past, this occurred because premature infants were exposed to high concentrations of oxygen when they were placed into incubators. Once the connection between this practice and blindness became widely known, hospitals changed their procedures. Another problem has been the very intensive lights in neonatal intensive care units, which were on 24 hours a day. These produced a new influx of retinopathy of prematurity (Dietz & Ferrell, 1993). Fortunately, many neonatal intensive care units now have lower levels of lighting. In a few instances, childhood accidents can produce blindness. To illustrate, the same falls, bicycle accidents, motor vehicle accidents, and so on, that could cause TBI or SCI could also, or instead, cause blindness by damaging the optic nerves and/or the optical cortex in the brain.

Technologies That Work

Vision Impairment

Students who are blind or have low vision often can succeed in an inclusive classroom *if* the technologies they need are made available. There is good news here for many schools. State rehabilitation agencies for people who are blind often will purchase the required products for the student. This ensures not only that the child or youth has the needed equipment (updated as appropriate) but also that the student has it at *home.* This can make a big difference.

Text to Speech (Speech Synthesis)

We discussed speech synthesis earlier in Chapters 3 and 4. When the student has speech synthesis enabled on his home PC, he can listen to e-mail, Web pages, and anything else you send to him in electronic format.

Speech synthesis also opens up many texts for students who are blind or have low vision. Today it is possible to acquire textbooks, articles, and other materials, directly from the publisher, at the time of publication, that are in "appropriate media" (meaning, can be used by students who are blind or have low vision). An excellent example is an electronic book, popularly called an "e-book" (Bowe, 2000c). Random House and other publishers of textbooks now routinely release books both in print and in electronic form (e.g., at a Web site or on disk). With e-books, making a text accessible to someone who is blind or has low vision is easy, fast, and inexpensive. That is because readers may readily convert text to speech, to large print, or to Braille. Materials that are "off copyright" (e.g., no longer protected by copyright and thus no longer subject to royalties to the author or the author's estate) are actually free; the complete works of Shakespeare, Dickens, and Wordsworth, to choose just three examples, are now available online at such sites as The E text Archives, *http://www.etext.org*, and The Internet Public Library, *http://www.ipl.org*.

Recordings for the Blind and Dyslexic (RFBD) is a very useful resource for curricular materials, including books. Students may register with RFBD for free materials. The organization offers books on tape as well as electronic books that may be listened to via speech synthesis. The American Printing House for the Blind offers Road Runner®, a portable device that lets students listen to text no matter where they may be. The product has "bookmarks" so students can easily return to read portions, adjustable volume and speed, and a choice of voices to listen to as well as earphones and a cable. Students download files from home or school PCs. The cost is about $300.

Kurzweil Educational Systems Group offers the "Kurzweil 1000" which convert texts to speech. The unit comes with optical character reader (OCR) software as well as a scanner. (The Kurzweil 3000 is similar, but is intended for persons with learning disabilities.) Costs vary, but generally are in the range of $2,500 to $7,500. The software itself retails for about $1,000. (When first introduced, as the Kurzweil Reading Machine, the OCR/scanner/speech synthesizer cost $35,000. Prices have fallen dramatically since then.) Many libraries have Kurzweil Personal Readers or Kurzweil 3000s.

For more information on the organizations, companies, and services listed in the Technologies That Work box, go to the Web Links module in Chapter 6 of the Companion Website.

Computer software that "talks" and also features large, bright images can assist children and youth who are blind or have low vision.

Screen Readers

How do people who are blind read computer screens? Most listen to it. Others feel it. All this is accomplished by software known as a "screen reader," a good name because that's what it does: It reads the contents on the screen. The user decides how the reading will take place: whether character formatting, font type and size, spacing, alignment, word spelling, and so on, will or will not be read. The user also selects the speed of the talking: 60 words per minute, 120 words per minute, or even faster. And the user determines the voice (male, female, child, etc.).

Screen readers read screens horizontally, from left to right. They try to speak out or send to a Braille machine everything they encounter, whether letter, number, or symbol. Screen readers handle letters and numbers well. They do not perform well with symbols. Pictures are impossible unless accompanied by a verbal description, known as "Alt Text" or long description ("longdesc"). These are simply small text files that describe the picture in words. The screen reader ignores the picture itself and reads the text file. Files in Word® or in WordPerfect® are usually easy for screen readers to handle. Files in PDF format are difficult. Neal Ewers has produced a brief orientation to screen readers. You can watch him on a video, read a transcript of the video, or purchase the video (1-608-262-7258). Neal gives an example of something he hears: "Character formatting, Times New Roman, 16 point, bolded style heading one line spacing single paragraph formatting, aligned left outline level one." From that, Neal knows that the screen reader is reading a text headline (the font is fairly large size and in bold). He can turn off all those formatting indicators and just listen to the headline itself. It should be obvious from this that considerable training and experience is needed to use screen readers effectively.

Windows® is a highly graphical user interface; so is the Web. Navigating either with the help of a screen reader can be challenging. If your student who is blind or has low vision is not an experienced user of screen readers, you should contact a vision teacher for assistance.

What if Neal were visiting a Web page that was filled with computer graphics, symbols, and pictures? Unless the Web page designer had offered alt text or other textual descriptions, the screen reader would simply say "symbol" each time it encountered an icon, leaving Neal confused.

If you have a student who uses a screen reader, you need to plan ahead. Visit the Web sites you will require or recommend for student use. Look for indications that the site is user friendly for people with screen readers. Two indications are a "Bobby Approved" seal, which indicates that the site passed the accessibility test at Wildfire's site (*http://www.wildfire.com* or *http://www.cast.org/bobby*) or a statement like "This site complies with W3C/WAI accessibility guidelines." Those guidelines (which are also the basis for the Bobby test of accessibility) were prepared by the World Wide Web Consortium's Web Accessibility Initiative, which explains the initials.

Enlargement

Some students who are blind or have low vision do well with enlargement of text. ALVA Access Group offers inLARGE®, software that enlarges text. There are also many closed circuit products that enlarge print in a textbook or handout. These are described at the technology pages of the National Federation of the Blind Web site (*http://www.nfb.org*) and that of the American Foundation for the Blind Web site (*http://www.afb.org*). You may also e-mail AFB at techctr@afb.net.

Braille

Many adults who are blind read Braille well. Far fewer PreK–12 students do. If you teach a student who knows Braille, or who is learning it from a vision teacher, you might look into Duxbury Systems (http://www.duxburysystems.com; 270 Littleton Road, Westford, MA 01886-3523). Duxbury is well-regarded for its variety of Braille translation software programs. Another good source of Braille-based technologies is Freedom Scientific (http://www.freedomscientific.com). This company also distributes the popular "Braille 'n Speak" unit that enables students who know Braille to take notes in class. It is made by Blazie Engineering (http://www.blazie.com). A modified version, called the "Braille 'n Speak Scholar," designed specifically for students, is distributed by the American Printing House for the Blind and other vendors. The Scholar has word processing (Grade I or Grade II Braille), file search/file organizing, talking phone directory, output in Braille or print (the Scholar translates Braille to print), a talking clock/calendar, and a talking scientific graphing calculator. A self-contained unit, the portable Scholar sells for about $1,000.

Low Tech

Not all technologies that help students who are blind or have low vision are high-technology products. Manipulatives are valuable teaching aids. These include raised-image maps (available from the American Printing House for the Blind). They also include concrete objects that children may feel and count. Wooden blocks are a good example. The Lighthouse has an excellent catalog of low-tech products, from beeping balls (for PE and for playing baseball, football, golf, etc.) to talking clocks and calculators.

Instructional Methods

The general rule in teaching blind or low-vision students in inclusive classrooms is they can succeed if the necessary technologies are provided (see "Technologies That Work: Vision Impairments"). In the early childhood and elementary levels particularly, the services of such related-services personnel as vision teachers and orientation and mobility specialists are required. Vision teachers convert materials as needed (enlarging some, creating Braille versions of others), and teach children Braille. Orientation and mobility specialists show children how to orient themselves ("Where am I?") and how to navigate around the school and the community.

Strategies in Early Childhood and Elementary School

At the elementary level, more than half (57%) of students with this label are placed in inclusive classrooms all or most of the school week, with another 17% spending at least part of the week in such environments (U.S. Department of Education, 2004, Table AB3). Thus, three out of every four (75%) are educated in regular classrooms in neighborhood schools at least part of the school week. The absolute number of such children, however, is small: Just 12,000 students between the ages of 6 and 11, inclusive, are blind or visually impaired.

Methods: Enriched Experiences. Many young children who are blind or have low vision were over-protected as infants, toddlers, and preschoolers. To adopt the term we introduced earlier in this chapter, they suffer from *experiential deprivation*. Accordingly, when they start kindergarten or first grade, they are lacking in some of the experiences that teachers expect children to have. Notably, many young children with vision impairments have not engaged in much physical play. They also may not have "explored the neighborhood" as much as have their sighted peers. Celeste (2002) reported, after surveying 84 families, that young children (aged four months to four years) who were blind or had low vision were most delayed in mobility milestones. Parents told Celeste that these young children did not walk independently, move easily around furniture, and/or walk up and down stairs as well as expected. Thus, an important method of teaching these children is to arrange for them to have those kinds of experiences.

Particularly valuable is *hands-on learning*. Young children who are blind or have low vision learn to "envision" the classroom, the globe, and other material objects, as well as people's faces, through the sense of touch. Note that Olivia's teachers (see "Teacher Strategies That Work: Collaboration for a Young Child Who Is Blind") regularly touched her and let her touch them, to "keep in touch" throughout the school day.

Methods: Orientation and Mobility Training. If you have a student in your class who is blind or has low vision, you need to make sure that the student acquires solid orientation and mobility skills. Experts in that field, known as *orientation and mobility specialists*, train young people who are blind or have low vision how to determine where they are ("orientation") and how to get where they want to go ("mobility"). They can also help, as can occupational and physical therapists, to teach the child other skills urgently needed at the early childhood/elementary level: how to take advantage of assistive technology products.

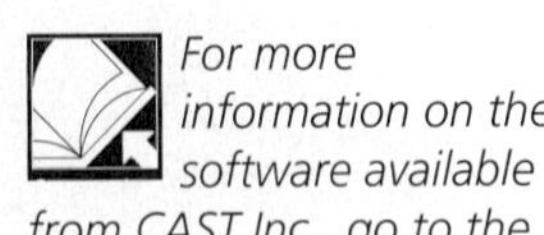

For more information on the software available from CAST Inc., go to the Web Links module in Chapter 6 of the Companion Website.

Methods: Assistive Technologies. Inclusion works for students who are blind or have low vision to the extent to which these children have and know how to use assistive-technology products. That may seem to be a sweeping statement, but it is not: Technology that is available today makes it possible for students who are blind or have low vision to "read" textbooks and other printed materials and to "write" their own materials as rapidly and as effectively as do students with unimpaired vision. The eReader[tm] software program from CAST Inc., for example, lets a student listen to test questions and to her answers. It highlights words as it speaks them. The software also enlarges text. This example shows how technology literally makes inclusion possible. The nearby box, "Technologies That Work: Vision Impairments," features **screen readers,** software that converts whatever is on a computer screen into speech. Screen readers open up the World Wide Web, e-mail, and other communications.

That is why studies such as one done by Kapperman, Sticken, and Heinze (2002) are worrisome. Surveying 60 teachers of students with visual impairments in Illinois, they discovered that *most* children and youth who needed alternative media were *not* given the assistive technologies that would have helped them. Students who were blind or had low vision and were served in inclusive classrooms were less likely than were their peers who were placed in resource rooms or separate classrooms to have such technologies. A major reason apparently was that the itinerant teachers who visited inclusive classrooms were not knowledgeable about assistive technologies. Studying this issue in Kentucky, other researchers found that teachers in fact lacked training about these products. Accordingly, only half of their students who were blind or had low vision have been provided with assistive technologies (Abner & Lahm, 2002).

A vision teacher can help you to identify promising technologies. A key is *how* the student best works. Those who have low vision frequently prefer to use it. You can help them by using sharp figure/ground contrast. Thus, handouts, tests, and other materials should have black images on a white background, or the reverse. Avoid black on grey, blue on yellow, and so on. Closed-circuit TV monitors and a variety of computer-based programs do a good job of enlarging text and images. Important in enlargement is the fact that most images, including the words on this page, are created by a large number of very small dots. Enlargement expands the space occupied by those dots. Inevitably this means expanding, too, the space between dots. That degrades the image, reducing the contrast between figure and ground.

Students who are blind generally prefer to listen to material. They prefer this to Braille for several reasons. First, more material can be converted to voice, quickly and easily, than is the case with Braille. Second, a tape or computer file that can be listened to is much smaller than is the same document in Braille. The textbook you are holding, converted to Braille, would fill several boxes. Third, Braille is a language and as such can take a year to two years to learn. Learning to understand speech on tape or on disk, by contrast, is a matter of a few weeks at most. However, some students both know and prefer Braille. The National Braille Press specializes in converting print to Braille. In some communities, you can also find volunteers or, occasionally, professionals to do the job locally. However, in most parts of the United States, there are shortages of Braille transcribers (e.g., Corn & Wall, 2002).

For more information on the National Braille Press, go to the Web Links module in Chapter 6 of the Companion Website.

Methods: Encouraging Self-Reliance. Especially at the early childhood/elementary level, teachers need to insist that students who are blind or have low vision do *all* of the work that is assigned. Many sighted people, including children, tend to volunteer to do things for people who are blind or have low vision. This tendency is so strong, and so prevalent, that many blind people come to rely on it. It is important that young children with visual impairments learn, at least in your classroom, that they are expected to perform, just as other students are.

Strategies in Middle School and High School

Half (53%) of secondary-age (12 to 17, inclusive) students with this label are taught in inclusive settings all or most of the school week; another 18% spend a large amount of time in such environments (U.S. Department of Education, 2004, Table AB4). As with elementary students, the absolute number of such individuals is, however, small.

Methods: Universal Design. The principles of universal design which were described earlier in Chapter 3 apply with even more force when a student is blind or has low vision. As the teacher of an inclusive classroom having such a student, you need to practice *redundancy.* As explained earlier, the principle of redundancy is to offer the same information in a variety of media. With respect to students who are blind or have low vision, you need to say what you write on a board or on a slide. You need to "video describe" what you are doing in the room ("I am holding up a flask to show the chemical reaction

Teacher Strategies That Work

Collaboration for a Young Child Who Is Blind

Olivia is a girl in her early teens. She is blind. When she was born, prematurely, she was placed in a neonatal intensive care unit. It was then that she was diagnosed with retinopathy of prematurity (ROP). What happened then illustrates the power of IDEA services to help children with disabilities. Debra Viadero, in an undated article for *Teacher Magazine Reader,* told what happened next:

Olivia's family enrolled her in an IDEA Part C early intervention program for infants and toddlers. A parent-infant teacher and a social worker visited the family's home to help Olivia. They touched and massaged her. They tied bells to her wrists and ankles so she could envision where her limbs extended into space. They put things in her crib so that when she moved she would feel them.

Olivia then entered an IDEA Part B preschool special education program that specializes in services for preschoolers who are blind or have low vision. Yes, her family said, this is not an inclusive setting. That was not the goal at this age. What her family wanted, and what the preschool program provided, were services that would prepare Olivia for integration later, in elementary school. Her parents learned Braille. Olivia's instruction at the preschool program focused upon making her socially observant—aware of other people, learning to face them when they spoke to her. (This is not automatic for children who are blind. Many turn an ear to the source of sound, rather than the face. Olivia did that. She had to be trained, over several weeks, to ignore that instinct.) The preschool program also taught Olivia to be tactually observant, meaning to pay attention to and learn how to interpret what she felt with her hands and fingers. Olivia also learned how to translate spoken descriptions of objects into mental images so that she could, for example, envision a cloud and "see" it emitting rain drops.

When Olivia entered first grade, she was ready for integration. The only child who was blind in a 450-student school, Olivia put to use what she had learned. A vision teacher came to her school every week. This professional taught Olivia how to read and write in Braille. She also taught Olivia the use of an abacus for counting. The vision teacher translated Olivia's books and stories into Braille. She helped Olivia learn to listen to books on tape. A second professional, an orientation and mobility specialist, also came to the school weekly. He helped Olivia to learn how to move around the classroom, then around the school, and finally around the neighborhood. Beginning in second grade, a third itinerant professional, an occupational therapist, visited Olivia's school weekly. This person worked with Olivia to strengthen her shoulder, arm, and finger muscles. The purpose was to make it possible for Olivia to type on a Braille writer. This is a machine much like those that court reporters use. Some upper body strength, more than most little girls have, is needed to depress its six buttons.

During each elementary grade, Olivia's teachers took small but essential steps to include Olivia. They spoke out loud anything they wrote on a board. They read out loud any handouts. From time to time, as they walked around the classroom, they would touch Olivia and let her touch them, to "stay in touch."

By the time Olivia was in middle school, she was fully prepared to compete successfully with her classmates. For Olivia, inclusion works because the necessary groundwork was done. Her story illustrates the fact that inclusion is sometimes most successful when young children "learn to swim" in a non-inclusive environment rather than immediately required to "sink or swim" in an inclusive setting.

I have been describing"). You need to post to a class Web site or hand out on a disk any paper materials that you provide for sighted students. If the information is in electronic format, your student who is blind or has low vision can convert it to the appropriate media. Thus, a student with low vision can enlarge it, a student who knows Braille can convert it to Braille, and a student who prefers to listen to it can convert it to speech. The general principle is to narrate verbally whatever sighted students are seeing in the classroom and to plan, in advance, for redundancy of any print materials.

One example of universal design in education is the use of a **listserv.** A listserv is a group of e-mail addresses saved to a common name. Thus, if you teach English Literature, you might enter the e-mail addresses of all students in your class into a group you name "EngLit12." Then, any time you want to e-mail all students, you need only compose one e-mail message, addressing it to "EngLit12." The software will automatically send a copy to every student on the list. You may also set up a monitored discussion group, using much the same approach. In this way, every student has the option of e-mailing all other students, or just one or two.

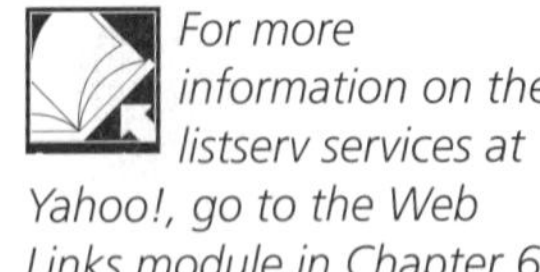

For more information on the listserv services at Yahoo!, go to the Web Links module in Chapter 6 of the Companion Website.

That greatly facilitates out-of-class discussion. Because the listserv is electronic, students who are blind or have low vision enjoy equal access to everything on the list. They can listen to, enlarge, or convert to Braille any message sent to the list. There are several commercial services which will set up a monitored listserv for you. One example is Yahoo! While America Online offers a similar service, its groups may be open only to subscribers to AOL.

Methods: Assistive Technologies. The importance of technology is, if anything, more striking at the secondary than at the early childhood/elementary level. This is a function of the fact that high-school students read far more materials, from many more sources, than do younger students. This means that **e-texts** (e-books) and other "appropriate media" materials, notably books on tape, are absolutely essential for these students to succeed at the secondary level. Recordings for the Blind and Dyslexic offers books on tape. With experience, students who are blind or have low vision learn to "scan" books on tape at very rapid speeds, as fast as 600 words per minute. They also learn to "read" textbooks as quickly as 200 to 300 words per minute. At those speeds, mental concentration has to be complete. Because of that level of focus, their ability to retain information is very good.

An e-text (e-book) is often provided by textbook publishers for schools which adopt printed texts. For example, after the state of California passed a law requiring publishers to offer both printed (bound) and electronic versions of texts approved for use by the state board of education, Random House, Prentice Hall, Allyn & Bacon, and other prominent book publishers rapidly acted to develop e-books—for all interested states, not just for California. Similarly, Barnes & Noble, the major bookstore chain, announced that its Web site (*http://www.bn.com*) would offer a wide range of e-texts. E-books of fiction and nonfiction often are available on the Web, particularly where copyrights have expired. There are two important advantages to electronic publishing:

1. E-texts may be listened to, enlarged, and converted to Braille.
2. E-texts may be searched, using the "search and replace" feature of popular word processors. Thus a student may use the search function in Word® to scan the text for every occurrence of a name or other word. This feature gives students who are blind or have low vision some of the same rapid access to a text that sighted students receive from visually scanning the text or from using an index.

Books and other materials that are not available electronically may be converted to Braille. The National Braille Press supplies Braille books, articles, and other documents to public schools from coast to coast. This not-for-profit organization charges about $1 per Braille page for the service. Teachers should bear in mind that several Braille pages are required for each printed page. NBP has computerized its operations, so even a textbook can be converted fairly quickly. Interested persons may visit the Web page, click on a hotlink to orders, describe the material to be converted, and receive an estimate on cost and on turnaround time.

Methods: Accessible Web Pages. If you teach a student who is blind or has low vision, you need to check out, in advance, any Web sites that you plan to assign to the students. Thus, before announcing a Webquest project (in which, for example, students are told to visit certain sites and then prepare a report on, say, Lewis and Clark's expeditions), it is essential that you check out the accessibility of those Web pages. Fortunately, this is relatively easy to do. Several "accessibility checkers" are available for your use.

- A very good one is offered by HiSoftware (*http://www.hisoftware.com*). The "AccVerify" tool from this company will review any uniform resource locator (URL) or uniform resource identifier (URI) on the Web. Within minutes, the company will send you an e-mail detailing the site's accessibility features. This includes identification of any barriers for people who are blind or have low vision, plus an explanation of each barrier.
- Another accessibility checker is "LIFT/NN" from the Nielsen Norman Group (*http://www.nngroup.com*). This software checks accessibility of Web sites and pages,

much as does AccVerify, and goes a step further: It can even fix some of the problems it encounters. This feature may appeal to you for improving your class Web page.

Two other Web page accessibility checkers are older but still useful.

- One more is "Bobby" from Watchfire (*http://www.watchfire.com*). A good way to use this tool is to click on "Use Bobby Trainer" at the site, then enter the URL/URI you wish to check. Doing so leads Bobby to produce a series of pages outlining the accessibility of the site.

All of these accessibility checkers build upon the principles of accessible Web page design that were developed by the World Wide Web Consortium's (W^3C) Web Accessibility Initiative (WAI). (Those principles are posted at *http://www.w3c.org/TR/2004/WD-WCAG20-20040311/*, the most recent update, as of March 11, 2004.)

If you encounter inaccessibility at any Web page that you wish to use with your students who are blind or have low vision, send an e-mail to the Web master responsible for that page. Most Web sites make this easy by offering an automatic e-mailer for you to use. Point out the error you found, suggest that the Web master visit the W^3C site to understand what the problem was and to see how it may be solved. Many Web Masters will fix access problems within a couple weeks. If this does not occur, and you still want to use the site for your students, you will need to do a "work around" for your students who are blind or have low vision. This may include assigning a sighted buddy to visit the site with this student, verbally explaining inaccessible material to the student who cannot see it.

Strategies in Transition to Adult Life

Students with vision impairments continue on to college at higher rates than do students with any other disability, with the possible exception of speech or language impairments (many of whom are declassified during the high-school years, making it difficult to track their progress; Blackorby & Wagner, 1996). Again, technology is key. So is orientation and mobility.

Methods: Transition to Postsecondary Education. Students with the classification "visual impairment, including blindness" are the most likely of all students with any classification to graduate from high school and to go to college (U.S. Department of Education, 2003; Valdes, Williamson, & Wagner, 1990). That is because most young people who are blind or have low vision master the skills required for academic success. It also reflects the power of today's technologies, such as the Braille 'n Speak, screen readers. Accordingly, time should be taken during the transition years (ages 14 to 18) to help the student to plan for an independent life at the college level. This should include at least one visit, preferably more, to the college at which admission is secured. A great many details must be mastered. The young person needs to learn the layout of the campus, the location of the dorm relative to the cafeteria and other landmarks of the campus, and the buildings and rooms in which classes will be held. All of this is very time-consuming. In addition, the student needs to be advised that the "rules" of accommodation at the college level differ greatly from those in PreK–12 schools. The major difference is that at the postsecondary level, the *student* is responsible for "self identifying" (telling college officials that she needs assistance) and for requesting needed accommodations; in elementary and secondary schools, those duties are handled by IEP teams, with parent assistance.

Methods: Transition to Independent Living. Students who continue to postsecondary education, as well as those who do not, need to master skills of living independently in the community. They must learn how to organize bills in their wallets or pockets so they know which is a \$20 bill, a \$10 bill, a \$5 bill or a \$1 bill. They also need to learn how to organize their kitchens so that cooking is easy and efficient. They also must learn how to relate well with other people, in particular how to ask for help and for directions. Vision teachers can help with this instruction. Time needs to be set aside for such training. That can be difficult for students who are pursuing, as many with visual impairments are, the standard curriculum with its heavy emphasis upon attaining learning standards and passing required tests. Krebs (2001) suggested that such instruction begin as early as seventh grade, with math word problems. Students should develop portfolios in which they document how they solve everyday problems involving money and other uses of math. Teachers and peers can model desired behaviors, including self-assessment. In cooperative learning groups, students who are blind or have low vision can work with sighted peers to imagine and then solve problems of everyday living.

Methods: Transition to Work. Youth and adults who are blind or have low vision frequently can secure government benefits that are more generous than those available to individuals with other disabilities. This tempts many not to work, even after completing college (Valdes et al., 1990). The fact is that adults with visual impairments usually can enjoy a much more rewarding quality of life through employment than is possible via government assistance. That is why Nagle (2001) recommended that educators work hand-in-glove with vocational rehabilitation counselors and other professionals to prepare young people who are blind or have low vision for success in work. She urged that part- or even full-time work be incorporated into the schedules of students, both to give them a taste of the world of work and to help them learn, first hand, the rewards of employment. Nagle was concerned that even young people with visual impairments who complete four years of college do not engage in paid employment as often as would be hoped. Helping more to get and keep jobs requires cooperation between educators and counselors both at the secondary level and during the college years.

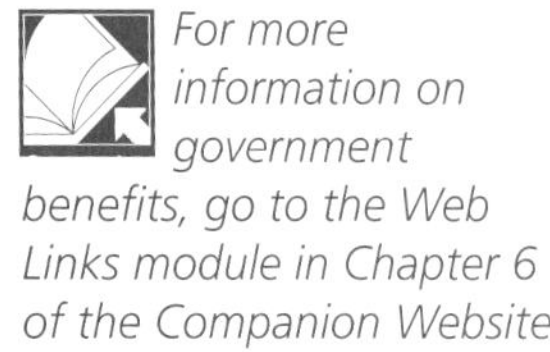

For more information on government benefits, go to the Web Links module in Chapter 6 of the Companion Website.

CHAPTER SUMMARY

- The disabilities in this chapter, taken together, account for only 10% of all students with disabilities.
- Students having physical impairments may have one of four labels: orthopedic impairment, traumatic brain injury, the other (primary) disability, or multiply disabled.

Orthopedic/Physical Disabilities

- Most students with physical disabilities learn in the same ways and at the same pace as do students with no disabilities.
- Pull-out service delivery models persist in many public schools because they are less costly than are push-in services.
- Cerebral palsy is the disability most likely to require a wide range of related services (physical therapy, occupational therapy, speech and language pathology, special transportation).
- Traumatic brain injuries can alter a student's personality and behavior patterns. In this respect, and also because most people with TBIs can walk, it differs from many other physical disabilities.
- A spinal cord injury differs from spina bifida principally in age at onset. SCI most often occurs during the teen years and early adulthood, while spina bifida is present at birth. One common result of this difference is people with SCI may struggle with self-perception while those with spina bifida tend to be comfortable with the condition, as they have never known another kind of life.
- Housing is probably the number-one worry for many people with physical disabilities. The supply of accessible and affordable housing in the United States is much too small to meet the demand.

Health Impairments

- Health conditions differ greatly one from another. Some are severe, some mild; some long-lasting, some sporadic; some visible, some not.

- Educators must take seriously the U.S. Department of Education's warning that harassment on the basis of disability is unacceptable.
- Counseling, social work services, family services and respite services can benefit families of young children with health disabilities. They can also help families of older children, but such services are less often provided in PreK–12 IDEA Part B schools than they are in IDEA Part C early intervention programs.
- Preparation for assuming responsibility for self-care is perhaps the most critical element of transition services for this population.

Blindness and Other Visual Impairments

- Children who are blind or visually impaired tend to learn as much, as rapidly, as do other students *if* schools provide them with appropriate technology. Particularly important are products that convert print to speech, to Braille, or to large print.
- Orientation training helps people who are blind or have low vision to identify where they are. Mobility training teaches them how to get around in a facility and in a community.
- A higher proportion of students who are blind or visually impaired continues on to college than is the case with students having any other disability label.
- A large variety of assistive technology products is available to meet the needs of students who are blind or have low vision. On the other hand, these students most need accessibility of information, whether in print or on the World Wide Web.

QUESTIONS FOR REFLECTION

1. How does cerebral palsy differ from other orthopedic impairments reviewed in this chapter?
2. What differentiates TBI from other physical conditions?
3. Where would you turn to get information about housing for persons with physical disabilities?
4. What is the number-one cause of AIDS in young children? What does this causative factor tell you about working with the child's family?
5. What does the fact that asthma is a "reversible" condition suggest to you as a teacher?
6. How would you help a student with epilepsy to decide whether or not to reveal the condition to others?
7. Which health condition discussed in this chapter is a leading cause of blindness?
8. What do orientation and mobility specialists do?
9. How do people who are blind use screen readers?
10. How could you use a Web page to make materials readily available to a student who is blind?

Chapter 7 *Autism and Severe/ Multiple Disabilities*

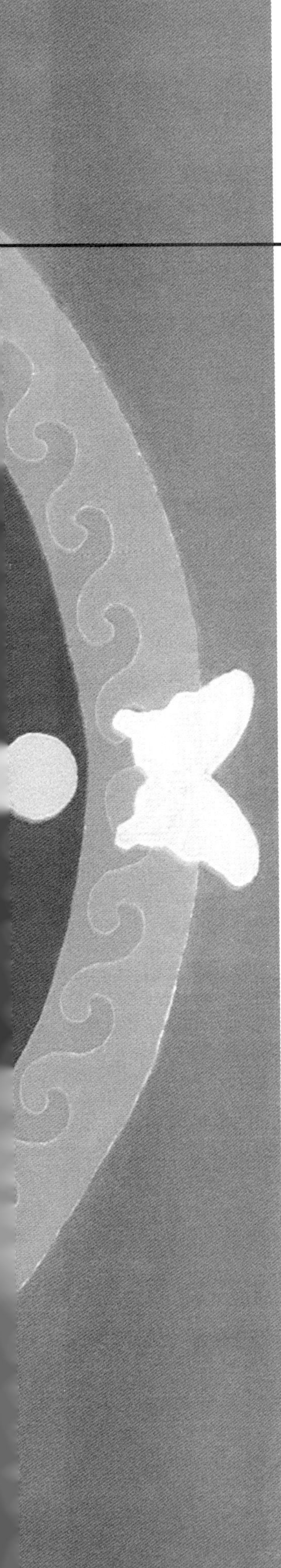

TERMS

functional curriculum
pervasive developmental disorders (PDD)
autism
Asperger's Syndrome
autistic savant behavior
applied behavior analysis (ABA)
stimulus control
successive approximations
sensory integration
severe disabilities
multiple disabilities
deaf-blindness
generalization
time delay
principle of partial participation
group home

CHAPTER FOCUS QUESTIONS

After reading this chapter, you should be able to answer such questions as:

1. What is a functional curriculum?
2. What considerations might lead an IEP team to place a student with severe disabilities in an inclusive classroom?
3. What features are characteristic of autism spectrum disorders?
4. Do childhood vaccinations cause autism spectrum disorders?
5. What is applied behavior analysis (ABA)?
6. What does "top-down" mean in curricula for students with severe or multiple disabilities?
7. What options are available to youth with severe or multiple disabilities after high school?

PERSONAL ACCOUNTS

Teacher gave positive report on teaching a child with pervasive developmental disorder (PDD), a form of autism spectrum disorders:

> *John's parents, an accountant (father) and homemaker (mother), as well as his grandparents, who live nearby, all learned applied behavior analysis (ABA) shortly after John was diagnosed at age 2.5. At that time, he was completely uninterested in playing with others and did not even seem to notice if another person was in the room with him. He preferred to engage in compulsive solitary activities, such as lining up objects or walking on his toes. John would tantrum for hours if interrupted in or prevented from doing these things. He did not have any conversational skills, did not use vocalizations to initiate or engage in interaction. Rather, his ways of communicating his needs and wants were crying and tantruming.*

I work with John at home for about 10 hours/week. I also work with him in school for 11 hours/week. (I also work with five other kids, but for a lot fewer hours.) John has averaged 30 hours/week of ABA since he was a little under 3 years of age. He is now 4 years old.

Today, John is a very verbal little boy who LOVES to talk. His mean sentence length is six words. However, he still has difficulty with pronouns (he will consistently say "Lauren's" rather than "yours" to refer to something of mine). He is very aware of people around him now and loves interacting with them. Eye contact is still very difficult for him, however. He can read at the second-grade level. He does not engage in any stereotypic or stimulatory behaviors in the classroom. The only times he tantrums now are when he's asked to help clean up the room.

—Lauren

Angela Policastro weighed 8 pounds, 9 ounces, at birth. She did not cry. Her skin was blue. She stopped breathing within minutes. Then her heart and kidneys ceased functioning. Because she was bleeding profusely, her brain did not get the oxygen it needed. Heroic efforts by a team of doctors and nurses kept Angela alive, but only her brain stem was undamaged. Angela lived for 404 days, all of them in a Connecticut hospital. For several years after her death, her mother Angie and father Bob continued to feel great pain. Perhaps the greatest source of their sorrow was that they had not been able to bring Angela home. There was no facility near the Policastro's home on Long Island that was equipped to help young children who are medically fragile and technology dependent. Over the next several years, Bob Policastro heard from hundreds of families that were also looking for a home for their children who were chronically ill or multiply disabled. That is why Bob lobbied state and county officials in New York to create a group home on Long Island. At last, in 2000, after nearly 10 years of trying, he succeeded.

Angela's House now is home to seven children ranging in age from 6 to 12. The five boys and two girls who live there have multiple disabilities. One boy had the umbilical cord wrapped around his neck at birth. That caused brain damage, cerebral palsy, seizures, congestive heart failure, and fluid-filled lungs. Another boy is blind, has cerebral palsy, and breathes only with great difficulty. A girl who weighs just 40 pounds despite being 12 years old has cerebral palsy, seizures, and blindness. Early in 2003, a second home, modeled after Angela's House, opened in eastern Long Island. It also houses seven children, these ranging in age from 4 to 13 years.

The 14 children who live in these two group homes attend special schools that provide a functional curriculum for them. Because most function cognitively at the equivalent of 6 to 9 months of age, this curriculum aims to train them to signal their needs and desires. The children learn very slowly, but they do learn. Their expressive communication is largely limited to kicking to the beat of a drum, squealing with delight at a bright light, and smiling at a familiar face. Occupational and physical therapists help them to maintain a healthy posture. The therapists and teachers find rewards both in the children's delight when they see something new and the parents' gratitude that the children are making progress (Myers, 2002; and Vargas, 2002).

The story about autism shows a child who was receiving an appropriate education in the least restrictive environment. The key words in IDEA are "appropriate" and "individualized"—words that IEP team members and teachers need to take seriously. The child Lauren worked with successfully benefited from one-on-one behavior modification, known as applied behavior analysis (ABA). It gave John what clearly was an education that was both appropriate and individualized. The issues raised in this vignette apply, as well, to students with multiple disabilities. As the second story shows, very individualized help is required for children with very severe medical and other needs. What is an "appropriate" education for a child who requires 24-hour nursing care to keep him alive? For students who are medically fragile and technology dependent, the least restrictive environment may be a separate school that has the trained staff and specialized equipment that are needed. Most children with multiple disabilities do not have such pressing needs. Many can participate in inclusive environments for all or much of the day. They may, however, require one-on-one assistance from teacher aides or volunteers.

INTRODUCTION

Chapter 7 addresses the challenges of teaching children with severe and multiple needs in an inclusive classroom. The conditions discussed in this chapter are all relatively low in prevalence. Autism, for example, represents about 2% of all school-age children and youth. Another 2% of children between 6 and 21 years of age, inclusive, are classified as having multiple disabilities. Just 1,600 are both deaf and blind. No statistics are reported on students with "severe" disabilities (U.S. Department of Education, 2004, Table AA3).

Students with the disabilities discussed in this chapter are less likely to be placed into inclusive classrooms than is the case with most other disabilities reviewed in this book. The proportions spending all or virtually all of the school week in regular classrooms are 25% (autism), 12% (multiple disabilities), and 18% (deaf-blindness). Correspondingly larger than usual proportions are educated outside of neighborhood schools: 12% (autism), 24% (multiple disabilities), and 30% (deaf-blindness). However, the numbers make clear that many children and youth with these severe conditions *are* placed into inclusive settings. That is why it is important for teachers and prospective teachers to learn techniques of instructing them in regular classrooms.

We begin with autism. This disorder exists along a spectrum. At one end are relatively mild "autistic-like" behaviors and at the other end is severe autism accompanied by mental retardation. While these students may have a wide range of needs, some, particularly children and youth with Asperger's syndrome, are appropriately placed into an inclusive setting. Other students with autism spectrum disorders may spend most of their time in a separate rather than an inclusive environment. Experts urge that they spend at least some of the school week in an inclusive environment, however, so they will see typical behavior on the part of other children, observe such behavior being reinforced, and be urged by classmates to exhibit such behavior themselves.

A wide variety of relatively uncommon conditions, many of them genetic in origin, account for what IDEA refers to as "multiple disabilities." Many students with this classification will be taught through an alternative scope and sequence known as a "functional curriculum." A **functional curriculum** focuses upon daily living skills much more than on academic content. In one version, known as the MOVE curriculum, the approach emphasizes that the typical developmental sequences, through which children, for example, crawl before they walk, is *not* necessarily appropriate. Rather, the critical question is "What do these students need to learn and do as adults?" The focus, experts say, should be upon those essential skills and knowledge, even if abilities that are foundational or developmental for most children never get mastered. Other alternative curricula teach students to travel in the community, shop at neighborhood schools, and do other things they will need for an independent life. These alternative curricula focus upon aspects of content subjects (English, math, etc.) that have real-world applications for these individuals.

Students who are both deaf and blind typically face real difficulties in the regular classroom. Today's technologies tend to address the needs of deaf students by offering information visually and those of blind students by providing it aurally. Neither type of solution, however, meets the needs of children and youth who are both deaf and blind.

A recurrent theme in this chapter will be the challenge of meeting the needs of students with autism, severe disabilities, multiple disabilities, and deaf-blindness in an inclusive setting. If an IEP team determines that a child with these kinds of conditions is

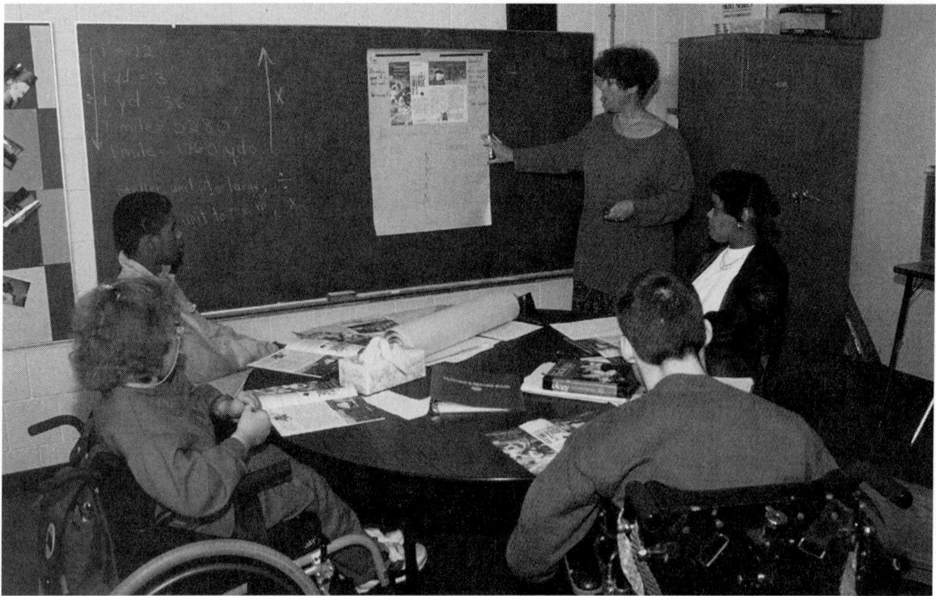

Separate classrooms are often appropriate for students having severe or multiple disabilities, because more individualized attention can be given and because the curriculum often focuses upon meeting special needs.

appropriately placed in an inclusive classroom, teachers must be prepared to depart from the standard curriculum in some significant ways. To take an example we will explore in this chapter, doing one-on-one discrete trials applied behavior analysis (ABA) with one child obviously takes you away from teaching the rest of the class.

Given the fact that many students with severe autism and severe or multiple disabilities need instruction that differs in significant ways from the standard curriculum, the question may arise: Are such children and youth properly placed into an inclusive classroom? The answer could be "Yes, at least for part of the school day." This may include "homeroom" activities at the beginning and end of the day, plus other activities such as field trips. Placement in an inclusive classroom for *part* but not necessarily all of the school day may make sense. In this way, children and youth share a "home" with age peers who do not have disabilities yet also receive an education appropriate to meeting their many needs. Such partial inclusion may be an appropriate solution for many students with autism or other severe and multiple disabilities who are not placed in regular classrooms full-time.

AUTISM SPECTRUM DISORDERS

Autism is one of a range of conditions collectively known as **pervasive developmental disorders (PDD).** The American Psychiatric Association's (APA) *Diagnostic and Statistical Manual,* 4th edition (*DSM-IV*) (1994) defines PDD as conditions in which physicians or other trained diagnosticians note the presence of characteristic behaviors that had an onset earlier than age three. In the area of social interaction, two of four defining features must be present: no attempt to share attention toward interesting people, objects, or events; failure to reciprocate when others attempt social interaction; non-use of typical interaction behaviors such as eye contact; and lack of age-appropriate peer relations. In the domain of communication, at least one of four behaviors must be noted: absent or severely delayed speech, particularly if not accompanied by gestures or other substitutes for speech; failure to begin or sustain a conversation; repetitive, stereotyped, or other idiosyncratic language; and no make-believe play or other age-appropriate imaginative behavior. With respect to preferred activities, at least one of five behaviors must be present: unusual preoccupation or fixation on one activity; inflexibility with respect to scheduling or other daily activities; stereotyped or repetitive behaviors; and fascination with parts of objects (color, shine, etc.) but not with the object itself. Finally, *DSM-IV* insists that the patient's condition is not bet-

A key to success for children and youth having physical disabilities is the ability to get around in the community, including, as needed, use of lift-equipped vans.

ter explained by Rhett's Disorder (see "Types," p. 247). As this lengthy list suggests, autism is a complex condition, one that can be challenging to diagnose.

Autism is a baffling disability. We do not understand much about people with severe autism, in large part because the very nature of the condition sharply constrains how much they can tell us about it. We also do not know what causes autism, in most instances. Lorna Wing (1998) and Uta Frith (1993) are among the top authorities on autism. Wing discussed the "theory of mind" idea with respect to Asperger's syndrome. Frith and Happe (1999) agreed that the central feature of autism probably is captured in the idea of "theory of mind": People with autism seem not to "get" the whole idea that their mental states (what they know, what they think) differ from those of other people. Stated differently, they lack empathy for others, in large part because they do not seem to recognize their own states of mind as being uniquely theirs. Wing and Frith have reported experiments showing that mental states most children have prior to the age of two are characteristic of people with autism at any age. That is, they do not seem to realize that others have different mental histories and perspectives than they do.

Looking at this from a developmental perspective, we can see that children generally make the leap from this mind-set when they are between 1.5 and 2 years of age. They suddenly realize that what they see, what they think, and what they feel are theirs alone. Most notably, they now recognize, their mothers and other care givers do *not* necessarily know what they know and feel what they feel. This dawning knowledge has two significant effects: First, it begins the process of making and keeping a mental, personal history. We do not remember, first-hand, what happened during the first two or three years of our lives; we do, however, have personal memories from three years of age and up. Second, it launches the "terrible twos" during which young children delight in disagreeing with and disobeying adults. A defining characteristic of autism spectrum disorders, then, is that people with these conditions did not make that leap.

Definitions

The U.S. Department of Education's (1999a) definition of **autism** reads:

> (i) Autism means a developmental disability significantly affecting verbal and nonverbal communication and social interaction, generally evident before age 3, that adversely affects a child's educational performance. Other characteristics often associated with autism are engagement in repetitive activities and stereotyped movements, resistance to environmental change or change in daily routines, and unusual responses to sensory experiences. The

> term does not apply if a child's educational performance is adversely affected primarily because the child has an emotional disturbance, as defined in paragraph (b)(4) of this section. (ii) A child who manifests the characteristics of "autism" after age 3 could be diagnosed as having "autism" if the criteria in paragraph (c)(1)(i) of this section are satisfied. (34 C.F.R. 300. 7[c][1])

A consensus statement produced by physicians and other experts in a meeting convened by the Cure Autism Now Foundation in 1997, citing *DSM-IV,* defined autism in these words:

> Autism is a neuropsychiatric syndrome characterized by onset prior to age 3 of severe abnormalities of reciprocal social relatedness; communication deficits (including deficits in language); and restricted, stereotyped patterns of interest and behaviors. Although autism has a wide spectrum of clinical presentations, it is distinct from other childhood neuropsychiatric disorders and primary forms of mental retardation. (*http://www.cureautismnow.org*)

Problems with These Definitions

The federal definition does not clearly identify mild versus severe forms of autism. It is much briefer than is the definition of Pervasive Developmental Disorders (PDD) found in *DSM-IV.* For this reason, it ignores several key aspects of autism, notably the lack of imagination. The reference to "paragraph (b)(4)" is erroneous. The actual definition for emotional disturbance appears in section 300.7(c)(4). That definition was provided in this book in Chapter 5.

The Department of Education's definition includes the familiar words "adversely affects a child's educational performance." What happens, however, if a child—perhaps one with Asperger's syndrome (see "Types," p. 247)—is achieving satisfactorily in school? Should IEP teams deny services under IDEA and consider, instead, eligibility under section 504? The definition refers to the behavioral characteristics of autism, notably the avoidance of eye contact (the non-use of eyes for communication) and the flapping of hands and fingers. What if those are only occasional and do not interfere with education? The definition incorporates the resistance to change that we often see in children having autism. However, persistent use of the techniques of ABA (see "Instructional Methods," p. 254) often succeeds in diminishing student displays of such behavior. You saw that in Lauren's story about John in the chapter-opening "Personal Accounts."

Prior to 1990, when autism was added as a separate category, many schools classified students with autism in the emotional or behavioral disorders category. That is now known to be erroneous. The definition makes note of this, clearly saying that autism is not an E/B disorder. Note that several of the characteristics the Department's definition attributes to autism are also mentioned in its definition of "severe disabilities" (p. 260). While autism is a severe disability, such overlap in definitions is less than helpful.

Characteristics and Types

In the 2002–2003 school year, 118,000 children and youth with the "autism" label who were between the ages of 6 and 21 inclusive participated in K–12 schools under IDEA (U.S. Department of Education, 2004, Table AA3). This was a 20% increase in one year, and more than twice the 53,500 reported just four years earlier (U.S. Department of Education, 2000b). Clearly, the numbers are rising rapidly. We do not know why. There is much else, too, that we do not know about autism spectrum disorders.

Characteristics

The federal definition implies certain characteristics. If you take another look at the definition, you will notice comments about communication, social interaction, repetitive (stereotypic) behaviors, rigidity, and responses to sensory input. Helpful in understanding all this is a three-prong explanation advanced by Frith (1993) and Wing (1998). Autism, they said, has three defining characteristics in the areas of *communication, socialization,* and *imagination*. Briefly, the theory suggests that in persons with autism interpersonal communication is severely impaired. Many people with autism do not speak at all. When they do talk, it is sometimes meaningless vocalizing (echolalia, for example, is the repeating of what was heard; thus, if you say "What is your name?" the child responds with "What is your name?"). In general, people with autism do not use eye contact as a method of communication, for example. That is why observers so often say, "She seemed to look right through me!" A related characteristic, one memorably reported by O. Ivar Lovaas (1987), is *overselectivity*. Lovaas described how one child focused upon her father's glasses. She did not recognize her father when shown a picture in which he was not wearing the glasses.

In the area of socialization, children with autism often play alone, years after other children have begun consistently to play in groups (Sigman & Ruskin, 1999). Frith (1993) introduced the term "autistic aloneness" to characterize such behavior. With respect to imagination, Frith noted that children with autism do not engage in pretend play. They also do not respond to something they find interesting by trying to gain an adult's attention to the same event or object.

Delays or deviations in speech and language development are among the first to be noticed (Wing, 1981, 1998). These may be attributable to the nature of autism as a disorder affecting "theory of mind." Developed by Uta Frith and others (e.g., Frith, & Happe, 1999), the idea is that, for whatever reason, persons with autism typically do not "get" the whole idea that their minds work differently from those of other people. If correct, this theory explains much that is baffling about autism. Why, for example, do so many children with autism have temper tantrums at the slightest change in daily routine? The "theory of mind" concept tells us that these children, unlike others, do not realize that teachers, parents, and others around them have knowledge, thoughts, feelings, and preferences different from their own. Thus, the whole idea that a teacher might alter a class schedule because the music teacher is sick is not something that children with autism can even begin to conceive. It is this theory of mind that is behind the screening instruments developed by Baron-Cohen and others (see "Diagnosis and Assessment," p. 252).

Parents and teachers routinely report that children and youth with autism spectrum disorders seem to be fascinated by one particular toy or movement, spending hour after hour in apparently pointless repetition of the same movements, with the same toy or object. Teachers and parents also note that any changes in usual activities can produce tantrums by the child. Anyone who watched the movie *Rain Man* can recall how Dustin Hoffman appeared to need to watch the TV program *The People's Court* at 4:00 each afternoon and how he tensed up when Tom Cruise moved a book from its usual location. The ways in which individuals with autism respond to sounds, sights, smells, and the feeling of touch is not well understood. However, some children and youth appear to be unusually sensitive to such sensory stimulation. Many children with autism exhibit some combination of abnormal sleep patterns, mood disorders, aggression, self-abuse, compulsive behaviors, or abnormal attention spans (Rapin, 1997).

We see many of these characteristics, in more muted form, in children and youth who have mild cases of autism (who may be labeled as having a "pervasive developmental disorder" [PDD] or "autistic-like" behavior). Some of these children speak. They may not, however, use the pronoun "I" and they may not discuss feelings. These patterns of expression seem to reinforce what Frith, Wing, and others have argued: that autism, even in mild forms, has "theory of mind" effects. One does not use "I" to refer to oneself unless one has a clear sense of being a distinct personality. Similarly, one would not discuss feelings if one thought that others invariably have the same feelings.

Types

Autism exists along a spectrum. The word "autism" and the words "full spectrum" typically are reserved for severe conditions. Asperger's syndrome is the term used when autism is present without mental retardation. People with Asperger's syndrome may have severe cases of autism, but their intelligence is generally within the typical range, and may even be superior. The words "autistic-like," applied to describe behavior and/or other symptoms, generally are used when autism is mild (Baron-Cohen, 1995).

Full-Spectrum Autism. Children who have full-spectrum, or "full-blown," autism are very severely impaired. A majority is also mentally retarded (Romanczyk, Weinter, Lockshin, & Ekdahl, 1999). Typically, persons with severe autism are regarded by others as fixated upon a few things. One father memorably described such rigidity of behavior by his son:

> At the age of four, Noah is neither toilet-trained nor does he feed himself. He seldom speaks expressively, rarely employs his less-than-a-dozen-words vocabulary. His attention span in a new toy is a matter of split seconds, television engages him only for an odd moment occasionally, he is never interested in other children for very long. His main activities are lint-catching, thread pulling, blanket-sucking, spontaneous giggling, inexplicable crying, bed-bouncing, eye-squinting, wall-hugging, circle-walking, and incoherent babbling addressed to his finger-flexing right hand. But two years ago, Noah spoke in complete sentences, had a vocabulary of well over 150 words, sang the verses of his favorite songs, identified the objects and animals in his picture books, was all but toilet-trained, and practically ate by himself. (Greenfield, 1972, 3–4)

These behaviors yield slowly, if at all, to sustained and intensive training (see "Instructional Methods," p. 254). That is why Cure Autism Now observes that "although many children make great strides, most will never marry, have a job or live independently. Half of all autistic children will never learn to speak" (*http://www.cureautismnow.org*).

Asperger's Syndrome. Asperger's syndrome is autism that is not accompanied by mental retardation (Wing, 1998). People with this disorder generally can be expected to be able to master some academic material, particularly information that is factual in nature (e.g., math, social studies, some science). However, as is the case with autism generally, people with Asperger's syndrome are sharply limited in empathy and, more broadly, in understanding that reality is perceived differently by different people (Safran, 2001). Bock and Myles (1999), in their overview of Asperger's syndrome, are emphatic about this lack of empathy being a defining characteristic of autism, including high-functioning autism. An excellent introduction to Asperger's syndrome for lay audiences is the article "Little Professor Syndrome" (Osborne, 2000).

Rhett's Disorder. The *DSM-IV* identifies Rhett's disorder as a condition in which physical development is normal early in life, after which all of the following occurs: Head growth slows notably until about age 4; the child loses skills until about age 2.5; the child loses interest in the surrounding environment; movement is uncoordinated; and receptive and expressive language both are very delayed or deviant in nature.

Pervasive Developmental Disorder. Educators often use the term "pervasive developmental disorder" or "PDD" to refer to children with mild symptoms of autism, in particular those who have very poor interpersonal relations. Thus, young children who consistently score low on "plays well with others" may sometimes be suspected of having PDD.

Autistic-Like Behaviors. You will sometimes see use of such terms as "autistic-like" behavior or "spectrum disorders." Both suggest that some children have conditions that are less severe than autism but that share some features with it. These various words and phrases generally refer to children and youth who share some characteristics with people who have autism, but who also have some features that we seldom see with severe-cases of autism. Teachers and therapists may use "autistic-like" to describe a child who does not interact well with others but who does do so on occasion. For all of these reasons, autism is often referred to as a spectrum disorder.

Commonalities. The three themes identified by Frith (1993)—communication, imagination, and socialization—are common to most types of autism. What varies is the extent to which those domains are disturbed. Thus, while about half of all persons with autism do not speak, muteness is far more prevalent among those with full-spectrum disorder than it is among those with autistic-like behaviors.

Studies have shown that many individuals with autism spectrum disorders have brain maps that are disordered in some way (e.g., Courchesne, 1989, 1995). In his review of the role of emotion in cognition, *The Feeling of What Happens: Body and Emotion in the Making of Consciousness,* Damasio (1999) explained that the human brain develops a model of the body, referred to as a "map." These mental patterns represent the body in the mind. The maps tell us where our bodies are in space, where each extremity is, and what sensations if any each is experiencing. In most of us, the body is mapped in the brain during the first several years of life. On occasion, however, the mapping is disrupted. Apparently, in some people with autism, the mapping occurs in the "wrong" areas of the brain. This is something reported by Tito Mukhopadhyay (see "Tito: A True Story About Autism," p. 251).

Differences. Asperger's syndrome is not accompanied by mental retardation. Most people with severe or "full-spectrum" autism are mentally retarded. Students with autistic-like behavior exhibit some behaviors that strike teachers and family members as "strange" but display other behaviors they consider "typical." By contrast, there is little that a person with full-spectrum autism does that most people would regard as "normal."

One difference that has attracted much attention is what is variously called **autistic savant behavior** or savant syndrome. Memorably displayed by Dustin Hoffman in *Rain Man* (where he instantly counted the number of toothpicks that fell on the floor and robotically recounted accident reports for each of several airline companies), savant behavior represents very unusual talents in a highly specific area. Thus, some people with autism can draw pictures of objects they have seen, with such accuracy in detail that the drawings are almost photographic in quality. Others can play a song after hearing it just once. Such abilities are rare. Some reports suggest that individuals with these talents practice them, devoting large amounts of time and energy to a very narrow interest. The displays of savant behavior that are seen by the public, as on an episode of *60 Minutes,* thus exaggerate the individual's inherent abilities. Even so, the competencies are unusual and striking.

Resources That Work

Autism

Newsweek magazine offered an outstanding cover story on autism in its July 31, 2000 issue. The story, "The Challenge of 'Mindblindness,'" by Geoffrey Cowley, is highly readable and filled with insights. Another article written for non-specialists, "Little Professor Syndrome" (Osborne, 2000) focuses upon Asperger's syndrome. The Web search engine Northern Light has performed a major service for teachers of children with autism by collecting at one site a large number of helpful Web pages about autism (*http://special.northernlight.com/autism/*). The federal government offers two Web sites about autism: *http://www.nimh.nih.gov/publicat/autism.cfm* (a publication about autism from the National Institutes of Health) and *http://www.cdc.gov/nceh/programs/cddh/dd/ddautism.htm* (information from the Centers for Disease Control and Prevention, or "CDC"). Two other sites, both by The Center of the Study of Autism, *http://www.autism.com* and *http://www.autism.org,* also offer a wealth of information. Also very helpful is the Web site of the Autism Society of America, *http://www.autism-society.org.*

Because autism is much misunderstood and treatment for it often hotly controversial, teachers need to be careful when seeking information about the disorder. In particular, Web sites that search engines such as Google™ locate tend to be those promoting alternative rather than mainstream points of view. Visitors should remind themselves that the word "alternative" means "little or no scientific evidence behind it." For example, widely held hopes that the hormone secretin might ameliorate the symptoms of autism remain unsupported by research. That is another reason to pursue a Web strategy suggested elsewhere in this book: begin with the most reputable sources. Links offered at such sites tend also to be trustworthy.

An excellent first-person account is offered by Maurice (1993). She tells how she and her family helped two of their children with autism to reach high levels of functioning. They adopted the applied behavior analysis (ABA) approach advocated by Lovaas. A highly regimented routine was followed in which the children were trained, again and again, in acceptable behavior. What makes her book, *Let Me Hear Your Voice,* different from many others is that she offers not just hope but a road map. The book has addresses and even phone numbers for resources that Maurice recommends to other families.

Co-Morbidity. As suggested earlier, autism is often co-morbid with mental retardation. Since Fragile X is one known cause of autism, the two obviously may be co-morbid (see Chapter 5).

Prevalence

The *26th Annual Report* (U.S. Department of Education, 2004, Table AA3) shows that 118,000 children between the ages of 6 and 21 inclusive were identified as having autism. That is about 2% of children having any label.

Teachers of inclusive classrooms are likely to see relatively few students with autism. Figure 7.1 shows that not only is the number of such children and youth quite small but, in addition, relatively modest proportions are placed into general classrooms all or most of the school week (that is, they spend less than 21% of the time outside of general classrooms).

The age distribution is revealing: The number of children with autism falls steadily with age. There are more children with this classification in the early elementary years than there are in the middle-school or high-school levels. Figure 7.2 shows the distribution of children with autism according to age. Notice that the numbers are much larger at the elementary than at the secondary level. That is what one would expect, given the fact that this label was first approved for use in 1990. That is, older children were not given this label. Rather, some were given the label "emotionally disturbed" and others were classified as "Other Health Impaired." The low prevalence numbers at the high-school level could also signal something parents report happening quite frequently: Adolescents are removed from the home and from public schools and placed into institutions. The Department's data include reports from public schools—but none from state hospitals or other institutions that do not provide special education services. Cowley (2000) noted that many young people with autism are institutionalized, some as early as age 13. This is an indication of the severity of autism. We will discuss it more under "Strategies in Middle School and Secondary School."

There is no apparent disproportionate representation of ethnic and racial minority groups among persons who have autism. The proportions who are of different races and ethnic groups are about the same as those of the nation as a whole (*26th Annual Report,* 2004, Table AA3). There *is* a gender difference, however, with boys outnumbering girls four to one. This seems to suggest an as-yet-unidentified sex-linked genetic component as one cause (Cowley, 2000).

FIGURE 7.1 Likelihood of Inclusive Placements: Autism

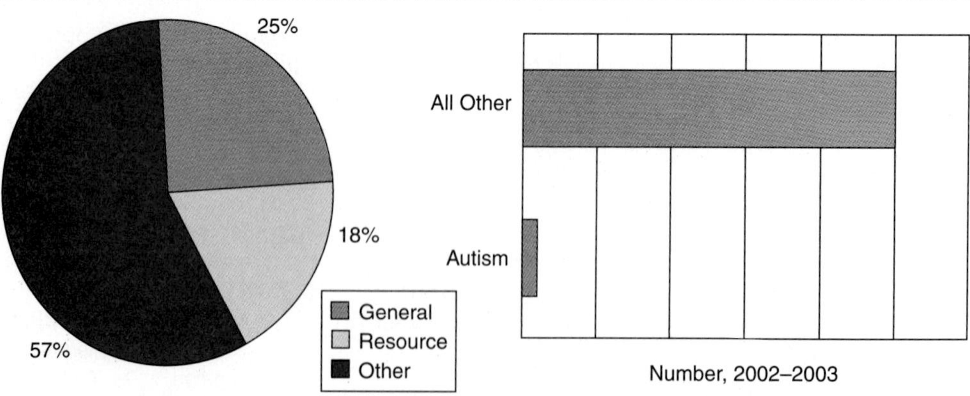

Students with the "autism" label are relatively few in number, at 118,000, according to the *26th Annual Report* (2004). About one in every four (25%) were placed in general classrooms all or most of the school week (spending less than 21% of the time in other settings). The two charts above illustrate these data.

Source: From the *26th Annual Report,* by the U.S. Department of Education, 2004, Washington, DC: Author.

FIGURE 7.2 Prevalence of Autism: Elementary and Secondary

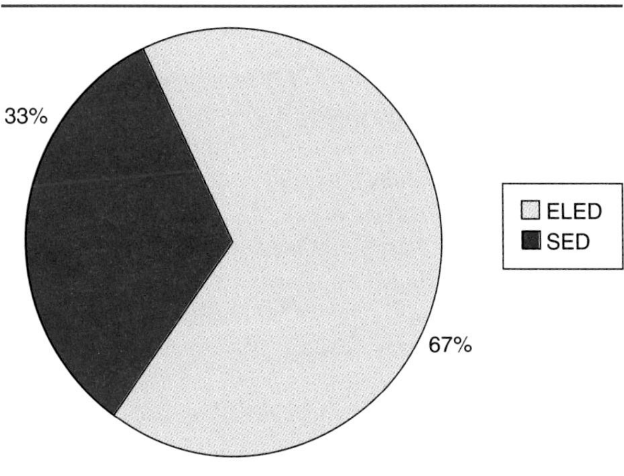

Source: From the *26th Annual Report,* by the U.S. Department of Education, 2004, Washington, DC: Author.

Reports of increasing numbers of children being identified as having PDD or autism, not just in K–12 schools but in physicians' offices as well, are disturbing. Once estimated to occur in one child per 2,000 (e.g., Bowe, 2000a), autism is now suspected to have an incidence of one per 500 or even one per 250 live births (Cure Autism Now Foundation, *http://www.cureautismnow.org*). If these reports of increased incidence are correct, autism is as common as other childhood medical disorders such as childhood-onset diabetes and leukemia. The new, higher reported rates are being investigated by the federal Centers for Disease Control and Prevention (CDC). The CDC effort is important because criteria for identification and practices for reporting vary widely from state to state. Initial findings suggest that much of the apparent increase in incidence, notably in California, may be due to mis-diagnosis. Alternatively, it may be that educators and physicians are becoming more adept at diagnosis.

TITO: A TRUE STORY ABOUT AUTISM

Tito Mukhopadhyay, age 15, took parents of children with autism and many experts by storm in mid- to late-2002 as he traveled around the U.S. with his mother, Soma. That was because Tito, diagnosed with autism at age 3, while living in India, appears to shatter widely held beliefs about the nature of autism—while explaining much-misunderstood characteristics of individuals with the condition. Tito's trip was sponsored by Cure Autism Now.

Tito seldom speaks. When he does, his voice is difficult to understand. He engages in repetitive flapping and rocking motions. In these and other ways, say authorities from the United Kingdom's Cambridge University to the University of California at San Francisco Medical School, he has a severe form of autism. As often occurs, Tito developed normally during his first 18 months of life, then regressed. For the next 8 years, his preferred activity was hiding in his room, watching a ceiling fan.

Yet Tito has a rich vocabulary. He types long, grammatically correct sentences, and sometimes writes by hand as well. He expresses feelings. Tito writes poetry and fiction. He grasps the idea that his mind works differently from those of typical people. Not only that, but he articulates the ways in which he thinks, feels, and acts. At one session in Los Angeles, after fluttering his fingers and flapping his arms, he calmly typed onto a laptop computer that in turn used speech synthesis to speak his words: "I am calming myself. My senses are so disconnected, I lose my body. So I flap. If I don't do this, I feel scattered and anxious" (quoted in Blakeslee, 2002, F1).

No one is touching Tito as he communicates. He types and writes by himself. For this reason, his abilities cannot be explained as can similar words and sentences "produced" by persons with autism with the "help" of facilitators in the now widely discredited method of facilitated communication. Research that appeared in the early and mid-1990s showed conclusively that the communications were actually coming, usually without conscious intent and even without conscious knowledge, from the facilitators rather than from persons with autism (e.g., Wheeler, Jacobson, Paglieri, & Schwartz, 1993).

His mother taught him English. At Soma's insistence, Tito began writing stories and poems. Soma stressed the importance of communicating feelings. She often would not give Tito his lunch or dinner until he had written a poem. Aware of the scathing criticism heaped upon facilitated communication, Soma demanded stories in which Tito discussed feelings and mental processes. A book of poems, essays, and stories that Tito wrote between the ages of 8 and 11, *Beyond the Silence,* was published in 2000 by the National Autistic Society, in the United Kingdom. Included is an essay in which he reports that "I hardly realized that I had a body except when I was hungry . . . I needed constant movement, which made me get the feeling of my body. The movement can be of a rotating type or just flapping of my hands. Every movement is proof that I exist. I exist because I can move." (quoted in Blakeslee, 2002, F4). In October 2003, another book, *The Mind Tree,* containing essays he wrote between the ages of 8 and 11, was published.

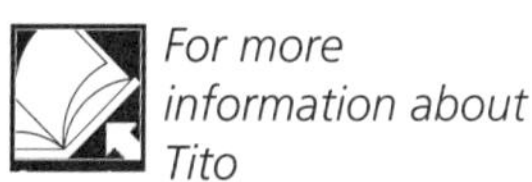

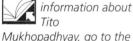

For more information about Tito Mukhopadhyay, go to the Web Links module in Chapter 7 of the Companion Website.

Although no less an authority on autism than Lorna Wing is reported to have vouched for the authenticity of Tito's writing, critics remain somewhat skeptical. Having been burned by early stories about "miracles" with facilitated communication, they wonder if Tito is too good to be true. Perhaps the stories that he tells are fiction, created because his mother would not feed him unless and until he wrote them. His mother's fixation upon proving that Tito had emotions and that his behavior was attributable to recognizable mental processes may be responsible for the fact that Tito articulates reasonable-sounding bases for his behavior. Or perhaps none of these speculations has any merit. It may simply be that Tito is one of a kind. If so, he tells us nothing about others who have autism.

Diagnosis and Assessment

Autism spectrum disorders can be difficult to diagnose with certainty, especially in the early childhood years. Often, several years pass between the initial appearance of symptoms and a definitive diagnosis. In addition, while *DSM-IV* outlines the criteria to be used, professionals vary greatly in how they interpret those guidelines. The American Psychiatric Association opened the door to such differences by listing 16 different behaviors, of which only five must be present for identification. Diagnosis is further complicated by the fact that about one-third of children eventually diagnosed with autism spectrum disorders appear to be without symptoms until about age 18 months or 2 years, at which point they begin to regress. The reversal in development can be sudden and precipitous. Toddlers who had begun speaking, who were toilet trained, and who had outgoing, even evanescent personalities abruptly cease speaking, stop using the bathroom, and withdraw from interpersonal contact. These changes understandably are traumatic for family members to observe.

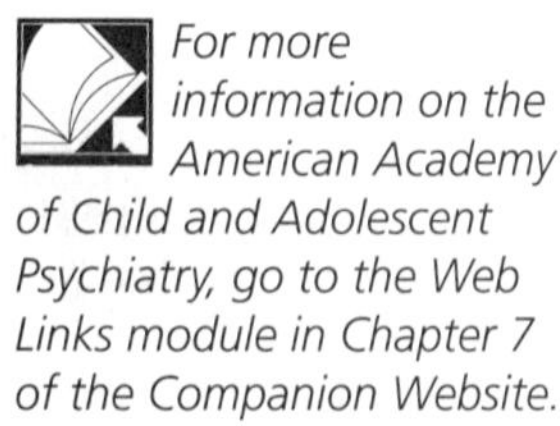

For more information on the American Academy of Child and Adolescent Psychiatry, go to the Web Links module in Chapter 7 of the Companion Website.

The American Academy of Child and Adolescent Psychiatry offers diagnosis guidelines in "Practice parameters for the psychiatric assessment of infants and toddlers (0–36 months)." As a medical condition, autism should be diagnosed by physicians or others highly trained in neurology. This includes child psychiatrists, pediatric neurologists, developmental pediatricians, neuropsychologists, and child psychologists. Because apparent non-responsiveness to speech is a defining characteristic of autism, professionals need to assess the child's hearing. Generally, pure-tone audiometry tested by a trained audiologist will suffice. A speech pathologist may also be consulted to assess the child's speech and language development and to help rule out other possible causes of speech and language delays and deviations from typical development.

The 1997 consensus statement from Cure Autism Now (*http://www.cureautismnow.org*) recommended use of the Checklist for Autism in Toddlers (CHAT). This is a screening tool that requires just 3 minutes to administer. Research suggests that the CHAT correctly identifies autism, Asperger's syndrome, and other PDD conditions (Baron-Cohen, Allen, & Gillberg, 1992; Baron-Cohen, Cox, & Baird, 1998). The panel urged that all children be screened by their pediatricians at 18 months of age using the CHAT, particularly if parents suspect autism spectrum disorders based upon communication skills. For children screened in by the instrument, follow-up testing of speech, language, and other development should be conducted. This is because some children later found to be developing normally may be wrongly identified by the CHAT. An autism-spectrum quotient (AQ) later was developed by Baron-Cohen and his colleagues. Impressive evidence has been reported that the instrument is useful (Baron-Cohen, Wheelwright, Skinner, Martin, & Clubley, 2001). This scale asks simple questions, such as whether the child is interested in fiction and in the personalities of people around her.

In your readings, you will often come across reports of the use of electroencephalograms (EEGs) or other such instruments and techniques, including functional brain imaging techniques such as single photon emission tomography, positron emission tomography, magnetoencephalography, or magnetic resonance spectroscopy. These are valuable research tools for exploring how people's minds work. At present, however, they are of limited utility in diagnosing autism spectrum disorders.

Causes

Experts do not know what causes autism spectrum disorders. There are associations with Fragile X, a genetic condition, but it is not clear whether Fragile X and autism have a shared, unknown, cause or whether some feature of Fragile X causes autism (Cohen & Volkmar, 1997). Similarly, there is a higher prevalence of autism in families having another child with autism. Frith (1993), for example, reported that when one child has autism the chances that a sibling does too are 50 to 100 times greater than is the case with unrelated children. This fact also suggests a genetic aspect. While this may be a genetic predisposition (meaning that something in the family's genes makes its children unusually susceptible to some environmental factor or factors such that the combination of genetic vulnerability and those environmental influences causes autism), scientists do not yet know what that aspect may be nor have they identified the environmental influences involved. Baron-Cohen and colleagues have reported that use of the AQ instrument reveals that unexpected numbers of parents of children with autism have unusual strengths in mathematics and physics (Baron-Cohen, Wheelwright, Skinner, Martin, & Clubley, 2001).

Many and varied possible causative factors have been identified in both lay and professional literature. Some of these have gained wide distribution. There is, for example, no reliable data suggesting a link between diet and autism. The theories advanced by Bruno Bettelheim, who famously said that mothers of children with autism were "refrigerator mothers" (Bettelheim, 1967), were long ago shown to be wrong.

Genetic Factors

Fragile X syndrome is one known cause of autism (National Fragile X Foundation, *http://www.fragilex.org*). This fact may help to account for the gender difference in autism, which is much more common among males than among females. Fragile X is a condition in which symptoms typically appear in males. Females, by contrast, usually are carriers (they do not exhibit symptoms themselves, but their male offspring may). Ridley (1999), reviewing new information about the genome, noted that the sex-linked nature of autism indicates a possible role for the X and Y sex chromosomes. However, definitive genetic causes have yet to be found. Population-based studies suggest that perhaps as few as one in ten children with autism spectrum disorders have an identifiable genetic condition (Cohen & Volkmar, 1997). Thus, most cases probably have other causes.

Environmental Factors

As suggested above, some factor or factors in the environment may be interacting in some as-yet-unknown way or ways with human genes so as to cause autism. Frith (1993) and Ridley (1999) concurred that when one child in a family has autism, not all of that child's siblings do. Much interest centers upon whether childhood vaccinations play a role. See "Research That Works: Autism and Vaccinations."

Instructional Methods

Applied behavior analysis (ABA), mentioned in "Resources That Work: Autism," is the most-validated instructional approach with children and youth having autism. This is intensive, one-on-one training. Few other interventions have been shown by impartial research to be effective.

Research That Works

Autism and Vaccinations

There is much discussion among parents about the possibility that childhood immunization for measles, mumps, and rubella (the MMR vaccine) may cause autism. A report on CBS's *60 Minutes* revealed widespread parental suspicions. Those doubts may be related to the fact that autism symptoms often appear shortly after young children are vaccinated. The connection was first suggested in a small study (N = 12 subjects) in 1998. The fact that this research reported only correlation, and not causation, seems to have made little difference to critics. The National Institutes of Health (NIH) and the Centers for Disease Control and Prevention (CDC), the major American authorities on health, dispute the allegations. Most physicians agree with NIH and CDC. The American Academy of Pediatrics (AAP) notes that the number of children who become ill from preventable illnesses is down 99% from the 1970s (*http://www.aap.org*). Vaccines successfully prevent 12 potentially serious diseases, among which are measles, mumps, rubella, diphtheria, polio, hepatitis B, hepatitis A, and chickenpox. The pediatricians are concerned that unfounded worries about vaccinations may cause American families to forego much-needed shots for their children.

The most controversial vaccine is MMR. A recent report (Madsen et al., 2002), published in the *New England Journal of Medicine,* found "no association between the age at the time of vaccination, the time since vaccination, or the date of vaccination and the development of autistic disorder," concluding that "this study provides strong evidence against the hypothesis that MMR vaccination causes autism" (p. 1477). The researchers conducted a retrospective review of the records of more than one-half million children, of whom 82% had received the MMR vaccination. They found only very small numbers diagnosed with autism (316 children) or other autism-spectrum disorders (422 children). Even this sophisticated study was not enough to silence the critics. One group of parents, the National Vaccine Information Center, of Vienna, VA, for example, said "this study was not good enough" (Barbara Loe Fisher, quoted in Ricks, 2002, p. A53). Another group, Safe Minds, is suing Eli Lilly & Co., makers of MMR vaccines.

NIH, CDC, AAP and other authorities also cite a large study in California which found no connection between the vaccines and autism. They also point to research reported in the prestigious journal *Lancet* showing that the mercury-based preservative thimersol, widely alleged to cause autism, does not. In any case, vaccines given to American children under 6 months of age no longer contain thimersol. The National Immunization Program (NIP) continues to recommend that young children receive this vaccine and also the DTP vaccine (which protects against diphtheria, tetanus, and pertussis; *http://www.cdc.gov/nip*).

As a result of widespread publicity about an alleged connection between vaccinations and autism, still-small but growing numbers of families are opting to not vaccinate their children. According to the NIP, 90% of school-age children in the United States have been vaccinated. However, decreases in rates of vaccination have been reported in 11 states, together with increases in cases of measles and other illnesses (e.g., McNeil, 2002).

Research continues on this very controversial topic (e.g., Allen, 2002). Hopefully, a cause or group of causes for autism will be identified soon and either the controversy evaporates in the face of that information or the vaccines are modified to remove the element(s) found to cause or contribute to autism spectrum disorders.

Strategies in Early Childhood and Elementary School

At the elementary level, of the 75,000 children aged 6 to 11 inclusive with the autism classification, 25% were taught in inclusive classrooms all or most of the school week during the 2002–2003 school year, with another 18% instructed in such settings as well as in resource rooms, according to the *26th Annual Report*. Almost half (46%) were educated in separate classrooms in neighborhood school buildings. As noted earlier, the number of children is higher at this level than at the secondary level (there are just 37,000 in the 12 to 17 inclusive age range). Thus, elementary teachers are more likely than are secondary teachers to find children with autism in their classrooms. This is particularly true because parents of younger children tend to be more enthusiastic about the potential benefits of inclusion than are parents of older children.

Methods: Positive Behavior Supports. Critical to determining how to intervene with a child or young person having autism spectrum disorders is to understand *why* behavior that strikes many people as bizarre is occurring. A *functional behavioral assessment* seeks to determine the function behavior serves for an individual. Positive behavior supports means much the same thing. The major difference is that educators use the term "functional behavioral assessment" when referring to children's *behavior management* but "positive behavior supports" with reference to children's *learning* (Chapter 9). In both cases, teachers look to determine when children display unacceptable behavior and try to determine the function that behavior serves for the child (that is, why the child produces that behavior). Such analyses are rarely more needed than they are with students having autism spectrum disorders. To illustrate, consider tantrums. When does a child act up? Specifically what precedes the tantrums? You may find that these occur when the child is expected to perform a task, such as reading a story. If so, the function of the tantrum may be to excuse the child from something he feels is not doable. Understood in this way, tantruming is simply a rather extreme instance of avoidance behavior. Such an analysis tells you to teach the child how to do the task and convince the student that he can in fact perform it satisfactorily. All of this introduces the idea of ABA.

Methods: Preschool Preparation for Inclusion in K–12 Schools. In his work with young children having autism, Lovaas (1987) stressed the importance of integrating the children at the first- or second-grade level, if not in kindergarten. This research is discussed below. His reports on those studies noted that exposure to the typical behaviors exhibited by children who do not have autism helps these children to change their behavior. Some experts are leery about the extent to which students with severe forms of autism spectrum disorders should be educated in inclusive classrooms. Others are enthusiastic. Koegel and Koegel (1995), for example, report that social interaction in particular improves when children are placed in inclusive settings.

The keys seem to be acquisition of skills and behaviors during the pre-inclusion years so that the child engages in reciprocal behavior as expected, relates to classmates, plays with others, and responds to multiple environmental stimuli. For this reason, it may be the case with children having full-spectrum autism as it is with most children who are blind (see Chapter 6) that inclusion is most likely to be successful if it is preceded by at least a year or two of non-inclusion. That year or those years in a separate setting should be devoted to intensive training on "how to swim" so that when the child enters the water, she is equipped for success. Stated differently, selecting *what will be taught* is as essential with this population as it is with children having mental retardation (see Chapter 5). Again, the basic reason is that instruction is so time-consuming. Some competencies and behaviors, in addition, are so important that they produce a ripple effect. Teaching those makes inclusion, at least for part of the day, possible.

Others insist that inclusion for most, if not all, of the day is appropriate. This may occur if the child's IEP identifies goals that can best be met in such a setting. To illustrate, Nickels (1996) described why inclusion was the appropriate choice for her son

Alex during his fifth-grade year, despite the fact that his academic competencies were generally at the first-grade level:

> Issues such as being aware and accepting of the real world; participating in part of an activity or project; taking directions and paying attention in large-group environments; learning to overcome and tolerate the distractions that such environments impose; learning to listen, follow along, finish a task, and take appropriate instructions from a peer helper or teacher and discriminate and respond on command; and learning to develop appropriate social responses and behaviors, to be a friend, and to spontaneously follow the natural rhythms and routines of normal life . . . These are the purposes of inclusive environments—the important skills and abilities that can be taught in general classrooms. (pp. 128–129)

Methods: Applied Behavior Analysis. Applied behavior analysis (ABA) may be characterized as a subset of behavior modification (Chapter 9). One way in which ABA differs from general behavior-modification techniques is that ABA generally is performed one-on-one. It involves repeated trials, or what is often called discrete trial training (DTT). The term refers to the fact that very specific ("discrete") behaviors are demanded in repeated trials in a way that more resembles training than teaching. To illustrate, a therapist first demonstrates the desired behavior (says "Thank you"). The therapist then says to the child, "Say 'thank you'." (The therapist does *not* discuss why the behavior is demanded, does not reason with the child to convince the child to respond, and so on. In these ways, ABA is training rather than teaching.) If the child responds appropriately, the therapist offers a reward (presentation reinforcement). This may be an M&M candy, it may be a sip of water, or it may be verbal praise. The key to success with these methods is to use a presentation reinforcer for which the child is willing to work. Sessions should also use as stimulus materials objects chosen by the *child;* research shows that student choice increases the quality of a student's participation and the pace of progress (Koegel & Koegel, 1995). In ABA, the trials continue until the student successfully performs the behavior, on demand, at a minimum level of competency (e.g., 90% of trials).

Lovaas (1987) used ABA in his work with young children having autism. This was ground-breaking research. He and students of his at UCLA provided very intensive discrete trials training in behavior and communication to preschool-age children with autism. The invasiveness of the approach needs to be appreciated. In Lovaas's project, students provided as many as 40 hours per week of one-on-one intervention. They continued this work for as many as five years, accumulating a total of 10,000 hours of instruction. Lovaas described the outcomes of these efforts as resulting, in many cases, in behavior that he said approached normal. Those claims startled other researchers. Some responded with harsh criticism of Lovaas's methods and data interpretation (e.g., Schopler, Short, & Mesibov, 1989). Notwithstanding their criticisms, Lovaas's research has stood the test of time. We now know that it works. We may not understand *why* it is effective. But some 20 years after he first demonstrated its effectiveness, the legitimacy of ABA with this population is now well-accepted. Lovaas illustrated the use of ABA to train young children to be less selective in the environmental stimuli to which they responded. To use an example he offered, a child learned to respond not only to her father's glasses but also to his face, his hair, his height, and his bearing. Professionals have picked up on the approach, giving it the rather cumbersome names of "stimulus control" and "within-stimulus prompting" (e.g., Koegel & Koegel, 1995, p. 11). The technique of **stimulus control** emphasizes environmental stimuli that the child has not been responding to and/or reinforces the child when he responds to those stimuli.

Methods: Successive Approximations. Another variation is the method of successive approximations, also known as *shaping*. Because many students with autism cannot produce the complete behavior that is desired, therapists and teachers reward approximations of that behavior. The method of **successive approximations** tells you to reinforce be-

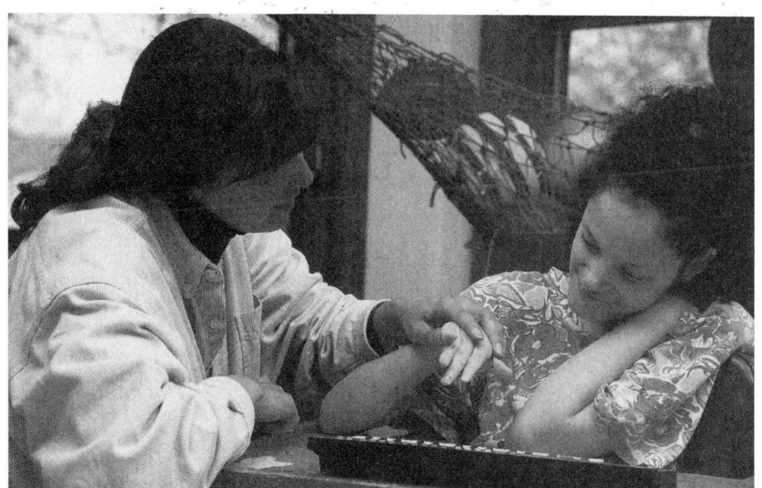

While communication boards help students to express themselves, care should be exercised by teachers and therapists not to influence the students' communication. In this instance, it would be preferable for the adult not *to place her hand over the child's hand.*

havior the child *can* give to you. Once that behavior appears regularly, you should no longer reinforce it. Rather, you withhold reinforcement until the child gives you more. Suppose, for example, that a child does not name a desired object. You would give the toy to the child after the child looks steadily at it. Some time later, just looking at the toy will not suffice. You would get the object only after the child asks for it, using words. Eventually, you would reinforce only a complete, grammatically correct request: "May I please have the red ball that's on the shelf?" Shaping is most used with behavior, for which reason we discuss it more fully in Chapter 9.

Method: Place "Interesting" and Desired Objects Out of Reach. In a related approach, teachers and therapists may increase the expressive communication of a student with autism by deliberately making a treasured toy or other much-desired object out of reach. They will refuse to give it to the child until the child requests it. The concept applies to many activities in the classroom. The underlying intent is to make *communication* by the child necessary. Koegel and Koegel (1995) related the technique to the more general approach of reducing learned helplessness in students having autism. The thrust, they suggested, should be on *motivating* the student to communicate. By showing children better ways than tantruming, self-stimulating, and so on, of indicating that they do not feel competent to do something, the Koegels said, teachers and therapists can encourage children to use less drastic and (to us) more understandable means of communication (e.g., "Help me").

Methods: Occupational and Physical Therapy. Some occupational and physical therapists design push-in and pull-out interventions for children and youth with autism spectrum disorder based upon a model they call **sensory integration.** Drawing upon theoretical work by A. Jean Ayres (1979) and others, they seek to assist students to bring together and make effective use of sensory information from hearing, vision, and touch. The allegation is made by Ayres and others that autism features sensory-integration problems in the brain. In other words, the body-mapping process is disordered in the brains of people with autism. Such mapping errors may be responsible for self-stimulation, rocking, flapping, and other physical behaviors that are seen in many people with autism. This theory has led to such interventions as swinging, brushing, and other activities designed to help children and youth to become more aware of their bodies and less hypersensitive to sensory input. There is very little objective research evidence in support of such interventions as brushing and swinging, that are based upon such data. Still, some therapists and teachers swear by them (Lord & McGee, 2001).

For more information on sensory integration, go to the Web Links module in Chapter 7 of the Companion Website.

Strategies in Middle School and Secondary School

Just 22% of students of secondary age (12 to 17 years, inclusive) who have the autism label were taught in inclusive environments all or most of the school week during the 2002–2003 academic year, plus another 19% who split time between regular classrooms and resource rooms. Nearly half (45%) were taught, instead, in separate (self-contained) classrooms, according to the *26th Annual Report* (U.S. Department of Education, 2004). As noted earlier, the number of students with this classification is much lower than is the case in elementary schools. Thus, a smaller proportion of a smaller population is included in high schools as compared to elementary schools. In part, this reflects the severity of autism.

Methods: Support for Inclusive Placements. It is important to recognize that some students with autism spectrum disorders, notably those with Asperger's syndrome, can be successfully integrated in middle school and high school. This is particularly true with respect to such subjects as math and science. To quote Baron-Cohen, Wheelwright, Skinner, Martin, and Clubley (2001), "Asperger Syndrome need not be any obstacle to achieving at the highest levels in these fields" (p. 14). We will revisit this issue when we look at the teaching of math and science in Chapter 15.

Methods: Functional Curriculum. As at the early childhood and elementary level, deciding *what* to teach is a key when working with children and youth having autism. Historically, it has been during the early secondary years that families have been forced to give up their goal of community living, making the difficult decision to place teens with autism into state hospitals or other residential facilities. While such placement may be appropriate in some instances, it can be avoided. If a major commitment is made during the middle-school and high-school years to prepare the student to function appropriately in the community. This means teaching behaviors that are expected in public settings. It also means teaching practical life skills. With many students having autism, such instruction is so time-consuming that little time remains available for more traditional academic instruction.

Methods: TEACCH. An approach built upon the idea that people with autism see the world differently than do others is TEACCH (*http://www.teacch.com*). The acronym stands for *T*reatment and *E*ducation of *A*utistic and related *C*ommunication handicapped *Ch*ildren. The method was developed in North Carolina, where it is used more in self-contained than in inclusive classrooms. With respect to students with autism who are included, the TEACCH approach emphasizes that children with autism have difficulty organizing. That is why the team at the University of North Carolina, Chapel Hill, urges teachers to structure the classroom. This includes such steps as minimizing distractions (e.g., mirrors, windows, more than one door in/out of the room) and organizing the student's day with schedules that are placed on notebook covers. Ring binders with folders for each subject are recommended. Those binders should have two pockets: one for assignments to be done and the other for finished work. In middle school and high school, the need for structure increases. This is because there are more classes, more teachers, and more rigid schedules. For this reason, the TEACCH team suggests that the students' lockers be well-organized, with reminders posted on the inside of the locker door about what to take at each period of the day.

The TEACCH Web site includes articles suggesting that students with autism may be excused from physical education classes. Article writers cite the fact that many children and youth with autism "hate PE" due to their movement-coordination difficulties. Other articles urge that middle-school and high-school students with autism, including those with Asperger's syndrome, be assigned a buddy. This student would accompany the child with autism to those activities which are relatively unstructured, including lunch, recess, and extracurricular activities. The buddy's role would be to assist in organizing and structuring social interactions. Several articles posted at the TEACCH site note that accommodations designed for students with learning disabilities, such as highlighted textbooks, often are useful for students with autism spectrum disorders.

Methods: Autism and the Arts. It is quite possible that most students with autism spectrum disorders who remain in inclusive settings into the secondary years are so-called "high-functioning" persons and/or people with Asperger's syndrome (Safran, 2001). Bock and Myles (1999) offered a thoughtful summary of what teachers should know about this syndrome. They pointed out that students with Asperger's syndrome have cognitive limitations. If the theory of mind developed by Frith (1993), Wing (1998), and others is correct, they likely will have great difficulty understanding the whole concept of creativity. This suggests that they will encounter problems not just with English literature but also with such "specials" as music and art.

Let us illustrate this with the example of poetry, something often taught in high-school English classes. It is the nature of poetry that readers are caused to look inward. The poet explores his own feelings and, by so doing, provokes us to examine our own. But, at least hypothetically, that is something that autism spectrum disorders prevent people from doing effectively. Stated differently, if the theory of mind is correct, autism defeats the whole exercise of reading poetry because autism interferes with the recognition of points of view.

Or consider prose fiction. This form of literature takes us outside of ourselves. It enables us to "visit" times and places we would not otherwise experience. That may be a far-away location (e.g., the South Seas) or a long-ago time (e.g., the Civil War), or both. In addition, good fiction frequently is firmly grounded in reality; that is one way writers of prose fiction succeed in making readers engage in "the willing suspension of disbelief" (to adopt Coleridge's very appropriate description of what readers of prose fiction do). For all these reasons, prose fiction is likely to be more readable for some people with autism, including Asperger's syndrome, than is poetry.

Strategies in Transition to Adult Life

Individuals with Asperger's syndrome often can secure paid employment in competitive settings, as, for example, computer programmers (Bock & Myles, 1999; Cowley, 2000). This possibility should prompt IEP teams to work closely with high-school students and their families, during the transition years (ages 14 to school exit) to *plan* how the housing, transportation, and other community resources can be mobilized to support a working adult who has autism or a similar spectrum disorder.

However, it can be difficult for many persons who are mentally retarded in addition to having autism to succeed in competitive employment. They may enjoy much more success in a supported employment environment, where ongoing help is available from trained counselors. Some may find community activity centers and other non-competitive environments to be most satisfying.

The fact that students with autism, including those who are not also mentally retarded, generally do not "get" the idea that people have different mental states is a central finding of research with this population. Teachers need to use this information in making decisions. Does it make sense, for example, to place a 16-year-old boy with autism into a driver education course? Driving requires people to respond to behavior, and to anticipate future behavior, by other drivers on the road. This means understanding other people's mind-sets.

Families that cope at home with the many demands placed upon them by a young child who has autism may give up these efforts when confronted with the much-greater burdens presented by an adolescent. The very nature of autism is that it sharply curtails an individual's ability to make judgments, especially about other people. Everyday interactions with people in the community may escalate into emergencies, as when an adolescent does not respond appropriately when told to wait in line, and so on. Eventually, crisis piles upon crisis, and the family determines that it must place the teen into a protective environment. Everyone involved, parents and educators alike, want to avoid institutionalization. The hope is that early and intensive intervention will assist growing numbers of people with autism to remain in the community.

SEVERE/MULTIPLE DISABILITIES

Many children and youth have more than one impairment. We have seen this repeatedly in previous chapters (see the "Co-Morbidity" sections in Chapters 3 to 6). State education departments and local school districts differ in how they report co-occurring disabilities. Many will classify a student according to what they regard as the primary impairment. Thus, a student who has a specific learning disability (SLD) and also an attention deficit hyperactivity disorder (ADHD) might be classified as SLD. To take another example, a child with Down Syndrome almost certainly has several disorders. Mental retardation is the most likely label to be used, but the child may also have a cardiac condition, hypotonia (low tension) in the muscles, and perhaps a hearing and vision impairment as well.

IDEA includes a category for "multiple disabilities." There is also a category for deaf-blindness. However, there is no category for a term sometimes used by educators, "severe disabilities."

The discussion here on severe and multiple conditions is fairly brief. This is because the individual disorders comprising multiple disabilities were discussed previously, because co-morbidity was described earlier for each category, and because previous chapters noted when disabilities tend to be severe rather than mild or moderate in nature (e.g., emotional disturbance and mental retardation both were characterized in Chapter 5 as being severe).

Definitions

The federal regulations for the Individuals with Disabilities Education Act (IDEA) do not offer a definition for severe disabilities. They do, however, define multiple disabilities and deaf-blindness. There is some overlap in those two definitions. We will address those duplications in the following section.

Until 1997, the U.S. Department of Education provided a definition of severe disabilities, for use in a discretionary program that no longer exists. The previous definition for **severe disabilities** was published at 34 C.F.R. 315.4(f):

> The term "children with severe disabilities" refers to children with disabilities who, because of the intensity of their physical, mental, or emotional problems, need highly specialized education, social, psychological, and medical services in order to maximize their full potential for useful and meaningful participation in society and for self-fulfillment. The term includes those children with disabilities with severe emotional disturbance (including schizophrenia), autism, severe and profound mental retardation, and those who have two or more serious disabilities such as deaf-blindness, mental retardation and blindness, and cerebral palsy and deafness. Children with severe disabilities may experience severe speech, language, and/or perceptual-cognitive deprivations, and evidence abnormal behavior such as failure to respond to pronounced social stimuli, self-mutilation, self-stimulation, manifestation of intensive and prolonged temper tantrums, and absence of rudimentary forms of verbal control; and may also have extremely fragile physiological conditions.

This definition was used for an IDEA Part D discretionary program demonstrating innovative ways of serving children and youth with severe impairments. As noted, the definition no longer appears in the federal rules.

There is, on the other hand, an IDEA category for **multiple disabilities.** The law itself offers no definition for that term. The Department's rules do:

> Multiple disabilities means concomitant impairments (such as mental retardation-blindness, mental retardation-orthopedic impairment, etc.), the combination of which causes such severe educational needs that they cannot be accommodated in special education programs solely for one of the impairments. The term does not include deaf-blindness. (34 C.F.R. 300.7[c][7])

The federal regulations define **deaf-blindness** in these words:

> Deaf-blindness means concomitant hearing and visual impairments, the combination of which causes such severe communication and other developmental and learning needs that they cannot accommodated in special education programs solely for children with deafness or children with blindness. (34 C.F.R. 300[c][2])

Problems with These Definitions

The definition for "children with severe disabilities" once used by the Department of Education is a wide-ranging one. It is also at times rather confusing. It includes autism and notes several behaviors characteristic of persons with autism, despite the fact that the rules continue to define autism separately. It also includes severe emotional disturbance, notwithstanding the fact that emotional disturbance is a separate category in IDEA and has its own definition (see Chapter 5). Other definitions for severe disabilities were offered by The Association for Persons with Severe Disabilities (TASH). TASH places more emphasis upon the types and extent of external support than upon personal characteristics of individuals with severe disabilities. According to the organization, individuals with severe disabilities need extensive and ongoing support in at least one major life activity (living at home, going to school, etc.).

For more information on TASH, go to the Web Links module in Chapter 7 of the Companion Website.

The definition for multiple disabilities is of little utility to teachers. In the author's experience, school districts typically use the term to refer to children and youth who need a variety of different services and/or to students who are both severely or profoundly mentally retarded and also have another significant condition, generally a physical (orthopedic) one. Most such students were born with the disabilities.

The definition for deaf-blindness is similarly unhelpful. It does not address the most common instances, that is, cases in which a student with one disability sustains an injury or illness that causes the other. It also makes no note of the fact that mental retardation often accompanies inborn (whether genetic or adventitiously caused) occurrences of both disabilities. One would expect the Department to address the latter issue because its definition for "multiple disabilities" explicitly excludes deaf-blindness. This book defines deafness (Chapter 4) and blindness (Chapter 6) elsewhere.

Characteristics and Types

Each of these categories is small relative to most IDEA classifications. Although the numbers of children and youth are low, the variety of conditions represented is sizeable. To illustrate, the National Organization for Rare Disorders (NORD; *www.rarediseases.org*) maintains in its database information on more than 800 conditions causing severe limitations in activity.

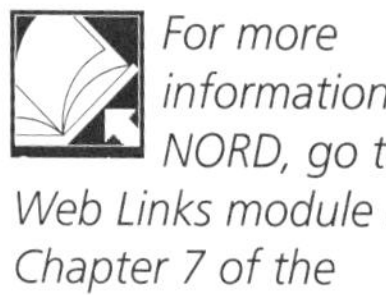

For more information on NORD, go to the Web Links module in Chapter 7 of the Companion Website.

Characteristics

Students with severe or multiple disabilities and those who are both deaf and blind share the defining characteristic that they require intensive care and highly individualized instruction. The nature of their educational needs is very different from that of their age peers. This is why so many are placed, not in inclusive classrooms but rather in separate classes and separate schools. This is not to say, however, that they cannot spend a good part of each day in an inclusive classroom.

The nature of "intensive care and highly individualized instruction" needs to be appreciated for its impact to be realized. Many of these students must be fed one-on-one, because of their mobility limitations, swallowing difficulties, and tongue thrusting. The same students may require 10 minutes for toileting, once or twice a day. Each activity requires additional time—from removing winter coats to opening a book to turning pages. In an inclusive classroom, it can easily require as much as an hour of a teacher's time, each day, just to provide custodial care that the child requires for basic needs. This does not even include instructional time.

In a separate classroom having, say, 10 students with severe disabilities, the time required for custodial care can add up to virtually the whole school day. At 30 minutes of a teacher's or an aide's time, per child, eating lunch would consume five hours' worth of staff time. The same students may require an hour and a half of staff time for toileting and diaper changes, once or twice a day. All of this means that each day must be orchestrated, much as a stage play is, so that time is freed up for instruction.

Types

The major types are those given in this section: severe disabilities, multiple disabilities, and deaf-blindness. Severe disabilities may be distinguished from multiple disabilities in that one condition alone creates the need for what we have called "intensive care and highly individualized instruction." Multiple disabilities, by contrast, may include several conditions, no one of which by itself requires such support.

One notable group of children and youth is referred to as "medically fragile/technology dependent" (Bowe, 2000b). These students have health impairments that are life-threatening. They may require one-on-one nursing care throughout the day, every day of the week. For this reason, they rarely are classified as Other Health Impaired (OHI) because that category is generally understood to refer to relatively mild or moderate conditions. Rather, educators may look at the many great needs of these students as justifying the label "multiple disabilities."

Commonalities. Many students with severe or multiple disabilities, and those who are both deaf and blind, typically are limited in expressive communication. Some are nonvocal. They need to be provided with means of communicating. Fortunately, a wide variety of low- and high-tech strategies are available. (See "Technologies That Work: Communication Devices," p. 269.) As noted earlier, students who have one recognized disability (e.g., specific learning disability) as well as a second condition, but whose combinations of impairments nonetheless do not rise to the level of "severe" may not be classified as having multiple disabilities. Rather, they may be identified in the "primary" category (in our example, SLD). For this reason, the category "multiple disabilities" tends to include children and youth who have needs that are severe.

Differences. Students who are deaf-blind generally are not also mentally retarded. This is the exception to the otherwise-pervasive rule that children and youth with multiple or severe disabilities tend to have mental retardation.

Co-Morbidity. It is clear from this discussion that severe and multiple disabilities may be co-morbid with mental retardation. On occasion, students who are both deaf and blind will have a third disability. Many with epilepsy would have frequent seizures were they not taking anti-seizure medication.

Prevalence

According to the *26th Annual Report* (U.S. Department of Education, 2004), a total of 131,000 students between the ages of 6 and 21 inclusive were classified as having multiple disabilities. There is no IDEA category specifically for students with severe disabilities. Deaf-blindness is very rare, with just 1,600 students identified in the *26th Annual Report*. Figures 7.3 and 7.4 show that multiple disabilities and deaf-blindness are less prevalent in regular classrooms than are most other disabilities.

FIGURE 7.3 Likelihood of Inclusive Placements: Multiple Disabilities

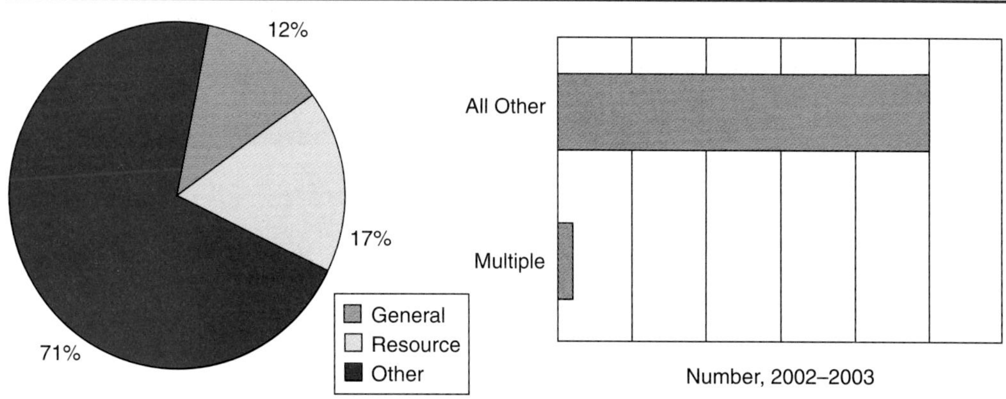

Students with the "multiple disabilities" label are rather few in number, at 131,000, according to the *26th Annual Report* (2004). Only one in every six (12%) were placed in general classrooms all or most of the school week (spending less than 21% of the time in other settings). The two charts above illustrate these data.

Source: From the *26th Annual Report,* by the U.S. Department of Education, 2004, Washington, DC: Author.

FIGURE 7.4 Likelihood of Inclusive Placements: Deaf-Blindness

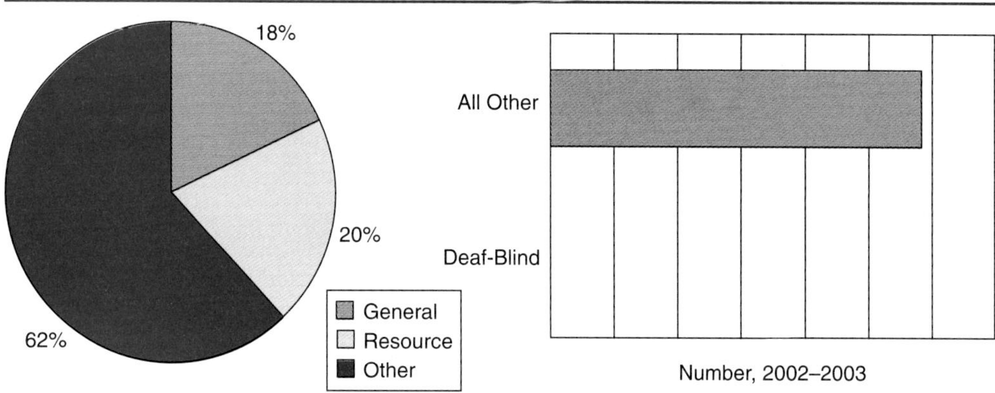

Students who are both deaf and blind are very few in number, at 1,600, according to the *26th Annual Report* (2004). Fewer than one in every five (18%) were placed in general classrooms all or most of the school week (spending less than 21% of the time in other settings). The two charts above illustrate these data.

Source: From the *26th Annual Report,* by the U.S. Department of Education, 2004, Washington, DC: Author.

Diagnosis and Assessment

Educators need not attempt to diagnose severe disabilities, because that category is not recognized in IDEA. Diagnosis and assessment should follow the guidelines outlined in previous chapters for instances in which severe versions of such conditions as severe mental retardation, emotional disturbance, and so on, are suspected. With respect to multiple disabilities, similar procedures apply: The two or more disabilities should be diagnosed and assessed as described in earlier chapters. Thus, a child who is or may be both mentally retarded and physically disabled would be evaluated according to the protocols in use for those two types of disabilities. A diagnosis of deaf-blindness requires testing both of hearing and of vision. Procedures for doing so were outlined earlier in Chapters 4 and 6.

In assessment, educators look at the educational implications of the conditions, asking, for example, whether a functional curriculum is required for a student who has multiple disabilities. If so, the IEP team needs to determine whether such an approach can be implemented in an inclusive classroom, at least for part of the school day. The consideration of educational aspects is particularly challenging with respect to deaf-blindness. Is there sufficient residual vision that allows the child to function as a person with low vision? If so, enlargement of materials may be a viable route for instruction. Is there enough residual hearing that the student functionally is hard of hearing, rather than deaf? If so, this student may benefit from auditory aids such as AM- or FM-equipped rooms.

Causes

Severe or multiple disabilities typically are caused by brain damage before, during, or shortly after birth. Some are inborn, caused by genetic syndromes. Often, a cause is difficult to pinpoint. At birth or shortly thereafter, the heart may fail, lungs fill with fluid, kidneys shut down, and the brain loses oxygen from loss of blood. Why all this happens remains a mystery. What is not a mystery is the result. Children may never talk, walk, feed themselves, or function mentally at higher than a 6-month-old level. They may require round-the-clock monitoring equipment and 24-hour nursing services.

Genetic Factors

Many genetic factors may be related to severe and multiple disabilities. These are too numerous to list here. Interested readers may visit NORD's Web site at *http://www.rarediseases.org*, using its search function to find information on any of the 800-plus conditions. Much information is provided online. Experience with the organization suggests that a request sent via surface mail will produce even more data on specific disorders by return mail.

Environmental Factors

One cause of severe or multiple disabilities is birth with the umbilical cord wrapped around the neck. This cuts off blood to the brain. As a result, the child has mental retardation, cerebral palsy, and other disorders. Another is a severe head injury, perhaps as the result of a fall. When a woman contracts measles while pregnant, the result may be maternal rubella. Rubella is known to cause mental retardation, deafness, blindness, cerebral palsy, and several other disabilities.

Students with severe and multiple disabilities may have great difficulty doing things that most other children and youth take for granted, such as eating lunch independently.

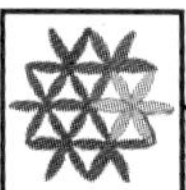

Student Strategies That Work

Internalizing Reinforcement

Children and youth can learn to self-monitor and self-reinforce, for which reason external monitoring and reinforcement are needed more to establish appropriate behavior than to maintain it long-term. Some students require years of external forces, while others respond within weeks or months. Evidence dating back a quarter century (e.g., Camp, Blom, Herbert, & Van Doornick, 1977) shows that talking to themselves is highly effective for many students with severe or multiple disabilities.

Students learn by being monitored and reinforced by others. They hear teachers, therapists, counselors, and others telling them to do something in a different way (to, for example, request assistance rather than starting a fight with a classmate). Over time, many internalize those statements, learning to tell themselves what to do ("Stop. Think. Ask for help."). They see professionals monitoring their behavior (when, for example, they meet with a teacher to go over what happened that day). In time, they learn to self-monitor ("I'm on task. I'm doing what I should be doing. I haven't gotten up in more than 20 minutes!"). They also hear adults praising good behavior and learn to self-praise ("I'm doing pretty good here. Just a few minutes more, and I'll be done!").

For students who do not themselves learn to self-monitor and self-reinforce, teachers and other adults may explicitly train them in those techniques. This is what Camp et al. (1977) did. Over just a few weeks, they taught young people specific self-reinforcement tactics—steps that the students continued to take months and even years later.

Because students with severe or multiple disabilities often require much more time and effort to accomplish things than do most others with disabilities, self-monitoring and self-reinforcement are needed more for motivation purposes than for behavior. Students need to track progress step by step, reminding themselves of the next steps, and praising themselves for the progress they are making. They also need to learn how to recognize when their best efforts are insufficient, and they must request an adult's assistance. Learning how to signal that they need help is one of the most important competencies some of these students can learn.

Instructional Methods

More than is the case with most disability categories discussed in this book, multiple disabilities and deaf-blindness present challenges in an inclusive classroom. The needs of these students may be so different from the needs of typical students that even if placement in an inclusive setting is made, what happens in that room may differ significantly for children and youth with multiple disabilities or deaf-blindness as compared to what occurs for other students. However, if the IEP team determined that an inclusive classroom was the right placement, it is likely that at least some class-wide instruction can be done. In particular, teachers should be alert to opportunities for cooperative learning and peer tutoring. That is because a major potential benefit of inclusion for students with multiple disabilities or deaf-blindness is exposure to role models displaying acceptable behavior.

Strategies in Early Childhood and Elementary School

According to the *26th Annual Report,* a total of 55,000 children aged 6 to 11 inclusive were classified as having multiple disabilities during the 2002–2003 school year. Of them, 12% spent all or virtually all of the school week in general classrooms. Another 17% split time between such settings and resource rooms. A plurality (47%) were in separate (self-contained) settings. No data were provided on severe disabilities, because that is not an IDEA category. A total of 675 children in the 6-to-11-inclusive age range were classified as deaf-blind. Of them, 20% were in general classrooms all or most of the school week, plus 23% who were in general classrooms part-time and in resource rooms part-time. About one in every three (35%) were in separate classrooms. As these numbers suggest, an unusually large proportion (22%) were educated in non-neighborhood programs, notably in day or residential schools. For example, there is a National Center for Deaf Blind Youths and Adults, located in Sands Point, NY, on the north shore of Long Island. HKNC works with state education agencies and local school districts to arrange for instruction and support services for deaf-blind children and youth.

For more information on the National Center for Deaf Blind Youths and Adults, go to the Web Links module in Chapter 7 of the Companion Website.

For more information on single-switch adaptors, go to the Web Links module in Chapter 7 of the Companion Website.

For more information on computer software that teaches cause and effect, go to the Web Links module in Chapter 7 of the Companion Website.

Methods: Teaching Cause and Effect. Many young children with severe or multiple disabilities, as well as many who are deaf-blind, have very few opportunities in everyday life to influence their environments. Whereas other children quickly learn cause and effect while toddlers or preschoolers (when, for example, they knock something off a table while crawling, walking, or running in the kitchen), young children with physical conditions may spend their entire days in one position, unable to touch or move anything in the home. For this reason, family members, early intervention personnel, preschool special educators, and others should create opportunities. One good way is to use single-switch adaptors for toys. Widely available, these adaptors let a child control the movement of a toy by touching a switch. This may be a large disk that is wired to the toy. The child may touch the disk with any body part she can control (a foot, a knee, an elbow, a wand attached to the head, etc.).

Low-tech aids teachers may use include velcro to attach drawings or pictures of story characters to a glove. As the story develops, children remove and re-position the characters, to show, for example, that two of them are talking. Students may use switches to control a blender as part of a lesson on cooking. High-tech products include computer software that teaches cause and effect, such as "101 Animations," which is a software program that activates cartoons when the student signals with a mouse click, a switch, touching a space bar, or touching a touch screen. The animations are both large and loud. IntelliTools offers "SwitchIt! Suite," a set of software programs that teach cause and effect.

Methods: Participation in Groups. Preschoolers typically engage in parallel play. They are just beginning to master turn-taking and other aspects of joint play. Possessions can become prized objects at this stage. For that reason, disputes over who can play with an object may lead to altercations. Young children with no disabilities learn to resolve such disputes as part of their group-play experiences in preschool, kindergarten, and the primary grades. Those who have severe or multiple disabilities may have few such experiences. Both at home and in school, their instruction frequently is one-on-one. They may need explicit teaching about how to play in groups. A good "technique" for gaining entry into a group is for the child to bring an "interesting" toy to the group and suggest ways to play with it. Children at this age tend to like puzzles and simple card games. They also enjoy construction with Lego™ blocks and other plastic or wooden pieces. Art work with crayons, paint, chalk, and collage materials can engage their attention for sustained periods of time (and they will want to keep what they produce!). All of these offer opportunities for you to teach a child with severe or multiple disabilities how to get other children to play.

Methods: Differentiating Instruction. How is a teacher of an inclusive classroom to provide the whole-class instruction required by most students and, at the same time, the one-on-one training needed by many children and youth who have multiple disabilities or are deaf-blind? At the early childhood and elementary level, you will need to engage the services of another adult. This may be a paraprofessional or a volunteer. Whoever you choose to assist you in the classroom, it is vital for you as the teacher to specify *exactly* what you want the assistant to do, how you want it done, and how you expect progress to be documented. The chapter on collaboration in this text (Chapter 12) offers a variety of strategies and tactics for effective supervision of aides in the classroom.

With respect to students with multiple disabilities or deaf-blindness, much instruction must be one-on-one. Children who are both deaf and blind lack any reliable means of communication at a distance. They can neither see you well enough nor hear you well enough to follow your whole-class teaching. That is why an aide must sit beside the child, translating your words into fingerspelling and sign language. The child and aide use the "hand-over-hand" method to communicate. In this approach, the child places his hands on top of the aide's hands. Whatever the aide spells on the fingers or signs with the hands will be sensed tactually by the student. Many children with multiple disabilities need one-on-one assistance for other reasons. They may, for example, need to have someone hold

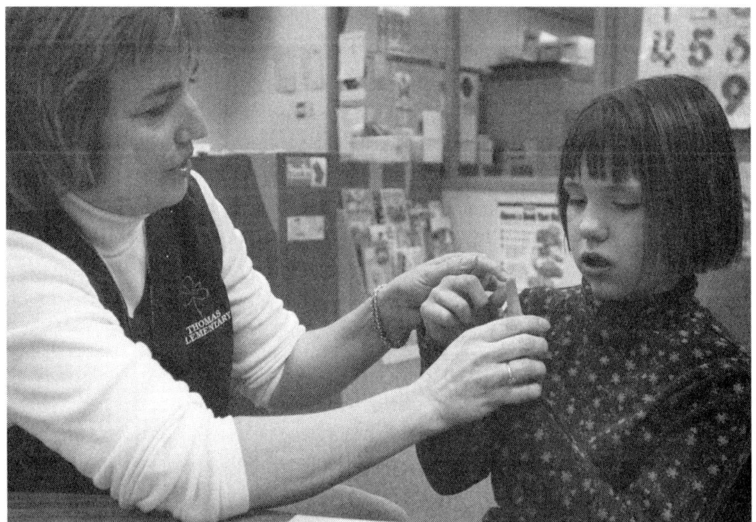

Fingerspelling and sign language can be effective means of expressive communication for students having severe or multiple disabilities. Here, a teacher helps a child form the sign for "word."

materials steady on the desk or wheelchair lapboard, turn pages, and provide other kinds of help.

Methods: The MOVE Curriculum. One approach, which was mentioned in the previous chapter, is the MOVE curriculum. With students having severe or multiple disabilities, MOVE may be *the* curriculum. That is, it serves as the core of instruction. Some students with these conditions have such limited cognitive abilities that little academic instruction is attempted.

For more information on the MOVE curriculum, go to the Web Links module in Chapter 7 of the Companion Website.

Mobility Opportunities Via Education (MOVE) is based on a "top-down" analysis of student needs. This is best explained by contrast to traditional curricula for teaching these students, which can be described as "bottom-up." In a top-down analysis, experts begin by asking the question, "What does this student need to be able to do in order to function as an adult?" In a bottom-up analysis, by contrast, planners begin by asking "What are the typical developmental stages that people go through?" The difference is revealing.

Take, for example, crawling. Teachers and therapists have learned that it can require several years to teach a child with severe or multiple disabilities to crawl (e.g., Snell, 1987). A top-down assessment will show that adults very rarely crawl. Accordingly, being able to crawl has minimal value in the MOVE curriculum. Research shows that students who never mastered crawling, but did master sitting independently, are able to function well as adults. The implication is obvious: Teaching children to crawl is both ineffective (it makes little difference in their daily lives) and inefficient (it consumes time that is better applied to other activities). That is why deciding *what* to teach is probably the single biggest decision educators and therapists must make. The MOVE curriculum was built upon such choices. It tells educators and therapists to instruct children in precisely those competencies that they will most need as adults (Snell & Brown, 2000). To appreciate the innovativeness of the MOVE curriculum, consider that many educators take the opposite approach. They begin by administering a test or instrument to assess what a child can and cannot do. They then teach those behaviors that the child failed to display. These teachers implicitly assumed that the "typical path of development" is the "right path"—and that, to resume our example, children should and indeed must learn to crawl before they stand.

Methods: Direct Instruction. Some young children require specialized teaching in order to master the prerequisites of reading, counting, and other skills. While this instruction may be embedded into family activities, more often it is offered in a special session. This is because it is time-consuming, because it requires the professional to have appropriate materials on hand, and because it is most successful when the activity has the child's full attention. Frequently used by teachers is a set of techniques collectively known as Direct Instruction

(DI). By (DI) (discussed in depth in the next chapter) we mean the explicit teaching of material, careful review by teachers of the kinds of mistakes children make, re-teaching of information as needed to help students to correct those mistakes, sustained practice of newly learned skills, and regular review to be sure that students retain learned information. These steps have a strong research basis (e.g., Gersten, Carnine, & Woodward, 1987).

One example of DI is DISTAR (Engleman, Haddox, and Bruder, 1986; Kuder, 1990). This is a commercial product offering "programmed instruction," that is, a highly structured curriculum. DISTAR uses a "say, show, do" approach. The teacher directs all activities. She might say, for example, "This is a _____." She will repeat that sentence, then ask the child to do so. She might show something. And she might ask the children to do something, such as choosing among three objects. DISTAR is so regimented that it generally is used in special, rather than in regular, sessions.

Methods: Teaching Methods of Communication. Several national organizations concerned about the adequacy of communication services and supports for children and youth with severe disabilities united in 2002 to issue a position statement in which they urged state departments of education and local IEP teams to adopt a broad definition for the term "communication" (National Joint Committee for the Communication Needs of Persons with Severe Disabilities, 2002). The committee noted that communication may take many forms. It may be intentional or not, may use conventional symbols or not, may follow linguistic rules or not, and may be spoken or not. A broad conceptualization of communication, then, encompasses the use of Picture Exchange Communication Systems (PECS), specialized symbol systems (Blissymbols), signs (American Sign Language), and other modalities. The deciding factor, argued the committee, should be the individual's preferences. The expected outcome should be functional, reflecting the individual's needs and desires. It is inappropriate to limit outcomes only to standard goals for speech and language because the bottom line for students with severe disabilities is the *effectiveness* of their communication. The operative question, then, is "Did the individual get the point across?" (Wehman, Sherron, & West, 1997; Wehmeyer & Schalock, 2001).

In the MOVE Curriculum, communication is first taught to young children with the use of objects. Thus, an actual Styrofoam cup represents the concept of "drink" as in "I want a drink." Later, the cup is cut so that just the bottom half remains. Even later, only the bottom of the cup is visible. Yet later a round image of that cup bottom, or a picture of a cup, is used. The child points to the image/picture to express the desire to drink something.

Students may also use sign language for receptive and/or expressive communication. Some signs, notably those for such things as COOKIES, MILK, BOOK, PICTURE, and the like have signs that directly relate to the referent. (The practice in delineating signs in print is to capitalize them.) Similarly, some actions, notably STOP, PAY, SIT, STAND, and the like are directly indicated by their signs. Since most children and youth with severe or multiple disabilities can hear well, you need not worry about signing everything you say; rather, signing the key ideas can suffice. A good example is the admonition to STOP AND LOOK before crossing a street. The sign for STOP has the edge of one hand hitting the palm of the other; the sign for AND connects two things; and the sign for LOOK has two fingers pointing in the direction(s) in which you want the student to look.

Students who are deaf and blind may sign as do children who are deaf. When others communicate to the deaf-blind student, a hand-over-hand method is used. The signer places his hands under those of the child. Words may be fingerspelled into the hands or words and phrases may be signed. Technologies are available which give these students information in a tactile mode. As Bruce (2002) has shown, teachers who receive training and follow-up coaching in the use of these kinds of technologies can implement them effectively in the classroom. For more information, see the nearby box, "Technologies That Work: Communication Devices."

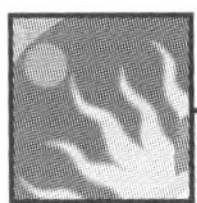

Technologies That Work

Communication Devices

A wide variety of communication products is available to help students with severe or multiple disabilities. Fewer, but a still impressive number, help persons who are both deaf and blind. Good ways to identify such products are the Web sites assitivetech.net (*http://www.assistivetech.net*) and ABLEDATA (*http://www.abledata.com*). These sites are, in effect, search engines specializing in assistive technologies. To illustrate their use, consider a situation in which you need to find a talking word processor for a child who does not speak intelligibly. At assistivetech.net, you will find 20 categories (Arts, Children and Families, Employment, Transportation, etc.). One is Communication. You may search within that category. Or, alternatively, you may elect to search by product name (if you know it), by function (in this case, communication), or by disability category (such as cerebral palsy or blindness). If, for example, you were aware that IntelliTools has a product called IntelliTalk, you would enter that product name. The site then would give you the following information:

Product Type:	Voice output software
Function:	Talking word processor
Features:	Talking word processor speaks letters, words, and sentences. Worksheets can be created so that learners cannot erase text or there are specific answer fields for the user. Onscreen keyboard. Pictures can be placed in text. Multiple voice output selections.
Options:	Available for Windows or Macintosh. Works with keyboard, IntelliKeys, or OnScreen keyboard.
Suggested Price:	$140.00
Vendor:	RJ Cooper & Associates Inc. 27601 Forbes Rd. #39 Laguna Niguel, CA 92677
Toll Free:	1-800-RJCooper (75266737)
Web site:	*http://www.rjcooper.com*

Severe and Multiple Disabilities

Many students with severe or multiple disabilities rely upon alternative and augmentative communication systems. These come in many varieties. They range from low-tech solutions such as PECS to high-tech products such as DynaVox®. In PECS, a set of pictures is used. These are assembled onto boards. Each board offers choices that a student is likely to want to make in a given setting. Thus, there may be a board for math, one for science, one for lunch, and so on. Key to the system is the selection and display of appropriate pictures. In the case of lunch, for example, there should be pictures to represent food and drink as well as self ("I") and intent ("want"). The child points to pictures in succession, while the teacher, therapist, or classmate watches. A manual is offered at *http://www.pecs.com*.

Deaf-Blindness

Students who are deaf-blind generally have *some* residual vision and/or hearing. These should be evaluated by specialists to determine the extent to which the residual abilities are useable in education. It may be, for example, that enough vision remains for enlargement of text and images to be a realistic option. If so, those alternatives should be explored. Far more communication options are available through hearing and vision than through touch.

Communication for people who are both deaf and blind challenges engineers and computer programmers. The fact is that today's technologies generally meet the needs of people who are blind by providing information in aural forms. Thus, students who are blind may listen to speech synthesis. Today's technologies usually meet the needs of people who are deaf by offering information in visual forms. Thus, students who are deaf may read instant messages and e-mail in lieu of hearing speech on the phone. These approaches generally have proven to be effective. However, they leave individuals who are deaf-blind out.

For this reason, thousands of products, software as well as hardware, may not be usable by students who are both deaf and blind. This includes much of what is on the World Wide Web. What is required for these persons is technologies that convert information so that it is understandable via the sense of touch. The American Printing House for the Blind (*http://www.aph.org*) offers raised-image maps and other tactile materials for use in schools. Braille-based technologies are available from the National Federation of the Blind (*http://www.nfb.org*) and from the American Foundation for the Blind (*http://www.afb.org*).

People who are both deaf and blind may use, for example, the Braille 'n Speak device for taking notes in class. This product lets the student take notes in Braille by keying on six levers on the machine's keyboard. Those notes may be read on a "paperless Braille" display (which raises and depresses small needles in each of six openings, one for each Braille cell). They may also be uploaded to a home PC. After being converted to text, they may be printed out (e.g., for a report that may be handed in to the teacher). For those with no functional hearing, Braille Lite (*http://www.blazie.com*) may be a more appropriate choice.

For more information on some of the organizations and products mentioned in the "Technologies That Work" box, go to the Web Links module in Chapter 7 of the Companion Website.

Strategies in Middle School and Secondary School

A total of 60,000 students in the 12 to 17 inclusive age range who had the "multiple disabilities" label were being educated during the 2002–2003 school year, according to the *26th Annual Report* (U.S. Department of Education, 2004, Table AB5). Of them, 11% were placed in general classrooms all or most of the school week, with another 19% splitting time between such settings and resource rooms. The plurality (45%) were in separate (self-contained) settings. An unusually large 25% were in non-neighborhood schools, generally state-supported day or residential programs. Among the 700 deaf-blind students in the same age range, 18% were in general classrooms, 20% split time between general settings and resource rooms, and 30% were in self-contained settings. As with early childhood and elementary school, no data were reported on severe disabilities because it is not an IDEA classification.

Methods: Embedding Instruction. For many students with severe or multiple disabilities, moving around is both difficult and time-consuming. This makes it essential for teachers to embed instruction whenever a "teachable moment" materializes. The principles of naturalistic instruction draw upon the fact that children and youth learn most when their interest is already engaged in a topic or activity. Embedding is minimally disruptive of ongoing classroom activities, because it usually may be performed by general educators, and because the activities occurring in typical preschool classrooms tend to lend themselves well to embedding (Horn, et al., 2000). Mark Wolery and his colleagues have shown that embedding may be done during art instruction, dramatic play, snack periods, and in-class transitions from one activity to another (Wolery & Gast, 2000). Ways teachers may do this include seating children with disabilities up front, using assistive technology devices as appropriate, providing performance cues, and physical assistance to children who need it. One teacher worked with technicians to suspend a padded swing from the ceiling. This enabled her to embed physical activity into her curriculum. She also uses bounce balls filled with rice, mobiles, and an air mattress in her classroom, so students can work on moving, balancing, sitting, and so on.

The same instruction (say, vocabulary development) may be embedded across activities so that repetition occurs naturally in a variety of settings. This promotes generalization of learning. By **generalization,** we mean that children who learn how to do something in one environment, from one adult, demonstrate the ability to perform that activity in at least one other setting, with at least one other adult. You may, for example, teach the many skills involved in planning a party (brainstorming ideas, making choices from alternatives, counting, buying things, making change, etc.) in your classroom. Students would then apply them in a class activity (shopping for the items required, decorating the room where the party will be held, etc.) that requires them to use those skills in other settings and with other people.

Wolery (2001) added that time delay procedures may also be embedded into classroom activities. In **time delay,** teachers and paraprofessionals provide prompts to young children to signal what the children are expected to do. Prompts include modeling, physical prompts, and other assistance. Gradually, prompts are delayed and then removed altogether. The techniques have been used to help children learn to answer questions, to put on their coats, to use spoons and other implements, and to label pictures. The guiding principle is to demonstrate the desired behavior, make sure the child can perform it, prompt for it when it is desired, and gradually phase out the prompts so that the child performs the activity when appropriate.

Methods: Functional Curriculum. The functional or alternative curriculum was introduced earlier (see Chapter 5 especially "Teacher Strategies That Work: Functional Curriculum," p. 166). Key to the approach is to identify, for each child, *specifically* what knowledge and skills are required for success in adult life. Those may then be taught *in situ* (that is, in the community where they will be used). Included in most iterations of alternative or functional curricula are such tasks as self-care, telling time, riding public transportation, ordering food at a fast-food restaurant, making change, budgeting scarce resources, opening and maintaining a checking account, paying rent and other regularly due bills, and the like. Many of these competencies involve academics, but at a practical level. Thus, self-care incorporates basic knowledge of health information, buying things involves math, paying bills involves reading, and so on.

A good resource on functional curricula is the Life Centered Career Education program. This approach is specific to preparing students for transition from school to work and to living independently in the community. Also very helpful for teachers is Wehman and Kregel's (1997) *Functional Curriculum for Elementary, Middle, and Secondary Age Students with Special Needs.* This book provides well-illustrated, in-depth presentations of methods for teaching functional academics (e.g., math and English specifically for everyday living), self-determination and other aspects of self-advocacy, peer relations, self-care, and living in the community. A critical component to a functional curriculum, according to Wehman and Kregel, is task analysis (see "Teacher Strategies That Work: Task Analysis," p. 274). In task analysis, educators separate out the various subtasks involved in any activity so that they may teach each separately. Wehman and Kregel urge teachers to begin with a broad instructional goal (e.g., traveling independently). They should then examine the community to identify where a given student is most likely to need to travel. The next step is to detail, one by one, the specific travel skills required to do that (Wehman and Kregel urge teachers to personally and physically do the traveling themselves, in advance, so as not to overlook any required steps). Teachers should then compare the list of skills with experts and with family members. The list then becomes the travel lesson. Wehman and Kregel encourage teachers to review and, if necessary, revise the list at least once annually.

For more information on the Life Centered Career Education Program, go to the Web Links module in Chapter 7 of the Companion Website.

Again and again, Wehman and Kregel emphasize that selecting *what* to teach is fundamental. The knowledge and skills should be practical for *that* student. The goals should be reachable by that particular student. Thus, if a student has struggled for a year or more to learn to tie shoelaces, without much observable progress, it might make more sense to provide him with loafers or other slip-on shoes and/or with sneakers that have velcro attachments, rather than continuing to train him to tie shoelaces. Another aspect of "what to teach" is setting priorities. Some competencies are more important than others. Some deserve all the time required to teach them. Others do not. Wehman and Kregel emphasize the need to prioritize, in conjunction with the student and his family.

Methods: Direct Instruction. The functional curriculum and the MOVE curriculum (which is also used in middle school and high school, as well as in early childhood and elementary school) both make heavy use of Direct Instruction. As we will see in greater detail in the next chapter, Direct Instruction features explicit teaching of material, review and re-teaching of mistakes children make, sustained practice of newly learned skills, and regular testing. The "explicit teaching" aspect is the most prominent. Teachers *teach* the students, directly and patiently, until material is learned. Periodic assessment identifies which tasks, if any, have yet to be mastered. That information then is retaught. Even after the student demonstrates success in the entire area of instruction, testing is periodically performed to ensure long-term retention (Gersten et al., 1987).

Methods: Positive Behavior Support. A related approach, mentioned earlier in the section on autism, is *positive behavior support.* As you will recall, this approach tells the teacher to be alert to the *antecedents* of unacceptable behavior. It is not enough to track the number of times that Marian cries. Rather, you as the teacher must also observe *when* she exhibits that behavior. It is also useful to document when she does *not* display that behavior. Because many students with severe and multiple disabilities are limited in expressive communication, it is not always possible to ask them to explain their behavior. The function of the behavior will become apparent if you study the situation with care. Marian may cry because she believes she is not capable of performing an assigned task.

The function of the crying, in that case, is to get her out of this requirement. This analysis tells you what to do, in this instance, ensuring that Marian receives whatever additional instruction or help she requires in order to be successful but, also and importantly, that she does complete the assignment. In short order, Marian will recognize that crying no longer achieves her goal.

Why do students sometimes behave in ways that do not seem to be appropriate? There may be many reasons. We have mentioned escape. One child literally chews on her sweater. This behavior baffled her teacher, until the educator understood the function it served for her. Because she almost always had something in her mouth, this child was able to deflect the questions the teacher asked in class to another student. Misbehavior may also be intended to gain attention, either from you or from peers, or perhaps both. Communication is a third possible function. Someone who does not know how to express a feeling or a desire may adopt a behavior that she does know how to perform, in the hopes that you and others will understand the intent behind the activity.

With many students who have severe or multiple disabilities, an effective way of quelling inappropriate behavior is to train the individual in acceptable ways of expressing those emotions or desires. A related tactic is to reinforce a behavior that interferes with the unacceptable activity. If, to illustrate, Howard routinely bothers other students during transition periods (when the class is wrapping up one activity but has yet to start another), you could assign him clean-up duties. Because he is occupied with collecting objects and returning them to storage components, he cannot at the same time pull Martha's hair and hide John's jacket.

Methods: Partial Participation. The **principle of partial participation** tells educators to find meaningful roles for students who cannot fully participate in an activity. Anderson (1992), who explored the concept as it applies to the teaching of art, emphasized the importance of finding a role that both the child with a disability and peers regard as valuable. This may be, to illustrate, playing the final flourish of drums in a song. It may be serving as time-keeper or moderator for a class debate. The child will feel that he has a meaningful part in the activity if he enjoys it and also if peers desire to play that role, as well. The principle of partial participation holds that students who are not able, because of the severity of their limitations, to take part fully in an activity should be given a meaningful but partial role to play. This should be an assignment that both the student and classmates regard as valuable. The point is to carve out a role so that the student is not relegated to passively observing the activity.

Methods: Medical Services in the Classroom. Because students with severe or multiple disabilities often have chronic health conditions, they may require considerable services from nurses and other medical personnel. This fact raises questions about the extent of a school's responsibilities. The landmark 1984 Supreme Court decision in *Irving Independent School District v. Tatro* (known as *Tatro*) established the ground rules. If the student needs medical services in order to benefit from instruction, if those services can be provided by nurses or other non-physicians, and if the family's health insurance does not cover the cost, the school district is responsible for paying. If, on the other hand, the family has medical insurance that covers such services, the school is permitted to arrange for covered costs to be billed to the health-care insurance provider. This may be Medicaid in the case of a child with a severe disability or multiple disabilities, especially if the family is of low-socioeconomic status (SES). A good review of the key court decisions over the past several decades was offered by Rapport (1996).

Methods: Supportive Living. Many families that have taken care of a child with severe or multiple disabilities find that they have become exhausted by middle school. Care for such a child is a 24-hour, 7-day-a-week job. Often, a first-floor room needs to be adapted to become the child's bedroom. Large, complex, and expensive equipment has to be installed in that room. Life involves constant trips to doctors' offices and visits from nurses, social workers, equipment technicians, and pharmacists. Another problem is that by the time the student reaches adolescence, she is much larger and weighs more than was the case in prior years. For all these reasons, families sometimes seek educator assistance in locating an alternative residential option. In some states, a **group home** specifically designed for children having severe or multiple disabilities is available. As shown in the chapter-opening story about Angela's House, these are single-family houses. They look like any other house. Located throughout the house are the ventilators, tracheal tubes for feeding, hospital beds, and wheelchairs these children need. The children who reside in the Long Island Angela's House all use diapers, despite the fact that they range in age from 6 to 12. Many require regular medication to control seizures. They are dressed, fed, cleaned and monitored by a staff of a dozen nurses and paraprofessionals. Most of the children go to a special school, which is run by United Cerebral Palsy or to another one administered by a consortium of local school districts. Nurses and specialized equipment surround them at school, as well. Medicaid covers most of the costs, both at Angela's House and at school (Myers, 2002).

Group homes also offer plentiful opportunities for adolescents and young adults to engage in group activities. Many individuals with severe or multiple disabilities prefer group to individual engagement (e.g., Lancioni, O'Reilly, & Oliva, 2002). This may be because they rarely are given chances to be part of a group. It may also be because they can achieve success in a group because they need perform only part of a larger task. It may also be because they enjoy the social aspects of group work. Whatever the reasons, group functions—from cleaning up, to making meals, to shopping, to traveling in the community—should be part of any transition program for students having severe or multiple disabilities.

Strategies in Transition to Adult Life

The functional or alternative curriculum is as valuable in planning and carrying out transition services as it is in other areas of PreK–12 education. For most students who have severe or multiple disabilities, and most who are both deaf and blind, transition to independent living is the most likely path. Fewer of these students than is the case with most other IDEA categories will go to college and fewer will work immediately after high school.

Methods: Plan for Group Home Living. Adults with multiple or severe disabilities often need supportive housing environments, as do some teens. In past years, this meant hospitalization or institutionalization. Today, in many states, group homes are a better option. In a group home, 7 to 12 adults reside in a typical one-family house. A staff of nurses, job coaches, and paraprofessionals come to the house for 8-hour shifts. Typically, rent and utilities are covered by the individual's monthly check from Social Security, under the Supplemental Security Income (SSI) program. Medicaid may also pay, especially for nursing services and for assistive technologies. The residents go to work, if they have a job, or to an activity center, five days a week. They keep their earnings, using them for clothes, movies, restaurant meals, and the like. In some states with many group homes, such as New York and Michigan, it is possible to find a group home that specializes in caring for individuals with multiple physical and mental disabilities. Even in those states, the waiting list to get into a group home can be lengthy. In New York, for example, it commonly is 7 years. That is why family members and educators put into a child's IEP, at the age of 14 when a transition plan is first written, information about what will be done to apply for a group home. That way, when the student ages out of special education at 21 or 22, she has risen on the list and can move promptly into a group home.

Methods: Teaching Self-Determination. A key concept of independent living is that even individuals who cannot do things for themselves generally can, and should, decide who will do those things, when, and how. This is an aspect of self-determination, which we discussed earlier in Chapter 5. With individuals who have multiple disabilities or are

Teacher Strategies That Work

Task Analysis

Marc Gold (1973) pioneered a method of deconstructing tasks into discrete components and teaching those, separately and then together. Today, the method is known as task analysis. It is a powerful tool for teaching students with mental retardation. Since many children and youth with severe or multiple disabilities are mentally retarded, and since those who are not often have limited motor skills, task analysis is a technique that can be effective even when other approaches for teaching competencies fail. It has particular value with many students who are medically fragile and technology dependent, such as those profiled in the chapter-opening story about group homes on Long Island.

Key to the method is to divide a task into its components. These are frequently more numerous than one might have suspected. Putting on a shirt, for example, might involve the successive performance of as many as a dozen different subtasks. The first several subtasks are needed to remove the shirt from a hanger. The next several involve grasping the shirt and positioning it. One continues through many steps, the last of which is inspection to ascertain that the shirt is properly put on (e.g., that the middle front, where the buttons are, is aligned with the belt around the slacks). What Gold (1973) did, and what many researchers and practitioners since him have done, is to teach each subtask separately until mastered. (It is sometimes preferable to begin with the final step, rather than the first one, so as it give the child the reinforcement of a task successfully completed.) Once a subtask has been learned, to criterion (e.g., 90% accuracy), the next subtask is taught. After that one is mastered, the next step may be to teach the two subtasks together.

Teachers who have used task analysis often report that the method is also applicable to their own lesson plans. They have learned to analyze what it is that they wish to teach. This assessment often reveals the presence of steps that they had overlooked. For this reason, task analysis may help them to improve their teaching.

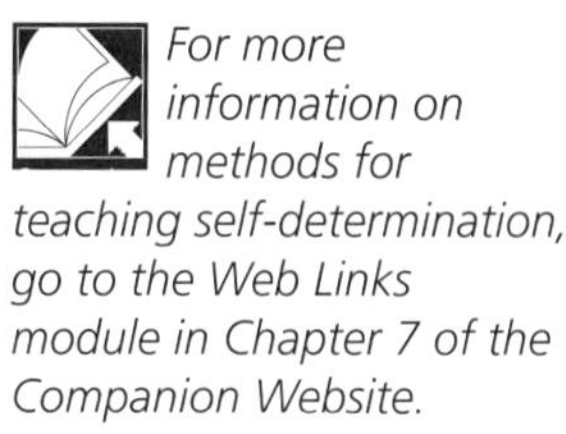

For more information on methods for teaching self-determination, go to the Web Links module in Chapter 7 of the Companion Website.

deaf-blind, a major need is for self-expression. They need to be able to convey their desires in a way that care givers can quickly and accurately understand them. Teachers may also consult the *Journal of Disability Policy Studies* special issue (vol. 13, no. 2) on self-determination. That issue included eight articles providing a wealth of useful information about self-determination and young people with disabilities. Emphasized again and again in the literature is the need for educators to help students to recognize what they can do by themselves, what they need help doing, and what they are unable to do even with assistance (Milthaug, 1998).

CHAPTER SUMMARY

Autism

- Autism is a complex and severe disability characterized by deficiencies in communication, imagination, and socialization.
- Autism ranges from severe (full-spectrum autism) to relatively mild (autistic-like behavior).
- The "theory of mind" is a powerful conceptualization of autism. It has led to the development of several instruments that quite reliably identify individuals who then are diagnosed by physicians as having autism.
- Asperger's syndrome is autism that is not accompanied by mental retardation.
- Research to date does not support the widespread belief that childhood vaccinations cause autism.
- Applied behavior analysis is one of several techniques that are of proven value in teaching students with autism.
- TEACCH (Treatment and Education of Autistic and related Communication handicapped Children) stresses the importance of organizing the environment and the schedule for students who have autism.

- If the theory of mind is correct, students with autism may have particular difficulty understanding fiction, because they may not comprehend that it is not a true story.

Severe and Multiple Disabilities

- There is no IDEA category for "severe" disabilities. Accordingly, the term is not defined in federal rules.
- The MOVE curriculum is a top-down approach that emphasizes teaching students skills and behaviors they need in order to function as adults.
- The principle of partial participation makes the important point that when students cannot fully take part in an activity, the roles they do assume should be meaningful to them and valued by their peers.
- DISTAR is a programmed instruction version of Direct Instruction.
- Task analysis is effective in identifying the sub-tasks that must be mastered in order for a student to successfully perform a task.
- Individuals who are both deaf and blind may have some residual capabilities in one or the other sense (enough vision to learn some things through sight, enough hearing to benefit from assistive listening technologies). Those who do not rely primarily upon the sense of touch. They will use hand-over-hand fingerspelling and sign language and will rely heavily on Braille and other tactile means of communication.
- Many young people with severe or multiple disabilities require substantial support after leaving high school. That is why group homes, which provide everyday help, can be appropriate residential options.
- Self-determination is a reachable goal for many young people with multiple disabilities or deaf-blindness.

QUESTIONS FOR REFLECTION

1. What does the American Psychiatric Association's definition of pervasive developmental disorder (PDD) suggest about the nature of autism?
2. How is the definition of autism that was developed by the U.S. Department of Education different from that of the APA in its *DSM-IV?*
3. What aspects of Greenfield's description of his son Noah are characteristic of autism?
4. What factors may contribute to the recent increase in reported instances of autism among children?
5. How does applied behavior analysis (ABA) differ from other kinds of behavior modification?
6. How might occupational and physical therapists help students who have disordered brain maps of their bodies?
7. Why does MOVE International insist on taking a "top-down" approach to the curriculum?
8. How does the MOVE curriculum differ from older approaches to teaching students with severe or multiple disabilities?
9. What aspects of a functional curriculum might you teach in an inclusive classroom at the middle- or high-school level?
10. Where can you learn more about teaching self-determination to students with multiple disabilities or deaf-blindness?

Part Three Endnotes

Making Inclusion Work . . . The Story So Far

In Part Three, we saw that making inclusion work involves these ideas:

- Collaborate with related–services personnel (occupational therapists, physical therapists, speech and language pathologists, etc.) to provide the full range of support that students with disabilities often require.
- Offer push-in related services when feasible for students with physical, health, and sensory disabilities, to avoid the problems associated with pull-out services.
- Act affirmatively to rid the school of any harassment on the basis of disability.
- Speak aloud every word and symbol that is written on a board, displayed on an overhead or a slide, and printed in a handout, so that students who are blind or have low vision may keep pace with instruction.
- Take advantage of today's technologies, which offer so much for students who are blind or have low vision.
- Celebrate the abilities of students with Asperger's syndrome in such areas as mathematics and science, which tend not to be limited by the condition.
- Use applied behavior analysis (ABA) as one as one of several techniques that are of proven value in teaching students with autism.
- Adopt, as appropriate, alternative curricula such as MOVE, to instruct students in life skills they need to function as adults.
- Follow the principle of partial participation so as to make sure that even students with severe disabilities can play meaningful roles in classroom and school activities.
- Offer information through the sense of touch, so that students who are both deaf and blind can benefit from instruction. This includes hand-over-hand fingerspelling and sign language as well as Braille and other tactile means of communication.
- Support young people with severe or multiple disabilities, and their families, in securing the support they need after leaving high school.
- Recognize that even people with severe or multiple disabilities can engage in self-determination, by learning how to direct the work of caregivers (deciding what is to be done, when, and how).

Part Four

Teaching in the Inclusive Classroom

Part Four focuses upon the techniques that educators use to make inclusion work. We begin with instructional strategies and tactics (Chapter 8). We then look at ways to manage behavior in the school and in the classroom (Chapter 9). Part Four concludes with an examination of assessment and evaluation (Chapter 10).

The material in Chapter 8 picks up on methods that were introduced earlier, when *Making Inclusion Work* discussed high- and low-prevalence disabilities in Parts Two and Three. The chapter adds new information about those tools, and places each technique into context. Featured in that chapter are writing behavioral objectives, using assistive technologies, individualizing instruction, and grouping.

Experienced teachers know that they cannot teach effectively until they have managerial control over the classroom. The same holds for schools themselves. Student behavior needs to comport with community standards—and support learning by *all* children and youth. That is why *Making Inclusion Work* devotes an entire chapter to behavior management. Featured in Chapter 9 are such tools as presentation (positive) reinforcement and discipline with dignity.

The final chapter of Part Four, Chapter 10, examines assessment and evaluation. Teachers participate in evaluation as members of IEP Teams. Much more often, they conduct assessments, notably of academic, social, and other progress toward IEP goals. That is why Chapter 10 identifies and briefly explains the major tools available to educators—from such widely used psychometric instruments as the Woodcock-Johnson to teacher-made tests. Educators are also responsible for making accommodations in testing. That role requires that teachers be familiar not only with the various accommodations that could be made, but also with how decisions are reached about which, if any, accommodations are appropriate for a given test and a given child.

Chapter 8 Planning for Universally Designed Instruction

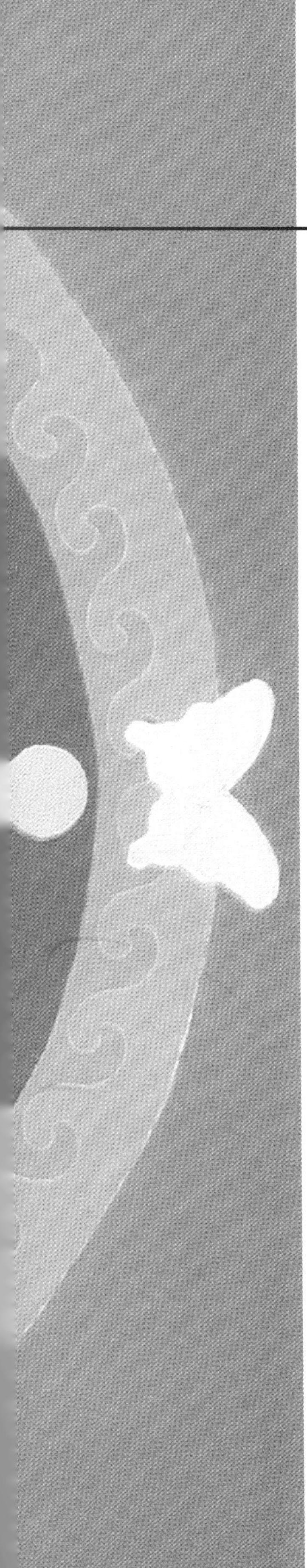

TERMS

socially mediated
behavioral terms
differentiated instruction
accommodations
listserv
screen readers
simulation
cooperative learning
problem-based learning
community-based instruction
class-wide peer tutoring (CWPT)
facilitation
constructivism

CHAPTER FOCUS QUESTIONS

After reading this chapter, you should be able to answer such questions as:

1. How do the new higher learning standards affect teachers of inclusive classrooms?
2. What can you learn about a given student's needs from his IEP?
3. How is universal design for education different from traditional approaches?
4. Why is grouping so strongly recommended to teachers of inclusive classrooms?
5. Why is *reciprocal* peer tutoring effective, according to research?
6. What is it about cooperative learning that teachers have found so helpful?
7. What aspects of Direct Instruction make this technique valuable for teachers?

PERSONAL ACCOUNTS

Peer tutoring is an excellent strategy for teachers individualizing instruction. Here, a teacher of first- and second- grade classes shows how she uses the technique:

> *I always try to give everyone opportunities to peer tutor. Jimmy is a perfect example. Jimmy has cerebral palsy. It's hard for him to project his voice in class. However, he can make himself heard in a pair or small group. I worked really hard to find some strength areas in Jimmy, and then spent more time preparing him on how to tutor. I would teach him a skill during extra help period and then assign him to teach a classmate how to perform that skill. This gave him a chance to lead and feel proud in front of his peers.*
>
> *William is another student who needs peer tutoring, but for a very different reason. I had William in my class last year, too, and I spent the whole year helping him to identify good choices and bad choices. He required praise almost every second to stay involved, to stay positive, and to stay safe (he's prone to violent behavior). At the beginning of this year, the other children were afraid of him. They would say, "He was always in trouble last year." He has extreme hyperactivity and impulsivity. William wants desperately to belong. That's why the positive words of others, and their practical suggestions in peer-tutoring sessions, helped him to become motivated to improve his behavior.*
>
> —Natasha

When inclusion does not work, it often is because instruction was not individualized appropriately. Below, a graduate student who worked as a teacher aide in an eighth-grade setting while pursuing her Master's degree told me about a real-world instance in which simple, and avoidable, errors were made:

> *One boy, let's call him "Mike," was in the lowest of the low placements: Life Skills. All his classes were self-contained except for lunch and gym. The school wants to move him to the high school next year. To fulfill his technology requirement, they placed him into the regular eighth-grade technology class. I went with him because he needed an aide. He lasted almost a week. Nothing was modified for him. So he went back to having an extra gym period instead. That lasted the rest of the first marking period and also the second. By the third marking period, the school decided that they were indeed promoting him to high school next year, so they put him back into the regular-education eighth-grade technology class. It was such a disaster! He stayed there until the end of the school year. He probably would have passed the class if anything had been modified. I, myself, had trouble comprehending all that was required of him because half the year was already gone and neither of us was in the class at that time. The classroom rules had already been set. The teacher had a very strict and disciplined way of teaching. Everything in Mike's IEP was ignored. It was very frustrating for me; I can't imagine how it must have been for him. But he plodded along, mostly out of fear, I think.*
>
> *I learned some lessons from this! First, only students who can benefit from inclusion should be placed into such settings. Second, modifications in instruction, methods, and materials that are needed to make the education "appropriate" must be provided! If this means training teachers, so be it. Third, schools should never assume that hiring a teacher assistant will "solve the problem." Fourth and finally, two wrongs (or three) do not make a right!*
>
> —Charlyn

These personal accounts highlight key ideas in this chapter. One is peer tutoring. As Natasha showed with Jimmy, peer tutoring offers students with disabilities often-rare opportunities to shine in an inclusive classroom. And, as Charlyn's story illustrated, planning is important. Few things are more disruptive for included students than is needless change. A few modifications, selected in advance, might have made inclusion work for Mike.

INTRODUCTION

In Chapter 8, we look at techniques that inclusion teachers use to individualize instruction, notably advance planning, universal design, and techniques for modifying materials and procedures. The focus is upon practical, readily adopted strategies and tactics. That is because research consistently has shown that schools and teachers are far more likely to follow research-based recommendations if this can be done quickly, with relatively little training, and without large amounts of time and effort (Fuchs, Fuchs, & Bahr, 1990; Ysseldyke, 2001).

As a teacher of an inclusive classroom, you will find that things go much more smoothly after some advance planning. In particular, you need to acquaint yourself with the needs of students who have disabilities. You also need to write behavioral objectives for each of the major goals in the students' IEPs. You may need to modify materials, perhaps even texts. Room set-up is another important step in advance planning.

The approach known as universal design is of proven value to teachers of inclusive classrooms. This is because universal design helps you to individualize instruction *before* and *while* you teach. It is often easier, as well as less costly, to take such steps than it is

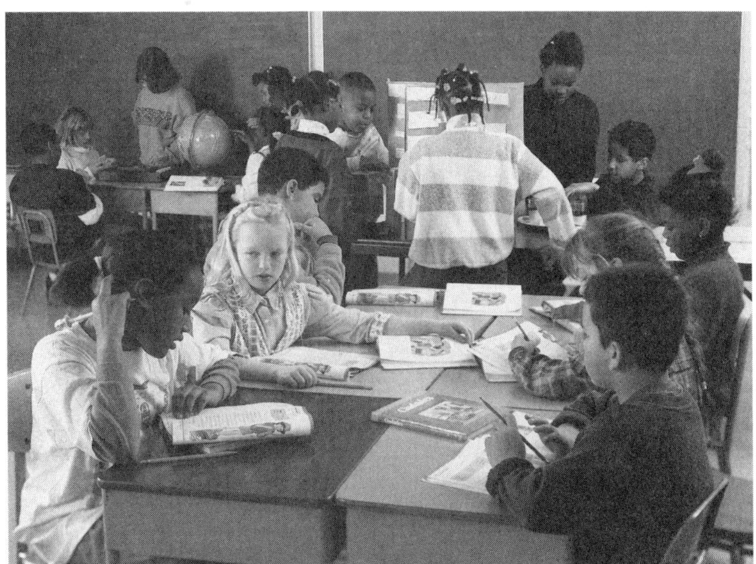

Grouping is an instructional technique that has a great deal of research behind it.

to rely upon more traditional accommodations. Both universal design and reasonable accommodations are ways of responding to IDEA's mandate to meet students' unique needs (see Chapters 1 and 2).

Such techniques as *peer tutoring* and *cooperative learning* help you to individualize instruction. This chapter offers in-depth reviews of those approaches, because of their demonstrated effectiveness not only with students who have disabilities (e.g., Fuchs et al., 2001) but also with English language learners who come from low-socioeconomic status (SES) homes (e.g., Greenwood, Arreaga-Mayer, Utley, Gavin, & Terry, 2001) and students who are at risk for school failure and dropping out (e.g., Gardner, Cartledge, Seidl, Woolsey, Schley, & Utley, 2001). Peer tutoring is easily and quickly adopted by classroom teachers (e.g., Fuchs et al., 2001). This is all very good news, indeed, for teachers who are challenged both to meet the special needs of students with disabilities *and* to help children and youth who have other kinds of needs. Some of the *same* strategies and tactics have been shown to improve outcomes for all of these kinds of learners. Teaching techniques of documented effectiveness are available for use with whole classes, with groups, or with individual students. All are appropriate for adoption by teachers in inclusive classrooms. One-on-one instruction, however, while it can be useful, should be a "last resort" by inclusion teachers because it is "extremely time-intensive" (Keel, Dangel, & Owens, 1999, p. 3).

TEACHING IN INCLUSIVE CLASSROOMS

Teaching an inclusive classroom is both like and not like teaching in a general classroom. The tail should not wag the dog: Although students with special needs are included, the essential nature of the classroom should remain intact. Notably, the content to be covered is not lessened. On the other hand, an inclusive classroom does feature a larger range of abilities and interests than does a typical non-inclusive classroom. Teaching techniques that may be helpful or interesting in a non-inclusive classroom generally are essential in an inclusive classroom.

Teaching an inclusive classroom is also like and not like teaching in a self-contained special-education classroom. Many of the approaches that are adopted by inclusive teachers originated in self-contained classrooms. Indeed, we know these techniques work with special-needs populations precisely because we have had decades of experience in using them in self-contained classes. However, inclusion classes are firmly based upon state learning standards. Teachers in separate classes frequently adopt curricula that are quite different. This is, indeed, one reason school districts maintain such classrooms: Some students need them. It is also why federal regulations require districts to make them available.

Standards and the Reform Curricula

The arrival of new and higher learning standards, coupled with annual state-wide and district-wide assessments, has spurred national and state teacher organizations to develop what Morocco (2001, p. 6) called "reform curricula" for teaching the key content subjects in elementary, middle, and high schools. These curricula are anchored on national standards. This book's Part Six: "Teaching in the Content Areas" describes the standards for English/Language Arts (Chapter 14); Math and Science (Chapter 15); and Social Studies (Chapter 16). These sets of standards have in common a consistent approach to PreK–12 education, despite the fact that they were created by widely diverse groups of subject-matter experts and classroom teachers. Simply put, these standards reject the idea of education as "transmission of knowledge" from teacher to student. They turn away from the notion of learning as something students do by themselves, alone.

Rather, these standards envision instruction that has students engaging in active and meaningful ("authentic") activities. The focus is upon the development, by all students, of skills and knowledge for "doing" content areas. That is, children and youth learn reading and writing *by* reading and writing. They learn history by *examining* source documents and by *simulating* past conditions and events. They learn math by *solving* problems that they believe are meaningful to them, that is, which are authentic. They learn science by performing experiments. These standards also encapsulate instruction that features students interacting with each other, participating together in heterogeneous pairs or small groups. That is because putting information into their own words helps students to master material. In more familiar terms, "The best way to learn something is to teach it!"

All of this is subsumed under the notion that learning is **socially mediated.** It is not passive. It is not something children and youth do well in isolation. Rather, "deep understanding" (Morocco, 2001, p. 7) comes as people try out their initial ideas on others, listen to different points of view, reflect further, and finally revise their understandings:

> Students with disabilities will improve their understanding in complex domains when they engage in instruction that reflects research-based principles of teaching for understanding. These principles include instruction designed around authentic tasks, opportunities to build cognitive strategies, learning that is socially mediated, and engagement in constructive conversations. As students with disabilities engage in instruction based on these principles, their additional learning needs become visible and teachers can respond through further domain-specific instructional support practices. (Morocco, 2001, p. 6)

Importantly for reform curricula, this is how professionals do their work. Scientists work collaboratively in their investigations. They discuss with their peers alternative ways to investigate problems. They try something, debate the meaning of results with colleagues, then try something else. The standards we will discuss in the chapters in Part Six all have this in common: Whether the standards are for English and language arts, mathematics, social studies, or some other subject, the expectation is that PreK–12 students will learn *both* the "ways of doing"/"ways of learning" *and* the state of the art in knowledge of these fields.

Students with disabilities who are included in regular classrooms can benefit from this new emphasis upon learning by doing. Hands-on instruction long has been recommended for children and youth having a wide variety of disabilities. The fact that cooperative learning is now in vogue similarly is very promising for such students. Experts have long expressed concern that successful employment requires teamwork, yet PreK–12 programs have given children and youth with disabilities very few opportunities to learn and practice cooperative teaming.

PLANNING

We look here at how teachers of inclusive classrooms prepare to teach, write instructional objectives and other plans, and set up the classroom. This section of the chapter opens with how schools "welcome" inclusion and support it. A school-wide climate is essential for inclusion to be successful. We then turn to the work of individual teachers as they prepare to teach students with disabilities, notably how they review IEPs and learn how other teachers approach instruction. We explore how to write instructional objectives and how to modify materials.

How Schools "Welcome" Inclusion

An essential ingredient for "making inclusion work" is a school-wide philosophy—and a set of implementing decisions—that support inclusion. The board of education, the superintendent, and the district director of special education must support inclusion. In most schools, the building principal is the key person. Think back to the "Tale of Two Schools" stories in Chapter 1. The principal of Hasta Vista School took a strong, personal interest in inclusion. She joined the district director of special education on visits to other school districts to study inclusion. She then invited teachers and therapists to visit inclusion schools, as well, and to give her advice on how to create an inclusion program at the Hasta Vista School. The principal began this process a full year before the first inclusion classes were created at the school. All of her decisions—involving teachers and therapists in making recommendations for "how to do inclusion," making inclusion classroom assignments voluntary, letting teachers self-nominate teams, offering inservice teacher training, and providing financial support—helped to pave the way for successful inclusion at Hasta Vista School. By contrast, the principal at the Forest Avenue School made critical decisions on her own, with no teacher input. She did this in April, intending for inclusion to begin the following September. The principal decided, arbitrarily, to implement inclusion in all classes in two entire grades (9 and 11). This meant that all children with disabilities in those two grades would be included, whether or not such placements were appropriate for them. Thinking about these two schools, we can readily imagine that a year later inclusion would be working at Hasta Vista School. We can also imagine, however, that it likely would fail at Forest Avenue School.

A school climate that supports inclusion has several features. First, teachers and therapists know that they can request, and expect to receive, what they need to do their jobs in inclusive classrooms. This means *inservice training* for educators on effective strategies and tactics for "making inclusion work." Such training should be offered during the school year, with release time, and/or during summer months, with extra pay. It means time to plan. Planning time needs to be built into the school week, because team members need uninterrupted time to make their partnerships work. It means that if teachers and therapists agree to push in support services (as opposed to pulling them out), the administration will make the necessary arrangements. It means the availability, of *peer coaches*—experienced inclusion teachers who can answer questions, offer advice, and trouble-shoot when problems arise. It also means the availability of the kinds of classroom *furnishings* that permit creation of small groups, provision of one-on-one instruction, and the like (see "Room Setup," p. 289). And it means the freedom to experiment and, on occasion, to fail.

Getting Started in an Inclusive Classroom

Teaching an inclusive classroom for the first time can be a daunting challenge. One big difference between an inclusive classroom and a non-inclusive classroom is the *range* of strengths and weaknesses of the students. This diversity makes whole-class instruction challenging. A second major difference is the extent to which inclusion teachers tend to

Forest Avenue School (left) and Hasta Vista School (right).

make use of use highly structured, *teacher-directed techniques,* in addition to the less regimented, student-focused facilitation that is favored by many general educators.

Figure 8.1 offers a flow chart illustrating the many steps involved in individualizing instruction. Some of these were discussed earlier in Chapter 2, notably identification, eligibility, and IEPs. Observe, in Figure 8.1, that the child's *needs* drive the entire process. This is notably *not* the child's label. Rather, it is the educational needs of the child, broadly defined, that is, academic needs, social development needs, life skills needs, and the like. The main questions that you want to answer as you read that IEP are given in the middle of Figure 8.1.

Reading the IEP

As you will recall, placement of a student into an inclusive classroom is made by a placement team (see Chapter 2). That team should not make such a placement if its members did not agree that an appropriate education could be provided in an inclusive setting and, more specifically, by you as a teacher. The presumption, then, is that the child belongs in your inclusive classroom. (If you disagree, you should tell the IEP team that, in your judgment, the placement was not an appropriate one.)

Ideally, you served on the IEP team and/or the placement team. If so, you are familiar with the child's strengths and weaknesses. If, however, you did not take part in such team sessions (which may occur, for example, if you are a newly hired teacher), you should familiarize yourself with the child's IEP and related documents. Those are available to you as the child's teacher. The IEP will document the child's current educational functioning (in other words, her needs), the goals for the child for the coming school year, the special-education and related services the child is to receive, and much more. Attached papers likely will include reports of prior teachers, results of psychological and other evaluations, and other materials that may be of assistance to you.

As you read, make notes. You will want to know, in as much depth as possible, what the child's unique needs are (see Figure 8.1). You will be responsible for meeting those needs, in cooperation with other professionals, with paraprofessionals, and with volunteers. If, for example, supplemental aids and services are to be provided to facilitate inclusion, you will want to be in touch with the itinerant teacher, assistive technology specialist, or other support personnel to plan delivery of these aids and services. Similarly, if related services are to be offered to the child, the IEP will tell you how often this will occur and for how long each time. You may wish to discuss this with the appropriate related-services professional(s). Among other things, you will want to talk about the advisability of push-in versus pull-out services. You may also wish to talk with the student's family members. Perhaps most important, you want to do some thinking. Reflecting upon your experience, your personal beliefs and preferences, and your knowledge of the skills of others who will be in the classroom (including paraprofessionals, volunteers, etc.), you

FIGURE 8.1 The Assessment Question Model

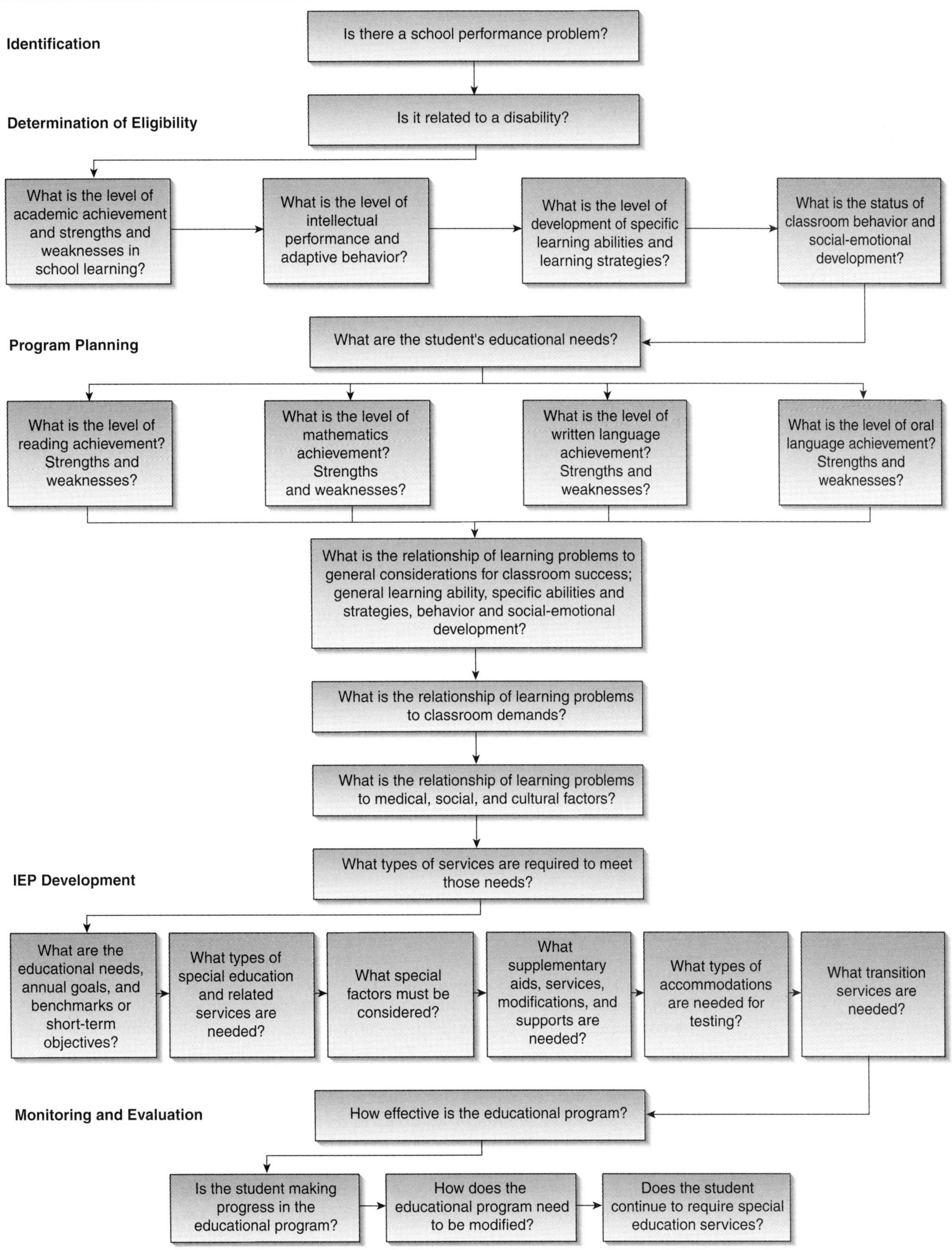

Source: From *Assessing students with special needs,* 5th ed. (p. 20, Figure 1-1), by J.A. McLoughlin and R.B. Lewis, 2001, Upper Saddle River, NJ: Prentice Hall. Copyright 2001 by Prentice Hall. Reprinted with permission.

will want to outline a plan that will help you to meet the needs of this child while also responding to the many needs of the other students in your class.

Field Visits

A good way to begin your preparation is to spend some time in regular and special classes at two *other* grade levels: the one below yours and the one above yours. You want to know where your students are coming from, and you want to know where they are going. What knowledge and skills are they being given at the lower grade level? Which ones will they need to be successful at the higher grade level?

If you are a special educator, you should spend more than half of this observation time in *general* classes. Both during teacher training and while teaching, some special educators lower their expectations, whether consciously or not. They do this because students with disabilities, in general, tend to function at lower levels than do most general-education students, and to learn more slowly. For teachers in inclusive classrooms, however, lowering expectation is dangerous. This is because success in an inclusive setting requires that children and youth with disabilities perform at a higher level than they would need to in a special environment. That holds not only for their success in your classroom, but also for their continued success next year. A key to successful teaching in inclusive classrooms is to *hold your expectations high—and support your students' efforts to reach those expectations.*

If you are a general educator, on the other hand, you should spend more than half of this observation time in *special* classrooms and/or resource rooms. You want to become familiar with alternative ways of adapting curricula, of modifying instruction, and of managing behavior. Which of the techniques you see in other classrooms strike you as promising? Take notes and ask your special education team member about them. In particular, be alert for strategies and tactics being used with special-education students that strike you as applicable for use with *other* students. You might be surprised how many such techniques you discover:

> Through our involvement in inclusive classrooms, we have seen (and heard from general education classroom teachers) that many of the strategies used to increase the social and curricular inclusion of students with disabilities are directly relevant to and supportive of many students without labels. (York, Doyle, & Kronberg, 1992, p. 4)

That is an important point. Many of the methods in this chapter are approaches that teachers have discovered work well with nondisabled students as well as those with disabilities.

Writing Instructional Objectives

Elementary and secondary education traditionally has focused on *groups* of children. States prepare curriculum guidelines for many thousands of students across a dozen grade levels. Schools create rules governing the behavior of hundreds of students. Teachers plan methods and materials for classes having two or three dozen students. All of these activities are conducted around groups. The education of children with disabilities is different: It is done one-by-one. Being able to deliver this level of individualized instruction is one of the most important competencies that teachers must master.

In his classic text, *Preparing Instructional Objectives* (1997), Mager insisted that instructional objectives be written in **behavioral terms.** That is, they should be presented as behaviors that the student will perform. The words used should be clear: They should mean the same thing to different people. Consider, for example, "Presented with a chart depicting eight differently colored objects, Shiran will correctly identify the three that are in primary colors." That objective talks about *behaviors* that Shiran will exhibit. Those behaviors will be visible to any observer. The only word in this instructional objective that we might disagree about is "identify"—it might be better to say "point to," so that the criterion behavior is explicit (see "Teacher Strategies That Work: Writing Behavioral Objectives").

Teacher Strategies That Work

Writing Behavioral Objectives

Change This . . .	To This . . .	Change This . . .	To This . . .
Will become more independent	Will put on coat before going outdoors in cold weather	Will pay attention	Will remain in seat during class time at least 90% of the time, unless excused by teacher
Will show improvement in math	Will correctly answer 8 of 10 two-digit addition problems	Will play well	Will offer to share toys when prompted by teacher, at least 75% of the time
Will become good speller	Will write correctly spelled words when spoken by teacher, with 80% accuracy or better		

Behavioral objectives should specify: (1) what the *child* will do and (2) under which *circumstances* and (3) with what level of *accuracy* or success. Very importantly, behavioral objectives do *not* talk about what teachers and other professionals will do (e.g., "Shiran will receive speech and language pathology services three times weekly, for 40 minutes each time"). Such statements do not help us to know how she is progressing. Equally as important, behavioral objectives are highly specific statements. An example of a bad behavioral objective is "Shiran will be more independent." Ask yourself, "What does 'independent' mean?" Then rewrite the objective, using *those* action-oriented terms.

To say that most teachers know about these techniques is not, sadly, to say that most practice them. This becomes an issue in teaching children with special needs. That is because special education places so much emphasis upon each child as an individual.

The big difference between writing instructional objectives for groups and writing them for particular children is that group goals are not applicable. IDEA forbids you as a teacher from setting goals for students with disabilities based upon class-wide goals. IEPs, after all, are *individualized* plans. The goals, assessment procedures, and reporting on progress all should be individualized. You should also write objectives for children's behaviors. That will be discussed later in Chapter 9.

Modifying Instruction

Planning to teach an inclusive classroom requires that you see what general education materials, methods, and procedures may need to be modified. This may include textbooks and assignments. Ideally, few modifications will be necessary. In most instances, though, some changes are appropriate.

Texts

Your preparation begins with an examination of the textbook(s) you plan to use. If any of your students are blind or have low vision, or have dyslexia or some other reading disability, you will want to find out if any texts are available in electronic form. Many publishers now offer "e-books" as well as bound books.

For more information on the Council for Exceptional Children, the AFB Directory of Services, the "Louis" catalog, and the CSMT, go to the Web Links module in Chapter 8 of the Companion Website.

If a text is widely adopted by special schools (e.g., schools for deaf children), you may be able to obtain text modifications and study guides from teachers at such a school. The Council for Exceptional Children is a good starting point to identifying such schools. So, too, is the Web site of your state department of education. The American Foundation for the Blind's *AFB Directory of Services* contains information about those state education departments. Also helpful is the American Printing House for the Blind's "Louis" catalog. The Clearinghouse for Specialized Media and Technology (CSMT) describes

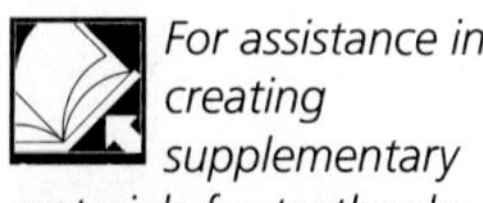
For assistance in creating supplementary materials for textbooks, go to the Web Links module in Chapter 8 of the Companion Website.

accessible versions of textbooks acquired by California schools pursuant to the California statute requiring publishers of school texts to deliver not only bound books but also e-texts.

Students with specific learning disabilities, mental retardation, and deafness or other hearing impairment often will benefit from supplementary materials. These include outlines (chapter heads and subheads) as well as definition sheets for key words and concept maps that show how different ideas discussed in a chapter relate to each other. Good textbooks come with these supplementary features. If the ones you plan to adopt do not, you will need to find or create them.

You will also need to provide *strategy instruction* for many of these students. They need explicit directions for making optimal use of concept maps, definition sheets, advance organizers, and the like. You need to plan such tutoring, including setting aside the required time early in the school year.

Ideally, in an inclusive classroom you should not have to simplify the text. On occasion, however, you will have a student who can succeed in an inclusive setting but requires simplified texts to do so. Simplifying a text is a time-consuming task, so you should do only as much of it as the IEP team determined was necessary. Among the steps you may take are

- Highlighting key words and passages (e.g., with a yellow highlighter)
- Rewriting passages into simpler English (shorter sentences, fewer unfamiliar words, etc.)
- Writing a study guide the student can use with the text. As you know from your own college work, study guides provide outlines, synopses, definitions, and self-monitoring tools (e.g., sample tests).

Assignments

The IEP may indicate that modifications of assignments will be provided. Some of these are straightforward, as when a blind child is to be permitted to turn in taped rather than

Teacher Strategies That Work

Outlining Texts

Many students with specific learning disabilities, and some others as well, fail to make effective use of the textual features that are used in today's textbooks. Research conducted by the Center for Applied Special Technology (CAST) showed the benefits of software that "pulls" the outline, heads, subheads, and other organizing features from a book chapter, and presents these to the student (Pisha & Coyne, 2001). The CAST team used Inspiration® software, but the strategy may be used without any computer programs (you may write by hand).

Consider the chapter you are now reading. This chapter contains several thousand words of text, in addition to heads, subheads, boxes, and other features. What Pisha and Coyne discovered when they worked with middle-school students having learning disabilities is that the students tended to ignore the "concept map" that these organizing features offered. By separating those features from the text, Pisha and Coyne highlighted them, making it much easier for the students to see the pattern. Below, we do this for heads and subheads of this chapter that are related to teacher planning:

Planning

How Schools "Welcome" Inclusion
Getting Started in an Inclusive Classroom
Reading the IEP
Field Visits
Writing Instructional Objectives
Modifying Instruction
  Texts
  Assignments
Room Setup

Notice that the outline makes clear that teachers need administrative support to succeed in inclusive classrooms and that they also have to engage in pre-teaching preparation, including reviewing children's IEPs and familiarizing themselves with classrooms at other grade levels. They also need to prepare individualized goals and objectives for included students and, often, to modify both texts and assignments. Finally, they need to give some thought to how their classrooms are designed. The outline helps us to "see the forest" as a whole; it also serves as a good reminder of the different ways in which planning helps teachers of inclusive classrooms. It is exactly this bird's-eye view that students with specific learning disabilities often do not obtain as they read a textbook. That is why outlining is a "strategy that works" in inclusive classrooms.

handwritten or typed papers. The IEP team may indicate that you should offer explicit instruction on completing assignments before making those assignments. Other interventions involve modifying time rather than response: Some IEPs will note that students should be granted additional time to complete assignments or that they should be given breaks so as to limit the length of time they must spend on the assignment in one sitting. Still others have to do with the way assignments are to be completed. Some IEPs will specify that a student may demonstrate knowledge by performing a target skill rather than by taking a pencil-and-paper test.

Instruction in classrooms today often features work in small groups. This includes cooperative learning, peer tutoring, inquiry-based learning, and the like. You should not assume that all children and youth with disabilities already know how to be good team members. They may have been instructed one-on-one in separate classrooms and/or in resource rooms, so they may come to you with little or no experience in working in pairs or small groups. If this is the case with a particular child, you may want to provide explicit instruction early in the school year on such things as listening attentively to the other student(s), showing respect for others' feelings and ideas, and performing the different roles played by team members (group leader, recorder, etc.).

Modifications in homework may include in-school homework periods, during lunch, recess, before- or after-school hours, and so on. Such steps often are feasible because teacher and peer support can be arranged. Students who are blind or have low vision, some with physical disabilities, and some with specific learning disabilities who require adaptive equipment that is not available at home may be permitted to do homework in alternative ways (e.g., taping an assignment). In more-demanding cases, you may work with the student's family to provide assistance at home. This may involve training a sibling, a parent, or some other person who resides in the student's home on how to help the student do homework (without overhelping).

If, after trying such minor modifications, you discover that a student cannot successfully complete assignments without more substantial modifications, your first option could be to offer strategy instruction on other processes, such as reading for meaning. A second might be to arrange peer tutoring or a "study buddy" who will provide assistance as required. A third, if these steps do not suffice, may be to request an itinerant teacher or a resource-room teacher to provide supplementary instruction and support on assignments. If, however, these interventions fail to meet the need, you should advise the IEP team that it should consider alternative measures.

Room Setup

You should examine the layout of the classroom you will use. Given the greater diversity of needs in an inclusive class, you probably will want to have a similarly broad range of options. This should include the traditional rows of seats facing in one direction. But it should also have small-group settings (table, four to eight chairs), dyads (two seats side-by-side or facing each other), and single-student positions (e.g., study carrels). This variety of physical features lets you conduct whole-class instruction, set up groups, and give students susceptible to distractions space to study or take tests where distractions are minimized. In addition, you should have physical separation between high-activity areas (e.g., for science experiments, art work, etc.) and low-activity spaces (e.g., for independent reading, test taking, etc.). By separating the two regions, you minimize the likelihood of children disrupting other students who are engaged in low-activity tasks.

Grouping is a very important set of techniques for teachers of inclusive classrooms. So is cooperative learning. Accordingly, it is important that you request, through your building principal, that you be given a variety of small, round tables. These may be collapsible tables if space is at a premium. Figures 8.2 and 8.3 may help you to plan your room layout. In Figure 8.2, you see the typical lecture layout. This is not an ideal arrangement for an inclusive classroom. In Figure 8.3, you see one possible layout that lends itself to small-group instruction.

If a student uses a wheelchair, you need to arrange the room so that clear pathways exist between the door and the student's study location/table/desk, as well as between

FIGURE 8.2 Sample Floor Plan for a General Education Classroom

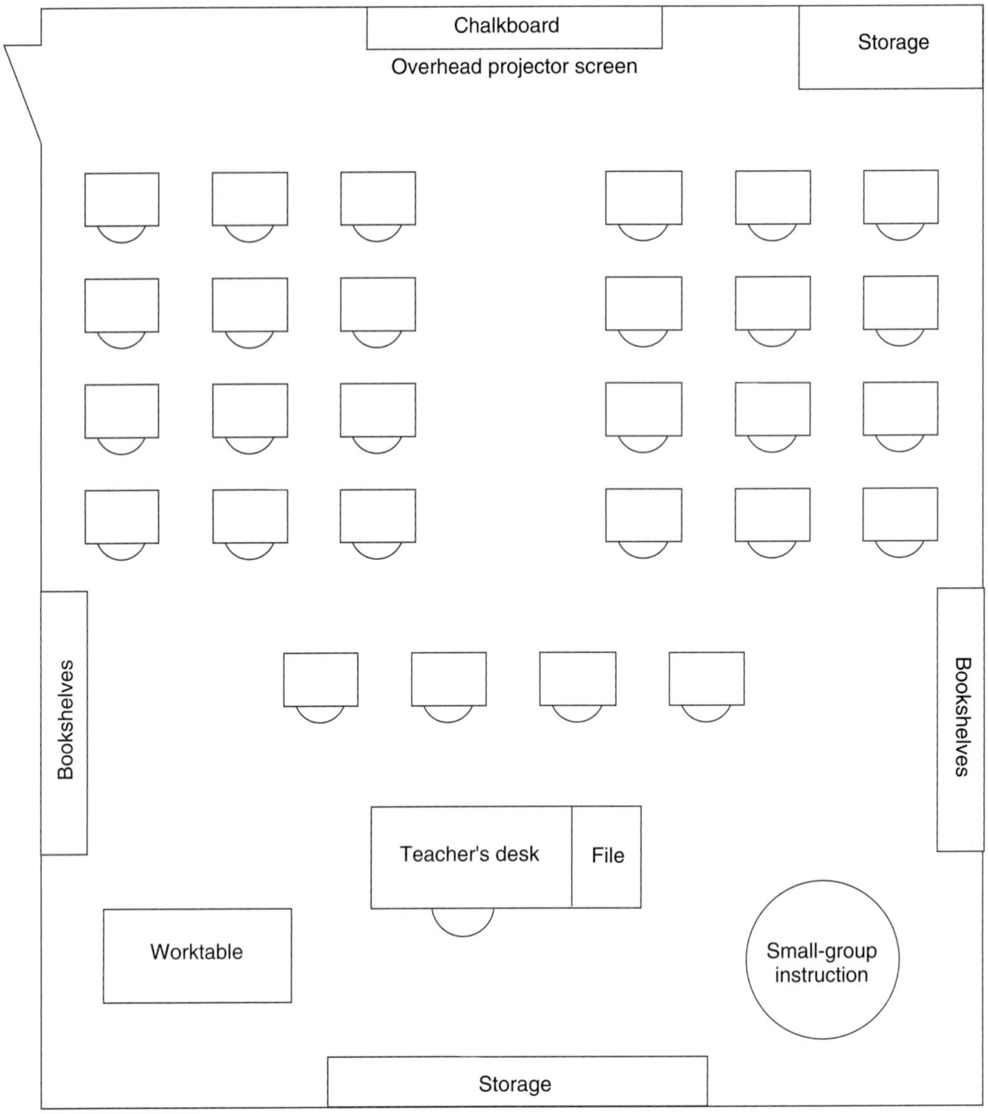

rows of desks. Controls for devices or systems that students are expected to use (this may include PCs, overhead projectors, laboratory devices, and the like) should be reachable from a wheelchair. Generally, this means they should be no more than 48" and no less than 35" above the floor (more than 48", the student can't reach high enough; less than 35", the student may tip over when trying to reach down). Placing wood boards under a desk raises the surface so that the wheelchair fits comfortably underneath. If a student has epilepsy that is not completely controlled by medication, you should look closely at protruding objects in the classroom. Any sharp ones should be removed or shielded. Deaf or hard of hearing students should not face a light source; their seats should be placed back-to-window. Students who are highly distractible should be located away from the door but relatively close to your main desk.

High-traffic areas in particular must be kept clear of congestion (Emmer, Evertson, & Worsham, 2000). This includes group-work areas and lab/science activity regions. Emmer et al. also suggested that teachers keep empty plenty of space on bulletin boards and walls. Although you probably will post classroom rules, current assignments, and the like, you should reserve room as a reward for students (after completing an arduous project, for ex-

FIGURE 8.3 Sample Floor Plan for an Inclusive Classroom

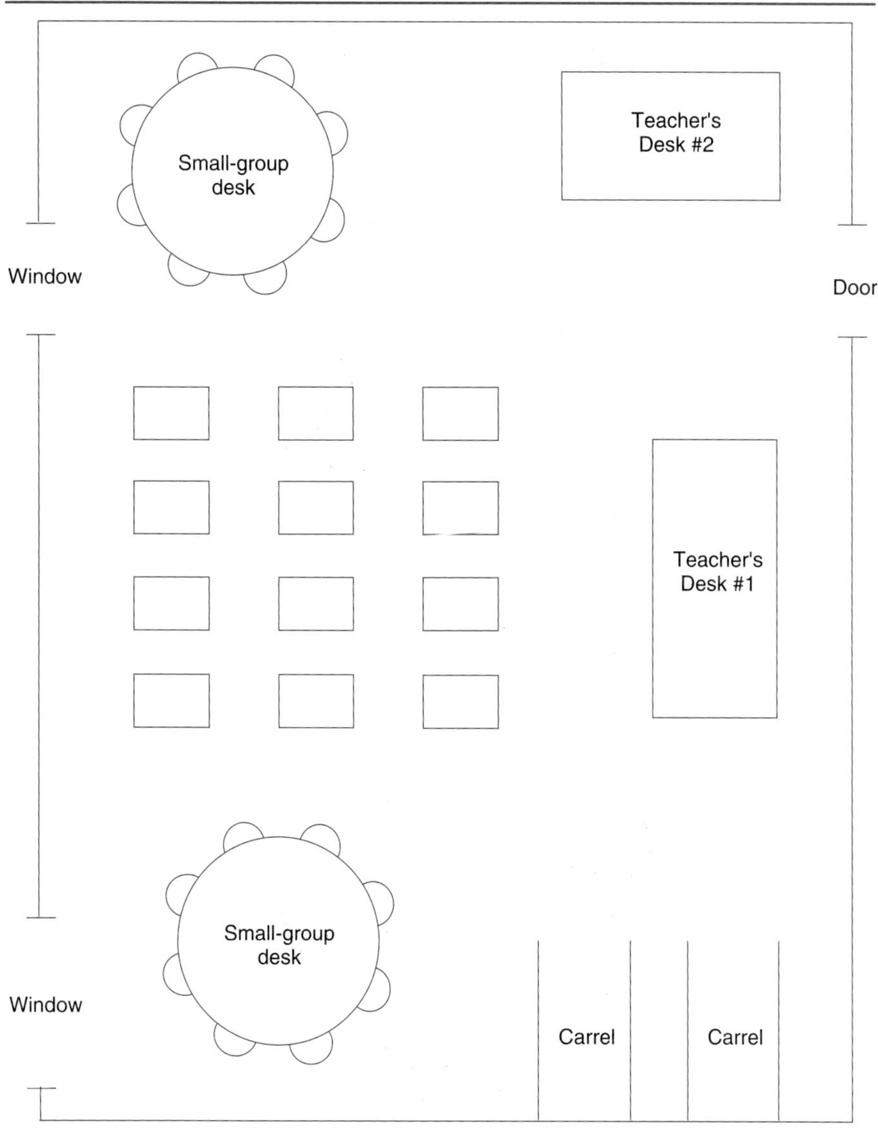

Source: Adapted from Mercer and Mercer (1998).

ample, you might allow them to decorate a bulletin board) and you also want to avoid distracting students with too many "busy" postings on the walls. Educators should also stand at each activity center, group-work area, etc., from time to time, so as to assess and re-assess traffic patterns, visibility of overheads, videos, etc., and distractions.

UNIVERSAL DESIGN

Universal design calls for teachers to take simple steps, in advance, so as to make education more accessible to students with varying needs and interests (Bowe, 2000c). The idea is to give each student what he needs or prefers, which, in turn, means making materials and other aspects of instruction available in different modalities. Fortunately, this is readily done using today's technologies.

An exciting new approach to teaching in inclusive classrooms is universal design. This is a way of preparing to teach, and a way of teaching. Generally, the idea is to design your

FIGURE 8.3 Instructional Options (*continued*)

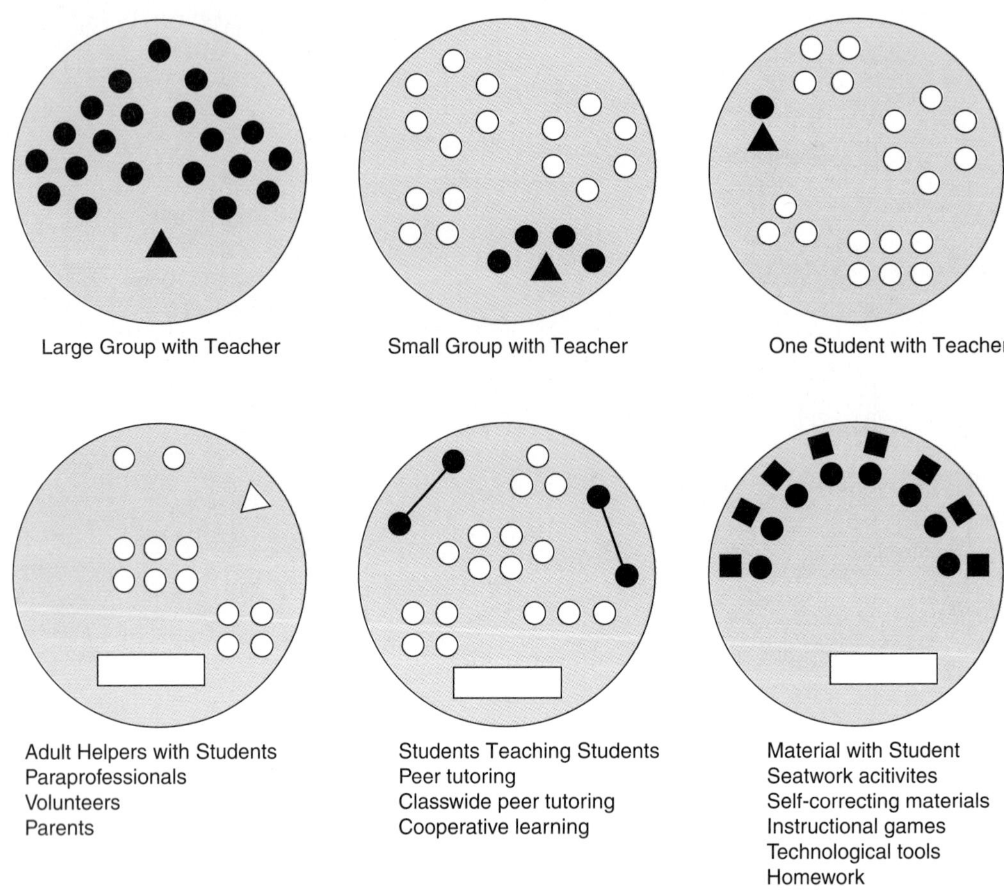

Source: Adapted from Mercer and Mercer (1998).

instruction *from* the start so as to respond to the diversity of needs, interests, and preferences that you will encounter in an inclusive classroom. To illustrate, consider how you might use organizing software, such as Inspiration®. You could create an outline of a chapter for your most-in-need students, calling it, say, "Chapter1." After saving it to that name, you add more depth, more details, and so on, that will appeal to more typical students. This outline you save as, say, "Chapter1A." You then continue, making the outline even more comprehensive, for use with your best students. Call that "Chapter1B." You now have three levels of the same chapter outline. These allow you to apply **differentiated instruction,** that is, to individualize your teaching/tutoring so as to respond to the varying needs of different students.

Applying Universal Design to Education

Bowe (2000c), faculty at the University of Connecticut (Scott, et al., 2001), and CAST (Pisha and Coyne, 2001) extended the concept to education. The three approaches are called, respectively, UDE (universal design in education), UDI (universal design for instruction), and UDL (universal design for learning). Bowe took principles of universal design that were developed for use in architecture and consumer product design and applied them to teaching. The seven principles were

1. Equitable use (everyone can use it, preferably in the same ways);
2. Flexibility in use (people have options about how they use it);
3. Simple and intuitive use (it works the way we expect it to);

A universally designed house.

4. Perceptible information (people can understand it even if they have sensory impairments);
5. Tolerance for error (we can "escape" from mistakes without penalty);
6. Low physical effort (using it does not require sustained strength); and
7. Size and space for approach and use (people using wheelchairs or walkers can get around easily and can use PCs, kiosks, and other devices).

The University of Connecticut's "Universal Design for Instruction" (Scott et al., 2001) adopted these same seven principles and added two more: (8) a community of learners (universally designed instruction promotes interaction between students and faculty) and (9) instructional climate (education is inclusive, welcoming all students). CAST's approach is perhaps best illustrated by the ways in which its researchers adapted social studies instruction at a local high school (see Chapter 16). They converted a social studies text to electronic form, which had two important benefits: First, students could listen to the text as well as, or instead of, reading it, and, second, the text was easily searchable using a "find" feature. "Teacher Strategies That Work: How to 'Do' Universal Design in Your Teaching" (see p. 306) summarizes 10 key techniques of UDE.

The Core Ideas of Universal Design for Teachers

Despite their differences, the three approaches emphasize the need for *teachers* to be proactive in advance of instruction. The essential idea is to create alternative versions of instructional materials and to allow students to adopt alternative ways of interacting with them. Universal design in education is a way of planning. The key is to ask the right questions. As a teacher in an inclusive classroom, you need to deal with a broader range of abilities and interests than do most teachers. Some students are visual learners; others learn better by listening. Some work best on their own; others like to work with a partner or two. Some are good with abstract ideas; others do better when concepts are translated into concrete realities.

Universal design encourages you as a teacher to ask questions such as: Can I make this more visual (perhaps by showing a video, displaying a map, using concept maps, etc.)? Can I offer an auditory learning experience (perhaps by letting students listen to

Manipulatives and other supports can make a big difference.

a politician's speech, singing a song popular in another culture, etc.)? Can I make this idea more concrete (perhaps by discussing school and class rules, talking about a recent event in the neighborhood, etc.)? Can I arrange for participatory learning (perhaps by assigning groups to investigate an issue, putting on a play in which students portray historical characters, etc.)? Can I use community-based learning opportunities (perhaps by taking students to a store where they order items and make change, visiting a local museum, etc.)?

There are other ways of making lectures accessible to students with special needs. Students with low vision, for example, appreciate being able to read large print. WordPerfect® lets you print out your lectures in fonts as large as 72 points. Here is an illustration of how large that is:

72 Point

Sophisticated technology is not required for educators to apply the teachings of universal design. When you write on a chalkboard, you must say out loud every word you write. That is redundancy. You should do the same thing when you display a PowerPoint® slide or an overhead transparency. This requires a few seconds to a minute of extra time. It just so happens that this additional time is exactly what many students with specific learning disabilities need (see Chapter 3). It also helps *any* student. If you display a slide or a transparency, or write on a chalkboard, but do not read the words out loud, many students, including those with no disabilities, are still reading the displayed information—and many are still copying it down into their notebooks. They are not ready for you to discuss the slide, overhead, or handwritten information. Speaking out loud what you write also gives information to students in the modalities they prefer because of learning style differences. Some do well with visual information, others with auditory information. That is why you should give the same information *both ways*. This is a good illustration of how the principles of universal design apply to and help *all* students. That makes these principles ideal for teachers of inclusive classrooms.

Advantages of Universal Design in Education

IDEA requires educators to meet students' unique needs. **Accommodations,** such as assistive technologies, help do that, usually while leaving the teacher's instruction unaltered. A sign-language interpreter, for example, is brought into the classroom to sign what the

Student Strategies That Work

Computers

Keyboarding: An Essential Skill

Students with disabilities need to develop keyboarding skills even more than do students with no disabilities. This is because so many assistive technology devices require keyboarding skill. It is also because students with specific learning disabilities, mild mental retardation, deafness and other hearing impairments, and many other conditions benefit greatly from the spell checkers and grammar checkers that are built into today's word processing software programs. These students can produce much better output on the computer than they could by hand—but only if they learn keyboarding skills.

At all levels, students should be taught techniques for reducing fatigue and preventing injury (e.g., carpal tunnel syndrome). These should become habit over time. They include sitting up straight, facing the keyboard and the screen, with feet flat on the floor. Breaks every 15 or 20 minutes are important. Typists should stand up, stretch, walk around, and in general do things very different than typing. After a short period (perhaps two minutes), they may return to keyboarding again.

Outlines/Advance Organizers

Many students, notably those with specific learning disabilities and those whose learning styles and preferences make them visual learners, benefit when they learn how to make optimal use of organizing tools. Inspiration Software has produced software tools that support visual learning by offering graphical ways of working with information and ideas. Inspiration® and Kidspiration™ support, respectively, middle/high school and early childhood/elementary students by pulling out the heads, subheads, and other organizing devices in textbooks and making these available in an outline view. Such outline views can also offer instant access to definitions of key terms. The programs can also be used to help students understand relationships better and to outline chapters as they read them. They offer causal diagrams, webs, concept maps, idea maps, and other support tools students may use to diagram and summarize information.

TABLE 8.1 Universal Design v. Assistive Technology

Universal Design	Assistive Technology
Responsibility of designers/developers	Responsibility of user or user's agent
Done while service or product is being developed	Done after product is finished, or while service is being delivered
Serves many people at once	Serves one individual user at a time
Renewable accessibility	Consumable accessibility
Allows for serendipity	Seldom is used in innovative ways

Source: From *Universal Design in Education* (Table 2.1), by F. Bowe, 2000, Westport, CT.: Greenwood Publishing Group, Reprinted with permission of the author and publisher.

teacher says. Such accommodations tend to be one-use adjustments. When the interpreter leaves the classroom, the accommodation she provides walks out, too. Consider, as well, such accommodations as Brailled reading materials and audio tape records in the classroom. Only one student benefits. Universal design, another way of meeting students' needs, by contrast, is a *many-use* adjustment of the instruction itself. Unlike the interpreter or a Braille textbook, a lecture on disk can be listened to by a student with a specific learning disability, one who is blind or has low vision, and one who is a visual learner (see Table 8.1).

Universal design is often an *any-time* technique. Many accommodations help a student at that time. They do not help other students who may have been too shy to request accommodations, nor do they help students in next year's class. Many universally designed interventions, by contrast, may be used at any time, even weeks or months after the lecture has been delivered. Lectures placed on disk or on a course Web page may also be used by children and youth who are blind or have low vision, at any time and at any location where they have a laptop or PC.

E-Texts

An exciting development is the recent emergence of e-texts. These are materials, including textbooks, that are published electronically. Electronically published texts may be "read" by students who are blind or have dyslexia by means of speech synthesis. The State of California in 1999 acted to require publishers whose texts are adopted by California public schools to publish those texts both in print and electronically (Assembly Bill AB 422). In 2000, Barnes & Noble announced that its Web site would begin offering a wide range of e-texts. Random House, the world's largest textbook publisher, announced that same summer that it would make a major investment in e-publishing. Not all printed texts are available in electronic format. The good news is that year after year, more and more are.

Why are e-texts so exciting? First, students can read them anywhere. They can read them online or download them to home PCs and to laptops. Second, these texts are *searchable*. This advantage is considerable when students are writing reports or other papers and when they are studying. The obvious application is to the study of literature, so we will discuss e-texts at length in Chapter 14. Third, e-texts may be listened to via text-to-speech (speech synthesis). This has obvious appeal to students whose learning styles are such that they learn better by listening than they do by reading. It helps students with specific reading disabilities, students who are blind or have low vision, and students who want to cram at the very last minute. Some students actually listen to lectures and handouts while driving to school to take a big exam (they have the laptop on the car seat beside them, with the speech synthesizer turned on). Finally, e-texts on laptops or on special readers are lightweight. The devices can hold a number of books. For this reason, carrying a dozen e-books is much easier than is carrying the same number of printed texts.

Interaction

A key principle of UDE, UDI, and UDL is to facilitate student and faculty interaction. Early 21st-century education differs dramatically from late 20th-century education in the ability of students and teachers alike to network even when they are not physically together. Teachers can facilitate such interaction by creating a **listserv**—a set of e-mail addresses collected into a program. For example, your American Literature class could have a listserv called "Litstu" into which you enter all student e-mail addresses, plus your own. You can send a message to all members of the listserv by addressing it to the listserv name (To: Litstu). Students can respond to the entire list or they can respond more privately just to the student posting a comment. Listservs make out-of-class student interaction available on an accessible basis to *all* students. That is much preferable to the traditional method of such interaction (voice phone calls), because those tend to leave out deaf students (not to mention students who are shy or withdrawn). And, because speech synthesizers may be used to read e-mails and messages posted to the listserv, students who are blind or have low vision as well as those with specific reading disabilities can be equal participants in the interactions.

This discussion of speech synthesizers, which are assistive technology devices, leads us to our next topic: assistive technology services and assistive technology devices. It is important for teachers of inclusive classrooms to become familiar with the potential that these offer to facilitate inclusion.

ASSISTIVE TECHNOLOGY

Assistive technology devices are products (hardware, software, firmware, etc.) that are designed for use by persons with disabilities so as to perform activities that they either could not otherwise do or could do only with great difficulty and/or personal assistance from someone else. Assistive technology services is the term we use to refer to locating such products, evaluating them, acquiring them, training teachers/students/family members on how to use them, and fixing them. IDEA requires that any child with a disability who needs assistive technology devices and/or services be provided with such in the child's IEP.

Assistive technologies help students with disabilities to read, write, perform mathematics, "do" science and social studies, and much else, including music and art. A wide variety of products are now available for helping people with special needs to function more independently. The key for educators is to know who keeps up with this flood of innovation and where to turn to get the newest information in a form that teachers can readily use.

Assistive technology devices can be simple and low-tech in nature. This includes velcro for fastening things, dycem for keeping items from slipping on a desk, and pen/pencil holders that make gripping easier. Assistive technology devices can also be complex and high-tech. There is, for example, a commercial copy machine that lets users speak commands, that talks back to users, and that also offers Brailled information. And there are many assistive technology devices that are mid-way between these two extremes. Thousands of assistive technology devices exist today and new products are being introduced daily. Prices change annually or even more frequently. Vendors go out of business from time to time; others are acquired by competing companies. That is why you should call upon assistive technology specialists for support.

Assistive Technology Specialists

Even with the help of resources such as *assistivetech.net*™, teachers of inclusive classrooms need support. That is where related-services personnel usually called "assistive technology specialists" come in. (Your school may have a somewhat different title for this person.) These individuals often are occupational therapists. Some are physical therapists. Some are neither but possess knowledge and skills in the area of assistive technology. The function of assistive technology specialists is to evaluate the needs of a child, research the technological options that are available for meeting these needs, select the most appropriate of these, and recommend acquisition. Usually this person reports her recommendations to the IEP team. On occasion, however, the inclusion classroom teacher will request and receive the report. The assistive technology specialist also trains people in the use of devices and software programs. This includes inclusive teachers, children with disabilities, and family members. Ideally, that training is not a one-time deal but rather continues as long as it is needed. Finally, because technology products inevitably will develop glitches or "bugs," or will for one reason or another fail to function properly, assistive technology specialists either repair the products or arrange for their repair by the manufacturer.

The Importance of Training

Perhaps the most critical function of the technology specialist is to train students in how to use assistive technology devices. You, as the inclusive classroom teacher, should also be trained on these products. You will need some knowledge in order to help your students and to solve common problems.

Some products require lengthy training for effective use. **Screen readers** are examples. Specialized classes lasting months often are needed before students who are blind or have low vision can navigate Windows® or Web environments using a screen reader. Speech synthesis (which talks for screen readers) usually requires much less training. However, for easy and rapid use, familiarity with the voice is required. Speech recognition requires training of a different kind: The user has to train the software to understand his voice. Depending on the software, anywhere from 20 minutes to several hours of training is necessary before the system can understand most of what a student says. (Children and youth should be warned that their voices change from time to time—they sound different early in the morning, soon after awakening, than they do in the afternoon; they sound different when they have a cold—and that such changes may produce less-than-expected recognition by the software.)

Training on technology is especially important for students who are blind or have low vision. They need to master screen readers, speech synthesis, Braille, and other alternative communication technologies. Braille alone comes in Grade I Braille, Grade II Braille, Nemeth Code (math Braille), and other varieties. That is an argument in favor of early intervention (birth to two inclusive) and preschool special education (ages 3 to 5 inclusive) in specialized (non-inclusive) environments. In order to succeed in inclusive settings in K–12 schools, these children need to have mastered these technologies already.

The Administration and Technology

School administrators play vital roles in assistive technology. They approve purchase of products and pay for them. They hire, and pay the salaries of, assistive technology specialists. They create and maintain a school-wide climate in which technology is welcomed, products are maintained, and updates/new versions are secured as needed.

For more information on Technology Standards for School Administrators, go to the Web Links module in Chapter 8 of the Companion Website.

Teachers in inclusive classrooms should make administrators aware of the Technology Standards for School Administrators that have been published by the International Society for Technology in Education. The standards are organized around several principles, including "Leadership and Vision" (creation and regular updating of a school-wide technology policy and plan), "Learning and Teaching" (emphasis on student-centered technologies and on professional development for educators), "Productivity and Professional Practice" (use of technology for administrative purposes), "Support, Management, and Operations" (allocation of financial, personnel, and other resources), "Assessment and Evaluation" (use of technology in testing and in management), and "Social, Legal, and Ethical Issues" (promotion of security, safety, etc., in use of technology).

If you decide to create a personal or class Web site, you will need the administration's permission to post it on a school server. Even if you place your Web site on a non-school server, you should secure advance permission from your assistant principal or principal. The administration's concerns likely will be with content and security. The box, "Technologies That Work: A Class Web Site," provides suggestions on creating and maintaining a personal/class Web site.

Preventing Technology Abandonment

A persistent problem in PreK–12 schools is that assistive technology devices that are acquired for use by students with special needs tend to be discarded shortly after purchase. This "technology abandonment" is usually quite avoidable. When it occurs, it usually reflects the fact that the user was not adequately consulted beforehand. The lesson is a clear one: Before acquiring any special-needs product, you and the school's technology specialist should work closely with the student. This is particularly urgent in instances in which the device is intended for personal communication. Speech synthesis, for example, serves as the child's voice. If the student is not comfortable with the speech, she will soon stop using it. Many programs are offered on the Web in downloadable test format. You can experiment with them for two weeks, or 30 days, free of charge. Examples are ALVA Access Groups' inLARGE® screen magnifier and outSPOKEN® speech synthesis program. These may be downloaded in time-sensitive formats from *http://www.aagi.com.*

Technology abandonment also happens when devices cannot be repaired easily and inexpensively. Educators have told me that electronic communicators sometimes are "balky" or "unstable"—they need to be fixed quite frequently. These products must also be programmed. Without the right programming, children will not be able to "say" what they want to say in each class, at lunch, at recess, and at home. Such frustrations may lead to technology abandonment. If an IEP team recommends acquisition of such a device, it is important that you as a teacher, working with an assistive technology specialist, arrange for the necessary programming and for regular maintenance and repair.

Finally, technology abandonment may occur if families are not brought into the decision-making process early. We turn now to that issue.

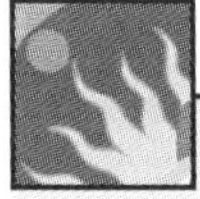

Technologies That Work

A Class Web Site

A class Web site offers many potential advantages for teachers of inclusive classrooms. A very important one is that materials posted at the site may be read by students using their personal adaptive equipment at home. This eliminates much adaptation on your part and much personal assistance on the part of paraprofessionals or other one-on-one aides who otherwise would have to read the materials for these students. You may post assigned readings at this site. You can use the Web site as an electronic bulletin board, posting outstanding student papers or projects at the site much as you do in your classroom with physical bulletin boards. You may design the site to facilitate student e-mails to you: just include a hotlink with your e-mail address. This offers one-click access for students while they are visiting the site. You can even post your tests at the class Web site.

Creating Web sites and Web pages has never been easier. It is no longer necessary to master the complex computer language known as Hyper Text Markup Language (HTML). You may create a personal Web site for each class/course you teach. Dreamweaver™ and Netscape Composer® permit you to use WordPerfect® and Word® to write documents. It takes a few hours to learn the mechanics of Dreamweaver or Composer. Thereafter, however, the programs are quite easy to use.

A related option is Blackboard®. Blackboard is specifically designed for educators. A 100-page instructor's manual is posted at the Web site. Blackboard lets you create, and post, instructional materials as well as announcements and other information, such as a course outline/schedule, assigned readings, and other documents.

For more information on Dreamweaver®, Netscape Composer®, and Blackboard®, go to the Web Links module in Chapter 8 of the Companion Website.

You can also offer hotlinks so that students may quickly visit recommended sites on the World Wide Web. Blackboard will also let you put your tests on the site. For these reasons, Blackboard offers a good supplement to a class Web page.

You may password-protect your entire site, so that only people who know the password may enter the class Web site. Alternatively, you can leave the site itself "open" but password-protect certain parts of the site (e.g., your lectures, tests). Blackboard allows you to require students also to have personal passwords in order to use all or parts of the site. In addition, you may use your own master password to protect materials you do not want anyone to alter. In effect, instructor password-protected materials are "read only" in nature: They may be changed only by you or by computer technicians authorized by your school or by the owner of the server you use.

While all this sounds reassuring, you should bear in mind that students are not always careful with passwords. You may find, to your surprise, that non-students have gained access to your site. In addition, instructor password-protected portions of the site are only as safe as is your own password. This means you should create an instructor password that is difficult for others to guess, and you should change it frequently.

With respect to tests, bear in mind that you cannot be certain who is actually taking a test on the Web site. It is possible for a student to sign on, using his password, but have a classmate or even a parent actually take the test. Unless you take steps to prevent it, students may print out as many copies of a test as they wish. This may lead to a situation in which the following year's class members have pirated copies of your tests. Unless you carefully protect any test posted at a Web site, you should regard the test as essentially being an open-book/take-home test and grade it as you would any other open-book or take-home test.

Families and Assistive Technology

You *must* involve family members as well as students with disabilities in decisions about technology. For some families, assistive technologies may be a source of shame and embarrassment (Bowe, 2000c). You may have to devote several meetings with family members to exploring, first, the need for technologies and, second, the options that are available. You may find it helpful to introduce family members to other families who have adjusted to assistive technologies and have discovered ways to minimize embarrassment. The "sale" usually occurs when family members *see* how much assistive technologies help children and youth with disabilities.

A question family members often ask is whether the assistive technology device(s) a school buys for a student's use may be brought home overnight, on weekends, and during the summer. This question generally is answered in the student's IEP. As United Cerebral Palsy Associations discovered when it surveyed schools and families, there is no good reason for a "no" answer. Children and youth are expected to do school-related work at home during the school year. A child who requires an assistive technology device to do

For more information on the United Cerebral Palsy Associations, go to the Web Links module in Chapter 8 of the Companion Website.

schoolwork during school hours most likely also needs it for homework. The case is even more compelling when the purpose of the assistive technology device is to enable the child to communicate. Thus, DynaVox® and DynaMyte® communication devices, which allow students with severe physical disabilities to express themselves, should be available to children both at home and at school, around the clock and around the year.

Another question is who keeps the device after the student leaves the school (moves, graduates). The school district purchased the device, so it owns it. The student must relinquish the product prior to leaving.

For more information on the companies and products mentioned in the section "Types of Assistive Technology Devices," go to the Web Links module in Chapter 8 of the Companion Website.

Types of Assistive Technology Devices

One way of organizing information about assistive technologies is to group them according to what they do, that is, function (e.g., a product that talks). Another is to look at them according to what disabilities they most often are used with (e.g., blindness, specific learning disabilities). A third is to examine them by subject matter (e.g., social studies). We will explore a few examples in each category. It should be understood that while I find these products to be interesting, I am not, and neither is Prentice Hall/Merrill Education, endorsing any of them.

Assistive Technologies by Function

Speech. Some students need to listen to information they cannot read or can only read with difficulty. JAWS (Job Access With Speech, from HenterJoyce) is a popular screen reader that supplies text-to-speech capabilities. ALVA Access Group sells the outSPOKEN® speech output software that reads text, Web pages, message boxes, warning dialogs, and tooltip text. It works on PCs and Macs. Cost varies, so contact the vendor. RJ Cooper & Associates offers "KeyRead," software that reads out loud information appearing on a computer screen (including Web pages). It is marketed for use by young children in the 5 to 10 age range. It is available for PC or Mac and the cost is $99. The same vendor sells "Hear-A-Story," software that speaks out loud stories that children type on the computer. It also lets them add sound effects to those stories. It is available for PC or Mac and the cost is $99.

The American Printing House for the Blind offers Road Runner®, a portable device that lets students listen to text no matter where they may be. The product has "bookmarks" so students can easily return to read portions, adjustable volume and speed, and a choice of voices to listen to as well as earphones and a cable. It works with PCs (you download files from the computer) and the cost is about $300.

For some students, devices are required that serve as their voices. Crestwood Communication Aids publishes a catalog that is distributed several times annually. It describes a wide variety of low-tech and some high-tech communication products. Mayer-Johnson sells "Speaking Dynamically Pro," described as a "multi-option speech system." It lets students use PCs or Macs as a communication device. Students who are deaf may use speech synthesis to create intelligible speech. The cost is about $350.

Hearing. Some students, notably those with quadriplegia or other physical conditions, need to be able to enter information by voice. Speech recognition software lets them talk and have their utterances "recognized" by the computer. ScanSoft markets Dragon NaturallySpeaking®, a very popular speech-recognition program (technology columnist John Williams [2000b] said it "is the most popular speech-recognition program among the disabled, hands down"). NaturallySpeaking works well with typical voices, but students whose speech is compromised may do better with VoiceXpress® (or with the older Dragon Dictate®). VoiceXpress allows students to dictate text into virtually any PC application, including Word® and WordPerfect® word-processing software. NaturallySpeaking retails for about $100 to $150 (depending upon features, such as size of its dictionary), while VoiceXpress is some $50 to $230 (there are specialized vocabulary add-ons).

Writing. For some students, writing is a slow and laborious process due to physical disabilities. Software known as "word-prediction" or "word-expansion" programs "guess" what the child or young person intends to write and completes the word/phrase/sentence. This can save hours on a student paper for children or youth with cerebral palsy and other physical disabilities. Aurora Systems sells "Aurora 3.0" for Windows, software that offers word prediction, spelling and homonym assistance, and speech synthesis. The cost is about $500. Mayer-Johnson's "Speaking Dynamically Pro" includes word-prediction software.

Other students need special input devices, including tactile keyboards. IntelliTools offers IntelliKeys® which is an expanded keyboard giving children larger targets for typing. It also permits mouse control from the keyboard (some people, notably those with cerebral palsy, cannot effectively use a mouse). Tactile overlays for keyboards that are made by IntelliTools are also distributed by the American Printing House for the Blind and by Don Johnston.

Cause and Effect. Some young children with physical disabilities such as cerebral palsy or quadriplegia get few opportunities to affect their environments. For this reason, they may be slow learning cause-and-effect. RJ Cooper & Associates offers "101 Animations," software that activates cartoons when the student signals with a mouse click, a switch, a space bar, or a touchscreen. The animations are both large and loud. It is available for PC or Mac and the cost is $99. IntelliTools has "SwitchIt! Suite," software to teach cause-and-effect. The cost is about $150.

Assistive Technologies by Disability

Specific Learning Disabilities. Thousands of books, including textbooks as well as classics of literature, are available from Recordings for the Blind and Dyslexic (RFBD). Students must register for RFBD's free service. Materials may be ordered in analog voice (real people reading books out loud) or in electronic format (readable using speech synthesizers).

E/B Disorders, ADHD, and TBI. Edmark sells "Strategy Series," software that teaches strategic thinking and problem-solving skills. It is available for PCs and Macs and the cost is $25. IEP Resources markets "Life Skill Game Package," board games for special education students age 10 and over. Six games cover self-control strategies, social skills, safety signs, functional words and symbols, and social skills at work. Brain Train sells "Brain Train Volume 1: Basic Cognitive Skills" (Enhanced Edition), described as cognitive/behavioral software offering exercises in visual and verbal memory and in basic vocational skills. It is available for PCs and the cost is $100.

A wide range of other programs for cognitive rehabilitation is available from IBM and from Life Sciences Associates.

EDUARDO: A TRUE STORY—PECS AND DYNAVOX®

Eduardo was 6 years old when he came to us. He didn't speak, rarely made eye contact, and didn't do any work on his own. He had an assistant, who was not trained in behavior modification. The assistant was all over him (holding his hand, holding his crayons, and basically doing the work for him). When I insisted that he do some work himself, Eduardo threw himself on the floor, screamed so loud that students in other rooms heard him. This was my introduction to autism.

Eduardo loved the computer. For a child who seemed not to know how to do anything, he could work the computer like a pro! Eduardo could start any game he wanted and play it. We used the Picture Exchange Communication System (PECS) with him. He told us what he wanted by using these pictures on his desk. There were pictures of a pencil, a ball, a computer, a book, a toilet, and the like, plus food and drink. Then, in your class on technology and special education, I learned about the DynaVox® machine. Eduardo didn't really like using it, except if he wanted to play or eat or if he wanted to watch a video tape. He would go to the typing section of the DynaVox® and type out "This film has been modified to fit your screen" or he would type out the FBI warning. This was his way of telling me that he wanted to watch a video. Another time, I told him to type "Mickey Mouse" on the DynaVox®. He typed the titles of 10 Disney movies. Not quite what I wanted, but close enough. At least he was responding to my request, in his own way. It seemed as if he acknowledged me then, and appreciated me being there.

—Maria

Blindness/Low Vision. ALVA Access Group (see "Speech,") offers inLARGE®, software that enlarges text. Duxbury Systems markets a variety of Braille translation software programs. These translate print to Braille. They are available for PCs or Macs and costs range from about \$600 to about \$750. Kurzweil Educational Systems Group offers the "Kurzweil 1000" which convert texts to speech. The unit comes with optical character reader (OCR) software as well as a scanner. (The Kurzweil 3000 is similar, but is intended for persons with learning disabilities.) Costs vary, but generally are in the range of \$2,500 to \$7,500. The software itself retails for \$1,000. (When first introduced, as the Kurzweil Reading Machine, the OCR/scanner/speech synthesizer cost \$35,000. Prices have fallen dramatically since then.) The very popular "Braille 'n Speak" unit that enables students who know Braille to take notes in class is made by Blazie Engineering. A modified version, called the "Braille 'n Speak Scholar," designed specifically for students, is distributed by the American Printing House for the Blind and other vendors. The Scholar has word processing (Grade I or Grade II Braille), file search/file organizing, talking phone directory, output in Braille or print (the Scholar translates Braille to print), a talking clock/calendar, and a talking scientific graphing calculator. A self-contained unit, the portable Scholar sells for about \$1,000. RFBD is a great resource for curricular materials, including books.

Physical Disabilities. Some students require communicators (devices that enable them to express themselves). DynaVox® and DynaMyte® are examples. The DynaMyte is the smaller and more portable of the two. DynaVox Systems, a unit of Sunrise Medical-DynaVox distributes them. ("Speaking Dynamically Pro" [see "Speech,"] is similar, but uses a personal computer while the DynaVox and DynaMyte are self-contained, all-in-one units.) Costs range from about \$6,400 to \$7,000; additional funds must be set aside to program the units so that children may "say" what they wish to communicate in different settings (e.g., in class, at lunch, in the rest room, at home).

Deaf/Hard of Hearing. Dozens of companies and organizations provide captioning services. These include the WGBH Education Foundation's Caption Center, the National Captioning Institute, and Vitac. If you have a video or film that you want to "open caption" (that is, to caption so that the captions are visible every time it is shown, with no decoding chips or devices required), you can contact the Captioned Media Program at *http://www.cfv.org*. In addition, software may be purchased enabling you to do your own captioning.

"HandTalk" is a Web-based resource that displays moving images of a person signing words/numbers. It is helpful when you forget the sign for something. Children who need to improve their sign receptive skills may also benefit from "Sign Link," a program that shows video clips of some 1,000 signs. It also has descriptions of American Sign Language (ASL) grammar. Available from a variety of vendors, it is compatible with PCs and its cost is \$60. A free Web site is HandSpeak, *http://www.handspeak.com*. You can choose, or type, a word or number, and watch a person sign it for you. You can also select stories and observe them being told in ASL.

Self Help for Hard of Hearing People (SHHH) has a technology specialist who can provide technical assistance and answer questions. So does the Alexander Graham Bell Association for the Deaf (AGBAD).

Technologies That Work

Captioning of Videos

Captioning used to be "an open secret" of people who are deaf or hard of hearing. Today, however, virtually every American has seen captions—in airport TVs, in hotel lobby TVs, in bars, even in the offices of United States Senators and Congresspersons. Your students may be intrigued by captioning.

What is called "pop-on" captions is also known as "canned" captions. These captions are produced ahead of screening. A program such as NBC's *Dateline* or *The West Wing* is taped months before it is shown on television. The captions are prepared in advance, too. Pop-on captions are usually very well done. All the words are spelled correctly. The captions are placed unobtrusively on the screen (they do not block information important to viewers).

By contrast, what is called "roll-up" captions are created in real time. Programs such as ABC's *Nightline* or *ABC Wide World of Sports* are broadcast live. The captions must be produced live, too. For this reason, errors often occur. These mistakes can be hilarious, or they can simply be annoying. Often, captions obscure other information (e.g., when a batter comes to the plate in a baseball game, his hitting statistics may not be visible because the same part of the screen is being used to display the captions).

There are no national standards for how good captioning has to be. Virtually all TV programming—taped or live, broadcast or cable—must be captioned by the beginning of 2006. The only exceptions have to do with local origination/public access programs, religious programming, and the like.

The rule in captioning is to present visually *everything* that hearing people hear. This can mean that captions appear on screen as rapidly as 200 words per minute. And because the captions disappear almost as rapidly as they appear, reading captions is even harder for deaf or hard of hearing students than is reading printed books.

For more information on the captioning your own videos and films, go to the Web Links module in Chapter 8 of the Companion Website.

For these reasons, it is a good idea to supplement captioning by providing explanations in sign language. Interpreters can explain information that is not clear from the captions.

Can you caption your own videos and films? Yes. The Captioned Media Program offers a lot of help, including sources of captioning software. So, too, does the WGBH Educational Foundation's National Center for Educational Media.

What about captioning of rich media? (Rich media are active-motion elements of a Web page: streaming video, animation, a Flash presentation, a QuickTime® video clip, and the like.) The NCAM distributes the Media Access Generator (MAGpie) multimedia authoring tool. With MAGpie, you can caption videos in QuickTime format, in the W3C's Synchronized Multimedia Integration Language (SMIL), and in Microsoft's Synchronized Accessible Media Interchange (SAMI) format. The NCAM site offers lots of technical assistance. It also has a FAQ (frequently asked questions) page.

Often used in schools today is RealPlayer®. You can turn captions on or off by selecting "View," and then "Preferences" and "Content," and finally "Settings"; just check "Use accessibility features when available" and captions will appear if they have been produced. RealPlayer is flexible enough to let you arrange captioning at the last minute. Text produced by the Computer Assisted Real Time (CART) captioner can be fed into the RealPlayer program, with little advance preparation.

Captions benefit not only students who are deaf and hard of hearing (see "Technologies That Work: Captions," in Chapter 4) but also those who are English language learners (ELL). They also help students whose learning preferences make them visual learners. The experience of watching a film or video that is captioned is different from the experience of watching one that is not captioned. When the offering is captioned, students find themselves focusing much more on content—because, like it or not, they find themselves reading the captions!

Assistive Technologies by Subject Matter

The National Center on Access to the General Curriculum at CAST and the National Center for Accessible Media (NCAM) at WGBH are two excellent resources for curricular adaptations. The team at CAST focuses upon the use of innovative pedagogies, such as redundancy, while the group at WGBH looks more at captions and video descriptions. WGBH's NCAM also has a CD-ROM access project. Following are other resources that may be of interest.

English/Language Arts. MindPlay offers "Word Hound," software for early childhood/elementary reading instruction. The program may be adjusted for a variety of special needs. There is also a Spanish/English version when this program is used with MindPlay's "Language Pack," which is sold separately. "Word Hound" focuses upon vocabulary development and word recognition. It is available for PCs or Macs and the cost is $50. MindPlay also has "Ace Reporter" (and a variety of other Ace programs) which teach reading for detail, reading for main idea, and critical thinking. It also is available for PCs or Macs and the cost is $50. Millennium Software sells "Labeling Tutor," software teaching children to associate words, sounds, and pictures. It is available for PCs or Macs and the cost is $120. For older students, MindPlay markets "Easy Street," a program teaching reading, math, and problem-solving skills involving labeling, counting, classification, matching, and using money to pay for items. It also is available for PCs or Macs and the cost is $50.

Math. Independent Living Aids offers "Talking Tape Ruler," a metal tape measure that speaks the measured length. The cost is $100. Crestwood Company sells "Cash Tray," a tray having 300 bills and 306 coins (replicas of U.S. currency) that may be used for learning math concepts. The cost is $35. Don Johnston markets "Blocks in Motion," colorful two-dimensional blocks (squares, triangles, circles, etc.) that students can use to build mazes, graphs, patterns, and so on. It is available for Macs and the cost is $80. The Attainment Company sells "Dollars and Cents CD-ROMs," talking software programs that teach money management. Three CD-ROMs are offered: First Money, Spending Money, and Making Change. They are available for PCs or Macs and the cost for each is about $100.

Metroplex Voice Computing offers programs for teaching math to students who are blind or have low vision. Most feature voice (speech synthesis). This includes MathPad by Voice® and MathTalk/ScientificNotebook®. For questions you can't answer and problems you can't solve, you may contact a secondary teacher of math at the Texas School for the Blind. Susan Osterhaus posts information to *http://www.tsbvi.edu/math*.

Science. The Annenberg/CPB Project distributes a 26-part series, *Cycles of Life: Exploring Biology* that is captioned. *Newton's Apple,* a 51-part series, is distributed by GPN Library at the University of Nebraska. The GPN also offers *Math in the Middle . . . Of Oceans,* a video for middle-school students about how math can be applied to understanding currents, waves, whales, sharks, and aquariums. MindPlay offers "Living Lab: Plants," software that lets students simulate a lab experiment. They may write hypotheses, conduct experiments, perform observations, and analyze results using this software. It is available for PCs and Macs and the cost is $50 (single user). The Lighthouse distributes a wide variety of products that could be used in science (they're primarily designed for use at home). WGBH Educational Foundation's National Center for Accessible Media (NCAM) has produced an innovative way of presenting a visual graph via audio. It is part of a biology simulation from Logal, Inc. You can download the prototype from the NCAM Photosynthesis Explorer Prototype section.

Social Studies. The American Printing House for the Blind offers large print and tactile maps. These are embossed on heavy white paper and measure 17″ by 15″. They vary in price, so contact the vendor. MindPlay markets "Race the Clock," software that teaches social-studies skills to students age 8 and up. It focuses upon states and state capitals, U.S. presidents, inventors/inventions, and events/dates. It is available for Macs and the cost is $49 (single user).

A program on CD-ROM, "Geographic Information Systems (GIS)," is offered by Environmental Systems Research Institute. With GIS, students may construct maps of their own and plug into those maps data the students have collected. Because this program uses many graphics, it may not be suitable for use by students who are blind.

Art. The American Printing House for the Blind offers *Art History Through Touch & Sound,* a multisensory system that uses sight, sound, and touch. Units are available for "The Building Blocks of Art," "The Art of Ancient Egypt," "European Modernism," and "African Art," each in printed pages using large print and Braille, plus cassette tapes offering narration and sound compositions that guide students through the tactile diagrams. The costs are about $100 for the complete kits; APH also provides additional manuals, teacher's supplement disks, and Braille teacher's supplements. The American Printing House for the

Blind distributes "ColorTest," a handheld talking color analyzer. It can distinguish more than 100 colors and nuances of colors. The device can help individuals who are color blind as well as those who are blind or have low vision. ColorTest also distinguishes between natural and artificial light and detects the brightness level. The cost is about $600.

Music. Synthesizers and computers are now widely used for music composition. These inexpensive products allow students to create music without having to write notes on paper. MIDI (musical instrument digital interface) is the key technology. Students may create, edit, and listen to their own compositions just by touching a few keys (Beckstead, 2001). Music educators teaching children and youth with disabilities need to make sure, in advance, that the programs are accessible. An assistive technology specialist could be called upon for advice and support.

Meeting Technology Learning Standards

Many state learning standards contain components related to technology. Math and science standards, in particular, refer to technology. Technology has become so pervasive in American culture, however, that it is much broader than just its uses in those fields.

Students in PreK–12 programs are expected to make use of calculation, measurement, and communication technologies. For many students, assistive technologies will be required. Thus, these children and youth must master not only the same technologies that other students learn, but assistive technologies as well.

At the early childhood/elementary level, teachers of inclusive classrooms need to recognize that today's young children are already experienced and, often, sophisticated users of technology. As the American Association for the Advancement of Science's (AAAS) Project 2061 team puts it:

> They ride in automobiles, use household utilities, operate wagons and bikes, use garden tools, help with the cooking, operate the television set, and so on. Children are also natural explorers and inventors, and they like to make things. Schools should give students many opportunities to examine the property of materials, to use tools, and to design and build things. Activities should focus on problems and needs in and around the school that interest the children and that can be addressed feasibly and safely.

At the middle-school level, students need to learn to appreciate the economic, social, ethical, and aesthetic aspects of technology. They need to recognize that technology has drawbacks as well as advantages. Our use of technologies has exacerbated Earth's environmental problems, notably with global warming. At the same time, the quality of life, especially in developed countries, is considerably higher because of technology. Middle-school students also need to learn about, and how to use, technologies of measurement (e.g., of volume, of distance, etc.), calculation (e.g., multiplication, division, etc.), and communication (e.g., the Web, e-mail, word processing).

At the secondary level, students must master application of technologies for solving problems. This includes doing their own experiments. They also need to develop deeper understandings of technologies, both for their future roles as citizens (in making the increasingly difficult decisions about deployment of technologies in the face of ethical and economic quandaries) and as workers (in their chosen fields).

The AAAS Project 2061 team recommends that students *use* technologies as the best way of learning about them. Discovery and project-based learning are obvious examples. Students should apply technologies to solve mathematical, scientific, and other problems. Teachers should also arrange for students to explore the history of technology so as to broaden their appreciation of how technology has affected human life on the planet and their understanding of the ethical issues we now face with advanced technologies.

Students with disabilities, as well as those with no disabilities, should be given these varied opportunities. The importance of technology for students with disabilities who are included in regular classrooms is, if anything, greater than that for other students. Children and youth who are blind or have low vision, for example, are routinely included today because technology makes it possible.

One way of introducing technology in an inclusive classroom is to discuss how "necessity is the mother of invention," as in these examples: In the late 1800s, Alexander Graham Bell invented the telephone as part of his quest to help his deaf wife; a century later, Vinton Cerf attached a protocol for e-mail into the first version of what later became the Internet because he wanted a way to communicate with his hard-of-hearing wife (Bowe, 2000c). Similarly, a low-tech innovation, the curb cut, has changed our lives, too. We can all ride bikes, push baby carriages, and move heavy objects around on college campuses and in many communities because curb cuts have been installed in sidewalks. They exist so that people using wheelchairs could navigate the campus. However, others benefit as well. Without those curb cuts, the 6-inch curbs separating sidewalks and streets would prevent bike riders, mothers with infants, and furniture movers from getting around easily. In these and many other ways, the lives of people with no disabilities are easier and more rewarding precisely because individuals with disabilities live among us.

Teacher Strategies That Work

How to "Do" Universal Design in Your Teaching

1. Offer a disk containing the lecture and advance-organizer information (outline, definitions, etc.) as well as paper-based advance organizers to students. It is important to make such disks and organizers available to *any* student. Some students with different learning styles may prefer, and learn better with, electronic information, despite the fact that these students do not have disabilities. In addition, making disks available to any student reduces the stigma that otherwise would be attached to "special help" given only to students with disabilities.
2. Write key words that you say on the board or on an overhead. Read out loud anything you write on the board or display in a slide. As you give students handouts, speak out loud the information that is printed on the sheets. The key is to give information *both* visually and auditorially, simultaneously.
3. Post key readings on your personal or a course Web page. With their adapted PCs at home, students with disabilities can easily access and use information on an accessible Web page. In addition, students who habitually lose papers, or are otherwise disorganized, will be relieved to know that they can always get another copy of something.
4. Pre-test any Web site you recommend for student use by visiting the site yourself. Is it accessible for people with disabilities? If you have doubts, visit Bobby at *http://www.cast.org/bobby* or *http://www.watchfire.com/bobby/* and enter the site's URL in the search box. Bobby will check the site's accessibility for you, one Web page at a time. If it turns out not to be accessible, you can e-mail the Web master, requesting that it be made accessible, and telling the Web master to consult W3C's site, *http://www.w3c.org/wai*, for guidance.
5. Prepare organizers, and teach students how to use heads, subheads, and the like. Many students with learning disabilities need help in making optimum use of such features in their texts.
6. Provide multiple ways for students to find meaning and thus motivate themselves. Unless you have compelling reasons not to, you should allow students to opt to work independently or as members of a team. You should permit them to show mastery of principles by applying those to favorite activities (e.g., calculate batting averages to demonstrate knowledge of adding, dividing, etc.), rather than by taking a test.
7. Consider creating and sponsoring a listserv, through which students may post comments, questions, and so on, to each other and to you. An alternative is a student-only listserv, which affords them privacy from you. Another variation is to ask students to exchange e-mail addresses. All of these options increase student interaction outside of class time. If one of your students uses a TTY (teletypewriter for the deaf) because she is deaf or hard of hearing, you should teach all your students how to use 7-1-1 to dial a statewide dual-party relay service. The operator they reach will type what they say to the student who is deaf and will speak out loud what that student types on his TTY. Relay services allow students who are deaf and those who are not to talk with each other on the phone (e.g., to help each other with homework).
8. Equip at least one PC in the classroom with text-to-speech (e.g., outSPOKEN®), speech recognition (e.g., NaturallySpeaking®), and a keyguard.
9. Use texts that are also offered as e-texts if available.
10. If you write your own software, make sure it is accessible. The Human Factors Engineering Society offers standards and guidelines (HFES 200.2) for such work at *http://www.hfes.org*.

INDIVIDUALIZING INSTRUCTION

Some of the strategies arose from the recent emphasis in general education upon inquiry-based activities (e.g., Koch, 2002; Singer, 1997). This strand has featured active participation by students to discover knowledge. Other techniques emerged from traditions in special education, notably Direct Instruction (Gersten, Carnine, & Woodward, 1987) and effective instruction (Mastropieri & Scruggs, 2000). This second strand has emphasized explicit instruction by teachers about fundamental skills and knowledge. Others emerged from the efforts of teachers and researchers to construct curricula that respond to the new, higher learning standards by fostering inquiry learning and problem solving. Morocco (2001) explained that a coming-together of these once-disparate traditions is both necessary and welcomed in inclusion classrooms:

> Confusions between theories of knowing and theories of pedagogy have led to the misconception that proponents of understanding as a constructive process think that explicit instruction in cognitive strategies has no place in teaching for understanding. To the contrary, explicit instruction plays a strong role in the development of cognitive tools that enable students to work toward understanding. (p. 8)

A third strand came out of efforts to help traditionally underserved populations to raise their academic achievement in light of the new, higher learning standards (Greenwood et al., 2001).

Helping us to bridge the gaps between these strands is work performed by the Research Institute to Accelerate Content Learning through High Support for Students with Disabilities in Grades 4–8 (REACH Institute), which was directed by Catherine Cobb Morocco at the Education Development Center of Newton, MA. The REACH Institute project emphasized what Morocco (2001) called "teaching for understanding" (p. 5). One of only a few sizable efforts to date to improve student outcomes on subject-matter content in inclusive classrooms, this 5-year project sought to enhance "deep understanding" (Morocco, 2001, p. 7) of English, math, science, and history by middle-school students having mild disabilities, notably specific learning disabilities. Morocco and her colleagues contended that only with such deep understanding could students with disabilities compete with non-disabled students in meeting the new, higher learning standards.

In this section, we first examine teaching techniques in whole-class, small-group, and one-on-one settings. These tactics allow teachers to *individualize instruction* (or, to use another term, *differentiate instruction*). We consider ways inclusion teachers can use *advance organizers, scaffolding,* and *modeling,* among other strategies. We look at how *problem-based instruction, community-based instruction,* and other techniques may enhance the authenticity of student projects, many of which are conducted in small groups. We then review *Direct Instruction (DI)*. Although our consideration of DI occurs in the context of one-on-one instruction, these tactics are of wide utility to teachers of inclusive classrooms in whole-class and small-group settings as well.

Whole-Class Instruction

Children with disabilities, as well as those with no disabilities, need and deserve *your* attention and instruction. Whenever feasible, then, you should teach them rather than assigning a paraprofessional to do so. While peer tutoring (see "Small-Group Instruction," p. 311) is of proven value in individualizing instruction, there are also strategies that you can use effectively in a whole-class setting. Prominent among these are assessing student competencies and knowledge prior to beginning a new instructional unit, explicitly teaching strategies students can use to perform inquiry-based learning, employing simulations, and using advance organizers and scaffolding. In addition, the techniques of universal design in education can be very helpful in whole-class instruction. Recommended techniques for whole-class instruction are summarized in Figure 8.4 and explained in detail as well.

FIGURE 8.4 Whole-Class Instruction

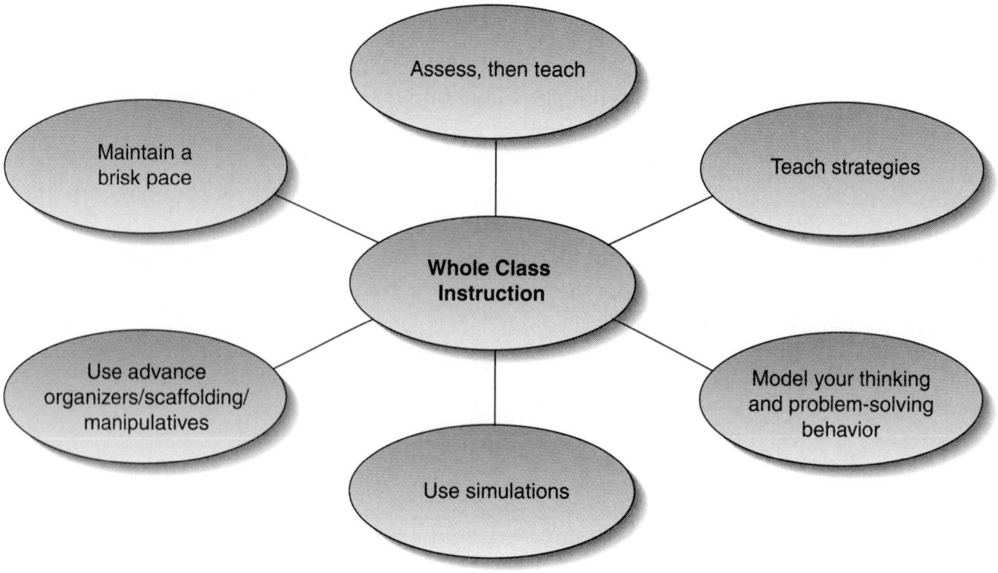

Assess, Then Teach

Special educators long have begun instruction by determining what competencies and knowledge students already possess (e.g., Gersten et al., 1987; Mercer & Mercer, 1998). By assessing before teaching, you learn what you need to instruct your students to know and do. Inclusive classrooms feature a very broad range of student abilities and needs. Teachers of inclusive classrooms do not have the luxury of "teaching to the middle"—neither do, for that matter, most other teachers in today's classrooms. The diversity of classrooms today mandates that teachers determine, rather than assume, where their students "are coming from" and what they are able to do.

Before-instruction assessment can take many forms. You could use a *pop quiz* for this purpose. Experts advise that you *not* use test results from pop quizzes as part of your grading rubric. This is because your purpose here is not to grade students but rather to determine your own teaching strategies and tactics (Tanner, 2001). Alternatively, you could administer a *student self-assessment* instrument, on which your students report upon their prior knowledge and skills. Even more simply, you could preview the following day's lesson unit by asking two or three questions, calling for a show of hands or brief oral responses. Precisely how you "assess, then teach" is less important than that you do it.

Teach Strategies

General educators, particularly in middle school and high school, frequently assume that their students possess knowledge about and skill in using academic tactics and strategies. Such assumptions often are unwarranted in inclusion classrooms (e.g., Ferretti, MacArthur, & Okolo, 2001). Research has shown that a major need of many children and youth with disabilities is in the area of selecting and using the appropriate strategies for each content area and problem. Students with specific learning disabilities, for example, are repeatedly shown in studies either to lack knowledge of appropriate strategies or, if they do know these, to fail to apply them suitably (e.g., Cawley et al., 2001; Maccini & Gagnon, 2000). Individuals with mental retardation are even less likely to know and use academic strategies (e.g., Butler et al., 2001; Parmar et al., 1996). Lederer (2000), teaching social studies to elementary students having learning disabilities, found that he had to spend a lot of time explicitly teaching how to ask good questions and make intelligent predictions about a text, how to monitor one's own learning, and how to summarize information. The well-developed techniques of explicit teaching or Direct Instruction is of obvious utility here (see "Use Direct Instruction," p. 318).

Model Your Thinking and Problem-Solving Behavior

In your whole-class instruction, you should verbalize your thoughts as you teach. If, for example, you are showing students how to examine an historical document, you should "talk out loud" as you study its internal consistency and as you compare it to other contemporary sources of information. To adopt another example, if you are demonstrating the solution to a geometry problem, you should explain *why* you take each step. And another: A great way to teach writing is to show students as you edit and revise your own writing. As is the case with many of the techniques presented in this chapter, modeling your thinking will benefit *all* students, not just those who have disabilities. To illustrate, children from low-SES homes often lack knowledge of problem-solving strategies, in large part because the adults in their homes did not discuss with them (as do many mid- and high-SES family adults). This is one reason such children often begin school with vocabularies half as large as those from mid-SES families (Children's Defense Fund, 2000; Greenwood et al., 2001).

Use Simulations

A **simulation** is a learning activity that offers an artificial reality. Popular computer games that require players to pretend to be city planners, for example, allow students to experiment with different designs for sewage systems (without putting anyone's health at risk!). Similarly, entire experiments can be performed on a personal computer (PC). Such simulations can save schools money they otherwise would spend on experimental supplies. Often, an even more compelling argument can be made: Some experiments are potentially dangerous to the experimenters; by simulating them on a PC, that danger is removed.

Simulations do not have to be computer-based. Teachers can make up situations of an almost infinite variety. Especially applicable are problems related to social studies (Chapin & Messick, 1996). You might require a group of students to pretend to be the Lewis and Clark expedition crew. Using only information available to the actual explorers, team members would need to plan their route, ensure an adequate supply of food and water, and find a reliable means of communicating their progress and findings back to the president in Washington, DC. As this example illustrates, simulations offer students opportunities to "experience" situations, without taking risks. A major advantage of simulations is that they can make the abstract seem much more concrete. Another is that they can provide almost immediate feedback. You might, for example, give the same assignment to two groups. Each would report back after completing the assignment. You might have each team critique the other group's methods. Finally, well-chosen simulations are accessible to students with special needs. A simulation of a musical composition, for example, can help a deaf student to "hear" it by watching it.

Use Advance Organizers/Scaffolding/Manipulatives

Three techniques that facilitate instruction are *advance organizers, scaffolding,* and *manipulatives*. Advance organizers help students to organize their study, by highlighting important ideas, outlining chapters, and so on. You have used advance organizers yourself in this text: The chapter-opening "Focus Questions" and "Personal Accounts," the "Chapter Summary" bulleted sections, and the chapter-ending "Questions for Reflection" components of each chapter all are examples of advance organizers. Scaffolding is structure, or "hooks," that let you move up and down the "structure" of your understanding as you construct it. Before beginning a lecture, give your students scaffolding to help them follow your remarks. These should be *both* oral and written. If you use PowerPoint® for this purpose, you *must* read out loud each word and number that is displayed. Examples of scaffolding appear in Chapter 14, on techniques for teaching English and language arts. For instance, the scaffolding about *Hamlet* summarizes the plot, identifies the major characters, and defines words that students often find challenging. Manipulatives are, as the name implies, objects you can hold in your hands. They can be remarkably effective in making abstract ideas concrete. The best science lectures, for example, make good use of props (e.g., models of molecules, models of internal organs, models of the solar system, etc.). The evidence is impressive that manipulatives really contribute to understanding by many students with disabilities (e.g., Mastropieri & Scruggs, 2000).

Advance organizers, scaffolding, and manipulatives are useful with *any* student. These techniques generally were developed in special education. There, they were shown to be particularly helpful for students having specific learning disabilities (e.g., Keel, Dangel, & Owens, 1999). However, students of all kinds benefit when they are given outlines, study guides, and the like. This is just another example of how many strategies and tactics developed in special education can be used in general classrooms, as well.

Teacher Strategies That Work

Scaffolding

Look, for a moment, at the scaffolding below (for *The Call of the Wild*). Notice the components of this scaffolding. Right below the title, we have the year of publication. A summary of the plot is then offered. The names of the key characters, together with thumbnail sketches, follow. Finally, words that are unfamiliar for most high-school students are listed and defined. Similarly structured scaffolding is provided for other works of literature in Chapter 14. Those are offered to help teachers but the structure can be used for students as well.

Scaffolding: *The Call of the Wild*

Title: *The Call of the Wild*
Author: Jack London
Published: 1903
Grade Levels: 7 and above
Difficulty: Modest (short at about 125 pages, few difficult words, little vernacular: The most challenging sentences are the statements of Perrault and Francois, e.g., "Some dam day heem keel dat Buck")
Summary: Buck is a family dog owned by Judge Miller, a wealthy landowner in central California. After being sold to become a sled dog, Buck is taken to the Alaskan wilderness during the late 1800s gold rush. His owners, Perrault and Francois, come to admire Buck. In time, as he learns the ways of the wild, Buck challenges and then kills the lead dog, Spitz. Midway through the book, Buck and the team he leads is sold to the incompetent Hal, Charles, and Mercedes. After these humans exhaust and nearly kill the dogs, John Thornton rescues Buck. While he comes to love Thornton, Buck is increasingly drawn to the life in the wild. After Thornton dies, Buck finally heeds the "call of the wild" and joins a wolf pack.
Characters: Judge Miller, Buck's original owner
Perrault, and Francois, Buck's first owners in the North.
Spitz, a vicious dog Buck hates, challenges, and finally kills
Sol-leks, Dave, and Billee, other dogs in the team
Hal, Charles, and Mercedes, Buck's next owners who do not know how to lead a dog team
John Thornton, strong man who rescues Buck from those owners
Vocabulary: harness and trace (how the dogs are attached to the sled)
haw and mush (commands to the dogs)
primordial (describing animals in the wild)
slipshod and slovenly (describing Hal and Charles)
wiliness and cunning (traits needed for survival in the North)

You can create scaffolding for your students for any of a wide variety of tasks and activities, following much the same format. Good scaffolds contain synopses or highlights, so that students immediately learn essential information. Definitions of key terms is another typical feature of scaffolds. Sometimes, a map or other drawing can be very useful. A variation on that idea is the "concept map" that is illustrated at the end of Chapter 15 (see "The 12 Fundamental Particles of the Universe"). Concept maps show how different ideas are related. That particular concept map shows that quarks come in six varieties (up, down, strange, etc.) and that quarks are different from leptons.

You can also teach your students how to *create their own scaffolds.* This is an effective strategy for learning. To illustrate, they might create a concept map of the chapter they are reading (heads, subheads, etc.). They might also create their own glossary of terms in the chapter. Writing their own summaries of the chapter is another excellent learning tool. Sometimes, noticing what they have highlighted (in the text) or taken notes about tells them what kind of information they need in their scaffolds. Finally, sharing scaffolds with other students can be helpful. After reading someone else's scaffold, a student will have questions. This can lead naturally to peer tutoring.

Maintain a Brisk Pace

Students with attention deficit disorders and emotional/behavioral disorders in particular will benefit from an unflagging pace of instruction. By keeping things moving, you minimize the likelihood students will become bored. You also reduce the temptation students have to become distracted by "more interesting" events and activities (Mastropieri & Scruggs, 2000; Taylor & Larson, 2000). On the other hand, you may worry that students who are deaf and who use interpreters in the classroom will fall behind if the pace of instruction is too rapid. You might be concerned that those with mental retardation will suffer from a too-fast pace. Notwithstanding these qualms, you should not slow down your overall pace. Rather, you should pause *between key ideas*. This is what students with specific learning disabilities and those with mental retardation need (see Chapters 3 and 5). It is what sign-language interpreters need (see Chapter 4). It is what English Language Learners need (see Chapter 11). No one is helped if you slow down by pausing between words, that is, within ideas. Doing so merely gives students a half-dozen or more discrete pieces of information to attend to and remember, rather than one important idea: It actually places a greater cognitive load on your students than does pausing between ideas.

Small-Group Instruction

The reform curricula place heavy emphasis upon student work in small groups. The key techniques for small-group instruction are offered in Figure 8.5 and explained in detail as well.

Small-group instruction is potentially very important for students with disabilities. Mary Wagner and her colleagues at SRI International (e.g., Valdes, Williamson, & Wagner, 1990), in their National Longitudinal Transition Study, made a major contribution by demonstrating that when high-school graduates or dropouts did not succeed in the world of work, it generally was *not* because they failed to perform job-related duties (e.g., data entry, word processing, factory floor machine operation, job site clean-up, etc.) but rather because they did not follow "unwritten rules" and otherwise get along well with co-workers. In retrospect, this finding should not have surprised special educators. We have tended to teach students with disabilities to master specific skills, one-by-one; we have *not* emphasized the teaching of skills needed for cooperative and collaborative activities. This has been especially true in inclusive settings: All too often, students with disabilities have worked in isolation, with support from an aide or teacher assistant. Occasionally, in fact, what these students were doing in the classroom was not even the same activity as what other children in the room were doing. Thus, it should be no surprise that when special-needs students enter the world of work, they continue to work alone, rather than as members of a team. This finding highlights one of the potential contributions grouping may make in education of students with disabilities. If we want these young people to be successful in workplaces that feature teaming, we need to give them teamwork experiences during their school years.

Grouping, as a technique, is strongly supported by educational research (see, for example, Springer, Stanne, & Donovan, 1999). Small groups have been found to help students to learn more, to like learning more, and to persist more in continuing their education beyond high school (e.g., Cohen, 1994; Slavin, 1995). The benefits associated with grouping are larger than those of many other teaching techniques. Grouping, as a technique, responds well to the learning preferences we see in many members of ethnic and racial minority groups and in many girls and young women (see Chapters 2 and 11). Finally, grouping is an effective part of a larger effort in education to move beyond teaching to facilitate student-directed learning.

In inclusive classrooms, it is often necessary for teachers to instruct students in the mechanics of group work. For example, when the assignment is to read a passage and discuss it, students with specific learning disabilities, mental retardation, and other conditions benefit greatly when provided with explicit instruction about, and prompts supporting their use of, techniques of successful group interaction. Lederer (2000) illustrated the approach when he taught students with learning disabilities to begin by recalling what

FIGURE 8.5 Small-Group Instruction

Create Cooperative Groups
Make the Groups Heterogeneous—And Change Them Often
Assign Projects That Require Students to Use the Processes and Tap the Knowledge of the Domain
Feature Problem-Based and Community-Based Instruction
Overprepare
Use Class-Wide Peer Tutoring
Provide Teacher-Made Advance Organizers/Scaffolding
Be Available
Require Students to Keep Journals—And Read Their Entries

they already know about a topic, then making predictions about a passage. He then told them to read the material, ask questions about it, discuss it among themselves, reread the passage, and summarize it.

Create Cooperative Groups

Cooperative learning is well-regarded by educational researchers. Ellis and Fouts (1997), for example, noted in their review of educational innovations that "cooperative learning has the best and largest empirical base" (p. 173) of any such technique. This is especially true at the secondary level, and particularly so in the sciences. Indeed, Slavin (1995) went so far as to celebrate cooperative learning (as contrasted to more competitive, lecture-based approaches) as "one of the greatest success stories in the history of educational research" (p. 43). The term was defined by Cooper and Mueck (1990) as a "structured, systematic instructional strategy in which small groups work together toward a common goal" (p. 68). They elaborated that cooperative learning features the teacher giving each group a goal to pursue, assigning tasks to each member of the group, holding each group member accountable for his own learning, and teaching techniques for effective group efforts.

By contrast, Cooper and Mueck explained, "collaborative" learning is less structured: it has group members themselves negotiating goals and deciding upon procedures. Thus, cooperative learning differs from collaborative learning primarily in the teacher's role: In cooperative learning, she creates a firm structure for the group, much more than characterizes collaborative learning. The social studies text by Chapin and Messick (1996), for example, repeatedly suggested that teachers decide which students are assigned to each group, what goals each group has, which approaches each takes, and what roles each group member plays. In collaborative groups, such decisions are made by group members themselves. Cooperative group structures are particularly suitable for younger students and for many children with special needs. They often need to be taught how to do group work, however. Rosenshine and Meister (1994) referred to this as "explicit teaching before reciprocal teaching" (p. 483). Regardless of which variation of the approach a teacher adopts, it is important that educators not interrupt or otherwise disturb the group as it works. That is, once you start each group working, you should let it complete its assigned task. Commented King-Sears (1997), "Teachers who monitored by interfering actively in the group's processing seemed to negate the idea that peers were expected to help each other" (p. 5).

Make the Groups Heterogeneous—And Change Them Often

The recommendation that groups be *heterogeneous* rather than homogeneous is virtually unanimous across disciplines. Experts in English and language arts, mathematics, science, social studies, music, and other content areas consistently urge teachers to pair unlike students rather than to use ability grouping, as you will see later in Part Six. Whether you create two-member, three-member, or larger groups, you should pair a student having a disability with a student having no disabilities, a high-achieving student with a lower-achieving one, a native English speaker with an English-learning student. Research is virtually unanimous on this point (e.g., Armstrong & Savage, 2002; Chapin & Messick, 1996; Parker, 2001; Springer, Stanne, & Donovan, 1999). In their text on secondary math instruction, Posamentier and Stepelman (1999), for example, do not even discuss the possibility of creating homogeneous groups.

Three to five members is a good size for small groups. Groups should remain intact for some time (e.g., at least a month). Short-term pairs and other small groups do not tend to work well, because members do not have time enough to "gel" as a team and because, knowing that the relationship will be a temporary one, members typically do not invest the time and energy required to get to know how to work cooperatively with each other (Posamentier & Stepelman, 1999; Singer, 1997). Given this fact, you should *re*-group frequently. No pair or other small group should remain together for more than about a month.

Assign Projects That Require Students to Use the Processes and Tap the Knowledge of the Domain

The best small-group assignments have a "fuzzy" character. There is no one correct solution. Rather, a range of answers, reached by a variety of approaches, may be appropriate. Such assignments generate genuine discussion and debate among students. They also mirror the kinds of problems adults encounter. In other words, these kinds of issues are authentic. Singer (1997) strongly urged social studies teachers to present such problems. So did Koch (2002), writing for science teachers. Morocco (2001) stressed that it is essential that students work on, and master, *both* the cognitive strategies for learning and the content knowledge of a discipline or domain. They will do so, she contended, if problems require them to ask questions, gather information, organize data, interpret findings, and synthesize information. Thus, students of history may create timelines to demonstrate how change occurred over time. Similarly, students of literature may collect and analyze samples of poetry by Robert Frost to show the use of irony. In both instances, children and youth learn content material *and* the investigative or analytic techniques of a domain.

Feature Problem-Based and Community-Based Instruction

Students will remain on task while in small groups if they perceive their work as being germane and meaningful to their lives. Students who are homeless, children from migrant families, students from low-SES homes, children who are slow learners, and many who are delinquent particularly need "relevant" instruction. They may be much more motivated to learn if they can see a direct connection to the "real world." This is true, as well, for many students with emotional/behavioral disorders or attention deficit disorders. Two approaches that add authenticity and practical importance to group projects are problem-based learning and community-based learning. These are so important in reform curricula that they deserve extended discussion.

Problem-Based Learning. Problem-based learning is what the name implies: Teachers pose "real-world" problems for students, who acquire information almost as a by-product of solving those problems. The idea is to appeal to student interest in practical applications. By giving students a problem or a puzzle that they want to solve, teachers motivate children and youth (Duch, Groh, & Allen, 2001; Koch, 2002).

The approach is similar in important ways to community-based instruction (see page 314). First, the emphasis in both approaches is upon teaching academics through practical applications. Second, problem-based learning, like community-based instruction, is inductive rather than deductive. That is, students acquire academic content by trying to solve a particular problem. The approach has obvious implications for teaching social studies (see Chapter 16). Problem-based learning also lends itself well to the constructivist, active-learning strategies that are being recommended for the teaching of math and science (see Chapter 15). It also ties in well with the "meaning" focus of whole language

(Chapter 14). The big difference between the two techniques is that problem-based learning is far less time-consuming than is community-based instruction, for which reason it may be more appealing to teachers who are pressed for time due to heightened learning standards.

When you ask students to bring to class newspaper ads promoting cars for sale versus cars for lease, you tap into their interest in eventually having their own cars. You can help them learn to become discerning auto shoppers. You can also teach them how to be sure they are comparing "apples to apples" and not "apples to oranges" by showing them how to figure out which is the better deal. Some ads use low percentage rates as a "come on," while others tout low purchase prices. Ads for auto leases must be distinguished from ads for auto sales. An essential skill for consumers is to be able to convert "oranges" to "apples" so as to be able to make informed choices. Students need to learn how to decide, for example, whether a closed-end lease or an open-end lease makes more sense for them; an open-end lease permits them to purchase the vehicle at lease end. However, because many leases set the lease-end price high in order to keep the monthly charges low, this may not be the best option.

Similarly, teens are constantly bombarded with print, radio, television, and Internet ads for clothing, videos, recordings, and the like. By posing a practical problem, and assigning students to come up with solutions, you both motivate them and help them to develop problem-solving skills. Students can then present their findings in class, after which spirited debates may ensue over who best solved the problem. This is particularly true because there is no one "right answer" for many problems; rather, there are several possible ways to solve those problems. Such problems are ideal for cooperative decision-making exercises.

For more information on The Telecommunications Research and Action Center, go to the Web Links module in Chapter 8 of the Companion Website.

Much the same can be said about many other consumer options. Telephone service, for example, now is marketed in very confusing ways. People are enticed by commercials and print advertisements offering 5 cents or 7 cents a minute. However, those rates may apply only at certain times (evenings, weekends) and there may be a monthly charge in addition to the per-minute fees. Often, which option is "right" will depend upon personal preferences. Still, it is easy to become confused by the many pricing plans. The Telecommunications Research and Action Center warns that deals which seem, on their face, to be attractive frequently turn out to be far worse than anyone might imagine. TRAC sells comparison charts, at $5 each, for local or long-distance rates.

Problem-based learning can be challenging for students with specific learning disabilities (SLD) or mental retardation (MR). Many children and youth with SLD, and even greater percentages of those with MR, do not immediately grasp the connections between the surface facts (the specific problem) and the underlying concepts (the principles behind the problem). However, students with both kinds of impairments *can* benefit from instruction on problem-solving. Children and youth with attention deficit disorders and emotional/behavioral disorders may be highly motivated by problem-based learning, especially if they are bored by more lecture- or text-based instruction on the same topics. These disabilities were discussed in Part Two, Chapters 3 and 5. The teacher's first job in problem-based learning is to pose questions that are interesting to the students (who thus find them motivating), answerable by those students (resources are available that students can use to work through the problems), and open-ended (require some thinking and some research to answer). The best such problems directly relate to the state curriculum/learning standards. Next, teachers need to identify, and, especially at the elementary level, assemble, the information and other resources students will need to solve the problem. Third, teachers can model problem-solving skills, e.g., by taking the class through their thinking processes as they solve similar problems. Instructors can also further the process by posing questions to students: "How do you know that?" "Why did you decide to do it that way?" and so on. Finally, and perhaps most importantly, the teacher needs to "step back" and let the students "do their thing."

Community-Based Instruction. Another approach pioneered in special education that has been shown to help in general education as well is **community-based instruction.** Sometimes called by the rather awkward term "situated learning" (Langone, 1998), it physically brings students to situations they need to learn about and teaches them essential skills *there*. It has been recommended for the teaching of science by Koch (2002) and for instruction in social studies by Singer (1997). These experts urged adoption of the strategy for *all students*. This approach, however, may be *necessary*, not just recommended, for some students who have mental retardation, autism, and emotional/behavioral disorders (see Chapters 5 and 7). This is because community-based instruction greatly reduces the intellectual burden of learning something in one time and place for use in another time and place. By contrast, what students learn in the classroom, away from the kinds of situations in which they will be expected to demonstrate knowledge, often is not generalized to those real-world settings. Children and youth with mental retardation and several other conditions often have difficulty generalizing. For these reasons, Kluth (2000) observed, use of community-based instruction quickly spread from special to general education. Today, she noted, it is recognized as helpful in inclusive classrooms because it responds to the wide range of abilities and interests typically found in such settings.

Community-based instruction includes excursions into town to shop. Such trips offer opportunities for instruction about planning, traveling, safety, budgeting, selecting items, and making change. Students can also learn a lot about self-determination: setting goals, choosing paths toward those goals, making choices, and expressing their desires clearly to members of the general public, notably including store clerks and bankers. Community-based instruction also lends itself nicely to self-regulation of behavior. Students with attention deficit disorders, autism, mental retardation, and emotional/behavioral disorders in particular may need considerable practice in monitoring and regulating their own behavior in public settings. Community excursions are a natural next step after students demonstrate mastery of such activities in the classroom.

Unfortunately, community-based instruction can be very time-consuming. This problem deserves some attention. Experts in field after field tell teachers and teachers-in-training to *facilitate* student learning, rather than direct it. Koch (2002), for example, addressing the teaching of science at the elementary level, urged educators to focus more on process than on content, on quality than on quantity, and on learning than on memorization. Similarly, Singer (1997), talking about the teaching of social studies at the secondary level, strongly advised educators to allow students to conduct projects through which they could discover important information. The "down side" to these strategies is that they take considerable time. Physics professor Richard Feynman (cited in Sykes, 1994) addressed the problem head-on when he noted that students will learn too few facts through experimentation, no matter how enlightening each experiment, simply because the school calendar offers time enough only for a few experiments.

The advent of standards-based testing exacerbates an already tense situation. Many teachers have found that they must cut back on, or even forego, community-based activities because of pressure to "teach to the test" (prepare students for high-stakes examinations). There simply is not enough time during the school year to both prepare students for tests related to the new, higher learning standards and, simultaneously, to help students to learn key information in the contexts in which they will be called upon, as adults, to use it, meaning, in the "real world."

The conflict may be exaggerated. Koch (2002), for example, drew a sharp distinction between "book learning" and "really knowing something"—between knowing the words in a question and remembering the words that go with them (the answers), on the one hand, and actually knowing the whole story because one has personally lived it. Many students with specific learning disabilities have told me that they do far, far better when they have experienced something themselves than when they have just studied it. To illustrate, the physics principle of conservation of matter is much better understood after doing an experiment involving ice melting into water than after reading a few pages in a textbook.

Overprepare

Inquiry-based learning, by its very nature, is unpredictable. You will not know in advance which aspects of a topic will intrigue your students, captivating them enough to set them

Teacher Strategies That Work

Community-Based Instruction

Going "out into the community" has much to recommend it. First, it can make instruction "come alive" by exposing students first-hand to subjects they otherwise would just read and talk about. Second, it often gives children and youth opportunities to learn by doing: They get to "do" science, political science, math, and so on. Third, it dramatically reduces the problem of generalizability. By teaching *in situ* (on site), where competency will be demanded from them, you alleviate the need for students to apply in one setting what they learned in another.

A good example of community-based instruction for students in an inclusive classroom is a visit to a nearby special school or adult services program. Suppose, to illustrate, that you have one student with cerebral palsy in your inclusive classroom. By taking the class to a local United Cerebral Palsy Association school/center, you can accomplish several important objectives. First, your non-disabled students will understand much more about the tremendous variety in which cerebral palsy comes: it ranges from mild to very severe. This will help non-disabled students to see their classmate as an individual. Second, your student with cerebral palsy could learn about local programs and events that may interest her. Some UCPA schools/programs offer driver education, for example, using hand controls for acceleration and braking. As this example suggests, your student may get to see a broad range of assistive technology devices that she otherwise would never know about.

Other good uses of community-based instruction have to do with transition (see Chapter 13). There is no more effective way to familiarize teens with the world of employment than in-person visits to local businesses, organizations, and agencies. Similarly, by visiting a local college, you can help your students to appreciate the logistical issues with which they will have to deal: where to live, where to secure personal necessities, and how to get around campus and around town. Finally, by escorting your class downtown, you can teach lessons about bus transportation, shopping, making change, and the like, that are much more meaningful ("authentic") than are classroom discussions or school-based mock exercises.

off on discovery learning. That is why you need to be prepared for a range of contingencies. Singer (1997) explained that teachers of social studies need to bring a variety of source documents and other materials with them when they introduce a new topic. He overplans lessons. During class discussion, he learns which students want to pursue which investigations. He gives them the tools they will need, placing the rest back into his bag. Concluded Singer

> I am convinced that most teachers need to plan even more than they do; that extensive advance planning is an essential feature of effective teaching; and that planning is where we, as teachers, get the chance to think and act as historians and social scientists. It is our opportunity to consider broader ideas, frame questions, suggest hypotheses, and research potential resources before we go into the classroom to teach about them. (p. 140)

Some teachers find the prospect of overpreparing to be intimidating. They realize that an open-inquiry approach demands that they know their content thoroughly. Wrote Woodward, Monroe, and Baxter (2001), "[T]eacher-guided discussions (or constructive conversations, as Morocco [2001] described them) . . . require a considerable amount of content and pedagogical knowledge, with few, if any, models for how to engage students with learning disabilities in these contexts" (p. 34). Singer argues that teaching through inquiry cannot be done well unless educators "overprepare" in advance of instruction.

Provide Teacher-Made Advance Organizers/Scaffolding

The scientific method is not instinctive in humans. It takes time to learn how to "think like a scientist." It also takes a lot of trial-and-error. Students with disabilities engaged in inquiry-based learning tend to do much better if educators give them, in advance, support in the form of prompts or reminders. Thus, Woodward, Monroe and Baxter (2001) offered a "problem-solving guide" for use by middle-school students who were attempting to solve math problems. Gradually, such scaffolding may be withdrawn. Eventually, without needing such support, students with disabilities as well as those with no disabilities do their investigations, discuss their findings, and report their conclusions.

Research That Works

Class-Wide Peer Tutoring

One highly effective small-group technique is known by a rather unwieldy term, **class-wide peer tutoring (CWPT).** This is so important that we discuss it at length. CWPT is a method of peer mediation and intervention that Greenwood (1997) defined as "an instructional strategy developed to help teachers individualize instruction, while still providing students with ample opportunity to become actively engaged during instruction" (p. 53). A notable feature of the method, as articulated by its proponents at the Juniper Garden Children's Project, in Kansas City, Kansas (Mortweet et al., 1999), is its *reciprocity:* students take turns being the "tutor" and the "tutee," which means that the student with a disability has a chance to teach non-disabled students. These opportunities can be very meaningful to special-needs students precisely because they are so rare. The reciprocal nature of CWPT also seems to have social skills benefits, because the experience of being "led" by students with special needs helps regular-education students to learn more about, and come to appreciate the positive characteristics of, students with disabilities. It can also help to combat racism and classism: Students who have been tutored by peers of other races and/or social classes are less likely to continue to hold stereotyped notions about those groups.

The Juniper Garden Children's Project has found that both general-education and special-education students benefit from peer tutoring. The gains for students with disabilities appear to come from their increased engagement as compared to teacher-led whole-class instruction. When one teacher works with 20 or 25 students, the students often lose focus. Such disabilities as mental retardation, attention deficit disorders, and specific learning disabilities are associated with difficulty in identifying and attending to the important data. That is why engagement is so critical. The increase in time-on-task that peer tutoring brings may be due to their knowledge that they will have a chance to teach and not just to learn. It may also be due to the fact that someone (albeit a fellow student) is watching them, and only them, during the instructional period.

In work reported by Mortweet et al. (1999), by Sideridis et al. (1997), and by Utley, Mortweet, and Greenwood (1997), Juniper Garden researchers have also noted gains for *general*-education students. These students tended to learn more than in teacher-led whole-class instruction, in part due to more time on task. The increased learning was modest in comparison to that secured by students having disabilities. Follow-up work (Gardner et al., 2001; Greenwood et al., 2001) suggests that the outcomes are not so modest after all. A side-benefit is that students with no disabilities may better understand, and appreciate, children and youth with disabilities, simply as a result of being tutored by someone with a disability.

Peer tutoring is an excellent supplement to whole-class instruction. It can be used with reading, spelling, math, and social studies (Mortweet, et al., 1999). What does the teacher do during such activities? The Juniper Garden researchers suggest that she meander around, offering help, answering questions, giving encouragement, and providing tokens to reinforce behavior. They urge that the teacher *not* disrupt the dyads. The intent is for the students to work together, independent of the teacher.

Fuchs et al. (2001) demonstrated that a variation on the method, which they called Peer-Assisted Learning Strategies, or PALS, is similarly effective with students of all ages. PALS features three kinds of activities. In "Partner Reading," each student reads aloud for about 5 minutes. When the lower-achieving member of the pair makes an error, the tutor immediately flags the mistake and encourages creative thinking to correct it. "Paragraph Shrinking," the second phase of PALS, has student pairs summarizing after each paragraph is read aloud. Again, the tutor stops the lower-achieving student right after any mistake and stimulates error-correction efforts. Finally, "Prediction Relay" requires students to make and (dis) confirm predictions.

We introduced cooperative learning earlier in this chapter. We have just discussed peer tutoring. You may be asking yourself, "How do the two differ?"

Cooperative learning has teams or other small groups *working together toward a common goal.* They are engaged in a group project. To pick up on an example given earlier, one student might be researching the biographical facts about explorers Lewis and Clark, another studying the geography west of the Mississippi River as it stood in the early 1800s, and a third examining the French-American relations of the time.

By contrast, peer tutoring has one student helping another. Both are working on the same facts and problems (e.g., both studying French and American foreign policy in 1800). Peer tutoring has one student giving one-on-one assistance to another student who is having difficulty with something.

Both techniques are well-regarded for use by teachers in inclusive classrooms and by teachers of other diverse groups of students. In particular, children and youth whose family cultures value group work may do better with these approaches than with more traditional, individual-achievement oriented strategies.

Be Available

Inquiry-based instruction gives students considerable latitude to pursue their own interests. This is good. However, it could also set some adrift—to stray far afield and to make a lot of mistakes. Particularly susceptible to such aimless drifting and errors are students with specific learning disabilities, many with attention deficit hyperactivity disorders, and many with mental retardation. They will often need not only advance organizers and scaffolding but also regular monitoring on your part. You need to make sure they remain on track. One method of doing this is student journal entries. We turn to that now.

Require Students to Keep Journals—And Read Their Journal Entries

Whether you teach social studies (Singer, 1997), science (Koch, 2002), math (Woodward et al., 2001), or some other subject, an excellent way to track student progress is to require children and youth to keep journals. Peters (1998), writing about science journals, pointed out something that should be obvious: These journal entries will only be made, and will only be effective as learning tools, if you (the teacher) read them. Each student's journal entries should be commented upon, even if briefly, to show that you appreciate the time and effort it took to perform the project and write the journal entry. Equally as important, if not more so, is that you use these entries as "eyes and ears" into your students' progress. Journal entries frequently reveal (usually unintentionally) what students really enjoy doing and what they do not quite understand. You can use this information in your teaching.

One-on-One Instruction

As mentioned earlier, one-on-one instruction is very time-consuming. Even if you gave each student just 20 minutes, in a class of 25 students you would need a full 8-hour day to do so. However, there are students, and there are times, when one-on-one instruction is both necessary and appropriate—when you know, based upon assessment, that this particular student needs intensive, personal help with this specific issue or problem. Research-recommended practices for one-on-one instruction are summarized in Figure 8.6.

Assess, Then Teach

This should be obvious. One-on-one instruction should begin with probes: Precisely what is the difficulty this student is encountering with this material? The reason for providing one-on-one instruction is because you have observed errors or other problems. Here, you narrow the issue down to specifics so that you can teach.

Teach Strategies

An excellent use of precious one-on-one time is to instruct students in the use of academic strategies. This is because an hour, or even 20 minutes, of such instruction can help the student achieve at higher levels for the rest of the school year. Students with disabilities often lack knowledge and/or skills about strategies useful in school. For some, this lack is *the* major cause for academic difficulties or failure. So common are these deficits that you can be sure that, whatever else the presenting problem may be, explicit instruction in learning strategies is very likely part of the solution.

Use Direct Instruction

Direct Instruction was introduced earlier in the text (see Chapter 3). We have mentioned it several times in this chapter, as well. This set of techniques is important enough to merit an extended discussion here. Special education has made extensive use of explicit teaching of what students need to learn. Direct Instruction is widely adopted by special educators because it is so often needed by students with disabilities, particularly mental

FIGURE 8.6 One-on-One Instruction

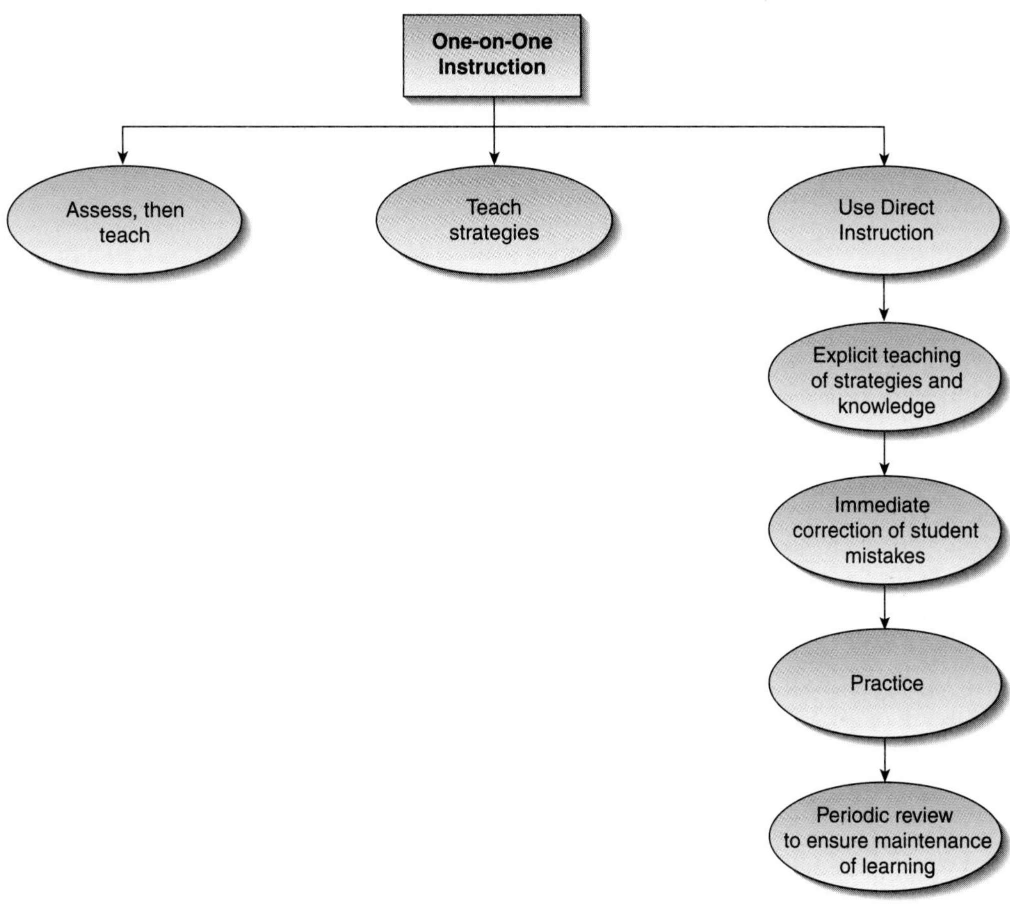

retardation. These students do not easily learn on their own. Still, Direct Instruction is somewhat controversial among general educators. That is because it seems to stand in sharp contrast to **facilitation,** in which teachers set the stage for students to learn material on their own. **Constructivism,** or the active discovery of information by students, is much the same. (We use the term "facilitation" to refer to what *teachers* do and "constructivism" to mean what *students* do.) Direct Instruction appears, on its face, to be non-constructivist. In actuality, however, constructivism and Direct Instruction complement each other when used by good teachers. Such educators might, for example, employ Direct Instruction to train students on fundamentals and then fade back, challenging the students to use those building blocks to learn on their own. Similarly, Direct Instruction may be used in one-on-one settings before and after facilitation/constructivism is used in whole-class or small-group instruction. These are reasons why King-Sears (1997) and other educators have insisted that inclusive teachers should employ *both* strategies. In some fields, notably social studies, Direct Instruction is widely used. Chapin and Messick (1996), for example, reported that some school districts go so far as to *require* teachers to practice a particular kind of Direct Instruction, notably the type advanced by Madeline Hunter (1982).

Direct Instruction Defined. What is Direct Instruction? Perhaps the simplest way to think of it is as explicit teaching of material, careful review by teachers of the kinds of mistakes children make, re-teaching of information as needed to help students to correct those mistakes, sustained practice of newly learned skills, and regular review to be sure that students retain learned information. The "explicit teaching" component features clear, unambiguous presentation of curriculum and materials on exactly the knowledge and skills

Teacher Strategies That Work

Strategy Instruction

Suppose you wanted to help a student with a specific learning disability to improve her reading skills. Teaching her strategies for effective reading is a good idea. Here are some suggestions:

Bring to her desk a passage she read earlier but evidently did not understand (she missed the test question based upon this material). Ask her to read it silently. Then ask her to read it out loud. [Recall from Chapter 3 that many students with specific learning disabilities have difficulty doing this. That is why you had her read silently first. You should indicate with your body language and by your tone of voice that you are going to be patient and accommodating as she reads out loud.] The oral reading reveals where the problems are.

If your student is an elementary or middle-school student, you should then suggest a strategy to her. Depending on her specific needs, this might be placing a ruler or similar device under the line she is reading, or it might be underlining words she is not sure about, or it may be reading each sentence twice. If your student is a high-school student, it would make more sense for you to ask the student, "What strategy do you think would help you here?" Adolescents tend to be more insightful about their own strengths and weaknesses than are younger children; teens also have had more experience, so have learned what does and does not work for them. As an alternative, you might have her listen as you read the passage. If so, you should "talk out loud" so she hears your mental processes and knows what strategies you are using and why you are adopting those.

When the two of you have agreed upon a successful strategy for her to use, teach your student to self-monitor her own use of the strategy. She might create a bookmark that reminds her of the steps, or she might write notes to herself before beginning to read. Give her practice at applying the strategy and at monitoring her use of it.

Suggest ways she could self-motivate to persist in her use of the strategy. This might be mental pats on the back. It might be permissions she gives herself to take a break, get a snack, and so on. Again, these rewards may be written on a bookmark or she may jot them down before beginning a reading assignment.

Teach your student how to recognize that the strategy is not working. (Few strategies work all the time!) Tell her what she can do in such instances (switch strategies, ask a peer, ask you, etc.).

that students require for academic success. The "careful review" part comprises item analysis and other probes that teachers use to discover not only how well a student is doing in general, but also precisely what kinds of thinking mistakes and knowledge gaps are lowering scores. The "re-teaching" element of Direct Instruction has the teacher focusing the child's attention upon those thought processes and that substantive information. The "sustained practice" factor of the approach incorporates immediate practice to establish competency. The final portion of Direct Instruction is periodic review and re-testing over long periods of time to maintain that achievement.

Components of Direct Instruction. The key parts of Direct Instruction, Gersten et al. (1987) reported, are (1) immediate correction of student mistakes, (2) practice, and (3) periodic review to ensure maintenance of learning. They found that teacher support for other teachers was a critical element. In particular, coaches (consulting teachers) gave very specific help to classroom teachers. This assistance took the form of identifying precisely what mistakes children were making and why they were making those mistakes. It also included correcting those errors. Gersten et al. offered the example of elementary school children beginning to learn subtraction. Second- and third-grade children take some time to pick up renaming in subtraction; that is, when subtracting "8" from "32" it is first necessary to rename the "2" as "12". (Teachers know that it *is* possible to subtract 7 from 4, resulting in −3. For most elementary students, however, this is an "impossible" problem.) A technique the coach might offer to the classroom teacher is to present students with "impossible" subtraction problems (e.g., subtract "7" from "4"). The teacher should tell students to cross out any problem that they believe cannot be done. Instruction is then offered to students on how to rename in subtraction.

A Strong Research Base. Researchers at the University of Oregon have spent more than a quarter century developing, testing, and implementing Direct Instruction. Russell Gersten,

Douglas Carnine, John Woodward, and their colleagues spent years working in neighborhood schools, side by side with classroom teachers, to refine the approach and to help teachers to acquire competency in it. Project Follow Through used Direct Instruction in low-income areas in East St. Louis, IL, rural South Carolina, and the Ocean Hill-Brownville section of New York City. Of particular importance to us in this book, implementation took place in general classrooms:

> In Follow Through, [separate] special education placements were actively discouraged. Even students entering with very weak academic skills, or those who appeared to learn slowly, were placed in regular classrooms where Direct Instruction techniques and curriculum were used. . . . No "pull-outs," no special testing, and no labeling of students took place. (Gersten, Carnine, & Woodward, 1987, p. 49)

Results have been documented by independent outside evaluators—and those results are quite impressive. Teachers trained in Direct Instruction became more effective educators. More to the point, children taught using this method achieved at high levels and maintained those levels.

Some Disadvantages of Direct Instruction. The flip side of Direct Instruction, as Gersten et al. (1987) reported in their useful summary of the first 20 years of research and implementation, is that effective use of Direct Instruction requires a real commitment on the part of teachers. They need intensive in-service training. They must also put up with weekly observations and documentation of outcomes by others. In addition, schools must make available consulting teachers who are relieved of classroom responsibilities in return for supporting a dozen or more working teachers. These are intrusive steps, both for individual teachers and for schools. Gersten et al. (1987) believed that teacher and administrator resistance have slowed deployment of Direct Instruction in the schools: "Becoming competent and comfortable with Direct Instruction takes considerably more time and effort than many teachers and administrators are willing to take" (p. 49). Recall that Fuchs, Fuchs, and Bahr (1990) and Ysseldyke (2001) commented that teachers tend to adopt research-based practices that are quickly and easily implemented.

New Uses for Direct Instruction. With many students having disabilities, Direct Instruction in *learning/studying* strategies can be very helpful. Students with specific learning disabilities, in particular, often need explicit instruction in, and considerable practice with, strategies. Similarly, those with emotional/behavioral disorders and many with attention deficit disorders need to learn, and practice, strategies for monitoring and controlling their own behaviors. All will benefit from training on how to take good notes. Direct Instruction naturally lends itself to such uses. First, teachers outline effective strategies. Students are then tested on their knowledge of these strategies and given opportunities to practice them. Periodic review sessions refresh their memories and speed up their application of the techniques. King-Sears (1997) made an important additional point:

> [L]ook at the cost-benefit for students. If they can spend one to two months of daily instruction learning a strategy they can use for the rest of the school year and the next school year and in out-of-school settings, too, what is the cost to them versus the benefit of the alternative of being tutored by someone who helps them pass each test and make the grade for each semester but doesn't teach them . . . how to learn by themselves? (p. 7)

In recent years, Gersten and his colleagues have applied Direct Instruction to the teaching of higher-order thinking skills, such as chemical interactions and analysis of poetry. Even in these areas, where several alternative answers might all be correct, Gersten et al. (1987) argued, "students need explicit instruction in the relevant facts and concepts before moving into the complex cognitive tasks involved [and] when teaching these more open-ended processes, instruction is somewhat more open-ended" (p. 55).

Teacher Strategies That Work

Direct Instruction

Suppose you were teaching a student how to subtract numbers that include decimals. The approach known as Direct Instruction tells you to follow these steps:

First, teach the student the essential elements (make sure columns are lined up, with the decimal points in the same vertical column; begin at the right and subtract the lower from the upper number in each column, renaming as necessary, for example, "2" becomes "12"; double-check that the decimal in the answer appears in the same column as it does in the other two horizontal lines). Teach each step explicitly and as clearly as possible, using manipulatives or whatever other support appears to be needed.

Second, give the student practice problems.

Third, do error analysis to identify where and why the student makes errors. Ask the student to "talk me through how you did this" to discover errors of thinking.

Fourth, re-teach the problem-solving steps the student had missed.

Fifth, re-test.

Sixth, repeat steps 2 to 5 as needed.

Seventh, periodically re-test to ensure that the student continues to know how to do these tasks.

Eighth, periodically test the student in different locales, in different ways (e.g., performance testing) to ensure that generalization occurs.

CHAPTER SUMMARY

Planning

- A school that values inclusion and wants it to succeed will provide teachers, therapists, and other educators with the support they need, including training, supplies, and planning time.
- Ideally, educators should have a say in who their collaborating teachers are. They should also have input on decisions about pulling out versus pushing in support services.
- Reviewing IEPs, talking with prior year teachers, and other steps to learn about individual students are essential preparatory measures for teachers of inclusive classrooms.
- Team members who are regular educators should visit classes having students with disabilities so as to become acquainted with methods of adapting instruction.
- Team members who are special educators should visit general classes so as to better appreciate the academic demands on special-education students in an inclusive classroom.
- Objectives (academic, behavioral) must be *individualized*. This is a major difference between a general classroom, where group objectives are the norm, and an inclusive classroom.

Universal Design

- Three approaches to universal design have been described in the literature. Universal design for instruction (UDI) adds two features to the seven contained in universal design in education (UDE), while universal design for learning (UDL) emphasizes making educational materials available in different formats and allowing students to interact with them in different ways.
- Universal design (under any of the three variations) greatly helps teachers to individualize instruction.
- Speech synthesis (computer talking) is used by screen-reader software to enable people who are blind or have low vision to "read" the contents of a computer screen.
- The main advantages of universal design over assistive technologies are that universal design offers many-user, any-time, and lower-cost adjustments.

Assistive Technology

- "Assistive technology devices" include hardware, software, and firmware. By contrast, "assistive technology services" include identifying, purchasing, and installing such devices.
- ABLEDATA and assistivetech.net™ are two sources of updated information on assistive technologies.

- Students may take assistive technology devices home on weekends and holidays, even all summer, if their IEPs contain such provisions.
- outSPOKEN® and KeyRead are two text to-speech software programs.
- The DynaVox® and DynaMyte® often are used as communication devices for children with severe physical disabilities who cannot speak intelligibly on their own.
- The Captioned Media Program (CMP) is a resource for information about captioning.
- Students should learn about technology and should use it for measuring, calculating, communicating, and other activities. To do so, many will need assistive technology devices and services.

Individualizing Instruction

- Texts may need to be modified or even simplified.
- Assignments may also need to be modified (where done, how done, with whom done).
- The classroom may need modifications (moving things around, making controls reachable).
- Scaffolding and advance organizers are useful for *any* student. They may be needed by students with disabilities.
- Problem-based learning can be highly motivating for students, because it lets them answer questions that are inherently meaningful to them in their own lives.
- Community-based instruction has much to recommend it. Unfortunately, it tends to be time-consuming and thus not adopted as often as it should be by teachers under pressure to teach to state learning standards.
- Peer tutoring can be effective in inclusive classrooms *if* it is reciprocal, that is, if students with disabilities have opportunities to tutor students with no disabilities as well as being tutored by them.
- The wide range of abilities and interests in inclusive classrooms make grouping an essential strategy. Another important advantage of group work is that it helps students to prepare for adult responsibilities. This is because much work today requires being an effective team member.
- In cooperative learning, teachers create structure for small groups. Such structure often is necessary for students with disabilities.
- The research evidence in favor of Direct Instruction is extensive and impressive. The "downside" is that it can be challenging for teachers to implement.
- Successful use of Direct Instruction requires that teachers receive training and that they gain experience with the method.

QUESTIONS FOR REFLECTION

1. What specific information that you need to teach an inclusive classroom is usually in an IEP?
2. If you will teach a 4th grade class, why should you visit a 3rd and a 5th grade class?
3. What mistakes do teachers often make when writing instructional objectives?
4. What is "redundancy" and why is it so important in universal design?
5. How does speech synthesis work? Who can it help?
6. How can e-texts help to make instruction more available to students with disabilities?
7. What must a teacher do in problem-based learning?
8. Why does community-based instruction increase the likelihood a student will generalize behavior?
9. What is the main difference between "cooperative" and "collaborative" learning?
10. Why has direct instruction proven to be so effective with many students having disabilities?

Chapter 9

Managing Behavior

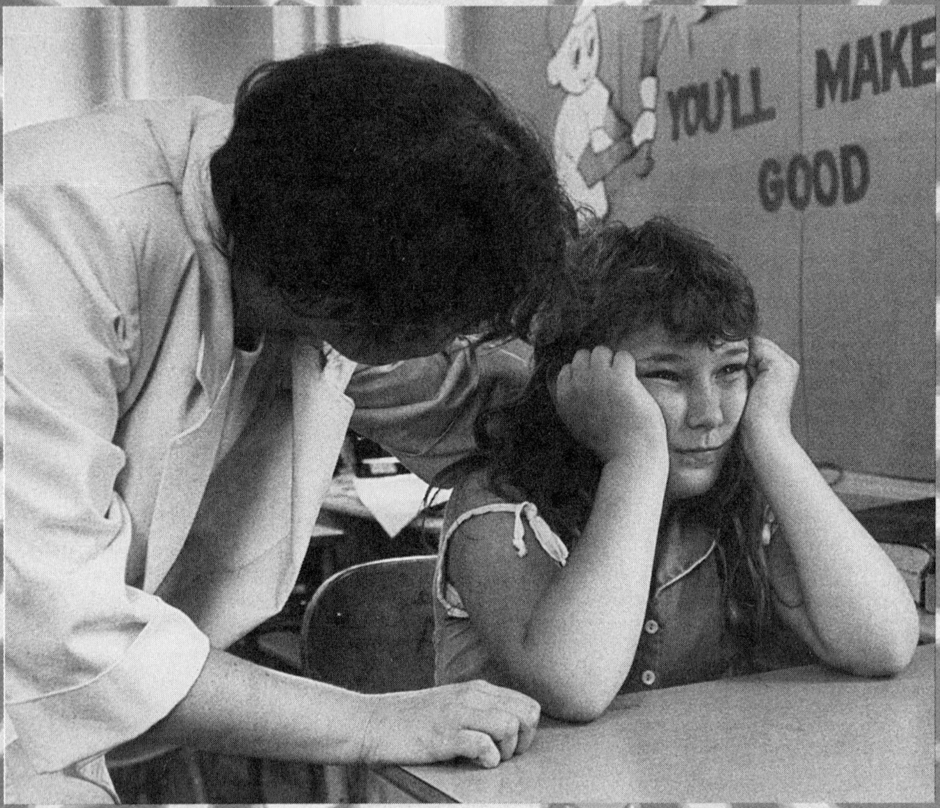

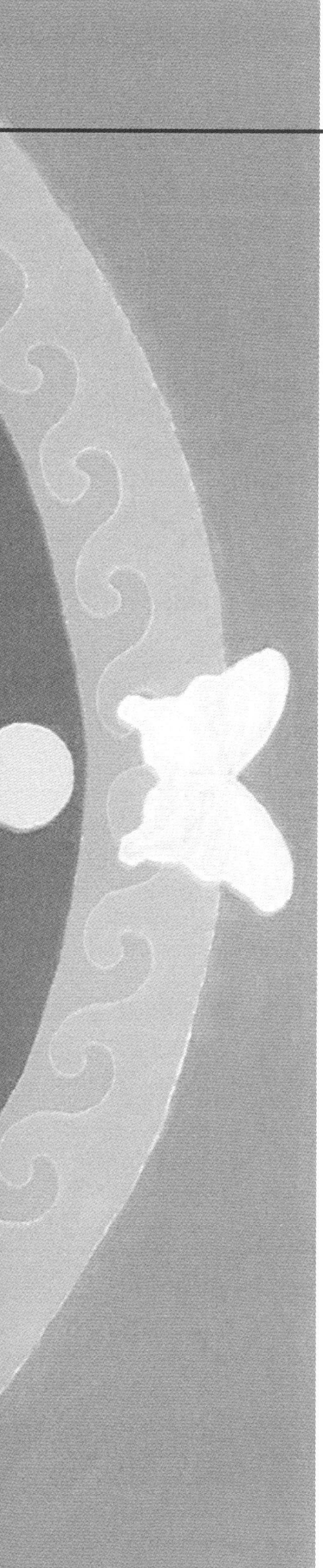

TERMS

transition periods
behavior modification
operant conditioning
presentation reinforcement
removal reinforcement
punishment
method of successive approximations
zone of proximal development
zero tolerance
positive-supports model
interim alternative placement
functional behavioral assessment

CHAPTER FOCUS QUESTIONS

After reading this chapter, you should be able to answer such questions as:

1. What makes for good classroom rules about student behavior?
2. What should educators do when teaching *new* behaviors?
3. How should educators maintain *learned* behaviors?
4. What are the pros and cons of positive supports versus zero-tolerance when it comes to discipline?
5. What do federal laws say about disciplining a student whose disability directly led to breaking school rules?
6. What is a "functional behavioral assessment" and how would you use one?
7. Why are self-advocacy and self-monitoring so critical for high-school students to learn?

PERSONAL ACCOUNTS

A teacher with a Master's degree in special education reported:

> *I am the teacher of a first-grade class of 18 children. One was classified in preschool as having emotional disturbance but for some reason was then declassified before coming to my class. Jamie clearly has many needs! A second child strikes me as having ADHD. However, she has not been diagnosed. Two of the other children in this class are English language learners (ELL). They, and the little boy with E/B disorders, are pulled out two to three times a week for out-of-class sessions. They not only miss important class time during these pull-out periods but they also disrupt the class when they return at different times throughout the day. All are functioning well below grade level.*
>
> *I took several steps in September. One was to request that the school provide me with a classroom aide. Just now, in March, I received one. This person is an art aide, not a teacher. Still, having an extra set of hands really helps! I also asked that the little girl be evaluated by the IEP team. Even now, in March, I am still waiting for that to happen. I also set up a strict behavior plan for the boy with E/B disorders. This is the only thing that began on time and is working well. Jamie has come a long, long way in nearly six months. It really makes*

a big difference that he knows exactly what I expect from him in each situation. He knows precisely what he is supposed to do. And he knows what will happen, both good and bad, depending on whether he does those things.

—Natasha

Another special educator shared this story:

When Will was placed into my fifth-grade classroom in November, the principal told me, "He's a live wire!" I soon found out why she said that. The very first day in class, Will spilled blue paint on one classmate and tripped another, causing her to sustain a cut on her forehead that required six stitches to close. Why was Will doing those things? No one could tell me—not the principal, not the previous teacher, not last year's teacher.

I decided to give Will a week while I studied his behavior. I created, on 8 × 10 cards, a set of six time sheets, one for each hour of the school day. I placed these in my left pocket. Whenever I had a chance, I pulled a card and made an entry, noting (a) what class activity was happening, (b) what Will was doing, and (c) what I thought might account for what Will was doing. After 5 days, I assembled all 30 cards and drew a chart showing the times of the day that Will was most likely to act out, the student(s) with whom he tussled, and what Will and other students had been doing at the time Will acted out.

I was rather amazed by what this experience taught me. Will acted out only *when he was working by himself on an assignment that would be graded. Not even once did he misbehave when engaged in a group activity on which he would not be assessed. From this I concluded that Will's aggressive behavior served the purpose of getting him excused from doing assigned work. Clearly, he must be fearful that even his best work would be graded low. Apparently, Will had made a calculation that misbehavior in class has less-severe consequences than does poor academic performance.*

The results of my functional behavioral assessment in hand, I met with Will. I told him that Steven, the best student in the class, would be available to him, as would I, any time he needed help. All Will had to do was to ask. I also told Will that if he needed additional time to complete an assignment, the same rule applied: Just ask. After making sure that Will understood these rules, I told him that continued misbehavior would not be tolerated in the classroom. I told him that henceforth, until further notice, 75% of his marking-period grade would be based upon how well he observed class rules (remaining in seat, no fighting, etc.).

My intent was to alter Will's calculations. I wanted him to see that behavior would play a larger part in his grades, at least temporarily, than would academics. At the same time, I wanted Will to alter his behavior—by asking for help rather than by acting up. If all goes well, next marking period I will make behavior and academics equal weight (50% each) and, later, reverse the current weighting (to 75% academics and 25% behavior). Hopefully, by mid-year, Will may no longer need these interventions.

—Amanda

These stories illustrate key ideas we will explore in this chapter. Natasha's experience exemplifies the fact that teachers of inclusive classrooms need to take steps to manage behavior, without waiting. Too often, much-needed assistance, in her case a teacher aide, arrives only after months of waiting. Natasha created a behavior management plan, and implemented it, even as she waited to get an aide. Amanda's story shows how eye-opening an objective analysis of behavior can be. By documenting when her student acted up, and when he did not, Amanda was able to identify the underlying purpose, for Will, of aggressive behavior. Had she not realized what function that behavior served for him,

Amanda likely would not have been able to control it. In this chapter, we will study behavior-management plans and functional behavior assessments as tools that teachers of inclusive classrooms may use to create an environment that is conducive to learning.

INTRODUCTION

A national survey of teachers found that their second highest-priority concern was managing children's behavior and managing the classroom (or, to use the researchers' term, "managing challenging behaviors"; Pearman, Huang, & Mellblom, 1997, p. 11). (The highest-priority worry, found the researchers, was finding enough time to teach children what they needed to learn.) Concerns about classroom and individual behavior are commonly reported in studies of inclusive teacher beliefs and needs (e.g., Austin, 2000). Many educators, both special and general, seek help in controlling the behavior of some students with disabilities in a large inclusive classroom.

As the Pearman et al. (1997) survey showed, teachers want and need knowledge and skills that will help them to be effective managers of student behavior. We address strategies and techniques for doing so in this chapter. Notable among the steps that experts recommend is planning what each adult in the room will do, what rules will be set for the class, and which students will be assigned duties during "transition periods" (the times between the end of one activity and the beginning of another). Also very important is behavior modification—the set of techniques for rewarding acceptable behavior and reducing unacceptable behavior. As valuable as those tools are, managing behavior involves more than behavior modification. When lessons are presented at the level where students are ready to learn (not too easy, not too hard), student behavior tends to be better. Teachers also need to be careful about the language they use, using words that describe behavior rather than criticize children.

A related topic has to do with discipline. Students with disabilities are entitled to due process before being disciplined for behavior that is related to their conditions. A functional behavioral assessment may be required before school-wide consequences are imposed upon children and youth who have disabilities. This chapter concludes with information about such measures and about other issues related to discipline.

PLANNING TO MANAGE YOUR CLASSROOM

Teachers of inclusion classrooms express interest in methods of managing the classroom, particularly with respect to controlling the behavior of students with attention deficit hyperactivity disorder (see Chapter 3) and with emotional/behavioral disorders (see Chapter 5), as well as "at-risk" students who may not do well at controlling their frustrations with out-of-school issues (see Chapter 11). There are techniques that are of proven value for such uses. First is to get the help you will need. This includes paraprofessionals who work in your classroom. It includes counselors and other related-services personnel who may "push in" to your classroom or "pull out" students for separate sessions. It also includes student peers.

The Need for Help in the Classroom

As a teacher of an inclusive classroom, you probably will benefit greatly from the assistance of a volunteer or paid assistant. Having another adult in the room by itself helps, simply because there is "another set of hands" to get things done. An obvious example has to do with **"transition periods"**—the time between the ending of one activity and

Working teachers report that having a male paraprofessional in the room can often alter student behavior, particularly of boys.

the beginning of another. As you are wrapping up a lesson, a paraprofessional or volunteer can be putting things away and setting up for the next activity. Another illustration has to do with supervision of small-group sessions. If your attention is being given to the group at one table, for example, it is good to know that another adult can monitor behavior by students at other tables. Many teachers find that a male paraprofessional, simply by being a man in a female-dominated school, can change the tone of a classroom. Young boys often modify their behavior when they are in the presence of a male adult. This is why the Woodward Center, a school for students with severe emotional or behavioral disorders in Freeport, New York, employs large numbers of male paraprofessionals (Joan Cottman, personal communication, November 18, 2002).

Ways Other Adults Support Teachers

Even if another adult is only present occasionally, you may benefit. That is because most teachers do *not* practice the techniques of behavior modification with anything approaching the proficiency they could, or think they do. Student teachers I help to prepare are routinely astonished to discover, after being observed, how little attention they actually were giving to behavior they wanted to see their children display, and how much attention they were displaying to unwanted behavior by those children. Both are violations of the teachings of behavior modification. Probably the most effective way for teachers to recognize what they are doing, as compared to what they had intended to do, is for *someone to record* what occurs in the classroom. A trained observer—it could be a school counselor, a teacher aide, or a volunteer—should tell you what you actually did in the classroom, even if just during a few weeks in the fall and another few weeks in the early spring. Even more effective is videotaping classes. Such feedback is essential for you to practice what you preach. How it is done matters less than that it be done. Experts strongly recommend that you have a co-teacher or other colleague monitor your classroom on occasion and remind you when you fail to adhere to your own rules (Martin & Pear, 2003).

Help is also needed when a teacher first implements a behavior-modification plan (see "Basics of Behavior Modification," p. 332). A cardinal principle of behavior modification is the establishment of a *baseline* measure—what happens and how frequently it occurs, *before* you implement a change. Someone, perhaps an aide or a volunteer, needs to record those occurrences. Finally, how will you know whether your new plan is working? Again, independent observations are critical. Someone needs to note how often "good" and "bad" behaviors occur, so that you can track student progress. It is usually not possible in a whole-class teaching situation for you to do that yourself.

Finally, you should avail yourself of the professional support of a school counselor. These professionals can be of assistance in several ways to teachers of inclusive classrooms. First, they can help you to understand students' motivations and behaviors. Second, they can make recommendations for controlling behavior in the classroom. Third, they are among the related-services personnel who may deliver services to students with disabilities, notably those who have emotional or behavioral disorders. Sciarra (2003) explained how school counselors may serve as consultants to teachers. He offered this example of how teachers may draw upon in-school resources such as counselors as well as upon local agencies:

> Mrs. G., the math teacher, comes to you, the school counselor, because one of her students, Ramon, is performing poorly in Algebra and has begun attention-seeking behaviors. The problem behavior was not present at the beginning of the school year but began about 2 months into the semester. From the school record, the consultant saw that Ramon's math grades, while not great, were always passing. Through talking with other teachers and from observation, the counselor concluded that this behavior was particular to math class. Since this was Algebra I, the working hypothesis became that Ramon was having difficulty doing more complex mathematical operations and that frustration over this resulted in his attention-seeking behaviors. The consultant considered two courses of action: one, a referral for an evaluation by the school psychologist to determine if Ramon had a learning disability in regards to math; two, tutoring to give Ramon extra help in understanding more complex operations. The consultant decided on recommending tutoring first, follow-up on the results of this, and then refer for an evaluation if tutoring did not seem to make a difference. The consultant knew that Mrs. G. herself would not be able to provide the tutoring since she was in charge of other after-school activities. However, the consultant was aware of an after-school tutoring program that took place through the local social services agency. The consultant suggested this course of action to Mrs. G., who agreed to contact Ramon's mother about his attending the after-school tutoring program. Mrs. G. and the consultant agreed to meet within a month's time to assess the effectiveness of the tutoring program.

For more on teacher-counselor consultation, see the nearby box, "Resources That Work: Teacher-Counselor Collaboration."

Ways Peers Support Students and Teachers

We saw earlier in Chapter 8 that peers can be invaluable in individualizing instruction for students in inclusive classrooms. Research shows that students doing peer tutoring, as well as those being tutored, display improved social skills (e.g., Blake, Wang, Cartledge, & Gardner, 2000). Thus, while a teacher can present a lesson for the whole class, a peer tutor can add instruction specific to the needs of *one* child. As it turns out, this has implications not only for teaching but also for managing behavior. When instruction is provided at a level at which the student is ready to learn, that student is both less frustrated and less bored. We will return to that topic later in this chapter (see "Vyogotsky's 'Zone of Proximal Development,'" p. 337).

Peers can help in classroom management, as well, sometimes as much as can adults. Many students, particularly teens with E/B disorders, respond better to their age peers than to adults, especially authority figures. Peers can model acceptable behavior. Peers can give approval that students value, sometimes even more than they appreciate adult approval. A third way peers can add value in the classroom is to teach students ways to behave. Children and youth often behave in unacceptable ways simply because they do not know other, more socially acceptable, ways of behaving. Finally, as Osterman (2000) has shown, peers are vital in creating a school community to which students, especially teens, feel attached. For that reason, they can help to prevent teenagers from dropping out of school.

Peers are particularly valuable in inclusive classrooms. When students with disabilities are placed in inclusive settings, they continue to observe appropriate behavior by their age peers. They remain under effective peer control, as well, because their age peers demand that they "behave." By contrast, when these students are removed from inclusive classrooms and placed in separate ("self-contained") settings, they observe the behavior, much of it inappropriate, of other students with disabilities. Indeed, they may be "egged

Resources That Work

Teacher-Counselor Collaboration

Collaboration with a school counselor can help teachers of inclusive classrooms in many ways. These include improving teacher-teacher relations, understanding reasons behind student misbehavior, changing student behavior in the classroom, training teachers in classroom management, and mediating conflicts.

First, school counselors can assist two teachers assigned to team-teach. As we will see later in Chapter 12 collaboration can be challenging. As professionals trained in helping people to get along and to reach compromises, counselors often are able to overcome teachers' resistance to change and to assist them in defining roles acceptable to both. Counselors can be particularly valuable in instances in which the teacher-teacher collaboration is not voluntary, that is, when team teaching is imposed upon the teachers by the administration. Under such circumstances, teachers may resent the outside interference. Those emotions may complicate the already difficult process of peer collaboration. Counselors function as consultants to the teachers. Sciarra (2003) noted that consultation does not involve personal issues. Counseling, on the other hand, does.

Second, because they often possess knowledge about a student's out-of-school circumstances, counselors may be able to employ systems theory to help troubled students to deal with their problems. As a "disinterested" third party, the counselor can objectively assess how a student's personal life affects his academic life. Thus, a counselor who is aware, from her own interactions with a student's family, that the parents have unrealistically high expectations for the child is in a position to understand more than the teacher might about why this child is chronically unhappy. That knowledge equips the counselor to work both with the family and with the student. In these instances, the counselor is engaging in counseling (because personal issues are unavoidable).

Third, counselors can provide counseling for students who exhibit inappropriate behavior. They can help both when students are unusually withdrawn and uncommunicative, as sometimes happens with girls, and when students resort to aggression to solve problems, as occurs more frequently with boys. The support services offered by school counselors may be push-in or pull-out. Both can help classroom teachers. By pushing in to the classroom, the counselor can observe the student in action—and can also see how the teacher handles episodes of student misbehavior. This first-hand observation can inform the counselor's understanding of the problems, faster and better in many instances that might occur were the teacher to verbally describe what happened in the classroom. Pull-out sessions may be necessary for one-on-one counseling with the student. These periods involve counseling (Sciarra, 2003).

Fourth, counselors can be invaluable for teachers who want to establish effective behavior-modification plans. As trained observers, counselors make excellent peers to record what a teacher does during a baseline period (before the plan is implemented). Similarly, as experts on behavior modification, counselors can instruct teachers in the nuances of creating, carrying out, and evaluating a behavior-modification plan.

Finally, school counselors are professional mediators. They can bring together family members and teachers to help resolve problems. They can also mediate between teachers and students. It is the nature of mediation that a third person must mediate, helping each party to identify what he most wants and assisting each to recognize what he is willing to give up in the interest of compromise (Sciarra, 2003).

---

on" by those peers to join them in such behavior. This is yet another reason why inclusion is an ideal worth striving to reach.

Begin Early

It is vital that preschool and elementary teachers of inclusive classrooms take proactive steps to manage behavior in the classroom. Research conducted by Forness and his colleagues (e.g., Forness, Kavale, & Lopez, 1993) has demonstrated that all too often teachers intervene much later than they should. The investigators found that even when behavior was identified as inappropriate in kindergarten, educators typically did not begin behavior modification or other intervention strategies until the end of the child's second-grade year. Kauffman (1999) concurred, saying that teachers in effect "prevent the prevention" of emotional and behavioral disorders (p. 448). By that he meant what Forness et al. also meant: Acts of omission may be as deleterious as acts of commission.

Kauffman, Forness, and other authorities strongly recommend that teachers be trained in recognizing behavior that is different from that of typical children and youth.

Educators must also learn how to discourage such acts. When teachers intervene at the first signs of unacceptable behavior, they send a strong message to young children. When, by contrast, they overlook inappropriate acts, the message they send is, in effect, "This is acceptable."

What is most important to teach students in the early years of school? Without much question, it probably is how to behave in acceptable ways. Many children and youth "act out" because they do not know other ways to respond to the frustration or anger they feel. Even first- and second-grade students can master the old standby "count to three" strategy. Direct Instruction (see Chapter 8) may be employed to teach such strategies. Regardless of how they are taught, the key is to teach them—early.

Also essential is to teach students how to make and keep friends. The skills that enable children and youth to "play well with others" (to quote an elementary-school report card item) are competencies that strengthen students' connections to school. Interventions that help young people to make effective use of free time may have another side-effect: keeping them from joining gangs (Decker & Curry, 2000). It is much easier to prevent students from engaging in gang activities than it is to dissuade them later, after they already have developed allegiance to a gang.

Rules

Rules are important in any classroom. Experts recommend that class rules be stated in positive terms (i.e., say what students *should* do, such as "Raise your hand to be recognized before speaking," rather than what they should not) and that they be few in number (five is probably enough, 10 is likely too many) (Kauffman, 2001; Mercer & Mercer, 1998). Curwin and Mendler (2001) suggested that you plan to spend a minute or two each day reviewing rules with your students. Clarity is essential: Students must understand these rules and know their consequences.

A related idea is "Do what you say, and say what you do." Do not make hollow threats. If you set a rule, and a child breaks it, you must follow through with the announced consequences. We saw, for example, in Chapter 3 that many students with attention deficit hyperactivity disorders also have oppositional defiant disorder (ODD). They have almost irresistible desires to defy authority. It is not difficult to imagine how ODD behavior emerges. In the home and in the classroom, adults often respond to the acting-out behavior characteristic of hyperactivity by imposing rules. The children may end up feeling like caged animals, surrounded everywhere by rules that say "Don't!" All too often, however, they soon learn that the rules have no "teeth"—parents and teachers alike repeatedly excuse the child. Over time, this produces in the child a disrespect for authority. The result is "out-of-control" behavior. The solution is simple to state, if sometimes difficult to execute: If you set a rule saying that a certain behavior will have a given consequence, you *must* impose that consequence following instances of that behavior. That being said, some bending of the rules can be helpful. Students who are hyperactive may perform better if allowed to get up and move about. As this example illustrates, you may decide to allow exceptions when those do not disrupt your classroom.

Keys to Effective Class Rules

A key is to make decisions about what behaviors you will accept in your classroom. Will you tolerate out-of-seat behavior by a student with ADHD, for example, that you will not allow other students to exhibit? Which presentation reinforcers (rewards) are you prepared to offer for good behavior? You need to acquire those (e.g., tokens, stars, M&M's). What consequences are you prepared to impose when rules are broken? If, to illustrate, you decide to remove children from situations they find reinforcing (e.g., hearing laughter from peers), where will you place these students? Do you have a suitable location in your classroom? Is there a spot in another room, such as a resource room, that might serve the purpose? Does your building have a time-out room? If so, what are the school's procedures for using it?

Teachers should review class rules with students at least once every school day.

Once you have made these basic decisions, you need to review your class roster. Which, if any, of your students may have difficulty understanding and/or following these rules? Students with mental retardation and specific learning disabilities, in particular, may require strategy instruction: You, a collaborating teacher, or a paraprofessional will need to teach them, explicitly and with plenty of practice opportunities, how to follow the rules. You may be aware that a particular student's family is having severe financial difficulties. Another may be a "disinterested student" or labeled a "slow learner;" He may resist your efforts to get him involved in instruction. Showing "tough love" by insisting that rules be followed despite the fact that you are aware of the student's problems may be your best way of helping him. This requires planning.

Class Rules and Discipline

Class rules are a key to effective discipline (see "Discipline," p. 343). Curwin and Mendler (2001) urged teachers to work with their students to create, together, *clear and unambiguous rules.* When students participate in writing these rules, they gain ownership over those rules and are much less likely to resist or ignore them. Rules should be stated in behavioral terms, e.g., "Trash is promptly placed into wastebaskets." Good rules tell students what to do (not just what *not* to do). These rules must be paired, said Curwin and Mendler, with *consequences.* In fact, they wrote, "Practically speaking, rules are far less important than consequences for a program to be successful" (Curwin & Mendler, 2001, p. 22). It must be clear to everyone, teacher and student, what will happen if a particular rule is broken. A progression of consequences makes sense, from simply restating the rule ("Shane, you know trash goes into the wastebasket") through restating the consequence ("Shane, if that trash is not immediately put where it belongs, the rule says you will stay after class to clean this room") to enforcing the consequence ("Shane, you will remain after class tomorrow to clean up. Advise your parents to pick you up no earlier than 5 p.m. tomorrow") to invoking the second-level consequence ("Shane, because of your repeated violations of this rule, I am calling your parents here for a meeting").

BEHAVIOR MODIFICATION

Special educators have learned to rely heavily on **behavior modification** techniques. The term usually refers to strategies and tactics teachers use in whole-class instruction. When used in a one-on-one situation, these approaches are called applied behavior analysis (ABA; see Chapter 7). The latter is a subset of the former.

To introduce behavior modification, recall that we all work for presentation reinforcements: pay, praise, recognition by our peers, the satisfaction of a job well done or of a mystery solved. Children are motivated by many of the same desires (Jensen, 1998). Conceptually, then, behavior modification is not artificial. No less than parents or bosses, teachers should offer children opportunities to earn what they will work to get: praise, social recognition, and pay (in the form of free time, tokens, etc.). The difference in the classroom is that behavior modification tells teachers to tie those rewards *explicitly and consistently* to displays by students of desired behavior. The approach emphasizes that long-lasting changes in behavior occur when students learn to self-motivate. That is, they move from relying on teacher praise and other external reinforcers to depending upon self-administration of rewards.

Some children and youth may appear to be unmotivated. This may be because of past failure. Behavior modification theory teaches that motivation depends both upon content beliefs ("I can learn this stuff") and context beliefs ("The strategies that I have acquired will work in this class, with this teacher"). When held, such beliefs activate intrinsic motivations. Students may not hold one or both tenets, in which case they may not put forth maximum effort in the classroom (Ford, 1992).

To continue in our introduction to behavior modification, consider the issue of punishment. We all seek to escape punishment. Levine (2002) went so far as to say that students strive the whole school day to avoid humiliation. For these reasons, teachers should strive to avoid punishing children whenever other options are available. Behavior modification theory stresses that teachers should *ignore* behavior they wish to extinguish, rather than punishing it. This can be easier said than done! Sometimes, inappropriate behavior cannot be ignored. As a rule, however, you should try ignoring misbehavior before you resort to punishment. In particular, you should not "punish the victim" for occasional breaches of classroom rules (Kerr & Nelson, 1998; Zirpoli & Melloy, 2001).

Quiet, Unobtrusive Steps

Often, simple adjustments are all that it takes. You do not even need to know the techniques of behavior modification to achieve some positive outcomes. When you teach while standing a few feet away from a student who sits in the back because he likes to read comics and sports magazines during class, you alter his behavior. You need do little else. You do not even need to say anything to the student. The simple fact that you are standing there changes that student's behavior. The student knows you can see what is on his desk. He also knows that the other students are looking steadily in his direction, as well. This knowledge alone will act to curb surreptitious pleasure reading.

Or consider "making a deal" with a very shy student. Suppose Elaine rarely speaks up in class. She has made it very clear to you that attention is the last thing she wants. Suspecting that she fears embarassing herself, you can tell her a day or two in advance that you will be calling upon her. By giving her advance notice, you afford her time to prepare her answer. That way, when you do call upon her, she can speak with confidence.

Basics of Behavior Modification

The most important kinds of behavior modification use what B. F. Skinner (1948, 1953) called **"operant conditioning."** This works on "operations"—things under our voluntary control. In general, Skinner taught us, we do more of what we are rewarded for doing. This immediately tells a teacher that behavior modification will not be effective *until and unless you know your students quite well.* You must know what they consider to be "rewards" before you can reinforce them. In **presentation reinforcement** (also called by the less-helpful term, positive reinforcement) you give them what they want when they give you what you want. The connection between the two events is called a *contingency.* In **removal reinforcement,** you take away something they do not like. The alternative

Technologies That Work

Self-Management

By comparison to other areas in education, there is relatively little technology for behavior management. The software that is available, however, can be helpful. Notable among the commercial programs on the market are tools for self-monitoring and self-management of behavior.

One example is KidTools, from the University of Missouri. This software is free to teachers planning to use it with students who have disabilities or are at risk of school failure. The First Step KidTools program focuses upon helping young children (7 to 10 years of age), while Second Step KidTools is intended for somewhat older students (11 to 14 years of age). Both let students select types of behavior to change and tools to use, including cards, charts, and so on, for self-monitoring.

Monitoring tools are available at three levels of control: external (teacher-based), shared (teacher- and child-based), and internal (self-based). Thus, at the first level, the teacher would use the tools (cards, charts, etc.) to monitor the child's behavior. At the second level, the child assumes some self-management responsibilities, in partnership with the teacher. Finally, at the third level, the child takes responsibility.

For more information on the products and companies mentioned in the Technologies That Work box, go to the Web Links module in Chapter 9 of the Companion Website.

The emphasis throughout is upon positive behavioral supports. Thus, children learn to think of behaviors in positive terms (starting good behavior), rather than negative ones (stopping bad behavior). This can be as difficult for children as for teachers, because our society's focus upon punishment for inappropriate behavior is so pervasive. New additions to KidTools include tools for time management, study skills, and organizational skills.

Software for learning how to solve problems is marketed by Edmark. The company's "Strategy Series" teaches strategic thinking and problem-solving skills.

Programs that help students to master life skills are provided by IEP Resources. These board games, "Life Skill Game Package," are for special-education students age 10 and over. Six games cover self-control strategies, social skills, safety signs, functional words and symbols, and social skills at work.

Targeting students with traumatic brain injuries, Brain Train markets "Brain Train Volume 1: Basic Cognitive Skills (Enhanced Editions)," described as cognitive/behavioral software offering exercises in visual and verbal memory and in basic vocational skills. Also helpful with the same population are cognitive rehabilitation programs from IBM and from Life Sciences Associates.

name for this, "negative reinforcement," confuses people. They tend to forget that *all* reinforcers increase the frequency of the behaviors they follow.

Punishment acts to *decrease* the frequency of behaviors it follows. However, people often respond to punishment by displaying what psychologists call "displacement"—they find other ways to express their feelings. That is why behavior modification theory tells educators to ignore, rather than punish, inappropriate behavior. If you ignore the unwanted behavior and, when it stops, reinforce the student for appropriate in-seat behavior, you will find that this often works—and does not produce the unwanted side-effects that punishment frequently does.

You can also modify someone's behavior by removing the "trigger" for that behavior. In Skinner's terms, you manipulate the *antecedent*. If, for example, Ramon laughs loudly when you make a pun, you can stop that behavior simply by not punning. If Marcia seems to be distracted by the beach-boy good looks of Frank, you could remove the trigger by seating them well away from each other.

To teach a *new* behavior, you should reinforce it immediately and consistently. But once it has been learned, you should switch to an unpredictable schedule of reinforcement. Such a variable schedule maintains learned behavior. It is precisely because they do not know when they will win that people gamble.

What do you do if your student simply cannot produce the behavior you want to reinforce? Suppose, for example, Lara never speaks up in class. She gives you nothing to reinforce. In these kinds of situations, you can use *shaping,* or the **method of successive approximations.** The idea is to find something you *can* reinforce. After that behavior

Teacher Strategies That Work

A-B-C

A good way to approach behavior modification is to think of your A-B-C's.

A is for "antecedent" what happened *before* the student misbehaved. You can remove the antecedent and thus prevent the reoccurrence of the undesired behavior. As painful as it may be to recognize this, one frequent antecedent to acting-out behavior is ineffective teaching on your part. Enliven your instruction and the misbehavior may be diminished.

B is for the behavior that you wish to alter. As you have just seen, much behavior is under the control of antecedents. Other behavior is under the control of consequences. The key for you as a teacher in an inclusive classroom is to recognize that you can alter behavior by altering antecedents and/or consequences.

C is consequences. Strictly speaking, a consequence is whatever happens *immediately following* the behavior. If you looked at the student who misbehaved, you gave that student attention. This is a C—a consequence. The fact that you did not intend to reward the misbehavior is beside the point. Your attention reinforced it. Stop attending and you may see the behavior decline in frequency. You may use presentation reinforcers as consequences in order to increase the frequency of desired behaviors. Thus, you would say "Good job!" to a student who finally shows some understanding of a difficult topic.

appears consistently, that is, at criterion (say, 90%), you cease reinforcing it. At that point, you demand further steps before you will grant the reward. You continue in this manner until the child finally is able to give you a complete, satisfactory response. To illustrate, you might reward Lara with a smile and a "Lara knows!" comment when her eyes light up with understanding. Later, you might reinforce her for raising her hand. Eventually, you will only reinforce her when she actually speaks, and even later, only when she produces complete sentences. To continue with an example related to behavior, you might at first reinforce Matthew for sitting quietly for 1 minute, then for 2, then for 5, and so on, until reaching the goal of one complete class period.

Regardless of the specific techniques you use, the goal is to fade your involvement. You want the student to assume responsibility. When the student effectively self-monitors and self-praises, you are relieved of those responsibilities. The development of self-regulation may be an important behavioral objective.

Presentation Reinforcement

When a drama teacher offers students a chance to perform in public a play they have studied, she is holding out the prospect of public recognition for their work. That is, the drama teacher is providing a reward at the end of a long period of conscientious study and practice. The same technique helps in inclusive classrooms, as well. The key to presentation reinforcement, as the technique is known, is a little research on the teacher's part. Watch the students during free time, such as recess. They will tend to do things that they enjoy doing. Some students are social, and use the time to talk with friends. Others are restive, and use free time to play, run, and swing. Yet others are studious, and use unassigned time for recreational and (we can hope!) serious reading. You can also learn much from informal conversation with your students, or from reports you get from their parents or other teachers. All of this information gives you a vital tool: Knowledge of what this particular student is willing to work to get. In presentation reinforcement, you present opportunities to do exactly those things, as a reward for good work in the classroom.

A word of caution: The presentation reinforcer should be appropriate to the behavior. You should have a "library" of reinforcers, ranging from simple verbal praise through permission to skip a quiz to bonus points or higher grades (or even beyond that, to tickets to a local concert). Common sense tells you to begin with the smallest presentation reinforcer that will get the job done. You should reserve the larger rewards for truly significant effort. A related concern is not to over-use any presentation reinforcer. Praise, like candy, can become less motivating over time.

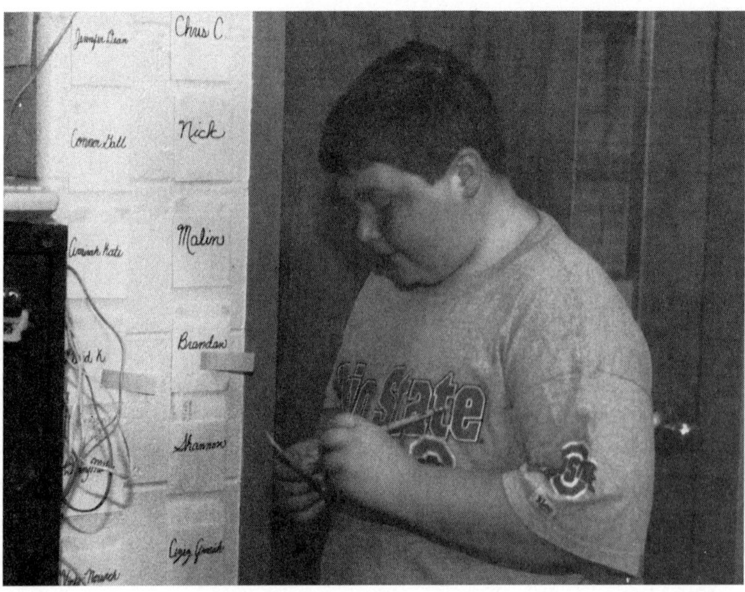

Posted stars, words of praise, and other presentation reinforcers can be highly effective.

Removal Reinforcement

When you relieve a well-performing student of the onerous burden of writing a book report, you are also practicing behavior modification. In this instance, you are using removal reinforcement. Also called by the more confusing, and less helpful, term "negative reinforcement," this technique rewards good behavior by taking away something the student will work to *avoid*. Again, the key is understanding your students. Earlier, we talked about a drama teacher and a public performance of a play. This works with students who volunteer for school plays. It may be exactly the wrong "reward" for others! Some children and youth will work to avoid being the center of attention. They don't want to be called upon in class and may even cringe if you publicly praise them. With such students, you want to find private ways to praise their work (such as a note given to them as they leave after the bell rings, or private e-mail messages). Because you did not embarrass them when they did good work, such students will tend to produce more such behavior.

Writing a Behavior Modification Plan

Teachers of inclusive classrooms often find behavior "contracts" or other written agreements to be helpful. To be effective, such contracts or plans should feature the same kinds of objective/observable and positive language that are found in instructional objectives (see "Writing Instructional Objectives," in Chapter 8). As with instructional objectives, behavioral objectives should be individualized. Your expectations will differ for Trish than for Sharlene, so the plans should differ, as well. The language used should describe the desired behavior in behavioral terms, for example, as behaviors the student will perform. The appropriate behavior should be specified in observable terms (so teacher and student can agree that they were indeed displayed). The conditions under which they will be produced must be spelled out. The level of success or accuracy needs to be written. A behavior modification plan, finally, must indicate the consequences that will attend success and failure. It should go without saying that the plan's success will depend largely upon the extent to which the teacher observes those consequences. If the student is successful, the teacher must produce the promised rewards. Equally as important, failures must be followed by the agreed-upon consequences.

To elaborate, rather than write that Ivan would receive counseling twice weekly for 30 minutes each time (which tells what professionals would do), your objectives should specify Ivan's target behaviors. Thus, "When he feels frustrated, Ivan will count silently to 10. If still frustrated, he will request permission to stand up and walk quietly around the room." Third, your decision making should reflect an understanding of the child. Just as two students who repeatedly make multiplication errors may do so for very different reasons, so, too, two young people who fight in class may have diverse motivations. You need to make some educated guesses about what is causing the problems in order to devise an appropriate intervention: You would act differently if the problem were a lack of knowledge about other ways of expressing frustration than if it were a desire to display dominance. There is a final similarity: Progress is readily and independently observed. You can count the number of times Ivan screams versus the number of times he silently paces the room. Another observer would agree with your tabulations.

Take, to illustrate, the case of a ninth-grader whose angry outbursts are to be reduced and, in time, eliminated. An effective behavior modification plan would indicate, in clear and objective language, exactly what behaviors Joshua may display when frustrated or angry. These are written in positive terms (e.g., "Joshua will raise his hand silently"). The raising of a hand is an observable behavior. Alternatively, the plan might specify that "Joshua will write in his journal the words, 'I am angry. Why am I angry? How do I think I should act now?'"). Each day, teacher and student will review the day's events (counting the number of times Joshua raised his hand and/or counting the number of times he wrote in his journal). Together, they will discuss what incidents enraged Joshua. Together, too, they will praise Joshua for following the plan. The written behavior modification plan also would note consequences for unacceptable responses to anger. Teacher and student would review those violations, as well. At the end of the week, Joshua's "score" would be tallied. He would either receive the rewards spelled out in the plan (e.g., being excused from one or more class assignments) or the consequences (perhaps an additional assignment).

Ideally, the raising of the hand and/or the writing of questions for himself should prompt Joshua to engage in critical thinking at the very time he is most tempted to act out. That itself is a positive outcome. However, thinking is not an observable behavior, for which reason it does not belong in the plan. It may, however, figure in your preparation, with the student, of the elements of that plan. An important objective of such plans typically is to help young people train themselves to pause, consider alternative reasons why something may have happened, and resist the urge to attribute adverse events to others' evil intentions. Good decision making begins with an accurate description of the problem (Franklin, 1998; Whaley, 1998).

BEYOND BEHAVIOR MODIFICATION

As important as are the techniques of behavior modification, there is more to controlling behavior and managing the classroom than is contained within the theory of behavior modification. An idea introduced earlier in Chapter 8 of teaching at the child's level has important implications for managing behavior. Teachers should also avoid gratuitous criticism of students. They should take advantage of the fact that inclusive classrooms include dozens of other potential "teachers" in the form of peers, particularly during transition periods. Teachers should keep activities brief, both to sustain attention to task and to avoid tiring and/or frustrating students. Finally, in middle school and high school, educators need to take steps to help students at risk of dropping out to remain members of the school community.

Vygotsky's "Zone of Proximal Development"

A key to classroom management is to plan instruction at a level that appeals to your students. The "Goldilocks Rule" applies: not to hard, not too easy, just right! This means teaching at what Vygotsky (1962, 1978) called the **"zone of proximal development,"** that is, the phase at which a child can master a task if provided appropriate help (Woolfolk, 2001). Vygotsky distinguished between the child's developmental level, by which he meant what the

Teacher Strategies That Work

Behavior Plans

There are several keys to an effective behavior plan.

First, the plan should be prepared by teacher and student, working together. Students are much more likely to follow a plan that they themselves helped to write. Teachers, too, need to have input into the plans. Among other things, they must give consent to the rewards that will be available to the student.

Second, the plan must specify, in objective terms, what the student will do. As with all instructional objectives, these should indicate (1) the behaviors to be exhibited, (2) the conditions or circumstances under which those behaviors will be displayed, and (3) the level or degree of accuracy that is required to meet the criterion.

Third, the plan needs to include agreed-upon consequences. Behavior-modification theory emphasizes the need to pay attention to (reward) behavior we want to see. For this reason, the plan should note the positive outcomes that will be associated with desired behavior. Usually, it is not necessary to add deleterious consequences for undesired behavior. The absence of positive outcomes generally is enough.

Fourth, there should be a time limit to the plan. For young children, plans may cover just one day, or even just a morning. In middle school and high school, plans may cover a week to six weeks.

Finally, the plan should be dated and signed by both parties.

Below is an illustration of a plan that follows these directions.

Mark's Behavior Plan

1. *Behavior Mark Will Exhibit*	Mark will set up for new activities as directed by Mrs. Askew. When Mrs. Askew signals him by removing and replacing her glasses, Mark will excuse himself from whatever he is doing and prepare the room for the next activity. Mrs. Askew will train Mark in this work.
2. *When Mark Will Do That*	Upon seeing the signal (Mrs. Askew with her glasses)
3. *How Often Mark Will Do It*	At least 80% of the time (four out of every five transition periods)
4. *Consequences*	Each day that Mark exceeds the 80% criterion for the week, he will receive five (5) Bonus Points. Those points are redeemable at week's end (2:30 p.m. Friday) as follows: 25 points = Mark is excused from doing two (2) homework assignments due the following week 20 points = Mark is excused from doing one (1) homework assignment due the following week 15 points = Mrs. Askew will buy Mark a soda and a candy bar 10 points = Mrs. Askew will buy Mark a soda 5 points = Mrs. Askew will buy Mark a candy bar

Signed: ________________ ________________

Mark Mrs. Askew

Dated: ________________ ________________

child was capable of doing without adult assistance, and the child's potential development, or what she could do with "a little help." The latter is the zone of proximal development.

Probably the most effective technique of discipline is to *teach at the student's level.* This way, the child is neither bored because the material is too easy nor frustrated because it is too hard. Curwin and Mendler (2001) highlighted this as a key, noting that student boredom is a major cause of misbehavior. We saw earlier in Chapter 8 that grouping and peer tutoring are two ways teachers can individualize instruction in an inclusive classroom, thus meeting the needs of more students and thereby reducing boredom.

We can look at Vygotsky's theories through a different lens. Piaget (1985) gave us the concept of *disequilibrium*. Children often struggle when they encounter new information. They become unsettled when they cannot readily place ideas into the mental schema they have developed. They are motivated, Piaget said, to resolve this disequilibrium. Teachers can help. You can show a child how to accommodate the new information into existing schema or, alternatively, how to change those schema or even develop new ones. Such suggestions are what Vygotsky had in mind when he talked about teachers intervening at the zone of proximal development.

The importance of all this for teachers is that the zone tells you when to step in to help a child. Vygotsky saw learning as a social endeavor, something children do with others, particularly with teachers. The key for teachers of inclusive classrooms is to *individualize instruction* by providing the help *each particular child needs,* when she needs it. Such individualization assists not only students with disabilities but others, as well. Migrant children, and children from homeless families, may have missed significant amounts of school. You need to know "where they are coming from" so that students are neither bored with too-easy work nor frustrated with too-difficult assignments.

Criticize Behavior, Not People

Experts recommend several strategies. One is to make sure that your language clearly distinguishes between the student and the behavior. You should make clear what behavior you accept and what behavior you do not accept. However, the words you use should not extend unnecessarily to the student himself or herself. Experts urge that you use sentences like "Jose, I'm delighted to see that your text is open to the right page" (which pinpoints the behavior) rather than structures like "Jose, I'm so impressed with you. You're such a great person" (which evaluates him as an individual). If you as the teacher assess the child himself, even positively, you suggest that a future evaluation may occur, as well. This may be threatening to a child. If, however, you make it clear that your assessments are strictly limited to behavior, the child may not feel as vulnerable. As was suggested earlier (see "Behavior Modification") it can be helpful to have an occasional lesson videotaped. In this way, you can monitor your actual, as opposed to your intended, observance of recommended techniques, including those that tell you to criticize behavior rather than people.

A related point: Avoid sarcasm. When you are sarcastic, there is an underlying hostility to your tone and to your words. Students may respond to that hostility by acting out, because they take offense at the sarcasm, viewing it as disguised criticism. Some students, especially younger ones and many who have mental retardation, will not understand the sarcasm. They will take your words at face value—completely misunderstanding your message.

Give the Student a Choice

Particularly with a student who has an emotional/behavioral disorder, it is critical that you never corner the student, leaving her with no options. Rather, your approach should always leave open the opportunity to make *some* choice. One way to do this is commonly referred to as "major option, minor option" or sometimes "major choice, minor choice." The behavior that you insist upon is the "major" option or choice. There is no negotiating on that behavior. However, the specific *way* in which the student complies, or the "minor" option or choice, can be left up to the student. For example, you might demand that a student complete a long-overdue essay on ethical choices. The student may opt to write that by hand or may write it on a computer. Or you may allow the student to decide whether to use a black or a blue pen to illustrate the essay. Those kinds of minor choices can help by defusing tension. The student can maintain her dignity by not acceding completely to your demands.

The Appeal of Short, Relevant Activities

Shorter rather than longer is a good rule to follow in controlling classroom behavior. Parents and educators know that young children have brief attention spans. Teachers may not recognize, however, that some older students also need relatively brief assignments and activities. This is particularly true of many who have E/B disorders or ADHD. These students tend to do much better if required to sustain attention for rather short periods of time. Researchers suggest that teachers consider abbreviating lessons, offering more short ones, breaking up into smaller sessions any lengthy test you administer National Center on Educational Outcomes, *http://www.education.umn.edu/NCEO.*

Granting permission to students to "be up and about" rather than sitting for long stretches may have the effect of "shortening" the perceived duration of an activity. As we saw earlier in Chapters 4 and 5, it is often appropriate for a teacher of an inclusive classroom to permit students with E/B disorders or ADHD to engage in physical activity. When you decide to grant such permission, you need to explain to the whole class that "Jeremiah has my approval to walk about—just ignore him when he does."

Similarly, activities that are perceived by students as being relevant to their out-of-school lives may seem "shorter" and more appealing than are those that strike the students

Research That Works

Positive Behavior Supports

The evidence that positive behavior supports, including teacher praise, works is impressive. Reviewing the research, Austin (2003) reached two major conclusions. First, he wrote, support for popular zero-tolerance policies is limited. In fact, Austin found studies suggesting that such rules may actually discriminate against students from minority groups as well as those with emotional or behavioral disorders. Austin decried "the knee-jerk response of school boards and school district administrators" (p. 3) to adopt zero-tolerance policies despite research showing that "programs that emphasize punishment, control, and containment are ineffective in preventing school violence and may even perpetuate such antisocial behaviors" (p. 6). Second, Austin discovered, the most effective practices were

> (a) the effective use of functional behavioral analysis and behavior intervention plans, (b) screening for risk factors, (c) teaching acceptance of diversity, (d) self-esteem building and social skills training, (e) conflict resolution through peer mediation, (f) the importance of family and community involvement, and (g) the classroom as community (pp. 8–9).

Building student self-esteem is a key component of positive behavior supports.

A good example of positive behavior supports is training based on the "think aloud" strategy. This approach has teachers and other adults talking as they mull over problems and make decisions. The theory behind it is the social learning theory of Albert Bandura (1977). Bandura showed that children engage in observational learning. That is, students can learn new behaviors by watching others perform those behaviors. The effectiveness of think-aloud tactics was shown in a summer camp for boys exhibiting aggressive behavior (Camp, Blom, Herbert, & Van Doornick, 1977). The boys were highly impulsive (acting without thinking). At the camp, they saw models being taught by adults how to think aloud, after which the models demonstrated that behavior and then were rewarded for doing so.

Another example of positive supports is school-to-life links that students find to be relevant. For many teens, school-to-work connections are particularly "relevant" (Hughes, Bailey, & Mechur, 2001). School-to-work programs characteristically involve brief visits to work sites and job shadowing, followed by paid or unpaid work experience that is linked to school instruction. Research summarized in the Hughes et al. report makes clear that student participation in school-to-work programs can reduce drop-out rates and increase college enrollment rates. It can also accelerate the development of maturity in young people. The benefits seem to be due to the fact that school-to-work programs offer learning in context ("situated learning" or *in situ* instruction). As we saw earlier in Chapter 8, such experiences have a "real-world" flavor that appeals to many teenagers. This kind of learning also reduces the burden on students of generalizing what they learn in one setting to another setting.

For more information on the Hughes, Bailey, and Merchur report, go to the Web Links module in Chapter 9 of the Companion Website.

as being irrelevant to the "real world." This is one reason why community-based instruction can be so effective, even when other methods of teaching are not (see Chapter 8). Even students with severe E/B disorders or ADHD can sustain appropriate behavior for long periods of time when their interest is piqued and the value of what they are learning is evident to them.

Controlling "Transition Time"

Further planning is required to eliminate as much "dead time" as you can. Research shows that students who are susceptible to acting out may be particularly tempted during "transition periods," or between the time that a teacher announces the end of one activity and before she declares the beginning of another one (Curwin & Mendler, 2001). With careful preparation, you can all but eradicate such periods. You can assign specific tasks, such as clean-up, to individual students, while you tell other students to prepare the area for the new activity. It is best not to trust your "spontaneous" decision making for such assignments. Rather, advance preparation is more likely to produce good results. Suppose, to illustrate, that Mohammed is particularly susceptible to acting out during unstructured time. You might plan to say, immediately before announcing the end of a class activity, "Mohammed, it's now time for you to place the crayons and paints back in their places!"

Preventing Delinquency and Dropping Out

Particularly in middle school and high school, part of the job of a teacher of an inclusive classroom is not simply to manage behavior in the classroom but more broadly to increase student involvement in, and connection to, the school itself. Elsewhere, we discuss methods of doing so, notably increasing the perceived relevance of instruction and the recruitment of peers to reach out to students who may be at risk of dropping out (see Chapters 5 and 11). To supplement such steps, you should reach out to community agencies. In particular, community mental-health agencies and state vocational-rehabilitation agencies have

Resources That Work

Classroom Management

Managing behavior and controlling the classroom challenge many teachers. They often ask professors for help. Here are some texts that working teachers have found to be particularly useful.

Zirpoli and Melloy's (2001) *Behavior Management: Applications for Teachers* takes a practical approach that many teachers value. The book describes problems that are common in today's classrooms and then offers tried-and-true strategies for solving them. A bit more theoretical in orientation, but still quite helpful, is Kerr and Nelson's (1998) *Strategies for Managing Behavior Problems in the Classroom.* This text shows how research in different fields of psychology, including psychotherapy as well as behavior modification, can be applied by classroom teachers.

Also useful is an article by Maag (2001). Recognizing that teachers often resist the entreaties of counselors and other professionals to employ the techniques of behavior modification, specifically to ignore rather than punish misbehavior, Maag quotes teachers' objections and, one by one, demolishes them. In particular, Maag shows, punishment often is ineffective. Not only does it not work, but it causes other problems, as students displace their still-smoldering emotions in other ways. Much better, Maag insists, is to ignore unacceptable behavior until it ceases. At that moment, teachers should praise the onset of acceptable behavior.

For problems related to discipline, many teachers have found Curwin and Mendler's (2001) *Discipline with Dignity* to be valuable. This text "cuts to the chase" to show how teachers can impose discipline without at the same time humiliating students. Many of their suggestions were reported in Chapter 5, where methods of teaching students with emotional/behavioral disorders were discussed. An issue of *Focus on Exceptional Children,* "Disciplining Students with Disabilities," concisely summarizes the legal and many of the procedural issues associated with discipline (Yell, Rozalski, & Drasgow, 2001).

staff members who are willing to visit schools to meet with and plan activities for students. Community resources can help you to prevent delinquency and to reduce dropping out by students with disabilities.

Delinquency is behavior that violates community norms and laws. Teachers can reduce delinquency in several ways. First, because delinquent behavior most often occurs in the after-school hours, they can offer meaningful in-school extracurricular activities. Giving young people reasons to stay off the streets is reason enough for schools to sponsor, and teachers to lead, after-school programs. For some students, particularly those with E/B disorders who are "school-phobic," after-school activities that are housed in *other* facilities may be even more appealing. This is one way in which community agencies can help. Young people who would resist in-school extracurricular activities, perhaps because they fear that their peers will think they are in detention, may welcome the very same activities in a non-school setting.

Curtailing and eventually preventing delinquent behavior was a long-time focus of researcher Hill Walker, of the University of Oregon. Walker found that praise by teachers for appropriate behavior and non-attention by teachers for inappropriate behavior are effective—especially when begun during the elementary school years (e.g., Sprague & Walker, 2000; Walker, 2000). The idea is to alter the child's behavior. Once children habitually display appropriate behavior, the next step involves teacher monitoring and occasional teacher intervention to help the child to maintain the behavior. This second phase is too often overlooked. Yet it is essential if students are to continue to display appropriate behavior as they move into new classrooms, work with new teachers, and encounter new temptations. After interviewing 277 young people who had been identified during their K–12 years as having specific learning disabilities or emotional disturbances, Scanlon and Mellard (2002) concurred, urging teachers to monitor student attendance and other behavior so as to identify those who may be engaging, or are at risk of engaging, in delinquent activities and who are at risk of dropping out of school.

A key component of such monitoring and as-needed intervention is to make good use of community agencies (Forness, Kavale, & Lopez, 1993). Teachers may turn to such resources in a time of crisis. However, connecting with non-school on a regular and routine basis may be more helpful. Teachers need to establish personal ties to community agency staff members. This involves identifying key professionals, visiting the agency, and remaining in touch via phone and e-mail. Each time teachers refer a student to the agency, it is essential that teachers monitor the student's use of the community resource. This may seem obvious. However, evidence presented at a U.S. Department of Health and Human Services conference (2001) indicates that teachers and community-agency staff rarely communicate. In fact, teachers seldom learn whether or not the student even kept the initial appointment, let alone returned for follow-up visits.

Community agencies can also help you to curtail dropping out. A major purpose of the new federal law, No Child Left Behind (P.L. 107-110), is to reduce drop-out rates. Those rates are highest among students with E/B disorders. They are also high among those with specific learning disabilities. (Students with other conditions drop out of school about as frequently as do non-disabled students.) The consequences of high drop-out rates can be disastrous. The U.S. Department of Education's *Twenty-First Annual Report to Congress* (1999c) reported, in its Section II module on incarcerated students, that large numbers of young people with E/B or SLD conditions have been jailed for breaking the law. In many instances, those violations followed long periods of being unable to secure gainful employment. A high-school diploma, after all, is a minimum requirement for most jobs. Unable to earn a living, many young people turn to a life of crime. One-Stop Career Centers can help. These are state, county, and local job-training agencies that have offices co-located in the same buildings, so as to be more convenient for clients. Many services at these centers are free. Importantly, all convey a central message: "Stay in school!" At such centers, young people will learn, from non-school authorities, that it is in their own best interest to secure a high-school diploma.

DISCIPLINE

Let us begin by making an observation that should prove to be comforting: The techniques that research has documented as being effective with students having disabilities are the *same* as those that have been shown to work with most students. There are some exceptions, which we will discuss below.

Discipline: The Basics

In their review of discipline issues, Yell, Rozalski and Drasgow (2001) correctly noted that "discipline involves more than just using procedures to control student misbehavior. It also is a means to teach students about the effects of their behavior on others and to help them learn to control and manage their own behavior" (p. 1). Research over many years gives teachers very specific, proven-effective techniques for managing a classroom and helping students to control their own behavior.

Other educators disagree. Discipline is inevitably a topic of controversy. My own beliefs and biases will be clear in what follows. I encourage you to read widely and to reflect upon your classroom experiences, so that you may draw your own informed conclusions.

These suggestions are sound for teachers of inclusive classrooms. Students with disabilities may need to be taught the rules more slowly, more frequently, and more explicitly than may some other students. They may require practice to be able to follow the rules consistently. However, it is important, wrote Curwin and Mendler (2001), that the same rules apply to students with and without disabilities. Because some previous teachers may have been overly accepting of misbehavior by some students, Curwin and Mendler recommended that teachers of inclusive classrooms recognize that, for them, discipline may be both challenging and draining. Accordingly, they suggested that teachers develop a support system for themselves, notably including other teachers who understand these demands and can help other teachers to meet them.

Controversies in Discipline

There are two general approaches to discipline in PreK–12 schools (Curwin & Mendler, 2001). We can call them the zero-tolerance and positive-supports models.

Zero Tolerance

The first approach, which gets by far the bulk of the publicity, is the **"zero-tolerance"** model. Featured in federal laws and rules such as the Safe and Drug-Free Schools program, the Gun-Free Schools Act, and similar edicts from Washington, zero-tolerance policies call for automatic penalties, up to and including expulsion from public education, for students discovered to be violating school rules about drugs, alcohol, and weapons. The emphasis is upon punishment that is swift and sure. As of 1996–1997 (the latest year for which data were available), 79% of PreK–12 schools had instituted zero-tolerance policies on violence, 91% had such rules in force for weapons of any kind, and 94% had such procedures in place for firearms (National Center for Education Statistics, 2001b).

According to the same source, states reported expelling 6,000 students that year for violating firearms rules. To place that number into context, bear in mind that the schools enrolled that year 46 million elementary and secondary students, thus, one student per 10,000 was expelled for gun violations that school year. The vast majority of PreK–12 students obey school rules the vast majority of the time.

For more information on government reports on school safety and school crime, go to the Web Links module in Chapter 9 of the Companion Website.

Positive Supports

The second approach, which is emphasized in *Discipline with Dignity* and which is also prominently featured in the Individuals with Disabilities Education Act (IDEA), looks to reinforce students for displaying good behavior. In other words, it tells teachers to "find children doing something right" and to reward them for that (Kauffman, 2001; Maag, 2001). This is combined with efforts to teach children acceptable behaviors, including suitable ways to respond to feelings of frustration and anger. These strategies are complemented by whole-school interventions that seek to minimize the number of incidents, before they even occur. The overall approach, which we will call the **"positive-supports model,"** is founded upon solid research showing that people in general, including students with disabilities, work for praise and other rewards, that when children misbehave in the classroom it is often because they *lack the skills* required to display more acceptable behaviors, and that preventive measures reduce temptations for and occurrences of misbehavior (Curwin & Mendler, 2001).

Discipline and Students with Disabilities

In general terms (there are exceptions), administrators and general educators are more comfortable with zero-tolerance approaches while special educators favor positive-supports techniques (Curwin & Mendler, 2001; Kauffman, 2001). Evidence of the effectiveness of zero-tolerance policies tends to be lacking, but evidence for positive-supports approaches is very broad and very deep (Forness, Kavale, & Lopez, 1993; U.S. Department of Health and Human Services, 2001). In a testimony presented to the U.S. House of Representatives, Skiba (2002, p. 1) concluded that "we currently have no evidence that suspension and expulsion make a positive contribution to school safety or have improved student behavior; they may in fact have significant unintended negative consequences for students and school climate."

With respect to inclusion, another important point to bear in mind is that zero-tolerance strategies may result in (unintentional) discrimination on the basis of disability. Students with mental retardation may simply not know how to behave in certain circumstances, such as when they are teased. Children and youth with E/B conditions, and some with AD/HD as well, may not be capable of controlling their behavior to the extent expected by school administrators. To suspend or expel such students after an episode or several, then, would be to remove them from an education on the basis of disability. That would be discrimination. Thus, the 1997 IDEA Amendments (PL 105-17) firmly rejected zero tolerance in favor of positive supports.

The positive-supports model is depicted in Table 9.1. Based upon an illustration in "Prevention Research & the IDEA Discipline Provisions: A Guide for School Administrators" (U.S. Department of Education, Office of Special Education Programs, 2000), it depicts preventive measures applicable to all students (bottom of the figure), general interventions useable with non-disabled children who are at risk for misbehavior, and in-

Teacher Strategies That Work

Discipline

As a teacher in an inclusive classroom, your most effective tool for classroom management is to provide an interesting, fast-moving environment in which students are able to learn in their own ways and at their own pace. In other words, individualizing instruction is a key to effective discipline.

Another key: posting and reviewing for a few moments, every day, the classroom rules that you and your students have agreed to follow.

A third: do what you say and say what you do. You must enforce classroom rules. Consequences must be effected, or they quickly become meaningless.

A fourth: explicitly teach students, as needed, how to follow rules and how to resist temptations. In many cases, students misbehave because they lack strategies for behaving in ways you find acceptable.

A fifth: minimize transition time. Be prepared with activities for students to do when one lesson ends and the next has not yet begun.

TABLE 9.1 Continuum of Effective Behavior Support

Level of Prevention	Targets	Interventions
Tertiary prevention	Students with chronic/intense problem behavior	Individualized interventions
Secondary prevention	At-risk students	Group interventions (classroom)
Primary prevention	All students	School-wide interventions

Source: From "Prevention Research & the IDEA Discipline Provisions: A Guide for School Administrators," U.S. Department of Education, Office of Special Education Programs. Retrieved March 26, 2004, from *http://www.ed.gov/offices/OSERS/OSEP/Products/adminbeh.web.pdf*

tensive measures suitable for use with students who persist in misbehavior. Primary prevention steps are intended to create a school climate where the rules are clear and where opportunities to break them are small in number. The idea is to stop problems before they occur. Secondary prevention works at the small-group level. It concentrates upon the relatively few students in any given school who are, for one reason or another, at risk for misbehavior. Members of this group typically have a history of misbehavior, usually minor. Finally, tertiary prevention is performed at the individual-student level. It is used with students who continue to act out despite primary- and secondary-prevention measures. Tertiary prevention measures are custom-designed for each student.

Discipline and IDEA

Discipline is one of the most controversial issues in inclusion and in special education. The controversy arose, in large part, because of language added to IDEA in 1997 (PL 105-17). Section 612 of IDEA, as amended in 1997, dealt with "State eligibility" (how a State becomes eligible for federal financial assistance under the Act). Section 612(a)(1) reads:

> Free appropriate public education—(A) in general—A free appropriate public education is available to all children with disabilities residing in the State between the ages of 3 and 21, inclusive, including children with disabilities who have been suspended or expelled from school.

This provision granted rights to children with disabilities that are *not* enjoyed by children who have no disabilities. The language means that even if a school expels a child with a disability, the State must educate that child, until the child either (a) is graduated from high school or (b) ages out at age 22. Recall that students with no disabilities and their families are left to fend for themselves after being expelled from a local school. Parents often enroll these students in private schools, at family expense. By contrast, under IDEA, students with disabilities were given the right to continue to receive a free appropriate public education at some school, somewhere, at state expense.

This section of IDEA excited much comment because it represented the first time a federal law ever extended to children with disabilities rights and privileges that clearly are beyond those granted under law to children with no disabilities. It was also controversial because it seems to fly in the face of the popular practice of "zero tolerance." What Congress intended was to recognize that expulsion of students with behavior problems may relieve pressure on teachers and schools but does nothing to help society at large: It "dumps" on the streets young people who qualify for few well-paying jobs (because they lack a high-school diploma). This argument could apply, as well, to many non-disabled students.

When Removal from School Is Permitted. School officials may remove a child (suspension, expulsion) for up to 10 school days, even if the parents object. Removal for more than 10 school days, however, is a "change in placement" and as such may only be made by the IEP Team. Parents must be notified, in writing and in advance, of any proposed change. They may challenge the school district, through mediation or due process (see Chapter 2). IDEA's "stay put" provision (section 615[j]) applies. That requirement says that the child remains in school, usually in the current placement, while the dispute is pursued.

If the IEP does not include a behavior management plan (e.g., specific procedures for using behavior modification), then the team must add one to the IEP. If the IEP does have such a plan, the team must review it and, if necessary, revise it (section 614[d][2][B]). In some cases, the child may be educated in an **interim alternative placement,** which may be a youth detention facility or even a jail or prison.

Exception for Weapons/Drugs. If a child with a disability brings to school a weapon or drugs, the school may remove the child for as many as 45 days. Notice the difference from "up from 10 school days" in the event of lesser offense. The "stay put" provision (section 615[j]) does *not* apply in incidences involving weapons/drugs. In general, education must be provided during the 45 days. This may include, if the IEP team so decides, instruction about weapons and/or drugs so as to prevent re-occurrence.

If the school officials believe that allowing the child to return after 45 days may be dangerous to the child or to others, they may ask an impartial hearing officer to extend the removal for another 45 days. That extension may be extended again, and again. However, the obligation of the State to educate remains (section 612[a][1]).

ROBERT: A TRUE STORY

A teacher related this story:

Last year, I worked as a teacher assistant in an inclusive classroom. Five classified students were integrated with 15 non-disabled young adolescents in this classroom. One was Robert.

Robert's problems at first seemed to be minor. He would begin seatwork by requesting permission to sharpen a pencil. Often, the pencil-sharpening took quite a while. I would tell him to resume his seat. Within a minute, Robert would stand up, saying that the pencil was broken. Or he would say that his eraser didn't work. At other times, Robert would begin seatwork assignments by saying that he had to go to the bathroom. Sometimes he would stand up, requesting permission to go to his locker because he had left his book there. I should have recognized all of these as variations on a theme. These were avoidance behaviors. For whatever reason, Robert didn't want to do the assigned work.

After a while, this behavior caught up with Robert. His grades suffered. Meanwhile, the constant complaining and classroom disruption had "turned off" his classmates. Robert became increasingly unpopular as the months went by. Even during recess periods, I could see how Robert's behavior was upsetting his peers. He would join a group for a game, only to demand that the rules be changed. If the others did not agree, Robert would invent an excuse and stomp off.

By mid-year, the combination of academic and personal problems were too much for the school to ignore. An IEP team meeting was called in January. The decision was made then to transfer Robert to a separate school, one that specialized in teaching students with emotional and behavioral disorders. As part of the transition process, I visited the school. There, I met with the school's director. She told me that young people like Robert frequently are underachievers in school, argumentative, and lacking in friends. "How do we make friends?" she asked me rhetorically. "We talk to people, we smile, we listen. Kids like Robert don't do those things."

Mrs. Osborne gave me an unforgettable parting message: Time is running out for Robert. Within just a few years, he will need to work. Unless he changes his behavior patterns, Robert will continually invent excuses for not doing his assigned work. He won't get along with co-workers. Likely, he will resist authority (the boss). What Robert needs, sooner rather than later, is a stiff dose of tough love. "To teach students like Robert, you first have to reach them," Mrs. Osborne said. The job of her school, she said, is to reach them. Then, hopefully, they can return to district, ready to learn.

—Rebecca

Functional Behavioral Assessments

Under IDEA, an initial step in meting out discipline for students with disabilities who break school rules is to conduct a functional behavioral assessment. As McLoughlin and Lewis (2001) explained in their text, *Assessing Students with Special Needs,* this is less of an undertaking than the rather forbidding name may suggest. A **functional behavioral assessment** is an informal examination of the child's needs and of possible supports to meet those needs. That is, it seeks to answer the questions: Why does the child behave as he does? Under which circumstances is his behavior particularly unsuitable? Under which does the child behave appropriately? By answering these questions, the team learns about antecedents and reinforcers that influence this student's behavior (see "Behavior Modification," p. 332). That information leads to the development of a plan to manage the behavior. Functional behavioral assessments came into use because special educators wanted to know why some students persisted in apparently inexplicable and even self-injurious behavior (Larson & Maag, 1998). Some children and youth with autism, for example, hit their heads hard enough and often enough to cause brain injuries. They bit their own arms. Because these students were non-speaking and largely non-communicative in other ways as well, educators were baffled. Behaviorists recommended that teachers focus upon the "function" that such behavior served for the individual. Self-injurious behavior, for example, may serve the function of getting the student excused from an onerous task. It may also give the student much-wanted attention from others.

While such extreme behaviors are not likely to occur in inclusive classrooms, the functional analysis approach may still be helpful. The key is planning. You should not act spontaneously, in the heat of the moment, because the motivations of your students may not be apparent until later, when you are removed from the situation and able to reflect. Rather, you should ask yourself, "What function does fighting serve for this student?" (Larson & Maag, 1998). If you assume, as did Larson and Maag, that all behavior is purposeful, then it follows that behavior you find unacceptable in the classroom must be serving some purpose for the student. This may be a good purpose (to stop others from teasing, to receive attention) but the behavior is not a good way to achieve it. By asking questions about the apparent intent of a behavior, you will be able to identify the purpose(s) it serves for the student. Then, you can offer alternative and far more acceptable ways for the student to achieve the same ends. By teaching the student these other ways of behaving, you can reduce or even eliminate much inappropriate behavior in your classroom.

All this implies that the key to a functional behavioral assessment is to seek insight into why a particular student behaves as he does. For example, fighting with Keyshawn might get Joey excused from cleaning up, which is doing something he hates. In this instance, the function was to get him out of a situation. Once you understand the behavior's function, you can approach the misbehavior much more effectively. You could, for example, plan to tell Joey that the interrupted work is due before he goes home in the afternoon. At the same time, you could teach Joey more appropriate ways of dealing with frustration. You could tell him, for example, that if an assignment upsets him, he should ask for assistance. These instructions lead naturally to behavioral objectives, for example, "Joey will raise his hand to request teacher assistance when he feels frustrated by a test or assignment."

Resources That Work

Discipline

The OSEP Center on Positive Behavioral Interventions and Supports (PBIS)

Behavioral Research and Training
5262 University of Oregon
Eugene, OR 97403-5262
http://www.pbis.org

PBIS specializes in giving schools capacity-building information and technical assistance in carrying out positive-supports strategies and tactics.

Center for Effective Collaboration and Practice (CECP)
1000 Thomas Jefferson Street, NW
Washington, DC 20007
http://www.air-dc.org/cecp

CECP focuses on children at risk of serious misbehavior and/or emotional disturbance. It links schools to resources about effective practices with such students.

IDEA Practices
http://www.ideapractices.org

IDEA Practices features links to federal and university sources of information about, among many other things, discipline and positive-supports techniques.

U.S. Department of Education
http://www.ed.gov/about/offices/list/OSERS/OSEP

The federal agency responsible for special education.

A Guide for Teachers

The Center for the Study and Prevention of Violence (2000), has issued a Planning Guide for schools to use in preventing and also in responding to violence in the schools. The Center recommended the creation of a Social Support Team comprised of at least three non-school professionals (who have ties to the community, yet maintain some distance from, and thus some objectivity about, the school) as well as school officials. This team would receive referrals from teachers, parents, and students. Those referrals would express concern that certain students were engaging in, or threatening to engage in, violent behavior. The team would evaluate these referrals and make recommendations for intervention.

Student Strategies That Work

Self-Advocacy

Particularly in middle school and high school, students need to learn and practice self-advocacy skills. This takes time and effort. Critical is understanding one's own self: strengths, weaknesses, needs, and resources. Students need to know what they can do without assistance, or with little outside help (strengths). They also need to recognize when and where they require support (weaknesses). On any tasks that they require a little or a lot of help from others, they must understand what it is that they need in order to be successful. Finally, it can be very beneficial for students to know, as well, what solutions are available and, among those, which they prefer. If you think about all of this, you will recognize that many adults have not mastered all of these elements that underlie effective self-advocacy. That should help you to appreciate the fact that it can and will challenge your students (Milthaug, 1998).

Students with disabilities in elementary, middle, and high schools benefit greatly from the requirement in federal laws, notably the IDEA and section 504, that professionals advocate on their behalf. Those laws do not require such third-party advocacy in the post–high-school years, however. Whether they go from school to work, to college, or to living in the community, young adults with disabilities will be required, as soon as they are graduated from or age out from high school, to advocate for themselves. That is why IDEA encourages IEP teams to invite students to take part in IEP meetings beginning as early as age 14. The law recognizes that young people need both training and experience in order to become effective self-advocates. Over time, they must learn how to set realistic goals, appreciate what is required for them to reach those goals, and learn how to be assertive in seeking the services and opportunities required Martin et al., 2001).

A good way to begin such instruction is for teachers to prepare students for their first IEP team meetings. By age 14, most students have matured sufficiently to understand the fact that decisions must be made and that if they do not speak up, others will make those decisions. Essential is understanding the political process, in this case, how an IEP team functions (who the key members are, what roles they play, etc.). Each year, the student should become more comfortable with the IEP team process and more competent in identifying her needs and in making the case for services and opportunities.

There are many ways in which students can develop, practice, and master self-advocacy skills. Seemingly small steps, from making a book report in class to role playing how historical characters made tough decisions to helping an after-school club decide what to do, all help students to develop the capacity to advocate for themselves. Critical is the ability to be assertive without being aggressive. Learning to be assertive without being aggressive is one part of such preparation. So, too, is learning how to communicate clearly, logically, and convincingly. This may happen in English classes. Learning the art of negotiation is also part of this work. Much of that kind of training can be provided in Social Studies units and classes.

CHAPTER SUMMARY

General

- Teaching strategies for inclusive classrooms come in two kinds: ways to help children learn and ways to control children's behavior.
- Teaching at a level where students are "ready to learn" (that is, in Vygotsky's "zone of proximal development") is a very effective way of controlling behavior in the classroom. Doing this in an inclusive classroom can be difficult. That is why inclusion teachers need to use a full range of strategies, from whole-class to small-group to one-on-one methods.

Behavior Modification

- Teaching children *how to learn* and *how to control their own behavior* are excellent uses of time in inclusive classrooms. That is because once students master these techniques, you and they are freed to focus upon academic content.
- Many behavior-modification tactics can be used in whole-class and small-group settings; these steps are not limited only to one-on-one instruction.
- "Removal reinforcement" is a better term than "negative reinforcement" because it clearly indicates that teachers take away something the student dislikes, thus increasing the likelihood of the student repeating desired behaviors.

Beyond Behavior Modification

- Vygotsky's "zone of proximal development" tells us to teach at the level where the child is ready to learn. Doing so is a highly effective tool for managing children's behavior.
- By criticizing behavior, rather than students, you avoid humiliating children. You also make it easier for children to act on your criticism in a positive manner.
- By offering hands-on, physically active, and community-based activities, at least occasionally, you can reduce acting-out behavior in your classroom.
- You should consult with school counselors and with community agencies for help in reducing delinquency and in preventing students from dropping out.

Discipline

- The key to successful discipline is to make following the rules rewarding for students. Research suggests that you "catch children doing something right" and reinforce them for that behavior. Educators call this the "positive supports" model of discipline.
- Zero tolerance may not be appropriate for students who either do not know what to do or who are unable, because of their disabilities, to consistently perform at expected levels of behavior.

QUESTIONS FOR REFLECTION

1. Why is it so important for you to model *your thinking* as well as your behavior?
2. How can a school counselor help you as a teacher?
3. If you must criticize, why should you criticize behavior rather than the person?
4. In what ways might a student assist you in changing another student's behavior?
5. How can you use "antecedent" control to manage a student's behavior?
6. What is "shaping" and how can you apply it to help a student master a difficult new behavior?
7. How could you use removal reinforcement to get a shy student to participate actively in class discussion?
8. Why do so many teachers persist in using punishment, despite overwhelming evidence against it?
9. What are the keys to effective school-wide and classroom discipline?
10. Why is instruction in self-advocacy so important for many students with disabilities?

Chapter 10 Assessment in the Classroom

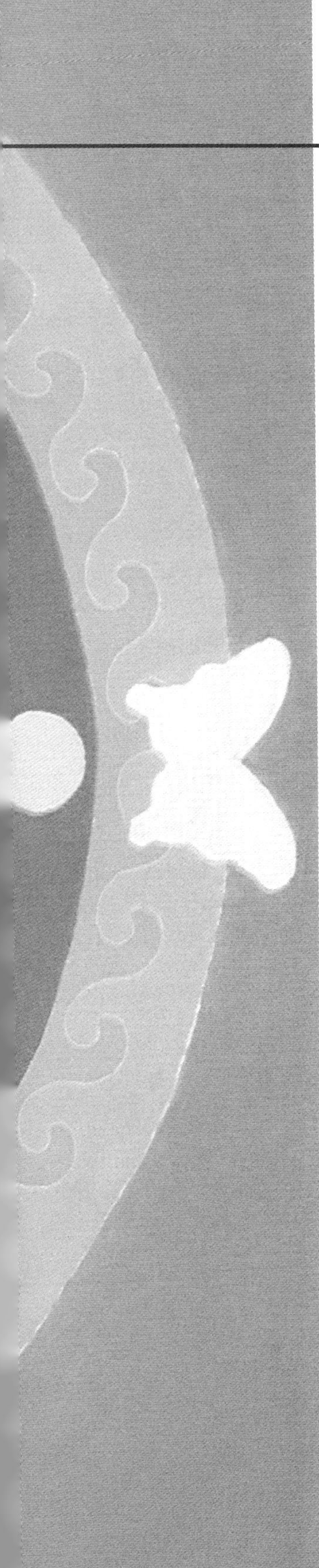

TERMS

assessment
observation
transdisciplinary play-based assessment
formative assessment
summative assessment
harassment
curriculum-based assessment (CBA)
curriculum-based measurement (CBM)
standardized tests
error analysis
task analysis
student self-assessment
rubric
authentic assessment
portfolios
high-stakes tests
accommodations
alternate assessments

CHAPTER FOCUS QUESTIONS

After reading this chapter, you should be able to answer such questions as:

1. What can you learn from observing students in an inclusive classroom?
2. What is curriculum-based assessment?
3. How can you use error analysis to improve your teacher-made tests?
4. What is authentic assessment and why can it help with students having severe disabilities?
5. What issues surround high-stakes testing of students with disabilities?
6. How do you determine whether or not to make test accommodations for students with disabilities?
7. How can you track a student's progress toward her IEP goals?

PERSONAL ACCOUNTS

Joelene, a fourth-grade special-education teacher working in an inclusive classroom, shared her experiences working with Karen, a more senior general educator:

> *The students with learning disabilities needed modified spelling tests. Karen [the general educator] disagreed, so we compromised one week. I gave half the words for the week and she gave the other half. Needless to say, they failed that week's spelling test, missing all of her words but few of mine. All I did was to speak clearly, repeat as often as needed, and allow more time for the test.*
>
> *Somehow, Karen got the idea that inclusion means that she can present lessons, give assignments, and make up tests just like she does with all her other students, but that if she* grades *the special-needs students differently, she's doing her job. Meanwhile, she doesn't even think she has to tell them about this modified grading system: She gives them the same point system ditto that everyone receives. Don't get me wrong: Karen is an effective teacher. But the students with special needs have auditory processing difficulties, so they are lost a lot of the time. As far as my "push-in" services in her classroom are concerned, I basically sit there*

> *and look pretty. She does not allow me any cooperative teaching. Rather, she does the teaching herself.*
>
> —Joelene

Meredith, a fifth-grade teacher shared this story, reminding me of the "Tale of Two Schools" section in Chapter 1:

> *My first year, when I was teaching fifth grade, the decision was made in central administration that almost all of the children in the self-contained class were ready for inclusion—with support. The teacher of the self-contained class and the psychologist felt that two of the eight students were still at risk if placed into an inclusion class. But once the ball got rolling, the "higher ups" decided that all eight should be included, because "how can we keep only two kids in a self-contained class?" Therefore, all eight came to us, four in each room. Eloise, the girl who was assigned to me, had an IQ of 58. The year before, her teacher believed that she had reached a plateau academically and would never learn much more. So there she sat, in a room full of high-functioning fifth graders. More often than not, she could not tell you what* day *it was. She could occasionally master simple, kindergarten math computations. She was, and still is, a wonderfully sweet young lady who is a pleasure to have in class. However, even a highly modified fifth-grade curriculum was completely out of her grasp. Last I heard, Eloise is now in seventh grade—and still doesn't know the months of the year.*
>
> —Meredith

These personal accounts illustrate issues we will consider in this chapter. Joelene's story illustrates a common misconception. It is far more important to provide modifications in instruction and in test administration than it is to adjust grading. If teachers of inclusive classrooms adapt their instruction so that all students learn, grading adjustments should not be required. Similarly, if teachers offer whatever test accommodations students with disabilities need so that the assessments fairly measure their knowledge, no alteration in grades should be necessary. The second story shows that assessments may be conducted inappropriately. In the instance recounted by Meredith, school officials used irrelevant criteria ("How can we keep only two kids in a self-contained class?") rather than suitable ones ("Is Eloise appropriately placed in this setting?") to make important educational decisions. The student paid a steep price for their failure to use assessment information to make sound placement choices.

INTRODUCTION

This chapter examines a wide range of assessment issues, including observations, portfolios, teacher-made tests, standardized and high-stakes testing, test accommodations, computer-based assessments, and grading. Finally, we discuss how teachers monitor and report progress that students with disabilities make toward their IEP goals. This range of topics reflects the many ways in which teachers of inclusive classrooms use assessments. First, recall that we saw earlier, in Chapter 2, how teachers serve as members of Individualized Education Program (IEP) teams that evaluate eligibility for services. The Individuals with Disabilities Education Act (IDEA) uses the term *evaluation* to refer to such eligibility determinations. We will use that word in this chapter for much the same purpose. Evaluation is the making of judgments about data. The word *assessment,* which is our focus in this chapter, refers to measurements of educational progress. Teachers of inclusive classrooms use assessments in several ways. First, they construct and administer teacher-made tests. Second, they help to administer state-wide and district-wide assessments. Third and finally, teachers of students with disabilities need to collect and report information that will assist IEP teams in assessing students' "adequate yearly progress" (AYP) toward IEP goals.

We open this chapter by exploring the many challenges of assessment with young children having disabilities. Testing young children can be problematic, for which reason observation is particularly important with children under age 9. The chapter then examines the role of assessment in IEPs. We then return to observation, this time to look at the role it can play for teachers of inclusive classrooms. Later, the chapter discusses teacher-made tests, most of which are curriculum-based rather than criterion-based instruments. That is, these tests are drawn from what the teacher covers in class. Test results compare students in that class to one another. Standardized tests, including state-wide and district-wide assessments, are then discussed. Typically, results on standardized tests compare students with large numbers of students in other classes, schools, and even states. The chapter continues by covering accommodations in assessments. It also reviews alternate assessments. (Issues related to testing English language learners [ELL] will be taken up in Chapter 11.)

This chapter concludes with three other topics: computer-based assessments, grading issues, and tracking student progress toward IEP goals. Increasingly, computers are being used to give both teacher-made and standardized tests. Grading is a sensitive issue in inclusive classrooms. As a teacher, you will be called upon to make decisions about what you will assess and how you will grade it, including whether you will use different criteria with students having disabilities than with those not having disabilities. Finally, an important role of teachers of inclusive classrooms is to document, on behalf of the IEP Team, how well a student is doing with respect to the goals set forth in his or her IEP. At the end of the chapter, we pick up on the "sample IEP" that was presented in Chapter 2. Figure 10.4, "Tracking Progress toward IEP Goals," shows how assessment is used to monitor student achievement during one school year.

ASSESSMENT

Assessment is the gathering of information to make decisions (McLoughlin & Lewis, 2001; Pierangelo & Giuliani, 2002; Salvia & Ysseldyke, 1998). Assessment includes measurement, evaluation, and grading. *Measurement* is the phase of assessment in which numbers are assigned. *Evaluation* is the making of judgments about those numbers. *Grading* is the conversion of those evaluations into symbols to communicate with students, families, and educators. Figure 10.1, "Assessment to Grading," illustrates the relationship between assessment, measurement, evaluation, and grading.

FIGURE 10.1 Assessment to Grading

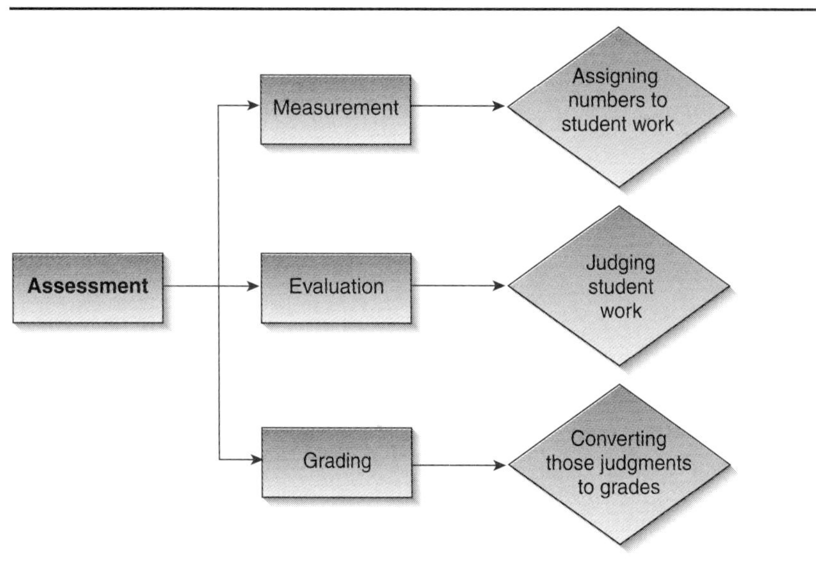

One-way mirrors permit unobtrusive observations to be performed.

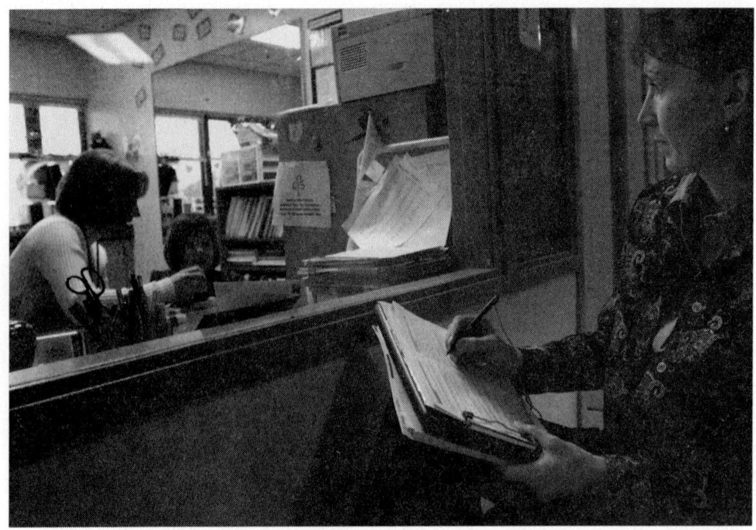

Suppose, to illustrate, that you gave a 20-item test of student knowledge of quadratic equations to Yolanda. Measurement tells you that Yolanda's score on your 20-item test is 14 correct responses. Deciding that 14 is a "good" score is evaluation. Translating it into a "B" is grading (Tanner, 2001). In this example, a test was administered. While educators typically think of tests when the word "assessment" is used, tests are only one kind of assessment. In fact, observation may be even more valuable for teachers. Below, we will discuss different kinds of assessments, including formative and summative assessment, observations, and tests, both teacher-made and published.

Assessment and Young Children

Before discussing formal assessments, such as major tests, which are often used with older elementary students as well as with middle-school and high-school students, we need to explore the challenges of assessment with young children. Early childhood special education covers the span from birth through age 8 (Bowe, 2000a, 2004).

With very young children (those under age 3), the principal means of assessment is **observation.** Trained observers, including teachers, speech/language pathologists, occupational and physical therapists, and others carefully observe the child. Family members, too, are asked to observe the child at home. This emphasis upon observation is by necessity. There are relatively few structured instruments, including tests, that may be used with infants and toddlers who have disabilities. Even standardized instruments designed for use with this population rely heavily upon reports from observations. Examples include the Bayley Scales of Infant Development, the Battelle Developmental Inventory, and the Kaufman Assessment Battery for Children. These instruments are described in Pierangelo and Giuliani's 2002 text on assessment in special education.

With preschool-age children (3 to 5 years of age, inclusive) having disabilities, another key principle is that observations and other assessments be conducted on multiple occasions and in different environments. Young children often behave differently at home than they do in a school or clinic. They display some behaviors when they are with family members that they do not show when they are with professionals, and vice versa. For these and other reasons, it is critical that decisions be based upon repeated measures that draw upon children's behavior in a variety of settings (Bowe, 2004). Linder (1993) has advanced a related procedure, **transdisciplinary play-based assessment.** In this approach, family members and professionals engage the young child in play. The method has several advantages. First, it is naturally collaborative in nature, allowing professionals from several fields to participate in assessment. Second, it features significant roles for parents and other family members. Transdisciplinary play-based assessment is an example of curriculum-based assessment (which we will discuss later in the chapter) because what is observed and measured is the child's emerging mastery of skills that are taught as part of the early childhood special education curriculum.

Children in kindergarten and the primary grades may be tested informally. Generally, teacher-made tests are used. Under the 2001 federal law, No Child Left Behind, standardized testing is to begin in third grade, effective with the 2005–2006 school year. The assessments are in the areas of math and reading. Beginning with the 2006–2007 school year, science tests will be added. These assessments are in addition to fourth- and eighth-grade tests given as part of the National Assessment of Educational Progress (NAEP). With third- and fourth-graders, particularly, test results should be interpreted in context. Not all children that young perform at optimal levels in highly structured settings. In addition, children aged 8, 9, and 10 vary greatly in development, much more so than do older children. Thus, some will respond well to the demands of formal assessments, but others will not. These facts argue for repeated measures (testing the child on different occasions) and for supplementing the assessments with teacher reports, observations, and other measures.

A good introduction to the many issues surrounding assessment with young children having disabilities is offered by Bondurant-Utz's (2002) *Practical Guide to Assessing Infants and Preschoolers with Special Needs.*

Assessments in IEPs

As you will recall, Chapter 2 outlined how educators prepare individualized education programs (IEPs). Essential to this work is assessment. First, IEP teams must determine the eligibility of each child believed to be a "child with a disability" as defined in IDEA. As we have seen in Chapters 3 to 7, assessments are vital in making those eligibility decisions, which the law refers to as evaluation. For example, students who are believed to have mental retardation are given individually administered tests of intelligence. They are also observed and their family members, past teachers, and other adults who know them complete rating scales. This information is brought together in making the eligibility decision.

Each child's IEP must also discuss how assessment of educational progress will be performed. This includes a description of test modifications that will be used with the student. In that section of the plan, the IEP team notes its consensus about whether any modifications or adaptations in testing will be provided in district-wide and state-wide assessments. If no modifications or adaptations are described in the IEP, *none may be offered.* Later in the plan, the IEP team describes the extent, if any, to which the student will not participate with children having no disabilities in district-wide and state-wide assessments. The presumption is that all students with disabilities will take such tests. If the IEP Team determines that the child will not participate in a particular assessment, or part of such an assessment, the IEP must contain a statement of why that assessment is not appropriate for the child—*and* how the child will be assessed (e.g., by means of alternate assessments). If, on the other hand, the student will take part in scheduled assessments, but requires changes in the way they are given, those individual modifications in the administration of assessments must be described in the student's IEP. Because large-scale assessments often take place in the spring, which is also the period in which IEPs typically are prepared, the opportunity exists for the IEP team to make decisions about participation in assessments and about test accommodations on a timely basis (i.e., shortly before the assessments are given; Shriner & DeStefano, 2003).

Teachers may provide adjustments as needed in teacher-made tests, even if the IEP is silent about district-wide and state-wide assessments. The requirement that accommodations for assessments be specified in the IEP applies only to large-scale assessments.

All IEPs of students aged 14 or older must include a statement of transition service needs. Assessment is necessary to outline those needs and assessment is necessary to identify appropriate services to meet them. Some students will participate in advanced-placement courses. Others will take part in a vocational education program. Finally, each student's IEP must offer a statement of how the child's progress toward annual goals will be measured and how the student's family members will be informed of that progress.

After the IEP is completed, a placement team (which may be the IEP Team) makes the placement decision. The chapter-opening "Personal Account" from Meredith illustrates an instance in which assessment information was disregarded in deciding upon placement, with dire consequences for a student. Instead of basing the placement decision upon Eloise's unique needs, which is what the law requires, the school based it upon other factors (administrative convenience).

Formative and Summative Assessments

Experts speak of formative assessment and summative assessment. According to Tanner (2001), in **formative assessment** "[I]t is primarily the instruction that we wish to make judgments about" (p. 36). Educators use results of pretests, reports from students, and their own observations to determine whether instruction is paced appropriately. That is, they will apply the "Goldilocks test"—not too fast, not too slow, but just right. They will decide to assign more, or less, or different homework based upon such findings. They may also discover that they need to re-teach particular concepts or operations. Students, too, may use information from such assessments to refocus their efforts so as to improve their learning. Thus, formative assessment is assessment of *process.*

Summative assessment, by contrast, looks at the *products* of instruction. It answers the question: "Did the students master the material?" and, by implication, "Did the teacher teach it?" Summative assessments occur as the final phase of a learning program, such as the end of a marking period or a school year. Typically, neither educators nor students apply results from summative assessments to alter current behavior. Rather, they use these outcomes as indicators of achievement. Generally, the results of summative assessment are used for communication about student performance (e.g., grades) and, often, teacher performance as well. However, they can, and appropriately may, be used to alter *next year's* instruction.

Students and teachers tend to pay much more attention to summative than to formative assessment. Ironically, formative assessment is actually more valuable to teachers and students than summative assessment. That is because formative assessment is done *during instruction,* so its results are applicable in the classroom. Teachers can, and should, use outcomes from formative assessments to change what they teach and how they teach. Students, similarly, can benefit more from the guidance they receive from formative assessment than they usually do from end-of-course grades. That is particularly the case with respect to diagnostic tests, which pinpoint the specific areas in which students need to improve.

Observation

A great deal of very useful information that will assist teachers in making decisions can be gathered by observation. By observing the child in the classroom, during recess, at lunch, and so on, teachers may accumulate a wealth of knowledge about a child's development. In fact, educators may acquire more information about a broader range of behavior by observation than by any other means of assessment.

Preparing to Observe

A good use of planning time is to set up observations. You may ask collaborating teachers, paraprofessionals, and volunteers to perform observations that will complement your own. What to observe depends upon who your students are and how they are doing. To illustrate, occasionally students with specific learning disabilities "give up" too easily. If you have such students in your inclusive classroom, you might want to watch closely to see if this occurs, not only during tests but also during lectures and class activities. Few tests, if any, get at such in-classroom behaviors. Observations, however, are a rich source of data. Sample observation report forms that you, collaborating teachers, paraprofes-

FIGURE 10.2 Observation Recording Form

Student ______________________ Date ______________

Reason for Observation ______________________________

Observer ______________________

Setting ______________________

Activity ______________________

Start Time __________ End Time __________

Observation Codes:

+ = on task

− = off task

P = inappropriate physical contact with other student

N = inappropriate noise

O = out-of-seat

Notes:

Below is a sample form, offered for illustrative purposes. Notice that 7 "observation periods" (which may be 5 min, 10 min, etc., in duration) are available for each school day. You would enter the codes above, as appropriate, to indicate observed behavior during the observation periods.

M	T	W	R	F
1				
2				
3				
4				
5				
6				
7				

sionals, and volunteers can use are offered in McLoughlin and Lewis (2001), Overton (2000), and Venn (2000). One appears in Figure 10.2. Commented McLoughlin and Lewis,

> Teachers are continually watching and listening to their students. They may not call this procedure observation, but by taking note of what their students say and do, teachers are conducting simple observations. When a potential problem is discovered during casual observation, more systematic observational procedures can be begun. Although observational techniques are often associated with the study of classroom conduct problems, they are just as appropriate for the study of academic, social, self-help, and vocational skills. Because observation involves the examination of student behaviors within the context of the natural environment, it produces information that often cannot be obtained from any other type of assessment procedure. (p. 111)

Systematic Observation

When important decisions are to be made on the basis of observations, more than one person should observe a student's behavior. You should select, or design, the instrument

Teachers can learn a lot about individual student strengths and weaknesses by observing during class activities.

co-teachers, paraprofessionals, and others will use (see Figure 10.2). Then you must train them in the use of this instrument. Interobserver reliability—that is, the agreement between different observers—becomes an issue if the reports from those observers diverge significantly in their ratings. In such instances, you should re-examine the forms, re-train the observers, and postpone decisions about the student until you have acceptable interobserver reliability (Venn, 2000).

Particularly helpful is the kind of systematic observation that is part of behavior modification (Overton, 2000). This is rigorous observation. Trained observers note on specially designed records exactly what a child does. Separate entries can be made as often as every 30 seconds. The data are then graphed to illustrate how the student's behavior changes over time. If, for example, a teacher wishes to reduce out-of-seat behavior, trained observers first would watch the student over a period of time, say a week, to establish "baseline behavior" (that is, the student's behavior prior to the onset of intervention). The teacher would then start to reinforce engaged, in-seat behavior and to ignore out-of-seat behavior. The observers would track how the student's behavior changed under these new conditions. Later, after the student has demonstrated consistent in-seat behavior, the teacher would switch to a program of intermittent and random reinforcement. Again, trained observers would document the extent to which the student was able to maintain in-seat behavior after that change. While the mechanics of such systematic observation are beyond the scope of this text, you may wish to look at texts on assessment for illustrations of forms observers could use for these purposes and for examples of how data are collected and reported (e.g., McLoughlin & Lewis, 2001; Overton, 2000; Tanner, 2001).

Observing and Assessing Small-Group Activity

Assessing student work in groups has become important, with inquiry learning and other group activities assuming prominence in reform curricula. This is best done through observation. You should develop a checklist for this purpose. Include on it such items as whether the group sustains its attention on germane topics, whether participants respect and support each other, and whether the group generates original solutions to problems. You should note both positive and negative behaviors. Evaluation comes later (Alleman & Brophy, 1999). Your intent with this observation form is to record information, not evaluate it. *Grading* students on group performance raises some difficult questions that we will explore in detail later (see "Grading," p. 376).

Observing and Reporting Harassment

Teasing of children and youth with disabilities by their non-disabled peers is a frequent concern of families (Palmer, Fuller, Arora, & Nelson, 2001). Such worries are so common that they deserve your attention. Defining clearly what teasing behaviors you consider to be unacceptable, and training adults in your classroom on recognizing these and responding appropriately to them, are both important. The U.S. Department of Education has referred to such teasing as "**harassment** on the basis of disability." The Department issued guidance for educators on July 25, 2000 (Cantu & Heumann, 2000; Reminder: Harassment Based on Disability is Wrong, Illegal *http://www.ed.gov/PressReleases/07-2000/0726_2.html*). This "Dear Colleague" letter included the statement by the directors of the Department's Office for Civil Rights (OCR) and Office for Special Education and Rehabilitative Services (OSERS): "We take these concerns very seriously (Cantu & Heumann, 2000, p. 1). It offered these examples of unacceptable behavior:

- Several students continually remark out loud to other students during class that a student is "retarded" or "deaf and dumb" and does not belong in the class. As a result, the harassed student has difficulty doing work in class and her grades decline.
- A student repeatedly places classroom furniture or other objects in the path of classmates who use wheelchairs, impeding the classmates' ability to enter the classroom.
- Students continually taunt or belittle a student with mental retardation by mocking and intimidating him so he does not participate in class. (pp. 3–4)

The Department's guidance noted that harassment on the basis of disability is parallel to harassment on the basis of race, origin, religion, or gender. It should be reported in the same way, to the same authorities. The only effective way of doing this is to observe—and to act on the basis of what you see. You should consult your building principal for details about local reporting procedures.

Other students may also be harassed. As we will see in Chapter 11, migrant children, children from homeless families, students who are gay or lesbian, and many who are teen mothers may be teased. Educators must be alert to these possibilities and immediately stop such harassment.

As a teacher of an inclusive classroom, it is your responsibility to *model* appropriate behavior. It is not enough for you to forestall and prevent inappropriate student behavior, nor is it sufficient for you to report instances of harassment. Rather, your example must be a positive one. The ways in which you address students with disabilities and the ways in which you talk about them send powerful signals to your students. They may not seem to attend to you all day, but you may be very sure that they notice your behaviors and your choice of language.

Curriculum-Based Assessment

Teacher-made instruments are of obvious appeal to educators because they are developed by classroom teachers specifically to assess knowledge of what is taught in the classroom. Another advantage of teacher-made assessments is that they can be performed *during* instruction. That is, they do not have to be separate activities, divorced from other things that happen in a classroom. Teacher-made assessments should be *frequent,* occurring twice or more weekly, so that the feedback you get from them may be put to use immediately to improve instruction (McLoughlin and Lewis, 2001). These kinds of assessments are often referred to as **curriculum-based assessment (CBA)** because they are based upon the curriculum as you follow it in your classroom.

Curriculum-Based Measurement

Curriculum-based measurement (CBM) is a subset of CBA. Some authorities use the term CBM to refer to *repeated* measures of student achievement within the curriculum. Whatever the words used, these techniques are powerful because they lead to changes in *teacher* behavior (Jones, Wilson, & Bhojwani, 1997). That is, educators alter the ways they teach, the materials they use, the pace of instruction, and much else, based, in large part, upon such assessments.

A few examples may help. The teacher may ask each child to read aloud for one minute. The educator records the number and type of errors made by each student. Those records tell the educator what to teach. This kind of diagnostic use of curriculum-based measurement illustrates a great strength—teachers learn not merely how well a student does overall but specifically where that student has difficulty. Even in a large class, such an assessment of all 30 students can be completed in 30 minutes.

Pop quizzes, too, can be curriculum-based assessments. Some experts suggest that if you use pop quizzes, the scores should *not* count toward student grades. Your interest is in assessing student progress so that you know what to teach. For example, Tanner (2001) commented, "'Pop quizzes' can probably be effective diagnostic and formative tools, but using them to grade learners makes little sense because they are typically administered when the students are still in the process of learning the material." (p. 36)

In CBA, data are gathered about student progress toward both short-term objectives and long-term goals. Recall that each student's IEP must not only state objectives and goals but must also indicate how progress toward them will be measured. This legal obligation is part of what drives special educators' use of CBA. They also use it to help them understand what children know, what they are learning, and what they are having difficulty with, so that lessons may be planned. Thus, CBA measures what is happening *while it is happening*. That is why CBA is one kind of formative assessment. CBA, then, is *ongoing*. It gives students and teachers alike regular feedback. CBA is founded upon the curriculum actually being followed in the classroom, for which reason Overton (2000) suggested that it could also be called *direct measurement*. Despite the fact that it can be used for short-term purposes (e.g., learning over the course of a week or a marking period), CBA is also tied to student long-term goals. In this way, CBA helps teachers to make sure that students are progressing toward the goals established for them in their IEPs.

Fuchs and Fuchs (1986) reported that CBA is highly effective. Other researchers have concurred (e.g., Shin, Deno, & Espin, 2000). CBA is particularly useful, the Fuchs found, if teachers did not make changes in curriculum, materials, or methods on the basis of judgment alone, but rather made them only after examining, and analyzing, objective data showing student achievement. In order to inform teaching, information should be collected before, during, and after lesson units. You need to have a baseline, or "starting point" (to know what your students don't know), then a "mid-course measure" (to see if you should change things), and an ending point (to satisfy yourself that they did learn the material). Because such numbers can be difficult to interpret when presented in raw form, Fuchs and Fuchs suggested that teachers *graph* the data. McLoughlin and Lewis (2001) concurred that only by graphing student data can teachers reliably track progress toward goals. Overton (2000) offered examples of how CBM data may be graphed.

Margaret King-Sears, at Johns Hopkins University, has been concerned that assessment differentiate between different kinds of students in an inclusive classroom (e.g., King-Sears, 1997). The "HALO" acronym captures this: Teachers should desegregate (that is, separate the scores and averages) according to *H*igh achievers, *A*verage students, *L*ow achievers, and *O*thers, including students with disabilities. Only if all four groups are showing satisfactory progress should teachers of inclusive classrooms conclude that learning has occurred.

Criterion-Referenced v. Norm-Referenced Assessments

Another term frequently used to refer to CBA/teacher-made assessments is "*criterion-referenced tests*"—tests that relate to (are "referenced" to) learning objectives ("criteria"). Teacher-made criterion-referenced tests, then, are assessments based upon the curriculum followed by the teacher. The teacher may prepare a 20-item test of long division, deciding that 16 (80%) or more correct answers constitutes a satisfactory score. By contrast, norm-referenced tests are tied to standards established by large numbers of students. The National Assessment & Educational Progress is an example of a norm-referenced test. What constitutes a satisfactory score depends on how the "norming group" did on the test. Thus, it is not the number of items correct that matters so much as how the student's performance compares to that of other students, e.g:, better than 80% of students in the norming group.

Resources That Work

Assessment

General

Assessment in Special Education: A Practical Approach (Pierangelo & Giuliani, 2002) is a good primer for teachers of inclusive classrooms. The book opens with a review of basic concepts in measurement (validity, reliability, etc.). It then explores how IEP teams use assessment. Individual chapters explore assessment of behavior, of achievement, of intelligence, of perceptual abilities, and of language. An appendix lists tests and offers addresses for test publishers. A second text of this kind, *Assessment in Special Education: An Applied Approach* (Overton, 2000), is also helpful. It covers much the same ground.

Self-Study Guides

The National Center on Educational Outcomes, at the University of Minnesota, offers self-study guides that help educators to plan and document student participation in high-stakes tests, plan and report accommodations made in such assessments, and plan and record alternate assessments. The fill-in blanks in the different guides provide step-by-step checklists for teachers to follow. The self-study guides are posted at *http://education.umn.edu/NCEO*.

State-Wide and District-Wide Assessments

Information about how your state is carrying out the requirements that all children in grades three–eight be tested in math and English and, beginning in 2006–2007, science as well, pursuant to the federal law No Child Left Behind Act of 2001 is available at *http://www.ccsso.org* (Council of Chief State School Officers; select "State Education Agencies" at the menu, which offers a direct link to each state's Web site). IDEA requires that students with disabilities participate in such required assessments. It also requires that such tests be non-discriminatory. Rules about test fairness are outlined by the U.S. Department of Education's Office for Civil Rights (OCR; 2000) in *The Use of Tests as Part of High-Stakes Decision-Making for Students* (*http://www.ed.gov/offices/OCR*).

Additional information on state accountability measures is offered at the Web sites of the Education Commission of the States (*http://www.ecs.org*), the National Conference of State Legislatures (*http://www.ncsl.org*), and the National Center on Educational Outcomes (*http://education.umn.edu/NCEO*).

Tests

Tests that teachers of inclusive classrooms may use are listed in *Tests in Print* and in *Mental Measurements Yearbook* (Impara & Plake, 1998), *Tests* (Maddox, 1997), *Special Educator's Complete Guide to 109 Diagnostic Tests* (Pierangelo & Giuliani, 1998), and other resources.

Standardized diagnostic instruments probably are of most interest to inclusion teachers. Chapter 7 of the Overton (2000) text and several chapters of the Pierangelo and Giuliani (1998) text offer helpful discussions of standardized tests. Both books identify tests you may use, explain what each test does, and discuss how to administer and score them.

Accommodations

Information about possible test accommodations is offered at the NCEO Web site (*http://education/umn.edu/NCEO*). You will find there an "online accommodations bibliography" that lets you enter a type of accommodation and learn what research relates to that accommodation. Adjustments for students with specific learning disabilities are described at *http://www.ldonline.org/ld_indepth* (LD Online). For more on research about test accommodations, see *http://www.aera.net* (the American Educational Research Association; Division D of AERA focuses upon measurement and methodology while Division H concentrates on evaluation).

Special Issues

Assessment of speech, language, and hearing is addressed in. Plante and Beeson's (1999) *Communication and Communication Disorders.* Morrison's (1995) *DSM-IV Made Easy: The Clinician's Guide to Diagnosis,* explains how to apply the American Psychiatric Association's criteria for such disabilities as pervasive developmental disorders and autism, attention deficit disorders and attention deficit hyperactivity disorders, and different kinds of emotional and behavioral disorders.

All norm-referenced tests have standardized procedures to be followed (Pierangelo & Giuliani, 2002). **Standardized tests** are formal evaluations with rules governing administration, timing, materials, scoring, and interpretation of results. They are widely used in making eligibility decisions (e.g., tests of intelligence, tests of perceptual ability). They are also used in public schools to measure achievement, as with the National Assessment of Educational Progress (*http://nces.ed.gov/nationsreportcard/*).

It is not necessary to be a psychologist to give most standardized tests. It *is* necessary, however, that you prepare carefully before doing so. Take the time to really understand each test you select or are assigned to proctor. You should become familiar enough with the materials that you can quickly and smoothly administer the test. The time you devote to this will pay dividends—and will help you if and when family members ask what the scores mean.

Teachers sometimes feel that norm-referenced tests are "better" or "preferable" as compared to criterion-referenced tests. That is only true, however, if norm-referenced tests are valid for use with the students you teach. At times, norm-referenced tests may not have been normed on populations that include sizeable numbers of students with disabilities. Thus, when norm-referenced tests are scored by comparing individual student results to the norm population, it is not clear what the "norm" (reference) is or should be for students with disabilities. In most cases, there *is* no norming group against which you can assess the scores of students with disabilities. (There is one notable exception to this: The Stanford Achievement Test—Hearing Impaired Version [SAT-HI]. This standardized test was normed on a population of students who were deaf or hard of hearing.)

Examples of norm-referenced tests include the Test of Early Reading Ability—2 (TERA-2), the Slosson Oral Reading Test—Revised (SORT-R), the Woodcock Reading Mastery Tests—Revised (WMRT-R), the KeyMath—Revised (KeyMath-R), and the Diagnostic Mathematics Inventory/Mathematics System (DMI/MS). Information about these tests is offered in Pierangelo and Giuliani (1998) and in Venn (2000).

Other Teacher-Made Assessments

A rich variety of options allows teachers of inclusive classrooms to assess student progress. Experts recommend a range of "error analysis" procedures, including some applicable to the teaching of English and language arts, some useful in math, and some helpful in other areas. Teachers may also require students to make and submit journal entries and other self-evaluations. Many teacher-designed assessments may be authentic, giving them an advantage over standardized tests (see "Authentic Assessment"). This includes performance assessments. Portfolios, too, may be authentic if well-planned and well-designed.

Teacher Strategies That Work

Curriculum-Based Assessment

Suppose you planned to teach a unit on Shakespeare's play *Hamlet.* How could you use CBA to make your teaching more effective?

You might begin a few days before actually starting the unit by giving your students a short quiz. That quiz would ask them if they have read or seen any Shakespearean plays. It might ask questions about how things were done in England and Europe in the late 1500s and early 1600s (How did people travel? How did they communicate at a distance? How much education did most people receive?). It might include a question about how students believe that people "learn their calling" or decide which careers make sense for them. It also might have an item asking students if they believe that suicide is ever an acceptable option and, if so, under what circumstances. Student answers to these questions will help you to target your teaching. You might decide, to illustrate, that you need to teach some history and geography before launching the unit on *Hamlet.*

Hamlet is a lengthy play, with many scenes in several acts. You may wish to test your students after each act, or even after some scenes. Again, your goal is to enhance your instruction by satisfying yourself that you may indeed move forward or by alerting you to the need to re-teach some ideas or to have students act out a scene.

You may do much of this ongoing assessment less formally, simply by asking questions and listening to your students' answers. And you may require students to keep logs, or journals (discussed later in the chapter), in which they write their thoughts and feelings as they study the play. You would learn from reading those journal entries which students misunderstood which words or events in the play and also which if any students were becoming upset about the play. That knowledge should shape your instruction. Student journals may not seem to be examples of CBA but they are, if you use them to help you to assess student progress through the curriculum.

Finally, you would give an end-of-unit examination. This would be an example of summative evaluation, because you would use it for grading and reporting purposes rather than for instruction purposes.

You should demonstrate cultural sensitivity and cultural competence in any teacher-made assessment. This means avoiding questions that unfairly discriminate against some students (e.g., those from low-socioeconomic status families). Test items containing fictional names should feature a variety of names that reflect cultural diversity (i.e., some "Jose" and "Jamal" and some "Tom" and "Margaret." It is particularly important that you take into consideration subjects that slow learners consider to be of high interest. Thus, if you make up a math test, you might include some items about sports, dancing, or whatever else especially interests your students. Consider scheduling teacher-made tests for morning rather than afternoon hours. Students with chaotic homes lives are likely to be less tired in the morning (Rafferty, 1999).

Error Analysis and Task Analysis

Error analysis, as the name suggests, is assessment by the teacher of the *kinds* of mistakes students make. The approach goes well beyond grading student work. It looks not at how a child or youth did overall but rather at where that student had difficulty. That is, error analysis looks for patterns in classwork and homework (Overton, 2000). One example is "miscue analysis" (Goodman, Goodman, & Hood, 1989), which examines the kinds and number of errors students make as they read aloud. We will discuss miscue analysis in our chapter on English and Language Arts (Chapter 14). A second illustration, this one having to do with math, is "error pattern analysis" (Venn, 2000). The educator examines student work to determine whether the child used the correct algorithm (e.g., did the child subtract in a subtraction problem?), the correct mechanics (e.g., did the child carry and/or regroup appropriately?), and the like.

A third variation is **task analysis.** In this application, teachers break down a task or behavior into its component parts. A key to task analysis is that the teacher recognizes, consciously, what skills and knowledge students require before they can perform a given task (Overton, 2000). One sub-task is then taught to mastery, after which a second sub-task is introduced. The two are then taught together until the student masters this two-step procedure. The teacher continues in this way for however many sub-tasks or steps are required. The major use of task analysis, then, is for *instructional* purposes rather than for assessment. The teacher endeavors to identify precisely where (in which subtask) a student has difficulty, so that the teacher knows exactly what to teach. However, task analysis can also be used in assessment. McLoughlin and Lewis (2001) offered suggestions, notably the use of criterion-referenced assessments for each subtask step that concerns the teacher. For example, a third-grade teacher might work backwards from writing skills that third-graders are expected to know until the task analysis identifies the component skills and knowledge a particular student does not yet possess. The tactic may be especially useful with migrant or homeless children who have erratic school-attendance patterns. It is vital for you to know exactly what these students do or do not know. You should then teach the key skills and knowledge to those students.

Teacher-student conferences are a *very* important component of any error analysis (Venn, 2000). By asking the student to "talk me through what you're doing," the educator can learn why the student is making the errors. The teacher can then point out the nature of the error. That should be followed by teacher modeling of the appropriate way to perform the task. Students should be asked to practice using that approach. Re-testing can then establish that the lesson was learned. Educators should periodically and unexpectedly re-test over a period of time to be sure that the new way of doing the task has indeed been mastered.

Journals. As we will see in Chapter 15, journal entries can be very revealing, especially to teachers of science. Teachers require students to produce journal entries following each experiment or field trip. By reading those entries, educators can tell if students are learning the necessary information. Journals lend themselves to science education because such instruction tends to be inquiry-based and thus unpredictable in scope and breadth. If 25 students do 25 different experiments, any educator would be hard-pressed to design a test

Teacher Strategies That Work

Outline for Journal Entries

- Descriptive Title (briefly identifies the entry, distinguishing it from other entries)
- Executive Summary (3 or 4 sentences in length, this section of the report gives a concise version of all significant information. In other words, someone who didn't have time to read the full report, but did read the executive summary, would learn virtually everything of interest)
- Question/Hypothesis (what question did you seek to answer? If an experiment, what was your hypothesis?)
- Resources/Reading (what literature did you read/what other resources did you use as background?)
- Materials/Supplies (what did you use in your project?)
- Procedures (what did you do, in order?)
- Findings/Data (what did you find out?)
- Interpretation (what does it mean? How does it relate to Resources/Reading, above?)
- Personal Reactions (did you enjoy this activity? Why or why not? If you did it again, would you do anything differently? If so, what? What is a logical next step to continue to investigate this topic area?)

that assessed their learning. Well-designed journal entries—each completed pursuant to teacher-set specifications—are, however, ideally suited to document such learning.

What should those specifications include? As illustrated in the box above, "Teacher Strategies That Work: Outline for Journal Entries," the format and content of journal entries will vary depending upon what the student is describing. In general, however, if you want children and youth to include the kinds of information that appears in that sidebar, you must tell them that, in advance.

Student Self-Assessment

Journal entries, as well as other student-generated reactions and comments, together comprise **student self-assessment.** The tactic may be used, as well, with portfolios. Whether students write reaction papers after reading stories, comment on their own revisions as they re-work writing samples, articulate their reasoning after completing a math problem, and so on, their observations can offer valuable insights that teachers can benefit from again and again (Venn, 2000). Particularly in an inclusive classroom, where some students with disabilities may feel isolated and/or overwhelmed, you should take advantage of every opportunity you get to "get into the minds" of your students. Venn provided this short list of good questions students might answer about their own writing:

What do I like best about this writing sample?

What was most important to me when I wrote this?

If I wrote this over again, what would I change?

Is this like my other writing? Why/Why not?

Has my writing changed since I wrote this? How?

Is this my best writing? Why/Why not? (p. 551)

Students everywhere tend to be very interested in grades. They continually monitor their own progress. This preoccupation with grades is well-known to working teachers. It is also an underutilized resource. You should give students, particularly in middle school and high school, an active role to play in their own grading. Make clear the grading rubric you intend to follow. A **rubric** is a rule for how something will be evaluated. You should explain, precisely, what kinds of work would merit an "A," a "B," and so on. If necessary, meet with students who express confusion about any parts of the rubric. Encourage them to use this rubric to monitor their progress. At unit's end, request that they write you a letter (which may be an e-mail) in which they express their self-evaluation (Hart, 1999). The teacher-student conference follows that letter. You will be pleasantly surprised how frequently you and your students concur on the grade: Protests and complaints about "subjective grading" will be few and far between. This is particularly important for teachers who make regular use of portfolios and projects, as assessment in those areas tends to be challenged more than in other areas (Venn, 2000).

Authentic Assessment

Authentic assessment is reality-based. It measures student knowledge and skills as these relate to activities in the "real world." The three key components of authentic assessment are (1) they are criterion-based, (2) they include multiple indicators, and (3) they are judged by standards that are reliable:

> Authentic assessment refers to the assessment of specific academic accomplishments that have meaning and value beyond the classroom. It is intended to foster a transfer of learning from the setting in which the learning occurred to all of the situations in which it will have application by making the assessment setting as similar as possible to the setting for which the learner is being prepared. (Tanner, 2001, p. 74)

Authentic assessment evaluates students by reference to a criterion established in advance. That criterion shows how student work will be assessed. Students may be given freedom to demonstrate knowledge of algebra by applying algebraic formulae to real-world problems, for example, told to figure out how much paint to buy to cover the four walls of a room that is 10 cubic feet in size. In this case, criteria might include such items as level of effort the student put in as reflected by the work product, amount of scholarly research involved, clarity of exposition, and so on. Remember, you must tell students, in advance, what criteria will be used and how each will be interpreted (e.g., "A 'superior' activity is one that shows imaginative application of algebraic functions, a 'satisfactory' activity is one that shows an obvious application, and a 'poor' activity is one that is not appropriate for the application of algebra. Superior = 2 points, Satisfactory = 1, Poor = 0."). Children should not be compared to each other. That is, norm-referenced criteria are not appropriate: "[R]anking is contrary to the spirit of authentic assessment" (Tanner, 2001, p. 80).

Finally, the standards used must be reliable. This can prove to be difficult, especially when a wide variety of activities is involved, as often occurs with authentic assessment. "Sometimes the instructor's judgments change from project to project, and sometimes multiple scorers who are assessing the same project do not agree on the quality of the effort" (Tanner, 2001, p. 81).

Historically, student work in physical education, art, music, and other "specials" has been authentically assessed. Thus, in physical education, children demonstrate that they have learned the rules of soccer by playing a game without violating those rules. In music, students show they have learned a composition by playing it. In art, young people prove that they have mastered material about art history by correctly identifying samples belonging to different periods. They may also create their own examples of realism, cubism, and so on, in art. All of these are authentic assessments. They are also examples of performance assessments, a topic to which we now turn.

Performance Assessments

A performance-based, or naturalistic, assessment requires students to demonstrate knowledge by applying it to real-life situations (Pierangelo & Giuliani, 2002). Thus, performance assessments can be, and should be, authentic. As Venn (2000) explained, "Performance assessment is authentic, curriculum-based assessment that emphasizes teacher observation and clinical judgment. . . . [P]erformance assessment . . . provides detailed information while avoiding use of traditional measures such as teacher-made tests" (p. 532). The appeal of performance tests for teachers of inclusive classrooms is that these procedures may avoid the "word problems" that plague so many students with disabilities in, for example, math (Berghoff, 2000). However, performance assessments, especially in math, sometimes require students to read complex material (Linn, 2000). For this reason, some students, notably those with specific learning disabilities, may require considerable instruction and practice on performance assessments (Woodward, Monroe, & Baxter, 2001). This suggests that teachers examine tests carefully before administering them to students with reading disabilities. If the intent is to have students show by performance that certain information is known, teachers will want to avoid defeating that purpose by giving test questions that are so word-heavy that students do not know what performance is desired.

Portfolios

Portfolios are collections of materials developed by students, usually independently but sometimes as members of groups, during the course of a school year. Portfolios, by definition, are to include more than one sample of a child's work. These work samples are often placed into very large folders or binders. Some educators consider portfolios, *ipso facto,* to be "authentic." Tanner (2001) insisted that this is not necessarily true: "[S]ome portfolio entries are no more authentic than the paper and pencil assessments they replace" (p. 78). This may happen if teachers evaluate portfolios on criteria other than those upon which they were developed. Consider, for example, portfolio entries prepared by students as illustrations of their creativity in art. Were the teacher to assess those entries as indications of interpersonal development or personal maturity, the portfolios would not be authentic, nor would they be valid assessments.

Criteria for Portfolios. Portfolio assessments can quickly become unwieldy unless teachers create, and enforce, firm guidelines. A rubric can help (see "Student Self-Assessment, p. 364).

You should create a standard tracking system that documents what materials were submitted by which students on what dates. A key is to record student proposals for portfolio entries, first drafts, revisions, your own comments on drafts, student reactions to their drafts, and the like. Even if all of these materials do not end up in the portfolio itself, you still need them to assess progress (see "Process v. Product Portfolios"). In addition to this management system, you need criteria for evaluating entries *and* the portfolio as a whole (see "Evaluation of Portfolios").

Structure of Portfolios. Portfolios may be organized in several different ways. Which you choose will depend upon your needs and your preferences. You can adopt a theme basis or you may decide to organize entries according to IEP goals (e.g., all entries related to the first goal are collected in one tab, entries connected to another goal in another tab, etc.). Alternatively, you may want to adopt a chronological order, particularly if this is to be a process portfolio.

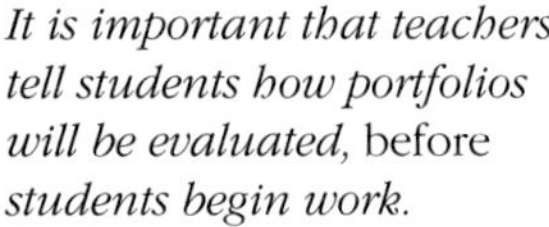
It is important that teachers tell students how portfolios will be evaluated, before *students begin work.*

Process v. Product Portfolios. In assessing portfolios, teachers should look both at *process* and *product* (Venn, 2000). In fact, process assessment is the more important of the two. When students enter first drafts, teacher comments, revisions, and reactions/comments into their portfolios, the pattern of learning becomes apparent. This kind of process portfolio automatically answers many of the questions future teachers will have (e.g., whether the student himself/herself did this work independently). A product portfolio, by contrast, contains only finished work. It leaves many important questions unanswered.

Electronic Portfolios. Portfolios may be *electronic* in whole or in part (Venn, 2000). An electronic portfolio can be assembled on a floppy disk, a CD-ROM, or a hard disk. This option is particularly attractive for process portfolios. The key is for each successive draft to be uniquely named. Thus, a first draft of a reaction paper to *The Adventures of Tom Sawyer* (see Chapter 14), might be named toms01.wpd. The second draft might be titled toms02.wpd, and so forth. Electronic portfolios have many advantages. First, they are, for all intents and purposes, of potentially unlimited size. Whereas binders, bags, and other containers in the physical world have defined storage limits, electronic media feature much greater capacities. Second, they can be multimedia in nature, including not only the written word but also hotlinks to Web sites the student found and used, video clips illustrating different aspects of the material, and so on. It is important that teachers, who may not be as fluent in the use of electronic media as are many of today's students, not be so dazzled by the technology that they overlook the basic rules for good portfolios. Electronic portfolios, no less than traditional paper ones, should comply with criteria established in advance for "complete," "original," and so on. The major disadvantage to electronic portfolios is that all educators who review it must have the requisite technical competencies.

Evaluation of Portfolios. You should establish criteria, in advance, for what kind of entries would be judged as being "complete," "partially complete," or "not attempted." That is, you need to specify how you will evaluate the creativity, level of effort, and so on, of portfolio entries. These criteria should be communicated to each student *before* the students begin work on their portfolios. Your evaluation system would indicate, for example, whether creativity will be rewarded, whether "neatness counts," and the like, as well as how much weight will be assigned to each component of the evaluation. Students need to be told, in advance, whether their reactions to their own creations, your teacher comments, and other "extraneous" papers will or will not be included in the portfolio (Tanner, 2001).

Many educators use rubrics, or rules explaining how work will be evaluated, to assess portfolio entries (McLoughlin & Lewis, 2001). A rubric might explain that "5" will be awarded for work of striking originality, "4" for work of better-than-average originality, "3" for average originality, and so on. Similar rules for neatness, factual accuracy, and so on, might be established. As we will observe later in Chapters 14 to 16, it is also important that teachers note, with respect to each portfolio entry, whether the work reflects the student's own efforts or, alternatively, whether it represents a final product to which the teacher had to contribute significantly (e.g., the student was not able to do this level of work without substantial adult assistance).

You may decide to evaluate entire portfolios differently than you evaluate particular entries. Portfolios of students with disabilities should also reflect IEP goals (McLoughlin & Lewis, 2001). For elementary teachers, then, one or several portfolios may document progress toward the child's annual goals. In high school, a number of portfolios will be needed. The point is that if portfolios are selected as the main, or a key, means of assessment, they must, taken as a whole, present a complete picture of the child's development in all IEP-related areas. Further, as we will recommend for teachers of English, math, and science, portfolios should include entries related to each learning standard established by the state department of education (see Chapters 14 and 15). Thus, for third-grade math, a complete portfolio would include entries reflecting mastery of the basics of multiplication as well as representation of mathematical ideas in various media, connections between mathematics, and other math operations and ideas. The *comprehensiveness* of the portfolio, viewed in its entirety, must be assessed against district and state learning standards. As you can see, criteria for evaluating entire portfolios may well differ from those used to evaluate distinct portfolio entries. Students should be advised in advance of *both* sets of criteria.

High-Stakes Tests

High-stakes tests are assessments, virtually all of them standardized, that have very significant consequences. This may include promotion from grade to grade. It may also encompass high-school graduation. There are stakes, too, for teachers and for schools. In many states, high-stakes assessments are used as one element in state evaluation of schools. Some school districts also reward or punish school administrators and teachers based, in part, upon the results of such tests (Gagnon, McLaughlin, & Rhim, 2000).

The high-stakes tests required by No Child Left Behind are criterion-referenced tests, not norm-referenced tests. This becomes clear when you recall that the tests are created to assess student performance as compared to state learning standards. Thus, these are standards-referenced tests. That is why giving a norm-referenced test, such as the NAEP, for purposes of measuring student achievement relative to state standards is inappropriate. Similarly, the NAEP and other national norm-referenced tests have items reflecting national, rather than state, content. That is why the new federal law requires that new tests be written that reflect specifically the content that is in a given state's learning standards. Stated differently, the law mandates these tests *actually* measure what they say they measure.

Some educators expressed surprise that the 1997 IDEA Amendments required that students with disabilities take whatever high-stakes assessments are offered to other PreK–12 students (see Figure 10.3, "IDEA on Participation in Assessments"). Participation in such stress-inducing tests was mandated by Congress. Federal policy makers regarded such participation as an "opportunity." Guidance offered by the U.S. Department of Education's Office for Civil Rights (OCR; 2000) explained:

FIGURE 10.3 IDEA on Participation in Assessments

Here is the statutory language, at section 612(a)(17) of the IDEA Amendments of 1997:

(17) Participation in Assessments.—

(A) In General—Children with disabilities are included in general State and district-wide assessment programs, with appropriate accommodations, where necessary. As appropriate, the State or local education agency.

(i) develops guidelines for the participation of children with disabilities in alternate assessments for those children who cannot participate in State and district-wide assessment programs; and

(ii) develops and, beginning no later than July 1, 2000, conducts those alternate assessments.

(B) Reports—The State educational agency makes available to the public, and reports to the public with the same frequency and in the same detail as it reports on the assessment of nondisabled children, the following:

(i) the number of children with disabilities participating in regular assessments.

(ii) the number of those children participating in alternate assessments.

(iii) (I) The performance of those children on regular assessments (beginning no later than July 1, 1998) and on alternate assessments (no later than July 1, 2000), if doing so would be statistically sound and would not result in the disclosure of performance results identifiable to individual children.

(II) Data relating to the performance of children described under subclause (I) shall be disaggregated—(aa) for assessments conducted after July 1, 1998; and (bb) for assessments conducted before July 1, 1998 if the State is required to disaggregate such data prior to July 1, 1998.

> [F]ederal laws generally require the inclusion of students with disabilities in state- and districtwide assessment programs, except as participation in particular tests is individually determined to be inappropriate for a particular student. Assessment programs should provide valuable information that benefits students, either directly, such as in the measurement of individual progress against standards, or indirectly, such as in evaluating programs. Given these benefits, exclusion from assessment programs, unless such participation is individually determined inappropriate because of the student's disability, would generally violate Section 504 and Title II [of the 1990 Americans with Disabilities Act, or ADA]. If a student with a disability will take the systemwide assessment test the student must be provided appropriate instruction and appropriate test accommodations. (pp. 61–62)

The last sentence is a very important one. Leaders of the American Educational Research Association (AERA), the American Psychological Association (APA), and the National Council on Measurement in Education (NCME) commented, in a jointly issued publication, *Standards for Educational and Psychological Testing* (2000), that high-stakes tests should cover *only* content that children and youth have had a chance to learn. The following year, AERA added, for emphasis, that curricula, materials, and courses must be upgraded to include the content that will be on high-stakes tests *before* decisions are made based upon student performance on such tests.

Assuming that students with disabilities do learn the content, and that the tests are non-discriminatory in nature, participation in high-stakes assessments can benefit the children and youth. This is so for several reasons. First, when students with disabilities take part in these tests, their scores are counted and reported. That fact means that school administrators, family members, and others in the local community will pay attention to their performance. Over time, this will lead to increased emphasis upon helping students with disabilities to achieve. By contrast, were these students to be excused from these high-stakes tests, there would be much less incentive on the part of educators and parents alike to raise their performance levels. Second, when children and youth with disabilities take part in large-scale assessments, data are generated which help district and state administrators to evaluate *programs*. This may lead to improvements in the quality of services provided to students with disabilities (Thurlow, 2000).

Educator Concerns About High-Stakes Tests

General and special educators alike have expressed misgivings about the recent surge of high-stakes tests in PreK–12 education. One frequently mentioned worry is that students with disabilities, English language learners, and other populations traditionally not included in such assessments tend to be ill-prepared for these tests. That is, the education

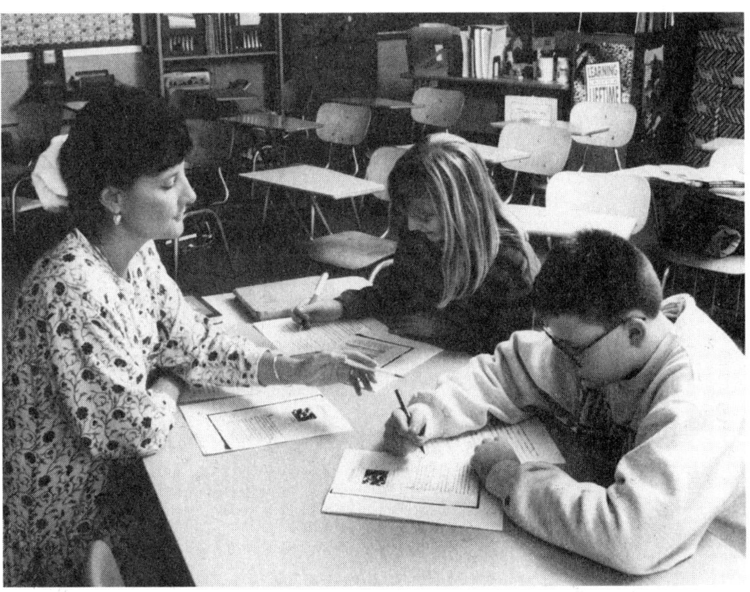

If a child's IEP specifies that test accommodations will be offered for high-stakes tests, then those adjustments must be provided.

they have been receiving generally was geared to their special needs (e.g., supplementary help with math and reading, bilingual instruction, etc.) rather than the content upon which high-stakes tests are founded. A second concern is that these students may do poorly on the tests. Recent reports (e.g., Johnson, Kimball, Brown, & Anderson, 2001; U.S. Department of Education, Office for Civil Rights, 2000) show that the lowest-scoring groups on statewide assessments, indeed, tend to be students with disabilities and bilingual-education students. A third area of concern is that the preparation required to help these students to get ready for high-stakes tests deprives these young people of the time they need for transition services (see Chapter 13).

Educational researchers have added concerns about the kinds of tests to be used, as well as how these would be interpreted. Linn (2000), for example, pointed out that scores on high-stakes assessments tend to rise during the first few years after a new test is adopted, for reasons unrelated to student performance (e.g., teachers learn from one year's test how to "teach to the test" better the following year, states make tests easier, etc.). Educators cannot conclude, therefore, that these higher scores necessarily mean better student learning nor that they show improvements in programs or teaching.

Another concern about high-stakes assessment is that the amount of information covered can be daunting. Many of these assessments are grounded upon the *same* kinds of facts as were at the core of the curriculum during the now-out-of-favor "education as transmission of knowledge from teacher to student" eras of past years. That is because test writers find it easier to assess factual knowledge than to measure process skills (e.g., Linn, 2000). Even new and non-traditional assessments now require students to possess a broad base of knowledge and skills. For example, the Comprehensive Social Studies Assessment Project (CSSAP), begun in 1997, seeks to design assessments for civics, economics, history, and geography at the elementary, middle- and high-school levels (see National Council for the Social Studies, *http://www.socialstudies.org*; Czarra, 1999). The CSSAP is intended to require high-level thinking because students must construct responses and must apply knowledge and skills in performance assessments. Only the portfolio assessment component of the CSSAP is to be based upon students' inquiry-based projects. In social studies, then, this means that no matter how much children and youth may benefit from the new active, hands-on, inquiry-based methods of instruction, they *still* must also master very sizeable amounts of specific pieces of information. The same is true in other content areas.

Will high-stakes testing ultimately help students with disabilities, as federal officials hope, or will it actually harm those young people? The evidence to date is inconclusive. On the one hand, educators are investing considerable resources to make sure that high-stakes tests are fair and that the accommodations students need are both available and effective (e.g., National Center on Educational Outcomes, *http://education.umn.edu/NCEO*). On the other hand, some trends are troubling. Large numbers of young people with disabilities are dropping out of school, either because they failed a high-stakes test or because they feared failing one. The American Council on Education's General Educational Development Testing Service reported in 2002 that unprecedented numbers of students with disabilities took the GED in 2001. To illustrate, twice as many persons in 2001 as in 2000 asked for accommodations for specific learning disabilities. In fact, in some states, *three times* as many persons requested such accommodations in 2001 as in 2000 (American Council on Education, 2002, Table 6). Comparing GED data to information about high-stakes tests, Amrein and Berliner (2003) discovered that states that had adopted high-stakes assessments tended to be the same states in which drop-out rates are rising. These reports are particularly portentous because the new assessments required by No Child Left Behind had not even begun.

Non-Discrimination in Testing

OCR's guidance (2000, p. 60) noted, "The regulations implementing Section 504 and Title II [of the ADA] specifically prohibit the use of 'criteria or methods of administration . . . that have the effect of subjecting qualified persons with disabilities to discrimination on the basis of disability' " (28 C.F.R. 35.130[b][3]; 34 C.F.R. 104.4[b][4]). This "effects test" looks at what the results are of test criteria and/or test procedures. The intent of the school district is irrelevant. Thus, it is not sufficient for educators to claim that they have non-discriminatory testing policies, nor to say that they have no desire to test students' disabilities rather than their knowledge and skills. What matters is the end result: Do test criteria and/or test procedures have the effect of discriminating? If the answer to that question is "Yes," then the criteria and/or procedures in question are illegal. OCR's guidance continued:

> Under Section 504, Title II, and the IDEA, tests given to students with disabilities must be selected and administered so that the test accurately reflects what a student knows or is able to do, rather than a student's disability (except where the test is designed to measure disability-related skills). This means that students with disabilities covered by these statutes must be given appropriate accommodations and modifications in the administration of the tests that allow the same constructs to be measured. Examples include oral testing, tests in large print, Braille versions of tests, individual testing, and separate group testing. (pp. 60–61)

To explain briefly, a test of a "disability-related skill" would be one that assessed hearing. IDEA requires that students with disabilities be tested fairly (section 614); so does section 504 (34 C.F.R. 104.35). Certainly, no deaf student should be tested (in a foreign language, music, or any other subject) by requiring her to listen to recorded passages. If the intent of the test is to measure hearing ability, then there is nothing discriminatory about its measuring a student's ability to hear. If, on the other hand, the purpose of the test is to assess knowledge of English literature, and the effect of the test, as given to a deaf student, is to measure, instead, her ability to hear test instructions, then the method of administration is discriminatory. High-stakes testing, by its very nature, is not intended to measure "disability-related skills"—any that does in fact do so would be discriminatory.

Test Accommodations

Accommodations in testing are adjustments made in response to the special needs of students with disabilities. A young person with a severe emotional/behavioral disorder who cannot successfully maintain attention for more than an hour might be given breaks, say, every 45 minutes, during important tests. As another example, students who are blind may be permitted to listen to questions, or use large-print tests, or to take tests in Braille. Similarly, students with specific learning disabilities may be offered additional test-taking time. Table 10.1 illustrates some possible test accommodations. Other ideas are outlined at *http://education.umn.edu/NCEO* (the National Center on Educational Outcomes). This source offers a useful "online accommodations bibliography" that lets you enter the type of accommodation you are interested in and investigate research studies on specific accommodations.

TABLE 10.1 Possible Test Accommodations

Site	Materials	Procedures
Special room	Brailled questions	Extra time
Special lighting	Large print	Morning only
Special acoustics	Index cards or other place keepers	No Monday tests (child may not take medication on weekends)
Special seat/carrel	Sections of a test (for abbreviated test sessions)	Directions read out loud
Small groups	Computer	Directions re-read each page
Adaptive furniture	speech output	Directions displayed on board/overhead
	speech input	Interpreter (deaf student)
	other adaptations	Scribe (student answers on test booklet, scribe copies onto answer sheets)

The intent, in each case, is to "level the playing field" by allowing students with disabilities to show what they know as well as what they can do. What levels the playing field is a judgment call. Having a sign-language interpreter to sign spoken test instructions that other students hear is not controversial when the test is of knowledge about geometry. However, if the student and/or the student's family also asks that the interpreter sign test questions as well, educators need to be sure that this additional intervention will not alter the nature of the test. It may well do that if the test is one intended to assess ability to read standard written English. In such a case, interpretation into American Sign Language (ASL) may not be appropriate. That is because ASL interpretation in that event alters the nature of the test. Watching someone sign a story in ASL is not the same as reading a printed version of that story. Similarly, when a student who has quadriplegia (a spinal-cord injury) asks for an adult to write answers on the test sheet, the request usually is an appropriate one. However, questions may be raised by some who object that the adult may provide undue advantages to the student. It would be better, and less controversial, to accommodate this student's needs by permitting him to use a PC to enter his own answers. Adaptations such as voice input or even mouthsticks allow this. Fewer objections will be raised when this student answers his own questions, albeit with assistive technology, than might arise when an adult writes answers for that student. The rule is to use the most direct alternative that will do the job (Thurlow, 2000).

Extended test-taking time (often requested for students with specific learning disabilities) or frequent breaks (sometimes sought for students with emotional/behavioral disorders) may be more controversial. Two questions that may arise are (1) How much additional test-taking time is enough? and (2) How many breaks are sufficient? Any accommodations in testing must be identified in the child's IEP. The child's IEP should answer questions about how much time is enough and how frequent breaks must be. An extra half hour may suffice for one student, while an additional two hours may be required for a second student. Similarly, one student may require breaks every 15 minutes, while another can sustain attention effectively for as long as two hours. Issues of possible unfair advantages should be referred to the building principal, who may in turn rely upon the judgment of the IEP team. (The principal is in a position that classroom teachers are not: As an administrator, the principal can explain to parents that there are legal obligations to which the school is subject and that the IEP team was the appropriate group to recommend how those duties should be fulfilled.)

The idea is for accommodations not to confer an unfair advantage upon students receiving these adaptations. A large study in Oregon, which examined whether accommodations offered any unintended advantages, showed that having questions read aloud assisted students with specific learning disabilities but did not help other students (Tindal, Heath, Hollenbeck, Almond, & Harniss, 1998). A later study researching the same kinds of alterations, this time in the state of Washington, also concluded that no unfair advantage was granted to students with disabilities (Johnson et al., 2001). Importantly, too, student opinion generally favors test accommodations that are perceived as being fair to everyone. To illustrate, Nelson, Jayanthi, Epstein, and Bursuck (2000) queried a large number of middle-school students, most having no disabilities, about a wide variety of test adaptations. Included were extra time, open-book tests, and take-home tests. Nelson et al. were surprised to discover that these students expressed only lukewarm interest in most such alterations. Most favored were open-book tests and untimed tests, because students thought these changes would help *them* as well as other students. We will have more to say on the theme of fairness in "Grading," on p. 376.

Accommodations may be made for students without disabilities, if permitted under state and local rules. A good example is to arrange for teen mothers to be tested in different locations so as to minimize teasing from other students.

Alternate Assessments

Some individuals will be excused altogether from certain tests. It would not make sense, for example, to administer a ninth-grade state-wide test in biology to a 15-year-old student whose IEP calls for her to master the skills of brushing her teeth and tying her shoelaces.

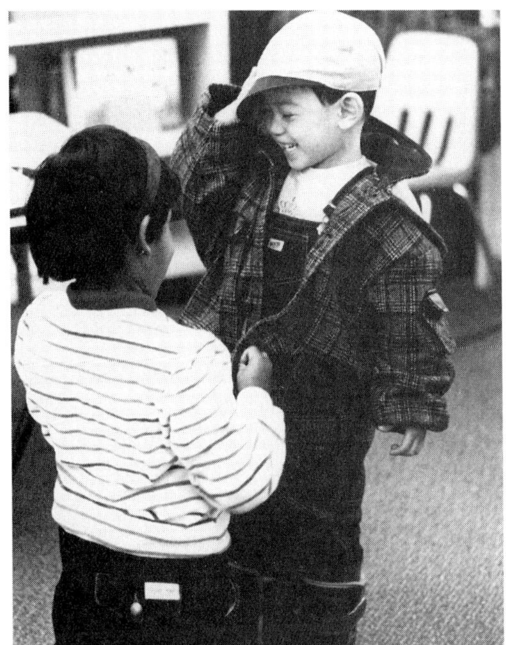

Alternate assessments may include such activities as "puts on own hat" and "assists others to put on own jacket."

IDEA anticipates that virtually all students with disabilities will participate in state-wide and district-wide testing. However, a small number will take **alternate assessments** (Warlick & Heumann, 2001). The fact that this option is to be made available only for a few students with disabilities is controversial. Education officials in New York told principals and teachers that IEP teams may arrange for alternate assessments for only 2% to 3% of PreK–12 children and youth with disabilities (NYS VESID, 1997). Given that about 11% of students with any classification have mental retardation (to take just one disability category), this means that *most* students with MR will *not* be excused from taking high-stakes and other state-wide or district-wide tests in New York State. That is, alternate assessments will be made available only to students with severe or profound mental retardation, students with severe forms of autism, and some students with multiple disabilities. Nationwide, the situation is similar. For that reason, and because most students qualifying for alternate assessments are *not* placed into inclusion classrooms (Ysseldyke & Olsen, 1999), our discussion will be a brief one.

Alternate assessments come in many forms. Teachers may review student records, including reports filed by physical therapists, occupational therapists, speech/language pathologists, and others, perhaps including family members, that document student achievement. These records may show that a given student has met an IEP goal. A second approach is to use portfolios. These first two approaches are variations on the "body-of-work" technique. A third technique is to ask the student to perform the goal behavior (see "Performance Assessments," p. 365). Yet another means of alternate assessment is for teachers to interview people who know the student well, asking for recollections of instances in which goal behavior was demonstrated. Ysseldyke and Olsen (1999) offered a good overview of the options available for alternate assessment. They urged that these be authentic. That is, given a choice, teachers should look for behaviors to be demonstrated in "real-life" (community) settings.

Critical to alternate assessments is an agreed-upon rubric for evaluating student work. This can be challenging. If educators assemble reports from teachers and other professionals, or if they review a portfolio containing student work, they need some means of determining whether the evidence gathered shows adequate yearly progress (AYP) toward the student's IEP goals. If, to illustrate, the student is to be evaluated with respect to the same domains of learning standards as are others, but to a different level of achievement, educators must decide how achievement will be measured and what levels of accomplishment are satisfactory. These decisions are best reached by a team. As with other instances of portfolio assessment (see "Evaluation of Portfolios," p. 367), team members need to decide *what* will be included in records to be reviewed or in the portfolio, how the *appropriateness* or *quality* of each entry will be assessed, and the extent to which the student's use of *assistance* from others will be a factor in evaluation. Helpful in assessing records or a portfolio is a *standard organization,* so that all sets of records or all portfolio entries are brought together in a consistent pattern. Also useful is a *rubric* to guide assessment. Thus, educators may first assemble three or four "samples" each representing a different level of achievement. These may illustrate "Not Evident" (the lowest level, in which AYP is not shown), "Emergent" (the second-lowest level, in which some but little evidence is apparent), "Supported Independent" (the third-lowest level, in which progress is shown but the student required considerable assistance), "Functional Independent" (the next-to-highest level, in which AYP with little need for assistance is evidenced), and "Independent" (the highest level). Each set of records or each portfolio should be evaluated by at least two educators. If they disagree, they should confer to try to reach consensus.

If you have a student who is not able to participate in high-stakes and other standardized assessments, even with test accommodations, this is an indicator that this child or youth may not be placed appropriately in an inclusive classroom. Serious questions must be asked in such an event. The idea of instructing students with severe disabilities about, and then assessing them in, such advanced academic subjects as algebra, biology, chemistry, geometry, English literature, and physics strikes many educators as being inappropriate. They argue that these students will benefit much more from instruction in daily living skills and other such functional curricula (e.g., Dever & Knapczyk, 1997; Beirne-Smith, et al., 2002). Such training seldom is provided in general classrooms. Further, unrealistically high academic standards may contribute to the high drop-out rates of students with emotional/behavioral disorders and specific learning disabilities, in particular (Blackorby & Wagner, 1996). These are important issues, which will be revisited when we discuss transition services in Chapter 13.

Technologies That Work

Universal Design and Assessment

The federally funded National Center on Educational Outcomes has explored universal design as it applies to assessment. The Center's initial findings are intriguing. Universal design, as explained in Chapter 8, is an approach in which educators take into consideration *in advance* the wide variety of needs students exhibit in today's schools. As related to the design of tests and other assessments, this means writing assessment instruments and procedures, from the ground up, to be useable with students with disabilities (and, as we will see in the next chapter, students who are LEP/ELL). Doing so requires test developers to express very precisely what it is they intend to measure. They must discard any items that they find are unfair for students with special needs and any items that require unusual or impossible accommodations.

For example, as we will see in Chapter 15, some social studies tests make use of maps and other graphics that cannot readily be converted to alternative media so as to be understood by students who are blind or have low vision. The principles of universal design require the developers of assessments to eliminate any unnecessary graphics and to construct questions so that they can be answered without the use of such graphics. Similarly, the concepts of universal design call upon test writers to use large font sizes and good contrast between figure and background (e.g., black words on white paper or white words on black paper). Test developers also must include students who have disabilities in the sample groups when assessments are pre-tested. Similarly, appropriate accommodations should be allowed, and used, during test try-outs. All of these steps are sensible. The fact that universal design, as a principle, is causing test developers to take such measures is encouraging.

Generally, universal design principles tell test developers to take into consideration the needs of students with disabilities *while first developing the instrument, when pretesting the assessment, and when preparing instructions for the published version.* These considerations must not wait until the test is completed. This is even more the case with respect to computer-administered tests than with paper-based tests because accommodations that can be provided on-site with pencil-and-paper assessments may not be available with computer-based tests. In addition, as we saw earlier, the ready availability of accommodations on computer is one of the factors driving educator adoption of computer-administered tests. Computer-based assessments that do not provide for such adjustments lose much of their appeal. For more on this issue, see Bowe (2000c) and Thompson, Johnstone, and Thurlow (2002).

Computer-Administered Testing

In recent years, the promise of computer-administered assessment to reduce the labor-intensiveness of test administration and to speed up scoring has captured the attention of educators. This is particularly true because states must develop high-stakes assessments without much financial assistance from the federal government. It is important that careful consideration of the pro's and con's precede a change to computer-based testing. Given the very rapid pace of change in computer-related products and services, this consideration must focus upon the current state of the art. What follows is accurate as of the date of publication of this book.

Advantages and Disadvantages

Computers permit easy and rapid scoring and grading of standardized tests. This is true for teacher-made tests, as well. You may use eReader, to take one example, to give a test to a student who is blind or has low vision or to one with dyslexia, a specific learning disability. eReader speaks out loud each word of each question, highlighting the words as it does. Students may also listen to their answers. Despite these apparent advantages, teachers must recognize that simply transferring pencil-and-paper tests to a computer often is a mistake. This is so for several reasons, other than the obvious one that students differ in their experience with computers (Thompson, Thurlow, Quenemoen, & Lehr, 2002):

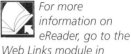

For more information on eReader, go to the Web Links module in Chapter 10 of the Companion Website.

1. People do not read and write on computers as they do with paper. Reading lengthy passages, as in document-based questions, is more difficult on a computer than it is on paper. This is why authors of Web pages and other documents intended for use on the Internet create them very differently from the ways authors of print materials do.
2. Taking a test on a computer requires use of the mouse, screen-navigation tools such as page-up and page-down commands, and other skills that are not required for pencil-and-paper tests.
3. Computers differ one from another. Some have large screens, others small ones. Some have high-resolution graphics cards, others do not. Some have high-speed Internet connections, others don't. All of this introduces variability in what is supposed to be a standardized test environment.
4. As a related concern, computers can and do crash. The general equivalent for pencil-and-paper tests is the non-delivery of test booklets on exam day. The difference with computers is that one machine may crash while others do not.
5. Schools differ in the extent to which they have on staff professionals who are skilled at keeping computers "up and running" and at solving hardware and software problems. One school giving a state-wide achievement test may have a group of highly skilled and experienced computer technicians. Another school administering the same test may not have any such staff members.

Educators and test developers must not allow their enthusiasm about computerizing assessment to cause them to overlook these issues. To elaborate on these serious matters, let us now turn to some pro's and con's of using computers to present tests to students of inclusive classrooms.

Advantages. Computer-based assessment offers several advantages over paper-based testing.

Speed and Familiarity. Many students today have grown up with computers. They are accustomed to writing with word-processing software, using the mouse with computer games, and searching for information on the Internet. In fact, they may be more comfortable with computers in these kinds of tasks than they are with pencils and paper. They may also be faster.

Built-In Accommodations. An important advantage of computer-administered tests is that PCs offer built-in accommodations. IBM-compatible PCs running Windows XP and

Macintoshes running OS X alike have important options for students with disabilities. Images on the screen, including words, may be enlarged. Font colors may be changed. Computer speech synthesis can be activated to speak out loud test questions. Speech recognition may be used to let students speak out loud their answers. Touch screens may be used to permit students to answer questions by touching icons on the screen. These built-in adaptations can be superior to in-person alternatives. A teacher's aide reading test questions out loud may inadvertently reveal his feelings about a question. A human scribe may be tempted to substitute her "better answer" for the one a student dictates. Either staff member may become impatient with a student who is slow to respond. Computers, by contrast, can read out loud each question in exactly the same non-revealing form, will enter whatever response the student gives, and will never become impatient.

Privacy. Students with disabilities may use accommodations on a computer in relative privacy as compared to use of in-person assistance. This fact may lessen embarrassment. Thus, a student who enlarges font sizes on a computer screen or who uses the keyboard number keys instead of the mouse to navigate around the screen may do so inconspicuously as compared to one who uses a magnifying device or requires a teacher assistant to turn pages of a test booklet.

Disadvantages. Computer-based assessment also has several disadvantages, as compared to paper-based assessments.

Student Non-Familiarity. Some students have had little experience on the computer with reading, writing, calculating, and other tasks required to pass tests. Some, notably many who have mental retardation, may not have mastered essential skills. In particular, they may not be comfortable with computer-based tests that display only parts of questions, expecting the student to scroll up and down to view the entire question and to answer it. Others, principally children and youth from low-socioeconomic status (SES) homes, may be much slower on a computer than with pencil and paper because they never use PCs at home. For these reasons, the "speed and familiarity" advantage listed above may not exist for these students.

Technical Expertise. The second advantage listed above ("built-in accommodations") is effective only if (a) the school's staff knows how to implement these accommodations (e.g., to call up "Accessories" in the Windows operating system), (b) the student knows how to use these accommodations, and (c) either the staff or the student, or both, know how to handle problems that may arise. The fact is that school staff and students vary greatly in these abilities.

Inaccessibility. Computer speech synthesizers and the screen readers that use them cannot handle images, icons, pictures, and other graphics that do not have "alt text" or "longdesc" tags (see Chapters 7 and 8 for explanations). For this reason, test items that present non-readable graphics discriminate against students who use such software. This is generally those who are blind, those who have low vision, and some who have specific learning disabilities.

As we have seen, some of the problems discussed here may be resolved by applying the principles of universal design to assessment (see "Technologies That Work: Universal Design and Assessment"). For teacher-made tests, a key is to prepare the test, from the beginning, for use by all of your students. Thus, if one of your students is blind, you would avoid asking questions that require interpretation of drawings and photographs, or, if such graphics were essential, you would offer accessible versions of them (e.g., a tactile, raised-image map).

GRADING

As a teacher in an inclusion classroom, you (and your team teacher, if you have one) should follow district policy on grading—for *all* your students. Variations from that policy should be made only in exceptional cases. IDEA's insistence on fair testing does *not* go so far as to call for special grading practices. The intent is for equity, not for favoritism, in testing (Thurlow, 2000). That being said, many teachers do adopt modifications in grading for *non*disabled students as well as for students with disabilities. For example, it can be entirely appropriate for the teacher to develop two rubrics for grading: one that considers spelling, punctuation, and so on, but not drawings and other appendices, and one that weighs such addenda but not spelling and punctuation. Assuming that both rubrics adhere to school policy, and that you explain both to your students, such variations can be both fair and suitable.

A wide range of other adjustments in grading is available. Teachers could decide to weight factors differently from usual practice (e.g., give greater weight than usual to "participates in class discussion," "submits all homework assignments on time," etc.). Teachers could assess students against themselves (e.g., "shows improvement"). Teachers could compare effort (e.g., giving higher grades to students believed to have worked harder in the course). A different kind of grading alternative is to provide addenda to letter and/or numerical grades. The teacher may add a note to a grade explaining how it was assigned, what considerations went into it, and the like. If district policy allows, elaborations upon simple letter grades can be helpful for all students. This is because grades are, by their very nature, abbreviated. There is much they don't reveal. If you take the time to explain, in advance, *how* the grades will be calculated and *why* points will be added/deducted, you may be pleasantly surprised with the results. Students and family members may more readily accept these annotated grades (e.g., Hart, 1999). Furthermore, students may be more motivated to improve, simply because they know much more exactly how to do that (Yell, 1999).

Adjustments in Grading?

More problematic is making grade decisions on *different* grounds for students with disabilities as opposed to students without disabilities. To begin our consideration of these issues, imagine that you have Melissa, a 14-year-old girl, in your class. She has no disabilities but comes from a single-parent household. Her mother, who is addicted to crack cocaine, is on welfare. Knowing all these facts, which certainly are unfortunate, should you *grade* Melissa differently? What about Katya, another 14-year-old in your class? Katya's circumstances are the same as Melissa's, but you do not know that; Katya prefers to keep this information to herself. The situations of Melissa and Katya introduce the whole idea of how appropriate it is for you as a teacher to assign grades, in part, based on non-academic information. Upon reflection, you may decide that such data should not factor into your grading.

Nonetheless, individualized grading plans have some appeal. One approach was tested by Munk and Bursuck (2001). Their study involved middle-school students with learning disabilities who were placed in inclusive settings. The Personalized Grading Plans (PGPs) for these students featured changed weights for assignments, credit for homework, credit for portfolio entries, and credit for class participation. Each child was given different weights, depending on that child's strengths and weaknesses. Munk and Bursuck reported that the modified grades resulted in better teacher-student and teacher-family communication about what the grades meant, and greater effort by the students in class. However, these outcomes may also have been due to the attention teachers and researchers gave to these students and their families (the so-called "Hawthorne Effect," where attention itself rather than other changes made seem to cause the results that are observed). In other words, the fact that teachers and university researchers met repeatedly with each student and each family, showing interest in ways to improve the grading rubric, itself may have produced the positive attitudes reported by students and families. Individualized grading rubrics make comparisons between students problematic—if a "B" for Vladimir reflects class participation and portfolio entries but the "B" for Darra is based upon her performance in class tests, is the teacher being fair to Darra? To Vladimir? To others in the class whose grading systems were not modified?

Many teachers feel tempted to give "special consideration" to students with special needs. That is an understandable emotion. After all, many such students do have to work harder, and longer hours, in order to pass their courses than is the case with non-disabled students. In addition, these teachers reason, many students came to their inclusion classes from special-education settings precisely *because* they had in an earlier year failed, or done very poorly in, general education environments. Finally, these teachers frequently find that students with disabilities already are lagging behind. Indeed, the National Longitudinal Transition Study (Valdes, Williamson, & Wagner, 1990) reported that most (60%) secondary students with learning disabilities had "C" or even lower grades.

I interviewed many hundreds of people with disabilities during the 1980s and 1990s over this exact issue—how they wished to be evaluated. By a margin of better than 20 to 1 (95%), they asked that they be assessed in exactly the *same* way that their non-disabled peers are assessed. This is a strong sentiment. Probing, I learned that they felt what should count is their *abilities,* that is, their performance. They wanted to be evaluated on that basis. They also said, very often, that if they are given extra "brownie points" just because they have disabilities, and/or because someone thought they "had to work harder for this," they would suffer for that later: In college or on the job, they would be at a disadvantage to competitors who did in fact know more and were in fact capable of doing more than they. As one person with a spinal-cord injury put it to me, "You'd be doing me no favors. I'd rather earn my own way." Many added another factor: If they were evaluated more leniently than were their non-disabled peers, that fact would quickly become known and would likely lead to a backlash. Said a young woman with cerebral palsy, "I really don't need to add jealousy [about assessment favoritism] to my list of problems. I'd much rather people saw me as someone holding my own" (Bowe, n.d.).

Research conducted by Bursuck, Munk, and Olson (1999) reached similar conclusions. They interviewed 275 high-school students, 257 with no disabilities and 15 with learning disabilities. The researchers asked these students to consider the following kinds of possible grading adjustments:

1. Give some students higher grades because they show improvement.
2. Give some students higher grades because they worked harder for them.
3. Give some students two grades for each subject (one for results, one for effort).
4. For some students, make assignments count toward grades, more than is done for other students.
5. For some students, require less learning for the same grade.
6. Use a different scale for some students than for others.
7. Pass some students under all circumstances (zero-fail policy).

Bursuck et al. found that *none* of these alternatives was favored by students without disabilities. Most were voted down by overwhelming margins. This reinforces what I was told in my own, less-formal interviews: people are concerned, rightly, that favoritism in assessment will be resented by peers. As for the students with learning disabilities surveyed by Bursuck et al., no conclusions could be drawn because the sample size was so small (N=15).

Deciding on Grading Practices

If you have a collaborating teacher, the two of you should review district policies and then discuss your philosophies and approaches to grading. By agreeing in advance on standards and procedures for grading, you remove the necessity for each of you independently to grade each student's every submission. Rather, you can divide the work, confident that your team member will apply the same grading rules that you do (Walther-Thomas, Korinek, & McLaughlin, 1999). That much is basic. Somewhat more controversial is the view that teachers in inclusion classrooms should adjust their instruction but usually *not* their grading patterns. You should meet the special needs of your students in the ways you teach, so that they learn, rather than in the way you evaluate their work.

TRACKING PROGRESS TOWARD IEP GOALS

A vital role of teachers of inclusive classes is to monitor the performance of students vis à vis those students' Individualized Education Programs (IEPs). Earlier in this book, we provided an illustration of an IEP for a hypothetical student, "Emil Gerardi" (see Figure 2.5 in Chapter 2). Let us see, here, how his teacher would track Emil's progress toward the goals established in that IEP.

Emil is 15 years old. His IEP notes that he requires behavior-modification interventions. The plan provides that during the 2003–2004 school year he was expected to be included in ninth-grade classes. However, he would be pulled out twice weekly for 30-minute counseling sessions. He would also participate in a work-study program every Friday afternoon. In Figure 10.4, his English teacher reports upon Emil's progress. To compile this report, Mrs. Blaylock consulted with Emil's other teachers and reviewed her own records of his work in ninth-grade English. Notice that she, and others, had to document what Emil did and where he spent his time. Mrs. Blaylock's report will be filed with Emil's IEP and combined with other documentation to produce a comprehensive record.

CHAPTER SUMMARY

Assessment

- In assessment, teachers collect information. In evaluation, they interpret those data. In grading, they communicate their judgments.
- Formative assessments help you improve the way you teach. Summative assessments tell you, and others, how well you did teach and how well your students learned.
- Purposeful observation can give a teacher a great deal of information, particularly about how students respond to instruction.
- Harassment on the basis of disability should be treated much as is harassment on any other basis.
- Curriculum-based assessment helps teachers to learn how students are progressing within the curriculum.
- Error analysis tells teachers precisely where students are having difficulty.
- Task analysis identifies the subtasks to be taught so that students can begin mastering material.
- Journal entries can be an effective way to track student progress, but only if they are well-designed and if teachers regularly review them.
- Performance assessment is almost always authentic (reality-based). Portfolios are not necessarily always authentic.
- A key to success with portfolios is devising criteria, in advance, for assessing them. The same applies to portfolios used for alternate assessments.
- Unfortunately, many standardized tests were never normed on populations including persons with disabilities.
- Test accommodations can be essential for students with disabilities who take high-stakes tests.

Computer-Administered Testing

- When tests are given on a computer, accommodations may be, as well. This may include accessibility features built into computer operating systems. It may also include special-purpose software such as CAST's eReader.
- Sometimes, computer administration of assessments can lead to problems. Two students taking the same test on different computers may not have the same experience. One, using a machine having a large screen, a high-speed Internet connection, and a state-of-the-art computer graphics card may have an unfair advantage over a student taking the test on a computer having a small screen, a dial-up Internet connection, and outdated graphics cards.

FIGURE 10.4 Tracking Progress Toward IEP Goals

Student's Name: Emil Gerardi D.O.B.:	4/14/89
Date of Latest Meeting to Prepare/Revise IEP:	4/3/04
Report Prepared by:	Lois Blaylock, Ninth-Grade English
Date of Progress Report:	5/20/04

I. Present Educational Performance

Emil has compiled an "A-" average in English this year, but his math and biology teachers report that his work in their classes is at the "C" level. He received a "P" in physical education and in music. It is my belief that Emil did much better in English than in other subjects because he enjoyed the literature we read this year: Salinger's *The Catcher in the Rye* and Mark Twain's *The Adventures of Huckleberry Finn.* These appealed to him, he told me, because Holden Caulfield and Huck Finn both had run-ins with authority figures, as Emil has.

Social/Emotional Development	Emil made some progress this year, but he continues to resist authority in his subject-matter classes.
Relations with Peers	Again, Emil has made progress, notably in curtailing the kinds of confrontations and fights he had last year. However, much progress remains to be made.
Relations with Adults	Emil relates much better to adults he knows well than to those with whom he has infrequent contact (see comments about Work/Study, in "III. Services" below).
Self-concept	Emil's self-image continues to be one of a misunderstood young man; when problems arise, it's always someone else's fault.
Adjustment to school	Emil is improving, but only when he's interested (as in English).

II. Goals

Emil passed the English achievement test but failed the other (in biology). He spent 70% of the school week in integrated environments; this was below the 80% goal in large part because of frequent referrals to the assistant principal's office for discipline.

III. Services

Emil attended only 75% of his scheduled 2 × 30 min/week counseling sessions.

Each of his subject-matter teachers received training in behavior-modification techniques. However, their implementation of those procedures was sporadic, resulting in the above-mentioned referrals to the A.P. Every Friday afternoon, Emil participated in a Work/Study program that exposed him to expectations of behavior in the workplace. According to the Work/Study program coordinator, Emil continues to have great difficulty accepting these demands for consistent and appropriate behavior.

IV. Extent, if Any, to Which the Child Will Not Participate with Nondisabled Children

Emil demonstrated some success in integrated programs this year. He should continue to receive such services next year. However, greater support for content teachers will be required for them to carry out behavior-modification strategies.

V. District-Wide and State Assessments

Emil received the required breaks during his two ninth-grade district-wide assessments. Extended test-taking time was granted, as well, for his content course tests and quizzes. Those will be needed next year, as well.

VI. Start Date and Duration

Emil will not receive extended school year (ESY) services, because his parents have arranged for his attendance at a sports camp during July and August 2004.

VII. Transition

Emil received the required counseling and participated in the Work/Study program. However, Emil elected not to attend his IEP team meeting this past March.

VIII. How Progress Will Be Measured and Parents Informed

Emil's parents were advised, via e-mail and/or phone messages from the school guidance counselor when Emil's behavior resulted in disciplinary action.

Emil's progress in his courses was reported on regular six-week report cards.

Grading

- In general, you should make accommodations in instruction. You should also make them in testing. However, you probably should *not* alter your grading schemes for students with special needs.

Tracking Progress Toward IEP Goals

- Progress toward IEP goals should be monitored by all teachers. Reports may be collected and summarized by one teacher. This information is needed by the IEP team to track the school's implementation of the plan as well as the student's progress toward IEP goals.

QUESTIONS FOR REFLECTION

1. What basic mistake was made by the veteran teacher with whom Joelene worked ("Personal Accounts")?
2. What is the difference between "formative" and "summative" assessments?
3. Why is observation a tool that is well-suited for assessing student behavior in small group activities?
4. What does research tell us about the effectiveness of curriculum-based assessment?
5. How could you use task analysis to find out why a student consistently fails tests on subtraction?
6. Why is authentic assessment becoming popular with many educators?
7. How could you evaluate a portfolio?
8. What are the major advantages and disadvantages of computer-administered assessments?
9. What options do you have for grading students with disabilities?
10. What kinds of information must be collected, by whom, to monitor a student's progress toward IEP goals?

Part Four Endnotes

Making Inclusion Work . . . The Story So Far

In Part Four, we saw that making inclusion work involves these ideas:

- Provide teachers, therapists, and other educators with the support they need, including training, supplies, and planning time.
- Prepare to teach by reviewing IEPs, talking with prior year teachers, visiting classes at lower and higher grade levels, and taking other steps to learn about individual students.
- Write objectives (academic, behavioral) that are *individualized* for each child.
- Use universal design principles to offer many-user, any-time, and low-cost adjustments as needed.
- Obtain technologies as needed for measuring, calculating, communicating, and other activities.
- Individualize instruction by modifying methods, materials, and even the classroom itself.
- Use problem-based and community-based instruction as appropriate to make learning meaningful to students.
- Adopt the well-researched tool of reciprocal peer tutoring.
- Teach at a level where students are "ready to learn" (that is, in Vygotsky's "zone of proximal development").
- Teach children how to learn and how to control their own behavior.
- Criticize behavior, rather than students, to avoid humiliating children.
- Make it rewarding for students to follow the rules.
- Catch children doing something right—and reinforcing them for that behavior.
- Use formative assessments to help you reinforce the way you teach and summative assessments to tell you, and others, how well you did teach and how well your students learned.
- Evaluate portfolios by devising criteria, in advance, for assessing them.
- Make adjustments in instruction and in testing, but probably not in grading.

Part Five

Other Aspects of Teaching in the Inclusive Classroom

Part Five takes up "other aspects" of teaching students with disabilities in general classrooms. First we explore status conditions and characteristics that are not disabilities but that often place children and youth at risk of school failure. Chapter 11 also discusses students who are gifted and/or talented. Some of these children and youth have disabilities. Sadly, the evidence is that these students tend not to be identified as gifted/talented as often as do children and youth with no disabilities.

In Chapter 12, we examine different models and approaches to collaboration—with fellow teachers, related-services personnel, paraprofessionals, family members, and students. Effective partnerships with others are critical to making inclusion work. As a lead-in to the next chapter, our review of collaboration includes discussion of school-community relations.

Finally, in this Part, the book takes up transition services. Chapter 13 focuses primarily upon the two kinds of transition that are mandated by the Individuals with Disabilities Education Act (IDEA): that between early intervention for infants and toddlers, on the one hand, and preschool services, on the other; and that between high school and life beyond high school. Other kinds of transition are briefly considered.

Chapter 11 *At-Risk, Culturally/Linguistically Diverse, and Gifted/Talented Students*

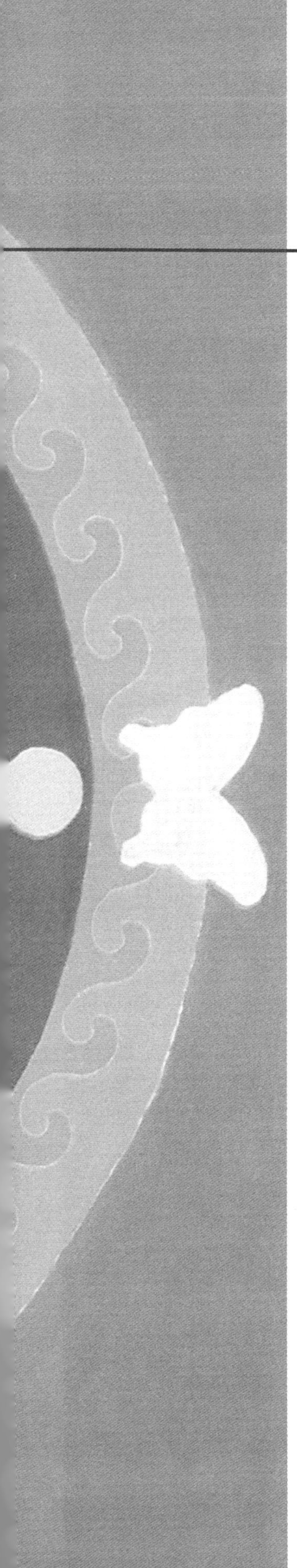

TERMS

at risk
poverty
Temporary Assistance to Needy Families (TANF)
homeless person
migrant children
slow learners
abuse
child abuse
sexual abuse
neglect
minority group
linguistic minority groups
gifted
talented

CHAPTER FOCUS QUESTIONS

After reading this chapter, you should be able to answer such questions as:

1. What is "poverty" and how does it relate to the income earned at a minimum-wage job over a year?
2. How does "child neglect" differ from "child abuse"?
3. Why must you be cautious about assuming a direct link between minority-group status and the cultural beliefs of a student and his family?
4. Americans of Hispanic origin tend to be of which two races?
5. What has been the impact of welfare reform with respect to teenage mothers?
6. What should you as a teacher do if a student tells you about plans to commit suicide?
7. How can teachers of inclusive classrooms support students who are gifted and/or talented, including those who have disabilities?

PERSONAL ACCOUNTS

Jane Santagello, a white non-Hispanic teacher with experience working in a suburban, mostly white school, began teaching this year in an urban area. Jane quickly became flustered when two African-American boys, Jamal and Kenyon, repeatedly interrupted her. She was also upset to see Maria and Manuel, two children whose families recently immigrated from Mexico, whispering to each other constantly. Jane's immediate reaction was to consider referring these four children for evaluation for special-education services. However, when she shared her concerns with Marcus Deaver, her mentor, who is an African American, she learned that a part of African-American culture is the "call-and-response" pattern seen so frequently in church settings. Marcus also told her that many people from Hispanic and/or Mexican cultures place great value upon collaboration and teamwork as effective problem-solving strategies. After learning these valuable lessons from Marcus, Jane found herself much more accepting of the behavior of these four children.

According to Cindy Little, managing editor of the periodical *Gifted Child Today,* children and youth who are potentially "dually eligible" (special education and gifted/talented programs) are more likely to be identified and served for their needs as students with disabilities than for their special abilities. That is, she believes that children who have disabilities often are not discovered also to have talents and gifts. This is particularly true of students with specific learning disabilities (SLD), because the dispersion of ability and achievement scores these children commonly get may be taken as indications of SLD but not of giftedness. Citing the example of actor Robin Williams ("Imagine being Robin Williams's fourth-grade teacher!"), Little was quoted as saying, "Uneven development is a red flag" and "It is worthwhile to look at the ones who act out" because they may be bored (quoted in Cosmos, 2002, pp. 1, 5). Little's comments call attention to the many unique needs of "twice-exceptional" children. We will discuss those needs toward the end of this chapter.

The status conditions discussed in this chapter have one thing in common: These are not disabilities. They only place students at risk if the climate at school, at home, and in the community is hostile and non-accommodating of differences. School cultures and policies that respond affirmatively to status conditions, environmental risk factors, and unusual abilities will do much to help many children and youth (Abedi, 2004).

INTRODUCTION

Chapter 11 focuses on teaching to meet the varied needs of children who are vulnerable in some way(s) but who do not qualify as a "child with a disability" under the Individuals with Disabilities Education Act (IDEA). Students who are at risk, who are culturally and/or linguistically diverse, and/or who are gifted/talented have several things in common with classified children.

1. *Causes.* Several of the disabilities discussed in this book may be caused by some of the factors discussed in this chapter. Thus, mental retardation and cerebral palsy are known to occur more frequently in families of low socioeconomic status (SES) than in families of middle or high SES. Similarly, genetics are known to play key roles in making children gifted and/or talented.
2. *Mis-classification.* Children from some of the backgrounds reviewed in this chapter may be erroneously labeled as being children with disabilities. For example, children who are linguistically diverse are sometimes wrongly classified as having speech or language impairments. (As explained earlier, in Chapter 4, if the determining factor is limited English proficiency, the child is not eligible under IDEA; see 34 C.F.R. 300.534 in the U.S. Department of Education's regulations for IDEA.) Students who are gifted and/or talented may be mis-classified in a different way: not identified and thus not provided with the services they need.
3. *Methods.* Strategies and techniques that are of proven utility with students having disabilities often are *also* effective with the kinds of children and youth discussed in this chapter. That is very fortuitous for educators. What they do in the classroom to facilitate inclusion can also improve outcomes by students who have needs that are not disability-related. In particular, many of the techniques of differentiated instruction that were discussed earlier in Chapter 8 can be helpful.

The bulk of this chapter focuses upon at-risk children and youth. The term **"at risk"** means "a set of presumed cause-and-effect dynamics that place the child or adolescent in danger of negative *future* events" (McWhirter, McWhirter, McWhirter, & McWhirter, 1998, p. 7; emphasis in original). The value of this definition is that it focuses our attention on the need, and also on the potential, to reduce that risk. The major such "future event" for our purposes here is not completing requirements for a high-school diploma. With respect to students who are gifted and/or talented, they may not reach their potential because schools did not respond to their needs.

We begin this chapter with students who live in *poverty.* Familial poverty is probably the single greatest risk factor for school failure. It is strongly associated with most of the other at-risk factors we will consider in this chapter. *Homeless and migrant* children fre-

Cultural sensitivity and cultural competence take many forms.

quently are in poverty. They are also at risk of not even being allowed to attend a neighborhood school, because their families lack a permanent address. We move then to examine *slow learners.* We do that because today's public schools are under growing pressure to raise academic standards for all students and, at the same time, to maintain or even raise the graduation rates. One group that may learn more slowly than would be expected from intelligence and other personal characteristics is that of children who have been *abused.* Drop-out rates are particularly high among many members of ethnic and racial *minority groups.* Worth special attention are students who present schools with challenges of *linguistic diversity.* Drop-out rates are also high among young women who become *pregnant*—and there is much that teachers can do to help those girls to avoid early pregnancies. Among boys, especially, dropping out is closely associated with *juvenile delinquency. Suicide* among children and youth is fortunately quite rare. It does occur more often than it should, however, and schools can take positive steps to prevent it. We conclude our review of at-risk behavior and conditions with *substance abuse,* particularly alcohol.

To a remarkable extent, at-risk factors (family poverty, homelessness, falling behind in school, abuse/neglect, minority-group status, linguistic diversity, teen pregnancy, juvenile delinquency, and substance abuse) tend to *occur together.* Stated differently, students who are "at risk" often display more than one of these kinds of status conditions or behavior. For example, substance abuse frequently leads to delinquent behavior. The National Institute on Drug Abuse, a federal agency that is part of the National Institutes of Health (NIH), reports on many of these interactions in its "Epidemiology of Youth Drug Abuse" reports (*http://www.nida.nih.gov*).

The state of the art today is that we *cannot* predict from the general to the specific. Stated differently, we cannot identify *individuals* at risk simply by examining broad trends. Indeed, it would be dangerous for you to attempt to do so. Rather, national data and trends in those data should be used as "indicators" that alert you to look more closely to see if in fact a particular child needs additional help.

The attitudes and actions of administrators, counselors, and teachers make school an uninviting place for some students. In fact, experts can make general predictions based on a school's characteristics. If the school adopts a rigorous and inflexible zero-tolerance policy, for example, and enforces it by expelling students after a single instance of unacceptable behavior, many students will feel unwelcome in that school and may, for this reason, become more at risk of dropping out of school (e.g., Leland, 2001).

This chapter concludes with discussion of students who are gifted and/or talented. Our focus here is upon what might be called "dually exceptional" or "twice-exceptional" students: those who have disabilities and are also gifted and/or talented. Teachers of inclusive classrooms need to be alert to the possibility that some children and youth who are included have special intellectual or other faculties. Overlooking their capabilities may result in their becoming frustrated and/or bored. Fortunately, techniques of differentiating instruction are as applicable to these students as to others who are included in general classrooms.

AT-RISK POPULATIONS

To be at risk, you will recall, is to be in jeopardy with respect to some future event, notably failure in school. The overall high-school drop-out rate in 1999 was about 11%, according to the National Center for Education Statistics (NCES; 2003). The rate varied greatly by race and ethnicity, from 7.3% among non-Hispanic whites to 11.0% among African Americans and 27.0% among persons of Hispanic origin (*http://nces.ed.gov/fastfacts/*). The word "dropout" is usually defined to mean someone who began ninth grade in a school district but did not complete twelfth grade in that district because she declined to continue in school. Drop-out rates declined throughout the 20th century. However, this century may be quite different. One reason is that we may have reached a "natural" drop-out rate beyond which further progress will be difficult. The major other reason is the newly established, much higher standards for graduation. Students who persisted through high school in years past, believing that they could make it, may give up in the face of much more rigorous demands.

That would be very unfortunate, indeed—for them and for all of us. Today's economy virtually demands a high-school diploma as the minimal entry standard for employment. Indeed, education attainment is the best predictor of subsequent employment and of economic stability (Entwisle, 1993). The NCES has offered some simple figures that illustrate the case. In 1950, when many of the grandparents of today's students were in the labor force, only about half of young adults held a high-school diploma. Both those with a high-school diploma, and those without one, were able to find work. By the early 1970s, when many parents of today's PreK–12 students were working, 84% of young adults were high-school graduates. At that time, it was possible, but difficult, for high-school dropouts to find jobs and they were limited largely to entry-level, low-paying jobs. Today, the labor market in many communities demands a high-school diploma even for minimum-wage jobs. As a result, high-school dropouts today are far more likely than are graduates to be unemployed or, if employed, to be making minimum wage. Life is highly stressful for dropouts, and things rarely get much better for them. That is why we find disproportionate numbers of dropouts among those arrested and incarcerated in the nation's prisons (NCES, *http://nces.ed.gov/fastfacts*; Office of Juvenile Justice and Delinquency Prevention, 1999).

In the interests of preventing school failure, teachers are expected to monitor the development of all children in their classes and, if they notice problems or potential problems, to initiate what special educators call *pre-referral intervention*. However, that term is misleading—and it suggests exactly the wrong goal. The intent is for teachers to find solutions in the school's *general* education services. Stated differently, the goal is to *obviate* (prevent) the necessity of a referral to special education. If you identify issues early enough, and mobilize appropriate resources effectively enough, you should succeed in retaining most of these students within the general education system—maximizing the students' opportunities for continued progress in school.

RISK FACTORS

What places students at risk of school failure? According to the National Dropout Prevention Center, at Clemson University, in South Carolina (*http://www.dropoutprevention.org*), the major factors are parental educational attainment (the less education on the part of the

TABLE 11.1 Early Indications of Possible At-Risk Status

Background Factors	Behavior Factors
Familial poverty	Excessive absenteeism
Parental under-education	Excessive tardiness
Single-parent household	Excessive disciplinary actions
Familial discord	Retentions

parents, the more likely dropping out becomes), family status (single-parent households are associated with higher risk of students dropping out), family discord (fighting between parents or between siblings and parents, etc., is associated with high drop-out rates), and familial poverty (low family income is positively correlated with high rates of dropping out). The Center also identified indicators of heightened risk. Notable among these are behaviors that teachers and administrators easily can track: absenteeism, tardiness, number of disciplinary actions, number of counseling visits, number of failing grades, low test scores, and number of retentions (being held back, or not promoted to the next grade). Table 11.1 summarizes these risk factors. Experts recommend early identification of students who appear to be in trouble, rapid mobilization of support services for these students, and active monitoring of their progress (Kauffman, 2001; Walker, 2000).

CHILDREN OF POVERTY

Low family income is a significant factor placing children and youth at risk of school failure. This should not be overemphasized. Perhaps nothing is more central to the American dream than the story of Horatio Alger, who rose from the depths of poverty and many other disadvantages to find success in work and in life. Most of us know people who may not have lived such a story-book life but nonetheless survived childhood poverty and went on to build a life that was firmly middle class or even upper class. That being said, on the whole, familial poverty brings with it a host of dangers, some of which place children at risk in school.

Definition

Poverty for a family of four in the United States in 2002 was defined as a family income from all sources of not more than $18,000 (Proctor & Dalaker, 2002). For a family of three, the level was just over $14,000 a year. To give these numbers some context, consider that an adult working 40 hours a week, 50 weeks a year, at $7/hour, or about minimum wage, would earn $14,000 a year. There are variations from state to state, and from urban to rural areas, reflecting differences in the cost of living. The median family income in 2002 was $42,400 (Income in the United States: 2002, at *http://www.census.gov/prod/2003pubs/p60-221.pdf*). This means that half of all households had incomes above that level and half below it.

Characteristics and Types

Familial poverty carries with it many implications. Children from such families are at risk for many reasons. They often suffer from malnutrition. Their parents frequently are not well-educated themselves, so they can offer only minimal help with homework. Many families living in poverty are, or until recently were, on public assistance. The welfare-reform effort launched by the 1996 Personal Responsibility and Work Opportunity Reconciliation Act has cut many of these families off from welfare. Able-bodied adults, usually mothers, were required by the **Temporary Assistance to Needy Families (TANF)** program, which replaced traditional welfare, to find and take a job within 2 years. Many did.

However, as a nationwide study by the Children's Defense Fund (CDF) illustrated, employment often did not lift them out of poverty. The Center asked questions of 5,000 families and individuals in 180 cities and towns across the nation. More than half (58%) of those who were working still had below-poverty incomes. Worse, about one in every three soon lost that job, frequently because of child-care problems. As a result of unpredictable incomes, many had to move. This meant that their children were removed from one school and placed into another. CDF's study shows that the "success story" of welfare reform has a dark underbelly (Children's Defense Fund, 2000).

When families live in poverty, other factors come into play. One is residence in older, less well-maintained buildings. These structures often have residual lead paint; as we saw earlier, lead paint is an important known cause of mental retardation. A second factor is erratic medical care. Families on public assistance generally qualify for Medicaid, the federal-state medical insurance program for the poor. As their incomes rise above poverty level and they leave welfare, however, their eligibility for Medicaid ceases. Unfortunately, many low-paying jobs and many part-time jobs carry with them no employer-provided medical insurance. The predictable result is that many of these families have no medical coverage. That translates, in turn, into delayed or even foregone medical care for their children. Cerebral palsy is known to be associated with low birth weight; that, in turn, is often a function of poor prenatal care and of poverty in the family. Illnesses that could be treated with no lasting effects instead produce disabilities. Measles, mumps, meningitis, and other childhood illnesses are known to cause hearing loss (including deafness), blindness, and other disabilities.

Prevalence

About one in every six school-age children, or 16%, live in low-SES families. These 12 million children and youth are "children of poverty." To place the number into context, consider that the total number of children with any disability discussed in this book is about six million. Most Americans who are poor are white. In 2001, 32 million white non-Hispanic persons and 8 million white Hispanic persons of all ages were poor, as against 8 million African-American individuals, 1.2 million Asian Americans, and 700,000 Native Americans (Proctor & Dalaker, 2002).

Causes

Many American families are of low SES, despite the economic growth of the country during the 1990s. The reasons they are poor are several. Prominent is the large number of single-parent households. Usually, these units are headed by women who either never married or were divorced. These women tend to be poorly educated. Large numbers became mothers while still teens themselves. Often these women can qualify only for low-paying jobs. Frequently, too, they can only work part time, because of difficulty in securing child-care services (Children's Defense Fund, 2000). In other cases, divorce results in a mother-child(ren) unit suddenly thrown into poverty. Even when two adult earners are present in the home, poverty may still occur, generally because one or both of the adults works part- rather than full-time, usually because of child-care needs. In some instances, illness or disability in the family may impoverish it by saddling the family with very high medical expenses.

Instructional Methods

Preschool services are available to 3-, 4- and 5-year-old children and their families, under the Head Start Act (PL 101-538). A smaller program, known as Early Head Start, helps even younger children and their families. At the elementary and secondary levels, remedial services are offered to students from low-SES families under Title I of Elementary and Secondary Education Act (ESEA) which was discussed earlier (see Chapter 1).

Early intervention, including early-childhood programming, can provide life-long benefits.

Strategies in Early Childhood and Elementary School

Methods: Early Intervention. We have known for many years that early intervention can ameliorate many of the effects of familial poverty. Head Start and Early Head Start programs provide preschoolers and infants/toddlers with a nutritious meal each day and with regular medical care. They also offer intellectual stimulation that may be lacking at home. Often, children benefit significantly. The fact that these effects tend to dissipate by the time the child turns 10 should not dissuade us from supporting such early childhood programs (Zigler & Valentine, 1979). Rather, they should inspire us to continue such efforts in elementary schools. This means ensuring that children are fed each day, seen periodically by a school nurse, and stimulated intellectually in class. It also means, as early intervention projects have shown, that teachers show parents how to support their children's learning (e.g., Bowe, 2000a).

Methods: Collaboration with Compensatory and Remedial Programs. Children from low-SES families who attend K–12 schools usually are eligible for Title I programs. Because teachers see these children every day, and can notice effects of familial poverty, educators often are the first line of defense for these vulnerable children. You can find out what resources your school offers and make sure that the family takes advantage of them. For example, not all children who are eligible for free or reduced-cost lunches are enrolled in those programs. Some schools are willing to make the school nursing staff available for periodic physical examinations of children who are known to come from families that do not have health insurance.

The reading, writing, mathematics, and other content-area specialists who are employed by schools using Title I funds are professionals with whom you should actively collaborate. As a teacher, you could make sure they know how eligible children are doing in your class, what needs they are displaying, and what abilities or talents you recognize them as having. You might ask the specialists to consult with you on ways you can enhance your own teaching.

Strategies in Middle School and High School

Methods: Preventing Dropout. Before- and after-school programs are as important at the secondary level as they are in elementary schools, if not more so. Young people living in households with low incomes are *five times* as likely to drop out of high school as were same-age peers from families with high incomes (National Center for Education

Statistics [NCES], 2001a). An important advantage of after-school supplementary activities is that these "keep the kids off the street." As illustrated throughout this chapter, poor children and children experiencing difficulty in school may be tempted to engage in harmful activities during the afternoon hours. Activities that teens find interesting, and which they perceive as being beneficial on the short as well as the long run, may steer them away from dropping out and from dangerous and deleterious after-school behavior.

Methods: Offering a "Carrot." Adolescents who come from poor families need to be made aware of opportunities for which they may qualify on the basis of family income. Notable among those are college scholarships. Teachers and counselors may foster in these young people the habit of thinking and planning for the long term. The realities of life at home may have exposed them principally to short-term thinking, that is, crisis management. For these teens to escape similar circumstances as adults, however, they need to adopt a long-term perspective and to appreciate the potential of further education for helping them to escape the cycle of poverty. Helping them to envision a future for themselves that is brighter than their present often helps to motivate these young people.

Strategies in Transition to Adult Life

Methods: Networking. It is urgent that teachers make clear to high-school students that dropping out is not an irreversible decision. Most young people know at least several dropouts. Ask them to communicate with these peers the fact that programs are available in the community for completion of requirements, for example, the GED. Dropouts may listen more to their still-in-school peers than to adults such as teachers and counselors.

HOMELESS OR MIGRANT CHILDREN

Paradoxically, an economically vibrant America in the 21st century is home to hundreds of thousands of temporarily or permanently homeless persons and to similarly large numbers of migrant families with children. Both homeless and migrant children are at high risk of school failure, particularly for dropping out of school. They are also at risk for disabilities, including mental retardation and learning disabilities (from exposure to lead paint in the shelters where they reside) and cancer (from pesticides in the fields they work).

Definitions

The major federal law on educating homeless children, the Stewart B. McKinney Homeless Assistance Act, recently amended as part of the Improving America's Schools Act (PL 103-382; 42 U.S.C. 11431-35), defines a **homeless person** as

1. an individual who lacks a fixed, regular, and adequate nighttime residence; and
2. an individual who has a primary nighttime residence that is
   - **a.** a supervised publicly or privately operated shelter designed to provide temporary living accommodations (including welfare hotels, congregate shelters, and transitional housing for the mentally ill);
   - **b.** an institution that provides a temporary residence for individuals intended to be institutionalized; or
   - **c.** a public or private place not designed for, or ordinarily used as, a regular sleeping accommodation for human beings. (Section 100(1)(1)(2), 42 U.S.C. 11302[a])

This definition excludes children placed in foster care, as well as anyone imprisoned or otherwise detained by federal or state law. Children of migrant workers may be considered to be homeless if they meet the above definition. However, many do reside in permanent residences and for that reason are not considered to be homeless.

The Interstate Migrant Education Council (*http://www.migedimec.org*) defined **migrant children** as the children of migrant workers who move from town to town, and state to state, seeking employment, generally in agricultural, fishing, or food processing work. Because they enroll, or seek to enroll, in several schools during any given school year, migrant children frequently interrupt their education or participate sporadically in school.

Characteristics and Types

Children who are homeless are disproportionally African American and Hispanic, are poor, and often lack basic skills (academic, emotional, gross and fine motor), for which reasons they are at risk of not completing high school (Williams & DeSander, 1999). These children are at risk for disabilities because of inadequate medical care, insufficient nutrition, and exposure to lead in the older buildings where they and their families seek shelter. In addition, their parents frequently lack a high-school education themselves, are preoccupied with meeting basic survival needs for the family, and often do not know their rights and their children's rights (Rafferty, 1999; Williams & DeSander, 1999). Young children who are homeless tend to be particularly delayed in language, social interaction and attention span. They often are retained (kept back in grade) because of low test scores (Tucker, 1999). Even a brief period of homelessness is "a major life event with devastating consequences for children" (Rafferty, 1999, p. 19). Nonetheless, many children who are homeless for long periods of time still manage to complete requirements for a high-school diploma; some become college graduates.

Bernstein (2001) offered an absorbing portrait of homeless children in a front-page article for the Sunday *New York Times*. She wrote about a 55-year-old grandmother struggling from a different shelter each morning to bring four young children, all clean, fed, and in uniforms, to their Manhattan school. Each evening, she waited in the shelter for their late bus, then took them to whatever shelter they had been assigned. Often she did not learn of that assignment until well after the children's bedtime. Such conditions clearly are not conducive to the timely completion of homework assignments.

Migrant labor tends to be seasonal. This fact forces migrant workers to move several times during any year as they seek employment. Children of migrant families also tend to be at risk because their parents typically lack formal education and are poor. Belton (2000) quoted one teen who was expected to prepare dinner for her family each day until, at age 10, she joined her parents in the fields: "I'd say in my mind, gosh, what you know in the morning was what you would know at the end of the day. There's no growth taking place here" (p. 464). Migrant children also may be anxious because of discontinuities between their personal and home experiences and what they see in school, because of language/communication differences between home and school, and because of cultural differences between parents and teachers (Brunn, 1999).

Prevalence

Counting homeless children is difficult. The best estimates, from the National Coalition for the Homeless, are that some 800,000 people are homeless on any given night and perhaps double that number is homeless at some time during any given year (National Coalition for the Homeless at *http://www.nationalhomeless.org*). According to the Interstate Migrant Education Council (2004), about 800,000 school-age children live in migrant families, many of which have no permanent housing.

Causes

Homelessness among children has many possible causes. Frequently, two factors act in concert. First, one or both parents may lose employment and thus the family may be forced to move out of an apartment or home. Second, affordable housing often is in short supply. While family poverty and the unavailability of low-cost apartments and other kinds of housing are the major factors, children sometimes become homeless for other reasons.

Some families expel children and youth who break family rules by, for example, abusing drugs. Such "throwaway children" sometimes include young women who become pregnant. For their part, children and youth may leave parents who abuse alcohol and/or drugs or who engage in physical, mental, or sexual abuse of their children. Finally, nature may play a role, as when tornadoes or hurricanes strike (Tucker, 1999).

Instructional Methods

Educators need to be sensitive to the fact that homeless and migrant students may have gaps in their education. That is why supplementary instruction can be very helpful. These children and youth may also be vulnerable to teasing from other students. Teachers should establish, and enforce, zero-tolerance policies on harassment.

Strategies in Early Childhood and Elementary School

Methods: Extra Services. The McKinney Act established, as national policy, that children who are homeless must neither be denied a free public education nor separated from neighborhood schools: "Homelessness alone should not be sufficient reason to separate students from the mainstream school environment" (Section 721[3]). At the elementary level, this policy calls upon schools to take steps to provide whatever remediation and tutoring in basic skills these children may need, to offer counseling, and to supply whatever special-education services these children may require. Belton (2000) suggested a simple service: allowing students to take school books with them as the family moves away after the end of the grape harvest, returning the books a few months later when the family returns for the beginning of the next season. It is often necessary to extend the school calendar with before-school and after-school activities as well as summer programs (Rafferty, 1999; U.S. Department of Education, 1995). This can be difficult for school systems, because the McKinney Act provides little funding for such activities.

Counseling may be particularly important for migrant children. The lives of migrant families, especially those who recently crossed the border from Mexico, can be traumatic. Each year, hundreds of migrants die in border crossings. The Center for Immigration Research, at the University of Houston, released an analysis of border deaths in March, 2001. The report showed that families may attempt to cross at remote, dangerous locations, due to the increased security measures taken by the United States at less treacherous sites in Texas, Arizona, New Mexico, and southern California. The result is that husbands and fathers, who often are the first to attempt such crossings, are dying in large numbers.

For more information on the report released by the Center for Immigration Research, go to the Web Links module in Chapter 11 of the Companion Website.

Methods: Preventing Stigma. Steps to help these children to avoid stigmatization may be vital. Reed-Victor and Pelco (1999) described how one bus driver altered his daily route so as to pick up homeless children first, in the mornings, and drop them off last, in the afternoons. He did this so that other children would not see that the children were homeless. At another school, secretaries hid student backpacks in the principal's office, so other children would not see that some children brought their belongings to school (fearing they would be stolen if left in the shelter).

Methods: Inter-Agency Collaboration. Volunteers from one church helped families to local housing and to secure household supplies and furnishings. Church members coordinated these efforts with local school officials, thus assuring that the many diverse needs of these families were met simultaneously (Quint, 1994). In another community, five family shelters cooperated with school officials to create shelter-based communities of learning that supplemented school-based programs (Nunez & Collignon, 1997). These efforts demonstrate how schools and other agencies can create bridges that meet the many needs of homeless families.

Strategies in Middle School and High School

Methods: Striking a Balance. Entwisle (1993) suggested that teachers hold homeless students to rigorous academic standards, insisting that they remain on task, that they complete homework, and that they show evidence of satisfactory progress toward goals. At the same time, teachers should be understanding of the extraordinary demands placed upon many of these children. Children residing in shelters may have no suitable space in which to do homework. Teens in migrant families often must join their parents in the fields. Others are told to have dinner ready when the adults return in the evenings. For these reasons, teachers need to demonstrate sensitivity and flexibility. They may, for example, arrange for peer tutoring during homeroom or study hall periods, so that much (if not all) homework may be completed at school.

Methods: Evaluations and Records. A major issue in high schools is the frequent unavailability of vital records. The peripatetic nature of homeless families (they move from shelter to shelter, from community to community) means, among other things, that evaluations and tests may be conducted in one school but not provided to the family. At times, the new school may not be able to secure those data either. That is why teacher-conducted assessments, even if informal, can be helpful (Reed-Victor & Pelco, 1999). Migrant families may not take records with them as they move from farm to farm. Many, lacking much formal education themselves, may not appreciate the importance of school records for their children.

Strategies in Transition to Adult Life

Methods: Information for Parents. According to Belton (2000), many migrant parents are astonished to learn about the wide variety of scholarships and loans available to help young people continue their education. When schools reach out to these parents, asking their advice and telling them about these opportunities, the change in attitude can be dramatic. Belton reports that "the overwhelming majority of parents emerge as ardent supporters of their children's education. Some of the strictest parents, ones who might not allow their children to date or to wear makeup, become parents who will drive in the middle of the night so that their children will be able to participate in late school functions" (p. 465).

SLOW LEARNERS

The heightened graduation requirements in many states place large numbers of students at risk for dropping out of school. Standards they could meet in past years, to qualify for, for example, a vocational diploma, may no longer even exist. Rather, all or virtually all students may now be expected to meet higher standards. In the recent past, about two-thirds of high-school graduates went on to some kind of post-secondary program (college or university, junior college, vocational/trade school, etc.). Today's raised academic standards for high-school graduation seem to envision virtually all continuing on to college. Accordingly, students for whom college never was a realistic expectation now are at greater risk of not graduating from high school. These facts illustrate an important truth: The status of being a "slow learner" is a school-defined status. It is not something inherent in the child.

Recall that children with intelligence quotients (IQs) of 70 or below could be classified as "mentally retarded" if they also displayed behavior that was characteristic of younger children (see Chapter 5). What about children with IQs between 70, on the lower end, and 85 on the upper end? These students have IQ scores that are below average. They are not mentally retarded, so they do not qualify (on that basis) for special education. However, their ability to learn is markedly lower than is that of students with IQs in the "normal range" (85 to 115). That is why they are often referred to as **"slow learners."**

Teaching this young man through his interests *will likely help him to learn.*

Definition

Slow learners are defined as students who can learn what other students do, but more slowly, with more effort, and with more assistance from teachers and others. While IQ scores in the range of 70 to 85 are a major part of our understanding of the term "slow learners," some students with higher IQs are also slow learners. These individuals may be fluent, even expert, in some areas of knowledge that are less-valued by the school. Here we see, yet again, that schools can place children at risk. By changing, schools may alleviate that risk.

Characteristics and Types

Slow learners tend to expend much more effort to learn and, despite this exertion, master only some of what is taught. This pattern repeats year after year. Accordingly, these students accumulate deficits. Many are kept back a year. Eventually, large numbers become frustrated or lose interest in school. They may do much better when information is presented in a way that captures their interest (Pressley & McCormick, 1995). For example, teaching math concepts in the context of real-world applications may be much more effective than teaching it in more traditional ways. If teachers do not take such affirmative steps, slow learners will often become distracted, because they do not understand what is being taught and because they fear embarrassment if they publicize this fact by asking questions. The result is a self-perpetuating cycle of ever-greater levels of school failure. The usual result is dropping out (McWhirter, et al., 1998).

Research reviewed by Pressley and McCormick (1995) offers real hope for teachers concerned about reaching slow learners. In study after study discussed by these authors, fluency and expertise in some area were shown to result much more from people's *interests* than from their general intelligence. Whether researchers looked at people who were good at betting on horse races, radiologists who were good at reading X-rays, or teachers who were good in the classroom, consistent findings emerged. The experts were intensely interested in what they were doing, and had invested large amounts of time in their specific endeavors. General intelligence explained much less of the differences between these experts and novices or less-skilled individuals. This research suggests that teachers identify student interests and then find ways to teach academic content *through* those interest areas. Math, for example, may be taught effectively by using sports-related exercises. Reading may be taught well by allowing students themselves to select the books they want to read. Doing all this does add to the teacher's workload. Over the course of a year, however, it may actually reduce that workload by obviating the need for repeated instruction or other remedial help.

Prevalence

Some 16% of all students (about one in every six) have IQs in the 70 to 85 range. Stated differently, nearly 9 million elementary and secondary students, out of the nation's 53 million, are slow learners. Figure 11.1 graphically illustrates how large this group is. Another way of appreciating the size of this group is to see that it is one-third larger than is the total of all PreK–12 students with disabilities (see Figure 11.2).

FIGURE 11.1 Prevalence: Slow Learners v. Students with Disabilities

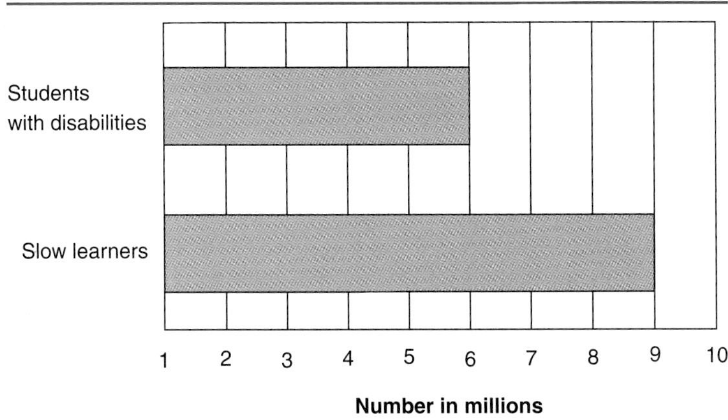

Source: From National Center for Educational Statistics (2003).

FIGURE 11.2 Estimates: K–12 Students

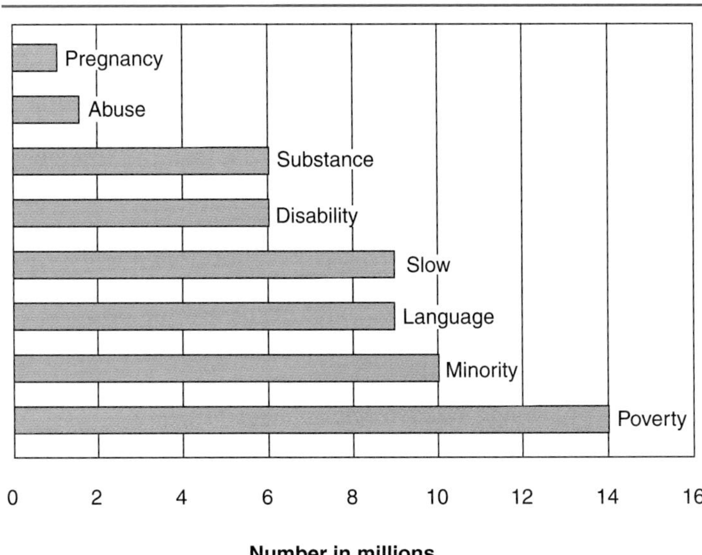

Source: From National Center for Educational Statistics (2003).

Causes

Not all students with IQs in this range are slow learners. It is also true that students with higher IQs can also be slow learners. Some children behave as "slow learners" because their backgrounds gave them knowledge and skills that differ from those that teachers expect to find in a given school's population. This may be because the family recently moved into the area, especially if they came from another country. Other children perform as slow learners because their family lives do not support their education (parents may be unavailable or unable to help with homework, may insist that children supervise younger siblings at home, etc.). Kaufman (2001) wrote movingly about being kept back in first grade, because her school did not accommodate her "immaturity." She was much more interested at that age in other people and in her relationships with them than she was in academic learning. Rather than adjusting—by, for example, teaching her academics through activities that tapped her interests and talents—the school labeled her a "slow learner" and forced her to repeat first grade.

Instructional Methods

Students who are slow learners need supplementary instruction. This may be particularly true in years in which they are expected to participate in district-wide and state-wide testing. Because many can blossom when allowed to focus upon areas of interest, they should be encouraged to pursue activities in which they show promise.

Strategies in Early Childhood and Elementary School

Methods: Stopping the Accumulation of Deficits. Smaller classes, more individualized instruction, and many community-based experiences may well assist slow learners to keep pace during the elementary years. Title I compensatory and supplementary programs often help these students. However, not all qualify for such assistance, which is limited to students who are classified as "disadvantaged," usually for reasons of familial poverty. Teachers must strive to ensure that these students master the basics at each grade level, so as to minimize the usual accumulation of deficits over time. Some of the techniques discussed in this book as helpful for students with mental retardation or specific learning disabilities also may be useful. Notable among these are the use of manipulatives (concrete materials) to teach conceptual knowledge and thinking skills, Direct Instruction (specific teaching followed by testing, review, and re-teaching), and peer tutoring (reciprocal and interactive tutoring by fellow students) (see Chapter 8).

Strategies in Middle School and High School

Methods: Support in Reaching Standards. Testing is much more heavily emphasized in high school than in elementary school. This greatly increases the pressure for achievement. While all students feel that pressure, few will find it as debilitating and discouraging as will slow learners. Teachers, counselors, and other school officials need to determine, on a child-by-child basis, whether the new, higher learning standards are appropriate goals or whether, instead, a vocational/trade sequence, combined with work-study opportunities, might better suit some slow learners. These slower tracks and more concrete learning opportunities may increase motivation and thus accomplishment by many students who are slow learners. Peer tutoring has potential as an intervention strategy. High-school students reading at second- to sixth-grade levels improved reading comprehension in a recent study of peer tutoring (Fuchs, Fuchs, & Kazdan, 1999).

Strategies in Transition to Adult Life

Methods: Helping Them to Find Their Niches. Individuals who were slow learners during the early childhood/elementary years and during high school may blossom as adults, when they finally can choose their own activities. These allow them to further develop their interests. Others, especially those who eventually dropped out of high school, may experience limited vocational success in today's economy. However, opportunities for employment exist as sanitation workers, janitors, fast-food and other service employees, cab drivers and long-haul truck drivers, and so on. Some of these jobs pay quite well, particularly because there often are more of them than there are job-seekers looking for them (this depends on the strength of the economy). Especially if these individuals have a spouse or partner who also works, it is quite possible for them to make a respectable living despite a modest academic record.

VICTIMS OF ABUSE

Child abuse and neglect, unfortunately, are persistent features of American life. In part, this seems to be a function of certain American values. The family, and the home, remain islands where privacy is respected. This community "hands-off" attitude gives abusers some latitude for their activities. The antiquated belief of some American males that they are inherently superior to women, simply because they are bigger and stronger, also contributes. Most directly, though, child abuse and neglect seem to vary according to two other variables: substance abuse, especially of alcohol, and familial poverty (National Clearinghouse on Child Abuse and Neglect Information, *http://www.calib.com/nccanch*). Educators should bear in mind that abuse in the home affects not only the child who is subjected to abuse, but siblings as well.

Definitions

According to the Child Abuse Prevention and Treatment Act (CAPTA; 42 U.S.C. 5106), as amended in 1996 by PL 104-235, the term "child" refers to persons under 18 years of age. Child abuse and neglect is "any recent act or failure to act on the part of a parent or caretaker which results in death, serious physical or emotional harm, sexual abuse or exploitation; an act or failure to act which presents an imminent risk of serious harm." Thus **abuse** is an overt act taken against another person. **Child abuse** refers to actions against children that have physical, emotional, and/or mental consequences. **Sexual abuse** is defined in the same law (CAPTA) as

> the employment, use, persuasion, inducement, enticement, or coercion of any child to engage in, or assist any other person to engage in, any sexually explicit conduct or simulation of such conduct for the purpose of producing a visual depiction of such conduct; the rape, and in cases of caretaker or inter-familial relationships, statutory rape, molestation, prostitution, or other form of sexual exploitation of children, or incest with children.

The Clearinghouse defined physical abuse as "the infliction of physical injury as a result of punching, beating, kicking, biting, burning, shaking or otherwise harming a child." It noted that these acts need not be intentional. They may result from unintentional overpunishing and/or overdisciplining a child. This source characterized emotional abuse as acts or failure to act that caused, or could have caused, serious behavioral, cognitive, emotional, or mental disorders.

The Clearinghouse defined child **neglect** as "failure to provide for the child's basic needs." It stated that neglect may be physical, educational, or emotional/mental. Physical neglect includes refusal of or delay in the provision of health care, abandonment of the child, or inadequate supervision. Educational neglect includes allowing children to be chronically absent from school as well as neglect of the child's special educational needs. Emotional neglect incorporates ignoring a child's need for affection, failing to provide needed psychological care, and allowing the child to abuse controlled substances. Each state defines these terms in its own way. Most, however, include the above elements in their state definitions (Clearinghouse, *http://www.calib.com/nccanch*).

Characteristics and Types

Children who have been sexually and/or physically abused often carry on their bodies physical evidence of such abuse, such as bruises or scars. Psychological and sexual abuse sometimes manifest themselves behaviorally in the children. For example, children may come to school early, leave late, and spend much of their time in school physically proximate to a trusted adult, usually a teacher. Neglect may be seen in the childrens' clothes (the same clothes being worn repeatedly, clothes that are not regularly cleaned, clothes with rips and tears, etc.) and in their appetites (either ravenously hungry during school hours or listless because of malnutrition). Children who have been abused or neglected also may be highly distractible, as they are anxious much of the time and so unable to focus on school work.

Prevalence

In 1998, some 1.4 million children in the United States received child protective services. They represented 2% of all children in the country. Estimating the number of instances of neglect and abuse that occurred in 1998 (some children receiving protection in 1998 had been harmed in an earlier year), the *Child Maltreatment 1998* report (U.S. Department of Health and Human Services, 2000) offered the following figures: 903,000 victims, of whom 53% were neglected, 23% were physically abused, 12% were sexually abused, and 6% were psychologically abused. In addition, 25% were abused and/or neglected in more than one way. Most frequently victimized were very young children under the age of three. By race/ethnicity, the rates of abuse and/or neglect ranged from a high of 2% of all African-American children and 2% of Native-American/Alaska Native children, to a low of 1% of Hispanic children and 0.8% of white children.

Causes

In most instances, we can only speculate about why adults abuse children or neglect them. The adults rarely volunteer this information. The statistics help us to get some sense of causation, however. Neglect is, as noted above, more common than abuse. Since women are the primary care givers of young children, it is not surprising that the most common form of child victimization is *neglect by a female parent.* Physical and sexual abuse, by contrast, were most commonly perpetrated by adult males, usually the father (Clearinghouse, *http://www.calib.com/nccanch*). Anecdotal evidence suggests that some of the reported neglect and abuse is related to adult substance abuse. In particular, mothers who use crack cocaine or other illegal drugs, or who drink excessively, may neglect their children in favor of their habits. When drunk or high on drugs, men and women may become violent. Babies who won't stop crying, including "colicky" babies, may exhaust parents,

Resources That Work

Abuse and Neglect

The major source for updated information about child abuse and neglect is the National Clearinghouse on Child Abuse and Neglect Information (*http://www.calib.com/nccanch*). The site maintains information on some 32,000 records of reported abuse and neglect. The U.S. Department of Health and Human Services annual publication, *Child Maltreatment,* which draws from the same database, offers a great deal of information. The Child Welfare League of America (*http://www.cwla.org/advocacy/*) is another good resource. A summary of state rules about reporting of abuse and neglect is offered at *http://www.smith-lawfirm.com/mandatory_reporting.htm*. Phone numbers are posted at How to Report Suspected Child Abuse and Neglect, *http://www.acf.hhs.gov/programs/cb/publications/rpt_abu.htm*. You may obtain other phone numbers and reporting information from your building principal.

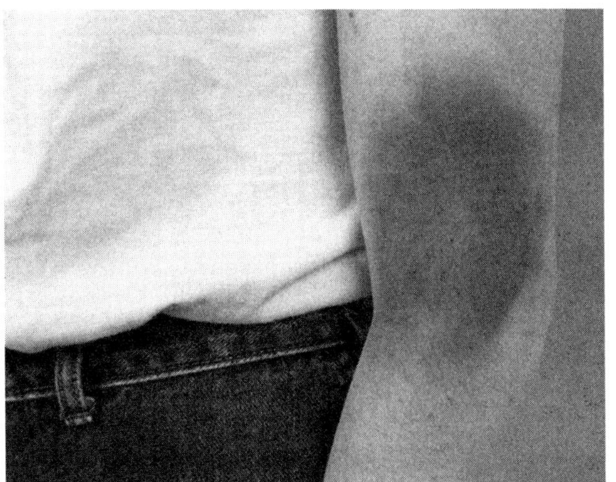

Teachers are required to report evidence of apparent abuse.

who then strike back. There are also numerous reports in both the media and in professional journals of neglect and abuse by poorly trained, poorly supervised workers in daycare facilities. Tragically, children who have disabilities already are at heightened risk for physical and mental abuse, and also for sexual abuse (Bowe, 2000a, b).

Instructional Methods

Strategies in Early Childhood and Elementary School

Methods: Report Suspicions. Every state requires teachers to report instances of suspected abuse. Typically, these state laws protect teachers who do so from retaliation; you may not be prosecuted by parents or other adults if as a teacher you acted on a reasonable basis for suspecting abuse or neglect (Lowenthal, 1996). The nearby box, "Resources That Work: Abuse and Neglect," offers information on how to report suspicious incidents. Although state laws vary considerably, most require teachers to be in possession of physical evidence of abuse and neglect or to have reason to believe a child who reports such abuse and neglect. This evidence need not be conclusive. The actual investigation and substantiation of the claims is made, not by teachers or other educators, but rather by representatives of county and state child protective services agencies. Your job as a teacher is to report your suspicions, usually in a toll-free phone call, to the appropriate investigative agencies (Lowenthal, 1996).

What do you look for? Abuse may be signaled by physical evidence, such as bruises on arms and legs. It may also be indicated if young children show evidence, perhaps in drawings or in things they say, of unusual knowledge about sexuality. As suggested earlier, neglect may be evidenced by a continually unkempt appearance, a persistent failure to maintain ordinary levels of cleanliness, and frequent hunger.

Strategies in Middle School and High School

Methods: Gain and Keep Trust. Abuse and neglect continue to be problems at the secondary level, despite the fact that teens are bigger and more sophisticated than are young children, thus more equipped to avoid and resist adults. Teachers and counselors are unlikely to know which teens are or were abused or neglected, unless the adolescents voluntarily impart this information. However, the effects of abuse and/or neglect at earlier ages often persist, having numerous deleterious effects on student learning in high school. Those effects may include an unwillingness to trust adults (including teachers), excessive shyness, and feelings of inferiority and of insecurity. In each instance, teachers should focus upon the problems they see students having. You may demonstrate that you, at least, can be trusted, that you respect student desires for privacy, and that you value the student as an individual.

Strategies in Transition to Adult Life

Methods: Recommend Counseling. Many adults who abuse or neglect children have a history of abuse and/or neglect themselves. This cycle of abuse and neglect is not inevitable, however. According to one source, most children who are abused/neglected do *not* repeat the behavior when they become adults (Clearinghouse, *http://www.calib.com/nccanch*). This is particularly true when adolescents and adults take advantage of counseling services. During the transition years (when students are 14 years of age or older), you as a teacher of an inclusive classroom may put students in touch with local counseling programs.

MINORITY GROUP STATUS

Minority groups are, by definition, populations that do not comprise a majority. In the United States today, the majority consists of Caucasian (white) persons, of individuals who speak English exclusively or primarily, and of people who consider themselves to be of middle socioeconomic status (SES). Thus, people who are non-white, who speak or prefer to speak languages other than English, and/or who consider themselves to be of lower or higher SES are, by definition, members of minority groups. For our purposes in this book, we will use the term **"minority group"** membership to refer to people who belong to one or more ethnic or racial minority groups. Our focus here is on racial minority groups. Later, we will look at linguistic minorities.

Schools in the United States are rapidly heading toward a "no-majority" situation in which no one ethnic or racial group comprises more than 50% of the school population. California has already reached it: There, most people belong to minority groups. In some cities, as many as 85% of all school children come from minority groups. Nationwide, the proportion today is 35%. Projections indicate that it will exceed 50% by the year 2040 (*Education Week,* 2000b). By that time there will be no racial/ethnic majority group as such. Rather, there will be several minority groups.

Definition

Majority and minority group status are defined along several demographic variables. About 65% of Americans of school age today are what demographics call "white non-Hispanic" individuals. They are, in other words, members of majority groups. The others, about one third in all, are African American, Asian American, Native American, or some other minority group. Among ethnic groups, persons of Hispanic origin may be of any race. When demographers talk about "persons of Hispanic origin," they refer to individuals who identify themselves as descended from at least some South American, Mexican, or Spanish persons. Other relatives may be white, non-Hispanic; some may be black.

Characteristics and Types

Many minority groups have cultural tenets that contribute to their members' success, both in school and in later life. Asian Americans, for example, often study together. When one member of the study group "can't see it," another volunteers a tutorial that helps the individual. Many African-American and Native-American individuals show a striking respect for other people by insisting that meetings begin, not at some pre-determined time as classes do in schools, but when all expected participants have arrived. There often are very strong extended families in minority communities. Korean-American families, for example, will make important decisions only after the entire family has been consulted. As these examples illustrate, minority-group status itself does not place students at risk for school failure. When problems arise, they are due, rather, to the *school's* inflexibility or unwillingness to accommodate differences.

Despite these facts, children of minority group status are more likely than are children in majority groups to come from poor families. In 2001, 23% of African Americans and 21% of white Hispanic Americans lived in poverty, versus 7.8% of white non-Hispanic individuals. Among the smaller minority groups, 26% of Native Americans and 11% of Asian Americans lived in poverty (Proctor & Dalaker, 2002). This is important information for educators, because poverty places children at risk for failure in school. Yet teachers must remember that correlation is not causation. To illustrate, the statistics given in this paragraph may be viewed from another perspective: 77% of African Americans, 79% of white Hispanic Americans, 74% of Native Americans, and 89% of Asian Americans do *not* live in poverty.

Stereotyping is dangerous. People differ greatly in the extent to which they identify with (i.e., consider themselves to belong to) minority groups. For example, one cannot assume that white Hispanic Americans identify with Spanish culture. People also differ greatly in the extent to which they adopt different cultures, which means that individual students may identify with *some* aspects of one culture and some of another (Sciarra, 1999). We will visit this issue again later (see p. 404, "Linguistic Diversity").

Prevalence

About 20 million American school children are members of one or more minority groups. They comprise 35% of all PreK–12 students. African Americans are by far the largest racial minority group in the United States and in the public schools. The fastest-growing group is that of Asian Americans. Of the estimated 20 million, half belonged to ethnic or racial minority groups as defined in this book. The other 10 million were persons of Hispanic origin (see p. 404, "Linguistic Diversity").

Causes

People are born into different ethnic and racial minority groups. Thus, being in a minority group is a "status" and not a condition. One cannot meaningfully discuss its "cause" except to discuss what causes people to consider themselves to belong to one or another minority group. Many children come from multiracial and/or multiethnic backgrounds. As Sciarra (1999) pointed out, they may consider themselves to be members of different cultures, or even to belong to a hybrid culture of their own creation. In this sense, causation refers to their own decisions about their preferred identities.

Instructional Methods

As a teacher, you should instruct students who are members of minority groups in the same ways as you teach those who belong to majority groups. *All* of your teaching, regardless of student group membership, should be informed by cultural competence and cultural sensitivity. We review these below.

Strategies in Early Childhood and Elementary School

Methods: Acquire Cultural Competence. You need to become culturally competent. This means that you infuse your instruction with behavior that responds to the different cultural backgrounds of your students. You must also foster understanding about and respect for other traditions in the children you teach. These steps will help minority group status children in your classrooms to be more successful. In turn, that will reduce overreferral of minority groups to special education. As you will recall from Chapter 1, such overreferral is widely recognized as a major problem in American education today.

For more information on the problems of overreferral of minority groups, go to the Web Links module in Chapter 11 of the Companion Website.

Strategies in Middle School and High School

Methods: Acquire Cultural Sensitivity. While it is important at the early childhood/ elementary level as well, designing educational activities that minority group children and youth find to be comfortable is urgently needed at the secondary level. This is because it is in high schools that the dominant culture finds its most complete realization (Duarte & Smith, 2000). This culture emphasizes *individual* achievement, in *competition,* and in *traditional tests.* For people who come from a Native American home or, to a lesser extent, an Hispanic American background, this focus may be uncomfortable. That is because other cultures stress *group* achievement, in *cooperation,* and in *practical activities* (e.g., Bowe, 2000a). Unless and until you acknowledge that many of your fondest beliefs are reflections of your own background, rather than immutable and universal truths, you will not be able to appreciate adequately the features and strengths of other cultures. By contrast, when you provide educational and assessment experiences that reward group cooperation and performance of socially important tasks—a good example is a class project to clean up a neighborhood—you will make high school more welcoming, and less hostile, to people from these cultures (National Clearinghouse for English Language Acquistion, at *http://ncela.gwu.edu*).

Strategies in Transition to Adult Life

Methods: Prepare Students for Diversity in College and the Workplace. Colleges and employers alike have taken major steps in recent years to become more diverse and, with that, more "diversity friendly." Both at the university level and in companies, there is growing recognition that diversity brings strength. These trends bode well for students who are minority-group members. Nonetheless, young people will be well-served if they acquire, during their school years, skills in behaving in ways expected by the dominant culture. Many successful adults switch easily between roles in different settings. They "code switch" between behaviors that are common at home and those that are expected in work settings. If your students who are members of minority groups have not yet become skilled at displaying behaviors that majority-group professors and employers expect, the transition years are good times to train them in those behaviors.

LINGUISTIC DIVERSITY

The term "linguistic diversity" does *not* refer only to students who speak *only* some language other than English. Most American school students, in fact, do speak *some* English. What places many of these students at risk is that they must master English on top of all the other knowledge and skills taught in school—and must do so rapidly enough to keep pace with their peers who are native speakers of English. Making their task much more difficult is the fact that researchers and educators have yet to identify truly effective ways of instructing students who are linguistically diverse.

Definition

Students are considered to belong to **linguistic minority groups** if they have a native language other than English, particularly if their parents speak only that other language. A less popular term (because it may be seen as disparaging, in that it describes people in deficit terms) is "limited English proficiency" (LEP). This refers to students who are not yet fluent in speaking, reading, and writing English, and to programs designed for such students. Some of these children are not proficient in *any* language. A different term, "English as a second language" (ESL), refers to programs designed for students who are proficient in some other language. The term "English language learners" (ELL) encompasses students in LEP and ESL programs.

Characteristics and Types

Spanish is the second-most spoken language in the country. Persons of Hispanic origin do not necessarily speak Spanish as their native language. In fact, according to the National Council of La Raza (NCLR), an organization promoting quality of life for Americans of Hispanic origin, the vast majority of Hispanic Americans aged five and over speak English well or very well. (The term "La Raza" means "the people" and is understood to refer, more specifically, to "the Hispanic people of the New World," according to the Council.) NCLR identifies the population of Hispanic Americans as Mexican American (63%), Central and South American (14%), Puerto Rican (11%), Cuban (4%), and other Hispanic (7%) (*http://www.nclr.org*).

In part because the Hispanic American population is so much younger on the whole than are other ethnic groups in the United States and in part because of relatively low rates of high-school graduation, annual incomes among Hispanic Americans are markedly lower than are those of most other groups. More than one out of every four (27%) Hispanic American families lived in poverty in 1997. Even in families having at least one adult worker, 25% had incomes under the poverty level (U.S. Bureau of the Census, 1998).

The third most "spoken" language in the United States, in fact, is American Sign Language, principally used by people who are deaf and their families (see Chapter 4). Other languages most often found in America include German, French, Portuguese, Mandarin Chinese, Japanese, Arabic, and Russian (U.S. Bureau of the Census, 2001). In some cities, such as New York, children in the public schools come from homes in which any of several dozen languages are spoken. This linguistic diversity is challenging to these school systems and to the teachers working there.

Prevalence

The United States now has millions of citizens who speak languages other than English. Most have at least minimal competency in English. They may be more comfortable in their native languages, however.

People Who Speak Spanish

In January 2003, the U.S. Bureau of the Census reported that the number of Americans of Hispanic origin had surpassed the number of African Americans for the first time ever: 37.0 million to 36.1 million. The population of persons of Hispanic origin grew an astonishing 58% between 1990 and 2000. The Hispanic population is densely clustered in five states: California, Texas, New York, Florida, and Illinois. However, Hispanics are a rapidly growing presence in such Midwestern states as Colorado. The U.S. Bureau of the Census annually conducts, as part of its March supplement to the Current Population Survey (CPS), an in-depth look at "foreign born" populations. The 2000 March CPS revealed that 28 million such persons reside in the United States. This is a remarkable 10% of the American population and represents an equally remarkable 43% growth since 1990. The growth was fueled by the explosive increase in the number of persons of Hispanic origin (*http://www.census.gov*).

Speakers of Other Languages

Much smaller numbers of Americans speak such other languages as French, German, Portuguese, Chinese, Japanese, Vietnamese, and so on. However, as is the case with Hispanic Americans, most of these children *can* and *do* also speak, read, and write English.

According to the U.S. Department of Education's National Center for Educational Statistics (2003), some two million students were Limited English Proficient (LEP) as of 2001–2002 (*http://nces.ed.gov/fastfacts/*). This is fairly consistent with data from the U.S. General Accounting Office (2001a), which reported that during the 1996–1997 school

TABLE 11.2 Region of Origin: Immigration

Origin	Number (Thousands)	Percent
Mexico	28,379	28%
East Asia	5,085	18
Europe	4,356	15
Caribbean	2,815	10
Central America	1,948	7
South America	1,876	7
South Asia	1,315	5
Middle East	1,035	4

Source: Camarota, 2003.

year, 3.4 million PreK–12 students were identified as Limited English Proficient. Overall, including Spanish speakers, some nine million PreK–12 students have native languages other than English, according to *Education Week* ("Children of Change," 2000b).

Causes

Immigration is the usual factor behind the presence in schools of children with native languages other than English. Table 11.2 identifies the major regions of origin for immigrants into the United States. Looking only at immigration since 1970, we see that the 10 major countries of origin are, in descending order: Mexico, China/Taiwan, Philippines, India, Vietnam, El Salvador, Korea, the Dominican Republic, Cuba, and Columbia.

Instructional Methods

Research does not yet firmly support any specific method of teaching ELL/LEP students. One basic fact is widely recognized: the brain is much more plastic, that is, amenable to change, during the early childhood and elementary than the secondary years. Thus, instruction in a language other than the child's native language logically should begin during the Pre–K years, and certainly by the elementary-school years (e.g., Ridley, 1999). Agreement seems to end at that point, however.

Strategies in Early Childhood and Elementary School

Methods: Try a Variety of Approaches. There is no consensus in American education about the best way to teach students who have native languages other than English. You might find out what policy has been adopted by your school district. In some states, and in some schools, "English immersion" is used. This approach exposes students to 100% English instruction throughout the school day. Some ELL or English as a Second Language (ESL) approaches also feature immersion in English, with periodic support provided in the native language. "Bilingual education," by contrast, is the term used to refer to a range of techniques which feature, rather than minimize, the native language. Two-way bilingual education, usually delivered by two teachers, each of whom conducts instruction in one language, is the purest form. More often seen are methods in which instruction in the native language gradually gives way to more and more instruction in English (Crawford, 1999; *Education Week,* 2000a: *http://www.edweek.org/context/topics/issuespage*). The nearby box, "Resources That Work: Teaching English to Speakers of Other Languages," offers some information sources on the teaching of English to people with other native languages.

The fact that educators have yet to agree on how to teach English to native speakers of other languages bodes ill for instruction of American students with other, much less common native languages. The history of teaching English to speakers of other languages

Resources That Work

Teaching English to Speakers of Other Languages

National Association for Bilingual Education
1030 15th Street NW
Washington, DC 20005
http://www.nabe.org

National Council of La Raza
1111 19th Street NW, Suite 1000
Washington, DC 20036
http://www.nclr.org

Teachers of English to Speakers of Other Languages, Inc.
700 S. Washington Street #200
Alexandria, VA 22314
http://www.tesol.org

in the public schools is not one inspiring confidence (Baker, 1996; Rossell & Baker, 1996). Brunn (1999) offered one discouraging example of how the lack of school policies on bilingual education can harm children. In that school, bilingual educators were separated from, and ignored by, other teachers. Some states, notably California and Arizona, recently have moved to ban bilingual education from the public schools, replacing it with a strict "English-only" policy. Sadly, however, the evidence that permitting only English in the schools will work where other approaches have failed is also not convincing. Efforts continue in several states to establish English as the "official language" and to eliminate ELL programs altogether.

Several methods recommended for use in special education may help with speakers of other languages. Working with ELL students from urban, low SES homes, Greenwood and his colleagues showed that several techniques applicable to teaching students with disabilities were also of value with non-disabled students who were at risk of academic failure. Specifically, they found that classwide peer tutoring (CWPT), using heterogeneous pairs or groups, fast-paced instruction, and cooperative learning approaches helped elementary ELL students improve outcomes in vocabulary and spelling (see Chapter 9).

Methods: Accept Code Switching Between, But Not Within, Sentences. Brice and Roseberry-McKibbin (2001) outlined some steps teachers can take to help bilingual children. They recommended that teachers respect and accept the children's native language (L1), including any code switching they may do. Code switching, as the term is used in bilingual education, is alternation of languages. However, Brice and Roseberry-McKibbin suggested that teachers permit code switching *only* between sentences. That is, any sentence begun in one language should be completed in the same language. They also recommended use of reiteration (asking the child to repeat what a teacher or aide says, using the target language [L2]), as well as heavy emphasis upon the teaching of vocabulary in the target language. Even with such adjustments by teachers, Baker (1996) suggested that schools allow as many as four or more years for children to acquire competency in L2. The U.S. General Accounting Office (2001a), surveying the state-of-the-art in bilingual education, concurred.

Strategies in Middle School and High School

Methods: Reduce Drop-out Rates. Hispanic Americans continue to graduate from high school at considerably lower rates than do white, non-Hispanic, or African Americans. Looking at Americans aged 25 and over, 55% of those who were Hispanic American, 87% of white non-Hispanic Americans, and 75% of African Americans were high-school graduates (U.S. Bureau of the Census, 1998). As of this writing, we have little information about high-school graduation and drop-out rates among recent immigrants from Vietnam, Croatia, and other countries.

Dropping out is most common among Latinos (boys and men of Hispanic origin), followed by Latinas (girls and women of Hispanic origin). Latino boys drop out at a 31% rate, far higher than the 12% rate among African American boys and the 8% rate among white non-Hispanic boys. Among girls, Latina girls drop out at a 26% rate, as compared to 13% of African American girls and 7% of white non-Hispanic girls (*http://www.census.gov*). Canedy (2001) suggested that conflicting cultural messages may be behind the high dropout rates among Hispanic young people, especially girls, who may be under some pressure to emulate their age peers from the country of origin, where few women complete much formal education. According to the National Council of La Raza, other factors contributing to high rates of dropping out include familial poverty and linguistic disadvantages (*http://www.nclr.org*).

Methods: Prepare Students to Meet the New, Higher Learning Standards. Students identified as LEP or ELL traditionally have been excluded from high-stakes tests, much as were students with disabilities. That is changing now. In most states, students classified as LEP/ELL are expected to take part in state-wide and district-wide assessment programs. The arguments in support of this are similar to those about students with disabilities, namely that only if these students are included in the assessments will schools fully recognize and respond to their unique needs. In response to these issues, the National Center on Educational Outcomes has prepared some materials on testing ELL students. These are posted at *http://education.umn.edu/NCEO/LEP*.

The key issue is the language in which tests should be provided for LEP/ELL individuals. Should the test be given in English or translated to the student's native language? The answer to that question has to do with the underlying purpose of the assessment. If the purpose is not related to language (e.g., if the intent is to assess a student's knowledge of algebra), then providing the test in the student's native language is a viable option for the school. Offering an interpreter to translate the test when it is administered is a second option, but is less desirable than is a translated test (largely because interpreters vary in quality). However, if the assessment is designed to measure a student's ability to read English, translation to the student's native language clearly would be inappropriate (as would be providing interpreter services). A second issue is the wording of questions, so that they do not pose unique problems for LEP/ELL students. For more information on these issues, consult *The Use of Tests as Part of High-Stakes Decision-Making for Students* (U.S. Department of Education, Office for Civil Rights, 2000) or visit the Office's Web site at *http://www.ed.gov/about/offices/list/OCR*.

The persistently high rates of dropping out among linguistically diverse students is especially troubling because state after state is now requiring these individuals to pass the same statewide tests that all students must pass to qualify for an academic diploma. Many states do offer some accommodations for at least some of these tests. Math tests, for example, might be offered in Spanish and other languages. In New York State, to illustrate, the 2001 Regents tests (which are required for academic diplomas) in math, biology, earth science, history, and geography were given in five alternate languages: Chinese, Haitian Creole, Korean, Russian, and Spanish. (Languages Other Than English, *http://www.emsc.nysed.gov/osa.hslote.html*). However, the State Education Department has indicated, as have education agencies in other states, that future versions of these tests will not necessarily be given in these or other "alternate" languages.

Strategies in Transition to Adult Life

Methods: Stress English Competency to Prepare Speakers of Other Languages. While Spanish is frequently understood and spoken at social service agencies and at community centers in many American cities, other languages are much less often used. Speakers of those languages also face other barriers. Young people whose families immigrated from Vietnam may encounter residual hostility in the community, particularly from American males who fought in Vietnam. The most searing issues for those whose families immigrated from Croatia or other areas in the Balkan region of Europe likely will come from within, rather than from outside, the family. These youth may have brothers, sisters, cousins, and other relatives who remain in danger. As these young Americans seek to mobilize public support for the protection of their relatives, they may find disinterest rather than sympathy. As this is written, American public opinion about Balkan conflicts continues to be divided, with apathy being the dominant emotion (e.g., Program on International Policy Attitudes, *http://www.pipa.org*).

TEEN PREGNANCY

When a young woman becomes pregnant while still in high school, the consequences often are grave. The young woman often drops out of school. She also delays or foregoes any plans she may have had for a college education. This means, in today's economy, that she sharply limits her future earning potential. Ann Crittenden (2001), in her major study, *The Price of Motherhood: Why the Most Important Job in the World Is Still the Least Valued,* concluded that having children may be the worst economic decision a woman could make, although it can also be deeply rewarding in other ways.

Definition

Teen pregnancy is a status. It refers to women under age 20 who are pregnant.

Characteristics and Types

While some pregnant teens defy all the stereotypes, certain tendencies are apparent. Teenage girls whose mothers were themselves pregnant as adolescents often have repeated the pattern.

Prevalence

According to the Office on Women's Health, a unit in the U.S. Department of Health and Human Services (HHS; *http://www.4woman.gov*), one million adolescent girls become pregnant each year. Of those pregnancies, 80% are unplanned and 50% result in abortions. As a result, 200,000 teens become mothers each year. The Centers for Disease Control and Prevention (CDC; *http://www.cdc.gov*) provided somewhat different statistics. CDC reported that 95% of the estimated one million annual pregnancies by teenage girls

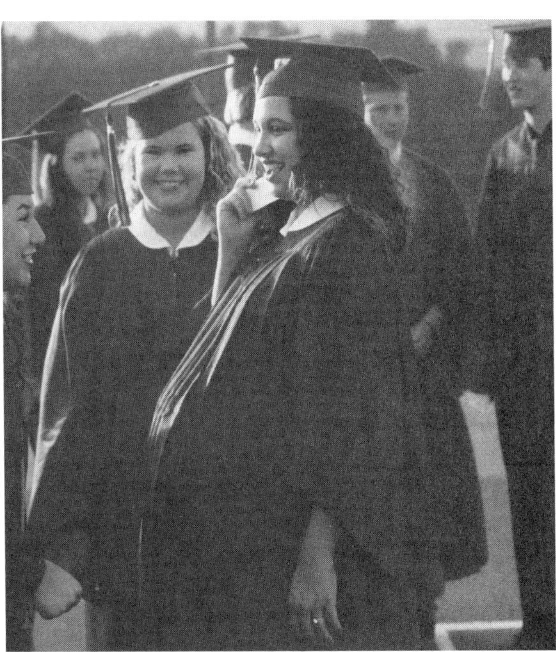

Teen mothers benefit greatly when they are graduated from high school.

are unplanned and one in three ends in abortion ("Teen Pregnancy" at *http://www.4woman.gov*). As these different data suggest, collecting information on what teens actually think and do in this area has been difficult. We can, however, safely estimate the annual prevalence at about 1 million. Some good news: teen pregnancy rates in 1997 were lower than at any time since 1976, according to a report ("Teen Pregnancy Rate Reaches a Record Low in 1997") released in 2001 by the Centers for Disease Control and Prevention.

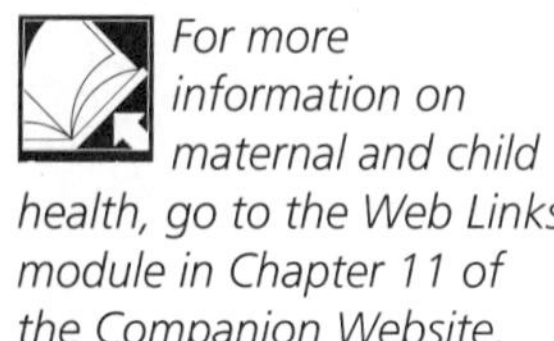

For more information on maternal and child health, go to the Web Links module in Chapter 11 of the Companion Website.

Causes

Pregnancy is caused by intimate sexual activities, notably intercourse. Adolescent girls may become pregnant despite using contraceptive measures; even the pill and condoms sometimes fail to prevent conception. Some may not use contraceptives at all, because of ignorance, carelessness, religious beliefs, or a desire to become pregnant.

Instructional Methods

Many schools offer sex education programs. If provided, these should begin early. In addition, teachers at the secondary level need to be flexible so as to prevent students from dropping out.

Strategies in Early Childhood and Elementary School

Methods: Begin Sex Education Early. Menarche (the onset of menstruation in puberty) often begins earlier today than was the case in the past. This may be due to better nutrition and to overall higher levels of public health. Whatever the causes, this fact means that educators need to address issues of sex education earlier than they once did. Sex education in the public schools is controversial. Different communities have different standards. In districts that provide such instruction at the elementary level, most begin in the fourth, fifth, and sixth grades (when bodies begin to develop). If your school has such a program, it is important that you choose your words with care. In general, the family remains the appropriate source of values education and of ethics. Educators, by contrast, should focus more upon factual material, helping young people to understand what is happening to their bodies.

Strategies in Middle School and High School

Methods: Continued Awareness Training. Teen pregnancy is a very appropriate topic for discussion at the middle- and high-school levels. Teens need to learn about the consequences of unprotected and even of "protected" sexual intercourse, as well as about methods of preventing pregnancy. This instruction may be offered in conjunction with information about sexually transmitted diseases, including HIV/AIDS. Adolescents also need to be appraised of the risks of teenage pregnancy to their babies. The rates of infant mortality (death) and morbidity (illness) both are much higher when the mother is a teenager than when she is in her 20s ("Teen Pregnancy," *http://www.4woman.gov*). Infants born to adolescent mothers tend to have low birth weight, which, as we saw earlier, is associated with a number of disabilities, notably cerebral palsy. All of this means that teachers present information that students, upon reflection, will consider to be arguments in favor of abstention (e.g., 4 Girls Health, at *http://www.4girls.gov*). Whether you as a teacher go a step further, to advocate abstention, is something you should discuss with your supervising teacher and principal.

Strategies in Transition to Adult Life

Methods: Keep Students in School. Drop-out rates among adolescent mothers are high. When the teen leaves school to care for her baby, the result more often than not is poverty. The father often is absent or contributing little to the support of the teen mother and the child. The girl may feel guilty no matter which decision she makes: if she stays home, foregoing employment, she suffers because she is not financially able to provide for the child and herself; if she goes to work, she may feel guilt for imposing upon her own parents or friends. When pregnancy is postponed at least until age 20, the situation tends to be markedly different. For example, 80% of children born to teenage mothers are poor, versus just 8% of children born to mothers in their twenties ("Teen Pregnancy," *http://www.4woman.gov*).

As is the case with dropping out of high school, leaving school because of pregnancy or childbirth is not necessarily an irreversible decision. Many high schools offer flexible schedules for teens who are pregnant or who are mothers. The often-devastating economic consequences of teen pregnancy argue for continuation and, indeed, expansion of such programs.

JUVENILE DELINQUENCY

In America today, juvenile delinquency seems to be most visible in gangs. Once the province of large urban areas, gangs have now spread to suburban and to many rural communities. In many instances, this is because gangs respond to adolescents' needs for friendship, excitement, and protection (Decker & Curry, 2000; Kauffman, 2001).

Definition

Delinquent behavior is antisocial conduct, generally violent in nature and targeted against people and/or property. When conducted by adolescents, it is referred to as "juvenile delinquency" (Kauffman, 2001). Theft is a common example. It is often motivated by a desire for drugs, alcohol, and other tangible objects, particularly those that impress their friends (Decker & Curry, 2000).

Characteristics and Types

Juvenile delinquents are generally boys. Many first engaged in antisocial or destructive behavior, albeit usually just once or twice, while still in elementary school. These students seem to be particularly resistant to efforts by adults to alter their behavior. By contrast, students who first engage in delinquent behavior in their late teens often cease those activities quickly and permanently (Kauffman, 2001). This is important information for educators: The real problem is among the younger students who persist in antisocial acts. Because much juvenile crime occurs in the afternoon hours (Center for the Study and Prevention of Violence, 2000), one indication that a student may be engaging in these activities is skipping the final class period or periods of a school day. Similarly, tardiness, absenteeism, and other forms of truancy may signal juvenile delinquency.

Prevalence

Prevalence and incidence figures for juvenile delinquency are highly variable. Different states define delinquency differently. Many acts of violence against people and property are not reported or, if reported, are not associated with individual perpetrators. Confidentiality rules protecting minors also confound the problem. Further clouding the issue: If a young person commits one act of delinquency during the course of a year, and never does so again, should we identify this person as delinquent? Kauffman (2001), citing the American Psychiatric Association and other sources, wrote that estimates range from a low of 6% to a high of 16% of boys and from a low of 2% to a high of 9% of girls.

Violence in American high schools, notably fistfights, occurs at a rate of about 15 per 1,000 students, according to an estimate by the U.S. General Accounting Office (2001b). The GAO surveyed building principals. If this is close to the actual rate, there would be some 200,000 such incidents annually among the nation's 13 million secondary students. That is an incident rate, not an estimate of the number of delinquent students.

Causes

Some young people become delinquents because of biological, social, and environmental factors, notably those which cause conduct disorders (see Chapter 5). In other cases, the "family-like" nature of a gang may attract adolescents who feel rejected or unappreciated by their biological families (Coleman, 1996). In yet other instances, familial poverty may combine with temptations to entice young people into alcohol and drug use, and particularly into drug selling. Criminal activities may be undertaken in order to support their families or themselves, or to feed a drug dependency (Kauffman, 2001).

Instructional Methods

Juvenile delinquency is preventable. A key is to provide discipline consistently, and to begin early. Also essential is to train children and youth in appropriate ways of dealing with frustration and anger. The Center for the Study and Prevention of Violence (2000) has issued a planning guide for schools to use in preventing and also in responding to violence in the schools. The Center recommended the creation of a social support team comprised of at least three non-school professionals (who have ties to the community, yet maintain some distance from, and thus some objectivity about, the school) as well as school officials. This team would receive referrals from teachers, parents, and students. Those referrals would express concern that certain students were engaging in, or threatening to engage in, violent behavior. The team would evaluate these referrals and make recommendations for intervention.

Referral introduces the idea of identifying potentially violent individuals. The Center cautioned against such "student profiling" (the term is reminiscent of "racial profiling" conducted by some highway patrol officers in some states). While it is true that *in retrospect* educators often are able to identify aggressive and antisocial acts by children, especially boys, as early as age 8 or 9, the state of the art is such that *prospective* identification remains fraught with dangers. There are too many false positives (children who are "identified" as potentially delinquent who never develop into dangers to themselves or others). It is far better to work with young children on an individual basis, treating each incident in isolation, than it is to label children prematurely as trouble-makers.

Strategies in Early Childhood and Elementary School

Methods: Offer Skills Training. Preventing delinquent behavior is a two-phase project, according to Hill Walker (Sprague & Walker, 2000; Walker, 2000). As was shown in Chapter 9 (see p. 342), Walker has demonstrated over a long career that behavior that is not acceptable may be altered. Intervention seems to most help children who do not have the social skills they need to get along with others and children who are already falling behind academically. The first step, according to Walker, involves the use of well-known interventions, notably (1) praise of appropriate behavior when it is exhibited and (2) ignoring inappropriate behavior when it appears. This is an intensive, but short-term process. Walker has written that he has become "painfully" aware of "the absolute necessity of following up target students and monitoring their behavior carefully within and across school years where they experience differing teachers, peers, and classroom ecologies" (Walker, 2000, p. 157). As did Kauffman (2001), Walker urged that schools place primary emphasis upon *prevention* and *immediate intervention,* on a school wide basis.

Methods: Offer Alternatives. Interventions that offer young people other ways of meeting peers, making friends, and using free time may be more effective than are efforts to prevent them from joining gangs. That was the conclusion reached by Decker and Curry (2000), who studied gang membership among 12- to 15-year-old students in middle school and alternative education centers. Decker and Curry noted that among these young students, involvement in gangs tends to be transient. That is, gangs seem to exert only tenuous control over young teens. Explaining their findings, Decker and Curry compared adolescent involvement in gangs to other activities of teenagers: "Adolescence is a time of fleeting allegiances, to friends, interests, and gangs" (p. 481). For this reason, interventions designed to break gangs' holds on young people may be highly effective.

Strategies in Middle School and High School

Methods: Provide After-School Activities. Because much juvenile delinquency occurs in the afternoon hours, when young people often are without adult supervision, after-school programs can be helpful in keeping students occupied in more productive endeavors. Working with adult male members of Mt. Olivet Church in Columbus, Ohio, a team of teacher-training students and their faculty members provided after-school peer tutoring for 15 African-American young males who were experiencing behavior problems. Interventions included reciprocal peer tutoring, reading instruction, and help in behavior management. Such techniques are discussed in Chapter 8 of this book. Results indicated that the students improved reading achievement, many significantly (Gardner, Cartledge, Seidl, Woolsey, Schley, & Utley, 2001).

Methods: Strengthen Ties to School. There is controversy about gang membership among older teens. While some researchers have reported findings similar to those obtained by Decker and Curry (2000) in their study of young gang members, others, studying older teens, have perceived gangs as well-organized, tightly controlled entities that effectively enforce discipline among members. For you as a teacher in an inclusive classroom, the key issue is the importance of gangs as providing "family-like" benefits (Coleman, 1996). The obvious implication: give your students family-like ties to the school, especially through clubs and other activities. That way, they will not need to turn to gangs to fulfill needs that their own families have not satisfied.

Strategies in Transition to Adult Life

Methods: Keep the Door Open. As is often the case with at-risk behavior, teachers and counselors need to emphasize, and re-emphasize with young people that delinquent behavior is not necessarily a terminal decision. Rather, it can be reversed. For example, students who are convicted of crimes may continue their education while incarcerated. They may also pursue a GED degree. Information about options frequently is not enough. Students often must be taught alternative behavior patterns that are more appropriate in meeting their needs and that are more acceptable to the community. The transition years are good times to teach those behaviors.

SUICIDE

Relatively few American school children attempt suicide; even fewer succeed. The good news is that the number of suicides annually among PreK–12 students is in the range of 1,000 (American Foundation for Suicide Prevention, *http://www.afsp.org*) to 5,000 (The Centers for Disease Control and Prevention, *http://www.cdc.gov*). To appreciate these figures, remember that some 53 million children and youth attend American public PreK–12 schools. While any number is too high, the fact that these estimates imply a rate of fewer than 1 per 10,000 students places the problem into perspective. The bad news is that the number of suicide *attempts* is several times this large. Again, any attempt, no matter how feeble, must be handled promptly and with sensitivity.

Definition

Suicide is the taking of one's life. It may be intentional or it may not be. Suicides are distinguished from *attempts* at suicide, which often are better understood as cries for help. In some instances, however, people may succeed where they intend to fail.

Characteristics and Types

Adolescents who attempt suicide may be depressed or otherwise mentally ill. They may also be mentally healthy but overwhelmed by temporary conditions or life events. It is difficult to generalize about these latter youth, because they have little in common other than the fact that they see no way out from under the weight of the circumstances in which they find themselves.

Prevalence

Attempts at suicide are very rare among children under 12 years of age, according to the American Foundation for Suicide Prevention (*http://www.afsp.org*). The organization has also reported that at every age, suicide is more common among males than females and that among boys and men, white non-Hispanics commit suicide far more often than do African Americans or white Hispanic Americans. In the school-age group, suicide is most frequent in the 15 to 19 age range. Boys of that age commit suicide at the rate of 17 per 100,000 population, girls at 4 per 100,000 population. The American Foundation for Suicide Prevention reported that 1,561 boys and 323 girls in the 15 to 19 age bracket committed suicide in 1993. It should be noted that one reason fewer adolescent females commit suicide is that their method of choice (drug overdoses) is much less often successful than is guns, the approach most used among boys (*http://www.afsp.org*).

Causes

Suicide often represents a cry for help. Usually, it is attempted only after teens make many efforts to reach out to parents, peers, teachers, and counselors. They may, for example, try to prevent parents from separating or divorcing. After failing at that, they may blame themselves for the dissolution of the family, and this self-blame may lead to a suicide attempt (Gould, Shaffer, & Fisher, 1998). Often, the adolescent does not really intend to kill himself or herself; rather, the attempt is to finally break through to communicate to people important in the teen's life (*http://www.afsp.org*). Suicides are more likely to be attempted when young people are abusing controlled substances and when they have anxiety/mood disorders (Center on Addiction and Substance Abuse, 2000). See "Substance Abuse," for more information.

Instructional Methods

Experts recommend that teachers as well as counselors should respond promptly to any suicide or attempt at suicide. They warn that adolescents may be particularly susceptible to suicidal behavior after an incident involving another member of the school community.

Strategies in Early Childhood and Elementary School

Methods: Be Willing to Listen. As mentioned earlier, suicide attempts among children of elementary-school age are very rare. For this reason, awareness and prevention programs seldom have much effect. The children tend to regard this issue as one not relevant to their lives. Rather, what may help are efforts to acquaint them with the fact that their teachers stand ready to listen when they are upset or worried about something. Children should also be reminded that counselors are employed by the local school district and are available, if needed.

Strategies in Middle School and High School

Methods: Be Alert for Copycat Actions. Attempts at suicide typically occur shortly after suicide or accidental death of a classmate. This should alert teachers and counselors to be especially vigilant in the days and weeks after a student dies. In some instances, teens who feel neglected and unpopular may be struck by the incredible amount of attention a classmate gets after committing suicide; the desire for attention may trigger a suicide attempt. Thus, teachers and counselors should watch closely students who are withdrawn and/or unpopular.

Among signs of near-term risk of suicide attempts, according to the American Foundation for Suicide Prevention, are history (a record of any prior attempt, particularly within the past year), depression and feelings of helplessness, divorce or death in the family within the past year, substance abuse, and, as already mentioned, any recent suicide or suicide attempt, either in the same high school or publicized in the media (*http://www.afsp.org*).

Teachers should take seriously any apparent or credible suicide threat. These must be reported to the appropriate authorities. You should check with your principal's office for specifics. Generally, teens who attempt suicide are hospitalized after the attempt. They are kept for observation and are discharged to the family only after a risk assessment has been performed. This includes the taking of a personal and family history (is there a history of suicides and/or suicide attempts in the family?), a psychological evaluation (is the individual depressed? etc.), an assessment of the family's ability to provide caring and responsible supervision, and the like. Families usually are asked if there are firearms in the home. If so, they are asked to remove them or, at minimum, to unload them and then lock them in some secure location (*http://www.afsp.org*).

Strategies in Transition to Adult Life

Methods: Point to Prospects for a Brighter Future. Responsibilities increase when adolescents leave high school for college or for work. In that sense, pressures only increase. However, counterbalancing those factors is the greatly increased level of independence that adults enjoy as compared to teenagers and the generally much higher level of maturity that adults bring to problems as compared to teens. For these reasons, it is responsible on the part of teachers and counselors to advise troubled teens that life will, indeed, "look a lot brighter in a few years." That is literally true. Evidence of it is readily at hand: Suicide rates among people in their 20s are dramatically lower than those among teens.

SUBSTANCE ABUSE

Experimentation is part of growing up. When it ranges as far as the use of substances, which are illegal for Americans of any age to possess, of abuse or those that are proscribed for minors, adolescents violate the law. Whether they place themselves at risk of physical, mental, or other harm depends largely upon which substances are abused, in what quantities, and how often. The good news is that overall use of controlled substances by PreK–12 students appears to have leveled off during the past few years (National Institute on Drug Abuse, *http://www.nida.nih.gov*). The bad news is that those are still, historically speaking, high levels.

The nature and hallucinatory effects of such drugs as heroin, cocaine (including the smokable crack cocaine), LSD, and marijuana are well-known. Information about these substances is readily obtained in local libraries, at many community service agencies, and on the Web (e.g., *http://www.cdc.gov*). One point that may be overlooked by parents and/or teachers who recall using some of these drugs themselves during the 1960s and 1970s: Today's versions of these substances are much stronger and thus far more dangerous.

Definition

Illegal drugs include heroin, cocaine, LSD, marijuana, and some much newer "club drugs" such as ecstasy. Ecstasy is a street name for a brain toxin that has the scientific name of methylenedioxymethamphetamine (MDMA). It is also popularly known by such names as X, XTC, Adam, clarity, and essence. Other substances which are legal for adults to use, but not for under-age individuals to consume, notably include alcohol.

Characteristics and Types

Students who abuse drugs often are novelty seekers. Others are rebelling. Yet others are following the crowd, seeking to be accepted. The substances that are abused vary, sometimes in waves. Thus, educators need to be alert to ever-newer drugs. In the late 1990s, ecstasy was popular. This is an illicit drug that is sold in small pills about the size of aspirin tablets; it can also be smoked, injected, or taken in liquid form. Less addictive than alcohol, it nonetheless can kill people. Ecstasy is in fact a brain toxin. The drug followed the usual course of illegal drugs in this country: It began as a party drug, quickly spread to upper-class teens in cities and suburban areas, and, as the price came down, made its way into middle-class and lower-class adolescent groups and individuals. As of 2001, each pill cost about $20 (Pratt, 2001; Szalavitz, 2000).

Prevalence

A major source for data on abuse of illegal drugs is the Monitoring the Future project (*http://www.nida.nih.gov/DrugPages/MTF.html*). According to this source, reported abuse of illegal drugs among teenagers has leveled off in recent years. Reports of use of cocaine (including crack cocaine), heroin, and similar "hard drugs" fell in 2003. Other studies also show declines over the past several years. It is important to bear in mind that these are self reports; if children and youth do not volunteer their use of illicit substances, data will not include them. In addition, "use" is defined differently in different surveys. Should we count someone as a "substance abuser" if he smoked one joint of marijuana eight months ago? What about someone who had a glass of wine with her family at a holiday dinner?

The drug of choice among adolescents continues to be alcohol. The Monitoring the Future project reported that 55% of high-school students reported having had at least some drinks during 2003. More disturbing, the data showed binge drinking (five or more drinks in a row, at least once in the preceding two weeks) was very high, at more than one out of every four young people.

No other drug is as popular among teenagers. Marijuana use (at least once during the past year) was reported by 15% of 12th-, 10th-, and 8th-graders. Hallucinogens (including LSD and ecstasy) fell sharply in 2003, according to the Monitoring the Future project. The decline in use of ecstasy was dramatic. In early 2001, use of ecstasy among teens was estimated at about 10%, but in some areas reported use was as high as 25% (Pratt, 2001). As a result of these data, the National Institute on Drug Abuse launched a new Web site specifically about ecstasy and related "club drugs"; the URL is *http://www.clubdrugs.org*. Evidently, these measures have had an effect: The Monitoring the Future project found that fewer than 2% of teens reported past-year use of the drug in 2003.

For our purposes here, in estimating the prevalence of substance abuse so that we can appreciate how many students this behavior places at risk, the best figures seem to be those for binge drinking during the two weeks prior to being asked. At the high-school level (these are rarely problems at lower levels of school), those figures suggest, given an enrollment of 13.5 million students in secondary schools (*http://nces.ed.gov*), a prevalence of some 3 million adolescents.

Causes

Controlled substances are illegal for a reason. They are dangerous and many are highly addictive. In some people, there is a genetic predisposition toward addiction. This is notably the case with alcohol. In addition, mental illness, chronic poverty, and a history of child abuse, among other factors reviewed in this chapter, place young people at risk for abuse of controlled substances. These are not causative relationships. That point needs to be stressed. Teens *can* "just say no"—they need to be given a reason or, preferably, many reasons. The most powerful of these, for most young people, is *hope*. They have, and they know they have, a future worth waiting for—and worth "saying no" for.

Instructional Methods

Knowledge helps in preventing substance abuse. In particular, educators can be successful by identifying and then exploding myths about various drugs. However, some approaches, notably that of Drug Abuse Resistance Education (DARE), are unproven.

Strategies in Early Childhood and Elementary School

Methods: Offer Factual Information. As with some other topics reviewed here (e.g., teen pregnancy), elementary students may not be in immediate need of instruction or intervention with respect to substance abuse. What they do need, and what can help them, is general factual information that helps to shape their core values. The idea that they are valuable beings (e.g., "I am somebody!" campaigns), that they are independent decision makers who will in future years be tempted in various ways but who will ultimately be responsible for their own actions, and the like are bedrock ideas that can be instilled during the elementary years.

The DARE program continues to be controversial (e.g., Coles, 1999; Barnard, 1997). The national organization has insisted upon tight control of local drug awareness projects. From its beginning in 1983, the DARE approved plan has featured neighborhood police officers lecturing in public-school classrooms. After much criticism, including (in some communities) withdrawal of permission to operate in the schools, DARE redesigned its curriculum. The new program, inaugurated in some seventh- and ninth-grade classrooms, features more activity by students themselves and less lecturing (Kalb, 2001). Only time will tell if the DARE message, long derided as simplistic and ineffective, will silence the critics.

Strategies in Middle School and High School

Methods: Explode Myths. A research-based report, *Preventing Drug Use Among Children and Adolescents* (National Institute on Drug Abuse, 1999) offers 14 specific techniques that have been shown to be effective (see "Teacher Strategies That Work: 14 Principles for Preventing Drug Use," p. 418). The publication is free (call 1-800-729-6686). A drug treatment hotline is also available nationally; the toll-free number for this confidential hotline is 1-800-662-HELP.

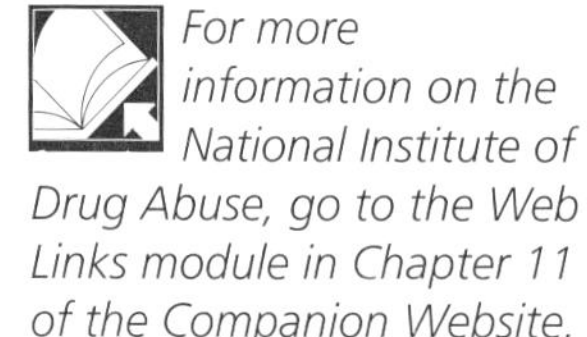
For more information on the National Institute of Drug Abuse, go to the Web Links module in Chapter 11 of the Companion Website.

The greater concern, simply because it is far more often abused by adolescents, with tragic consequences, is alcohol. This is particularly true of teens old enough to drive. Teachers and counselors need to appeal to the idea that when drivers drink, they are placing not only themselves at risk but other people and property as well. In addition, the fact that judgment is impaired when people are "under the influence" needs to be emphasized. The American Foundation for Suicide Prevention has reported that substance abuse, including alcohol abuse, has been associated with 42% of suicides among males and 12% among females (*http://www.afsp.org*). It is likely that a great many of those people, had they been sober, would not have taken their lives.

Strategies in Transition to Adult Life

Methods: Focus on Alcohol, the #1 Drug of Choice. Drinking is even more frequent among college students than among high-school students. Abuse of illegal drugs is also higher at this level of education than in high schools. All of this suggests that teachers and counselors at the secondary level reinforce student understanding that they are responsible for *their own* behavior. A sense of responsibility will serve them well in college (Center on Addiction and Substance Abuse, *http://www.casacolumbia.edu*).

GIFTED AND TALENTED

Students with superior intellectual capabilities (those who are gifted) and children and youth with unusual abilities in art, music, athletics, leadership, and other areas (those who are talented) frequently require differentiated instruction in order to reach their potentials. There is much that teachers of inclusive classrooms can do to help these children and

Teacher Strategies That Work

14 Principles for Preventing Drug Use

1. Enhance protective factors (such as adult monitoring, strong family ties) while reducing risk factors (such as failure in school, poor coping skills).
2. Target all forms of drug abuse, including alcohol and inhalants.
3. Teach skills about resisting drugs when offered or available.
4. Include peer discussion and other interactive activities, not just lectures.
5. Bring parents and other caregivers into the program.
6. Repeat interventions throughout students' school careers.
7. Focus on families, not just children and not just parents.
8. School programs should complement (work with) community prevention programs.
9. Norms against drug use should be strengthened in the community.
10. Target all populations, including those who are potential dropouts.
11. Adapt the school program to fit the specifics of drug abuse problems in the community.
12. For children and youth at high risk, begin earlier and do more.
13. Tailor interventions to the age and development level of the audience.
14. Realize that communities can save $4 to $5 for every dollar spent on drug use prevention.

Source: Preventing Drug Use Among Children and Adolescents, National Institute on Drug Abuse, 1999, Washington, DC: National Institutes of Health.

youth. The words "differentiated instruction" hold the key: As you saw earlier in Chapter 8, there are well-documented techniques you may use to individualize learning opportunities. Many are applicable to gifted and talented students, just as they are for children and youth who are at risk and for students with disabilities.

There is no federal mandate to identify nor to serve gifted/talented students. States vary widely in what they authorize and what they require. School districts, too, differ considerably in what they do for these children and youth. Federal funding, under the Jacob K. Javits Gifted and Talented Act (20 U.S.C. 7253), most recently reauthorized as part of the No Child Left Behind Act of 2001, provides just $11 million a year for gifted/talented programs. To place that number into perspective, consider that annual spending under IDEA exceeds $9 billion. Students with disabilities are roughly twice as numerous as are gifted and talented children and youth, yet federal allotments for those with disabilities are larger by a factor of *800*. Spending by states and local school districts are proportionally similar. Another way to show the disparity is this: Just 2 cents out of every $100 spent on PreK–12 education goes to programs for gifted and/or talented students.

The fact that state laws are permissive rather than mandatory, and the fact that programs for students with gifts and/or talents are chronically underfunded, reflect historical controversy in this area. Gifted/talented education has been dogged with accusations of elitism and political incorrectness and by charges that acceleration (skipping grades) and enrichment (pull-out) programs are ineffective, unnecessary, or both. These and other aspects of education for gifted and talented students are discussed in depth elsewhere (e.g., Clark, 2002).

Definitions

The term **"gifted"** usually refers to people who have IQs in the superior ranges. Statistical theory suggests that about 2% to 3% of the American school population has IQs that are two or more standard deviations above the mean. Given a mean score of 100 and a standard deviation of 15 points, this means IQs above 130. The word **"talented"** is much less susceptible to tight definitions. It usually refers to individuals with startling abilities, including but not limited to those whose talents are evident from an early age (prodigies).

The Javits Act definition, contained in Section 9101(a)(22) of No Child Left Behind, reads:

> The term "gifted and talented," when used with respect to students, children, or youth, means students, children, or youth who give evidence of high achievement capability in

> areas such as intellectual, creative, artistic, or leadership capacity, or in specific academic fields, and who need services or activities not ordinarily provided by the school in order to fully develop those capabilities.

The Marland Report of 1972, which is widely credited with spurring PreK–12 programs for gifted and talented children, also emphasized that only those students who need special services should be identified:

> Gifted and talented children are identified by professionally qualified persons as those who, by virtue of outstanding abilities, are capable of high performance. These are children who require differentiated educational programs and services beyond those normally provided by the regular program in order to realize their contribution to self and society. Children capable of high performance include those with demonstrated achievement and/or potential ability in any of the following areas: (1) general intellectual ability; (2) specific academic aptitude; (3) creative or productive thinking; (4) leadership ability; (5) visual and performing arts; and (6) psychomotor ability (Marland, 1972, p. 2).

Characteristics and Types

Students who are gifted and/or talented vary greatly. Stereotyping is as dangerous with this population as with any other discussed in this book. With that disclaimer in mind, we can examine general characteristics of each group.

Those who are gifted tend to be unusually interested in cause-and-effect, in problem-solving, and in abstract reasoning. Typically, they become bored if not challenged. Gifted children and youth often have a strong sense of humor. They tend to be curious and persistent in seeking answers. Many have large vocabularies, vivid imaginations, and potent memories. Many are highly creative. They tend to learn well on their own and to display a wide range of interests.

Students who are talented may or may not also be gifted. Talents may be highly specialized, such that a child who is gifted in music is not also advanced in reading and writing. Commonly, students with unusual talents spend very substantial amounts of time perfecting their skills. They may hold themselves to high standards and even be perfectionists.

Prevalence

Few Census Bureau or U.S. Department of Education surveys offer statistical information about the number of PreK–12 students who are gifted and/or talented. One recent estimate, contained in a Senate bill introduced in March 2003, is 3 million children and youth. Section 501, intended to reauthorize the Javits Gifted and Talented Act, pointedly noted that state and district reports on students served by gifted/talented programs continue to show that these programs tend to neglect traditionally underserved children and youth: "Gifted and talented students are from all cultural, racial, and ethnic backgrounds, and socioeconomic groups. Some such students have disabilities and for some, English is not their first language. Many students from such diverse backgrounds have been historically underrepresented in gifted education." For this reason, there may be more than 3 million school-age students who are potentially eligible for gifted/talented programs. For statistical information about your state, contact the Council of State Directors of Programs for the Gifted (Texas Education Agency, 1701 North Congress Avenue, Austin, TX 78701) and the National Association for Gifted Children (1707 L Street NW, #550, Washington, DC 20036).

For more information on the National Association for Gifted Children, go to the Web Links module in Chapter 11 of the Companion Website.

Instructional Methods

While most teachers receive preservice and/or inservice training about methods of instruction for students who are linguistically and culturally diverse, few are given support on how to teach gifted and/or talented students. Two guiding principles are essential for teachers of inclusive classrooms. First is to become familiar with characteristics and other indications of possible giftedness and talent. That is because classroom teachers often are the first to recommend children for identification and assessment as gifted/talented. Second is to focus upon strengths more than upon weaknesses. Teachers should provide accommodations that are required because of disability (e.g., scaffolding and text-to-speech for those with reading disabilities, frequent breaks for those with ADHD or emotional disorders, occupational therapy sessions for children and youth with physical disabilities), but once that is done, the emphasis should be upon developing the student's abilities and talents. Children and youth who are gifted and/or talented and also have disabilities generally will become frustrated and/or bored with routine drill-and-practice exercises (Weinfeld, Barnes-Robinson, Jeweler, & Shevitz, 2002).

Strategies in Early Childhood and Elementary School

The discovery learning approaches favored by many early childhood educators often work well with young children who are gifted and/or talented. Play, especially, should be encouraged. A stimulating environment, one that offers many options and supports many different activities, is very important. However, with this age group, teachers need to offer some supporting structures (e.g., intermediate goals, timelines, etc.). Interdisciplinary instruction can also be effective, as when children with gifts in music use their talents to master mathematics. Multi-sensory instruction, including hands-on use of manipulatives, can be effective (Clark, 2002). Other ideas are offered by the Web sites of elementary schools with gifted/talented programs (see the "County" resources list at *http://pegagus.cc.ucf.edu/~multicul/res/gifted.htm*).

Strategies in Middle School and High School

Mentorship can be highly effective with students who are gifted and/or talented. A "big brother" or "big sister" with similar gifts or talents can stimulate children's growth while also serving as a role model. At these age levels, students should be offered increased opportunities for independent study (e.g., research projects, Webquests). Teachers, too, can make frequent use of parallel talk and self talk (see Chapter 8) to model successful strategies. Heterogeneous groups, in which a gifted/talented student is paired with a less-advanced peer, can help. Although such cooperative learning is somewhat controversial among experts in gifted/talented education (in "Gifted Education: An Endangered Species," at *http://www.gifteddevelopment.com*, for example, Linda Silverman claims that "there is no evidence that the gifted profit from heterogeneous groups" [p.2]), the fact remains that even very gifted or talented individuals can benefit from being required to explain "obvious" ideas or steps so that others can understand and follow them. Collaboration between teachers of inclusive classrooms, special educators, and teachers of gifted/talented children and youth is essential (Cline & Hegeman, 2000).

Strategies in Transition to Adult Life

Students who are gifted and/or talented should be encouraged to continue their education on a life-long basis. College and post-graduate education are typical transition goals for those who are gifted, while specialized post-secondary training is common for those who are talented. Support is available from such organizations as American Mensa (201 Main Street #1101, Fort Worth, TX 76102-3105), the Camelopard Society (PO Box 16898, San Diego, CA 92116), and the International High Five Society (3546 Devon Hill Road, Toledo, OH 43606-1102).

The National Research Center on the Gifted and Talented, comprised of three universities (Connecticut, Virginia, and Yale) and 300 collaborating school districts, promises to offer practical guidelines on transition as well as other aspects of educating students who are gifted and/or talented, including those with disabilities (*http://www.gifted.uconn.edu*). The recently funded center focuses upon practical issues facing teachers and students. In particular, it examines ways the standard curriculum may be modified so as to rectify the traditional mismatch between gifted/talented students and the material they study in regular and inclusive classrooms.

CHAPTER SUMMARY

At Risk

- "At risk" means cause-and-effect dynamics that put students in danger of negative *future events* (McWhirter, McWhirter, McWhirter, & McWhirter, 1998, p. 7).
- A school's climate or environment may place students unnecessarily at risk.

Poverty and Homeless/Migrant Children

- Family poverty is a major risk factor, largely because of malnutrition and inadequate medical care.
- Adolescents need to learn that the "safety net" of welfare has dramatically changed with TANF, placing teens who become pregnant at greater risk of poverty than was the case until just a few years ago.
- Homeless or migrant children may be at risk if schools are rigid about requiring proof of a permanent home address or if schools do not act affirmatively to prevent other children from teasing these students.
- Teachers who look for, and teach to, student interests may help "slow learners" to blossom.

Abuse and Neglect

- Suspected child abuse or neglect must be reported to the appropriate investigative agencies.

Ethnic/Racial Minority Groups

- Culturally sensitive and culturally competent teachers make schools more welcoming for members of minority groups.
- We cannot be satisfied with our limited success to date in teaching students of linguistic minority groups.

Delinquency

- Research shows that students who first engage in delinquent behavior when they are teens often can be quickly returned to "the straight and narrow," but that those who begin such behavior as young children may require much more intensive and more long-term interventions.

Suicide and Drug/Alcohol Abuse

- Suicide prevention efforts are particularly urgent after someone in the school has attempted to or succeeded at committing suicide.
- Alcohol continues to be the "drug of choice" for most adolescents, although ecstasy recently gained popularity.

Gifted/Talented

- There is no mandate to identify, nor to provide appropriate services to, students who have gifts and/or talents. States and school districts vary widely in what they offer.
- Teachers play important roles in identifying students who may be gifted and/or talented and in referring them for formal evaluation. Teachers may also differentiate instruction in the classroom with discovery learning, mentorship, parallel talk, and self talk.

QUESTIONS FOR REFLECTION

1. What factors keep so many Americans in poverty, despite a long-lasting strong economy?
2. Why are so many children homeless?
3. How could you take advantage of the fact that many high-school students know at least one dropout?
4. What teaching approaches discussed in this book may help slow learners?
5. What proportions of PreK–12 students in your area are members of ethnic and/or racial minority groups? Which groups? What does this information suggest for the way you teach (see the story of Jane and Marcus, in this chapter)?
6. How can reflecting on *your own* culture help you to become more competent in teaching children who adhere to the teachings of other cultures?
7. Why is becoming a teen mother such a risky behavior for both parent and child?
8. Which of the several approaches to teaching ELL students strikes you as most promising?
9. Why is "student profiling" (akin to racial profiling) a bad idea, according to the Center for the Prevention and Study of Violence?
10. Why are the gifts and talents of students with learning disabilities often overlooked?

Chapter 12

Collaboration

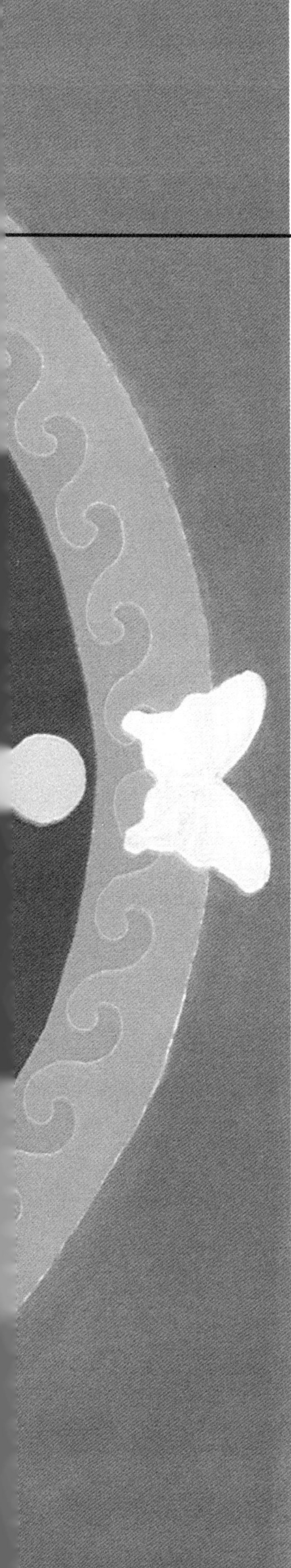

TERMS

collaboration
co-teaching
consultation
adapted physical education
art therapy
block scheduling
paraprofessionals

CHAPTER FOCUS QUESTIONS

After reading this chapter, you should be able to answer such questions as:

1. What distinguishes collaboration from consultation?
2. Which team member is more likely to feel she has much to lose from collaboration: the general educator or the special educator? Why?
3. How does the differing kinds of preparation they received often lead general and special educators to teach differently?
4. What advantages are associated with pull-out related services? With push-in services?
5. Which roles should a professional teacher not relinquish to a paraprofessional?
6. When should IEP teams invite representatives of community agencies to IEP meetings?
7. How are teacher-family relations affected by the changing nature of families?

PERSONAL ACCOUNTS

Kelly, a new teacher of an inclusive high-school biology class, reflected on some real political realities:

> *In the perfect inclusion classroom, two teachers work together toward a common goal. The special education teacher should not stick out. The general teacher in my experience is the lead teacher; I am merely a resource, keeping everyone on task, making sure notes are being written down, modifications are implemented, and so on. I do not teach except when the regular education teacher is absent. The regular biology teacher teaches by straight lecture, with a few diagrams here and there and sometimes a 3-D model. I give the regular education teacher tips on reaching students with disabilities, but they still struggle. When I taught a separate special education biology class, I used hands-on experiences, videos, graphic organizers, diagrams, repetition, and colors to distinguish things. I know these tactics work. However . . . Since this is my first year, I watch what I say. Even though my regular education teacher listens to my suggestions and sometimes carries them out (he has an open mind), I will wait to open my mouth more once I feel more comfortable. As the years go on and I work more with him, I am positive that we will find the right "groove" that will be most beneficial to him, to me, and especially to the students with disabilities.*
>
> —Kelly

Carmela, a graduate student, did half of her student teaching in an inclusive classroom. This was for a 7-week period from September to late October.

> *There are three classified students in this class. I am particularly concerned about one of them. He needs a great deal of one-on-one time to help him focus and complete his work. My cooperating teacher is certified in elementary education. There is a special educator who comes to our class for 90 minutes each day and a teaching assistant who comes in the mornings to help with reading. Other than those people, the teacher and I are the only adults there. My primary responsibility is this one boy. I will be leaving in two weeks, when my student-teaching assignment ends. I am very worried that this boy is going to have a great deal of trouble when I leave. What I cannot understand is how the school thought that 7 weeks of me assisting him made this an "appropriate" placement for him for the school year!*
>
> —Carmela

These stories highlight some political aspects of teaching in inclusive classrooms. As Kelly observed, when the two teachers are of unequal status, one may be subservient to the other. Carmela's story, on the other hand, illustrates the lengths to which some schools go in order to save money. In her case, the school assigned a "free" student teacher to work with a general educator. Other ways in which political realities influence collaboration will be discussed in the pages that follow.

INTRODUCTION

The term **collaboration** means cooperative partnerships between two or more individuals. When two people collaborate, they jointly make decisions (Turnbull & Turnbull, 2001; Walther-Thomas, Korinek, & McLaughlin, 1999). Teachers in inclusion classrooms typically forge and maintain collaborative working relationships with many persons, among them other teachers, related-services personnel, paraprofessionals, and volunteers. Less often, they work collaboratively with students and with families.

Collaboration between workers, as an approach to completing tasks, began in business and industry. There is considerable evidence that when people collaborate successfully in the workplace, teams outperform individuals, even high-achieving workers, when tasks require wide-ranging knowledge and varied skills (e.g., Katzenbach & Smith, 1994; Vroom & Deci, 1972). In education, too, when general and special educators, as well as related-services personnel, administrators, "para's," and volunteers work together well, as members of smoothly functioning teams, the chances of success with inclusion increase significantly (Austin, 2000; Cole & McLeskey, 1997; Hunt, Soto, Maier, & Doering, 2003; Turnbull & Turnbull, 2001). By contrast, when these adults do not collaborate effectively, inclusion is likely to fail (Fuchs & Fuchs, 1996; Garshelis & McConnell, 1993).

Co-teaching (Friend & Cook, 2003) refers to joint instruction by two equal partners. In this book, we use "co-teaching" and "collaboration" interchangeably, to mean the same thing. Collaboration (co-teaching) features people deciding for themselves the structure, process, and content of what they do. Collaborative learning was distinguished in Chapter 8 from cooperative learning, which has students working together under *teacher*-set rules. The words "collaborative" and "cooperative" have the same meanings in this chapter, where we discuss teachers' work, as they did in the earlier chapter, where we talked about students' work. Educators generally use the term collaboration when discussing professionals teaching and the term cooperative when referring to students learning.

There is another important term: **consultation.** When teachers work in a consultative mode, one (usually the general educator) is the primary instructor while the other (typically the special educator) is the secondary educator. That is, consultation has one person teaching most students while the other modifies instruction for some students. That is what Kelly reported doing during her first year as a teacher in an inclusive classroom. Histori-

Collaboration has two professionals working hand-in-hand, jointly teaching.

cally, the word "consultation" held another meaning: a special educator would come in to the school as a consultant to train general educators. As a consultant, the special educator had no direct teaching responsibility.

This chapter opens by discussing collaboration between general and special educators in an inclusive classroom. This is, without question, the kind of collaboration that is most important for success with inclusion. For that reason, we devote the bulk of the chapter to it. We then examine collaboration between those teachers and such related-services personnel as speech/language pathologists and counselors. Strategies for working with paraprofessionals and volunteers follows. We then look at collaboration with students and with families.

COLLABORATION BETWEEN TEACHERS

Collaborating teachers typically describe their partnership as a "marriage" because they share responsibility for the "home" (classroom)—the layout of the furnishings, the supplies, the daily routine, and the children. As with any marriage, participants may experience nervousness at the beginning, but find that with open and sustained communication, flexibility, and mutual understanding and respect, they can make it work. Support from fellow teachers is one of the most important contributors to satisfaction on the job, according to recent surveys of special education teachers (e.g., Gersten, Keating, Yovanoff, & Harniss, 2001).

Keys to Successful Collaboration

Collaboration (co-teaching) is challenging, especially at the beginning. It is most likely to work when collaborators communicate openly and frequently with each other, when they appreciate each other's beliefs and worries, when they are flexible, when they are willing to learn from each other, and when they carve out (and are given, by school administrators) enough time to make the partnership work.

Initial Worries About Collaboration

Special educators tend to feel vulnerable when entering the partnership (Cole & McLeskey, 1997). This is because the change from a special classroom to an inclusive classroom is far more dramatic than is that from a general classroom to an inclusive classroom. Special educators typically must give up their own rooms. They often must, or feel they must, surrender their identities. As collaborators in an inclusive classroom, they must work daily with 25 or 30 students, not with 8 to 12. Especially at the secondary level, they must become fluent in a subject matter (math, chemistry, history, etc.) rather than remain a generalist who can teach some content in many disciplines. The sense of vulnerability these worries produce may be why special educators often are sensitive to the fact that "the little things are just as important. This includes physical space issues such as a desk, a chair, a place to put their things, and a file cabinet" (Cole & McLeskey, 1997, p. 9). Principals and other administrators who demonstrate sensitivity to teachers' concerns and needs, who offer support and training when needed, and who supply the resources that teachers require to do their jobs greatly alleviate the initial stress that so many special educators report (Gersten et al., 2001).

General educators, too, may approach collaboration with some worries and doubts. Typically, general educators express concerns about lack of knowledge about how to reach students with special needs. The initial thought is to "leave that to the special educator." Frequently, general educators must adopt small-group and even one-on-one teaching techniques in lieu of their accustomed teacher-led whole-class lecture methods. Thus, especially on the secondary level, they may feel some trepidation about making such fundamental changes in the ways they teach (Cole & McLeskey, 1997). These concerns naturally open the door for respect to develop between special and general educators (see "Mutual Understanding and Respect," p. 429). If teamed teachers acknowledge each other's skills and defer to each other's expertise, the partnership will be off to a good start.

Communication

As with any marriage, teacher-teacher collaboration requires a lot of communication. The partners need a great deal of planning time when they first begin to collaborate. Assuaging the doubts mentioned above is a big part of this early work. The box, "Teacher Strategies That Work: Discussion Topics for Collaboration," identifies some issues around which this communication may occur. Although the time required for communication between them drops after the first few weeks and months, it remains a daily necessity throughout the school year (Austin, 2000).

Collaborating teachers strongly recommend that the key decisions on how to present themselves in the classroom be made *before* the first day of class. Said a math teacher interviewed by Cole and McLeskey (1997),

At times, one collaborating teacher leads the lesson while another provides support. Here, the teacher on the left stands ready to refocus the attention of a student with attention deficit hyperactivity disorder by, for example, gently tapping on the desk.

> We are co-teachers from the word go, from the ground up. . . . We tell students, "We are your teachers." We put the names up on the board, they stay up there all year long, and we go right into what the class is about and what they are going to experience this year, and we don't say another word about the roles we might play. We don't even explain it. I can't recall anyone asking, "Why are there two teachers in here?" They just kind of sit in here, and there are two teachers! (p. 9)

Being "co-teachers from the word go" does not just happen. It requires a great deal of communication between the partners. Hunt et al. (2003) recommend formal structures for such communication. Their "Unified Plan of Support" features regularly scheduled meetings (monthly, for about 90 minutes each time), built-in accountability systems (agreed-upon criteria for success and ways to assess progress), and flexibility to change as events demand (fall-back arrangements). The Plan also incorporates academic and social supports for students who are included in general classrooms. Those supports involve family members as well as other educators. For these reasons, Hunt et al. urge that communication among adults be all-encompassing, bringing in parents, siblings, coaches, extracurricular club leaders, related-services personnel, and any others whose work helps or could help students to succeed. Written plans are prepared for each student, spelling out the roles and responsibilities of all adults. The plans also detail student expectations (to meet academic goals, to participate in class discussion, etc.).

Mutual Understanding and Respect

A *sine qua non* (literally, "without which, none" or freely translated, "something you got to have!") of successful collaboration between teachers is that they understand and respect

Teacher Strategies That Work

Discussion Topics for Collaboration

1. What are the needs of the students we will be teaching this year? (This requires a review of IEPs and other pupil-personnel documents. Do either/both of us think that further assessment, early in the school year, is necessary so we know what to teach, and how?)
2. What are each of our expectations for how much, and how quickly, these students will learn? (We need to agree upon these, after reviewing documentation on the children, so that we can set realistic goals for at least the first marking period. If we hold very different expectations, we won't be able to make collaboration work.)
3. What substantive knowledge do each of us possess and which teaching techniques are each of us skilled in using, that could help those students to learn those things? (Can we do the things you most enjoy doing, and those I like, too? Are there any conflicts between those?)
4. Are each of us comfortable with the idea of helping the other acquire that knowledge and those skills during the course of the year? (Is the general-education team member prepared to devote the time and energy required to learn how to modify instructional materials and methods and how to carry out behavior-modification techniques? Is the special-education team member amenable to learning much more about math/biology/language arts/etc. and ways of teaching them? If so, we will teach each other as the year proceeds. If not, we should recognize that we're going to have to be unequal partners this year.)
5. How will we begin? Do we want to "pilot" first, so as to work out how best we can team up? In one pilot lesson, we might teach in a consultative mode (one of us taking primary instructional responsibility while the other provides support, examples, etc., while walking from seat to seat). In another unit, we might adopt in a cooperative mode (both of us assuming equal roles in instructing and also in modifying). (The ideal is collaboration but we may not be ready to do that early in the school year.)
6. What do each of us believe about class rules? How can we take advantage of the fact that two of us are in the room to minimize non-instructional time (e.g., classroom management) and maximize academic time? (Rules can be contentious unless we resolve the issue now.)
7. How do we want to communicate with parents? This includes reporting children's progress to parents as well as responding to parental questions and concerns. (Are each of us comfortable with more-frequent communications with parents than is usual in general education?)

each other. Accomplishing this takes time. General and special educators come to the partnership from very different backgrounds. Typically, general educators see themselves as *facilitators* who point students in the right direction, provide needed materials, teach the "big ideas," and then stand ready to answer questions as needed. Special educators, by contrast, tend to function as *instructors* who directly teach students virtually all of what the children are expected to learn (Cole & McLeskey, 1997). It should be evident that meshing those styles can be challenging.

To oversimplify matters, general educators tend to think in terms of whole-class and group instruction. They frequently favor indirect teaching methods. They want children to *learn*. That often means discovery learning, in which teachers present children with a new concept and invite them to discover its features and make-up, largely on their own. This approach is particularly popular in the teaching of science. The underlying assumption behind teacher facilitation is that children are ready to learn and that they do best when guided and encouraged. Ruiz (1989), writing about instruction for English-language learners insisted that open-ended, unstructured opportunities are essential and that children may actually be harmed if they are limited to Direct-Instruction, highly structured experiences. Part of the reason why general educators tend to function in these ways is the fact that they often were not trained in Direct-Instruction, special-needs assessment, materials modification, and the like. They quite naturally resist what they are not comfortable doing (Austin, 2000; Villa, Thousand, Nevin, & Malgeri, 1996).

Special educators, by contrast, generally think in terms of individual children, rather than in whole classes or in groups. They favor more teacher-centered methods. They *teach* children. They break down large ideas or topics ("task analysis") and teach each, one by one. The underlying assumption is that children with special needs are not likely to discover these features on their own. Children with mental retardation, for example, usually do better if assignments are broken down into discrete, step-by-step activities. Similarly, many children with emotional/behavioral disorders need the constant presence of a trained adult to remain focused on the task (see Chapter 5). Also weighing on the minds of many special educators is time. Children with special needs often require so long to master knowledge and skills that precious little time is available for discovery learning.

There is yet another concern. In order for students to engage in discovery learning, the teacher must be thoroughly conversant in the subject matter. Whereas it is theoretically possible in a structured environment for a teacher to "learn on the fly" so he can "stay one week ahead" of the students, this is much less feasible in an unstructured setting, simply because students may wander far afield from "this week's content" and ask questions that a teacher not thoroughly conversant with the content may not be able to answer. Such worries could quite naturally lead any educator to resist indirect teaching methods. Austin (2000) interviewed 139 collaborating teachers in 20 school districts in northern New Jersey in 1999. Most were secondary-school teachers of social studies, science, English, and math. One anonymous teacher told Austin: "I'm not an English teacher; I'm a special ed. teacher. I'm not a physics teacher; I'm a special ed. teacher. I do what I do best and I think they're expecting me to get up and teach physics" (p. 153). This comment reflects the self-perception of some special educators. Most such teachers, like Kelly who has taught biology both in a separate classroom and in an inclusive classroom, are knowledgeable both in content areas and in adapting curricula, methods, and materials (see "Personal Accounts," p. 425).

These problems can be solved. The key is mutual respect. The two teachers need to help each other. When general and special educators collaborate as team teachers, they can effectively guide students. Students who struggle with math may learn significantly more in a team-teaching classroom than in a traditional classroom (Rosman, 1994). The difference in Rosman's study was that general and special educators planned and delivered instruction together. They supported each other, to the students' benefit.

Willingness to Learn

When a special and a general educator become team members, each needs to be amenable to deferring to the other's expertise but also, and this is crucial, willing to learn from the other. As the year proceeds, the special educator should pick up more and more nuances of subject matter information and the general educator should become more and more skilled in behavior modification and in test/material modification. General educators can learn, from collaborating special educators, about assessment and diagnosis and about Direct Instruction. Special educators, for their part, can also gain appreciation for the potential of students to *learn*—leading to comfort in suppressing their own urge to *teach* everything. It should be evident that acquiring new skills and knowledge—on top of everything else a teacher must do—is a *major commitment*. It will only happen with mutual admiration and respect, and with genuine support from the partner.

General educators in Austin's study tended to defer to special educators on matters of discipline and modification of materials and tests. Special educators, in turn, tended to defer to general educators on issues of content (subject matter). Austin was encouraged to learn that both general and special educators reported *learning from each other* during the school year: "Special education co-teachers most often identified an increase in content expertise as the principal professional benefit of co-teaching whereas general educators typically cited contribution to skills in curriculum modification and classroom management" (Austin, 2000, p. 136). One technique general educators reported as valuable was that of advance organizers (see Chapter 8). In this approach, as you will recall, a teacher provides the student, before the lesson begins, with an outline of the lecture, definitions of key words, and similar "hooks" so as to help the student prepare to learn. While this method has been widely used in special education, it is, as the general educators Austin interviewed learned, also helpful to many students who do not have disabilities. Other "lessons learned" reported by teachers in Austin's study are described here:

> All but one of the co-teachers interviewed stated that they felt the collaborative teaching strategies they were using were effective in teaching students without disabilities in their classes. The most common explanations for the effectiveness of co-teaching with these students included: (a) the reduced student-teacher ratio, (b) the benefit of another teacher's expertise and viewpoint, (c) the value of remedial strategies and review for all students, and (d) the opportunity to learn about and appreciate different learning styles. (pp. 140–141)

Flexibility

Flexibility is another hallmark of successful teacher-teacher collaboration. Both general and special educators must relinquish sole decision-making power about virtually everything (from how the physical layout of the room is set up to what color chalk to use). Team members will find themselves, at different times, playing many roles: that of a facilitator, that of a teacher, that of a learner, that of an interior designer, that of a disciplinarian, and that of a supervisor. While flexibility is essential for all teachers, it is particularly critical for educators who collaborate with other teachers in the inclusive classroom.

One aspect of flexibility is the willingness to alter plans as required. Once both educators are convinced that the arrangements they made at the beginning are no longer effective, or no longer needed, they must be willing to acknowledge reality, even if this means another round of intense meetings to plan new strategies and tactics. If, for example, a student with attention deficit hyperactivity disorder (ADHD) or one with an emotional/behavioral disorder (E/B) is not responding positively to the teachers' structure and procedures in the classroom, a change may be required. Perhaps one team member will focus upon classroom management and discipline, freeing the other to concentrate upon instruction. If, on the other hand, such divided responsibilities prove to be ineffective, the change may result in both teachers becoming disciplinarians as well as educators.

Cole and McLeskey (1997), after interviewing collaborating teachers, reported on one school's flexible approach to collaboration:

> Prior to development of the inclusive school program, "compensatory and support" programs were viewed primarily as support services provided by the teacher of students with disabilities to allow students with mild disabilities to succeed in the general education classroom. These programs did not question the curriculum, instruction, or classroom organization of the general education classroom. Thus, "the problem" was perceived to reside within the student, and the role of the teacher of students with disabilities was viewed as making sure the student could fit into the general education classroom.

> As partnerships developed, teachers concluded quickly that this perspective had to change. They found that though students with mild disabilities indeed lacked some of the skills manifested by typical students, these deficits could be addressed best by changing the general education classroom and assisting students with disabilities within these settings to gain the skills necessary to succeed. Thus, as part of these partnerships, teachers worked to *transform* the general education classroom to better meet the needs of *all* students. The partnerships often resulted in significant changes in the curriculum of the general education classroom, methods of delivering instruction, and classroom organization. Classes also often became more student-centered and less teacher- or content-centered. (p. 6; emphasis in original)

Time

Collaboration is time-consuming. Indeed, Pearman, Huang, and Mellblom (1997), in their study of 558 teachers and administrators in K–12 schools, reported that the number-1 concern of teachers was "time pressure" (p. 11). That is why a resource such as Nelson's text, *Time Management for Teachers* (1995), should be on your "must-read" list. The principles are easier to learn about than to practice. Basically, teachers need to set priorities—and to follow them! Priority setting may involve organizing a "to do" list into three categories: (A) urgent and important, (B) important but not urgent, and (C) routine. The discipline is in forcing yourself to do the "A" items *first*—each and every day. You must resist the temptation to do "C" items simply because they are quickly and easily accomplished, rewarding you with the pleasure of crossing them off the list.

Another key technique of time management is to do first those things that *only* you can do. Things that can be delegated should be. Cole and McLeskey (1997) quoted a general education (math) teacher as saying about his collaborating special-education team member: "[M]y partner will say 'Okay, I'll make the test out and make sure we cover this,' and there is no conversation about what should be on it, because I feel like the marriage has really settled in and we have become one" (p. 8). In this instance, the math teacher delegated a task. He did so appropriately, recognizing that his partner was capable of doing it.

Clearly, teachers from such divergent backgrounds as general and special education should not be expected to work out these two philosophies of instruction quickly and easily. Recall that "Teacher Strategies That Work: Discussion Topics for Collaboration" illustrates some topics for early planning sessions. Whether during the summer months before school begins, or in September, teachers need considerable time to identify each other's strengths and preferences, to determine what modifications in the curriculum and methods will be required to meet the special needs of the children, to discuss the use of directive versus facilitative techniques, and to work out agreements on how to handle many other matters. When team members know each other, respect each other, and get along well, they can discuss these potentially divisive issues in a friendly, non-confrontational manner, and reach a consensus.

When Austin explored what kinds of support team members needed in order to collaborate effectively, he found very substantial majorities identifying planning time as a key support. Yet fewer than half (47%) said that their administrations gave them such planning time. They wanted to have scheduled "free" periods *during the school year*. Few expressed interest in paid planning time during summer months.

There are time-management benefits, some unexpected, that come with collaboration. Collaborating teachers find that they actually have more time to work with individual students and more time to do what they do best, because there is "another teacher here" who can shoulder some of the administrative burdens (copying papers, taking attendance, etc.) and some of the teaching load (handling a disciplinary problem while the lesson goes on; Cole & McLeskey, 1997).

Making Collaboration Work

Teachers frequently say that additional factors are involved in successful teacher-teacher collaboration. These include the volitional nature of the partnership, practicing what they

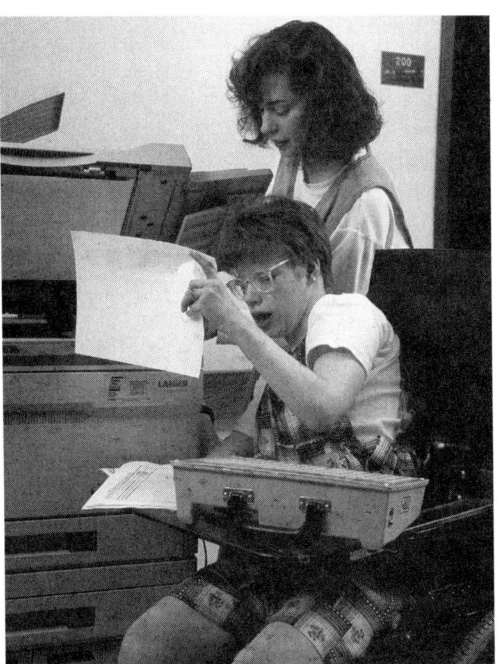

Paraprofessionals perform many tasks in support of classroom teaching, among them copying work for a student with a physical disability.

preach, inservice training, and forming truly collaborative partnerships, especially at the secondary level where forging equal roles can be challenging.

Tapping Each Others' Strengths

Perhaps your collaborating partner has a background in art and/or physical education. If so, she would know that a wide variety of teacher-made and commercial adaptations help students with cerebral palsy and other physical or health conditions. Anderson's (1992) *Art for All the Children* text featured ways to individualize instruction by taping or rubber banding art supplies such as brushes to provide larger, more easily grasped surfaces. Anderson also recommended use of orthoplast ("a special plastic material that can be molded when warm"; p. 277). If heated in an oven or even in warm water, it can be shaped so as to exactly fit a child's hand. Once it cools, it has much strength. She also suggested Velcro wrist straps, attached with rubber bands, to assist a child to hold an instrument. Velcro or dycem can also be placed under supplies to keep them from slipping on desks or drawing surfaces. Paint and water containers may be weighted by placement of gravel inside, making them less susceptible to being overturned. Because children who are blind or have low vision may position their eyes very close to the surface to see art or read materials, Anderson (1992) warned that these students are at greater than usual risk for inhaling and/or tactually absorbing toxic substances. She recommended that art teachers check the child's IEP records for information about allergies and other known susceptibility to toxic substances, that art rooms be well ventilated, and that protective eye gear be worn to protect against chemical splashes. Anderson also pointed out that blindness or low vision makes it necessary for children to be given tactually perceptible working surfaces. Their art paper might be placed into a flat tray, for example, with the tray's raised edges serving as indicators of where the paper begins and ends. On the paper itself, tape or glue may be used to provide raised surfaces that give the child reference points (e.g., where she stopped the day/week before). See the box, "Teacher Strategies That Work: Collaborating with a Creative Art Therapist," later in this chapter.

Formal and informal play opportunities as well as games are important (Clements, 1995). This begins at the early childhood level, simply because young children learn most everything while being physically active (Bowe, 2000a). With infants, toddlers, and preschoolers, swimming (aquatics) is becoming more and more popular (e.g., Suomi and Suomi, 2000). Again, your partner's interests and skills, this time in swimming, may prove valuable.

Choosing Your Partner (If Possible)

Selection of team members is a critical first step in inclusion. Interviews with working teachers (e.g., Austin, 2000; Cole & McLeskey, 1997) reveal that the identity of the team member is very high on the list of important factors. Teachers bring it up within the first few minutes of these interviews. When researchers talk with teachers who feel that inclusion has not worked for them, they find that educators often begin by talking about their partners. Frequently, they report that they had no choice in the matter: They were assigned someone to work with. They say team members were paired by building administrators simply because their daily schedules matched. Or they say that the principal assigned only new teachers to inclusion teams. Any of these errors can set up inclusion for failure. Researchers urge that teachers should *volunteer* for team teaching and be able to identify teachers they want to work with (King-Sears, 1997; Walther-Thomas, Bryant, & Land, 1996). Both veteran and new educators should participate as collaborating teachers. As one teacher put it:

> It makes all the difference in the world who the partner is. If you had come to me and asked me to do this interview a year ago, my responses would have been quite different on a lot of these questions because last year I worked with two people and neither one of them put the energy or selflessness into the job that this woman I'm working with this year does. (Anonymous, quoted in Austin, 2000, p. 150)

Doing What You Say You Will Do

Collaborating teachers often report divergences between their intentions and their actual actions. Austin found that while most (about 90%) of the teachers he interviewed said that daily planning sessions are essential for effective team teaching, just over half (about 58%) said that they actually did meet daily with their partners. Similarly, while the vast majority of interviewed teachers believed that both partners should share classroom-management responsibilities, including discipline, fewer said this happened in actual practice. More disturbing was the finding that, although virtually all of the teachers said they expected their partners to give them feedback, just one out of every five special educators reported actually receiving regular feedback from their general-education partners. Educators find that, with feedback, they become much more consistent over time, actually doing what they said they would do. As a result, they become better, and more satisfied, collaborating teachers.

Preparation

New collaborating teachers frequently identify inservice preparation needs. Prominent among them is "formal training in conflict resolution and collaboration skills" (Cole & McLeskey, 1997, p. 10). Educators typically report that their undergraduate and graduate teacher preparation did not equip them in those areas. Special educators commonly were prepared to teach in a separate classroom or in a resource room. General educators usually were trained in content areas and in child and adolescent development. Neither background featured much preparation in teamwork. That is why inservice training in such techniques is potentially of great value for inclusion teachers. It helps not only in teacher-teacher collaboration but also in teacher-therapist, teacher-paraprofessional, teacher-student, and teacher-parent collaboration. Particularly valued are opportunities to observe other teachers in action (Gersten et al., 2001).

College and university teacher-preparation programs typically have *separate* faculties for general and for special education. Collaboration between those faculties often is limited. If professors expect teachers in training to value and practice collaboration, we need to model it ourselves.

Collaboration at the Secondary Level

Preparation may be particularly helpful in assisting secondary teachers to make their partnership collaborative rather than consultative. Virtually all (97%) of the teachers Austin (2000) interviewed reported satisfaction with the ways in which they were working together. However, he discovered that nearly half of the general educators, but *none* of the

Teacher Strategies That Work

Models for Co-Teaching

Collaborating teachers may divide responsibilities in any one or combination of ways (Friend & Cook, 2003). These include

Team Teaching—Both educators teach the entire class. One may lecture while the other demonstrates (e.g., carries out a physics experiment). One may present concepts, the other examples. This set-up may be most feasible in inclusive classrooms where behavior management is seldom an issue.

One Teach, One Roam—In this arrangement, the second teacher moves around the classroom, checking on seat work, nudging inattentive students back to task, dispensing verbal or token rewards, and so on. This plan can be particularly effective in inclusive classrooms where at least one student has ADHD or an E/B disorder.

Station Teaching—Each educator teaches in his part of the room, generally at tables or other designated group work spaces. This model works well for small-group sessions, such as discovery-learning activities or student debate preparations.

Parallel Teaching—Friend and Cook (2003) distinguish this model from station teaching in that parallel teaching has both educators conducting the same instruction. This model lowers the student-to-teacher ratio, producing smaller groups and thus greater opportunities for individualization of instruction.

One Teach, One Tutor—Under this arrangement, one educator teaches a lesson while the other provides one-on-one tutoring and support. This plan may be most effective with students having severe disabilities. Children and youth with mental retardation, autism, deafness, and so on, may need the intensive support this model offers. Note that in this case it is a teacher doing the tutoring, not a paraprofessional.

One Teach, One Observe—This model is particularly useful when educators need to monitor student behavior. The observing teacher records what happens (see Chapter 9). This frees the other educator to focus exclusively upon instruction. This model may also be used by student teachers to learn how experienced educators work.

special educators, believed that "I do more than my partner." This finding illustrates the difficulty team members often have in dividing the work equally. Although they called themselves, and were called by their administrators, "collaborating" teachers, Austin found that they were more likely functioning in a consultation mode. As explained earlier in this chapter, the consultative approach has one teacher (here, the general educator) determining most of syllabus and the other (here, the special educator) modifying materials, and so on, for the special-needs students. Consultation is not a teacher-recommended approach (Cole & McLeskey, 1997; King-Sears, 1997). It may be that educators require a full school year, or even longer, to develop into truly collaborating partners.

Austin's study involved more secondary than elementary teachers. There have been few efforts to explore collaboration at the high-school level (Villa, Thousand, Nevin, & Malgeri, 1996). This fact makes the work of Boudah, Schumacher, and Deshler (1997) noteworthy. They monitored collaboration in four secondary classes of English, math, and science, comparing them to four other secondary classes teaching similar content but in non-collaborative ways. None of the teachers had been trained in collaboration at the time the study began. The researchers watched as, first, one teacher assumed the instruction role (teaching the content) while the partner played the mediator role (adapting materials, paraphrasing ideas, teaching individual students strategies to use, etc.). Typically, the general educator stood in the front of the room and the special educator at the back or beside the desk of one or more students. Over time, as Boudah et al. taught these educators better ways to collaborate, the two teachers learned how to become much more equal partners. Both stood at the front of the room and at different times both navigated among student desks to offer help on strategies, give prompts, and so on. This "role exchange" (p. 299), with the general educator adapting instruction and the special educator presenting the main content, marked a high level of collaboration.

While the teachers were generally satisfied with the experiment, Boudah and his colleagues were not. They expressed concern about the large proportion of class time that was spent in non-instructional activities (e.g., maintaining order). Given that the students had mild (not severe) disabilities and given that the situation was an experiment (meaning the teachers had university researchers to train and support them, something most secondary teachers do not get), it was evident to Boudah et al. that collaborative instruction at the high-school level is going to be more complex, and more demanding, than is generally acknowledged. Even with university trainers offering help on an ongoing basis, these secondary-school teachers spent a distressingly small amount of class time actually teaching the subject. The students spent correspondingly little time actively engaged in content learning.

For all of these reasons, Boudah et al. recommended that considerable additional research be done on how to make collaboration effective at the secondary level and that teacher preparation programs do far more to prepare teachers-in-preparation to be effective collaborators. Until we know more about how to "do" inclusion, they suggested, schools adopting inclusion programs should continue to offer resource room and other pull-out services. They should not move to full inclusion "cold turkey." This is so because of the high level and continuing nature of student needs to acquire and master competency in learning strategies. There simply does not appear to be time during class at the secondary level to teach these students *both* the content material *and* effective learning techniques, especially when the teachers have not been prepared to do both simultaneously.

What Does Research Show?

The literature on collaborative teaching, to date, is more prescriptive than analytical. Articles in professional journals tend to describe what teachers do and recommend best practices. The focus of studies to date is more on the process of collaboration than on the effects of collaboration on student achievement (Boudah et al., 1997, Welch, 2000). There

Technologies That Work

Collaboration

Educators may use today's technologies to facilitate collaboration. Particularly helpful are Internet-based tools that allow teachers to work together at a distance.

Perhaps the simplest tool for teacher-teacher collaboration is the editing functions built into most popular word-processing software packages. Word® and WordPerfect® both permit a second person to edit what a first author writes, using different font colors, highlighting, and other tools. The edited manuscript then can be returned, as an e-mail attachment, to the first author, who may elect to accept or challenge the alterations. The necessary tools are accessed via buttons displayed in the tool bar that typically appears at the top, bottom, or side of the screen.

Conference calls once had to be arranged through a telephone-company operator. Today, three or more people may be connected on a call by any of the participants, at the touch of a few buttons. Instant-messaging and e-mail communications technologies, similarly, permit text-based conferencing. Any user of instant messaging services may invite one or more persons into a chat room to discuss a matter. One advantage of these text-based services is that the entire conversation may be stored, verbatim, and may be sent to participants after the session concludes.

Yahoo!® and other Internet service providers offer "groups" (also known as "listservs"). These are controlled groups. Members may send e-mails to all other members by addressing messages to the group e-mail address rather than individual member e-mail addresses. Groups are discussion forums. Teachers of inclusive classrooms, for example, could set up a listserv at which they could talk about mutual concerns.

A related approach is electronic grading. Here, two educators work collaboratively, perhaps via e-mail, possibly with the assistance of Blackboard® or some other interactive software program, to decide upon student grades.

If one of the participating educators has a disability, materials and conversations can be made accessible for them. Voice-based calls, for example, now may be captioned by such services as CaptionFirst™. Text-to-speech capabilities are built into Windows XP® and are commercially available that speak out loud whatever text is displayed on a screen. Such speech synthesis helps educators who have reading disabilities or are blind. IBM, at its Hawthorn research laboratory, is investigating other ways in which users who have disabilities may increase the accessibility of interactive and collaborative technologies, including groups and Web-based content. Being explored are adaptations to change text size, line spacing, and between-character spacing, all of which assist users who have low vision.

For more information on CaptionFirst™, go to the Web Links module in Chapter 12 of the Companion Website.

have been a few research studies, however. Welch (2000) gathered student outcome data to show that students with specific learning disabilities gained in reading and spelling when taught by collaborating teachers. However, Welch conceded that "it is not possible to discern whether student achievement in this study would have occurred anyway, as no comparison group was utilized" (p. 373). Reviewing a large number of such investigations, Murawski and Swanson (2001) concluded that the evidence on collaborative teaching is suggestive, rather than conclusive. Noting that only 6 out of 89 articles reviewed contained enough data to permit the statistical re-analysis process known as meta-analysis to be done, they conceded that, nonetheless, what data are available suggest that collaboration may well have a potential for positive results on student outcomes.

Collaboration can have practical benefits. Teachers in inclusive classrooms should work with others to instruct students in the proper use of equipment. This will reduce the likelihood of injury. Educators need to exercise unusual care in music, art, and physical education because of the potential for danger. Art involves use of scissors and other instruments that may be used as weapons, as well as glue and other materials that may be toxic if used in inappropriate ways (e.g., sniffed). Some musical instruments, including the mallets used by percussionists, potentially are weapons as well. Sports, too, feature baseball bats and other objects that students may use to hurt other children, or even themselves. Teachers need to set firm rules regarding these materials and instruments, and enforce them vigorously. In each instance, specialists in those areas (music, art, and physical educators) can offer valuable information.

WORKING WITH RELATED-SERVICES PERSONNEL

Special educators are accustomed to working with speech/language pathologists, counselors, occupational and physical therapists, orientation and mobility specialists, and other related-services personnel (Bowe, 2000b). General educators tend to be much less familiar with these professionals and what they do. For this reason, brief explanations are offered before collaboration between educators and related-services personnel is addressed.

Kinds of Related Services

The most common related service is *speech and language pathology* services. These are provided by speech/language pathologists. In years past, pathologists focused mostly on remediation of speech problems. More recently, they have become more active in dealing with language difficulties. The professional organization representing these pathologists is the American Speech-Language-Hearing Association; it still goes by its old acronym "ASHA." Children with mental retardation, deafness or other hearing impairment, cerebral palsy, autism, and other disabilities often receive speech/language pathology services.

For more information on ASHA, go to the Web Links module in Chapter 12 of the Companion Website.

Another related service is *counseling*. Children with emotional/behavioral disorders, many who have attention deficit hyperactivity disorder, and students with traumatic brain injury often receive counseling services. In addition, students with *any* disability may benefit from counseling immediately prior to and during the transition years, for example, ages 14 to 18 or whenever they leave school. Any such student may also be referred for counseling services for non-disability reasons. Students aged 15 who have cerebral palsy are, after all, still 15 years old and for that reason alone may be helped by a counselor. The American School Counselor Association represents school-based counselors.

For more information on the American School Counselor Association, go to the Web Links module in Chapter 12 of the Companion Website.

Less frequent in the schools are *physical therapy* (PT) and *occupational therapy* (OT) services. This is simply because physical conditions are relatively uncommon among school-age children and youth. In general, physical therapists focus upon gross-motor activities and strive to prevent muscle atrophy (wasting away). Occupational therapists, by contrast, tend to concentrate upon fine-motor activities, particularly "practical" things such

For more information on the American Physical Therapy Association and the American Occupational Therapy Association, go to the Web Links module in Chapter 12 of the Companion Website.

as buttoning a shirt, eating food with utensils, and the like. Students with cerebral palsy, spinal cord injuries, traumatic brain injuries, and muscular dystrophy often benefit from PT and OT services. The American Physical Therapy Association and the American Occupational Therapy Association represent physical and occupational therapists (Bowe, 2000b).

Orientation and *mobility specialists* and "*VI Teachers*" may assist children who are blind or have low vision. These professionals perform different functions. Orientation and mobility is all about knowing where you are and knowing how to get from Point A to Point B. This includes orienting the child to the neighborhood around the school and to the school itself. It also involves training the student how to get from one classroom to another and how to get to the cafeteria, rest rooms, and so on. Visual impairment teachers, commonly called VI Teachers, adapt instructional materials. They may convert teacher handouts into Braille. They may also train a child in the use of a Braille writer or other note-taking device.

For more information on RID, go to the Web Links module in Chapter 12 of the Companion Website.

Students who are deaf or hard of hearing often use *interpreters* in the classroom. These related-services personnel are trained in methods of visual communication. They can play many roles in the inclusive classroom. First, they can translate what teachers say into "English on the hands" or, as it is sometimes called, Signed English. Notice that the word "translate" was used, rather than the term "interpret": That is because interpreters can also do something different—they can interpret the English words you speak into another language, that of American Sign Language (ASL). Interpretation is chosen over translation when a student is more fluent with ASL than with English, which often is the case if one or both parents of the child is/are also deaf. Fingerspelling, or "spelling in the air," is used both with translation and with interpretation. Interpreters often fingerspell words that do not have well-known signs. The Registry of Interpreters for the Deaf (RID) represents sign-language interpreters. Additional information about working with interpreters was offered earlier in Chapter 4.

Physical education comprises physical and motor fitness, motor skills and patterns, health issues, and skills in aquatics, dance, and individual or group games or sports. **Adapted physical education** includes the above, and adds assessment and instruction by qualified personnel that implement and comply with individualized education programs (IEP's), including instruction in a least restrictive environment (LRE).

Adapted physical educators (sometimes referred to as special physical educators) are professionals who are trained not only in sport and physical education but also in special education. Some have taken undergraduate or graduate courses similar to those taken by occupational and physical therapists (Clements, 1995). Adapted physical educators train PE teachers how to adjust activities so as to enable the whole class to take part. They also use assistive technology devices and different materials, as appropriate, to meet special needs (Adapted Physical Education, at *http://ncperid.usf.edu/index.html*).

Creative art therapists are special educators with additional training in using expressive arts to offer children opportunities to communicate. The American Art Therapy Association (AATA) defines **art therapy** as "the therapeutic use of art making, within a professional relationship, by people who experience illness, trauma, or challenges in living, and by people who seek personal development. Through creating art and reflecting on the art products and processes, people can increase awareness of self and others, cope with symptoms, stress and traumatic experiences; enhance cognitive abilities; and enjoy the life-affirming pleasures of making art" (*AATA Newsletter,* Spring 2002, p. 3). Abuse (sexual, physical, emotional) may be detected from a child's drawings (Anderson, 1992). These professionals can also help students having emotional needs. Training is required before teachers can interpret children's use of colors and shapes for their drawings (Anderson, 1992). If you believe a child is trying to communicate important and/or painful information, consultation with a professional may be appropriate. AATA is a useful resource. If you contact AATA, you will be given the name and phone number of the state association president of the state where you teach; from that person, in turn, you can learn who are licensed/certified creative art therapists in your local area. See the box on p. 441, "Teacher Strategies That Work: Collaborating with a Creative Art Therapist."

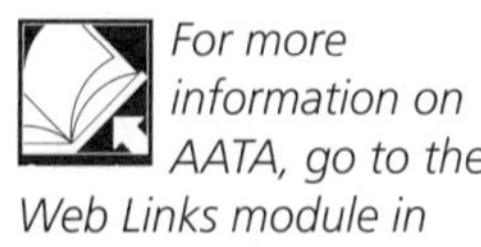
For more information on AATA, go to the Web Links module in Chapter 12 of the Companion Website.

Finally, you may have opportunities to work with specialists in the area of *gifted and talented* education. Giftedness and talent are perhaps more valued in the expressive arts than elsewhere in American society. Even during the Civil War and the Reconstruction, Thomas Wiggins (known as "Blind Tom") was able to rise above race and disability, due to his amazing abilities in music. In more recent years, Ray Charles and Stevie Wonder have done much the same. Athletes who are deaf have played at the professional level in baseball and basketball.

The special abilities of children with disabilities should be recognized. A good way of doing that is to feature those students in class productions and other activities. Students with disabilities generally receive so few opportunities to excel and be recognized for outstanding achievements that any such opportunities should be seized by the teacher. In the area of fine art, VSA arts (formerly Very Special Arts) offers numerous opportunities throughout the year and across the country to recognize original art work, as well as other expressive creations, by children, youth, and adults with disabilities (*http://www.vsaarts.org*). VSA arts sponsors several "Young Soloists Awards" each year to recognize musicians with disabilities who are under 25 years of age. These may be vocalists or instrumentalists. Young Soloists evenings are held in Washington, DC, each March. Some metropolitan areas have additional resources. In Philadelphia, for example, USArtists runs a special needs program that includes a juried and invitational exhibit called "Extraordinary Art—Beyond the Museum" (*http://www.palaestra.com/artfeature.html*). The Special Olympics provides events for the showcasing of abilities in sports and exercise. The close-knit deaf community holds its own state, national, and international competitions (in baseball, basketball, tennis, wrestling, etc.) through the USA Deaf Sports Federation (USADSF); the USADSF sends American teams to the quadrennial international Deaflympics.

For more information on the Special Olympics and USADSF, go to the Web Links module in Chapter 12 of the Companion Website.

The box on the next page, "Teacher Strategies That Work: Related Services," summarizes the main types of related services that are used in PreK–12 schools and suggests questions you might ask about how you could support related-services personnel. As an inclusion teacher, you should seek out your school's related-services personnel and establish working relationships with those who are or will be providing services to students in your classroom.

To illustrate, consider how related-services personnel can assist teachers of inclusive classrooms to implement the "principle of partial participation" (Anderson, 1992, p. 297). This approach calls for educators to identify things children cannot do or can only do in part, and then to structure activities so that these children can contribute to the best of their abilities. In music, art, and physical education, the method features task analysis by the teacher, followed by planning for students to perform components of activities, with whatever assistive technology devices they may require. Task analysis involves scrutiny of the steps involved in a particular task and identification of precisely the subtasks that the student cannot do or can do only with assistance: "In a task analysis, *all* of the steps necessary for meeting a particular behavioral objective are recorded in terms of *observed* behavior and in terms of the most logical sequential order in which these steps can be placed" (Anderson, 1992, p. 293; emphasis in original). Teachers should complete each step themselves and also watch someone else completing them in order to be sure they thoroughly understand the various steps involved. The principle of partial participation calls for the teacher or therapist to determine what the student *can* do, alone or with help. The teacher/therapist then does the other components herself or arranges for them to be done by someone else.

Issues in Teacher–Related-Services Personnel Collaboration

School counselors, speech-language pathologists, occupational therapists, physical therapists, and other related-services personnel may need to adjust their practices so as to collaborate effectively with classroom teachers. Educators, too, must be flexible. At least four potential problems may plague such relationships (Brown, Pryzwansky and Schulte, 2001). First, teacher-therapist collaboration is time-consuming. Educators may feel that they do not have the required time for such collaboration. Similarly, therapists who once

Teacher Strategies That Work

Related Services

Profession	Services	Teacher Questions/Roles
Speech Pathology	Remediation of speech problems (e.g., stuttering)	"What should I say and do in my classroom?"
	Remediation of language problems (e.g., aphasia)	"What teaching tools and materials do you recommend I use?"
	Feeding (e.g., students with cerebral palsy)	"Show me how to do it."
Occupational Therapy	Recommend assistive technologies (e.g., DynaMyte[TM])	"Show me how it works, and what to do if it doesn't."
	Solve practical problems (e.g., feeding, typing)	"Tell me what to do in my classroom."
Physical Therapy	Recommend assistive technologies (e.g., wheelchairs)	"Show me how it works and what to do if it doesn't."
	Maintain functioning (e.g., muscle strength)	"What should I do in my classroom?"
Orientation and Mobility	Travel training	"What should I do?"
Visual Impairment Teacher (VI Teacher)	Instructional modifications	"Show me how to make handouts and other materials accessible to students who are blind or have low vision."
Interpreting	Translation services	"Tell me what to do and what not to do."
Art Therapy	Self-expression	"Show me how to use art to help Ed express his feelings."

used recess, art, and other "special" periods for one-on-one assistance to students may feel that today's greater emphasis upon academics deprives them of the time they need for such sessions. Second, teachers typically were prepared to view a student having problems in class as a person in need of a technical service. For this reason, educators may refer students for evaluation and treatment. Teachers may not start, as experts recommend, by examining their own practices in the classroom and considering what changes might assist the child. Related-services personnel, for their part, are more likely to view themselves as therapists who receive referrals from teachers. Third, school administrators may impose teacher-therapist collaboration, depriving the process of the volitional nature that both professionals may feel is essential for success. Fourth and finally, teachers and therapists alike who are insecure about their status may hide behind their titles and professional stature, refusing to admit the need for outside help.

In response to these problems, Brown et al. (2001) developed what they called the "15-minute consultation" process. The intent is to catch teachers "on the fly" (Sciarra, 2003, 129), offering assistance during an educator's available time. The approach features several steps. In the first, the related-service professional (in this case, the school counselor) identifies the teacher's difficulty as primarily a function of knowledge, skill, confidence, and/or objectivity. Next, the counselor or other professional assess the educator as being primarily task-oriented or process-oriented. (Brown et al. expect teachers typically to be task-oriented, meaning that they prefer that the related-service professional offer a solution rather than seek to explore the problem together.) Third, the counselor or other professional makes a recommendation, always with the caveat that it is a seat-of-the-pants proposal. Finally, both parties agree upon a plan and upon respective responsibilities for carrying it out. While this approach will produce some mis-diagnoses of problems, and thus mis-identification of solutions, it does have the advantage of responding to the realities of the hectic school day.

Teacher Strategies That Work

Collaborating with a Creative Art Therapist

According to the American Art Therapy Association (AATA), art therapists are trained both in art and in therapy. Their preparation includes extensive course work in human development, psychological theories, clinical practice, and art (art traditions, multicultural perspectives on art, and spiritual uses of art). Creative art therapists have additional training in special education. These professionals typically are certified as classroom teachers under state rules for certification in the area of special education. They are also certified, or licensed, as clinical practitioners in the area of art therapy. The question we raise here is how can a teacher of an inclusive classroom collaborate with a creative art therapist?

Draw-a-Person, House-Tree-Person, and Kinetic Family Drawings may be used by art therapists to provide teachers with insights into the special needs of children and youth (Handler, 1996). Kramer and Schehr (1983) illustrated one approach to such collaboration in their article, "An Art Therapy Evaluation Session for Children." At the request of a general educator, the art therapist asks that the child draw a picture of his choice. After completing this task, the child is given a choice of paint or clay and encouraged to do whatever he wishes to do with the materials. The therapist evaluates the drawing and the painting/sculpture, noting product (no product, stereotypical product, chaotic or aggressive product, etc.), and the child's attitudes during the session (toward the therapist, toward his art work, toward the materials, and toward suggestions or offers of help). The resulting report is discussed with the teacher. Together, the two professionals decide how to use the information (e.g., Is professional counseling indicated? Should referral to a child-study team be made?). Notice that the quality of the art work itself is irrelevant. Creative art therapy is about expression and understanding. It is not about helping children and youth to become better artists.

Art therapists may also guide teachers of inclusive classrooms in the selection of art materials. Some are toxic. Only talc-free, premixed clays should be used. Lead-free liquid glazes should be used; alternatively, finished pieces should be painted with acrylics or tempera instead of glazing. Colorants that contain carcinogenic nickel, cadmium, uranium, chromates, or talc should be avoided (Jacobs & Milton, 1994).

Creative art therapists may also offer teachers ideas for the curriculum. To illustrate, the New York State Art Teachers Association produced, in 2002, "Visual Arts Curriculum Companion," a standards-based core PreK–12 curriculum for the visual arts. As another example, the Visual Arts Department, Jersey City (NJ) Public Schools, prepared, one year earlier, an "Art Therapy Program."

Finally, art therapists may teach or co-teach in general classrooms. Henley (1997) described one year when he was both therapist and teacher in an alternative high school. His students had emotional and behavioral disorders, several were substance abusers, and many had been abused or neglected at home. He memorably described how he used drawings and other art-based activities to help the teenagers to understand themselves better, to express their feelings, and to improve their academic performance.

For more information on the "Visual Arts Curriculum" and the "Art Therapy Program," go to the Web Links module in Chapter 12 of the Companion Website.

Art offers opportunities for collaboration between therapists and teachers.

Push-In v. Pull-Out of Related Services

Even when you engage in whole-class teaching, many students with special needs will require help from related-services personnel. The usual practice is for children to be "pulled out" for related services. That is, at the times and on the days when a child is scheduled to receive speech and language pathology services, occupational and physical therapy services, counseling, and the like, the child is removed from the classroom and taken to a therapy room or other location, where those services were delivered.

Another approach is "push-in" (the professional enters the classroom and the child remains there). At the scheduled time, the related-services worker enters the inclusive classroom. He works with the child right in that classroom.

Pull-out and push-in were discussed briefly in Chapter 6 because students with physical, sensory, and health disabilities make extensive use of related services. The focus in the current chapter is upon how push-in and pull-out affect teacher-therapist collaboration.

To introduce this extended discussion of push-in and pull-out, consider the experience of Natasha, a first-grade teacher of an inclusive classroom:

> One of my students was a child who has cerebral palsy, together with several secondary conditions, such as learning disabilities and speech/language impairment. I think the regular classroom was the right setting for this boy. However, making inclusion "work" for him was trying, to say the least! He was taken out of my classroom almost half of every school day. He met with an occupational therapist, a physical therapist, a speech pathologist, and a resource teacher—each one and every time on a "pull-out" basis. To say this was disruptive for me, and for his academic learning, is to understate the case. The constant pull-out exhausted him. Plus, every time he re-entered my classroom, I or someone else had to "catch him up to speed." This child needed much more structure than the school gave him. I approached each of the related-services specialists, trying to solve this problem. Most were at the school on a part-time basis, however, so it was hard even to schedule meetings, let alone planning sessions. This may be why only one of the four agreed to my request to provide push-in services instead of pull-out. I learned from this experience! This year, I insisted that related-services personnel get my prior approval for any pull-out sessions and that these be the exception, rather than the rule. My students this year are doing much, much better. There are fewer disruptions for the children, plus I can give each of them far more structure.

Natasha's experiences are not uncommon. Pull-out services have been controversial for years. Title I services for students from economically and educationally disadvantaged homes routinely are delivered by pull-out. An early study (Carter, 1984) found that Title I services were only marginally effective, largely because the teaching techniques used by pull-out staff differed so much from the methods used by general educators in general classrooms. Johnson, Allington, and Afflerbach (1985), digging more deeply into the same issues, concluded that the disparity of instructional approaches produced cognitive confusion in the students. These researchers reported that remedial teachers seldom reviewed or extended the instruction provided by the general educators. If these problems sound familiar, they should: They are common issues in inclusion, too.

Advantages of Push-In

When related services are pushed in, the therapist's arrival minimizes transition time. There is no "free time" for the child, and thus no temptation to act out. Second, the child does not move from room to room, so no instructional time is lost in transit. Finally, the fact that the therapist comes into the classroom on a general basis facilitates teacher-therapist communication. As a result, the therapist may (indeed, should) configure the therapy, when possible, to extend instruction. If, for example, a first-grade class is working on a "Four Seasons" unit, a physical therapist could help the child through movements that "imitate" nature ("falling leaves," "blossoming flowers," etc.). Similarly, and equally as important, the therapist may adopt the behavior-management techniques that the teacher is using. This ensures that the child continues to be under a consistent management strategy. Such an approach also facilitates generalization learning by the child: The child learns to generalize responses, in this case from teacher to therapist.

As these considerations show, push-in avoids some drawbacks of pull-out. First, the pull-out time begins a "transition period"—a time when the child may feel "free" of adult supervision. As experienced teachers well know, children who are susceptible to acting out find such "free time" to be all but irresistible. Children with emotional/behavioral disorders and attention deficits are particularly vulnerable during transition times. A good teaching technique is to minimize transition times during the school day. A second problem with pull-out is that the child must spend time moving from the classroom to the related-services location; instructionally speaking, this is "dead time." It may only be a few minutes, but when it occurs several times each week for the entire school year, those minutes add up, frequently to hours. Third, the physical separation of teacher and therapist leads to other separations as well. The therapist does not become familiar with the teacher's goals and objectives with the child and does not see how the teacher manages behavior in the classroom. Meanwhile the teacher does not see how the therapist works with the child.

To illustrate, one teacher reported on working collaboratively with a speech/language pathologist. Each week, she gave this professional a copy of the "advance organizer" she prepared for her students with learning disabilities. Among other things, those sheets listed vocabulary words being taught that week. She asked the speech/language pathologist to consider incorporating the same terms in her own work. She also asked the pathologist to show the teacher assistant assigned to the classroom how to prompt and model the articulation of these words during class time. In this way, the "speech path" push-in periods reinforced the content being taught during other periods and vice versa.

Advantages of Pull-Out

Today, pull-out still occurs with many children. Its main advantages are one-on-one treatment and fewer distractions during therapy. Economic considerations are also noteworthy. When a therapist can work with three students at the same time, there may be savings of time and money. That is less likely to occur with push-in, simply because any given general classroom probably has only one student who requires that therapist's services. As a result, to see three students, the therapist needs to devote (and bill for) three class periods, not one.

It is possible for pull-out services to be improved in much the same ways. The therapist, for example, could come to the classroom and escort the child to the therapy location. This removes the "free time" feeling on the child's part and thus reduces the temptation to act out. The therapist could make productive use of transit time, by talking with the child during the trip. And therapists and teachers could collaborate in weekly sessions in which they exchange information about teaching goals, behavior-management techniques, and so on, so as to make their respective efforts more consistent. If these things happen, pull-out services will take on many of the favorable characteristics ascribed above to push-in services.

Block Scheduling

Block scheduling—the rearrangement of time periods so as to create a large chunk, or "block," of time during the school day—offers promise to alleviate the drawbacks of pull-out related services. In block scheduling, the teacher(s) and therapist(s) examine the weekly schedules of each special-needs child in the classroom. Where possible, twice-weekly or thrice-weekly related-services periods of two or more children are combined. This produces considerably longer, but less-frequent, "blocks" of time that teacher and therapist may use for collaboration. That is, they may work as equal partners, jointly planning how to use the time. In some cases, the availability of a large block of time (albeit just once a week) allows for out-of-school, community-based instruction and therapy (see the discussion of "community-based instruction," in Chapter 8).

To illustrate, an occupational therapist could teach travel skills while the class makes a field trip to a local park. At the secondary level, work-study experiences may be scheduled in this way. If block scheduling appeals to you, ask the IEP team to specify the level of service in words like "once or twice weekly for a total of 100 minutes." Such wording gives you the flexibility to use, or not use, block scheduling.

It should be noted that, other than such uses, block scheduling is an approach that enjoys little support in the research literature (e.g., "Making Time Count," 2001).

WORKING WITH PARAPROFESSIONALS

The wide range of abilities in an inclusive classroom makes it necessary, in many instances, for several adults to be present in the classroom. In addition to **paraprofessionals,** you should actively seek volunteers and student teachers from nearby colleges. These people are required for many reasons. Children with physical disabilities often need one-on-one assistance at many times during the day, for such basic things as opening textbooks and turning pages, writing notes and test answers, going to the bathroom, and so on. Students with emotional/behavioral disorders and many with attention deficit disorders need frequent reinforcement. Someone should be near the student to offer it. In addition, an adult needs to record student behaviors so that you may determine the effectiveness of different instructional techniques.

Despite these realities, you should strive to teach every student in your class. Unlike teacher aides, teacher assistants, and volunteers, you are a professional educator certified by the state education agency to provide instruction in the public schools. As such, you are the highest-trained (not to mention highest-paid) adult in your classroom. Children with special needs, particularly those who have disabilities, are the most-in-need of the students in that room. Accordingly, when you can, you should avoid "handing off" children to paraprofessionals.

In far too many school districts, inclusion, as practiced, features a certified teacher instructing *non*-disabled children while a "para" works with the student(s) with disabilities. A moment's reflection will reveal the absurdity of this arrangement: The neediest children are taught by the least-trained and lowest-paid adults in the room. Teachers in secondary schools should be particularly careful about training and supervising paraprofessionals. These individuals often possess only a high-school diploma. They may not know enough about English, math, social studies, science, or other subject matters to be effective at the secondary level.

The Need for a School Policy on Paraprofessionals

The school should have a school-wide policy on paraprofessionals. Sadly, most schools have not taken this fundamental step. Riggs and Mueller (2001) recommended that paraprofessionals themselves, together with teachers and administrators, work as a team to develop the policy. This policy should outline qualifications required for all para's, detail the job descriptions of paraprofessionals, explain what training will be offered to them, and describe how para's will be evaluated.

Most school districts likely will require at least a high-school diploma, but some may also call for at least some postsecondary education. As an example, para's assigned to classrooms for young children may be expected to possess a Child Development Associate (CDA) certificate. The CDA is a credential awarded after course work in child development and child care (Bowe, 2000a). While the precise nature of assignments for paraprofessionals will vary from classroom to classroom, the general scope of those responsibilities should be noted in the policy statement. Figure 12.1 offers some specifics that a policy may include. The policy should continue with specifics about training available for para's—on what topics, at what frequency intervals, and from whom (Riggs & Mueller, 2001). How paraprofessionals will be evaluated, and by whom, should be explicitly stated in the school's policy. Usually, para's are evaluated by the same teams that assess teachers. However, the classroom teacher should have considerable input to such evaluations.

What Makes a Good Paraprofessional?

The ideal traits of a paraprofessional assigned to an inclusive classroom include the willingness to accept supervision, the ability to follow directions with precision and with con-

FIGURE 12.1 Roles Played by Paraprofessionals

1. Administrative support for teachers: copying, distributing papers/supplies/tests, etc.
2. Classroom set-up for different activities: moving furniture, etc.
3. Classroom management: monitor student behavior, reinforce suitable behaviors, and record results/report to teachers about children's progress and problems
4. Student assistance: turn pages/take notes for students with physical limitations, etc.
5. Elaboration/review: amplify and illustrate what teachers say during a lesson
6. Instruction: after being briefed by a teacher, lead a group while the teacher leads another group.

sistency, and the discipline to document what she does throughout the day. The first characteristic is essential: There should be no confusion in the mind of a para who is the teacher and who is the assistant. The second is also very important: Much of the value of a paraprofessional comes from doing exactly what the teacher wants done, the way the teacher wants it done, and with whom the teacher wants it done. Finally, para's who keep thorough notes, not only on what they do but also how each student responded, add much value in an inclusive classroom.

Selecting, Training, and Supervising Paraprofessionals

Whenever possible, teachers should participate in the selection of paraprofessionals (French, 2001). As with all working relationships in PreK–12 education, partnerships are most successful when professionals have a say in who their partners are. When choosing among candidates, you should pay particular attention to the following.

The three keys to successful teacher-paraprofessional collaboration are (1) that you prepare paraprofessionals so that they become skilled in doing what you want them to do, (2) that you supervise them throughout the school day to make sure that they consistently do those things, and (3) that you reward them for their work. In a large study of teachers, administrators, and paraprofessionals, Wallace, Shin, Bartholomay, and Stahl (2001) found consistency in reports of the importance of teacher training, supervising, and supporting paraprofessionals.

Few para's are trained in theory and methods of instruction. However, if you tell them exactly what you want them to do (and point out clearly what you do *not* want them doing), they can make a big difference in your ability to teach an inclusive class. Often, it helps not merely to explain, in words, what you want; you should demonstrate it. Modeling is, after all, one of the teaching techniques you learned in your teacher preparation courses. It works as well with para's as well as with students. You should also ask them to monitor student work. This extra pair of eyes and ears can give you valuable information about student needs and progress. Finally, your communication with para's should not all be one-way: Ask your para's for input and feedback. As is true with anyone, they will do better work if they feel they have a say in it.

Telling paraprofessionals what you want is not enough. You need to supervise them closely, and frequently. A good way to do this is to provide them with *written* instructions. You should review these with them in advance, orally. Instruction sheets should have plenty of "white space" on them. Para's should use this space to write notes documenting what was done (e.g., checking off activities as they are performed) and what students did (e.g., attending behavior, response accuracy, etc.).

In most schools, paraprofessionals are paid at or near minimum wage (e.g., about $7 or $8 an hour). There is little you can do, as a classroom teacher, about such compensation. However, paraprofessionals often report that other forms of compensation are also important to them. Prominent among these is the respect that you as a teacher show them.

Also frequently mentioned is the praise that you give them when they do something right. Even such "small" gestures as adding a nameplate to the classroom door so that the para's name is publicly identified with the class can be very reinforcing for paraprofessionals (Giangreco, Edelman, & Broer, 2001; Wallace, et al., 2001).

The Para's Role

The role of a paraprofessional is to carry out activities that you have assigned, to report to you on progress and problems, and to assist you in your own work by gathering materials, copying handouts, and the like. Teachers retain responsibility for planning lessons, individualizing instruction, assessing student progress, collaborating with parents and other professionals, and delivering instruction. Paraprofessionals may *assist* in all of these roles. That is, para's may make recommendations for lessons, may suggest ways to individualize instruction, may grade student work contingent upon teacher review and final grading, may convey teacher-approved messages to parents and professionals, and may teach in groups or one-on-one under the supervision of the teacher (see Figure 12.1). Research has shown (e.g., French, 2001) that when the roles and responsibilities for paraprofessionals are not explicit, role confusion results. "For example, some teachers reported that paraprofessionals created their own plans, determined behavioral approaches for students, and consulted with other professionals about student needs. These types of planning and decision-making tasks are never appropriate for nonprofessionals . . . " (French, 2001, p. 52).

When armed with explicit and specific instructions, para's can provide much-needed and very valuable assistance in the classroom. This is particularly true with respect to individualizing instruction (see Chapter 8). Without the support of paraprofessionals, modifying instruction in inclusive classrooms is often not possible. Having said this, the flip side of the same coin is that when para's are inadequately prepared and poorly supervised, they just "hover" rather than help (Giangreco, Edelman, Luiselli, & MacFarland, 1997; Marks, Schrader, & Levine, 1999). Frequently, they will yield to the temptation to do, themselves, the work you assigned to students, just "to get it over with." That defeats your whole purpose.

WORKING WITH REPRESENTATIVES OF OTHER AGENCIES

Some students require services from agencies other than public schools. This may be the case, for example, with children who are homeless and youth who have emotional/behavioral disorders. The most important fact for educators to know about such services is that they are *not* services to which these children and youth are entitled. There is no "zero reject" principle in social services comparable to that in education. The second-most important fact for teachers to bear in mind is that they must not fall victim to the fallacy that simply referring a family and/or a student to a non-educational agency for services solves problems. Researchers consistently report that students with emotional disorders, in particular, often fail to follow up on such referrals. The result is a series of assumptions: The school assumes the community mental health agency now owns the problem, and the agency assumes the school still owns it. The reality is that the student has fallen between the cracks.

Interagency responsibilities are to be detailed in the IEPs of students aged 16 or over. In general, this means that educators discuss with family members, and with the young person with a disability, what kinds of support services, preparation, and other assistance may be required during the post–high-school years. In particular, representatives of state vocational rehabilitation agencies may be invited to join IEP meetings to talk about job training services and representatives of Social Security Administration district determination offices may be asked to outline Supplemental Security Income (SSI) benefits and procedures. As this discussion reveals, interagency responsibility issues are most directly related to transition. That is why we will discuss them in Chapter 13.

COLLABORATING WITH STUDENTS

IDEA requires that students aged 14 and over, and even students under age 14 if appropriate, be invited to participate in IEP team meetings (Section 614[d][1][B]). This is because adolescents may have strong views about their own education. They also tend to have hopes and dreams of their own, which may differ from those of their parents.

When we talk about student involvement and about teacher-student collaboration, we are discussing self-determination (Turnbull & Turnbull, 2001). The Turnbulls defined self-determination as "choosing how to live one's life consistent with one's own values, preferences, strengths and needs" (p. 13). The Arc, a national organization representing parents (primarily) of persons with mental retardation, defined it this way: "acting as the primary causal agent in one's life and making choices and decisions regarding one's quality of life free from undue external influence or interference" (Self Determination, at *http://TheArc.org/sdet/sdet.html*). Both definitions feature the idea that while persons with special needs may not necessarily make all decisions about their lives, nor do everything for themselves, they do have the right to make the "big decisions" and to select who will act on their behalf and consult with them about other decisions and do things for them.

For inclusion teachers, collaboration with students features respect from teacher to student. It incorporates teacher recognition that this is, after all, the student's life, so no one has a greater stake in it than does the student himself. When teachers are serving as IEP team members, they should be sure, as per IDEA's requirement, that individuals aged 14 or over (and, if appropriate, under) are both invited to attend IEP team meetings and given opportunities during such meetings for meaningful participation.

The Importance of Peers

The peers of students with disabilities play vital roles in making inclusion work. When they accept students who have disabilities, the results are positive all around. The school becomes a more inviting place. Students with disabilities have a greater sense of belonging. The classroom, too, becomes a more comfortable environment. Students' engagement increases and, with it, so does their achievement. By contrast, when peers reject students with disabilities, the isolation of these students from the school community grows. Their engagement in academic learning declines. The classroom becomes a more risky site. Reviewing an extensive body of research on these issues, Karen Osterman (2000, p. 336) concluded that "rejection is consistently and repeatedly associated with negative effects" and that dropping out is a frequent consequence.

What can teachers do to promote positive peer relationships? Cooperative learning (see Chapter 8) facilitates student-to-student bonding: "The importance of cooperation in contrast with competition to enhance overall student motivation is well-developed. Cooperative learning is also particularly significant for the development of peer relations" (Osterman, 2000, p. 349). She added that when teachers give students other opportunities to speak up in whole-class and small-group settings, students' sense of belonging increases. One positive outcome she identified from her review of the literature is that teacher referrals of children and youth for disciplinary action dropped sharply. Concurring, Pavri (2001) described loneliness as having "devastating consequences" (p. 52) on children with disabilities. She recommended that teachers provide social-skills training on initiating, continuing, and ending conversations, assertiveness training on acceptable ways of advocating for one's needs, and conflict-resolution strategies for resolving student-student disputes. She added that cooperative learning and heterogeneous groups help, as well.

WORKING WITH FAMILIES

Collaboration between teachers and families is vital to the success of inclusion. Experts in special education and the family (e.g., Grove & Fisher, 1999; Turnbull & Turnbull, 2001) have deplored the very limited ways in which educators and family members collaborated in years past. They urged teachers to create more positive relations with families. These same authorities preferred the term "family" over the more common "parents" for several reasons. First, not all families will be represented at school by parents. Some families will elect to send grandparents, while others may opt to have an entire family council speak on their behalf. While there are exceptions, the former is most likely to occur among African Americans and the latter among Korean Americans (see Chapter 2). Second, the word "parent" has taken on the meaning of "mother" in special-education literature, by default, because mothers have been far more active as advocates in the public schools than have fathers. Third and most important, the term "family" is understood by special educators and inclusion teachers as being, defined by family members themselves. That is, a family consists of whatever people the family says it does (Bowe, 2000a; Turnbull & Turnbull, 2001).

There is another, more sensitive, issue. While most families can be depended upon to advocate for children, this is not always the case. Some family members are "in denial" about the disability. Other family members may seek IEP approval of actions that serve the members more than the children. An example mentioned several times in this book is family pressure on the IEP team and the school district to place a child into an inclusive classroom when, in fact, an appropriate education is not available there for that child. In such instances, teachers should bear in mind that the IEP is a document outlining services *for the child*. Sometimes (fortunately, not often) it is necessary that someone protect a child against her own family. IDEA envisions IEP teams in that role. That is why IEP teams, acting through school districts, may take families to mediation and then to due process to contest family requests or demands (see Chapter 2). As uncomfortable as such situations may be, teachers should speak out at IEP team meetings if they see that family members are acting in a manner contrary to the best interests of a child (Bowe, 2004).

The Early Childhood Special Education Model

True collaboration between educators and families is the ideal of early intervention and preschool special-education programs. Especially in programs serving infants and toddlers, the goal is for families to be fully involved, as equal partners, in all decisions. Early interventionists look to the family to set the key goals, both for themselves and for their young children. Professionals then identify strategies and tactics, including educational methodologies, suitable for reaching those goals. Families are regularly and thoroughly informed about progress made by their children. In fact, early intervention programs often sponsor sibling programs, child care facilities, and respite services so that family members can participate in the program. They also open their doors during evening and weekend hours so that family members can attend meetings (Bowe, 2000a).

The Realities of K–12 School-Family Relations

That level of family-program cooperation remains more an ideal than a reality in most PreK–12 schools. Family members often report that elementary schools and, especially, high schools are much less flexible toward and welcoming of families (e.g., Grove & Fisher, 1999; Turnbull & Turnbull, 2001). This may be because public schools traditionally have had an uneasy relationship with families, particularly parents of children with disabilities. For example, parents advocating for inclusion often report that schools "rarely [identify] a contact person within the system to facilitate inclusive education" (Grove & Fisher, 1999, p. 212). Family members also report that they must educate teachers and administrators about inclusion. Said one parent interviewed by Grove and Fisher (1999,

p. 213), "They're not experts. We (the parents) are the teachers of the teacher, teachers of the therapists. If there is a problem, they call us."

The National Council on Disability (NCD; 1993), a small federal "watchdog" agency, reported some time ago that public policy must change so that relationships between neighborhood schools and families having children with disabilities become less adversarial. Little has changed, however. The problem is partly a function of the rights IDEA gives to parents and partly because of the nature of due process proceedings in general (National Council on Disability, 2000; Turnbull & Turnbull, 2000; Yell, 1998). Administrators of neighborhood public schools sometimes view families as adversaries rather than as partners. When they do, the message to teachers working for those administrators is "You better not give aid and comfort to the enemy!" Teachers become fearful that if they give information to family members, their principals or even superintendents may exact revenge upon them.

Building Better Relations in K–12 Schools

How can we improve family-school relations in PreK–12 programs? The fact of the matter is that families of children in early intervention (birth to age two, inclusive) and preschool special education programs have the *same* rights as do parents of children with disabilities who attend K–12 schools. This suggests that the adversarial nature of school-family relations is not a necessary one. That being noted, what can educators in K–12 schools learn from the experiences of teachers and other professionals working in early childhood special education settings?

Educators should view family members as *partners* deserving of the same kinds of courtesies that professionals extend to one another, notably regular communication, mutual understanding, mutual respect, flexibility, willingness to learn, and willingness to devote the time necessary to make the partnership work (see "Collaboration Between Teachers," p. 427). No administrator should seek vengeance on a teacher for "sharing too much" with family members. When family members understand the "just good enough" nature of an "appropriate" education, the limits of school resources, the time constraints on teachers, and other realities, they tend to ameliorate their expectations. Similarly, when they sense that school officials are being candid and open, rather than evasive and secretive, family members tend to reciprocate. In fact, many families demonstrate real compassion for inclusion teachers. The most commonly cited worry of family members with a child having a severe disability, according to a recent study, was that the child's many needs might overwhelm general educators (Palmer, Fuller, Arora, & Nelson, 2001). All of this suggests that educators be open and honest with family members, frankly acknowledging limitations and soliciting family cooperation in meeting childrens' needs.

The adversarial nature of due process may never completely go away from K–12 schools. Teachers should bear in mind that the privileges of pursuing mediation, administrative law proceedings, and litigation are granted by IDEA *both* to school systems and to families. These steps, then, remain as options for both sides. The goal is to avoid needing to use those options.

There is much you as a teacher in an inclusive classroom can do to assuage family fears. Sharing with family members your training and experience will help. As mentioned earlier, parents of children having severe disabilities often worry that the many demands such students place on educators will overwhelm teachers. You can demonstrate that this is not the case. A second concern mentioned by these family members is that non-disabled children in the inclusive classroom will mistreat, tease, or even abuse their children. By acknowledging the logic of this fear, but showing family members how you will deal with it, you can assuage those worries, too. A third issue with many families is that the inclusive classroom is ill-suited to meet the needs of students with severe disabilities for instruction in how to live independently (Palmer, et al., 2001). By demonstrating to family members that you and your collaborating teacher have worked out plans for meeting special needs, including protection from ridicule and abuse, you can gain their trust and increase their confidence that inclusion is a viable option for them and for their children.

A Family Systems Approach

Turnbull and Turnbull (2001) urged that teachers move away from a narrow view of "parents and children" and toward a more comprehensive "family systems" theory. They defined "family systems" as referring to educator recognition of the many pressures to which families respond. This includes internal dynamics, cultural factors, religious beliefs, economic issues, personal convictions about child-rearing, and much else. Such a framework opens teachers' eyes to the potential contributions of family members to the child's total education and development. A family-systems approach also focuses teacher attention on the valuable roles that persons other than parents may play. Notably this includes foster parents, adoptive parents, grandparents, members of the extended family such as uncles and aunts. It also includes siblings, both younger and older than the child with a disability. The Turnbulls were particularly eloquent on the contributions made by their daughters Amy and Kate in the development of their son Jay, who has a disability. Their thesis was that if teachers recognize the many varied resources offered by the family as a whole, and work hand-in-hand with the family to bring those resources to bear upon the education and development of a child with a disability, everyone benefits.

A family systems approach recognizes that not all families are in a position to be effective advocates for their children with disabilities as much as some families were in years past. Indeed, we have IDEA today precisely because family members in Pennsylvania and in Washington, DC, persisted in legal and political battles with public school systems. Those battles culminated in the consent decrees *PARC* and *Mills* that convinced the U.S. Congress to enact what later was named IDEA (see Chapter 1). However, the reality for many families early in the 21st century is that dual careers rob parents of the time required to advocate for their children as much as they may wish. Another aspect of family systems theory that relates to this is the fact that not all families feel comfortable, for cultural reasons or because of lack of formal education, in disputing educators' decisions. The Turnbulls pointed out in their book that even The Arc, one of the oldest and largest family-based organizations in the disability field, is comprised almost entirely of family members who are of middle to upper socioeconomic status (SES).

For all these reasons, professionals should not make the assumption that they need not advocate for children because "that's the family's job" nor that family members should become "teachers at home": not all family members can fulfill either role. The Turnbulls suggested that educators provide "information exchanges" rather than "family training sessions" as one step toward showing that they recognize these realities.

CHAPTER SUMMARY

Collaboration Between Teachers

- Collaborating partners make all key decisions as a team.
- Consultative teachers, by contrast, play a secondary role in support of the "primary" teacher.
- The transition from traditional to collaborative roles often is more jarring for special educators than for general educators.
- Collaborative partners often come to the partnership with very different tendencies and biases. Special educators typically *teach* while general educators commonly *facilitate student learning*. These and other variations in approach can make the first weeks and months of collaboration challenging. Ultimately, however, teachers report that they learn from each other, to their benefit.
- Skill in time management is a key for successful collaboration. Teachers are well-advised to invest time and energy into mastering proven techniques of making the best use of limited time.
- General and special educators alike often are surprised to see just how effective "special-education" techniques can be when teaching students with no disabilities.

- Collaboration at the secondary level frequently challenges teachers. This is because of the short class periods, the subject-focus orientation of high-school general educators, and the demanding nature of student work.

Collaboration with Related-Services Personnel

- The most-used related service is speech/language pathology. It is often written into the IEPs of students identified as having speech or language impairments (SLI), mental retardation (MR)—two of the "Big Four" labels—as well as less-common conditions such as autism or hearing loss.
- Push-in facilitates teacher-therapist communication and collaboration and reduces transition time. However, it can be more costly for schools than is pull-out.
- Block scheduling (less frequent but longer periods of related services) has important advantages. Among other things, it can free related-services personnel to accompany a class on a field trip. There are disadvantages, as well.

Collaboration with Paraprofessionals

- It is vital that schools establish clear policies governing the work of paraprofessionals in inclusive classrooms. Administrators, teachers, and "para's" themselves all need to know what is expected and what is forbidden.
- The key to supervising paraprofessionals is to give them explicit instructions and then to supervise them throughout the school day.

Collaboration with Students

- Students with disabilities have as much a right to self-determination as do students with no disabilities. Even if children and youth cannot physically do something, they usually can choose who will do it and how. It is important for teachers to respect the right to self-determination on the part of students with disabilities.

Collaboration with Families

- Experience in early childhood special education (early intervention and preschool special education) shows that programs and families can in fact work cooperatively, notwithstanding the fact that due process remains an option for both.
- The principles of successful teacher-teacher collaboration—mutual understanding and respect, flexibility, regular communication, and the like—apply just as strongly to teacher-family collaboration.

QUESTIONS FOR REFLECTION

1. Which of the many kinds of collaboration discussed in this chapter is most critical for successful inclusion? Why?
2. What worries might a general educator have when beginning to teach an inclusive class?
3. Discovery learning is a technique much used in the teaching of science, as well as other subjects. Why might some special educators have doubts about its use with students who have disabilities?
4. Chapter 1 featured a "Tale of Two Schools." Re-read the two memos. What mistakes can you identify now in the decisions made by the principal of the Forest Avenue School about collaboration?
5. What are some ways teachers and other professionals might collaborate effectively?
6. Why do administrators often resist push-in, despite its many potential benefits?
7. What are paraprofessionals often tempted to do that teachers do not want them to do?
8. What decisions by a family might be counter to the best interests of that family's child?
9. What is "family systems" theory and how can it contribute to better teacher-family relations?
10. Re-read Chapter 2 on due process. What specific aspects of those procedures might contribute to the often-reported "adversarial" relationship between schools and families?

Chapter 13 Transition: Early Childhood and High School

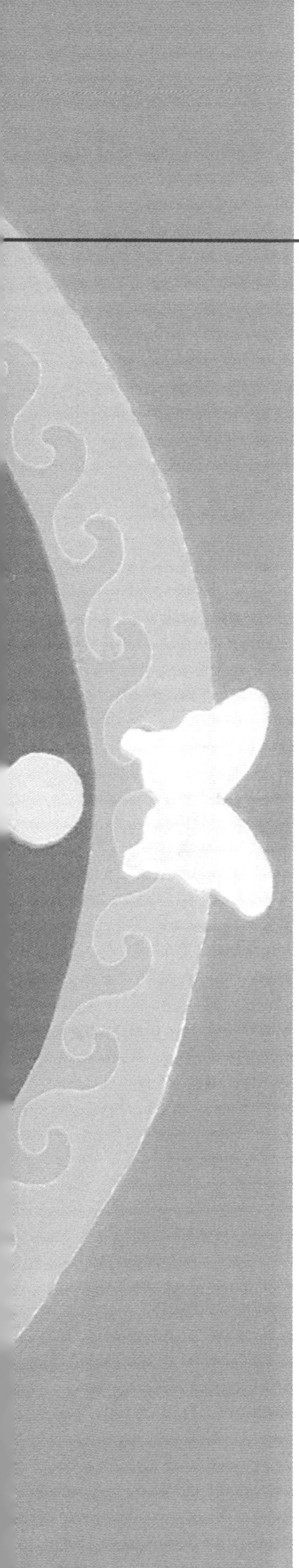

TERMS

transition services

Individualized Plans for Employment (IPEs)

self-determination

CHAPTER FOCUS QUESTIONS

After reading this chapter, you should be able to answer such questions as:

1. What are "transition services" and why are they so important?
2. Why does IDEA mandate transition services for children about to turn 3 years of age?
3. Why have educators generally not done well on transition for teenagers with disabilities?
4. What kinds of transition services do students with specific learning disabilities or emotional/behavioral disorders most need for success in postsecondary programs?
5. What are One-Stop Career Centers and how can they help young people get jobs?
6. What do teachers and students in inclusive classrooms need to know about Supplemental Security Income?
7. What does the law mean by "interagency agreements" in transition?

PERSONAL ACCOUNTS

Deserie discussed how she teaches transition in a local junior high school (middle school):

> *I teach a group of eight 13-, 14-, and 15-year-olds with mental retardation. We work four or five sites each year, spending 8 to 10 weeks at each: McDonald's, Marriott, Kmart, a local library, and other sites. By now, we have partnerships with more than 30 companies.*
>
> *During class, we work on social skills, responsibility, and maintaining a neat/clean appearance. We also review money handling, eye contact, and other skills they need to master. Money handling is the most difficult skill, one only a few of these students can do well. So, each student has a "bank" (plastic jar) in class. Throughout the day, as they earn money for appropriate behavior, teamwork, participation in class discussion, and so on, they collect coins. We bake brownies in class and sell those to other students during the week. The students handle all transactions. Money raised is used once a month when we all go out for lunch (to practice our ordering, table manners, and appropriate community behavior). All extra money goes to an end-of-year class trip.*
>
> *Each Friday we count our money. When students have earned more than $1, they can trade for other coins (e.g., many pennies for one quarter)—if they count correctly! I have a class store with items such as school supplies and*

garage sale products (mostly donated by teachers). They can buy these with their earned money.

At McDonald's, we cleaned the dining room, filled up condiment containers, and handed food to drive-through customers. At the Marriott, we worked in the laundry room (washing, drying, and folding linens) and in the restaurant (setting tables, stocking products). At Kmart, we did stocking, bagging, cleaning, and organizing work.

At the library, we re-shelved books, cleaned, and organized supplies. We always debrief after a work day (often on the bus coming back to school). In addition, students work one period every day in our school café: preparing cookies, bagging vegetables, setting up the food racks of chips, filling soda machines, etc.).

The students learn a lot over the 3 years they participate in this transition program. When they reach high school, they will be paid wages for the work they do. Our transition program also exposes the community to our incredible students. Residents see these young people in a work situation, hopefully easing their inclusion into society.

—Deserie

Deborah Leuchovius, of St. Paul, Minnesota, told a U.S. government panel about the impact of transition services on her 17-year-old son, Freddy:

Freddy was born with spina bifida and has a number of complicated health conditions. Freddy uses a ventilator and attends school accompanied by a home care nurse. Frequent surgeries to replace an intraventricular shunt have resulted in brain injury partially paralyzing the left side of his body (he was already paraplegic) as well as having significant nonverbal learning disabilities . . . he is currently receiving transition services to help him develop computer skills that will prepare him for employment. He already has a summer job lined up working for the school district doing data processing. I tell you this because I want to make the point that although Freddy's individual needs, strengths, and interests are complex and unique, our special education and transition experiences mirror the struggles reported by families across the country. At the same time, our experience reflects what I have learned from researchers about best practice in transition. To put it simply, when the services Freddy receives reflect best practice, he has been successful; when they don't, he has not.

For more information on Ms. Leuchovius's testimony, go to the Web Links module in Chapter 13 of the Companion Website.

These perspectives illustrate the wide range of transition services. For some students, the focus is upon daily living skills and basic work competencies. Deserie's students learn about expected employee behavior (being on time, well-groomed, courteous, etc.). Freddy Leuchovius, by contrast, is preparing for a professional job, one that requires sophisticated technologies, both to do the job itself and also to meet his special needs. These two stories highlight the importance, for students with disabilities, of preparation for life beyond high school, specifically for employment.

INTRODUCTION

Transition, particularly the key transition from school to life after high school, is our topic in Chapter 13. We will look briefly, too, at other kinds of transition, notably that from early intervention to preschool special education. The key for you as a teacher in an inclusive classroom is to become acquainted with the "worlds" your students will enter after they leave your program. What you learned earlier (Parts Two and Three) about students with disabilities will help, as well. You might reflect on their needs for extended and specific instruction in daily-life activities, self-determination and self-advocacy, self-care, career exploration, and vocational skills. Ask yourself about the relative importance of those, for these students, vis à vis the academic standards now in place in your state. The new, higher learning standards, and the emphasis schools are placing upon those standards, are appropriate for some children and youth. For other students, however, there is a risk that the increased amounts of time devoted to test preparation may reduce the amount of time available for other kinds of transition, notably transition from school to work and transition from school to independent living. You may wish to visit local schools and see how secondary educators are managing the often-conflicting responsibilities between helping students to meet state learning standards, on the one hand, and assisting them to create lives they will find meaningful and rewarding, on the other.

This chapter opens with a brief overview of transition. Following that is a discussion of the first kind of transition services that are required by the Individuals with Disabilities Education Act (IDEA): transition from early intervention programs to preschool special education programs. We then turn our focus to the second type of transition services IDEA mandates: transition from school to life beyond high school. In general, students take one or more of three paths in that second transition: school to postsecondary education, school to work, and school to independent living. We will explore each in depth. The chapter concludes with an examination of the interagency linkages required for students beginning at age 16—how you can connect with colleges, job-training programs, and others to help your students effect successful transitions.

WHAT IS TRANSITION?

Transition services, as used in this book, primarily refers to services that educators offer to high-school age students with disabilities to prepare them for life after high school. There are exceptions. One is the transition from early intervention programs to preschool. The other is transition that is not discussed in IDEA, notably transition from preschool to kindergarten, transition from elementary school to middle school, and transition from middle school to high school. We will discuss these other transitions separately.

IDEA specifies that one purpose of the Act's Part B is to "prepare them for employment and independent living" (Section 601[d][1][A]). This means helping students with disabilities to learn how to make informed decisions, to advocate for themselves, to, in other words, become empowered. Many young people with disabilities have been "over protected" by parents and, often, by teachers as well. Now that they are nearing adulthood, they urgently need to learn how to assume responsibility for their own actions and for their own decisions. They must understand their rights in the workplace, in the community, and in such places of public accommodation as hotels and doctor's offices. Even if they are not able to feed, dress, or otherwise take care of themselves, they need to determine what will be done, and how, on a day-to-day basis. That is a big part of empowerment. It is also a component of what we called, in the previous chapter, "self-determination." We call all of the steps mentioned in this paragraph "transition services."

Definition

In IDEA, section 602, this definition of "transition services" is offered:

> The term "transition services" means a coordinated set of activities for a student with a disability that
>
> **a.** is designed within an outcome-oriented process, which promotes movement from school to post-school activities, including post-secondary education, vocational training, integrated employment (including supported employment), continuing and adult education, adult services, independent living, or community participation;
>
> **b.** is based upon the individual student's needs, taking into account the student's preferences and interests; and
>
> **c.** includes instruction, related services, community experiences, the development of employment and other post-school adult living objectives, and, when appropriate, acquisition of daily living skills and functional vocational evaluation.

This transition is a forward-looking one. The focus in transition planning is not just on a student's current needs, but also on her future needs. The idea is to offer support, while

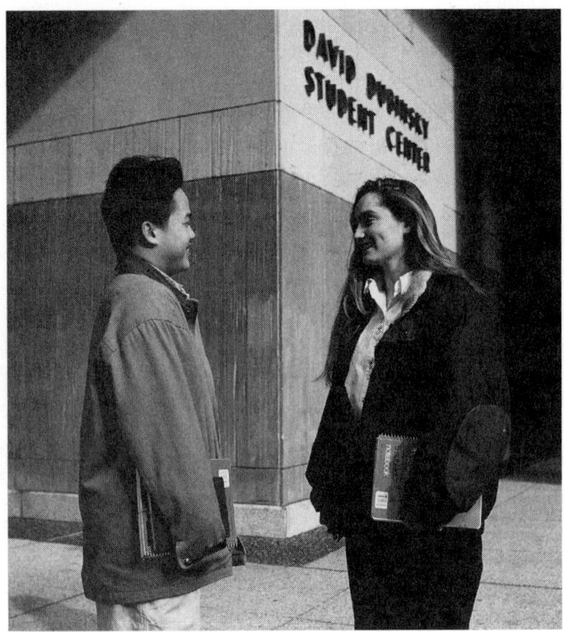

Transition to postsecondary education is one, but only one, of three general paths that transition services delivered in the secondary years may take (the other two are transition to work and transition to independent living).

services continue to be free of charge to the family (that is, while the student remains eligible under IDEA), so that once the student loses IDEA eligibility upon high-school graduation or upon attaining the age of 22, she is prepared to face life as an adult. This introduces a point that is important for families to understand: While services under IDEA are guaranteed to be (1) provided if needed, (2) appropriate, (3) timely, and (4) free to the family, *none* of these four characteristics necessarily applies to services provided to youth and adults outside of IDEA. Vocational and other adult services may not be offered no matter how much they are needed, may not be particularly useful, may be not provided when needed, and may not be paid for by any public agency. That is why the IEP team may arrange as many services as possible during the K–12 years, while these services remain free to the family.

Ideally, school-to-life-beyond-high-school transition services should begin during the middle-school years. The law calls for transition services to begin by age 14, but notes that they may start earlier than that. For example, during grades six through eight students may learn how to travel in the community, navigate architectural and other barriers, and buy things in community stores (Beakley & Yoder, 1998). Equally important, they learn to decide whether to travel, whether and how to file complaints about illegal barriers, and which things are needed vs. merely wanted. Also, critical decisions are made during eighth grade, notably the election of college-preparatory or other courses of study. By engaging in career exploration and other pre-transition activities prior to age 14, students become ready to make those kinds of life-altering decisions. Expressed differently, a major purpose of transition, and, indeed, high school in general, is to guide students through the choices they must make and to teach them the skills they must possess for success as adults (Halpern, 1999). That is what "prepare them for employment and independent living" means, and it is what we mean, in this book, by "transition services."

TRANSITION FROM EARLY INTERVENTION TO PRESCHOOL

IDEA requires transition services to facilitate smooth movement of very young children and their families between the early intervention programs authorized by the law's Part C and the preschool special education programs in Part B. This is a major transition for family members. That is because early intervention services are provided by different agencies than are preschool special education services, services are offered at different locations, service plans are different, and services for families differ as well (Bowe, 2004).

How Early Intervention Differs from Preschool

The early intervention centers that serve very young children from birth until the children turn 3 years of age are not operated by public school districts. Rather, they are funded by state and county governments, generally by departments of health. These centers tend to remain open year-round, closing (in most cases) only the last two weeks of August and the final two weeks of December. Preschools, by contrast, generally are part of the public school system. They follow the school year (September to June), although they may offer special-education services during summer months. Some, however, are not part of the local school district, notably Head Start preschool programs and private preschool centers.

Early intervention programs provide many services in the home (Bowe, 2004). Specialists visit the family at home, delivering their services both to the child and to other family members. In fact, early intervention often is delivered *primarily* in the home. Preschool programs, by contrast, usually provide services only at school.

Early intervention centers provide services to infants and toddlers pursuant to Individualized Family Services Plans (IFSPs), which differ in some respects from the Individualized Education Programs (IEPs) that are used in preschool programs (see Chapter 2). A service coordinator is named in, and helps to implement, the IFSP. That is because early intervention features services that are provided by many different agencies (health, housing, child protection services, Social Security, and many others). A key role of the service coordinator is to assist the family in navigating around all these different agencies. There is no need for a service coordinator in preschool, and none is named in an IEP, because only one agency (the school) is involved.

As the name suggests, IFSPs offer much more emphasis upon services for family members other than the child with a disability than is the case with IEPs. Early intervention centers may deliver services to parents and siblings directly, even if such services will provide only indirect benefits to the infant or toddler with a disability. By contrast, IEPs focus upon the child. Services are designed for, and delivered to, children with disabilities. Although IEPs may describe some family services such as family counseling (identifying these as "related services"), the emphasis is clearly upon educating the child.

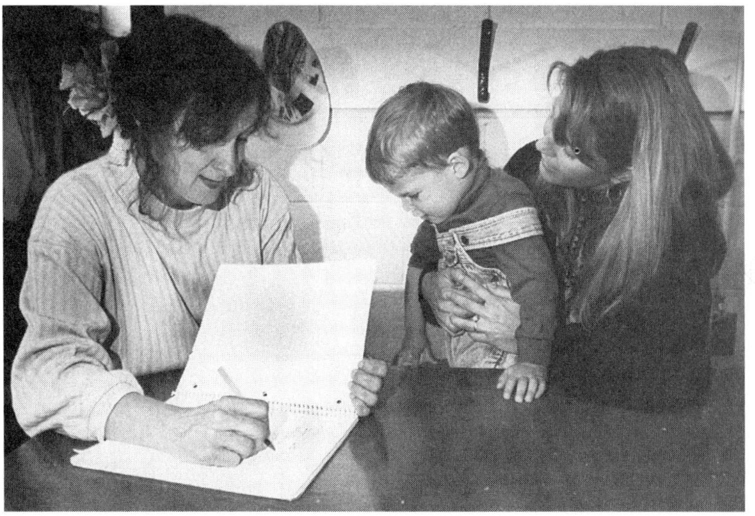

Transition from early intervention (IDEA Part C) to preschool (IDEA Part B) occurs once a young child reaches 2.5 years of age.

Making a Smooth Transition

IDEA, in section 637, calls upon early intervention professionals to begin transition planning by the time a child reaches 2.5 years of age. Such planning must begin no later than three months before the child reaches 3 years of age. This schedule allows three to six months for planning the transition. The first step is for early intervention personnel to discuss the upcoming transition with family members: Do they wish to enroll the child in preschool special education services? Do they consent for the early intervention center to transfer the child's records to the local preschool? Do they have any concerns or questions about preschool services? If the option is available, would they prefer a public preschool, a Head Start preschool, or some other preschool? The second step is, assuming family approval, to arrange for the family and early intervention staff (usually including the service coordinator) to visit the preschool. At that meeting, educators offer family members a tour, answer family questions, and initiate the process of preparing an IEP.

The law allows some options that could smooth this transition. First, family members may elect to continue working with an IFSP rather than using an IEP. If this decision is made, the IFSP is amended by adding information about the child's educational needs. Any IFSP used after the child turns 3 years of age will not contain the name of a service coordinator, because children aged 3 and over are not entitled to a service coordinator. Second, young children may begin preschool services earlier than, or even after, they turn 3. This may be convenient for family members and preschool educators alike. Thus, if a child turns 3 years of age in July, it may be easier if he continues in early intervention for another two or three months, and begins preschool in September. Alternatively, if a child turns 3 in November, it may make sense for him to start preschool a few months before that birthday. IDEA offers the flexibility for all these contingencies.

Other Transitions

The transition from preschool to kindergarten is an important one, especially if kindergarten is an all-day program (Fromberg, 1995). IDEA does not require any particular services at this transition point. Another important transition is that from elementary school to middle school. So, too, is the change from middle school to high school. IDEA imposes no specific requirements about those transitions, either. These are illustrations of how transition is broader than just what the law requires. Educators may take whatever measures appear to be appropriate for a given child or youth. In particular, it may be helpful if one of a student's middle-school or high-school teachers assumed a "key teacher" role, assisting as the student adjusts to having as many as six or even more teachers.

TRANSITION FROM SCHOOL TO POSTSECONDARY PROGRAMS

College differs from high school in several important respects. First, students themselves are responsible for everything that IEP teams do for high-school students with disabilities. While children and youth attending public schools enjoy rights whether or not they explicitly request them, this is not the case for college students, who must "self-identify" as requiring support services in order to receive them. The transition phase during high school is a good time to acquaint students with the fact that they must specifically request, and advocate for, any support services they may need in college (e.g., interpreters, note takers, personal attendants, etc.).

Many students with disabilities begin college without the necessary study and time-management skills. That is why special "pre-college" programs may help. The HEATH Resource Center lists dozens of summer programs for students with disabilities (*http://www.heath.gwu.edu/bookstore/pre-college.html*). Most are targeted toward students with specific learning disabilities, attention deficit disorders, and other high-prevalence conditions. These pre-college programs (which cost between $1,500 and $5,000 on average) feature instruction on study skills, practice with self-advocacy, and the like, together with orientation to that particular college's facilities and programs. However, most postsecondary institutions in the United States do *not* offer comprehensive pre-college programs for incoming students who have disabilities. Working to help more do so is the National Center for the Study of Postsecondary Educational Supports, at the University of Hawaii. That center also provides technical assistance to secondary educators about transition from school to postsecondary education.

For more information on the National Center for the Study of Postsecondary Educational Supports, go to the Web Links module in Chapter 13 of the Companion Website.

Just 14% (one out of every seven) students with disabilities who are graduated from high school enroll in a postsecondary program within two years of leaving secondary school. Even five years post-high-school, the proportion is just 27% (Blackorby & Wagner, 1996). These percentages contrast with the 53% and 68%, respectively, for students with no disabilities (Bullis & Cheney, 1999). The story becomes even more bleak when one looks further to see what happens during the freshman and subsequent college years: More students with disabilities than students without disabilities drop out with no degree

Technologies That Work

Universal Design and Technology in Transition

Education today increasingly is being delivered electronically. Most jobs today require the use of at least some information technologies. Much independent living does, too. For these reasons, it is now vital that transition services include instruction and a lot of practice in using information technologies.

Technology in Education

Colleges increasingly allow students to apply online, register for courses on the Web, and contact their professors via e-mail. On some campuses, in fact, the word "allow" should read "require": more and more, college students are expected to have laptop computers, e-mail accounts, and the like. Many professors post required readings on the Web, rather than (or in addition to) handing them out in class. The Web is rapidly replacing the library as the place to start research for term papers. The largest private university in the United States has few students on campus. Rather, most students pursuing degrees at the University of Phoenix are telecommuting students—they take all their courses electronically, logging on from home or from work from as far away as Maine or Florida.

Technology in the Workplace

The proportion of workers employed in the manufacturing sector of the economy—that is, people who are engaged in making things—has remained below 20% for more than a generation. Many employees use high technology to do their jobs. The fastest-growing part of the economy is the services sector. Services workers do not "make" anything; rather, they provide direct services to customers (food, laundry, financial advice, help in arranging travel, education and training, etc.). Services jobs, particularly in the information services segment, usually require people to use technologies. Drivers of UPS and FedEx trucks, for example, use handheld communicators to report deliveries. Cab and limousine drivers often receive instructions via pagers or other communication devices. Office workers and travel agents spend most of the work day in front of personal computers. Very few Americans still work on farms. Even there, information technologies are becoming unavoidable: farmers now buy and sell products electronically, check commodity prices on the Web, and e-mail with their suppliers and customers.

Technology and Independent Living

Increasingly, people get air and other transportation, reserve seats at theaters and restaurants, and manage their financial affairs with PCs and PC-based electronic services. Web sites such as *www.bigyellow.com* (an electronic White and Yellow Pages site) or *www.switchboard.com* (another searchable directory) are being used, rather than printed white and yellow phone books, to find information about stores and products.

What all of this means is that transition from school to postsecondary education, from school to work, and from school to independent living is most likely to be successful if the individual acquires competency in using information and communication technologies, during the school years. For students with disabilities, this often means becoming fluent in the use of assistive technology devices, as well. For these reasons, transition services in secondary school increasingly must include training in use of today's technologies.

For more information on the University of Phoenix, go to the Web Links module in Chapter 13 of the Companion Website.

(HEATH Resource Center, *http://www.heath.gwu.edu*). Transition services that improve both academic skills and daily living skills are essential to enable students to persist in, and be graduated from, postsecondary programs.

Physical and Sensory Disabilities

Finding and using accessible facilities and services can be a challenge. Although the Americans with Disabilities Act (ADA) and section 504 of the Rehabilitation Act require colleges to make some dorm buildings and rooms accessible, there may not be a sufficient supply of such facilities. Off-campus housing rarely is accessible. The ADA and section 504 also mandate that public transportation services colleges provide to students be offered to students with disabilities. Usually, this means that some (rather than all) college vans or buses will be lift-equipped. Students who use wheelchairs will need to plan in advance, making sure that a lift-equipped vehicle runs at times that will get them to class on time. Most campuses have "special services coordinators," sometimes called "504 coordinators," who will work with students, upon request, to make these kinds of arrangements. The phrase "upon request" bears repeating: Students have to step forward, identify themselves as needing support services, and officially request assistance.

College and university students who are deaf or hard of hearing need to request interpreting services, captioning services (notably CART, for "computer assisted real time" captioning), note-taking, tutoring, and other services. Students must specify which, if any, of these services is needed. Similarly, students who are blind or have low vision need to request (again, explicitly) whatever support services they may need (e.g., notetakers, Braille printers on campus, etc.).

Specific Learning Disabilities, ADHD, and E/B Disorders

Students with these disabilities frequently require support services of a different kind. They may need counseling to help them to maintain focus over a full semester (some college courses have just one exam in four months, a marked contrast to the typical high-school course which includes tests at least once every six weeks). Those with attention deficit disorders and attention deficit hyperactivity disorder may need to receive counseling about the importance of continuing to take prescribed medication. Once they reach 18 years of age, especially once they leave home for college, they may be tempted to stop. This may have deleterious consequences on their learning. Students with emotional and behavioral disorders in particular may need instruction and supervised practice in "reading" the emotions and behaviors of their fellow students and of professors. Parents report that such social skills are much-needed by many young people with disabilities (e.g., Kolb & Hanley-Maxwell, 2003).

Students with emotional/behavioral (E/B) disorders and related mental-health needs particularly need transition-related assistance. Examining transition issues for these populations, Bullis and Cheney (1999) presented a bleak picture. They observed that "few continue their education after leaving high school" (p. 2)—noting that the National Longitudinal Transition Study (NLTS; Blackorby & Wagner, 1996) found that only 17% of students identified as having E/B disorders enrolled in any postsecondary program within two years, and 26% within five years—and that a "majority are arrested at least once upon leaving school" (p. 6). Bullis and Cheney (p. 9) added, "This population poses incredibly demanding and all too real service delivery challenges that seem at times to consume every working and waking hour" [of transition staff members' time]. Students with E/B disorders have the highest rates of dropping out during the secondary years. The NLTS reported those at 59% (Blackorby & Wagner, 1996). Non-completion of high school precludes continued education at the postsecondary level (U.S. Department of Education, 2000b).

Students with specific learning disabilities have the most support once they get to college, as compared to students with other disabilities (HEATH Resource Center, (*http://www.heath.gwu.edu*). However, according to the NLTS, just 14% matriculated in college within two years after leaving high school and 30% had done so within five years. These proportions are barely above those for students with E/B disorders. Again, high rates of dropping out during the high-school years are partially to blame (U.S. Department of Education, 2000b). According to the NLTS, 36% of students with specific learning disabilities dropped out of school after beginning ninth grade (Blackorby & Wagner, 1996).

The G.E.D. as a Bridge to Postsecondary Education

The General Educational Development (G.E.D.) Testing Service, a unit of the American Council on Education, reported providing more than 14,000 modifications for individuals with disabilities in 2001. Most requested was additional time. About 4,000 took Braille, large print, or audiocassette versions of the test. Most (about two out of every three) of those taking the G.E.D. said they did so to qualify for postsecondary education. The Service reported that requests for other editions of the G.E.D. doubled between 2000 and 2001, while requests for accommodations related to learning disabilities increased by 162% (American Council on Education, 2002).

Secondary students who have disabilities need to be aware that the G.E.D. Testing Service offers helpful modifications, such as those mentioned above. Also available is the use of a scribe to write answers, use of a calculator, a private room, and supervised breaks. However, students should not be misled. The G.E.D. is a difficult test to pass, even with those modifications. The current G.E.D. tests, introduced in 2002, are designed so that as many as 40% of high-school graduates would fail the examination (American Council on Education, 2002).

An Example

In an interesting twist, The College Connection, in Baltimore, Maryland, offers transition services to secondary and postsecondary students with disabilities on the campus of a community college, rather than in a high school. This approach may be particularly viable for students with E/B disorders who were, in the words of Bullis and Cheney (1999), "highly 'school-phobic' and had an aversion to being at and around [high] schools" (p. 9). The project serves 18- to 21-year-olds who continue to need transition services, regardless of whether or not they are still in high school. These services include not only support for college work but also services facilitating transition from school to work and from school to independent living (Baltimore County Public Schools/CCBC-Essex, 7201 Rossville Blvd., Baltimore, MD 21237).

College-age students with disabilities must arrange for residential, transportation, and other support services. There is no longer an IEP team for the students to call upon.

TRANSITION FROM SCHOOL TO WORK

The rules of school and of places of work differ. Young people need to learn about the expectations of the workplace, particularly the "unwritten rules" that are so critical to success in many vocations. In some companies, for example, "The customer is always right" (so, too, is the boss!). Many young people have difficulty accepting these ideas. Dress codes are an obvious example of how students and workers are held to different standards. Other examples include attendance and punctuality rules. As Deserie showed in the chapter-opening vignette, explicit training and lots of experience will help students to learn about and become versed in, and skilled at complying with, the expectations of the workplace. All of these, it is worth noting, are *non-vocational issues*. When workers with disabilities are fired, it often is not because they lacked vocational skills. Rather, it is because they did not fulfill expectations about observing unwritten rules and about being good team members (Blackorby & Wagner, 1996).

Transition from school to work is best planned through phased-in transition services. In some states, transition begins in middle school with collection of basic information about the student, including age, abilities, interests, and needs. This is sometimes referred to as a "Level I" assessment. Then, in eighth grade, vocational evaluations may be administered to identify aptitudes and interests with respect to different career paths. That is a "Level II" assessment. For students who have multiple needs, including those with severe disabilities, a "Level III" assessment may also be conducted. In those evaluations, the individual's fine-motor control, reach, strength, and other capabilities are assessed, as are the person's ability to learn specific tasks, to perform those tasks consistently, and to remember multi-step procedures. Perhaps most important, students should *work* during the secondary years and should secure competitive employment, with the assistance of transition specialists, prior to high-school graduation (Wehman, 2002).

Beginning at age 14 and continuing until high-school graduation, experiences in being a team member, in working toward shared goals, and in completing tasks on a timely basis are offered both within the school and in work-study programs. Starting in ninth grade, or after the decision is made to prepare for college, for work, and/or for independent living, transition services become more specialized. In the case of transition from school to work, these include in-school work opportunities (e.g., in running a school "store"), work-study programs, and after-school supervised jobs.

Just as are students in postsecondary programs, workers with disabilities are expected to "self-identify" and to request accommodations they need. This means they need to master self-advocacy skills. Also useful, as we saw in Chapter 8, because they help to develop skills and competencies in team work, are experiences with peer tutoring and other group projects.

For more information on the research done at the University of Illinois and University of Minnesota, go to the Web Links module in Chapter 13 of the Companion Website.

What other specific skills do students most need to acquire in order to succeed in the world of work? "Student Strategies That Work" outlines the major ones that were identified by researchers at the University of Illinois *http://www.ed.uiuc.edu/sped/tri* and at the University of Minnesota *http://ici.umn.edu/ncset*. Notice that most are not job-specific skills (e.g., typing speed, skill in using a fork lift, etc.). Rather, most have to do with *behavior* that is expected on the job.

Particularly in need of support in displaying appropriate self-advocacy skills in the workplace are students with E/B disorders and other mental-health conditions. In their overview of transition issues related to students with emotional and behavioral disorders, Bullis and Cheney (1999) observed that few students identified as having E/B disorders (as well as other students who are not so identified but who display antisocial behaviors) continue their education beyond high school. They added that "vocational and transition services offered to adolescents and young adults with EBD during and after the secondary years are apt to be the last set of coordinated educational and social services they are likely to receive" (p. 2). This fact places the burden clearly on the shoulders of secondary educators. The Natural Longitudinal Transition Study (Blackorby & Wagner, 1996) reinforced the point by reporting that 59% of school leavers who had been given E/B labels while in

Student Strategies That Work

Critical Competencies for Employment

1. Have and produce as needed key documents (Social Security card, birth certificate, driver's license or other ID card with picture, etc.).
2. Complete application and other employment forms.
3. Set realistic goals (recognize the educational, skill, and other requirements of different kinds of jobs, and connect that information to personal aspirations).
4. Know how to conduct a job search (using electronic and printed want ads and other resources, tap, word-of-mouth, get assistance from relatives and neighbors, etc.).
5. Prepare for an interview (research the company, anticipate interview questions, practice answers to such questions, etc.).
6. Attend regularly, be punctual, and advise supervisor of any unavoidable absence/lateness.
7. Dress appropriately and maintain good hygiene.
8. Demonstrate courteous and appropriate verbal behavior in person, on the phone, in e-mail, etc.
9. Know how to use appropriate means of transportation.
10. Know what job accommodations are needed and how to recommend these to supervisors.

school were unemployed three to five years after leaving high school. That number was even higher than the 53% rate that obtained when students were two years out of high school. The median hourly wage of those who were working was at about minimum wage.

For more information on the TransCen Inc., the Center for Workforce Development, and the National Center on Secondary Education and Transition, go to the Web Links module in Chapter 13 of the Companion Website.

Focusing on these problems, and offering technical assistance to schools, are TransCen Inc., of Rockville, Maryland, the Institute for Educational Leadership's Center for Workforce Development, and the new (2001) National Center on Secondary Education and Transition.

A new resource, "Working @ IT," provides an annual program that is free to high schools in North America. Juniors and seniors use the program to help decide what careers are right for them. The sponsor, DeVry Institute of Technology, specializes in business and technology fields, but the program also covers careers in medicine and communications. DeVry educational representatives offer the interactive program, which is a 45- to 90-minute interactive session.

For more information on the Working @ IT and DeVry, go to the Web Links module in Chapter 13 of the Companion Website.

Rights in the Workplace

Individuals with disabilities enjoy certain civil rights in employment. The Americans with Disabilities Act (ADA), in title I, requires most employers having 15 or more workers to supply reasonable accommodations that are needed (e.g., sign-language interpreter, application forms on disk or in large print, etc.) for interviews, for training, and for work. The application forms and other employment documents may not require people to reveal medical data, including disability status. Rather, these papers may allow applicants to volunteer information about accommodations they believe will help them to do the job. Employers are not permitted to refuse to hire someone just because of a disability or just because an accommodation would be needed. Rather, decisions must be based upon the applicant's ability to do the job, with or without accommodations. These are important rights.

For more information on equal employment rights, go to the Web Links module in Chapter 13 of the Companion Website.

Three U.S. Supreme Court decisions have somewhat narrowed the scope and reach of the ADA's title I. If an individual has a disability such as epilepsy, but has medication that effectively controls that condition (seizures are few and far between), the person may not qualify as an "individual with a disability" because the condition does not "significantly affect major life activities"—which is an element of the first part of the ADA's three-part definition of "individual with a disability" (quoting from the EEOC's definition: "has a physical or mental impairment that substantially limits one or more of the major life activities of that individual"). Major life activities include keeping house, working, going to school, and the like. Similarly, someone who has a disability but who uses an assistive technology device that effectively accommodates for the condition may not be eligible under title I, for the same reason. The EEOC's guidance about the ADA reflects these court-ordered changes.

The ADA, in title II, also requires nondiscrimination on the basis of disability in employment by federal and state government agencies. This includes One-Stop Career Centers

Resources That Work

One-Stop Career Centers

Located in most major metropolitan areas, and in every state, are One-Stop Career Centers that cater to the needs of job seekers with and without disabilities. So-called "core services" are available to anyone. People may find out about job vacancies and career options, may explore employment trends, may receive training on conducting a job search, and may be taught how to write a resume and/or interview with an employer. Importantly, the Centers provide free access to PCs, fax and copy machines, and other essential office functions that make job searches so much easier. (Many Centers charge nominal fees for copy paper, phone charges, etc.). Additional, so-called "intensive services" are offered to individuals for whom core services are not sufficient to obtain a job. These include individualized assistance in all aspects of the job search, from customization of resumes to development of individualized career plans. "Training services" are available only for individuals who qualify under particular programs (as many persons with disabilities do under the Rehabilitation Act). One-Stop Career Centers also offer support services, such as interpreting or notetaking, as needed.

For most individuals, the first step is to identify a local One-Stop Career Center. They usually are not listed as such in the White Pages, nor in government-agencies Blue Pages. Rather, students should visit the Web site *http://www.ttrc.doleta.gov/ETA,* which contains listings of all Centers. Students may also look under Rehabilitation or Training in phone books or on the Web, calling the phone numbers given until they learn the location of the One-Stop Career Center. The second step is to call the Center and inquire about an orientation session. After attending that session, students generally are "on their own" in using Center services. They can sign up for workshops, use the business machines, and so on. If they need accommodations, they should request these. In the event that such requests are denied, they may ask to talk with the Center's Equal Opportunity Officer.

(see "Resources That Work: One-Stop Career Centers"). It also includes state colleges, universities, and community colleges, as well as public schools and public libraries.

An Example

In Sturgis, South Dakota, the Brown High School Transition Team teaches students how to send resumes (complete with cover letter) in response to job ads, fill out an application, request a needed accommodation, and so on. The year-long course, offered for high-school credit, also helps students with cognitive disabilities to appreciate what impacts their disabilities have on employment and to discuss those impacts in job interviews. In addition, the team provides training in independent living. Coordinator Chrissy Peterson notes that the Sturgis school district covers 3,000 square miles but has just 2,900 K–12 students. Some students and family members travel as many as 100 miles a day, round trip, to get to school. In such a rural area, students with disabilities require considerable assistance in solving the many transition-related matters (transportation, housing, food, etc.; Meade School District, 1230 Douglas, Sturgis, SD 57785-1869).

TRANSITION FROM SCHOOL TO INDEPENDENT LIVING

Some students will neither go to college nor begin work immediately following high school. For these students, transition to a life of relative independence requires much planning and work. Similar support is needed by many students who *do* go to college or to work. They need instruction on how to use public transportation, manage money, self-advocate in the community, and much else. What Deserie teaches her students is a good example of transition from school to independent living as well as transition from school to work (see "Personal Accounts," at the beginning of this chapter).

Deserie's students have mental retardation (MR). Young people with mild or moderate MR can learn to function quite independently, but they require considerable support to do

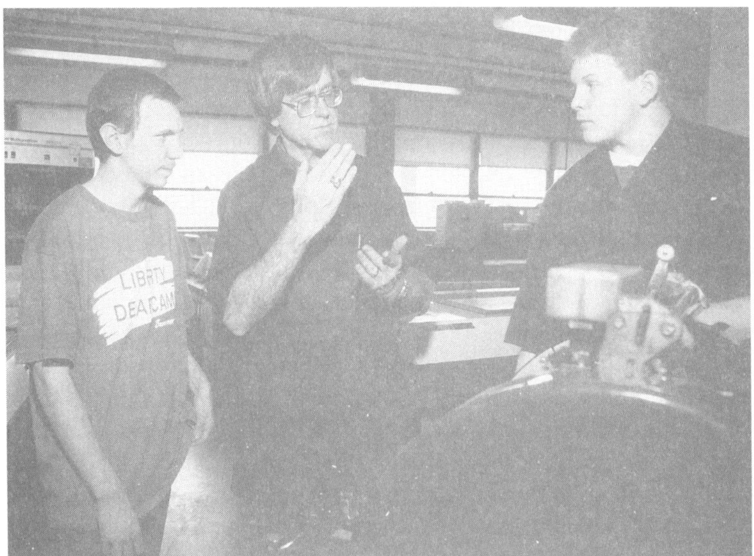

Transition from school to work may be facilitated by support staff, including, here, a sign-language interpreter.

so. Notice, in the chapter-opening vignette, that Deserie teaches her students social skills, personal responsibility, maintaining a neat/clean appearance, and handling money. All of that comes under the rubric of "transition from school to independent living." The skills involved in managing money (from buying things to making change to handling checking and savings accounts) are so critical that researchers have conducted many dozens of studies looking for better ways to teach individuals with MR about money management. An excellent overview of these research projects is offered by Browder and Grasso (1999). Their review article is valuable because it describes, and offers references to, 43 research studies on many aspects of teaching money management to students with disabilities.

Also in great need for transition services are students with E/B disorders and other social/behavioral needs. Reported Bullis and Cheney (1999) in their review of transition for these populations, "Perhaps the most prominent characteristic of persons with EBD is poor social skills" (p. 2). They added, "only a small segment secure support services from community-based social service agencies" (p. 6). Echoing Forness and others (e.g., Forness, Kavale, & Lopez, 1993; Forness, Kavale, King, & Kasari, 1994), Bullis and Cheney emphasized the need to serve students who display socially unacceptable behaviors but are not labeled E/B:

> Adolescents whom the public schools do not formally label as EBD, but who may present patterns of antisocial behavior (criminality, alcohol and substance abuse, aberrant sexual behaviors, school failure) or who receive a psychiatric label from a community-based agency pose thorny service delivery challenges as they typically are not afforded special education or transition services in any consistent and effective manner. (p. 2)

Independent Living Centers

About 600 independent living centers are available to offer support to persons with disabilities. These centers are located in every state. Each major metropolitan area has at least one, as do many counties in the nation. Despite the name, these programs do not offer residential housing. Rather, they provide information and referral, advocacy, peer counseling, and other services to help people with disabilities to locate accessible and affordable housing in the community, to find accessible public transportation, and to advocate for removal of architectural and other barriers in the community.

The Independent Living Resource Utilization (ILRU) Program, in Houston, TX, publishes an annual directory of independent living centers: *http://www.ilru.org* and 2323 South Shepherd #1000, Houston, TX 77010. The publication costs about $10. Some centers have their own Web sites. You can link to those through ILRU's Web site.

Supplemental Security Income

Many high-school age students qualify for Supplemental Security Income (SSI), usually because their families are of low socioeconomic status (SES). Upon turning 18, they will be considered by the Social Security Administration (SSA) to be a "family of one"—meaning that they can qualify on the basis of their own earned income and personal assets. Thus, an 18-year-old who was not eligible in past years because of high family income may suddenly become eligible. Many college students with disabilities rely upon SSI checks to pay daily living expenses while they continue their education. In addition, SSI eligibility usually brings with it coverage by Medicaid, the federal-state medical insurance program for people who are poor.

Numerous and complex rules govern initial and continued eligibility for SSI/Medicaid. If a young person earns more than about $800 per month, he/she may not qualify for SSI, or, if on SSI rolls, lose that eligibility. Brief explanations of these rules appear at *http://www.socialsecurity.gov/work.* Notice, especially, the "Red Book on Employment Support" (*http://www.socialsecurity.gov/work/ResourcesToolKit/redbook.html*). This electronic book outlines how SSA cooperates with rehabilitation agencies, job training organizations, and others to help individuals become gainfully employed. The major recent change in SSI is the advent of the Ticket to Work and Work Incentive Improvement Act (PL 106-170). Under this law, individuals may earn more than previously allowed and still receive Medicaid coverage. People looking for jobs may now arrange for services from providers other than state rehabilitation agencies. (Those alternative providers, as well as rehabilitation agencies, may be reached through One-Stop Career Centers; see p. 464, "Resources That Work: One-Stop Career Centers"). A different federal agency, the U.S. Department of Health and Human Services, through its Healthy & Ready to Work program, offers more information at *http://www.mchbhrtw.org.*

Young people with disabilities need to understand the limits of assistance that is available through SSI. While a monthly check in the amount of $500 or so may seem to be a lot of money for a teenager still living at home, a few moments' reflection will reveal how little it actually is. Even if a young person worked, earning up to the allowable limit (about $800/month), and qualified for a check from SSI as well, the quality of life these funds would support is a restricted one. When one adds up rent, utilities, and food (the bare necessities) one has little if anything left over. By contrast, if the young person were to secure a well-paying job, a much higher quality of life would become possible.

A new online resource, "SSIManager Software Internet Application," at *http://www.ssimanager.com,* lets people track their SSI payments, earned income, impairment-related work expenses, and much else. The site includes a section on "Support for Transitioning Students" which tracks student earned income exclusions.

An Example

The 18-21 Transition Program, in Boulder, CO, provides support services, not in school but rather in the community, in such areas as riding the bus, shopping for groceries, finding a place to live, developing social skills, opening and maintaining a checking account, and managing time (Boulder Valley School District, Special Education Department, 6600 East Arapahoe Rd., Boulder, CO 80303).

INTERAGENCY LINKAGES

IDEA, in describing IEP team responsibilities, notes that IEP teams should write any "interagency responsibilities or any needed linkages" in the IEP (section 614[d]). This requirement calls for several steps on your part. First, you need to identify *non-school* resources that the student needs in order to complete transition training. Second, you need to establish linkages with those resources. Usually this means finding out who the appro-

Resources That Work

Interagency Coordination

How do educators identify and locate the other organizations and agencies with which they need to forge the "interagency cooperation" that IDEA calls for on behalf of students aged 16 and over? Here are some resources that will help you. Many others are mentioned throughout the chapter. Make a point of "visiting" them on the Web.

With respect to colleges and universities, an excellent starting point is the American Council on Education (ACE; *http://www.ace.org*). The council maintains information on colleges and universities throughout the country. Another site of importance is the HEATH Resource Center, at George Washington University (*http://www.heath.gwu.edu*). This center is funded by the U.S. Department of Education to serve as a resource on higher education and individuals with disabilities. One of its many offerings is an annual report on pre-college programs that are designed to help young people with disabilities (especially specific learning disabilities) to prepare for college (*http://www.heath.gwu.edu/bookstore/pre-college.html*). The HEATH center formerly was affiliated with ACE.

In addition, a professional organization called AHEAD (*http://www.ahead.org*) has as its members people who provide accommodations for college students with disabilities on college campuses throughout the nation. The AHEAD board and its staff can direct you to the "504 coordinators" at the colleges and universities that interest you and your student. Because these persons make adjustments for college students with disabilities on their campuses, they are very familiar with "what's possible here" and what is not. You may also contact state rehabilitation agency counselors. These counselors have had experience working with college students with disabilities. They likely know which college and university programs do well with such students, and which do not.

Many individuals with disabilities who continue on to postsecondary education programs, and many who want to go directly to work, benefit from assistance from state rehabilitation agencies. These agencies are funded by state and federal governments to provide counseling and other support for youth and adults with disabilities. You can locate your state rehabilitation agency(ies) in the government-agencies Blue Pages of your local telephone directory. (Some states have two such agencies: one for clients who are blind and one for clients with all other disabilities.) You may also visit the Department of Labor's Web site *http://www.ttrc.doleta.gov/ETA*, which includes listings of One-Stop Career Centers. State rehabilitation agencies are located at such Centers. So are many job-training agencies. These facts make One-Stop Career Centers key resources for transition services. Under the 1998 Workforce Investment Act (PL 105-220) organizations and agencies other than state rehabilitation agencies may offer job training for people with disabilities. Your local One-Stop Career Center can direct you to these alternative providers of vocational services.

Some of these same young people with disabilities, but many others as well, are interested in or already beneficiaries of Supplemental Security Income (SSI). The local resources that can help you with SSI are known as state disability determination offices. These are financed by the Social Security Administration (SSA). You can locate those determination offices at *http://www.socialsecurity.gov/work*.

Two national advocacy groups are particularly interested in transition and in interagency agreements. One is the Arc (*http://www.thearc.org*) which represents families having members with mental retardation. Another is United Cerebral Palsy Associations (*http://www.ucpa.org*). Both URLs can help you to identify state and local affiliates of these organizations.

---

priate individuals are and securing their contact information (phone, e-mail, etc.). Second, you need to assess the suitability of the resources, including the appropriateness of the key people, for meeting a particular student's needs. Third, you need to introduce the student to these people and to support his efforts to answer questions. There are other steps, as well. In general, you need to identify resources, evaluate them, and make them available to students. Representatives from agencies and organizations that are expected to assist students during the post-high school years should be invited to IEP meetings when students are 16 years of age or older.

Postsecondary Institutions

In the case of someone planning to go to college, you need to help the student to identify colleges and universities that are suitable for all the usual reasons (selectivity, cost, geographical location, etc.). If the student requires accommodations in order to succeed at the postsecondary level, another consideration arises: Are those colleges and universities prepared to make the necessary adjustments (to provide notetakers, interpreters, lift-equipped vans, etc.)? The box "Resources That Work: Interagency Coordination," p. 467, offers helpful information, notably about the HEATH Resource Center. Once students have narrowed down their choices, a good next step is contacting the campus "504 coordinators" (also called "special services coordinators"): These are the people who actually hire tutors, note-takers, interpreters, and the like, who locate accessible housing on or off campus, and who schedule special transportation. On some campuses, an office staffed by several professionals fulfills these functions. They are often willing to come to area high schools to meet with prospective students and to answer questions. They also make themselves available, by appointment, when students visit the campus.

Employment Agencies

Many of the key agencies are working together in what are known as "One-Stop Career Centers"—a variety of job training and related agencies that were told by the Workforce Investment Act of 1998 (PL 105-220) to cooperate in making their services convenient to young people who seek to become employed (see p. 464, "Resources That Work: One-Stop Career Centers"). The fact that these agencies now are co-located (sharing office space as well as pooled phone numbers and other contact addresses such as cross-linked Web sites) makes it easier for transition workers in public schools to involve representatives of these agencies in transition programming. In addition, because the agencies that comprise One-Stop Career Centers must comply with title II of the ADA, students can be assured that they will not be subjected to discrimination on the basis of disability. Title II requires state agencies to make services available to individuals with disabilities on the same basis as they do for persons with no disabilities. In addition, state agencies must provide whatever "reasonable accommodations" (materials in Braille or large print, sign-language interpreter services, etc.) are required.

One such agency is the state rehabilitation agency. These agencies are funded by federal and state legislatures to provide support for people with disabilities in the job hunt and in the early work years. A good use of time is to familiarize yourself with state rehabilitation agencies, the role and function of rehabilitation counselors, and the plans they write, **Individualized Plans for Employment (IPEs).** Counselors may even begin writing IPEs while young people are still in high school. Formerly known as Individualized Written Rehabilitation Plans, or IWRPs, these plans are similar in some respects to IEPs. They outline services that the agency and the individual (called a "client") agree upon, explain who will pay for these (often, the agency will pay only part of the costs), identify who will provide the services, and detail how the client can appeal adverse decisions. For example, an IPE may indicate that the state rehabilitation agency will contribute part of the cost of a college education. Alternatively, it may signify that this agency will pay much of the cost of attending a technical/vocational school, or other trade school, as an alternative to college. Note the big difference from IDEA: Services for young people while they are still in PreK–12 programs are free to the individual and to her family, but similar services after young people leave PreK–12 programs may no longer be free. Rehabilitation counselors are available to attend IEP meetings to begin the school-agency coordination that will facilitate the student's transition.

Social Security and Health Insurance Providers

Another agency with which to connect students who are interested is the Social Security Administration (SSA). This is because SSA administers the Supplemental Security Income (SSI) program.

There are pro's and con's to enrolling on SSI. A major pro is the availability of Medicaid coverage. An important con is the fact that disincentives exist that discourage SSI recipients from pursuing gainful employment, despite program changes designed to minimize such disincentives. Staff members at local centers for independent living (IL) can address these issues with high-school students. IL staff frequently agree to visit local schools to explain government programs. Other resources include The Arc and the Consortium for Citizens with Disabilities. The latter is an umbrella association which joins The Arc to other advocacy organizations such as United Cerebral Palsy Associations. Students and family members should thoroughly explore all options prior to making decisions.

Another option, one particularly attractive for students with health impairments (see Chapter 6) is the Children's Health Insurance Program (CHIP; sometimes referred to as the State Children's Health Insurance Program, or SCHIP).

For more information on the centers, organizations, and programs regarding health care coverage, go to the Web Links module in Chapter 13 of the Companion Website.

"DOING" TRANSITION

For more information on Web sites about transition, go to the Web Links module in Chapter 13 of the Companion Website.

For more than 30 years, researchers have demonstrated how transition from school to post-school environments can be effected. Much of what we know is now available on the Web. The keys to success are not many, and they are not complex. The fact that few schools "do" transition as Deserie has (see the opening vignette for this chapter) is, therefore, somewhat puzzling (Hasazi, Furney, & DeStefano, 1999; Repetto & Correa, 1996; Valdes, Williamson, & Wagner, 1990).

The failures we keep seeing in the schools seem to be traceable to two factors. First, educators, as a group, tend not to take the time that is necessary to investigate the "worlds" beyond the public schools. In particular, teachers often violate the most fundamental principle of biofeedback: In order to know what to do with this year's class, you need to find out what happened to last year's class (and the classes before that). This means that schools should contact recent graduates, the colleges they went to, the companies they worked for, and the neighborhood stores and facilities they visited in their post-school years. It means asking how many were successful in postsecondary programs and, of those who did not complete their studies there, what specific factors impeded them? The answers will tell you much of what you need to teach this year's students. Similarly, how many found gainful employment within a year or two following graduation? How many remain employed? Of those who have not been successful in the world of work, what factors seem to be at root? Again, the answers will tell you what to teach your current students. Finally, how independent are former students? Are they able to live on their own? Do their parents report that they are functioning well without continuous parental intervention? The answers to these questions, too, inform your present efforts.

The second major causative factor behind the persistent failure of public schools to effect successful transitions for adolescents with disabilities seems to be that educators tend to focus upon academics virtually to the exclusion of everything else. Particularly now that higher learning standards have taken effect, the attitude in the nation's secondary schools seems to be that the purpose of high school is to get young people ready for college. The fact that just 50% of secondary students actually enroll in postsecondary programs within two years, and 68% within five years, means that substantial numbers of young people do *not* follow the presumptive route of going directly from secondary school to postsecondary programs. As discussed earlier in the chapter, this is even more true of students with disabilities. The National Longitudinal Transition Study (NLTS; Blackorby & Wagner, 1996) demonstrated that just 14% of students with disabilities had matriculated at a postsecondary program within two years of leaving high school and 27% within five years. Thus, *the overwhelming majority* of secondary students with disabilities do *not* go from high school to college. These facts raise serious questions. If educators spend the bulk of their time during the four secondary years preparing students for college, they of necessity spend little time preparing students for other post-school environments, notably those of working and living independently.

Successful transition, argued transition expert Jim Martin, begins with trusting teens with disabilities to lead their own transition planning (Martin, Marshall, and DePry, 2001). The law requires that students with disabilities take part in IEP team meetings "when appropriate," by which it generally means when they reach age 14 or over and possess the mental capacity to plan their own futures. No one has more at stake than do students.

For more information on empowerment, go to the Web Links module in Chapter 13 of the Companion Website.

For more information on the two fact sheets on transition for special educators and specialists, go to the Web Links module in Chapter 13 of the Companion Website.

Martin observed that by offering opportunities to become actively involved in transition planning, the IEP team signals to the student that an important crossroads has come. In Florida, Sheila Gritz adopted Martin's approach to empowering teens with disabilities. She found that teaching a semester-long course on self-determination and transition planning, prior to the IEP team meeting, helped students to acquire the skills they would need to be successful in the process ("New Ideas for Planning Transitions to the Adult World," 2000). Twenty teens told a national conference in Washington, DC, the same thing: "Listen to us! We want control over our own transition process. . . . We want the opportunity to live our own lives, have a voice, learn how to be self-determined and [to] self-advocate for our education and the transition to what is next" (quoted in Thomas, 2000).

The Transition-Related Personnel Competencies Project, at the University of Illinois, in cooperation with the Division on Career Development and Transition of the Council for Exceptional Children (CEC), has produced two brief fact sheets: "Transition-Related Planning, Instruction, and Service Responsibilities for Secondary Special Educators" and "Transition Specialist Competencies."

Here are some of the project team's suggestions:

- Adopt a student-led process, including self-determination
- Develop educational experiences that correspond with post-school goals
- In the IEP, specify responsibilities for each such experience
- Evaluate progress at least annually, including student evaluation of his progress
- Teach academic skills in the context of real-life experiences
- Teach social skills for school, work, and community living
- Involve post-school agencies, such as state rehabilitation agencies, as early as age 16
- Involve parents throughout, especially during the first several years.

Self-determination is central to all kinds of school-to-postschool transition. Involving students in decision making throughout the transition process is a key idea. This includes the initial decision whether to pursue school-to-postsecondary education, school-to-work, and/or school-to-independent living transition. It also incorporates the major decisions within each strand of transition. Such approaches as community-based instruction (situated learning) pave the way for success in transition, because learning occurs outside of the school. We will see, in Chapter 16, how social studies classes and units can be used to teach the kinds of social skills and civic responsibilities that support successful inclusion. Family members should be involved in this planning, particularly during IEP team meetings. Interagency cooperation, including between schools and rehabilitation agencies, is taken up later under "Transition from School to Work."

Assessing Progress in Transition

Measuring achievement in transition is somewhat different from assessment in other areas. The best way to know if a student is becoming ready to make a transition is to test that transition. Many postsecondary institutions offer activities for high-school students. Your students may enroll for one non-credit summer course at a local community college following the high-school sophomore year and for another following the junior year. Ideally, students would live on campus so as to experience a wide range of challenges (housing, food, transportation, etc.). The College Connection (see "Transition from School to Postsecondary Programs") is an example of a transition program actually operated on a college campus. Similarly, to see if students are prepared to make the transition from school to work, they should work. The activities that Deserie described in the chapter-opening vignette are excellent examples. Gradually, over the secondary-school years, the student should participate in a variety of increasingly challenging jobs. With respect to transition from school to independent living, you and other educators can require from students increasing self-sufficiency during the high-school years. You can ask families to do likewise at home.

The principle of biofeedback is vital to evaluation of progress in transition. A good idea is to "feed back" into transition activities the results of these trials and experiences. What your previous students were, and were not, able to do tells you what to teach future students.

If you find that progress is slower than you had hoped, and that "time is running out" because the end of high school is approaching, you might talk with your fellow teachers about integrating transition into their content courses. We will explain more about this in the Part Six chapters on teaching content subjects.

Issues in Transition

Transition services are most contentious for students who are not expected to continue on to college. (College-bound students certainly need and should receive transition services. Those services are rather easily integrated into their college-prep programs. For non–college-bound students, however, transition services may well necessitate delivery of a different curriculum. That makes these somewhat controversial.) The IDEA Amendments of 1997 heightened attention to transition services for non–college-bound students by adding new language to the law's first statement of purpose. Section 601(d)(1)(A) says that Part B, which deals with elementary and secondary education for children with disabilities, is intended to, among other things, "prepare them for employment and independent living."

That change in the law occurred at the very time that state after state was raising academic standards, particularly at the high-school level. This renewed emphasis upon academics may not be appropriate for students who do not anticipate going to college. In fact, the additional time high-school teachers now spend preparing students for tougher district-wide and state achievement tests may actually deprive non–college-bound students of the opportunity to learn what they urgently need to learn. This includes the skills of self-care and of self-determination. That is why Congress added the new words to section 601(d)(1)(A): do not overlook employment and independent living.

Notable in this respect is the *22nd Annual Report to Congress* (U.S. Department of Education, 2000b) finding that *just 26% of students with disabilities aged 17 or older were graduated from high school with a standard (academic) diploma* in 1997–1998 (the most recent year for which data were available). Thus, three quarters of students with disabilities who left secondary schools were not eligible for postsecondary education (unless they secured a G.E.D.). A high-school diploma increasingly is required, as well, for employment. Young people exiting high school without such a degree will need support to secure employment. They have to learn how to navigate a job market that is unfriendly for persons lacking academic diplomas. They must also learn to manage on a tight budget, because their earnings likely will be limited. School-to-work and school-to-independent living transition services can provide the needed support.

A good foundation for students who are not expected to go to college is offered in Wehman and Kregel's (1997), *Functional Curriculum for Elementary, Middle, and Secondary Age Students with Special Needs*. A somewhat more practical version is provided by Wehman, Sherron, and West (1997) in *Exceptional Individuals in School, Community, and Work*. Also helpful are the texts on teaching persons with mental retardation by Dever and Knapczyk (1997) and by Beirne-Smith et al. (2002).

Clearly, transition planning can be complex. The nearby box, "Teacher Strategies That Work: Transition Plan," illustrates how the many aspects of transition services may be brought together. With admirable brevity, the plan shows how Cindy Doe, age 16, will be assisted in her education, community experiences, employment, daily living, and other important aspects of the transition from school to work and independent living.

Self-Determination and Self-Advocacy

Critical skills for students with disabilities to acquire, with your help, are those of self-determination and self-advocacy. The term **self-determination** refers to making key decisions about one's own life. Articles that provide teachers with important information

Teacher Strategies That Work

Transition Plan

Statement of Needed Transition Services

Name: Cindy Doe
Date: 5/1/00
Age: 16
Age to Graduate: 22
Person Responsible for Coordinating Transition: Jill Smith, Teacher

Postsecondary goals: Supported employment in clerical setting; supported living in hometown; involvement in integrated clubs and religious organizations; more friends

Course of study and needed transition services: Vocational education (clerical) with direct instruction and behavioral supports. Also classes in consumer sciences, applied academics

Transition Area and Related Activities	Responsible Person	IEP Goal	Start: End:
1. Instruction:			
1. Applied math and English	Pat Claire - math teacher	1.1, 1.2	9/00–6/01
2. Clerical vocational education	Joe Gonzalez - VOED teacher	3.3	9/00–6/01
3. Employability skills	Jill Smith - SPED teacher	3.2	9/00–6/01
4. Social skills training	Joe Lyon - teacher	4.1	9/00–6/01
2. Community Experiences:			
1. Job shadowing in clerical settings	Jeff Ringles - work study	3.4	9/00–6/01
2. Visits to clubs and church groups	Julie Doe - parent		9/00–6/01
3. Community work experiences	Jeff Ringles - work study	3.5	9/01–6/03
4. Supported employment	Jack Point - VR counselor		9/03–6/04
5. Summer camp	Julie Doe - parent		8/00–9/00
3. Development of Employment and Adult Living Objectives:			
1. Job placement and training	Jack Point - VR counselor		5/03–9/03
2. Development of a PASS plan	Sally Fort - Social Security		5/03–9/03
3. Development of residential plan	Fred Fryman - MR/DD		9/02–5/03
4. Development of ongoing supports	Fred Fryman - MR/DD		5/03–9/03
4. Related Services:			
1. Behavioral plan	Leonard James - Beh Spec.	4.2	By 9/00
2. Augmentative communication training	Jackie Speaker - O.T.		9/00–5/01
5. Daily Living Skills:			
1. Provide mobility training	Jeff Plant - Friend		4/01–5/01
2. Provide training in home safety	Jill Smith - SPED teacher	4.4	1/01–5/01
6. Linkages with Adult Services:			
1. Vocational rehabilitation services	Jack Point - VR counselor		Age 16
2. Developmental disability services	Fred Fryman - MR/DD		Age 16
3. Social Security	Sally Fort - Social Security		Age 16
4. Residential services	Fred Fryman - MR/DD		Age 18
5. Case management services	Fred Fryman - MR/DD		Age 16
7. Functional Vocational Evaluation:			
1. Situational assessments in a variety of class, home, work, and leisure environments	Jeff Ringles - work study coordinator		9/00–5/01
2. Career portfolio	Sam Smith - guidance counselor		

Comments: Cindy will need a calm and nondistracting environment and ongoing supports.

Source: From *Transition planning: A Guide for Parents and Professionals* (p. 30), by R. Baer, R. McMahan, and R. Flexer, 1999, Kent, Ohio: Kent State University.

include those by Marshall, Marshall, and DePry (2001) and by Wehmeyer and Schalock (2001).

Central to instruction about self-determination is helping students to understand their own needs and limitations. Early childhood and elementary students may not appreciate these, meaning that teachers and family members need to make most key decisions. However, beginning in middle school and certainly in high school, students should be given opportunities to make decisions for themselves. A first step, explained Marshall et al. (2001), is to set personal short- and long-term goals. Students need to learn how to make progress toward those goals and how to measure that progress over time. They must acquire skills in adjusting strategies and tactics so as to remain on target toward their goals. At times, they may need to re-reevaluate and even change those goals. Throughout, students need to recognize which steps they can do alone, which they can do with assistance, and which they cannot do at all (Milthaug, 1998). They should be granted by family members and teachers alike increasing independence in making decisions about who should assist them, when, and how.

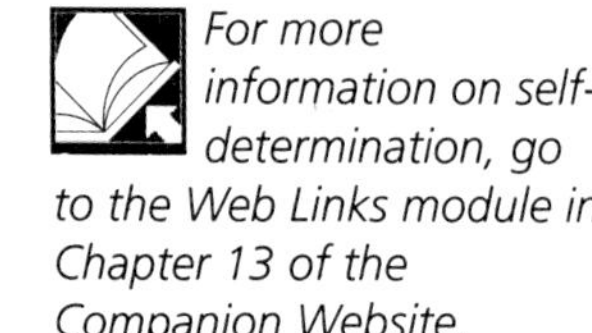

For more information on self-determination, go to the Web Links module in Chapter 13 of the Companion Website.

It is not always realistic to expect that middle-school students should be held accountable for the consequences of their own decisions. Some lack the life experience to appreciate what those consequences might be, while others have not been required by family members nor by previous teachers to assume such responsibility (Wehmeyer and Schalock, 2001). By the time young people reach high school, however, it is essential that they realize those consequences. Good decisions cannot be made unless responsibility is accepted for the consequences those decisions produce. As Martin et al. (2001) convincingly argued, high-school-age students, including those with mental retardation, can and should assume the risks that come with self-determination. This is important at the secondary level because once they leave high school, these young people will be expected to be both responsible and accountable. You need to prepare them—and to urge their other teachers, counselors, and other professionals to offer them additional opportunities to learn personal responsibility.

Self-advocacy is standing up for one's rights and requesting what one needs. Individuals with disabilities enjoy certain civil rights in 21st-century America, including the right to non-discriminatory treatment in service programs, in transportation, in housing, and in employment. Virtually all of these rights are enforced, primarily, through self-advocacy. That is, people have to complain when rights are violated (Bowe, 2000b). Training in self-advocacy includes instruction in what those rights are and how to file complaints. A good way to begin such instruction is to prepare students for their first IEP team meetings. They may need several weeks to several months of preparation in order to understand the IEP process, learn what their options are, recognize their preferences, and learn to advocate for those. Later, as they participate in work-study, job-search, and other transition activities, they need to know what their rights are (e.g., for accommodations they need) and how to advocate for these rights.

Learning to be assertive without being aggressive is one part of such preparation. So, too, is learning how to communicate clearly, logically, and convincingly. Learning the art of negotiation is also part of this work. Much of this kind of instruction can be provided in social studies classes (see Chapter 16). If not, it must be offered during transition programming.

CHAPTER SUMMARY

Transition

- The major transition is from high school to life beyond high school: postsecondary education, work, and/or independent living.
- The other transition for which IDEA services are required is from early intervention (birth to 2 inclusive) to preschool special education (3 to 5 inclusive).

Transition at Age 3

- Early intervention personnel secure family permission to begin the transition for young children. This includes family concurrence on transfer of records from the early intervention program to the preschool.
- If the family agrees, a meeting is then convened by the early intervention staff so that families may visit preschools and an individualized education program may be prepared.

Transition from High School to Life Beyond High School

- It is important for families and young people with disabilities to realize that services after students age out of IDEA services generally are not free. This fact reinforces the point that needed support should be provided during the PreK–12 years, while they remain free to the family, to the extent possible.
- Teachers may become familiar with nearby postsecondary programs, places of employment, and community stores and facilities. Knowledge of these programs and facilities helps you to prepare students for transition.
- The new, higher learning standards are consuming class time that otherwise might be used for transition services. In some instances, for some students, decisions must be made: a class, two classes, or even more of academics may have to be sacrificed so that a student acquires the real-world knowledge she will need in order to succeed after high school.

Transition from School to Postsecondary Education

- Unlike PreK–12 students, postsecondary students must actively request services and accommodations.
- To date, most students with disabilities have not continued on to postsecondary education. Rather, they have transitioned from school to work and/or from school to independent living.

Transition from School to Work

- When young people with disabilities fail in the workplace, it generally is because of behavior issues rather than because of inability to do the job itself. This is why transition services must emphasize behaviors that are expected in the world of work.
- Work today increasingly is done by *teams* rather than by individuals working alone. It is urgent that students with disabilities (whom we traditionally taught, for the most part, one-on-one) learn to be good team members.
- State rehabilitation agencies and other job-training programs have come together in One-Stop Career Centers, which are located in all 50 states and in most U.S. metropolitan areas.

Transition from School to Independent Living

- Living independently requires knowledge and skills in the areas of money management, transportation, housing, and many others. Students who go on to postsecondary programs and/or to work often need training in these areas.
- Located in most major metropolitan areas and many counties are centers for independent living. These not-for-profit organizations offer advocacy services, peer counseling, and other kinds of assistance that often makes the difference between living independently and continuing to depend upon others.
- Supplemental Security Income (SSI) provides monthly checks and medical insurance to individuals with disabilities who are living in below-poverty circumstances. However, SSI only brings people up to a subsistence level of living. To go beyond that, people need to get good jobs.

Interagency Linkages

- Transition often cannot be planned without cooperation with non-school agencies. This is particularly true for transition from school to postsecondary programs and transition from school to work.
- You need to identify resources, locate the right people within each, and (as appropriate) either invite those persons to an IEP meeting or arrange for the student to meet with them.

"Doing" Transition

- Critical components of transition services include training in self-determination and in self-advocacy.

QUESTIONS FOR REFLECTION

1. Do you think Deserie's transition program is a successful one? Why or why not?
2. Describe in your own words the apparent conflict between the new, higher learning standards and transition services.
3. Why do infants and toddlers and their families have service coordinators, but preschoolers and their families do not?
4. What does the principle of biofeedback tell us about transition services?
5. Why is training in self-determination so central a component to successful transition?
6. Why do experts recommend that much transition-related instruction take place in the community?
7. Why are transition services sometimes controversial?
8. How is the provision of accommodations (such as interpreters) different in postsecondary education as compared to PreK–12 schools?
9. Students with which disabilities tend to have the least success in employment and independent living?
10. What services do centers for independent living provide?

Part Five Endnotes

Making Inclusion Work . . . The Story So Far

In Part Five, we saw that making inclusion work involves these ideas:

- Examine the school's climate to be sure that it does not unnecessarily place students at risk.
- Accommodate students who have no permanent home address (those who are homeless or are migrant children)
- Take steps to become culturally sensitive and culturally competent, especially with respect to cultures that are prominent in the local community.
- Make special efforts to identify, and to provide appropriate services to, students who have gifts and/or talents, *including* those who also have disabilities.
- When possible, be collaborative with other professionals, rather than consultative.
- As appropriate, use "special-education" techniques when teaching students who have no disabilities.
- Use push-in as well as push-out, acknowledge the advantages and disadvantages of each.
- Give paraprofessionals explicit instructions and then supervising them throughout the school day.
- Respect the right of persons with disabilities, including those with severe limitations, to self-determination.
- Make time, despite the new, higher learning standards, for instruction and "real-life" experiences that are essential for success in transition.
- Tap One-Stop Career Centers and local centers for independent living to support school-based transition services.

Part Six

Content-Area Instruction

Part Six of *Making Inclusion Work* offers three chapters on the teaching of content subjects in inclusive classrooms. These chapters cover a broad range, from the early childhood years (birth to age 8) through high school. Each opens with a summary of national standards in the content area(s). Teachers in inclusive classrooms, no less than educators in other classrooms, must help students to reach the new, higher learning standards and to pass the high-stakes tests that state departments of education are requiring for high-school graduation. The chapters of Part Six continue with brief discussions of the teaching of the content area(s) involved—English and Language Arts in Chapter 14, math and science in Chapter 15, and social studies in Chapter 16. Subject-area content material is included in these chapters because research shows that some special educators express concern about the depth of their preparation in content subjects (e.g., Austin, 2000; Cole & McLeskey, 1997). We then explore issues and strategies for teaching content in inclusive classrooms, placing as much emphasis upon middle school and high school as elementary school, because texts used to prepare teachers to work with students having disabilities often neglect the higher grade levels.

Chapter 14 focuses upon instruction in reading, writing, and public speaking. Competencies in those areas are essential if students are to be successful in inclusive classes not just in English/Language Arts but in other content subjects as well. Students who may have difficulty in English often can do well in math and science. This includes children and youth with autism as well as many with specific learning disabilities. That is one reason Chapter 15 discusses those subjects together. Many of the same methods are used in math and in science, another reason to present those subjects together. Social studies (history, political science, geography, etc.) are reviewed in Chapter 16. A unique feature of social studies is that the content lends itself well to instruction that helps students to reach transition-related goals.

Chapter 14 Language Arts and English

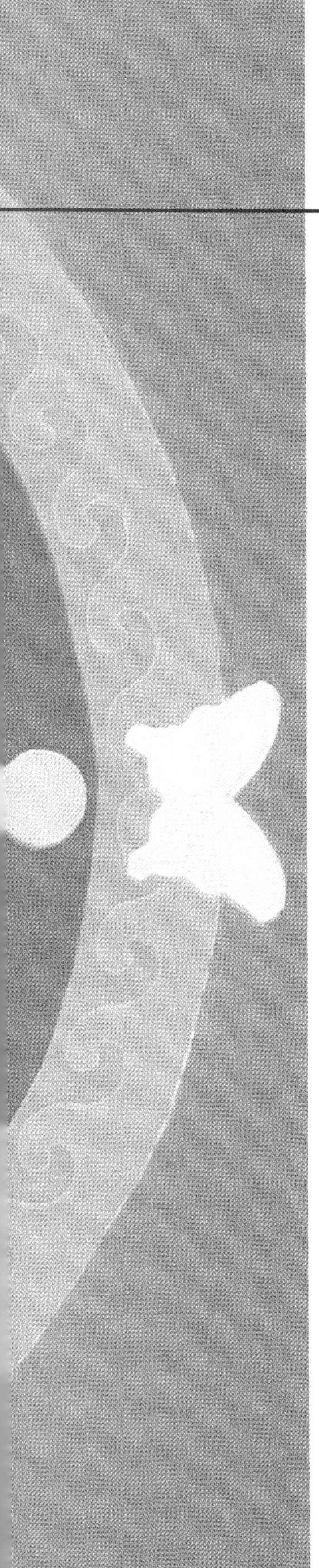

TERMS

language arts | literacy | miscue analysis

CHAPTER FOCUS QUESTIONS

After reading this chapter, you should be able to answer such questions as:

1. Where are national standards for English and Language Arts made available?
2. Why is phonics a necessary component of the teaching of reading in inclusive classes?
3. Why are grouping and direct instruction important techniques in language arts and English?
4. How can technology help students with disabilities to write?
5. What techniques of "universal design in education" are applicable to the teaching of English?
6. Why should secondary teachers of English consider adopting such works as Shakespeare's *Richard III*, Carson McCullers' *The Heart Is a Lonely Hunter*, and Steinbeck's *Of Mice and Men?*
7. How can classics such as *The Call of the Wild, Tom Sawyer*, and *Hamlet* be taught to inclusive classes?

PERSONAL ACCOUNTS

A teacher comments about how she teaches English to students in fourth grade:

> *I have seen enough successes to know that an integrated whole language/phonics approach is the way to go. In our classroom, there is a large poster I made which announces our "Reading Detective Club." (This was inspired by the work of the Goodmans.) The picture is of a person reading a book. We can see in the person's head three circles: one for meaning (semantic cues), one for language (syntactic cues), and one for phonics (graphophonic awareness). The poster is a reminder to use all the pieces.*
>
> *Whole language does not mean disregard for phonics. I consider myself a whole language teacher and I use phonics. However, when phonics is taught in isolation, it is of no benefit for a child who struggles with a learning disability. Instead, teachers need to ask questions: What kinds of things are happening when the reader samples the text? What kinds of miscues are occurring? Are these showing a reader attempting to make predictions? In my classroom, I use miscue analysis as a tool to guide reading instruction.*

> *Last year, a little girl entered my classroom with very, very limited reading skills. She has a low IQ and is diagnosed with Fragile X syndrome. Her learning difficulties were, and continue to be, considerable. It was only by integrating phonics instruction into a holistic approach that this little girl began to read. In the spring, she picked up a simple* Henry and Mudge *storybook that she had never read before and ran over to me. With surprise and delight, she shouted: "I can read it! I can read this book, Mrs. R!"*
>
> —Lori

A sixth-grade teacher shared her experiences in teaching a student with specific learning disabilities how to prepare an effective speech:

> *My student Alyssa, who is 12, wrote just three sentences when asked in September to describe her summer. I realized that her learning disabilities probably were making it hard for her to organize her thoughts. So I introduced her to the organizing software package known as Inspiration™. First, we selected a template that provided a graphic outline of a character study. In this case, the character was Alyssa herself. The template prompted her to enter information about herself (what she likes to do, etc.), about her family and friends, and about her activities over the previous summer months. It turned out that Alyssa had a lot to say! She entered enough information to completely fill the graphic organizer. Then Alyssa clicked on the "outline" button to reveal a detailed outline for her essay. She printed that out. With the outline by her side, Alyssa wrote a well-organized and quite comprehensive description of the many things she had done that summer.*
>
> *While grading her essay, I pulled out the original "essay" she had produced without the help of the software. The difference was just staggering. This experience made me realize how valuable this graphic organizer software can be in spurring students with learning disabilities to produce what they are capable of writing!*
>
> —Jaime

INTRODUCTION

Chapter 14 opens our three-chapter exploration of strategies and tactics for teaching content subjects in inclusive settings. English and language arts is a good topic with which to begin, because it offers us the opportunity to examine very different kinds of content. The term "English" is often used to refer to the content area studied in secondary schools, specifically to literature. The **"language arts"** are listening, speaking, reading, writing, viewing, and visually representing information (Tompkins, 2002). We begin by examining recommended standards for these subjects.

At the early childhood/elementary level, and to a lesser extent at the middle-school level, the focus generally is upon the foundation skills of literacy, reading, and writing. These are developed through listening to and reading children's literature, particularly stories students themselves select as being meaningful to their lives. At the secondary level, however, teachers tend to emphasize the classics of American and English literature. Increasingly, high-school curricula include multicultural texts (by such authors as Maya Angelou, Sandra Cisneros, Gabriel Garcia Marquez, and Nadine Gordimer). With respect to students with disabilities, English and language arts content at the lower grade levels tends to be appropriate. Indeed, students with specific learning disabilities and deafness very much need and greatly benefit from such instruction. However, the secondary-school concentration on literature may be problematic for students with some disabilities. Some with autism may have difficulty with fiction and poetry, for example, while many with mental retardation or deafness may lack the skills to make sense of Elizabethan English or to appreciate the nuances of F. Scott Fitzgerald's prose.

Making our task as teachers of inclusive classrooms more difficult than it needs to be is the fact that the professional literature offers much guidance for inclusion teachers at the elementary but very little for teachers at the secondary level. Journals and books about special education focus almost exclusively on elementary levels of instruction, while journals and texts about language arts and English seldom even mention disabilities. To give preservice teachers the information they need, this chapter will emphasize the teaching of English and literature at the secondary level, although it does not neglect early childhood/elementary and middle-school education.

NATIONAL STANDARDS

The National Council of Teachers of English (NCTE; 1111 W. Kenyon Road, Urbana, IL 61801-1096; 1-800-369-6283) and the International Reading Association (IRA) have offered 12 standards. These feature readings in a broad variety of texts (fiction, nonfiction, classic literature, materials from different historical periods and from different geographical regions, and contemporary works) and from a wide spectrum of sources (libraries, databases, video, computer networks, people, artifacts). In writing, students are to learn how to fine-tune their expressive communication so as to reach different audiences for different purposes. The NCTE/IRA Standards for the English Language Arts are available in a range of formats. "Standards in Practice" are offered for grades K–5, 6–8, 9–12. Standards for teaching literature are available for elementary, middle, and high-school levels. There are also standards for writing and for teacher preparation. These are all recommended standards, intended for use by educators at state and local levels in developing their own standards. The emphasis clearly is upon reading diverse materials and writing for different purposes and for different audiences. Competencies in those areas are vital for success in other subject areas as well, notably social studies and science.

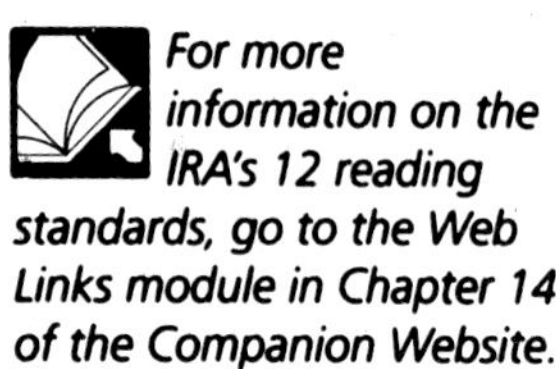

For more information on the IRA's 12 reading standards, go to the Web Links module in Chapter 14 of the Companion Website.

EARLY CHILDHOOD AND ELEMENTARY

Reading and writing are of urgent importance for students with disabilities, particularly for those placed into inclusive environments. It is the nature of schools that *virtually everything else* is taught through reading and writing. That is why the expert Gail Tompkins (2001) urged, in her popular text for elementary and middle-school teachers, *Literacy for the 21st Century,* that elementary and middle-school teachers set aside several hours in every school day for reading and writing.

Teaching Reading and Literacy

The field we used to know as "reading" has become a lively one, as advocates of "literacy" have invigorated a generation of teachers with a mission. The new emphasis is upon the "creation of meaning" and away from the mechanics of reading. Phonics (sound-symbol correspondence and the rules of spelling) instruction has been controversial in recent years (e.g., Strickland, 1998). In many schools, however, it continues to be one part of a "comprehensive" approach to teaching reading. This is part of what Yale's Sally Shaywitz referred to when she talked about "not our mother's phonics" (see Chapter 3). Tompkins (2001) used the word "balanced" to make much the same point as Shaywitz (1998) does with the term "comprehensive": that phonics, albeit presented in natural contexts, remains an integral element of instruction.

Early Literacy

Literacy, Tompkins contended, is the ability to use reading (and writing) in everyday life, with the emphasis upon work and other out-of-school activities that matter to children and adults. The current popularity of literacy represents a rejection of older approaches that taught the mechanics of reading, largely in isolation from real-world applications. If, as literacy advocates insist, reading is at the bottom of the creation of meaning, then it is best taught as part of activities children find to be meaningful in their own lives. This may mean that students select stories and books that interest them. It may also mean that teachers encourage groups of children to react to what they read by drawing parallels between literature and their own everyday lives. Strickland (1998) put it well when she suggested that teachers should help children work "from whole to part to whole"—that is, teachers should give children meaningful texts, then extract parts of it for intensive study, and finally help students to generalize from the material and give other examples of the language elements being studied.

A related way to view this approach to literacy is to focus upon metacognitive strategies students use to construct meaning. Metacognition is "thinking about thinking" (see Chapter 3). Students draw from their knowledge and experience to decide what is, and is not, important in a given text. They summarize that content in their own words. Students then make inferences and ask questions, specifically with respect to prediction: They state what they think will happen in the story. As they read and re-read, they monitor their own comprehension. Working together in small groups and in whole-discussions, they get answers to their questions, share their understandings, and verify or refute their predictions.

These competencies are of great importance in reform curricula. Science, social studies, and other content areas are taught today by having students read a remarkable variety of materials, ranging from historical documents to scientific journal articles. Reading is not confined to textbooks. Rather, primary (original) sources are examined. So, too, are secondary sources such as biographies. (Textbooks, by contrast, are tertiary sources.) The aim is for students to achieve "deep understanding" (Morocco, 2001, p. 7) of imagery, metaphor, and point of view, not to mention maps, diagrams, and formulas. Dole, Duffy, Roehler, and Pearson (1991) noted that readers need to master five strategies: deciding what is important in a text, summarizing that information, drawing inferences from it, asking good questions about it, and monitor their own comprehension of it. This is what literacy is all about.

What Shaywitz et al., (1998, 2004) and Tompkins (2001) warned us about, however, is that we cannot just assume that the foundation skills of decoding the written word will take care of themselves. Stated differently, students cannot bring meaning to a text they do not understand. To adopt an analogy, if teachers need to spend time helping students with nails and hammers, screws and screwdrivers, nuts and bolts, they should do so. Otherwise, the house these students construct will collapse. This is why more traditional Direct-Instruction techniques (see Chapter 8) still have a place in the teaching of English and language arts, alongside constructivist approaches.

Reading Recovery

Working in New Zealand as a teacher of young children, then a special educator, and later a university trainer of educators, Marie Clay developed a well-articulated set of procedures for identifying the difficulties that some children encountered in learning to read and write and then for remediating those problems. In *An Observation Survey of Early Literacy Achievement* and in *Reading Recovery: A Guidebook for Teachers in Training,* Clay (1993a, 1993b) presented her recommendations. She intended the two books to be used together: Teachers should conduct observations during and especially at the end of the child's first year of formal schooling, then perform the interventions described in the second book early in the child's second year of school. Noting that 80% to 90% of young children will not require these interventions, Clay urged kindergarten and first-grade teachers to conduct careful, individualized observations of 5- and 6-year-old children as they read and write. The key is understanding what strategies the child has adopted, so you know what to change and what to teach. Teachers should begin with trade books or stories the child can read and watch very closely as the child reads them. *Reading Recovery* is filled with specifics of strategies teachers can give to young readers. (American readers should be aware that they will encounter some sentences that appear to be odd. Clay, for example, speaks of "tuition to detail" by which she means "fixating on details" and about "reception teachers" by which she means first-year teachers. These minor differences in the use of English should not dissuade educators from giving Clay's ideas a chance. Clay argued that most "early reading failures" would benefit "very quickly, on average in 12 to 15 weeks" (1993b, p. 8) from one-on-one, highly individualized instruction. That assertion is controversial, because independent research has yet to support such expectations with respect to students with disabilities.

Phonemic Awareness and Phonics

We mentioned phonemic awareness and phonics earlier in Chapter 3. That brief discussion noted that we would explore those terms in greater detail here in Chapter 14. To begin: What is the difference between the two? *Phonemic awareness* is a mental ability, one most of us possess at birth, that equips us to pull apart the different phonemes in the speech we hear and to put together different phonemes to make the words we speak. Phonemes are the smallest units of sound. There are 44 phonemes. *Phonics,* by contrast, is a method of teaching, one we use to instruct children to "sound it out" when they encounter new words on a page.

Reading, in Shaywitz's (1998) view, is a hierarchy of mental tasks. At bottom is phonemic awareness. Built upon that level are the higher-order tasks of semantics (meaning), syntax (structure), and discourse (connected sentences). If you think of reading in this way, it is clear that some kind of phonics needs to be part of the teaching of reading to students with reading disabilities. Ken Goodman (1986) disagreed, seeing phonemic awareness (or, as Lori put it in the chapter-opening vignette, graphophonic awareness), semantics, and syntax as three equally valid cuing systems that are used to create meaning. He did not envision them in a hierarchy. What experts do agree upon is that phonics be taught, as should all of reading, in context, that is, as a part of *meaningful* reading. The aim is for students to read for reasons that they find relevant, that is, to accomplish something important to them. This "balanced" approach steers teachers away from drill-and-practice exercises that are isolated from real-world applications.

Experts also concur that teachers should let young readers *try something.* Let them make mistakes. For you as a teacher, this is an opportunity for assessment. The mistakes they make tell you what you need to teach. Vygotsky (1962, 1978) told us to begin where the child is. We discussed his "zone of proximal development" earlier in this book. That is what this is about. Teachers should encourage children to do a great deal of independent reading, including material that may be "above grade level." If it interests them, they will pursue it. (There is no other way to explain the extraordinary popularity of J. K. Rowling's *Harry Potter* series. Many avid readers of these books are, by any objective measures, "too young" for such difficult material.) Inevitably, students will encounter problem-words they don't know, sentence constructions they cannot decipher, and so on. That is when you step in as the teacher (Atwell, 1998).

Phonemic Awareness/Phonics and Students with Specific Learning Disabilities. Phonemic awareness is *the* great challenge of the largest contingent of included students, those with dyslexia and other reading disabilities. Even at the secondary level, individuals with specific learning disabilities may require explicit instruction as well as sustained practice in the basics of phonics, simply because their brains are wired in such a way that putting phonemes together, and using them to read, does not come naturally. This matters because, as we saw earlier in Chapter 3, students with dyslexia and other learning disabilities comprise some two-thirds (62%) of secondary students having any disability (U.S. Department of Education, 1999c, Tables AA2–AA4). Dyslexia causes students to err when they *say* words they are reading (when reading out loud). That is, students with dyslexia

Teacher Strategies That Work

Phonemic Awareness

Strategy	Explaining the Strategy	Example	Why It Works	Special Considerations/ Possible Accommodations
Phoneme Isolation	Teach students to recognize sounds within words	"Tell me the first sound in *paste.*" (/p/)	Some students with LD need explicit instruction in how to segregate phonemes	Direct Instruction tells you to teach this skill, give the student many practice opportunities, test knowledge, re-teach as needed, and test periodically thereafter.
Phoneme Identity	Teach students to recognize the common sound in different words	"Tell me the sound that is the same in *bike, boy,* and *bell.*" (/b/)	This gives children another way to learn to segregate phonemes	If student cannot do this, ask audiologist to test hearing.
Phoneme Characterization	Teach children to recognize the word with the odd sound in a sequence of 3 or 4 words	"Which word does not belong? *bus, bug, car* (car)	As above	As above
Phoneme Blending	Teach children to combine sounds to form a recognizable word	"What word is made up of these sounds? /s/ /k/ /u/ /l/ (school)	This task forces children to consciously blend phonemes	Phoneme blending helps with decoding
Phoneme Segmentation	Teach students to break a word into its sounds by tapping out,counting, or otherwise marking each sound	"How many phonemes are there in the word *ship?*" (3: /sh/ /i/ /p/)	This helps children to spell	Direct Instruction may be needed to teach variations (e.g., the same letters may represent different graphemes)
Phoneme Deletion	Teach children to recognize what word remains when a phoneme is removed	"What is *smile* without /s/?" (mile)	This helps children to write	Use non-words (e.g., *blig,* asking children to remove the /l/)

often have great difficulty with the *most basic* tasks of reading (Wadlington, 2000). However, they tend to do well (indeed, many do very well!) in understanding ideas. Shaywitz (1996) told the story of an adult with a reading disability who could and did master a demanding medical-school curriculum, yet was embarrassingly unable to pronounce the words he was reading. This illustrates the problem. It should also alert us not to underestimate the intelligence or the reading skills of students with dyslexia, but rather to recognize that their needs are very specific (hence the term "specific learning disabilities").

The No Child Left Behind Act of 2001 (PL 107–110) contains a Reading First program designed to ensure that children learn to read no later than third grade. This program is to be provided in general education and in inclusive classrooms, rather than in special education. The emphasis must be on early and intensive intervention, rather than on identifying children as having learning disabilities, suggested Lyon, et al. (2001). Their review of literature suggested that *prevention* of reading disabilities would be far more effective than would be remediation.

Teacher Strategies That Work

Phonics

Strategy	Explaining the Strategy	Example	Why It Works	Special Considerations/ Possible Accommodations
Analogy Phonics	Teach students to recognize new words by analogy to known words	Teach *brick* by showing that /ick/ is also in the known word *kick*	This helps children to both segregate and blend phonemes	Direct-Instruction may be needed to teach variations (e.g., the same letters may represent different graphemes)
Analytic Phonics	Teach students to analyze letter-sound relations in words they know	Teach that /f/ is in *finger, fine,* and *fair*	Students learn how to look at what they already know as sources of new information	Use non-words (e.g., *blig,* asking children to remove the /l/)
Embedded Phonics	Embed phonics in incidental and assigned reading	Say "sound it out" when student asks your help	Motivation may be greater with meaningful reading than with explicit lessons on phonics	Consult a speech/ language pathologist for assistance
Phonics Through Spelling	Teach students to segment words into phonemes, and to select letters for those phonemes	Allow "invented" spelling	This lets children write much earlier than they could if they had to spell well	Once the skill is mastered, you should insist upon accurate spelling
Synthetic Phonics	Teach children to blend the sounds to form recognizable words	Blend /b/ and /oo/ and /k/ to create *book*	Children can blend two- or three-phonemes but may have difficulty with more	Teach children to read larger sub-units of longer words, so that they need only blend two or three such units

Phonics and Students Who Are Deaf. Students who have hearing impairments, particularly those who are deaf, tend not to benefit much from phonics. This makes sense once you think about it. A young child encountering the printed word "elephant" for the first time, but knowing phonics, can "sound it out," producing the triumphant shout, "*Oh!*" as the connection is made between the printed word and the often-heard sounds. Hearing students, in other words, know their words; they just have to learn how to recognize them on a page.

Deaf students, by contrast, do not enjoy a personal history of having heard many thousands of spoken words. Simply sounding out printed words produces a string of sounds that, never having been heard, holds no meaning. One strategy is that students who are deaf or hard of hearing be instructed in *Latin word roots.* Easterbrooks (2001) reported upon other language-instruction practices recommended by "veteran teachers" of deaf and hard of hearing students. Included were modeling appropriate language, hands-on activities, visual aids and prompts, and peer-to-peer tutoring. These teachers tended to favor educator-directed rather than student-initiated instruction (e.g., Direct-Instruction versus facilitated learning). In addition, the PBS series "*Reading Rainbow,*" which is captioned, offers more than 150 episodes that encourage beginning readers to learn good reading habits. These are available from PBS itself and also from GPN Educational Media at the University of Nebraska.

For more information on how to access Reading Rainbow *episodes, go to the Web Links module in Chapter 14 of the Companion Website.*

Teacher Strategies That Work

Collaboration

Both general and special educators should use *miscue analysis* with oral reading
Both general and special educators should analyze student writing samples to identify mis-learned or unlearned rules of grammar and syntax
Both general and special educators should prepare *scaffolding* to guide student writing, especially of factual or fictional stories and of lecture/reading notes
Enlist the collaborative support of speech/language pathologists to give students who are deaf or hard-of-hearing extra help on vocabulary
Enlist the collaborative support of vocational rehabilitation counselors to help teach high-school students how to write material related to employment
Call upon occupational therapists and (for students who are blind) orientation and mobility specialists to teach survival words and phrases "in the community"
Use *planned serendipity* to select readings that will heighten class sensitivity to the needs of included students
General educators should consult with special educators before assigning reading that may cause difficulty for included students (e.g., *Of Mice and Men*)

Survival Words and Phrases

Which words *must* students learn? This question becomes a critical one when teaching students who are deaf or hard of hearing, who have mental retardation, and who have learning disabilities. There is considerable consensus around certain "survival" words and phrases. Polloway and Polloway (1981) listed many of the most important of these. Tables 4.1 and 4.2, in Chapter 4, have some of their recommendations. Notice that most of these words and phrases are important for safety and for getting around in the community. Elementary-school teachers should take whatever steps are necessary to ensure that children with disabilities master these words and phrases. University of Texas special-education professor David Katims (1999) was particularly adamant on this point with respect to instruction for students with mental retardation: "[T]he lack of content on literacy instruction for people with mental retardation in contemporary textbooks is deplorable" (p. 14).

In this, as in so many areas, collaboration between educators and related-services personnel is essential. One technique introduced earlier in this book that is directly applicable to the teaching of survival words and phrases is *community-based instruction,* or, as Langone (1998) called it, "situated learning" (see Chapter 8). The idea is to take students out into the community and teach them essential words and phrases as they find them (e.g., on street signs). The task of generalizing instruction is made much easier in this way. Orientation and mobility specialists, occupational therapists, and speech/language pathologists can assist teachers in such field-based instruction. The box above, "Teacher Strategies That Work: Collaboration," offers some suggestions.

Strategies for Teaching Reading

Scaffolding. Yopp and Yopp (2001) performed a real service to elementary teachers of inclusive classrooms in their *Literature-Based Reading Activities.* This 170–page text features scaffolding for many dozens of stories and books often read in elementary grades. *Scaffolding* is teacher-provided structure. It may be an outline that students may use in reading, or in writing. This chapter offers examples of scaffolding: the "Focus Questions" and the "Questions for Reflection" that open and close the chapter. Scaffolding thus may include definitions of key words, names and roles of fictional characters, and the like. Later in this chapter, you will see such scaffolding for many of the classics taught in middle school and in high school. Children and adolescents with mental retardation and those with learning disabilities such as dyslexia, as well as many with other disabilities, will benefit from such scaffolding.

Supplemental Activities. Yopp and Yopp (2001) also offered a rich variety of pre-reading activities (including questionnaires), during-reading exercises (such as literature maps), and post-reading projects (including Venn diagrams). These exercises are helpful for any student, including one with a disability.

Disability-Specific Interventions. In general terms (there are exceptions), students with emotional/behavioral disorders and those with attention deficits need *frequent breaks* while reading. They often benefit, as well, from learning experiences that allow them to get out of their seats and "*do* something." Individuals who are deaf or hard of hearing generally need vocabulary support, especially in the form of clear definitions of words they do not yet know. With respect to Shakespeare and other literature that is difficult to read, they may also require assistance with understanding the structure and syntax of the material. Students who have autism may be unable to grasp the basic idea that fiction is a creation of one human mind. They may read *Tom Sawyer,* for example, and come away convinced that it is a factual/historical account of a group of boys in post-Civil War Missouri. Poetry presents a problem of another order. While prose fiction takes us to "worlds" we might never otherwise "visit," poetry by its very nature is designed to take us into ourselves. That is, quite simply, a mental task beyond the capability of many people with autism. Dennis et al. (2001), for example, documented great difficulty by high-functioning children with autism with metaphors and inferential meanings of words. However, research has shown that they can comprehend elements of stories they read and can demonstrate that understanding through art (Colasent & Griffith, 1998).

Grouping. Children with all of these conditions likely will benefit from *group work,* especially from teacher-, aide-, and/or peer-provided tutoring. Perhaps in no area is group work more critical to successful inclusion than in the case of reading. Educational research convincingly shows that small groups help students learn more and enjoy learning (see the summary offered by Springer, Stanne, & Donovan, 1999). This is particularly true of *cooperative learning,* in which students work together under broad guidance from teachers (Ellis & Fouts, 1997). As defined by Cooper and Mueck (1990), cooperative learning is a "structured, systematic instructional strategy in which small groups work together toward a common goal" (p. 68). The teacher(s) provide each group with a goal and each group member with a specific task. This structure is particularly needed by younger students with disabilities. Mortweet et al. (1999) suggested that teacher(s) move from group to group, offering assistance, posing and also answering questions, and dispensing tokens to reinforce appropriate behavior.

Grouping tends to enhance engagement in the task and facilitates immediate one-on-one assistance precisely when needed. As we discussed earlier in Chapter 8, you should insist on two-way peer tutoring. Heterogeneous groups are recommended (e.g., Schumm, Moody, & Vaughn 2000). Students with learning disabilities may excel as peer tutors, explaining and illustrating obscure ideas; the fact that they have difficulty speaking out loud the words that they read should not dissuade you from giving them opportunities to tutor other students. Many individuals with attention deficits, similarly, are capable of real insights that could help other students to grasp difficult concepts. Some such students are highly creative. In these ways, the "regular" students in your class may come to recognize strengths in your "included" students.

Assessing Student Progress in Reading

At the elementary level, teachers need to analyze student performance so as to identify strengths and weaknesses. Formative evaluation looks diagnostically at student work so that teachers can adjust methods and materials. One such tool is miscue analysis. Teachers also need to track progress over marking periods and over whole school years. Summative evaluation documents student progress over these time periods. Portfolios are one way of showing what students have learned.

Miscue Analysis. A means of assessing reading skills is miscue analysis. Developed by Ken and Yetta Goodman (Goodman, Goodman, & Hood, 1989), **miscue analysis** is used with oral reading. As students read out loud, teachers note what mistakes they make. The Goodmans are the researchers Lori mentioned in the chapter-opening vignette. The Goodman approach uses copy editors' marks to code student errors. They urge teachers to pay particular attention to miscues that are *not* spontaneously and immediately corrected by students. The Goodman system differentiates between three categories of miscues. In grapheme-related errors, students do not make the appropriate connection between letters/words on a page and the sounds these represent; in other words, the failure in these cases is one of phonemic awareness. With respect to syntax-related errors, student mistakes show misunderstandings about how prefixes, suffixes, phrases, and clauses convey meaning. In pragmatics-related errors, students demonstrate a lack of real-world knowledge, that is, how language is used by members of the society.

Another method is to present students with nonsense words in grammatical sentences. That is what Debra Goodman did in *The Reading Detective Club* (1999). Good readers can figure out the part of speech (noun, adjective, etc.) of each nonsense word. Their ability to do this shows you that they have mastered key aspects of grammar and syntax. Students who are deaf or hard of hearing may have difficulties with such tasks. See the box, "Teacher Strategies That Work: Miscue Analysis with Deaf Students."

You might ask students with specific learning disabilities (SLD) to read out loud. However, when you do so, you should bear in mind that dyslexia, by its very nature, is known to cause difficulties in this task (see Chapter 3). What you may hear as the student reads out loud are dyslexia-caused problems. Because these may embarrass the student, you should avoid requiring children and youth with SLD to read aloud before the whole class. Rather, you should limit such assignments to more private settings, such as one-on-one sessions with you or with a related-services professional. Wadlington (2000) offered additional suggestions on teaching language arts to students with dyslexia (see Chapter 3).

Portfolios. Teachers may collect, in a large folder or bin, samples of each student's work. These samples should be chosen to illustrate progress related to state learning standards and the curriculum. At the elementary level, items may include book reports and journal entries documenting completion of assigned reading and of elective reading, test papers showing mastery of read materials, and the like. The principles of authentic assessment should be followed, notably criteria to be used in selecting items and in evaluating them (see Chapter 10). It is important that chosen items relate to *each* learning standard. If a child has not met a particular standard, that fact should be evident in the file. If extensive teacher correction and repeated attempts were required to produce an item that is included in the portfolio, that fact should also be noted. In these ways, portfolios may be used diagnostically. The child's future teachers can learn about the child's needs by reviewing the portfolio.

Accommodations, when appropriate to meet unique needs, may be helpful in high-stakes testing.

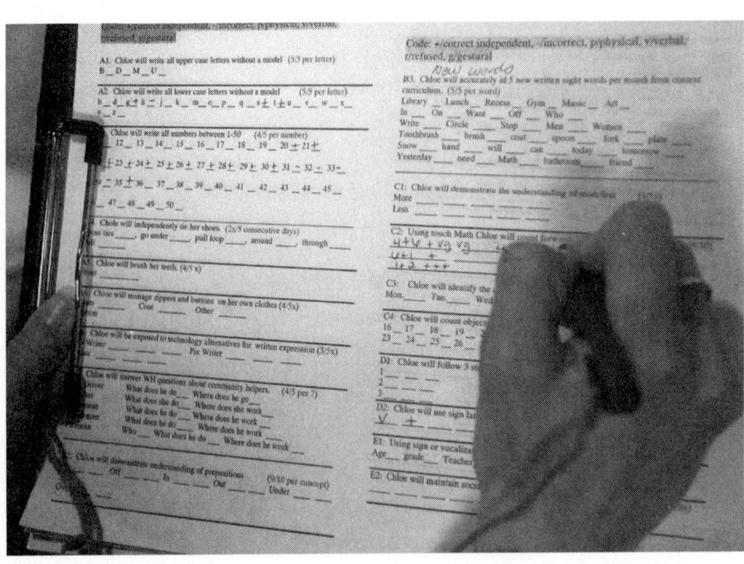

Teacher Strategies That Work

Miscue Analysis with Deaf Students

Miscue analysis can also help with students who are deaf or hard of hearing. After using the Goodmans's techniques with deaf students for nine years, Chaleff and Ritter (2001) recommended the approach, with some changes. First, sessions should be videotaped. Second, teachers should be alert for children fingerspelling rather than signing words (this may indicate that the child knows the letters but may not understand the word). Chaleff and Ritter suggested that two miscue-analysis tactics be added: repeating and pausing. When students who are deaf or hard of hearing repeat words or phrases, and when they pause during reading, these events should be recorded just as are omissions, self-corrections, repetitions, insertions, and the like. Chaleff and Ritter offered a 10-point procedure. Most steps should be familiar to readers who are familiar with miscue analysis. The items are based upon Figure 1 in Chaleff and Ritter:

1. Choose a book on the student's reading level.
2. Create or secure a typed copy of the text (to use in recording miscues).
3. Videotape the child reading (because teachers don't always catch everything that is signed).
4. Have the student read out loud (signing).
5. Record what is said/signed.
6. Ask the child to retell the story.
7. Probe miscues and any signs/fingerspelling you did not clearly understand.
8. View the videotape (see point 3, above), recording additional miscues.
9. Analyze.
10. Create goals and objectives for instruction. (p. 193)

Teacher Strategies That Work

Reading Recovery v. Miscue Analysis

We talked about Marie Clay's "Running Record," the assessment part of "Reading Recovery," earlier in this chapter. We have now discussed the Goodmans's "miscue analysis." You may be wondering about the similarities and differences.

Reading Recovery began in New Zealand. Clay developed and publicized her efforts in the late 1960s and into the early 1980s. Miscue analysis started in the United States. Ken Goodman, Yetta Goodman, and their colleagues published information about the approach in the late 1960s and into the late 1980s.

Clay's Reading Recovery and the Goodmans' miscue analysis are based upon *teacher observation* of children as they read out loud. Both make use of trade books and other materials that are at the child's developmental level in reading. That is, they use whole-language texts. Both call upon teachers to carefully record what the child says and does. Both protect children's feelings by conducting sessions in private (not within hearing of other children). Both are approaches that are well supported by an impressive body of research.

The two strategies differ in some respects. First, Reading Recovery is designed to be used with very young children (ages 6 or 7) who are struggling to read after completing one year of school. It is a short-term intervention (perhaps three or four months). Miscue analysis may be used with children of any age, although it is most used during the elementary years. There is no specific time frame for using it. Second, Reading Recovery does not involve taping the reader. Miscue analysis does. Third, Reading Recovery looks for errors. Miscue analysis, by contrast, does not regard all miscues as mistakes. Rather, miscues are considered to be neutral and items to be analyzed to understand the strategy the child is using to construct meaning. Some miscues show strength.

Tests. Teacher-made and standardized tests are also appropriate ways to assess student progress. Reading is one of the areas (math is the other) in which children in grades 3 through 8 are to be assessed each year, under the No Child Left Behind Act of 2001. The purposes of these annual tests are to show that students are progressing satisfactorily *and* that schools and teachers are following the curriculum. These statewide tests are norm-referenced, summative-evaluation instruments. They rarely offer diagnostic information. Teacher-made tests may be used as formative-evaluation tools, if the tests assess particular competencies (comprehension of the plot, description of the main characters, identification of the setting, etc.).

Teaching Writing

Instruction in writing begins at the elementary levels with the building blocks of printing and cursive writing and moves gradually toward the construction of clear and grammatical sentences, paragraphs, and essays. Students may start with short, factual stories. With scaffolding provided by teachers, the students should also learn how to take good notes. At the middle-school and high-school levels, the focus shifts to the finer points of narration, persuasion, tone, and character. Students should also learn how to write poems and short stories. Tompkins (2001) recommended use of *block scheduling,* a technique introduced earlier in Chapter 8. Uninterrupted time, preferably several hours in duration during each school day, is necessary. Writing cannot be learned, Tompkins asserted, in small chunks of time.

"Kid writing" (Tompkins, 2002, p. 176)—if accepted and encouraged by teachers—is a way to begin. Young children typically scatter letters around a page, only later learning to write in a straight horizontal plane. They will use invented spelling (Tompkins, 2001, p. 177). A key is indulgence on your part: The children need to recognize that it is acceptable for their writing to appear very different from yours. They do not have to be neat. They need not spell accurately, at this age. Stated differently, the message is that you are giving them permission to experiment.

Direct Instruction

An essential tool for the teaching of writing in inclusive classrooms is Direct Instruction. This is, you may recall, a combination of explicit teaching, careful review of mistakes, reteaching as needed, practice, and regular review: Of these steps, Gersten et al. (1987) found, the most critical are, in descending order: (1) immediate correction, (2) practice, and (3) periodic review. Close supervision alone is not enough; the writing itself should be meaningful to the student (Ruiz, 1989). We saw the emphasis upon meaningful instruction earlier, in our discussion of the teaching of reading.

Discovery Learning

How can teachers help young children who have not yet mastered the mechanics of writing, grammar, and spelling, learn to write? One approach is to just let them write—and learn those mechanics as they discover the need for them. The box, "Teacher Strategies That Work: Literacy in an Inclusive Third-Grade Classroom," which is based upon a year-long participatory research project by a doctoral student, illustrates the approach.

Atwell's (1998) *In the Middle* on teaching writing to middle-school students begins by assessing where students are. This is a widely recommended strategy (see Chapter 8). Atwell invites other teachers "to come out from behind their own big desks" (p. 4) and *try something*. Teachers should turn the classroom into a workshop. By that she means allowing students to choose, for themselves, what to write about, how to write about it, and for whom to write it—all choices that Atwell had as a writer but that PreK–12 students typically do not. She assigned *herself* the same writing assignments she gave her students. She didn't like doing them! That, in turn, led to the workshop idea: Teachers and students write together, commenting on each others' work. Atwell found that all of her students benefitted—and that she became a far better teacher.

Marie Ponsot and Rosemary Deen's (1982) *Beat Not the Poor Desk* is a text on methods of teaching writing. This one focuses upon reaching students of different abilities, particularly those known to previous teachers as "poor writers." I have also found that Kinneavy and Warriner (1998), in their *Elements of Writing,* provide many avenues of attack on the writing endeavor. Although not written specifically for use by inclusion teachers, their text nonetheless is invaluable for such professionals, because it focuses on the specific knowledge and skills necessary for good writing and offers a wealth of practice exercises. Whether you use this text, or another, the central point is that students with disabilities tend to need more instruction, and more practice, in writing than is generally the case with students who have no disabilities.

Teacher Strategies That Work

Literacy in an Inclusive Third-Grade Classroom

Bizzaro (2000) watched as Jenna, an 8-year-old African-American girl with low vision, asthma, and other physical conditions learned to read and write in a neighborhood third-grade classroom. Jenna's literacy portfolio for that year opens with an autobiographical story, in which she describes herself as "a girl who has black hair and glasses" and "a girl who likes basketball and play at her house" (sic). The collaborating teachers structured the day to include some shared reading, class discussion about the story, student writing, and student sharing of what they wrote. Virtually every school day students wrote something. They made entries into their journals, they wrote down things they had said in class discussion, and they wrote during "free time" about any topic of interest. Mrs. Kiellor allocated about an hour a day for journal and other writing. She encouraged students to experiment in their writing and to circle any words they thought they misspelled. She wanted them to engage in inventive spelling. Misspelled words became parts of weekly spelling tests. Mrs. Kiellor also taught them to write first drafts, to share these with each other, and to edit them.

When several children elected to write poems, Mrs. Kiellor gave a lesson on poetry. She later read them a mystery, a horror story, and a news story. Mrs. Kiellor helped them to discover the key elements of these genres. She then encouraged students to reread these stories on their own. They were urged to make predictions, to analyze characters, and to write summaries of the stories. Several girls opted to write their own mysteries; the boys chose to write horror stories. They also wrote "literature response journals" in which they commented on mysteries and other stories they read on their own. These journal entries were read aloud in heterogeneous groups. Commented Bizzaro, "Students routinely appropriated literary genres, themes, and stylistic devices from each other, modifying and expanding upon them as they saw fit. During their journal interactions, they networked and exchanged information through their stories" (p. 131).

Jenna gradually began to write about her feelings, not just factual information such as her gender or hair color. Using an illuminated magnifier, she read along as classmates read orally. Later, she read aloud herself. Her portfolio gradually grew, as she wrote expository pieces, poems, and stories. Her spelling continuously improved. So did her oral reading, as she came to "say it with expression" (p. 160). As did her peers, she learned punctuation when she saw a need for it. Similarly, she grew in her writing to be able to develop multidimensional characters, to include narrative details a reader or listener would need to make sense of the story, and a discernible beginning/middle/end for her creations.

Technologies That Work

Software for English/Language Arts

Young Children

"Word Hound" is software for early childhood/elementary reading instruction. It is marketed by MindPlay. The program helps young children vocabulary development and word recognition.

"Labeling Tutor" teaches children to associate words, sounds and pictures. Millennium Software is the source.

Older Children

"Ace Reporter," and other "Ace" software programs, teach middle-school and high-school students how to read for detail, read for main ideas, and engage in critical thinking. MindPlay is the source.

"Easy Street" is software teaching reading, math and problem-solving skills involving labeling, counting, classification, matching, and using money to pay for items. It is available from MindPlay.

For more information on software created by MindPlay and Millennium Software, go to the Web Links module in Chapter 14 of the Companion Website.

Writing about the teaching of Spanish-speaking students, Vernon and Ferreiro (1999) showed that early writing stimulates phonemic awareness and thus improves reading. Their findings have important implications for instruction of students with learning disabilities, many of whom struggle with phonemic awareness. If indeed the first-hand experience of transcribing sounds to letter combinations helps students to increase phonemic awareness, which appears to be quite likely, then writing in kindergarten and

Technologies That Work

Assistive Technologies

Students with physical disabilities such as cerebral palsy and quadriplegia, too often have been excused from writing at all; today's technologies make such exclusions inexcusable. With the aid of assistive technology devices such as augmentative and assistive communication systems (DynaMyte™ and DynaVox™ among them), even students with severe cerebral palsy can compose essays and book reports. These machines allow students to use different methods of input. They may write using a stylus, a head wand, or a pointer. Alternatively, they may enter text using computer speech recognition. Many of these programs can accept dictation of continuous speech. The student just talks into a microphone, and the software does the rest: It enters the words that are spoken. This software even checks spelling. Although the programs supposedly allow people to speak at "conversational speed," reality is that most users do not achieve speeds of better than 30 to 40 words per minute (wpm). That is because error correction is inevitable. On average, about one word out of every 20 will be entered incorrectly by the speech-recognition software. Fixing these errors is time-consuming. Still, 30 wpm is amazingly fast compared to other methods of input that many students having physical disabilities can use. For all of these reasons, it is no longer necessary to excuse such students from performing the same writing tasks that are assigned to other students.

Students with dyslexia and other reading disabilities may have bad, even atrocious spelling. This is because of the way their brains are wired. Even as adults, they will need to rely on rote memory, rather than on phonemic awareness, to spell accurately. Many use the spell checkers embedded in popular word-processing software programs. As a teacher, you should not expect too much from spell checkers. They are of rather limited help because they do not actually correct mis-spellings. Rather, they offer a list of possible words (via a drop-down menu), requiring the writer to know which is the desired word. Even then, the correct word appears on that list only if the initial letters are spelled correctly.

Inspiration™ and its counterpart for younger children, Kidspiration™, can help students with limited skills to write. These "organization" programs are particularly helpful for students with specific learning disabilities and many who are deaf. The templates that are provided with the program greatly assist writers in organizing essays (e.g., comparisons, character descriptions, etc.). See "Resources That Work: Writing and SLD."

For more information on Inspiration™ and Kidspiration™, go to the Web Links module in Chapter 14 of the Companion Website.

first grade should be encouraged (Yopp & Yopp, 2000). An approach pioneered by Samuel Orton, popularly referred to as "Orton-Gillingham" or "Gillingham-Stillman," helps students with learning disabilities to read words, then sentences, and then stories, using phonics, much repetition, and multisensory (visual, auditory, tactile) input (see Tierney, Readence, & Disner, 1995 for a discussion).

Assessing Student Progress in Writing

At the elementary level, teachers need to analyze student performance so as to identify strengths and weaknesses. Formative evaluation looks diagnostically at student work so that teachers can adjust methods and materials. One such tool is miscue analysis. Teachers also need to track progress over marking periods and over whole school years. Summative evaluation documents student progress over these time periods. Portfolios are one way of showing what students have learned.

Portfolio. You might require each student, early in the school year, to generate a portfolio of writing for you to examine. If so, choose fairly broad topics, since your interest is not in what they write but rather in *how* they write. Some example topics are "What I Did on My Summer Vacation," "What My Mother Means to Me," and, with older students, "My Favorite Author and My Favorite Book," "How I Keep Up with Political News," and the like. With younger children, oral dictation may be the method of output; someone, either a teacher aide or a volunteer, may transcribe the stories. Older children write by themselves. Once you have the material on paper, spend an evening or two analyzing it. Ask yourself, "What rules must have been used to produce this output?" Look for misunderstood or never-learned rules of grammar, of syntax, of spelling, and, with older students, of organization. This analysis tells you what you need to teach.

Resources That Work

Writing and SLD

A very helpful resource for teaching writing, particularly for students with specific learning disabilities (SLD), is the organizing software program called Inspiration™. This program offers a wide variety of "templates" (organizing rubrics) that guide students in outlining what they wish to write. There are templates for essays on literature (e.g., character descriptions, plot descriptions), science, social studies, and other subject areas. Particularly useful are compare/contrast templates. Students may insert text into boxes, bubbles, and so on, as they write. Once the graphic organizer is filled, students open the "outline" display to reveal a textual outline. They use this to write the essay. For many students, the result of using Inspiration to organize their thoughts before writing is a much richer, much longer, and much more cohesive essay than they typically produce without the assistance of this software.

Younger students (those in fifth or lower grades) may prefer Kidspiration™ instead. This version of the program features more graphics, pictures, and other symbols than does Inspiration™. In addition, Kidspiration has an easy-to-use text-to-speech (speech synthesis) capability. This lets children listen to the material as they organize it.

As this example illustrates, portfolios can be used to monitor and evaluate student progress. At the elementary level, items may include thank-you letters and "what I did on vacation"-type essays as well as creative writing (poems, songs, short stories). Criteria for selection and for evaluation should be established at the beginning of the school year (e.g., legible print or cursive writing, good spelling, well-formed sentences, etc.). To be most informative, portfolios should include not only samples of student writing but also annotations about those items. A well-written letter, for example, is best appreciated if the person reading it knows whether the student produced this version on the first draft or whether many drafts and much teacher assistance was required to produce this version.

Tests. Teacher-made and standardized tests are also appropriate ways to assess student progress. Writing may be assessed by requiring the student to generate an essay in response to a particular question. Inevitably, there is some subjectivity to evaluating written work. Errors of measurement may be reduced by having evaluators agree in advance upon standards to be used, giving evaluators sample essays that illustrate grading standards, and offering evaluators practice at applying those standards.

MIDDLE SCHOOL AND HIGH SCHOOL

As the focus in reading shifts from short essays and stories to book-length fiction, the challenge for teachers of inclusive classes increases. With respect to students who are deaf or hard of hearing, the introduction of book-length works, especially those dating from other eras and those making extensive use of idioms and vernacular speech, greatly magnifies the difficulties with vocabulary that is characteristic of students with hearing loss. Peer tutoring, speech and language pathology services, the assistance of a teacher aide, and other interventions may well be necessary so these students can make their way through the prose. Students with attention deficits and those with emotional/behavioral disorders may have great difficulty sustaining attention for book-length works. You may need to break up the reading into small chunks (perhaps a chapter at a time). You may also need to design active-learning opportunities, where students can make things or act out scenes (Wood & Nichols, 2000). Similarly, in the teaching of writing, the emphasis in middle school and high school turns away from the simple mechanics of writing and toward persuasion, organization, and writing for specific audiences and purposes.

Teaching Literature

Universal design in education (see Chapter 8) lends itself well to the teaching of the classics that children read in K–12 schools. As explained in the box on p. 495, "Technologies That Work: Universal Design and the Classics of Literature," technology helps educators to make these materials more accessible to students with disabilities, including those who have dyslexia or vision impairments. That is why it is much easier today to teach the classics to many of these students than it was in years past.

Recognizing the difficulties many middle-school and high-school students have in reading literature, Lederer (2000) recommended the use of what he called "reciprocal teaching"—a variation on what we have called guided discovery learning (see Chapter 8). Lederer worked with small groups of students with and without disabilities in an active discussion of texts. He taught them how to ask good questions about what they were reading, how to summarize text, how to predict what might happen next in a story, and how to help each other to develop deeper understandings of texts. Gradually, Lederer faded his support. He continually emphasized that the group work was *not* a competition, either within the group or against other groups. Rather, the aim was for each student individually to assume ever-greater personal responsibility for his learning and for helping others to learn.

Selecting texts that students find meaningful in their own lives is a well-accepted technique. Some classics help students with disabilities to develop insights into their own lives. J. D. Salinger's classic coming-of-age story, *The Catcher in the Rye* (1951), is an obvious example. Students with such disabilities as ADHD and emotional disturbance may relate very powerfully to Holden Caulfield's sense of alienation. A major advantage is that *The Catcher in the Rye* is one of the easiest-to-read classics in American literature. You might require included students to write a few pages of reaction, focusing upon their *personal* and *emotional* responses to the book. Some teachers say, for example, that Holden seems headed for a nervous breakdown. You might ask students to comment on whether his perception of the world is seriously "off." (If they are willing to share their thoughts with the class, that might offer an opportunity for group discussion and lead to greater insights by non-disabled students into the realities of living with a disability.)

The Scarlet Letter is another example. As do many students with disabilities, Hester Prynne had to deal with prejudice. Her response to public disapproval was to become defiant. Hester even took pride in the "A" she was forced to wear. Hawthorne's story ends without telling us how Hester's daughter Pearl will deal with that prejudice. Will Pearl harbor anger about what happened to her mother, or will she move beyond that? Adolescents with visible disabilities can use this classic as a springboard to an examination of their own attitudes toward their disabilities and toward society's perceptions of them.

Disabilities in Literature: Planned Serendipity

In teaching an inclusion class, you should take advantage of opportunities to use literature you assign to further non-disabled students' understanding of and appreciation about special needs. Fortunately, a rich body of literature affords you such chances. Many of these have film versions, as well, some of which are captioned. Any experienced teacher knows that today's video generation, reared on MTV and *Sesame Street,* will understand and appreciate literature with much greater ease if given the opportunity, first, to watch the story on video or film. Finally, as you read the discussions which follow, bear in mind that much literature is a source of trepidation for many students. Being able to read and understand these classics, on any level, could be a source of confidence and satisfaction for many included students.

Richard III. If you teach Shakespeare to a class that includes a student who has a physical disability, consider adopting one of Shakespeare's early plays, *The Tragedy of King Richard III.* (It is available as an e-text from, among other sites, that at the University of Virginia.) What a story this is! Set in England at the end of the late 1400s War of the Roses—between the forces of York, who wore white roses, and those of Lancaster, who wore red roses—*Richard III* takes us to the assumption to the throne of the great Queen Elizabeth II, who presided over a time of peace and prosperity as well as a unified royal family. In addition to teaching history, the play gives us links to geography (the towns of Lancaster and York in southeastern Pennsylvania), commerce (the ocean liner Queen Elizabeth II), and famous lines ("A horse! a horse! my kingdom for a horse!").

Richard III is, nonetheless, at bottom a story of character. Richard, leader of the red-rose Lancaster forces, had a hunchback. Shakespeare presented this as one reason why

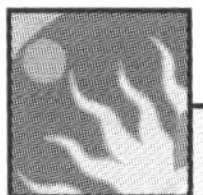

Technologies That Work

Universal Design and the Classics of Literature

One technique introduced earlier (in Chapter 8) is that of *universal design.* The approach, you will recall, features work by the instructor to make the course easier and more accessible for all students, including those with special needs.

A notable example of universal design in education that is useful in the teaching of language arts and English is *e-texts.* These are textbooks, poems, articles, and the like, that are published electronically. Electronically published books may be read in two principal ways: (1) online, that is, on the World Wide Web, and (2) off-line, that is, on CD-ROMs or after downloading them. Since e-texts are so readily applicable to the teaching of literature, both methods will be discussed here.

To date, most literature that is available electronically is that which is "off copyright" (e.g., publishers no longer owe royalties to the author). Much of what is read at the secondary level falls in to this category. One site, the Electronic Text Center at the University of Virginia (*http://www.etext.lib.virginia.edu/books*) has more than 1,000 books and other works, virtually all in two formats: online (readable in your browser by visiting the site) and downloadable. This site offers the Microsoft Reader® for downloading, free of charge. In late 2000, the site claimed to be shipping 250,000 books per month, an indication of the popularity of e-texts. Among the English classics available at this site are Louisa May Alcott's *Little Women* (1869), Emily Bronte's *Wuthering Heights* (1847), and Lewis Carroll's *Alice's Adventures in Wonderland* (1866), Herman Melville's *Moby-Dick, or, The Whale* (1851), and many of Shakespeare's plays (*Hamlet, The Merchant of Venice,* etc.)

A similar site is maintained at the University of Pennsylvania: http://digitallibrary.upenn.edu/books.

Other sites include Project Gutenberg (*http://www.gutenberg.net*), BookDigital (*http://www.bookdigital.com*), Barnes & Noble online (*http://www.bn.com*), BiblioBytes (*http://www.bb.com*), and the well-known Recordings for the Blind & Dyslexic (*http://www.rfbd.org*). Some texts are available from RFB&D that are not available from other sources, simply because many authors and publishers are willing to forego royalties in the interest of making materials available to this not-for-profit organization.

Reading literature online is much like reading it in print, with some notable exceptions. One good one is the use of *hotlinks.* These make it possible, and easy, for the reader to navigate from the text to virtually any site on the Web. If, for example, you are reading Jane Austen's *Emma* and you want to explore the author's own life to discover parallels to the novel, you can easily do that (several sites, including that at the University of Virginia, provide helpful links). Then, with a click or two on the computer mouse, you are back at the novel itself. On the downside, reading on a computer screen is more difficult than is reading on a printed page. That is why material written specifically for the Web tends to be short (e.g., about 500 to 1,000 words) and choppy (e.g., with lots of one- or two-sentence paragraphs). Books were not written for this medium. That means they can be challenging to read online.

The real advantages of electronic publishing come when books are read off-line. By downloading a text—say, *Emma*—and then opening it with a word processor, such as Microsoft Word® or Corel WordPerfect®, you can make use of powerful *search functions.* Continuing with the Jane Austen example, suppose you were studying the topic of money in *Emma.* Being aware that Austen's father was a minister and the family was decidedly middle-class, you could use the search button to identify virtually every reference to finances in the novel. There are a lot of those references. While one could locate most of them simply by reading the novel, chances are quite good that one would overlook some critical instances; with the search function, this task becomes much less onerous, freeing the researcher to think about what is said and what it means. This is particularly true because the search engine will locate references to money in places the reader might overlook, not expecting to find them there. As an example, a human reader would look for financial terms in dialogue and in textual descriptions of houses and their contents. She likely would not expect to find them in an author's descriptions of protagonists. However, Austen sometimes uses attitudes toward money to define character, that is, as a moral compass. The computer will pick this up, even if the human researcher does not. Similarly, if one were to research the setting for *Emma* (which was written after Austen returned to the much-loved Hampshire of her early years), one could search for descriptions of Highbury, the locale for virtually all of the action in this novel. Again, one could do this manually, by re-reading each page of the novel, but being human we would overlook some clues.

E-texts can also be read aloud, by a speech synthesizer, making the story accessible to people who are blind or have such reading disabilities as dyslexia. The word-processor functions of "thesaurus" may be used to identify synonyms and antonyms and to secure definitions. The spell checker is also available. You may create a *listserv* (e-mail list) through which students may exchange messages as they study a text. E-mail may be listened to rather than read, and it may be displayed or printed in large type, thus facilitating access for students who have vision impairments. The technologies of e-texts, spell checkers, listservs, and e-mail may be used by *all* students, not just those with special needs.

he is, to put it mildly, bloodthirsty: Action, Richard tells us, especially battle, is much to be preferred over quiet and peace, the better so he would not need to think too much about his physical deformities. He used his cunning mind and his silky tongue to win over those he did not simply kill. Step one in Richard's journey was to position himself to become King of England. Following the battle of Tewksbury in 1471, he proposed to the royal Anne, so as to solidify his leadership of the House of York. He did this *after* killing her father, father-in-law, and her husband, the Prince of Wales (which was the point, really). How he then got Anne to accept his proposal of marriage is a study in the powers of persuasion that has few parallels in all of literature.

Step two was to leap from prince-in-waiting to the kingship itself. Richard quickly had Anne killed, so that he could position himself to marry Elizabeth, of the House of Lancaster, and thus unite behind himself the warring forces of the white and red roses. He sought to marry her after killing Elizabeth's relatives, including two princes who were in line for the throne. (Is there *any* more satanic lead character anywhere in western literature?) Before he could win Elizabeth, however, Henry Tudor, Earl of Richmond and leader of the House of Lancaster, challenged him. Richard, the play tells us, fought like 10 men. His horse was killed underneath him. Richard fought on, all the while shouting that memorable line about "my kingdom for a horse!" The play ends with Henry killing Richard, marrying Elizabeth, and ushering in one of the great eras of the United Kingdom.

This play is a good selection for an inclusion English class because it forces students to confront a widely held but generally unspoken thought: that people with physical disabilities are bitter about them, and thus secretly vengeful. *Richard III* causes adolescents, famous for admiring physical perfection, to confront their often unexamined biases about the human body, including their less-conscious tendency to look down on anyone not possessing physical attractiveness. The included student, too, is given by class study of this play a natural opportunity to tell her classmates about how she feels about the disability. All of this can advance the class's movement toward one of the most cherished goals of inclusion: acceptance of people with disabilities.

Moby-Dick. Another frequently read classic, Herman Melville's *Moby-Dick,* or *The Whale,* presents less-direct illustrations of the same widespread assumption of many non-disabled Americans: that people with disabilities tend to be vengeful. As recently as the 1990s, this perception was resurrected in the motion picture *A Fish Called Wanda,* as a character who stutters delighted in "Revenge!" against his tormenter. In Melville's classic, Ishmael's physical disability seems to motivate him on his relentless pursuit of the whale. The reality is that most Americans with disabilities adjust well to their conditions and are not consumed with thoughts of revenge. While *Moby-Dick* perpetuates the stereotypes, reading it together in an inclusive classroom offers you, as the teacher, a chance to dispel the popular myth that people with disabilities are consumed with thoughts of vengeance.

The Heart Is a Lonely Hunter. If, on the other hand, you have a student with a hearing loss in your class, consider teaching Carson McCullers' classic novel *The Heart Is a Lonely Hunter.* Published in 1940 and set in the Deep South, this is a coming-of-age tale about a young girl, Mick Kelly, encountering the darker sides of adult life. This novel features a deaf man as a major character. John Singer is described as intelligent and sensitive, despite the fact that he neither hears nor speaks intelligibly.

This wonderfully written novel offers inclusion teachers an opportunity to guide students through an exploration of what it means to be alone and isolated in society. McCullers is at pains to help us see that the "obvious" reason "Mister Singer" commits suicide is wrong. He shoots himself soon after learning that his long-time friend, Spiros Antonapoulous, has died. McCullers warns us away from the idea that Singer commits suicide because he now had no other deaf people with whom to socialize. She dispels this theory by setting up a scene in which Singer encounters and has a brief conversation with three adults who are deaf. This meeting occurs right after Singer learns of Antonapoulous's death and just a day before Singer commits suicide. What the scene tells us is that being around others who are deaf that is, people with whom he can sign, is not enough, for John Singer, to give meaning to his life. Antonapoulous meant far more to Singer than that. The relationship was in some ways almost like a marriage: The two men had spent virtually all of their time, away from work, together. It was that much-deeper connection that Singer missed and without which life had no meaning.

If you adopt this book for class use, be sure to call student attention to the differences in the quality of life for people who are deaf today as compared to 1940. Most characters in *The Heart Is a Lonely Hunter* communicated with Singer by writing notes to him; Singer responded the same way. There simply were no other options. Today, however, people who are deaf can communicate with hearing people in a wide variety of ways. Making and receiving phone calls is both possible and easy. AOL's Instant Messager™ and similar services make interpersonal communication through the Internet just as available to people who are deaf as to persons who are not. In addition, deaf people today have access to interpreted events, captioned television, and even captioned first-run movies. It is still true, nonetheless, for all of these differences, that people who are deaf, just like people who are hearing, find meaning in deeply satisfying interpersonal relations and feel great loss if those are taken away.

Of Mice and Men. Another book that has disability as a topic is John Steinbeck's *Of Mice and Men*. One of the two protagonists in this 1937 book is mentally retarded. Steinbeck helps us to see how Lennie Small, like so many people who are mentally retarded, has difficulty with short-term memory and needs help with daily living (notably things most of us consider to be "common sense"). Yet he possesses positive traits as well; as the other protagonist, George Milton, notes, Lennie does good work. The title refers to "the best laid schemes o' mice an' men" but also to the mice that Lennie likes to pet. That desire foreshadows the book's ending. If you believe that your students are not ready, emotionally and/or intellectually, to recognize that most people with mental retardation are not, as Lennie was, a danger to society, you have a decision to make. You may elect to teach this book, so that your students read it under your guidance, recognizing that Lennie's huge size and great strength differentiate him from the vast majority of people with mental retardation. Alternatively, you may decide that discretion is the better part of valor. You do no favors for an included student who is mentally retarded if you give immature fellow students an excuse to harass him. Will your students understand why George has to kill Lennie? Will they see not only that Lennie is different from their classmate(s) with mental retardation but also that societal resources for people with mental retardation today are greater by an order of magnitude than they were in the 1930s and that such extreme measures are no longer appropriate? Those considerations may guide you in making your decision.

The Classics

In middle school and at the secondary level, instruction in English features the study of classics of literature. While there is much variation from state to state, and school district to school district, in which classics are studied at what grade levels, there are some books that are so widely adopted that they merit examination here. We begin with books frequently read at the middle-school level, notably *The Call of the Wild* and *The Adventures of Tom Sawyer,* and continue with literature often studied at the secondary level, including *The Great Gatsby* and *Hamlet*. In each instance, our interest is in how these might be taught in *inclusive classrooms*. That is, our focus is upon how teachers, including collaborating teachers, may adapt instruction so as to assist students with special needs. The scaffolding of each may prove useful as you teach these classics.

Universal Design and Assistive Technologies. Each of the classics discussed in this section is available from Recordings for the Blind & Dyslexic in the traditional human-recordings form and, increasingly, in electronic form as well. Some are available as e-texts from other sources as well (e.g., Shakespeare's plays). That is important for educators working to include students who are blind or have such reading disabilities as dyslexia (see the box on p. 492, "Technologies That Work: Assistive Technologies"). This section also includes *advance organizers* for each classic. These offer the title, author, and date of publication, a plot summary, and some key vocabulary. Finally, with organizers or anything else you write on a blackboard or display on an overhead or with PowerPoint™ you should be *redundant:* Speak out loud what you write and write the important words that you speak. You should also make use of *grouping* and of *peer tutoring*. These techniques, introduced earlier in this text, have been shown to increase student engagement. That is especially important if your inclusive class has students with emotional or behavioral disorders, attention deficits, or learning disabilities (Mortweet et al., 1999).

The Call of the Wild. Jack London's classic story of a pampered family dog who learns to live in the wild and later elects to live that new life is one of the shortest, easiest-to-read classics of American literature. *The Call of the Wild* takes as its theme the idea that dogs will revert to their heritage as wild animals (see the "scaffolding" for this book in Chapter 8). Class discussion could revolve around the extent to which students believe that the dogs, and for that matter, cats, in their neighborhoods are "truly" wild, and are only superficially domesticated. The book also offers you an opportunity to help young readers to consider *anthropomorphism,* or the giving by authors of human characteristics to animal characters. Jack London gives Buck, Spitz, Dave, and Billee human-like character traits. Most students with disabilities can participate on equal terms in such class discussions.

For students who are blind or have low vision, you could bring *manipulatives* into instruction by purchasing a set of toy animals (preferably dogs) and string that you would use to create harnesses for the dogs and traces connecting them. An alternative is to buy a toy Santa Claus sled, complete with reindeer; the basic concept of animals pulling a sled is what you need. Most published editions of *The Call of the Wild* include illustrations that will guide you in creating these manipulatives. By letting students who are blind or have low vision run their fingers along the traces, and feel the harnesses on the dogs, you can help them to envision key scenes in the book. The same set-up offers students who are mentally retarded an opportunity to "act out" some of these scenes.

Another helpful activity is to have the children watch as a dog is released from any harness/rope and allowed to chase a squirrel or other neighborhood animal. The transformation of the dog from a quiescent pet to an excited hunter illustrates London's central contention in *The Call of the Wild.* You can probably think of other opportunities to demonstrate that London was correct in saying that, given the chance, dogs will quickly revert to their wild state. These activities also give students with attention deficits or emotional/behavioral disorders opportunities for active learning, which will benefit them.

With students who are deaf or hard of hearing, extensive support on vocabulary may be necessary. While this is one of the easiest classics for middle-school and high-school students to read, the fact remains that hearing loss generally has very significant effects on children's vocabulary. The syntax and grammar of this book may also present challenges to deaf or hard-of-hearing students, notwithstanding the fact that, compared to other classics often read by adolescents, the sentences in *The Call of the Wild* are comparatively short and simple.

Adventures of Tom Sawyer. Samuel L. Clemens, writing as Mark Twain, created the archetype of American small-town boyhood in this 1876 classic. (A counterpart about girls, Louisa May Alcott's *Little Women,* appeared at about the same time. You might assign it to be read alongside *Tom Sawyer,* asking students to compare Civil War-era perceptions of boys and girls, particularly with respect to societal expectations, as well as the relative "wildness" of the Mississippi River area at that time versus the comparatively "staid" nature of New England.) One exercise you might assign is for students to identify the many superstitions Tom and the other boys picked up from the adults around them and to research their factual basis, or lack thereof. Students with learning disabilities such as dyslexia can do well in such assignments, because they tend to perform better at comprehending ideas than at the more basic aspects of reading (see Chapter 3).

Other than constructing a "cave" in a "mountain" to illustrate Tom and Becky in the cavern, an "island" to show their pirate adventures, or a "graveyard" to illustrate Tom, Huck, and the boys' witnessing of Injun Joe's murder of "young Dr. Robinson," there are not many ways to use manipulatives with *Tom Sawyer*. Acting out these scenes gives students with attention deficits or emotional disabilities chances to be "up and around," thus reducing unwanted out-of-seat behavior. Despite the fact that this is one of the easiest-to-read classics assigned in middle school and high school, students who are deaf or hard of hearing likely will need extensive assistance with the vocabulary.

Scaffolding: *Tom Sawyer*

Title: *The Adventures of Tom Sawyer*
Author: Samuel L. Clemens (Mark Twain)
Published: 1876
Grade Levels: 7 and above
Difficulty: Modest [short at about 200 pages, few difficult words, some vernacular in dialogue, e.g., "warn't it," "middling warm," "spunk water"]
Summary: Tom is an orphan living with his Aunt Polly in St. Petersburg, MO (the author's home town of Hannibal). It is a small, isolated community near the Mississippi River. The entire book is a picaresque series of boyhood adventures; Tom never grows up. One theme is the lesson Tom learns when he convinces others to pay him for the "privilege" of painting Aunt Polly's fence: "He had discovered a great law of human action, without knowing it—namely, that in order to make a man or a boy covet a thing, it is only necessary to make the thing difficult to attain."
Characters: Tom Sawyer
Aunt Polly, Tom's only living relative (his mother is dead; his father is never mentioned)
Becky Thatcher, a blonde girl Tom likes, daughter of Lawyer Thatcher
Huckleberry Finn, son of the town drunk, who is homeless
Joe Harper, another friend of Tom's
Jim, an African-American adult who befriends Tom
Injun Joe, a villain who kills Dr. Robinson
Widow Douglas, a strict woman Tom goes to live with
Vocabulary: juvenile pariah (how Huck is introduced)
adamantine (hard as steel; how Aunt Polly's resolve to punish Tom is described)
dilapidated (worn out)
immunity (freedom from punishment)
discordant (harsh)

The Great Gatsby. The challenge of this book, and its fascination, is the reader's search for the truth as narrator Nick Carraway gradually peels the onion on the story of James Gatz, son of an unsuccessful farmer, as he creates the persona of "Jay Gatsby" and later an extravagant lifestyle on Long Island as part of his obsessive pursuit of Daisy Fay Buchanan. Students with learning disabilities may appreciate the rich irony of this story, where nothing is as it seems, because it so much mirrors how they themselves see the world. Tom Buchanan is a character with whom some students with emotional/behavioral disorders or attention deficits may identify, increasing their interest in the tale. Tom has many emotional and behavioral "episodes" in the story.

Students with all of these disabilities may appreciate the splendid writing in this book, the many instances in which the reader must set down the book to smile, or even to gasp, at Fitzgerald's deft touch with the English language. His introduction of Gatsby, at the very end of Chapter 1, as Nick first glimpses him, is just perfect. The many descriptions of Daisy's voice, scattered throughout the novel, are evocative jewels (". . . her low, thrilling voice. It was the kind of voice that the ear follows up and down, as if each speech is an arrangement of notes that will never be played again."). These gems may pass unnoticed, however, by students who are deaf, as they struggle simply to understand the text. This story is much too subtle and ambiguous to be assigned to the vast bulk of students with mental retardation.

Scaffolding: *The Great Gatsby*

Title:	*The Great Gatsby*
Author:	F. Scott Fitzgerald
Published:	1925
Grade Levels:	11 and 12
Difficulty:	Challenging despite the fact that the vocabulary is not difficult and the sentences are not complex. Rather, it is the elusiveness of the story's "truth" that baffles many young readers.
Summary:	Nick Carraway, the book's narrator, introduces us to Jay Gatsby (we do not learn his real name, James Gatz, until half-way through the book) and to Tom and Daisy Buchanan, all of whom live on Long Island during the Jazz Age (early 1920s). There is an unreality to Gatsby's life and an unending speculation about how he came into the vast wealth he so ostentatiously displays. The core of the story is Jay's pursuit of Daisy, symbolized by his "trembling" fixation on the green light near her house. Gradually, Nick lets us in on some dark secrets of Gatsby's past and then ends the tale with Gatsby's death, friendless and alone.
Characters:	Nick Carraway, the story's narrator Jay Gatsby, the title character who is obsessed with Daisy Daisy Buchanan, Tom's wife Tom Buchanan, Jay's antagonist Jordan Baker, Daisy's friend
Vocabulary:	caterwauling (shrill) decadent (jaded) disillusion (disappoint) mesmerize (fascinate) pastoral (rural, farm-like) sardonic (sarcastic) swindle (steal from)

Hamlet. The setting for most of the action is the Royal Castle of Elsinore, in Denmark, circa 1600. That is 400-plus years ago and on another continent. Attracting and keeping interest thus is one of the teacher's greatest challenges. The language is another; Shakespeare's English is not our English. My experience is that the "famous lines" in Shakespeare's plays tend to be motivational for adolescent readers, who recognize that "educated adults" should know them. Some, however, will require some teacher explanation:

Hamlet (talking about his mother): "Frailty, thy name is woman!" Hamlet is saying Gertrude is inexcusably weak. He feels betrayed that his mother could marry Claudius, almost immediately after the death of King Hamlet.

The Ghost (the late King Hamlet): "of life, of crown, of queen, at once dispatch'd." Hamlet's father succinctly summarizes the reasons Hamlet should avenge his murder.

Hamlet (after hearing the Ghost): "There are more things in heaven and earth, Horatio, than are dreamt of in your philosophy." Hamlet is reflecting the belief, common at the time, that ghosts exist.

Hamlet (talking about Denmark to Rosencrantz and Guildenstern, who say they are happy to be back in Denmark): "Why, then, 'tis none to you; for there is nothing either good or bad, but thinking makes it so: to me it is a prison." Hamlet regards Denmark as a "prison" because of his father's murder.

Hamlet (to himself): "To be or not to be: that is the question." He is musing about his own will to live. This is certainly the play's most famous line. In part, that is because it encapsulates the vacillation he displays throughout most of the play.

Hamlet (to himself): "I will speak daggers to her, but use none." Preparing to confront his mother, he reminds himself to obey the Ghost's injunction to "leave her to heaven." He will not harm his mother, but limit himself to words: to "speak daggers" means he will tell Gertrude how angry he is toward her.

Hamlet (to Horatio): "Alas! poor Yorick. I knew him, Horatio." Hamlet is showing that he is resigned to life being both short and unfair.

Scaffolding: *Hamlet*

Title: *Hamlet*
Author: William Shakespeare
Published: about 1601
Grade Levels: 11 and 12
Difficulty: Challenging, because although it is English, it is a different English than today's students know.
Summary: The Ghost (Hamlet's late father) urges Hamlet to exact revenge upon Claudius, Hamlet's uncle and the new king. The Ghost cautions him, though, not to harm Gertrude, Hamlet's mother. Vacillating and debating with himself throughout the play, Hamlet ultimately resolves to kill Claudius. Before he can, however, Ophelia's brother Laertes duels with Hamlet. At the end, dying, Hamlet tell Horatio to tell the story of what has happened in Denmark.
Characters: Hamlet, Prince of Denmark. His father, King Hamlet, has just died and his mother, Queen Gertrude, has just married his uncle, Claudius, who then became King. Claudius is the killer of King Hamlet.
Horatio. Hamlet's dependable friend. At the play's end, Horatio is the person Hamlet selects to tell the world what really happened in Denmark.
Ophelia. She is an innocent young woman Hamlet loves. Her dominating father, Polonius, is an advisor to Claudius. Her brother Laertus is protective of her. Ophelia suffers greatly in the play.
Vocabulary: rank (foul smelling)
knave (bad person, fool)
augury (fortune, prophecy)
insinuation (hinting, indirectly)
conjunctive (connecting, necessary)
dally (waste time, put off acting)
union (pearl, with which the drink is poisoned)
envenomed (the sword is poisoned, tipped with venom)

To keep students with attention deficits or emotional disorders involved in *Hamlet,* you might give them a treat like Tom Stoppard's *Rosencrantz & Guildenstern Are Dead* (Grove Press, 1991). No writer has ever mimicked Shakespeare's dialog as did Stoppard. This modern comedy makes wicked fun of Shakespeare's play, describing Hamlet's saga from the point of view of two bumbling commoners, Rosencrantz and Guildenstern, who are minor characters in Shakespeare's play. An alternative for students of lower academic achievement is to let them read the version of *Hamlet* in Richard Armour's (1957) *Twisted Tales from Shakespeare.* Armour's parodies aim straight for an adolescent's sense of humor. Students who are deaf or hard-of-hearing and those who have mental retardation very likely will find this play (or any other Shakespearean play, for that matter) to be extremely difficult. Youth with mental retardation may also be given brief, simple summaries of the play (see "Scaffolding: Hamlet").

For students with learning disabilities such as dyslexia, who often are very good at conceptual thinking, you might give this assignment: "It has been said that the real tragedy of *Hamlet* is that the prince died just when he had matured to the point where he was ready to be a great king. Quoting from the play, support or refute that statement."

Connect the Plays to 20th-Century Figures. A good motivational tool is to tie the play to more modern events with which students are familiar. (It may well be necessary first to make them "familiar" with historical figures. I never cease being amazed how many high-school students lack awareness even of very recent history!) Hamlet, as a vacillating figure, can be tagged with the chorus (a take-off on the Nike slogan) "Just do it, Hamlet!" (Murphy, personal communication, 2004).

Another modern parallel is that of Ophelia with Marilyn Monroe. Constance Collier, the great drama coach who worked with Katharine Hepburn, among others, was reported (by Truman Capote in the piece, "A Beautiful Child," in his 1975 book, *Music for Chameleons* [Random House]) to have made the following comment about Monroe (Norma Jean Baker): "She could be the most exquisite Ophelia." You could encourage students to draw on their knowledge about Norma Jean Baker, especially her poverty-stricken childhood with a

Teacher Strategies That Work

Murphy's Recommendations

Murphy, who prepares teachers of English at the middle-school and secondary levels, has recommended stories, films, and texts that offer "serendipitous" opportunities for students to learn about and discuss disability (personal communication, 2004). She reported that she and the preservice teachers she works with built a unit around William Gibson's (1960) play about Helen Keller, *The Miracle Worker,* with Mark Medoff's play/movie about an angry deaf woman, "Children of a Lesser God," and the Hollywood Film's movie "Mr. Holland's Opus"—all of which deal with deafness. She added that Chris Crutcher's (1987) story, *The Crazy Horse Electric Game,* which tells the tale of a young man with a promising baseball career who becomes disabled in a water skiing accident, and Robert Cormier's (1998) *Heroes,* which recounts the lives of two badly wounded World War II veterans, encourage students to talk about how people can re-create their lives after debilitating injuries.

Dr. Murphy specializes in the teaching of Shakespeare. She recommends this way of teaching Shakespeare: "Do scenes. Period. It works!" (personal communication, 2004). A good place to start is the Drama Teacher's Resource Room, at *http://www3.sk.sympatico.ca/erachi/.* This site offers tips on rehearsing plays and a good glossary of drama terms. "Doing scenes" makes sense because Shakespeare was, after all, a writer of *plays.* He intended them to be seen and heard, not read. She reported success with methods outlined in the Folger Library's *Shakespeare Set Free* publications. For example, *Shakespeare Set Free: Teaching Hamlet and Henry IV, Part I* (1994) makes the point:

> Shakespeare study can and should be active, intellectual, energizing, and a pleasure for teacher and student. This is not about *acting.* It's about *doing.* When students get his language in their mouths and take on the work of actors, directors, and scholars, they find themselves engaged in the very best kind of close reading . . . This is the learning process. This is also *very* good teaching. . . . [W]e have good evidence that students who learn Shakespeare through the *process* of performance and through the *process* of a collaborative investigation of the play with their teacher and their classmates have a much greater understanding of Shakespeare's language than students who sit and have things explained to them. . . . (p. xiii; emphasis in original)

"Do scenes!" urges Maureen O. Murphy, a Shakespeare scholar.

Dr. Murphy also recommended the "adapted classics" also included in the Simon & Schuster Folger Library series. An example is *The Tragedy of Julius Caesar: An Adapted Classic* (1992). This text includes the play, but each page also offers short definitions for words that may not be familiar to high-school students. There are brief synopses offered before and after each scene. Large print is also used, which helps students with low vision.

Similarly, the *Folger Library General Reader's Shakespeare: Hamlet* (1992) offers the play on odd-numbered pages, with even-numbered (facing) pages having definitions of such terms. Because of the way books are laid out, this gives students at-a-glance assistance: As the book sits on a table or lap, the left-hand pages contain definitions of words appearing in the right-hand pages that have Shakespeare's language.

deranged mother and her well-publicized travails as an adult—you may find Joyce Carol Oates's novel *Blonde* (Ecco Press, 2000) to be especially revealing about her character—to compare the two women and then agree or disagree with Collier's comment. Murphy (personal communication, 2001) concurred that today's high-school students tend to "have great empathy for Ophelia: What forces drive her to madness and suicide? What forces in our world drive young people to similar actions? Can we help? How?" She added that student study of the "Ophelia complex" might help them gain insight into the character. Mary Pipher's (1999) *Reviving Ophelia,* especially, but also Sara Shandler's (1995) *Ophelia Speaks,* offer informa-

Teacher Strategies That Work

English/Language Arts

Include *phonemic awareness* as part of a comprehensive approach to reading

Elementary teachers must ensure that **all** students learn survival words and phrases (Polloway & Polloway, 1981), especially through *community-based learning*

Classwide peer tutoring, particularly if it is reciprocal, is an excellent strategy for learning both reading and writing

Scaffolding can help young students to learn how to write stories and how to take notes

Use *block scheduling* in middle school and high school to carve out time periods of sufficient length to teach reading and writing

Give students with attention deficits, emotional disorders, or mental retardation *short* assignments in reading and writing, with frequent breaks

Offer students who are deaf/hard of hearing, who have attention deficits, or who have emotional disorders opportunities to act out stories they are reading

Use *manipulatives* for students with hearing loss or mental retardation

tion about this "teenage girl as victim" phenomenon. Another possibility is to read, or watch the movie based upon Jeffrey Eugenides's (1993) *The Virgin Suicides.* This is a story of four sisters who self-destruct as their youthful ideals erode. Then-teen heartthrob Kirsten Dunst stars in the movie, which may make the film an appealing way to study Ophelia's character.

Assessing Student Progress in Literature

Students are assessed annually in reading through grade 8, under federal law. Many states impose a reading test as a requirement for high-school graduation. These summative-evaluation instruments are helpful in showing that students have mastered material. They are not, however, useful diagnostically. Portfolios, if assembled pursuant to the principles of sound authentic assessment, can help to pinpoint student strengths and weaknesses.

Portfolios. Test papers showing student mastery of assigned literature, results from annual assessments of reading (grades 7 and 8), a playbill showing the student had an acting role in a school play, a tearsheet of a student-written review of a play or movie based on a classic of literature, and book reviews written for class all are examples of work that may be included in a portfolio. It is vital that portfolio entries correspond to state learning standards. Thus, if students are expected to have read well-known minority writers, women writers, and writers from, say, South America, the portfolio should include at least one entry in each area. Dr. Murphy recommended that student reflection be required for all portfolio entries: Why did they pick this piece? What were they trying to achieve with it? Do they believe they were successful in doing so?

Tests. Teacher-made and standardized tests are also appropriate ways to assess student progress. These tests generally are of little diagnostic (formative evaluation) value. They can, however, provide a basis for summative evaluation of student progress.

Teaching Writing

Direct Instruction is often as necessary at the secondary level as at the elementary. Teaching the tools of the trade—organizing, proofreading, and, most important, re-writing—combined with line-by-line review, re-teaching, practice, and regular review probably are best accomplished in small groups. Gersten et al. (1987), in their review of a quarter-century of research and practice with Direct Instruction, showed that it is as applicable to higher-order writing, such as poetry or persuasion writing, as it is to the basics of spelling, number agreement, and syntax. At the middle-school and high-school levels, the emphasis is upon writing *for a purpose.* Book reports, business proposals, resumes, and the like have their own formats.

These must be learned. The writing of fiction and of poetry introduces yet other skills. All of these can be learned not only through instruction but also with considerable practice. Direct Instruction, combined with small-group work in which students help each other, can be very useful. Again, as in the elementary grades, *block scheduling* is an administrative measure that can be used to carve out the time that is required. If some students must forego some "specials" in order to free up this time, that seems to be an appropriate trade off.

The Kinneavy and Warriner (1998) text, *Elements of Writing,* offers chapters on the many techniques required for successful writing at the middle-school and high-school levels, as it does at the elementary-school level. Students need to learn when and how to cite references, how to handle quotations, how to structure different kinds of letters (personal, business, etc.). They also need to learn the difference between reporting and persuasion: how to write a narrative that presents facts and how to weave arguments in such a way as to sell an opinion to a reader. Writing instructions is a good exercise for learning to communicate clearly. It forces students to identify topics of interest to intended readers (e.g., how to fix a flat bicycle tire, for eighth-graders), to collect needed facts, to organize steps in a logical order, to write clearly and unambiguously, to revise, and to proofread. The strategies and tactics appropriate to such writing are illustrated by Kinneavy and Warriner.

For students with hearing impairments, particularly deafness, the grammar and syntax of writing are often challenging, even after these students enter high school. Their vocabularies tend to be still quite impoverished. Even with good instruction, many adolescents who are deaf will write at a fifth- or sixth-grade level. They need, more than anything else, (1) a wealth of reading, so they learn grammar, syntax, and vocabulary in context, (2) explicit instruction in the rules of writing well, and (3) plenty of practice.

These issues highlight the complex nature of writing. As anyone who has done much writing is aware, the well-known fact that the human mind can focus on and remember between six and nine items of information at any one time has a practical impact: Good writing requires several drafts. (This is why so many writers say that the real work of writing is re-writing.) If a student is concentrating upon content, making sure to "cover" the topic, she will of necessity neglect grammar and style: There will be simple errors of writing. Once the content is "down," organizing it in a logical sequence requires that the essay be re-written: Even the best writers have difficulty dealing simultaneously with content and organization. A logical final step in composing an essay is to double-check spelling (especially words that are not flagged by word-processing programs as misspelled) and grammar (particularly agreement in number, e.g., "he" goes with "is" and not "are," etc.).

However difficult it may be, mastery of the tools of writing is an essential competency for secondary students. They need these skills in mathematics (Woodward, Monroe & Baxter, 2001), social studies (Singer, 1997), science (Koch, 2002), and other content areas. Students must be able to write persuasive essays, concise summaries of project activities and findings, factual reports on events (the classic who, what, where, when, how, and why of journalism), and a range of other products. They need these not just as adults but as students in high school.

Disability-Specific Issues in Writing

Students with specific learning disabilities (SLD) may spell very badly and may submit poorly organized essays and papers. Both types of problems relate to the nature of SLD (see Chapter 3). However, the spell checker and grammar checker that is part of Word® and WordPerfect® (as well as other popular word-processing programs) can help—if the student is taught how to use these and is encouraged to do so. The substance of what students with SLD say, including the accuracy of information and the creativity of expression, should not be affected by the condition.

You may find that students with emotional/behavioral (E/B) disorders and many with attention deficit disorders (ADD) or attention deficit hyperactivity disorders (ADHD) turn in work before it is ready to be submitted. They may not devote the necessary time to researching material, nor to editing their work. These problems illustrate the impulsivity that often accompanies these disabilities. You should firmly return the papers to them, indi-

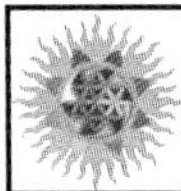

Lesson Plans That Work

Writing Well

If you are teaching writing in a middle-school or high-school classroom, you might group students into heterogeneous reciprocal peer tutoring dyads (a strong writer paired with a weak writer). You might assign one dyad to prepare a cover letter (to accompany a resume) in response to a job ad. Another dyad might be asked to write a proposal for consideration by the board of education (to, for example, increase the district's budget for field trips). A third dyad might be asked to write a speech nominating someone for public office. There are many other possible assignments. You may ask the dyads to recommend their own projects.

You should give each dyad a rubric for writing well. This might feature the following:

- Organization: Is it logical? Does it pave the way for each new idea? Is there a clear beginning, middle, and end?
- Clarity: Does it say what it says without excess verbiage? Is active voice used when appropriate? Are words used that the intended audience certainly or very probably knows? Are direct, simple sentences used rather than compound-complex sentences?
- Accuracy: Are the statements made correct? Are claims documented?
- Appropriateness to Intended Audience: Does the piece speak to the intended audience in appropriate ways (e.g., one speaks differently to the board of education than to peers in a class)?
- Interest Level: Are the words chosen, the examples selected, and so on, lively enough to engage the audience? Sometimes, surprising your audience is a good way to get and keep its attention.
- Appropriateness for the Purpose: Do the format, layout, and so on, comply with conventions for the type of writing being done (one uses different styles of writing for formal, discursive, investigative, and other kinds of writing)?
- Spelling and Grammar: Are all words spelled correctly? Are all sentences grammatical?

You would ask each member of the dyad to read the other's piece, checking the above elements. Students may request your involvement if *both* members of the dyad agree to make that request.

You might select, at random, one or two persons to read out loud. (Students should not know in advance which dyad would be chosen, nor which member of that dyad.) Other students would be invited to comment on the extent to which the piece responded to the elements in the rubric.

---

cating that you expect more complete products. Nothing about these conditions prevents people from giving you work that reflects the level of attention to detail that you demand from others.

Children and youth with mental retardation may produce written work that falls short of what the same students could deliver orally. Often it is not realistic to expect people with moderate to profound mental retardation to express themselves clearly and well on paper. Rather, you should encourage them to show you what they have in mind (demonstrate it, e.g., by play acting) or to tell it to you orally.

Students who are deaf or have other hearing impairments typically have great difficulty with the written word. Their written work may feature very limited vocabularies as well as ungrammatical sentences. Spell checkers and grammar checkers may be of limited use to these students. This is because the software flags what it considers to be errors but does not actually correct mistakes. Rather, users are given options in a drop-down menu. Deaf children and youth may not know which option to select. Thus, the material they submit may not meet your standards notwithstanding the level of effort they put into the project. You should encourage them to work with a "writing buddy" who can assist them in the writing endeavor. You should also arrange for tutoring and other kinds of additional support.

The written work of students who are blind or have low vision may be of high quality if these individuals are provided with the appropriate assistive technologies. There are newspaper editors who are blind—a position one would not casually associate with blindness. The technology has advanced that far! See Chapters 6 and 8 for more information on technology and blindness.

Public Speaking. A key competency in the English/language arts curriculum is writing persuasive pieces (speeches, opinion-editorial or "op-ed" pieces, advertising, etc.). These skills can be taught as part of the social studies curriculum. The elements of persuasive writing were presented in Kinneavy and Warriner's (1998) *Elements of Writing*. A controversy

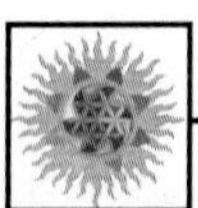

Lesson Plans That Work

Public Speaking

Young people with disabilities tend to have far fewer opportunities to write and present public speeches than is generally true of their age peers. Yet, people with disabilities, as well as persons with other special needs (see Chapter 11), may be strongly motivated to become effective public speakers so that they might influence public opinion and thereby change laws and social mores. For these reasons, teaching students with disabilities how to write and make speeches is a good use of time in an English classroom.

The art of public speaking has two key elements. The first is writing the speech. Suggestions given in the previous box, "Lesson Plans That Work: Writing Well," apply. In particular, the speech writer must be very clear about the intended audience, the purpose of the speech, the occasion, and the time of day the speech will be given. A speech made to a community group will be written differently from a speech presented to fellow students. One that urges action must be written differently from one that presents information. An award-acceptance speech differs from a nomination speech. A dinner speech needs some elements that differ from the components of a convention speech.

For students with disabilities, opportunities for public speaking may be priceless preparation for a life of advocacy.

The fact that speeches are given orally imposes some requirements on, and offers some opportunities for, the speech writer. In particular, the writer and the audience are face-to-face, in the same room at the same time. This means that emotions can be signaled in an unambiguous way (humor, sarcasm, and other tools of communication may work far better in a speech than in an article). Speeches may be *interactive* if the writer takes care to build into the speech natural pauses and questions (e.g., the "call-and-respond" pattern found in sermons written for delivery in many African-American churches). Students who are not confident about the intelligibility of their speech should be especially careful to create natural pauses so audience members may offer suggestions (e.g., to speak louder, to draw closer to the microphone, etc.). Speeches address many people simultaneously, rather than, as is the case with an article, one-by-one. This fact means that the speech writer has an opportunity to take advantage of the sociology of groups (e.g., appealing to emotions that may galvanize people to look to each other to act on some issue or problem). Audience members cannot discover the length of the presentation as easily as can readers with a printed article, the speaker must give them clues (e.g., "I have five points to make about this. First, . . . Second, . . . " and "In conclusion, let me say . . . ").

Speeches need not necessarily be delivered in the speaker's own voice. They may be signed. Schools for deaf students typically offer courses in public speaking during which students learn how to sign clearly and effectively to a large audience. If, as is likely, an interpreter voices for the speaker who is deaf, the student should supply the interpreter with an advance copy of the speech. This way, the voicing will be much more smooth. Assistive technology devices can also be used in public speeches. Physicist Stephen Hawking uses a computer speech synthesizer as his voice during public lectures. If one of your students does, he needs to be careful to make sure that the artificial voice is both loud and clear.

That much being said, in some cases students with disabilities may be more effective, and more satisfied with the results, if they participate on a team that together prepares the presentation and chooses a member to deliver it. This is particularly true for many young people with mental retardation. The opportunity to influence what is said can be a treasured one. The feeling of contentment after a speech is well received may be no less for being vicarious. Often, individuals with disabilities are motivated to make public speeches because they want to change society. For this reason, the tools of advocacy rhetoric are important for students with disabilities to learn (see "The Social Activist Framework," in Chapter 16). I have learned a few lessons over the years about such speeches. First, members of the general public (whether or not they acknowledge it) often expect individuals with disabilities to be angry and resentful about their conditions (shades of *The Hunchback of Notre Dame* and Ahab in *Moby-Dick!*). Accordingly, I find that if I surprise them by displaying an equanimity and a sense of humor about my disability, I can predispose them to react favorably to my presentation. Second, I find that if I take care to connect what I want to benefits for *them* as non-disabled persons, I usually get a better reception. Finally, if I give the audience steps they can take, without investing too much time and effort, I can get them to act.

in this area is whether to acknowledge opposing views. Some experts argue that you need to "inoculate" your audience against alternative points of view. Others say that you should stick to your case, because you have limited time to inform and influence people. Another controversy is whether you should "stoop" so low as to appeal to base human emotions. The tactics you may use include

- Identifying a topic that matters (to you, to others in your community/state/nation/etc.)
- Identifying your audience (you will write/speak differently to peers than to bankers, for example)
- Deciding what your goal is (to influence attitudes? to provoke people to act?)
- Stating your opinion (clearly and accurately)
- Presenting facts that support your position and showing why these are persuasive
- Optional: Presenting facts that undermine your position and showing why they are not persuasive
- Optional: Appeals to emotion (patriotism, pride, etc.)
- Take-home message (summarize what you want people to think and/or do)

Teachers could ask students to bring to class samples of advertising from newspapers and magazines. They could also bring op-ed pieces. Some may tape TV commercials. These examples of persuasive writing should be analyzed. How effective are the samples? Of those most students agree are indeed persuasive, what elements make them so? Of those they find unpersuasive, what aspects undermined the case?

For more on public speaking, see the nearby box, "Lesson Plans That Work: Public Speaking."

Assessing Student Progress in Writing

At the middle-school and high-school levels, teachers need to assess different kinds of student writing. Standards should be established at the beginning of each school year. Students need to be told not only what kinds of writing will be evaluated but how each will be graded.

Portfolios. Because creative writing, business writing, scientific writing, and other kinds of writing are included in most state learning standards for middle-school and high-school students, samples of each are needed for a portfolio. As at the elementary level, annotations explaining how a piece of writing came to be helps others to evaluate student work. Was a given writing sample produced independently? In a group? With teacher help? Was the writing assigned or was it volitional on the student's part? Was the writing actually used in the student's life outside the school? Details like these help evaluators to assess student work.

Tests. Teacher-made and standardized tests may assess student progress in writing. Some teachers give separate grades for student writing. One grade relates to the content (acceptable for English 11, for example). The other grade applies to the writing itself (grammar, syntax, spelling, etc.). Standardized tests have strict time limits. Teacher-made tests sometimes do and sometimes don't. Some teachers allow students to submit drafts for editing before a final version is graded.

CHAPTER SUMMARY

- Journal articles tend to ignore the teaching of Language Arts and English at the secondary level. Texts, too, usually emphasize instruction at the elementary level.
- Phonemic awareness is a mental capacity, one we use to pull out phonemes from words we hear and to create spoken words from discrete phonemes.
- Phonics, by contrast, is a teaching method, one that asks children to sound words out in order to make the connection between spoken and printed words.

Much literature now may be read online.

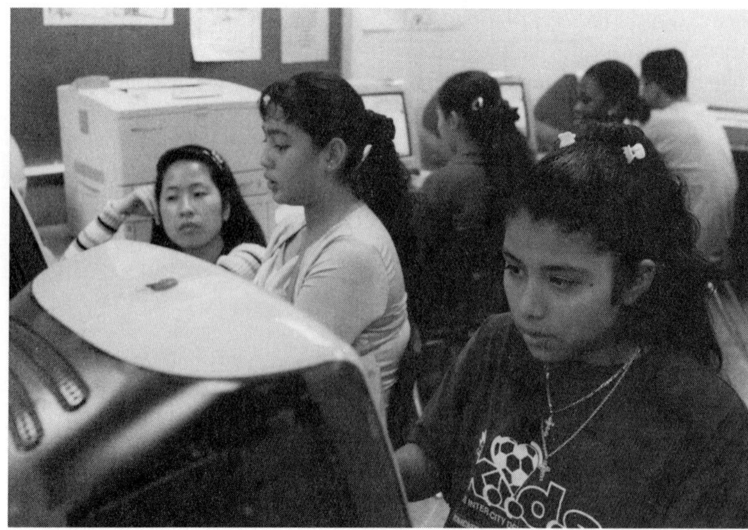

- Literacy is the ability to use reading and writing for practical purposes.
- Miscue analysis is an assessment tool that examines mistakes students make, especially those they do not immediately and independently correct by themselves.
- Community-based instruction takes students out into the community to learn on-site. This greatly eases the mental burden of generalizing instruction.
- Scaffolding is a teaching technique that gives students "hooks" such as plot outlines, thumbnail sketches of key characters, definitions of new words, and so on.
- Cooperative learning, in which teachers give students structure for their work in groups, has been shown by much research to be effective in inclusive English and language arts classrooms.
- *Richard III* forces students to confront their stereotypes about physical perfection and its corollary that people with physical imperfections are bitter and vengeful.
- The everyday lives of deaf people in America today are vastly richer and more rewarding than those of the characters in the 1940 novel, *The Heart Is a Lonely Hunter.*
- Direct Instruction in the mechanics of writing continues to be necessary through the secondary years, with many students having disabilities.

QUESTIONS FOR REFLECTION

1. How could you use miscue analysis to help a student with dyslexia?
2. How is today's phonics different from "our mother's phonics" (quoting Shaywitz)?
3. What problems prevent many deaf students from benefitting from instruction in phonics?
4. How would you use Direct Instruction to teach writing at the elementary level?
5. How would you use the scaffolding in this chapter to teach *Tom Sawyer?*
6. What is it about *The Great Gatsby* that confuses many young readers?
7. What do teachers do in cooperative learning?
8. Why is it especially important for students with disabilities to master public speaking?
9. Why should inclusion teachers of English be careful with *Of Mice and Men* and, to a lesser extent, *The Heart Is a Lonely Hunter?*
10. What advantages might accrue to students reading *Hamlet* as an e-text?

Chapter 15

Math and Science

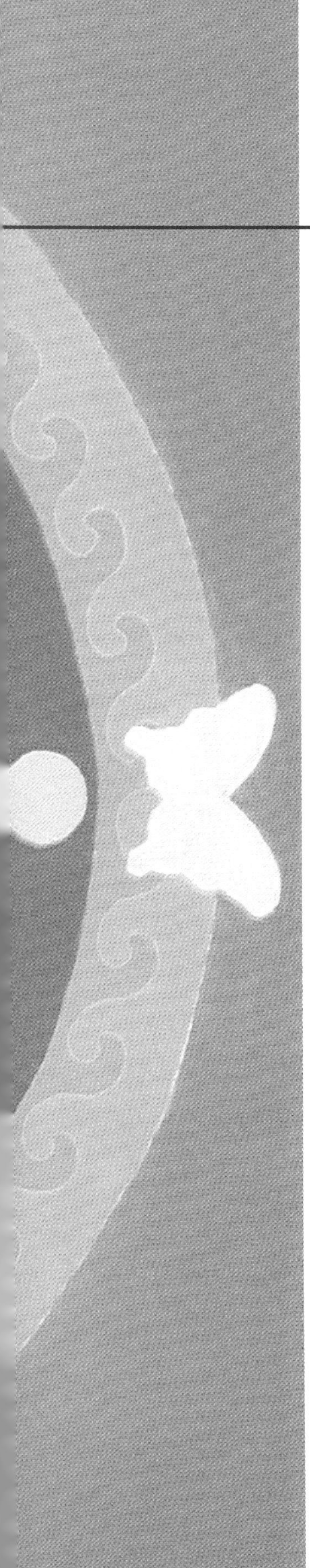

TERMS

guided discovery learning — directed discovery learning

CHAPTER FOCUS QUESTIONS

After reading this chapter, you should be able to answer such questions as:

1. Why is math and science instruction in inclusive classrooms more challenging for teachers than it needs to be?
2. Should students who have not yet mastered basic knowledge and skills be permitted to take inclusive math courses at the secondary level?
3. Why do experts recommend that math teachers assess the knowledge and skills of students with disabilities prior to teaching those students?
4. What guiding principles behind math and science standards can be implemented in conjunction with the "Direct Instruction" approach favored by many special educators?
5. What specific teaching techniques are recommended for inclusion teachers of math and science?
6. What concerns have been expressed by middle-school and high-school teachers of inclusion math and science classes about texts they use as resources (e.g., teacher-training course textbooks)?
7. What are your responsibilities as an educator when a student appears not to be appropriately placed in a secondary inclusion class for science?

PERSONAL ACCOUNTS

An inclusive classroom teacher told me about her experiences teaching "J" math and science:

> *"J" was a 10-year-old boy in my fifth-grade class. He was a very well-behaved young man who worked arduously. Labeled as learning-disabled, J had a lot of difficulty with math. I always used manipulatives during my math lessons. I did this because I learned that many of the techniques I acquired as a special educator work, too, for non-disabled students. Teaching through manipulatives is one of these. Technically, I use puzzles, models, and demonstrations to meet the special needs of students with disabilities, but in reality all the children gain from them.*
>
> *J was pulled out every school day for 40 minutes for resource-room instruction, which included math. Even so, I had to take J aside after each lesson and re-teach it. I broke ideas down into smaller, more manageable parts. We color-coded and highlighted materials. We played games. My approach to*

teaching math is to introduce an idea in whole-class instruction, then break the class into groups. Manipulatives are used in the lecture and made available for students to use as they wish. The special-education students often do get the manipulatives for use in group work. I also practice, practice, practice! All to no avail with J! It was quite frustrating, for him and for me, because he never could recall previously taught concepts—no matter what strategies we used! Every once in a while there would be a breakthrough. These were few and far between, though. As the year progressed, and the math became more abstract, J needed more one-on-one attention. We met early in the morning for private tutoring.

Science was J's favorite subject. He readily participated in all science activities. J devoured the information! Because we didn't have a lot of materials, the inclusion class by necessity worked cooperatively. I paired J with a student who performed better academically and also had the patience to work with him. This helped a lot! Most science lessons were hands-on experiments. J loved "getting his hands dirty"—this worked out perfectly, since it was one of the ways he learned best. J was given a study guide one week prior to every test or quiz. The study guide was due a few days before the test. Thus, it forced him to study ahead of time. J was more independent during science than during any other subject, even though he had a partner during science.

Next year, J will have a modified math curriculum. I believe he will see more success. He definitely belongs in an inclusive setting. He just needs more intense instruction when it comes to math. So, at year's end, I met with J's teacher-to-be for sixth grade. She will work closely with a special educator. I warned her that J is famous for telling you he understands something he doesn't, so she must check his work closely. I added that she must stand near him; teacher proximity works with J! I suggested that she pair him with more capable students for cooperative learning experiences. This summer I am tutoring J to help him get ready for sixth grade, but also because I find it so rewarding to work with him.

—Kelly

A secondary teacher of science, who had invited me to an IEP meeting, reported,

You would have been so disappointed at the IEP meeting. The meeting began late, and was very rushed. In fact, the parent was not even given time to ask any questions. (Isn't that illegal?) From what I've seen, the parent is expected to just sit in on the meeting, like a formality or something, and isn't really viewed as a resource. At the meeting, the psychologist made "suggestions" for the student's placement next year. In fact, she only talked with this young woman once this year. This psychologist is a take-charge woman. She's very dominating. But if she doesn't really know this kid, why does everyone defer to her? She said the student should be placed in a self-contained classroom next year. I was shocked. My gut tells me inclusion is the best placement for this child, especially because this is where the content on the state tests is most completely taught. I worked as a teacher in a self-contained classroom a couple years ago—it is a whole other ball game! But what can I say? I'm a new teacher in the district. I guess my biggest disappointment so far is being introduced to the politics of education and seeing so many children who need so much more support than they are getting. But instead of looking at the child's needs, people around here just look to what the psychologist wants to do.

—Mel

These stories illustrate some of the challenges of teaching Math and Science, especially in Middle School and High School.

INTRODUCTION

Chapter 15 explores the many issues surrounding the teaching of math and science in inclusive classrooms. We begin by outlining national standards. National organizations offer support for teachers of inclusive classrooms in helping students to meet these standards. Nonetheless, many special educators are concerned about whether students with disabilities will be able to achieve at the high levels envisioned in national standards. We then look at early childhood/elementary education, examining methods of adapting instruction and of performing assessments of student progress, first for math and then for science. Finally, the chapter explores issues related to teaching math and science in middle schools and secondary schools. Inclusion has been notably less successful to date at those levels than at the elementary level, in part because preservice and inservice teacher preparation has been lacking. Hence, Chapter 15 goes into considerable detail to provide middle-school and high-school teachers with the knowledge they need to make inclusion work.

NATIONAL STANDARDS

A recent study of math competency among students with disabilities concluded that the available evidence has "ominous implications" that these students may not be able to meet the national standards set by the National Council of Teachers of Mathematics (NCTM, 2000) any time soon (Cawley, Parmar, Foley, Salmon, & Roy, 2001, p. 325). Cawley and his colleagues reported that their own research and that of others cast serious doubt upon the prospect that students with specific learning disabilities or mild mental retardation could satisfy the problem-solving or even the computational proficiency requirements in the standards. The situation, sadly, is even more dire for many students with severe disabilities (e.g., Browder et al., 2004).

For more information on the national standards set by NCTM and the NSES, go to the Web Links module in Chapter 15 of the Companion Website.

Similarly, many special educators are concerned about standards for science education in PreK–12 schools. The National Science Education Standards (NSES) developed by the National Research Council (NRC) of the National Academy of Sciences contain very little about teaching students with special needs. Project 2061 (named for the year Halley's comet is expected to return to earth's orbit) of the American Association for the Advancement of Science (AAAS) is another effort to reform science education. It first set some "science literacy" goals, in *Science for All Americans,* after which the Project worked with teachers to translate those goals into expectations about what students should know in PreK–2 and in

For more information on Project 2061, go to the Web Links module in Chapter 15 of the Companion Website.

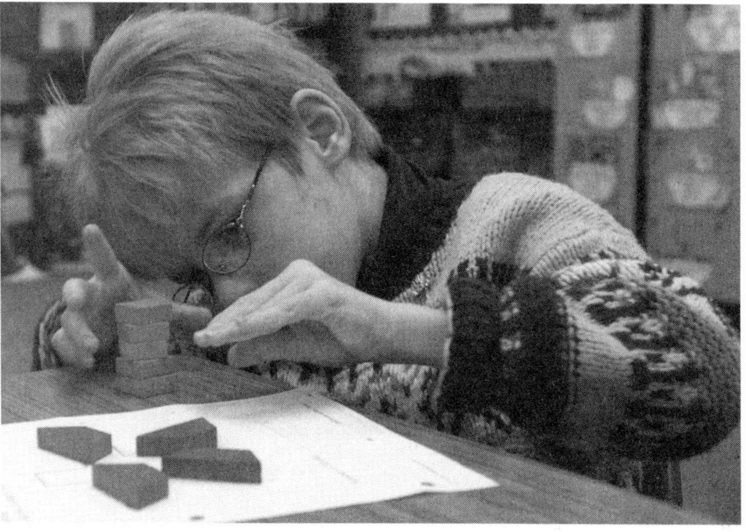

Manipulatives are key to teaching Math and Science.

Grades 2, 5, 8, and 12. The Project then developed "reform tools" for educators to use in their own districts. The documents do include some provisions relating to students with disabilities. Much more, however, is needed, particularly at the secondary level.

Inclusion teachers may find much-needed help on the World Wide Web. The box below, "Resources That Work: Math and Science on the Web," offers some useful sites.

Math

Under the No Child Left Behind Act of 2001, students in Grades 3 to 8 are to be tested annually in the area of math. Children and youth with disabilities are to be included in these assessments. This annual testing raises the pressure on inclusive teachers and students alike. The assessments, as well as those used in secondary grades, are to be developed at the state level. However, they should relate to the math standards developed by the

Resources That Work

Math and Science on the Web

Note: Before recommending any Web site for use by students who use screen readers (because of blindness or low vision), be sure to check out the site first with "Bobby"—log onto *http://www.watchfire.com/bobby*, type in the site's URL, and note the results. If more than a few problems are reported, the site should not be used. Rather, you should e-mail the site's Webmaster to explain the accessibility issues and to recommend that he take advantage of the Web accessibility resources at *http://www.w3.org/wai.*

Materials and Modifications

http://www.etacuisenaire.com ETA/Cuisenaire. A source for manipulatives usable in math education (500 Greenview Court, Vernon Hills, IL 60061–1862).

http://www.mathforum.org Math Forum. A leading Web site for math and math education.

http://www.tsbvi.edu Texas School for the Blind and Visually Impaired, Austin, TX. Outstanding resource on blindness and low vision, with extensive online and hotlinked materials and resources.

http://www.ldonline.org/ld_indepth/math_skills LD Online's page on mathematics.

http://www.pbs.org/teachersource/math.htm Public Broadcasting Service (PBS). Math lessons. See "/science" for other content subjects.

Standards

http://standards.nctm.org The Principles and Standards for School Mathematics, by the National Council of Teachers of Mathematics.

http://www.nap.edu/readingroom/books/nses/html National Science Education Standards. A printed version is also available at *http://books.nap.edu/catalog/4962.html*.

http://www.project2061.org The American Association for the Advancement of Science (AAAS) Project 2061. Contains goals and related materials for the project.

Books

Mathematics on the Internet: A Resource for K–12 Teachers, by J.A. Ameis, 2000, Upper Saddle River, NJ: Prentice Hall, Merrill Education.

The Internet and Web Design for Teachers: A Step-by-Step Guide to Creating a Virtual Classroom, by D.S. Anderson, 2001, New York: Addison-Wesley Educational Publishers.

Science on the Internet: A Resource for K–12 Teachers by J.V. Ebenezer and E. Lau, 1999, Upper Saddle River, NJ: Prentice Hall, Merrill Education.

Other

http://www.nctm.org Home page of the National Council of Teachers of Mathematics.

http://www.enc.org Eisenhower National Clearinghouse, Columbus, OH. Located at The Ohio State University, this federally funded site features exemplary materials on the teaching of math and science. The site itself is accessible for people with disabilities; there is, for example, a text version in addition to the graphics-rich standard version. The site offers a section on assessment.

http://www.iit.edu/~smile Smile Program Mathematics Index. The Science and Mathematics Initiative for Learning Enhancement, at Illinois Institute of Technology. This site offers more than 200 lesson plans that were developed by K–12 teachers attending summer workshops at the college. Subjects include biology, chemistry, mathematics, and physics. Most are middle-school or high-school lessons.

http://www.aaas.org Home page of the American Association for the Advancement of Science.

NCTM. These standards are described by the NCTM (2000) itself as "highly ambitious" (p. 3). They are. You can review the standards and see how they apply at different grade levels by visiting the NCTM standards Web site at *http://standards.nctm.org*.

Not all students with disabilities will have problems meeting these standards. Some are gifted in math and may also be talented in math-related activities, such as music and computer science (see Chapter 11). Individuals like Andrew Wiles (see p. 520, "Professionals at Work: What Do Mathematicians Do?") have a very unusual gift for numbers and for dealing with abstract ideas and symbols. Such talents likely are present at birth. They may be inborn, too, in people who have disabilities. If one of your students with a disability is gifted in this way, you should arrange for opportunities for the child or youth to display her talents. Persons with disabilities often do not receive public recognition for their abilities. This holds as much for middle school and high school as it does for early childhood and elementary school.

Most children and youth with disabilities—as is the case with their non-disabled peers—are neither gifted nor talented in math-related activities. The new standards clearly give teachers of inclusive classrooms a "wake-up call" on the urgency of helping students to master math. We begin our response to that wake-up call by reviewing the standards, noting how little has been done by math educators and special educators alike to show teachers how to modify instruction and, if necessary, to adapt assessment. We look first at the six NCTM principles, then at the five sets of content standards, and finally at the five process standards.

Principles

There are six key principles in the NCTM *"Principles and Standards for School Mathematics"* (2000), the first of which ("equity") emphasizes the need for high levels of achievement by *all* students (see the nearby box, "Resources That Work: NCTM [2000] Principles for School Mathematics"). The "curriculum" principle calls teacher and student attention to "important" mathematical ideas and skills, that is, those which have real-world applications. The principle of "teaching" tells educators to adopt some ideas special educators have long advocated, notably the thesis that teachers must understand individual students before they can teach those students effectively. The "learning" principle emphasizes discovery learning, for example, actively "learning math" rather than passively "being taught math." The principle of "assessment" highlights the need to use test, observation, and other assessment data both to help students and to improve programs. Finally, the "technology" principle recognizes the obvious: The availability of calculators, personal computers, and other technologies significantly alters the ways math is taught and learned in PreK–12 schools.

Cutting shapes is a good way to teach about angles.

Content

The NCTM (2000) standards feature content standards in the areas of measurement, data analysis and probability, numbers and operations, algebra, and geometry. Meeting the standards will require performance at increasingly challenging levels as students move through early childhood/elementary, middle, and secondary grades. Measurement is self explanatory: It is the ability to measure objects and fluids. Data analysis and probability are content areas often used in research: the formulation of an hypothesis, the design of a study to gather data, the collection of those data, data analysis (statistics), and data interpretation. Numbers and operations have to do with ways numbers may be represented and manipulated in mathematical operations. Algebra and geometry are traditional "math" subjects in American high schools. Algebra uses symbols to stand for unknown quantities and features operations performed via equations. Geometry concerns measurement and spatial relationships. Some state curriculum standards will also include trigonometry and calculus. Trigonometry has to do with triangle and angle measurement; it is a branch of geometry that is used in physics, engineering, and chemistry. Calculus, which many high-school students take, extends algebra and geometry to determining rates of change and measurement of non-standard shapes. It is much-used in chemistry (e.g., to determine the rate of change of a chemical reaction), physics (to measure the speed of a falling body), biology (to calculate the rate of growth of a colony of bacteria), social studies (to make statistical predictions), and engineering (to design aircraft).

Processes

Students are expected to demonstrate competency in the "processes" of mathematics, including problem solving, reasoning and proof, communication, connections, and representation. Briefly, problem solving emphasizes the *use* of mathematical knowledge and skills to solve problems, notably those the students will encounter as adults. The "reasoning and proof" process has to do with proving or disproving propositions. The process of "communication" has to do with explaining math ideas and how to solve problems to teachers, peers, and others. "Connections" relates to the ability to see how math concepts relate to each other and to the ability to apply math knowledge and skills to non-mathematical situations. The "representation" process has to do with using different ways to represent mathematical, physical, and other ideas and phenomena.

Concerns About These Standards

In order for students with disabilities who are being taught in inclusive classes to meet the high academic standards of the NCTM, general and special educators across the nation will need to collaborate. They must plan instructional modifications, materials adaptations, and assessment accommodations for use in inclusive classrooms. This is even more essential in math than it is in most other subject areas. National leadership that teachers of many

Resources That Work

NCTM (2000) Principles for School Mathematics

Equity. Excellence in mathematics education requires equity-high expectations and strong support for all students.

Curriculum. A curriculum is more than a collection of activities: It must be coherent, focused on important mathematics, and well articulated across the grades.

Teaching. Effective mathematics teaching requires understanding what students know and need to learn and then challenging and supporting them to learn it well.

Learning. Students must learn mathematics with understanding, actively building new knowledge from experiences and prior knowledge.

Assessment. Assessment should support the learning of important mathematics and furnish useful information to both teachers and students.

Technology. Technology is essential in teaching and learning mathematics; it influences the mathematics that is taught and enhances students' learning.

Source: Principles and Standards of School Mathematics (p.11), NCTM, 2000, Reston, VA: Author.

other content subjects can rely upon continues to be lacking in the area of mathematics. One review of standards-related activities concluded

> None of the various documents of NCTM or other standards groups describe how programs will be modified consistent with the developmental characteristics of students with mild disabilities to assure the attainment of high level standards. Similarly, the special education community has yet to address procedures to modify the combined effects of instructional, curriculum, or assessment practices in a manner that demonstrates enhanced performance of students with mild disabilities as evidence that they can and have responded to higher standards. (Cawley et al., 2001, p. 323)

Special educators have expressed other doubts about the NCTM standards. In particular, they have objected that not enough is yet known about teaching higher-order math skills to students with disabilities (e.g., Thornton, Langrall, & Jones, 1997). The emphasis in special education has been upon basic knowledge and skills, including number line, computation, and the like. Thornton et al. pointed out that very little research has been done on problem solving and reasoning ability in the area of mathematics on the part of students with disabilities. They conceded, however, that continued emphasis on drill-and-practice and on the basics of elementary math probably would not be appropriate. Fortunately, the AAAS, working with the Education Development Center (EDC), has helped make the NCTM more aware of special needs. As a result, a number of changes have been made in the *Principles and Standard for School Mathematics,* notably new statements about the importance of raising expectations for students with disabilities and tapping technology for accommodations that students may need to succeed in mathematics classes.

Science

The National Research Council (NRC, 1996) has created the *National Science Education Standards* (NSES), a synopsis of which was provided by Peters (1998). As noted earlier, AAAS (1993), through its Project 2061, has developed a set of "benchmarks" as well *(http://www.project2061.org).* Project 2061 sets goals that most teachers can agree with—students should see the relevance of what they learn, learning science should be as much as possible like "doing science" is for real scientists (that is, discovery-oriented, collaborative, etc.), teaching science should focus on solving problems and performing tasks, and so on. The AAAS documents do not propose standards as such. Rather, they provide guidelines for setting goals for science and technology education.

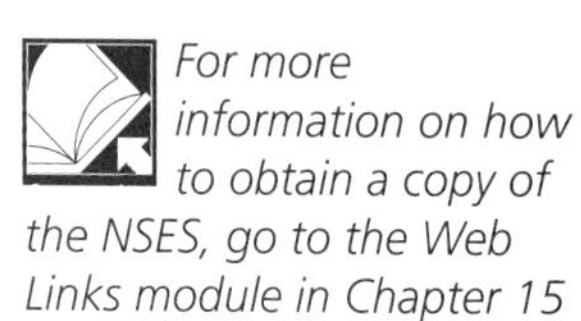

For more information on how to obtain a copy of the NSES, go to the Web Links module in Chapter 15 of the Companion Website.

Fortunately for teachers, these sets of proposed education goals are in agreement in many respects. Both stress inquiry-based learning, both emphasize the relevance to students' lives of science education, and both call for meeting the needs of all students (including children and youth with disabilities) in instruction and assessment.

Still, inclusion classroom teachers of science likely will be frustrated with the standards movement. National science standards materials *(http://www.nap.edu/readingroom/books/nses.html)* largely ignore the needs of these teachers. Student progress toward the goals set by AAAS's Project 2061 seldom is measured by statewide assessment instruments. In fact, as Andrew Ahlgren, the associate director of Project 2061, has conceded, most standardized tests, including of course those used for high-stakes assessment, have not been aligned with Project 2061 goals. AAAS's Natalie Nielsen (2001) quoted Ahlgren as acknowledging that there is "no useful synthesis of the latest thinking on assessment, much less practical advice on how to judge alignment of assessment with learning goals" (p. 2). For all these reasons, collaboration between general and special educators is needed to ensure that standards-based teaching techniques are developed that meet the special needs of students with disabilities.

Here, we examine the national science standards developed by the NRC. This is because those standards seem more likely to be used as a basis for state assessments than are the benchmarks of Project 2061.

Content

The NSES Science Content Standards include entries on physical science, life science, and earth and space science standards, science and technology standards, and history and nature of science standards, among others. These are further divided into content standards for K–4, 5–8, and 9–12. The NSES content standards are described as "minimum indicators of success, something that every student can and should achieve" (Peters, 1998, p. 2).

Teaching

The NSES documents include Science Teaching Standards as well as Standards for Professional Development for Teachers of Science. The teaching standards emphasize inquiry-based instruction and the professional development standards stress the need for teachers to remain current with the ever-evolving knowledge base as well as with new teaching methods.

Assessment

The assessment standards cover teacher-made tests and observations, district/state/national standardized tests, and sample assessments of student achievement. These are parameters for state education officials to use in developing the actual assessment instruments that schools and students will use.

Concerns About These Standards

Special educators often express worry that students with disabilities, especially those with mental retardation (MR) and specific learning disabilities (SLD), may not function independently enough to be able to participate meaningfully in discovery learning. Some with MR will not know how to design their own inquiries, or how to follow the many steps such investigations involve (Parmar, Cawley, & Frazita, 1996). Those with SLD may make many more mistakes if "left to themselves" than if given firm and continuous guidance (Steeves & Tomey, 1998). Some teachers also have concerns about the safety and well-being of students with physical or health impairments, and those with autism, in relatively unstructured learning environments. Perhaps the greatest area of concern, however, is that special educators with an interest in science education have been afforded few opportunities to become involved in standards writing. Fortunately, AAAS, with EDC, pressed the case. See "Appendix E: Science for All: Including *Each* Student" in the *NSTA Pathways to the Science Standards* elementary and secondary guides. These appendices were written by EDC's Babette Moeller and Ellen Wahl.

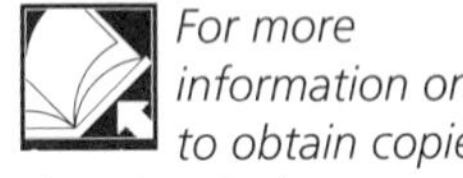

For more information on how to obtain copies of the NSTA Pathways to the Science Standards, *go to the Web Links module in Chapter 15 of the Companion Website.*

Assessment that is built into ongoing activities may not even be recognized as such by the students.

EARLY CHILDHOOD AND ELEMENTARY

Students with disabilities, English language learners, and other students are being tested yearly on math knowledge and skills, but not on science, in Grades 3 to 8, under federal law. (Although the No Child Left Behind Act does not require testing on science until 2007, many states already test students in some of these grades in basic science knowledge and skills.) These high-stakes tests increase anxiety for teachers and students alike. In New York State, where such tests have been administered to fourth-grade students, educators and children alike have reported feeling the pressure. Said one educator about the 10-year-olds she teaches, "It hits them like a bomb the minute they walk into fourth grade. It's way too early to put this amount of pressure on them" (Anonymous, quoted in Goodnough, 2001). Students with disabilities may well feel even more pressure. In this section of the chapter, we discuss resources that will help teachers of inclusive classrooms to prepare students to meet national standards for math and science. We then review what research tells us about effective teaching strategies and methods. We look first at math and then at science.

Teaching Math

Special education teacher-training programs typically provide instruction on the teaching of math at the early childhood/elementary level. Accordingly, special educators who serve on collaborative teams in elementary classrooms generally have preparation for adapting instruction and modifying materials. General education teacher-training programs, by contrast, seldom give more than lip service to such issues. The situation is much worse at the secondary level, as we will see later in this chapter.

The texts teachers use to prepare for teaching math often fail to meet the needs of inclusive teachers. Concluded one review,

> The present authors examined the teachers' manuals of selected elementary series written before and after the standards to determine their implications for students with disabilities. In one series, the recommendations to the teacher for "at-risk" students were the same in both editions. In fact, the pictures of the students were the same. No changes had been made. None of the recommendations clearly supported the obvious need to adapt the levels and types of mathematics to address the needs of *all* students. (Cawley et al., 2001, p. 324, emphasis in original)

My own observations support their contentions. While writing this book, I examined the contents of popular texts adopted by teacher-training programs in colleges and universities across the country. An example is *Learning Mathematics in Elementary and Middle Schools* (Cathcart, Pothier, Vance, & Benzuk, 2001). The text is intended for use in preservice and inservice training for elementary and middle-school teachers. It offers more than 400 pages of information about helping students to meet the new standards. Although the content coverage is very good, the closest this book comes to showing teachers how to do this in an inclusive classroom is this statement: "It is important for all teachers to have high expectations for each child and to work toward assuring the learning of each child" (p. 17). Tucker, Singleton, and Weaver (2002), in their *Teaching Mathematics to All Children,* provide much more in the way of specifics, a wealth of innovative tactics for teaching number line, addition, subtraction, multiplication, division, fractions, decimals, and geometry. This text likely will prove more helpful to inclusive teachers of mathematics. Sadly, most other popular texts do not meet the needs of teachers of inclusive classrooms.

Strategies

Direct Instruction and *advance organizers,* two techniques introduced earlier in Chapter 8, are applicable to the teaching of math at the elementary level. *Discovery learning,* or teacher facilitation (Bruner, 1960), is also appropriate for this purpose. Direct Instruction features explicit teaching, practice, regular review, and periodic assessment. These techniques are as helpful in teaching higher-order thinking skills as they are in teaching students about computation (Gersten et al., 1987). Such advance organizers as "concept

Professionals at Work

What Do Mathematicians Do?

A good way to get into the mind of a mathematician is to view the PBS *Nova* program, "The Proof." In the course of one short hour, you watch as a prominent mathematician, Andrew Wiles, and his colleagues, discuss Wiles' lifelong search for a "proof" of Fermat's Last Theorem. Mathematicians had tried for 300 years, but failed, to solve it. Fermat claimed that for the family of equations

$$x^n + y^n = z^n$$

where "n" is a positive integer larger than two, it is impossible to find a solution. Thus, for example, if "n" were 3, that is, if each variable (x, y, z) were cubed, or if "n" were 4—or *any* positive integer, up to infinity—people cannot prove that the formula is incorrect. (The formula *does* work for squared numbers; thus, $3^2 + 4^2$ does indeed equal 5^2 because $9 + 16 = 25$, but that was not "interesting" for Wiles, as it was known. A proof for Fermat's theorem was not known, and thus was interesting for mathematicians like Wiles.)

From the time he was 10 years old, Wiles wanted to solve the problem. For seven long years, he worked on this theorem. We see, in the *Nova* program, that he spent most of his work day alone. He worked in an upstairs office in his home. His wife did not understand what he was doing. It was a lonely endeavor, interspersed with occasional conferences with colleagues around the world. At one point, he thinks he has it, so he makes a major speech presenting his solution. Only later does another mathematician show that Wiles made a critical mistake in his calculations. We watch as an embarrassed Wiles spends months more on the problem. He finally comes up with a solution—and this one stands the test of his colleagues' criticism.

One could ask why an intelligent person would spend many years on such an impractical matter. Wiles explained himself to *Nova* in this way: "Pure mathematicians just love to try unsolved problems—they love a challenge." The value of "doing math," for mathematicians, often has nothing whatsoever to do with any real-world applications of what they learn.

This does not mean, of course, that the rest of us do not benefit. We do—modern civilization would be inconceivable without the contributions of mathematicians. What the *Nova* program shows us, though, is that we benefit *despite* rather than because of the motivations of mathematicians. ("The Proof," *http://www.pbs.org/wgbh/nova/proof/wiles.html*)

maps" or "figures, lines, arrows, and spatial configurations to show how content ideas and concepts are organized and related" have been recommended by Guastello, Beasley, and Sinatra (2000, p. 357). These advance organizers can help students decide what strategy to use in solving a particular problem. A graphic depicting the problem to be solved can help students with specific learning disabilities and mental retardation to determine quickly whether they need to add, subtract, multiply, or divide. In the nearby box, "Lesson Plans That Work," a teaching strategy recommended by Tucker et al. (2002) is presented using the framework offered in the "methods" chapter of this book (Chapter 8).

Manipulatives are of obvious use in the teaching of math. We discussed this in some detail in Chapter 8. Error analysis, which was discussed in Chapter 10, is a key to teaching math in inclusive classrooms. Often referred to by math experts as "*error pattern analysis*" (e.g., Venn, 2000), this strategy tells you to see if the student applied the right algorithm (e.g., did the child multiply in a multiplication problem?), the correct mechanics (e.g., did the child first multiply the digits in the right-most column?), and the like. It is an essential tool for teachers of math in inclusive classrooms, because it is usually the only way you will find out precisely where your students with disabilities are encountering difficulties.

Community-based instruction and problem-based instruction (see Chapter 8) are two other useful strategies. Jerome Bruner's emphasis upon helping students to construct their own knowledge suggests that teachers plan real-life problems that students can solve. Students with emotional/behavioral disorders and attention deficit disorders, as well as many with mental retardation and specific learning disabilities, will often benefit from seeing

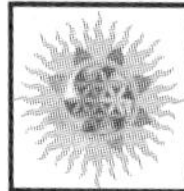

Lesson Plans That Work

Number Sense for Early Childhood/Elementary Classes

Assess, Then Teach. Open by asking the children if they can tell you how many stars are on your slide (or, if you prefer, overhead transparency). You should show 9 stars in a horizontal row. Likely, they will guess different numbers. Your next slide (transparency) should display 9 stars grouped in three horizontal rows of three stars per row. Ask the children how many stars there are. (If one or more children cannot tell you, make a note to provide follow-up instruction later.) Introduce the concept of grouping.

Teach Strategies. Tell the students what you did was to create smaller, more easily recognized bundles of stars. Illustrate with a third slide (transparency) in which you have two stars in one row and two stars in the next row. Show them that the same grouping idea works with (successively) three, four, and five stars on one row. Then introduce the idea of adding. Display a slide (transparency) having three stars. Place one more star to the right; this produces "3 + 1" or "4". If your students can visualize four stars as "four" then show them that five is "4 + 1".

Model Your Thinking and Problem-Solving Behavior. Pull up a slide (transparency) displaying 12 stars in one horizontal row. Say, "This is too many to be able to count easily. So I am going to move four of them into one bunch, four into another bunch, and four into a third bunch." Display a slide (transparency) showing these "bunches." Do the same with three stars in each of four bunches. Then (if your students can visualize six stars as "6"), two bunches of six stars each. Explain your strategy.

Use Simulations. The above *is* a simulation.

Small Groups. Create heterogeneous pairs. Give each pair a set of 5 *manipulatives* (crayons, paper clips, whatever is handy). Ask each group to find three different ways of grouping those (viz.: 4 + 1, 3 + 2, 2 + 2 + 1). Tell the class you will call upon each pair to report, but that the person in each pair that will talk will be chosen at random. (This tells the children to be sure *each* pair member is prepared to report.) Walk around, being available to ask leading questions or give suggestions, but do not interfere with the dyads' work.

One-on-One Instruction. After the exercise is over, provide one-on-one instruction to any student who was not able to do the small-group work. If there are more than a few such students, ask higher-achieving students to provide peer tutoring, under your supervision.

---

how they can use math to do things of interest to them. These students may find community learning opportunities to be far more motivating than in-class paper-and-pencil calculations (see Chapter 5).

The first step, regardless of which strategy(ies) teachers adopt, is to *assess* the knowledge and skills of included students. Research shows that educators cannot assume that students with special needs have mastered material taught in lower grades. Even if we look at students with mild disabilities such as specific learning disabilities, we find data suggesting that basic skills may not have been mastered. Concluded Cawley et al. (2001) from their review of research,

> The background literature of special education has long shown that students with mild disabilities (a) demonstrate levels of achievement approximating 1 year of academic growth for every 2 or 3 years they are in school; (b) exit school achieving approximately 5th- to 6th-grade levels; and . . . Data from a Connecticut report indicate that some 20% to 30% of all students with disabilities taking state mastery tests at Grades 4, 6, and 8 score above the statewide average for all students. (p. 312; references omitted)

Helping us to meet these challenges is a model math lesson offered in a recent text on methods of teaching students with mild disabilities (Mercer & Mercer, 1998). The Mercers' approach borrows heavily from Direct Instruction (Gersten et al., 1987). They recommended that teachers continue, after assessing students' strengths and weaknesses, by explaining to children and youth the *relevance* to their present and future lives of the material about to be taught. Educators should then *model* the skill/strategy being taught, "thinking out loud" so as to show students the metacognitive aspects of the activity. The next step is for children and youth to do problems themselves, using teacher-made scaffolding. Teachers should limit themselves to guidance and leading questions ("What did we say the first step was?"). This is followed by *student practice* leading to mastery. Teachers should look closely at student errors. These mistakes often reveal where children and youth lack knowledge and/or skills. (If this step sounds familiar, it should: It is similar to the "miscue analysis" of the Goodmans that we discussed in Chapter 14.) Teachers then should give students *additional instruction* and practice in areas of weakness. Finally, teachers should pave the way for student *generalization* of learning, by giving them more difficult problems of the same kind and by asking them to explain how they would use these skills and knowledge in the "real world."

A key technique recommended by the Mercers is to *model* the behavior desired. Teachers should demonstrate how a math operation is carried out, explaining orally each step of the process. Modeling the metacognitive strategies is especially helpful for students who have difficulty with metacognition, notably those with specific learning disabilities. The use of *manipulatives,* or concrete objects that students can count, measure, and so on, is also highly recommended for inclusive teachers (Mercer & Mercer, 1998). One source for manipulatives usable in math education is ETA/Cuisenaire. Other teaching ideas are illustrated in math instruction videos offered by the Annenberg/CPB Math and Science Project. These include *Teaching Math: A Video Library,* K–4 and *Teaching Math: A Video Library,* 5–8.

For more information on ETA/Cuisenaire and the Annenberg/CPB Math and Science Project, go to the Web Links module in Chapter 15 of the Companion Website.

Teaching Students with Specific Learning Disabilities. Children with SLD often can do well in elementary math (Carnine, 1997). Beginning with *manipulatives* was recommended by Garnett (n.d., *http://www.ldonline.org*) and by Steeves and Tomey (1998). Wrote Garnett, "The fact that concrete materials can be moved, held, and physically grouped and separated makes them much more vivid teaching tools than pictorial representations." Pictures or graphs can also be used to reinforce understanding of the basic concepts being learned. Teachers can then guide students to symbolic representations of the same ideas, such as in mathematical symbols. Finally, students can tackle math problems at the abstract level, without aid of manipulatives, pictures, or symbols. Other experts made similar recommendations, such as Maccini and Gagnon (2000).

Although some students with SLD have dyscalculia, or math disability, the more common case is that students' *language* difficulties affect their learning of math. Only by examining student work carefully will you be able to determine if dyslexia/reading disability is causing the student's problems or if these problems are truly math-specific, such as deficits in number sense (Gersten & Chard, 1999). In any event, *constant monitoring* of what children are doing is a core element of careful teaching. Teachers should ask children to "talk me through how you are doing this" so that the child's metacognitive strategies become evident. Garnett, as well as Steeves and Tomey, recommended that teachers pay careful attention to whether children overlook key elements of an expression (e.g., the minus sign), and to whether they "lazily read" a word problem and thus misunderstand what the problem calls for them to do. Take, for example, this math problem: "Tiki has three times as many marbles as Jenny does. He gives Jenny five marbles. She now has nine marbles. How many did she have at the beginning?" A "lazy" reading of this problem picks up the first two numbers (3 and 5) and the math word "times." The student thinks this is a multiplication problem and thus produces the result of "15" ($3 \times 5 = 15$). By having children "talk through the problem," teachers make students read more carefully. Once children begin trying to solve the problem, teachers will hear what mistakes they are making—as they are making them. The techniques of Direct Instruction (see Chapter 8) can then be applied: teaching the concepts explicitly, immediate correction of student errors, lots of practice, and periodic review to make sure students retain the information.

Elementary students with SLD often use the wrong strategy to solve a problem. A research study of culturally diverse fourth-graders with SLD looked at knowledge of the number system and of the relation of numbers to quantity, as well as skill at problem solving. Given a word problem requiring simple subtraction ("Joe's house is 17 miles from Grandmother's house. Jane's house is 21 miles from Grandmother's house. How far is Jane's house from Joe's house?"), several SLD students used their fingers to measure distance, for example, "three fingers." Others added when subtraction was required. Some used the most recently taught strategy (they had just learned multiplication) despite the fact that none of the problems in the study required them to multiply numbers. Although drawings (helpful ones!) were given with each problem, the SLD students did not use the drawings to solve the problems. Asked about their use of inappropriate strategies, the students told the researchers that they had not been taught how to use diagrams or pictures, how to decide which math process to apply to a problem, and so on. (Rodriguez, Parmar, & Singer, 2001). These findings further illustrate the need for teachers to assess student knowledge prior to teaching and then to examine student work closely in order to diagnose difficulties in learning math.

Teaching Students with Mental Retardation. Research has demonstrated that children with mild MR can master basic math skills (such as multiplication) and can succeed in problem-solving tasks (including word problems). Direct Instruction featuring time delay was used successfully to teach multiplication facts to elementary-age students with mild MR. Time delay is a technique in which the teacher presents a problem, asks for a response, then waits X seconds. If students correctly answer after waiting the required number of seconds, they are rewarded. If they miss the question or fail to wait, they are reprimanded. Whalen, Schuster, and Hemmeter (1996) and Mattingly and Bott (1990) showed that these approaches helped children to achieve mastery-level learning, maintain that achievement level over as long as 22 weeks, *and* generalize to other settings and with other teachers. These are impressive findings.

Teachers of children with MR, together with researchers in the field, recently have moved to embrace discovery-learning (constructivist) approaches to the teaching of math to students with MR. Hypothesizing that the well-documented difficulties these students often encounter with problem-solving and reasoning tasks (e.g., Parmar et al., 1996) may be traceable to their problems in reading and their inability to come up with appropriate strategies to solve problems, researchers have sought to make use of technology to enhance student learning. Mastropieri, Scruggs, and Shiah (1997), for example, used a computer program that featured animation, strategy instruction, and minimal reading. All written instructions were verbalized by speech synthesis software ("computer talk"; see Chapter 8). Problems were displayed graphically using animation. The steps to be followed remained on screen throughout the session.

Teachers should adopt *both* traditional Direct Instruction *and* newer constructivist approaches when teaching students with mental retardation (Butler, Miller, Lee, & Pierce, 2001). Butler et al. suggested that teachers begin by assessing student knowledge. This is a frequently recommended technique. Educators then should offer strategy instruction. Breaking into small groups for cooperative learning, students then would engage in problem-solving activities. For more ideas, see Browder and Grasso (1999).

Whatever approaches you use, you should bear in mind that *manipulatives* are essential in teaching children with MR. These children may not do well with abstract ideas but they can learn elementary-level math if taught with concrete materials, plenty of practice, and much patience (Beirne-Smith, Ittenbach, & Patton, 2002). Dice used in games offer opportunities for counting and simple multiplication. Wooden blocks of different sizes and colors may be used to teach the concept of "counting apples and apples, not apples and oranges." However, some care is required: Children with MR may mis-learn a lesson with such manipulatives. If you were to use green blocks to teach the number 4, for example, they may actually learn "4" as signifying "green." This makes it necessary for teachers to *vary* manipulatives; for example, use differently colored blocks when the intent is to teach number but same-colored ones when the purpose is to teach colors. Whenever possible, instruction should be offered in meaningful contexts, notably the environments in which students will be expected to use knowledge and skills as adults.

Teaching Students with Other High-Prevalence Disabilities. Teaching in meaningful contexts, breaking up instruction into short "chunks," making certain that materials and activities are age-appropriate, teaching what students are able to learn without being bored (too easy) or frustrated (too hard), and using the principles of behavior modification to control behavior are all techniques introduced in Chapter 9 that can be used in math instruction with students having attention deficit disorders (ADHD) or emotional/behavioral (E/B) disorders. Instruction that students perceive as being relevant to their lives will keep their interest. Teaching in small units will reduce frustration and promote attention. Physical activities can also be helpful, because they give students with ADHD or E/B disorder opportunities to get up and move around without disrupting the class.

Teaching Students with Visual Impairments. Students who are blind or have low vision (see Chapter 6) can master mathematics content at the elementary level if provided with appropriate adaptations. The most important of these is that the teacher verbalize *everything* she writes or displays in the classroom. This is, of course, a key tool of universal design (Chapter 8). Also essential are *manipulatives.* Whenever possible, these students should be able to touch and feel what other students see. Thus, countable objects, foldable papers, commercial or teacher-made raised maps (which offer tactual highlights of key features), and the like are essential. As we saw earlier in Chapter 8, manipulatives help *all* students; they are an excellent example of adaptations first developed for use in special education that later were discovered to be useful in general education as well.

Teachers can quickly and easily adapt any teacher-made handouts to very large print by using the "font" function in any good word-processing program. Many copy machines have an enlargement button. Educators can make pictures of roads, houses, and so on, tactually perceptible by adding strips of scotch tape or rubber, or by gluing small pieces of wood to boards or paper. Magnets can be very helpful. You should be creative in finding resources. In many classrooms, for example, the windows are bifurcated with wooden or metal dividers. It just so happens that these are perfectly suited to serve as tactile rectangles. Students can measure length, width, circumference, diameter, and even do geometry—on the window pane! Some classroom floors, too, are made of tiles which can be counted, measured, and so on, in much the same way.

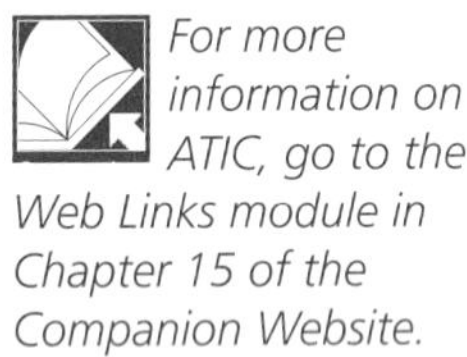

For more information on ATIC, go to the Web Links module in Chapter 15 of the Companion Website.

The Accessible Textbook Initiative and Collaboration Project (ATIC) of the American Printing House for the Blind is an outstanding resource. It offers texts on math, including algebra, in Braille, large type, and/or voice. Another excellent resource for teachers is the Web site of the state agency, Texas School for the Blind and Visually Impaired (*http://www.tsbvi.edu*). It has a frequently updated special section on the teaching of math (*http://www.tsbvi.edu/math*) that teachers having students who are blind or visually impaired should visit regularly. Another good resource is Metroplex Voice Computing Inc. They offer programs developed by Henry Gray, a math professor at Southern Methodist

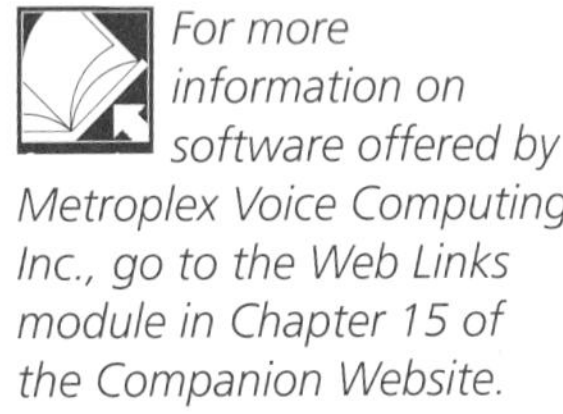

For more information on software offered by Metroplex Voice Computing Inc., go to the Web Links module in Chapter 15 of the Companion Website.

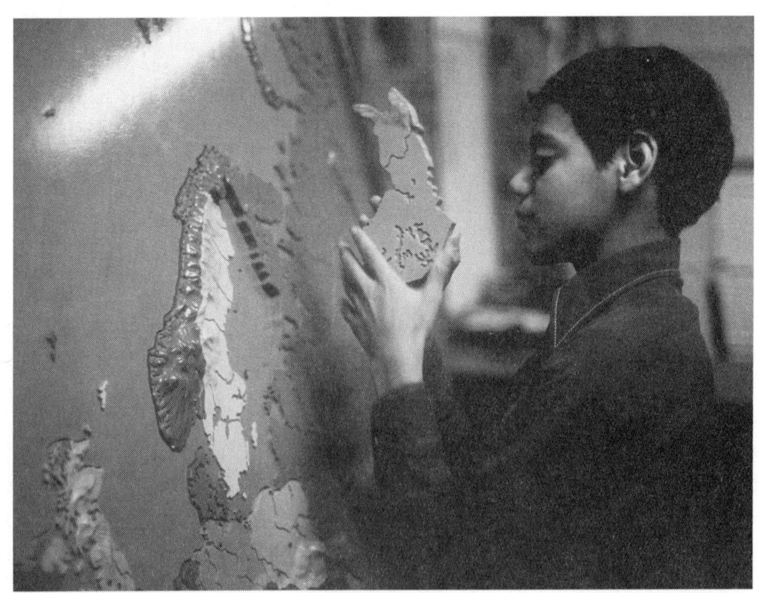

Tactile maps help students who are blind or have low vision.

University, including MathTalk for the Visually Impaired® and its many successors (ArithmeticTalk®, VoiceEZMathType®, and MathBrailleTalk®).

Teaching Students with Other Low-Prevalence Disabilities. Students with physical or health impairments generally have no disability-related problems in elementary math. It is important, however, that teachers work with related-services personnel to (a) minimize pull-out time, which limits class time for instruction of these students, and (b) ensure that students have whatever assistive technology devices and assistive technology services they need to do their math work. Children with physical disabilities get too few opportunities to influence their environment. Accordingly, teachers should use manipulatives they *can* manipulate whenever possible. This will help them to learn cause-and-effect as well as math (Bowe, 2000b). Deaf students are visual learners. Those who use American Sign Language (ASL) will benefit if you *write* all technical terms on the blackboard or on PowerPoint® or other slides. Not all such words have ASL signs. The student and interpreter may need to "invent" signs. All videos or films screened for students should be captioned. If you want to use one that is not currently captioned, contact the Captioned Media Program. Children with autism likely will do well in math, unless significant MR is also present as a secondary condition. Those with Asperger Syndrome are particularly apt to be good at math (Baron-Cohen, Wheelwright, Skinner, Martin, & Clubley, 2001; Safran, 2001).

For more information on the Captioned Media Program, go to the Web Links module in Chapter 15 of the Companion Website.

Assessing Student Progress in Math

Mercer and Mercer (1998) organized the math sections of their text on methods of instructing students with mild disabilities in this way: Chapter 11 "Assessing Math"; Chapter 12 "Teaching Math." That sequence makes sense. As we saw earlier, teachers of inclusive classrooms need to assess student knowledge and skills in math before attempting to teach them. A first step is to review student performance on the annual math tests that are required by the No Child Left Behind Act for students in grades 3 to 8. A second is to talk with the child's previous teachers. A third is to review the child's IEP. Even after taking all these steps, you may wish to administer diagnostic tests in September and periodically throughout the school year. A WGBH-TV production, *Mathematics Assessment: A Video Library K–12,* accompanied by print materials, guides teachers on NCTM-related assessments. The materials are available from the Annenberg/CPB Math and Science Project.

For more information on materials offered by Annenberg/CPB Math and Science Project, go to the Web Links module in Chapter 15 of the Companion Website.

Teacher-Made Tests. Teacher-made tests are essential not only for initial diagnosis but also for ascertaining progress. Curriculum-based assessment (CBA) and curriculum-based measurement (CBM) have much research behind them (Chapter 10). CBA, you will recall, is a broad category of observations of student performance with respect to a curriculum, while CBM, one kind of CBA, is *repeated* assessment of student progress. These are well-accepted procedures for use with students having disabilities, as shown in a review of literature by Fuchs and Fuchs (1996) and a report by Shin, Deno, and Espin (2000).

Children with SLD often have difficulty with "word problems" even if they can do the same mathematical operations to correctly answer similar questions posed in other ways (e.g., in numbers). Thus, if the teacher's intent is to assess knowledge and skills in math, word problems should be composed with care (e.g., avoid using math words that are not relevant to the problem, e.g., "times" when you do not mean to signal that the student should multiply). Students who are blind or have low vision should be granted double time for taking tests. They should also be permitted to use talking calculators and other adaptive devices. With these accommodations, most blind or low-vision students should be able to take teacher-made and standardized tests in mathematics.

Performance tests can be particularly helpful in lieu of multiple-choice or short-essay questions. Give the child a problem to solve and whatever manipulatives are needed to solve it. The child's actions constitute a performance assessment. Performance tests can be, and should be, authentic assessments (see Chapter 10).

Portfolios. Samples of student work should illustrate progress toward and mastery of state learning standards and of the curriculum. They should not consist solely of the student's best work. It is important that chosen items relate in some way to each NCTM content standard (measurement, data analysis and probability, numbers and operations, algebra, and geometry) and process standard (problem solving, reasoning and proof, communication, connections, and representation). If a student did not independently meet a state and/or national math standard, this should be clear to readers of the file. A fourth-grade teacher needs to know if a student's portfolio of work in third grade reflects genuine mastery by the student of all key skills or if, alternatively, the child was only able to produce some portfolio entries after many tries and with substantial teacher support.

Standardized and High-Stakes Tests. Standardized tests are also appropriate ways to assess student progress. These statewide tests are summative-evaluation instruments. They rarely offer reliable diagnostic information. Whenever indicated in their IEPs, students should be allowed adaptations in testing, including extra time, use of calculators, answering out loud, dictating to a scribe, and so on. The general rule is that the adaptation should not give the student with a disability an advantage over other students, nor should it obviate the test itself. These issues were discussed in Chapter 10.

With respect to standardized tests, Cawley et al. (2001) urged teachers to be very cautious: "The majority of instruments utilized to assess the mathematics performance of students with disabilities are inadequate with respect to content validity" (p. 313). For that reason, they preferred the Arithmetic Appraisal Battery (AAB; United Educational Services, 1995). The AAB offers word problems of various kinds (start unknown, extraneous information, etc.), giving teachers valuable information about the *types* of difficulties students are having. Pierangelo and Giuliani's (1998) *Special Educator's Complete Guide to 109 Diagnostic Tests* has a unit on "Arithmetic/Mathematics Assessment" which discusses several useful tests. Each is described, together with strengths and weaknesses. The Key Math Diagnostic Arithmetic Tests—Revised (Key Math-R), for example, can be used at the elementary level to assess student mastery of numbers, addition, subtraction, multiplication, and division. The test manual tells teachers what to do when the test shows deficiencies. The Enright Diagnostic Inventory of Basic Arithmetic Skills (Enright) is helpful with respect to computation skills of elementary students (Pierangelo & Giuliani, 1998). The Test of Mathematical Abilities—2 (TOMA-2) can be used with children in grades 2 to 12 to assess math vocabulary, computation, and general knowledge. Math quotients and age equivalents may be derived. The test is especially helpful in determining whether a given student is ready for the curriculum in a particular grade (Pierangelo & Giuliani, 1998).

Teaching Science

Science texts, whether designed for teacher training or for student use, tend to give little attention to students with special needs. *Science in Elementary Education* (Peters & Gega, 2002) is one of the better ones. Yet even this 600-page text devoted just a few pages to meeting the needs of students with disabilities. (Competing texts provided even less coverage.) The Peters and Gega book discussed visual impairment, hearing impairment, physical disabilities, and mental retardation. Three of the four are low-prevalence disabilities. For this reason, even the very short discussion offered in the text is of limited utility to most teachers of inclusive classrooms, who are much more likely to see students with specific learning disabilities, emotional/behavioral disorders, attention deficit disorders, and physical/health conditions. That is true even though some of the suggestions are helpful, for example, to use manipulatives to help blind and visually impaired students to understand scientific principles and knowledge.

Joseph Abruscato's *Teaching Children Science* (2001) devoted five pages to methods of teaching science to students with blindness and other visual impairments, deafness and hearing impairment, emotional/behavioral disorders, and physical disabilities. Notably lacking is any discussion of specific learning disabilities, attention deficit disorders, or mental retardation, all of which are very prevalent in PreK–12 programs.

At the early childhood/elementary level, it is vital that teachers convey to students a sense of wonder and excitement about science. Koch has argued that stories about real scientists "doing science" can inspire elementary children (Koch, 2002). Children naturally ask good questions about nature, people, and events. Virtually every day, teachers can use the "ordinary" experiences of elementary children to stimulate interest in science. The key seems to be asking good questions. Richard Feynman, one of the 20th century's great scientists, traced his passion to the way his father stimulated him to ask questions (Sykes, 1994). Koch (2002) has offered methods elementary teachers may use to help students learn the key skill of asking good questions. She proposed that hands-on experiences with manipulatives, combined with teacher-led discussion and reflection, are "especially vital" (p. 20) for students with disabilities.

Koch (2002) provided a chart summarizing the key content areas of elementary science. The box on p. 528, "Resources That Work," reprinted from her text, is quite helpful. At the left of the figure are the three main NSES categories for elementary science (life science, physical science, and earth/space science). Koch suggested that teachers conceive of two organizing themes, "systems" and "interactions and patterns of change," for each.

Strategies

Albert Einstein was widely reported to have had some kind of a learning disability (e.g., Bronowski, 1973). The physicist often identified as Einstein's successor, Stephen Hawking, has ALS (Lou Gehrig's disease). As these famous examples illustrate, persons with disabilities may be gifted and talented in science (see Chapter 11). As with math, this holds as much for middle school and secondary school as it does for early childhood and elementary school. If one of your students is gifted in science, you might want to put her in touch with the American Association for the Advancement of Science's Office of Opportunities in Science. This office, directed by Virginia Stern, was recently recognized by President Bush for providing outstanding mentoring programs for prospective scientists with disabilities.

For more information on the American Association for the Advancement of Science's Office of Opportunities in Science, go to the Web Links module in Chapter 15 of the Companion Website.

Science instruction today emphasizes discovery learning, also called inquiry learning (Abruscato, 2001; Peters & Gega, 2002). The techniques of discovery learning that Bruner (1960) and others pioneered often are highly appropriate for students with disabilities as

Professionals at Work

What Do Scientists Do?

Christopher Sykes taped physicist Richard Feynman, his colleagues, and his family members for a series of BBC television programs. He compiled many of the transcripts into a book, *No Ordinary Genius* (1994). I found the book to be engaging, in large part because everyone spoke "plain English," knowing that they were addressing a lay audience. The pages of this book are filled with stories about how scientists "do science." Reported Feynman's wife,

> When Richard works, when he gets a new idea, he's way off. He's just so excited. He paces around, he talks aloud too. He worries day and night, and then suddenly—"Oh, no! It doesn't work!" And if it really and truly doesn't work, that's it. On the rare occasions when something works—it doesn't happen very often—then it's really something! (Sykes, 1994, p. 151)

Concurred his colleague David Goodstein,

> The way I work, and the way every scientist I know works, there are very intense periods of time when you forget to eat, you forget to sleep, you forget your wife, and your students, and everything else, and you get consumed by a problem until you solve it—or else decide that you can't solve it, and give up. Most of the rest of the time is quite routine, and your life is like everybody else's. (Sykes, 1994, p. 150)

Resources That Work

Early Childhood/Elementary Science Topics

	Systems	*Interactions and Patterns of Change*
Life science	Ourselves Human body systems Plants Animals Habitats	The five senses Life cycles Tropisms Food chains
Physical science	Properties of matter: ■ Solids, liquids, gases ■ Sinking and floating ■ Solutions and suspensions Simple machines	Matter and its changes: ■ Chemical and physical change ■ Heat energy Electricity and magnetism Light energy and color Sound energy
Earth science	Solar system Dinosaurs	Weather and seasonal change Earth motions Rocks, soil, erosion Earthquakes and volcanoes Environmental science: ■ Oil spills ■ Conservation and recycling ■ Air and water pollution Moon phases

Source: From *Science Stories,* 2nd ed. (Figure 14.1, p. 319), by J.A. Koch, 2002, Boston: Houghton Mifflin Co. Copyright © by Houghton Mifflin Company. Used with permission.

well as for those with no disabilities. Teachers should model discovery learning. Koch (2002) recommended that *teachers themselves* keep science journals, into which they write the questions they ask as they go through the day and the ways they seek to answer those questions. These journal entries become a constantly renewed source of the "science stories" that teachers can tell students, inspiring them to think scientifically. However, some included students may be limited in their ability to benefit from such indirect instruction. What should teachers of inclusive classrooms do in such cases?

Direct Instruction is a technique that can be very useful as a supplement for discovery learning with students having many different kinds of disabilities (see Chapter 8). We need to dispel the common notion that Direct Instruction is always counter to discovery learning. In fact, the two can be complementary (Maccini & Gagnon, 2000). Teachers can model a discovery process and then challenge students to come up with their own variations on that process to solve other problems. Similarly, teachers can employ Direct Instruction to teach basic knowledge and skills, after which students engage in discovery learning, whether guided or not. Koch (2002) has noted that discovery learning includes such processes as "teacher talk" (talking out loud so students can follow your thinking), "student talk" (asking students to talk out loud so you can follow their thinking), and scaffolding.

Guided discovery learning (Carin, 1997) is suitable for students who have difficulties with metacognition (e.g., many who have specific learning disabilities) and for students who often cannot sustain attention for long periods of time (e.g., many who have attention deficit disorders or emotional/behavioral disorders). In guided discovery learning, a teacher or a peer helps students by asking leading questions, and, as necessary, by discouraging students from pursuing approaches that are not fruitful. Some sample questions are "Is there a pattern here?" "Can you predict the next one?" "Is there a different way to do this?" For many students with mental retardation, guided discovery will not be enough. Rather, they may require **directed discovery learning,** in which a teacher or peer takes them step-by-step through the discovery process. Carin (1997) recommended that teachers maintain high expectations for children and youth with disabilities, but that they modify materials, methods, content, and assessment to meet student needs, including, as necessary, considerable support services.

As with math, *manipulatives* can be very helpful in teaching science to elementary inclusive classrooms. In the teaching of science, manipulatives are the materials necessary to the scientific investigation (Koch, 2002). If, for example, you were to tell students that 1,000 cubic centimeters of water is the same as 1,000 milliliters of water (that is, that both "1,000 cubic centimeters" and "1,000 milliliters" are accurate ways to describe "1 liter"), you would confuse many students with SLD, deafness, and MR. However, if you were to bring cylinders marked with milliliters and various containers such as coffee cans or cookie tins, your students could see for themselves—and they would not soon forget the lesson.

Teaching Students with Specific Learning Disabilities. Advance organizers of all kinds (graphic organizers, content maps, etc.) can be very helpful for children and youth with SLD. Peer tutoring and cooperative learning can also be effective with SLD students, particularly if individual accountability is emphasized along with group rewards (Jones, Wilson, & Bhojwani, 1997). All of these techniques can help students to overcome their tendencies to "read lazily" and for that reason misunderstand problems (see "Strategies," p. 532). Carin (1997) recommended use of concrete and relevant materials, short activities, immediate feedback, and multisensory activities for teaching science to students with SLD. Those are all methods that were introduced earlier in this text.

Teaching Students with Mental Retardation. Manipulatives and real-life relevant activities are helpful with students having MR. Children and youth with MR should be shown equipment and trained in its use before any device is used in the classroom or in a lab (Carin, 1997). In addition, giving students with MR opportunities to learn science *in vivo* (in real life) is highly appropriate. Community-based instruction minimizes demands on these children and youth to generalize, simply because teaching and learning occur "out there" where students will be expected to demonstrate knowledge and skills (see Chapter 8).

Teaching Students with Other High-Prevalence Disabilities. Advance training with equipment is also recommended for students with emotional/behavioral disorders and those with attention deficit disorders, who may be impulsive unless cautioned about any dangers. You may also want to offer high-activity lessons rather than sedentary, lecture-based classes. Keeping instruction brief and to the point will also help (see Chapter 3).

Teaching Students with Visual Impairments. Advance training on equipment is recommended with students who are blind or have low vision, as well. They need to feel each key component of a device and learn how it operates because they cannot always see machines in operation. In class, teachers should articulate all key concepts and ideas, so that students with visual impairments can follow through their ears alone lectures that other students both hear and see (Carin, 1997). The American Printing House for the Blind's ATIC project can provide Brailled, large-type, and/or voiced versions of many science texts.

For more information on ATIC, go to the Web Links module in Chapter 15 of the Companion Website.

Teaching Students with Other Low-Prevalence Disabilities. A key in teaching students with physical impairments is to ensure adequate space for mobility, whether wheelchairs, walkers, crutches, or other devices are used. The AAAS Office of Opportunities in Science has publications that will help in designing or adapting physical space. Students with epilepsy most likely have seizure-controlling medication. In the unlikely event of a seizure, you should examine your classroom and/or lab to see if sharp edges can be

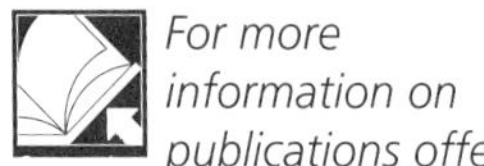

For more information on publications offered by the AAAS Office of Opportunities in Science, go to the Web Links module in Chapter 15 of the Companion Website.

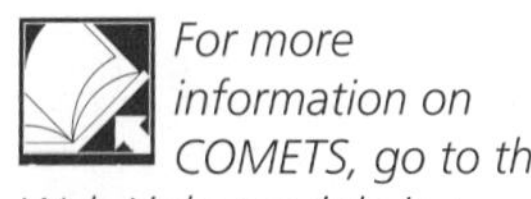
For more information on COMETS, go to the Web Links module in Chapter 15 of the Companion Website.

padded or rounded and other protruding objects removed. Students who are deaf or hearing impaired should be able to do well in science, given that information is consistently made available in visual forms (Chiappetta & Koballa, 2002). A good source of materials is the Clearinghouse on Mathematics, Engineering, Technology, and Science (COMETS) at the Rochester Institute of Technology. Those who have autism may resist discovery learning. If that occurs, it may be because of the "theory of mind" deficits that we discussed earlier in Chapter 7. However, if you firmly instruct them to engage in such activities, and if you give them step-by-step instructions for doing those, they should succeed. Indeed, Baron-Cohen and his colleagues (2001) went so far as to state that there is nothing about autism that prevents achievement, even excellence, in the physical sciences and mathematics. T. J. Publishers offers a small text of signs for science.

Assessing Student Progress in Science

Teachers may conduct formative evaluation (assessments during the course of instruction) by requiring and reviewing journal entries, by administering teacher-made tests, and by observation. As we recommended be done with respect to math, teachers should evaluate student knowledge of science in advance of instruction (e.g., in September of any school year). This may be done by reviewing IEP documents, by talking with prior year teachers, and by administering start-of-year teacher-made tests. It may also be done via observation. As suggested earlier in Chapter 9, observation is perhaps the most important means of assessment. By watching closely as students do assignments, by examining test papers, and the like, as well as by "walking around" during class time, you can learn a great deal about the children you teach. That knowledge should inform your instruction.

Journals. An effective way of tracking student progress in science is to require them to complete daily or weekly journals documenting what they did and what they learned. These entries are useful only if students are required to make such entries and

Student Strategies That Work

Science

A woman with cerebral palsy, recalling her school years, commented on how students with disabilities can often "add value" to science classes:

While our society often views disability as a deficit, when it comes to science, the experience of disability can, in fact, be an asset. The experience of having a disability can lead to the development of ways of being in and exploring the world, and a set of skills, attitudes, and interests that can be extremely beneficial to the pursuit of science. People with disabilities often devise innovative ways of exploring materials and their environment involving senses, parts of the body, and/or creative instruments not typically used by nondisabled people for such exploration. . . . For wheelchair users, viewing the world at eye level, i.e., from the seated position, can lead to a different, interesting perspective on the world compared to those who stand; and rolling rather than walking can foster an important understanding of such concepts as gravity, speed, and friction. . . . From figuring out how to distinguish different denominations of money when you cannot see to developing ways to button your shirt sleeves when you have no use of your fingers to devising schemes to assess the exact moment that your parents arrive home when you cannot hear them at the door, disability breeds creativity and all students can benefit from it.

Although we tend to stereotype scientists as isolated, eccentric individuals locked up in their laboratories, making discoveries on their own, in fact many scientific endeavors require collaboration, cooperation, and interdependence. While our culture and schools continue to foster traditional American values of independence, individualism, and competition, the experience of disability can teach important lessons about giving and receiving help, interdependence, and the value of clear, direct communication that can serve one well in the laboratory.

—Marilyn Rousso

Source: From *Thoughts and Deeds*, by N. Kreinberg and E. Wahl, Eds., 1997, Washington, DC: American Association for the Advancement of Science. Reprinted with permission.

Stephen Hawking uses text-to-speech software to speak for him.

only if teachers regularly read and respond to them. The key for educators is to notice when journal entries reflect misinformation, lack of knowledge, boredom, or other problems. Teachers should comment to the students about each week's journal entries. As needed, educators should also intervene, immediately, to provide corrective instruction, additional practice, or more motivating lessons. Peters (1998) quoted one science teacher as saying, "Students in my class now do not even realize they are being assessed since it is just a normal part of every activity—writing a summary about the nature walk in their journal, creating a new animal based on what they found out about adaption . . . " (p. 21).

Teacher-Made Tests. *Performance assessments* can be especially useful in testing children's knowledge of science. Done right, they neatly avoid "word problems" which cause difficulty for some students as well as multiple-choice questions which confuse others. Stated the National Standards for Science Education (1996), "Assessment tasks must be appropriately modified to accommodate the needs of students with physical disabilities, learning disabilities, or limited English proficiency" (p. 85). Tests that assess knowledge and skills in ways other than word problems are examples of such modified assessments.

Portfolios. Journal entries can be collected into a portfolio. In addition, samples of student work from throughout the school year may be placed into the portfolio. It is important that *all* areas of student performance (e.g., such processes as designing a plan for research, collecting data, reporting, etc., as well as such content issues as knowledge about evolution, gravity, etc.) be represented in the portfolio. Incomplete portfolios are of limited utility because they do not contain a comprehensive record of student learning.

Standardized and High-Stakes Tests. As noted earlier, the national testing program begun under the No Child Left Behind Act does not require annual testing in grades 3 to 8 in the area of science, as it does in the area of math. However, many states require science assessments in at least one elementary grade. You should check with your building principal about such testing. Any modifications or accommodations that are entered into the child's IEP are to be provided during such assessments.

MIDDLE SCHOOL AND HIGH SCHOOL

Research into issues related to the teaching of math and science at the middle-school and high-school levels has been minimal by comparison to research on the same topics with respect to elementary grades. Teacher training for special educators, too, has given much more emphasis to the teaching of these subjects at the elementary than at higher levels of public education (e.g., Hallahan & Kauffman, 2000; Mercer & Mercer, 1998; Turnbull, Turnbull, Shank, Smith, & Leal, 2002). For these reasons, teachers of inclusive math and science classes in middle school and high school must show much personal initiative. They cannot depend as much as can elementary teachers upon expert guidance.

Annual math testing continues through Grade 8, under the No Child Left Behind Act. Many states also test students in each of the high-school science areas (typically biology, chemistry, and physics). At the secondary level, in particular, these assessments take on the character of "high-stakes" tests in that promotion from grade to grade and high-school graduation depend, in part, upon passing such tests.

Teaching Math

For more information on the NCTM standards, go to the Web Links module in Chapter 15 of the Companion Website.

Even more than is the case at the elementary level, special and general educators at the middle-school and high-school levels will need to collaborate to modify teaching materials and methods and assessment procedures in order to meet the NCTM standards (see "Math," p. 514). Teachers will have to overcome some formidable obstacles to do so. As we saw earlier, collaboration in high school can be a challenging task because class periods are short, because general educators rarely have been trained about adapting instruction to meet special needs nor about handling discipline problems in the classroom, and because the level of academic performance expected from the students may be high relative to their achievements up to that point.

Further, few textbooks tell teachers how to adapt math instruction (e.g., Cathcart et al., 2000; Huetinck & Munshin, 2000). The AAAS Project 2061 has conducted "Standards-Based Evaluations" of texts used to teach science and math in PreK–12 schools. One criterion, "Criterion VII.3 Supporting All Students" has, as Indicator 4, the following: "The material includes specific suggestions on how teachers can modify activities for students with special needs, interests, or abilities." Text after text failed to meet that indicator. Project 2061 is one of very few efforts currently underway that offers real help to teachers of math in inclusive classrooms. AAAS has a long tradition of active involvement in these areas. This is fortunate for anyone interested in inclusion, because few other associations bring together experts on math and on disability to address problems of teaching math to students with special needs.

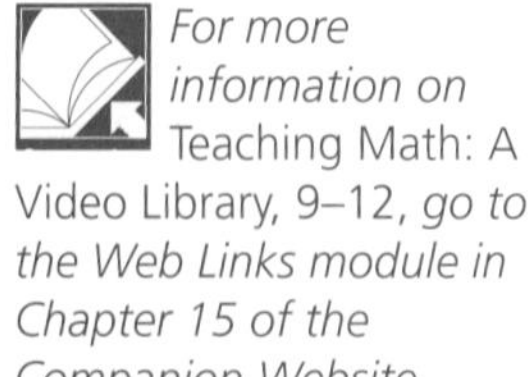

For more information on Teaching Math: A Video Library, 9–12, *go to the Web Links module in Chapter 15 of the Companion Website.*

In addition, texts on adapting instruction for students with disabilities tend to limit their discussion to topics of interest to elementary teachers. The Mercer and Mercer (1998) 'methods' text, for example, gave thorough coverage to number line, addition, subtraction, multiplication, division, fractions, and decimals—all suitable for elementary grades—but virtually no attention to algebra, geometry, or other middle-school and high-school subjects. Much the same is true of other methods textbooks. One result of all this is that special educators, as a group, tend to be underprepared to teach math in inclusive classrooms, particularly at the secondary level. This problem of personnel preparation concerned Jones et al. (1997), who noted, "Descriptions of the constructivist approach depict situations in which (a) teachers possess a considerable knowledge of their subject matter; (b) teachers are able to draw on that knowledge to facilitate student learning under conditions that require a great deal of extemporaneous decision making. . . . " (p. 160). Fortunately, *Teaching Math: A Video Library, 9–12,* offered by the Annenberg/CPB Math and Science Project can help.

Strategies

The math standards of the NCTM, (2000) anticipate that middle-school students will be introduced to irrational numbers (such as pi and the square root of 2). Irrational numbers are those that cannot be written as terminating or repeating decimals. You never get to the end of them! A good example of an irrational number is pi. Pi is the ratio of the circumference of any circle to its diameter. Pi times the radius squared equals the area of a circle. We usually approximate pi as 3.14159, but it continues forever: one could write it as 3.14159265358793 . . . and still not be done! In addition to such topics as irrational numbers, the NCTM standards envision high-school students mastering algebra to solve number-theory problems, vectors as ways to represent magnitude and direction, and matrices as ways to solve linear equations. To illustrate, here is a verbatim entry in the NCTM (2000) standards materials on secondary math:

> Being able to operate with algebraic symbols is also important because the ability to rewrite algebraic expressions enables students to reexpress functions in ways that reveal different types of information about them. For example, given the quadratic function $f(x) = x^2 - 2x - 3$ . . . students should be able to reexpress it as $f(x) = (x - 1)^2 - 4$, a form from which they can easily identify the vertex of the parabola. And they should also be able to express the function in the form $f(x) = (x - 3)(x + 1)$ and thus identify its roots as $x = 3$ and $x = -1$. (*http://standards.nctm.org/document/chapter7/alg.htm*)

The key to solving such equations is to know the rules, or steps, to follow. If you do not know those, the paragraph above might as well be gibberish. Clearly, homework—and a lot of it!—will be necessary. O'Melia and Rosenberg (1994) offered helpful suggestions on cooperative teams on homework. If you discover that despite your best efforts, and despite consulting widely with your colleagues, the homework you assign and other efforts you make to teach important material to a particular student fail to meet that student's needs, you should bring those concerns to the IEP team, together with your recommendations.

Manipulatives and real-world relevance are as helpful at this level as in elementary school. William Byrne, a math teacher in Chicago, offered this example:

> "If one pipe can drain a swimming pool in four hours and another, smaller, pipe could do so in seven hours, how long would it take to drain the pool if both pipes were used?" (*http://www.iit.edu/~smile/ma8904.html*) Swimming being a popular activity for many teens, and dreams of owning one's own pool being common, this problem has some relevance for students' lives. Byrne suggested that the teacher bring to class a plastic container holding some 2 to 3 liters of water, several four-foot plastic tubes of different inside diameter (e.g., one-half inch, one-quarter inch, etc.), a stopwatch, and several pails for holding water. He recommended that teachers ask students first to estimate the time required for each tube. ("Estimation" is a key competency in the national standards.) Suppose experiments show that the draining times required are 25 and 40 seconds, respectively, for each of the two tubes. Accordingly, a formula suggests itself: $(1 \div 25 + 1 \div 40) \div 1$ sec $= 1 \div X$ sec, where X is the time to drain the pool when both tubes are used. This exercise is far more useful in an inclusive classroom than is instruction from a textbook about formulas for generating proportions.

Teaching Advanced Mathematics in Inclusion Classrooms. The formula above is an algebraic formula. So is the quadratic equation given earlier ($x^2 - 2x - 3 = 0$). Algebra is taught beginning in eighth grade. Typically, it is followed by geometry, trigonometry, and, often, calculus. What does research tell us about how inclusion teachers of these content subjects can be successful? The literature is scant. Maccini, McNaughton, and Ruhl (1999) found just six published studies on the teaching of algebra: four at the secondary level and two at the postsecondary level. One of the few germane contributions since was the effort by Woodward, Monroe, and Baxter (2001) with middle-school students on problem solving. Van Hiele's (1996) text on teaching geometry, *Structure and Insight: A Theory of Mathematics Education* was recommended by Whitton (personal communication, 2001). Van Hiele begins by describing the cognitive growth of PreK–12 students so that teachers may recognize what concepts their students understand. He then outlines teaching phases through which students move from one cognitive level to the next. In the following paragraphs we summarize these and other tactics that research has supported for use in inclusive classrooms.

Safety rules and equipment are essential during experiments.

A key is to teach *strategies.* Students with disabilities can perform at a high level in advanced mathematics if they know and use appropriate strategies. For algebra, this means recognizing relationships and creating an appropriate equation for solution of a given problem. To do that, they first must recognize the problem as one calling for algebra and, further, one requiring use of a specific formula or procedure. Second, *diagrams* or *pictures* can be very helpful in visualizing the problem. Students with disabilities who skip this step tend to do much worse than do students who take the time to visualize the problem for which a solution is being sought. Third, as is so often the case in special education, *manipulatives* can be invaluable. There is something about being able to see, touch, hold, and manipulate concrete objects that tends to make problems much more understandable. Looking at a windowpane, for example, helps students to visualize the fact that angles in rectangles are always 90 degrees. Fourth, *simplifying the problem* can help. Faced with a word problem having very large numbers, students often find that re-stating the issue with smaller numbers helps them to envision how it may be solved. It is less intimidating to attack "$2x + 6 = 15$" than "$2x + 67 = 225$," yet the ways the problem may be solved are the same. A related strategy is to simplify the wording (many word problems contain irrelevant statements and many others use language that is less direct than it could be).

Fifth, *estimations* or guesses made before the problem is solved help prevent "silly mistakes": By supposing beforehand that the answer is in the range of 6 to 8, students can quickly recognize that they made an error somewhere if their calculations produce an answer of 28. (It may have been that they added instead of subtracting, or perhaps they overlooked a decimal, etc.) Sixth, as this suggests, *self-monitoring/self-regulation* is essential: Students must check on their thinking as well as their work. A good way to do this is to use an index card listing the steps to follow to solve a problem. Checking the solution by doing calculations in reverse, or by comparing the final answer to the estimate, is self-monitoring. This is an advantage of heterogeneous grouping: Students with lower abilities can check their work, step-by-step, against that of a peer who is better at geometry and thereby discover the source of the error.

For teachers, the literature strongly recommends *explicit instruction on strategies.* More than is the case with most non-disabled students, young people with disabilities need and benefit from precisely taught strategies (e.g., Maccini et al., 1999). Second, researchers suggest that you ask students to *think out loud* while they work on problems.

Student and Teacher Strategies That Work

Advanced Mathematics

Student Techniques

Review strategies
Diagram or draw the problem
Use manipulatives to represent the problem
Simplify the problem (numbers and/or wording)
Make predictions or estimations
Self-monitoring (e.g., using an index card)

Teacher Techniques

Explicitly teach problem-solving strategies
When working with students, ask them to articulate their thinking as they work
Model your own thinking as well as your problem-solving actions
Create heterogeneous cooperative learning groups
Assign problems that are relevant to students' lives
Make available good computer software programs

This may give you your best clues as to precisely where they are having problems. Researchers also recommend that you *model* your own thinking as well as your own problem solving when you teach. Students need to follow your train of thought as well as your actual math. Creating *heterogeneous cooperative groups* gives students a partner to learn with. As we just saw, listening to how another person sees the problem, or solves it, sometimes "makes the difference." Also suggested, whenever feasible, is selection of *authentic* problems. All of us find it more motivating to learn and use algebra, geometry, and trigonometry to solve problems that matter to us or that we can easily imagine might someday help us in "real life" than problems that seem to have no real-world relevance (Miller & Mercer, 1997). Finally, and obviously, you should make available to your students *computer programs* that call for advanced mathematics. Good computer software offers rich graphics that enticingly simulate a problem and also provide many more practice problems than can be included in any published book.

Teaching Students with Specific Learning Disabilities. Teachers in middle school and high school are well advised, as are elementary teachers, to "assess before teaching anything" in an inclusive classroom. In their literature review, Cawley et al. (2001) offered this sobering assessment:

> [Students with such mild conditions as specific learning disabilities] demonstrate that on tests of minimum competency at the secondary level, their performance is lower for mathematics than it is for other areas. . . . [They] attained only one-grade equivalent level in mathematics from Grade 7 through Grade 12. . . . [O]n a test of *minimum competency* for students in the 11th grade, 48% of students with learning disabilities passed the language/reading component, but only 16% of the students passed the mathematics component. (p. 312; emphasis in original; references omitted)

Given that these students continue to do poorly in basic math, middle-school and high-school teachers face a quandary: Should they allow such students to take the standard math courses, such as algebra and geometry, or should they hold these students back for additional remedial instruction? Experts recommend the former. Students with SLD may actually do better in advanced math courses than in elementary courses, so they should be given that opportunity. This is for two reasons: First, these students often excel in understanding concepts, which higher math requires, and second, the computation skills required for success in algebra, geometry, trigonometry, and so on, often are modest (e.g., solving "$x^2 + 6 = 15$" requires subtracting 6 from each side and then taking the square root of 9). Suggestions for teaching math to adolescents with SLD have been offered by Miller, Butler, and Lee (1998) and by Maccini and Hughes (1997). Instruction for SLD students in algebra was reviewed by Maccini et al. (1999). Many of the techniques they reported as being successful with students having SLD appear in the nearby box, "Student and Teacher Strategies That Work: Advanced Mathematics."

Particularly helpful to this population, among the strategies in that box, are teacher monitoring (asking students to "talk the problem and your solution out loud so I can hear you think") and authenticity. Bottge (1999) argued that it is a disservice to these students to continue context-less and thus meaningless instruction on computation and withhold authentic instruction in interesting material. In his research, he found that middle-school students with learning disabilities achieved well with what he called "contextualized problem-solving instruction" (similar to what we have called, in Chapter 8, problem-based instruction and community-based instruction): "The results of this study support the practice of situating problems in a meaningful context for improving the math problem-solving skills of low- and average-achieving students" (p. 90). Kate Garnett agreed:

> [Students who] may be remedial math students during the elementary years when computational accuracy is heavily stressed . . . can go on to join honors classes in higher math where their conceptual prowess is called for. Clearly, these students should not be tracked into low level secondary math classes where they will only continue to demonstrate these careless errors and inconsistent computational skills while being denied access to higher-level math of which they are capable. (*http://ldonline.org/ld_indepth/math_skills/garnett.html*)

While Bottge urged middle-school teachers to connect math ideas to real-world applications (such as building a skateboard), Garnett called for use of manipulatives and motivational materials such as games, intensive practice in short doses, student self-monitoring of progress, and frequent teacher requests for the student to "talk me through what you're doing now." She also advised that peer tutoring (see Chapter 8) could be very helpful: "having students regularly 'play teacher' can be not only enjoyable but necessary for learning the complexities of the language of math."

There is some disagreement among experts, however, about the advisability of including students with SLD in general math classes at the secondary level. Special educators note that these students tend to require careful instruction and plenty of practice. The NCTM math standards, by contrast, encourage independent discovery learning and self-regulation. In a review of issues surrounding standards-based instruction and youth with learning disabilities, Jones and colleagues (1997) concluded, "The premise that secondary students with LD will construct their own knowledge about important mathematical concepts, skills, and relationships, or that in the absence of specific instruction or prompting they will learn how or when to apply what they have learned is indefensible, illogical, and unsupported by empirical investigations" (p. 161). These are strong words. Jones et al. based their criticism upon research, which they cited, showing that many SLD students are not ready to undertake the kind of self-directed learning that the NCTM encourages. They added, "By the time students with LD become adolescents, they have typically endured many years of failure and frustration . . . [they] generally expect to fail in the future and give up readily when confronted with difficult tasks" (p. 152). For all of these reasons, the facilitative or student-directed approaches recommended by the NCTM may not be appropriate for many youth with SLD.

Cooperative learning, including peer tutoring, helps many students with SLD to master mathematics at the secondary level. Jones et al. (1997), citing considerable research evidence, commented that cooperative learning is of demonstrated effectiveness for teaching mathematics skills to SLD students. They added, "Several of these studies also consistently revealed that low-achieving students in cooperative learning programs enjoyed greater social acceptance by their higher achieving peers and reported higher levels of self-esteem than did low-achieving students in traditional instructional programs" (p. 158). Jones et al. also supported *strategy instruction,* in which teachers specifically train students with SLD about strategies for solving problems in math:

> Teachers manage the instruction of strategies by overtly modeling strategies and then leading students through their applications. Students verbalize their applications of strategies and monitor their own progress. The teachers also provide the students with many opportunities to determine which strategies are appropriate . . . (p. 159).

As we saw earlier (see, "Elementary," p. 519), many students with SLD adopt the wrong strategy when confronted with word problems in math.

Teaching Students with Mental Retardation. The professional literature offers very scant guidance for secondary teachers of math who find themselves teaching inclusive classrooms having students with MR. Butler et al. (2001), surveying research reports from 1989 to 1998, found studies on teaching students with MR about addition, subtraction, and multiplication, but none relating to instruction in algebra, geometry, or trigonometry. Even the few studies that are of relevance to secondary teachers of math offer limited guidance. Browder and Grasso (1999) reviewed 43 studies of teaching money skills to students with MR. Most involved students in middle school or high school.

Much research on effective teaching has studied groups comprised of students with SLD and students with mild MR. Looking at students aged 8 to 14 as they worked on four math domains, including basic match concepts, problem solving, fractions, and listening vocabulary, Parmar, Cawley, and Miller (1994) found significant differences in achievement between students with MR and those with SLD. This casts serious doubt upon some professional literature reports of methods of instructing students. You should read such articles with care, because the efficacy of techniques with students having MR may be overstated in some reports. Meanwhile, texts on instruction of such students (e.g., Beirne-Smith et al. [2002], Dever & Knapczyk [1997]) do not even discuss such advanced mathematics.

None of this is to say that adolescents with mild MR cannot learn in inclusive math classrooms. The research record is impressive in showing that skills and knowledge some educators might think of as being beyond the grasp of these students can in fact be developed by them, given enough time and the right kinds of instruction. Butler et al. (2001) reported upon several studies showing that students with mild MR not only could master multiplication facts but could generalize their knowledge to other situations and teachers long after instruction ceased. This is encouraging. Nonetheless, inclusive classroom teachers should also ask themselves, "Even if some elements of geometry could be taught to this student, *should* they be?" Put differently, the fact that a student can learn and perform basic square-root facts (e.g., "the square root of 9 is 3," etc.) does not in itself mean much. You need to ask yourself, "Does this student understand what a square root is?" and "How will she use this skill?" These are questions of practicality. In many cases, the answers will be positive, in which case you may proceed with confidence. In some instances, however, asking these questions will cause you to re-examine the appropriateness of continuing. The IEP team is the group to handle those kinds of issues.

Teachers in middle schools and high schools need to help IEP team members to appreciate the very abstract nature of much of advanced mathematics. Many youth with MR can understand information on a concrete level but not at a symbolic one (Dever & Knapczyk, 1997). Algebra, geometry, and trigonometry are symbolic and highly abstract. All three subjects, accordingly, may be inappropriate for many children and youth with MR. If an IEP team on which you serve, or for which you consult, is considering placement of a student with MR into an inclusive math class, you should help the IEP team members to realize how challenging such a placement may be, not to mention legally inappropriate (see Chapter 2). We cannot say, "Never place a child with MR into a geometry class." Rather, such decisions must be made by IEP teams on a child-by-child basis. Your expert input to the team is important.

Teaching Students with Other High-Prevalence Disabilities. Youth with attention deficit disorders or emotional/behavioral disorders may become frustrated with middle-school and high-school mathematics unless instruction is closely tied to real-life problems and unless math activities that allow students to be physically active are included in the curriculum. In a review of math strategies for secondary schools, Maccini and Gagnon (2000) further recommended that teachers structure the learning environment, give frequent praise for appropriate behavior, and limit each instructional session to one main idea or operation.

Another technique suggested by Maccini and Gagnon (2000) is time-out from reinforcement to help control behavior. Time-out removes the student from an environment in which he might be reinforced for inappropriate behavior (e.g., eliciting laughter from peers) and places him in an environment devoid of such possibilities (a time-out room). Time-out is a tried-and-true technique, but it must be used with care. This means imposing it only on rare occasions, restricting it to short periods of time (e.g., five minutes), and coaching the student before permitting return to the classroom (e.g., "What will you do when you get back?") (Kerr & Nelson, 1998). The need for time-out will be reduced if teachers make instruction interesting, age-appropriate, and at least somewhat physical in nature.

Cole and McLeskey (1997) reported upon one way to make a high-school math course more relevant to an inclusive class. Two teachers at a local high school (identified as "Gary" and "Adam") noticed that workers in area businesses consulted manuals throughout the day. These workers realized that their jobs were too complex for simple memorization to suffice. Yet, Gary and Adam knew, the "general math" class they would teach in September featured just such memorization. So, with the students' help, the teachers completely changed the course, basing it around a "Math Manual" written by the students themselves. A big part of each student's grade was her contribution to the "Math Manual." Tests now told students not to answer test questions but simply to write the page number in the manual where the answers could be found. Class time was used for hands-on activities that mirrored what employees do in the workplace, including collaboration between "workers." Gary and Adam were delighted with the results: "We are both pleasantly surprised at the capability of these students. When we raised our expectations of them, we found that we can go higher, faster; that we can go into things that we never even ventured into last year" (quoted in Cole & McLeskey, 1997, p. 13).

Teaching Students with Visual Impairments. Earlier, we recommended the Web site *http://www.tsbvi.edu/math* as a resource for teachers who have students with blindness or other visual impairments. A secondary math teacher at the Texas School for the Blind and Visually Impaired, Susan A. Osterhaus, is nationally known for sharing her expertise in this area. Ms. Osterhaus strongly recommended that teachers choose their words very carefully, making sure to speak out loud everything they write/show as well as what they do physically. She also suggested singing or otherwise presenting rhythmically important heuristics (e.g., the FOIL approach to multiplication of binomials could be taught as a cheerleaders' cheer: First, Outside, Inside, Last!).

Osterhaus called upon inclusive teachers to work closely with Visual Impairment Teachers (VI Teachers). These related-services professionals can recommend manipulatives for classroom use, can Braille class handouts, and can train the students in the Nemeth Code, which is a variation on Braille to accommodate mathematics symbols and technical expressions. It uses the same six cells that are used for Braille. Osterhaus stressed the necessity to make sure that all graphics have high-contrast colors (remember: most students who are blind or have low vision can see *something;* it is important, whenever possible, to let them use their residual vision). Trigonometry today is done with calculators and PC programs. While this is a big advance over the traditional reliance upon time-consuming work on slide rules, it raises questions about the accessibility of programs to users of screen readers.

For more information on other resources that provide adapted materials for those with vision impairment, go to the Web Links module in Chapter 15 of the Companion Website.

Teaching Students with Other Low-Prevalence Disabilities. Students with physical or health impairments should not have disability-related difficulties with secondary math. The

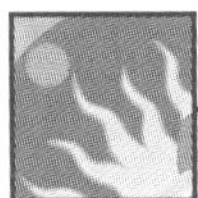

Technologies That Work

Math and Science Education

Speech synthesis (text to speech) is an excellent tool for enabling students with visual impairments, specific learning disabilities, mental retardation, and others to "do math and science"—but it is essential that some basic rules be observed. First, if you point your students to any Web sites, be sure they are compatible with screen readers. You can check those at *http://www.watchfire.com/bobby*. Second, in materials you create, be careful about columns of numbers. The speech synthesizer will read from left to right, horizontally. Column data that make sense when viewed may not be comprehensible when heard.

Math

"Lemonade Stand" at *http://www.lemonadegame.com* is designed for Grades 4 to 8. Students decide how to operate a business profitably. It is based upon the computer game by the same name.

"Baseball and Geometry" tells teachers and students how to use measurements of a baseball field to design a scale model field: *http://www.ehr.nsf.gov/pres_awards/bestlessons/Allison_Vail.html*.

A good site is "Dr. Math" at *http://mathforum.org/dr.math/*. It has an "Ask Dr. Math" service and a FAQ (Frequently Asked Questions) section, about math topics (e.g., "About Pi"). It also has a "Teacher2Teacher" service for educators.

"Algebra Online" offers free tutoring, live chat, and other forms of help: *http://www.algebra-online.com*.

"Math Explorer" at *http://www.resource2000.org/math_explorer.htm* is also valuable. This site has many dozens of hotlinks to math education sites (on algebra, long division, trigonometry, etc., plus math games and practical math).

"History of Mathematics" is self-explanatory: *http://www.groups.dcs-st-and.ac.uk/~history/index.html*.

Science

"Visual Physics" is a site offering simulations created by high-school students. You can choose "force" or some other concept in physics: *http://library.thinkquest.org/10170/main/htm*.

"Hands on Physics" (Grades 10 to 12) offers experiments for which students can use readily available and inexpensive supplies: *http://www.concord.org/HOP*.

"Physics 2000" (Grades 9 to 12) provides simulations (Java applets) of physics concepts: *http://www.colorado.edu/physics/2000*.

"Interactive Physics and Math with Java" (Grades 9 to 12): *http://www.physics.voguelph.ca/apples*.

"Teachers.First.com—Biology: High School" at *http://www.teachersfirst.com/introphysics/cisalerl* offers hundreds of hotlinks, ranging from a site about cloning (the Dolly lamb) to one about how our eyes perceive color. The site is frequently updated, but inevitably some links do not work.

"Teachers.First.com—Chemistry Resources" is a less comprehensive collection of hotlinks, this time for chemistry: *http://www.teachersfirst.com/cnt-chem.htm*.

"Teachers.First.com—Earth Science: Middle & High School" is a rich compendium of hotlinks to a vast range of topics: *http://www.teachersfirst.com/matrix.htm*. You can learn about dinosaurs, volcanos, and even birds and bears.

---

major concern with some such conditions, such as asthma, cancer, AIDS, and other health impairments, is prolonged absence from school, which of course results in their missing vital instruction. As for students who are deaf or hard of hearing, competency in mathematics typically exceeds that in reading and language arts. However, it is essential for teachers that they make *visible* the metacognitive patterns they use to solve problems. That is, when you model a procedure, be very sure that your thoughts as well as your actions are visible to the student; often, this means "thinking out loud" while an interpreter translates your words into sign language. It also means clearly and explicitly writing not only solutions but also intermediate steps, whether you use a blackboard, a PowerPoint®, or other slide, or other kinds of writing. Youth with Asperger Syndrome, a form of autism, can do very well indeed in higher mathematics (e.g., Safran, 2001). However, children with other forms of autism may find the kinds of mathematics taught in middle school and high school to be challenging (see Chapter 7).

Assessing Student Progress in Math

As at the elementary level, teachers should monitor students on a day-to-day basis to assess progress. They may do this with teacher-made tests and by observation. Any modifications or accommodations that are entered into student IEPs should be provided during such assessments (see "Standardized and High-Stakes Tests," p. 540).

Teacher-Made Tests. The real value of CBA/CBM assessment of student mastery of the curriculum, reported Jones et al. (1997), "can be attributed to the effects it appears to have on teachers' instructional behavior" (p. 159). That is, educators do things differently as a result of assessments. This is something experts repeatedly mention. Teachers need to monitor student performance closely and make instructional modifications frequently. In addition, educators in middle schools and high schools may wish to emphasize *authentic assessment* strategies. This is because solving realistic math problems has obvious relevance to student interests. The real-world connections of such measures may increase motivation of students with emotional/behavioral disorders and attention deficit disorders in particular.

Portfolios. Jones et al. (1997) added that they were skeptical about the ability of assessments of any kind to measure student achievement in constructivist classrooms: "[P]recise, meaningful, and measurable learning objectives may not be established" (p. 160). They argued that this was because of the relatively unstructured nature of such classrooms. If students choose to do very different things, how is the teacher to assess performance? Portfolios may be one answer to this dilemma, but only if teachers develop meaningful criteria for portfolio entries. The other kind of solution, which Jones et al. recommended, was teacher-made CBA testing.

Standardized and High-Stakes Tests. Standardized tests should not be used for diagnostic purposes, especially not with students having learning disabilities (Jones et al., 1997). Rather, such assessments should be performed as summative-evaluation measures, that is, to provide broad-brush portraits of student achievement over long periods of time. It is very important that any appropriate adaptations be provided for students during such tests.

Today's math instruction places far more emphasis upon problem solving and other applications of math knowledge and skills than it does upon basic computations. Accordingly, calculators are expressly permitted under the NCTM standards. The NCTM (2000) noted that calculators are approved for use *by any student* in responding to problem-solving questions, for example, because they would relieve the tedium of performing routine calculations that are of little relevance to those questions. Similarly, calculators can be used for estimation and for pattern discovery. Accordingly, whenever calculator use is indicated in a child's IEP, there should be no question as to their acceptability as adaptations in assessments.

As appropriate, and if specified in their IEPs, students should be allowed to listen to questions/instructions being read aloud, dictate answers to a scribe, and the like (see Chapter 10). These adaptations do not give students advantages over other students in math assessments. Extra time should be allowed, particularly if skills and knowledge that are not inherently time-sensitive are being assessed (e.g., problem-solving skills). For students with ADHD or E/B disorders, test sessions may be broken into small units (e.g., 30 minutes in the morning, 30 minutes in the afternoon, over 3 days, for a 3-hour standardized test).

The Test of Mathematical Abilities—2 (TOMA-2) can be used with children in grades 2 to 12 to assess math vocabulary, computation, and general knowledge. Math quotients and age equivalents may be derived. The test is especially helpful in determining whether a given student is ready for the curriculum in a particular grade (Pierangelo & Giuliani, 1998).

Teaching Science

Science is a subject in which many students with disabilities can succeed and, indeed, excel. For those with severe conditions, however, some cautionary comments are in order. The explosion of knowledge in the sciences strains credulity. The sheer volume of information in, say, biology, as compared to what was known 20 or 30 years ago, is staggering. Physicists now try to understand the world of quantum mechanics, where nothing is as it seems. Even Richard Feynman, who won a Nobel Prize for his work on quantum mechanics, confessed late in his career, "I still don't understand quantum mechanics!" (quoted in Sykes, 1994, p. 141). Wonderful for helping teachers to pick up on the current state-of-the-art in different branches of science is Bill Bryson's (2003) *A Short History of Nearly Everything.* In just 550-odd pages, and in an engaging style, Bryson reviews biology, chemistry, physics, geology, and much else.

Meanwhile, it has become impossible to "do" physics without first mastering advanced mathematics. Thorne (1994), for example, reported that Einstein could not complete his general theory of relativity until he learned some very complicated formulas of differential geometry, and this was back in 1912! Astronomy is no longer studied solely by the naked eye looking through a telescope, no matter how powerful. Rather, it is frequently done through computer modeling. That, of course, means that what are examined are not stars or other physical bodies but rather computer-generated images. In this as in so many other areas, much of today's science is much more abstract, much more mathematical, and much more removed from everyday experience than was the case in years past (see, for example Ridley, 1999; Siegfried, 2000).

The cognitive load on today's science students is much heavier than was the case in years past. We know much more today than we did in years past, too, about atoms (biology), neurotransmitters (chemistry), and neutrinos (physics). Science educators should ensure that IEP team members are at least aware of this increased cognitive load. They need to recognize that it poses major challenges for many students with disabilities. Even "minimum indicator" standards (National Science Education Standards, at *http://www.nap.edu/readingroom/books/nses.html*) will be a real reach for many such students. Children and youth with specific learning disabilities, and those who are deaf, for example, typically need much longer to read material than do other students. The amount of reading required in today's science courses is massive by comparison with that of just a few years ago. Just the number of scientific terms, each with its own definitions, has mushroomed over the past few decades. The very abstract nature of much of today's science places some knowledge beyond the grasp of students who do not devote the sustained attention required to understand it, which, sadly, includes many with ADHD or E/B disorders. These cautionary comments apply with even intensity with respect to students with MR. As you saw earlier in Chapter 2, one cannot simply say that students with MR or any other disability should not be placed into inclusive high-school science courses. Rather, decisions must be based upon individual children's needs and must be made on a case-by-case basis.

Relatively few teacher-training science texts offer more than minimal guidance for inclusion teachers. One that does is Arthur Carin's (1997) *Teaching Modern Science.* Carin provided a full chapter (Chapter 9) on adaptations for students with physical, sensory, health, mental, and emotional disorders, as well as for students who are gifted or talented, complete with specific recommendations. As mentioned earlier, Joseph Abruscato's (2001) text, *Teaching Children Science,* has some useful information. Both cover middle-school (as well as elementary) science. Neither, however, explores high-school sciences. For that, you may find Chiappetta and Koballa (2002) of interest. *Science Instruction in the Middle and Secondary Schools* has, in Chapter 3 (pp. 47–52), a discussion of teaching adolescents with SLD, E/B disorders, physical impairments, vision and hearing loss, and health disabilities. They recommended that teachers articulate *exactly* what they write (e.g., "from pH 4.3 to pH 7.1" and not "from this pH to that") so that students who are blind and those with SLD can follow the lecture. They also suggested that educators write scientific terms on the blackboard because many do not have sign equivalents in ASL.

Strategies

Small-group instruction is of very great utility in the teaching of science (Springer, Stanne, & Donovan, 1999) and, as we saw earlier in Chapter 8, particularly with students who have disabilities. Armstrong and Savage (2002) in their text, *Teaching in the Secondary School: An Introduction,* devoted a whole chapter (Chapter 9) to the approach. That is because grouping is a technique that is recommended for general secondary education, just as it is for special education and for inclusive education. In high-school science classes, small groups promote cooperative and collaborative learning. The fact that the scientific endeavor is highly collaborative (scientists typically work in teams, rather than individually) makes such instruction even more valuable and relevant. Whenever possible, you should encourage middle-school and high-school science students to work together in their inquiries, experiments, and reports. Such activities help students to reach NSES and Project 2061 goals related to understanding how scientists do their work. You might arrange for cooperative peer groups (see Chapter 8) to review basic concepts and procedures before students begin major discovery-learning projects. However, you probably want groups to be "cooperative" rather than "collaborative." That is because collaborative groups set their own agenda, procedures, and so on—which as anyone who has served on a committee knows can be very time consuming!—but cooperative groups take their cues about what to do and how to do it from teacher directions, saving much class time. The nearby box, "Lesson Plans That Work: Inertia," offers a model lesson adapted from one in Chiappetta and Koballa (2002) that uses the techniques recommended in Chapter 8.

An essential tool for the teaching of science in inclusive classrooms at this level, as in elementary schools, is Direct Instruction. This is explicit teaching followed by careful review of mistakes, re-teaching as needed, practice, and regular review (Gersten, et al., 1987). We suggested earlier that Direct Instruction can, and should, supplement inquiry learning (discovery learning). That holds as much in middle school and high school as it does at the elementary level. Direct Instruction is a method that is recommended for use in *general* education as well. For example, Armstrong and Savage's (2002) text, *Teaching in the Secondary School* contains a chapter (Chapter 8) on Direct Instruction. Noting that

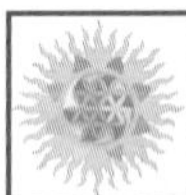

Lesson Plans That Work

Inertia

Assess, Then Teach. Ask students what they know about inertia. Discuss how it means that a body at rest "wants" to remain at rest, while one in motion "wants" to continue in motion. Ask whose theories contributed to our understanding of inertia (Newton's first law).

Teach Strategies. Studying inertia requires the development of hypotheses. We need to make predictions. To do an experiment and *then* make guesses would violate the scientific method. Ask students to propose ways in which inertia could be investigated. For each good suggestion, ask for hypotheses about what would happen. This brings up the issue of materials needed to conduct an experiment. As high-school students, they need to design studies that involve available and affordable supplies.

Model Your Thinking and Your Problem-Solving Behavior. Select a hanging bar or a coat hanger on a door or some other well-secured protruding object in the room. Attach to it a light string or heavy thread (you want something that will break). Attach the string, as well, to a weight (a good one is a small barbell weight, but anything circular will do). Attach a second string/thread to the bottom of the weight. Make a prediction about what would happen if you yanked on the bottom string/thread. Ask for comments on your prediction. Then make a prediction about what would occur if you pulled, slowly and consistently, on that bottom string/thread. Again, ask for comments.

Use Simulations. First, yank quickly. (The bottom string should break, but not the top one.) Ask for explanations. Encourage students to be innovative in proposing creative explanations that make sense under the laws of physics. Next, put a new string/thread where the broken one was. This time, pull slowly and steadily. (The upper string should break, but not the bottom one.) Ask for explanations.

Small Groups. Ask heterogeneous pairs to repeat the experiment. It would be good if other supplies were available in sufficient number that many pairs could work simultaneously. After the pairs have themselves done similar experiments, ask them to propose what they believe are the most logical explanations. (Newton's first law explains that when you yank, the lower string has to overcome the inertia of *both* the weight and the upper string, so it breaks. When you pull slowly, however, the barbell weight moves down with your pulling. This adds stress to the upper string, which breaks.)

One-on-One Instruction. Provide yourself, or ask a mid- or high-achieving student to provide tutoring to any student who does not understand what happened in the experiments.

it has also been called mastery learning, explicit teaching, systematic teaching, among other names, these authors commented that Direct Instruction is especially well-suited to instances where students must master new information. They remarked favorably upon the method's emphasis upon teachers breaking content down into manageable units, teachers checking on student comprehension at frequent intervals, students demonstrating knowledge before additional material is introduced, and students engaging in controlled practice. They urged teachers to *model* the metacognitive (thinking) processes needed to perform tasks and to *make explicit* for students exactly what they are expected to learn and do. Koch (2002) cautioned that excessive Direct Instruction may produce passive learners who do not really understand the material. She emphasized the need for "teacher talk" to help students follow their teachers in exploring materials, images, and ultimately, ideas.

"Concept mapping" is an approach recommended for science instruction of students who are low-achieving (e.g., Guastello, Beasley, & Sinatra, 2000). These are examples of advance organizers. They are also known as semantic maps (what you might think of as "organizational charts for scientific terms") and as graphic organizers. As articulated by Guastello et al., concept maps use boxes, arrows, and so on, to graphically depict relationships between ideas and words. They illustrated the approach with a concept map of "The Circulatory System." Using that name as the top box, they placed immediately under it three other boxes: "The Blood," "The Heart," and "Blood Vessels." These three second-level boxes were connected to the main box ("The Circulatory System") by arrows. Each, in turn, was then connected to tertiary boxes. For example, "The Heart" was tied by arrows to: "Atria," "Ventricles," and "Septum." Similarly, "Blood Vessels" (a second-level box) was connected to "Arteries," "Veins," "Capillaries," and "Pulse." In that way, many scientific terms were related, making student learning easier. In this book, we have used the table of contents for each chapter as a concept map. Two are offered in nearby boxes.

Teaching Students with Specific Learning Disabilities. Youth with specific learning disabilities (SLD) can do well in science, especially if given continuing support. This may take the form of Direct Instruction, supplemented by scaffolding and/or advance organizers (see Chapter 8). To illustrate, McCleery and Tindal (1999) provided prompts telling SLD students what to write in their lab reports. These prompts were both general (e.g., prompts for completing a lab report on a scientific experiment) and specific

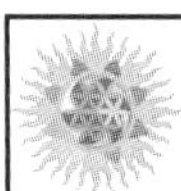

Lesson Plans That Work

Direct Instruction in Secondary Schools

Armstrong and Savage (2002) recommend that you structure lesson plans along these lines:

1. Maintain a tight focus on academic content and skills. *Teach* what you want students to know and do.
2. Formally present the information in a logically organized fashion. Highlight reasons students should pay attention to it (why it is or will be relevant to them). Motivate them to learn, too, by increasing their confidence that they will understand the material because it is so clearly laid out in your lecture. Stated differently, the material should be at Vygotsky's zone of proximal development (what students are ready to learn, with your help). It should anticipate areas of confusion and clear those up immediately. It should also be to the point, with no unnecessary digressions.
3. Ask students to demonstrate their understanding of each step before proceeding to the next step.
4. Ask many rhetorical questions (recall questions) along the lines of "Now, why did we say that?"
5. Offer controlled practice in the skills being taught before allowing students to begin applying content information. You might model what you want and then ask them to do it too.
6. Require students to apply new knowledge. They might be assigned to use information and/or skills in a different context or to solve a different kind of problem. Monitor them closely during these applications, to make sure they actually learned the material.

Concept Map: Space Science

SPACE

Visible Space	**Invisible Space**
Stars	Black Holes
Planets	Neutrinos
Other Interstellar Bodies	Other "Dark Matter"

Scientists have been able to observe evidence for about half of the predicted mass of the universe. The other half, however, remains impervious to their every effort at detection. Indirect evidence is strong that neutrinos (particles that interact hardly at all with matter) and black holes (collapsed stars or other bodies that have great gravitational pull) exist and comprise some of the "invisible" matter of space (Kunzig, 2001; Thorne, 1994). Neutrinos pass through us, and everything else, by the billions, every second. They have a tiny amount of mass. Because there are billions of them, they might represent 20% of the elusive "dark matter" scientists have been seeking so assiduously (Kunzig, 2001). Most "dark matter"—so–called because it does not reflect light—remains a mystery: no one knows what it is.

(e.g., prompts for entering information into the report sections on statement of the problem, tools used, measurements made, data collected, and conclusions). McCleery and Tindal reported that the students benefitted considerably from this help, especially because their science teachers failed to specify what was desired (e.g., students were told to write reports on their experiments but were not told how to organize/write those reports). Students with SLD often need concrete, to-the-point guidance from their teachers.

Teaching Students with Mental Retardation. Youth with mental retardation (MR) tend to have a strong sense that events are outside of their control. That is, these individuals have an external locus of control. They often believe that things "just happen"—they do not necessarily wonder, as do typical young people, why something occurred and whether it could be prevented from recurring (Beirne-Smith, Ittenbach, & Patton, 2002). For these reasons, the very foundation of discovery learning in science is of tenuous application with this population. Obvious adaptations include *directed discovery* in which a teacher or a peer firmly points the student in the desired directions and *guided discovery* in which less authoritative support is given than is the case in directed discovery learning.

Teaching Students with Other High-Prevalence Disabilities. Seating assignments for students and standing patterns for teachers can help to control unwanted behavior by students with ADHD or E/B disorders. As was suggested earlier, when teachers are physically proximate to students who are inclined to act out, such behavior tends to be curtailed. Thus, these students might be seated in front-row desks. Alternatively, when a teacher senses that a student might act out, he could physically move to a site near that student's desk, and teach from that position.

For more information on ATIC, go to the Web Links module in Chapter 15 of the Companion Website.

Teaching Students with Visual Impairments. The suggestions offered in the "Elementary" section of this chapter hold, as well, for middle school and high school. However, because of the much more abstract nature of science in advanced courses (as compared to that taught in elementary classes), it is even more vital that teachers speak out loud *every* word that is written or displayed in class. These students must be able to, in effect, "hear you think." In addition, the American Printing House for the Blind's ATIC project should be consulted for accessible materials, including textbooks.

Concept Map: The 12 Fundamental Particles of the Universe

Leptons		Quarks	
Electron	Electron neutrino	Up	Down
Muon	Muon neutrino	Charm	Strange
Tau	Tau neutrino	Top	Bottom

The "standard model" of physics divides all matter into 12 particles that—at least for now—can't be divided into anything smaller. Ordinary matter is comprised of the particles in the top row. The heavier particles below were abundant right after the Big Bang, but now they're produced only at high energies—by cosmic rays, for instance, or in accelerators. Neutrinos aren't stable parts of atoms; they are produced only when other particles decay.

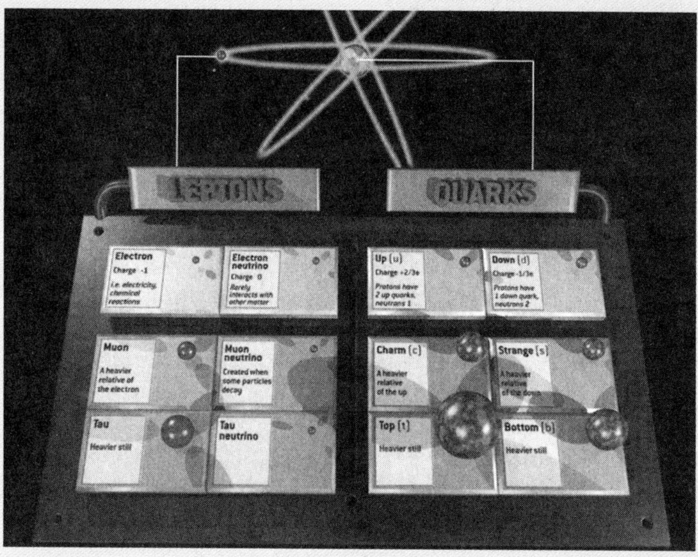

Source: Based on a graphic by Matt Zang, in "The Unbearably Unstoppable Neutrino," by R. Kunzig, 2001, *Discover, 22*(8), p. 37. Reprinted with permission of artist and with permission of *Discover.*

Teaching Students with Other Low-Prevalence Disabilities. Science instruction for students with physical or health impairments is much like that for any students. With respect to students who are deaf or hard of hearing, several projects funded by the National Science Foundation (NSF) offer real guidance for teachers. A clearinghouse of materials of all kinds is available at Rochester Institute of Technology (RIT). Another NSF-funded effort is the Distance Learning Science Project at the Marie H. Katzenbach School for the Deaf, in Trenton, NJ. This project demonstrated the use of video conferencing to deliver six science lessons per year, over a three-year period. The lessons follow the New Jersey state science standards. As at the elementary level, students with autism may have difficulty grasping the rationale for and processes of discovery learning. However, many, particularly those with Asperger Syndrome, should be able to complete their work satisfactorily, especially that which involves factual information and discrete data.

For more information on the clearinghouse of materials at RIT and the Distance Learning Science Project, go to the Web Links module in Chapter 15 of the Companion Website.

Assessing Student Progress in Science

Journals. Progress in high-school science depends heavily upon understanding abstract ideas. For this reason, teachers may find that *student journals* can reveal what young people do and do not understand. By requiring students to complete journal entries every week, and by reading and commenting on those entries, teachers can learn a great deal about gaps in knowledge, misunderstandings, and the like—in time to correct these. Particularly in physics, but also in biology and chemistry, hard thinking is required before students can let go of intuitive but erroneous ideas. There often is too little time during class for teachers to recognize such errors, particularly in large classes. That is why individual student journals can be so useful to educators. This is particularly true with respect to the problem-solving standards. You need to understand your students' thinking processes in order to assess how well you are teaching each of them to solve mathematical and scientific problems.

To take a basic example, most middle-school and high-school students will have great difficulty thinking about time as a dimension. For most of us, time is a constant. It flows in only one direction and does so at a constant pace. Until Einstein showed that time is relative, the concept that time is (as are height, width, and length) a dimension was beyond the comprehension even of the world's smartest people.

Teacher-Made Tests. Because so much science instruction is discovery-based, teacher-made tests are essential—standardized tests are unlikely to assess what students learn in their projects. As we have stressed in this book, teachers should use tests to supplement daily observations.

Portfolios. The same factor argues strongly for the use of portfolios. No matter how diverse student projects may be, portfolios can represent their achievements. As at the elementary level, it is essential both that these portfolio entries reflect all key science standards *and* that they indicate, in some way, whether the student himself produced the displayed work independently, or needed considerable help from others to complete it.

Electronic portfolios can be very helpful assessment tools in the teaching of science. Students who use graphics and multimedia to "bring material alive" can demonstrate a deeper understanding of ideas than may be possible via more traditional paper-based portfolio entries.

For more information on Project 2061, go to the Web Links module in Chapter 15 of the Companion Website.

Standardized and High-Stakes Tests. Tests in biology, chemistry, and physics typically are required, along with passing grades in courses, for high-school graduation in many states. Because so much is at stake in such tests, it is urgent that teachers and administrators ensure that whatever accommodations students need be provided; otherwise, they may not be able to demonstrate their knowledge through these assessments. The AAAS Project 2061 has recognized this as an important consideration in assessing student learning in science.

CHAPTER SUMMARY

Standards

- The national math standards, from the National Council of Teachers of Mathematics (NCTM), are described, even by the NCTM itself, as "highly ambitious." Teachers of inclusive classes and special educators worry that many students with disabilities may not be prepared to meet such high standards.
- Two organizations—the American Association for the Advancement of Science (AAAS), through its Project 2061, and the National Academy of Sciences (NAS)—have published recommended science standards. The NAS standards, called the National Science Education Standards (NSES), form the basis for many state standards on science education.
- Both the national math standards and the two national science standards emphasize inquiry learning (discovery learning) over more traditional methods of instruction. Some educators worry that many students with disabilities have not been prepared for such independent study.

Math

- Few teacher-training textbooks offer more than minimal guidance on teaching math to students with disabilities. This is particularly a problem at the secondary level, because texts that are written specifically for special educators rarely discuss higher mathematics.
- Experts recommend Direct Instruction, advance organizers, and discovery learning for instruction of math to included students. They note that Direct Instruction and discovery learning can be, and indeed should be, complementary rather than contradictory.
- Teacher assessment of student knowledge and skills is an essential first step in teaching math to included students. Research shows that educators cannot assume prior knowledge.
- Mercer and Mercer (1998) recommended that teachers of math show how lessons are relevant to students' lives, then model mathematics thinking and problem solving, after which students should work on problems (with teacher guidance). Frequent monitoring and assessment of progress are necessary.
- Students with specific learning disabilities may have math disabilities but the more common problem is one of language and reading disabilities affecting math as well as English/language arts.
- Strategy instruction is highly recommended to teachers of inclusion classrooms, both at the elementary and the secondary level.
- Few standardized tests in math have content validity, especially with respect to constructivist curricula where students engage in discovery learning.

Science

- Only a few teacher-training texts in the area of science education provide more than a page or so of guidance on teaching science to students with disabilities. This is particularly a problem with respect to high-school science.
- "Guided" and "directed" discovery learning are recommended for use by teachers of inclusive science classes. In guided discovery learning, teachers and/or peers offer suggestions for included students. In directed discovery learning, teachers and/or peers actually do the "discovering" and the included student (usually one with a severe disability) in effect "comes along on the journey."
- Also highly recommended are advance organizers of all kinds, including concept maps and graphic organizers. Anything you can do to make science less abstract and more concrete should help.
- Community-based instruction is often recommended for inclusive science education, because it minimizes the need for student generalization of knowledge and skills and because it offers an immediacy that makes learning more vivid. In addition, it helps students with E/B disorders and ADHD because it is by its very nature "active learning" and for this reason works better than do sedentary in-class lectures.
- Journal entries are an excellent means both of instruction and of assessment. While they demand additional time from teachers, the investments are well worthwhile because they help teachers understand students.
- Manipulatives are highly recommended, even for advanced science classes, because they can help make information "real" and thus enhance learning.
- Strategy instruction is recommended to teachers of inclusive science classes for the same reason it is suggested to teachers of math: Many students with disabilities, particularly those with SLD, often adopt the wrong strategy for solving problems or investigating phenomena.
- Knowledge has advanced in science as in no other area of study. Accordingly, the cognitive load upon today's students is much greater than it was in years past. Teachers may need to make sure that IEP team members are aware of these demands upon students, especially at the secondary level.

QUESTIONS FOR REFLECTION

1. Why do researchers believe that the national math standards have "ominous implications" (Cawley et al., 2001) for included students?
2. Where is a lot of information about standards-based science education available, free of charge?
3. What processes of mathematics are emphasized more in today's standards than in years past?
4. What are the key features of the Mercer and Mercer (1998) "model math lesson plan"?
5. What do experts recommend that teachers of students having specific learning disabilities do to help those children and youth learn math?
6. How do "guided" and "directed" discovery learning differ from "regular" discovery learning?
7. How can teachers of science interest students who have E/B disorders or ADHD disabilities?
8. Why do experts recommend grouping, including cooperative learning, for science instruction?
9. How can science teachers make the curriculum more "relevant" for students with disabilities?
10. What steps do experts recommend in the teaching of science to students with mental retardation?

Chapter 16

Social Studies

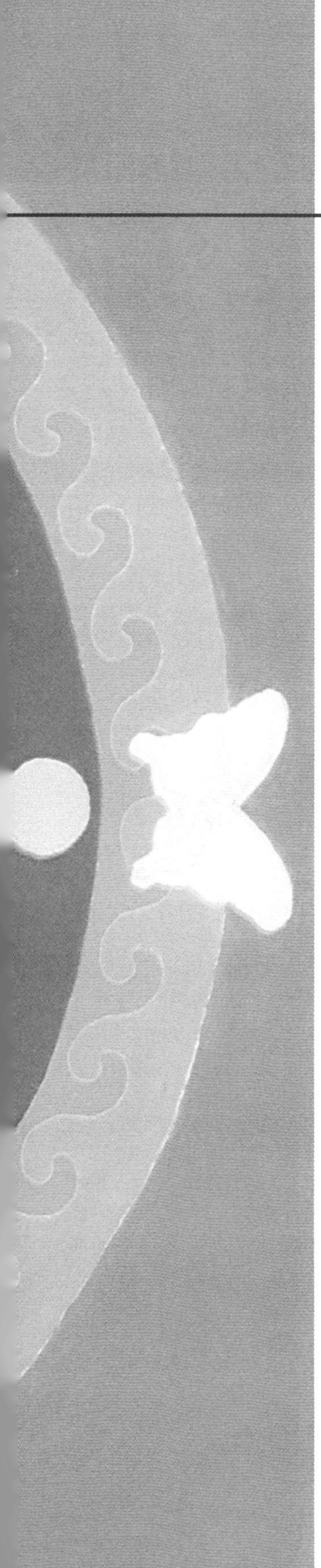

TERMS

Social Studies | Frameworks

CHAPTER FOCUS QUESTIONS

After reading this chapter, you should be able to answer such questions as:

1. How can units in social studies help many students to reach their IEP goals?
2. What kinds of strategy instruction can help students with disabilities to succeed in social studies?
3. What is "self-determination" and how can it be developed by children and youth with severe disabilities?
4. Which aspects of social studies textbooks are most troublesome for students with disabilities?
5. How can the biographies of historical figures help students learn about why historians differ in their interpretations of source materials?
6. What techniques can help youth with specific learning disabilities to master social studies?
7. How can students learn to advocate for community change?

PERSONAL ACCOUNTS

Singer, who helps to prepare social studies teachers for secondary schools, spent a year teaching social studies in a New York City high school. He shared this story:

> *I was teaching 11th-grade United States History at a NYC school that has a large inclusion program. There were four students with special needs in my classes. One had spina bifida, one had cerebral palsy, and the other two had specific learning disabilities. The two with physical conditions (spina bifida and cerebral palsy) had one-on-one aides assigned to work with them. I made the decision to deploy those two aides to assist* any *student who needed help. Since most instruction was delivered through student-directed group projects, the aides supported the groups to which the included students were assigned.*
>
> *These four students were told they were "excused" from taking the statewide social studies test known as the Regents Examination. I objected to this. I told the school counselors that these students had prepared for the exam and should be permitted to take it, alongside their classmates. To make a long story short, the four took the Regents. Three passed it. The fourth failed it because he only answered two out of the three required essays. He told the counselor he was tired, so the counselor let him give up.*
>
> —Alan Singer

A new social studies teacher told about her first few weeks on the job:

> *I have global history and geography for ninth-graders and a social studies class for 12th-graders. Some of the students have emotional/behavioral disorders or attention deficit disorders. Others have specific learning disabilities and one has a speech impairment. Several use English as a second language. We spent most of the first week getting to know each other. One thing I did was to give a multiple intelligences test (Howard Gardner). We displayed the results, which showed that the students learn in very different ways. I made a chart, "How Am I Smart?" so they could see that each has areas of strengths and special ways of learning.*
>
> *What this told me to do was to create options. Different strokes for different folks! Some students prefer to get information from visuals, so I have pictures and transparencies. Another student, who always seems "spaced out" in class, comes to life on the Internet, so I have him research stuff there and present his findings to the class. Other kids like to work with a partner.*
>
> *They all love games, so I have a "Jeopardy!" type game that offers answers from history. What always seems to get my students going, regardless of learning style, is doing a role-playing activity in the beginning of class. I might assign each of them a specific role, and then I interview them as if I were a reporter (or they interview each other). This helps them to understand what life was like "back then" in a fun way where they don't have to do what they dread—sitting in a chair, reading a textbook, and answering questions. One girl asked me, "Are we doing something fun today?" I asked her what her idea of fun was. She replied, "Not learning!" Responses like that stimulate me because they challenge me to do something to make them feel differently about learning social studies.*
>
> —Olga

These stories illustrate how teachers of inclusive classrooms adopt a variety of methods, most of which involve activities, and teach the Social Studies.

INTRODUCTION

Chapter 16 opens with a brief review of national standards for social studies, including history, civics, economics, and geography. This is followed by "frameworks" through which early childhood/elementary social studies may be taught. Each (the citizenship, scientific, and social activist frameworks) is described with Web sites for further information. We then focus upon techniques of teaching social studies, and assessing student progress, at the early childhood/elementary level. The chapter then turns to middle school and high school. Our presentation there is divided, as is the secondary curriculum, into the different social sciences. Thus, suggestions on teaching history, civics, economics, and geography are offered separately.

NATIONAL STANDARDS

Social studies teachers help students to meet state learning standards that are based upon one broad set of national standards (for social studies) and four more content-specific ones (for geography, civics, economics, and history). Historians were primarily responsible for the multiplicity of standards, following heated debate in the field (Chapin & Messick, 1996; Singer, 1997).

Social Studies

The National Council for the Social Studies defines **social studies** as "the integrated study of the social sciences and humanities to promote civic competence" (*http://www.socialstudies.org/about/background.html*). NCSS offered *Expectations of Excellence: Curriculum Standards for Social Studies* that are organized around seven specific and three broad themes or "thematic strands." At least one strand, and preferably several, should be explored during each social studies lesson. The first seven strands below are the specific themes; the three broad themes follow:

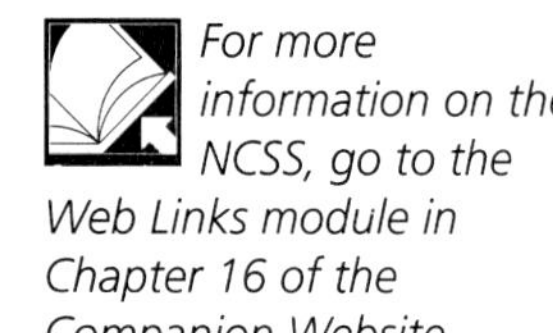
For more information on the NCSS, go to the Web Links module in Chapter 16 of the Companion Website.

I. Culture (Examination of different cultures and how they change over time; multiculturalism)
II. Time, Continuity, and Change (History and how each of us is connected to the past)
III. People, Places, and Environments (Geography and how it changes over time)
IV. Individual Development and Identity (Human psychology and development)
V. Individuals, Groups, and Institutions (Why people create groups and how those groups affect people)
VI. Power, Authority, and Governance (What power is and how it is attained and used)
VII. Production, Distribution, and Consumption (How goods and services are produced and sold)
VIII. Science, Technology, and Society (Coping with technological change)
IX. Global Connections (Interdependence in health care, human rights, the environment, etc.)
X. Civic Ideals and Practices (Balancing rights and responsibilities)

These themes draw from all of the various social sciences (anthropology, economics, political science, psychology, and sociology). These fields each have their own methods of gathering data, as well as their own knowledge bases. They often are referred to collectively as the "soft sciences" (by comparison to the "hard sciences" of physics, biology, and chemistry). The main difference is that progress in the soft sciences has been much more gradual, and halting, than that in the hard sciences, probably because certainty is much more elusive. Scientists can elucidate precise laws in physics for example, using these to make remarkably accurate predictions. Discovering similarly universal rules for sociology has proven to be a much more challenging task.

Anthropology and archaeology examine relics from the past and/or from geographically remote locations and from these attempt to reconstruct and understand the past and contemporary exotic cultures. Economics studies supply and demand, attempts to predict economic recessions and expansions, tries to understand how individuals make economic decisions, and strives to bring all this together so as to make recommendations for microeconomic and macroeconomic policies. Political science observes the behavior of people with respect to government and elections. Psychology studies human behavior,

Teacher Strategies That Work

Early Introduction to Social Studies

A first-grade teacher illustrated why it's never too early to begin teaching what we call social studies:

> *At the beginning of the school year, I spent a lot of time helping the students get to know each other's strengths and weaknesses. In fact, our whole first month was taught through feelings and appreciating differences. My first-graders really benefit from this! Now, the children seek each other out when they need help. If one student feels less confident in drawing, he or she will ask another for help. The students love the opportunity to help someone else. They always volunteer!*
>
> —Natasha

Magnifying glasses help students to read maps. For children and youth who have vision disabilities, they can be essential.

notably how individuals meet their needs. Sociology looks at how groups behave and how they influence behavior by individuals.

Strand I (Culture) relates to anthropology, Strand II (Time, Continuity, and Change) to history, Strand III (People, Places, and Environments) to geography, Strand IV (Individual Development and Identity) to psychology, Strand V (Individuals, Groups, and Institutions) to sociology, Strand VI (Power, Authority, and Government) to political science, and Strand VII (Production, Distribution, and Consumption) to economics. Performance expectations feature "essential skills" students should develop during the PreK–12 years. Thus, students should be able to explain, with examples, how groups, societies, and cultures have changed over time and how these influence the ways individuals perceive reality. Similarly, students should be capable of showing relations between music, folk tales, art, and language, on the one hand, and culture and behavior, on the other.

History

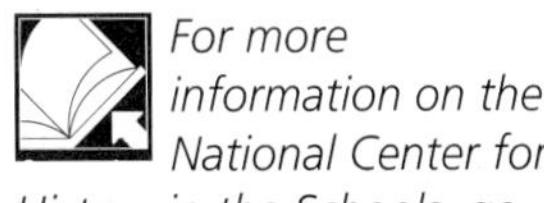

For more information on the National Center for History in the Schools, go to the Web Links module in Chapter 16 of the Companion Website.

The National Center for History in the Schools, which is located at UCLA, has proposed national history standards. The standards are divided into History (K–4), United States History (5–12) and World History (5–12). The Center is also working with San Diego State University on a federally funded project to develop a Web-based model curriculum for world history ("An Architecture for World History").

The World History (5–12) standards are presented with some 250 pages of examples of knowledge students should attain. These are divided into eight historical eras and 39 "understandings" standards. United States History (5–12) has 31 standards. Even History (K–4) envisions student achievement over large realms of knowledge. Chapin and Messick (1996), in their text on elementary social studies, claimed that "an average fifth-grade teacher would have to teach nothing but history all day long for 3 years to meet the fifth-grade standards" (p. 136). While they may have overstated the case, their central point is valid: The content students are expected to master in social studies consists of a very impressive body of knowledge. This raises serious questions for teachers of inclusive classrooms. While all teachers need to think hard about what content to teach, educators responsible for teaching students with special needs may need to zero in on what *really* matters. If, to illustrate, one believes that history should be studied so as to develop wisdom (e.g., not repeat past mistakes), as Parker (2001) contended is the case, then teachers of inclusive classrooms need to ask themselves: "What historical information lends itself to the development of such judgments?"

Resources That Work

Social Studies on the Web

General

A mind-boggling number of resources on the World Wide Web may be used in social studies. Boals has collected hundreds of hotlinks for History/Social Studies K–12 teachers at *http://myexecpc.com/~dboals/*. These include entries in archaeology, government, non-western history, and religion/ethics/philosophy. The site is best visited over a weekend, or during the summer, because there is just so much information there, and because some URLs are no longer current.

"A Thousand Years" at *http://csmonitor.com/atcsmonitor/specials/athousandyears.framset.html* lets students see changes over the past 1,000 years in such areas as science/technology, the environment, and work/money.

History

"Resource 2000—Government & History" at *http://www.resource2000.org/government_&_history.htm* is a valuable source of hotlinks organized by topic (e.g., prehistory, Rome, Age of Industry, etc.).

"The History Channel" Web site (*http://www.historychannel.com/index.html*) is a helpful site that links teachers and students to TV programs of interest. Many of these programs are closed captioned.

An impressive set of links on prehistory is offered at "Prehistory" *http://history.evansville.net/prehist.html*.

"20th Century War Maps," a collection of maps, at *http://baby.indstate.edu/gga_cart/sucar20.html*.

"1492: An Ongoing Voyage," about Columbus's voyage, at *http://www.ibiblio.org/expo/1492.exhibit/Intro.html*.

"Investigating the Vietnam War," about the Vietnam War, at *http://www.spartacus.schoolnet.co.uk/vietnam.html* explores that conflict and offers hotlinks to sites with related material.

Famous speeches are collected at *http://usinfo.state.gov/usa/infousa/facts/speeches.htm*. Included are many inaugural addresses by U.S. Presidents, Patrick Henry's "Give Me Liberty or Give Me Death" speech, Lincoln's Gettysburg Address, Martin Luther King, Jr.'s "I Have a Dream" speech, and many others.

Famous documents and speeches are at *http://www.mddbweb.com/CurSocStud.html*. This site includes the Constitution, presidential addresses, and landmark court cases.

The Library of Congress (humongous resources!) at *http://www.loc.gov*. Among the pages is "America from the Great Depression to World War II" at *http://lcweb2.loc.gov/ammem/fsowhome.html*. This page has 100,000-plus photographs from the 1930s and 1940s. Another page is "Thomas," the legislative documents site. Thomas lets you look up all public laws enacted since 1973. You can also see bills (including those never passed) from more recent Congresses, including the current one. Thomas lets you search by keyword, Senate or House sponsor name, bill number, and so on. Once you find a law or bill that interests you, Thomas connects you to stories about it in the *Congressional Quarterly* and other sites: http://thomas.loc.gov.

Archaeology and Anthropology

Human evolution is explored at *http://www.mc.maricopa.edu/academic/cult_sci/anthro/origins/asm97.html*. The site features natural selection, the role of the environment, and other factors about human genetics, enabling students to study the question, "So what is race?"

A "geological time machine" is offered at *http://www.ucmp.berkeley.edu/help/timeform.html*. Students may "travel" through prehistoric time periods and may connect to a host of related links.

"The Evidence for Human Evolution" site at *http://www.talkorigins.org/faqs/homs/* offers an overview of the fossil record as contrasted to the claims made by creationism advocates.

The "radiocarbon Web-info" site at *http://www.c14dating.com* features an explanation of the use of Radioactive Carbon 14 (C14) for dating ancient artifacts.

Vital Statistics

Interested in comparing your country to another? You may find *http://www.your-nation.com* to be helpful. Students may find it fascinating to explore their countries of origin (or their parents'/grandparents').

The Atmosphere

The National Oceanographic and Atmospheric Administration (NOAA) is a major source of online information about geography. *http://www.noaa.gov* offers, for example, "Live from the Storm," a site that allows students to "visit" as experts use satellites and other technologies to track dangerous storms (*http://passporttoknowledge.com/ptk_storm.html*). Students "fly" through Hurricane Dennis and into the eye of the storm.

Similarly, "What is an El Nino?" (*www.pmel.noaa.gov/tao/elnino/el-nino-story.html*) allows students to watch an animation showing changes in sea surface temperatures in the Pacific Ocean.

Global environmental changes, and the choices we must make, are explored through five question areas:

(1) What is the environment worth? (2) New uncertainties, new risks, new science? (3) Environmental decisions: who knows best? (4) When do people trust policy-makers? and (5) Avoiding soft disasters: new approaches for environmental decision making at *http://www.gecko.ac.uk/doc-a/index.html*. ("Soft disasters" are slow-developing ones, that is, disasters we can avert with advance planning.)

(continued)

Space

The National Aeronautics and Space Administration (*http://www.nasa.gov*) offers a wealth of resources.

NASA Television is broadcast over the Web (*http://www.nasa.gov/ntv/ntvweb.html*). Educators may record and use tapes one year after they are broadcast on PBS (the "PBS extended rights" period).

Geography and Maps

Historical maps are at *http://www.lib.utexas.edu/maps/map_sites/hist_sites.html*.

The GeoNet game requires players to defend the United States from aliens who claim we don't know enough about our planet to run it: *http://www.eduplace.com/geo/indexhi.html*.

The standard for comprehensiveness, if not always ease of use, has been set by the Central Intelligence Agency in its *World Factbook* (*http://www.odci.gov/cia/publications/factbook/index.html* or *http://www.cia.gov*). Also very useful are maps provided by the National Geographic Society at *http://www.nationalgeographic.com/xpeditions*. The site also offers "Resources" including lesson plans you can use.

The Mapmaking Project (*http://collections.ic.gc.ca/teach/mapmaking/intro.htm*) lets students do research and brainstorm before drawing maps. The U.S. Department of State has a Geographic Learning Site which offers geography information and maps (*http://geography.state.gov/htmls/statehome.html*). Teachers may click on K–4, 5–8, or 9–12. You may also click on "Cool Sites" for hotlinks to maps. Students may order up local maps at *http://maps.yahoo.com* and at *http://www.mapquest.com*, among many other sites. Driving directions between any two reasonably contiguous locations may also be obtained, free of charge, at either site.

A map of the world, explorable in different ways, is provided by the Xerox Corporation's Palo Alto Research Center at *http://pubweb.parc.xerox.com/map*.

"Maps of Ancient Earth" at *http://www.dinosauria.com/dml/maps.htm* lets students explore tectonics and other changes over long periods of history. Particularly good at showing how what are now South and North America were contiguous with Europe and Africa during the Mesozoic and Jurassic eras.

"Teaching with Historic Places" (TwHP) at *http://www.cr.nps.gov/nr/twhp/* features National Park Service National Register of Historic Places sites, including national parks. Lesson plans are also featured.

Economics

A well regarded resource for K–12 teachers is *http://EcEdWeb.unomaha.edu/teach.htm*. This Economics Education Web site has a wealth of materials and information.

The World Game of Economics (*http://www.worldgameofeconomics.com*) is self-explanatory.

The *Wall Street Journal's* Classroom Edition site (*http://www.wsjclassroomedition.com*) is another helpful resource on the teaching of economics. It includes sample lesson plans.

Source: Thanks to A. J. Singer for many of these URLs. His Web site, "Hofstra Social Studies Educators," offers lesson plans and activities, as well as a host of hotlinks: *http://www.geocities.com/athens/academy/5753/*.

Civics and Government

For more information on CIVITAS and the Center for Civic Education, go to the Web Links module in Chapter 16 of the Companion Website.

The Center for Civic Education, has offered CIVITAS, "a framework for civic education." (*http://www.civiced.org/civitasexec.html*). This framework opens with a rationale for studying civics and government in PreK–12 schools, continues with goals and objectives, and concludes with scope-and-sequence statements. The bulk of the material is given over to "Civic Knowledge," a review of the history of Western political thought, the nature of propaganda, the role of the press, and civic disobedience. It is distributed by the National Council for the Social Studies.

CIVITAS describes each subject in three phases. First is a "historical perspective." That is followed by a "contemporary perspective" and then by "the role of the citizen." The emphasis clearly is upon United States political structures and institutions, although CIVITAS considers China as an example of a non-Western approach to government. Sample lessons are offered (e.g., "What Responsibilities Accompany Our Rights?"). Also provided for teachers is a "matrix of teaching strategies" that suggests how documents, other primary sources, literature and drama, group work, and simulations may be used to teach, for example, units on Nazi concentration camps and "Rock Music and the Collapse of Communism" (which could be interesting!).

Geography

A set of 18 geography standards developed in a Geography Education Standards Project involving the American Geographical Society, the Association of American Geographers, the National Geographic Society, and the National Council for Geographic Studies has been proposed by the Council (*http://www.ncge.org/publications/tutorial/standards*). These 1994 standards have to do with reading maps, understanding geographical regions on Earth, recognizing the geosystems that affect life on this planet, comprehending how people's behavior influences and is influenced by the environment, and realizing what steps must be taken to preserve the habitability of Earth in the years to come. Students examine why deforestation occurs and what effects it has on the Earth, where fossil fuels are found and how long known deposits are expected to support current rates of fuel consumption, what current ozone levels are and what these imply for the future of life on the planet, and many other topics. Computer technology greatly expands the scope and reach of geography topics students may explore. In particular, *The World Factbook* (*http://www.odci.gov/cia/publications/factbook/index.html*) has a stupendous wealth of information. Similarly, computer games such as the popular series "Where in ___ is Carmen Sandiego?" can assist students to develop geographic knowledge and skills.

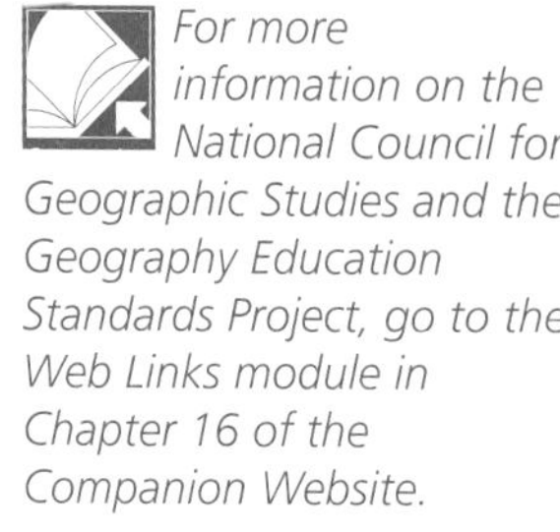

For more information on the National Council for Geographic Studies and the Geography Education Standards Project, go to the Web Links module in Chapter 16 of the Companion Website.

For more information on The World Factbook, go to the Web Links module in Chapter 16 of the Companion Website.

Economics

The National Council for Economic Education, the National Association of Economics Educators, and the Foundation for Teaching Economics jointly developed Voluntary National Content Standards in Economics (*http://www.economicsamerica.org/standards*). The materials include "Contents" (the 20 standards) and "Handbook" (explanations). Both are downloadable. You can also get copies from the Council. The key ideas explored in the standards include

For more information on the National Council for Economic Education and the Voluntary National Content Standards in Economics, go to the Web Links module in Chapter 16 of the Companion Website.

Production (scarcity, choice)

Decision making (weighing costs, benefits)

Allocation of goods and services (market economies, command economies, etc.)

Barter (voluntary exchanges of goods and services)

Markets (buyers and sellers)

Pricing (supply and demand)

Competition

Economic institutions (labor unions, banks)

Interest rates

Labor (earned incomes)

Entrepreneurs

Government

Online lessons are offered in connection with each of the standards. Some of the topics explored are "Are the Best Things in Life Free?" "Rationing Transplants: An Ethical Problem," "The Opportunity Costs of a Lifetime," and "$10 Billion to Host the Winter Olympic Games: Is it Worth It?"

EARLY CHILDHOOD AND ELEMENTARY SCHOOL

At the early childhood/elementary level, social studies often are taught in an integrated fashion. History, economics, civics, and geography come together in a seamless whole. During the early childhood years, themes are developed—getting along with others, following class rules, meeting people in the neighborhood, and so on—which in later years become "subjects" for study. The chapter-opening vignette from Natasha illustrates this. Many early childhood/elementary teachers teach other subjects, such as English/language arts and math, *through* social-studies content areas. Teachers of inclusive classrooms also need to take advantage of the fact that social studies offer a natural context in which to help students to develop much-needed self-determination and self-advocacy skills. Our review of early childhood/elementary social studies follows the unitary nature of instruction at this level. Later, when we turn to middle school and high school, we will examine the main strands of the social studies separately—history, civics/government, geography, and economics.

Teaching Social Studies

Early childhood/elementary social studies may be taught in any one or more of a variety of ways. We can call them **frameworks** or ways of approaching the content. Good teachers will use more than one of these frameworks. The techniques discussed in Chapter 8 may be used with any of these frameworks. Thus, you should make liberal use of simulations, manipulatives, reciprocal classwide peer tutoring, problem-based learning, community-based instruction, and other strategies and tactics in social studies just as you do in other subject areas.

Other techniques are more specific to the teaching of social studies. One is to assign the *reading of fiction and biographies*. Students may learn much more about the Revolutionary War by reading the fictional story of Johnny Tremain than by reading accounts in history books. Similarly, children may understand the American civil-rights movement much more fully by reading simple biographies of Martin Luther King, Jr., Malcolm X, and Cesar Chavez than by studying textbook summaries. These are two ways in which the teaching of English and language arts (see Chapter 14) may be integrated into the teaching of social studies.

Strategies

The Citizenship Framework. Probably the most traditional approach is the "cultural heritage" or "citizenship transmission" framework. The focus is upon teaching students about American history, values, and institutions, and preparing children to be active citizens in a democratic society. Teachers can use the classroom, the school, and the community to provide concrete experiences through which students may learn abstract ideas. The approach is the one featured by the NCSS at its Web site: "The basic purpose of the social studies is to teach students the content knowledge, intellectual skills, and civic values necessary for fulfilling the duties of citizenship in a participatory democracy" (*http://www.socialstudies.org* or *http://www.ncss.org*). It may be particularly suited to students with mental retardation, autism, and other disabilities, especially where IEP goals feature development of abilities to interact effectively with others, understand and follow rules, and participate actively as a member of a community.

Some Web sites that you may find helpful with this way of teaching social studies include the Children's Express site at *http://cenews.org*. Voting-related sites include *http://vote.com*, *http://voter.com*, and *http://voxcap.com*. The Congressional "Thomas" site is invaluable for studying federal laws: *http://thomas.loc.gov*.

The Scientific Framework. A second general strategy for teaching social studies is to emphasize the social sciences. Children learn what kinds of questions scientists ask in anthropology, archaeology, economics, psychology, and sociology. They study the research methodologies these scientists follow. Students then are given opportunities to conduct their own inquiries. They may examine artifacts at a local museum. They may interview fellow students to learn about different cultural traditions. They may create a class business selling, for example, hand-painted T-shirts. The main objective in each case is for children to gain experience with the methods used in the social sciences. While simplified versions of these methodologies are used, the essential elements nonetheless do represent a way of thinking, one that is not instinctive for most people. Social scientists generally begin with a question ("Why did the Titanic sink?" or "What factors caused the Great Depression?"). They then make an informed guess as to what the answer may be. This guess is a hypothesis. Evidence is then gathered in support or in opposition to that hypothesis. The social sciences diverge here, using different data-collection methods. A conclusion is then drawn: The hypothesis is supported or it is refuted. For teachers of social studies at the early childhood/elementary level, a great deal of support for student learning is needed, especially on gathering information. Teachers at the secondary level need to bear in mind that student questionnaires and interview forms need to be written with care, or they will produce useless data.

The scientific approach to social studies may appeal to students who enjoy active learning, including those who want to "get out there and *do* something!" For this reason, it may be useful for children with specific learning disabilities, attention deficit disorders, emotional/behavioral disorders, deafness or blindness, especially when IEP goals relate to reading, writing, problem solving, technology, and decision making.

Some Web sites that may help you teach social sciences include the National Oceanographic and Atmospheric Administration at *http://noaa.gov*, Maps of Ancient Earth at *http://dinosauria.com/dml/maps.htm*, and the National Council for Economics Education at *http://www.EcEdWeb.unomaha.edu/K-12/home.cfm*.

The Social Activist Framework. A third overall approach to the teaching of social studies is the "social criticism" or "reform" model. The goal is to guide students in a critical examination of the environments in which they live. If, for example, they believe that some school rules are not fair, or if they want to raise voter participation in their community, or if they want the state to adopt new regulations governing the use of cell phones in cars (to name just three examples), this approach would guide students to recognize why the current policy is in place, who is in a position to change it, and how those policy makers may be influenced. The method may appeal most strongly to students who feel that they and/or their family members have been discriminated against and those who have other reasons for being dissatisfied with the status quo. Some who may be attracted to this approach include students who are homeless, those who come from low-socioeconomic status (SES) homes and/or from migrant families, those who are members of ethnic or racial minority groups, those who are gay or lesbian, and others who are for one reason or another vulnerable in today's society. These individuals often need to become effective self-advocates (Chapter 11). Students with disabilities may be, as well. We will examine this approach in more detail later in this chapter (see p. 562, "Middle School and High School").

Some Web sites that may help you teach through an activist framework include Speak-Out at *http://www.speakout.com* and Awesome Library's current events page at *http://www.awesomelibrary.org/classroom/Social_Studies/ Current_Events/Current_Events.htm*.

Perspectives. The social studies are united in that they observe the behavior of human beings: over time (history), in different environments (geography), and under various schemes of government (political science). Social scientists ask what effects different systems of production and distribution have upon economic well-being (economics) and why people create and treasure different cultures (sociology). At the early childhood/elementary level, these topics usually are taught in a very immediate, concrete way—by focusing on students and their own lives, their school, and their community. This immediacy of focus makes early childhood/elementary social studies a hospitable "home" for work on IEP goals (see Chapter 2). Students whose IEPs call for them to learn expressive and communication skills, develop interpersonal skills, read and write for a variety of purposes, interact cooperatively with others, and/or become aware of life style and career choices can make progress toward these goals within the early childhood/elementary social studies curriculum.

Ford, Davern, and Schnorr (2001) offered suggestions on helping students with disabilities to do these things. Noting that many IEPs set goals in the areas of language and literacy (communication, reading, writing), mathematics and technology (problem solving,

Resources That Work

Books by Eve Bunting for Teaching Human and Civil Rights

Singer (1997) recommended several works by the author Eve Bunting for teaching young children about human rights:

Train to Somewhere, by E. Bunting, R. Himler, Illustrator, New York: Clarion Books, 1996. This story about an orphan girl in the late 1800s acquaints children with foster care and adoption.

Fly Away Home, by E. Bunting, R. Himler, Illustrator, New York: Clarion Books, 1991. In this story about homelessness, Andrew and his father live surreptitiously in an airport.

Terrible Things, by E. Bunting, S. Gammell, Illustrator, New York: Harper & Row, 1980. A rabbit is left alone, defenseless, after other animals are taken from the forest. This story is an allegory of the Holocaust, showing why we must look after one another and the rights of all of us.

---

money management, time management), personal/social development (decision making, interpersonal skills, self management), and school/community/work (classroom and school routines, use of community resources, and career/vocational exploration), Ford et al. stated that while IEP goals should "be at the center of curriculum planning" this does not mean that they should "be confused with activities. Students may be meaningfully involved in an extensive array of activities in classes such as social studies. . . ." (p. 217). They were correct. Social studies, by its very nature, involves considerable reading. In well-run classrooms, social studies also features cooperative learning and other small-group activities that develop expressive and receptive communication skills. Being group members fosters interpersonal relations skills. Inquiry-based (or, as Singer [1997] calls it, document-based) instruction requires students to solve problems. And the study of civics (government) at the early childhood/elementary level typically begins with classroom routines ("Why do we have rules?"), continues with school issues ("Who runs our school?"), and proceeds out into the community ("Who are the people in our community?"). All of this makes the social studies an ideal environment for instruction that will help students with disabilities to meet their IEP goals.

Ferretti, MacArthur, and Okolo (2001) described the research literature on teaching social studies in inclusive classrooms as "scant" (p. 67). For this reason, we give extended coverage to their study (see p. 562 "Middle School and High School") and, here, to one by Lederer (2000). Methods for teaching social science were investigated in a New Mexico elementary school by Lederer. Working with 25 students having learning disabilities who were placed in inclusive fourth-, fifth-, and sixth-grade classrooms, Lederer created heterogeneous groups to conduct what he called "reciprocal teaching." He began by teaching students how to ask questions, summarize information, make predictions, and clarify statements. For example, he asked them to "pretend that they were the teacher and had to think of three good questions to ask" (p. 94). Lederer emphasized that the children were to work together and that no competition was intended, either within groups or between groups. Each group chose a discussion leader who guided the group to answer five questions about a passage. Lederer provided the students with a worksheet that prompted them to ask questions, monitor their understanding, and summarize their discussions. Results indicated that students with learning disabilities, as well as those with no disabilities, did better on comprehension assessments than did students in control groups. Even 30 days after completion of the project, students continued to show improvement.

Teaching Students with Specific Learning Disabilities. Explicit instruction about inquiry-based methods and about cooperative learning often is required for students with specific learning disabilities (SLD) to be able to participate effectively in the relatively unstructured social studies reform curricula (Lederer, 2000). Ferretti and his colleagues, whose work we will discuss later, came to similar conclusions. They did, however, express grave reservations about the dense and often indecipherable writing in social studies textbooks, which raise unnecessary barriers for students with SLD. Teachers of inclusive classrooms at the elementary level should post classroom rules and discuss them often (civics), use story maps and other organizing devices (history), and adopt manipulatives such as textured artifacts (geography), according to Taylor and Larson (2000).

Teaching Students with Mental Retardation. There should be a *use* for whatever is taught that is at least potentially available to students with mental retardation (MR). That is, functional applications should guide teacher decision making about what to include in the curriculum (Taylor & Larson, 2000). With respect to history, students with mild MR may benefit from class re-enactments of key historical events (e.g., Boston Tea Party) and from other teacher efforts to make abstract concepts more concrete (e.g., visits to historical sites). Taylor and Larson added that repetition of important content often is necessary. Social studies offer a natural context to help elementary students to begin to develop competencies in self-determination and self-advocacy. As we saw in Chapter 13, the concepts that all of us have choices, and that choices have consequences, need to be developed. This is particularly true for students with MR. At the elementary level, these skills can be taught, and used, in deciding whether to participate in a class project (e.g., a student "store"), which roles to accept (e.g., a class play), and which class and school rules to obey. Instruction in choice making should begin in the primary grades but the connections between those choices and their consequences should not be applied until students have matured enough to understand the risks they assume with certain decisions. Rather, the early childhood/elementary years should be used to introduce the idea that self-determination is itself a choice and that part of "growing up" is making decisions for oneself and taking responsibility for them (Wehmeyer and Schalock, 2001).

Teaching Students with Other High-Prevalence Disabilities. Role playing and simulations could be useful as ways to keep the interest of students who may otherwise become distracted. Taylor and Larson (2000) added that teachers should emphasize cooperative learning, and de-emphasize competition, so that students with emotional/behavioral disorders or attention deficit disorders are less likely to become frustrated. Recall that Lederer stressed with his students that the reciprocal teaching (cooperative learning) he wanted them to engage in was "a group activity and not a contest with other groups" (Lederer, 2000, p. 95).

Teaching Students with Visual Impairments. The kinds of source documents that Singer (1997) and others recommend teachers use, as well as Web sites, need to be reviewed. If necessary, accommodations should be arranged. Some, such as magnifying glasses, are readily available (e.g., *http:www.lighthouse.org* or even a local arts supply store). Others, notably electronic aids, may be secured on the Web (e.g., *http://www.nfb.org*). Yet others, such as raised relief versions of historical maps, are more difficult to obtain. A very helpful resource is the Accessible Textbook Initiative and Collaboration Project, at the American Printing House for the Blind (APH). APH, has the Macmillan/McGraw-Hill series, *Adventures in Time and Place,* which covers communities (third grade), regions (fourth grade), U.S. (fifth grade), and world (sixth grade) history. Also recommended is the Texas School for the Blind.

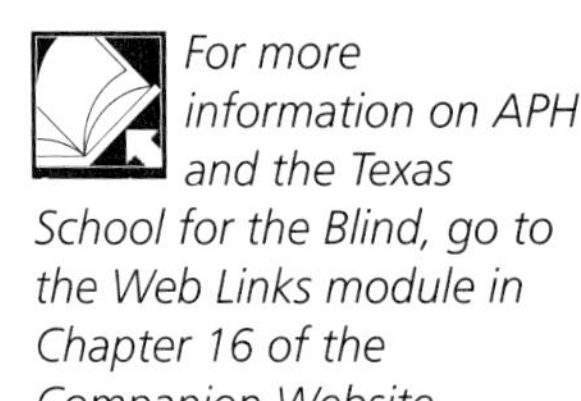

For more information on APH and the Texas School for the Blind, go to the Web Links module in Chapter 16 of the Companion Website.

Teaching Students with Other Low-Prevalence Disabilities. Students with physical or health impairments should encounter no particular problems in early childhood/elementary social studies. Teachers should recognize that many deaf or hard of hearing students will find texts and other social studies material difficult to read, in large part because of the very substantial number of names of people, places, and things. The fact that class lectures feature the same multiplicity of words is also troublesome. (One cannot lipread words one does not already know.) Children with autism need to learn that routines can and do vary from time to time, and that rules sometimes do change. Learning to cope with

The ability to speak persuasively can be invaluable.

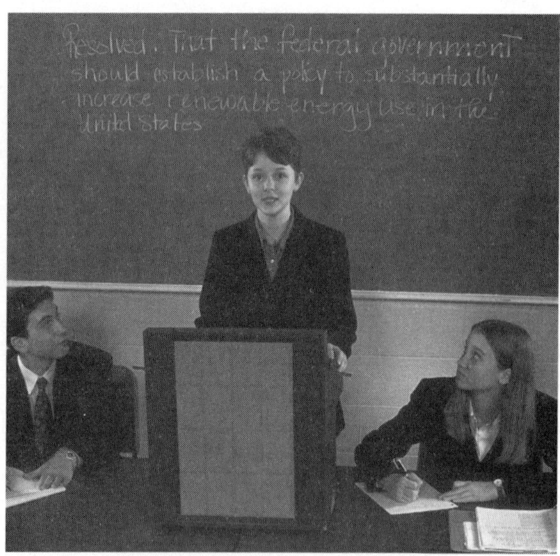

changes in daily routines can be taught in connection with early childhood/elementary civics/government lessons about class, school, and community rules.

Assessing Student Progress in Social Studies

Yell (1999) was one of many social studies teachers to recommend the use of journal entries for assessment. His aim was to employ "multiple types of assessment at multiple points during my units" and "to make assessments a part of the learning experience for students as opposed to something that only occurred following a learning experience" (p. 326). Because students can make such entries using whatever assistive technologies they need (e.g., typing, speech recognition, etc.), journal entries are a good vehicle for assessments. In addition, journal entries are relatively unobtrusive. They become part of the routine of instruction, so much so that students may not even be aware that they are being assessed.

Teachers of third- and fourth-grade classes who have students who are blind should check, in advance, with National Assessment of Educational Progress (NAEP) officials to (1) determine if any graphical or other visual materials will be used and (2) what accommodations NAEP plans so as to allow students who are blind or have low vision to understand the questions that use such materials and to answer those questions. The NAEP tests on history and geography achievement are administered to fourth-grade students. However, because making needed adjustments sometimes requires quite some time, third grade is not too early to bring up these issues.

MIDDLE SCHOOL AND HIGH SCHOOL

As do other content subjects, the social studies become much more complex and challenging at the higher levels of PreK–12 education. There is a difference, however. Social studies is an appropriate context within which to help youth to prepare for transition to the adult world. We devoted Chapter 13 to transition. One question raised there was: When during the school day can we teach students these vital skills? A major part of the answer is: in social studies.

Individuals with disabilities may be gifted or talented in areas related to civics and government. Franklin Delano Roosevelt was no less inspiring a president for using a wheelchair (see *FDR's Splendid Deception* by Hugh Gallagher [1985]). Paul Hearne became student body government president at Hofstra University during his undergraduate years, despite the fact that he used a wheelchair due to a rare neurological condition. The Gallaudet uprising of 1988, when deaf students successfully protested the appointment by the school's board of trustees of yet another of a long line of non-deaf presidents, was led by Gregory Hlibok, who is deaf. The examples go on and on. If one of your students is unusually skillful in politics and related fields, you should look for opportunities to help this student to receive appropriate recognition and also to lend his talents to activities beyond the school.

Teaching Social Studies

We begin with a major problem area: textbooks students with disabilities often cannot understand. Later, we will look at making decisions about what to cover (history), making maps and other graphics accessible to students who are blind or have low vision (geography), and other issues.

The Problem of Textbooks

Social studies texts used in middle schools and high schools are, almost without exception, major obstacles to the success of inclusion. Particularly in the areas of history and economics, these texts become longer each year. They present other problems, as well. Paxton (1999) decried the "anonymous, authoritative style of writing" (p. 315) which leaves out everything that is personal about history. In a thorough review of such texts, he found them to be "dull," "erroneous," "overly broad," and "difficult to understand" (pp. 323–324). It is often said that newspapers are the first draft of history. Today, to be strictly accurate, we probably should say that CNN televised broadcasts are the first drafts, with newspapers the second drafts, and news magazines the third draft. Regardless, we can say one thing about these "drafts": They are lively. They are filled with controversies. To illustrate, Fox Cable News pointedly and repeatedly calls CNN a biased source of information (saying it is too liberal). That it is possible to "do" great history from original material cannot be doubted. William Manchester (1974) magnificently did so in *The Glory and the Dream,* a history of the United States between 1932 and 1972. This history is packed with unforgettable details that bring to life the controversies of our recent past. Manchester had opinions and he was not shy about expressing them. Why is it, then, that we cannot seem to achieve a similarly honest look at history in the social studies textbooks? Why did Paxton (1999), when reviewing these texts, resort to sarcasm: "Critics both ancient and modern have labored under the fundamental misconception that accomplished historical writing is, or ever was, a lucid combination of fact and truth, unblemished by the interpretations and beliefs" (pp. 315–316) of historians?

Experts on inclusion have expressed similar concerns: "[T]he textbook, which is the *de facto* social studies curriculum, has come under increasing scrutiny. Social studies textbooks often lack conceptual coherence, sacrifice depth for breadth of coverage, attempt to cover too much information in the allotted pages, and fail to provide contextual information and other conceptual scaffolds that would facilitate comprehension" (Ferretti et al., 1991, p. 59). Lederer (2000) joined the chorus:

> [S]ocial studies texts are difficult to comprehend for several reasons. Because textbooks tend to be written to accommodate many diverse interests, they are often written in a manner in which important concepts are not presented in a logically ordered fashion. Furthermore, explanations, as well as causes and effects, may not follow closely in the text or may be omitted altogether. Moreover, information that is presented is often not elaborated on or presented in a fashion that would allow readers to make connections to prior knowledge. . . . textbooks tend to make comparisons that are easy for adults to understand but difficult for students to understand. (p. 93)

Some Solutions to These Problems

Fortunately, the principles of universal design in education can help us to resolve some of these problems. High-school students with specific learning disabilities told Pisha and Coyne (2001) that the text they used in their 11th-grade United States history course was "confusing" and "busy"; they objected to the graphics and sidebars that appeared on almost every page of *The American Nation* (Boyer, 1998). Pisha, who was director of research at the Center for Applied Special Technologies (CAST), and Coyne, who was on the staff at CAST, responded by developing an electronic version of the textbook. Graphics and sidebars were removed from the electronic "pages"—they were "hidden" from view but could be called up, at any time, by clicking on hotlinks. The text was linked to CAST's eReader software, introduced earlier (it is a speech-synthesis program that speaks out loud any text on a screen, including material on Web sites). The students reported that they found the "plain-text" version much less cluttered and much easier to read, particularly since they could listen to it.

That solved one problem. Probing further, Pisha and Coyne learned, to their surprise, that these students seldom used the organizing features of the Boyer text. They did not pay much attention to, nor benefit from, the heads and subheads, the different sizes and styles of type, and the boldface/italic fonts that the publisher used to structure the material. Their failure to tap these organizing tools is an example of the difficulties children and youth with specific learning disabilities often display in the overall area of learning strategies (see Chapter 3). In response, Pisha and Coyne created an "outline view" of each book chapter. The outline view contained *only* the heads, subheads, and key vocabulary. By calling up the outline view, students could see, at a glance, how the material was organized. By clicking on any element on this "page," they could retrieve the full text of that section.

The students told Pisha and Coyne that they seldom used dictionaries or other resources while studying the Boyer textbook. The CAST researchers created a "unified resource page" (p. 201) that pulled together, in one place, all resources relating to key terms or concepts. This included the definitions for these words and hotlinks to Web sites related to the topics.

Finally, Pisha and Coyne gave these students access to concept-mapping software that facilitates student use of the historical material they are learning. Such software makes it much easier for students to monitor their own learning and present their findings and conclusions.

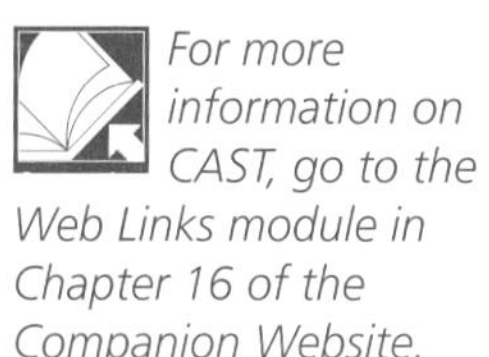
For more information on CAST, go to the Web Links module in Chapter 16 of the Companion Website.

The work at CAST is available for social studies teachers everywhere. Whether other social studies/history textbooks are made available in electronic form is up to the publishers. As we saw earlier, some states now require publishers of textbooks that are adopted in the state's public schools to provide not only bound (printed) texts but also e-texts. You can often find out which social studies, history, and other texts are available in electronic form by visiting the publishers' Web sites.

Other Adaptations

Other ways to support the reading of social studies materials were reviewed earlier. Briefly, you should offer advance organizers, concept maps, and other kinds of scaffolding. Make sure each lesson clearly identifies the "big idea" and shows how the details relate to that theme. Strive for clarity, avoiding unnecessary jargon and technical terms. Pace your instruction so as to pause between ideas (but not between words within an idea). Be redundant (say what you write, write names and terms that you speak). Study guides can help not only students with disabilities but others as well. Encourage your students to keep journals, writing journal entries to record their changing views as well as their emotional reactions to what they learn.

Lederer's (2000) solution to the difficulties his students encountered in reading text passages was to enlist peer support: He showed team members how to read, discuss, and reread documents. He also provided his students with prompts that reminded them to ask questions, make predictions, outline the passage (by writing headlines and subheads), discuss it among themselves, and then summarize it. Another approach, recommended by Singer (1997) and others, involves the creation of virtual texts. You assemble your own "textbook" by selecting and compiling materials your students can read with more success than they can a standard textbook. Singer (1997) pointed to the "Archiving Early America" site (*http://earlyamerica.com*). This site has a treasure trove of newspapers, maps, and so on, that students can analyze. Singer also edited a virtual text on slavery (Singer, 2001). You

Social studies is greatly enriched by Internet sites as those described in this chapter.

can also create your own high-interest, low-vocabulary versions of the text. However, as noted earlier in this book, doing this is very time-consuming. You must also weigh the fact that district-wide and state-wide tests, which students with disabilities are required to take, very likely will use language comparable to that of the standard texts.

History

The cognitive load on today's students is much heavier than was the case in years past. Consider, as a case in point, something as "simple" as Darwin's "theory of evolution." Historian of science Ernst Mayr (2002) recently demonstrated that it is actually five distinct theories, not just one: the theory of common descent, the theory of multiplication of species, the theory of gradualism, the theory of natural selection, and the theory of evolution itself. Similar advances in knowledge have expanded other areas of the social studies, as well.

Due, in part, to the heavy demands they must meet in history, students with emotional/behavioral disorders, some with attention deficit disorders, and many with other disabilities may need a "hook" to capture their interest.

A good way to "make history come alive" is to use the past to shed light upon the present. There has been much controversy recently, for example, about "Kennewick Man" and the implications of those bones for the legitimacy of claims made by Native Americans. The archaeological record suggests that Polynesians, not the ancestors of today's Native Americans, were the original settlers of what is now America (see *http://www.kennewick-man.com*). Students of Polynesian and Native American heritage may hold diametrically opposing views on the record and what it means. This opens the door for discussions about, among other things, America 9,000 years ago (American history; geography); how we can determine the heritage of Kennewick man (archaeology, anthropology); the role of the U.S. Department of the Interior in overseeing Native American reservations (civics/governmental institutions); and why Kennewick man is said to be so important to Polynesians and Native Americans (culture, sociology).

Reparations: A Current Controversy Offering a Glimpse of the Past

The idea of reparations for African Americans is much in the news, as advocates continue to press the case for slavery compensation. Randall Robinson's *The Debt: What America Owes to Blacks* (1999) claimed that trillions of dollars were due to survivors of slaves. Supporters contend that other groups have received reparations (e.g., Japanese Americans who were interred during World War II), while opponents point out that no African American now alive was ever a slave nor has any white American still living in the United States ever owned slaves. One way to begin class discussion about reparations is to read Mark Twain's (Samuel Clemens's) *The Adventures of Huckleberry Finn.* This novel ends with Huck freeing Jim. The historical record shows that Clemens had concluded, by the time he wrote *Huckleberry Finn,* that America owed reparations to the former slaves. This is evidenced in a 1885 letter he wrote to Dean Wayland of the Yale School of Law, in which he offered to pay the expenses of a black law student: "We have ground the manhood out of them and the shame is ours, not theirs, & we should pay for it" (Born to Trouble, Adventures of Huck Finn, at *http://www.pbs.org/wgbh/cultureshock/beyondhuck.html;* see also *http://library.yale.edu,* for Yale's Beinecke Rare Book and Manuscript Library). *Huckleberry Finn* is a much more controversial novel than is *Tom Sawyer,* which we discussed earlier in Chapter 14. In particular, students may become very uncomfortable about seeing the "N word" on virtually every page. That, itself, should be discussed in class. Singer (1997) recommended debate on a similar issue: whether or not historical documents containing words we now find offensive should be edited for political correctness. He illustrated with a speech by Sojourner Truth and with subsequent edits to remove from that speech the offensive "N word." The Summer/Fall 2001 issue of *Social Science Docket* (Singer, 2001) presents source documents and essays on a range of issues related to slavery, literature, and race. All of these areas allow students to grapple with lively controversies while also confronting their feelings about "political correctness" versus "historical integrity."

Strategies

Disability History. Students with disabilities who are placed into inclusive classrooms may be particularly interested in disability history. A good starting point is the Disability Social History Project, at *http://www.disabilityhistory.org/dshp.html.* It offers a link to "Disabled Women on the Web" and historical material on "Disability Militancy in the 1930s" and "U.S. Campaigns for the Handicapped." The Smithsonian National Museum of American History features an exhibit on the history of disability rights at *http://www.americanhistory.si.edu/disabilityrights/exhibit/html.* Teacher resources and course packages are offered at the Disability History Museum at *http://www.disabilitymuseum.org.* A calendar noting key dates in disability history is offered for purchase at the Colorado Cross-Disability Coalition, at *http://www.colorado2.com/ccdc.* Few other resources so easily let teachers and students identify dates on which significant events in disability history may be celebrated.

For more information on ClearVue/eav Inc. and DeBeck Educational Video, go to the Web Links module in Chapter 16 of the Companion Website.

Captioned Videos and Films. Videos, particularly if they are captioned, are an obvious way to increase interest and reach students with different needs and learning styles. ClearVue/eav Inc. offers *Geography in U.S. History,* a captioned video which combines geography with history. It is intended for use in grades 10 to 12. DeBeck Educational Video distributes *Cranberry Bounce,* a captioned video that shows a re-enactment of the first Thanksgiving at Plymouth. Students in grades K–9 learn about seasons on a cranberry farm as well as history.

Small-Group Projects. Few research projects have examined the teaching of history in inclusive classrooms. For this reason, we give an extended discussion to one recent such effort. Ferretti et al. (2001) used project-based instruction of history in fifth-grade inclusion classrooms. The students had specific learning disabilities, mild mental retardation, and/or attention deficit disorders. There were 18 students with disabilities and 27 other students. The project is best described as field intervention research. That is, the researchers actually taught the unit and conducted the evaluations. This is similar to what Lederer (2000) did with elementary students.

Heterogeneous groups engaged in cooperative learning about 19th-century westward migration. The unit helped students to construct a narrative because, the researchers argued, "history is fundamentally a narrative—the story of people who encountered a problem that required them to take some action" (p. 63). Contending that deep understanding is socially mediated (Morocco, 2001), Ferretti et al. (2001) assigned groups to examine and interpret historical evidence and then to create multimedia products demonstrating their knowledge. The researchers provided support for students with disabilities, notably a narrative framework that guided students to collect data about "the following narrative components: the people, the problems they faced in their homeland, the reasons for their decision to move west, the challenges they faced on the trip, and the outcomes that occurred when they reached their destination" (p. 63). Both the cooperative learning groups and the multimedia presentations were organized around these elements. Ferretti et al. also taught students how to analyze, interpret, and communicate historical information.

The researchers provided extensive support for group cooperation. The driving concept was "constructive conversation" (p. 63), by which they meant "students' questions and interpretations could be addressed and their thinking extended in discussion with other students. All group activities involved oral reading of the evidence and group discussion so that information and ideas could be shared" (p. 63). A lot of emphasis was placed upon peers interacting with peers.

Progress was assessed via multiple-choice questions and interviews. The interviews took place before and after the interventions. Both methods of historical inquiry and content knowledge were assessed. In addition, student attitudes were measured. Finally, the researchers observed once weekly throughout the eight-week unit.

Results indicated that students with and without disabilities improved from pre-test to post-test. Those with no disabilities gained much more. Analysis revealed that students learned most about the nature of historical evidence, notably about how historians detect bias in documents and other materials. Stated the researchers, "Our data are consistent with the conclusion that students with disabilities can understand authentic historical practices and meet the demands of rigorous curricula" (p. 67).

Teaching Students with Specific Learning Disabilities. After teaching history to 18 students with SLD, Ferretti et al. (2001) concluded that "Our findings are generally consistent with previous research documenting the effectiveness of project-based investigations for all students" (p. 67). They added that "students with disabilities can understand authentic historical practices and meet the demands of rigorous criteria" although they "may need more explicit instruction to use the narrative framework to organize and understand the content" (p. 67). This is, indeed, "promising," to adopt the word Ferretti and his colleagues used. Similarly, Lederer (2000) was successful in improving outcomes for students with learning disabilities by providing explicit teaching about cooperative learning and by offering extensive scaffolding that guided students in their group work. Both studies emphasized the importance of supporting students with SLD in organizing and in presenting their findings.

Teaching Students with Mental Retardation. Historians and other advocates of the study of history frequently quote the old maxim "those who don't know history are condemned to repeat it" and refer to the "wisdom" that students hopefully will attain by the study of history (e.g., Parker, 2001). What has not been shown convincingly is that knowing the many thousands of discrete facts about United States and World History leads to such understanding. Teachers in inclusive classrooms who have students with MR have to think long and hard about precisely what history is really worth knowing. That is because the amount of information such students can learn is sharply limited (see Chapter 5). To appreciate the dilemma, consider this all-but-impossible question: "If you had to select just 20 facts to teach about history, what would they be?" Focusing upon important *recent* history that conceivably could affect the student's future makes sense. You might explain the fact that history shows that trends and fads tend to reappear/recycle, and discuss how history teaches us that we almost always have to "go back and fix it" because we seldom get it right the first time.

Resources That Work

Secondary Sources

Concluded one study of teaching history in an inclusive classroom: "[F]ew students understood the concept of bias or reasons why historians' interpretations differ" (Ferretti, et al., 2001, p. 67).

A good way to address this important area is to read biographies. These are, to use the vernacular, "secondary sources." (Primary sources are original reports, secondary sources are interpretations and explanations about primary sources, and tertiary sources are textbooks that draw heavily upon secondary sources as well as some primary sources.) To coin a phrase, there is nothing wrong with studying secondary sources in secondary schools.

Take, for example, William T. Sherman. Was he an ogre? A racist? Or a great war strategist? The debate still rages. You might not know it, though, from the United States history texts used in middle schools and high schools, many of which blandly say that his "march through Georgia" left thousands of acres burning. If you teach in a Southern state, the portrait drawn in texts adopted by your school may be based upon Michael Fellman's (1995) *Citizen Sherman* of a murdering racist who destroyed the South. But another historian, Lee Kennett (2001), who teaches at the University of Georgia, found the same Sherman to be a world-class military strategist who went out of his way to avoid killing or otherwise harming blacks. Sherman, in Kennett's *Sherman: A Soldier's Life,* pioneered the tactics that much later won America the Gulf War: dismantling the enemy's infrastructure and thus its ability to fight back. Kennett shows that General Sherman freed the slaves he found on the southern plantations he burned.

An attempt to balance these contrasting portraits was offered by S. P. Hirshson (1997) in *The White Tecumseh.*

A sympathetic portrait of one of Sherman's opponents, Thomas J. ("Stonewall") Jackson, who led Confederate troops, *Standing Like a Stone Wall: The Life of General Thomas J. Jackson,* was written by James I. Robertson, Jr. (2001). Intended for readers age 12 or over, it is an outstanding secondary source on the Civil War. Robertson is also the author of a 950-page biography of Jackson that was written for professional historians and graduate students in history; he drew upon that work in writing *Standing Like a Stone Wall.*

You might assign one of these books to each of three good readers, telling them to then lead a group that would work together to prepare a 10-minute oral argument answering the question, "Sherman: Genius or Devil?" It may be the last time you have to tell your students that there is a story behind every story in the history books: The events of the past, no less than those we live through today, are surrounded by controversy. What history teaches may depend upon is who is speaking/writing.

You may follow the lead of Lederer (2000) and that of Ferretti et al. (2001) by providing students with scaffolding and prompts. What questions should they ask of the text(s) they read? How can group members discuss the material among themselves? How can they develop persuasive arguments that will convince the rest of the class that their interpretation is correct? What rubric should other class members follow in evaluating the three competing presentations?

While the suggestions of Taylor and Larson (2000), such as repeating key information, making abstract information concrete, and emphasizing material that students with MR can use in their everyday lives, are as relevant here as in early childhood/elementary schools, the ability of middle-school and high-school teachers to follow these suggestions is much more limited. In middle-school and especially in high-school history classes, the sheer volume of material makes repetition a dubious tactic (covering the content is challenging enough without it). One may find it difficult, too, to imagine how such concepts as "republican form of government" can be made concrete. Secondary social studies is replete with such abstract ideas. And aside from the basics, it is not easy to identify what aspects of United States and/or World History would actually have practical, everyday meaning for individuals with MR.

Teaching Students with Other High-Prevalence Disabilities. Cooperative learning and other team-based activities may appeal to students with attention deficit disorders or emotional/behavioral disorders simply because these are hands-on, active pursuits. The fact that overt competition is reduced, by comparison to traditional lecture methods, is helpful as well.

Teaching Students with Visual Impairments. The greater reliance in middle-school and high-school history upon source documents makes it even more imperative at these levels than at the elementary level that students who are blind or have low vision are provided with appropriate adaptive devices and software. This is an issue in assessment as well as in instruction. It is imperative that students be able to "see" what other students see. In particular, it is sadly true that many Web sites are not accessible to users of screen readers (see "Resources That Work: Social Studies on the Web," p. 555).

Teaching Students with Other Low-Prevalence Disabilities. If your class makes trips to local sites of historical interest, you must check beforehand to see if the sites are accessible. Historical landmarks are exempted from building accessibility laws and rules to the extent to which accessibility modifications might impair the historical nature or status of the structure. However, renovations and additions to existing buildings generally are accessible. Students who are deaf or hard of hearing may find history to be problematic because of the very large number of new names and words that must be learned. In the classroom, every such word must be spelled out on the fingers. Those that are mentioned frequently in class may eventually be given "homemade signs" that are agreed upon between student and interpreter.

Assessing Student Progress in History

Singer (1997) was caustic about the social studies questions asked of 8th-and 12th-graders taking the NAEP (National Assessment of Educational Progress) examinations and other social studies assessments. He made the valid point that questions calling for recall of factual information reveal very little, if anything, about student understanding of and ability to use materials and procedures in the social sciences. He told the story of teaching one child who learned the material but failed tests because he could not read fluently. Singer's solution to problems like this was similar to Yell's (see "Early Childhood and Elementary," p. 557): make assessment part of learning itself, not something separate. Singer supported use of portfolios and wrote that student self-evaluation should be part of the overall assessment process.

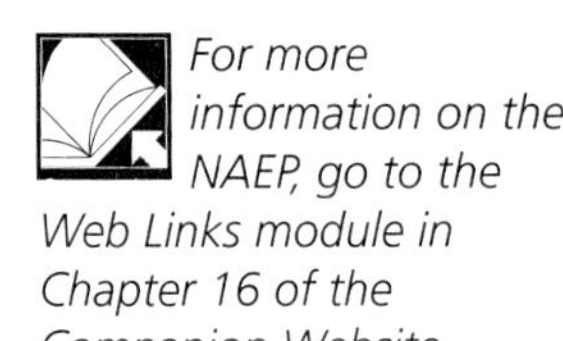
For more information on the NAEP, go to the Web Links module in Chapter 16 of the Companion Website.

The CSSAP asks open-ended questions, some of which use maps and other graphical materials for students to analyze. Czarra (1999), for example, displayed "Sample Questions from a CSSAP High School History Text Booklet" about immigration into the United States (1820–1920) which include a graph showing immigration by decade. Students are asked to give examples of "push factors" and "pull factors" affecting immigration. They are then to identify countries from which people emigrated and to offer reasons why they did. The questions are fairly straightforward and thus should not present undue problems for students with specific learning disabilities, attention deficit disorders, or other mild disabilities. Students with MR likely will find them challenging. Fortunately for students who are blind or have low vision, the bar chart is not needed to answer the questions that are asked. This will not always be the case, however. You should check well in advance with district or state testing officials about plans to use charts or other graphical materials in assessments. You should also inquire about staff support.

Civics and Government

The study of controversial issues is a good way to make civics and government "come alive." American government has adapted to the multicultural nature of society by adopting a variety of "affirmative action" measures designed to protect minority-group members from discrimination. Other than those measures, the U.S. government generally reflects the heritage of the early settlers, namely, the Magna Carta and other European forms of government. Americans tend to accept these traditions without much scrutiny. Here is one thought-provoking idea: Do these institutions reflect "white privilege"? A related question is, Do the social studies regard people from ethnic and racial minority groups as actors or as subjects? That is, do social studies "study" minority groups but not majority groups? Should social studies similarly "study" whites? "White" institutions? *White Reign* claims there should indeed be white studies (Kincheloe, Steinberg, Rodriguez, & Chennault, 1998). Your students may be as uncomfortable questioning white privilege as they are discussing the "N word" and slavery. But, as Singer (1997) argued, it is not the purpose of social studies to make our students feel comfortable.

Asking interesting questions is a good strategy. Why is it, for example, that the citizens of New Hampshire are more active in civic affairs than are people in most other states? In some New Hampshire towns, as many as 8% of all adults serve on some board or commission. New Hampshire residents are twice as likely as are citizens of all states to report participation in civic activities. To illustrate, there is a waiting list for every committee in the city of Portsmouth. Exploring these issues, Lewin (2001) suggested that the small size of communities in New Hampshire is part of the story. So, too, is the fact that the state has no income tax and no state sales tax. Accordingly, its state and county governments are small, making town governance unusually important. Projects students may find interesting involve discovering the extent of civic involvement of adults in your town—and developing recommendations to increase that level of participation.

Strategies

Challenging Beliefs. One strategy that may appeal to students is to upset their preconceptions about what is natural and normal. Reading William Golding's (1962) classic novel about boys stranded on an island, *Lord of the Flies* is an excellent beginning. Left to their own devices, without adult supervision, the boys created a culture and a government (of sorts) that are uncomfortable in what they reveal about human nature. The book can be a springboard for discussions ranging from "Why Do We Have Rules?" to "Is there anything disabling about obesity?"

Making Government "Real." Another is to teach government through projects and illustrations that are germane to your students. A good example is the role of the courts in deciding how to interpret the U.S. Constitution's ban on "cruel and unusual punishment" for individuals with mental retardation who are convicted of serious crimes. (For an intriguing story about how the Constitution came to be written, see Berkin [2003]. Her *A Brilliant Solution: Inventing the American Constitution* is wonderful on the behind-the-scenes haggling among Jefferson, Franklin, and others to hammer out this document.)

Teacher Strategies That Work

Making Government Real

The Arc, a national parent-led organization representing 140,000 Americans interested in mental retardation, has become increasingly convinced that adults with MR should not be executed under any circumstances. In March 2001, for example, the association's president wrote to the governor and board of pardons in Nevada, requesting that they commute the death sentence of a man there. Karen Staley also wrote, just two days earlier, to a district attorney in Oklahoma, requesting that he not seek the death penalty in a case involving an adult with MR. See The Arc's Web site: *http://www.thearc.org/nevius.htm*. The Arc believes that MR by its very nature presents so many problems in capital punishment cases that the death penalty becomes, in such instances, a cruel and unusual punishment. The Arc's position, adopted in its current form in 1998, is controversial. It reads:

> Existing case-by-case determinations of competence to stand trial, criminal responsibility and mitigating factors at sentencing have proven insufficient to protect the rights of individuals with mental retardation.
>
> The presence of mental retardation by definition raises so many possibilities of miscommunication, misinformation, and an inadequate defense that the imposition of the death penalty is unacceptable.
>
> People with mental retardation shall be exempt from the death penalty, but not from other appropriate punishment, on a case-by-case basis. (*http://www.thearc.org*)

The U.S. Supreme Court ruled on June 4, 2001, in *Penry v. Johnson,* that MR must be considered as a possible mitigating circumstance. Thus, the Court moved toward the Arc's position that capital punishment may indeed be "cruel and unusual punishment" for persons with MR. One year later, the Court effectively outlawed the death penalty for persons with mental retardation in its *Atkins vs. Virginia* decision.

In the United States, we have three co-equal branches of government: the legislative, the executive, and the judicial. Of the three, the judicial branch is the most shrouded in mystery. One way to explicate its function is to explore the role courts play in resolution of complex issues. To illustrate, consider the Constitution's prohibition of "cruel and unusual punishment"—what this means has varied over time. We can see that in a series of cases involving persons with mental retardation who were convicted of serious crimes. Putting aside for the moment questions of innocence versus guilt, let us assume that an individual were in fact guilty. Should he be treated any differently from the ways society deals with others convicted of similar crimes? For most of America's history, the answer to that question was "No." Recently, however, a national consensus has begun to form around the idea that the answer probably should be "Yes." You can help your students work through the questions such cases raise. The box, "Teacher Strategies That Work: Making Government Real" provides background information.

The nearby box, "Lesson Plans That Work," offers a sample lesson plan on the courts, using this Supreme Court case. Note: The Constitution appears in most encyclopedias. A handy and inexpensive pocket version is published by the U.S. Government Printing Office.

For more information on how to contact the U.S. Government Printing Office, go to the Web Links module in Chapter 16 of the Companion Website.

Social Activism. Students with disabilities, as well as many "at-risk" youth (see Chapter 11), need to become skilled self-advocates. The reality of America in the early years of the 21st century leaves them no choice. Civil-rights laws for people with disabilities are, virtually without exception, "complaint-driven" statutes (Bowe, 2000b, p. 272). For example, the Americans with Disabilities Act (PL 101-336) calls for most stores, sporting establishments, hotels, restaurants, and other "places of public accommodations" to make their physical facilities accessible to and useable by persons with disabilities. This includes individuals who use wheelchairs, those who need interpreters, and those who require Brailled or other alternative-media print resources. These requirements have been law for more than a decade. However, there are millions of such establishments in thousands of communities across our country. Experience has shown that individuals with disabilities cannot expect all local places of public accommodation to make appropriate alterations on their own initiative. Rather, what is frequently required is for a local citizen with a disability to request such changes. If those requests are ignored, the individual needs to use the complaint

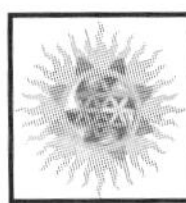

Lesson Plans That Work

The Role of the Courts

Assess, Then Teach. Ask students if they recall language in the U.S. Constitution about "cruel and unusual punishment." (It is in the VIIIth Amendment—"Excessive bail shall not be required, nor excessive fines imposed, nor cruel and unusual punishments inflicted"). Ask if students think the meaning of this term might change over time (e.g., mean something different today from what it meant in, say, 1865). This should lead to a discussion of the fact that judges, including Supreme Court Justices, do reflect the times in which they live.

Teach Strategies. Since this is the U.S. Constitution, questions about "cruel and unusual punishment" would be litigated in federal courts. These include district courts, courts of appeals, and the U.S. Supreme Court. (Questions about a state constitution would be reviewed by state courts.) The key to thinking about the meaning of "cruel and unusual punishment" is to consider what we would think of as "usual" punishment. This itself is controversial. Federal courts bring two opposing attorneys before the bench, each arguing a different interpretation.

Use Simulations. We will do that in groups, next.

Small Groups. While not "small" in the usual sense, breaking the class into three groups allows for a "mock court" session. One team should take the position that execution is cruel and unusual. The second team should argue that it is not. The third team serves as the jury. Ask the competing teams to develop arguments that present the most convincing case for their interpretation. These teams should also choose a litigator (the "attorney" who speaks for the group). Spell out the criteria the "jury" should use, for example, the strength of the case, the clarity of the presentation, and so on.

One-on-One Instruction. You, a collaborating teacher, or a peer tutor should offer explicit instruction for any student(s) who do not understand some aspect of the lesson.

procedures provided under the Act. Generally, the fact of filing a complaint triggers action. Similarly, it is one thing for federal and state law to ban acts of discrimination against gays and lesbians. It is quite another, as we saw earlier, for such acts actually to cease.

Social studies, particularly at the secondary level, is an appropriate subject through which students may learn self-advocacy skills. This is because secondary social studies routinely includes examination of politics, the sociology of culture, and other related issues—*and* regularly features student-initiated projects as course activities. Helping teachers to guide students in their exploration of social issues is NCSS's *Handbook on Teaching Social Issues* (Evans, Newman, & Saxe, 1996).

Paolo Freire (1995) argued that students are experts on their own lives, just as teachers are on subject matter content. The two must work together, then, so that children and youth may take possession of content and use it to empower themselves. Singer (1997), in his text on teaching social studies in secondary schools, endorsed this approach, saying that social-studies educators should encourage students who desire social change to equip themselves to advocate for such change. This view of social studies as "transformative" (Singer, 1997, p. 81) brings social studies alive because students acquire the knowledge and skills they need to become social activists. Sites of possible interest include the "African American Web Connection" at *http://www.aawc.com*; it offers links to all kinds of information about African-American culture. Another site, Native Americans and Indigenons Peoples Links, at *http://neravt.com/left* does much the same on Native American culture.

Politics: Making It Work for You

Politics is not exclusively the domain of elected officials. Rather, it is a domain of knowledge and skills available to all of us. People who feel oppressed need to understand how to use politics to improve their lives. The "bible" of politics is Machiavelli's *The Prince*. This slim text is often read in secondary schools, as well it should be. Machiavelli offered advice to landowners and provincial princes of the Dark Ages, which was his time (1469—1527), yet the perceptions of how politics works are timeless. Much less often read, which is a shame, is Saul Alinksy's *Rules for Radicals* (1971). This enthralling and empowering guide was written in a direct, no-nonsense style that recalls *The Prince*. Alinksy's *Rules* is also product of a time (the late 1960s). Alinsky, who died just a year after this book was published, knew that many young people at the time were desperate to change America. Richard Nixon was in the White House, the Vietnam War was at its height, and the student rebellions at Berkeley and Columbia were vivid, recent memories. Alinksy addressed his

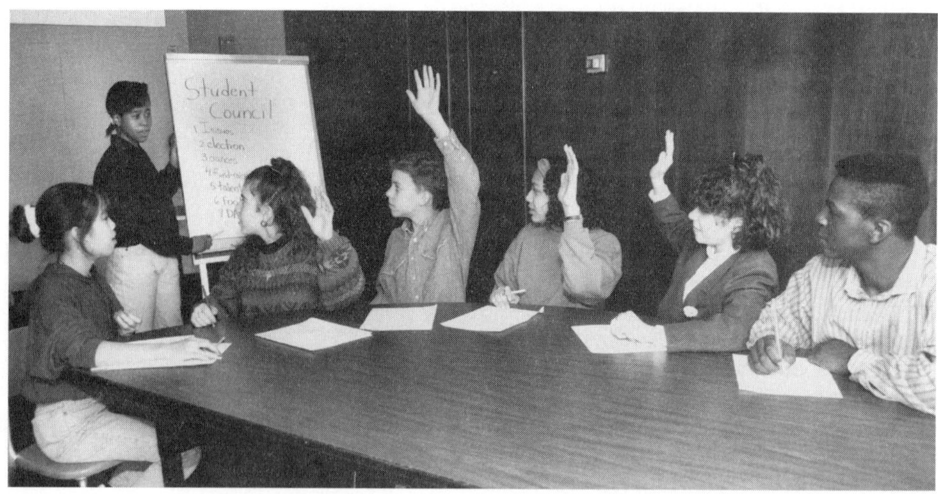

Participating in student government is a good way to learn civics.

primer toward "realistic radicals" who wanted to alter the status quo. I was one: in the mid-1970s, I went to Washington determined to create some civil rights for Americans with disabilities. We enjoyed none at the time. *Rules for Radicals* was my handbook.

Alinsky's "rules" as well as his sardonic sense of humor come through in his dictums. One, "If the real radical finds that having long hair sets up psychological barriers to communication and organization, he cuts his hair" (p. xix). A second, "There can be no such thing as a successful traitor, for if one succeeds he becomes a founding father" (p. 34). A third, "The ninth rule of the ethics of means and ends is that any effective means is automatically judged by the opposition as being unethical" (p. 35). And finally, "*The Prince* was written by Machiavelli for the Haves on how to hold power. *Rules for Radicals* was written for the Have-Nots on how to take it away" (p. 3). These "rules" were vividly illustrated with stories from Alinksy's colorful career as a civic organizer in Chicago and New York.

Although dated, Eugene Burdick's novel, *The Ninth Wave* (1956) may be useful. This is a coming-of-age story about a young man, Mike Freesmith, while he was attending Stanford University. The title refers to an observation he and other Californians made, namely that the Pacific Ocean along the Long Beach and Bakersfield beaches produces waves, every ninth of which was said to be bigger than the preceding eight. The biggest of them all was the ninth ninth wave. There was, Mike thought, no rational reason why this should be so. It just was. So, too, are the laws of human relations. The key, he realized, was to see people as they were, not as one wishes they were and not as they want to be seen. As the story evolves, the Stanford student learns the fundamental realities of political science. Mike is interested in getting what he wants. He's in a hurry. He has no time for theory. Rather, he does things with his fellow students, professors, and others, and observes the results. Thus, "Freesmith's First Principle of Human Behavior: One person can make a decision faster than a group" (p. 45). The novel is less a *How to Win Friends and Influence People* (Carnegie, 1994) than it is a "How to Get Yours."

You could assign a group of students to read these three books and summarize the "lessons" to be learned. A good next step might be to create two role-playing teams, one of "Haves" and one of "Have-Nots," each of which would show the class how the principles might play out in real life. How would Dale Carnegie, Saul Alinksy, and the fictional Mike Freesmith each approach a common problem, such as getting the school administration to upgrade the quality of food in the cafeteria? You could have the class indicate, after the two presentations, which tactics they believe will be effective in today's world. If you give them a rubric, they can also evaluate the competing presentations.

Teaching Students with Specific Learning Disabilities. Concept maps may be particularly useful in helping students with SLD to comprehend how government works at various levels (federal, state, local; legislative, executive, judicial; etc.).

Teaching Students with Mental Retardation. As at the early childhood/elementary level, the civics framework is a useful one for teaching students with MR about rules and how to follow them. In middle school and high school, they should also learn how to present their needs to decision makers. They can also learn how to organize. Many states have chapters of People First, a major consumer organization comprised largely of persons with MR. The first statewide group was created in Oregon. Today, there are chapters in England, Canada, and other English-speaking countries. Educators also need to remember that individuals with MR can vote in national, state, and local races in most states. They need preparation to discharge this civic responsibility.

For more information on People First in the United States and other countries, go to the Web Links module in Chapter 16 of the Companion Website.

Teaching Students with Other High-Prevalence Disabilities. Students with emotional/behavioral disorders or with attention deficit disorders may find civics/government to be annoying (because the content may strike them as personally intrusive, being as it is about following rules). However, they may enjoy high-activity methods of instruction, which let them "get out and *do* something!"

Teaching Students with Visual Impairments. The Web sites of federal agencies generally are accessible to people using screen readers. State, county, and local government Web sites tend to be much less accessible. However, printed materials at all levels of government usually are made available, upon request, in large-print and other alternative formats.

Teaching Students with Other Low-Prevalence Disabilities. Most county and local government offices, as well as state and federal offices, are accessible to and usable by people who use wheelchairs and other mobility devices. Individuals who are deaf or hard of hearing may find Web sites and e-mail the most accessible ways of communicating with various units of government. However, most also have Telecommunications Devices for the Deaf (TTY's) on at least one phone line or can be called through dual-party relay services (TDI Inc., *http://www.tdi.org*).

Assessing Student Progress in Civics/Government

An appropriate measure to include in assessments of students with mental retardation, emotional/behavioral disorders, and attention deficit disorders is the extent to which they learn and follow class, school, and town rules. This is civics at the level where they learn and live. The observations you make as you teach, and the records you keep of your own and school disciplinary actions may contribute to your assessments. You may also ask students to self-evaluate, perhaps sending you an e-mail toward the end of each 6-week marking period, in which they express their views on the extent to which they complied with appropriate class and school rules.

Geography

Singer (1997) advocated teaching geography in the context of reasons to learn it. Study of North America, for example, might be linked to an examination of different forms of government in Canada, the United States, and Mexico. An interesting account of the three North American countries, including some very readable stories on recent history, appears in DePalma (2001), *Here: A Biography of the New American Continent.* A unit on North America thus could connect civics/government to geography. The on-again, off-again efforts by residents of Quebec to separate themselves from the rest of Canada are illustrated with fascinating stories in DePalma's book. These tales lead naturally to questions about where Quebec is located vis à vis other parts of Canada and, for that matter, Northern states of the United States.

For more information on the Environmental Systems Research Institute, go to the Web Links module in Chapter 16 of the Companion Website.

A set of excellent tools for teaching geography is offered by Environmental Systems Research Institute. This is Geographic Information Systems (GIS), which is available on CD-ROM. GIS lets students create maps and use them to display information the students have collected. Those data may be manipulated mathematically. The program is particularly good at handling map overlays (e.g., a topographical map and a surface features map). A good way to get started is to read "GIS in K–12 Education," a white paper posted at ESRI's Web site. Note: because GIS is dynamic and makes extensive use of graphics, configuring it for use by students who are blind or have low vision may be difficult. If you have such students, contact ESRI and/or the American Printing House for the Blind.

For more information on the companies and organizations discussed in the "Technologies That Work," go to the Web Links module in Chapter 16 of the Companion Website.

Strategies

Making It Concrete. Geography includes local geography, of course, and this may be highly appropriate for some students with disabilities. Likely, you didn't really get to know where everything in town was until you started riding your bike around town or driving (somehow, we don't really pay attention when someone else does the driving). For this reason, many children and youth under age 16 or 17 may not really know the "lay of the land" locally. Such knowledge is valuable. It is also part of transition (see Chapter 13). This

Technologies That Work

Software for Social Studies

Large-print and tactile maps are available from The American Printing House for the Blind. Embossed on heavy white paper and measuring 17" × 15", they vary in price.

Students may construct their own maps using a program on CD-ROM, "Geographic Information Systems (GIS)," offered by Environmental Systems Research Institute. Be warned, however, that those maps may not be readable for students who are blind or have low vision.

"Race the Clock," software that teaches social studies skills to students age 8 and up, is distributed by MindPlay. You can use it to teach states, state capitals, U.S. presidents, inventors/inventions, and events/dates.

is because learning one's way around town is an essential part of both the employment and independent-living objectives in many transition plans. Accordingly, community-based instruction that features exploring neighborhoods in the area be a good way to teach geography.

Comparative Geography. Another way to make geography "come alive" in an inclusive classroom is to compare the civil rights of persons with disabilities in different countries. Suppose, to pick up again on the North America example, your class were to compare rights and opportunities in the United States to those in Canada and Mexico. Using the Web and following up leads by e-mail, your students would acquire information that is in itself interesting in many ways. In Canada, efforts have been made to replicate some American laws, notably the Americans with Disabilities Act. At least some parts of large cities in Canada are reasonably accessible to users of wheelchairs. In Mexico, by contrast, there are few if any civil rights for people with disabilities and accessibility is the exception rather than the rule.

For more information on United Learning, go to the Web Links module in Chapter 16 of the Companion Website.

Captioned Videos and Films. United Learning offers a four-part series, *How Geography Defines a Culture* (about how cultures reflect geography), *Physical Geography* (about how physical features on earth affect human/cultural geography), and *Basics of Geography* (about climate, natural resources, water and landforms). All are captioned.

Teaching Students with Specific Learning Disabilities. Maps can be very confusing for some students with SLD. Young people with SLD may not make effective use of color and may not even look at map legends. Accordingly, explicit instruction in how to read maps may be required.

Teaching Students with Mental Retardation. Local geography can be highly useful for children and youth with MR. They need to learn how to get to key places (grocery store, fast-food restaurant, etc.), on foot and via public buses. This can further transition goals. Considerable time may be required for travel training to be successful. Virtually all of this training should be on-site, that is, in the community (Dever & Knapczyk, 1997).

Teaching Students with Other High-Prevalence Disabilities. Students with the inattentive variety of attention deficit disorders (ADHD/I) may need training that helps them to consciously attend to where they are, where they park the car, and so on. Students with emotional/behavioral disorders and many with the hyperactive variety of attention deficit disorders (ADHD/HI) need training and plenty of practice in following the unwritten rules of community living, particularly standing in line. Youth with autism may require even more such training.

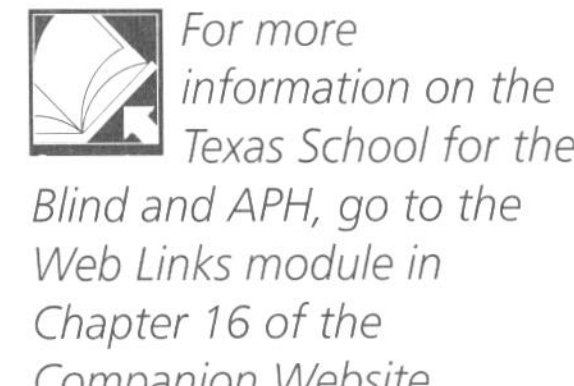

For more information on the Texas School for the Blind and APH, go to the Web Links module in Chapter 16 of the Companion Website.

Teaching Students with Visual Impairments. Raised-relief maps and other materials useful in teaching geography to students who are blind or have low vision are available from special schools such as the Texas School for the Blind and the American Printing House for the Blind. If you visit the APH site, look for its catalog of accessible textbooks, using the "GEOGRAPH.TXT" code. Experts called "orientation and mobility specialists" are widely available to train people who are blind or have low vision how to get around—at home, in the school, in the neighborhood, and in the larger community.

Teaching Students with Other Low-Prevalence Disabilities. Students using wheelchairs and other mobility devices need to be trained about the availability (or, in some communities, unavailability) of lift-equipped public buses and of dial-a-ride door-to-door taxi services. There are specific rules that govern the provision of such services (Bowe, 2000b). Notably, dial-a-ride services are available on a subscription basis and generally only for instances in which an individual is unable to use lift-equipped public buses.

Assessing Student Progress in Geography

A set of "Sample Questions from a CSSAP Middle School Geography Test Booklet" was presented in Czarra (1999). These presented a map of the Yangtze river, plus a larger map of China. Students were directed to answer three multiple-choice questions by marking answer sheets. Better for students with specific learning disabilities or attention deficit disorders would be to permit answers directly on the test sheet (to eliminate unintentional errors). The CSSAP then asks essay questions, one of which calls for students to identify two groups supporting or opposing the Three Gorges Project to dam the river and then to give two arguments for and two against damming. Judging from these questions, the level of difficulty likely is too high for most students with mental retardation. The clarity and detail of the maps are insufficient for students who are blind or low vision to be able to use effectively. Magnification devices could be used. A better approach for these students, but much more difficult to implement, would be raised maps which tactually highlight important features.

Experienced teachers of social studies, including Singer, favor the use of portfolios to assess student progress. As explained in Chapter 8, portfolio assessment has much to recommend it. Students may assemble evidence of accomplishment throughout the school year. Teachers need to develop criteria with which to evaluate those portfolio entries—and to communicate those criteria to students early in the school year.

Economics

The teaching of economics at the middle school and secondary levels is conceptual rather than analytic. In particular, the advanced mathematics that economists use to develop and test their models are skimmed over at best. Rather, the emphasis is upon the basic ideas of macroeconomics (international, national, and large business economics) and microeconomics (personal and interpersonal economics). Even so, the material can be challenging for many teenagers who are just beginning to grasp the value of money and of material objects in their own lives and have not yet thought seriously about macroeconomic issues.

Strategies

Many economics concepts are highly abstract in nature. They can best be taught in inclusive classrooms by means of *simulations* and *manipulatives*. Thus, instruction about money could be introduced through barter: Students can exchange items, gradually coming to agreement about how many of X is equivalent to how many of Y. (Historically speaking, barter emerged before money did.) Such exercises also can teach such economics concepts as decision making (how and why people reach economic decisions, such as how much a new or used car is worth), markets, and pricing.

Teaching Practical Math in Inclusion Classrooms. Many students will benefit greatly from instruction in real-world applications of mathematics. Particularly needed are skills in

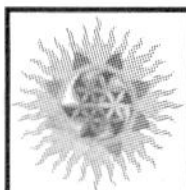

Lesson Plans That Work

Balancing a Checkbook

Assess, Then Teach. Open by asking what students know about checkbooks. What does it mean to "balance a checkbook"? Note that adults do that several times a month, if not every week. Why is it important to balance a checkbook?

Teach Strategies. The keys to success in balancing checkbooks is to keep records of *all* transactions involving the checking account. This includes bank fees, cash withdrawals, deposits, and other transactions that do not actually involve writing checks. Record-keeping is 90% of the job. The rest has to do with addition and subtraction.

Model Your Thinking and Problem-Solving Behavior. Using an overhead or a PowerPoint® slide, as well as deposit slips, hand-written notes to yourself and so on, demonstrate how you balance a (hypothetical) checkbook. As you do each step, explain *why* as well as how you do it. Articulate orally anything that is written/displayed visually, and vice versa.

Use Simulations. The above *is* a simulation.

Small Groups. Assign students to heterogeneous dyads. Give each pair a hypothetical checkbook complete with an opening balance and a variety of deposit and withdrawal notations. Offer advance organizers/scaffolding (e.g., "Did you make note of that ATM withdrawal you made?"). Instruct the pairs to determine today's actual balance and what the balance will be in a week (after deposits have cleared, etc.). Explain that you will call on one member of each pair, at random, to give the current balance and the next-week balance, and to explain how those were calculated. (Announcing that you will pick at random from each dyad makes the teams responsible to ensure that each member is prepared.) Ask the pairs to engage in peer tutoring, helping team members as needed, so that the team ends up with the right numbers. Wander around the room as they work, being available to answer questions but do not interfere with the teams.

One-on-One Instruction. As needed, afterwards, provide direct instruction in which you teach strategies and problem-solving behaviors to students whose work in the dyads demonstrated that they need this additional help.

managing money (Browder & Grasso, 1999). Units on balancing a checkbook, making a budget, and the like help students to reach their IEP goals. These are also key elements of many transition plans. That is why nearby boxes offer sample lesson plans in these areas. These instructional units tap some key teaching tactics introduced earlier in Chapter 8.

Teaching Students with Specific Learning Disabilities. Economics texts tend to be dry and dense. Students with SLD may need auxiliary materials such as concept maps to comprehend textual material. We discussed some of these issues earlier.

Teaching Students with Mental Retardation. The sample lesson plans about checkbooks and budgeting can be of direct benefit to transition-age students with MR. Note, also, that a "next dollar strategy" is often taught to these young people (Browder & Grasso, 1999). To illustrate: If the student orders a Happy Meal® at McDonalds™ and is told the cost is $3.79, the "next dollar strategy" tells her to hand the employee four one-dollar bills. This avoids the necessity on the part of the customer to count coins. It shifts that responsibility to the employee (actually, in McDonalds™ restaurants, to the cashier's machine). This strategy, and other ways of working with money, can be taught as part of economics while also helping the student to reach transition goals.

Teaching Students with Other High-Prevalence Disabilities. Students with ADHD and emotional/behavioral disorders may benefit from instruction which gives them opportunities to try out and apply economics concepts. This "active" learning may reduce undesired behaviors.

Teaching Students with Visual Impairments. Well-developed strategies for organizing money (e.g., placing all $10 bills together, and separating those from $5 bills and, in turn, from $1 bills as well) are available for use. These may be taught by VI Teachers or, alternatively, a VI Teacher can train the student's inclusive classroom teachers how to train him in these techniques.

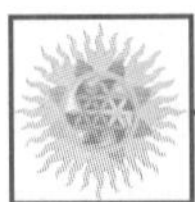

Lesson Plans That Work

Making and Keeping a Budget

Assess, Then Teach. Open by encouraging group discussions about budgets. Why do families make budgets? What can we learn by creating a budget and seeing how we do after a month? After 6 months? What does it mean to "stick to the budget"?

Teach Strategies. Successful budgeting requires (1) Collecting key information about fixed costs (how much rent costs, how much utilities cost, etc.) and about variable costs (how much we tend to spend on take-out lunches, on clothes, etc.); (2) Adding, subtracting, multiplying, and dividing; and (3) Making adjustments.

Model Your Thinking and Problem-Solving Behavior. Let students watch as you create a hypothetical budget showing entries for rent, utilities (telephone, heat, electricity, water, cable TV, etc.), car payments, gasoline, lunch money, clothing, insurance, food, household cleaning supplies, etc. Demonstrate two scenarios: (1) You make your budget, with $150 to spare that month. Let students see your pleasure and your decision making about how to use that money (e.g., save it, reward yourself with a spending spree, and so on), and (2) You break your budget, overspending by $400. Encourage students to help you think of ways to fix the problem (e.g., work extra hours, cut back this month on discretionary spending, etc.). Show students how to extend the budget to an annual one, using a calculator, and how to estimate costs.

Use Simulations. The above *is* a simulation.

Small Groups. Assign students to heterogeneous dyads. Give each pair the list of budget items you used (rent, utilities [telephone, heat, electricity, water, cable TV, etc.], car payments, gasoline, lunch money, clothing, insurance, food, household cleaning supplies). Give each pair two "net earned income" numbers: "$1,250/month" and "$2,000/month"). *Optional:* Give them copies of newspaper ads for cars, rental apartments, and so on, so they may make decisions based on locally prevailing prices.

Alternative. Assign them, a week earlier, to cut out such ads and bring them to school. Instruct the pairs to come up with a monthly *and* an annual budget for each, justifying differences they decide to make depending upon earned income. Explain that you will call upon one member of each pair, at random, to give the current balance and the next-week balance, and to explain how those were calculated. Ask the pairs to engage in peer tutoring, helping team members as needed, so that good decisions are made. Wander around the room as they work, being available to answer questions but do not interfere with the teams.

One-on-One Instruction. As needed, afterwards, provide Direct Instruction in which you teach the steps or decision-making strategies that caused difficulties for your students.

Teaching Students with Other Low-Prevalence Disabilities. Students who are deaf tend to do better in math than they do in reading, but even in math their achievement levels usually do not go above the equivalent of eighth grade. Thus, they can master the material in the two sample lessons in this chapter (on balancing a checkbook and making/keeping a budget) but may encounter considerable difficulty with the more abstract math of other aspects of economics (e.g., macroeconomics, monetary policy, fiscal policy, etc.). Students with autism who are not also mentally retarded may excel in economics, because of its basis in math.

Assessing Student Progress in Economics

Perhaps the best way to measure student achievement in economics is to offer "real-life" tests, as were suggested in the two "lesson plans" on balancing a checkbook and on budgeting. Such assessments may be more fair to students with mental retardation, emotional/behavioral disorders, deafness, and other disabilities than are traditional paper-and-pencil word-based tests.

CHAPTER SUMMARY

Social Studies

- The National Council for the Social Studies (NCSS) offers broad national standards that cover content and methods in the areas of anthropology, economics, political science, psychology, sociology, and history.

- Teaching social studies through the "framework" of civics makes sense at the early childhood/elementary level. It is particularly suitable for students who have mental retardation or emotional/behavioral disorders because the emphasis is upon following rules people create.
- An alternative is to emphasize the scientific aspects of the social studies, including introduction to the various methods social sciences use to collect and analyze data.
- The "social activist" framework is probably better suited for use in secondary schools, but it can be applied (as can the civics framework) to help students, particularly those with severe disabilities, to begin to develop competencies in self-determination.
- Social studies is a "natural home" for instruction in knowledge and skills identified in students' IEPs.

  This includes expressing needs, getting along with others, and reading for a purpose.
- Explicit instruction, and lots of supervised practice, is often required for students with disabilities to master the skills they need to participate meaningfully in groups and on projects.
- Probably the biggest issue in social studies education at this level is textbooks that are largely inaccessible. Some important progress is being made, notably through universal design techniques, but much more is needed. The ATIC project at the American Printing House for the Blind is a hopeful sign of needed progress.

Civics and Government

- Civics and government can "come alive" for students through simulations and projects in which the rights and responsibilities of persons with disabilities are explored.
- As mentioned earlier, the "social-activist" framework can be usefully employed in middle-school and high-school social studies. Such an approach can help adolescents deal with needs they have because of familial poverty, homelessness, and other factors that may place them at risk for school failure.

Geography

- Making geography accessible to students who are blind or have low vision requires the use of raised relief maps and other adaptive devices and procedures, as well as accessible textbooks.
- Manipulatives and simulations can both "make economics come alive" in inclusive classrooms.
- Economics can also be made more accessible to students by focusing upon real-world applications, such as dividing biweekly checks into categories (fixed expenses, discretionary expenses, savings, etc.).

QUESTIONS FOR REFLECTION

1. What questions should social studies teachers working in inclusion classrooms ask about social studies content, particularly in history, that teachers of non-inclusion classes may not need to ask?
2. Why does social studies lend itself so readily to the teaching of self-determination?
3. In what ways might biographies and fiction help students to learn social studies?
4. The ways in which work is done varies from anthropology to psychology to economics to geography. What aspects of the scientific method are *common* to these disciplines?
5. What tactics did Lederer (2000) find effective for teaching social studies in an inclusive classroom?
6. What questions should teachers having students who are blind ask about published texts and assessments in the social studies? What sources offer accessible texts and related materials?
7. How can social studies texts, especially in history, be made easier to read and understand?
8. What other techniques have been suggested for increasing student access to social studies materials?
9. What did Ferretti and his colleagues learn about teaching history in an inclusive classroom?
10. How can high-school civics help students to learn self-advocacy skills?

Part Six Endnotes

Making Inclusion Work . . . The Story Concludes

In Part Six, we saw that making inclusion work involves these ideas:

- Help included students to use language for purposes they regard as relevant in their own lives, which is what we mean when we talk about "literacy." Students need to begin reading trade books and writing stories early in their elementary school years.
- Teach students phonemic awareness, particularly those who have specific learning disabilities, and teach phonics as well. Teachers with students who are deaf or hard of hearing need to recognize that phonics will be of little help, so greater emphasis will be needed upon sight reading and other visual means of instruction.
- Use block scheduling, so as to free up uninterrupted class time for instruction in reading, writing, and other academic skills.
- Insist that *all* students write. Some with physical disabilities will need adaptive devices to do so, while some with specific learning disabilities will need scaffolding.
- Use portfolio and journal entries as means to monitor student progress throughout the year.
- Assign some readings that have disability themes and/or characters with disabilities, as ways to increase sensitivity and awareness of non-disabled students while giving students with disabilities opportunities to articulate their feelings and concerns.
- Take advantage of e-texts, screen readers, and other technologies to make literature equally accessible to students with special needs.
- Adopt "act out a scene" and other participatory activities so as to keep the attention of students with emotional/behavioral disorders or attention deficit disorders.
- Support included students in problem-solving activities for math and science, including modeling teacher thinking and problem-solving skills, making sure that information is offered in more than one modality (hearing, seeing, touching, etc.) and that manipulatives as well as activities that students regard as relevant to their lives are used.
- Provide scaffolding, advance organizers, modeling, and peer tutoring for discovery learning.
- Train students how to make good use of heads, graphics, fonts, colors, maps, charts, and figures so as to comprehend texts in math and science.
- Use concept maps, Direct Instruction and other techniques to teach students effective strategies.
- Take advantage of social studies units and classes to teach skills that included students will need in order to transition successfully from school to postsecondary education, work, and independent living.
- Find, from the American Printing House for the Blind and the Texas School for the Blind and Visually Impaired, technologies to make geography accessible to students who are blind or have low vision.
- Make sure that statewide and other high-stakes assessments are accessible to students with disabilities.
- Use software (e.g., Inspiration®) that creates concept maps and outlines to help students with specific learning disabilities to master challenging material.
- Empower included students by instructing them, during social studies units, in techniques used by civil-rights movements, in strategies for self-advocacy, and in tactics for persuading different audiences.

Glossary

A

Abuse Children may be abused physically, sexually, emotionally, and in other ways by parents or other adults. Such acts are judged by their consequences, not by the adults' intent. Neglect is a variation on abuse, where nurturing, food, and so on, are withheld.

Accommodations In testing, arrangements such as additional time or permission to use an assistive technology device or to have use of a person to read questions or write answers. In other situations, too, accommodations are (usually) one-time adjustments that make an otherwise inaccessible event or program accessible for people with disabilities. An example is sign-language interpretation of spoken information.

Adapted physical education An individually modified program that includes physical education (physical and motor fitness and skills and skill in aquatics, dance, and individual or group games or sports) and adds assessment and instruction by qualified personnel that implements and complies with individualized education programs (IEPs), including instruction in a least restrictive environment (LRE).

Advance organizers Self-study questions, outlines, graphic representations, definitions, and other supports provided to students by their teachers in advance of lessons.

Alternate assessment An alternative approach in determining that students who cannot participate in standardized tests have met IEP goals. The process may include reviewing records, interviewing teachers/therapists/parents, and asking the student to perform the goal behavior.

American Sign Language (ASL) A distinct language, with its own rules of grammar, syntax, and so on. It is often used together with fingerspelling, which is (literally) spelling in the air.

Anxiety disorder Disturbance of mental functioning that includes extreme anxiety (such as, separation anxiety) as well as atypical eating patterns (such as bulimia nervosa and anorexia nervosa).

Aphasia A language disorder characterized by difficulties naming things and/or finding words.

Applied behavior analysis (ABA) Behavior modification as done one-on-one with students. It features the immediate presentation of reinforcers (often, food and praise) when students do what is expected.

Appropriate The standard set by IDEA, according to *Rowley* (1982), under which the child is "benefitting" from an education if he is promoted from grade to grade. A "good enough" standard.

Apraxia An impairment caused by an injury (lesion) in the motor-control pathways of the brain.

Art therapy A therapeutic use of art, as distinguished from art education, which seeks to improve students' performance in art.

Articulation The production of sounds, as part of speech.

Asperger syndrome So-called "high-functioning" autism, or autism not accompanied by mental retardation. There is some disagreement among experts as to whether the two terms (Asperger syndrome and high-functioning autism) are synonymous or whether there is some, rather subtle, difference between them.

Assessment An ongoing process in which educators collect and analyze information so as to make decisions.

Assistive technology devices Special-purpose technologies, ranging from simple, low-tech products such as splints to help someone with a spinal cord injury to grasp a pen to complex, high-tech devices such as a Dynavox® augmentative communication tool that assists someone with cerebral palsy to communicate to others. Assistive technology devices may be related services when used in special environments and may be supplementary aids and services when used in regular environments.

Assistive technology services Steps taken to identify, acquire, fit, repair, etc., an assistive technology device.

At risk In general education, students who are "at risk" are in possible danger of not completing K–12 education due to possible future events. In special education, the meaning is somewhat different: Children who are "at risk" do not have disabilities nor do they have developmental delays. However, because of environmental and/or biological factors, it is possible that in the future they may develop a disability and/or a delay. These children are not eligible for IDEA Part B services. (They may be eligible for IDEA Part C services, as "infants or toddlers with a disability," if the state recognizes at-risk status as qualifying for such services.)

Attention deficit hyperactivity disorders (ADHD) ADHD-HI is the "primarily hyperactive and impulsive" version of attention deficits, while ADHD-I is the "primarily inattentive" version. Both are types of Attention Deficit Hyperactivity Disorder, as defined by the American Psychiatric Association in its *DSM-IV* manual.

Augmentative and alternative communication (AAC) AAC products offer people "augmentative" (supplementary) and "alternative" (replacement) means of communication. For example, the DynaVox® machine speaks out loud the message entered by touching on the machine's surface.

Authentic assessment Authentic assessments connect student behavior to the "real world"— they are based on what students will need to do at work, in college, and so on, as adults.

Autism The severe communication-, socialization-, and imagination-related condition that usually occurs at about the age of two. It is the most severe of the "spectrum" of "pervasive developmental disorders."

Autistic savant behavior A few people with autism display unusual abilities, typically in very circumscribed areas. They may, for example, be able to play a song on a piano after hearing it just once. This rare talent is referred to as "savant" behavior.

Automaticity The speed of processing. When material is over-learned (e.g., simple multiplication tables), students display automaticity in responding.

B

Behavior modification A set of techniques to reinforce desired behavior and to extinguish undesired behavior. These techniques include positive (presentation) reinforcement, negative (removal) reinforcement, and the like. Generally, researchers tell us to attend to behavior we want to see more of and to ignore behavior we want to see less of.

Behavioral terms Words that mean the same thing to different people and refer to actions that may be observed. For example, "Given a list of 20 words, 10 correctly spelled and 10 incorrectly spelled, Mark will circle those that are accurately spelled." In that sentence, Mark's behavior is to "circle" 10 words.

Blindness People who are blind have vision that measures, using Snellen charts, at 20/200 or worse, or have sharply constrained fields of vision (to a very narrow range).

Block scheduling Combining several sessions into one, so that the twice-weekly physical therapy sessions of one child, or several, are combined into a single, longer, once-weekly session.

C

Central auditory processing disorders Some children hear well but when speech information traverses the VIIIth nerve to the brain, and is interpreted in the auditory cortex, it may not be understood.

Child abuse The term used to refer to acts against children, usually by adults, that have negative consequences for the child. Abuse may be physical, sexual, or emotional in nature. Sometimes the term encompasses child neglect. See also, *abuse* and *neglect.*

Child Find The steps—from locating children through screening them—that IDEA requires state agencies to take so that no infant, child, or youth with a disability who needs early intervention or special education is overlooked.

Child with a disability IDEA's guarantee of a free, appropriate public education applies only to children who meet eligibility requirements. Under Part B, those are "children with disabilities." They are between the ages of 3 and 18 or 21 (whenever they leave secondary school), they have a disability on the law's list of qualifying conditions, and they need special education and related services.

Class-wide peer tutoring A technique in which all students in a class pair off, one by one, to tutor each other in turn. The method features strong teacher guidance for the tutoring pairs.

Clinical judgment This term is used when a substantial portion of the work to classify a student is comprised of a professional's judgment, rather than standardized assessments.

Cochlear implants Electronic devices that are surgically inserted into the skull, with an external wire leading to batteries. These devices stimulate the cochlea, or "snail" in the body, enabling people to hear better than they could with hearing aids.

Collaboration A general educator and a special educator share full responsibility for the classroom and for all students. Ideally, neither thinks that one does most of the work. Rather, they are, and believe they are, equal partners.

Communication disorders A broad term encompassing impairments of speech, language, and hearing.

Community-based instruction Teaching children in the setting(s) in which they will be expected to use what they learn. Sometimes referred to as "situated learning," for example, learning in the situation.

Co-morbid/co-morbidity Co-occurrence. For example, attention deficit disorders often are co-morbid with oppositional defiant disorders.

Conduct disorder (CD) Behavior in which an individual deliberately disregards societal rules, producing damage to property and/or injury to people, often because she decides, instead, to follow the rules of a gang or other group.

Constructivism The active discovery of factual information by students (who "construct knowledge"). It is set against traditional lectures, where teachers impart knowledge. The role of teachers in constructivism is described by the term *facilitation.*

Consultation One certified teacher works with special-needs students while the other continues to be the "primary" teacher in the classroom. In the consultative model, as usually practiced, the general educator makes the major decisions about content, materials, methods, and so on, and the special educator adapts those, as needed, and presents modified instruction to students who have disabilities.

Continuum of alternative educational placement options The continuum ranges from general classrooms, on the left, to home/hospital settings, on the right. IDEA requires that the full continuum be made available, to the extent needed by any individual child.

Cooperative learning Students helping each other, under supervision of a teacher. Each student remains responsible for his own learning.

Co-teaching When two educators collaborate as equal partners and share all aspects of instruction.

Counseling Professional services offered by school counselors, guidance counselors, psychologists, and others, including social workers, that assist students in understanding themselves, making plans, and changing their own behavior.

Culturally competent Someone possessing the skills and knowledge to create classrooms and lessons that students coming from different cultural backgrounds find welcoming.

Culturally sensitive Someone possessing self-awareness of one's own culture and sensitivity to other cultural tenets and behaviors as equally deserving of respect.

Curriculum-based assessment (CBA) Observation and other measures of what children learn, while they are learning it. Curriculum-based measurement (CBM) is a subset of CBA in which repeated measures are taken over time (see *formative assessment*).

Curriculum-based measurement. One kind of curriculum-based assessment (see *curriculum-based assessment*).

D

Deaf-blindness The occurrence in the same individual of severe hearing and visual impairments. Typically, people who are classified as deaf-blind have some residual vision and/or hearing, but a few are both profoundly deaf and totally blind.

Deaf culture A set of beliefs holding that individuals who are deaf are primarily users of a different language (American Sign Language) and inheritors of a cultural tradition.

Deafness The inability to understand conversational speech through the ear alone. Officially, according to the U.S. Department of Education, it is "a hearing impairment that is so severe that the child is impaired in processing linguistic information through hearing, with or without amplification, that adversely affects a child's educational performance."

Declassification Removal of a child from special education when it is determined by the IEP team that she no longer needs special education and related services, that is no longer eligible under IDEA.

Deductive reasoning Beginning with a rule and generating, from it, discrete examples or applications. Contrasts with *inductive reasoning*.

Developmentally delayed The term we use to describe an instance in which a child is developing through typical stages but more slowly than expected; an example might be a child aged 8 who still clings to the mother's clothes when near strangers.

Differentiated instruction This is a form of individualizing instruction, when the teacher differentiates materials, methods, and so on, according to the needs of the child. Thus, for one student, the teacher might use a simple outline of a book chapter, while for another student, the teacher might use a much more detailed outline.

Direct Instruction (DI) Specific teaching of something, starting with a review of previously learned material that relates to the topic, usually featuring step-by-step instruction as well as guided practice, and finishing with a review. Contrast to "discovery learning" and to "facilitation."

Directed discovery learning A variation on *discovery learning* in which teachers and/or peers direct a student's inquiry. More structured than guided discovery learning and much more structured than discovery learning.

Discovery learning Also called "inquiry-based learning," this approach sees the teacher as a facilitator of student-directed learning. Popularized by Jerome Bruner, the technique is founded upon a belief that people learn better when they discover things for themselves than when they are passively told about them. Two variations: *directed discovery learning* and *guided discovery learning*.

Down syndrome Mental retardation (usually moderate), plus cardiac conditions, and frequently impairments of hearing and of vision, due to division errors during cell reproduction or to other mutations involving the 21st chromosome.

Due process The procedural safeguard rules that apply to parents and their children who have special needs. Both IDEA and section 504 offer due-process rights, including a "private right of action," that is, the right to go to court to enforce civil rights.

Dyscalculia A specific learning disability that interferes with learning and using numbers and, more generally, mathematics.

Dysgraphia A specific writing disability that interferes with writing the letters of the alphabet and sentences.

Dyslexia A reading disability. As is dyscalculia, it is a specific learning disability (SLD). Often used, instead of *dyslexia,* is *reading disabilities*.

E

Early childhood Generally, this term refers to children between the ages of 3 and 8 inclusive. Those age 3 to 5 are preschoolers, while those age 6 to 8 attend the primary grades (up to and including third grade).

Early intervention Generally, proactive steps taken to prevent or ameliorate problems (e.g., effects of familial poverty). The term is also defined in IDEA as authorized services for children from birth until age 3 and their families.

Eating disorders These include bulimia nervosa (compulsive eating, usually followed by disgorging) and anorexia nervosa (extreme dieting). Both are described in the *DSM-IV* (American Psychiatric Association, 1994).

Elaboration An adult explains, justifies, and/or otherwise articulates reasons behind a decision, rather than just telling a child "No!"

Embedding A technique of inserting special education and related services into child-chosen activities, so that instruction is offered unobtrusively.

Emotional disturbance Behavior that is very different from that displayed by age peers in similar circumstances.

Error analysis In error analysis, teachers go beyond grading student work to assess *what kinds of mistakes* those students made. "Miscue analysis" is an example.

E-texts Books, plays, articles, and other works that are made available electronically.

Experiential deprivation Family members at times will forbid a child with a disability from participating in activities that other children of the same age typically engage in, thus depriving the child with a disability from those experiences.

Extended school year (ESY) ESY Services that are offered during summer months as well as during the "school year."

Evaluation Tests, observations, and other steps to help the IEP team to determine whether a child is eligible for special services.

F

Facilitation The practice, common in general classrooms, of teachers setting out "interesting" materials and then unobtrusively allowing students to teach themselves. Contrast to *Direct Instruction*.

Family services The IDEA, Part C (Infants and Toddlers), authorizes services that are provided to the family itself, in addition to services offered to young children. When professionals offer counseling, respite care, and child-care instruction to parents and other adults in the family, this is referred to as family services.

504 children A term sometimes used to refer to "individuals with a disability" who are being served in public schools pursuant to section 504, rather than the IDEA.

Formative assessment Collection of data while an activity is taking place, for the purpose of assessing progress and deciding whether to alter the way something is being taught. (In contrast to *summative assessment.*)

Fragile X syndrome The leading inherited cause of mental retardation among males. It is rare among females. The syndrome may also cause specific learning disabilities and some other conditions.

Frameworks General approaches to, or ways of organizing, social studies instruction.

Free appropriate public education An education that is provided free of charge to parents by public schools and that meets each of a child's unique needs. Often abbreviated as "FAPE."

Full inclusion The placement of all children with disabilities into general education classrooms throughout the school day. In this interpretation, the continuum of alternative placement options ceases to exist: All services are delivered in general classrooms.

Functional behavioral assessment An examination of a child's needs, establishment of goals, and delineation of services, including any behavior modification so the child may receive an appropriate education. A functional behavior analysis should be included as part of the preparation of the IEP of any child who has emotional/behavioral disorders or some other condition (such as attention deficit hyperactivity disorder) and for that reason requires instruction and/or related services, including counseling, to deal with unsuitable classroom behavior.

Functional curriculum A curriculum that emphasizes practical knowledge and skills, much more than academics. Intended for students with mental retardation and others with severe conditions, it is also known as an "alternative" curriculum and (by the Council for Exceptional Children) an "independence" curriculum.

G

Generalizing The ability of a child or youth to respond in the same ways and to produce the same behaviors when in the presence of different people and when in different locations. Traditionally, many special-needs students have had great difficulty learning to generalize. They would learn something in the classroom but not show evidence of it at home, and vice versa.

Gifted The term used to refer to children and youth who have very superior intellectual abilities. The word *"talented"* (see definition below), by contrast, refers to those who have unusual abilities in other areas, such as art, music, and sports.

Graphemes The written representation of the sounds of speech (*phonemes*).

Group home A building, usually a single- or two-family house, that is used as a residence for several adults who have disabilities. A group home is located in a regular neighborhood. Group homes thus are residential options that are much more integrated into the community than are institutions and hospitals.

Group instruction Groups, which may be small or large, are formed. A teacher may move from group to group, or one teacher may work with one group, another with a second group. Grouping allows for different things to be taught, for the speed at which material is presented to vary, and/or for the methods of instruction to differ.

Guided discovery learning A variation on *"discovery learning"* in which a teacher and/or peer offers suggestions to a student in her discovery learning. More structured than discovery learning but less so than *directed discovery learning.*

H

Harassment Harassment on the basis of disability includes the same kinds of behavior as are seen in harassment on the basis of gender, race, and other characteristics: persistent teasing, interfering with free movement, and so on.

Hard of hearing People who can understand some conversational speech, especially with the help of hearing aids or other assistive listening devices and systems.

Hearing The sensory faculty that lets us hear environmental sounds, including speech, and to make sense of it.

High-stakes tests High-stakes tests are those which have important consequences. A test that must be passed before permission is granted for promotion to the next grade is an example.

Homeless person Under the Stewart B. McKinney Homeless Assistance Act, an individual who lacks a fixed, regular, and adequate nighttime residence or has a primary nighttime residence that is in a shelter or a temporary housing institution.

I

Identification The steps, including "Child Find" and teacher identification, to locate children who may be eligible for services under the IDEA.

Incidence The number of new instances in a given year. Thus, the incidence of mental retardation is the number of new occurrences (usually, by birth) during a particular year. Contrast to *prevalence.*

Inclusion The placement of special-needs students in general classrooms for all or most of the school day. Inclusion permits these students to be "pulled out" as needed for related services such as speech and language pathology services; *full inclusion* by contrast insists that such services be "pushed in."

Individualization IDEA principle that all major decisions about children with disabilities must be made on a case-by-case basis. Making decisions about groups of these children is not lawful.

Individualized Education Program The annual planning document that outlines the unique needs of a child, describes the services to be provided, and articulates the goals to be met. The name of the plan is frequently abbreviated as "IEP."

Individualized Education Program team The IEP team consists of a representative of the local school district, the child's teacher(s)— general as well as special educators—and others who are needed to assess a child's needs and to devise a plan of action. The child's parents may attend and participate in all IEP team meetings. Once the child reaches age 14, the child himself or herself may attend and take part in these meetings.

Individualized Plan for Employment IPEs are the service plans prepared by state rehabilitation counselors and clients. These plans outline services to help an individual with a disability to become employable or to become more independent. Formerly known as Individualized Written Rehabilitation Plans (IWRP's), the documents were renamed by PL 105-220, the Rehabilitation Act Amendments of 1998.

Individuals with a disability Section 504 of the 1973 Rehabilitation Act prohibits discrimination on the basis of disability against people who "qualify" for services (in this case, for a public education) and satisfy at least one of three criteria: they have a permanent medical condition that substantially limits major life activities; they once had such a condition; or they are falsely believed to have one now. Notably, the definition of "individuals with a disability" does *not* require that people "need special education and related services," nor that they have a condition on some list; nor is there an age limitation in the definition. (Note: the U.S. Department of Education's regulations for section 504 continue to use the outdated term "individuals with handicaps.")

Individuals with Disabilities Education Act IDEA is the nation's landmark special-education law. The statute guarantees all "children with disabilities" a free and appropriate education at public expense. Part A of IDEA presents the law's purposes and defines key terms. Part B governs elementary and secondary education for children with disabilities. Part C outlines early intervention and preschool services for infants, toddlers, and preschoolers with disabilities. Part D authorizes research, training, and demonstration projects.

Inductive reasoning Beginning with specific instances and creating, from them, a rule. Contrasts with *deductive reasoning.*

Infants or toddlers with disabilities Under Part C, early intervention services are assured for young children who are under the age of three, have a state-defined developmental delay or a state-listed disability, and need early intervention services.

Interim alternative placement A different placement that is chosen after a child or youth proves to be a danger to himself and/or others, or to disrupt the classroom, to such an extent that removal from the current educational placement is required. A juvenile detention center or even a county jail could serve as an interim alternative placement.

Itinerant teacher An educator who travels between different school buildings, providing periodic tutoring or other instruction to students.

L

Labels In special education, the words used to refer to different eligibility criteria. Thus, the label "mental retardation" is used to refer to behavior characteristic of significantly younger children, IQ scores of 70/75 or below, and an age at onset prior to 18.

Language A rule-based system of putting words and word units together to convey meaning.

Language arts The six language arts are listening, talking, reading, writing, viewing, and visually representing.

Least restrictive environment (LRE) The placement setting where (a) an appropriate education is made available for a child with a disability and (b) integration with non-disabled children is available. Abbreviated "LRE."

Linguistic minority groups In the United States, groups of individuals whose primary language is not English.

Listserv Software that links e-mail addresses of teacher and students, enabling any to initiate messages to all and all to respond.

Literacy The ability to use reading and writing for real-world, practical purposes.

Low vision People whose vision, measured using Snellen charts, is better than that of people who are blind, but worse than 70/200. In general, people with low vision can make effective use of their residual vision.

M

Mainstreaming An early interpretation of LRE in which children with disabilities were integrated with children having no disabilities during non-academic activities in school.

Manifestation determination An answer to the question: "Was this behavior caused by the disability, or not?" That is, was the behavior a manifestation of the disability?

Manipulatives As the name suggests, these are "touchable" concrete objects. Many children with mental retardation or specific learning disabilities find that they can grasp otherwise elusive concepts when they learn these through manipulatives.

Mediation Discussions aimed at reaching a compromise, led by a trained mediator.

Mental illness Disorders of mental functioning, including loss of contact with reality, depression, and a wide variety of neuroses and psychoses. In education, a more narrow term, "emotional or behavioral disorders" is used.

Mental retardation (MR) Significantly subaverage intelligence combined with behavior that is normal but is generally characteristic of younger individuals.

Metacognition Awareness of one's own learning and thinking processes, that is, "thinking about thinking."

Method of successive approximations Also known as "shaping," this teaching technique suggests that the educator reward behavior that the child *can* exhibit. As the child becomes capable of performing ever-more appropriate behavior, the teacher should cease reinforcement of less-appropriate behavior. Over time, this method helps children and youth to acquire the ability to display fully acceptable behaviors.

Migrant children The children of migrant workers, generally in agricultural fields, and those eligible for the federal Title I Migrant Education Program.

Mild Children and youth with "mild" disabilities usually can succeed in inclusive or general classrooms, if they are provided with supplementary aids and services, tutoring, and other support services. By contrast, students with *severe disabilities* often are challenging to integrate into such settings.

Minority groups Demographic groups that comprise fewer than 51% of the population. In this text, the term refers to ethnic and racial minority groups. Persons who belong to linguistic minority groups are discussed separately.

Miscue analysis A technique in which teachers note children's behavior during oral reading. It is one variation on *error analysis*. However, not all miscues are errors.

Mnemonics Memory tricks involving the first letters of steps to be taken. Thus, STEP might be a mnemonic for *S*tudy the problem, *T*ranslate it to numbers, *E*xecute the calculation, and *P*roduce the answer.

Mood disorders Mood disorders include depression, manic-depression, and other serious mental disorders. These are described in the *DSM-IV* (American Psychiatric Association, 1994).

Morphemes The smallest units of meaning.

Multiple intelligences A theory advanced by Howard Gardner to highlight his contention that the construct of a general intelligence is inadequate for understanding human abilities.

N

Native language The language used in the child's home. If the child's parents are deaf, for example, this may be American Sign Language. If family members primarily speak Portuguese, the native language of the child is Portuguese.

Neglect The withholding of food, medical care, attention, and so on, from a child. Neglect is a form of *abuse*. The difference is that with abuse, something bad is done to the child while in neglect something good is not done.

Number sense This is a fundamental facility with numbers. It includes knowing the ideas behind counting (that things exist in categories and may be counted, for example, one apple plus two apples equals three apples, but one apple and one pear equal two pieces of fruit).

O

Observation Observations by teachers may be informal (walking around the classroom, watching students) or formal (using checklists, rating scales, etc.). The intent is to gather information which informs teaching.

Occupational therapy Noninstructional services provided to children and youth with disabilities to perform goal-directed activities of a sensorimotor, cognitive, or psychosocial nature, including gross- and fine-motor coordination, problem-solving, self-control, and self-expression.

Operant conditioning The change of behavior that is voluntary (under our control).

Oppositional defiant disorder (ODD) Behavior in which an individual seems compelled to disobey rules, despite knowing that this will bring adverse consequences. Often associated with ADHD.

Orthopedic impairment The term used in IDEA to refer to such physical conditions as cerebral palsy, muscular dystrophy, spinal cord injury, and the like.

Other Health Impaired (OHI) The OHI classification, in IDEA, includes attention deficit hyperactivity disorders as well as such health conditions as asthma and epilepsy.

P

Parallel talk An adult provides words for what a child is doing.

Paraprofessional "Para's" are non-certified individuals who assist certified teachers in the classroom. In some schools, the terms "teacher aide" or "teacher assistant" is used to refer to these people.

Peer tutoring One student instructs another. Usually, a well-achieving student works with a struggling student. Ideally, both benefit, as suggested by the saying, "To really learn something, teach it."

Pervasive developmental disorder (PDD) Term often used to refer to "autistic-like behavior" or "mild autism." The term is defined in the American Psychiatric Association's *DSM-IV* by reference to behaviors observed by a physician or other trained professional as having first appeared during the early childhood years.

Phonemes The smallest units of speech sound. A phoneme cannot further be divided. Example: /p/.

Phonemic awareness A set of abilities to combine and separate phonemes. It is a fundamental skill, probably one we are born with and one we perform with little cognitive effort. Sometimes called "phonological awareness."

Phonics A method of reading instruction which emphasizes the sounding out of words. The assumption is that children have heard those words, many times, and simply need to connect the written/printed version of the word (which is new to them) to the sound(s) of the word (which is well-known to them).

Phonology The study of sounds used in speech. A *phoneme* is the smallest unit of sound.

Physical therapy Non-instructional services provided to children and youth with disabilities to retain or improve gross-motor function and to prevent muscle atrophy.

Placement team The team making placement decisions consists of parents, who by law have the right to take part in those decisions, and any other persons "knowledgeable about the child, the meaning of the evaluation data, and the placement options" (34 C.F.R. 300.552). The placement team may be, but does not need to be, the IEP team.

Portfolios A portfolio is a collection of work products, such as writing samples, that represent student work over a period of time, usually one school year.

Positioning Term often used to describe how educators, occupational therapists, physical therapists and others 'position' the trunk, limbs, and head of a child or youth with a physical disability so as to facilitate breathing, eating, and other behaviors. The word is most often used with respect to wheelchair seating and students with cerebral palsy.

Positive supports model The discipline model that tells teachers to "catch children doing something right" and then reinforce them for it. Contrast to *zero tolerance*.

Poverty When people live in poverty, they have incomes from all sources that are lower than "the poverty level" for a given year. Recently, that was $14,000 for a family of three.

Pragmatics The often-unspoken rules for appropriate social use of language. My students talk differently to me, their professor, than they do to each other, for example.

Preference IDEA establishes a preference in favor of integration. That is, if an appropriate education is available in more than one setting, the law prefers that the child be placed in the more integrated of those. IDEA permits this preference to be "rebutted" (set aside) if the result of integration would be an inappropriate education.

Pre-referral intervention Relatively small changes made in the general classroom to see if they suffice to meet the need; the idea is to try minor alterations before attempting the larger ones known as "special education" and "related services." Often, a school-based "child study team" including a psychologist, a social worker, and so on, will assist the teacher in selecting, carrying out, and assessing such pre-referral interventions.

Presentation reinforcement Giving a student something she will work to get, as a reward for doing what you wanted in the classroom.

Prevalence The number of instances in existence. Thus, the prevalence of mental retardation is the total number of persons who are mentally retarded. Contrast with *incidence*.

Principle of partial participation Planning to provide that a child or youth with a disability who cannot fully take part in a given activity is able, nonetheless, to assume a role of some kind, one that is meaningful to the student.

Problem-based learning The approach in which teachers pose problems of practical significance, challenging students to research the issues and develop their own solutions.

Prosody The alteration in frequency (pitch) that people use to signal questions, statements, and so on, in speech.

Punishment Verbal or even physical actions taken after a student misbehaves. The intent is to reduce the frequency of such misbehavior. Researchers caution that punishment is often not effective.

R

Reading disabilities (RD) Specific learning disabilities that affect basic reading skills and reading comprehension. RD includes dyslexia.

Rebuttable presumption IDEA's least restrictive environment (LRE) preference is not absolute; rather, it may be, indeed must be, treated as subordinate to the law's primary principle, that of appropriateness.

Referral After failing to meet a child's needs with pre-referral interventions, the teacher may ask the IEP team to step in. A referral is a request for a formal assessment of the child's eligibility for services under IDEA.

Reflective practitioner A teacher or other professional who actively and regularly reflects upon what he has done, what happened, and how to do better next time.

Regular Education Initiative (REI) An early interpretation of LRE, in which children having mild disabilities were integrated with non-disabled children throughout the school day.

Related services Non-instructional support services, such as assistive technology devices and services, speech and language pathology, occupational and physical therapy, counseling, and the like.

Removal reinforcement Increasing the frequency of behaviors by removing something students dislike.

Resource rooms These are classrooms, usually small ones, in which a special educator, perhaps with an aide, offers individualized instruction specifically on a particular student's needs. Typically, a handful of students will visit the resource room two or three times a week, being pulled out from their usual classroom.

Respite services Family services provided so that family members "get a break" from caring for a child or youth with a disability.

Rubric An outline of how an essay, a portfolio, or some other assessment will be evaluated. Thus, an "A" essay on the Lewis & Clark expedition would identify the key actors, explain why the expedition was launched, sketch the route taken, and summarize what the explorers learned.

S

Scaffolding Providing a student with a structure, to enhance learning. This structure may include an outline of the plot of a story, a list of key characters, and so on.

Schizophrenia A serious mental illness characterized by inappropriate emotions and speech as well as by disturbed connections to reality. It is described in the *DSM-IV* (American Psychiatric Association, 1994).

Screen readers Software programs that "read" a computer screen out loud so that a child or youth who is blind or has low vision may understand what is displayed. Typically, screen readers give the user control over the speed, pitch, and other characteristics of the computer's "voice."

Section 504 This non-discrimination statute was the final sentence of the Rehabilitation Act when it was passed in 1973. Unlike IDEA, it does not provide federal funding for services. Rather, it bans discrimination on the basis of disability.

Self-advocacy Knowing what one needs and what one's rights are, and advocating for those needs to be met and rights to be respected.

Self-determination The making of decisions and the assumption of responsibility for them. Self-determination may include deciding who does things for the students, when, and how.

Self talk An adult talks while doing something, thus enabling the child to "see inside the brain" of an adult making a reasoned decision.

Semantics The choice of words to express the exact meaning you intend.

Sensory integration An approach to teaching students with autism or other pervasive developmental disabilities (PDDs) that considers inability to integrate sensory information to be a concern and attempts to assist children to do that.

Service coordination Support for families as they seek services from a variety of government agencies on behalf of infants and toddlers.

Severe disability A disability that poses numerous and/or complex barriers to inclusion. Children and youth with "severe" disabilities can often succeed in inclusive or general classrooms, but only after being given extensive support services. By contrast, those who have "mild" disabilities are much easier to integrate into such settings.

Sexual abuse Any of a wide variety of acts that involve children as participants or observers of sexual acts, including molestation and other sexual exploitation.

Simulations Artificial renderings or depictions of events or processes. Students may simulate a chemistry experiment by using a computer software program, for example.

Slow learners Students who are underachieving academically, despite intelligence at or near average levels. This basket term encompasses children and youth with a wide variety of school-related problems.

Social Studies Instruction civics, geography, history, and related subjects.

Socially mediated The concept that deep understanding emerges as students articulate their initial thoughts, react to others' ideas, and refine our thinking.

Social work services Related services that are provided by social workers on behalf of the family and/or infants/toddlers or children with disabilities.

Socioeconomic status (SES) Low, mid, and high levels of family wealth and income. You will sometimes see the term social class, which refers to much the same thing.

Special education Specially designed (custom designed) instruction that responds to a child's unique needs.

Special factors In the 1997 IDEA Amendments, IEP teams were required, for the first time, formally to consider such "special factors" as the linguistic and communication needs of children who are deaf, the possible use of Braille for children who are blind, and behavioral supports for students with emotional disturbance.

Specific learning disabilities (SLD). A classification used in IDEA, and defined there. The category includes reading disabilities, such as dyslexia, and other learning disabilities.

Speech The oral production of sounds to communicate.

Speech-language pathology Related services that are provided by speech-language pathologists. The American Speech-Language-Hearing Association (ASHA) prefers this term to "speech therapy."

Speech or language impairment (SLI) The SLI category is used in IDEA for students whose primary disabilities are in the areas of speech and/or language.

Speech recognition The ability of a computer to "hear" and "understand" the spoken word. Also called speech-to-text.

Speech synthesis Computer talk: speech-synthesis software converts digital ones and zeroes into material that speech-synthesis hardware can speak aloud. Both software and hardware are required. Software includes *screen readers* that identify synthesizer-readable information and other software that follows user instructions (e.g., to use a female voice with a Spanish accent, to speak out all punctuation marks, etc.). The hardware includes such peripherals as a Sound Blaster™ sound card, which greatly improves the intelligibility of the computer voice, and a speaker that produces the sound. Also called text-to-speech.

Standardized tests Highly structured assessments that feature tight control over how tests are administered and scored.

Stimulus control Focusing the child's attention on stimuli in the environment to which the child has not yet been responding and prompting the child to respond to them.

Student self-assessment Self-monitoring and self-evaluation by students.

Stuttering A speech dysfluency characterized by great difficulty starting to say certain words or sounds.

Summative assessment Collection of data after an activity has ended, for the purpose of determining whether or not it was successful and, if so, to what extent. (Contrast to *formative evaluation.*)

Supplemental Security Income SSI is a federal-state minimum-income program for people who are poor and have disabilities. Eligible persons receive monthly checks and usually qualify for Medicaid as well.

Supplementary aids and services Additional support services that may be required to assist a child to benefit from education. These may include itinerant teacher services, resource room services, use of applied behavior analysis, test modifications, use of assistive technology services and assistive technology devices, and similar steps intended to assist the child to benefit from instruction.

Supports Types and degrees of assistance that teachers, family members, and others offer to help individuals with disabilities.

Supported education The term adopted by Hamre-Nietupski, MacDonald, and Nietupski (1992) to articulate the fact that *supplementary aids and services,* and other supports, are what makes inclusion possible.

Syntax The way language uses word order to signify meaning.

T

Talented Term used to refer to children and youth who have unusual abilities in such areas as art, music, athletics, and so on.

Task analysis Breaking down tasks into sub-tasks and teaching those sub-tasks.

Team teaching Two (usually) or more teachers work together in one classroom. Variations include *collaboration* and *consultation*.

Technology abandonment Term used when a student ceases using a device or software program, generally from frustration or a conviction that it is not helpful.

Temporary Assistance to Needy Families (TANF) The program that replaced traditional welfare, which was known as Aid to Families with Dependent Children (AFDC). TANF is temporary for recipients, where as AFDC often was permanent.

Testing Tests may be formal and standardized, or they may be informal and teacher designed. Testing is one form of assessment.

Time delay Prompts giving children clues about desired behaviors are delayed, thereby offering them opportunities to make the correct responses.

Title I This is the major federal financial assistance program designed to help schools provide supplemental instruction to children from low-SES families. Occasionally, you will see the term "Chapter 1" used, instead.

Transdisciplinary play-based assessment Developed and promoted by Toni Linder, this approach has family members and professionals involving young children in structured play activities.

Transition periods Times of change, as when a child moves from early intervention services to preschool. The IDEA requires educator action at some but not all transition periods. See *transition services.*

Transition services Instruction and other support to help a student move successfully from one stage to another. In IDEA, two kinds of transition are highlighted. The first is between early intervention services provided under Part C and preschool special education services offered under Part B. The second is between secondary school and adult life. The IDEA requires the current providers of service (under Part C, early interventionists; under Part B, special educators) to deliver free and appropriate services to children prior to the transition event. That is, early interventionists help infants and toddlers and their families to prepare for preschool special education or other public services, while special educations prepare adolescents with disabilities for post–high-school experiences such as work, college, and living in the community.

Traumatic brain injuries (TBI) Injuries to the brain, generally from accidents or falls, that have a variety of short- and long-term effects. The term is not used when brain injury is caused by illness. Nor is it adopted when injuries are pre-, peri-, or postnatal in origin (e.g., occur prior to, during, or immediately after birth).

U

Unique needs A particular child's needs, as those relate to his or her disability(ies). The term *appropriate* is defined in IDEA as services that are "designed to meet their unique needs" (with the word "their" referring to children with disabilities). The intent is to communicate the idea that each child is an individual, and should be treated as such. Decisions, including placements, that are based only on the child's disability and not on the needs of the child are not lawful.

Universal design In education, the development and then the presentation of information by the teacher in a variety of modalities and using a rich mix of techniques. Contrasted to *accommodation,* which is during-presentation or after-the-fact adjustment to allow a student to participate in the classroom. In universal design, the teacher makes information available to students in the modalities those students need or want to receive it. Universal design features planning by the teacher, in advance, so that the need for accommodations during delivery of instruction may be minimized.

V

Visitability In architecture, the design of a house so that it may be visited by someone using a wheelchair or other mobility device (e.g., it has one entrance that is wheelchair-accessible).

Visual impairment, including blindness The term used in IDEA to encompass the range of impairments from low vision on the upper end to blindness on the lower end.

Z

Zero reject The IDEA principle that no child with a disability will be denied a public education.

Zero tolerance The discipline model that sets explicit consequences for misbehavior. Contrast to *positive supports.*

Zone of proximal development For Vygotsky (1962), this is where the child is ready to learn, with a teacher's guidance. It is developmentally appropriate for the child.

References

Abedi, J. (2004). The No Child Left Behind Act and English language learners: Assessment and accountability issues. *Educational Researcher, 33*(1), 4–14.

Abner, G. H., & Lahm, E. A. (2002). Implementation of assistive technology with students who are visually impaired: Teachers' readiness. *Journal of Visual Impairment and Blindness, 96*(2), 98–105.

Abruscato, J. (2001). *Teaching children science: Discovery methods for the elementary and middle grades.* Needham Heights, MA: Allyn & Bacon.

ACES-ASCA Joint committee on the elementary school counselor. (1996). The elementary school counselor: Preliminary statement. *Personnel and Guidance Journal, 61,* 658–661.

Adams, M. J., Foorman, B. R., Lundberg, I., & Beeler, T. (1998). *Phonemic awareness in young children.* Baltimore: Paul H. Brookes Publishing.

Adapted Physical Education. (2004). Retrieved April 11, 2004, from *http://ncperid.usf.edu*

Alcott, L. M. (1890). *Little women.* Boston: Roberts Brothers. (Circa 1869: New York: Grosset & Dunlap.)

Algozzine, B., Beattie, J., Audette, B., & Lambert, M. (2000). Students with learning disabilities and literacy issues. In Wood, K. D., & Dickinson, T. S. (Eds.), *Promoting Literacy in Grades 4–9* (pp. 155–171). Needham Heights, MA: Allyn & Bacon.

Alinksy, S. D. (1971). *Rules for radicals: A pragmatic primer for realistic radicals.* New York: Random House.

Alleman, J., & Brophy, J. (1999). The changing nature and purpose of assessment in the social studies classroom. *Social Education, 65*(6), 334–337.

Allen, A. (2002, November 10). The not-so-crackpot autism theory. *New York Times Magazine,* Section 6, 67–69.

American Academy of Child and Adolescent Psychiatry. (1997). Practice parameters for the psychiatric assessment of infants and toddlers (0–36 months). *Journal of the American Academy for Child and Adolescent Psychiatry, 36* (Suppl 10), 21S–36S.

American Academy of Child and Adolescent Psychiatry. (2000). *Children and firearms.* Retrieved April 10, 2004, from *http://www.aacap.org/publication/factsfam/firearms.html*

American Academy of Pediatrics. (2000). Diagnosis and evaluation of the child with attention-deficit/hyperactivity disorder (AC0002). *Pediatrics, 105*(5), 1158–1170.

American Academy of Pediatrics. (2004). Retrieved April 12, 2004, from *http://www.aap.org*

American Art Therapy Association. (2002, Spring). Art therapy: Definition of the profession. *American Art Therapy Association Newsletter, XXXV*(2), p. 3.

American Association for the Advancement of Science. (1993). *Benchmarks for science literacy.* Retrieved April 5, 2004 from *http://www.project2061.org*

American Association for the Advancement of Science. (1998). *Science for all americans.* Retrieved April 10, 2004 from *http://www.project2061.org/tools/sfaa*

American Association of Colleges for Teacher Education. (1999). *Teacher education pipeline IV: Schools, colleges, and departments of education.* Washington, DC: Author.

American Association on Mental Retardation. (1992). *Mental retardation: Definition, classification, and systems of support* (9th ed.). Washington, DC: Author.

American Association on Mental Retardation. (2001, September/October). Request for comments on proposed new edition of *Mental Retardation: Definition, Classification, and Systems of Supports. News & Notes, 1,* 9–12.

American Council on Education, General Educational Development Testing Service. (2002). *Who took the GED?* Washington, DC: Author.

American Educational Research Association, American Psychological Association, and National Council on Measurement in Education. (1999). *Standards for educational and psychological testing.* Washington, DC: American Psychological Association.

American Federation of Teachers, AFL-CIO. (2000). *Survey and analysis of salary trends 1998.* Washington, DC: Author (555 New Jersey Avenue NW, Washington, DC 2001). Online at *http://www.aft.org/research/survey/tables/table 1-2.html*

American Foundation for Suicide Prevention. (2001). About suicide: Youth. Retrieved April 9, 2004 from *http://www.afsp.org/index-1.htm*

American Psychiatric Association. (1994). *Diagnostic and statistical manual of mental disorders* (4th ed.). Washington, DC: Author.

American Psychological Association. (1996). *Manual of diagnosis and professional practice in mental retardation.* Edited by J. W. Jacobson and J. A. Mulick. Washington, DC: Author.

American Speech Hearing Language Association. (2004). Retrieved March 10, 2004, from *http://www.asha.org*

Amrein, A. L., & Berliner, D. C. (2003, February). The effects of high-stakes testing on student motivation and learning. *Educational Leadership,* 32–38.

Anastasi, A., & Urbina, S. (1997). *Psychological testing* (7th ed.). Upper Saddle River, NJ: Prentice Hall.

Anderson, F. E. (1992). *Art for all the children: Approaches to art therapy for children with disabilities.* Springfield, IL: Charles C. Thomas.

The Arc's Self-Determination Program. Retrieved April 10, 2004 from *http://www.thearc.org/sdet/sdet.html*

Armour, R. W. (1957). *Twisted tales from Shakespeare.* New York: McGraw-Hill.

Armstrong, D. G., & Savage, T. V. (2002). *Teaching in the secondary school: An introduction.* Upper Saddle River, NJ: Merrill/Prentice Hall Education.

Armstrong, T. (1995). *The myth of the ADD child.* New York: Dutton Press.

Artiles, A. J., & Trent, S. C. (1994). Overrepresentation of minority students in special education: A continuing debate. *Journal of Special Education, 27*(4), 410–437.

Asch, A. (1993). The human genome and disability rights: Thoughts for researchers and advocates. *Disability Studies Quarterly, 13*(3), 3–5.

Assembly Bill AB 422, "Instructional materials; disabled students." Chapter 379. (Adds Section 67302 to the Education Code, State of California.) Signed by Governor Gray Davis, September 15, 1999.

Atwell, N. (1998). *In the middle: New understandings about writing, reading, and learning* (2nd ed.). Portsmouth, NH: Boynton/Cook.

Austin, V. L. (2000). Co-teachers' perceptions of the collaborative instruction of elementary and secondary students with and without disabilities in inclusive classrooms. Unpublished doctoral dissertation, Fordham University, New York, New York. An article describing this study appeared as Teachers' beliefs about co-teaching, *Remedial and Special Education, 22*(4), 245–263. (Page numbers cited in the text are those of the manuscript version.)

Austin, V. L. (2003). Fear and loathing in the classroom. *Journal of Disability Policy Studies, 14*(1), 17–22.

Ayres, A. J. (1979). *Sensory integration and the child.* Los Angeles: Western Psychological Services.

Bagheri, M. M., Burd, L., Martsolf, J. T., & Klug, M. G. (1998). Fetal alcohol syndrome: Maternal and neonatal characteristics. *Journal of Perinatal Medicine, 26,* 263–269.

Baker, K. (1996). What bilingual education research tells us. In Amselle, J. (Ed.), *The Failure of Bilingual Education.* Washington, DC: Center for Equal Opportunity.

Bandura, A. (1977). *Social learning theory.* Upper Saddle River, NJ: Prentice Hall.

Banikowski, A. K., & Mehring, T. A. (1999). Strategies to enhance memory based on brain research, entire issue. *Focus on Exceptional Children, 32*(2).

Barkley, R. A. (1990). *Attention deficit hyperactivity disorder: A handbook for diagnosis and treatment.* New York: Guilford Press.

Barnard, N. (1997, December 26). Pupils "brainwashed" by U.S. drugs project. *New York Times,* The Times Educational Supplement, no. 4252, p. 3.

Barnes, K. J., Schoenfeld, H. B., & Pierson, W. P. (1997). Inclusive schools: Implications for occupational therapy. *Physical Disabilities: Education and Related Services, 15*(2), 37–52.

Baron-Cohen, S. (1995). *Mindblindness: An essay on autism and theory of mind.* Boston: MIT Press/Bradford Books.

Baron-Cohen, S., Bolton, P., Wheelwright, S., Short, L., Mead, G., Smith, A., & Scahill, V. (1998). Autism occurs more often in families of physicists, engineers, and mathematicians. *Autism, 2,* 296–301.

Baron-Cohen, S., Wheelwright, S., Skinner, R., Martin, J., & Clubley, E. (2001). The autism-spectrum quotient (AQ): Evidence from Asperger syndrome/high-functioning autism, males and females, scientists and mathematicians. *Journal of Autism and Developmental Disabilities, 31*(1), 5–17.

Bauer, C. R. (1999). Perinatal effects of prenatal drug exposure: Neonatal aspects. *Clinics in Perinatology, 26,* 87–106.

Baumeister, A. A. (1987). Mental retardation: Some conceptions and dilemmas. *American Psychologist, 42,* 796–800.

Baumohl, J. (Ed.). (1996). *Homelessness in America.* Phoenix, AZ: Onyx Press.

Beakley, B., & Yoder, S. (1998). Middle schoolers learn community skills. *Teaching Exceptional Children, 30*(3), 16–21.

Bean, R.M., & Wilson, R.M. (1989). Using closed-captioned television to teach reading to adults. *Reading Research Instruction, 28*(4), 27–37.

Beirne-Smith, M., Ittenbach, R. F., & Patton, J. R. (2002). *Mental retardation.* Upper Saddle River, NJ: Prentice Hall, Merrill Education.

Bellamy, G. T., Horner, R., & Inman, D. (1979). *Vocational training for severely retarded adults.* Baltimore: Brookes.

Belton, P. (2000). The children who pick our grapes. *Peace Review, 12*(1), 463–466.

Bender, W. N. (1998). *Learning Disabilities: Characteristics, identification, and teaching strategies* (3rd ed.). Needham Heights, MA: Allyn & Bacon.

Berghoff, B. (2000). New ways of thinking about assessment and curriculum, entire issue. *Focus on Exceptional Children, 32*(7).

Berkin, C. (2003). *A brilliant solution: Inventing the American constitution.* Fort Washington, PA: Harvest Books.

Bernstein, N. (2001, March 25). For family in shelter system, living from bench to bench. *New York Times,* pp. 1, 36.

Bettelheim, B. (1967). *The empty fortress.* New York: Free Press.

Bizzaro, J. R. (2000). *Becoming literate in an inclusive environment: A study of the ways in which students in an inclusionary program construct their understanding of literacy and become members of their learning community.* Unpublished doctoral dissertation, Hostra University Department of Literacy Studies, School of Education and Allied Human Services.

Blackorby, J., & Wagner, M. (1996). Longitudinal postschool outcomes of youth with disabilities: Findings from the National Longitudinal Transition Study. *Exceptional Children, 62*(5), 399–413.

Blake, C., Wang, W., Cartledge, G., & Gardner, R. (2000). Middle school students with serious emotional disturbances serve as social skills trainers and reinforcers for peers with SED. *Behavioral Disorders, 25*(4), 280–298.

Blakeslee, S. (2002, November 19). A boy, a mother and a rare map of autism's world. *New York Times,* pp. F1, F4.

Bloom, L. (1988). What is language? In Lahey, M. (Ed.), *Language Disorders and Language Development.* New York: Macmillan.

Boals, D. (2004). History/social studies for K-12 teachers. Retrieved April 1, 2004, from *http://myexecpc.com/~dboals*

Board of Education, Hendrick Hudson School District, v. Rowley. 458 U.S. 176, 181 (1982).

Bock, S. J., & Myles, B. S. (1999). An overview of characteristics of Asperger syndrome. *Education and Training in Mental Retardation and Developmental Disabilities, 34*(4), 511–520.

Bondurant-Utz, J. (2002). *Practical guide to assessing infants and preschoolers with special needs.* Upper Saddle River, NJ: Merrill/Prentice Hall Education.

Bos, C. S., & Vaughn, S. (2002). *Strategies for teaching students with learning and behavior problems* (5th ed.). Boston: Allyn & Bacon.

Bottge, B. A. (1999). Effects of contextualized math instruction on problem solving of average and below-average achieving students. *Journal of Special Education, 33*(2), 81–92.

Boudah, D. J., Schumacher, J. B., & Deshler, D. D. (1997). Collaborative instruction: Is it an effective option for inclusion in secondary classrooms? *Learning Disability Quarterly, 20*(4), 293–316.

Bowe, F. G. (n.d.). *Interviews with individuals with physical, sensory, health, and emotional disabilities: Boston, St. Louis, Atlanta, New York, Baltimore, Detroit, Minneapolis, and Denver.* Unpublished manuscript.

Bowe, F. G. (1978). *Handicapping America: Barriers to disabled people.* New York: Harper & Row.

Bowe, F. G. (Ed.). (1988b). *Toward equality: Education of the deaf.* Report of the Commission on Education of the Deaf, U.S. Congress. Washington, DC: Government Printing Office.

Bowe, F. G. (1998). Language development in deaf children. *Journal of Deaf Studies and Deaf Education, 3*(1), 73–78.

Bowe, F. G. (2000a). *Birth to five: Early childhood special education* (2nd ed.). Albany, NY: International Thomson Learning, Delmar.

Bowe, F. G. (2000b). *Physical, sensory, and health disabilities.* Columbus, OH: Prentice Hall, Merrill Education.

Bowe, F. G. (2002a). *Broadband and Americans with disabilities.* Silver Spring, MD: National Association of the Deaf. Retrieved April 5, 2004 from *http://www.newmillenniumresearch.org/disability.pdf*

Bowe, F. G. (2002b). Enhancing reading ability to prevent students from becoming "low functioning deaf" as adults. *American Annals of the Deaf, 147*(5), 22–27.

Bowe, F. G. (2000c). *Universal design in education: Teaching nontraditional students.* Westport, CT: Greenwood Publishing Group.

Bowe, F. G. (2004). *Birth to eight: Early childhood special education* (3rd ed.). Clifton Park, NY: International Thomson Learning, Delmar.

Boyer, P. (1998). *The American nation.* Austin, TX: Holt, Rinehart & Winston.

Braden, J. P. (1994). *Deafness, deprivation, and IQ.* New York: Plenum Press.

Breggin, P. R. (1998). *Talking back to Ritalin.* New York: Common Courage Press.

Brice, A., & Roseberry-McKibbin, C. (2001). Choice of languages in instruction. *Teaching Exceptional Children, 33*(4), 10–16.

Bricker, D. (2000). Inclusion: How the scene has changed. *Topics in Early Childhood Special Education, 20*(1), 14–19.

Bricker, D., Pretti-Frontczak, K., & McComas, N. R. (1998). *An activity-based approach to early intervention* (2nd ed.). Baltimore: Brookes.

Brody, G. H., & Flor, D. L. (1997). Maternal psychological functioning, family processes, and child adjustment in rural, single-parent, African-American families. *Developmental Psychology, 33*(6), 1000–1011.

Brody, H. (2000). *The placebo response: How you can release your body's inner pharmacy for better health.* New York: HarperCollins.

Bronowski, J. (1973). *The ascent of man.* Boston: Little Brown.

Brotherson, M. J., Sheriff, G., & Milburn, P. (2001). Elementary school principals and their needs and issues for inclusive early childhood programs. *Topics in Early Childhood Special Education, 21*(1), 31–45.

Browder, D., Flowers, C., Ahlgrim-Delzell, L., Karvonen, M., Spooner, F., & Algozinne, R. (2004). The alignment of alternate assessment content with academic and functional curricula. *Journal of Special Education, 37*(4), 211–223.

Browder, D. M., & Grasso, E. (1999). Teaching money skills to individuals with mental retardation: A research review with practical applications. *Remedial and Special Education, 20,* 297–308.

Brown, D. (2000). *Learning a living: A guide to planning your career and finding a job for people with learning disabilities, attention deficit disorder, and dyslexia.* Bethesda, MD: Woodbine House.

Brown, D., Pryzwansky, W. B., & Schulte, A. C. (2001). *Psychological consultation: Introduction to theory and practice* (5th ed.). Boston, MA: Allyn & Bacon.

Brown, L., Schwartz, P., Udvari-Solner, A., Kampschroer, E., Johnson, F., Jorgensen, J., & Gruenewald, L. (1991). How much time should students with severe intellectual disabilities spend in regular classrooms and elsewhere? *Journal of The Association for Persons with Severe Handicaps, 16,* 39–47.

Brown v. Board of Education of Topeka, Kansas. 347 U.S. 483 (1954).

Bruce, S. M. (2002). Impact of a communication intervention model on teachers' practice with children who are congenitally deaf-blind. *Journal of Visual Impairment and Blindness, 96*(3), 154–168.

Bruner, J. (1960). *The process of education.* Cambridge, MA: Harvard University Press.

Brunn, M. (1999). The absence of language policy and its effects on the education of Mexican migrant children. *Bilingual Research Journal, 23*(4), 319–344.

Bryan, T., Pearl, R., & Herzog, A. (1989). Learning disabled adolescent's vulnerability to crime: Attitudes, anxieties, and experiences. *Learning Disabilities Research, 5,* 51–60.

Bryson, B. (2003). *A short history of nearly everything.* New York: Broadway Books.

Bullis, M., & Cheney, D. (1999). Vocational and transition interventions for adolescents and young adults with emotional or behavioral disorders, entire issue. *Focus on Exceptional Children, 31*(7).

Burdick, E. (1956). *The ninth wave.* Boston: Houghton Mifflin.

Bureau of Justice Statistics. (1998). 1973–1997 National Crime Victimization Survey. Washington, DC: U.S. Department of Justice.

Bursuck, W. D., Munk, D. D., & Olson, M. M. (1999). The fairness of report card grading adaptations: What do students with and without learning disabilities think? *Remedial and Special Education, 20*(2), 84–92, 105.

Bussing, R., Zima, B. T., & Forness, S. R. (1998). Children who qualify for LD and ADHD programs: Do they differ in level of ADHD symptoms and comorbid psychiatric conditions? *Behavioral Disorders, 23,* 85–97.

Butler, F. M., Miller, S. P., Lee, K., & Pierce. T. (2001). Teaching mathematics to students with mild-to-moderate mental retardation: A review of the literature. *Mental Retardation, 39*(1), 20–31.

Byrne, W. (2004). Math lessons (draining a swimming pool). Retrieved April 11, 2004, from *http://iit.edu/~smile/ma8904.html*

Callahan, J. (1990). *Don't worry, he won't get far on foot.* New York: Random House, Vintage Books.

Camarota, S. A. (2003). 800,000+ entered annually in late 90's. Retrieved April 11, 2004 from *http://www.cis.org/articles/20013/illegalsrelease.html*

Camp, B. W., Blom, G. E., Herbert, R., & Van Doornick, W. J. (1977). "Think aloud": A program for developing self-control in young aggressive boys. *Journal of Abnormal Child Psychology, 5,* 157–169.

Campbell, C. (1993). Strategies for reducing parental resistance to consultation in the schools. *Elementary School Guidance and Counseling, 28,* 83–91.

Canedy, D. (2001, March 25). Troubling label for Hispanics: "Girls most likely to drop out." *New York Times,* pp. 1, 24.

Cantu, N. V., & Heumann, J. E. (2000, July 25). *Dear colleague letter.* Washington, DC: U.S. Department of Education, Office for Civil Rights and Office of Special Education and Rehabilitative Services (400 Maryland Avenue SW, Washington, DC 20202).

Carbone, E. (2001). Arranging the classroom with an eye (and ear) to students with ADHD. *Teaching Exceptional Children, 34,* 2, 72–81.

Carin, A. A. (1997). *Teaching modern science* (7th ed.). Upper Saddle River, NJ: Merrill/Prentice Hall Education.

Carle, E. (1994). *The very hungry caterpillar.* New York: Philomel Books.

Carnahan, I. (2003, November 10). Desegregation's broken promises. *Forbes,* 114, 119–120.

Carnegie, D. (1994). *How to win friends and influence people.* Reissue edition. New York: Pocket Books.

Carnine, D. (1997). Instructional design in mathematics for students with learning disabilities. *Journal of Learning Disabilities, 30*(2), 130–141.

Carter, L. F. (1984). The sustaining effects study of compensatory and elementary education. *Educational Researcher, 13*(7), 4–13.

Cathcart, W. G., Pothier, Y. M., Vance, J. H., & Benzuk, N. S. (2001). *Learning mathematics in elementary and middle schools.* Upper Saddle River, NJ: Merrill/Prentice Hall Education.

Cawley, J., Parmar, R., Foley, T. E., Salmon, S., & Roy, S. (2001). Arithmetic performance of students: Implications for standards and programming. *Exceptional Children, 67*(3), 311–328.

Celeste, M. (2002). A survey of motor development for infants and young children with visual impairments. *Journal of Visual Impairment and Blindness, 96*(3), 169–174.

Center for Civic Education. (2004). Home page. Retrieved April 11, 2004, from *http://www.civiced.org*

Center for the Study and Prevention of Violence. (2000). *Safe communities—safe schools Planning Guide.* Boulder, CO: Author.

Center on Addiction and Substance Abuse. (2000). *Substance abuse and learning disabilities: Peas in a pod or apples and oranges?* New York: Columbia University Press. Online at: *http://www.casacolumbia.org/publications1456*

Centers for Disease Control and Prevention. (2004). *CMV virus.* Retrieved March 30, 2004 from *http://www.cdc.gov/ncidod/diseases/cmv.htm*

Chaleff, C. D., & Ritter, M. H. (2001). The use of miscue analysis with deaf readers. *The Reading Teacher, 55*(2), 190–200.

Chapin, J. R., & Messick, R. G. (1996). *Elementary Social Studies: A Practical Guide* (3rd ed.). White Plains, NY: Longman.

Chiappetta, E. L., & Koballa, T. R. (2002). *Science Instruction in the Middle and Secondary Schools* (5th ed.). Upper Saddle River, NJ: Merrill/Prentice Hall Education.

Children and Adults with Attention Deficit Disorders. (2001). Facts About ADD (CH.A.D.D., 8181 Professional Place #201, Landover, MD 20785). Retrieved April 10, 2004 from *http://www.chadd.org/fs/fs1.pdt*

Children's Defense Fund. (2000). *Families struggling to make it in the workforce: A post welfare report.* Washington, DC: Author.

Chomsky, N. (1965). *Aspects of the theory of syntax.* Cambridge, MA: MIT Press.

Chomsky, N. (1972). *Language and mind.* New York: Harcourt Brace Jovanovich.

Clark, B. (2002). *Growing up gifted: Developing the potential of children at home and at school* (6th ed.). Upper Saddle River, NJ: Merrill/Prentice Hall Education.

Clay, M. M. (1993a). *An observation survey of literacy achievement.* Portsmouth, NH: Heinemann.

Clay, M. M. (1993b). *Reading recovery: A guidebook for teachers in training.* Portsmouth, NH: Heinemann.

Clements, R. L. (1995). *Games and great ideas: A guide for elementary school physical educators and classroom teachers.* Westport, CT: Greenwood Press.

Cline, S., & Hegeman, K. (2000). Gifted children with disabilities. *Gifted Child Today, 24*(3), 16–24.

Cohen, D., & Volkmar, F. (Eds.). (1997). *Handbook of autism and pervasive developmental disorders.* (2nd ed.). New York: John Wiley & Sons.

Cohen, E. (1994). Restructuring the classroom: Conditions for productive small groups. *Review of Educational Research, 64*(1), 1–35.

Cohen, M. K., Gale, M., & Meyer, J. M. (1994). *Survival guide for the first year special education teacher* (Rev. ed.). Reston, VA: Council for Exceptional Children.

Colasent, R., & Griffith, P. L. (1998). Autism and literacy: Looking into the classroom with rabbit stories. *The Reading Teacher, 51*(5), 414–420.

Cole, C. M., & McLeskey, J. (1997). Secondary inclusion programs for students with mild disabilities, entire issue. *Focus on Exceptional Children, 29*(6).

Coleman, M. C. (1996). *Emotional & behavioral disorders: Theory and practice.* Needham Heights, MA: Allyn & Bacon.

Coles, A. D. (1999, January 20). Discontented, some districts shifting gears on anti-drug programs. *Education Week, 18*(19), 5.

Cook, L. H., & Boe, E. E. (1995). Who is teaching students with disabilities? *Teaching Exceptional Children, 28*(1), 70–72.

Cooper, J., & Mueck, R. (1990). Student involvement in learning: Cooperative learning and college instruction. *Journal of Excellence in College Teaching, 1*(1), 68–76.

Copeland, L. I. (1998, November 26). Echo in the sounds of silence: For a stutterer, words are a barrier to communication. *Washington Post,* Article 328035.

Cormier, R. (1998). *Heroes: A novel.* New York: Delacorte Press.

Corn, A. L., & Wall, R. S. (2002). Training and availability of Braille transcribers in the United States. *Journal of Visual Impairment and Blindness, 96*(4), 223–232.

Cosmos, C. (2002). Imagine teaching Robin Williams—Twice-exceptional children in your school. *CEC Today, 9*(4), 1, 5.

Cottman, J. (2002). Personal communication, November 18.

Courchesne, E. (1989). Pathophysiologic findings in nonretarded autism and receptive developmental language disorder. *Journal of Autism and Developmental Disabilities, 19*(1), 1–17.

Courchesne, E. (1995). New evidence of cerebellar and brainstem hypoplasia in autistic infants, children, and adolescents: The MR imaging study by Hashiomoto and colleagues. *Journal of Autism and Developmental Disabilities, 25*(1), 19–22.

Council for Exceptional Children. (2000). *What every special educator must know.* Reston, VA: Author.

Council for Learning Disabilities. (1997). Infosheet: What do we know about the characteristics of learning disabilities? Retrieved April 11, 2004 from *http://www.semo.edu/provost/courses/exe628.htm*

Cowley, G. (2000, July 31). The challenge of "mindblindness." *Newsweek,* 46–54.

Cravchik, A., & Goldman, D. (2000). Neurochemical individuality: Genetic diversity among human dopamine and serotonin receptors and transporters. *Archives of General Psychiatry, 57*(12), 1105–1114.

Crawford, J. (1999). *Bilingual education: History, politics, theory and practice* (4th ed.). Los Angeles: Bilingual Educational Services.

Crealock, C., & Bachor, D. (1995). *Instructional strategies for students with special needs.* Scarborough, Ontario: Allyn & Bacon.

Crittenden, A. (2001). *The price of motherhood: Why the most important job in the world is still the least valued.* New York: Metropolitan Books.

Crutcher, C. (1987). *The crazy horse electric game.* New York: Bamtam Doubleday Dell.

Cure Autism Now. (1997). Autism screening and diagnostic evaluation: CAN consensus statement by the CAN consensus group (1997). Retrieved April 9, 2004 from *http://www.cureautismnow.org*

Curwin, R. L., & Mendler, A. N. (2001). *Discipline with dignity.* Upper Saddle River, NJ: Merrill/Prentice Hall Education.

Czarra, F. (1999). Breaking new ground: The comprehensive social studies assessment project (CSSAP). *Social Education, 65*(6), 360–364.

Dalaker, J., & Naifeh, M. (1998). *Poverty in the United States: 1997.* Current Population Reports, (pp. 60–201). Washington, DC: U.S. Bureau of the Census.

Dales, L., Hammer, S. J., & Smith, N. J. (2001). Time trends in autism and in MMR immunization coverage in California. *Journal of the American Medical Association, 285*(9), 1183–1185.

Damasio, A. (1999). *The feeling of what happens: Body and emotion in the making of consciousness.* New York: Harcourt.

D'Arcangelo, M. (1999). Learning about learning to read: A conversation with Sally Shaywitz. *Educational Leadership, 57*(2). Online at *http://www.ascd.org*

Dattilo, J., & Hoge, G. (1999). Effects of a leisure education program on youth with mental retardation. *Education and Training in Mental Retardation and Developmental Disabilities, 34*(1), 20–34.

Davila, R. R., Williams, M. L., & MacDonald, J. T. (1991, September 16). Clarification of policy to address the needs of children with attention deficit disorders within general and/or special classrooms. Unpublished memorandum. Available from U.S. Department of Education, Office of Special Education and Rehabilitative Services, Washington, DC 20202, or online at *http://www.add.org/content/legal/memo.htm*

Decker, S. H., & Curry, G. D. (2000). Addressing key features of gang membership measuring the involvement of young members. *Journal of Criminal Justice, 28,* 473–482.

Denckla, M. B., & Cutting, L. E. (1999). History and significance of rapid automatized naming. *Annals of Dyslexia, 49,* 29–42.

Dennis, M., Lazenby, A. L., & Lockyer, L. (2001). Inferential language in high-function children with autism. *Journal of Autism and Developmental Disorders, 31*(1), 47–54.

Deno, E. (1970). Special education as development capital. *Exceptional Children, 37*(3), 229–237.

DePalma, A. (2001). *Here: A biography of the new American continent.* New York: Public Affairs.

Desai, S. S. (1997). Down syndrome: A review of the literature. *Oral Surgery, Oral Medicine, Oral Pathology, Oral Radiology, and Endodontics, 84,* 279–285.

Deschenes, C., Ebeling, D., & Sprague, J. (1994). *Adapting curriculum and instruction in inclusive classrooms: A teacher's desk reference.* Bloomington, IN: Center for School and Community Integration, Institute for the Study of Developmental Disabilities.

Deshler, D.D., Ellis, E.S., & Lenz, B.K. (Eds.) (1996). *Teaching adolescents with learning disabilities: Strategies and methods.* (2nd ed.). Denver: Love Publishing.

Developing quality IEPs: A case-based tutorial. Upper Saddle River, NJ: Merrill/Prentice Hall Education.

Dever, R. B., & Knapczyk, D. R. (1997). *Teaching persons with mental retardation: A model for curriculum development and teaching.* Madison, WI: Brown & Benchmark.

deVilliers, P. A., Buuck, M., Findlay, L., & Shelton, J. (1994). *A language arts curriculum for deaf students.* Northampton, MA: Clarke School for the Deaf.

Dew, D. W. (Ed.). (1999). *Serving individuals who are low-functioning deaf.* Report of the 25th Institute on Rehabilitation Issues. Washington, DC: George Washington University.

Dewey, J. (1963). *Experience and education.* New York: Collier/Macmillan.

DiCarlo, C. F., Stricklin, S., & Banajee, M. (2001). Effects of manual signing on communication verbalizations by toddlers with and without disabilities in inclusive classrooms. *The Journal of the Association for Persons with Severe Handicaps, 26*(2), 68–92.

Dietz, S. J., & Ferrell, K. A. (1993). Early services for young children with visual impairment: From diagnosis to comprehensive services. *Infants and Young Children, 6*(1), 68–76.

Dimitrovsky, L., Spector, H., Levy-Shiff, R., & Vakil, E. (1998). Interpretation of facial expressions of affect in children with learning disabilities with verbal or nonverbal deficits. *Journal of Learning Disabilities, 31,* 286–292, 312.

Ding, Y., et al. (2002). Evidence of positive selection acting at the human dopamine receptor D4 gene locus. *Proceedings of the National Academy of Sciences, 99*(1), 309–314.

Dole, J. A., Duffy, G. C., Roehler, L. R., & Pearson, P. D. (1991). Moving from the old to the new: Research on reading comprehension instruction. *Review of Educational Research, 61,* 239–264.

Duarte, E. M. (1998). Expanding the borders of liberal democracy: Multicultural education and the struggle for cultural identity. *Educational Foundations, 12*(2), 5–30.

Duarte, E. M., & Smith. S. (Eds.). (2000). *Foundational perspectives in multicultural education.* New York: Longman.

Duch, B. J., Groh, S. E., & Allen, D. E. (2001). *The power of problem-based learning: A practical "how-to" for teaching undergraduate courses in any discipline.* Sterling, VA: Stylus Publishing. Online at *http://www.styluspub.com*

Dunst, C. J., Bruder, M. B., Trivette, C. M., Raab, M., & McLean, M. (2001). Natural learning opportunities for infants, toddlers, and preschoolers. *Young Exceptional Children, 4*(3), 18–25.

Dunst, C. J., Herter, S., Shields, H., & Bennis, L. (2001). Mapping community-based natural learning opportunities. *Young Exceptional Children, 4*(4), 16–25.

Easterbrooks, S. R. (2001). Veteran teachers of children who are deaf/hard of hearing describe language instructional practices: Implications for teacher preparation. *Teacher Education and Special Education, 24*(2), 116–127.

Easterbrooks, S. R., & Baker, S. K. (2001). Enter the matrix! Considering the communication needs of students who are deaf or hard of hearing. *Teaching Exceptional Children, 33*(3), 70–76.

Ebenezer, J. V., & Lau, E. (1999). *Science on the Internet: A resource for K–12 teachers.* Upper Saddle River, NJ: Merrill/Prentice Hall Education.

Education Week. (2000a). English-language learners. Retrieved April 12, 2004 from *http://www.edweek.org/context/ topics/issuespage.cfm?id=8*

Education Week. (2000b). "Children of change" series. Retrieved March 30, 2004 from *http://www.edweek.org/ew/ ew_printstory.cfm?slug=04centoverview.h20*

Education Week (2004). *Brown at 50.* Available online at: *http://www.edweek.com/sreports/special_reports_article. cfm?slug=brown.htm*

Edyburn, D. L. (2000). Assistive technology and students with mild disabilities, entire issue. *Focus on Exceptional Children, 32*(9).

Ehrenreich, B. (1990). *Fear of falling: The inner life of the middle class.* New York: HarperCollins.

Ehrenreich, B. (2001). *Nickel and dimed: On (not) getting by in America.* New York: Metropolitan Books.

Elementary and Secondary Education Act. 20 U.S.C. 2701 *et seq.*

Elliott, J., Algozzine, B., & Ysseldyke, J. E. (1997). *Time savers for educators.* Longmont, CO: Sopris West.

Ellis, A., & Fouts, J. (1997). *Research on educational innovations* (2nd ed.). Larchmont, NY: Eye on Education.

Ellis, E. S., & Colvert, G. (1996). Writing strategy instruction. In Deshler, D. D., Ellis, E. S., & Lenz, B. K. (Eds.), *Teaching Adolescents with Learning Disabilities.* Denver: Love Publishing Company.

Emmer, E. T., Evertson, C., & Worsham, M. E. (2000). *Classroom management for secondary teachers* (5th ed.). Needham Heights, MA: Allyn & Bacon.

Engleman, S., Haddox, P., & Bruder, E. (1986). *Teaching your child to read in 100 easy lessons.* New York: Simon & Schuster.

Entwisle, D. R. (1993). Schools and the adolescent. In Feldman, S., & Elliot, G. R. (Eds.). *At the Threshold: The Developing Adolescent* (pp. 197–224). Cambridge, MA: Harvard University Press.

Epilepsy Foundation of America. (2004). Retrieved April 11, 2004 from *http://www.efa.org*

Epstein, M., Munk, D., Bursuck, W., Polloway, E., & Jayanthi, M. (1999). Strategies for improving home-school communication about homework for students with disabilities. *The Journal of Special Education, 33*(3), 166–176.

Eugenides, J. (1993). *The virgin suicides.* New York: Farrar Straus Giroux.

Evans, M. D., Newman, M., & Saxe, D. W. (1996) *NCSS handbook on teaching social issues.* Silver Spring, MD: National Council for the Social Studies.

Fellman, M. (1995). *Citizen Sherman: A life of William Tecumseh Sherman.* New York: Random House.

Felton, R. H. (2001). Students with three types of severe learning disabilities: Introduction to the case studies. *Journal of Special Education, 35*(3), 122–124.

Fennick, E. (2001). Coteaching: An inclusive curriculum for transition. *Teaching Exceptional Children, 33*(6), 60–66.

Ferretti, R. P., MacArthur, C. D., & Okolo, C. M. (2001). Teaching for historical understanding in inclusive classrooms. *Learning Disability Quarterly, 24*(1), 59–72.

Fitzgerald, F. S. (1925). *The great Gatsby.* New York: Charles Scribner's Sons.

Flexer, R.W., Simmons, T. J., Luft, P., & Baer, R. (2001). *Transition planning for secondary students with disabilities.* Upper Saddle River, NJ: Merrill/Prentice Hall Education.

Foegen, A., & Deno, S. L. (2001). Identifying growth indicators for low-achieving students in middle school mathematics. *Journal of Special Education, 35*(1), 4–16.

Folger Library General Reader's Shakespeare: Hamlet. (1992). New York: Simon & Schuster, Washington Square Press.

Ford, A., Davern, L., & Schnorr, R. (2001). Learners with significant disabilities: Curricular relevance in an era of standards-based reform. *Remedial and Special Education, 22*(4), 214–222.

Ford, M. (1992). *Motivating humans.* Newbury Park, CA: Sage Publications.

Forness, S. R., & Kavale, K. A. (2000). Emotional or behavioral disorders: Background and current status of the E/BD terminology and definition. *Behavioral Disorders, 25*(3), 264–269.

Forness, S. R., Kavale, K. A., King, B. H., & Kasari, C. (1994). Simple versus complex conduct disorders: Identification and phenomenology. *Behavioral Disorders, 19,* 306–312.

Forness, S. R., Kavale, K. A., & Lopez, M. (1993). Conduct disorders in school: Special education eligibility and comorbidity. *Journal of Emotional and Behavioral Disorders, 1,* 101–108.

Foster, W. P. (2004). The decline of the local: A challenge to educational leadership. *Educational Administration Quarterly, XL*(2), 176–191.

Frank, A. R., & Sitlington, P. L. (2000). Young adults with mental disabilities—Does transition planning make a difference? *Education and Training in Mental Retardation and Developmental Disabilities, 35*(2), 119–134.

Franklin, A. J. (1998). Treating anger in African American men. In Pollack, W. S., & Levant, R. F. (Eds.), *New Psychotherapy for Men* (pp. 239–258). New York: Wiley.

Freire, P. (1995). *A pedagogy of hope.* New York: Continuum.

French, N. K. (2001). Supervising paraprofessionals: A survey of teacher practices. *Journal of Special Education, 35*(1), 41–53.

Friend, M., & Cook, L. (2003). *Interactions: Collaboration skills for school professionals.* Boston, MA: Allyn & Bacon.

Frith, U. (1993, June). Autism. *Scientific American,* 108–114.

Frith, U., & Happe, F. (1999). Theory of mind and self-consciousness: What is it like to be autistic? *Mind & Language, 14,* 1–22.

Fromberg, D. P. (1995). *The full-day kindergarten: Planning and practicing a dynamic themes curriculum* (2nd ed.). New York: Teachers College Press.

Fuchs, D., & Fuchs, L. (1994). Inclusive schools movement and the radicalization of special education reform. *Exceptional Children, 60*(4) 94–309.

Fuchs, D., & Fuchs, L. (1996). Consultation as a technology and the politics of school reform. *Remedial and Special Education, 17*(6), 386–392.

Fuchs, D., Fuchs, L., & Bahr, M. (1990). Mainstream assistance teams: A scientific basis for the art of consultation. *Exceptional Children, 57*(2), 128–139.

Fuchs, D., Fuchs, L. S., Mathes, P. G., Lipsey, M. E., & Eaton, S. (2000). A meta-analysis of reading differences with and without the disabilities label: A brief report. *Learning Disabilities, 10,* 1–3.

Fuchs, D., Fuchs, L. S., Thompson, A., Svenson, E., Yen, L., Al Otaiba, S., Yang, N., McMaster, K. N., Prentice, K., Kazdan, S., & Salenz, L. (2001). Peer-assisted learning strategies in reading: Extensions for kindergarten, first grade, and high school. *Remedial and Special Education, 22*(1), 15–21.

Fuchs, L., & Fuchs, D. (1986). Effects of systematic formative evaluation: A meta-analysis. *Exceptional Children, 53*(3), 199–208.

Fuchs, L., & Fuchs, D. (2001). Principles for sustaining research-based practice in the schools: A case study. *Focus on Exceptional Children, 33*(6), 1–14.

Fuchs, L. S., Fuchs, D., & Kazdan, S. (1999). Effects of peer-assisted learning strategies on high school students with serious reading problems. *Remedial and Special Education, 20*(5) 309–318.

Fujiura, G. T., & Yamaki, K. (2000). Trends in demography of childhood poverty and disability. *Exceptional Children, 66*(2), 187–199.

Gagnon, J. C., McLaughlin, M. J., & Rhim, L. M. (2000). *Standards-driven reform policies at the local level: Report on a survey of local special education directors in large districts.* College Park, MD: University of Maryland Institute for the Study of Exceptional Children and Youth.

Galaburda, A. M., Menard, M. T., & Rosen, G. D. (1994). Evidence for aberrant auditory anatomy in developmental dyslexia. *Proceedings of the National Academy of Sciences, 91,* 8010–8013.

Gallagher, H. G. (1985). *FDR's splendid deception.* New York: Dodd, Mead.

Gardner, H. (1983). *Frames of mind: The theory of multiple intelligences.* New York: Basic.

Gardner, H. (2000). *Intelligence reframed: Multiple intelligences for the 21st century.* New York: Basic.

Gardner, R., Cartledge, G., Seidl, B., Woolsey, M. L., Schley, G. S, & Utley, C. A. (2001). Mt. Olivet after-school program: Peer-mediated interventions for at-risk students. *Remedial and Special Education, 22*(1), 22–33.

Garnett, K. (n.d.) Math learning disabilities. Retrieved April 11, 2004 from *http://ldonline.org/ld_indepth/math_skills/garnett.html*

Garshelis, J. A., & McConnell, S. R. (1993). Comparison of family needs assessed by mothers, individual professionals, and inter-disciplinary teams. *Journal of Early Intervention, 17*(1), 36–49.

Garza, T. (1991). Evaluating the use of captioned video materials in advanced foreign language learning. *Foreign Language Annals, 24*(3), 239–258.

Geography Education Standards Project. (1994). *The eighteen national geography standards.* Retrieved April 11, 2004, from *http://www.ncge.org/publications/tutorial/standards/*

Gersten, R., Carnine, D., & Woodward, J. (1987). Direct instruction research: The third decade. *Remedial and Special Education, 8*(6), 48–56.

Gersten, R., & Chard, D. (1999). Number sense: Rethinking arithmetic instruction for students with mathematical disabilities. *Journal of Special Education, 33*(1), 18–28.

Gersten, R., Keating, T., Yovanoff, P., & Harniss, M. K. (2001). Working in special education: Factors that enhance special educators' intent to stay. *Exceptional Children, 67*(4), 549–567.

Gersten, R., & Woodward, J. (1994). The language-minority student and special education: Issues, trends, and paradoxes. *Exceptional Children, 60*(4), 310–322.

Giangreco, M. F., Edelman, S. W., & Broer, S. M. (2001). Respect, appreciation, and acknowledgment of paraprofessionals who support students with disabilities. *Exceptional Children, 67*(4), 485–498.

Giangreco, M. F., Edelman, S. W., Luiselli, T. E., & MacFarland, S. Z. C. (1997). Helping or hovering? Effects of instructional assistant proximity on students with disabilities. *Exceptional Children, 64*(1), 7–18.

Gibb, G. S., & Dyches, T. T. (2000). *Guide to writing quality individualized education programs.* Needham Heights, MA: Allyn & Bacon.

Gibson, W. (1960). *The miracle worker: A play in three acts.* New York: S. French.

Gifted education: An endangered species. (2004). Retrieved April 11, 2004, from *http://www.gifteddevelopment.com*

Glanz, J. (2000, July 16). Amid race profiling claims, Asian-Americans avoid labs. *New York Times,* pp. 1, 14–15.

Gold, M. W. (1973). Vocational habilitation for the mentally retarded. In Ellis, N. R. (Ed.), *International Review of Research in Mental Retardation.* (Vol. 6, pp. 237–263). New York: Academic Press.

Gold, M. W. (1980). *Try another way training manual.* Champaign, IL: Research Press.

Golding, W. (1962). *Lord of the flies.* New York: Coward-McCann.

Goodman, D. (1999). *The reading detective club: Solving the mysteries of reading, A teacher's guide.* Portsmouth, NH: Heinemann.

Goodman, J. (1992). *When slow is fast enough: Educating the delayed preschool child.* New York: Guilford Press.

Goodman, K. S. (1986). *What's whole about whole language?* Portsmouth, NH: Heinemann.

Goodman, K. S., Goodman, Y. M., & Hood, W. J. (1989). *The whole language evaluation book.* Portsmouth, NH: Heinemann.

Goodnough, A. (2001, June 14). Strains of fourth-grade tests drives off veteran teachers. *New York Times.* Retrieved July 31, 2002 from *http://www.nystimes.com/search/ardire.html*

Gould, M. S., Shaffer, D., & Fisher, P. (1998). Separation/divorce and child and adolescent completed suicide. *Journal of the Academy of Child and Adolescent Psychiatry, 37,* 155–162.

Graczyk, M. (2000, August 9). Two killers executed in Texas. Associated Press Newswire.

Green, M., et al. (1999). *Diagnosis of attention deficit/hyperactivity disorder: Technical review 3.* Rockville, MD: Agency for Health Care Policy and Research, U.S. Department of Health and Human Services.

Greenfield, J. (1972). *A child called Noah.* New York: Holt, Rinehart & Winston.

Greenspan, S. (1997). Dead manual walking? Why the 1992 AAMR definition needs redoing. *Education and Training in Mental Retardation and Developmental Disabilities, 32,* 179–190.

Greenwood, C. R. (1997). Classwide peer tutoring. *Behavior and Social Issues, 7*(1), 53–57.

Greenwood, C. R., Arreaga-Mayer, C., Utley, C. A., Gavin, K. M., & Terry, B. J. (2001). Classwide peer tutoring learning management system: Applications with elementary-level English language learners. *Remedial and Special Education, 22*(1), 34–47.

Grove, K. A., & Fisher, D. (1999). Entrepreneurs of meaning: Parents and the process of inclusive education. *Remedial and Special Education, 20*(4), 208–215.

Grove, N., & Dockrell, J. (2000). Multisign combinations by children with intellectual impairments: An analysis of language skills. *Journal of Speech, Language, and Hearing Research, 43*(2), 309–320.

Guastello, E. F., Beasley, T. M., & Sinatra, R. C. (2000). Concept mapping effects on science content comprehension of low-achieving inner-city seventh graders. *Remedial and Special Education, 21*(6), 356–365.

Gutierrez-Clellan, F. (1999). Mediating literacy skills in Spanish-speaking children with special needs. *Clinical Forum, 30*(3), 285–292.

Guyer, B. P. (2000). (Ed.). *ADHD: Achieving success in school and in life.* Needham Heights, MA: Allyn & Bacon, 2000.

Hall, B. J., Oyer, H. J., & Haas, W. H. (2001). *Speech, language, and hearing disorders: A guide for the teacher.* Needham Heights, MA: Allyn & Bacon.

Hallahan, D. P., & Kauffman, J. M. (2000). *Exceptional learners* (8th ed.). Needham Heights, MA: Allyn & Bacon.

Hallahan, D. P., Kauffman, J. M., & Lloyd, J. W. (1999). *Introduction to learning disabilities.* Needham Heights, MA: Allyn & Bacon.

Halpern, A. (1999). Transition: It is time for another rebottling? Paper presented at the 1999 annual OSEP project directors' meeting, Washington, DC. Retrieved April 11, 2004 from *http://www.ed.uiuc.edu/sped/tri/halpern99.htm*

Hamre-Nietupski, S., Dvorsky, S., McKee, A., Nietupski, J., Cook, J., & Costanza, C. (1999). Going home: General and special education teachers' perspectives as students with moderate/severe disabilities return to rural neighborhood schools. *Education and Training in Mental Retardation and Developmental Disabilities, 34*(3), 235–259.

Hamre-Nietupski, S., McDonald, J., & Nietupski, J. (1992). Integrating elementary students with multiple disabilities: Challenges and solutions. *Teaching Exceptional Children, 24*(3), 6–11.

Handler, L. (1996). The clinical use of drawings: Draw-a-Person, House-Tree-Person, and Kinetic Family Drawings. In C.E. Newmark (Ed.). *Major Psychological Assessment Instruments.* 2nd ed. Boston: Allyn & Bacon.

Harrington, R. C. (2001a). Adolescent depression: Same or different? *Archives of General Psychiatry, 58*(1), 21–22.

Harrington, R. C. (2001b). Childhood depression and conduct disorder: Different routes to the same outcome? *Archives of General Psychiatry, 58*(3), 237–238.

Harry, B., Kalyanpur, M., & Day, M. (1999). *Building cultural reciprocity with families: Case studies in special education.* Baltimore, MD: Brookes Publishing.

Hart, D. (1999). Opening assessments to our students. *Social Education, 65*(6), 343–345.

Hasazi, S. B., Furney, K. S., & DeStefano, L. (1999). Implementing the IDEA transition mandates. *Exceptional Children, 65*(4), 555–566.

Hatton, D. D., Bailey, D. B., Roberts, J. P., Skinner, M., Mayhew, L., Clark, R. D., Waring, E., & Roberts, J. E. (2000). Early intervention services for young boys with Fragile X syndrome. *Journal of Early Intervention, 23*(4), 235–251.

Hawthorne, N. (1859). *The scarlet letter.* Boston: Ticknor, Reed, and Fields. Bantam Books edition published 1965. New York: Bantam Books.

Heller, K. W., Fredrick, L. D., Dykes, M. K., Best, S., & Cohen, E. T. (1999). A national perspective of competencies for teachers of individuals with physical and health disabilities. *Exceptional Children, 65*(2), 219–234.

Henderson, C. (1999). *College freshmen with disabilities: Statistical year 1998.* Washington, DC: American Council on Education, HEATH Resource Center.

Heumann, J. E., & Warlick, K. R. (2001). *Guidance on including students with disabilities in assessment programs.* Memorandum. Washington, DC: Office of Special Education and Rehabilitation Services.

Hirshson, S. P. (1997). *The white tecumseh: A biography of General William T. Sherman.* New York: John Wiley & Sons.

Hobbs, N. (Ed.). (1975). *Issues in the classification of children.* San Francisco: Jossey-Bass.

Holicky, R. (2000). Richard Castaldo after Columbine. *New Mobility, 11*(78), 24–26.

Horn, E., Lieber, J., Li, S., Sandall, S., & Schwartz, I. (2000). Supporting young children's IEP goals in inclusive settings through embedded learning opportunities. *Topics in Early Childhood Special Education, 20*(4), 208–223.

Horner, B. R., & Scheibe, K. E. (1997). Prevalence and implications of attention-deficit hyperactivity disorder among adolescents in treatment for substance abuse. *Journal of the American Academy of Child and Adolescent Psychiatry, 36*(1), 30–36.

Huang, H-S., & Eskey, D.E. (2000). The effects of closed-captioned television on the listening comprehension of intermediate English as a second language (ESL) students. *Educational Administration Abstracts, 35*(1). Retrieved January 22, 2004, from *http://ejournals.ebsco.com/direct.asp?ArticleID=G6W90G6GLAPG09RY7T6*

Huetinck, L., & Munshin, S. N. (2000). *Teaching mathematics for the 21st century: Methods and activities for grades 6–12.* Upper Saddle River, NJ: Merrill/Prentice Hall Education.

Hughes, K. L., Bailey, J. R., & Mechur, M. J. (2001). *School-to-work: Making a difference in education.* New York: Columbia University Teachers College.

Human Rights Watch, (2001). Retrieved May 30, 2004, from *http://www.hrw.org/reports/2001/ustat/ustat0301-01.htm*

Hunt, P., Soto, G., Maier, J., & Doering, K. (2003). Collaborative teaming to support students at risk and students with severe disabilities in general education classrooms. *Exceptional Children, 69*(3), 315–332.

Hunter, M. (1982). *Mastery teaching.* El Segundo, CA: TIP Publications.

Impara, J. C., & Plake, B. S. (Eds.). (1998). *The thirteenth mental measurements yearbook.* Lincoln, NE: Buros Institute of Mental Measurements.

International Dyslexia Society. (Formerly Orton Dyslexia Society.) Retrieved April 11, 2004, from *http://www.interdys.org*

Interstate Migrant Education Council. (2004). Retrieved April 11, 2004 from *http://www.migedimec.org*

Jacobs, J., & Milton. I. (1994). The art of art therapy may be toxic. *Art Therapy, 11*(4), 271–277.

Jacobson, J. W., & Mulick, J. A. (Eds.). (1996). *Manual of diagnosis and professional practice in mental retardation.* Washington, DC: American Psychological Association.

Jamison, K. R. (1993). *Touched with fire: Manic-depressive illness and the artistic temperament.* New York: Free Press/Macmillan.

Jennings, J. F. (2000). Title I: Its legislative history and its promise. In Borman, G., Stringfield, S., & Slavin, R. (Eds.), *Title I: Compensatory Education at the Crossroads.* Hillsdale, NJ: Lawrence Erlbaum Associates.

Jensema, C. J. (1998). Viewer reaction to different television captioning speeds. *American Annals of the Deaf, 143*(4), 318–324.

Jensema, C. J., & Burch, R. (1999). *Caption speed and viewer comprehension of television programs. Final report.* Silver Spring, MD: Institute for Disability Research and Training, Inc.

Jensen, E. (1998). *Teaching with the brain in mind.* Alexandria, VA: Association for Supervision and Curriculum Development (1250 N. Pitt Street, Alexandria, VA 22314-1453); online at *http://www.ascd.org*

Jensen, P. S., Vitiello, B., Leonard, H., & Laughren, T. P. (1994). Child and adolescent psychopharmacology: Expanding the research base. *Psychopharmacology Bulletin, 30,* 3–8.

Johnson, E., Kimball, K., Brown, S. O., & Anderson, D. (2001). A statewide review of the use of accommodations in large-scale, high-stakes assessments. *Exceptional Children, 67*(2), 251–264.

Johnson, P., Allington, R., & Afflerbach, P. (1985). The congruence of classroom and remedial reading instruction. *Elementary School Journal, 85*(4), 465–477.

Jones, E. D., Wilson, R., & Bhojwani, S. (1997). Mathematics instruction for secondary students with learning disabilities. *Journal of Learning Disabilities, 30*(2), 151–163.

Kalb, C. (2001, February 26). DARE checks into rehab. *Newsweek,* 56.

Kamens, M. W., Loprete, S. J., & Slostad, F. A. (2003, September). Inclusive classrooms: What practicing teachers want to know. *Action in Teacher Education, 25*(1), 20–26.

Kantrowitz, B., & Underwood, A. (1999, November 23). Dyslexia and the new science of reading. *Newsweek,* 73–79.

Kapperman, G., Sticken, J., & Heinze, T. (2002). Survey of the use of assistive technology by Illinois students who are visually impaired. *Journal of Visual Impairment and Blindness, 92*(2), 106–108.

Katims, D. (1999, June/July). Standards fail to address literacy needs of individuals with mental retardation. *CEC Today,* 14.

Katzenbach, J. R., & Smith, D. K. (1994). *The wisdom of teams: Creating the high-performance organization.* New York: Harper Business.

Kauffman, J. M. (1993). How might we achieve the radical reform of special education? *Exceptional Children, 60*(1), 6–16.

Kauffman, J. M. (1999). How we prevent the prevention of emotional and behavioral disorders. *Exceptional Children, 65*(4), 448–468.

Kauffman, J. M. (2001). *Characteristics of emotional and behavioral disorders of children and youth* (7th ed.). Upper Saddle River, NJ: Merrill/Prentice Hall Education.

Kaufman, J. S. (2001). The classroom and labeling: "The girl who stayed back." In Hudak, G. M., & Kihn, P. (Eds.), *Labeling: Pedagogy and Politics* (pp. 41–54). New York: RoutledgeFalmer.

Keel, M. C., Dangel, H. L., & Owens, S. H. (1999). Selecting instructional interventions for students with mild disabilities in inclusive classrooms, entire issue. *Focus on Exceptional Children, 31*(8).

Keilitz, I., & Dunivant, N. (1986). The relationship between learning disability and juvenile delinquency: Current state of knowledge. *Remedial and Special Education, 7,* 18–26.

Kelly, J. P. (1985). Auditory system. In Kandel, E. R., & Schwartz, J. H. (Eds.), *Principles of Neural Science.* New York: Elsevier.

Kendall, E., Shum, D., Halson, D., Bunning, S, & The, M. (1997). The assessment of social problem-solving ability following traumatic brain injury. *Journal of Head Trauma Rehabilitation, 12*(3), 68–78.

Kennett, L. (2001). *Sherman: A soldier's life.* New York: HarperCollins.

Kennewick Man. (2004). Retrieved April 11, 2004, from *http://www.kennewick-man.com*

Kerr, M. M., & Nelson, C. M. (1998). *Strategies for managing behavior problems in the classroom* (3rd ed.). Upper Saddle River, NJ: Merrill/Prentice Hall.

Kincheloe, J. L., Steinberg, S. R., Rodriguez, N. M., & Chennault, R. E. (Eds.). (1998). *White reign: Deploying whiteness.* New York: St. Martin's Press.

King, S. H. (1993). The limited presence of African American teachers. *Review of Educational Research, 64*(2), 115–149.

King-Sears, M. E. (1997). Best academic practices for inclusive classrooms. *Focus on Exceptional Children, 29*(7), 1–22.

King-Sears, M. E., & Cummings, C. S. (1996). Inclusive practices of classroom teachers. *Remedial and Special Education, 17*(4), 217–225.

Kinneavy, J. L., & Warriner, J. E. (1998). *Elements of writing.* Austin, TX: Holt, Rinehart and Winston.

Klein, D. N., Lewinsohn, P. M., Seeley, J. R., & Rohde, P. (2001). A family study of major depressive disorder in a community sample of adolescents. *Archives of General Psychiatry, 58*(1), 13–20.

Kleinman, J., Marciano, P. L., & Ault, R. L. (2001). Advanced theory of mind in high-functioning adults with autism. *Journal of Autism and Developmental Disorders, 31*(1), 29–36.

Kluth, P. (2000). Community-referenced learning and the inclusive classroom. *Remedial and Special Education, 21*(1), 19–26.

Koch, J. A. (2002). *Science stories: A science methods book for elementary school teachers* (2nd ed.). Boston: Houghton Mifflin Co.

Koegel, R. L., & Koegel, L. K. (Eds.). (1995). *Teaching children with autism: Strategies for initiating positive interactions and improving learning opportunities.* Baltimore, MD: Paul H. Brookes Publishing Co.

Kohn, A. (1993). *Punished by rewards: The trouble with gold stars, incentive plans, A's, praise, and other bribes.* Boston: Houghton-Mifflin.

Kolb, S. M., & Hanley-Maxwell, C. (2003). Critical social skills for adolescents with high incidence disabilities: Parental perspectives. *Exceptional Children, 69,* 163–179.

Kolko, D. J., Bukstein, O. G., & Barron, J. (1999). Methylphenidate and behavior modification in children with ADHD and comorbid ODD or CD: Main and incremental effects across settings. *Journal of the American Academy of Child and Adolescent Psychiatry, 38*(5), 578–586.

Kotulak, R. (1993, April 13). Research discovers secrets of how brain learns to talk. *Chicago Tribune,* Section 1, pp. 1–4.

Kramer, E., & Schehr, J. (1983). An art therapy evaluation session for children. *American Journal of Art Therapy, 23,* 3–12.

Kranz, C. (2002, January 28). Blind girl's teacher wins inclusion award. *Cincinnati Enquirer.* Retrieved April 9, 2004 from *http://enquirer.com/editions/2002/01/28/loc_blind_girls_teacher.html*

Krauss, R. M. (1998). Why do we gesture when we speak? *Current Directions in Psychological Science, 7,* 54–59.

Kravetz, S., Faust, M., Lipshitz, S., & Shalhav, S. (1999). LD, interpersonal understanding, and social behavior in the classroom. *Journal of Learning Disabilities, 32,* 248–255.

Krebs, C. S. (2001). Learning to solve word problems in a middle school vision class. *Journal of Visual Impairment and Blindness, 92*(12), 757–760.

Kreinberg, N., & Wahl, E. (Eds.). (1997). *Thoughts and deeds: Equity in mathematics and science education.* Washington, DC: American Association for the Advancement of Science, The Collaboration for Equity.

Krents, H. (1972). *To race the wind.* New York: Putnam Publishing Group.

Kuder, S. D. (1990). Effectiveness of the DISTAR reading program for students with learning disabilities. *Journal of Learning Disabilities, 23*(1), 69–71.

Kunzig, R. (2001). The unbearably unstoppable neutrino. *Discover, 22*(8), 32–40.

Lamison-White, L. (1997). *Poverty in the United States: 1996.* Current Population Reports (pp. P60–198). Washington, DC: U.S. Bureau of the Census.

Lancioni, G. E., O'Reilly, M. F., & Oliva, D. (2002). Engagement in cooperative and individual tasks: Assessing the performance and preferences of persons with multiple disabilities. *Journal of Visual Impairment and Blindness, 96*(1), 50–53.

Langone, J. (1998). Managing inclusive instructional settings: Technology, cooperative planning, and team-based organization, entire issue. *Focus on Exceptional Children, 30*(8).

Larson, P. J., & Maag, J. W. (1998). Applying functional assessment in general education classrooms. *Remedial and Special Education, 19*(6), 338–349.

Lederer, J. M. (2000). Reciprocal teaching of social studies in inclusive elementary classrooms. *Journal of Learning Disabilities, 33*(1), 91–106.

Leland, J. (2001, April 8). Zero tolerance changes life at one school. *New York Times,* section 9, pp. 1, 6.

Lerman, R. I. (1996). The impact of the changing U.S. family structure on child poverty and income inequality. *Economica, 63*(249), 119–139.

Lerner, J. W. (1989). Educational interventions in learning disabilities. *Journal of the American Academy of Child and Adolescent Psychology, 28,* 326–331.

Lerner, J. W., Lowenthal, B., & Lerner, S. R. (1995). *Attention deficit disorders: Assessment and teaching.* Pacific Grove, CA: Brooks/Cole.

Levine, M. D. (2002). *A mind at a time.* New York: Simon & Schuster.

Lewin, T. (2001, August 26). One state finds secret to strong civic bonds. *New York Times,* pp. 1, 18.

Linder, T. (1993). *Transdisciplinary play-based assessment.* (Rev. ed.). Baltimore, MD: Brookes.

Linn, R. L. (2000). Assessments and accountability. *Educational Researcher, 29*(2), 4–16.

Lipsky, D., & Gartner, A. (1996). Inclusion, school restructuring, and the remaking of American society. *Harvard Educational Review, 66*(4), 762–796.

Livingstone, M. S., Rosen, G. D., Dislane, F. W., & Galaburda, A. M. (1991). Physiological and anatomical evidence for a magnocellular defect in developmental dyslexia. *Proceedings of the National Academy of Sciences, 88*(18), 7943–7947.

Logan, K. R., and Stein, S. S. (2001). The research lead teacher model: Helping general education teachers deal with classroom behavior problems. *Teaching Exceptional Children, 33*(3), 10–15.

Lohrmann-O'Rourke, S., & Zirkel, P. A. (1998). The case law on aversive interventions for students with disabilities. *Exceptional Children, 65*(1), 101–123.

London, J. (1903). *The call of the wild.* Puffin Classics edition published 1982. New York: Viking Penguin.

Lord, C., & McGee, J. P. (2001). *Educating children with autism.* Washington, DC: National Academy Press.

Lovaas, O. I. (1987). Behavioral treatment and normal educational and intellectual functioning in young autistic children. *Journal of Consulting and Clinical Psychology, 55*(1), 3–9.

Lowenthal, B. (1996). Educational implications of child abuse. *Intervention in School and Clinic, 32*(1), 21–25.

Lubman, D. (1999, October). Classroom acoustics. *Universal Design, 4*(4), 1, 8.

Luckasson, R., Borthwick-Duffy, S., Buntinx, W., Coulter, D., Craig, E. M., Reeve, A., Schalock, R. L., Snell, M. E., Spitalnik, D. M., Spreat, S., & Tasse, M. J. (2002). *Mental retardation: Definitions, classification, and systems of support* (10th ed.). Washington, DC: American Association on Mental Retardation. Online at *http://www.aamr.org/Bookstore/MR/mental_definition.shtml*

Luckasson, R., Coulter, D., Polloway, E., Reiss, S., Shalock, R., Snell, M., Spitalnik, D., & Stark, J. (1992). *Mental retardation: Definitions, classification, and systems of support* (9th ed.). Washington, DC: American Association on Mental Retardation.

Luckner, J., Bowen, S., & Carter, K. (2001). Visual teaching strategies for students who are deaf or hard of hearing. *Teaching Exceptional Children, 33*(3), 38–44.

Lyon, G. R. (2002, June 6). Learning disabilities and early intervention strategies: How to reform the special education referral and identification process. Testimony before the Subcommittee on Education Reform, U.S. House of Representatives. For copies, contact the Committee on Education and the Workforce, Ford House Office Building, Washington, DC 20515.

Lyon, G. R., Fletcher, J. M., Shaywitz, S. E., Shaywitz, B. A., Torgesen, J. K., Wood, F. B., Schulte, A., & Olson, R. (2001). Rethinking learning disabilities. In Finn, C. E., Rotherham, A. J., & Hokanson, C. R. (Eds.), *Rethinking special education for a new century.* Washington, DC: Thomas B. Fordham Foundation and Progressive Policy Institute.

Maag, J. W. (2001). Rewarded by punishment: Reflections on the disuses of positive reinforcement in schools. *Exceptional Children, 67*(2), 173–186.

MacArthur, C. A., Graham, S., Haynes, J. B., & DeLaPaz, S. (1996). Spelling checkers and students with learning disabilities: Performance comparisons and impact on spelling. *Journal of Special Education, 30*(1), 35–57.

Maccini, P., & Gagnon, J. C. (2000). Best practices for teaching mathematics to secondary students with special needs, entire issue. *Focus on Exceptional Children, 32*(5).

Maccini, P., & Hughes, C. R. (1997). Mathematics interventions for adolescents with learning disabilities. *Learning Disabilities Research & Practice, 12,* 168–176.

Maccini, P., McNaughton, D., & Ruhl, K. (1999). Algebra instruction for students with learning disabilities: Implications from a research review. *Learning Disabilities Quarterly, 22*(1), 113–126.

Mace, R., et al. (1997, April 1). The principles of universal design. Version 2.0. One-page publication available from Center for Universal Design, School of Design, North Carolina State University, Box 8613, Raleigh, NC 27695-8613.

Maddox, T. (Ed.). (1997). *Tests: A comprehensive reference for assessments in psychology, education, and business.* Austin, TX: PRO-ED.

Madsen, K. M., et al. (2002). A population-based study of measles, mumps, and rubella vaccination and autism. *New England Journal of Medicine, 347*(19), 1477–1482.

Mager, R. F. (1997). *Preparing instructional objectives: A critical tool in the development of effective instruction* (3rd ed.). Atlanta, GA: Center for Effective Performance.

Maheady, L., Harper, G. F., & Mallette, B. (2001). Peer-mediated instruction and interventions and students with mild disabilities. *Remedial and Special Education, 22*(1), 4–14.

"Making Time Count." (2001). A policy brief. San Francisco, CA: WestEd. Online at *http://web.wested.org/online-pubs/making_time_count.pdf*

Mamlin, N. (1999). Despite best intentions: When inclusion fails. *Journal of Special Education, 33*(1), 36–49.

Manchester, W. (1974). *The glory and the dream: A narrative history of America, 1932–1972.* Boston: Little Brown.

Marks, S. U., Schrader, C., & Levine, M. (1999). Paraeducator experiences in inclusive settings: Helping, hovering, or holding their own? *Exceptional Children, 65*(3), 315–328.

Marland, S. P. (1972). *Education of the gifted and talented* (Vol. 1). Washington, DC: Government Printing Office.

Maroney, S. A. (2000). What's good? Suggested resources for beginning special education teachers. *Teaching Exceptional Children, 33*(1), 22–27.

Marschark, M. (2001). *Language development in children who are deaf: A research synthesis.* Alexandria, VA: National Association of State Directors of Special Education [1800 Diagnonal Road, #320, Alexandria, VA 22314].

Marschark, M., Lang, H. G., & Albertini, J. A. (2001). *Educating deaf students: From research to practice.* New York: Oxford University Press.

Marszalek, J. F. (1993). *Sherman: A soldier's passion for order.* New York: Free Press.

Martin, G., & Pear, J. (2003). *Behavior modification: What it is and how to do it* (7th ed.). Upper Saddle River, NJ: Prentice Hall/Merrill Education.

Martin, J., Marshall, L., & DePry, R. (2001). Participatory decision-making: Innovative practices that increase student self-determination. In Flexer, R., Simmons, T., Luft, P., & Bart, R. (Eds.), *Transitions planning across the life span.* Columbus, OH: Merrill/Prentice Hall Education.

Martin, S. L., Ramey, C. T., & Ramey, S. (1990). The prevention of intellectual impairment in children of impoverished families: Findings of a randomized trail of educational day care. *American Journal of Public Health, 80* (7), 844–847.

Mastropieri, M. A., & Scruggs, T. E. (2000). *The inclusive classroom: Strategies for effective instruction.* Upper Saddle River, NJ: Merrill/Prentice Hall Education.

Mastropieri, M. A., Scruggs, T. E., & Shiah, R. (1997). Can computers teach problem-solving strategies to students with mild mental retardation? A case study. *Remedial and Special Education, 18,* 157–163.

Mattingly, J. C., & Bott, D. A. (1990). Teaching multiplication facts to students with learning problems. *Exceptional Children, 56,* 438–449.

Mayes, S. D., Calhoun, S. L., & Crowell, E. W. (2000). Learning disabilities and ADHD: Overlapping spectrum disorders. *Journal of Learning Disabilities, 33,* 417–424.

Mayr, E. (2002). *What evolution is.* New York: Basic Books.

McCarney, S. B., & Cummins, K. K. (1988). *The pre-referral intervention manual: The most common learning and behavior problems encountered in the educational environment.* Columbia, MO: Hawthorne Press.

McCleery, J. A., & Tindal, G. A. (1999). Teaching the scientific method to at-risk students and students with learning disabilities through concept anchoring and explicit instruction. *Remedial and Special Education, 20* (1), 7–18.

McCullers, C. (1940). *The heart is a lonely hunter.* Boston: Houghton Mifflin.

McGill, T., & Vogtle, L. K. (2001). Driver's education for students with physical disabilities. *Exceptional Children, 67* (4), 455–466.

McKinley, A. M., & Warren, S. F. (2001). The effectiveness of cochlear implants for children with prelingual deafness. *Journal of Early Intervention, 23* (4), 252–263.

McLoughlin, J. A., & Lewis, R. B. (2001). *Assessing students with special needs.* (5th ed.). Upper Saddle River, NJ: Merrill/Prentice Hall Education.

McNeil, D. (2002, November 30). When parents say no to child vaccinations. *New York Times,* Section A, p. 1 from *http:www.nytimes.com*

McNeil, J. (1993). *Americans with disabilities: 1991–1992. Data from the survey of income and program participation.* Current Population Reports, P70-33. Washington, DC: Department of Commerce, Bureau of the Census.

McNeil, J. (1997). *Americans with disabilities: 1994–1995.* Current Population Reports, (pp. 70–61). Washington, DC: Department of Commerce, Bureau of the Census.

McWhirter, J. J., McWhirter, B. T., McWhirter, A. M., & McWhirter, E. H. (1998). *At-risk youth: A comprehensive response.* Pacific Grove, CA: Brooks/Cole.

Medoff, M. H. (1980). *Children of a lesser god: A play in two acts.* Clifton, NJ: J. T. White.

Meltzer, L. (1993). *Strategy assessment and instruction for students with learning disabilities.* Austin, TX: PRO-ED.

Melville, H. (1851). *Moby-Dick; or, the whale.* New York: Modern Library (1992) and New York: W. W. Norton & Company (1967).

Mercer, C. D., & Mercer, A. R. (1998). *Teaching students with learning problems* (5th ed.). Upper Saddle River, NJ: Prentice Hall, Merrill Education.

Microsoft. (2004). Speech recognition. Retrieved April 11, 2004, from *http://www.microsoft.com/office/evaluation/indepth/speech.asp*

Miller, J. M., Miller, A. L., Yamagata, T., Bredberg, G., & Altschuler, R. A. (2002). Protection and regrowth of the auditory nerve after deafness. *Audiology & Neuro-Otology, 7,* 175–179.

Miller, L. L., & Felton, R. H. (2001). "It's one of them. . . I don't know": Case study of a student with phonological, rapid naming, and word-finding deficits. *Journal of Special Education, 35* (3), 125–133.

Miller, S. P., Butler, F. M., & Lee, K. (1998). Validated practices for teaching mathematics to students with learning disabilities: A Review of literature. *Focus on Exceptional Children, 31,* whole issue.

Miller, S. P., & Mercer, C. D. (1997). Educational aspects of mathematics disabilities. *Journal of Learning Disabilities, 30,* 47–56.

Mills, P. E., Cole, K. N., Jenkins, J. R., & Dale, P. S. (2002). Early exposure to direct instruction and subsequent juvenile delinquency: A prospective examination. *Exceptional Children, 69* (1), 85–96.

Mills v. Board of Education of the District of Columbia, 348 F. Supp. 866 (D.D.C., 1972). Civil action 193–71.

Milthaug, D. (1998). Your right, my obligation? *Journal of the Association for Persons with Severe Disabilities, 23,* 41–43.

Mitchell, L. M., & Buchele-Ash, A. (2000). Abuse and neglect of individuals with disabilities: Building protective supports through public policy. *Journal of Disability Policy Studies, 10* (2), 225–243.

Monitoring the Future. (2004). Retrieved April 11, 2004, from *http://www.nida.nih.gov/DrugPages/MTF.html*

Moores, D. F. (1993). Total inclusion/zero reject models in general education: Implications for deaf children. *American Annals of the Deaf, 138* (3), 251.

Morocco, C. C. (2001). Teaching for understanding with students with disabilities: New directions for research on access to the general education curriculum. *Learning Disabilities Quarterly, 24* (1), 5–13.

Morocco, C. C., Hindin, A., Mata-Aguilar, C., & Clark-Chiarelli. (2001). Building a deep understanding of literature with middle-grade students with learning disabilities. *Learning Disability Quarterly, 24* (1), 47–58.

Morrison, G. M., & D'Incau, B. (2000). Developmental and service trajectories for students with disabilities recommended for expulsion from school. *Exceptional Children, 66* (2), 257–272.

Morrison, J. (1995). *DSM-IV made easy: The clinician's guide to diagnosis.* New York: Guilford Press.

Morse, T. E., & Schuster, J. W. (2000). Teaching elementary students with moderate intellectual disabilities how to shop for groceries. *Exceptional Children, 66* (2), 273–288.

Mortweet, S. L., Utley, C. A., Walker, D., Dawson, H. L., Delquadri, J. C., Reddy, S. S., Greenwood, C. R., Hamilton, S., and Ledford, D. (1999). Classwide peer tutoring: Teaching students with mild mental retardation in inclusive classrooms. *Exceptional Children, 65* (4), 524–536.

Mt. Sinai School of Medicine. (2003). Research and training center on community integration of individuals with traumatic brain injury. Retrieved April 1, 2004, from *http://www.mssm.edu/tbinet*

Munk, D. M., & Bursuck, W. D. (2001). Preliminary findings on personalized grading plans for middle school students with learning disabilities. *Exceptional Children, 67*(2), 211–234.

Murawski, W., & Swanson, H. (2001). A meta-analysis of co-teaching research. *Remedial and Special Education, 22*(5), 258–275.

Murphy, M.O. (2004). Personal communication, March 31.

Myers, D. P. (2002, June 18). A little girl's legacy. *Newsday,* pp. B6–B7, B9–B10.

Nagel, D. R., Schumaker, J. B., & Deshler, D. D. (1986). *The FIRST-letter mnemonic strategy.* Lawrence, KS: Edge Enterprises.

Nagle, K. M. (2001). Transition to employment and community life for youths with visual impairments: Current status and future directions. *Journal of Visual Impairment and Blindness, 95*(2), 725–738.

National Alliance of Black School Educators and Council for Exceptional Children. (2002). *Addressing over-representation of African American students in special education.* Washington, DC: NASBE (310 Pennsylvania Avenue SE, Washington, DC 20003; *http://www.nasbse.org*).

National Assessment of Educational Progress. (2004). Online at: *http://nces.ed.gov/nationsreportcard/*

National Center for the Dissemination of Disability Research. (2002). *Technical brief number 3: Underachieving students.* Retrieved April 10, 2004 from *http://www.ncddr.org/du/products/focus/focus3/*

National Center for Education Statistics. (2000). *State profiles of public elementary and secondary education,* 1996–1997. Washington, DC: Author (400 Maryland Avenue SW, Washington, DC 20202). Online at *http://nces.ed.gov/pubs2000/stateprofiles*

National Center for Education Statistics. (2001a). *Digests of educational statistics, 2000.* Retrieved from *http://nces.ed.gov/programs/digest/d00/* Note, also "Dropout rates" at *http://nces.ed.gov/fastfacts*

National Center for Education Statistics. (2001b). *Violence prevention: NCES fast facts.* Retrieved April 10, 2004 from *http://nces.ed.gov/fastfacts*

National Center for Education Statistics. (2003). *Digest of education statistics, 2002.* NCES Publication # 2003-060. Washington, DC: U.S. Department of Education.

National Center for Health Statistics. (1997). *Vital statistics of the United States.* Hyattsville, MD: Author.

National Center for Health Statistics. (1998). *Data file documentation, national health interview survey, 1996.* Hyattsville, MD: Author.

National Center for Health Statistics. (2001). *Dropout rates in the United States: 1999.* Hyattsville, MD: Author.

National Center for Injury Prevention and Control. (2001). *Traumatic brain injury in the United States: Assessing outcomes in children.* Washington, DC: Centers for Disease Control and Prevention.

National Center on Accessing the General Curriculum. (2004). Retrieved May 28, 2004, from *http://www.east.org/ncac*

National Center on Educational Outcomes. (2001). Crosswalk of Title I and IDEA Assessment and Accountability Provisions for Students with Disabilities. Minneapolis, MN: Author. Online at *http://education.umn.edu/NCEO/OnlinePubs/Crosswalk.htm*

National Clearinghouse for English Language Acquisition and Language Instruction Education Programs. (2004). Retrieved April 11, 2004, from *http://ncela.gwu.edu*

National Clearinghouse on Child Abuse and Neglect. (n.d.). National Child Abuse and Neglect Data System (NCANDS). P.O. Box 1182, Washington, DC 20013–1182.

National Coalition for the Homeless. (2004). Retrieved April 11, 2004, from *http://www.nationalhomeless.org*

National Council for Economic Education, National Association of Economics Educators, and the Foundation for Teaching Economics. (2003). *Voluntary national content standards in economics education.* New York: National Council for Economics Education (1140 Avenue of the Americas, New York, NY 10036). Retrieved April 11, 2004, from *http://www.ncee.net/ea/program.php?pid=19*

National Council for the Social Studies. (1994). *Curriculum standards for social studies.* Washington, DC: Author.

National Council for the Social Studies. (2003). *Expectations of excellence: Curriculum standards for social studies.* Retrieved April 11, 2004, from *http://www.ncss.org*

National Council of La Raza. (2001). Twenty most frequently asked questions about the Latino community. Retrieved April 10, 2004, from *http://www.nclr.org/about/nclrfaq.html*

National Council of La Raza. (2004). Retrieved April 10, 2004, from *http://www.nclr.org*

National Council of Teachers of Mathematics. (2000). *Principles and standards of school mathematics.* Reston, VA: Author.

National Council on Disability. (1993). *Serving the nation's students with disabilities: Progress and prospects.* Washington, DC: Author.

National Council on Disability. (2000). *Back to school on civil rights.* Washington, DC: Author.

National Down Syndrome Society. (n.d.). Facts about Down syndrome. Retrieved April 9, 2004, from *http://ndss.org*

National Dropout Prevention Center. (2004). Retrieved April 11, 2004, from *http://www.dropoutprevention.org*

National Fragile X Foundation. (n.d.). Facts about fragile X. Retrieved April 11, 2004 from *http://www.fragilex.org*

National Immunization Program. (2004). Retrieved April 11, 2004 from *http://www.cdc.gov/nip*

National Institute on Drug Abuse. (1999). *Preventing drug use among children and adolescents: A research-based guide.* Washington, DC: National Institutes of Health.

National Institute on Drug Abuse. (2000). *Monitoring the future survey.* Washington, DC: National Institutes of Health.

National Institutes of Health. (2004). Epidemiology of youth drug abuse. Retrieved April 10, 2004, from *http://nces.ed.gov/fastfacts/display.asp?id=16*

National Organization for Rare Disorders. (2004). Retrieved March 9, 2004, from *http://www.rarediseases.org*

National Reading Panel. (2000). *Report of the National Reading Panel: Teaching children to read.* Retrieved April 11, 2004, from *http://www.nochd.nih.gov/publications/nrp/report.htm*

National Research Council. (1996). *National science education standards.* Washington, DC: National Academy Press. *http://www.nap.edu/readingroom/books/nses.html*

National Science Teachers Association. (2001). *NSTA pathways to the science standards.* Arlington, VA: Author.

National study of inclusive education. (1995). New York: City University of New York, Graduate School and University Center, National Center on Educational Restructuring and Inclusion.

Nelson, I. (1995). *Time management for teachers.* London: Kogan Page Ltd.

Nelson, J. S., Jayanthi, M., Epstein, M. H., & Bursuck, W. D. (2000). Student preferences for adaptations in classroom testing. *Remedial and Special Education, 21*(1), 41–52.

New Ideas for Planning Transitions to the Adult World. (2000). *Research connections in special education, 6,* whole issue. Reston, VA: Council for Exceptional Children, ERIC/OSEP Special Project.

New York State Department of Education. (2004). Languages other than english. Retrieved March 19, 2004, from *http://www.emsc.nysed.gov/osa.hslote.html*

New York Times. (2004). Education Life, January 26 (whole issue).

New York State, Office of Vocational and Educational Services for Individuals with Disabilities (NYS VESID). (1997). *The learning standards and alternate performance indicators for students with severe disabilities.* Albany, NY: Author.

Newacheck, P. W., & Halfon, N. (1998). Prevalence and impact of disabling chronic conditions in childhood. *American Journal of Public Health, 88*(4), 610–617.

Nickels, C. (1996). A gift from Alex—The art of belonging. In Koegel, L. K., Koegel, R. L., & Dunlap, G. (Eds.), *Positive Behavioral Supports* (pp. 123–144). Baltimore, MD: Paul H. Brookes Publishing Company.

Nielsen, D. C., & Luetke-Stahlman, B. (2002). Phonological awareness: One key to the reading proficiency of deaf children. *American Annals of the Deaf, 147*(3), 11–19.

Nielson, N. (2001). Aligning assessment with learning goals. Retrieved April 11, 2004 from *http://www.enc.org/topics/assessment*

"No Right Is More Precious": Voting Rights and People with Intellectual and Developmental Disabilities. *Policy Research Brief, 11*(1), entire issue. Available from: Research and Training Center on Community Living, Institute on Community Integration, University of Minnesota, 109 Pattee Hall, 150 Pillsbury Drive S. E., Minneapolis, MN 55455.

Nuland, S. B. (1997). *The wisdom of the body.* New York: Alfred A. Knopf.

Nunez, R. D., & Collignon, K. (1997). Creating a community of learning for homeless children. *Educational Leadership, 55*(2), 56–60.

Obiakor, F. (1999). Teacher expectations of minority exceptional learners: Impact on "accuracy" of self-concepts. *Exceptional Children, 66*(1), 59–63.

Odden, A., Monk, D., Nakib, Y., & Pincus, L. (1995, October). The story of the education dollar: No academy awards and no fiscal smoking guns. *Phi Delta Kappan, 73,* 161–172.

Office of Juvenile Justice and Delinquency Prevention. (1999). OJJDP statistical briefing book. Retrieved April 10, 2004 from *http://www.ojjdp.ncjrs.org/ojstatbb/index.html*

O'Melia, M. C., & Rosenberg, M. S. (1994). Effects of cooperative homework teams on the acquisition of mathematics skills by secondary students with mild disabilities. *Exceptional Children, 60*(6), 538–548.

Open eBook Authoring Group. (1999). Open eBook Publication Structure 1.0. Final version. Retrieved April 7, 2004 from *http://www.openebook.org*

Osborne, J. (2000, June 18). Little professor syndrome. *New York Times Magazine,* pp. 55–60, 74. See, also: *http://www.nytimes.com/library/magazine/home/20000618magasperger.html* Retrieved April 10, 2004.

Osterhaus, S. A. (2004). Teaching math. Retrieved April 9, 2004, from *http://www.tsbvi.edu/math*

Osterman, K. F. (2000). Students' need for belonging in the school community. *Review of Educational Research, 70*(3), 323–367.

Oswald, D. P., Coutinho, M. J., & Best, A. M. (2001). Community and school predictors of over representation of minority children in special education. Retrieved April 10, 2004 from *http://www.civilrightsproject.harvard.edu/research/books/special_ed.php*

Overton, T. (2000). *Assessment in special education: An applied approach* (3rd ed.). Upper Saddle River, NJ: Merrill/Prentice Hall Education.

Pajer, K., Gardner, W., Rubin, R. T., Perel, J., & Neal, S. (2001). Decreased cortisol levels in adolescent girls with conduct disorder. *Archives of General Psychiatry, 58* (3), 297–302.

Palmer, D. S., Borthwick-Duffy, S. A., & Widaman, K. (1998). Parent perceptions of inclusive practices for their children with significant cognitive disabilities. *Exceptional Children, 64* (2), 271–282.

Palmer, D. S., Fuller, K., Arora, T., & Nelson, M. (2001). Taking sides: Parent views on inclusion for their children with severe disabilities. *Exceptional Children, 67* (4), 467–484.

Palmer, J. (1993). *Anatomy for speech and hearing.* Baltimore, MD: Williams & Wilkins.

The PAR^{2}A Center. (2004). *Paraprofessionals.* University of Colorado at Denver, 1380 Lawrence Street, Suite 650, Denver, CO 80204.

Parette, P. (1999). Transition and assistive technology planning with families across cultures. *Career Development for Exceptional Individuals, 22* (2), 213–231.

Park, J., Turnbull, A. R., & Turnbull, H. R. (2002). Impacts of poverty on quality of life in families of children with disabilities. *Exceptional Children, 68* (2), 151–170.

Parker, W. C. (2001). *Social studies in elementary education.* (11th ed.). Upper Saddle River, NJ: Prentice Hall.

Parmar, R., Cawley, J. F., & Frazita, R. R. (1996). Word problem solving by students with and without mild disabilities. *Exceptional Children, 62,* 45–49.

Parmar, R., Cawley, J. F., & Miller, J. H. (1994). Differences in mathematics performance between students with learning disabilities and students with mild retardation. *Exceptional Children, 60* (6), 549–563.

Paton, J. W. (n.d.) Central auditory processing disorders (CAPD's). Retrieved April 9, 2004 from *http://www.ldonline.org/ld_indepth/process_deficit/capd_paton.html*

Patterson, G., & Capaldi, D. M. (1991). Antisocial parents: Unskilled and vulnerable. In Cowan, P. A., & Hetherington, E. M. (Eds.), *Family Transitions* (p. 195–218). Hillsdale, NJ: Lawrence Erlbaum Associates.

Paul, P. V., & Quigley, S. P. (1994). *Language and deafness* (2nd ed.). San Diego, CA: Singular Publishing.

Paulesu, E., Demonet, J. F., et al. (2001). Dyslexia: Interaction of genes with culture. *Science, 291* (5511), 2165–2167.

Paull, S. (1986). Balancing a checkbook: Children using mathematics skills. *Arithmetic Teacher, 33* (9), 32–33.

Pavri, S. (2001). Loneliness in children with disabilities: How teachers can help. *Teaching Exceptional Children, 33* (6), 52–58.

Paxton, R. J. (1999). A deafening silence: History textbooks and the students who read them. *Review of Educational Research, 69* (3), 315–339.

Pearman, E. L., Huang, A. M., & Mellblom, C. I. (1997). The inclusion of all students: Concerns and incentives of educators. *Education and Training in Mental Retardation and Developmental Disabilities, 32* (1), 11–20.

Pelham, W. E., Wheeler, T., & Chronis, A. (1998). Empirically supported psychosocial treatments for attention deficit hyperactivity disorder. *Journal of Clinical Child Psychology, 27*(2), 190–205.

Pennsylvania Association for Retarded Children v. Commonwealth of Pennsylvania, David H. Kurtzman, et al. 334F. Supp. 1257 (E. D. Pa. 1972), civil action no. 71–42 (3 Judge Court, E.D. Pennsylvania, 1971), order, injunction, and consent agreement.

Peters, J. M. (Ed.). (1998). *A sampler of national science education standards*. Upper Saddle River, NJ: Merrill/Prentice Hall Education.

Peters, J. M., & Gega, P. C. (2002). *Science in elementary education* (9th ed.). Upper Saddle River, NJ: Prentice Hall.

Piaget, J. (1985). *The equlibrium of cognitive structures: The central problem of intellectual development*. Chicago: University of Chicago Press.

Pierangelo, R., & Crane, R. (2000). *The special education yellow pages*. Upper Saddle River, NJ: Merrill/Prentice Hall Education.

Pierangelo, R., & Giuliani, G. (1998). *Special educator's complete guide to 109 diagnostic tests: How to select and interpret tests, use results in IEPs, and remediate specific disabilities*. West Nyack, NY: Center for Applied Research in Education.

Pierangelo, R., & Giuliani, G. A. (2002). *Assessment in special education*. Boston, MA: Allyn & Bacon.

Pinker, S. (1994). *The language instinct: How the mind creates language*. New York: HarperCollins Perennial.

Pipher, M. (1995). *Reviving Ophelia: Saving the selves of adolescent girls*. New York: Ballantine.

Pisha, B., & Coyne, P. (2001). Smart from the start: The promise of universal design for learning. *Remedial and Special Education, 22*(4), 197–203.

Pittman, P., & Huefner, D. S. (2001). Will the courts go bi-bi? IDEA 1997, the courts, and deaf education. *Exceptional Children, 67*(2), 187–198.

Plante, E., & Beeson, P. M. (1999). *Communication and communication disorders: A clinical introduction*. Needham Heights, MA: Allyn & Bacon.

Polloway, E. A., and Polloway, C. H. (1981). Survival words for disabled readers. *Academic Therapy, 16*(4), 443–448.

Ponsot, M., & Deen, Rosemary. (1982). *Beat not the poor desk: writing: What to teach, how to teach it, and why*. Montclair, NJ: Boynton/Cook.

Posamentier, A. S., & Stepelman, J. (1999). *Teaching secondary mathematics* (5th ed.). Upper Saddle River, NJ: Prentice Hall.

Prater, M. A. (1999). Characterization of mental retardation in children's and adolescent literature. *Education and Training in Mental Retardation and Developmental Disabilities, 34*(4), 418–431.

Pratt, C. (2001, January 14). Awash in ecstasy. *Newsday*, pp. A5, A46–A47.

Pressley, M., & McCormick, C. (1995). *Advanced educational psychology for educators, researchers, and policymakers*. New York: HarperCollins.

Prevalence of mental retardation and/or developmental disabilities: Analysis of the 1994/1995 NHIS–D. *MR/DD Data Brief, 2*(1), whole issue. Available from: Institute on Community Integration, University of Minnesota, 109 Pattee Hall, 150 Pillsbury Drive S. E., Minneapolis, MN 55455.

Proctor, B. D., & Dalaker, J. (2002). *Poverty in the United States: 2001*. Current Population Reports (pp. 60–219). Washington, DC: U.S. Government Printing Office. Project 2061 (2004). Retrieved May 30, 2004, from *http:// www.project2061.org*

The Proof. (n.d.) PBS "Nova" series. For video, contact *http://www.pbs.org/wgbh/proof*

Quesnel, S., & Malkin, D. (1997). Genetic predisposition to cancer and familial cancer syndromes. *Pediatric Clinics of North America, 44*(4), 791–808.

Quint, S. (1994). *Schooling homeless children: A working model for America's public schools*. New York: Teachers College Press.

Rafferty, Y. (1999). Legal issues in educating homeless children: Past accomplishments and future challenges. *Journal for a Just and Caring Education, 5*(1), 19–33.

Rapin I. (1997). Autism. *New England Journal of Medicine, 337*(2), 97–104.

Rapport, M. J. (1996). Legal guidelines for the delivery of special health care services in schools. *Exceptional Children, 62*(6), 537–549.

Reed-Victor, E., & Pelco, L. E. (1999). Helping homeless students build resilience: What the school community can do. *Journal for a Just and Caring Education, 5*(1), 51–71.

Rehabilitation Act. Most recently amended in 1998 by PL 105–220.

Reichman, A. (2001). Personal communication, March 15.

Repetto, J., & Correa, V. (1996). Expanding views on transition. *Exceptional Children, 62*(6), 551–563.

Report of the Surgeon General's Conference on Children's Mental Health: A national action agenda. (2000). Washington, DC: U.S. Department of Health and Human Services.

Richters, J., Arnold, L. E. A., Jensen, P. S., Abikoff, H., Conners, C. K., Greenhill, L., Hechtman, L., Hinshaw, S., Pelham, W. E., & Swanson, J. (1995). NIMH collaborative multisite, multimodal treatment study of children with ADHD. I. Background and rationale. *Journal of the American Academy of Child & Adolescent Psychiatry, 34*, 987–1000.

Ricks, D. (2002, November 7). Study: autism, vaccine not tied. *Newsday*, p. A53.

Ridley, M. (1999). *Genome: The autobiography of a species in 23 chapters*. New York: HarperCollins.

Riggs, C. G., & Mueller, P. H. (2001). Employment and utilization of paraeducators in inclusive settings. *Journal of Special Education, 35*(1), 54–62.

Roberts, R. E., Attkisson, C. C., & Rosenblatt, A. (1998). Prevalence of psychopathology among children and adolescents. *American Journal of Psychiatry, 155*(6), 715–725.

Robertson, J. I. (2001). *Standing like a stone wall: The life of General Thomas J. Jackson*. New York: Atheneum.

Robey, R. R. (1998). A meta-analysis of clinical outcomes in the treatment of aphasia. *Journal of Speech-Language-Hearing Research, 41*(1), 172–187.

Robin, A. L. (1998). *ADHD in adolescents: Diagnosis and treatment*. New York: Guilford Press.

Robinson, L. M., Skaer, T. L., Sclar, D. A., & Galin, R. S. (2002). Is attention deficit hyperactivity disorder increasing among girls in the U.S.? Trends in diagnosis and the prescribing of stimulants. *CNS Drugs, 16* (2) 129–137.

Robinson, R. (1999). *The debt: What America owes to blacks*. New York: Penguin Putnam, Dutton/Plume.

Rodis, P., Garrod, A., & Boscardin, M. L. (Eds.). (2001). *Learning disabilities and life stories*. Needham Heights, MA: Allyn & Bacon.

Roditi, B. (1993). Mathematics assessment and strategy instruction: An applied developmental approach. In Meltzer, L. J. (Ed.), *Strategy assessment and instruction for students with learning disabilities* (pp. 293–320). Austin, TX: PRO-ED.

Rodriguez, D., Parmar, R. S., & Singer, B. R. (2001). Fourth-grade culturally and linguistically diverse exceptional students' concepts of number line. *Exceptional Children, 67* (2), 199–210.

Rogner, B.M. (1992). *Adult literacy: Captioned videotapes and word recognition*. Unpublished doctoral disseration, The Urban Institute, Cincinnati, OH. Retrieved March 28, 2004, from *http://www.robson.org/gary/captioning/rogner-abstract.html*

Roizen, N. J. (1997). New advancements in medical treatment of young children with Down syndrome: Implications for early intervention. *Infants and Young Children, 9*(4), 36–42.

Romanczyk, R. G., Weinter, T., Lockshin, S., & Ekdahl, M. (1999). Research in autism: Myths, controversies, and perspectives. In Zager, D. B. (Ed.). *Autism: identification, education, and treatment* (2nd ed., pp. 23–61). Mahwah, NJ: Lawrence Erlbaum Associates.

Rosenshine, B., & Meister, C. (1994). Reciprocal teaching: A review of the research. *Review of Educational Research, 64*, 479–530.

Rosenshine, B., & Stevens, R. (1986). Teaching functions. In Whittrock, M. C. (Ed.), *Handbook of research on teaching* (3rd ed., pp. 376–391). New York: Macmillan.

Rosman, N. J. S. (1994). *Effects of varying the special educator's role within an algebra class on math attitude and achievement*. Vermillion: University of South Dakota. (ERIC Document Reproduction Service No. ED381 993.)

Rossell, C. H., & Baker, K. (1996). *Bilingual education in Massachusetts: The emperor has no clothes*. Boston, MA: Pioneer Institute.

Ruiz, N. T. (1989). An optimal learning environment for Rosemary. *Exceptional Children, 56* (2), 130–144.

Sacks, O. (1995). *An anthropologist on Mars*. New York: Knopf.

Safer, D. J., Zito, J. M., & Fine, E. M. (1999). Increased methylphenidate usage for attention deficit disorder in the 1990s. *Pediatrics, 98*, 1084–1088.

Safran, S. (2001). Asperger syndrome: The emerging challenge to special education. *Exceptional Children, 67*(2), 151–160.

Salend, S., & Taylor, L. (1993). Working with families: A cross-cultural perspective. *Remedial and Special Education, 14*, 25–39.

Salinger, J. D. (1951). *The catcher in the rye*. Boston: Little Brown.

Salvia, J., & Ysseldyke, J. (1998). *Assessment*. (7th ed.). Boston: Houghton Mifflin Company.

Sander, B. (1972). When are speech sounds learned? *Journal of Speech and Hearing Disorders, 37*, 55–63.

Savage, N. (2001). A leg to stand on: Will artificial limbs get better than the real thing? *Discover, 22* (4), 24–25.

Scanlon, D., & Mellard, D. F. (2002). Academic and participation profiles of school-age dropouts with and without disabilities. *Exceptional Children, 68* (2), 239–258.

Schemo, D.J. (2004, March 2). Schools, facing tight budgets, leave gifted programs behind. *New York Times*, A1, A18.

Schleier, C. (2000, May). Overcoming: Nothing got in his way: The remarkable story of Ronan Tynan. *Biography Magazine*, see also: *http://www.drronantynan.net*

Schopler, E., Short, A., & Mesibov, G. (1989). Relation of behavioral treatment to "normal functioning": Comment on Lovaas. *Journal of Consulting and Clinical Psychology, 57* (1), 162–164.

Schumm, J. S., Moody, S. W., & Vaughn, S. (2000). Grouping for reading instruction: Does one size fit all? *Journal of Learning Disabilities, 33*, 477–496.

Schweinhart, L., Weikart, D., & Larner, M. (1986). Consequences of three preschool curriculum models through age 15. *Early Childhood Research Quarterly, 1*, 15–45.

Sciarra, D. (1999). *Multiculturalism in counseling*. Itasca. IL: F.E. Peacock.

Sciarra, D. (2003). *School counseling*. Pacific Grove, CA: Brooks/Cole. (Page numbers cited in the text are those of the manuscript version.)

Sciarra, D., & Ponterotto, J. (1991). Counseling the Hispanic bilingual family: Challenges to the therapeutic process. *Psychotherapy, 28*(3), 473–479.

Scott, S. S., McGuire, J., & Foley, T. E. (2001). *Universal design for instruction: An exploration of principles for anticipating and responding to student diversity in the classroom*. Storrs, CT: Center on Postsecondary Education and Disability.

Seefeldt, C. (2001). *Social Studies for the preschool/primary child*. (6th ed.). Upper Saddle River, NJ: Merrill/Prentice Hall Education.

Self-Determination. (2004). Retrieved April 11, 2004, from *http://TheArc.org/sdet/sdet.html*

Seymour, E., & Hewitt, N. (1997). *Talking about leaving: Why undergraduates leave the sciences*. Boulder, CO: Westview.

Shakespeare set free: Teaching Hamlet and Henry IV, Part I. (1994). New York: Simon & Schuster, Washington Square Press.

Shandler, S. (1999). *Ophelia speaks: Adolescent girls write about their search for self*. New York: HarperCollins Harperperennial Library.

Shaywitz, B. A., et al. (2004). Development of left occipotemporal systems for skilled reading in children after a phonologically based intervention. *Biological Psychiatry, 55*(9), 926–934.

Shaywitz, S. E. (1996). Dyslexia. *Scientific American, 275,* 98–104.

Shaywitz, S. E. (1998). Dyslexia. *New England Journal of Medicine, 338,* 307–312.

Shaywitz, S. E., & Shaywitz, B. A. (1993). Learning disabilities and attention deficits in the school setting. Chapter 8 in Meltzer, L. J. (Ed.), *Strategy Assessment and Instruction for Students with Learning Disabilities* (pp. 221–241). Austin, TX: PRO-ED.

Shaywitz, S. E., et al. (1998). Functional disruption in the organization of the brain for reading in dyslexia. *Proceedings of the National Academy of Sciences, 95*(5), 2636–2641.

Shin, J., Deno, S. L., & Espin, C. (2000). Technical adequacy of the maze task for curriculum-based measurement of reading growth. *Journal of Special Education, 34*(3), 164–173.

Shriner, J. G., & DeStefano, L. (2003). Participation and accommodation in state assessment: The role of Individualized Education Programs. *Exceptional Children, 69*(2), 147–161.

Sideridis, G. D., Utley, C., Greenwood, C. R., Delqadri, J., Dawson, H. L., Palmer, P., & Reddy, S. (1997). Classwide peer tutoring: Effects on the spelling performance and social interactions of students with mild disabilities and their typical peers in an integrated instructional setting. *Journal of Behavioral Education, 7,* 435–462.

Siegfried, T. (2000). *The bit and the pendulum: From quantum computing to M theory—The new physics of information.* New York: John Wiley & Sons.

Sigman, M., & Ruskin, E. (1999). Continuity and change in the social competence of children with autism, Down syndrome, and developmental delays. *Journal of Autism and Developmental Disorders, 24,* 647–657.

Silver, L. B. (1998). *The misunderstood child* (3rd ed.). New York: Times Books.

Silver, L. B. (1999). *Dr. Larry Silver's advice to parents on ADHD* (2nd ed.). New York: Times Books.

Silver, L. B. (2001, November 2001). What are learning disabilities? Retrieved April 10, 2004 from *http://www.ldonline.org/ld_indepth*

Silver, L. B. (2002). Update on ADHD medications. Retrieved April 10, 2004 from *http://www.ldonline.org/ld_indepth/add_adhd/adhd_medications-update.html*

Singer, A. J. (1997). *Social studies for secondary schools: Teaching to learn, learning to teach.* Mahwah, NJ: Lawrence Erlbaum Associates.

Singer, A. J. (2004). Hofstra New Teachers Network. Retrieved April 11, 2004, from *http://www.geocities.com/Athens/Troy/6931/ntntoc.htm*

Singer, A. J. (Ed.). (2001). *Social science docket, 1*(2). Published by Department of Curriculum and Teaching, Hagedorn Hall, Hofstra University, Hempstead, NY 11549.

Singh, N. N., Oswald, D. P., & Ellis, C. R. (1998). Mental retardation. In Ollendick, T. H., & Herson, M. (Eds.), *Handbook of Child Psychopathology.* New York: Plenum Press.

Skiba, R. (2002). Testimony: "state and local level special education programs that work and federal barriers to innovation." Hearing May 8 before the Subcommittee on Education Reform, Committee on Education and the Workforce, U.S. House of Representatives. Retrieved April 10, 2004 from *http://www.house.gov/ed_workforce/hearings/107th/edr/ idea5802/skiba.htm*

Skinner, B. F. (1948). *Walden two.* New York: Macmillan.

Skinner, B. F. (1953). *Science and human behavior.* New York: Macmillan.

Skinner, D., Bailey, D. B., Correa, V., & Rodriguez, P. (1999). Narrating self and disability: Latino mothers' construction of identities vis à vis their child with special needs. *Exceptional Children, 65*(4), 481–495.

Slavin, R. (1995). *Cooperative learning: Theory, research, and practice* (2nd ed.). Boston: Allyn & Bacon.

Smith, C. R. (1998). *Learning disabilities: The interaction of learner, task, and setting* (4th ed.). Needham Heights, MA: Allyn & Bacon.

Smith, J. D., & Hilton, A. (1997). The preparation and training of the educational community for the inclusion of students with developmental disabilities: The MRDD position. *Education and training in mental retardation and developmental disabilities, 32*(1), 3–10.

Smith, R. C. (1996). *A Case about Amy.* Philadelphia, PA: Temple University Press.

Snell, M. E. (1987). *Systematic instruction of persons with severe handicaps.* Columbus, OH: Merrill.

Snell, M. E., & Brown, F. (Eds.). (2000). *Instruction of students with severe disabilities* (5th ed.). Upper Saddle River, NJ: Merrill/Prentice Hall Education.

Snow, C. E., Burns, S., & Griffin, P. (Eds.). (1999). *Preventing reading difficulties in young children.* Washington, DC: National Academy Press. Online at *http://www.nap.edu/catalog/6023.html*

Sonnenschein, J. L. (1983). *Basic achievement skills individual screener.* Cleveland: The Psychological Corporation.

Sorrells, M. A., Rieth, H. J., & Sindelar, P. T. (2004). *Critical issues in special education: Access, diversity, and accountability.* Boston: Allyn & Bacon.

Spanos, G., & Smith, J. (1990). *Closed captioned television for adult LEP literacy learners.* ERIC Digest. Washington, DC: National Center for ESL Literacy Education. (EDRS No. ED 321 623).

Specific learning disabilities: Finding common ground. (2002). Washington, DC: U.S. Department of Education, Office of Special Education Programs. Online at: *http://www.lda.org.site*

Sprague, J., & Walker, H. (2000). Early identification and intervention for youth with antisocial and violent behavior. *Exceptional Children, 66*(3), 367–379.

Springer, L., Stanne, M. E., & Donovan. S. S. (1999). Effects of small-group learning on undergraduates in science, mathematics, engineering, and technology: A meta-analysis. *Review of Educational Research, 69*(1), 21–51.

Stainback, W., & Stainback, S. (1991). A rationale for integration and restructuring: A synopsis. In J. W. Lloyd, N. N. Singh, & A. C. Repp (Eds.), *The Regular Education Initiative: Alternative Perspectives on Concepts, Issues and Modes* (pp. 225–239). Sycamore, IL: Sycamore.

State, M. W., King, B. H., & Dykens, E. (1997). Mental retardation: A review of the past 10 years. Part II. *Journal of the*

American Academy of Child and Adolescent Psychiatry, 36, 1664–1671.

Steeves, K. J., & Tomey, H. A. (1998). Mathematics and dyslexia. Retrieved April 10, 2004 from *http://ldonline.org/ld_indepth/mdath_skills/ida_math_fall98.html*

Steinbeck, J. (1937). *Of mice and men.* New York: Covici, Friede, Inc. Penguin Books edition, 1978.

Stewart, J. (2001). Blackboard bungle: Why California's kids can't read. *LA Weekly.* Retrieved April 10, 2004 from *http://www.kidsource.com/kidsource/content/whole.l.html*

Stiller, C. (1992). Aetiology and epidemiology. In Plower, P., & Pinkerton, C. (Eds.), *Paediatric Oncology: Clinical Practice and Controversies.* London: Chapman and Hall Medical.

Stoppard, T. (1967). *Rosencrantz & Guildenstern are dead.* New York: Grove Press.

Story, M. F., & Mueller, J. L. (1998). Measuring usability: The principles of universal design. In J. Reagan & L. Trachtman (Eds.), *Designing for the 21st Century: Proceedings* (pp. 126–129). Raleigh, NC: Center for Universal Design, North Carolina State University.

Strickland, D. S. (1998). *Teaching phonics today: A primer for educators.* Newark, DE: International Reading Association.

Stronge, J. H., & Hudson, K. S. (1999). Educating homeless children and youth with dignity and care. *Journal for a Just and Caring Education, 5*(1), 7–18.

Stuckless, E. R., & Birch, J. (1966). The influence of early manual communication on the linguistic development of deaf children. *American Annals of the Deaf, 106,* 436–480.

Swanson, H. L., & Hoskyn, M. (1998). Experimental intervention research on students with learning disabilities: A meta-analysis of treatment outcomes. *Review of Educational Research, 68*(3), 277–321.

Sykes, C. (1994). *No ordinary genius: The illustrated Richard Feynman.* New York: W. W. Norton & Company.

Tanner, D. E. (2001). *Assessing academic achievement.* Boston: Allyn & Bacon.

Taylor, H. E., & Larson, S. M. (2000). *Teaching elementary social studies to students with mild disabilities.* Social Education, 64(4), 232–235.

Taylor, S. (1988). Caught in the continuum: A critical analysis of the principle of least restrictive environment. *Journal of the Association for Persons with Severe Handicaps, 13*(1), 41–53.

TDI, Inc. (2004). Home page. Retrieved April 11, 2004, from *http://www.tdi.org*

TEACCH. (2004). Retrieved April 11, 2004, from *http://www.teacch.com*

Teen pregnancy rate reaches a record low in 1997. (2001, June 12). Press release. Centers for Disease Control and Prevention. Retrieved April 10, 2004 from *http://www.cdc.gov/nchs/releases/01news.trendpreg.htm*

Thomas, K. (2000, June 21). Disabled youths seek power over education. *USA Today,* online edition.

Thompson, S. J., Johnstone, C. J., & Thurlow, M. L. (2002). *Universal design applied to large-scale assessments.* Synthesis Report 44. Minneapolis, MN: University of Minnesota, National Center for Educational Outcomes. Retrieved December 31, 2002, from *http://education.umn.edu/NCEO/OnlinePubs/Synthesis44.html*

Thompson, S. J., Thurlow, M. L., Quenemoen, R. F., & Lehr, C. A. (2002). *Access to computer-based testing for students with disabilities.* NCEO Synthesis Report 45. Minneapolis, MN: University of Minnesota, National Center on Educational Outcomes. Retrieved December 29, 2002, from *http://education.umn.edu/NCEO/OnlinePubs/Synthesis45. html*

Thorndike, R. L., Hagen, E. P., & Sattler, J. M. (1986). *The Stanford-Binet Intelligence Scale: Fourth Edition, Guide for Administering and Scoring.* Chicago, IL: Riverside Publishing Company.

Thorne, K. S. (1994). *Black holes & time warps: Einstein's outrageous legacy.* New York: W. W. Norton & Company.

Thornton, C. A., Langrall, C. W., & Jones, G. A. (1997). Mathematics instruction for elementary students with learning disabilities. *Journal of Learning Disabilities, 30* (2), 142–150.

Thurlow, M. L. (2000). Standards-based reform and students with disabilities: Reflections on a decade of change, entire issue. *Focus on Exceptional Children, 33* (3).

Tierney, R. J., Readence, J. E., & Disner, E. K. (1995). *Reading strategies and practices.* Boston: Allyn & Bacon.

Timothy, W. v. Rochester (NH) School District. (1989). 875 F. 2d 954 (1st Circuit), cert. denied 110 S. Ct. 519.

Tindal, G., Heath, B., Hollenbeck, K., Almond, P., & Harniss, M. (1998). Accommodating students with disabilities on large-scale tests: An experimental study. *Exceptional Children, 64,* 439–450.

Tindall-Ford, S., Chandler, P., & Sweller, J. (1997). When two sensory modes are better than one. *Journal of Experimental Psychology,* 3 (4), 257–287.

Tompkins, G. E. (2001). *Literacy for the 21st century: A Balanced Approach* (2nd ed.). Upper Saddle River, NJ: Merrill/Prentice Hall Education.

Tompkins, G. E. (2002). *Language arts: Content and teaching strategies* (5th ed.). Upper Saddle River, NJ: Merrill/Prentice Hall Education.

Toscano, R.M., McKee, B., & Lepoutre, D. (2002). Success with academic English: Reflections of deaf college students. *American Annals of the Deaf, 147* (1), 5–23.

Tournaki, N. (2003). The differential effects of teaching addition through strategy instruction versus drill and practice to students with and without learning disabilities. *Journal of Learning Disabilities, 36*(5), 449–458.

Townsend, B. L. (2000). The disproportionate discipline of African American learners: Reducing school suspensions and expulsions. *Exceptional Children, 66* (3), 381–391.

Toy, A. (1994). Stigma. *New Mobility, 5* (18), 11–12.

The Tragedy of Julius Caesar: An adapted classic. (1992). New York: Simon & Schuster, Globe Book Company.

Trent, J. W. (1994). *Inventing the feeble mind: A history of mental retardation in the United States.* Berkeley, CA: University of California Press.

Trueman, M., & Hartley, J. (1996). A comparison between the time-management skills and academic performance of mature and traditional-entry university students. *Higher Education, 32,* 199–215.

Tucker, B. F., Singleton, A. H., & Weaver, T. L. (2002). *Teaching mathematics to all children.* Upper Saddle River, NJ: Merrill/Prentice Hall Education.

Tucker, P. D. (1999). Providing educational services to homeless students: A multifaceted response to a complex problem. *Journal for a Just and Caring Education,* 5 (1), 88–107.

Turnbull, A., & Turnbull, H. R. (1997). *Families, professionals, and exceptionality* (3rd ed.). Upper Saddle River, NJ: Merrill/Prentice Hall Education.

Turnbull, A., & Turnbull, H. R. (2001). *Families, professionals, and exceptionality: Collaborating for empowerment* (4th ed.). Upper Saddle River, NJ: Merrill/Prentice Hall Education.

Turnbull, H. R., & Turnbull, A. (2000). *Free appropriate public education: The law and children with disabilities* (6th ed.). Denver, CO: Love.

Turnbull, H. R., Turnbull, A., Shank, M., Smith, S., & Leal, D. (2002). *Exceptional lives: Special education in today's schools* (3rd ed.). Upper Saddle River, NJ: Merrill/Prentice Hall Education.

Turner, J. E., Husman, J., & Schallert, D. L. (2002). The importance of students' goals in their emotional experience of academic failure: Investigating the precursors and consequences of shame. *Educational Psychologist, 37*(2), 79–89.

Twain, M. (1884). *Adventures of Huckleberry Finn*. Riverside Press edition, 1958. Cambridge, MA: Riverside Press.

Twain, M. (1917). *Adventures of Tom Sawyer*. New York: Harper.

United Cerebral Palsy Associations. (2004). Retrieved April 11, 2004 from *http://www.ucpa.org*

U.S. Architectural and Transportation Barriers Compliance Board. (1999, November 16). Americans with Disabilities Act accessibility guidelines for buildings and facilities; Notice of Proposed Rulemaking. *Federal Register*. Online at *http://www.access-board.gov*

U.S. Bureau of the Census. (1998). *U.S. population estimates by sex, race, and hispanic origin with median age: 1990 to 1998*. Washington, DC: Government Printing Office.

U.S. Bureau of the Census. (2000). *Poverty in the U.S.: 1999. Publication P60–210*. Washington, DC: U.S. Department of Commerce. Online at *http://www.census.gov/prod/2000pubs*

U.S. Bureau of the Census. (2001). *First Census 2000 Results—Resident population and apportionment counts*. Washington, DC: U.S. Department of Commerce. *http://www.census.gov/main/www/cen2000.html*

U.S. Bureau of the Census. (2003). *Hispanics outnumber blacks*. Retrieved April 9, 2004, from *http://www.census.gov/population/cen2000/phc-t1/tab01.pdf*

U.S. Bureau of the Census. (2004). *Income in the United States, 2002*. Retrieved April 12, 2004, from *http://www.census.gov/prod/2003pubs/p60-221.pdf*

U.S. Department of Education. (1992a, September 29). Assistance to states for the education of children with disabilities program and preschool grants for children with disabilities: Final rule. *Federal Register*, 44794–44852.

U.S. Department of Education. (1992b, October 30). Deaf students education services; policy guidance. *Federal Register*, 49274–49276.

U.S. Department of Education. (1993a, February 10). Invitation to comment on the regulatory definition of "serious emotional disturbance" and the use of this term in the Individuals with Disabilities Education Act. *Federal Register*, 7938.

U.S. Department of Education. (1993b). *1990 Elementary and secondary school civil rights survey: National summaries*. Washington, DC: Author (Office for Civil Rights).

U.S. Department of Education. (1995). *Report to Congress: A compilation and analysis of reports submitted by states in accordance with Section 722(d)(3) of the education for homeless children and youth program*. Washington, DC: Author.

U.S. Department of Education. (1997a). *Nineteenth annual report to Congress on the implementation of the Individuals with Disabilities Education Act*. Washington, DC: Author.

U.S. Department of Education. (1997b). *OSEP data dictionary*, Office of Special Education Programs. Washington, DC: Author.

U.S. Department of Education. (1998). *Twentieth annual report to Congress on the implementation of the Individuals with Disabilities Education Act*. Washington, DC: Author.

U.S. Department of Education. (1999a, March 12). Assistance to states for the education of children with disabilities and the early intervention program for infants and toddlers with disabilities: Final regulation. *Federal Register*, 12405–12672.

U.S. Department of Education. (1999b). *OSEP brief: Regular education teachers as IEP team members*. Washington, DC: Author.

U.S. Department of Education. (1999c). *Twenty-first annual report to Congress on the implementation of the Individuals with Disabilities Education Act*. Washington, DC: Author.

U.S. Department of Education. (2000a). *A Guide to the individualized education program*. Washington, DC: Author. Online at *http://www.ed.gov/pubs/edpubs.html* or *http://www.ed.gov/offices/OSERS*

U.S. Department of Education. (2000b). *Twenty-second annual report to Congress on the implementation of the Individuals with Disabilities Education Act*. Washington, DC: Author. Online at *http://www.ed.gov/offices/OSERS/OSEP/Products/OSEP2000AnlRpt/index.html*

U.S. Department of Education. (2001). *Twenty-third annual report to Congress on the implementation of the Individuals with Disabilities Education Act*. Washington, DC: Author. Online at *http://www.ed.gov/offices/OSERS/OSEP/Products/OSEP2001AnlRpt/index.html*

U.S. Department of Education. (2002). *Twenty-fourth annual report to Congress on implementation of the Individuals with Disabilities Education Act*. Washington, DC: Author.

U.S. Department of Education. (2003). *Twenty-fifth annual report to Congress on implementation of the Individuals with Disabilities Education Act*. Washington, DC: Author. Portions online at *http://www.ideadata.org*

U.S. Department of Education. (2004). *Twenty-sixth annual report to Congress on implementation of the Individuals with Disabilities Education Act*. Washington, DC: Author. Portions online at *http://www.ideadata.org*

U.S. Department of Education and U.S. Department of Justice. (2000). *2000 annual report on school safety*. Washington, DC: Authors.

U.S. Department of Education, National Center for Education Statistics. (2004). *Indicators of school crime and safety, 2003*. Retrieved April 11, 2004, from *http://nces.ed.gov/pubs2004/crime03/*

U.S. Department of Education, Office for Civil Rights. (1994). *Elementary and secondary school compliance reports*. Washington, DC: Author. Online at *http://www.ed.gov/offices/OCR*

U.S. Department of Education, Office for Civil Rights. (2000). *The use of tests as part of high-stakes decision-making for students: A resource guide for educators and policy-makers.* Washington, DC: Author.

U.S. Department of Education, Office of Special Education Programs. (2000). *Prevention research & the IDEA discipline provisions: A guide for school administrators.* Retrieved April 10, 2004 from *http://www.ed.gov/offices/OSERS/OSEP/Products/adminbeh.web.pdf*

U.S. Department of Health and Human Services. (2000). *Child maltreatment 1998: Reports from the states to the national child abuse and neglect data system.* Washington, DC: U.S. Government Printing Office.

U.S. Department of Health and Human Services. (2001). *Report of the Surgeon General's conference on children's mental health: A national action agenda.* Washington, DC: U.S. Government Printing Office.

U.S. Department of Labor. (2000). *Futurework: Trends and challenges for work in the 21st century.* Washington, DC: Author.

U.S. General Accounting Office. (2001a). *Public education: Meeting the needs of students with limited English proficiency.* Washington, DC: Author. Report GAO-01-226.

U.S. General Accounting Office. (2001b). *Student Discipline: Individuals with Disabilities Education Act.* Washington, DC: Author. Report GAO-01-210.

U.S. General Accounting Office. (2002). *Special education: Grant programs designed to serve children ages 0–5.* Washington, DC: Author. Report GAO-02-394.

Utley, C. A., Mortweet, S. L., & Greenwood, C. R. (1997). Peer-mediated instruction and interventions. *Focus on Exceptional Children, 29*(5), 1–23.

Vaidya, C. J., Austin, G., Kirkorian, G., Ridlehuber, H. W., Desmond, J. E., Glover, G. H., & Gabrielli, J. D. E. (1998). Selective effects of methylphenidate in attention deficit hyperactivity disorder: A functional magnetic resonance study. *Proceedings of the National Academy of Sciences, 95,* 14494–14499.

Valdes, K., Williamson, B., & Wagner, M. (1990). *The longitudinal transition study of special education students: Statistical almanac (Vol. 1).* Menlo Park, CA: SRI International.

Valente, W. D., & Valente, C. M. (2001). *Law in the schools* (5th ed.). Upper Saddle River, NJ: Prentice Hall.

Van Hiele, P. (1996). *Structure and insight: A theory of mathematics education.* Orlando, FL: Academic Press.

Vargas, T. (2002, December 8). A place to "watch their children grow." *Newsday,* G23.

Venn, J. J. (2000). *Assessing students with special needs* (2nd ed.). Upper Saddle River, NJ: Merrill/Prentice Hall Education.

Vernon, M. (1967). Relationship of language to the thinking process. *Archives of General Psychiatry, 16,* 325–333.

Vernon, M., & Prickett, H. (1976, March). Mainstreaming: Issues and a model plan. *Audiology, Hearing, and Education.*

Vernon, S. A., & Ferreiro, E. (1999). Writing development: A neglected variable in the consideration of phonological awareness. *Harvard Educational Review, 69*(1), 395–415.

Villa, R. A., Thousand, J. S., Nevin, A. I., & Malgeri, C. (1996). Instilling collaboration for inclusive schooling as a way of doing business in public schools. *Remedial and Special Education, 17*(3), 169–181.

Voelker, R. (2002a, July 17). Improved care for neglected population must be "rule rather than exception." *Journal of the American Medical Association, 288*(3), 299–302.

Voelker, R. (2002b, July 24/31). Putting mental retardation and mental illness on health care professionals' radar screen. *Journal of the American Medical Association, 288*(4), 433–435.

Vroom, H. V., & Deci, E. L. (1972). An overview of work motivation. In Deci, E. L., Von Haller Gilmer, B., & Karn, H. W. (Eds.), *Readings in Industrial and Organizational Psychology* (pp. 308–333). New York: McGraw-Hill.

Vygotsky, L. (1962). *Thought and language.* New York: Wiley.

Vygotsky, L. (1978). *Mind in society: The development of higher psychological processes.* Cambridge, MA: Harvard University Press.

Wadlington, E. (2000). Effective language arts instruction for students with dyslexia. *Preventing School Failure, 44,* 61–65.

Wald, J. L. (1996). *Culturally and linguistically diverse professionals in special education: A demographic analysis.* Reston, VA: Council for Exceptional Children, National Clearinghouse for Professions in Special Education.

Walker, H. (2000). Investigating school-related behavior disorders: Lessons learned from a thirty-year research career. *Exceptional Children, 66*(2), 151–161.

Wallace, T., Shin, J., Bartholomay, T., & Stahl, B. J. (2001). Knowledge and skills for teachers supervising the work of paraprofessionals. *Exceptional Children, 67*(4), 520–533.

Walther-Thomas, C., Bryant, M., & Land, S. (1996). Planning for effective co-teaching: The key to successful inclusion. *Remedial and Special Education, 17*(4), 255–264, Cover 3.

Walther-Thomas, C., Korinek, L., & McLaughlin, V. L. (1999). Collaboration to support students' success. *Focus on Exceptional Children, 32*(3), entire issue.

Wasserman, R., et al. (1999). Identification of attentional and hyperactivity patterns in primary care: A report from Pediatric Research in Office Settings and the Ambulatory Sentinel Practice Network. *Pediatrics, 103*(3). Online at *http://www.pediatrics.org/cgi/content/full/103/3/e38*

Wauters, L. N., Knoors, H. E. T., Vervloed, M. P. J., & Aarnoutse, C. A. J. (2001). Sign facilitation in word recognition. *Journal of Special Education, 35*(1), 31–40.

Wechsler, D. (1991). *The Wechsler Intelligence Scale for Children-Third Edition-WISC-III.* San Antonio, TX: Psychological Corporation.

Wehman, P. (2002). *Individual transition plans: The teacher's curriculum guide for helping youth with special needs.* Austin, TX: PRO-ED.

Wehman, P., & Kregel, J. (Eds.). (1997). *Functional curriculum for elementary, middle, and secondary age students with special needs.* Austin, TX: Pro-Ed.

Wehman, P., Sherron, P. D., & West, M. D. (1997). *Exceptional individuals in school, community, and work.* Austin, TX: PRO-ED.

Wehmeyer, M. L. (1994). Perceptions of self-determination and psychological empowerment of adolescents with mental retardation. *Education and Training in Mental Retardation and Developmental Disability, 29,* 9–21.

Wehmeyer, M. L., & Schalock, R. L. (2001). Self-determination and quality of life: Implications for special education services and supports. *Focus on Exceptional Children, 33*(8), whole issue.

Weinberg, N. Z. (1997). Cognitive and behavioral deficits associated with parental alcohol use. *Journal of the American Academy of Child and Adolescent Psychiatry, 36,* 1177–1186.

Weiner, B. (1985). An attributional theory of achievement motivation and emotion. *Psychological Review, 92,* 548–573.

Weinfeld, R., Barnes-Robinson, L., Jeweler, S., & Shevitz, B. (2002). Academic programs for gifted and talented/learning disabled students. *Roeper Review, 24*(4), 226–233.

Weiss, K. R. (2000, January 9). New test-taking skill: Working the system. *Los Angeles Times,* online edition.

Wekselman, K., Spiering, K., Hetteberg, C., Kenner, C., & Flandermeyer, A. (1995). Fetal alcohol syndrome from infancy through childhood: A review of the literature. *Journal of Pediatric Nursing, 10,* 296–303.

Welch, M. (2000). Descriptive analysis of team teaching in two elementary classrooms: A formative experimental approach. *Remedial and Special Education, 21*(6), 366–376.

Wenz-Gross, M., & Siperstein, G. N. (1998). Students with learning problems at risk in middle school: Stress, social support, and adjustment. *Exceptional Children, 65*(1), 91–100.

Weyandt, L. L. (2001). *An ADHD primer.* Needham Heights, MA: Allyn & Bacon.

Whalen, C., Schuster, J. W., & Hemmeter, M. L. (1996). The use of unrelated instructive feedback when teaching in a small group instructional arrangement. *Education and Training in Mental Retardation and Developmental Disabilities, 31,* 188–201.

Whaley, A. L. (1998). Cross-cultural perspectives on paranoia: A focus on the Black American. *Psychiatric Quarterly, 69,* 325–343.

What's Best for Matthew. (2000). [CD-ROM]. Needham Heights, MA: Allyn & Bacon.

Wheeler, D., Jacobson, J., Paglieri, R., & Schwartz, A. (1993). An experimental assessment of facilitated communication. *Mental Retardation, 31*(1), 49–60.

Whinnery, K. W., & Barnes, S. B. (2002). Mobility training using the MOVE curriculum. *Teaching Exceptional Children, 34*(3), 44–50.

White, A. H. (2002). Assessing semantic-syntactic features of verbs from thirteen verb subsets. *American Annals of the Deaf, 147*(1), 65–78.

White, S. R., & Yadao, C. M. (2000). Characterization of methylphenidate exposures reported to a regional poison control center. *Archives of Pediatric and Adolescent Medicine, 154,* 1199–1203.

Wicks-Nelson, R., & Israel, A. C. (2000). *Behavior disorders of childhood* (4th ed.). Upper Saddle River, NJ: Prentice Hall.

Wilens, T. E. (1998). ADHD and risk for substance use disorders. In National Institute of Mental Health, National Institute on Drug Abuse, Office of Medical Applications of Research. (Eds.), *Diagnosis and treatment of attention deficit hyperactivity disorder: Programs and abstracts: NIH consensus development conference.* (pp. 181–186). Bethesda, MD: National Institutes of Health.

Will, M. C. (1986). Educating children with learning problems: A shared responsibility. *Exceptional Children, 52*(5), 411–415.

Williams, B. T., & DeSander, M. K. (1999). Dueling legislation: The impact of incongruent federal statutes on homeless and other special-needs students. *Journal for a Just and Caring Education, 5*(1), 34–50.

Williams, J. M. (2000a). How stuttering has changed my life. *Business Week.* Retrieved April 12, 2000, from *http://www.businessweek.com*

Williams, J. M. (2000b). Straight talk about naturally speaking. *Business Week.* Retrieved December 27, 2000, from *http://www.businessweek.com*

Williams, J. R. (1998). *Guidelines for the use of multimedia in instruction.* Proceedings of the Human Factors and Ergonomics Society 42nd Annual Meeting, 1447–1451.

Wilson, G. L. (2003). Personal communication, October 25.

Wilson, W. M. (1992). The Stanford-Binet: Fourth edition and Form L-M in assessment of young children with mental retardation. *Mental Retardation, 30*(2), 81–84.

Winchester, S. (2001). *The map that changed the world: William Smith and the birth of modern geology.* New York: HarperCollins.

Wing, L. (1981). *Early childhood autism: Clinical, educational, and social aspects.* (3rd. ed.) New York: Pergamon Press.

Wing, L. (1998). The history of Asperger syndrome. In Schopler, E., Mesibov, G. B., & Kunce, L. J. (Eds.), *Asperger Syndrome or high-functioning autism?* (pp. 11–28). New York: Plenum.

Wingert, P., & Kantrowitz, B. (1997, October 27). Why Andy couldn't read. *Newsweek,* 56–64.

Wolery, M. (2001). Embedding time delay procedures in classroom activities. In M. Ostrosky and S. Sandall (Eds.). *Teaching Strategies: What to Do to Support Young Children's Development.* Longmont, CO: Sopris West.

Wolery, M., & Gast, D. L. (2000). Classroom research for young children with disabilities: Assumptions that guided the conduct of research. *Topics in Early Childhood Special Education, 20*(1), 49–55.

Wolfe, M. P. (2001). Reflections on the most important educational developments of the 20th century: Kappa Delta Pi laureates. *The Educational Forum, 65*(2), 146–163.

Wolfensberger, W. (1972). *The principle of normalization in human services.* Toronto, Canada: National Institute on Mental Retardation.

Wong, H. K., & Wong, R. T. (1998). *The first days of school: How to be an effective teacher.* Sunnydale, CA: Wong Publications.

Wood, K. D., & Nichols, W. D. (2000). Helping struggling learners read and write. In Wood, K. D., & Dickinson, T. S. (Eds.), *Promoting literacy in grades 4–9* (pp. 233–249). Needham Heights, MA: Allyn & Bacon.

Woodward, J., Monroe, K., & Baxter, J. (2001). Enhancing student achievement on performance assessments in mathematics. *Learning Disability Quarterly, 24*(1), 33–46.

Woolfolk, A. (2001). *Educational psychology* (8th ed.). Needham Heights, MA: Allyn & Bacon.

Xin, Y. P., & Jitendra, A. K. (1999). The effects of instruction in solving mathematical word problems for students with learning disabilities: A meta-analysis. *Journal of Special Education, 32*(4), 207–225.

Yell, M. (1995). Least restrictive environment, inclusion, and students with disabilities: A legal analysis. *Journal of Special Education, 28*(4), 389–404.

Yell, M. L. (1998). *The law and special education.* Upper Saddle River, NJ: Merrill/Prentice Hall Education.

Yell, M. L., Rozalski, M. E., & Drasgow, E. (2001). Disciplining students with disabilities. *Focus on Exceptional Children, 33*(9), whole issue.

Yell, M. M. (1999). Multiple choice to multiple rubrics: One teacher's journey in assessment. *Social Education, 65*(6), 326–329.

Yopp, H. K., & Yopp, R. H. (2000). Supporting phonemic awareness development in the classroom. *The Reading Teacher, 54,* 130–143.

Yopp, R. H., & Yopp, H. K. (2001). *Literature-based reading activities* (3rd ed.). Boston: Allyn & Bacon.

Yore, L. D. (2000). Enhancing science literacy for all students with embedded reading instruction and writing-to-learn activities. *Journal of Deaf Studies and Deaf Education, 5,* 105–122.

York, J., Doyle, M. B., & Kronberg, R. (1992). A curriculum development process for inclusive classrooms. *Focus on Exceptional Children, 25*(4), 1–16.

Ysseldyke, J. (2001). Reflections on a research career: Generalizations from 25 years of research on assessment and instructional decision making. *Exceptional Children, 67*(3), 295–309.

Ysseldyke, J., & Olsen, K. (1999). Putting alternative assessments into practice: What to measure and possible sources of data. *Exceptional Children, 65*(2), 175–185.

Yuker, H. E. (1994). Variables that influence attitudes toward people with disabilities: Conclusions from the data. *Journal of Social Behavior and Personality, 9*(5), 3–22.

Zeller, T. (2001, March 18). Migrants take their chances on a harsh path of hope. *New York Times,* the Nation Section, 14.

Zigler, E., & Valentine, J. (1979). *Project Head Start: A Legacy of the War on Poverty.* New York: Free Press.

Zigmond, N. (2000). Reflections on a research career: Research as detective work. *Exceptional Children, 66*(3), 295–304.

Zigmond, N. (2001). Special education at a crossroads. *Preventing School Failure, 45*(2), 70–74.

Zigmond, N., Jenkins, J., Fuchs, L., Deno, S. Fuchs, D., Baker, J., Jenkins, L., & Coutinho, M. (1995). Special education in restructured schools: Findings from three multi-year studies. *Phi Delta Kappan, 76,* 531–540.

Zirpoli, T. J., & Melloy, K. J. (2001). *Behavior management: Applications for teachers* (3rd ed.). Upper Saddle River, NJ: Merrill/Prentice Hall Education.

Zito, J. M., Safer, D. J., dosReis, S., Gardner, J. F., Boles, M., & Lynch, F. (2000). Trends in the prescribing of psychotropic medications to preschoolers. *Journal of the American Medical Association, 283,* 1025–1030.

Name Index

Subject Index